Mastering
Modern World History

Palgrave Master Series

Accounting
Accounting Skills
Advanced English Language
Advanced Pure Mathematics
Arabic
Basic Management
Biology
British Politics
Business Communication
Business Environment
C Programming
C++ Programming
Chemistry
COBOL Programming
Communication
Computing
Counselling Skills
Counselling Theory
Customer Relations
Database Design
Delphi Programming
Desktop Publishing
e-Business
Economic and Social History
Economics
Electrical Engineering
Electronics
Employee Development
English Grammar
English Language
English Literature
Fashion Buying and Merchandising
   Management
Fashion Marketing
Fashion Styling
Financial Management
Geography
Global Information Systems

Human Resource Management
International Trade
Internet
Java
Language of Literature
Management Skills
Marketing Management
Mathematics
Microsoft Office
Microsoft Windows, Novell NetWare
   and UNIX
Modern British History
Modern European History
Modern German History
Modern United States History
Modern World History
The Novels of Jane Austen
Organisational Behaviour
Pascal and Delphi Programming
Personal Finance
Philosophy
Physics
Poetry
Practical Criticism
Practical Grammar
Psychology
Public Relations
Shakespeare
Social Welfare
Sociology
Statistics
Strategic Management
Systems Analysis and Design
Team Leadership
Theology
Twentieth-Century Russian History
Visual Basic
World Religions

www.palgravemasterseries.com

Palgrave Master Series
Series Standing Order ISBN 0–333–69343–4
(*outside North America only*)

You can receive future titles in this series as they are published by placing a standing order. Please contact your bookseller or, in the case of difficulty, write to us at the address below with your name and address, the title of the series and the ISBN quoted above.

Customer Services Department, Macmillan Distribution Ltd, Houndmills, Basingstoke, Hampshire, RG21 6XS, UK

Mastering
Modern World History

Fifth edition

Norman Lowe

palgrave
macmillan

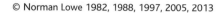
First edition published 1982
Second edition published 1988
Third edition published 1997
Fourth edition published 2005
Fifth edition published 2013

Published by
PALGRAVE MACMILLAN

Palgrave Macmillan in the UK is an imprint of Macmillan Publishers Limited, registered in England, company number 785998, of Houndmills, Basingstoke, Hampshire RG21 6XS.

Palgrave Macmillan in the US is a division of St. Martin's Press LLC, 175 Fifth Avenue, New York, NY 10010.

Palgrave Macmillan is the global academic imprint of the above companies and has companies and representatives throughout the world.

Palgrave® and Macmillan® are registered trademarks in the United States, the United Kingdom, Europe and other countries

ISBN: 978–1–137–27694–0

This book is printed on paper suitable for recycling and made from fully managed and sustained forest sources. Logging, pulping and manufacturing processes are expected to conform to the environmental regulations of the country of origin.

A catalogue record for this book is available from the British Library.

A catalog record for this book is available from the Library of Congress.

10   9   8   7   6   5   4   3   2
22 21 20 19 18 17 16 15 14

Printed in China

For Jane

Contents

PART II   THE RISE OF FASCISM AND GOVERNMENTS OF THE RIGHT

PART III   COMMUNISM – RISE AND DECLINE

List of figures

List of maps

List of tables

List of illustrations

Acknowledgements

The author and publishers wish to thank the following for permission to reproduce copyright material:

Guardian News & Media Ltd. for Map 11.4 from *The Guardian*, 25 September 1995, Copyright Guardian News & Media Ltd. 1995; Guardian News & Media Ltd. for Map 11.5 from *The Guardian*, 1 May 1996, Copyright Guardian News & Media Ltd. 1996; Guardian News & Media Ltd. for Map 24.6 from *The Guardian*, 20 April 1996, Copyright Guardian News & Media Ltd. 1996; Hodder Education for Figures 6.1 and 10.1 based on J. B. Watson, *Success in Modern World History Since 1945*, John Murray (1989), pp. 3 and 150. © Margaret Watson 1989. Reproduced by permission of Hodder Education; Oxford University Press for Maps 6.6, 7.2 and 22.1 from *Our World this Century* by D. Heater (OUP, 1992), copyright © Oxford University Press 1982, reprinted by permission of Oxford University Press.

The following photograph sources are acknowledged for Illustrations included throughout the book:

Camera Press, 23.1; Corbis Images, 6.3, 7.2, 14.3, 19.1, 22.1, 23.2; Getty Images, 2.1, 6.1, 6.2, 7.1, 12.1, 12.2, 14.1, 14.2, 17.1, 25.1; International Planned Parenthood Federation, 28.1; Press Association, 8.1, 20.1.

Preface to the fifth edition

This fifth edition of *Mastering Modern World History* is designed to meet the needs of students following AS and A-level History courses. The questions are mostly in the current styles of the three examination boards, AQA, Edexcel and OCR. I hope that the book will be useful for GCSE students and that it will provide an introduction to the study of twentieth- and early twenty-first-century world history for first-year undergraduates. The general reader who wants to keep abreast of world affairs should also find the book helpful.

So much has happened since I put the finishing touches to the fourth edition in 2005, and the pace of change seems to be quickening. This makes it more difficult to get a stable perspective on the state of the modern world. The historian has to trace a careful way through all the available sources of information, and try to be as objective as possible in getting as close as possible to the truth. The problem of course is that it is difficult to be completely objective: writers from different cultures, religions, states and political groups will produce widely differing accounts of the same events, and so we are faced with many conflicting theories and interpretations. After reviewing, for example, the different theories about what really caused the First World War, or about whether colonialism was a 'good thing' or not, history teachers are sometimes asked questions like: 'Yes, that's all very interesting, but what's the right answer? What's the truth?' However, as AS- and A-level students go deeper into their study of history, they will, hopefully, develop skills of analysis and argument as well as a critical and sceptical approach to historical controversy. They will come to realize that it is sometimes impossible to decide what 'the truth' is – all we can say is what our view of the truth is, based on our study of the different interpretations.

Inevitably this edition is much longer than its predecessor. There is a new chapter on Latin America, and new sections dealing with important events and developments since 2005. The associated website (www.palgrave.com/masterseries/Lowe) contains a selection of source-based questions. New sections include:

- The 2008 financial crisis and its aftermath
- The Arab Spring
- The European Union in crisis
- Islamism
- The Afghanistan situation
- Iran and North Korea
- Somalia and the Sudan
- The new China and the other BRIC countries (Brazil, Russia and India)

I am most grateful to my friends Glyn Jones, formerly of Bede College, Billingham, and Michael Hopkinson, formerly Head of History at Harrogate Grammar School, who read the new sections and made many helpful suggestions, and the Reverend Melusi Sibanda, who once again gave me invaluable help in sorting out the problems of Africa. I must also thank Suzannah Burywood, Della Oliver, Tina Graham and Juanita Bullough for their help, encouragement and guidance. And finally I would like to thank my wife Jane, who, as usual, was able to suggest many improvements to the text.

NORMAN LOWE
September 2012

Part I

War and International Relations

The world in 1914: outbreak of the First World War

1.1 PROLOGUE

Under cover of darkness late on the night of 5 August 1914, five columns of German assault troops, which had entered Belgium two days earlier, were converging on the town of Liège, expecting little resistance. To their surprise they were halted by determined fire from the town's outlying forts. This was a setback for the Germans: control of Liège was essential before they could proceed with their main operation against France. They were forced to resort to siege tactics, using heavy howitzers. These fired shells up into the air and they plunged from a height of 12 000 feet to shatter the armour-plating of the forts. Strong though they were, these Belgian forts were not equipped to withstand such a battering for long; on 13 August the first one surrendered and three days later Liège was under German control. This was the first major engagement of the First World War, that horrifying conflict of monumental proportions which was to mark the beginning of a new era in European and world history.

1.2 THE WORLD IN 1914

(a) Europe still dominated the rest of the world in 1914

Most of the decisions which shaped the fate of the world were taken in the capitals of Europe. Germany was the leading power in Europe both militarily and economically. She had overtaken Britain in the production of pig-iron and steel, though not quite in coal, while France, Belgium, Italy and Austria–Hungary (known as the Habsburg Empire) were well behind. Russian industry was expanding rapidly but had been so backward to begin with that she could not seriously challenge Germany and Britain. But it was outside Europe that the most spectacular industrial progress had been made during the previous 40 years. In 1914 the USA produced more coal, pig-iron and steel than either Germany or Britain and now ranked as a world power. Japan too had modernized rapidly and was a power to be reckoned with after her defeat of Russia in the Russo-Japanese War of 1904–5.

(b) The political systems of these world powers varied widely

The USA, Britain and France had *democratic forms of government*. This means that they each had a parliament consisting of representatives elected by the people; these parliaments had an important say in running the country. Some systems were not as democratic as they seemed: Germany had an elected lower house of parliament (Reichstag), but real power lay with the Chancellor (a sort of prime minister) and the Kaiser (emperor). Italy was a monarchy with an elected parliament, but the franchise (right to vote) was limited to wealthy people. Japan had an elected lower house, but here too the franchise was restricted, and the emperor and the privy council held most of the power. The governments in Russia and Austria–Hungary were very different from the democracy of the West. The Tsar (emperor) of Russia and the Emperor of Austria (who was also King of Hungary) were *autocratic* or *absolute rulers*. This means that although parliaments existed, they could only advise the rulers; if they felt like it, the rulers could ignore the parliaments and do exactly as they wished.

(c) Imperial expansion after 1880

The European powers had taken part in a great burst of imperialist expansion in the years after 1880. *Imperialism* is the building up of an empire by seizing territory overseas. Most of Africa was taken over by the European states in what became known as the 'the Scramble for Africa'; the idea behind it was mainly to get control of new markets and new sources of raw materials. There was also intervention in the crumbling Chinese Empire; the European powers, the USA and Japan all, at different times, forced the helpless Chinese to grant trading concessions. Exasperation with the incompetence of their government ment caused the Chinese to overthrow the ancient Manchu dynasty and set up a republic (1911).

(d) Europe had divided itself into two alliance systems

The Triple Alliance:	Germany
	Austria–Hungary
	Italy
The Triple Entente:	Britain
	France
	Russia

In addition, Japan and Britain had signed an alliance in 1902. Friction between the two main groups (sometimes called 'the armed camps') had brought Europe to the verge of war several times since 1900 (Map 1.1).

(e) Causes of friction

There were many causes of friction which threatened to upset the peace of Europe:

- There was naval rivalry between Britain and Germany.
- The French resented the loss of Alsace–Lorraine to Germany at the end of the Franco-Prussian War (1871).
- The Germans accused Britain, Russia and France of trying to 'encircle' them; the Germans were also disappointed with the results of their expansionist policies (known as *Weltpolitik* – literally 'world policy'). Although they had taken possession of some islands in the Pacific and some territory in Africa, their empire was small in comparison with those of the other European powers, and not very rewarding economically.

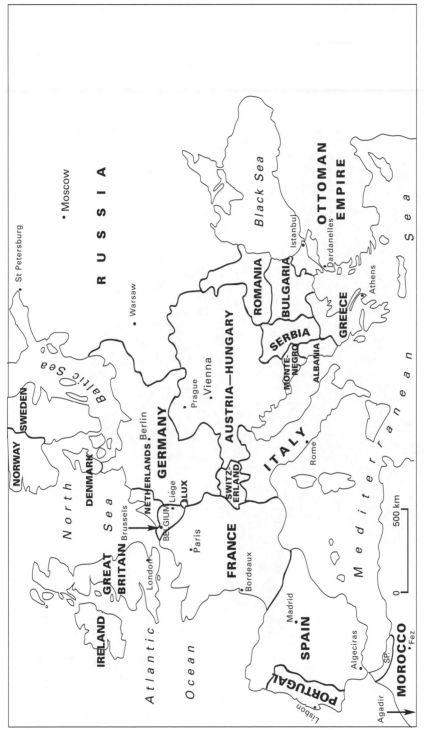

Map 1.1 Europe in 1914

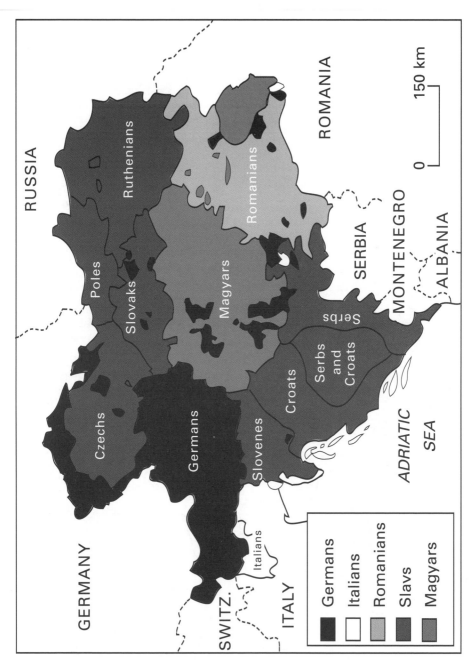

Map 1.2 **Peoples of the Habsburg Empire**

RUSSIA

ROMANIA

150 km

0

SERBIA

MONTENEGRO

ALBANIA

ADRIATIC
SEA

Ruthenians

Romanians

Poles

Slovaks

Magyars

Czechs

Germans

Serbs

Serbs
and
Croats

Croats

Slovenes

GERMANY

SWITZ.

Italians

ITALY

Germans

Italians

Romanians

Slavs

Magyars

- The Russians were suspicious of Austrian ambitions in the Balkans and worried about the growing military and economic strength of Germany.
- Serbian *nationalism* (the desire to free your nation from control by people of another nationality) was probably the most dangerous cause of friction. Since 1882 the Serbian government of King Milan had been pro-Austrian, and his son Alexander, who came of age in 1893, followed the same policy. However, the Serbian nationalists bitterly resented the fact that by the Treaty of Berlin signed in 1878, the Austrians had been allowed to occupy Bosnia, an area which the Serbs thought should be part of a Greater Serbia. The nationalists saw Alexander as a traitor; in 1903 he was murdered by a group of army officers, who put Peter Karageorgević on the throne. The change of regime caused a dramatic switch in Serbian policy: the Serbs now became pro-Russian and made no secret of their ambition to unite all Serbs and Croats into a large South Slav kingdom (Yugoslavia). Many of these Serbs and Croats lived inside the borders of the Habsburg Empire; if they were to break away from Austria–Hungary to become part of a Greater Serbia, it would threaten to break up the entire ramshackle Habsburg Empire, which contained people of many different nationalities (Map 1.2). There were Germans, Hungarians, Magyars, Czechs, Slovaks, Italians, Poles, Romanians, Ruthenians and Slovenes, as well as Serbs and Croats. If the Serbs and Croats left the fold, many of the others would demand their independence as well, and the Hapsburg Empire would break up. Consequently some Austrians were keen for what they called a 'preventive war' to destroy Serbia before she became strong enough to provoke the break-up of their empire. The Austrians also resented Russian support for Serbia.

Arising from all these resentments and tensions came a series of events which culminated in the outbreak of war in late July 1914.

1.3 EVENTS LEADING UP TO THE OUTBREAK OF WAR

Time chart of main events

Europe divides into two armed camps:

1882	Triple Alliance of Germany, Austria–Hungary and Italy
1894	France and Russia sign alliance
1904	Britain and France sign 'Entente Cordiale' (friendly 'getting-together')
1907	Britain and Russia sign agreement.

Other important events:

1897	Admiral Tirpitz's Navy Law – Germany intends to build up fleet
1902	Britain and Japan sign alliance
1904–5	Russo-Japanese War, won by Japan
1905–6	Moroccan Crisis
1906	Britain builds first 'Dreadnought' battleship
1908	Bosnia Crisis
1911	Agadir Crisis
1912	First Balkan War

1913	Second Balkan War	
1914	28 June	Archduke Franz Ferdinand assassinated in Sarajevo
	28 July	Austria–Hungary declares war on Serbia
	29 July	Russia orders general mobilization of troops
	1 August	Germany declares war on Russia
	3 August	Germany declares war on France
	4 August	Britain enters war
	6 August	Austria–Hungary declares war on Russia.

(a) The Moroccan Crisis (1905–6)

This was an attempt by the Germans to expand their empire and to test the recently signed Anglo-French 'Entente Cordiale' (1904), with its understanding that France would recognize Britain's position in Egypt in return for British approval of a possible French takeover of Morocco; this was one of the few remaining areas of Africa not controlled by a European power. The Germans announced that they would assist the Sultan of Morocco to maintain his country's independence, and demanded an international conference to discuss its future. A conference was duly held at Algeciras in southern Spain (January 1906). The British believed that if the Germans had their way, it would lead to virtual German control of Morocco. This would be an important step on the road to German diplomatic domination and it would encourage them to press ahead with their *Weltpolitik*. The British, who had just signed the 'Entente Cordiale' with France, were determined to lead the opposition to Germany at the conference. The Germans did not take the 'Entente' seriously because there was a long history of hostility between Britain and France. But to the amazement of the Germans, Britain, Russia, Italy and Spain supported the French demand to control the Moroccan bank and police. It was a serious diplomatic defeat for the Germans, who realized that the new line-up of Britain and France was a force to be reckoned with, especially as the crisis was soon followed by Anglo-French 'military conversations'.

(b) The British agreement with Russia (1907)

This was regarded by the Germans as another hostile move. In fact it was a logical step, given that in 1894 Russia had signed an alliance with France, Britain's new partner in the 'Entente Cordiale'. For many years the British had viewed Russia as a disgraceful example of corrupt, anti-democratic aristocratic government. Worse still, the Russians were seen as a major threat to British interests in the Far East and India. However, the situation had recently changed. Russia's defeat by Japan in the war of 1904–5 seemed to suggest that the Russians were no longer much of a military threat. The outbreak of revolution in Russia in January 1905 had weakened the country internally. The Russians were keen to end the long-standing rivalry and anxious to attract British investment for their industrial modernization programme. In October 1905, when the tsar granted the Russian people freedom of speech and the right to have an elected parliament, the British began to feel more kindly disposed towards the tsarist system. It made agreement possible and the two governments were able therefore to settle their remaining differences in Persia, Afghanistan and Tibet. It was not a military alliance and not necessarily an anti-German move, but the Germans saw it as confirmation of their fears that Britain, France and Russia were planning to 'encircle' them.

(c) The Bosnia Crisis (1908)

The crisis over Bosnia, a province of Turkey, brought the tension between Austria–Hungary and Serbia to fever pitch. In 1878 the Congress of Berlin had reached the rather confusing decision that Bosnia should remain officially part of Turkey, but that Austria–Hungary should be allowed to administer it. In 1908 there was a new government in Turkey, dominated by a group of army officers (known as Young Turks), who resented the Austrian presence in Bosnia and were determined to assert Turkish control over the province. This gave the Austrians the chance to get in first: they announced the formal annexation (takeover) of Bosnia. This was a deliberate blow at the neighbouring state of Serbia, which had also been hoping to take Bosnia since it contained about three million Serbs among its mixed population of Serbs, Croats and Muslims. The Serbs appealed for help to their fellow Slavs, the Russians, who called for a European conference, expecting French and British support. When it became clear that Germany would support Austria in the event of war, the French drew back, unwilling to become involved in a war in the Balkans. The British, anxious to avoid a breach with Germany, did no more than protest to Austria–Hungary. The Russians, still smarting from their defeat by Japan, dared not risk another war without the support of their allies. There was to be no help for Serbia; no conference took place, and Austria kept Bosnia. It was a triumph for the Austro-German alliance, *but it had unfortunate results*:

- Serbia remained bitterly hostile to Austria, and it was this quarrel which sparked off the outbreak of war.
- The Russians were determined to avoid any further humiliation and embarked on a massive military build-up and modernization of the army, together with an improvement in their railway system to allow faster mobilization. They intended to be prepared if Serbia should ever appeal for help again.

(d) The Agadir Crisis (1911)

This crisis was caused by further developments in the situation in Morocco. French troops occupied Fez, the Moroccan capital, to put down a rebellion against the Sultan. It looked as if the French were about to annex Morocco. The Germans sent a gunboat, the *Panther*, to the Moroccan port of Agadir, hoping to pressurize the French into giving Germany compensation, perhaps the French Congo. The British were worried in case the Germans acquired Agadir, which could be used as a naval base from which to threaten Britain's trade routes. In order to strengthen French resistance, Lloyd George (Britain's Chancellor of the Exchequer) used a speech which he was due to make at the Lord Mayor of London's banquet at the Mansion House, to warn the Germans off. He said that Britain would not stand by and be taken advantage of 'where her interests were vitally affected'. The French stood firm, making no major concessions, and eventually the German gunboat was removed. The Germans agreed to recognize the French protectorate (the right to 'protect' the country from foreign intervention) over Morocco in return for two strips of territory in the French Congo. This was seen as a triumph for the Entente powers, but in Germany public opinion became intensely anti-British, especially as the British were drawing slowly ahead in the 'naval race'. At the end of 1911 they had built eight of the new and more powerful 'Dreadnought'-type battleships, compared with Germany's four.

(e) The First Balkan War (1912)

The war began when Serbia, Greece, Montenegro and Bulgaria (calling themselves the Balkan League) launched a series of attacks on Turkey. These countries had all, at one time, been part of the Turkish (Ottoman) Empire. Now that Turkey was weak (regarded by the other powers as 'the Sick Man of Europe'), they seized their chance to acquire more land at Turkey's expense. They soon captured most of the remaining Turkish territory in Europe. Together with the German government, Sir Edward Grey, the British Foreign Secretary, arranged a peace conference in London. He was anxious to avoid the conflict spreading, and also to demonstrate that Britain and Germany could still work together. The resulting settlement divided up the former Turkish lands among the Balkan states. However, the Serbs were not happy with their gains: they wanted Albania, which would

Map 1.3   **The Balkans in 1913 showing changes from the Balkan Wars (1912–13)**

give them an outlet to the sea, but the Austrians, with German and British support, insisted that Albania should become an independent state. This was a deliberate Austrian move to prevent Serbia becoming more powerful.

(f) The Second Balkan War (1913)

The Bulgarians were dissatisfied with their gains from the peace settlement and they blamed Serbia. They had been hoping for Macedonia, but most of it had been given to Serbia. Bulgaria therefore attacked Serbia, but their plan misfired when Greece, Romania and Turkey rallied to support Serbia. The Bulgarians were defeated, and by the Treaty of Bucharest (1913), they forfeited most of their gains from the first war (see Map 1.3). It seemed that Anglo-German influence had prevented an escalation of the war by restraining the Austrians, who were itching to support Bulgaria and attack Serbia. In reality, however, *the consequences of the Balkan Wars were serious*:

- Serbia had been strengthened and was determined to stir up trouble among the Serbs and Croats living inside Austria–Hungary;
- the Austrians were equally determined to put an end to Serbia's ambitions;
- the Germans took Grey's willingness to co-operate as a sign that Britain was prepared to be detached from France and Russia.

(g) The assassination of the Austrian Archduke Franz Ferdinand

This tragic event, which took place in Sarajevo, the capital of Bosnia, on 28 June 1914, was the immediate cause of Austria–Hungary's declaration of war on Serbia, which was soon to develop into the First World War. The Archduke, nephew and heir to the Emperor Franz Josef, was paying an official visit to Sarajevo when he and his wife were shot dead by a Serb terrorist, Gavrilo Princip. The Austrians blamed the Serb government and sent a harsh ultimatum. The Serbs accepted most of the demands in it, but the Austrians, with a promise of German support, were determined to use the incident as an excuse for war. On 28 July, Austria–Hungary declared war on Serbia. The Russians, anxious not to let the Serbs down again, ordered a general mobilization (29 July). The German government demanded that this should be cancelled (31 July), and when the Russians failed to comply, Germany declared war on Russia (1 August) and on France (3 August). When German troops entered Belgium on their way to invade France, Britain (who in 1839 had promised to defend Belgian neutrality) demanded their withdrawal. When this demand was ignored, Britain entered the war (4 August). Austria–Hungary declared war on Russia on 6 August. Others countries joined later.

The war was to have profound effects on the future of the world. Germany was soon to be displaced, for a time at least, from her mastery of Europe, and Europe never quite regained its dominant position in the world.

1.4   WHAT CAUSED THE WAR, AND WHO WAS TO BLAME?

It is difficult to analyse why the assassination in Sarajevo developed into a world war, and even now historians cannot agree. Some blame Austria for being the first aggressor by declaring war on Serbia; some blame the Russians because they were the first to order full mobilization; some blame Germany for supporting Austria, and others blame the British for not making it clear that they would definitely support France. If the Germans had known this, so the argument goes, they would not have declared war on France, and the fighting could have been restricted to eastern Europe.

The point which is beyond dispute is that the quarrel between Austria–Hungary and Serbia sparked off the outbreak of war. The quarrel had become increasingly more explosive since 1908, and the Austrians seized on the assassination as the excuse for a preventive war with Serbia. They genuinely felt that if Serb and Slav nationalist ambitions for a state of Yugoslavia were achieved, it would cause the collapse of the Habsburg Empire; Serbia must be curbed. In fairness, they probably hoped the war would remain localized, like the Balkan Wars. The Austro-Serb quarrel explains the outbreak of the war, but not why it became a world war. *Here are some of the reasons which have been suggested for the escalation of the war.*

(a)   The alliance system or 'armed camps' made war inevitable

The American diplomat and historian George Kennan believed that once the 1894 alliance had been signed between France and Russia, the fate of Europe was sealed. As suspicions mounted between the two opposing camps, Russia, Austria–Hungary and Germany got themselves into situations which they could not escape from without suffering further humiliation; war seemed to be the only way for them to save face.

However, many historians think this explanation is not convincing; there had been many crises since 1904, and none of them had led to a major war. In fact, *there was nothing binding about these alliances.* When Russia was struggling in the war against Japan (1904–5), the French sent no help; nor did they support Russia when she protested at the Austrian annexation of Bosnia; Austria took no interest in Germany's unsuccessful attempts to prevent France from taking over Morocco (the Morocco and Agadir Crises, 1906 and 1911); Germany had restrained Austria from attacking Serbia during the Second Balkan War. Italy, though a member of the Triple Alliance, was on good terms with France and Britain, and entered the war *against* Germany in 1915. No power actually declared war because of one of these treaties of alliance.

(b)   Colonial rivalry in Africa and the Far East

Again, the argument that German disappointment with their imperial gains and resentment at the success of other powers helped cause the war is not convincing. Although there had certainly been disputes, they had always been settled without war. In early July 1914 Anglo-German relations were good: an agreement favourable to Germany had just been reached over a possible partition of Portuguese colonies in Africa. However, there was one side effect of colonial rivalry which did cause dangerous friction – this was naval rivalry.

(c)   The naval race between Britain and Germany

The German government had been greatly influenced by the writings of an American, Alfred Mahan, who believed that sea power was the key to the successful build-up of a great empire. It followed therefore that Germany needed a much larger navy capable of challenging the world's greatest sea power – Britain. Starting with Admiral Tirpitz's Navy Law of 1897, the Germans made a determined effort to expand their navy. The rapid growth of the German fleet probably did not worry the British too much at first because they had an enormous lead. However, the introduction of the powerful British 'Dreadnought' battleship in 1906 changed all this because it made all other battleships obsolete. This meant that the Germans could begin building 'Dreadnoughts' on equal terms with Britain. The resulting naval race was the main bone of contention between the two right up to 1914. For many of the British, the new German navy could mean only one thing: Germany intended making war against Britain. However, early in 1913 the Germans had actually reduced naval spending in order to concentrate more on strengthening the army. As Winston Churchill correctly pointed out, in the spring and summer of 1914, naval rivalry had ceased to be a cause of friction, because 'it was certain that we (Britain) could not be overtaken as far as capital ships were concerned'.

(d) Economic rivalry

It has been argued that the desire for economic mastery of the world caused German businessmen and capitalists to want war with Britain, which still owned about half the world's tonnage of merchant ships in 1914. Marxist historians like this theory because *it puts the blame for the war on the capitalist system.* But critics of the theory point out that Germany was already well on the way to economic victory; one leading German industrialist remarked in 1913: 'Give us three or four more years of peace and Germany will be the unchallenged economic master of Europe.' On this argument, the last thing Germany needed was a major war.

(e) Russia made war more likely by supporting Serbia

Russian backing probably made Serbia more reckless in her anti-Austrian policy than she might otherwise have been. Russia was the first to order a general mobilization, and it was this Russian mobilization which provoked Germany to mobilize. The Russians were worried about the situation in the Balkans, where both Bulgaria and Turkey were under German influence. This could enable Germany and Austria to control the Dardanelles, the outlet from the Black Sea. It was the main Russian trade route, and Russian trade could be strangled (this happened to some extent during the war). Thus Russia felt threatened, and once Austria declared war on Serbia, saw it as a struggle for survival. The Russians must also have felt that their prestige as leader of the Slavs would suffer if they failed to support Serbia. Possibly the government saw the war as a good idea to divert attention away from domestic problems, though they must also have been aware that involvement in a major war would be a dangerous gamble. Shortly before the outbreak of war, one of the Tsar's ministers, Durnovo, warned that a long war would put a severe strain on the country and could lead to the collapse of the tsarist regime. Perhaps the blame lies more with the Austrians: although they must have hoped for Russian neutrality, they ought to have realized how difficult it would be for Russia to stay neutral in the circumstances.

(f) German backing for Austria was crucially important

It is significant that Germany restrained the Austrians from declaring war on Serbia in 1913, but in 1914 encouraged them to go ahead. The Kaiser sent them a telegram urging them to attack Serbia and promising German help without any conditions attached. This was like giving the Austrians a blank cheque to do whatever they wanted. The important question is: *Why did German policy towards Austria–Hungary change?* This question has caused great controversy among historians, and several different interpretations have been put forward:

1   After the war, when the Germans had been defeated, the Versailles Treaty imposed a harsh peace settlement on Germany. The victorious powers felt the need to justify this by putting all the blame for the war on Germany (see Section 2.8). At the time, most non-German historians went along with this, though German historians were naturally not happy with this interpretation. After a few years, opinion began to move away from laying sole blame on Germany and accepted that other powers should take some of the blame. Then in 1967 a German historian, Fritz Fischer, caused a sensation when he suggested that Germany should, after all, take most of the blame, because they risked a major war by sending the 'blank cheque' to Austria–Hungary. He claimed that Germany deliberately planned for, and provoked war with Russia, Britain and France in order to make Germany the dominant power in the world, both economically and politically, and also as a way of dealing with domestic tensions. In the elections of 1912, the German Socialist Party (SPD) won over a third of the seats in the Reichstag (lower house of parliament), making it the largest single party. Then in January 1914, the Reichstag passed a vote of no confidence in the Chancellor, Bethmann-Hollweg, but he remained in office because the Kaiser had the final say. Obviously a major clash was on the way between the Reichstag, which wanted more power, and the Kaiser and Chancellor, who were determined to resist change. A victorious war seemed a good way of keeping people's minds off the political problems; it would enable the government to suppress the SPD and keep power in the hands of the Kaiser and aristocracy.

Fischer based his theory partly on evidence from the diary of Admiral von Müller, who wrote about a 'war council' held on 8 December 1912; at this meeting, Moltke (Chief of the German General Staff) said: 'I believe war is unavoidable; war the sooner the better.' Fischer's claims made him unpopular with West German historians, and another German, H. W. Koch, dismissed his theory, pointing out that nothing came of the 'war council'. However, historians in Communist East Germany supported Fischer because his theory laid the blame on capitalists and the capitalist system, which they opposed.

2   Other historians emphasize the time factor involved: the Germans wanted war not only because they felt encircled, but because they felt that the net was closing in on them. They were threatened by superior British naval power and by the massive Russian military expansion. German army expansion was being hampered by opposition from the Reichstag which refused to sanction the necessary tax increases. On the other hand the Russians had been helped by huge loans from the French government. Von Jagow, who was German Foreign Minister at the outbreak of war, reported comments made earlier in 1914 in which Moltke stated that there was no alternative for the Germans but to make 'preventive' war in order to defeat their enemies before they became too powerful. The German generals had decided that a 'preventive' war, *a war for survival*, was necessary, and that it must take place before the end of 1914. They believed that if they waited longer than that, Russia would be too strong.

3   Some historians reject both points 1 and 2 and suggest that Germany did not want a major war at all; the Kaiser, Wilhelm II, and Chancellor Bethmann-Hollweg believed that if they took a strong line in support of Austria, that would *frighten the Russians into remaining neutral* – a tragic miscalculation, if true.

(g)   The mobilization plans of the great powers

Gerhard Ritter, a leading German historian, believed that the German plan for mobilization, known as the *Schlieffen Plan*, drawn up by Count von Schlieffen in 1905–6, was extremely risky and inflexible and deserved to be seen as the start of disaster both for

Germany and Europe. It gave the impression that Germany was being ruled by a band of unscrupulous militarists.

A. J. P. Taylor argued that these plans, based on precise railway timetables for the rapid movement of troops, accelerated the tempo of events and reduced almost to nil the time available for negotiation. The Schlieffen Plan assumed that France would automatically join Russia; the bulk of German forces were to be sent by train to the Belgian frontier, and through Belgium to attack France, which would be knocked out in six weeks. German forces would then be switched rapidly across Europe to face Russia, whose mobilization was expected to be slow. Once Moltke knew that Russia had ordered a general mobilization, he demanded immediate German mobilization so that the plan could be put into operation as soon as possible. However, Russian mobilization did not necessarily mean war – their troops could be halted at the frontiers; unfortunately the Schlieffen Plan, which depended on the rapid capture of Liège in Belgium, involved the first aggressive act outside the Balkans, when German troops crossed the frontier into Belgium on 4 August, thus violating Belgian neutrality. Almost at the last minute the Kaiser and Bethmann tried to avoid war and urged the Austrians to negotiate with Serbia (30 July), which perhaps supports point 3 above. Wilhelm suggested a partial mobilization against Russia only, instead of the full plan; he hoped that Britain would remain neutral if Germany refrained from attacking France. But Moltke, nervous of being left at the post by the Russians and French, insisted on the full Schlieffen Plan; he said there was no time to change all the railway timetables to send the troop trains to Russia instead of to Belgium. It looks as though *the generals had taken over control of affairs from the politicians*. It also suggests that a British announcement on 31 July of her intention to support France would have made no difference to Germany: it was the Schlieffen Plan or nothing, even though Germany at that point had no specific quarrel with France.

Doubt was cast on this theory by an American military expert and historian, Terence Zuber, in his book *Inventing the Schlieffen Plan* (2002). Using documents from the former East German military archive, he argued that the Schlieffen Plan was only one of at least five alternatives being considered by the German high command in the years after 1900. One alternative dealt with the possibility of a Russian attack at the same time as a French invasion; in this case the Germans would transfer considerable forces by train to the east while holding the French at bay in the west. Schlieffen actually carried out a military exercise to test this plan towards the end of 1905. Zuber concluded that Schlieffen never committed himself to just one plan: he thought war in the west would begin with a French attack and never intended that the Germans should send all their forces into France to destroy the French army in one huge battle. It was only after the war that the Germans tried to blame their defeat on the rigidity and the constraints of the so-called Schlieffen Plan, which had, in fact, never existed in the form they tried to make out.

(h)   A 'tragedy of miscalculation'

Another interpretation was put forward by Australian historian L. C. F. Turner. He suggested that the Germans may not have deliberately provoked war and that, in fact, war was not inevitable, and it should have been possible to reach agreement peacefully. The war was actually caused by a 'tragedy of miscalculation'. Most of the leading rulers and politicians seemed to be incompetent and made bad mistakes:

- The Austrians miscalculated by thinking that Russia would not support Serbia.
- Germany made a crucial mistake by promising to support Austria with no conditions attached; therefore the Germans were certainly guilty, as were the Austrians, because they risked a major war.

- Politicians in Russia and Germany miscalculated by assuming that mobilization would not necessarily mean war.
- If Ritter and Taylor are correct, this means that the generals, especially Moltke, miscalculated by sticking rigidly to their plans in the belief that this would bring a quick and decisive victory.

No wonder Bethmann, when asked how it all began, raised his arms to heaven and replied: 'Oh – if I only knew!'

Nevertheless, probably a majority of historians, including many Germans, accept Fritz Fischer's theory as the most convincing one: that the outbreak of war was deliberately provoked by Germany's leaders. For example, in *The Origins of World War I*, a collection of essays edited by Richard Hamilton and Holger H. Herwig (2002), the editors examine and reject most of the suggested causes of the war discussed above (alliance systems, mobilization plans, threat of socialism) and reach the conclusion that ultimate responsibility for the catastrophe probably rests with Germany. The Kaiser and his leading advisers and generals believed that time was running out for them as Russia's vast armament plans neared completion. It was a war to ensure survival, rather than a war to secure world domination, and it had to take place before Germany's position among the Great Powers deteriorated too far for the war to be won. Herwig argues that the German leaders gambled on a victorious war, even though they knew it was likely to last several years. As for world domination – that might well come later. In the words of Moltke, the Germans took this gamble in 1914 in order to fulfil 'Germany's preordained role in civilization', which could 'only be done by way of war'.

In 2007 a new collection of essays edited by Holger Afflerbach and David Stevenson appeared. Entitled *An Improbable War*, the book focused on the single issue: the degree of probability and inevitability in the outbreak of the conflict. Not surprisingly, no consensus was reached, but there was a clear leaning towards the view that in the circumstances that existed in 1914, war was certainly not inevitable, though it was possible. Some of the contributors moved in new directions. For example, Samuel Williamson, a leading expert on the Habsburg Empire, believes that the government in Vienna had not taken a decision to attack Serbia before the assassinations at Sarajevo, because they had other political priorities. Thus the murders of Franz Ferdinand and his wife really did provide the decisive moment: without that there would have been no decision for war in Vienna and therefore no general conflict. Nor does he believe that German pressure and promises of support were important – the Austrian leaders made their own decisions. Another contributor, John Rohl, was more traditional: he argues that the German leaders deliberately started the war and that Wilhelm II bears the main responsibility because of his duplicity and his recklessness.

It is also possible to argue that if Russia's rearmament was indeed making the Germans so nervous, then Russia should bear at least equal responsibility for the outbreak of war. This is the conclusion reached in a new analysis by historian William Mulligan in his book *The Origins of the First World War* (2010). He argues that Russia's defeat by Japan in 1905 had fatal consequences for the peace of Europe. It sparked off a revolution in Russia which severely weakened the government, and it forced the Russians to focus their foreign policies towards the Balkans instead of in the direction of the Far East. This foreign policy had two main aims: the desire for peace and the necessity of winning back their lost prestige. Until 1911 the desire for peace was paramount. But in that year the Russian leading minister, Pyotr Stolypin, who favoured peace, was assassinated, and the government began to succumb to the growing jingoistic public opinion which demanded that action should be taken to increase Russian prestige. Consequently, following the Balkan Wars of 1912 and 1913, in February 1914 the tsar promised to help the Serbs in the event of an attack by Austria–Hungary, and signed a naval agreement with Britain which, it was hoped, would help safeguard Russian access to the Mediterranean, if the Germans and Turks should ever try to block the Dardanelles. Mulligan argues that these new policies had 'a devastating impact on German foreign policy, bringing about an important shift in German thinking about the international system'. The naval agreement outraged the Germans, who saw it as a betrayal by the British; and the promise of backing for Serbia convinced the Germans that it was vital for them to support Austria–Hungary. Together with the vast Russian military expansion, all this was enough to galvanize the Germans into risking a war for survival, before Russia became any stronger. Perhaps the most sensible conclusion is that Germany, Russia and Austria–Hungary must both share the responsibility for the outbreak of war in 1914.

FURTHER READING

Afflerbach, H. and Stevenson, D. (eds), *An Improbable War? The Outbreak of World War One and Political Culture before 1914* (Berghahn, 2007).
Clark, C., *The Sleepwalkers: How Europe Went to War in 1914* (Allen Lane, 2012)
Fischer, F., *Germany's Aims in the First World War* (Norton, new edition, 2007).
Hall, R.C., *The Balkan Wars 1912-1913:Prelude to the First World War* (Routledge, 2000).
Hamilton, R. and Herwig, H. H., *The Origins of World War I* (Cambridge University Press, 2002).
Henig, R., *The Origins of the First World War* (Routledge, 3rd edition, 2001).
Mulligan, W., *The Origins of the First World War* (Cambridge University Press, 2010).
Strachan, H., *The First World War*, Vol. 1: *To Arms* (Oxford University Press, 2001).
Taylor, A. J. P., *The First World War* (Penguin, New Impression edition, 1974).
Turner, L. C. F., *Origins of the First World War* (Edward Arnold, 1970).
Zuber, T., *Inventing the Schlieffen Plan* (Oxford University Press, 2002).

QUESTIONS

1 Explain why relations between the European states were so full of tensions in the early years of the twentieth century.
2 How far would you agree that the arms race was only one of many causes of the First World War?
3 To what extent was Germany responsible for the outbreak of the First World War?

◣ There is a document question about Germany and the origins of the First World War on the website.

2

The First World War and its aftermath

SUMMARY OF EVENTS

The two opposing sides in the war were:

The Allies or Entente Powers:

Britain and her empire (including troops from Australia, Canada, India and New Zealand)
France
Russia (left December 1917)
Italy (entered May 1915)
Serbia
Belgium
Romania (entered August 1916)
USA (entered April 1917)
Japan

The Central Powers:

Germany
Austria–Hungary
Turkey (entered November 1914)
Bulgaria (entered October 1915)

The war turned out to be quite different from what most people had anticipated. It was widely expected to be a short, decisive affair, like other recent European wars – all over by Christmas 1914. This is why Moltke was so worried about being left at the post when it came to mobilization. However, the Germans failed to achieve the rapid defeat of France: although they penetrated deeply, Paris did not fall, and *stalemate quickly developed on the western front*, with all hope of a short war gone. Both sides dug themselves in and spent the next four years attacking and defending lines of trenches.

In eastern Europe there was more movement, with early Russian successes against the Austrians, who constantly had to be helped out by the Germans. This caused friction between Austrians and Germans. But by December 1917 the Germans had captured Poland (Russian territory) and forced the Russians out of the war. Britain, suffering heavy losses of merchant ships through submarine attacks, and France, whose armies were paralysed by mutiny, seemed on the verge of defeat. Gradually, however, the tide turned; the Allies, helped by the entry of the USA in April 1917, wore down the Germans, whose last despairing attempt at a decisive breakthrough in France failed in the spring of 1918. The success of the British navy in blockading German ports and defeating the submarine threat by defending convoys of merchant ships was also telling on the Germans. By late summer 1918 they were nearing exhaustion. *An armistice (ceasefire) was signed on 11 November*

1918, though Germany itself had hardly been invaded. A controversial peace settlement was signed at Versailles the following year.

2.1   1914

(a)   The western front

On the western front the German advance was held up by unexpectedly strong Belgian resistance; it took the Germans over two weeks to capture Brussels, the Belgian capital. This was an important delay because it gave the British time to organize themselves, and left the Channel ports free, enabling the British Expeditionary Force to land. Instead of sweeping round in a wide arc, capturing the Channel ports and approaching Paris from the west (as the Schlieffen Plan intended, if indeed the Germans *were* attempting to carry out the plan – see Section 1.4(g)), the Germans found themselves just east of Paris, making straight for the city. They penetrated to within twenty miles of Paris, and the French government withdrew to Bordeaux; but the nearer they got to Paris, the more the German impetus slowed up. There were problems in keeping the armies supplied with food and ammunition, and the troops became exhausted by the long marches in the August heat. In September the faltering Germans were attacked by the French under Joffre in *the Battle of the Marne* (see Map 2.1); they were driven back to the River Aisne, where they were able to dig trenches. *This battle was vitally important; some historians regard it as one of the most decisive battles in modern history*:

- It ruined the Schlieffen Plan once and for all: France would not be knocked out in six weeks, and all hopes of a short war were dashed.

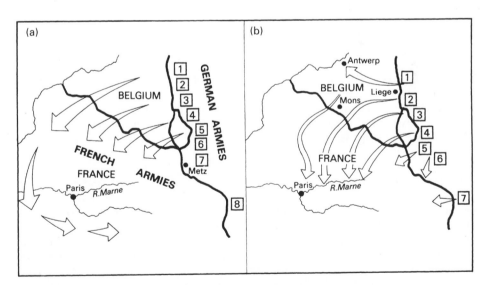

Map 2.1   **The Schlieffen Plan**

The Schlieffen Plan intended that the German right wing would move swiftly through Belgium to the coast, capture the Channel ports, and then sweep round in a wide arc to the west and south of Paris, almost surrounding the French armies – see (a). In practice, the Plan failed to work out. The Germans were held up by strong Belgian resistance; they failed to capture the Channel ports, failed to outflank the French armies, and were halted at the First Battle of the Marne – see (b).

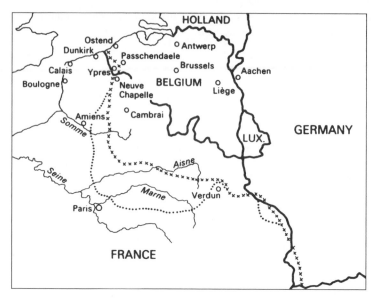

······ Limit of the German advance in 1914

×××××× The trench line for most of the war

Map 2.2   **The western front**

- The Germans would have to face full-scale war on two fronts, which they had probably never intended.
- The war of movement was over; the trench lines eventually stretched from the Alps to the Channel coast (see Map 2.2).
- There was time for the British navy to bring its crippling blockade to bear on Germany's ports.

The other important event of 1914 was that although the Germans captured Antwerp, the British Expeditionary Force held grimly on to Ypres. This probably saved the Channel ports of Dunkirk, Calais and Boulogne, making it possible to land and supply more British troops. Clearly the war was not going to be over by Christmas – it was settling down into a long, drawn-out struggle of attrition.

(b)   The eastern front

On the eastern front the Russians mobilized more quickly than the Germans expected, but then made the mistake of invading both Austria and Germany at the same time. Though they were successful against Austria, occupying the province of Galicia, the Germans brought Hindenburg out of retirement and defeated the Russians twice, at *Tannenburg* (August) and *the Masurian Lakes* (September), driving them out of Germany. *These battles were important*: the Russians lost vast amounts of equipment and ammunition, which had taken them years to build up. Although they had six and a quarter million men mobilized by the end of 1914, a third of them were without rifles. The Russians never recovered from this setback, whereas German self-confidence was boosted. When Turkey entered the war, the outlook for Russia was bleak, since Turkey could cut her main supply and trade route from the Black Sea into the Mediterranean (Map 2.3). One bright spot for

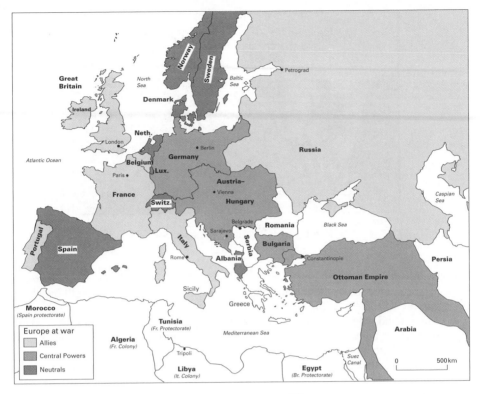

Map 2.3 **Europe at War**

the Allies was that the Serbs drove out an Austrian invasion in fine style at the end of 1914, and Austrian morale was at rock bottom.

2.2 1915

(a) Stalemate in the west

In the west the stalemate continued, though several attempts were made to break the trench line. The British tried at Neuve Chapelle and Loos, the French tried in Champagne; the Germans attacked again at Ypres. But, like all the attacks on the western front until 1918, these attempts failed to make a decisive breakthrough. *The difficulties of trench warfare were always the same*:

- There was barbed wire in no-man's land between the two lines of opposing trenches (Figure 2.1), which the attacking side tried to clear away by a massive artillery bombardment; but this removed any chance of a quick surprise attack since the enemy always had plenty of warning.
- Reconnaissance aircraft and observation balloons could spot concentrations of troops on the roads leading up to the trenches.
- Trenches were difficult to capture because the increased firepower provided by magazine rifles and machine-guns made frontal attacks suicidal and meant that cavalry were useless.

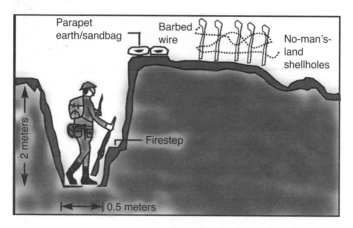

Figure 2.1   **Trench cross-section**

- Even when a trench line was breached, advance was difficult because the ground had been churned up by the artillery barrage and there was more deadly machine-gun fire to contend with.
- Any ground won was difficult to defend since it usually formed what was called a *salient* – a bulge in the trench line. The sides, or flanks, of these salients were vulnerable to attack, and troops could be surrounded and cut off.
- During the attack on Ypres in 1915, the Germans used poison gas, but when the wind changed direction it was blown back towards their own lines and they suffered more casualties then the Allies, especially when the Allies released some gas of their own.

(b)   The east

In the east, Russia's fortunes were mixed: they had further successes against Austria, but they met defeat whenever they clashed with the Germans, who captured Warsaw and the whole of Poland. The Turkish blockade of the Dardanelles was beginning to hamper the Russians, who were already running short of arms and ammunition. It was partly to clear the Dardanelles and open up the vital supply line to Russia via the Black Sea that the *Gallipoli Campaign* was launched. This was an idea strongly pressed by Winston Churchill (Britain's First Lord of the Admiralty) to escape from the deadlock in the west by eliminating the Turks. They were thought to be the weakest of the Central Powers because of their unstable government. Success against Turkey would enable help to be sent to Russia and might also bring Bulgaria, Greece and Romania into the war on the Allied side. It would then be possible to attack Austria from the south.

The campaign was a total failure; the first attempt, in March, an Anglo-French naval attack through the Dardanelles to capture Constantinople, failed when the ships ran into a series of mines. This ruined the surprise element, so that when the British attempted landings at the tip of the Gallipoli peninsula, the Turks had strengthened their defences and no advance could be made (April). Further landings by Australian and New Zealand troops (Anzacs) in April and by British troops in August were equally useless, and positions could only be held with great difficulty. In December the entire force was withdrawn. *The consequences were serious*: besides being a blow to Allied morale, it turned out to be the last chance of helping Russia via the Black Sea. It probably made Bulgaria decide to join the Central Powers. A Franco-British force landed at Salonika in neutral Greece to try and

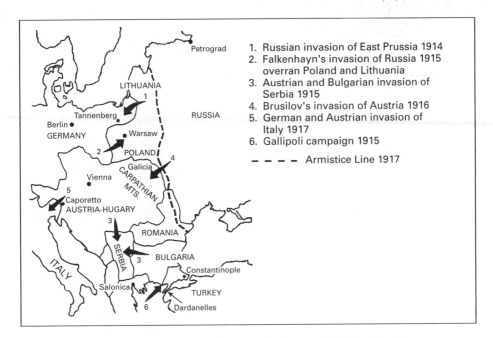

1. Russian invasion of East Prussia 1914
2. Falkenhayn's invasion of Russia 1915 overran Poland and Lithuania
3. Austrian and Bulgarian invasion of Serbia 1915
4. Brusilov's invasion of Austria 1916
5. German and Austrian invasion of Italy 1917
6. Gallipoli campaign 1915

– – – – Armistice Line 1917

Map 2.4   **War on the Eastern, Balkan and Italian Fronts**

relieve Serbia, but it was too late. When Bulgaria entered the war in October, Serbia was quickly overrun by Bulgarians and Germans (see Map 2.4). The year 1915 was therefore not a good one for the Allies; even a British army sent to protect Anglo-Persian oil interests against a possible Turkish attack became bogged down in Mesopotamia as it approached Baghdad; it was besieged by Turks at Kut-el-Amara from December 1915 until March 1916, when it was forced to surrender.

(c)   Italy declares war on Austria–Hungary (May 1915)

The Italians were hoping to seize Austria–Hungary's Italian-speaking provinces as well as territory along the eastern shore of the Adriatic Sea. *A secret treaty was signed in London* in which the Allies promised Italy Trentino, the south Tyrol, Istria, Trieste, part of Dalmatia, Adalia, some islands in the Aegean Sea and a protectorate over Albania. The Allies hoped that by keeping thousands of Austrian troops occupied, the Italians would relieve pressure on the Russians. But the Italians made little headway and their efforts were to no avail: the Russians were unable to stave off defeat.

2.3   1916

(a)   The western front

On the western front, 1916 is remembered for two terrible battles, *Verdun* and *the Somme*.

1   *Verdun* was an important French fortress town against which the Germans under Falkenhayn launched a massive attack (February). They hoped to draw all the best

French troops to its defence, destroy them and then carry out a final offensive to win the war. But the French under Pétain defended stubbornly, and in June the Germans had to abandon the attack. The French lost heavily (about 315 000 men), as the Germans intended, but so did the Germans themselves, with over 280 000 men killed and no territorial gains to show for it.

2 *The Battle of the Somme* was a series of attacks, mainly by the British, beginning on 1 July and lasting through to November. The aim was to relieve pressure on the French at Verdun, take over more of the trench line as the French army weakened, and keep the Germans fully committed, so that they would be unable to risk sending reinforcements to the eastern front against Russia. The attack began disastrously: British troops found themselves walking into deadly machine-gun fire; on the very first day 20 000 were killed and 60 000 injured. Yet Haig, the British Commander-in-Chief, did not call off the attack – it continued at intervals for over four months. At the end of it all, the Allies had made only limited advances varying between a few hundred yards and seven miles, along a 30-mile front. *The real importance of the battle was the blow to German morale*, as they realized that Britain (where conscription was introduced for the first time in May) was a military power to be reckoned with.

Losses on both sides, killed or wounded, were appalling (Germans 650 000; British 418 000; French 194 000). The Allied generals, especially Haig, came under severe criticism for persisting with suicidal frontal attacks. In spite of the failures and the appalling casualties, both British and French generals remained convinced that mass infantry charges – the 'big push' – were the only way to make a breakthrough. None of them showed any sign of producing alternative tactics, and tens of thousands of lives were sacrificed for no apparent gain. It was after one of the disastrous attacks in 1915 that a German officer remarked that the British army were 'lions led by donkeys'. Haig came in for the most serious criticism – for the majority of historians, he became the epitome of Allied incompetence and lack of imagination. One historian, W. J. Laffin, went so far as to call his book about the war *British Butchers and Bunglers of World War 1* (1988), and for him the chief 'donkey' was Haig. J. P. Harris, in *Douglas Haig and the First World War* (2008), is rather more balanced. He argues that Haig certainly found it difficult to cope with the unprecedented situation that he found himself in on the western front and he misjudged the strength of the German forces. He was slow to see beyond the tactic of the 'big push' and must therefore bear much of the responsibility for the massive casualties. However, he did eventually show himself to be receptive to new techniques and strategies and played a vital role in the 1918 campaign which brought the final collapse of German forces.

The horrors of the Somme also contributed to the fall of the British prime minister, Asquith, who resigned in 1916 after criticism of British tactics mounted. And yet the events of 1916 *did* contribute towards the eventual Allied victory; Hindenburg himself admitted in his memoirs that the Germans could not have survived many more campaigns with heavy losses like those at Verdun and the Somme.

(b)   David Lloyd George becomes British prime minister (December 1916)

Taking over from Asquith as prime minister, *Lloyd George's contribution to the Allied war effort and the defeat of the Central Powers was invaluable.* His methods were dynamic and decisive; already as Minister of Munitions since May 1915, he had improved the supply of shells and machine-guns, encouraged the development of new weapons (the Stokes light mortar and the tank), which Kitchener (Minister of War) had turned down, and taken control of mines, factories and railways so that the war effort could be properly centralized. As prime minister during 1917, he set up a small *war cabinet*, so that quick decisions could be taken. He brought shipping and agriculture under government control and introduced the Ministry of National Service to organize the mobilization of men into the army. He also played an important part in the adoption of the convoy system (see Section 2.4(e)).

(c) In the east

In June 1916 the Russians under Brusilov attacked the Austrians, in response to a plea from Britain and France for some action to divert German attention away from Verdun. They managed to break the front and advanced 100 miles, taking 400 000 prisoners and large amounts of equipment. The Austrians were demoralized, but the strain was exhausting the Russians as well. The Romanians invaded Austria (August), but the Germans swiftly came to the Austrians' rescue, occupied the whole of Romania and seized her wheat and oil supplies – not a happy end to 1916 for the Allies.

2.4 THE WAR AT SEA

The general public in Germany and Britain expected a series of naval battles between the rival Dreadnought fleets, something like the Battle of Trafalgar (1805), in which Nelson's British fleet had defeated the combined French and Spanish fleets. But both sides were cautious and dared not risk any action which might result in the loss of their main fleets. The British Admiral Jellicoe was particularly cautious; Churchill said he 'was the only man on either side who could have lost the war in an afternoon'. Nor were the Germans anxious for a confrontation, because they had only 16 of the latest Dreadnoughts against 27 British.

(a) The Allies aimed to use their navies in three ways

- to blockade the Central Powers, preventing goods from entering or leaving, slowly starving them out;
- to keep trade routes open between Britain, her empire and the rest of the world, so that the Allies themselves would not starve;
- to transport British troops to the continent and keep them supplied via the Channel ports.

The British were successful in carrying out these aims; they went into action against German units stationed abroad, and at the *Battle of the Falkland Islands*, destroyed one of the main German squadrons. By the end of 1914 nearly all German armed surface ships had been destroyed, apart from their main fleet (which did not venture out of the Heligoland Bight) and the squadron blockading the Baltic to cut off supplies to Russia. In 1915 the British navy was involved in the *Gallipoli Campaign* (see Section 2.2(b)).

(b) The Allied blockade caused problems

Britain was trying to prevent the Germans from using the neutral Scandinavian and Dutch ports to break the blockade; this involved *stopping and searching all neutral ships* and confiscating any goods suspected of being intended for enemy hands. The USA objected strongly to this, since they were anxious to continue trading with both sides.

(c)   The Germans retaliated with mines and submarine attacks

These tactics seemed to be the only alternative left to the Germans, since their surface vessels had either been destroyed or were blockaded in port. At first they respected neutral shipping and passenger liners, but it was soon clear that the German submarine (U-boat) blockade was not effective. This was partly because they had insufficient U-boats and partly because there were problems of identification: the British tried to fool the Germans by flying neutral flags and by using passenger liners to transport arms and ammunition. On 7 May 1915 the British liner *Lusitania* was sunk by a torpedo attack. In fact the *Lusitania* was armed and carrying vast quantities of weapons and ammunition, as the Germans knew; hence their claim that the sinking was not just an act of barbarism against defence-less civilians.

This had important consequences: out of almost two thousand dead, 128 were Americans. President Wilson therefore found that the USA would have to take sides to protect her trade. Whereas the British blockade did not interfere with the safety of passengers and crews, German tactics certainly did. For the time being, however, American protests caused Bethmann to tone down the submarine campaign, making it even less effective.

(d)   The Battle of Jutland (31 May 1916)

This was the main event at sea during 1916; it was the only time in the entire war that the main battle-fleets emerged and engaged each other; the result was indecisive. The German Admiral von Scheer tried to lure part of the British fleet out from its base so that that section could be destroyed by the numerically superior Germans. However, more British ships came out than he had anticipated, and after the two fleets had shelled each other on and off for several hours, the Germans decided to retire to base, firing torpedoes as they went. On balance, the Germans could claim that they had won the battle since they lost only 11 ships to Britain's 14. The real importance of the battle lay in the fact that *the Germans had failed to destroy British sea power*: the German High Seas Fleet stayed in Kiel for the rest of the war, leaving Britain's control of the surface complete. In desperation at the food shortages caused by the British blockade, the Germans embarked on 'unrestricted' submarine warfare, and this was to have fatal results for them.

(e)   'Unrestricted' submarine warfare (began January 1917)

As the Germans had been concentrating on the production of U-boats since the Battle of Jutland, this campaign was extremely effective. They attempted to sink all enemy and neutral merchant ships in the Atlantic; although they knew that this was likely to bring the USA into the war, they hoped that *Britain and France would be starved into surrender* before the Americans could make any vital contribution. They almost did it: the peak of German success came in April 1917, when 430 ships were lost; Britain was down to about six weeks' corn supply, and although the USA came into the war in April, it was bound to be several months before their help became effective. However, the situation was saved by Lloyd George, who insisted that the Admiralty adopt a convoy system. A convoy was a large number of merchant ships sailing together, so that they could be protected by escorting warships. This drastically reduced losses and meant that the German gamble had failed. *The submarine campaign was important because it brought the USA into the war.* The British navy therefore, helped by the Americans, played a vitally important role in the defeat of the Central Powers; by the middle of 1918 it had achieved its three aims.

2.5   1917

(a)   In the west

On the western front, 1917 was a year of Allied failure. A massive French attack in Champagne, under Nivelle, achieved nothing except mutiny in the French army, which was successfully sorted out by Pétain. From June to November the British fought *the Third Battle of Ypres*, usually remembered as *Passchendaele*, in appallingly muddy conditions; British casualties were again enormous – 324 000 compared with 200 000 Germans – for an advance of only four miles. More significant was *the Battle of Cambrai, which demonstrated that tanks, used properly, might break the deadlock of trench warfare.* Here, 381 massed British tanks made a great breach in the German line, but lack of reserves prevented the success from being followed up. However, the lesson had been observed, and *Cambrai became the model for the successful Allied attacks of 1918.* Meanwhile the Italians were heavily defeated by Germans and Austrians at Caporetto (October) and retreated in disorder. This rather unexpectedly proved to be an important turning point. Italian morale revived, perhaps because they were faced with having to defend their homeland against the hated Austrians. The defeat also led to the setting-up of an *Allied Supreme War Council.* The new French premier, Clemenceau, a great war leader in the same mould as Lloyd George, rallied the wilting French.

(b)   On the eastern front

Disaster struck the Allies when *Russia withdrew from the war (December 1917).* Continuous heavy losses at the hands of the Germans, lack of arms and supplies, problems of transport and communications and utterly incompetent leadership caused two revolutions (see Section 16.2), and the Bolsheviks (later known as communists), who took, over power in November, were willing to make peace. Thus in 1918 the entire weight of German forces could be thrown against the west; without the USA, the Allies would have been hard pressed. Encouragement was provided by the British capture of Baghdad and Jerusalem from the Turks, giving them control of vast oil supplies.

(c)   The entry of the USA (April 1917)

This was caused partly by the German U-boat campaign, and also by the discovery that Germany was trying to persuade Mexico to declare war on the USA, promising her Texas, New Mexico and Arizona in return. The Americans had hesitated about siding with the autocratic Russian government, but the overthrow of the tsar in the March revolution removed this obstacle. *The USA made an important contribution to the Allied victory*: they supplied Britain and France with food, merchant ships and credit, though actual military help came slowly. By the end of 1917 only one American division had been in action, but by mid-1918 over half a million men were involved. Most important were the psychological boost which the American potential in resources of men and materials gave the Allies, and the corresponding blow it gave to German morale.

2.6 THE CENTRAL POWERS DEFEATED

(a) The German spring offensive, 1918

This major German attack was launched by Ludendorff in a last, desperate attempt to win the war before too many US troops arrived, and before discontent in Germany led to revolution. It almost came off: throwing in all the extra troops released from the east, the Germans broke through on the Somme (March), and by the end of May were only 40 miles from Paris; the Allies seemed to be falling apart. However, under the overall command of the French Marshal Foch, they managed to hold on as the German advance lost momentum and created an awkward bulge.

(b) The Allied counter-offensive begins (8 August)

Launched near Amiens, the counter-attack involved hundreds of tanks attacking in short, sharp jabs at several different points along a wide front instead of massing on one narrow front. This forced the Germans to withdraw their entire line and avoided forming a salient. Slowly but surely the Germans were forced back until by the end of September the Allies had broken through the Hindenburg Line. Though Germany itself had not yet been invaded, Ludendorff was now convinced that they would be defeated in the spring of 1919. He insisted that the German government ask President Wilson of the USA for an armistice (ceasefire) (3 October). He hoped to get less severe terms based on Wilson's 14 Points (see Section 2.7(a)). By asking for peace in 1918 he would save Germany from invasion and preserve the army's discipline and reputation. Fighting continued for another five weeks while negotiations went on, but eventually *an armistice was signed on 11 November.*

(c) Why did the war last so long?

When the war started the majority of people on both sides believed that it would be over by Christmas. However, Britain's Secretary for War, Lord Kitchener, himself a successful general, told the cabinet, much to its collective dismay, that it would last nearer three years than three months. Though he did not live to see the end of the war (he was drowned in 1916 on his way to Russia, when his ship struck a mine and sank), he was one of the few who had judged the situation correctly. There are several reasons why the conflict lasted so long. The two sides were fairly evenly balanced, and although the main theatre of war was in Europe, it quickly became a global conflict. Other countries that had not been in the original alliance systems, decided to join in, some because they saw it as a chance to gain new territory, and others waited to see which side looked the more likely to win, and then joined that side. For example, Italy (May 1915), Romania (August 1916), the USA (April 1917) and Japan joined the Allied side, while Turkey (November 1914) and Bulgaria (October 1915) joined the Central Powers. To complicate matters further, troops from the British Empire – from India, Australia, New Zealand, Canada and South Africa – all played their part in the fighting, which eventually spread into the eastern Mediterranean, Asia and Africa.

The main countries involved in the war had very strongly held war aims which they were absolutely determined to achieve. The Germans, anxious to protect themselves from becoming 'encircled', aimed to take territory from Poland in the east and Belgium in the west to act as buffer zones against Russia and France. The French were obsessed with taking back Alsace-Lorraine, which the Germans had taken in 1871. The British would never allow Belgium, a country so near to their coast, to be controlled by a hostile power like Germany. Austria–Hungary was desperate to preserve its empire against the ambitions of Serbia. Right from the beginning these competing war aims meant that it would be almost impossible to reach an acceptable negotiated solution.

Once stalemate had been reached on the western front with troops bogged down in lines of trenches, the Allies were faced with difficult problems: the weapons available to the Central Powers as they defended their trenches were more deadly than those available to the attackers. German troops, using fixed machine-guns in trenches protected by barbed wire, had a huge advantage over the attackers, who relied too much on preceding artillery bombardments (see Section 2.2 for more about the problems of trench warfare). Another remarkable factor prolonging the war was the way in which propaganda helped to motivate and encourage the general public as well as the military on both sides. Morale was boosted and support for the war sustained by newspapers, posters, films and advertisements directed at all classes in society to make them proud of their own country and way of life, while spreading stories of horror and atrocity about the enemy. In Germany, in spite of food shortages, labour unrest and a general war-weariness, public support for the war continued. The defeat of Russia encouraged the German generals to continue the struggle and launch what turned out to be a last desperate attempt to break through on the western front in spring 1918, before too many American troops arrived on the scene. A combination of all these factors meant that there would have to be a fight to the finish until one side or the other was either overrun and occupied by the enemy, or was so completely exhausted that it could not carry on fighting.

(d) Why did the Central Powers lose the war?

The reasons can be briefly summarized:

1 Once the Schlieffen Plan had failed, removing all hope of a quick German victory, it was bound to be a strain for them, *facing war on two fronts*.

2 *Allied sea power was decisive*, enforcing the deadly blockade, which caused desperate food shortages among the civilian population and crippled exports, while at the same time making sure that the Allied armies were fully supplied.

3 The German submarine campaign failed in the face of *convoys* protected by British, American and Japanese destroyers; the campaign itself was a mistake because it brought the USA into the war.

4 The entry of the USA brought *vast new resources* to the Allies and made up for the departure of Russia from the war. It meant that the Allied powers were able to produce more war materials than the enemy, and in the end this proved decisive.

5 Allied political leaders at the critical time – Lloyd George and Clemenceau – were probably more competent than those of the Central Powers. The unity of command under Foch probably helped, while Haig learned lessons, from the 1917 experiences, which proved to be crucial to the allied victory in the final stages of the war. In fact some historians believe that the criticisms levelled at Haig are unfair. John Terraine was one of the first to present a defence of Haig, in his book *Douglas Haig: The Educated Soldier* (1963). Recently Gary Sheffield has gone further: in *The Chief: Douglas Haig and the British Army* (2011) he argues that, given the fact that the British had no experience of trench warfare, and that they were the junior partners to the French, Haig learned remarkably quickly and proved to be an imaginative commander. Haig made four outstanding contributions to the Allied victory. First, he took a leading part in reforming the army and preparing it for a major war before 1914. Then, between 1916 and 1918 he was responsible for transforming the

British Expeditionary Force from an inexperienced small force into a mass war-winning army. Thirdly, his battles in 1916 and 1917 (the Somme, Arras and Third Ypres), though his troops suffered heavy losses, played a vital role in wearing down the Germans, whose losses were also heavy. Finally Haig's generalship was a crucial component of the Allied victory in 1918. He had learned lessons about the effective use of tanks, and the avoidance of salients by using small groups of infantry attacking at different points along the trench line; his idea of transporting infantry in buses to accompany the cavalry was very effective. Eventually, too, there was a great improvement in the coordination between infantry, artillery and aerial observation. In the words of Gary Sheffield: 'Douglas Haig might not have been the greatest military figure Britain has ever produced, but he was one of the most significant – and one of the most successful.'

6   The continuous strain of heavy losses told on the Germans – they lost their best troops in the 1918 offensive and the new troops were young and inexperienced. At the same time the forces available to the Allies were increasing as more Americans arrived, bringing the total of American troops to around two million. From July 1918 onwards the Germans were forced into their final retreat. An epidemic of deadly Spanish flu added to their difficulties and morale was low as they retreated. Many suffered a psychological collapse: during the last three months of the war some 350 000 German troops actually surrendered.

7   Germany was badly let down by her allies and was constantly having to help out the Austrians and Bulgarians. The defeat of Bulgaria by the British (from Salonika) and Serbs (29 September 1918) was the final straw for many German soldiers, who could see no chance of victory now. When Austria was defeated by Italy at Vittorio-Veneto and Turkey surrendered (both in October), the end was near.

The combination of military defeat and dire food shortages produced a great war-weariness, leading to mutiny in the navy, destruction of morale in the army and revolution at home.

(e)   Effects of the war

The impact of the war was extraordinarily wide-ranging, which was not surprising given that it was the first 'total war' in history. This means that it involved not just armies and navies but entire populations, and it was the first big conflict between modern, industrialized nations. New methods of warfare and new weapons were introduced – tanks, submarines, bombers, machine-guns, heavy artillery and mustard gas. With so many men away in the armed forces, women had to take their places in factories and in other jobs which had previously been carried out by men. In the Central Powers and in Russia, the civilian populations suffered severe hardships caused by the blockades. In all the European states involved in the war, governments organized ordinary people as never before, so that the entire country was geared up to the war effort. The conflict caused a decline in Europe's prestige in the eyes of the rest of the world. The fact that the region which had been thought of as the centre of civilization could have allowed itself to experience such appalling carnage and destruction was a sign of the beginning of the end of European domination of the rest of the world. The effects on individual countries were sometimes little short of traumatic: the empires which had dominated central and eastern Europe for over two hundred years disappeared almost overnight.

1   The most striking effect of the war was the appalling death toll among the armed forces. Almost 2 million Germans died, 1.7 million Russians, 1.5 million French, over a million Austro-Hungarians and about one million from Britain and her

empire. Italy lost around 530 000 troops, Turkey 325 000, Serbia 322 000, Romania 158 000, the USA 116 000, Bulgaria 49 000 and Belgium 41 000. And this did not include those crippled by the war, and civilian casualties. A sizeable proportion of an entire generation of young men had perished – the 'lost generation'; France, for example, lost around 20 per cent of men of military age. However, military historian Dan Todman, in *The First World War: Myth and Memory* (2005), argues that as time has passed, the public perception of the war has changed. He produces evidence suggesting that the 'lost generation' interpretation is something of a myth. Certainly casualties were severe but were not the wholesale destruction of a generation that was claimed. According to Todman, overall, just 12 per cent of fighting men died. Although some 20 000 British soldiers were killed on the first day of the Battle of the Somme, this was not typical of the war as a whole. In the circumstances, Todman insists, Haig had no alternative – his was the only rational strategy, and in the end, whatever the criticisms, the war *was* won. Still, many find it difficult to put aside the long-held perception of the war as a 'futile mud- and bloodbath', and no doubt historians will continue to find it a controversial topic.

2   In Germany, hardship and defeat caused a revolution: the Kaiser Wilhelm II was compelled to abdicate and a republic was declared. Over the next few years the Weimar Republic (as it became known) experienced severe economic, political and social problems. In 1933 it was brought to an end when Hitler became German Chancellor (see Section 14.1).

3   The Habsburg Empire collapsed completely. The last emperor, Karl I, was forced to abdicate (November 1918) and the various nationalities declared themselves independent; Austria and Hungary split into two separate states.

4   In Russia the pressures of war caused two revolutions in 1917. The first (February–March) overthrew the tsar, Nicholas II, and the second (October–November) brought Lenin and the Bolsheviks (Communists) to power (see Sections 16.2–3).

5   Although Italy was on the winning side, the war had been a drain on her resources and she was heavily in debt. Mussolini took advantage of the government's unpopularity, to take over control – Italy was the first European state after the war to allow itself to fall under a fascist dictatorship (see Section 13.1).

6   On the other hand, some countries outside Europe, particularly Japan, China and the USA, took advantage of Europe's preoccupation with the war to expand their trade at Europe's expense. For example, the USA's share of world trade grew from 10 per cent in 1914 to over 20 per cent by 1919. Since they were unable to obtain European imports during the war, Japan and China began their own programmes of industrialization. During the 1920s the Americans enjoyed a great economic boom and their future prosperity seemed assured. Within a few years, however, it became clear that they had made the mistakes of over-confidence and over-expansion: in October 1929 the Wall Street Crash heralded the beginning of a severe economic crisis which spread throughout the world and became known as 'the Great Depression' (see Section 22.6).

7   Many politicians and leaders were determined that the horrors of the First World War should never be repeated. President Woodrow Wilson of the USA came up with a plan for a League of Nations, which would settle future disputes by arbitration and keep the world at peace through a system of 'collective security' (see Chapter 3). Unfortunately the job of the League of Nations was made more difficult by some of the terms of the peace settlement reached after the war, and the peace itself was unstable.

8   In his recent book *The Great War and the Making of the Modern World* (2011), Jeremy Black makes the point that the war led to the final stage of the partition of

Africa, when the peace settlement placed Germany's colonies in Africa under the control of the League of Nations. The League allowed them to be 'looked after' by various member states. This meant that in practice, for example, Britain acquired Tanganyika, while Britain and France divided Togoland and the Cameroons between them, and South Africa gained German South West Africa (Namibia).

2.7 THE PROBLEMS OF MAKING A PEACE SETTLEMENT

(a) War aims

When the war started, none of the participants had any specific ideas *about what they hoped to achieve*, except that Germany and Austria wanted to preserve the Habsburg Empire, and thought this required them to destroy Serbia. As the war progressed, some of the governments involved, perhaps to encourage their troops by giving them some clear objectives to fight for, began to list their *war aims*.

British prime minister Lloyd George mentioned (January 1918) the defence of democracy and the righting of the injustice done to France in 1871 when she lost Alsace and Lorraine to Germany. Other points were the restoration of Belgium and Serbia, an independent Poland, democratic self-government for the nationalities of Austria–Hungary, self-determination for the German colonies and an international organization to prevent war. He was also determined that Germany should pay reparations for all the damage they had done.

American President Woodrow Wilson stated US war aims in his *famous 14 Points* (January 1918):

1   abolition of secret diplomacy;
2   free navigation at sea for all nations in war and peace;
3   removal of economic barriers between states;
4   all-round reduction of armaments;
5   impartial adjustment of colonial claims in the interests of the populations concerned;
6   evacuation of Russian territory;
7   restoration of Belgium;
8   liberation of France and restoration of Alsace and Lorraine;
9   readjustment of Italian frontiers along the lines of nationality;
10 self-government for the peoples of Austria–Hungary;
11 Romania, Serbia and Montenegro to be evacuated and Serbia given access to the sea;
12 self-government for the non-Turkish peoples of the Turkish Empire and permanent opening of the Dardanelles;
13 an independent Poland with secure access to the sea;
14 a general association of nations to preserve peace.

These points achieved publicity when the Germans later claimed that they had expected the peace terms to be based on them, and that since this was not the case, they had been cheated.

(b)   Differing Allied views about how to treat the defeated powers

When the peace conference met (January 1919) it was soon obvious that a settlement would be difficult because of basic disagreements among the victorious powers:

1 *France* (represented by Clemenceau) wanted a harsh peace, to ruin Germany economically and militarily so that she could never again threaten French frontiers. Since 1814 the Germans had invaded France no fewer than five times. At all costs France's security must be secured.

2 *Britain* (Lloyd George) was in favour of a less severe settlement, enabling Germany to recover quickly so that she could resume her role as a major customer for British goods. Also, a flourishing German economy was vital if reparations were to be paid. However, Lloyd George had just won an election with slogans such as 'hang the Kaiser', and talk of getting from Germany 'everything that you can squeeze out of a lemon and a bit more'. The British public therefore expected a harsh peace settlement.

3 *The USA* (Woodrow Wilson) was in favour of a lenient peace, though he had been disappointed when the Germans ignored his 14 Points and imposed the harsh *Treaty of Brest–Litovsk* on Russia (see Section 16.3(b)). He wanted a just peace: although he had to accept British and French demands for *reparations* (compensation for damages) and *German disarmament*, he was able to limit reparations to losses caused to civilians and their property, instead of 'the whole cost of the war'. Wilson was also in favour of *self-determination*: nations should be freed from foreign rule and given *democratic governments of their own choice*.

By June 1919 the conference had come up with *the Treaty of Versailles for Germany*, followed by other treaties dealing with Germany's former allies. The Treaty of Versailles in particular was one of the most controversial settlements ever signed, and it was criticized even in the Allied countries on the grounds that it was too hard on the Germans, who were bound to object so violently that *another war was inevitable*, sooner or later. In addition, many of the terms, such as reparations and disarmament, proved *impossible to carry out*.

Illustration 2.1   **The three leaders at Versailles: (*left to right*) Clemenceau, Wilson and Lloyd George**

(a) The terms

1 *Germany had to lose territory in Europe*:

- Alsace–Lorraine to France;
- Eupen, Moresnet and Malmédy to Belgium;
- North Schleswig to Denmark (after a plebiscite, i.e. a vote by the people);
- West Prussia and Posen to Poland, though Danzig (the main port of West Prussia) was to be a free city under League of Nations administration, because its population was wholly German.
- Memel was given to Lithuania.
- The area known as the Saar was to be administered by the League of Nations for 15 years, when the population would be allowed to vote on whether it should belong to France or Germany. In the meantime, France was to have the use of its coal mines.
- Estonia, Latvia and Lithuania, which had been handed over to Germany by Russia by the Treaty of Brest–Litovsk, were taken away from Germany and set up as independent states. This was an example of *self-determination* being carried into practice.
- Union (*Anschluss*) between Germany and Austria was forbidden.

2 *Germany's African colonies were taken away* and became 'mandates' under League of Nations supervision: this meant that various member states of the League 'looked after' them.

3 *German armaments were strictly limited* to a maximum of 100 000 troops and no conscription (compulsory military service), no tanks, armoured cars, military aircraft or submarines, and only six battleships. The Rhineland was to be permanently demilitarized. This meant that all German territory on the left bank of the Rhine, together with a 50-kilometre strip on the right bank, was to be closed to German troops and was to be occupied by Allied troops for at least ten years.

4 *The War Guilt clause* fixed the blame for the outbreak of the war solely on Germany and her allies and proposed that the ex-Kaiser should be put on trial for war crimes.

5 *Germany was to pay reparations* for damage done to the Allies; the actual amount was not decided at Versailles, but it was announced later (1921), after much argument and haggling, as £6600 million.

6 *A League of Nations* was formed; its aims and organization were set out in the *League Covenant* (see Chapter 3).

The Germans had little choice but to sign the treaty, though they objected strongly. The signing ceremony took place in the Hall of Mirrors at Versailles, where the German Empire had been proclaimed less than 50 years earlier.

(b) Why did the Germans object, and how far were their objections justified?

1 It was a dictated peace
The Germans were not allowed into the discussions at Versailles; they were simply presented with the terms and told to sign. Although they were allowed to criticize the

treaty in writing, all their criticisms were ignored except one (see Point 3 below). Some historians feel that the Germans were justified in objecting, and that it would have been reasonable to allow them to take part in the discussions. This might have led to a toning-down of some of the harsher terms. It would certainly have deprived the Germans of the argument much used by Hitler, that because the peace was a 'Diktat', it should not be morally binding. On the other hand, it is possible to argue that the Germans could scarcely have expected any better treatment after the harsh way they had dealt with the Russians at Brest–Litovsk – also a 'Diktat' (see Section 16.3(b)).

2 Many provisions were not based on the 14 Points

The Germans claimed that they had been promised terms based on Wilson's 14 Points, and that *many of the provisions were not based on the 14 Points*, and were therefore a swin-dle. This is probably not a valid objection: the 14 Points had never been accepted as offi-cial by any of the states involved, and the Germans themselves had ignored them in January 1918, when there still seemed a chance of outright German victory. By November, German tactics (Brest–Litovsk, the destruction of mines, factories and public buildings during their retreat through France and Belgium) had hardened the Allied attitude and led Wilson to add *two further points*: Germany should pay for the damage to civilian popula-tion and property, and should be reduced to 'virtual impotence'; in other words, Germany should be disarmed. The Germans were aware of this when they accepted the armistice, and, in fact, most of the terms did comply with the 14 Points and the additions.

There were also objections on specific points:

3 Loss of territory in Europe

This included Alsace–Lorraine and especially West Prussia, which gave Poland access to the sea. However, both were mentioned in the 14 Points. Originally Upper Silesia, an industrial region with a mixed population of Poles and Germans, was to be given to Poland, but this was the one concession made to the German written objections: after a vote among the population, Germany was allowed to keep about two-thirds of the area. In fact most of the German losses could be justified on grounds of nationality (Map 2.5). Where the Germans did have genuine cause for protest was on the question of national self-determination. Right from the start of the peace conference the Allies had emphasized that all nationalities should have the right to choose which country they wanted to belong to. This principle had been applied in the case of non-Germans; but the settlement left around a million Germans under Polish rule, and almost three million in the Sudetenland controlled by the new state of Czechoslovakia. In addition, Austria was a completely German state with a population of some seven million. All these Germans wanted to become part of Germany, but the unification of Germany and Austria was specifically forbidden in the agreement, probably because that would have made Germany larger and more powerful even than in 1914.

4 Loss of Germany's African colonies

The Germans probably had good grounds for objection to the loss of their African colonies, which was hardly an 'impartial adjustment'. The mandate system allowed Britain to take over German East Africa (Tanganyika) and parts of Togoland and the Cameroons, France to take most of Togoland and the Cameroons, and South Africa to acquire German South West Africa (now known as Namibia); but this was really a device by which the Allies seized the colonies without actually admitting that they were being annexed (Map 2.6).

5 The disarmament clauses were deeply resented

The Germans claimed that 100 000 troops were not enough to keep law and order at a time of political unrest. Perhaps the German objection was justified to some extent, though the

| Territory lost by Germany | Former territory of tsarist Russia | Austria-Hungary until 1918 |

●●●●●●●●●●●●● Curzon Line – proposed by Britain (Dec. 1919) as Poland's eastern frontier. Russian territory east of the line was seized by Poland in 1920

Map 2.5 **European frontiers after the First World War and the Peace Treaties**

≡≡≡ German colonies taken away as mandates by the
≡≡≡ Versailles Treaty, 1919

Map 2.6 **Africa and the Peace Treaties**

French desire for a weak Germany was understandable. The Germans became more aggrieved later, as it became clear that none of the other powers intended to disarm, even though Wilson's Point 4 mentioned 'all-round reduction of armaments'. However, disarmament of Germany was impossible to enforce fully, because the Germans were determined to exploit every loophole.

6 'The War Guilt' clause (Article 231)
The Germans objected to being saddled with the entire blame for the outbreak of war. There are some grounds for objection here, because although later research seems to indicate Germany's guilt, it was hardly possible to arrive at that conclusion in the space of six weeks during 1919, which is what the Special Commission on War Responsibility did. However, the Allies wanted the Germans to admit responsibility so that they would be liable to pay reparations.

7 Reparations

Reparations were the final humiliation for the Germans. Though there could be little valid objection to the general principle of reparations, many historians now agree that the actual amount decided on was far too high at £6600 million. Some people thought so at the time, including J. M. Keynes, who was an economic adviser to the British delegation at the conference. He urged the Allies to take £2000 million, which he said was a more reasonable amount, which Germany would be able to afford. The figure of £6600 million enabled the Germans to protest that it was impossible to pay, and they soon began to default (fail to pay) on their annual instalments. This caused resentment among the Allies, who were relying on German cash to help them pay their own war debts to the USA. There was international tension when France tried to force the Germans to pay (see Section 4.2(c)). Eventually the Allies admitted their mistake and reduced the amount to £2000 million (*Young Plan, 1929*), but not before reparations had proved disastrous, both economically and politically.

The Germans clearly did have some grounds for complaint, but it is worth pointing out that the treaty could have been even more harsh. If Clemenceau had had his way, the Rhineland would have become an independent state, and France would have annexed the Saar.

2.9 THE PEACE TREATIES WITH AUSTRIA–HUNGARY

When Austria was on the verge of defeat in the war, *the Habsburg Empire disintegrated* as the various nationalities declared themselves independent. Austria and Hungary separated and declared themselves republics. Many important decisions therefore had already been taken before the peace conference met. However, the situation was chaotic, and the task of the conference was *to formalize and recognize what had taken place.*

(a) The Treaty of St Germain (1919), dealing with Austria

By this treaty Austria lost:

- Bohemia and Moravia (wealthy industrial provinces with a population of 10 million) to the new state of Czechoslovakia;
- Dalmatia, Bosnia and Herzegovina to Serbia, which, with Montenegro, now became known as Yugoslavia;
- Bukovina to Romania;
- Galicia to the reconstituted state of Poland;
- the South Tyrol (as far as the Brenner Pass), Trentino, Istria and Trieste to Italy.

(b) The Treaty of Trianon (1920), dealing with Hungary

This treaty was not signed until 1920 because of political uncertainties in Budapest (the capital); the Communists, led by Béla Kun, seized power but were later overthrown.

- Slovakia and Ruthenia were given to Czechoslovakia;
- Croatia and Slovenia to Yugoslavia;
- Transylvania and the Banat of Temesvar to Romania.

Both treaties contained the League of Nations Covenant.

These settlements may seem harsh, but it has to be remembered that much of what was agreed had already happened; on the whole they did keep to the spirit of self-determination. More people were placed under governments of their own nationality than ever before in Europe, though they were not always as democratic as Wilson would have liked (especially in Hungary and Poland). However, there were some deviations from the pattern; for example the three million Germans (in the Sudetenland) who now found themselves in Czechoslovakia, and the million Germans who were placed under Polish rule. The Allies justified this on the grounds that the new states needed them in order to be economically viable. It was unfortunate that both these cases gave Hitler an excuse to begin territorial demands on these countries.

The treaties left both Austria and Hungary with serious economic problems

Austria was a small republic, its population reduced from 22 million to 6.5 million; most of its industrial wealth had been lost to Czechoslovakia and Poland. Vienna, once the capital of the huge Habsburg Empire, was left high and dry, surrounded by farming land which could hardly support it. Not surprisingly, Austria was soon facing a severe economic crisis and was constantly having to be helped out by loans from the League of Nations. Hungary was just as badly affected, her population reduced from 21 million to 7.5 million, and some of her richest corn land lost to Romania. Matters were further complicated when all the new states quickly introduced tariffs (import and export duties). These hampered the flow of trade through the whole Danube area and made the industrial recovery of Austria particularly difficult. In fact there was an excellent economic case to support a union between Austria and Germany.

2.10   THE SETTLEMENT WITH TURKEY AND BULGARIA

(a)   The Treaty of Sèvres (1920), dealing with Turkey

Turkey was to lose Eastern Thrace, many Aegean islands and Smyrna to Greece; Adalia and Rhodes to Italy; the Straits (the exit from the Black Sea) were to be permanently open; Syria became a French mandate, and Palestine, Iraq and Transjordan British mandates. However, the loss of so much territory to Greece, especially Smyrna on the Turkish mainland, outraged Turkish national feeling (self-determination was being ignored in this case). Led by Mustafa Kemal, the Turks rejected the treaty and chased the Greeks out of Smyrna. The Italians and French withdrew their occupying forces from the Straits area, leaving only British troops at Chanak. Eventually a compromise was reached and the settlement was revised by the *Treaty of Lausanne* (1923), by which Turkey regained Eastern Thrace including Constantinople, and Smyrna (Map 2.7). Turkey was therefore the first state to challenge the Paris settlement successfully. One legacy of the Treaty of Sèvres which was to cause problems later was the situation in the mandates. These were peopled largely by Arabs, who had been hoping for independence as a reward after their brave struggle, led by an English officer, T. E. Lawrence (Lawrence of Arabia), against the Turks. Nor were the Arabs happy about the talk of establishing a Jewish 'national home' in Palestine (see Section 11.2(a)).

(b)   The Treaty of Neuilly (1919), dealing with Bulgaria

Bulgaria lost territory to Greece, depriving her of her Aegean coastline, and also to Yugoslavia and Romania. She could claim, with some justification, that at least a million Bulgars were under foreign governments as a result of the Treaty of Neuilly.

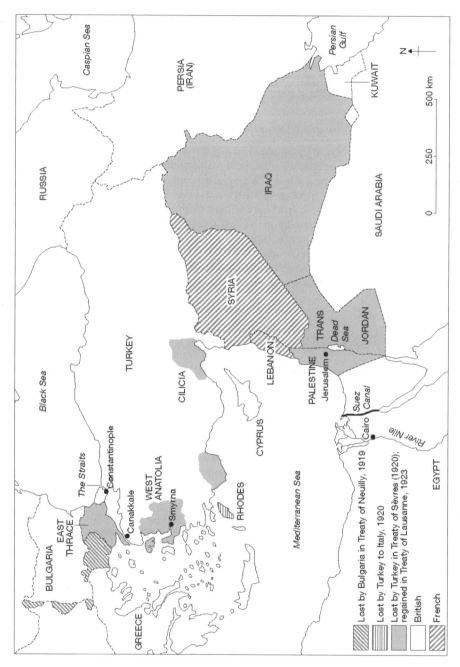

Map 2.7 **The treatment of Turkey (Treaty of Sèvres) and Bulgaria (Treaty of Neuilly)**

Lost by Bulgaria in Treaty of Neuilly, 1919

Lost by Turkey to Italy, 1920

Lost by Turkey in Treaty of Sèvres (1920); regained in Treaty of Lausanne, 1923

British

French

In conclusion, it has to be said that this collection of peace treaties *was not a conspicuous success*. It had the unfortunate effect of dividing Europe into the states which wanted to revise the settlement (Germany being the main one), and those which wanted to preserve it. On the whole the latter turned out to be only lukewarm in their support. The USA failed to ratify the settlement (see Section 4.5) and never joined the League of Nations. This in turn left France completely disenchanted with the whole thing because the Anglo-American guarantee of her frontiers given in the agreement could not now apply. Italy felt cheated because she had not received all the territory promised her in 1915, and Russia was ignored, because the powers did not want to negotiate with its Bolshevik government.

Germany, on the other hand, was only temporarily weakened and was soon strong enough to challenge certain of the terms. In fact it is possible to argue that Germany was weakened less than her enemies. Much of France, Poland and the Balkans had been ravaged by occupying troops, whereas German territory was virtually untouched. After all, no enemy troops had set foot on German soil and not surprisingly it was soon widely accepted in Germany that their armies had not been defeated. Returning German soldiers were welcomed back as heroes, fresh and undefeated from the battlefield. German industry was able to switch back to peacetime production remarkably quickly, and by 1921 was producing three times as much steel as France.

All this tended to sabotage the settlement from the beginning, and it became increasingly difficult to apply the terms fully. Clearly, since Germany was still the strongest power in Europe economically, the great failing of the peace settlement was that it left the Germans with a sense of resentment and grievance, but did not leave them too weak to retaliate and seek revenge. These weaknesses were widely recognized at the time, even among allied delegates at the conference. Harold Nicolson, a British diplomat at the conference, wrote: 'If I were the Germans, I shouldn't sign for a moment.' John Maynard Keynes, a senior British delegate and economic adviser, was so disillusioned with the way things were going that he resigned in protest and came home. But it is easy to criticize after the event; Gilbert White, one of the American delegates, put it well when he remarked that, given the intricacy of the problems involved, 'it is not surprising that they made a bad peace: what is surprising is that they managed to make peace at all'. With the availability of new sources, many historians find themselves in sympathy with this assessment, and argue that the settlement can now be seen 'as a workable compromise', and perhaps the best that could have been achieved under difficult circumstances. True, there were some mistakes, but the peacemakers cannot be blamed for Hitler's rise to power, and certainly not for the Second World War. For example P. M. H. Bell, in his book *Origins of the Second World War in Europe* (2007), argues that in the early 1920s, Europe, including Germany, was beginning to recover well from the after-effects of the war. The tragedy was that 'the outline of a successful European recovery was cut off in its prime by the great depression and its dreadful consequence, the advent of Hitler'.

FURTHER READING

Beckett, I. F. W., *The Great War, 1914–1918* (Longman, 2000).

Black, J., *The Great War and the Making of the Modern World* (Continuum, 2010).

Harris, J. P., *Douglas Haig and the First World War* (Cambridge University Press, 2008).

Laffin, W. J., *British Butchers and Bunglers of World War 1* (Alan Sutton, 1988).

Macfie, A. L., *The End of the Ottoman Empire* (Longman, 1998).

Palmer, A., *Twilight of the Habsburgs* (Weidenfeld & Nicolson, 1994).

Sharp, A., *The Versailles Settlement: Peacemaking in Paris, 1919* (Palgrave Macmillan, 2008).

Sheffield, G., *Forgotten Victory: The First World War, Myth and Realities* (Headline, 2001).

Sheffield, G., *The Chief: Douglas Haig and the British Army* (Aurum Press, 2011).

Stevenson, D., *1914–1918: The History of the First World War* (Penguin, 2005).

Stevenson, D., *With Our Backs To The Wall: Victory and Defeat in 1918* (Allen Lane, 2011).

Watson, A., *Enduring the Great War: Combat, Morale and Collapse in the German and British Armies, 1914–1918* (Cambridge University Press, 2008).

QUESTIONS

1 Assess the reasons why the First World War was not 'over by Christmas' 1914.
2 Explain why the 1919 Peace Settlement provoked so much opposition among the Germans.
3 To what extent was the Paris Peace Settlement shaped by the principle of self-determination?

◤ There is a document question about the First World War on the website.

Chapter 3

The League of Nations

The League of Nations formally came into existence on 10 January 1920, the same day that the Versailles Treaty came into operation. With headquarters in Geneva in Switzerland, one of its main aims was to settle international disputes before they got out of hand, and so prevent war from ever breaking out again. After some initial teething troubles, the League seemed to be functioning successfully during the 1920s; it solved a number of minor international disputes, as well as achieving valuable economic and social work; for instance, it helped thousands of refugees and former prisoners of war to find their way home again. In 1930 supporters of the League felt optimistic about its future; the South African statesman Jan Smuts was moved to remark that 'we are witnessing one of the great miracles of history'. However, during the 1930s the authority of the League was challenged several times, first by the Japanese invasion of Manchuria (1931) and later by the Italian attack on Abyssinia (1935). Both aggressors ignored the League's orders to withdraw, and for a variety of reasons it proved impossible to force them to comply. After 1935, respect for the League declined as its weaknesses became more apparent. During Germany's disputes with Czechoslovakia and Poland, which led on to the Second World War, the League was not even consulted, and it was unable to exert the slightest influence to prevent the outbreak of war. After December 1939 it did not meet again, and it was dissolved in 1946 – a complete failure, at least as far as preventing war was concerned.

3.1 WHAT WERE THE ORIGINS OF THE LEAGUE?

The League is often spoken of as being the brainchild of the American President Woodrow Wilson. Although Wilson was certainly a great supporter of the idea of an international organization for peace, the League was the result of a coming together of similar suggestions made during the First World War, by a number of world statesmen. Lord Robert Cecil of Britain, Jan Smuts of South Africa and Leon Bourgeois of France put forward detailed schemes showing how such an organization might be set up. Lloyd George referred to it as one of Britain's war aims, and Wilson included it as the last of his 14 Points (see Section 2.7(a)). Wilson's great contribution was to insist that the League Covenant (the list of rules by which the League was to operate), which had been drawn up by an international committee including Cecil, Smuts, Bourgeois and Paul Hymans (of Belgium) as well as Wilson himself, should be included in each of the separate peace treaties. This ensured that the League actually came into existence instead of merely remaining a topic for discussion.

The League had two main aims:

- To maintain peace through **collective security**: if one state attacked another, the member states of the League would act together, collectively, to restrain the aggressor, either by economic or by military sanctions.
- To encourage **international co-operation**, in order to solve economic and social problems.

3.2 HOW WAS THE LEAGUE ORGANIZED?

There were 42 member states at the beginning and 55 by 1926 when Germany was admitted. It had five main organs.

(a) The General Assembly

This met annually and contained representatives of all the member states, each of which had one vote. Its function was to decide general policy; it could, for example, propose a revision of peace treaties, and it handled the finances of the League. Any decisions taken had to be unanimous. One of the advantages of the League Assembly was that it gave small and medium-sized states a chance to raise issues that concerned them and have their say on world developments.

(b) The Council

This was a much smaller body, which met more often, at least three times a year, and contained four permanent members – Britain, France, Italy and Japan. The USA was to have been a permanent member but decided not to join the League. There were four other members, elected by the Assembly for periods of three years. The number of non-permanent members had increased to nine by 1926. It was the Council's task to deal with specific political disputes as they arose; again, decisions had to be unanimous.

(c) The Permanent Court of International Justice

This was based at the Hague in Holland and consisted of 15 judges of different nationalities; it dealt with legal disputes between states, as opposed to political ones. It started to function in 1922 and by 1939 it had dealt successfully with 66 cases, winning respect for the idea that there was a place for a generally accepted code of legal practice in international politics.

(d) The Secretariat

This looked after all the paperwork, preparing agendas, and writing resolutions and reports so that the decisions of the League could be carried out. This acted as a sort of international civil service whose members came from over 30 different countries. Like the Court of Justice, the Secretariat won respect for the high quality of its organisation and administration.

(e) Commissions and committees

A number of these were formed to deal with specific problems, some of which had arisen from the First World War. The main commissions were those which handled the mandates, military affairs, minority groups and disarmament. There were committees for international labour, health, economic and financial organization, child welfare, drug problems and women's rights.

The main function of the League was meant to be **peacekeeping.** It was intended that it would operate in the following way: all disputes threatening war would be submitted to the League, and any member which resorted to war, thus breaking the Covenant, *would face collective action by the rest*. The Council would recommend 'what effective military, naval or air force the members should contribute to the armed forces'.

3.3 SUCCESSES OF THE LEAGUE

(a) It would be unfair to dismiss the League as a total failure

Many of the committees and commissions achieved valuable results and much was done to foster international co-operation. One of most successful was *the International Labour Organization (ILO)* under its French socialist director, Albert Thomas. Its purpose was to improve conditions of labour all over the world by persuading governments to:

- fix a maximum working day and week;
- specify adequate minimum wages;
- introduce sickness and unemployment benefit;
- introduce old-age pensions.

It collected and published a vast amount of information, and many governments were prevailed upon to take action.

The Refugee Organization, led by Fridtjof Nansen, a Norwegian explorer, solved the problem of thousands of former prisoners of war marooned in Russia at the end of the war; about half a million were returned home. After 1933, valuable help was given to thousands of people fleeing from the Nazi persecution in Germany.

The Health Organization did good work in investigating the causes of epidemics, and it was especially successful in combating a typhus epidemic in Russia, which at one time seemed likely to spread across Europe.

The Mandates Commission supervised the government of the territories taken from Germany and Turkey, while yet another commission was responsible for administering the Saar. It did this very efficiently, and concluded by organizing the 1935 plebiscite in which a large majority voted for the Saar to be returned to Germany.

Not all were successful, however; *the Disarmament Commission* made no progress in the near-impossible task of persuading member states to reduce armaments, even though they had all promised to do so when they agreed to the Covenant.

(b) Political disputes resolved

Several political disputes were referred to the League in the early 1920s. *In all but two cases, the League's decisions were accepted.*

- In the quarrel between Finland and Sweden over *the Aaland Islands*, the verdict went in favour of Finland (1920).
- Over the rival claims of Germany and Poland to the important industrial area of *Upper Silesia*, the League decided that it should be partitioned (divided) between the two (1921).
- When *the Greeks invaded Bulgaria*, after some shooting incidents on the frontier, the League swiftly intervened: Greek troops were withdrawn and damages were paid to Bulgaria.
- When *Turkey claimed the province of Mosul*, part of the British mandated territory of Iraq, the League decided in favour of Iraq.
- Further afield, in South America, squabbles were settled between *Peru and Colombia* and between *Bolivia and Paraguay*.

It is significant, however, that none of these disputes seriously threatened world peace, and none of the decisions went against a major state that might have challenged the League's verdict. In fact, during this same period, *the League found itself twice overruled by the Conference of Ambassadors, based in Paris*, which had been set up to deal with problems arising out of the Versailles Treaties. There were first the rival claims of Poland and Lithuania to Vilna (1920), followed by *the Corfu Incident* (1923); this was a quarrel between Mussolini's Italy and Greece. The League made no response to these acts of defiance, and this was not a promising sign.

3.4 WHY DID THE LEAGUE FAIL TO PRESERVE PEACE?

At the time of the Corfu Incident in 1923 (see (d) below), many people wondered what would happen if a powerful state were to challenge the League on a matter of major importance, for example, by invading an innocent country. How effective would the League be then? The former British prime minister, Lord Balfour, remarked: 'The danger I see in the future is that some powerful nation will pursue a realpolitik ... as in the past. I do not believe we have yet found, or can find, a perfect guarantee against such a calamity.' Unfortunately several such challenges occurred during the 1930s, and on every occasion the League was found wanting.

(a) It was too closely linked with the Versailles Treaties

This initial disadvantage made the League seem like an organization created especially for the benefit of the victorious powers. In addition it had to defend a peace settlement which was far from perfect. It was inevitable that some of its provisions would cause trouble – for example, the disappointing territorial gains of the Italians and the inclusion of Germans in Czechoslovakia and Poland.

(b) It was rejected by the USA

The League was dealt a serious blow in March 1920 when the US Senate rejected both the Versailles settlement and the League. The reasons behind their decision were varied (see Section 4.5). The absence of the USA meant that the League was deprived of a powerful member whose presence would have been of great psychological and financial benefit.

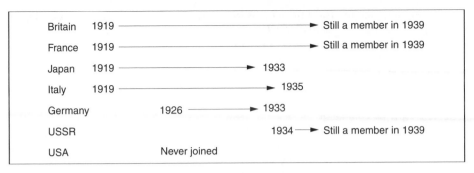

Figure 3.1   **Great power membership of the League of Nations**

(c)   Other important powers were not involved

Germany was not allowed to join until 1926 and the USSR only became a member in 1934 (when Germany left). So for the first few years of its existence the League was deprived of three of the world's most important powers (see Figure 3.1).

(d)   The Conference of Ambassadors in Paris was an embarrassment

This gathering of leading ambassadors was only intended to function until the League machinery was up and running, but it lingered on, and on several occasions it took precedence over the League.

- In 1920 the League supported Lithuania in her claim to Vilna, which had just been seized from her by the Poles; but when the Conference of Ambassadors insisted on awarding Vilna to Poland, the League allowed it to go ahead.
- A later example was *the Corfu Incident* (1923): this arose from a boundary dispute between Greece and Albania, in which three Italian officials working on the boundary commission were killed. Mussolini blamed the Greeks, demanded huge compensation and bombarded and occupied the Greek island of Corfu. Greece appealed to the League, but *Mussolini refused to recognize its competence to deal with the problem.* He threatened to withdraw Italy from the League, whereupon the Ambassadors ordered Greece to pay the full amount demanded.

At this early stage, however, supporters of the League dismissed these incidents as teething troubles.

(e)   There were serious weaknesses in the Covenant

These made it difficult to ensure that decisive action was taken against any aggressor. It was difficult to get unanimous decisions; the League had no military force of its own, and though Article 16 expected member states to supply troops if necessary, a resolution was passed in 1923 that each member would decide for itself whether or not to fight in a crisis. This clearly made nonsense of the idea of collective security. Several attempts were made to strengthen the Covenant, but these failed because a unanimous vote was needed to change it, and this was never achieved. The most notable attempt was made in 1924 by the

British Labour prime minister, Ramsay MacDonald, a great supporter of the League. He introduced a resolution known as *the Geneva Protocol*. This pledged members to accept arbitration and help any victim of unprovoked aggression. With supreme irony, the Conservative government which followed MacDonald informed the League that they could not agree to the Protocol; they were reluctant to commit Britain and the Empire to the defence of all the 1919 frontiers. A resolution proposed by one British government was thus rejected by the next British government, and the League was left, as its critics remarked, still 'lacking teeth'.

Reasons for this apparently strange British attitude include the fact that British public opinion was strongly pacifist, and there was a feeling that Britain was now so militarily weak that armed interventions of any sort should be avoided. Many other League members felt the same as Britain; and so, perversely, they were all basing their security on a system whose success relied on their support and commitment, but which they were not prepared to uphold. The attitude seemed to be: leave it to the others.

(f)   It was very much a French/British affair

The continued absence of the USA and the USSR, plus the hostility of Italy, made the League very much a French/British affair. But as their rejection of the Geneva Protocol showed, the British Conservatives were never very enthusiastic about the League. They preferred to sign *the Locarno Treaties* (1925), outside the League, instead of conducting negotiations within it (see Section 4.1(e)).

None of these weaknesses necessarily doomed the League to failure, however, provided all the members were prepared to refrain from aggression and accept League decisions; between 1925 and 1930 events ran fairly smoothly.

(g)   The world economic crisis began in 1929

The situation really began to drift out of control with the onset of the economic crisis, or the Great Depression, as it was sometimes known. It brought unemployment and falling living standards to most countries, and caused extreme right-wing governments to come to power in Japan and Germany; together with Mussolini, they refused to keep to the rules and took a series of actions which revealed the League's weaknesses (points (h), (i) and (j)).

(h)   The Japanese invasion of Manchuria (1931)

In 1931 Japanese troops invaded the Chinese territory of Manchuria (see Section 5.1); China appealed to the League, which condemned Japan and ordered her troops to be withdrawn. When Japan refused, the League appointed a commission under Lord Lytton, which decided (1932) that there were faults on both sides and suggested that Manchuria should be governed by the League. However, Japan rejected this and withdrew from the League (March 1933). The question of economic sanctions, let alone military ones, was never even raised, because Britain and France had serious economic problems. They were reluctant to apply a trade boycott of Japan in case it led to war, which they were ill-equipped to win, especially without American help. Japan had successfully defied the League, whose prestige was damaged, though not yet fatally.

(i) The failure of the World Disarmament Conference (1932–3)

This met under the auspices of the League, and its failure was a grave disappointment. The Germans asked for equality of armaments with France, but when the French demanded that this should be postponed for at least eight years, Hitler was able to use the French attitude as an excuse to withdraw Germany from the conference and later from the League.

(j) The Italian invasion of Abyssinia (October 1935)

This was the most serious blow to the League's prestige and credibility (see Section 5.2(b)). The League condemned Italy and introduced economic sanctions; however, these were not applied to exports of oil, coal and steel to Italy. So half-hearted were the sanctions that Italy was able to complete the conquest of Abyssinia without too much inconvenience (May 1936). A few weeks later sanctions were abandoned, and *Mussolini had successfully flouted the League*. Again Britain and France must share the blame for the League's failure. Their motive was the desire not to antagonize Mussolini too much, so as to keep him as an ally against the real danger – Germany. But the results were disastrous:

- Mussolini was annoyed by the sanctions anyway, and began to draw closer to Hitler;
- small states lost all faith in the League;
- Hitler was encouraged to break the Versailles Treaty by introducing conscription (March 1935) and sending German troops into the demilitarized zone of the Rhineland (March 1936). Neither matter was raised at the League Council, mainly because France and Britain were afraid that Hitler would reject any decision that went against Germany, and they were reluctant to be forced into military action against the Germans.

After 1935, therefore, the League was never taken seriously again. The real explanation for the failure of the League was simple: when aggressive states such as Japan, Italy and Germany defied it, the League members, especially France and Britain, were not prepared to support it, either by decisive economic measures or by military action. *The League was only as strong as the determination of its leading members to stand up to aggression*; unfortunately, determination of that sort was sadly lacking during the 1930s.

However, some historians believe that the League should not be dismissed as a complete failure and a total irrelevance in world history. Ruth Henig, for example, feels that 'it is high time that these verdicts are challenged and that the League is seen for what it was, a bold step towards international cooperation which failed in some of its aims but succeeded comprehensively in others'. And challenge them she did, by publishing a book, *The League of Nations* (2010), to mark the ninetieth anniversary of its beginning. She argues that its creation 'marked an important step on the road to our contemporary global system of international organisation, coordinated through the United Nations, which was built on the foundations of the League's experience'. Expectations of what the League might achieve were far too high and completely unrealistic. How could it possibly have been expected to deal with aggressors when it had no army of its own and no mechanism to compel member states to provide their troops? In fact its great contribution was that it provided the first experimental phase, the blueprint for a second, more effective and longer-lasting form of international co-operation – the United Nations (UN). The Assembly, the Council and the Secretariat were adopted as a basis by the UN. The UN International Court of Justice reproduced almost identically the League's Permanent Court. The International Labour Organization is still operating today. Many other UN bodies, such as the Economic and Social Council and World Health Organization, were built on the foundations of the pioneering work carried out by the League agencies before 1939. Ruth Henig concludes that 'the creation of an international body in 1920 promoted international collaboration and compromise, and was a dynamic step forward in international diplomacy ... Rather than dwell on its weaknesses or condemn its failings, we should applaud the League's successes, while continuing to learn important lessons from its history.'

FURTHER READING

Fitzsimmons, O., *Towards One World* (London University Tutorial Press, 1974).
Henig, R., *The League of Nations* (Haus Publishing, 2010).
Overy, R., *The Inter-War Crisis, 1919–1939* (Longman, 1994).

QUESTIONS

1 How successful was the League of Nations in resolving international disputes in the 1920s?
2 Assess the reasons why there were no major international conflicts during the 1920s.
3 Explain why the League of Nations was hailed as a success during the 1920s but was considered a failure by 1936.
4 How far would you agree that the League of Nations was 'a complete failure, a total irrelevance in world history'?

◥ There is a document question about the League of Nations and its problems on the website.

International relations, 1919–33

SUMMARY OF EVENTS

International relations between the two world wars fall into two distinct phases, with the division at January 1933, the fateful month in which Adolf Hitler came to power in Germany. Before that, there seemed reasonable hope that world peace could be maintained, in spite of the failure of the League of Nations to curb Japanese aggression in Manchuria. Once Hitler was firmly in control, there was little chance of preventing a war of some sort, either limited or full-scale, depending on one's interpretation of Hitler's intentions (see Section 5.3). The first phase can be divided roughly into three:

- 1919–23
- 1923–9
- 1930–3

(a) 1919 to 1923

In the aftermath of the First World War, relations were disturbed by problems arising from the peace settlement, while the newborn League of Nations struggled to sort things out.

- Both Turkey and Italy were dissatisfied with their treatment; Turkey was prepared to defy the settlement (see Section 2.10). The Italians, soon to come under the rule of Mussolini (1922), showed their resentment first by the seizure of Fiume, which had been awarded to Yugoslavia, and then in the Corfu Incident (see Section 3.4(d); later, Italian aggression was turned against Abyssinia (1935).
- The problem of German reparations and whether or not she could afford to pay caused strained relations between Britain and France, because of their different attitudes towards German recovery. France wanted a weak Germany; Britain wanted an economically strong Germany which would be able to buy British exports.
- An attempt by Lloyd George to reconcile France and Germany at the 1922 Genoa Conference failed miserably.
- Relations deteriorated still further in 1923 when French troops occupied the Ruhr (an important German industrial region) in an attempt to seize in goods what the Germans were refusing to pay in cash. This succeeded only in bringing about the collapse of the German currency.
- Meanwhile the USA, while choosing to remain politically isolated, exercised considerable economic influence on Europe by, among other things, insisting on full payment of European war debts.

- Russia, now under Bolshevik (Communist) rule, was viewed with suspicion by the western countries, several of which, along with Japan, intervened against the Bolsheviks in the civil war which ravaged Russia during 1918–20.
- The new states which came into existence as a result of the war and the peace settlement – these included Yugoslavia, Czechoslovakia, Austria, Hungary and Poland – all had serious problems and were divided among themselves. These problems and divisions had important effects on international relations.

(b)   1924 to 1929

There was a general improvement in the international atmosphere, caused partly by changes in political leadership. In France, Edouard Herriot and Aristide Briand, in Germany Gustav Stresemann, and in Britain James Ramsay MacDonald, came to power, and all were keen to improve relations. The result was *the Dawes Plan*, worked out in 1924 with American help, which eased the situation regarding German reparations; 1925 saw the signing of *the Locarno Treaties*, which guaranteed the frontiers in western Europe fixed at Versailles: this seemed to remove French suspicions of German intentions. Germany was allowed to join the League in 1926 and two years later, 65 nations signed *the Kellogg–Briand Pact*, renouncing war. The 1929 *Young Plan* reduced German reparations to a more manageable figure; all seemed set fair for a peaceful future.

(c)   1930 to 1933

Towards the end of 1929 the world began to run into economic difficulties, which contributed towards a deterioration in international relations. It was partly for economic reasons that Japanese troops invaded Manchuria in 1931; mass unemployment in Germany was important in enabling Hitler to come to power. In this unpromising climate, the World Disarmament Conference met in 1932, only to break up in failure after the German delegates walked out (1933). With such a complex period, it will be best to treat the various themes separately.

4.1   WHAT ATTEMPTS WERE MADE TO IMPROVE INTERNATIONAL RELATIONS, AND HOW SUCCESSFUL WERE THEY?

(a)   The League of Nations

The League played an important role, settling a number of international disputes and problems (see Chapter 3). However, its authority tended to be weakened by the fact that many states seemed to prefer signing agreements independently of the League, which suggests that they were not exactly brimming with confidence at the League's prospects. Nor were they prepared to commit themselves to providing military support in order to curb any aggressor.

(b)   The Washington Conferences (1921–2)

The purpose of these meetings was to try to improve relations between the USA and Japan. The USA was increasingly suspicious of growing Japanese power in the Far East, and of Japanese influence in China, especially bearing in mind that during the First World War, Japan had seized Kiaochow and all the German islands in the Pacific.

- To prevent a naval building race, it was agreed that the Japanese navy would be limited to three-fifths the size of the American and British navies.
- Japan agreed to withdraw from Kiaochow and the Shantung province of China, which she had occupied since 1914.
- In return she was allowed to keep the former German Pacific islands as mandates.
- The western powers promised not to build any more naval bases within striking distance of Japan.
- The USA, Japan, Britain and France agreed to guarantee the neutrality of China and to respect each other's possessions in the Far East.

At the time, the agreements were regarded as a great success, and relations between the powers involved improved. In reality, however, Japan was left supreme in the Far East, possessor of the world's third largest navy, which she could concentrate in the Pacific. On the other hand, the navies of Britain and the USA, though larger, were spread more widely. This was to have unfortunate consequences for China in the 1930s when the USA refused to become involved in checking Japanese aggression.

(c) The Genoa Conference (1922)

This was the brainchild of the British prime minister Lloyd George; he hoped it would solve the pressing problems of Franco-German hostility (the Germans were threatening to stop paying reparations), European war debts to the USA and the need to resume proper diplomatic relations with Soviet Russia. Unfortunately the conference failed: the French refused all compromise and insisted on full reparations payments; the Americans refused even to attend, and the Russians and Germans withdrew, moved to Rapallo, a resort about 20 miles from Genoa, and signed a mutual agreement there (see Section 4.3(b)). When, the following year, the Germans refused to pay the amount due, French troops occupied the Ruhr, and deadlock quickly developed when the Germans responded with a campaign of passive resistance (see Section 14.1(c) for full details).

(d) The Dawes Plan

Worked out at a conference in London in 1924, this was an attempt to break the general deadlock. The three newcomers to international politics, MacDonald, Herriot and Stresemann (German Foreign Minister 1924–9), were eager for reconciliation; the Americans were persuaded to take part, and the conference was chaired for part of the time by the American representative, General Dawes. No reduction was made in the total amount that the Germans were expected to pay, but it was agreed that they should pay annually *only what they could reasonably afford until they became more prosperous*. A foreign loan of 800 million gold marks, mostly from the USA, was to be made to Germany. The French, now assured of at least some reparations from Germany, agreed *to withdraw their troops from the Ruhr*. The plan was successful: the German economy began to recover on the basis of the American loans, and international tensions gradually relaxed, preparing the way for the next agreements.

(e) The Locarno Treaties (1925)

These were a number of different agreements involving Germany, France, Britain, Italy, Belgium, Poland and Czechoslovakia. The most important one was that *Germany, France* and Belgium promised to respect their joint frontiers; if one of the three broke the agreement, Britain and Italy would assist the state which was being attacked. Germany signed agreements with Poland and Czechoslovakia providing for arbitration over possible disputes, but Germany would not guarantee her frontiers with Poland and Czechoslovakia. It was also agreed that France would help Poland and Czechoslovakia if Germany attacked them. The agreements were greeted with wild enthusiasm all over Europe, and the reconciliation between France and Germany was referred to as the 'Locarno honeymoon'. It was regarded as Stresemann's greatest success to date. Later, historians were not so enthusiastic about Locarno; there was one glaring omission from the agreements – no guarantees were given by Germany or Britain about *Germany's eastern frontiers with Poland and Czechoslovakia*, the very areas where trouble was most likely to arise. By ignoring this problem, the British gave the impression that they might not act if Germany attacked Poland or Czechoslovakia. For the time being though, as the world enjoyed a period of great economic prosperity, such uneasy thoughts were pushed into the background and Germany was allowed to enter the League in 1926 with a seat on the Permanent Council. Stresemann and Briand (French Foreign Minister 1925–32) met regularly and had friendly discussions; often Austen Chamberlain (British Foreign Minister 1924–9) joined them. The three of them were jointly awarded the Nobel Peace Prize. In September 1926 Stresemann and Briand reached agreement on the withdrawal of French troops from the Rhineland. This 'Locarno spirit' culminated in the next piece of paper-signing.

(f) The Kellogg–Briand Pact (1928)

This was originally Briand's idea; he proposed that France and the USA should sign a pact renouncing war. Frank B. Kellogg (American Secretary of State) proposed that the whole world should be involved; eventually 65 states signed, agreeing *to renounce war as an instrument of national policy*. This sounded impressive but was completely useless because no mention was made of sanctions against any state which broke its pledge. Japan signed the Pact, but this did not prevent her from waging war against China only three years later.

(g) The Young Plan (1929)

The aim of this new initiative was to settle the remaining problem of reparations – the Dawes Plan had left the total amount payable uncertain. In the improved atmosphere, the French were willing to compromise, and a committee chaired by an American banker, Owen Young, decided to reduce reparations from £6600 million to £2000 million, to be paid on a graded scale over the next 59 years. This was the figure that Keynes had urged at Versailles, and its acceptance ten years later was an admission of error by the Allies. The plan was welcomed by many in Germany, but the Nazi party campaigned against accepting it, because they thought it offered Germany far too little. They wanted a much quicker and a much more radical revision of the peace settlement. Even before there was time to put the Young Plan into operation, a series of events following in rapid succession destroyed the fragile harmony of Locarno:

1 First came the death of Stresemann (October 1929), reportedly from overwork at the age of only 51. Tragically this removed one of the outstanding 'men of Locarno', a German leader who aimed at peaceful change in Europe and hoped that his country's economic recovery would be successful enough to prevent the extremists of both right and left from gaining power in Germany.

2   The Wall Street Crash on the American stock exchange in the same month soon developed into a worldwide economic crisis – the Great Depression, and by 1932 there were over six million people unemployed in Germany. Hope was kept alive by *the Lausanne Conference* (1932), at which Britain and France released Germany from most of the remaining reparations payments. However, in January 1933 Hitler became German Chancellor, and after that, international tension mounted.

(h)   The World Disarmament Conference (1932–3)

Although all member states of the League of Nations had undertaken to reduce armaments when they accepted the Covenant, only Germany had made any moves towards disarmament, as Stresemann regularly pointed out. In fact the rest seem to have increased their arms expenditure – between 1925 and 1933 world expenditure on arms rose from $3.5 billion to around $5 billion. The World Disarmament Conference met in Geneva to try and work out a formula for scaling down armaments. But if no progress could be made during the Locarno honeymoon, there was little chance of any in the disturbed atmosphere of the 1930s. The British said they needed more armaments to protect their empire. The French, alarmed by the rapid increase in support for the Nazis in Germany, refused either to disarm or to allow Germany equality of armaments with them. Hitler, knowing that Britain and Italy sympathized with Germany, withdrew from the conference (October 1933), which was doomed from that moment. A week later Germany also withdrew from the League.

In retrospect, it can be seen that the statesmen of the world had only limited success in improving international relations. Even the 'Locarno spirit' proved an illusion, because so much depended on economic prosperity. When this evaporated, all the old hostilities and suspicions surfaced again, and authoritarian regimes came to power, which were prepared to risk aggression.

4.2   HOW DID FRANCE TRY TO DEAL WITH THE PROBLEM OF GERMANY BETWEEN 1919 AND 1933?

As soon as the First World War ended, the French, after all they had suffered in two German invasions in less than 50 years, wanted to make sure that the Germans never again violated the sacred soil of France; this remained the major concern of French foreign policy throughout the inter-war years. At different times, depending on who was in charge of foreign affairs, the French tried different methods of dealing with the problem:

- trying to keep Germany economically and militarily weak;
- signing alliances with other states to isolate Germany, and working for a strong League of Nations;
- extending the hand of reconciliation and friendship.

In the end, all three tactics failed.

(a)   Trying to keep Germany weak

1   Insistence on a harsh peace settlement
At the Paris peace conference the French premier, Clemenceau, insisted on a harsh settlement.

- In order to strengthen French security, the German army was to number no more than 100 000 men and there were to be severe limitations on armaments (see Section 2.8(a)).
- The German Rhineland was to be demilitarized to a distance of 50 kilometres east of the river.
- France was to have the use of the area known as the Saar, for 15 years.

Britain and the USA promised to help France if Germany attacked again. Although many French people were disappointed (Foch wanted France to be given the whole of the German Rhineland west of the river, but they were only allowed to occupy it for 15 years), it looked at first as though security was guaranteed. Unfortunately French satisfaction was short-lived: the Americans were afraid that membership of the League might involve them in another war, and preferred a policy of isolation. Consequently they rejected the entire peace settlement (March 1920) and abandoned their guarantees of assistance. The British used this as an excuse to cancel their promises, and the French understandably felt betrayed.

2   Clemenceau demanded that the Germans should pay reparations
The figure to be paid for reparations (money to help repair damage) was fixed in 1921 at £6600 million. It was thought that the strain of paying this huge amount would keep Germany economically weak for the next 66 years – the period over which reparations were to be paid in annual instalments – and consequently another German attack on France would be less likely. However, financial troubles in Germany soon caused the government to fall behind with its payments. The French, who claimed to need the cash from reparations to balance their budget and pay their own debts to the USA, became desperate.

3   Attempts to force the Germans to pay
The next prime minister, the anti-German Raymond Poincaré, decided that *drastic methods were needed to force the Germans to pay* and to weaken their powers of revival. In January 1923, French and Belgian troops occupied the Ruhr (the important German industrial area which includes the cities of Essen and Dusseldorf). The Germans replied with passive resistance, strikes and sabotage. A number of nasty incidents between troops and civilians resulted in the deaths of over a hundred people.

Although the French managed to seize goods worth about £40 million, the whole episode caused galloping inflation and the collapse of the German mark, which by November 1923 was completely valueless. It also revealed the basic difference between the French and British attitudes towards Germany: while France adopted a hard line and wanted Germany completely crippled, Britain now saw moderation and reconciliation as the best security; she believed that an economically healthy Germany would be good for the stability of Europe (as well as for British exports). Consequently Britain strongly disapproved of the Ruhr occupation and sympathized with Germany.

(b)   A network of alliances and a strong League

At the same time, *the French tried to increase their security by building up a network of alliances*, first with Poland (1921) and later with Czechoslovakia (1924), Romania (1926) and Yugoslavia (1927). This network, known as the 'Little Entente', though impressive on paper, did not amount to much because the states involved were comparatively weak. What the French needed was a renewal of the old alliance with Russia, which had served them well during the First World War; but this seemed out of the question now that Russia had become communist.

The French worked for a strong League of Nations, with the victorious powers acting as a military police force, compelling aggressive powers to behave themselves. However, in the end it was the much vaguer Wilson version of the League that was adopted. French disappointment was bitter when Britain took the lead in rejecting the Geneva Protocol, which might have strengthened the League (see Section 3.4(e)). Clearly there was no point in expecting much guarantee of security from that direction.

(c) Compromise and reconciliation

By the summer of 1924, when the failure of Poincaré's Ruhr occupation was obvious, the new premier, Herriot, *was prepared to accept a compromise solution* to the reparations problem; this led to the Dawes Plan (see Section 4.1).

During the Briand era (he was Foreign Minister in 11 successive governments between 1925 and 1932), *the French approach to the German problem was one of reconciliation.* Briand persevered with great skill to build up genuinely good relations with Germany, as well as to improve relations with Britain and strengthen the League. Fortunately Stresemann, who was in charge of German foreign policy from November 1923 until 1929, believed that the best way to foster German recovery was by co-operation with Britain and France. The result was the Locarno Treaties, the Kellogg–Briand Pact, the Young Plan and the cancellation of most of the remaining reparations payments (see previous section). There is some debate among historians about how genuine this apparent reconciliation between France and Germany really was. A. J. P. Taylor suggested that though Briand and Stresemann were sincere, 'they did not carry their peoples with them'; nationalist feeling in the two countries was so strong that both men were limited in the concessions they could offer. The fact that Stresemann was secretly determined to get the frontier with Poland redrawn to Germany's advantage would have caused friction later, since Poland was France's ally. He was equally determined to work for union with Austria and a revision of the Versailles terms.

(d) A tougher attitude towards Germany

The death of Stresemann in October 1929, the world economic crisis and the growth of support in Germany for the Nazis, alarmed the French, and made them adopt a tougher attitude towards Germany. When, in 1931, the Germans proposed an Austro-German customs union to ease the economic crisis, the French insisted that the matter be referred to the International Court of Justice at the Hague, on the grounds that it was a violation of the Versailles Treaty. Though a customs union made economic sense, the court ruled against it, and the plan was dropped. At the World Disarmament Conference (1932–3) relations worsened (see Section 4.1), and when Hitler took Germany out of the Conference and the League, all Briand's work was ruined. The German problem was as far from being solved as ever.

4.3 HOW DID RELATIONS BETWEEN THE USSR AND BRITAIN. GERMANY AND FRANCE DEVELOP BETWEEN 1919 AND 1933?

For the first three years after the Bolsheviks came to power in Russia (November 1917), relations between the new government and the western countries deteriorated to the point of open war. This was mainly because the Bolsheviks tried to spread the revolution further, especially in Germany. As early as December 1917, they began to pour floods of propaganda into Germany in an attempt to turn the masses against their capitalist masters. Lenin called together representatives from communist parties all over the world to a conference in Moscow in March 1919. It was known as the Third International, or Comintern. Its aim was to bring the world's communists under Russian leadership and show them how to organize strikes and uprisings. Karl Radek, one of the Russian Bolshevik leaders, went secretly to Berlin to plan the revolution, while other agents did the same in other countries. Zinoviev, the chairman of the Comintern, confidently predicted that 'in a year the whole of Europe will be Communist'.

This sort of activity did not endear the communists to the governments of countries like Britain, France, the USA, Czechoslovakia and Japan. These states tried rather half-heartedly to destroy the Bolsheviks by intervening in the Russian civil war to help the other side (known as the Whites) (see Section 16.3(c)). The Russians were not invited to the Versailles Conference in 1919. By the middle of 1920, however, circumstances were gradually changing: the countries which had interfered in Russia had admitted failure and withdrawn their troops; communist revolutions in Germany and Hungary had failed; and Russia was too exhausted by the civil war to think about stirring up any more revolutions for the time being. At the Third Comintern Congress, in June 1921, Lenin acknowledged that Russia needed peaceful coexistence and co-operation in the form of trade with, and investment from, the capitalist world. The way was open for communications to be re-established.

(a) The USSR and Britain

Relations blew hot and cold according to which government was in power in Britain. The two Labour governments (1924 and 1929–31) were much more sympathetic to Russia than the others.

1   After the failure to overthrow the communists, Lloyd George (British prime minister 1916–22) was prepared for reconciliation. This corresponded with Lenin's desire for improved relations with the west so that Russia could attract foreign trade and capital. The result was *an Anglo-Russian trade treaty* (March 1921), which was important for Russia, not only commercially, but also because Britain was one of the first states to acknowledge the existence of the Bolshevik government; it was to lead to similar agreements with other countries and to full political recognition.

The new rapprochement (drawing together) was soon shaken, however, when at the Genoa conference (1922), *Lloyd George suggested that the Bolsheviks should pay war debts* incurred by the tsarist regime. The Russians were offended; they left the conference and signed the separate Treaty of Rapallo with the Germans. This alarmed Britain and France, who could see no good coming from what Lloyd George called 'this fierce friendship' between the two 'outcast' nations of Europe.

2   Relations improved briefly in 1924 when MacDonald and the new Labour government gave *full diplomatic recognition to the communists*. A new trade treaty was signed and a British loan to Russia was proposed. However, this was unpopular with British Conservatives and Liberals who soon brought MacDonald's government down.

3   *Under the Conservatives (1924–9), relations with Russia worsened.* British Conservatives had no love for the communists, and there was evidence that Russian propaganda was encouraging the Indian demands for independence. Police raided the British Communist Party headquarters in London (1925) and the premises of Arcos, a soviet trading organization based in London (1927), and claimed to have

found evidence of Russians plotting with British communists to overthrow the system. The government expelled the mission and broke off diplomatic relations with the Russians, who replied by arresting some British residents in Moscow.

4   *Matters took a turn for the better in 1929* when Labour, encouraged by the new pro-western Foreign Minister, Maxim Litvinov, resumed diplomatic relations with Russia and signed another trade agreement the following year. But the improvement was only short-lived.

5   The Conservative-dominated National government, which came to power in 1931, *cancelled the trade agreement* (1932), and in retaliation the Russians arrested four Metropolitan-Vickers engineers working in Moscow. They were tried and given sentences ranging from two to three years for 'spying and wrecking'. However, when Britain placed an embargo on imports from Russia, Stalin released them (June 1933). By this time Stalin was becoming nervous about the possible threat from Hitler, and was therefore prepared to take pains to improve relations with Britain.

(b)   The USSR and Germany

The USSR's relations with Germany were more consistent and more friendly than with Britain. This was because the Germans saw advantages to be gained from exploiting friendship with the USSR, and because the Bolsheviks were anxious to have stable relations with at least one capitalist power.

1   *A trade treaty was signed (May 1921)*, followed by the granting of Russian trade and mineral concessions to some German industrialists.

2   *The Rapallo Treaty, signed on Easter Sunday 1922* after both Germany and Russia had withdrawn from the Genoa conference, was an important step forward:

- Full diplomatic relations were resumed and reparations claims between the two states cancelled.
- Both could look forward to advantages from the new friendship: they could co-operate to keep Poland weak, which was in both their interests.
- The USSR had Germany as a buffer against any future attack from the west.
- The Germans were allowed to build factories in Russia for the manufacture of aeroplanes and ammunition, enabling them to get round the Versailles disarmament terms; German officers trained in Russia in the use of the new forbidden weapons.
- In return, the Russians would supply Germany with grain.

3   *The Treaty of Berlin (1926)* renewed the Rapallo agreement for a further five years; it was understood that Germany would remain neutral if Russia were to be attacked by another power, and neither would use economic sanctions against the other.

4   *About 1930, relations began to cool* as some Russians expressed concern at the growing power of Germany; the German attempt to form a customs union with Austria in 1931 was taken as an ominous sign of increasing German nationalism. Russian concern changed to alarm at the growth of the Nazi party, which was strongly anti-communist. Though Stalin and Litvinov tried to continue the friendship with Germany, they also began approaches to Poland, France and Britain. In January 1934, Hitler abruptly ended Germany's special relationship with the Soviets by signing a non-aggression pact with Poland (see Section 5.5(b)).

(c)   The USSR and France

The Bolshevik takeover in 1917 was a serious blow for France, because Russia had been an important ally whom she relied on to keep Germany in check. Now her former ally was calling for revolution in all capitalist states, and the French regarded the Bolsheviks as a menace to be destroyed as soon as possible. The French sent troops to help the anti-Bolsheviks (Whites) in the civil war, and it was because of French insistence, that the Bolsheviks were not invited to Versailles. The French also intervened in the war between Russia and Poland in 1920; troops commanded by General Weygand helped to drive back a Russian advance on Warsaw (the Polish capital), and afterwards the French government claimed to have stemmed the westward spread of Bolshevism. The subsequent alliance between France and Poland (1921) seemed to be directed as much against Russia as against Germany.

Relations improved in 1924 when the moderate Herriot government resumed diplomatic relations. But the French were never very enthusiastic, especially as the French Communist Party was under orders from Moscow not to co-operate with other left-wing parties. Not until the early 1930s did the rise of the German Nazis cause a change of heart on both sides.

4.4   THE 'SUCCESSOR' STATES

One important result of the First World War in eastern Europe was the break-up of the Austro-Hungarian or Habsburg Empire, and the loss of extensive territory by Germany and Russia. A number of new national states were formed, of which the most important were Yugoslavia, Czechoslovakia, Austria, Hungary and Poland. They are sometimes known as the 'successor' states because they 'succeeded' or 'took the place of' the previous empires. Two of the guiding principles behind their formation were *self-determination* and *democracy*; it was hoped that they would act as a stabilizing influence in central and eastern Europe and as a buffer against potential attacks from communist Russia.

However, they all developed serious problems and weaknesses:

- There were so many different nationalities in the region that it was impossible for them all to have their own state. Consequently it was only the larger national groups which were lucky enough to have their own homeland. Smaller nationalities found themselves once again under what they considered to be 'foreign' governments, which, so they claimed, did not look after their interests – for example, Croats in Yugoslavia, Slovaks and Germans in Czechoslovakia, and Germans, White Russians and Ukrainians in Poland.
- Although each state began with a democratic constitution, Czechoslovakia was the only one in which democracy survived for a significant length of time – until the Germans moved in (March 1939).
- They all suffered economic difficulties, especially after the onset of the Great Depression in the early 1930s.
- The states were divided by rivalries and disputes over territory. Austria and Hungary had been on the losing side in the war and greatly resented the way the peace settlement had been forced on them. They wanted a complete revision of the terms. On the other hand, Czechoslovakia and Poland had declared themselves independent shortly before the war ended, while Serbia (which became Yugoslavia) had been an independent state before 1914. These three states were represented at the peace conference and were, on the whole, satisfied with the outcome.

(a) Yugoslavia

With a population of around 14 million, the new state consisted of the original kingdom of Serbia, plus Montenegro, Croatia, Slovenia and Dalmatia; it was known as the Kingdom of the Serbs, Croats and Slovenes until 1929, when it took the name Yugoslavia (Southern Slavs). The new constitution provided for an elected parliament, which was dominated by the Serbs, the largest national group. The Croats and the other national groups formed a permanent opposition, constantly protesting that they were being discriminated against by the Serbs. In 1928 the Croats announced their withdrawal from parliament and set up their own government in Zagreb; there was talk of proclaiming a separate Republic of Croatia. The king, Alexander (a Serb), responded by proclaiming himself a dictator and banning political parties; it was at this time that the country was renamed Yugoslavia (June 1929).

Soon afterwards, *Yugoslavia was badly hit by the depression*. Largely agricultural, the economy had been reasonably prosperous during the 1920s; but in the early 1930s world agricultural prices collapsed, causing widespread hardship among farmers and workers. In 1934, King Alexander was assassinated in Marseilles as he was arriving for a state visit to France. The murderer was a Macedonian who was connected with a group of Croat revolutionaries living in Hungary. For a time, tensions were high, and there seemed to be danger of war with Hungary. However, the new king, Peter II, was only 11 years old, and Alexander's cousin Paul, who was acting as regent, believed it was time to compromise. In 1935 he allowed political parties again, and in August 1939 he introduced a semi-federal system which enabled six Croats to join the government.

In foreign affairs the government tried to stay on good terms with other states, signing treaties of friendship with Czechoslovakia (1920) and Romania (1921) – a grouping known as the 'Little Entente'. Further treaties of friendship were signed with Italy (1924 – to last for five years), Poland (1926), France (1927) and Greece (1929). In spite of the treaty with Italy, the Yugoslavs were deeply suspicious of Mussolini. He was encouraging the Croat rebels and was tightening his grip on Albania to the south, threatening to encircle Yugoslavia.

Disappointed with the economic help they had received from France, and nervous of Mussolini's intentions, *Prince Paul, the regent, began to look towards Nazi Germany for trade and protection*. In 1936 a trade treaty was signed with Germany; this led to a significant increase in trade, so that by 1938, Germany was taking over 40 per cent of Yugoslavia's exports. Friendship with Germany reduced the threat from Mussolini, who had signed the Rome–Berlin Axis agreement with Hitler in 1936. In 1937 therefore, Italy signed a treaty with Yugoslavia. As the international situation deteriorated during 1939, Yugoslavia found itself uncomfortably aligned with the Axis powers.

(b) Czechoslovakia

Like Yugoslavia, *Czechoslovakia was a multinational state*, consisting of some 6.5 million Czechs, 2.5 million Slovaks, 3 million Germans, 700 000 Hungarians, 500 000 Ruthenians, 100 000 Poles and smaller numbers of Romanians and Jews. Although this might look like a recipe for instability, the new state worked well, being based on a solid partnership between Czechs and Slovaks. There was an elected parliament of two houses, and an elected president who had the power to choose and dismiss government ministers. Tomáš Masaryk, president from 1918 until his retirement in 1935, was half Czech and half Slovak. It was the only example in eastern Europe of a successful western-style liberal democracy. On the whole, relations between the different nationalities were good, although there was some resentment among the German-speaking population who lived in

Bohemia and Moravia and along the frontiers with Germany and Austria (an area known as the Sudetenland). They had previously been citizens of the Habsburg Empire and complained at being forced to live in a 'Slav' state where they were discriminated against, or so they claimed.

Czechoslovakia was fortunate that it contained about three-quarters of the industries of the old Habsburg Empire. *There were successful textile and glass factories, valuable mineral resources and rich agricultural lands.* The 1920s was a period of great prosperity as production expanded and Czechoslovakia became a major exporting country. *Unfortunately the depression of the early 1930s brought with it an economic crisis.* The surrounding states of central and eastern Europe reacted to the depression by increasing import duties and reducing imports, demand for Czech manufactures fell, and there was severe unemployment, especially in the industrial areas where the Sudeten Germans lived. Now they really had something to complain about, and both they and the Slovaks blamed the Czechs for their problems.

This coincided with the rise of Hitler, who inspired imitation movements in many countries; in Czechoslovakia the Sudeten Germans formed their own party. After Hitler came to power in Germany, the party, under the leadership of Konrad Henlein, became bolder, organizing rallies and protest demonstrations. In the 1935 elections they won 44 seats, making them the second largest party in the lower house of parliament. The following year, Henlein began to demand self-government for the German-speaking areas. But Hitler was determined on more: by 1938 he had decided that the Sudetenland must become part of Germany, and that the state of Czechoslovakia itself must be destroyed.

Meanwhile the Czech Foreign Minister, Edvard Beneš, had taken great trouble to build up a system of protective alliances for his new state. He was the instigator of the 'Little Entente' with Yugoslavia and Romania (1920–1) and he signed treaties with Italy and France in 1924. Benes was involved in the Locarno agreements of 1925, in which France promised to guarantee Czechoslovakia's frontiers and Germany promised that any frontier disputes would be settled by arbitration. The growing success of Henlein and his party rang alarm bells; Benes looked desperately around for further protection and an agreement was signed with the USSR (1935). The two states promised to help each other if attacked. But there was one vital proviso: help would be given only if France assisted the country under attack. Tragically, neither France nor Britain was prepared to give military support when the crisis came in 1938 (see Section 5.5(a)).

(c) Poland

Poland had previously existed as an independent state until the late eighteenth century, when it was taken over and divided up between Russia, Austria and Prussia. By 1795 it had lost its independent status. The Poles spent the nineteenth and early twentieth centuries struggling for liberation and independence; the Versailles settlement gave them almost everything they wanted. The acquisition of West Prussia from Germany gave them access to the sea, and although they were disappointed that Danzig, the area's main port, was to be a 'free city' under League of Nations control, they soon built another modern port nearby at Gdynia. However, there was the usual nationalities problem: out of a population of 27 million, only 18 million were Poles. The rest included 4 million Ukrainians, a million White Russians, a million Germans and almost 3 million Jews.

A democratic constitution was introduced in March 1921, which provided for a president and an elected parliament of two houses. Since there were no fewer than 14 political parties, the only way to form a government was by a coalition of several groups. Between 1919 and 1926 there were 13 different cabinets, which lasted on average just a few months. It was impossible to get a strong, decisive government. By 1926 many people felt that the democratic experiment had been a failure; Marshal Józef Piłsudski, founder of the Polish Socialist Party and the man who had declared Polish independence at the end of the war, led a military coup. In May 1926 he overthrew the government and became prime minister and minister for war. He acted as a virtual dictator in a right-wing, authoritarian and nationalist regime until his death in 1935. The same system then continued with Ignatz Moscicky as president and Józef Beck as foreign minister. However, no effective measures had been taken to deal with the economic crisis and high unemployment, and the government became increasingly unpopular:

The Poles were involved in several frontier disputes with neighbouring states:

- Both Poland and Germany claimed Upper Silesia, an important industrial area.
- Poland and Czechoslovakia both wanted Teschen.
- The Poles demanded that their frontier with Russia should be much further eastwards instead of along the Curzon Line (see Map 2.5).
- The Poles wanted the city of Vilna and its surrounding area, which was also claimed by Lithuania.

The government wasted no time: taking advantage of the civil war in Russia (see section 16.3(c)), they sent Polish troops into Russia and quickly occupied Ukraine, capturing Kiev, the capital (7 May 1920). Their aims were to liberate Ukraine from Russian control and to take over White Russia. The invasion caused outrage among the Russians and rallied support for the Communist government. The Red Army counter-attacked, drove the Poles out of Kiev and chased them back into Poland all the way to Warsaw, which they prepared to attack. At this point France sent military help, and together with the Poles, they drove the Russians out of Poland again. In October 1920 an armistice was agreed, and in March 1921 the Treaty of Riga was signed; this gave Poland a bloc of territory all the way along her eastern frontier roughly a hundred miles wide. During the fighting, Polish troops also occupied Vilna; they refused to withdraw and in 1923 the League of Nations recognized it as belonging to Poland. However, these activities soured Poland's relations with Russia and Lithuania, leaving her with two bitterly hostile neighbours.

The other two frontier disputes were settled less controversially. In July 1920 the Conference of Ambassadors (see Section 3.4(d)) divided Teschen between Poland and Czechoslovakia. In March 1921 a plebiscite was held to decide the future of Upper Silesia, in which 60 per cent of the population voted to be part of Germany. However, there was no clear dividing line between the Germans and the Poles. Eventually it was decided to divide it between the two states: Germany received about three-quarters of the territory, but Poland's share contained the vast majority of the province's coal mines.

France was Poland's main ally – the Poles were grateful to the French for their help in the war with Russia – and the two signed a treaty of friendship in February 1921. Hardly had one threat been neutralized when an even more frightening one appeared – Hitler came to power in Germany in January 1933. But to the surprise of the Poles, Hitler was in a friendly mood – in January 1934 Germany signed a trade agreement and a ten-year non-aggression pact with Poland. Hitler's idea was apparently to bind Poland to Germany against the USSR. Foreign Minister Beck took advantage of the new 'friendship' with Hitler at the time of the 1938 Munich Conference to demand and receive a share of the spoils – the rest of Teschen (which had been divided between Poland and Czechoslovakia in July 1920) – from the doomed Czechoslovakia. Within four months he was to find that Hitler's attitude had changed dramatically (see Section 5.5(b)).

(d) Austria

Set up by the Treaty of St Germain in 1919 (see Section 2.9), the republic of Austria soon found itself faced by *almost every conceivable problem except that of nationalities* – the vast majority of people were German-speaking:

- It was a small country with a small population of only 6.5 million, of which about a third lived in the capital – the huge city of Vienna, which, it was said, was now 'like a head without a body'.
- Almost all its industrial wealth had been lost to Czechoslovakia and Poland; although there were some industries in Vienna, the rest of the country was mainly agricultural. There were immediate economic problems of inflation and financial crises and Austria had to be helped out by foreign loans arranged by the League of Nations.
- Most Austrians felt that the natural solution to the problems was union (*Anschluss*) with Germany; the Constituent Assembly, which first met in February 1919, actually voted to join Germany, but the Treaty of St Germain, signed in September, vetoed the union. The price exacted by the League in return for the foreign loans was that the Austrians had to promise not to unite with Germany for at least 20 years. Austria was forced to struggle on alone.

Under the new democratic constitution there was to be a parliament elected by proportional representation, a president, and a federal system which allowed the separate provinces control over their internal affairs. There were two main parties: the left-wing Social Democrats and the right-wing Christian Socials. For much of the time between 1922 and 1929 Ignaz Seipel, a Christian Social, was Chancellor, though Vienna itself was controlled by the Social Democrats. There was a striking contrast between the work of the Social Democrats in Vienna, who set up welfare and housing projects for the workers, and the Christian Socials in the rest of the country, who tried to bring economic stability by reducing expenditure and sacking thousands of government officials.

When the economic situation did not improve, *the conflict between right and left became violent*. Both sides formed private armies: the right had the 'Heimwehr', the left the 'Schutzband'. There were frequent demonstrations and clashes, and the right accused the left of plotting to set up a communist dictatorship. Encouraged and supported by Mussolini, the Heimwehr announced an anti-democratic fascist programme (1930). The world depression affected Austria badly: unemployment rose alarmingly and the standard of living fell. In March 1931 the government announced that it was preparing to enter a customs union with Germany in the hope of easing the flow of trade and therefore the economic crisis. However, France and the other western states took fright at this, suspecting that it would lead to a full political union. In retaliation, France withdrew all its funds from the leading Austrian bank, the Kreditanstalt, which teetered on the verge of collapse; in May 1931 it declared itself insolvent and was taken over by the government. Only when Austria agreed to drop its plans for a customs union did the French relent and make more cash available (July 1932). Clearly Austria was scarcely a viable state economically or politically, and it seemed as though the country was descending into anarchy as ineffective governments came and went. A further complication was that there was now an Austrian Nazi party, which was campaigning for union with Germany.

In May 1932 Engelbert Dollfuss, a Christian Social, became chancellor; he made a determined effort to bring the country to order: he dissolved parliament and announced that he would run the country by decree until a new constitution had been prepared. The Schutzband was declared illegal and the Heimwehr was to be replaced by a new paramilitary organization – the Fatherland Front. The Austrian Nazi party was banned and dissolved. *Unfortunately these policies had catastrophic results.*

- The ban on the Austrian Nazi party caused outrage in Germany, where Hitler was now in power. The Germans launched a vicious propaganda campaign against Dollfuss and in October 1933, Austrian Nazis tried to assassinate him. He survived, but tensions remained high between Germany and Austria. The problem for many Austrians was that although they wanted union with Germany, they were appalled at the idea of becoming part of a Germany run by Hitler and the Nazis.
- His attacks on the socialists backfired on Dollfuss. The Schutzband defied the ban: in February 1934 there were anti-government demonstrations in Vienna and Linz and three days of running battles between demonstrators and police. Order was restored, but only after some 300 people had been killed. Many socialists were arrested and the Social Democrat party was declared illegal. This was a serious mistake by Dollfuss – with careful handling, the socialists might well have been strong allies in his attempt to defend the republic against the Nazis. In the event, many of them now joined the Austrian Nazis as the best way of opposing the government.
- Dollfuss relied for support on Italy, where Mussolini was still nervous about Hitler's intentions. Mussolini had made it clear that he backed Dollfuss and an independent Austria. In March 1934 they signed the 'Rome protocols' – these included agreements on economic co-operation and a declaration of respect for each other's independence. Even Hitler at this point had promised to respect Austrian independence – he was afraid of alienating Italy and was prepared to wait.
- Impatient at the delay, the Austrian Nazis launched an attempted coup (25 July 1934). Dollfuss was shot and killed, but the affair was badly organized and was soon suppressed by government forces. Hitler's role in all this is still not clear; what is certain is that the local Nazis took the initiative, and although Hitler probably knew something about their plans, he was not himself prepared to help them in any way. When Mussolini moved Italian troops up to the frontier with Austria, that was the end of the matter. Clearly the Austrian Nazis were not strong enough to bring about a union with Germany without some outside support; so long as Italy supported the Austrians, their independence was assured.

Kurt Schuschnigg, the next Chancellor, worked hard to preserve the alliance with Italy, and even signed an agreement with Germany in which Hitler recognized Austrian independence and Schuschnigg promised that Austria would follow policies in line with her nature as a German state (July 1936). One such policy allowed the Austrian Nazi party to operate again, and two Nazis were taken into the cabinet. But time was running out for Austria, as Mussolini began to draw closer to Hitler. After his signing of the Rome–Berlin Axis (1936) and the Anti-Comintern Pact with Germany and Japan (1937), Mussolini was less interested in backing Austrian independence. Once again it was the Austrian Nazis who took the initiative, early in March 1938 (see Section 5.3(b)).

(e) Hungary

When the war ended in November 1918, the republic of Hungary was declared, with Michael Karolyi as the first president. Neighbouring states took advantage of the general chaos to seize territory which the Hungarians thought should rightly belong to them – Czech, Romanian and Yugoslav troops occupied large swathes of territory. In March 1919, Karolyi was replaced by a left-wing government of communists and socialists led by Béla Kun, who had recently founded the Hungarian Communist Party. Kun looked for help to Vladimir Lenin, the new Russian communist leader; but the Russians, having themselves suffered defeat at the hands of the Germans, were in no state to provide military support. The government's attempts to introduce nationalization and other socialist measures were bitterly opposed by the wealthy Magyar landowners. When Romanian troops captured Budapest (August 1919), Kun and his government were forced to flee for their lives.

After a confused period, the initiative was seized by Admiral Horthy, commander of the Austro-Hungarian fleet in 1918; he organized troops, order was restored and elections held in January 1920 were won by the right. The situation improved when the Romanians, under pressure from the Allies, agreed to withdraw. A stable government was formed in March 1920. It was decided that Hungary should be a monarchy with Admiral Horthy acting as Regent until it was decided who should be king. However, the country was deeply divided over the issue; when the most likely candidate, the last Habsburg emperor Karl, died in 1922, no further attempts at restoration were made. However, Horthy continued to be Regent, a title he held until Hungary was occupied by the Germans in 1944.

The new government soon suffered a stunning blow when it was forced to sign the Treaty of Trianon (June 1920), agreeing to massive losses of territory containing about three-quarters of Hungary's population – to Czechoslovakia, Romania and Yugoslavia (see Section 2.9(b)). From then on, Hungarian foreign policy centred on one major aim: to get a revision of the treaty. The 'Little Entente' members (Czechoslovakia, Romania and Yugoslavia), which had taken advantage of her weakness, were seen as the major enemy; Hungary was prepared to co-operate with any state that would back them. Treaties of friendship were signed with Italy (1927) and Austria (1933), and after Hitler came to power, a trade treaty was signed with Germany (1934).

During the 1920s and 1930s all the governments were right-wing, either conservative or nationalist. Admiral Horthy presided over an authoritarian regime in which the secret police were always active and critics and opponents were liable to be arrested. In 1935, Prime Minister Gombos announced that he wanted to co-operate more closely with Germany. Restrictions on the activities of Jews were introduced. At the time of the Munich crisis (September 1938) Hungary took advantage of the destruction of Czechoslovakia to demand and receive a sizeable strip of South Slovakia from Czechoslovakia, to be followed in March 1939 by Ruthenia. The following month Hungary signed the anti-Comintern Pact and withdrew from the League of Nations. She was now well and truly tied up with Hitler and Mussolini. In fact, in the words of historian D. C. Watt, 'it is difficult to write about the regime in command of Hungary at this time with anything but contempt'.

4.5 UNITED STATES FOREIGN POLICY, 1919–33

The USA had been deeply involved in the First World War, and when hostilities ceased, she seemed likely to play an important role in world affairs. President Woodrow Wilson, a Democrat, was a crucial figure at the peace conference; his great dream was the League of Nations, through which the USA would maintain world peace. He embarked on a gruelling speaking tour to rally support for his ideas. However, the American people were tired of war and suspicious of Europe: after all, the American population was made up of people who had moved there to get away from Europe. The Republican Party in particular was strongly against any further involvement in European affairs. To Wilson's bitter disappointment the US Senate voted to reject both the Versailles peace settlement and the League of Nations. From 1921 until early 1933 the USA was ruled by Republican governments which believed in a policy of *isolation*: she never joined the League and she tried to avoid political disputes with other states and the signing of treaties – for example, no American representative attended the Locarno Conference. Some historians still blame the failure of the League on the absence of the USA. And yet in spite of their desire for isolation, the Americans found it impossible to avoid some involvement in world affairs, because of overseas trade, investment and the thorny problem of European war debts and reparations. American isolationism was probably more concerned with keeping clear of political problems in Europe than with simply cutting themselves off from the world in general.

1   During the prosperous years of the 1920s, Americans tried to *increase trade and profits by investment abroad*, in Europe, Canada, and in Central and South America. It was inevitable therefore, that the USA should take an interest in what was happening in these areas. There was, for example, a serious dispute with Mexico, which was threatening to seize American-owned oil wells; a compromise solution was eventually reached.

2   *The Washington Conferences (1921–2)* were called by President Harding because of concern at Japanese power in the Far East (see Section 4.1(b)).

3   *Allied war debts to the USA caused much ill-feeling.* During the war the American government had organized loans to Britain and her allies amounting to almost 12 billion dollars at 5 per cent interest. The Europeans hoped that the Americans would cancel the debts, since the USA had done well out of the war (by taking over former European markets), but both Harding and Coolidge insisted that repayments be made in full. The Allies claimed that their ability to pay depended on whether Germany paid her reparations to them, but the Americans would not admit that there was any connection between the two. Eventually Britain was the first to agree to pay the full amount, over 62 years at the reduced interest rate of 3.3 per cent. Other states followed, the USA allowing much lower interest rates depending on the poverty of the country concerned; Italy got away with 0.4 per cent, but this predictably caused strong objections from Britain.

4   *Faced with the German financial crisis of 1923, the Americans had to change their attitude* and admit the connection between reparations and war debts. They agreed to take part in the Dawes and Young Plans (1924 and 1929), which enabled the Germans to pay reparations. However, this caused the ludicrous situation in which America lent money to Germany so that she could pay reparations to France, Britain and Belgium, and they in turn could pay their war debts to the USA. The whole set-up, together with American insistence on keeping high tariffs, was a contributory cause of the world economic crisis (see Section 22.6), with all its far-reaching consequences.

5   *The Kellogg–Briand Pact (1928)* was another notable, though useless, American foray into world affairs (see Section 4.1(f)).

6   *Relations with Britain were uneasy*, not only because of war debts, but because the Conservatives resented the limitations on British naval expansion imposed by the earlier Washington agreement. MacDonald, anxious to improve relations, organized a conference in London in 1930. It was attended also by the Japanese, and the three states reaffirmed the 5:5:3 ratio in cruisers, destroyers and submarines agreed at Washington. This was successful in re-establishing friendship between Britain and the USA, but the Japanese soon exceeded their limits.

7   *The USA returned to a policy of strict isolation* when the Japanese invaded Manchuria in 1931. Although President Hoover condemned the Japanese action, he refused to join in economic sanctions or to make any move which might lead to war with Japan. Consequently Britain and France felt unable to act and the League was shown to be helpless. Throughout the 1930s, though acts of aggression increased, the Americans remained determined not to be drawn into a conflict.

FURTHER READING

Cohrs, P. O., *The Unfinished Peace after World War 1: America, Britain and the Stabilisation of Europe, 1919–1932* (Cambridge University Press, 2006).

Henig, R., *Versailles and After, 1919–33* (Routledge, 2nd edition, 2011).

Marks, S., *The Illusion of Peace: International Relations in Europe, 1918–1933* (Macmillan, 2nd edition, 2003).

Overy, R. and Wheatcroft, A., *The Road to War: The Origins of World War II* (Vintage, 2009).

Steiner, Z., *The Lights that Failed: European International History 1919–1933* (Oxford University Press, 2005).

QUESTIONS

1 Assess the reasons why there were no major wars during the 1920s.
2 How far can it be said that the USA followed a policy of strict isolation in foreign affairs during the 1920s and early 1930s, and what effects did this policy have on international relations?
3 How did the fact that Russia was a Communist state affect international relations between 1920 and 1939?

There is a document question about German foreign policy and international relations, 1920–32 on the website.

5

International relations, 1933–9

SUMMARY OF EVENTS

This short period is of crucial importance in world history because it culminated in the Second World War. Economic problems caused the Locarno spirit to fade away, and the new rule seemed to be: every country for itself. Affairs were dominated by the three aggressive powers – Japan, Italy and Germany; their extreme nationalism led them to commit so many acts of violence and breaches of international agreements that in the end, the world was plunged into total war.

Japan became the first major aggressor with its successful invasion of the eastern part of China, known as Manchuria, in 1931. Both Hitler and Mussolini took note of the failure of the League of Nations to curb Japanese aggression. Hitler, by far the most subtle of the three, began cautiously by announcing the reintroduction of conscription (March 1935). This breach of Versailles caused Britain, France and Italy to draw together briefly in suspicion of Germany. At a meeting held in Stresa (on Lake Maggiore in northern Italy), they condemned Hitler's action, and soon afterwards (May) the French, obviously worried, signed a treaty of mutual assistance with the USSR.

However, *the Stresa Front*, as it was called, was only short-lived: it was broken in June 1935 when the British, without consulting France and Italy, signed *the Anglo-German Naval Agreement*; this allowed the Germans to build submarines – another breach of Versailles. This astonishing move by Britain disgusted France and Italy and destroyed any trust which had existed between the three of them. Mussolini, encouraged by Japanese and German successes, now followed suit with his successful invasion of Abyssinia (October 1935), which met only half-hearted resistance from the League and from Britain and France.

March 1936 saw Hitler sending troops into the Rhineland, which had been demilitarized by the Versailles Treaty; Britain and France again protested but took no action to expel the Germans. An understanding then followed (October 1936) between Germany and Italy, Mussolini having decided to throw in his lot with Hitler; it was known as *the Rome–Berlin Axis*. The following month Hitler signed *the Anti-Comintern Pact* with Japan. (The Comintern, or Communist International, was an organization set up in 1919 by Lenin with the aim of helping communist parties in other countries to work for revolution.) During the summer of 1936 the Spanish Civil War broke out when right-wing groups (Nationalists) tried to overthrow the left-wing Republican government. The conflict quickly developed an international significance when both Hitler and Mussolini, flexing their military muscles, sent help to Franco, the Nationalist leader, while the Republicans received Soviet help (see Section 15.3(c)). Predictably, Britain and France refused to intervene and by 1939 Franco was victorious.

In 1937 the Japanese took full advantage of Europe's preoccupation with events in Spain to embark on a full-scale invasion of northern China. The resulting Sino-Japanese War eventually became part of the Second World War.

By this time it was clear that the League of Nations, working through collective security, was totally ineffective. Consequently Hitler, now sure that the Italians would not object, carried out his most ambitious project to date – the annexation of Austria (known as the *Anschluss* – 'forcible union') in March 1938. Next he turned his attentions to Czechoslovakia and demanded the *Sudetenland*, an area containing three million Germans, adjoining the frontier with Germany. When the Czechs refused Hitler's demands, the British prime minister, Neville Chamberlain, anxious to avoid war at all costs, took up Hitler's invitation to a conference at Munich (September 1938), at which it was agreed that Germany should have the Sudetenland, but no more of Czechoslovakia.

War seemed to have been averted. But the following March, Hitler broke this agreement and sent German troops to occupy Prague, the Czech capital. At this, Chamberlain decided that Hitler had gone too far and must be stopped. When the Poles rejected Hitler's demand for Danzig, Britain and France promised to help Poland if the Germans attacked. Hitler did not take these British and French threats seriously, and grew tired of waiting for Poland to negotiate. After signing *a non-aggression pact with Russia* (August 1939), the Germans invaded Poland on 1 September. Britain and France accordingly declared war on Germany.

5.1 RELATIONS BETWEEN JAPAN AND CHINA

(a) The Japanese invasion of Manchuria in 1931

The motives behind this were mixed (see Section 15.1(b)). The Japanese felt it was essential to keep control of the province because it was a valuable trade outlet. China seemed to be growing stronger under the rule of Chiang Kai-shek, and the Japanese feared this might result in their being excluded from Manchuria. At the League of Nations, Sir John Simon, the British Foreign Secretary, presented a strong defence of Japan's actions. Japan had been involved in the province since the 1890s, and was given Port Arthur and a privileged position in South Manchuria as a result of the Russo-Japanese War (1904–5). Since then, the Japanese had invested millions of pounds in Manchuria in the development of industry and railways. By 1931 they controlled the South Manchurian Railway and the banking system; they felt they could not stand by and see themselves gradually squeezed out of such a valuable province with a population of 30 million, especially when the Japanese themselves were suffering economic hardship because of the Great Depression. The Japanese announced that they had turned Manchuria into the independent state of Manchukuo under Pu Yi, the last of the Chinese emperors. This fooled nobody, but still, no action was taken against them. The next Japanese move, however, could not be justified, and could only be described as flagrant aggression.

(b) The Japanese advance from Manchuria

In 1933 the Japanese began to advance from Manchuria into the rest of north-eastern China, to which they had no claim whatsoever. By 1935 a large area of China as far as Beijing (Peking) had fallen under Japanese political and commercial control (see Map 5.1), while the Chinese themselves were torn by a civil war between Chiang Kai-shek's Kuomintang government and the communists led by Mao Zedong (Mao Tse-tung) (see Section 19.3).

JAPANESE EXPANSION
1931–42

MILES
0   5000

USSR

MONGOLIA

USSR

MANCHURIA
1931-32

MANCHUKUO
1934

SAKHALIN

KURIL IS.

Vladivostok

Mukden

KOREA

JAPAN

C H I N A

Peking
1937

Tokyo

Pacific Ocean

Kaifeng
1938

Hankow

1938

Shanghai
1937

Chungking

Yang Tse

Nanchang
1939

RYUKYU
IS.

OKINAWA

Swatow
1938

Canton
1938

FORMOSA

INDIA

Hong
Kong 1941
(British)

BURMA
1942

Hanoi

HAINAN

Mariana
Is

Rangoon

SIAM

FRENCH
INDO-CHINA

PHILIPPINE IS.
(USA)

Guam
(USA)
1941

ANDAMAN
IS
(British)
1942

1940-41

JAPANESE MANDATE
FROM 1920

N
BORNEO
1942
BRUNEI

MINDANAO
1941

Caroline Is

SARAWAK
1942

MALAYA 1941-42
1942

Singapore
15-2-42

BORNEO
1942

D U T C H

SUMATRA

New
Britain

1942

Solomon Is.
(British)
1942

E A S T   I N D I E S

NEW
GUINEA

1941

JAVA

TIMOR
1942

Coral
Sea

Darwin

Indian Ocean

AUSTRALIA

Map 5.1 **Japanese expansion 1931–42**

(c) Further invasions

After signing the Anti-Comintern Pact with Germany (1936), the Japanese army seized the excuse provided by an incident between Chinese and Japanese troops in Peking to begin an invasion of other parts of China (July 1937). Although the prime minister, Prince Konoye, was against such massive intervention, he had to give way to the wishes of General Sugiyama, the war minister. By the autumn of 1938 the Japanese had captured the cities of Shanghai, Nanking (Chiang Kai-shek's capital) and Hankow, committing terrible atrocities against Chinese civilians. However, complete victory eluded the Japanese: Chiang had reached an understanding with his communist enemies that they would both co-operate against the invaders. A new capital was established well inland at Chungking, and spirited Chinese resistance was mounted with help from the Russians. However, Japanese troops landed in the south of China and quickly captured Canton, but Chiang still refused to surrender or accept Japanese terms.

Meanwhile the League of Nations had again condemned Japanese aggression but was powerless to act, since Japan was no longer a member and refused to attend a conference to discuss the situation in China. Britain and France were too busy coping with Hitler to take much notice of China, and the Russians did not want full-scale war with Japan. The USA, the only power capable of effectively resisting Japan, was still bent on isolation. Thus, on the eve of the Second World War, the Japanese controlled most of eastern China (though outside the cities their hold was shaky) while Chiang held out in the centre and west.

5.2 MUSSOLINI'S FOREIGN POLICY

In the early days of Mussolini's regime (he came to power in 1922 – see Section 13.1(e)), Italian foreign policy seemed rather confused: Mussolini knew what he wanted, which was 'to make Italy great, respected and feared', but he was not sure how to achieve this, apart from agitating for a revision of the 1919 peace settlement in Italy's favour. At first he seemed to think an adventurous foreign policy was his best line of action, hence the Corfu Incident (see Section 3.4(d)) and the occupation of Fiume in 1923. By an agreement signed at Rapallo in 1920, Fiume was to be a 'free city', used jointly by Italy and Yugoslavia; after Italian troops moved in, Yugoslavia agreed that it should belong to Italy. After these early successes, Mussolini became more cautious, perhaps alarmed by Italy's isolation at the time of Corfu. After 1923 his policy falls roughly into two phases with the break at 1934, when he began to draw closer towards Nazi Germany.

(a) 1923–34

At this stage Mussolini's policy was determined by rivalry with the French in the Mediterranean and the Balkans, where Italian relations with Yugoslavia, France's ally, were usually strained. Another consideration was the Italian fear that the weak state of Austria, along her north-eastern frontier, might fall too much under the influence of Germany; Mussolini was worried about a possible German threat via the Brenner Pass. He tried to deal with both problems mainly by diplomatic means:

1   *He attended the Locarno Conference (1925)* but was disappointed when the agreements signed did not guarantee the Italian frontier with Austria.
2   *He was friendly towards Greece, Hungary, and especially Albania*, the southern neighbour and rival of Yugoslavia. Economic and defence agreements were signed,

with the result that Albania was virtually controlled by Italy, which now had a strong position around the Adriatic Sea.

3 *He cultivated good relations with Britain*: he supported her demand that Turkey should hand over Mosul province to Iraq, and in return, the British gave Italy a small part of Somaliland.

4 *Italy became the first state after Britain to recognize the USSR*; a non-aggression pact was signed between Italy and the USSR in September 1933.

5 He tried to bolster up Austria against the threat from Nazi Germany by supporting the anti-Nazi government of Chancellor Dollfuss, and by signing trade agreements with Austria and Hungary. When Dollfuss was murdered by the Austrian Nazis (July 1934), Mussolini sent three Italian divisions to the frontier in case the Germans invaded Austria; the Nazis immediately called off their attempt to seize power in Austria. This decisive anti-German stand improved relations between Italy and France. However, though he was now highly respected abroad, Mussolini was getting impatient: his successes were not spectacular enough.

(b) After 1934

Mussolini gradually shifted from extreme suspicion of Hitler's designs on Austria to grudging admiration of Hitler's achievements and a desire to imitate him. After their first meeting (June 1934), Mussolini described Hitler contemptuously as 'that mad little clown', but he later came to believe that there was more to be gained from friendship with Germany than with Britain and France. The more he fell under Hitler's influence, the more aggressive he became. His changing attitude is illustrated by events:

1 When Hitler announced the reintroduction of conscription (March 1935), *Mussolini joined the British and French in condemning the German action and guaranteeing Austria (the Stresa Front, April 1935)*. Both British and French carefully avoided mentioning the Abyssinian crisis, which was already brewing; Mussolini took this to mean that they would turn a blind eye to an Italian attack on Abyssinia, regarding it as a bit of old-fashioned colonial expansion. The Anglo-German Naval Agreement signed in June (see Section 5.3(b), Point 6) convinced Mussolini of British cynicism and self-interest.

2 *The Italian invasion of Abyssinia (Ethiopia)* in October 1935 was the great turning point in Mussolini's career. Italian involvement in the country, the only remaining independent state left in Africa, went back to 1896, when an Italian attempt to colonize it had ended in ignominious defeat at Adowa. *Mussolini's motives for the 1935 attack were*:

- Italy's existing colonies in East Africa (Eritrea and Somaliland) were not very rewarding, and his attempts (by a treaty of 'friendship' signed in 1928) to reduce Abyssinia to a position equivalent to that of Albania had failed. The Emperor of Abyssinia, Haile Selassie, had done all he could to avoid falling under Italian economic domination.
- Italy was suffering from the depression, and a victorious war would divert attention from internal troubles and provide a new market for Italian exports.
- It would please the nationalists and colonialists, avenge the defeat of 1896 and boost Mussolini's sagging popularity.

3 The Italian victory over the ill-equipped and unprepared Ethiopians was a foregone conclusion, though they made heavy weather of it. *Its real importance was that it*

demonstrated the ineffectiveness of collective security. The League condemned Italy as an aggressor and applied economic sanctions; but these were useless because they did not include banning sales of oil and coal to Italy, even though the resulting oil shortage would have seriously hampered the Italian war effort. The League's prestige suffered a further blow when it emerged that the British Foreign Secretary, Sir Samuel Hoare, had made a secret deal with Laval, the French prime minister (December 1935), to hand over a large section of Abyssinia to Italy; this was more than the Italians had managed to capture at that point (see Map 5.2). Public opinion in Britain was so outraged that the idea was dropped.

4 *Reasons for this weak stand against Italy* were that Britain and France were militarily and economically unprepared for war and were anxious to avoid any action (such as oil sanctions) that might provoke Mussolini into declaring war on them. They were also hoping to revive the Stresa Front and use Italy as an ally against the real threat to European peace – Germany; so their aim was to appease Mussolini. *Unfortunately the results were disastrous*:

- The League and the idea of collective security were discredited.
- Mussolini was annoyed by the sanctions anyway, and began to be drawn towards friendship with Hitler, who had not criticized the invasion and had not

Map 5.2   **The position of Abyssinia and the territories of Britain, France and Italy**

Source: Nichol and Lang, *Work Out Modern World History* (Macmillan, 1990), p. 47

applied sanctions. In return, Mussolini dropped his objections to a German takeover of Austria. Hitler took advantage of the general preoccupation with Abyssinia to send troops into the Rhineland.

5   When the Spanish Civil War broke out in 1936, *Mussolini sent extensive help to Franco, the right-wing Nationalist leader*, hoping to establish a third fascist state in Europe and to get naval bases in Spain from which he could threaten France. His justification was that he wanted to prevent the spread of communism.

6   An understanding was reached with Hitler known as *the Rome–Berlin Axis.* Mussolini said that the Axis was a line drawn between Rome and Berlin, around which 'all European states that desire peace can revolve'. In 1937 Italy joined *the Anti-Comintern Pact* with Germany and Japan, in which all three pledged themselves to stand side by side against Bolshevism. This reversal of his previous policy, and his friendship with Germany, were not universally popular in Italy, and disillusionment with Mussolini began to spread.

7   *His popularity revived temporarily with his part in the Munich agreement of September 1938* (see Section 5.5), which seemed to have secured peace. But Mussolini failed to draw the right conclusions from his people's relief – that most of them did not want another war – and he committed a further act of aggression.

8   *In April 1939 Italian troops suddenly occupied Albania*, meeting very little resistance. This was a pointless operation, since Albania was already under Italian economic control, but Mussolini wanted a triumph to imitate Hitler's recent occupation of Czechoslovakia.

9   Carried away by his successes, *Mussolini signed a full alliance with Germany, the Pact of Steel (May 1939)*, in which Italy promised full military support if war came. Mussolini was committing Italy to deeper and deeper involvement with Germany, which in the end would ruin him.

5.3   WHAT WERE HITLER'S AIMS IN FOREIGN POLICY, AND HOW SUCCESSFUL HAD HE BEEN BY THE END OF 1938?

(a)   Hitler aimed to make Germany into a great power again

He hoped to achieve this by:

- destroying the hated Versailles settlement;
- building up the army;
- recovering lost territory such as the Saar and the Polish Corridor;
- bringing all German-speaking peoples inside the Reich; this would involve annexing Austria and taking territory from Czechoslovakia and Poland, both of which had large German minorities as a result of the peace settlement.

There is some disagreement about what, if anything, Hitler intended beyond these aims. Some historians believe that annexing Austria and parts of Czechoslovakia and Poland was only a beginning, and that Hitler planned to follow it up by seizing the rest of Czechoslovakia and Poland, and then conquering and occupying Russia as far east as the Ural Mountains. 'National boundaries', he said, 'are only made by man and can be changed by man.' The changes of boundary which Hitler had in mind would give the Germans what he called *Lebensraum* (living space). He claimed that Germany's population was much too large for the area into which it was constrained; more land was needed to provide food for the German people as well as an area in which the excess German population could settle and colonize. Certainly Hitler had made clear his hatred of what he called 'Jewish Bolshevism'. This suggests that war with the USSR was unavoidable at some point, in order to destroy communism. The next stage would be to get colonies in Africa and naval bases in and around the Atlantic.

Other historians disagree about these further aims; back in 1961 A. J. P. Taylor claimed that Hitler never had any detailed plans worked out for acquiring *Lebensraum* and never intended a major war; at most he was prepared only for a limited war against Poland. 'He got as far as he did because others did not know what to do with him', concluded Taylor. Martin Broszat, writing in 1983, also believed that Hitler's writings and statements about *Lebensraum* did not amount to an actual programme which he followed step by step. It is more likely they were a propaganda exercise designed to attract support and unite the Nazi party. More recently Mark Mazower, in his book *Hitler's Empire: Nazi Rule in Occupied Europe* (2008), suggests that there is very little evidence that Hitler had given much serious thought to the problems of creating and organising a Nazi empire in Europe.

(b) A series of successes

Whatever the truth about his long-term intentions, Hitler began his foreign policy with an almost unbroken series of brilliant successes, which was one of the main reasons for his popularity in Germany. By the end of 1938 almost every one of the first set of aims had been achieved, without war and with the approval of Britain. Only the Germans in Poland remained to be brought within the *Reich*. Unfortunately it was when he failed to achieve this by peaceful means that Hitler took the fateful decision to invade Poland.

1 Given that Germany was still militarily weak in 1933, *Hitler had to move cautiously at first*. He withdrew Germany from the World Disarmament Conference and from the League of Nations, on the grounds that France would not agree to Germany having equality of armaments. At the same time he insisted that Germany was willing to disarm if other states would do the same, and that he wanted only peace. This was one of his favourite techniques: to act boldly while at the same time soothing his opponents with the sort of conciliatory speeches he knew they wanted to hear.

2 *Next Hitler signed a ten-year non-aggression pact with the Poles (January 1934)*, who were showing alarm in case the Germans tried to take back the Polish Corridor. This was something of a triumph for Hitler: Britain took it as further evidence of his peaceful intentions; it ruined France's Little Entente (see Section 4.2(b)), which depended very much on Poland; and it guaranteed Polish neutrality whenever Germany decided to move against Austria and Czechoslovakia. On the other hand, it improved relations between France and Russia, who were both worried by the apparent threat from Nazi Germany.

3 In July 1934 Hitler suffered a setback to his ambitions of an *Anschluss* (union) between Germany and Austria. The Austrian Nazis, encouraged by Hitler, staged a revolt and murdered the Chancellor, Engelbert Dollfuss, who had been supported by Mussolini. However, when Mussolini moved Italian troops to the Austrian frontier and warned the Germans off, the revolt collapsed. Hitler, taken aback, had to accept that Germany was not yet strong enough to force the issue, and he denied responsibility for the actions of the Austrian Nazis.

4 *The Saar was returned to Germany (January 1935)* after a plebiscite (referendum) resulting in a 90 per cent vote in favour. Though the vote had been provided for in the peace settlement, Nazi propaganda made the most of the success. Hitler announced that now all causes of grievance between France and Germany had been removed.

5   Hitler's first successful breach of Versailles came in March 1935 when he announced *the reintroduction of conscription*. His excuse was that Britain had just announced air force increases and France had extended conscription from 12 to 18 months (their justification was German rearmament). Much to their alarm, Hitler told his startled generals and the rest of the world that he would build up his peace-time army to 36 divisions (about 600 000 men) – six times more than was allowed by the peace treaty. The generals need not have worried: although the Stresa Front (consisting of Britain, France and Italy) condemned this violation of Versailles, no action was taken; the League was helpless, and the Front collapsed anyway as a result of Hitler's next success.

6   Shrewdly realizing how frail the Stresa Front was, Hitler detached Britain by offering to limit the German navy to 35 per cent of the strength of the British navy. Britain eagerly accepted, signing *the Anglo-German Naval Agreement (June 1935)*; British thinking seems to have been that since the Germans were already breaking Versailles by building a fleet, it would be as well to have it limited. Without consulting her two allies, Britain had condoned German rearmament, which went ahead with gathering momentum. By the end of 1938 the army stood at 51 divisions (about 800 000 men) plus reserves, there were 21 large naval vessels (battleships, cruisers and destroyers), many more under construction, and 47 U-boats. A large air force of over 5000 aircraft had been built up.

7   Encouraged by his successes, Hitler took the calculated risk of *sending troops into the demilitarized zone of the Rhineland (March 1936)*, a breach of both Versailles and Locarno. Though the troops had orders to withdraw at the first sign of French opposition, no resistance was offered, except the usual protests. At the same time, well aware of the mood of pacifism among his opponents, Hitler soothed them by offering a peace treaty to last for 25 years.

8   Later in 1936 Hitler consolidated Germany's position by reaching an understanding with Mussolini (*the Rome–Berlin Axis*) and by signing *the Anti-Comintern Pact with Japan* (also joined by Italy in 1937). Germans and Italians gained military experience by helping Franco to victory in the Spanish Civil War. One of the most notorious exploits in this war was the bombing of the defenceless Basque market town of Guernica by the German Condor Legion (see Section 15.3).

9   *The Anschluss with Austria (March 1938)* was Hitler's greatest success to date (see Section 4.4(d) for the situation in Austria). Matters came to a head when the Austrian Nazis staged huge demonstrations in Vienna, Graz and Linz, which Chancellor Schuschnigg's government could not control. Realizing that this could be the prelude to a German invasion, Schuschnigg announced a referendum about whether or not Austria should remain independent. Hitler decided to act before it was held, in case the vote went against union; German troops moved in and Austria became part of the Third Reich. It was a triumph for Germany: it revealed the weakness of Britain and France, who again only protested. It showed the value of the new German understanding with Italy, and it dealt a severe blow to Czechoslovakia, which could now be attacked from the south as well as from the west and north. All was ready for the beginning of Hitler's campaign to get the German-speaking Sudetenland, a campaign which ended in triumph at the Munich Conference in September 1938.

Before examining the events of Munich and after, it will be a good idea to pause and consider why it was that Hitler was allowed to get away with all these violations of the Versailles settlement. The reason can be summed up in one word – *appeasement*.

(a)   What is meant by the term 'appeasement'?

Appeasement was the policy followed by the British, and later by the French, of *avoiding war with aggressive powers such as Japan, Italy and Germany, by giving way to their demands*, provided they were not too unreasonable.

There were two distinct phases of appeasement

1. *From the mid-1920s until 1937*, there was a vague feeling that war must be avoided at all cost, and Britain and sometimes France drifted along, accepting the various acts of aggression and breaches of Versailles (Manchuria, Abyssinia, German rearmament, the Rhineland reoccupation).
2. When Neville Chamberlain became British prime minister in May 1937, he gave appeasement new drive; he believed in taking the initiative – he would find out what Hitler wanted and show him that reasonable claims could be met *by negotiation rather than by force*.

The beginnings of appeasement can be seen in British policy during the 1920s with the Dawes and Young Plans, which tried to conciliate the Germans, and also with the Locarno Treaties and their vital omission – Britain did not agree to guarantee Germany's eastern frontiers (see Map 5.3), which even Stresemann, the 'good German', said must be revised. When Austen Chamberlain, the British Foreign Minister (and Neville's half-brother), remarked at the time of Locarno that no British government would ever risk the bones of a single British grenadier in defence of the Polish Corridor, it seemed to the Germans that Britain had turned her back on eastern Europe. Appeasement reached its climax at Munich, where Britain and France were so determined to avoid war with Germany that they made Hitler a present of the Sudetenland, and so set in motion the destruction of Czechoslovakia. Even with such big concessions as this, appeasement failed.

Map 5.3   **Hitler's gains before the Second World War**

(b) How could appeasement be justified?

At the time appeasement was being followed, there seemed to be many very good things in its favour, and the appeasers (who included MacDonald, Baldwin, Simon and Hoare as well as Neville Chamberlain) were convinced that their policy was right:

1 *It was thought essential to avoid war,* which was likely to be even more devastating than ever before, as the horrors of the Spanish Civil War demonstrated. The great fear was the bombing of defenceless cities. Memories of the horrors of the First World War still haunted many people. Britain, still in the throes of the economic crisis, could not afford vast rearmament and the crippling expenses of a major war. British governments seemed to be supported by *a strongly pacifist public opinion.* In February 1933, in a much-publicized debate, the Oxford Union voted that it would not fight for King and Country. Baldwin and his National Government won a huge election victory in November 1935 shortly after he had declared: 'I give you my word of honour that there will be no great armaments.'

2 *Many felt that Germany and Italy had genuine grievances.* Italy had been cheated at Versailles and Germany had been treated too harshly. Therefore the British should show them sympathy – as far as the Germans were concerned, they should try and revise the most hated clauses of Versailles. This would remove the need for German aggression and lead to Anglo-German friendship.

3 Since the League of Nations seemed to be helpless, Chamberlain believed that the only way to settle disputes was by *personal contact between leaders*. In this way, he thought, he would be able to control and civilize Hitler, and Mussolini into the bargain, and bring them to respect international law.

4 *Economic co-operation between Britain and Germany would be good for both*. If Britain helped the German economy to recover, Germany's internal violence would die down.

5 *Fear of communist Russia* was great, especially among British Conservatives. Many of them believed that the communist threat was greater than the danger from Hitler. Some British politicians were willing to ignore the unpleasant features of Nazism in the hope that Hitler's Germany would be *a buffer against communist expansion westwards*. In fact, many admired Hitler's drive and his achievements.

6 Underlying all these feelings was the belief that Britain ought not to take any military action in case it led to *a full-scale war, for which Britain was totally unprepared*. British military chiefs told Chamberlain that Britain was not strong enough to fight a war against more than one country at the same time. Even the navy, which was the strongest in the world apart from the American navy, would have found it difficult to defend Britain's far-flung Empire and at the same time protect merchant shipping in the event of war against Germany, Japan and Italy simultaneously. The air force was woefully short of long-range bombers and fighters. The USA was still in favour of isolation and France was weak and divided. Chamberlain speeded up British rearmament so that 'nobody should treat her with anything but respect'. The longer appeasement lasted, the stronger Britain would become, and the more this would deter aggression, or so Chamberlain hoped.

(c) What part did appeasement play in international affairs, 1933–9?

Appeasement had a profound effect on the way international relations developed. Although it might have worked with some German governments, with Hitler it was doomed to failure. Many historians believe that it convinced Hitler of the complacency and weakness of Britain and France to such an extent that he was willing to risk attacking Poland, thereby starting the Second World War.

It is important to emphasize that appeasement was mainly a British policy, with which the French did not always agree. Poincaré stood up to the Germans (see Section 4.2(c)), and although Briand was in favour of conciliation, even he drew the line at the proposed Austro-German customs union in 1931. Louis Barthou, foreign minister for a few months in 1934, believed in firmness towards Hitler and aimed to build up a strong anti-German group which would include Italy and the USSR. This is why he pressed for Russia's entry into the League of Nations, which took place in September 1934. He told the British that France 'refused to legalize German rearmament', contrary to the Versailles Treaties. Unfortunately Barthou was assassinated in October 1934, along with King Alexander of Yugoslavia, who was on a state visit to France. They were both shot by Croat terrorists shortly after the king had arrived in Marseilles. Barthou's successor, Pierre Laval, signed an alliance with Russia in May 1935, though it was a weak affair – there was no provision in it for military co-operation, since Laval distrusted the communists. He pinned his main hopes on friendship with Mussolini, but these were dashed by the failure of the Hoare–Laval Pact (see Section 5.2(b)). After this the French were so deeply split between left and right that no decisive foreign policy seemed possible; since the right admired Hitler, the French fell in behind the British.

Examples of appeasement at work

1 *No action was taken to check the obvious German rearmament.* Lord Lothian, a Liberal, had a revealing comment to make about this, after visiting Hitler in January 1935: 'I am convinced that Hitler does not want war … what the Germans are after is a strong army which will enable them to deal with Russia.'

2 *The Anglo-German Naval Agreement* condoning German naval rearmament was signed without any consultation with France and Italy. This broke the Stresa Front, gravely shook French confidence in Britain, and encouraged Laval to look for understandings with Mussolini and Hitler.

3 There was only *half-hearted British action against the Italian invasion of Abyssinia.*

4 The French, though disturbed at the German reoccupation of the Rhineland (March 1936), *did not mobilize their troops.* They were deeply divided, and ultra cautious, and they received no backing from the British, who were impressed by Hitler's offer of a 25-year peace. In fact, Lord Londonderry (a Conservative, and Secretary of State for Air from 1931 to 1935), was reported to have sent Hitler a telegram congratulating him on his success. Lord Lothian remarked that German troops had merely entered their own 'back garden'.

5 *Neither Britain nor France intervened in the Spanish Civil War*, though Germany and Italy sent decisive help to Franco. Britain tried to entice Mussolini to remove his troops by officially recognizing Italian possession of Abyssinia (April 1938); however, Mussolini failed to keep his side of the bargain.

6 Though both Britain and France protested strongly at the *Anschluss* between Germany and Austria (March 1938), many in Britain saw it as *the natural union of one German group with another.* But Britain's lack of action encouraged Hitler to make demands on Czechoslovakia, which produced Chamberlain's supreme act of appeasement and Hitler's greatest triumph to date – Munich.

5.5 MUNICH TO THE OUTBREAK OF WAR: SEPTEMBER 1938 TO SEPTEMBER 1939

This fateful year saw Hitler waging two pressure campaigns: the first against Czechoslovakia, the second against Poland.

(a) Czechoslovakia

It seems likely that Hitler had decided to destroy Czechoslovakia as part of his *Lebensraum* (living space) policy, and because he detested the Czechs for their democracy, for the fact that they were Slavs, and because their state had been set up by the hated Versailles settlement (see Section 4.4(b) for the situation in Czechoslovakia). Its situation was strategically important – control of the area would bring great advantages for Germany's military and economic dominance of central Europe.

1 The propaganda campaign in the Sudetenland
Hitler's excuse for the opening propaganda campaign was that 3.5 million Sudeten Germans, under their leader Konrad Henlein, were being discriminated against by the Czech government. It is true that unemployment was more serious among the Germans, but this was because a large proportion of them worked in industry, where unemployment was most severe because of the depression. The Nazis organized huge protest demonstrations in the Sudetenland, and clashes occurred between Czechs and Germans. The Czech president, Edvard Beneš, feared that Hitler was stirring up the disturbances so that German troops could march in 'to restore order'. Chamberlain and Daladier, the French prime minister, were afraid that if this happened, war would break out. They were determined to go to almost any lengths to avoid war, and they put tremendous pressure on the Czechs to make concessions to Hitler.

Eventually Beneš agreed that the Sudeten Germans might be handed over to Germany. Chamberlain flew to Germany and had talks with Hitler at Berchtesgaden (15 September), explaining the offer. Hitler seemed to accept, but at a second meeting at Godesberg only a week later, he stepped up his demands: he wanted more of Czechoslovakia and the immediate entry of German troops into the Sudetenland. Beneš would not agree to this and immediately ordered the mobilization of the Czech army. The Czechs had put great effort into fortifying their frontiers with Germany, Austria and Hungary, building bunkers and anti-tank defences. Their army had been expanded, and they were hopeful that with help from their allies, particularly France and the USSR, any German attack could be repulsed. It would certainly not have been a walkover for the Germans.

2 The Munich Conference, 29 September 1938
When it seemed that war was inevitable, Hitler invited Chamberlain and Daladier to a four-power conference, which met in Munich. Here a plan produced by Mussolini (but actually written by the German Foreign Office) was accepted. The Sudetenland was to be handed over to Germany immediately, Poland was given Teschen and Hungary received South Slovakia. Germany, along with the other three powers, guaranteed the rest of Czechoslovakia. Neither the Czechs nor the Russians were invited to the conference. The Czechs were told that if they resisted the Munich decision, they would receive no help from Britain or France, even though France had guaranteed the Czech frontiers at Locarno. Given this betrayal by France and the unsympathetic attitude of Britain, Czech military resistance seemed hopeless: they had no choice but to go along with the decision of the conference. A few days later Beneš resigned.

The morning after the Munich Conference, Chamberlain had a private meeting with Hitler at which they both signed a statement, the 'scrap of paper', prepared by Chamberlain, promising that Britain and Germany would renounce warlike intentions against each other and would use consultation to deal with any problems that might arise. When Chamberlain arrived back in Britain, waving the 'scrap of paper' for the benefit of the newsreel cameras, he was given a rapturous welcome by the public, who thought war had been averted. Chamberlain himself remarked: 'I believe it is peace for our time.'

However, not everybody was so enthusiastic: Churchill called Munich 'a total and unmitigated defeat'; Duff Cooper, the First Lord of the Admiralty, resigned from the cabinet, saying that Hitler could not be trusted to keep the agreement. They were right.

3 The destruction of Czechoslovakia, March 1939

As a result of the Munich Agreement, Czechoslovakia was crippled by the loss of 70 per cent of her heavy industry, a third of her population, roughly a third of her territory and almost all her carefully prepared fortifications, mostly to Germany. Slovakia and Ruthenia were given self-government for internal affairs, though there was still a central government in Prague. Early in 1939 Slovakia, encouraged by Germany, began to demand complete independence from Prague and it looked as if the country was about to fall apart. Hitler put pressure on the Slovak prime minister, Father Jozef Tiso, to declare independence and request German help, but Tiso was ultra-cautious.

It was the new Czech president, Emil Hacha, who brought matters to a head. On 9 March 1939 the Prague government moved against the Slovaks to forestall the expected declaration of independence: their cabinet was deposed, Tiso was placed under house arrest, and the Slovak government buildings in Bratislava were occupied by police. This gave Hitler his chance to act: Tiso was brought to Berlin, where Hitler convinced him that the time was now ripe. Back in Bratislava, Tiso and the Slovaks proclaimed independence (14 March); the next day they asked for German protection, although, as Ian Kershaw points out (in *Hitler, 1936–1945: Nemesis*), this was only 'after German warships on the Danube had trained their sights on the Slovakian government offices'.

Next, President Hacha was invited to Berlin, where Hitler told him that in order to protect the German Reich, a protectorate must be imposed over what was left of Czechoslovakia. German troops were poised to enter his country, and Hacha was to order the Czech army not to resist. Goering threatened that Prague would be bombed if he refused. Faced with such a browbeating, Hacha felt he had no alternative but to agree. Consequently, on 15 March 1939 German troops occupied the rest of Czechoslovakia while the Czech army remained in barracks. Bohemia and Moravia (the main Czech areas) were declared a protectorate within the German Reich, Slovakia was to be an independent state but under the protection of the Reich, and Ruthenia was occupied by Hungarian troops. Britain and France protested but as usual took no action. Chamberlain said the guarantee of Czech frontiers given at Munich did not apply, because technically the country had not been invaded – German troops had entered by invitation. Hitler was greeted with enthusiasm when he visited the Sudetenland.

However, the German action caused a great outburst of criticism: for the first time even the appeasers were unable to justify what Hitler had done – he had broken his promise and seized non-German territory. Even Chamberlain felt this was going too far, and his attitude hardened.

(b) Poland

After taking over the Lithuanian port of Memel (which was admittedly peopled largely by Germans), Hitler turned his attentions to Poland.

1 Hitler demands the return of Danzig

The Germans resented the loss of Danzig and the Polish Corridor, at Versailles, and now that Czechoslovakia was safely out of the way, Polish neutrality was no longer necessary. In April 1939 Hitler demanded *the return of Danzig and a road and railway across the corridor, linking East Prussia with the rest of Germany*. This demand was, in fact, not unreasonable, since Danzig was mainly German-speaking; but with it coming so soon after the seizure of Czechoslovakia, the Poles were convinced that the German demands were only the preliminary to an invasion. Already fortified by a British promise of help 'in the event of any action which clearly threatened Polish independence', the Foreign Minister, Colonel Beck, rejected the German demands and refused to attend a conference; no doubt he was afraid of another Munich. British pressure on the Poles to surrender Danzig was to no avail. Hitler was probably surprised by Beck's stubbornness, and was still hoping to remain on good terms with the Poles, at least for the time being.

2 The Germans invade Poland

The only way the British promise of help to Poland could be made effective was through an alliance with Russia. But the British were so slow and hesitant in their negotiations for an alliance that Hitler got in first and signed *a non-aggression pact with the USSR*. They also reached a secret agreement *to divide Poland up between Germany and the USSR* (24 August). Hitler was convinced now that with Russia neutral, Britain and France would not risk intervention; when the British ratified their guarantee to Poland, Hitler took it as a bluff. When the Poles still refused to negotiate, a full-scale German invasion began, early on 1 September 1939.

Chamberlain had still not completely thrown off appeasement and suggested that if German troops were withdrawn, a conference could be held – there was no response from the Germans. Only when pressure mounted in parliament and in the country did Chamberlain send an ultimatum to Germany: if German troops were not withdrawn from Poland, Britain would declare war. Hitler did not even bother to reply; when the ultimatum expired, at 11 a.m. on 3 September, Britain was at war with Germany. Soon afterwards, France also declared war.

5.6 WHY DID WAR BREAK OUT? WERE HITLER OR THE APPEASERS TO BLAME?

The debate is still going on about who or what was responsible for the Second World War.

- The Versailles Treaties have been blamed for filling the Germans with bitterness and the desire for revenge.
- The League of Nations and the idea of collective security have been criticized because they failed to secure general disarmament and to control potential aggressors.
- The world economic crisis has been mentioned (see Sections 14.1(e–f) and 22.6(c)), since without it, Hitler would probably never have been able to come to power.

While these factors no doubt helped to create the sort of atmosphere and tensions which might well lead to a war, something more was needed. It is worth remembering also that by the end of 1938, most of Germany's grievances had been removed: reparations were largely cancelled, the disarmament clauses had been ignored, the Rhineland was remilitarized, Austria and Germany were united, and 3.5 million Germans had been brought into the Reich from Czechoslovakia. Germany was a great power again. So what went wrong?

(a) Were the appeasers to blame?

Some historians have suggested that appeasement was largely responsible for the situation deteriorating into war. They argue that *Britain and France should have taken a firm line with Hitler before Germany had become too strong:* an Anglo-French attack on western Germany in 1936 at the time of the Rhineland occupation would have taught Hitler a lesson and might have toppled him from power. By giving way to him, the appeasers increased his prestige at home. As Alan Bullock wrote, 'success and the absence of resistance tempted Hitler to reach out further, to take bigger risks'. He may not have had definite plans for war, but after the surrender at Munich, he was so convinced that Britain and France would remain passive again, that he decided to gamble on war with Poland.

Chamberlain has also been criticized for choosing the wrong issue over which to make a stand against Hitler. It is argued that German claims for Danzig and routes across the corridor were more reasonable than the demands for the Sudetenland (which contained almost a million non-Germans). Poland was difficult for Britain and France to defend and was militarily much weaker than Czechoslovakia. Chamberlain therefore should have made his stand at Munich and backed the Czechs, who were militarily and industrially strong and had excellent fortifications.

Chamberlain's defenders, on the other hand, claim that his main motive at Munich was to give Britain time to rearm for an eventual fight against Hitler. Arguably Munich did gain a crucial year during which Britain was able to press ahead with its rearmament programme. John Charmley, in his book *Chamberlain and the Lost Peace* (1989), argues that Chamberlain had very little option but to act as he did, and that Chamberlain's policies were far more realistic than any of the possible alternatives – such as building up a Grand Alliance, including Britain, France, Poland, Czechoslovakia, Romania and the USSR. This idea was suggested at the time by Churchill, but Andrew Roberts (2006) argues that this was never a serious possibility because of the many points of disagreement between them. Chamberlain's most recent biographer, Robert Self (2007), believes that he had very few viable alternatives and deserves great credit for trying to prevent war. Surely any 'normal' leader, like Stresemann, for example, would have responded positively to Chamberlain's reasonable policies; sadly Hitler was not the typical German statesman. Having said all this, arguably Britain and France must at least share the responsibility for war in 1939. As Richard Overy pointed out in *The Origins of the Second World War* (2nd edition, 1998):

> It must not be forgotten that war in 1939 was declared by Britain and France on Germany, and not the other way round. Why did the two western powers go to war with Germany? Britain and France had complex interests and motives for war. They too had to take decisions on international questions with one eye on public opinion and another on potential enemies elsewhere. ... British and French policy before 1939 was governed primarily by national self-interest and only secondarily by moral considerations. In other words, the British and French, just like the Germans, were anxious to preserve or extend their power and safeguard their economic interests. In the end this meant going to war in 1939 to preserve Franco-British power and prestige.

(b) Did the USSR make war inevitable?

The USSR has been accused of making war inevitable by signing the non-aggression pact with Germany on 23 August 1939, which also included a secret agreement for Poland to be partitioned between Germany and the USSR. It is argued that Stalin ought to have allied with the west and with Poland, thus frightening Hitler into keeping the peace. On the other hand, the British were most reluctant to ally with the Russians; Chamberlain distrusted them (because they were communists) and so did the Poles, and he thought they were militarily weak. Russian historians justify the pact on the grounds that it gave the USSR time to prepare its defences against a possible German attack.

(c) Was Hitler to blame?

During and immediately after the war there was general agreement outside Germany that Hitler was to blame. By attacking Poland on all fronts instead of merely occupying Danzig and the Corridor, Hitler showed that he intended not just to get back the Germans lost at Versailles, but to destroy Poland. Martin Gilbert argues that his motive was to remove the stigma of defeat in the First World War: 'for the only antidote to defeat in one war is victory in the next'. Hugh Trevor-Roper and many other historians believe that *Hitler intended a major war right from the beginning.* They argue that he hated communism and wanted to destroy Russia and control it permanently. In this way, Germany would acquire *Lebensraum*, but it could only be achieved by a major war. The destruction of Poland was an essential preliminary to the invasion of Russia. The German non-aggression pact with Russia was simply a way of lulling Russian suspicions and keeping her neutral until Poland had been dealt with.

Evidence for this theory is taken from statements in Hitler's book *Mein Kampf* (*My Struggle*) and from the Hossbach Memorandum, a summary made by Hitler's adjutant, Colonel Hossbach, of a meeting held in November 1937, at which Hitler explained his expansionist plans to his generals. Another important source of evidence is Hitler's *Secret Book*, which he finished around 1928 but never published.

If this theory is correct, appeasement cannot be blamed as a cause of war, except that it made things easier for Hitler. Hitler had his plans, his 'blueprint' for action, and this meant that war was inevitable sooner or later. Germans, on the whole, were happy with this interpretation too. If Hitler was to blame, and Hitler and the Nazis could be viewed as a kind of grotesque accident, a temporary 'blip' in German history, that meant that the German people were largely free from blame.

Not everybody accepted this interpretation. A. J. P. Taylor, in his book *The Origins of the Second World War* (1961), came up with the most controversial theory about the outbreak of the war. He believed that *Hitler did not intend to cause a major war, and expected at the most, a short war with Poland.* According to Taylor, Hitler's aims were similar to those of previous German rulers – Hitler was simply continuing the policies of leaders like Bismarck, Kaiser Wilhelm II and Stresemann; the only difference was that Hitler's methods were more ruthless. Hitler was a brilliant opportunist taking advantage of the mistakes of the appeasers and of events such as the crisis in Czechoslovakia in February 1939. Taylor thought the German occupation of the rest of Czechoslovakia in March 1939 was not the result of a sinister long-term plan; 'it was the unforeseen by-product of events in Slovakia' (the Slovak demand for more independence from the Prague government). Whereas Chamberlain miscalculated when he thought he could make Hitler respectable and civilized, Hitler misread the minds of Chamberlain and the British. How could Hitler foresee that the British and French would be so inconsistent as to support Poland (where his claim to land was more reasonable) after giving way to him over Czechoslovakia (where his case was much less valid)?

Thus, for Taylor, Hitler was lured into the war almost by accident, after the Poles had called his bluff. 'The war of 1939, far from being premeditated, was a mistake, the result on both sides of diplomatic blunders.' Many people in Britain were outraged at Taylor because they thought he was trying to 'whitewash' Hitler. But Taylor was not defending Hitler; just the opposite, in fact – Hitler was still to blame, and so were the German people, for being aggressive. 'Hitler was the creation of German history and of the German present. He would have counted for nothing without the support and cooperation of the German people. ... Many hundred thousand Germans carried out his evil orders without qualm or question.'

Most recent interpretations have tended to play down Taylor's 'continuity' theory and highlight the *differences in aims between earlier German rulers on the one hand, and Hitler and the Nazis on the other*. Until 1937, Nazi foreign policy could be seen as typically conservative and nationalistic. It was only when all the wrongs of Versailles had been put right – the main aim of the conservatives and nationalists – that the crucial differences began to be revealed. The Hossbach memorandum shows that Hitler was preparing to go much further and embark on an ambitious expansionist policy. But there was more to it even than that. As Neil Gregor points out (2003), what Hitler had in mind was 'a racial war of destruction quite unlike that experienced in 1914–18'. It began with the dismemberment of Poland, continued with the attack on the USSR, and culminated in an horrific genocidal war – the destruction of the Jews and other groups which the Nazis considered inferior to the German master race; and the destruction of communism. 'Nazism was a destructive new force whose vision of imperial domination was radically different' from anything that had gone before.

Another explanation of why Hitler decided to risk war in September 1939 was put forward by Adam Tooze in his book *The Wages of Destruction: The Making and Breaking of the Nazi Economy* (2006). His theory is that Hitler was afraid that the longer he delayed the inevitable war, the greater the danger that Britain and France would overtake German rearmament. According to Tooze, 'Hitler knew that he would eventually have to confront the Western powers. And in the autumn of 1939 he attacked Poland because he had decided that he was willing to risk that wider war sooner rather than later. ... The military advantage that Germany currently enjoyed over its enemies was fleeting.' Germany had been steadily rearming, even before Hitler came to power. From 1936, when the Four Year Plan was introduced, until 1939, no less than two thirds of all investment in industry was for producing war materials. Richard Overy points out that in 1939 about a quarter of the industrial workforce was employed on military orders, 'a figure unmatched by any other state in Europe'. The problem was that the German armaments industry was running short of raw materials, mainly because Germany's shortage of foreign exchange made it impossible to import sufficient quantities of iron and copper ore. Throughout the interwar period the Reichsmark was chronically overvalued, making exports uncompetitive. Hitler complained that Germany's enemies, egged on by their Jewish backers, had closed their borders to German exports. To make matters worse, in response to the German occupation of Prague, in March 1939 President Roosevelt of the USA placed punitive tariffs on imports from Germany. As Tooze explains:

> Hitler might have wished to fight the big war against Britain and France at a moment of his choosing at some point in the early 1940s, but by early 1939 the pace of events had rendered such long-term plans impractical. With America, France and Britain appearing to grow ever closer together, there was no time to lose. If Hitler's sworn enemies were improvising, so would he. It was time to wager everything. Otherwise, faced by a global coalition animated by its implacable Jewish enemies, Germany would face certain ruin.

What conclusion are we to reach? Today, over forty years after Taylor published his famous book, very few historians accept his theory that Hitler had no long-term plans for war. Some recent writers believe that Taylor ignored much evidence which did not fit in with his own theory. It is true that some of Hitler's successes came through clever opportunism, but there was much more behind it than that. Although he probably did not have a long-term, detailed step-by-step plan worked out, he clearly had a basic vision, which he was working towards at every opportunity. That vision was a Europe dominated by Germany, and it could only be achieved by war. This is why there was so much emphasis on rearmament from 1936 onwards. Clearly Hitler intended much more than self-defence.

There can be little doubt, then, that Hitler *was* largely responsible for the war. The German historian Eberhard Jäckel, writing in 1984, claimed that

> Hitler set himself two goals: a war of conquest and the elimination of the Jews. … [his] ultimate goal was the establishment of a greater Germany than had ever existed before in history. The way to this greater Germany was a war of conquest fought mainly at the expense of Soviet Russia … where the German nation was to gain living space for generations to come. … Militarily the war would be easy because Germany would be opposed only by a disorganized country of Jewish Bolsheviks and incompetent Slavs.

So it was probably not a *world* war that Hitler had in mind. Alan Bullock believed that he did not want a war with Britain; all he asked was that the British should not interfere with his expansion in Europe and should allow him to defeat Poland and the USSR in separate campaigns. Richard Overy agrees, pointing out that there is no evidence that Hitler ever thought of declaring war on Britain and France. He hoped to keep the war with Poland localized and then turn to the main campaign – the destruction of the USSR. Hitler was responsible for the war because he failed to realise that as far as Britain and France were concerned, the attack on Poland was one step too far.

Hitler's most recent biographer, Ian Kershaw, sees no reason to change the general conclusion that Hitler must take the blame:

> Hitler had never doubted, and had said so on innumerable occasions, that Germany's future could only be determined through war. … War – the essence of the Nazi system which had developed under his leadership – was for Hitler inevitable. Only the timing and direction were at issue. And there was no time to wait.

FURTHER READING

Bell, P. M. H., *The Origins of the Second World War in Europe* (Longman, 3rd edition, 2007).

Broszat, M., *The Hitler State* (Longman, 1983).

Bullock, A., *Hitler: A Study in Tyranny* (Penguin, new edition, 1990).

Charmley, J., *Chamberlain and the Lost Peace* (Hodder & Stoughton, 1989).

Doig, R., *Co-operation and Conflict: International Affairs, 1990–1962* (Hodder & Stoughton, 1995).

Fewster, S., *Japan, 1850–1985* (Longman, 1988).

Gregor, N. (ed.), *Nazism: A Reader* (Oxford University Press, 2000).

Gregor, N., 'Hitler's Aggression: Opportunistic or Planned?', *Modern History Review,* 15:1 (September 2003).

Henig, R., *Versailles and After* (Routledge, 2nd edition, 2005).

Henig, R., *The Origins of the Second World War* (Routledge, 2nd edition, 2005).

Jackel, E., *Hitler in History* (University Press of New England, 1984).

Kershaw. I., *Hitler, 1889–1936: Hubris* (Allen Lane/Penguin, new edition, 2001).

Kershaw, I., *Hitler, 1936-1945: Nemesis* (Allen Lane/Penguin, new edition, 2010).

Martel, G. (ed.), *The Origins of the Second World War Reconsidered: The A.J.P. Taylor Debate after 25 Years* (Routledge, 2nd edition, 1999).

Mazower, M., *Hitler's Empire: Nazi Rule in Occupied Europe* (Allen Lane/Penguin, 2008).

McDonough, F., *The Origins of the Second World War: An International Perspective* (Continuum, 2011).

Overy, R. J., *1939: Countdown to War* (Allen Lane, 2009).

Steiner, Z., *The Triumph of the Dark: European International History 1933–1939* (Oxford University Press, 2010).

Taylor, A. J. P., *The Origins of the Second World War* (Penguin, new edition, 2011).

Tooze, A., *The Wages of Destruction: the Making and Breaking of the Nazi Economy* (Penguin, 2007).

Watt, D. C., *How War Came* (Heinemann, 1990).

QUESTIONS

1 'Hitler alone caused the Second World War in 1939'. How far do you agree?
2 'Hitler's foreign policy successes between 1935 and 1939 were the result of his own tactical skills and his ability to exploit the weaknesses of his opponents.' How far would you agree with this view?
3 Examine the evidence for and against the view that Hitler had no clear long-term plans for war.
4 'Hitler had one simple over-riding aim in foreign policy – expansion in the East.' Explain why you agree or disagree with this statement.
5 How far was appeasement to blame for the outbreak of the Second World War?

There is a document question about Hitler's aims in foreign policy on the website.

Chapter 6

The Second World War, 1939–45

Unlike the 1914–18 war, the Second World War was a war of rapid movement; it was a much more complex affair, with major campaigns taking place in the Pacific and the Far East, in North Africa and deep in the heart of Russia, as well as in central and western Europe and the Atlantic. *The war falls into four fairly clearly defined phases*:

1   Opening moves: September 1939 to December 1940
By the end of September the Germans and Russians had occupied Poland. After a five-month pause (known as the 'phoney war'), German forces occupied Denmark and Norway (April 1940). In May, attacks were made on Holland, Belgium and France, who were soon defeated, leaving Britain alone to face the dictators (Mussolini had declared war in June, just before the fall of France). Hitler's attempt to bomb Britain into submission was thwarted in *the Battle of Britain* (July to September 1940), but Mussolini's armies invaded Egypt and Greece.

2   The Axis offensive widens: 1941 to the summer of 1942
The war now began to develop into a worldwide conflict. First Hitler, confident of a quick victory over Britain, launched an invasion of Russia (June 1941), breaking the non-aggression pact signed less than two years earlier. Then the Japanese forced the USA into the war by attacking the American naval base at Pearl Harbor (December 1941), and they followed this up by occupying territories such as the Philippines, Malaya, Singapore and Burma, scattered over a wide area. At this stage of the war there seemed to be no way of stopping the Germans and Japanese, though the Italians were less successful.

3   The offensives held in check: summer 1942 to summer 1943
This phase of the war saw three important battles in which Axis forces were defeated.

- In June 1942, the Americans drove off a Japanese attack on *Midway Island*, inflicting heavy losses.
- In October, the Germans under Rommel, advancing towards Egypt, were halted at *El Alamein* and later driven out of North Africa.
- The third battle was in Russia, where by September 1942, the Germans had penetrated as far as *Stalingrad* on the river Volga. Here the Russians put up such fierce resistance that in the following February the German army was surrounded and forced to surrender.

Meanwhile the war in the air continued, with both sides bombing enemy cities, while at sea, as in the First World War, the British and Americans gradually got the better of the German submarine menace.

4 The Axis powers defeated: July 1943 to August 1945

The enormous power and resources of the USA and the USSR, combined with an all-out effort from Britain and her Empire, slowly but surely wore the Axis powers down. Italy was eliminated first, and this was followed by an Anglo-American invasion of Normandy (June 1944) which liberated France, Belgium and Holland. Later, Allied troops crossed the Rhine and captured Cologne. In the east, the Russians drove the Germans out and advanced on Berlin via Poland. *Germany surrendered in May 1945 and Japan in August, after the Americans had dropped an atomic bomb on Hiroshima and one on Nagasaki.*

6.1 OPENING MOVES: SEPTEMBER 1939 TO DECEMBER 1940

(a) Poland defeated

The Poles were defeated swiftly by the German *Blitzkrieg* (lightning war), which they were ill-equipped to deal with. It consisted of rapid thrusts by motorized divisions and tanks (*Panzers*) supported by air power. The *Luftwaffe* (the German air force) put the Polish railway system out of action and destroyed the Polish air force. Polish resistance was heroic but hopeless: they had no motorized divisions and they tried to stop advancing German tanks by massed cavalry charges. Britain and France did little to help their ally directly because French mobilization procedure was slow and out-of-date, and it was difficult to transport sufficient troops to Poland to be effective. When the Russians invaded eastern Poland, resistance collapsed. *On 29 September Poland was divided up between Germany and the USSR* (as agreed in the pact of August 1939).

(b) The 'phoney war'

Very little happened in the west for the next five months. In the east the Russians took over Estonia, Latvia and Lithuania and invaded Finland (November 1939), forcing her to hand over frontier territories which would enable the Russians to defend themselves better against any attack from the west. Meanwhile the French and Germans manned their respective defences – the Maginot and Siegfried Lines. Hitler seems to have hoped that the pause would weaken the resolve of Britain and France and encourage them to negotiate peace. This lack of action pleased Hitler's generals, who were not convinced that the German army was strong enough to attack in the west. It was the American press which described this period as the 'phoney war'.

(c) Denmark and Norway invaded, April 1940

Hitler's troops occupied Denmark and landed at the main Norwegian ports in April 1940, rudely shattering the apparent calm of the 'phoney war'. Control of Norway was important for the Germans because Narvik was the main outlet for Swedish iron-ore, which was vital for the German armaments industry. The British were interfering with this trade by laying mines in Norwegian coastal waters, and the Germans were afraid that they might try to take over some of Norway's ports, which they were in fact planning to do. Admiral Raeder, the German navy chief, realized that the fjords would be excellent naval bases from which to attack Britain's transatlantic supply lines. When a British destroyer chased the German vessel *Altmark* into a Norwegian fjord and rescued the 300 British prisoners aboard, Hitler decided it was time to act. On 9 April, German troops landed at Oslo, Kristiansand, Stavanger, Bergen and Trondheim; although British and French troops arrived a few days later, they were unable to dislodge the Germans, who were already well established. After a temporary success at Narvik, all Allied troops were withdrawn by early June because of the growing threat to France itself. *The Germans were successful* because the Norwegians had been taken by surprise and their troops were not even mobilized; local Nazis, under their leader Vidkun Quisling, gave the invaders every assistance. The British had no air support, whereas the German air force constantly harassed the Allies. *This Norwegian campaign had important results*:

- Germany was assured of her bases and her iron-ore supplies, but had lost three cruisers and ten destroyers. This made the German navy less effective at Dunkirk than it might have been (see (d) below).
- It showed the incompetence of Chamberlain's government. He was forced to resign and *Winston Churchill became British prime minister*. Although there has been criticism of Churchill's mistakes, there is no doubt that he supplied what was needed at the time – drive, a sense of urgency, and the ability to make his coalition cabinet work well together.

(d) Hitler attacks Holland, Belgium and France

The attacks on Holland, Belgium and France were launched simultaneously on 10 May, and again *Blitzkrieg* methods brought swift victories. The Dutch, shaken by the bombing of Rotterdam, which killed almost a thousand people, surrendered after only four days. Belgium held out for longer, but her surrender at the end of May left the British and French troops in Belgium perilously exposed as German motorized divisions swept across northern France; only Dunkirk remained in Allied hands. The British navy played the vital role in evacuating over 338 000 troops – two-thirds of them British – from Dunkirk between 27 May and 4 June. This was a remarkable achievement in the face of constant *Luftwaffe* attacks on the beaches. It would perhaps have been impossible if Hitler had not ordered the German advance towards Dunkirk to halt (24 May), probably because the marshy terrain and numerous canals were unsuitable for tanks.

The events at Dunkirk were important: a third of a million Allied troops were rescued to fight again, and Churchill used it for propaganda purposes to boost British morale with the 'Dunkirk spirit'. In fact it was a serious blow for the Allies: the troops at Dunkirk had lost all their arms and equipment, so that it became impossible for Britain to help France.

The Germans now swept southwards: *Paris was captured on 14 June and France surrendered on 22 June*. At Hitler's insistence the armistice (ceasefire) was signed at Compiègne in the same railway coach that had been used for the 1918 armistice. The Germans occupied northern France and the Atlantic coast (see Map 6.1), giving them valuable submarine bases, and the French army was demobilized. Unoccupied France was allowed its own government under Marshal Pétain, but it had no real independence and collaborated with the Germans. Britain's position was now very precarious. Lord Halifax, the Foreign Secretary, allowed secret enquiries to be made via Washington about what German peace terms would be; even Churchill thought about the possibility of a negotiated peace.

(e) Why was France defeated so quickly?

1   *The French were psychologically unprepared for war, and were bitterly divided between right and left.* The right was fascist in sympathy, admired Hitler's achievements in Germany and wanted an agreement with him. The communists, following

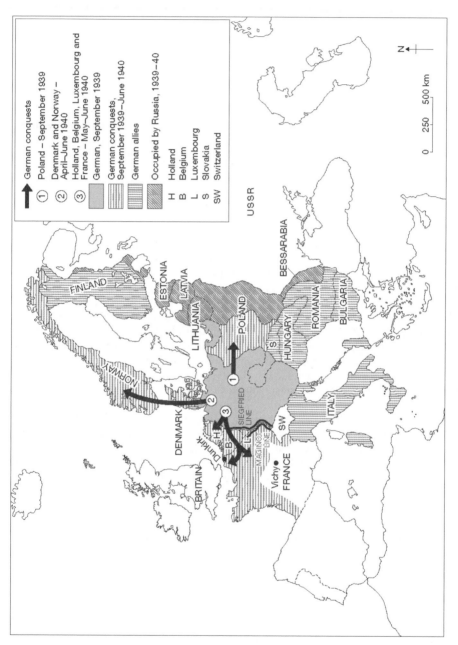

Map 6.1 **The beginning of the war in Europe – main German thrusts, 1939–40**

the non-aggression pact between Germany and the USSR, were also against the war. The long period of inaction during the 'phoney war' allowed time for a peace party to develop on the right, headed by Laval. He argued that there was no point in continuing the war now that the Poles, whom they were supposed to be helping, had been defeated.

2   *There were serious military weaknesses.*

- France had to face the full weight of an undivided German offensive, whereas in 1914 half the German forces had been directed against Russia.
- The French High Command was content to sit behind the Maginot Line, a line of defences stretching from the Swiss to the Belgian frontiers. Unfortunately the Maginot Line did not continue along the frontier between France and Belgium, partly because that might have offended the Belgians, and because Pétain believed that the Ardennes would be a strong enough barrier; but this was exactly where the Germans broke through.
- France had as many tanks and armoured vehicles as Germany, but instead of being concentrated in completely mechanized armoured divisions (like the Germans), allowing greater speed, they were split up so that each infantry division had a few. This slowed them to the speed of marching soldiers (infantry).
- The German divisions were supported by combat planes, another area neglected by the French.

3   *The French generals made fatal mistakes.*

- No attempt was made to help Poland by attacking Germany in the west in September 1939, which might have had a good chance of success.
- No troops were moved from the Maginot Line forts (most of which were completely inactive) to help block the German breakthrough on the River Meuse (13 May 1940).
- There was poor communication between the army and air force, so that air defence to drive German bombers off usually failed to arrive.

4   *Military defeats gave the defeatist right the chance to come out into the open and put pressure on the government to accept a ceasefire.* When even the 84-year-old Pétain, the hero of Verdun in 1916, urged peace, Prime Minister Reynaud resigned and Pétain took over.

(f)   The Battle of Britain (12 August to 30 September 1940)

This was fought in the air, when Goering's *Luftwaffe* tried to destroy the Royal Air Force (RAF) *as a preliminary to the invasion of Britain.* The Germans bombed harbours, radar stations, aerodromes and munitions factories; in September they began to bomb London, in retaliation, they claimed, for a British raid on Berlin. The RAF inflicted heavy losses on the *Luftwaffe* (1389 German planes were lost as against 792 British); when it became clear that British air power was far from being destroyed, Hitler called off the invasion. *Reasons for the British success were*:

- Their chain of new radar stations gave plenty of warning of approaching German attackers.

- The German bombers were poorly armed. Though the British fighters (Spitfires and Hurricanes) were not significantly better than the German Messerschmitts, the Germans were hampered by limited range – they could only carry enough fuel to enable them to stay in the air about 90 minutes.
- The switch to bombing London was a mistake because it relieved pressure on the airfields at the critical moment.

The Battle of Britain was probably the first major turning point of the war: for the first time the Germans had been checked, demonstrating that they were not invincible. Britain was able to remain in the struggle, thus facing Hitler (who was about to attack Russia) with *the fatal situation of war on two fronts*. As Churchill remarked when he paid tribute to the British fighter pilots: 'Never in the field of human conflict was so much owed by so many to so few.'

(g) Mussolini invades Egypt, September 1940

Not wanting to be outdone by Hitler, Mussolini sent an army from the Italian colony of Libya which penetrated about 60 miles into Egypt (September 1940), while another Italian army invaded Greece from Albania (October). However, the British soon drove the Italians out of Egypt, pushed them back far into Libya and defeated them at Bedafomm, capturing 130 000 prisoners and 400 tanks. They seemed poised to take the whole of Libya. British naval aircraft sank half the Italian fleet in harbour at Taranto and occupied Crete. The Greeks forced the Italians back and invaded Albania. Mussolini was beginning to be an embarrassment to Hitler.

6.2 THE AXIS OFFENSIVE WIDENS: 1941 TO THE SUMMER OF 1942

(a) North Africa and Greece

Hitler's first moves in 1941 were to help out his faltering ally. In February he sent Erwin Rommel and the Afrika Korps to Tripoli, and together with the Italians, they drove the British out of Libya. After much advancing and retreating, by June 1942 the Germans were in Egypt approaching El Alamein, only 70 miles from Alexandria (see Map 6.2).

In April 1941 Hitler's forces invaded Greece, the day after 60 000 British, Australian and New Zealand troops had arrived to help the Greeks. The Germans soon captured Athens, forcing the British to withdraw, and after bombing Crete, they launched a parachute invasion of the island; again the British were forced to evacuate (May 1941).

The campaigns in Greece had important effects:

- It was depressing for the Allies, who lost about 36 000 men.
- Many of the troops had been removed from North Africa, thus weakening British forces there just when they needed to be at their most effective against Rommel.
- More important in the long run was that Hitler's involvement in Greece and Yugoslavia (which the Germans invaded at the same time as Greece) may well have delayed his attack on Russia. This was originally planned for 15 May and was delayed for five weeks. If the invasion had taken place in May, the Germans might well have captured Moscow before the winter set in.

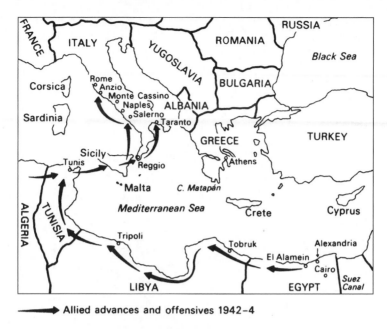

Allied advances and offensives 1942–4

Map 6.2 **North Africa and the Mediterranean**

(b) The German invasion of Russia (Operation Barbarossa) began on 22 June 1941

Hitler's motives seem to have been mixed:

- He feared that the Russians might attack Germany while his forces were still occupied in the west.
- He hoped that the Japanese would attack Russia in the Far East.
- The more powerful Japan became, the less chance there was of the USA entering the war (or so Hitler thought).
- But above all there was his hatred of communism and his desire for *Lebensraum* (living space).

According to historian Alan Bullock, 'Hitler invaded Russia for the simple and sufficient reason that he had always meant to establish the foundations of his thousand-year *Reich* by the annexation of the territory lying between the Vistula and the Urals.' It has sometimes been suggested that the attack on Russia was Hitler's greatest mistake, but in fact, as Hugh Trevor-Roper pointed out, 'to Hitler the Russian campaign was not a luxury: it was the be-all and end-all of Nazism; it could not be delayed. It was now or never.' Hitler did not expect a long war; he told one of his generals: 'We have only to kick in the door and the whole rotten structure will come crashing down.'

The German attack was three-pronged:

- in the north towards Leningrad,
- in the centre towards Moscow,
- in the south through the Ukraine.

- - - - Line of the German advance in December 1941

········· German line in November 1942

Map 6.3   **The Russian front**

It was *Blitzkrieg* on an awesome scale, involving close on 5.5 million men, and 3550 tanks supported by 5000 aircraft and 47 000 pieces of artillery. Important cities such as Riga, Smolensk and Kiev were captured (see Map 6.3). The Russians had been caught off their guard, in spite of British and American warnings that a German attack was imminent. Stalin apparently believed that Hitler could be trusted to honour the Nazi–Soviet non-aggression pact, and was extremely suspicious of any information which came from Britain or the USA. The Russians were still re-equipping their army and air force, and many of their generals, thanks to Stalin's purges, were inexperienced (see Section 17.3(b)).

However, the German forces failed to capture Leningrad and Moscow. They were severely hampered by the heavy rains of October, which turned the Russian roads into mud, and by the severe frosts of November and December when in some places the temperature fell to minus 38°C. The Germans had inadequate winter clothing because Hitler had expected the campaigns to be over by the autumn. Even in the spring of 1942 no progress was made in the north and centre as Hitler decided to concentrate on a major drive south-eastwards towards the Caucasus to seize the oilfields.

(c)   The USA enters the war, December 1941

The USA was brought into the war by the Japanese attack on Pearl Harbor (their naval base in the Hawaiian Islands) on 7 December 1941 (see Illus. 6.1). Until then, the

Illustration 6.1   **Pearl Harbor, 7 December 1941: US warships lie in ruins after the Japanese air attack**

Americans, still intent on isolation, had remained neutral, though after *the Lend-Lease Act (April 1941)*, they had provided Britain with massive financial aid.

Japanese motives for the attack were tied up with her economic problems. The government believed they would soon run short of raw materials and cast longing eyes towards territories such as Britain's Malaya and Burma, which had rubber, oil and tin, and towards the Dutch East Indies, also rich in oil. Since both Britain and Holland were in no fit state to defend their possessions, the Japanese prepared to attack, though they would probably have preferred to avoid war with the USA. However, relations between the two states deteriorated steadily. The Americans assisted the Chinese, who were still at war with Japan; when the Japanese persuaded Vichy France to allow them to occupy French Indo-China (where they set up military bases), President Roosevelt demanded their withdrawal and placed an embargo on oil supplies to Japan (26 July 1941). Long negotiations followed in which the Japanese tried to persuade the Americans to lift the embargo. But stalemate was reached when the Americans insisted on a Japanese withdrawal both from Indo-China and from China itself. When the aggressive General Tojo became prime minister (16 October), war seemed inevitable.

The attack was brilliantly organized by Admiral Yamamoto. There was no declaration of war: 353 Japanese planes arrived undetected at Pearl Harbor, and in two hours, destroyed 350 aircraft and five battleships; 3700 men were killed or seriously injured. Roosevelt called 7 December 'a date which will live in infamy'.

Pearl Harbor had important results:

- It gave the Japanese control of the Pacific, and by May 1942 they had captured Malaya, Singapore, Hong Kong and Burma (all part of the British Empire), the Dutch East Indies, the Philippines, and two American possessions, Guam and Wake Island (see Map 6.4).
- It caused Hitler to declare war on the USA.

Declaring war on the USA was perhaps Hitler's most serious mistake. He need not at this stage have committed himself to war with the USA, in which case the Americans might well have concentrated on the Pacific war. However, the Germans had already assured the Japanese that they would come to Japan's aid if she was ever at war with the USA. Hitler assumed that President Roosevelt of the USA would declare war on Germany sooner or later, so he wanted to get Germany's declaration of war in first, to show the German people that he, and not the Americans, controlled events. In fact the US Congress was naturally

Map 6.4 **The war in the Pacific**

determined to have their revenge on Japan, but was still reluctant to get involved in Europe. Roosevelt would have had a difficult job to persuade Congress to declare war on Germany; Hitler's action saved him the trouble.

As it was, Germany was now faced with the immense potential of the USA. This meant that with the vast resources of the USSR and the British Commonwealth as well, the longer the war lasted, the less chance there was of an Axis victory. It was essential for them to deliver swift knock-out blows before the American contribution became effective.

(d) Brutal behaviour by Germans and Japanese

The behaviour of both Germans and Japanese in their conquered territories was ruthless and brutal. The Nazis treated the peoples of eastern Europe as sub-humans, fit only to be slaves of the German master-race. As for the Jews – they were to be exterminated (see Section 6.8). As American journalist and historian William Shirer put it:

Nazi degradation sank to a level seldom experienced by man in all his time on earth. Millions of decent, innocent men and women were driven into forced labour, millions were tortured in the concentration camps, and millions more still (including nearly six million Jews) were massacred in cold blood or deliberately starved to death and their remains burned.

This was both amoral and foolish: in the Baltic states (Latvia, Lithuania and Estonia) and in the Ukraine, the Soviet government was so unpopular that decent treatment would have turned the people into allies of the Germans.

The Japanese treated their prisoners of war and the Asian peoples badly. Again this was ill-advised: many of the Asians, like those in Indo-China, at first welcomed the Japanese, who were thought to be freeing them from European control. The Japanese hoped to organize their new territories into a great economic empire known as a *Greater East Asia Co-prosperity Sphere*, which would be defended by sea and air power. However, harsh treatment by the Japanese soon turned the Asians against rule from Tokyo, and determined resistance movements began, usually with communist involvement.

6.3 THE OFFENSIVES HELD IN CHECK: SUMMER 1942 TO SUMMER 1943

In three separate areas of fighting, Axis forces were defeated and began to lose ground:

- Midway Island
- El Alamein
- Stalingrad

(a) Midway Island, June 1942

At Midway Island in the Pacific the Americans beat off a powerful Japanese attack, which included five aircraft carriers, nearly 400 aircraft, 17 large warships and an invasion force of 5000 troops. The Americans, with only three carriers and 233 planes, destroyed four of the Japanese carriers and about 330 planes. *There were several reasons for the American victory against heavier odds*:

- They had broken the Japanese radio code and knew exactly when and where the attack was to be launched.
- The Japanese were over-confident and made two fatal mistakes: they split their forces, thus allowing the Americans to concentrate on the main carrier force; and they attacked with aircraft from all four carriers simultaneously, so that when they were all rearming, the entire fleet was extremely vulnerable.

At this stage the Americans launched a counter-attack by dive-bombers, which swooped unexpectedly from 19 000 feet, sinking two of the carriers and all their planes.

Midway proved to be a crucial turning point in the battle for the Pacific: the loss of their carriers and strike planes seriously weakened the Japanese, and from then on the Americans maintained their lead in carriers and aircraft, especially dive-bombers. Although the Japanese had far more battleships and cruisers, they were mostly ineffective: the only way war could be waged successfully in the vast expanses of the Pacific was by air power operating from carriers. Gradually the Americans under General MacArthur began to recover the Pacific islands, beginning in August 1942 with landings in the Solomon Islands. The struggle was long and bitter and continued through 1943 and 1944, a process which the Americans called 'island hopping'.

(b) El Alamein, October 1942

At El Alamein in Egypt Rommel's Afrika Korps were driven back by the British Eighth Army, commanded by Montgomery. This great battle was the culmination of several engagements fought in the El Alamein area: first the Axis advance was temporarily checked (July); when Rommel tried to break through he was halted again at Alam Halfa (September); finally, seven weeks later in the October battle, he was chased out of Egypt for good by the British and New Zealanders.

The Allies were successful partly because during the seven-week pause, massive rein-forcements had arrived, so that the Germans and Italians were heavily outnumbered – 80 000 men and 540 tanks against 230 000 troops and 1440 tanks. In addition, Allied air power was vital, constantly attacking the Axis forces and sinking their supply ships as they crossed the Mediterranean, so that by October there were serious shortages of food, fuel oil and ammunition. At the same time the air force was strong enough to protect the Eighth Army's own supply routes. Montgomery's skilful preparations probably clinched the issue, though he has been criticized for being over-cautious, and for allowing Rommel and half his forces to escape into Libya.

However, there is no doubt that *the El Alamein victory was another turning point in the war*:

- It prevented Egypt and the Suez Canal from falling into German hands.
- It ended the possibility of a link-up between the Axis forces in the Middle East and those in the Ukraine.
- More than that, it led on to the complete expulsion of Axis forces from North Africa. It encouraged landings of British troops in the French territories of Morocco and Algeria to threaten the Germans and Italians from the west, while the Eighth Army closed in on them from Libya. Trapped in Tunisia, 275 000 Germans and Italians were forced to surrender (May 1943), and the Allies were well-placed for an invasion of Italy.

The desert war had been a serious drain on German resources that could have been used in Russia, where they were badly needed.

(c) Stalingrad

At Stalingrad the southern prong of the German invasion of Russia, which had penetrated deeply through the Crimea, capturing Rostov-on-Don, was finally checked. *The Germans had reached Stalingrad at the end of August 1942*, but though they more or less destroyed the city, the Russians refused to surrender. In November they counter-attacked ferociously, trapping the Germans, whose supply lines were dangerously extended, in a large pincer movement. With his retreat cut off, the German commander, von Paulus, had no reasonable alternative but to surrender with 94 000 men (2 February 1943).

If Stalingrad had fallen, the supply route for Russia's oil from the Caucasus would have been cut off, and the Germans had hoped to advance up the River Don to attack Moscow from the south-east. This plan had to be abandoned; but more than this was at stake – *the defeat was a catastrophe for the Germans*: it shattered the myth that they were invincible, and boosted Russian morale. They followed up with more counter-attacks, and in July 1943, in a great tank battle at Kursk, they forced the Germans to keep on retreating. Early in 1944 the Germans had to abandon the siege of Leningrad and to retreat from their position west of Moscow. It was now only a matter of time before the Germans, heavily outnumbered and short of tanks and guns, were driven out of Russia.

6.4 WHAT PART WAS PLAYED BY ALLIED NAVAL FORCES?

The previous section showed how the combination of sea and air power was the key to success in the Pacific war and how, after the initial shock at Pearl Harbor, the Americans were able to build up that superiority in both departments, which was to lead to the eventual defeat of Japan. At the same time the British navy, as in the First World War, had a vital role to play: this included protecting merchant ships bringing food supplies, sinking German submarines and surface raiders, blockading Germany, and transporting and supplying Allied troops fighting in North Africa and later in Italy. At first success was mixed, mainly because the British failed to understand the importance of air support in naval operations and had few aircraft carriers. Thus they suffered defeats in Norway and Crete, where the Germans had strong air superiority. In addition the Germans had many naval bases in Norway, Denmark, France and Italy. In spite of this the British navy could point to some important achievements.

(a) British successes

1 *Aircraft from the carrier* Illustrious *sank half the Italian fleet at Taranto (November 1940)*. The following March five more warships were destroyed off Cape Matapan.
2 *The threat from surface raiders was removed* by the sinking of the *Bismarck*, Germany's only battleship at the time (May 1941).
3 *The navy destroyed the German invasion transports* on their way to Crete (May 1941), though they could not prevent the landing of parachute troops.
4 *They provided escorts for convoys carrying supplies to help the Russians.* These sailed via the Arctic to Murmansk in the far north of Russia. Beginning in September 1941, the first 12 convoys arrived without incident, but then the Germans began to attack them, until convoy 17 lost 23 ships out of 36 (June 1942). After this disaster, Arctic convoys were not resumed until November 1943, when stronger escorts could be spared. Altogether 40 convoys sailed: 720 out of a total of 811 merchant ships arrived safely, with valuable cargo for the Russians; this included 5000 tanks, 7000 aircraft and thousands of tons of canned meat.

5 *Their most important contribution was their victory in the Battle of the Atlantic* (see below).
6 *Sea and air power together made possible the great invasion of France in June 1944* (see below, Section 6.6(b)).

(b) The Battle of the Atlantic

This was the struggle against German U-boats attempting to deprive Britain of food and raw materials. At the beginning of 1942 the Germans had 90 U-boats in operation and 250 being built. In the first six months of that year the Allies lost over 4 million tons of merchant shipping and destroyed only 21 U-boats. Losses reached a peak of 108 ships in March 1943, almost two-thirds of which were in convoy. However, after that the number of sinkings began to fall, while the U-boat losses increased. By July 1943 the Allies could produce ships at a faster rate than the U-boats could sink them, and the situation was under control.

The reasons for the Allied success were:

- more air protection was provided for convoys by long-range Liberators;
- both escorts and aircraft improved with experience;
- the British introduced the new centimetric radar sets, which were small enough to be fitted into aircraft; these enabled submarines to be detected in poor visibility and at night.

The victory was just as important as Midway, El Alamein and Stalingrad: Britain could not have continued to sustain the losses of March 1943 and still remained in the war.

6.5 WHAT CONTRIBUTION DID AIR POWER MAKE TO THE DEFEAT OF THE AXIS?

(a) Achievements of Allied air power

1 *The first significant achievement was in the Battle of Britain (1940)*, when the RAF beat off the *Luftwaffe* attacks, causing Hitler to abandon his invasion plans (see Section 6.1(f)).
2 *In conjunction with the British navy, aircraft played a varied role*: the successful attacks on the Italian fleet at Taranto and Cape Matapan, the sinking of the German battleship *Tirpitz* by heavy bombers in Norway (November 1943), the protection of convoys in the Atlantic, and anti-submarine operations. In fact, in May 1943 Admiral Doenitz, the German navy chief, complained to Hitler that since the introduction of the new radar devices, more U-boats were being destroyed by aircraft than by naval vessels.
3 *The American air force together with the navy played a vital part in winning the Pacific war against the Japanese.* Dive-bombers operating from aircraft carriers won *the Battle of Midway Island in June 1942* (see Section 6.3(a)). Later, in the 'island-hopping' campaign, attacks by heavy bombers prepared the way for landings by marines, for example at the Mariana Islands (1944) and the Philippines (1945). American transport planes kept up the vital flow of supplies to the Allies during the campaign to recapture Burma.
4 *The RAF took part in specific campaigns which would have been hopeless without them*: for example, during the war in the desert, operating from bases in Egypt and

Palestine, they constantly bombed Rommel's supply ships in the Mediterranean and his armies on land.

5   *British and Americans later flew parachute troops in, to aid the landings in Sicily (July 1943) and Normandy (June 1944)*, and provided air protection for the invading armies. (However, a similar operation at Arnhem in Holland in September 1944 was a failure.)

(b)   Allied bombing of German and Japanese cities

The most controversial action was the Allied bombing of German and Japanese cities. The Germans had bombed London and other important British cities and ports during 1940 and 1941, but these raids dwindled during the German attack on Russia, which required all the *Luftwaffe's* strength. The British and Americans retaliated with what they called a 'strategic air offensive' – this involved massive attacks on military and industrial targets in order to hamper the German war effort. The Ruhr, Cologne, Hamburg and Berlin all suffered badly. Sometimes raids seem to have been carried out to undermine civilian morale, as when about 50 000 people were killed during a single night raid on Dresden (February 1945).

Early in 1945 the Americans launched a series of devastating raids on Japan from bases in the Mariana Islands. In a single raid on Tokyo, in March, 80 000 people were killed and a quarter of the city was destroyed. There has been debate about how effective the bombing was in hastening the Axis defeat. It certainly caused enormous civilian casualties and helped to destroy morale, but critics point out that heavy losses were also suffered by air-crews – over 158 000 Allied airmen were killed in Europe alone.

Others argue that this type of bombing, which caused the deaths of so many innocent civilians (as opposed to bombings which targeted industrial areas, railways and bridges), was morally wrong. Estimates of German civilian deaths from Allied bombing vary between 600 000 and a million; German raids on Britain killed over 60 000 civilians. In 2001 Swedish writer Sven Lindqvist, in his book *A History of Bombing*, suggested that what he called 'the systematic attacks on German civilians in their homes' should be viewed as 'crimes under international humanitarian law for the protection of civilians'. However, Robin Niellands (2001) defended the bombing, pointing out that this is what could be expected to happen during a total war – in the context of what the Germans had done in eastern Europe and the Japanese in their occupied territories, this was the necessary 'price of peace'.

This was by no means the end of the controversy: in 2002 a German historian, Jorg Friedrich, in his book *Der Brand (The Fire)*, published an account of the horrific suffering inflicted by Allied bombers on German citizens; an English translation came out in 2007. He blamed specifically Churchill and Arthur 'Bomber' Harris, the head of Bomber Command. Friedrich clearly believed that these bombing raids were war crimes. Many British historians immediately condemned Friedrich's book. Corelli Barnett called it 'a historical travesty' designed to move the spotlight away from Nazi atrocities. To mark the appearance of the English edition, York Membery, writing in *History Today* (January 2007), sought the views of some leading British historians. Richard Overy suggested that while it was time for a proper assessment of the bombing strategy, Friedrich played down the contribution of the Americans and felt that the general tone of his book was unhelpful. Overy went on to argue that the bombing was neither immoral nor strategically useless. Adam Tooze, an expert on the Nazi economy, wrote: 'unfortunately, if you start a war with Britain as Germany deliberately did, then this is the kind of war you have to be prepared to fight'. Bruce Kent, a peace campaigner and former secretary of CND, pointed out that the bombing raids probably were war crimes, but that the Nazis themselves were the first to begin bombing innocent civilians in Guernica (during the Spanish Civil War),Warsaw and Rotterdam.

As to the question of whether the bombing helped to shorten the war, it used to be thought that the campaign had little effect until the autumn of 1944. However, evidence from German archives shows that the RAF attack on the Ruhr in the spring of 1943 had an immediate effect on production. From July 1944, thanks to the increasing accuracy of the raids and the use of the new Mustang fighter escorts, which could outmanoeuvre all the German fighters, the effects of the bombings reached disaster proportions; synthetic oil production fell rapidly, causing acute fuel shortages. In October the vital Krupp armaments factories at Essen were put out of action permanently, and the war effort ground to a halt in 1945. By June 1945 the Japanese had been reduced to the same state.

In the end, therefore, after much wasted effort early on, *the Allied strategic air offensive was one of the decisive reasons for the Axis defeat*: besides strangling fuel and armaments production and destroying railway communications, it caused the diversion of many aircraft from the eastern front, thus helping the Russian advance into Germany.

6.6 THE AXIS POWERS DEFEATED: JULY 1943 TO AUGUST 1945

(a) The fall of Italy

This was the first stage in the Axis collapse. British and American troops landed in Sicily from the sea and air (10 July 1943) and quickly captured the whole island. This caused *the downfall of Mussolini, who was dismissed by the king*. Allied troops crossed to Salerno, Reggio and Taranto on the mainland and captured Naples (October 1943).

Marshal Badoglio, Mussolini's successor, signed an armistice and brought Italy into the war on the Allied side. However, the Germans, determined to hold on to Italy, rushed troops through the Brenner Pass to occupy Rome and the north. The Allies landed a force at Anzio, 30 miles south of Rome (January 1944), but bitter fighting followed before Monte Cassino (May) and Rome (June) were captured. Milan in the north was not taken until April 1945. The campaign could have been finished much earlier if the Allies had been less cautious in the early stages, and if the Americans had not insisted on keeping many divisions back for the invasion of France. *Nevertheless, the elimination of Italy did contribute towards the final Allied victory*:

- Italy provided air bases for bombing the Germans in Central Europe and the Balkans;
- German troops were kept occupied when they were needed to resist the Russians.

(b) Operation Overlord, 6 June 1944

Operation Overlord – the invasion of France (also known as the Second Front) – began on 'D-Day', 6 June 1944. It was felt that the time was ripe now that Italy had been eliminated, the U-boats brought under control and Allied air superiority achieved. The Russians had been urging the Allies to start this Second Front ever since 1941, to relieve pressure on them. The landings took place from sea and air on a 60-mile stretch of Normandy beaches (code-named Utah, Omaha, Gold, Juno and Sword) between Cherbourg and Le Havre (see Map 6.5). There was strong German resistance, but at the end of the first week 326 000 men with tanks and heavy lorries had landed safely (see Illus. 6.2).

It was a remarkable operation: it made use of prefabricated 'Mulberry' harbours, which were towed across from Britain and positioned close to the Normandy coast, mainly at

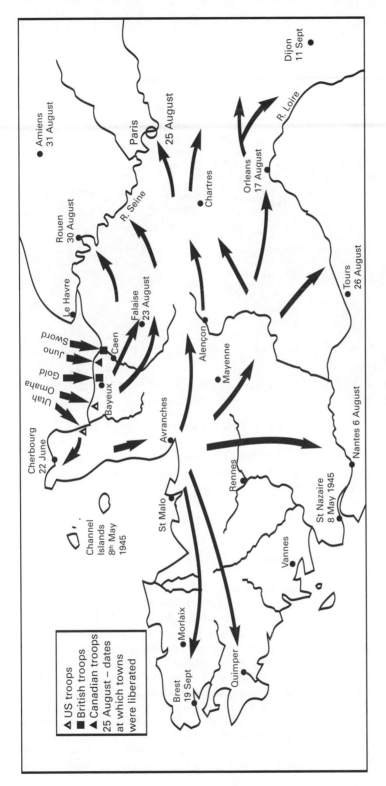

Map 6.5   **The D-Day landings – 6 June 1944**

US troops
British troops
Canadian troops
25 August – dates
at which towns
were liberated

Amiens
31 August

Paris

25 August

Dijon
11 Sept

R. Loire

Chartres

Orleans
17 August

Rouen
30 August

R. Seine

Le Havre

Falaise
23 August

Caen

Sword
Juno
Gold
Omaha
Utah

Bayeux

Alençon

Mayenne

Tours
26 August

Cherbourg
22 June

Avranches

Nantes 6 August

Channel
Islands
8th May
1945

Rennes

St Malo

St Nazaire
8 May 1945

Vannes

Morlaix

Quimper

Brest
19 Sept

Illustration 6.2 **D-Day, 6 June 1944: US assault troops landing in Normandy**

Arromanches (Gold beach), and of PLUTO – pipelines under the ocean – carrying motor fuel. Eventually over 3 million Allied troops were landed. Within a few weeks most of northern France was liberated (Paris on 25 August), putting out of action the sites from which the German V1 and V2 rocket missiles had been launched with devastating effects on south-eastern Britain. In Belgium, Brussels and Antwerp were liberated in September.

(c) 'Unconditional surrender'

With the Germans forced to retreat in France and in Russia, there were people on both sides who hoped that there might be an armistice followed by a negotiated peace; this was the way in which the First World War had been brought to an end. However, Hitler himself always talked of a fight to the death, and there were serious differences between the Allies themselves over the question of peace negotiations. As far back as January 1943, President Roosevelt announced that the Allies were fighting for '*the unconditional surrender of Germany, Italy and Japan*'. Churchill and most of his staff were dismayed by this because they felt that it ruined all chances of a negotiated peace. Members of the British secret service were actually in touch with their German opposite numbers and with members of the German resistance to the Nazis, who hoped to persuade the German generals to help them overthrow Hitler. This, they believed, would lead to the opening of peace negotiations. The Nazi leaders were delighted with Roosevelt's announcement; Goebbels remarked: 'I should never have been able to think up so rousing a slogan. If our western enemies tell us, we won't deal with you, our only aim is to destroy you, how can any German, whether he likes it or not, do anything but fight on with all his strength?'

Many leading Americans, including General Eisenhower, were against 'unconditional surrender' because they realized that it would prolong the war and cause further unnecessary loss of life. Several times in the weeks before D-Day, the American chiefs of staff put pressure on Roosevelt to change his mind, but he stubbornly refused, in case this was taken by the Axis powers as a sign of weakness. The policy was continued by Roosevelt until his death in April 1945, and by his successor, Harry S. Truman. No attempts were made to negotiate peace with either Germany or Japan until they had both surrendered. Thomas Fleming, writing in *History Today* (December 2001), calculated that in the period from D-Day until the end of the war in August 1945, close on two million people were killed. Many of these lives could perhaps have been saved if there had been the prospect of a negotiated peace to encourage the German resistance to overthrow Hitler. As it was, concludes Fleming, the policy of unconditional surrender was 'an ultimatum written in blood'.

(d)   The assault on Germany

With the success of the Second Front, the Allies began to gather themselves together for the invasion of Germany itself. If they had expected the German armies to fall apart rapidly, they must have been bitterly disappointed. The war was prolonged by desperate German resistance and by further disagreements between the British and Americans. Montgomery wanted a rapid thrust to reach Berlin before the Russians, but Eisenhower favoured a cautious advance along a broad front. *The British failure at Arnhem in Holland* (September 1944) seemed to support Eisenhower's view, though in fact the Arnhem operation (an attempt by parachute troops to cross the Rhine and outflank the German Siegfried Line) might have worked if the troops had landed nearer the two Rhine bridges.

Consequently Eisenhower had his way and Allied troops were dispersed over a 600-mile front (see Map 6.6), *with unfortunate results*:

- Hitler was able to launch an offensive through the weakly defended Ardennes towards Antwerp;
- the Germans broke through the American lines and advanced 60 miles, causing a huge bulge in the front line (December 1944).

Determined British and American action stemmed the advance and pushed the Germans back to their original position. But *the Battle of the Bulge*, as it became known, was important because Hitler had risked everything on the attack and had lost 250 000 men and 600 tanks, which at this stage could not be replaced. Early in 1945, Germany was being invaded on both fronts, from east and west. The British still wanted to push ahead and take Berlin before the Russians, but supreme commander Eisenhower refused to be hurried, and Berlin fell to Stalin's forces in April. *Hitler committed suicide and Germany surrendered.*

The question has sometimes been asked: why did the Germans keep on fighting to the bitter end in 1945 long after it must have been obvious that the war was lost? Why was there not some sort of popular uprising to force the government to start peace negotiations? Adam Tooze believes that one of the reasons was that a large section of German society was completely committed to the war effort, and actually took or suggested many of the initiatives which made it possible for Germany to fight to the death. Ian Kershaw has addressed these questions in his recent book *The End: Hitler's Germany 1944–45* (2011). In his view, the main reason is obvious: it lies in the nature of the Nazi regime and in Hitler's belief that relations between states were a life and death struggle for survival and supremacy. Hitler's attitude was completely irrational: either Germany would be totally

Map 6.6 **The defeat of Germany, 1944–5**

Source: D. Heater, *Our World This Century* (Oxford, 1992), p. 90

victorious – the most powerful state in the world – or Germany would be destroyed. There could be no compromise. When it was all over, many Germans tried to blame the Allied policy of 'unconditional surrender' for their determination to fight on. However, Kershaw is adamant that the reason the Germans fought on has to be found inside Germany itself. Many Germans kept going because they were afraid of the enemy, especially the Russians, but also because they were afraid of Nazi officials. The Nazis hanged or shot people they described as defeatists, deserters and cowards, and generally bullied and terrorised the civilian population. Kershaw is not convinced by historians who claim that the Nazi regime was based overwhelmingly on popular consent. He concludes that terror was a vital element in sustaining the regime, just as it had been even in the years of peace before 1939.

(e) The defeat of Japan

On 6 August 1945 *the Americans dropped an atomic bomb on Hiroshima, killing perhaps as many as 84 000 people and leaving thousands more slowly dying of radiation poisoning*. Three days later they dropped an atomic bomb on Nagasaki, which killed perhaps another 40 000; after this the Japanese government surrendered. The dropping of these bombs was one of the most controversial actions of the entire war. President Truman's justification was that he was saving American lives, since the war might otherwise drag on for another year. Many historians believe that the bombings were not necessary, since the Japanese had already put out peace feelers in July via Russia. One suggestion is that the real reason for the bombings was to end the fighting swiftly before the Russians (who had promised to enter the war against Japan) gained too much Japanese territory, which would entitle them to share the occupation of Japan. The use of the bombs was also a deliberate demonstration to the USSR of the USA's enormous power.

6.7 WHY DID THE AXIS POWERS LOSE THE WAR?

The reasons can be summarized briefly:

- shortage of raw materials;
- the Allies learning from their mistakes and failures;
- the Axis powers taking on too much;
- the overwhelming impact of the combined resources of the USA, the USSR and the British Empire;
- tactical mistakes by the Axis powers.

(a) Shortage of raw materials

Both Italy and Japan had to import supplies, and even Germany was short of rubber, cotton, nickel and, after mid-1944, oil. These shortages need not have been fatal, *but success depended on a swift end to the war,* which certainly seemed likely at first, thanks to the speed and efficiency of the German *Blitzkrieg*. However, the survival of Britain in 1940 was important because it kept the western front alive until the USA entered the war.

(b) The Allies soon learned from their early failures

By 1942 they knew how to check *Blitzkrieg* attacks and appreciated the importance of air support and aircraft carriers. Consequently they built up an air and naval superiority which won the battles of the Atlantic and the Pacific and slowly starved their enemies of supplies.

(c) The Axis powers simply took on too much

Hitler did not seem to understand that war against Britain would involve her empire as well, and that his troops were bound to be spread too thinly – on the Russian front, on both sides of the Mediterranean, and on the western coastline of France. Japan made the same mistake: as military historian Liddell-Hart put it, 'they became stretched out far beyond their basic capacity for holding their gains. For Japan was a small island state with limited industrial power.' In Germany's case, Mussolini was partly to blame: his incompetence was a constant drain on Hitler's resources.

(d) The combined resources of the USA, the USSR and the British Empire

These resources were so great that the longer the war lasted, the less chance the Axis had of victory. The Russians rapidly moved their industry east of the Ural Mountains and so were able to continue production even though the Germans had occupied vast areas in the west. By 1945 they had four times as many tanks as the Germans and could put twice as many men in the field. When the American war machine reached peak production it could turn out over 70 000 tanks and 120 000 aircraft a year, which the Germans and Japanese could not match. Albert Speer, Hitler's armaments minister from 1942, gave the impression that he had worked some sort of miracle, enabling Germany's arms production to keep pace with that of the enemy. However, Adam Tooze has shown that Speer was more successful as a self-publicist than as an armaments minister. He claimed credit for successful policies that were actually started before he took over; he blamed everybody else when his policies failed, and continued right to the end to produce a stream of false statistics.

(e) Serious tactical mistakes

- The Japanese failed to learn the lesson about the importance of aircraft carriers, and concentrated too much on producing battleships.
- Hitler should have defeated Britain before invading the USSR, which committed Germany to a war on two fronts. German plans for the invasion of Britain were vague and improvised, and they underestimated the strength of the enemy. Britain was saved for the Allies and was able to be used later as the base from which to launch the D-Day landings.
- Hitler failed to provide for a winter campaign in Russia and completely underestimated Russian resourcefulness and determination. The deeper the German army advanced into Soviet territory, the more its supply and communication lines became exposed to enemy counter-attacks. Hitler also became obsessed with the idea that the German armies must not retreat; this led to many disasters in Russia, especially Stalingrad, and left his troops badly exposed in Normandy (1944). This all helped to hasten defeat because it meant that scarce resources were being wasted.
- Hitler made a fatal mistake by declaring war on the USA after Japan's attack on Pearl Harbor.
- Another serious mistake was Hitler's decision to concentrate on producing V-rockets when he could have been developing jet aircraft; these might well have restored German air superiority and prevented the devastating bomb attacks of 1944 and 1945.

(f) Nazi racial policy

Nazi treatment of Jews, gypsies and homosexuals in occupied territories of the USSR alienated many of the conquered peoples who, with decent treatment, could have been brought on board to fight the Stalinist regime. Soviet rule was especially unpopular in the Ukraine.

6.8 THE HOLOCAUST

As the invading Allied armies moved into Germany and Poland, they began to make horrifying discoveries. At the end of July 1944 Soviet forces approaching Warsaw came upon the extermination camp at Majdanek near Lublin. They found hundreds of unburied corpses and seven gas chambers. Photographs taken at Majdanek were the first to reveal to the rest of the world the unspeakable horrors of these camps. It later emerged that over 1.5 million people had been murdered at Majdanek; the majority of them were Jews, but they also included Soviet prisoners of war, as well as Poles who had opposed the German occupation. This was only one of at least 20 camps set up by the Germans to carry out what they called the 'Final Solution' (*Endlosung*) of the 'Jewish problem'. Between December 1941, when the first Jews were killed at Chelmno in Poland, and May 1945 when the Germans surrendered, some 5.7 million Jews were murdered, along with hundreds of thousands of non-Jews – gypsies, socialists, communists, homosexuals and the mentally handicapped.

How could such a terrible atrocity have been allowed to happen? Was it the natural culmination of a long history of anti-Semitism in Germany? Or should the blame be placed fairly and squarely on Hitler and the Nazis? Had Hitler been planning the extermination of the Jews ever since he came to power, or was it forced on him by the circumstances of the war? These are some of the questions that historians have wrestled with as they try to explain how such a monstrous crime against humanity could have taken place.

Earlier interpretations of the Holocaust can be divided into two main groups.

- *Intentionalists* – historians who believed that responsibility for the Holocaust rests on Hitler, who had hoped and planned to exterminate the Jews ever since he came to power.
- *Functionalists* – historians who believed that the 'Final Solution' was in a sense forced on Hitler by the circumstances of the war.
- There is also a small group of misguided writers with anti-Semitic sympathies, who try to play down the significance of the Holocaust. They have variously argued that the numbers of dead have been greatly exaggerated; that Hitler himself was unaware of what was happening; and that other Nazis, such as Himmler, Heydrich and Goering, took the initiative; a few have even denied that the Holocaust ever took place at all. All these writers have now been largely discredited.

(a)   The intentionalists

They argue that Hitler was personally responsible for the Holocaust. Right from his early days in Vienna he had been venomously anti-Semitic; in his book *Mein Kampf* (*My Struggle*) he blamed the Jews for Germany's defeat in the First World War and for all her problems since. In his speech to the Reichstag in January 1939 Hitler declared: 'if international finance Jewry inside and outside Europe should succeed in plunging the nations once more into a world war, the result will be, not the bolshevization of the earth, and thereby the victory of Jewry, but the annihilation of the Jewish race in Europe'. The intentionalists stress the continuity between his ideas in the early 1920s and the actual policies that were carried out in the 1940s. As Karl Dietrich Bracher puts it, although Hitler may not have had a master plan, he certainly knew what he wanted, and it included the annihilation of the Jews; the Final Solution 'was merely a matter of time and opportunity'. Critics of this theory question why it took until the end of 1941 – almost nine years after Hitler came to power – before the Nazis began to murder Jews. Why did Hitler content himself with anti-Jewish legislation if he was so determined to exterminate them? In fact, following *Kristallnacht* – an attack on Jewish property and synagogues throughout Germany in November 1938 – Hitler ordered restraint and a return to non-violence.

(b)   The functionalists

They believe that it was the Second World War which aggravated the 'Jewish problem'. About three million Jews lived in Poland; when the Germans took over the western part of

Poland in the autumn of 1939, and occupied the rest of Poland in June 1941, these unfortunate people fell under Nazi control. The invasion of the USSR in June 1941 brought a further dimension to the 'Jewish problem', since there were several million Jews living in the occupied republics of the western USSR – Belorussia and Ukraine. The functionalists argue that it was sheer pressure of numbers that led the Nazi and SS leaders in Poland to press for the mass murder of Jews. Hitler's views were well known throughout Nazi circles; he simply responded to the demands of the local Nazi leaders in Poland. Hans Mommsen, one of the leading functionalists, believes that Hitler was 'a weak dictator' – in other words, more often than not, he followed the promptings of others rather than taking initiatives himself (see Section 14.6(d)) for more about the 'weak dictator' theory). As late as 2001 Mommsen was still suggesting that there was no clear evidence of any genocidal bent before 1939.

According to Ian Kershaw in his biography of Hitler (published in 2000), 'Hitler's personalized form of rule invited radical initiatives from below and offered such initiatives backing, so long as they were in line with his broadly defined goals.' The way to advancement in Hitler's Third Reich was to anticipate what the Führer wanted, and then 'without waiting for directives, take initiatives to promote what were presumed to be Hitler's aims and wishes'. The phrase used to describe this process was 'working towards the Führer'. The intentionalists are not impressed with this interpretation because they feel it absolves Hitler from personal responsibility for the atrocities committed during the war. However, this conclusion does not necessarily follow: many of these initiatives would not even have been proposed if his subordinates had not been well aware of the 'Führer's will'.

Some historians feel that the intentionalist *v.* functionalist debate is now somewhat dated and that both approaches can be misleading. For example, Allan Bullock in *Hitler and Stalin* (1991), pointed out that the most obvious interpretation of the genocide was a combination of both approaches. Richard Overy in *The Dictators* (2004) claims that

> both approaches to the hunt for genocide divert attention from the central reality for all Jews after 1933: whether or not the later genocide was explicit or merely implicit in the anti-Jewish policies of the 1930s. ... the vengeful and violent xenophobia promoted by the regime had the Jews as its primary object throughout the whole life of the dictatorship.

What were Hitler's motives? Why was he so obsessively anti-Jewish? It is clear from a secret memorandum which Hitler wrote in 1936, however crazy it may appear today, that he genuinely perceived the Jews as a threat to the German nation. He believed that the world, led by Germany, was on the verge of a historic racial and political struggle against the forces of communism, which he saw as a Jewish phenomenon. If Germany failed, the German *Volk* (people) would be destroyed and the world would enter a new Dark Age. It was a question of German national survival in the face of a worldwide Jewish conspiracy. In the words of Richard Overy:

> The treatment of the Jews was intelligible only in the distorted mirror of German national anxieties and national aspirations. The system deliberately set out to create the idea that Germany's survival was contingent entirely on the exclusion or, if necessary, the annihilation of the Jew.

It was the convergence of Hitler's uncompromising anti-Jewish prejudice and his self-justification, together with the opportunity for action, which culminated in the terrible 'apocalyptic battle between "Aryan" and "Jew"'.

(c)   The 'Final Solution' takes shape

Alan Bullock argued that the best way to explain how the Holocaust came about is to combine elements from both intentionalists and functionalists. From the early 1920s Hitler had committed himself and the Nazi party to destroying the power of the Jews and driving them out of Germany, but exactly how this was to be done was left vague. 'It is very likely', writes Bullock, 'that among the fantasies in which he indulged privately … was the evil dream of a final settlement in which every man, woman and child of Jewish race would be butchered. … But how, when, even whether, the dream could ever be realized remained uncertain.'

It is important to remember that Hitler was a clever politician who paid a lot of attention to public opinion. During the early years of his Chancellorship, he was well aware that the so-called 'Jewish question' was not a main concern of most German people. Consequently he would go no further than the Nuremberg Laws (1935) (see Section 14.4(b), Point 11), and even they were introduced to satisfy the Nazi hardliners. Hitler allowed *Kristallnacht* to go ahead in November 1938 for the same reason, and to test popular feeling. When public opinion reacted unfavourably, he called an end to violence and concentrated on excluding Jews as far as possible from German life. They were encouraged to emigrate and their property and assets were seized. Before the outbreak of war, well over half a million Jews had left the country; plans were being discussed to forcibly remove as many Jews as possible to Madagascar.

It was the outbreak of war, and in particular the invasion of Russia (June 1941), that radically changed the situation. According to Richard Overy, this was seen not as an accidental or unplanned opportunity for a more vigorous anti-Jewish policy, but as 'an extension of an anti-Semitic Cold War that Germany had been engaged in since at least her defeat in 1918'. The occupation of the whole of Poland and large areas of the USSR meant that many more Jews came under German control, but at the same time the conditions of war meant that it was almost impossible for them to emigrate. In Poland, around two and a half million Jews were forcibly moved from their homes and herded into overcrowded ghettos in cities such as Warsaw, Lublin and Łódź. In 1939, for example, 375 000 Jews lived in Warsaw; after they captured the city, the Germans built a wall round the Jewish districts. Later, Jews from other parts of Poland were moved into Warsaw, until by July 1941, there were about 445 000 Jews crammed into this small ghetto. Nazi officials complained about the problems of coping with such large numbers of Jews – conditions in the ghettos were dreadful, food was deliberately kept in short supply and there was the danger of epidemics. Eventually 78 000 died from disease and starvation.

In December 1941, soon after Germany had declared war on the USA, Hitler stated publicly that his prophecy of January 1939, about the annihilation of Europe's Jews, would soon be fulfilled. The following day Goebbels wrote in his diary: 'The World War is here, the extermination of the Jews must be the necessary consequence.' There is no firm evidence as to exactly when the decision was taken to begin the implementation of the 'Final Solution' – to kill the Jews – but it was arguably in the autumn of 1941.

The decision was the result of a combination of various developments and circumstances:

- Hitler's self-confidence was at a new high point after all the German victories, especially the early successes of Operation Barbarossa.
- Hitler had already made it clear that the war in the east was something new. As Alan Bullock puts it: it was 'a racist–imperialist adventure … an ideological war of destruction, in which all the conventional rules of war, occupation and so on, were to be disregarded, political commissars shot out of hand and the civilian population made subject to summary execution and collective reprisals'. It was only a short

step further to carry out the extermination of the Jews. In the words of Richard Overy: 'This was consistent with the long history of his anti-Semitism, which was always expressed in the idiom of war to the death.'

- It would now be possible to carry out the Final Solution in Poland and the USSR, *outside* Germany. Hitler would have no need to worry about German public opinion; there could be strict censorship of all news reporting in the occupied territories.

The Nazis wasted no time; as their forces advanced deeper into the USSR, communists and Jews were rounded up for slaughter both by SS units and by the regular army. For example, in two days at the end of September 1941, some 34 000 Jews were murdered in a ravine at Babi Yar, on the outskirts of Kiev in Ukraine. At Odessa in the Crimea at least 75 000 Jews were killed. Any non-Jew who tried to hide or protect Jews in any way was unceremoniously shot along with the Jews and communists.

In January 1942, soon after the first Jews had been sent to the gas chambers at Chelmno in Poland, a conference was held at Wannsee (Berlin) to discuss the logistics of how to remove up to 11 million Jews from their homes in all parts of Europe and transport them into the occupied territories. At first the general idea seemed to be to kill off the Jews by forced labour and starvation, but this soon changed to a policy of systematically destroying them before the war ended. Hitler did not attend the Wannsee Conference; he kept very much in the background as regards the Final Solution. No order for its implementation signed by Hitler was ever found. This has been taken by a few historians as evidence that Hitler ought not to be blamed for the Holocaust. But this position is difficult to sustain. Ian Kershaw, after an exhaustive consideration of the evidence, comes to this conclusion:

There can be no doubt about it: Hitler's role had been decisive and indispensable in the road to the 'Final Solution'. ... Without Hitler and the unique regime he headed, the creation of a programme to bring about the physical extermination of the Jews would have been unthinkable.

(d) Genocide

As the extermination programme gained momentum, the Jews from eastern Europe were taken to Belzec, Sobibor, Treblinka and Majdanek in eastern Poland; most of those from western Europe went to Auschwitz-Birkenau in south-west Poland (see Map 6.7). Between July and September 1942, some 300 000 Jews were transported from the Warsaw ghetto to the Treblinka extermination camp. By the end of 1942 over 4 million Jews had already been put to death. Even though the fortunes of war began to turn against the Germans during 1943, Hitler insisted that the programme should continue; and continue it did, long after it was perfectly clear to everybody that the war would be lost. In April 1943 the remaining Jews of the Warsaw ghetto rose in revolt; the rising was brutally crushed and most of the Jews were killed. Only about 10 000 were still alive when Warsaw was liberated in January 1945. In July 1944, after German forces had occupied Hungary, about 400 000 Hungarian Jews were taken to Auschwitz. As Russian forces advanced through Poland, the SS organized forced marches from the death camps into Germany; most of the prisoners either died on the way, or were shot when they arrived in Germany. On 6 August 1944, with the Russians only about a hundred miles away, the Germans moved 70 000 Jews from the Łódź ghetto, south-west of Warsaw, and took them to Auschwitz, where half of them were immediately sent to the gas chambers.

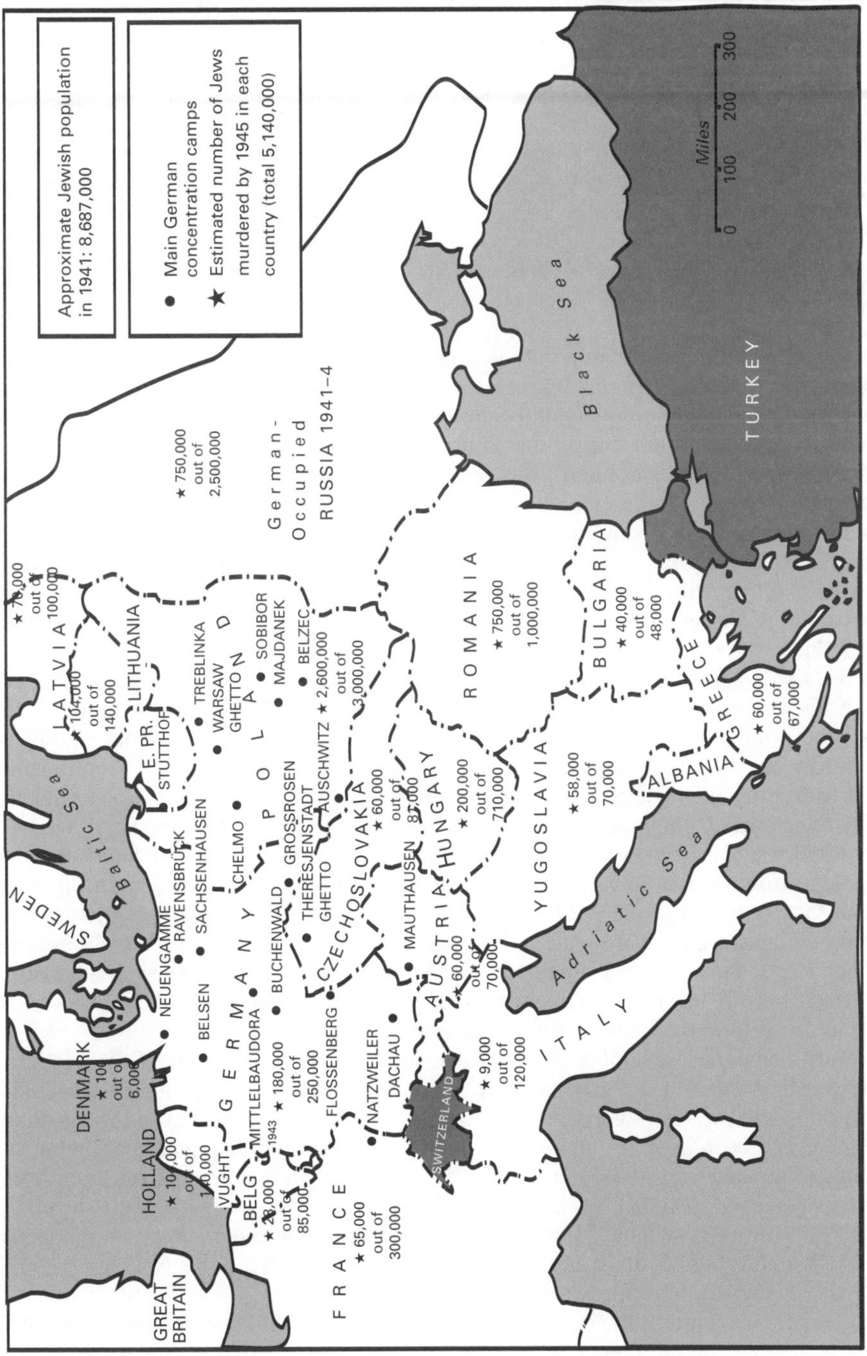

Map 6.7 The Holocaust

Legend

Approximate Jewish population in 1941: 8,687,000

● Main German concentration camps

★ Estimated number of Jews murdered by 1945 in each country (total 5,140,000)

Map labels

GREAT BRITAIN

HOLLAND
★ 10,000 out of 16,000

DENMARK
★ 100 out of 6,000

SWEDEN

Baltic Sea

BELG.
★ 20,000 out of 85,000

VUGHT- 1943

G E R M A N Y

MITTLELBAUDORA
★ 180,000 out of 250,000

BELSEN

NEUENGAMME

RAVENSBRÜCK

SACHSENHAUSEN

E. PR. STUTTHOF

LATVIA
★ 104,000 out of 140,000

LITHUANIA
★ 70,000 out of 100,000

German- Occupied RUSSIA 1941–4
★ 750,000 out of 2,500,000

BUCHENWALD

GROSSROSEN

THERESJENSTADT

FLOSSENBERG

NATZWEILER

DACHAU

P O L A N D

CHELMO

WARSAW GHETTO

TREBLINKA

SOBIBOR

MAJDANEK

BELZEC

AUSCHWITZ
★ 2,600,000 out of 3,000,000

GHETTO

CZECHOSLOVAKIA
★ 60,000 out of 87,000

MAUTHAUSEN

AUSTRIA
★ 60,000 out of 70,000

HUNGARY
★ 200,000 out of 710,000

ROMANIA
★ 750,000 out of 1,000,000

Black Sea

TURKEY

BULGARIA
★ 40,000 out of 48,000

YUGOSLAVIA
★ 58,000 out of 70,000

GREECE
★ 60,000 out of 67,000

ALBANIA

Adriatic Sea

ITALY
★ 9,000 out of 120,000

SWITZERLAND

FRANCE
★ 65,000 out of 300,000

Miles
0   100   200   300

Alan Bullock provided this chilling description of what happened when each new batch of Jews arrived at one of the death camps:

> They were put through the same ghastly routine. White-coated doctors – with a gesture of the hand – selected those fit enough to be *worked* to death. The rest were required to give up all their clothing and possessions and then in a terrified column of naked men and women, carrying their children or holding their hands and trying to comfort them, were herded into the gas-chambers. When the screaming died down and the doors were opened, they were still standing upright, so tightly packed that they could not fall. But where there had been human beings, there were now corpses, which were removed to the ovens for burning. This was the daily spectacle which Hitler took good care never to see and which haunts the imagination of anyone who has studied the evidence.

What sort of people could carry out such crimes against humanity? Historian Daniel Goldhagen, in his book *Hitler's Willing Executioners*, published in 1997, suggests that the German people were uniquely anti-Semitic and were collectively responsible for the many atrocities committed during the Third Reich. These included not just the 'Final Solution' of the 'Jewish problem', but also the euthanasia programme in which some 70 000 people deemed to be mentally handicapped or mentally ill were killed, the cruel treatment of the Polish people during the occupation, and the appalling way in which Russian prisoners of war and the civilian populations were treated. Michael Burleigh (2010) goes along with Goldhagen, suggesting that there was a sort of inherent anti-Semitism in the German people which the Nazis had only to tap into; there was no need to stir it up.

While Goldhagen's theory perhaps goes too far, there is no doubt that large numbers of ordinary Germans were willing to go along with Hitler and the other leading Nazis. Perhaps they were convinced by the arguments of men like Himmler, who told a group of SS commanders: 'We had the moral right, we had the duty to destroy this people which wanted to destroy us.' The SS, originally Hitler's bodyguard regiments, along with the security police, camp commandants and guards, and local *gauleiters* (governors), were all deeply implicated, and so was much of the Wehrmacht (the German army), which became increasingly ruthless and barbaric as the war in the east progressed. Leaders of big business and factory owners were willing to take advantage of the cheap labour provided by the camp inmates; others were grateful to get their hands on confiscated Jewish property and other assets; medical experts were prepared to use Jews in experiments which caused their deaths. At all levels of German society there were people who happily took the chance to profit from the fate of the helpless Jews.

But such behaviour was not confined to the Germans: many Polish and Soviet citizens willingly collaborated in the genocide. Only three days after the invasion of the USSR began, 1500 Jews were savagely murdered in Lithuania by local militias, and soon thousands more had been killed by non-Germans in Belorussia and Ukraine. Ion Antonescu, the ruler of Romania from 1941 until 1944, was not bullied into deporting Romanian Jews: Romania was never occupied by Germans, and the initiative was taken by the Romanians themselves. However, without Hitler and the Nazis to provide the authority, the legitimacy, the backing and the drive, none of this would have been possible. Romania, though not actually occupied, was firmly within Germany's orbit.

On the other hand it must be remembered that many Germans courageously risked their lives to help Jews, giving them shelter and organizing escape routes. But it was a very dangerous business – such people themselves often ended up in concentration camps.

Illustration 6.3   **Bodies at the Belsen concentration camp**

Similarly in Poland, there were many people who were willing to help Jewish fugitives. In a recent book, historian Gunnar Paulsson suggests that in Warsaw there was a network of perhaps 90 000 'decent and honest people' – over 10 per cent of the city's population – who were directly or indirectly involved in assisting Jews in a variety of ways. This challenges the usual view that the Poles quietly went along with the mass extermination of their Jewish compatriots.

6.9   WHAT WERE THE EFFECTS OF THE WAR?

(a)   Enormous destruction

There was enormous destruction of lives, homes, industries and communications in Europe and Asia.

Almost 40 million people were killed: well over half of them were Russians, 6 million were Poles, 4 million Germans, 2 million Chinese and 2 million Japanese. Britain and the USA got off comparatively lightly (see Figure 6.1).

A further 21 million people had been uprooted from their homes: some had been taken to Germany to work as slave labourers, and around seven million of these were still in Germany; some had been put into concentration camps, and some had been forced to flee from invading armies. The victorious powers were left with the problem of how to repatriate them (arrange for them to return home).

Large parts of Germany, especially her industrial areas and many major cities, lay in ruins. Much of western Russia had been completely devastated, and some 25 million people were homeless. France had suffered badly too: taking into account the destruction of housing, factories, railways, mines and livestock, almost 50 per cent of total French

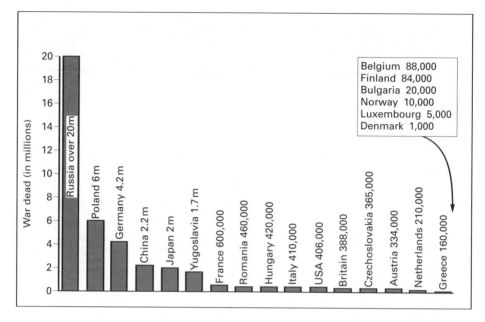

Figure 6.1   **Second World War dead**

Source: based on J. B. Watson, *Success in Modern World History Since 1945*, John Murray (1989), p. 3.
© Margaret Watson 1989. Reproduced by permission of Hodder Education.

wealth had been lost. In Italy, where damage was very serious in the south, the figure was over 30 per cent. Japan suffered heavy damage and a high death toll from bombings.

Though the cost was high, it did mean that the world had been rid of Nazism, which had been responsible for terrible atrocities. The most notorious was **the Holocaust** – *the deliberate murder in extermination camps of over five million Jews and hundreds of thousands of non-Jews*, mainly in Poland and Russia (see Section 6.8).

(b)   There was no all-inclusive peace settlement

This was different from the end of the First World War, when an all-inclusive settlement was negotiated at Versailles. This was mainly because the distrust which had re-emerged between the USSR and the west in the final months of the war made agreement on many points impossible.

However, a number of separate treaties were signed:

- *Italy* lost her African colonies and gave up her claims to Albania and Abyssinia (Ethiopia).
- *The USSR* took the eastern section of Czechoslovakia, the Petsamo district and the area round Lake Ladoga from Finland, and held on to Latvia, Lithuania and Estonia, which they had occupied in 1939.
- *Romania* recovered northern Transylvania, which the Hungarians had occupied during the war.
- *Trieste*, claimed by both Italy and Yugoslavia, was declared a free territory protected by the United Nations Organization.
- Later, at San Francisco (1951), *Japan* agreed to surrender all territory acquired during the previous 90 years, which included a complete withdrawal from China.

However, *the Russians refused to agree to any settlement over Germany and Austria*, except that they should be occupied by Allied troops and that East Prussia should be divided between Russia and Poland.

(c)   The war stimulated important social changes

In addition to the population movements during the war, once hostilities were over, many millions of people were forced to move from their homes. The worst cases were probably in the areas taken from Germany by Russia and Poland, and in the German-speaking areas in Hungary, Romania and Czechoslovakia. About ten million Germans were forced to leave and make their way to West Germany so that no future German government would be able to claim those territories. In some countries, especially the USSR and Germany, extensive urban redevelopment took place as ruined cities had to be rebuilt. In Britain the war stimulated, among other things, the Beveridge Report (1942), a plan for introducing a Welfare State.

(d)   The war caused the production of nuclear weapons

The first ever use of these weapons, on Hiroshima and Nagasaki, demonstrated their horrifying powers of destruction. The world was left under the threat of a nuclear war that might well have destroyed the entire planet. Some people argue that this acted as a deterrent, making both sides in the Cold War so frightened of the consequences that they were deterred or discouraged from fighting each other.

(e)   Europe's domination of the rest of the world ended

The four western European states which had played a leading role in world affairs for most of the first half of the twentieth century were now much weaker than before. Germany was devastated and divided, France and Italy were on the verge of bankruptcy; although Britain seemed strong and victorious, with her empire intact, the cost of the war had been ruinous. The USA had helped to keep Britain going during the war by sending supplies, but these had to be paid for later. As soon as the war was over, the new US president, Truman, abruptly stopped all further help, leaving Britain in a sorry state: she had overseas debts of over £3000 million, many of her foreign investments had been sold off, and her ability to export goods had been much reduced. She was forced to ask for another loan from the USA, which was given at a high rate of interest; the country was therefore closely and uncomfortably dependent on the USA.

(f)   Emergence of the superpowers

The USA and the USSR emerged as the two most powerful nations in the world, and they were no longer as isolated as they had been before the war. The USA had suffered relatively little from the war and had enjoyed great prosperity from supplying the other Allies with war materials and food. The Americans had the world's largest navy and air force and they controlled the atomic bomb. The USSR, though severely weakened, still had the largest army in the world. Both countries were highly suspicious of each other's intentions now that the common enemies, Germany and Japan, had been defeated. The rivalry of these two superpowers in the Cold War was the most important feature of international relations for almost half a century after 1945, and was a constant threat to world peace (see Chapter 7).

(g) Decolonization

The war encouraged the movement towards decolonization. The defeats inflicted on Britain, Holland and France by Japan, and the Japanese occupation of their territories – Malaya, Singapore and Burma (British), French Indo-China and the Dutch East Indies – destroyed the tradition of European superiority and invincibility. It could hardly be expected that, having fought to get rid of the Japanese, the Asian peoples would willingly return to European rule. Gradually they achieved full independence, though not without a struggle in many cases. This in turn intensified demands for independence among the peoples of Africa and the Middle East, and in the 1960s the result was a large array of new states (see Chapters 24–5). The leaders of many of these newly emerging nations met in conference at Algiers in 1973 and made it clear that they regarded themselves as *a Third World*. By this they meant that *they wished to remain neutral or non-aligned* in the struggle between the other two worlds – communism and capitalism. Usually poor and under-developed industrially, the new nations were often intensely suspicious of the motives of both communism and capitalism, and they resented their own economic dependence on the world's wealthy powers.

(h) The United Nations Organization (UNO)

This emerged as the successor to the League of Nations. Its main aim was to try to maintain world peace, and on the whole it has been more successful than its unfortunate predecessor (see Chapters 3 and 9).

FURTHER READING

Bankier, D., *The Germans and the Final Solution: Public Opinion under Nazism* (Blackwell, 1992).
Beevor, A., *Stalingrad* (Penguin, 1998).
Beevor, A., *Berlin – The Downfall, 1945* (Penguin, 2003).
Beevor, A., *D-Day: The Battle for Normandy* (Viking, 2009).
Bloxham, D., *The Final Solution. A Genocide* (Oxford University Press, 2009).
Bracher, K. D., *The German Dictatorship* (Penguin, 1985 edition).
Browning, C., *The Origins of the Final Solution* (Heinemann, 2003)
Bullock, A., *Hitler and Stalin – Parallel Lives* (HarperCollins, 1991).
Burleigh, M., *Moral Combat: A History of World War II* (Harper, 2009).
Davies, N., *Rising '44: The Battle for Warsaw* (Macmillan, 2003).
Davies, N., *Europe at War 1939–1945: No Simple Victory* (Pan, 2nd edition, 2007).
Friedlander, S., *The Years of Extermination: Nazi Germany and the Jews 1939–1945* (Weidenfeld & Nicholson, 2007).
Friedrich, J., *The Fire: The Bombing of Germany 1940–1945,* translated from the German by Allison Brown (Columbia University Press, 2007).
Gilbert, M., *Second World War* (Phoenix, new edition, 2000).
Goldhagen, D., *Hitler's Willing Executioners* (Vintage, 1997).
Jones, M., *Leningrad: State of Siege* (John Murray, 2008).
Kershaw, I., *Hitler, 1936–1945:Nemesis* (Allen Lane/Penguin, 2000).
Kershaw, I., *Hitler* (Allen Lane, 2009).
Kershaw, I., *The End: Hitler's Germany, 1944–1945* (Allen Lane/Penguin, 2011).
Lindqvist, A., *A History of Bombing* (Granta, 2001).
Lipstadt, D., *Denying the Holocaust* (Plume, 1995).
Longerich, P., *The Unwritten Order: Hitler's Role in the Final Solution* (Tempus, 2000).

Mazower, M., *Hitler's Empire: Nazi Rule in Occupied Europe* (Allen Lane, 2008).

Merridale, C., *Ivan's War: The Red Army 1939–1945* (Faber, 2005).

Mommsen, H. (ed.), *The Third Reich Between Vision and Reality* (Oxford University Press, 2001).

Neillands, R., *Arthur Harris and the Allied Bombing Offensive, 1939–45* (John Murray, 2001).

Overy, R. J., *Russia's War, 1941–1945* (Penguin, 1997).

Overy, R. J., *The Dictators* (Allen Lane, 2004).

Overy, R. J., *Why the Allies Won* (Pimlico, 2006).

Overy, R. J., *The Third Reich: A Chronicle* (Quercus, 2010).

Parker, R. A. C., *The Second World War: A Short History* (Oxford paperbacks, 3rd edition, 2001).

Paulsson, G. S., *Secret City: The Hidden Jews of Warsaw, 1940–1945* (Yale University Press, 2002).

Rees, L., *Auschwitz: The Nazis and the Final Solution* (BBC Books, 2005).

Roberts, A., *The Storm of War: A New History of the Second World War* (Penguin, 2010).

Tooze, A., *The Wages of Destruction: The Making and Breaking of the Nazi Economy* (Penguin, 2007).

Wint, G., *The Penguin History of the Second World War* (Penguin, 3rd edition, 1999).

QUESTIONS

1   Explain why Germany was successful in the Second World War up to the end of 1941, but suffered ultimate defeat in 1945.

2   'Retreats and defeats marked the first two years of the war for Britain.' How far would you agree with this opinion?

3   Explain why you agree or disagree with the view that the Allied victory in the Second World War was secured mainly because of the contribution of the USSR.

There is a document question on Hitler's thoughts about the future on the website.

The Cold War: problems of international relations after the Second World War

SUMMARY OF EVENTS

Towards the end of the war, the harmony that had existed between the USSR, the USA and the British Empire began to wear thin and all the old suspicions came to the fore again. Relations between Soviet Russia and the West soon became so difficult that, although no actual fighting took place directly between the two opposing camps, the decade after 1945 saw the first phase of what became known as *the Cold War*. This continued, in spite of several 'thaws', until the collapse of communism in eastern Europe in 1989–91. What happened was that instead of allowing their mutual hostility to express itself in open fighting, *the rival powers attacked each other with propaganda and economic measures, and with a general policy of non-cooperation.*

Both superpowers, the USA and the USSR, gathered allies around them: between 1945 and 1948 the USSR drew into its orbit most of the states of eastern Europe, as communist governments came to power in Poland, Hungary, Romania, Bulgaria, Yugoslavia, Albania, Czechoslovakia and East Germany (1949). A communist government was established in North Korea (1948), and the Communist bloc seemed to be further strengthened in 1949 when Mao Zedong (Mao Tse-tung) was at last victorious in the long-drawn-out civil war in China (see Section 19.4). On the other hand, the USA hastened the recovery of Japan and fostered her as an ally, and worked closely with Britain and 14 other European countries, as well as with Turkey, providing them with vast economic aid in order to build up an anti-communist bloc.

Whatever one bloc suggested or did was viewed by the other as having ulterior and aggressive motives. There was a long wrangle, for example, over where the frontier between Poland and Germany should be, and no permanent settlement could be agreed on for Germany and Austria. Then in the mid-1950s, after the death of Stalin (1953), the new Russian leaders began to talk about 'peaceful coexistence', mainly to give the USSR a much-needed break from its economic and military burdens. The icy atmosphere between the two blocs began to thaw: in 1955 it was agreed to remove all occupying troops from Austria. However, relations did not improve sufficiently to allow agreement on Germany, and tensions mounted again over Vietnam and the Cuban missiles crisis (1962). The Cold War moved into a new phase in the later 1960s when both sides took initiatives to reduce tensions. Known as *détente,* this brought a marked improvement in international relations, including the signing of the Strategic Arms Limitation Treaty in 1972. *Détente* did not end superpower rivalry, and the Soviet invasion of Afghanistan in 1979 heightened international tensions once more. The Cold War came to an end in 1989–91 with the collapse of the Soviet Union.

(a)   Differences of principle

The basic cause of conflict lay in the differences of principle between the communist states and the capitalist or liberal-democratic states.

- *The communist system* of organizing the state and society was based on the ideas of Karl Marx; he believed that the wealth of a country should be collectively owned and shared by everybody. The economy should be centrally planned and the interests and well-being of the working classes safeguarded by state social policies.
- *The capitalist system*, on the other hand, operates on the basis of private ownership of a country's wealth. The driving forces behind capitalism are private enterprise in the pursuit of making profits, and the preservation of the power of private wealth.

Ever since the world's first communist government was set up in Russia (the USSR) in 1917 (see Section 16.2(d)), the governments of most capitalist states viewed it with mistrust and were afraid of communism spreading to their countries. This would mean the end of the private ownership of wealth, as well as the loss of political power by the wealthy classes. When civil war broke out in Russia in 1918, several capitalist states – the USA, Britain, France and Japan – sent troops to Russia to help the anti-communist forces. The communists won the war, but Joseph Stalin, who became Russian leader in 1929, was convinced that there would be another attempt by the capitalist powers to destroy communism in Russia. The German invasion of Russia in 1941 proved him right. The need for self-preservation against Germany and Japan caused the USSR, the USA and Britain to forget their differences and work together, but as soon as the defeat of Germany was clearly only a matter of time, both sides, and especially Stalin, began to plan for the post-war period.

(b)   Stalin's foreign policies contributed to the tensions

His aim was to take advantage of the military situation to strengthen Russian influence in Europe. As the Nazi armies collapsed, he tried to occupy as much German territory as he could, and to acquire as much land as he could get away with from countries such as Finland, Poland and Romania. In this he was highly successful, but the West was alarmed at what they took to be Soviet aggression; they believed that he was committed to spreading communism over as much of the globe as possible.

(c)   US and British politicians were hostile to the Soviet government

During the war, the USA under President Roosevelt sent war materials of all kinds to Russia under a system known as 'Lend-Lease', and Roosevelt was inclined to trust Stalin. But after Roosevelt died, in April 1945, his successor Harry S. Truman was more suspicious and toughened his attitude towards the communists. Some historians believe that Truman's main motive for dropping the atomic bombs on Japan was not simply to defeat Japan, which was ready to surrender anyway, but to show Stalin what might happen to Russia if he dared go too far. Stalin suspected that the USA and Britain were still keen to destroy communism; he felt that their delay in launching the invasion of France, the Second Front (which did not take place until June 1944), was deliberately calculated to keep most of the pressure on the Russians and bring them to the point of exhaustion. Nor did they tell Stalin about the existence of the atomic bomb until shortly before its use on Japan, and they rejected his request that Russia should share in the occupation of Japan. *Above all, the West had the atomic bomb and the USSR did not.*

Which side was to blame?

During the 1950s, most western historians, such as the American George Kennan (in his *Memoirs, 1925–50* (Bantam, 1969)), *blamed Stalin.* During the mid-1940s Kennan had worked at the US embassy in Moscow, and later (1952–3) he was US Ambassador in Moscow. He argued that Stalin's motives were sinister, and that he intended to spread communism as widely as possible through Europe and Asia, thus destroying capitalism. Kennan advised a policy of 'containment' of the USSR by political, economic and diplomatic means. The formation of NATO (see Section 7.2(i)) and the American entry into the Korean War in 1950 (see Section 8.1) were the West's self-defence against communist aggression.

On the other hand, Soviet historians, and during the 1960s and early 1970s some American historians, argued that *the Cold War ought not to be blamed on Stalin and the Russians.* Their theory was that Russia had suffered enormous losses during the war, and therefore it was only to be expected that Stalin would try to make sure neighbouring states were friendly, given Russia's weakness in 1945. They believe that Stalin's motives were purely defensive and that there was no real threat to the West from the USSR. Some Americans claim that the USA should have been more understanding and should not have challenged the idea of a Soviet 'sphere of influence' in eastern Europe. The actions of American politicians, especially Truman, provoked Russian hostility unnecessarily. This is known among historians as the *revisionist* view; one of its leading proponents, William Appleman Williams, believed that the Cold War was mainly caused by the USA's determination to make the most of its atomic monopoly and its industrial strength in its drive for world hegemony.

The main reason behind this new view was that during the late 1960s many people in the USA became critical of American foreign policy, especially American involvement in the Vietnam War (see Section 8.3). This caused some historians to reconsider the American attitude towards communism in general; they felt that American governments had become obsessed with hostility towards communist states and they were ready to take a more sympathetic view of the difficulties Stalin had found himself in at the end of the Second World War.

Later a third view – known as the *post-revisionist* interpretation – was put forward by some American historians, and this became popular in the 1980s. They had the benefit of being able to look at lots of new documents and visit archives which had not been open to earlier historians. The new evidence suggested that the situation at the end of the war was far more complicated than earlier historians had realized; this led them to take a middle view, arguing that *both sides should take some blame for the Cold War.* They believe that American economic policies such as Marshall Aid (see Section 7.2(e)) were deliberately designed to increase US political influence in Europe. However, they also believe that although Stalin had no long-term plans to spread communism, he was an opportunist who would take advantage of any weakness in the West to expand Soviet influence. The crude Soviet methods of forcing communist governments on the states of eastern Europe were bound to lend proof to claims that Stalin's aims were expansionist. With their entrenched positions and deep suspicions of each other, the USA and the USSR created an atmosphere in which every international act could be interpreted in two ways. What was claimed as necessary for self-defence by one side was taken by the other as evidence of aggressive intent, as the events described in the next section show. But at least open war was avoided, because the Americans were reluctant to use the atomic bomb again unless attacked directly, while the Russians dared not risk such an attack.

When the Cold War came to an end with the collapse of eastern European communism and the Soviet Union in 1989–91, a number of new Cold War histories appeared reviewing both its causes and effects. In 2006 John Lewis Gaddis restated his belief that Russian attempts to dominate the world had been the cause. American policy had been right because it ended in victory, for which Ronald Reagan and Margaret Thatcher must take much of the credit: 'the universal acceptance of capitalism, the discrediting of dictatorships and the globalisation of democratisation under benevolent American leadership'. In the same year O. A. Westad set out the rival view: he pointed out that the collapse of communism stemmed from the decision of the Chinese communists to abandon socialist economics and change to a form of capitalism, albeit a different one from that in the West. The Chinese had been pressurising other communist states to do the same; it was this, together with the Soviet involvement in Afghanistan from 1979 onwards, that weakened and finally brought down the USSR.

7.2 HOW DID THE COLD WAR DEVELOP BETWEEN 1945 AND 1953?

(a) The Yalta Conference (February 1945)

This was held in Russia (in the Crimea) and was attended by the three Allied leaders, Stalin, Roosevelt and Churchill, so that they could plan what was to happen when the war ended (see Illus. 7.1). *At the time it seemed to be a success*, *agreement being reached on several points*.

Illustration 7.1 **Churchill, Roosevelt and Stalin at Yalta, February 1945**

- A new organization – to be called *the United Nations* – should be set up to replace the failed League of Nations.
- *Germany was to be divided into zones* – Russian, American and British (a French zone was included later) – while Berlin (which happened to be in the middle of the Russian zone) would also be split into corresponding zones. Similar arrangements were to be made for Austria.
- Free elections would be allowed in the states of eastern Europe.
- Stalin promised to join the war against Japan on condition that Russia received the whole of Sakhalin Island and some territory in Manchuria.

However, there were ominous *signs of trouble over what was to be done with Poland*. When the Russian armies swept through Poland, driving the Germans back, they had set up a communist government in Lublin, even though there was already a Polish government-in-exile in London. It was agreed at Yalta that some members (non-communist) of the London-based government should be allowed to join the Lublin government, while in return Russia would be allowed to keep a strip of eastern Poland which she had annexed in 1939. However, Roosevelt and Churchill were not happy about Stalin's demands that Poland should be given all German territory east of the rivers Oder and Neisse; no agreement was reached on this point.

(b) The Potsdam Conference (July 1945)

The atmosphere here was distinctly cooler. The three leaders at the beginning of the conference were Stalin, Truman (replacing Roosevelt, who had died in April) and Churchill, but Churchill was replaced by Clement Attlee, the new British Labour prime minister, after Labour's election victory.

The war with Germany was over, but no agreement was reached about her long-term future. The big questions were whether, or when, the four zones would be allowed to join together to form a united country again. She was to be disarmed, the Nazi party would be disbanded and its leaders tried as war criminals. It was agreed that the Germans should pay something towards repairing the damage they had caused during the war. Most of these payments (known as 'reparations') were to go to the USSR, which would be allowed to take non-food goods from their own zone and from the other zones as well, provided the Russians sent food supplies to the western zones of Germany in return.

It was over Poland that the main disagreement occurred. Truman and Churchill were annoyed because Germany east of the Oder–Neisse Line had been occupied by Russian troops and was being run by the pro-communist Polish government, which expelled some five million Germans living in the area; this had not been agreed at Yalta (see Map 7.1). Truman did not inform Stalin about the exact nature of the atomic bomb, though Churchill was told about it. A few days after the conference closed, the two atomic bombs were dropped on Japan and the war ended quickly on 10 August without the need for Russian help (though the Russians had declared war on Japan on 8 August and invaded Manchuria). They annexed south Sakhalin as agreed at Yalta, but they were allowed no part in the occupation of Japan.

(c) Communism established in eastern Europe

In the months following Potsdam, the Russians systematically interfered in the countries of eastern Europe to set up pro-communist governments. This happened in Poland, Hungary, Bulgaria, Albania and Romania. In some cases their opponents were imprisoned

Key labels within map:

NORWAY

FINLAND — from Finland

SWEDEN

Leningrad

DENMARK

ESTONIA

LATVIA

EAST PRUSSIA

LITHUANIA

U.S.S.R.

Stettin

GERMANY

Berlin

R. Oder

POLAND

R. Neisse

Warsaw

from Poland

CZECHOSLOVAKIA

from Czechoslovakia

FRANCE

Vienna

AUSTRIA

from Romania

HUNGARY

Trieste — from Italy

ITALY

ROMANIA

YUGOSLAVIA

BULGARIA

ALBANIA

GREECE

TURKEY

Land taken by Poland from Germany: territory east of the *Oder–Neisse* line and part of East Prussia

Land acquired by the USSR during the war

Occupation zones in Germany and Austria:
1 Russian   3 French
2 British   4 American

Map 7.1 **Europe after 1945**

or murdered; in Hungary for example, the Russians allowed free elections; but although the communists won less than 20 per cent of the votes, they saw to it that a majority of the cabinet were communists. Stalin frightened the West further by a widely reported speech in February 1946 in which he said that communism and capitalism could never live peacefully together, and that future wars were inevitable until the final victory of communism was achieved. However, Russian historians have claimed that the speech was reported in

Map 7.2 **Central and eastern Europe during the Cold War**

Source: D. Heater, *Our World This Century* (Oxford, 1992), p. 129

the west in a misleading and biased way, especially by George Kennan, who was the US *chargé d'affaires* in Moscow.

Churchill responded to all this in a speech of his own at Fulton, Missouri (USA), in March 1946, in which he repeated a phrase he had used earlier: 'From Stettin in the Baltic to Trieste in the Adriatic, *an iron curtain has descended across the continent*' (see Map 7.2). Claiming that the Russians were bent on 'indefinite expansion of their power and doctrines', he called for *a Western alliance* which would stand firm against the communist threat. The speech drew a sharp response from Stalin, who revealed his fears about Germany and the need to strengthen Soviet security. The rift between East and West was steadily widening and Stalin was able to denounce Churchill as a 'warmonger'. But not everybody in the West agreed with Churchill – over a hundred British Labour MPs signed a motion criticizing the Conservative leader for his attitude.

(d)   The Russians continued to tighten their grip on eastern Europe

By the end of 1947 every state in that area with the exception of Czechoslovakia had a fully communist government. Elections were rigged, non-communist members of coalition governments were expelled, many were arrested and executed and eventually all other political parties were dissolved. All this took place under the watchful eyes of secret police and Russian troops. In addition, Stalin treated the Russian zone of Germany as if it were Russian territory, allowing only the Communist Party and draining it of vital resources.

Only Yugoslavia did not fit the pattern: here the communist government of Marshal Tito had been legally elected in 1945. Tito had won the election because of his immense prestige as leader of the anti-German resistance; it was Tito's forces, not the Russians, who had liberated Yugoslavia from German occupation, and Tito resented Stalin's attempts to interfere.

The West was profoundly irritated by Russia's treatment of eastern Europe, which disregarded Stalin's promise of free elections, made at Yalta. And yet they ought not to have been surprised at what was happening: even Churchill had agreed with Stalin in 1944 that much of eastern Europe should be a Russian sphere of influence. Stalin could argue that friendly governments in neighbouring states were necessary for self-defence, that these states had never had democratic governments anyway, and that communism would bring much-needed progress to backward countries. It was Stalin's methods of gaining control which upset the West, and they gave rise to the next major developments.

(e)   The Truman Doctrine and the Marshall Plan

1   The Truman Doctrine
This sprang from events in Greece, where communists were trying to overthrow the monarchy. British troops, who had helped liberate Greece from the Germans in 1944, had restored the monarchy, but they were now feeling the strain of supporting it against the communists, who were receiving help from Albania, Bulgaria and Yugoslavia. Ernest Bevin, the British Foreign Minister, appealed to the USA and Truman announced (March 1947) that the USA 'would support free peoples who are resisting subjugation by armed minorities or by outside pressures'. Greece immediately received massive amounts of arms and other supplies, and by 1949 the communists were defeated. Turkey, which also seemed under threat, received aid worth about $60 million. The Truman Doctrine made it clear that the USA had no intention of returning to isolation as she had after the First World War; she was committed to *a policy of containing communism*, not just in Europe, but throughout the world, including Korea and Vietnam.

2   The Marshall Plan

Announced in June 1947, this was an economic extension of the Truman Doctrine. American Secretary of State George Marshall produced his *European Recovery Programme (ERP)*, which offered economic and financial help wherever it was needed. 'Our policy', he declared, 'is directed not against any country or doctrine, but against hunger, poverty, desperation and chaos.' Western Europe was certainly suffering from all of these problems, exacerbated by the coldest winter for almost 70 years (1947–8). One of the aims of the ERP was to promote the economic recovery of Europe, but there was more behind it than humanitarian feeling. A prosperous Europe would provide lucrative markets for American exports; but its main aim was probably political: communism was less likely to gain control in a flourishing western Europe. By September, 16 nations (Britain, France, Italy, Belgium, Luxembourg, the Netherlands, Portugal, Austria, Greece, Turkey, Iceland, Norway, Sweden, Denmark, Switzerland and the western zones of Germany) had drawn up a joint plan for using American aid. During the next four years over $13 billion of Marshall Aid flowed into western Europe, fostering the recovery of agriculture and industry, which in many countries were in chaos because of war devastation. During the same period the communist parties in western Europe suffered electoral defeat, most notably in France and Italy, which had seemed the most likely states to go communist.

Most American historians have claimed that Europe's rapid recovery from impending economic and political disaster was due entirely to the Marshall Plan, which was held up as a perfect example of humanitarian intervention. In his history of the Plan, published in 2008, Greg Behrman follows the same line: Marshall and his assistants were heroes and America saved Europe from economic disaster and a communist takeover. In another 2008 publication, Nicolaus Mills also sees the Plan as a model of how to go about helping states struggling with exhaustion, poverty and economic chaos. However, he admits that European leaders themselves played an important part in their countries' recovery. In fact, European historians have rejected the view that Europe was saved solely by the Marshall Plan. They point out that European economies recovered so quickly after 1947 that the conditions for recovery must already have been in place. Although $13 billion sounds an awful lot of money, Marshall Aid averaged only about 2.5 per cent of the total national income of the 16 countries involved. This raises the question: if Marshall Aid had not been available, would western Europe have turned communist, either from electoral choice or by Soviet invasion? The overwhelming evidence suggests that the communists' popularity was already in decline before American aid began to arrive. And most historians agree that Stalin was more concerned to protect Soviet security than to start launching wholesale invasions of western Europe.

The Russians were well aware that there was more to Marshall Aid than pure benevolence. Although in theory aid was available for eastern Europe, Russian Foreign Minister Molotov denounced the whole idea as 'dollar imperialism'. He saw it as a blatant American device for gaining control of western Europe, and worse still, for interfering in eastern Europe, which Stalin considered to be Russia's sphere of influence. The USSR rejected the offer, and neither her satellite states nor Czechoslovakia, which was showing interest, were allowed to take advantage of it. *The 'iron curtain' seemed a reality*, and the next development only served to strengthen it.

(f)   The Cominform

This – the Communist Information Bureau – was the Soviet response to the Marshall Plan. Set up by Stalin in September 1947, it was an organization to draw together the various European communist parties. All the satellite states were members, and the French and Italian communist parties were represented. Stalin's aim was to tighten his grip on the satellites: to be communist was not enough – *it must be Russian-style communism*. Eastern Europe was to be industrialized, collectivized and centralized; states were expected to trade primarily with Cominform members, and all contacts with non-communist countries were discouraged. When Yugoslavia objected she was expelled from the Cominform (1948), though she remained communist. In 1947 *the Molotov Plan* was introduced, offering Russian aid to the satellites. Another organization, known as *Comecon (Council of Mutual Economic Assistance)*, was set up to co-ordinate their economic policies.

(g) The communist takeover of Czechoslovakia (February 1948)

This came as a great blow to the Western bloc, because it was the only remaining democratic state in eastern Europe. There was a coalition government of communists and other left-wing parties, which had been freely elected in 1946. The communists had won 38 per cent of the votes and 114 seats in the 300-seat parliament, and they held a third of the cabinet posts. The prime minister, Klement Gottwald, was a communist; President Beneš and the foreign minister, Jan Masaryk, were not; they hoped that Czechoslovakia, with its highly developed industries, would *remain as a bridge between east and west*.

However, a crisis arose early in 1948. Elections were due in May, and all the signs were that the communists would lose ground; they were blamed for the Czech rejection of Marshall Aid, which might have eased the continuing food shortages. The communists decided to act before the elections; already in control of the unions and the police, they seized power in an armed coup. All non-communist ministers with the exception of Beneš and Masaryk resigned. A few days later Masaryk's body was found under the windows of his offices. His death was officially described as suicide. However, when the archives were opened after the collapse of communism in 1989, documents were found which proved beyond doubt that he had been murdered. The elections were held in May but there was only a single list of candidates – all communists. Beneš resigned and Gottwald became president.

The western powers and the UN protested but felt unable to take any action because they could not prove Russian involvement – the coup was purely an internal affair. However, there can be little doubt that Stalin, disapproving of Czech connections with the West and of the interest in Marshall Aid, had prodded the Czech communists into action. Nor was it just coincidence that several of the Russian divisions occupying Austria were moved up to the Czech frontier. The bridge between East and West was gone; *the 'iron curtain' was complete*.

(h) The Berlin blockade and airlift (June 1948–May 1949)

This brought the Cold War to its first great crisis. It arose out of *disagreements over the treatment of Germany*.

1 At the end of the war, as agreed at Yalta and Potsdam, *Germany and Berlin were each divided into four zones*. While the three western powers did their best to organize the economic and political recovery of their zones, Stalin, determined to make Germany pay for all the damage inflicted on Russia, treated his zone as a satellite, *draining its resources away to Russia*.

2 *Early in 1948 the three western zones were merged to form a single economic unit*, whose prosperity, thanks to Marshall Aid, was in marked contrast to the poverty of the Russian zone. The West wanted all four zones to be re-united and given self-government as soon as possible; but Stalin had decided that it would be safer for

Russia if he kept the Russian zone separate, with its own communist, pro-Russian government. The prospect of the three western zones re-uniting was alarming enough to Stalin, because he knew they would be part of the Western bloc.

3   *In June 1948 the West introduced a new currency and ended price controls in their zone and in West Berlin.* The Russians decided that the situation in Berlin had become impossible. Already irritated by what they saw as an island of capitalism a hundred miles inside the communist zone, they felt it impossible to have two different currencies in the same city, and they were embarrassed by the contrast between the prosperity of West Berlin and the poverty of the surrounding area.

The Russian response was immediate: *all road, rail and canal links between West Berlin and West Germany were closed*; their aim was to force the West to withdraw from West Berlin by reducing it to starvation point. The western powers, convinced that a retreat would be the prelude to a Russian attack on West Germany, were determined to hold on. They decided to fly supplies in, rightly judging that the Russians would not risk shooting down the transport planes. Truman had thoughtfully sent a fleet of B-29 bombers to be positioned on British airfields. Over the next ten months, 2 million tons of supplies were airlifted to the blockaded city in a remarkable operation which kept the 2.5 million West Berliners fed and warm right through the winter. In May 1949 the Russians admitted failure by lifting the blockade.

The affair had important results:

- The outcome gave a great psychological boost to the western powers, though it brought relations with Russia to their worst ever.
- It caused the western powers to co-ordinate their defences by the formation of NATO.
- It meant that since no compromise was possible, Germany was doomed to remain divided for the foreseeable future.

(i)   The formation of NATO

The formation of the North Atlantic Treaty Organization (NATO) took place in April 1949. The Berlin blockade showed the West's military unreadiness and frightened them into making definite preparations. Already in March 1948, Britain, France, Holland, Belgium and Luxembourg had signed *the Brussels Defence Treaty*, promising military collaboration in case of war. Now they were joined by the USA, Canada, Portugal, Denmark, Iceland, Italy and Norway. All signed *the North Atlantic Treaty*, agreeing to regard an attack on any one of them as an attack on them all, and placing their defence forces under a joint NATO command organization which would co-ordinate the defence of the west. This was a highly significant development: the Americans had abandoned their traditional policy of 'no entangling alliances' and for the first time had pledged themselves in advance to military action. Predictably Stalin took it as a challenge, and tensions remained high.

(j)   The two Germanies

Since there was no prospect of the Russians allowing a united Germany, the western powers went ahead alone and set up *the German Federal Republic, known as West Germany (August 1949)*. Elections were held and Konrad Adenauer became the first Chancellor. The Russians replied by setting up their zone as *the German Democratic*

Republic, or East Germany (October 1949). Germany remained divided until the collapse of communism in East Germany (November–December 1989) made it possible early in 1990 to re-unite the two states into a single Germany (see Section 10.6(e)).

(k) More nuclear weapons

When it became known in September 1949 that the USSR had successfully exploded an atomic bomb, an arms race began to develop. Truman responded by giving the go-ahead for the USA to produce *a hydrogen bomb* many times more powerful than the atomic bomb. His defence advisers produced a secret document, known as NSC-68 (April 1950), which shows that they had come to regard the Russians as fanatics who would stop at nothing to spread communism all over the world. They suggested that expenditure on armaments should be more than tripled in an attempt to defeat communism.

It was not only the Russians who alarmed the Americans: *a communist government was proclaimed in China (October 1949)* after the communist leader Mao Zedong (Mao Tse-tung) had defeated Chiang Kai-shek, the nationalist leader, who had been supported by the USA and who was now forced to flee to the island of Taiwan (Formosa). *When the USSR and communist China signed a treaty of alliance in February 1950*, American fears of an advancing tide of communism seemed about to be realized. It was in this atmosphere of American anxiety that the Cold War spotlight now shifted to Korea, where, in June 1950, troops from communist North Korea invaded non-communist South Korea (see Section 8.1).

7.3 TO WHAT EXTENT WAS THERE A THAW AFTER 1953?

There is no doubt that in some ways East–West relations did begin to improve during 1953, though there were still areas of disagreement and the thaw was not a consistent development.

(a) Reasons for the thaw

1 The death of Stalin

The death of Stalin was probably the starting point of the thaw, because it brought to the forefront new Russian leaders – Malenkov, Bulganin and Khrushchev – who wanted to improve relations with the USA. Their reasons were possibly connected with the fact that by August 1953 the Russians as well as the Americans had developed a hydrogen bomb: the two sides were now so finely balanced that international tensions had to be relaxed if nuclear war was to be avoided.

Nikita Khrushchev explained the new policy in a famous speech (February 1956) in which he criticized Stalin and said that *'peaceful coexistence' with the West was not only possible but essential*: 'there are only two ways – either peaceful coexistence or the most destructive war in history. There is no third way.' This did not mean that Khrushchev had given up the idea of a communist-dominated world; this would still come, but it would be achieved when the western powers recognized the superiority of the Soviet economic system, not when they were defeated in war. In the same way, he hoped to win neutral states over to communism by lavish economic aid.

2 McCarthy discredited

Anti-communist feelings in the USA, which had been stirred up by Senator Joseph McCarthy, began to moderate when McCarthy was discredited in 1954. It had gradually become clear that McCarthy himself was something of a fanatic, and when he began to accuse leading generals of having communist sympathies, he had gone too far. The Senate condemned him by a large majority and he foolishly attacked the new Republican President Eisenhower for supporting the Senate. Soon afterwards Eisenhower announced that the American people wanted to be friendly with the Soviet people.

(b) How did the thaw show itself?

1 The first signs

- The signing of the peace agreement at Panmunjom ended the Korean War in July 1953 (see Section 8.1(c)).
- The following year the war in Indo-China ended (see Section 8.3(c–e)).

2 The Russians made important concessions in 1955

- They agreed to give up their military bases in Finland.
- They lifted their veto on the admission of 16 new member states to the UN.
- The quarrel with Yugoslavia was healed when Khrushchev paid a visit to Tito.
- The Cominform was abandoned, suggesting more freedom for the satellite states.

3 The signing of the Austrian State Treaty (May 1955)
This was the most important development in the thaw. At the end of the war in 1945, Austria was divided into four zones of occupation, with the capital, Vienna, in the Russian zone. Unlike Germany, she was allowed her own government because she was viewed not as a defeated enemy but as a state liberated from the Nazis. The Austrian government had only limited powers, and the problem was similar to the one in Germany: whereas the three western occupying powers organized the recovery of their zones, the Russians insisted on squeezing reparations, mainly in the form of food supplies, from theirs. No permanent settlement seemed likely, but early in 1955 the Russians were persuaded, mainly by the Austrian government, to be more co-operative. They were also afraid of a merger between West Germany and western Austria.

As a result of the agreement, all occupying troops were withdrawn and Austria became independent, with her 1937 frontiers. She was not to unite with Germany, her armed forces were strictly limited and she was to remain neutral in any dispute between East and West. This meant that she could not join either NATO or the European Economic Community. One point the Austrians were unhappy about was the loss of the German-speaking area of the South Tyrol, which Italy was allowed to keep.

(c) The thaw was only partial

Khrushchev's policy was a curious mixture, which western leaders often found difficult to understand. While making the conciliatory moves just described, he was quick to respond to anything which seemed to be a threat to the East, and he had no intention of relaxing Russia's grip on the satellite states. The Hungarians discovered this to their cost in 1956 when *a rising in Budapest against the communist government was ruthlessly crushed by Russian tanks* (see Sections 9.3(e) and 10.5(d)). Sometimes he seemed to be prepared to see how far he could push the Americans before they stood up to him:

- *The Warsaw Pact (1955)* was signed between Russia and her satellite states shortly after West Germany was admitted to NATO. The Pact was a mutual defence agreement, which the West took as a gesture against West Germany's membership of NATO.

- The Russians continued to build up their nuclear armaments (see next section).
- The situation in Berlin caused more tension (see below).
- The most provocative action of all was when Khrushchev installed Soviet missiles in Cuba, less than a hundred miles from the American coast (1962).

The situation in Berlin

The western powers were still refusing to give official recognition to the German Democratic Republic (East Germany), which the Russians had set up in response to the creation of West Germany in 1949. In 1958, perhaps encouraged by the USSR's apparent lead in some areas of the nuclear arms race, Khrushchev announced that the USSR no longer recognized the rights of the western powers in West Berlin. When the Americans made it clear that they would resist any attempt to push them out, Khrushchev did not press the point.

In 1960 it was Khrushchev's turn to feel aggrieved when an American U-2 spy plane was shot down over a thousand miles inside Russia. President Eisenhower declined to apologize, defending America's right to make reconnaissance flights. Khrushchev stormed out of the summit conference which was just beginning in Paris, and it seemed that the thaw might be over.

In 1961 Khrushchev again suggested, this time to the new American president, John F. Kennedy, that the West should withdraw from Berlin. The communists were embarrassed at the large numbers of refugees escaping from East Germany into West Berlin – these averaged about 200 000 a year and totalled over 3 million since 1945. When Kennedy refused, *the Berlin Wall was erected (August 1961)*, a 28-mile-long monstrosity across the entire city, effectively blocking the escape route (see Map 7.3 and Illus. 7.2).

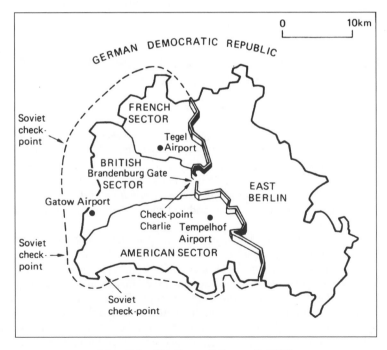

Map 7.3 **Berlin and the wall, 1961**

Illustration 7.2   **The Berlin Wall: an 18-year-old East Berliner lies dying after being shot during an escape attempt (*left*); he is carried away by East Berlin guards (*right*)**

7.4   THE NUCLEAR ARMS RACE AND THE CUBAN MISSILES CRISIS (1962)

(a)   The arms race begins to accelerate

The arms race between East and West arguably began in earnest towards the end of 1949 *after the Russians had produced their own atomic bomb*. The Americans already had a big lead in bombs of this type, but the Russians were determined to catch up, even though the production of nuclear weapons placed an enormous strain on their economy. When *the Americans made the much more powerful hydrogen bomb* towards the end of 1952, the Russians did the same the following year, and had soon developed a bomber with a range long enough to reach the USA.

The Americans remained well ahead in numbers of nuclear bombs and bombers, but it was the Russians who took the lead in August 1957 when they produced *a new type of weapon – the intercontinental ballistic missile (ICBM)*. This was a nuclear warhead carried by a rocket so powerful that it could reach the USA even when fired from inside the USSR. Not to be outdone, the Americans soon produced their version of an ICBM (known as Atlas), and before long they had many more than the Russians. The Americans also began to build nuclear missiles with a shorter range; these were known as Jupiters and Thors, and they could reach the USSR from launching sites in Europe and Turkey. When *the Russians successfully launched the world's first earth satellite (Sputnik 1) in 1958*, the

Americans again felt that they dared not be left behind; within a few months they had launched an earth satellite of their own.

(b) The Cuban missiles crisis, 1962

Cuba became involved in the Cold War in 1959 when Fidel Castro, who had just seized power from the corrupt, American-backed dictator Batista, outraged the USA by nationalizing American-owned estates and factories (see Section 8.2). As Cuba's relations with the USA worsened, those with the USSR improved: in January 1961 *the USA broke off diplomatic relations with Cuba*, and the Russians increased their economic aid.

Convinced that Cuba was now a communist state in all but name, the new US president, John F. Kennedy, approved a plan by a group of Batista supporters to invade Cuba from American bases in Guatemala (Central America). The American Central Intelligence Agency (CIA), a kind of secret service, was deeply involved. There was a general view in the USA at this time that it was quite permissible for them to interfere in the affairs of sovereign states and to overthrow any regimes which they felt were hostile and too close for comfort (see Chapter 26). The small invading force of about 1400 men landed at *the Bay of Pigs* in April 1961, but the operation was so badly planned and carried out that Castro's forces and his two jet planes had no difficulty crushing it. Later the same year, *Castro announced that he was now a Marxist and that Cuba was a socialist country.* Kennedy continued his campaign to destroy Castro, in various ways: Cuban merchant ships were sunk, installations on the island were sabotaged and American troops carried out invasion exercises. Castro appealed to the USSR for military help.

Khrushchev decided to set up nuclear missile launchers in Cuba aimed at the USA, whose nearest point was less than a hundred miles from Cuba. He intended to install missiles with a range of up to 2000 miles, which meant that all the major cities of the central and eastern USA such as New York, Washington, Chicago and Boston would be under threat. This was a risky decision, and there was great consternation in the USA when in October 1962, photographs taken from spy planes showed a missile base under construction (see Map 7.4). *Why did Khrushchev take such a risky decision?*

- The Russians had lost the lead in ICBMs, so this was a way of trying to seize the initiative back again from the USA. But it would be wrong to put all the blame for the crisis on the USSR.
- In 1959 the Americans had signed an agreement with Turkey allowing them to deploy Jupiter nuclear missiles from bases in Turkey. This was *before* any top-level contacts between Castro and the Russians had taken place. As Khrushchev himself put it in his memoirs, 'the Americans had surrounded our country with military bases, now they would learn what it feels like to have enemy missiles pointing at you'.
- It was a gesture of solidarity with his ally Castro, who was under constant threat from the USA; although the Bay of Pigs invasion had been a miserable failure, it was not the end of the US threat to Castro – in November 1961 Kennedy gave the go-ahead for a secret CIA operation known as Operation Mongoose which aimed to 'help Cuba overthrow the Communist regime'. Hopefully, the Russian missiles would dissuade such an operation; if not, they could be used against invading American troops.
- It would test the resolve of the new, young, American President Kennedy.
- Perhaps Khrushchev intended to use the missiles for bargaining with the West over removal of American missiles from Europe, or a withdrawal from Berlin by the West.

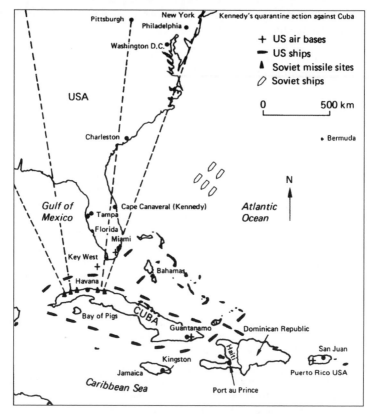

Map 7.4 **The Cuban missiles crisis, 1972**

Kennedy's military advisers urged him to launch air strikes against the bases. General Maxwell Taylor urged Kennedy to launch a full-scale invasion of Cuba; but he acted more cautiously: he alerted American troops, began a blockade of Cuba to keep out the 25 Russian ships which were bringing missiles to Cuba and demanded the dismantling of the missile sites and the removal of those missiles already in Cuba. The situation was tense, and the world seemed to be on the verge of nuclear war. The Secretary-General of the UN, U Thant, appealed to both sides for restraint.

Khrushchev made the first move: he ordered the Russian ships to turn back, and eventually a compromise solution was reached. Khrushchev promised to remove the missiles and dismantle the sites; in return Kennedy promised that the USA would not invade Cuba again, and undertook to disarm the Jupiter missiles in Turkey (though he would not allow this to be announced publicly). Castro was furious with Khrushchev for 'deserting' him apparently without consulting the Cubans, and Cuban–Soviet relations were extremely cool for several years.

The crisis had only lasted a few days, *but it was extremely tense and it had important results*. Both sides could claim to have gained something, but most important was that both sides realized how easily a nuclear war could have started and how terrible the results would have been. It seemed to bring them both to their senses and produced a marked relaxation of tension. *A telephone link (the 'hotline') was introduced between Moscow and Washington* to allow swift consultations, and in July 1963, the USSR, the USA and Britain signed *a Nuclear Test Ban Treaty*, agreeing to carry out nuclear tests only underground to avoid polluting the atmosphere any further.

At first Kennedy's handling of the crisis was highly praised. Most American commentators argued that by standing up to the Russians and by resisting pressure from his own army Chiefs of Staff for a military response, Kennedy defused the crisis and achieved a peaceful settlement. The president's brother Robert was one of his chief supporters, particularly in his book *Thirteen Days* (1969). In order to lay all the blame for the crisis on the USSR, the Americans emphasized that Khrushchev and various Russian diplomats had repeatedly lied, insisting that they had no intention of building missile bases in Cuba. However, some later historians were more critical of Kennedy. A few accused him of missing a chance to solve the problem of Cuba once and for all – he ought to have called Khrushchev's bluff, attacked Cuba and overthrown Castro. Others criticized Kennedy for causing the crisis in the first place by placing nuclear missiles in Turkey and repeatedly trying to destabilize the Castro regime. It was also pointed out that since Soviet long-range missiles could already reach the USA from Russia itself, the missiles in Cuba did not exactly pose a new threat.

(c) The race continues into the 1970s

Although in public the Russians claimed the outcome of the missiles crisis as a victory, in private they admitted that their main aim – to establish missile bases near the USA – had failed. Even the removal of American Thors and Jupiters from Turkey meant nothing because the Americans now had another threat – *ballistic missiles (known as Polaris, later Poseidon) which could be launched from submarines (SLBMs)* in the eastern Mediterranean.

The Russians now decided to go all-out to catch up with the American stockpile of ICBMs and SLBMs. Their motive was not just to increase their own security: they hoped that if they could get somewhere near equality with the Americans, there would be a good chance of persuading them to limit and reduce the arms build-up. As the Americans became more deeply involved in the war in Vietnam (1961–75), they had less to spend on nuclear weapons, and slowly but surely the Russians began to catch up. By the early 1970s they had overtaken the USA and her allies in numbers of ICBMs and SLBMs. They had brought out a new weapon, *the anti-ballistic missile (ABM)*, which could destroy incoming enemy missiles before they reached their targets.

However, the Americans were ahead in other departments – they had developed an even more terrifying weapon, *the multiple independently targetable re-entry vehicle (MIRV)*; this was a missile which could carry as many as 14 separate warheads, each one of which could be programmed to hit a different target. The Russians soon developed their version of the MIRV, known as the SS-20 (1977). These were targeted on western Europe, but were not as sophisticated as the American MIRV and carried only three warheads.

At the end of the 1970s the Americans responded by developing *Cruise missiles, which were based in Europe*; the new refinement was that these missiles flew in at low altitudes and so were able to penetrate under Russian radar.

And so it went on; by this time both sides had enough of this horrifying weaponry to destroy the world many times over. The main danger was that one side or the other might be tempted to try and win a nuclear war by striking first and destroying all the other side's weapons before they had time to retaliate.

(d) Protests against nuclear weapons

People in many countries were worried at the way the major powers continued to pile up nuclear weapons and failed to make any progress towards controlling them. Movements were set up to try to persuade governments to abolish nuclear weapons.

In Britain *the Campaign for Nuclear Disarmament (CND)*, which was started in 1958, put pressure on the government to take the lead, so that Britain would be the first nation to abandon nuclear weapons; this was known as *unilateral disarmament* (disarmament by one state only). They hoped that the USA and the USSR would follow Britain's lead and scrap their nuclear weapons too. They held mass demonstrations and rallies, and every year at Easter they held a protest march from London to Aldermaston (where there was an atomic weapons research base) and back.

No British government dared take the risk, however. They believed that unilateral disarmament would leave Britain vulnerable to a nuclear attack from the USSR, and would only consider abandoning their weapons as part of a general agreement by all the major powers (*multilateral disarmament*). During the 1980s there were protest demonstrations in many European countries, including West Germany and Holland, and also in the USA. In Britain many women protested by camping around the American base at Greenham Common (Berkshire), where the Cruise missiles were positioned. The fear was that if the Americans ever fired any of these missiles, Britain could be almost destroyed by Russian nuclear retaliation. In the long run, perhaps the enormity of it all and the protest movements did play a part in bringing both sides to the negotiating table. And so the world moved into the next phase of the Cold War – *détente* (see Sections 8.6 and 8.7 for détente and the end of the Cold War).

FURTHER READING

Aylett, J. F., *The Cold War and After* (Hodder & Stoughton, 1996).
Behrman, G., *The Most Noble Adventure: The Marshall Plan and the Reconstruction of Postwar Europe* (Aurum, 2008).
Dockrill, M., *The Cold War 1945–63* (Macmillan, 1998).
Foss, C., *Fidel Castro* (Alan Sutton, 2006).
Gaddis, J. L., *The United States and the Origins of the Cold War, 1941–1947* (Columbia University Press, 1972).
Gaddis, J. L., *The Cold War: A New History* (Allen Lane, 2006).
Lovell, S., *The Shadow of War: Russia and the USSR, 1941 to the Present* (Wiley-Blackwell, 2011).
Lowe, P., *The Korean War* (Macmillan, 2000).
McCauley, M., *Origins of the Cold War, 1941–1949* (Longman, 3rd edition, 2008).
Mills, N., *Winning the Peace: The Marshall Plan and America's Coming of Age as a Superpower* (Wiley, 2008).
Skierka, V., *Fidel Castro: A Biography* (Polity, 2004).
Taylor, F., *The Berlin Wall* (Bloomsbury, 2006).
Westad, O. A., *The Global Cold War* (Cambridge University Press, 2006).
Williams, W. A., *The Tragedy of American Diplomacy* (World Publishing, revised edition, 1962).

QUESTIONS

1 In what ways did the Marshall Plan, the dividing of Berlin, the communist takeover of power in Czechoslovakia, and the formation of NATO contribute to the development of the Cold War?
2 How accurate is it to talk about a 'thaw' in the Cold War in the years after 1953?
3 What were the causes of the Cuban missiles crisis? How was the crisis resolved and what were its consequences?

4   Assess the reasons why Berlin was a major source of tension in the Cold War from 1948 to 1961.
5   How important was the Marshall Plan in bringing about the recovery of Western Europe between 1947 and 1951?

There is a document question about the causes of the Cold War on the website.

Chapter

8

The spread of communism outside Europe and its effects on international relations

SUMMARY OF EVENTS

Although the first communist state was set up in Europe (in Russia in 1917), communism was not confined to Europe; it later spread to Asia where several other communist states emerged, each with its own brand of Marxism. As early as 1921, encouraged by the Russian Revolution, the Chinese Communist Party (CCP) had been formed. At first it co-operated with the Kuomintang (KMT), the party trying to govern China and to control the generals, who were struggling among themselves for power. As the KMT established its control over more of China, it felt strong enough to do without the help of the communists and tried to destroy them. Civil war developed between the KMT and the CCP.

The situation became more complex when the Japanese occupied the Chinese province of Manchuria in 1931 and invaded other parts of China in 1937. When the Second World War ended in the defeat and withdrawal of the Japanese, the KMT leader Chiang Kai-shek, with American help, and the communists under their leader Mao Zedong (Mao Tse-tung), were still fighting it out. At last, *in 1949, Mao triumphed*, and Chiang and his supporters fled to the island of Taiwan (Formosa); the second major country had followed Russia into communism (see Section 19.4). In 1951 the Chinese invaded and occupied neighbouring Tibet; an uprising by the Tibetans in 1959 was crushed, and the country has remained under Chinese rule ever since.

Meanwhile communism had also gained a hold in **Korea**, which had been controlled by Japan since 1910. After the Japanese defeat in 1945, the country was divided into two zones: the north occupied by the Russians, the south by the Americans. The Russians set up a communist government in their zone, and since no agreement could be reached on what government to have for the whole country, Korea, like Germany, remained divided into two states. *In 1950 communist North Korea invaded South Korea.* United Nations forces (mostly American) moved in to help the south, while the Chinese helped the north. After much advancing and retreating, the war ended in 1953 with South Korea still non-communist.

In **Cuba**, early in 1959, Fidel Castro drove out the corrupt dictator Batista. Although Castro was not a communist to begin with, the Americans soon turned against him, particularly in 1962 when they discovered that Russian missiles were based on the island (see Section 7.4(b)). These were later removed after a tense Cold War crisis which brought the world to the brink of nuclear war.

In **Vietnam**, a similar situation to that in Korea occurred after the Vietnamese had won their independence from France (1954): the country was divided, temporarily it was thought, into north (communist) and south (non-communist). When a rebellion broke out in the south against a corrupt government, communist North Vietnam gave military assistance to the rebels; the Americans became heavily involved, supporting the South Vietnamese government to stop the spread of communism. In 1973 the Americans withdrew from the struggle, following which the South Vietnamese forces

rapidly collapsed, and the whole country became united under a communist government (1975). Before the end of the year, neighbouring **Cambodia** and **Laos** had also
become communist.

In **South America**, which had a tradition of right-wing military dictatorships, communism made little headway, except in **Chile**, where in 1970 a Marxist government was
democratically elected, with Salvador Allende as president. This was an interesting but
short-lived experiment, since in 1973 the government was overthrown and Allende killed.

Africa saw the establishment of governments with strong Marxist connections in
Mozambique (1975) and **Angola** (1976), both of which had just succeeded in winning
independence from Portugal. This caused more western alarm and interference (see
Sections 24.6(d) and 25.6).

During the second half of the 1970s a more consistent thaw in the Cold War began,
with *the period known as détente (a more permanent relaxation of tensions)*. There were
several hiccups, however, such as the Russian invasion of Afghanistan (1979), before
Mikhail Gorbachev (who became Russian leader in March 1985) made a really determined effort to end the Cold War altogether, and some arms limitations agreements were
signed.

Then the international situation changed dramatically: in 1989 communism began to
collapse in eastern Europe; by 1991 the communist bloc had disintegrated and East and
West Germany were re-united. Even the USSR split up and ceased to be communist.
Although communism still remained in China, Vietnam and North Korea, the Cold War
was well and truly over.

8.1 THE WAR IN KOREA AND ITS EFFECTS ON INTERNATIONAL RELATIONS

(a) Background to the war

The origins of the war lay in the fact that Korea had been under Japanese occupation since
1910. When the Japanese were defeated (August 1945), the USA and the USSR agreed to
divide the country into two zones along the 38th parallel (the 38-degree-north line of latitude), so that they could jointly organize the Japanese surrender and withdrawal – Russia
in the north (which had a frontier with the USSR) and the Americans in the south. As far
as the Americans were concerned, it was not intended to be a permanent division. The
United Nations wanted free elections for the whole country and the Americans agreed,
believing that since their zone contained two-thirds of the population, the communist north
would be outvoted. However, the unification of Korea, like that of Germany, soon became
part of Cold War rivalry: no agreement could be reached, and the artificial division continued (see Map 8.1).

Elections were held in the south, supervised by the UN, and *the independent Republic
of Korea, or South Korea* was set up with Syngman Rhee as president and its capital at
Seoul (August 1948). The following month, the Russians created *the Democratic People's
Republic of Korea, or North Korea* under the communist government of Kim Il Sung, with
its capital at Pyongyang. In 1949 Russian and American troops were withdrawn, leaving
a potentially dangerous situation: most Koreans bitterly resented the artificial division
forced on their country by outsiders, but both leaders claimed the right to rule the whole
country. Before very long it was clear that Syngman Rhee was a ruthless authoritarian,
while Kim Il Sung was even worse: he seemed to be modelling himself on Stalin, arresting and executing many of his critics. Without warning, North Korean troops invaded
South Korea in June 1950.

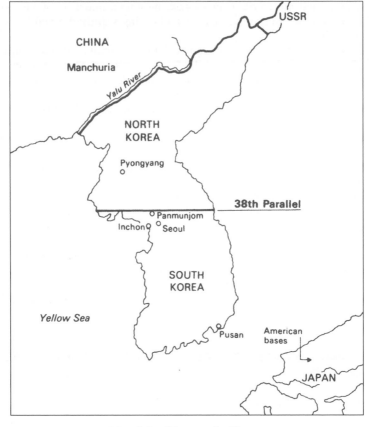

Map 8.1 **The war in Korea**

(b) Why did the North Koreans invade the South?

Even now it is still not clear how the attack originated, or whose idea it was. *The following suggestions have been offered*:

- It was Kim Il Sung's own idea, possibly encouraged by a statement made by Dean Acheson, the American Secretary of State, earlier in 1950. Acheson was talking about which areas around the Pacific the USA intended to defend, and for some reason he did not include Korea.
- Kim Il Sung may have been encouraged by the new Chinese communist government, who were at the same time massing troops in Fukien province facing Taiwan, as if they were about to attack Chiang Kai-shek.
- Perhaps Stalin and the Russians were responsible, wanting to test Truman's determination; they had supplied the North Koreans with tanks and other equipment. A communist takeover of the south would strengthen Russia's position in the Pacific and be a splendid gesture against the Americans, to make up for Stalin's failure in West Berlin.
- The communists claimed that South Korea had started the war, when troops of the 'bandit traitor' Syngman Rhee had crossed the 38th parallel.

Probably the most widely accepted view nowadays is that Kim Il Sung himself pressed the idea of a campaign to unify the peninsula, and that both the USSR and China approved the plan and promised help in the way of war materials, but made it clear that they had no desire themselves to become directly involved.

(c)　The USA takes action

There were several reasons for President Truman's decision to intervene:

- He was convinced that the attack was Stalin's doing; he took it as a deliberate challenge and saw it as part of a vast Russian plan to spread communism as widely as possible.
- Some Americans saw the invasion as similar to Hitler's policies during the 1930s. Appeasement of the aggressors had failed then, and therefore it was essential not to make the same mistake again.
- Truman thought it was important to support the United Nations Organization, which had replaced the League of Nations. The League had failed to preserve peace because the great powers – and especially the USA – had not been prepared to back it. Truman was determined that the USA should not repeat that fatal mistake.
- Truman was a Democrat president, and he and his party were coming under severe criticism from the Republicans for their failure to take action against what they saw as the dangerous spread of world communism. A Republican senator, Joseph McCarthy, claimed that the State Department was 'infested' with communists who were, in effect, working for the USSR (see Section 23.3). Truman was anxious to show that this claim was preposterous.

American policy therefore changed decisively: instead of just economic help and promises of support, Truman decided it was essential for the West to take a stand by supporting South Korea. American troops in Japan were ordered to Korea even before the UN had decided what action to take. The UN Security Council called on North Korea to withdraw her troops, and when this was ignored, asked member states to send help to South Korea. This decision was reached in the absence of the Russian delegation, who were boycotting meetings in protest against the UN refusal to allow Mao's new Chinese regime to be represented, and who would certainly have vetoed such a decision. In the event, the USA and 14 other countries (Australia, Canada, New Zealand, Nationalist China, France, the Netherlands, Belgium, Colombia, Greece, Turkey, Panama, the Philippines, Thailand and Britain) sent troops, though the vast majority were Americans. All forces were under the command of American General MacArthur.

Their arrival was just in time to prevent the whole of South Korea from being overrun by the communists. By September, communist forces had captured the whole country except the south-east, around the port of Pusan. UN reinforcements poured into Pusan and on 15 September, American marines landed at Inchon, near Seoul, 200 miles behind the communist front lines. Then followed an incredibly swift collapse of the North Korean forces: by the end of September UN troops had entered Seoul and cleared the south of communists. Instead of calling for a ceasefire, now that the original UN objective had been achieved, Truman ordered an invasion of North Korea, with UN approval, aiming to unite the country and hold free elections. The Chinese Foreign Minister Zhou Enlai (Chou En-lai) warned that China would resist if UN troops entered North Korea, but the warning was ignored. By the end of October, UN troops had captured Pyongyang, occupied two-thirds of North Korea and reached the River Yalu, the frontier between North Korea and China.

The Chinese government was seriously alarmed: the Americans had already placed a fleet between Taiwan and the mainland to prevent an attack on Chiang, and there seemed every chance that they would now invade Manchuria (the part of China bordering on North Korea). In November therefore, the Chinese launched a massive counter-offensive with over 300 000 troops, described as 'volunteers'; by mid-January 1951 they had driven the UN troops out of North Korea, crossed the 38th parallel and captured Seoul again. MacArthur was shocked at the strength of the Chinese forces and argued that the best way to defeat communism was to attack Manchuria, with atomic bombs if necessary. However, Truman thought this would provoke a large-scale war, which the USA did not want, so *he decided to settle for merely containing communism*; MacArthur was removed from his command. In June UN troops cleared the communists out of South Korea again and fortified the frontier. Peace talks opened in Panmunjom and lasted for two years, ending in July 1953 with an agreement that the frontier should be roughly along the 38th parallel, where it had been before the war began.

(d) The results of the war were wide-ranging

1 For Korea itself it was a disaster: the country was devastated, about four million Korean soldiers and civilians had been killed and five million people were homeless. The division seemed permanent; both states remained intensely suspicious of each other and heavily armed, and there were constant ceasefire violations.

2 Truman could take some satisfaction from having contained communism and could claim that this success, plus American rearmament, dissuaded world communism from further aggression. However, many Republicans felt that the USA had lost an opportunity to destroy communism in China, and this feeling contributed towards some of the later excesses of McCarthyism (see Section 23.3).

3 The UN had exerted its authority and reversed an act of aggression, but the communist world denounced it as a tool of the capitalists.

4 The military performance of communist China was impressive; she had prevented the unification of Korea under American influence and was now clearly a world power. The fact that she was still not allowed a seat in the UN seemed even more unreasonable.

5 The conflict brought a new dimension to the Cold War. American relations were now permanently strained with China as well as with Russia; the familiar pattern of both sides trying to build up alliances appeared in Asia as well as Europe. China supported the Indo-Chinese communists in their struggle for independence from France, and at the same time offered friendship and aid to under-developed Third World countries in Asia, Africa and Latin America; 'peaceful coexistence' agreements were signed with India and Burma (1954).

Meanwhile the Americans tried to encircle China with bases: in 1951 defensive agreements were signed with Australia and New Zealand, and in 1954 these three states, together with Britain and France, set up *the South East Asia Treaty Organization (SEATO)*. However, the USA was disappointed when only three Asian states – Pakistan, Thailand and the Philippines – joined SEATO. It was obvious that many states wanted to keep clear of the Cold War and remain uncommitted.

Relations between the USA and China were also poor because of the Taiwan situation. The communists still hoped to capture the island and destroy Chiang Kai-shek and his Nationalist Party for good; but the Americans were committed to defending Chiang and wanted to keep Taiwan as a military base.

(a) Why did Castro come to power?

The situation which resulted in Fidel Castro coming to power in January 1959 had built up over a number of years.

1   *There was long-standing resentment among many Cubans at the amount of American influence in the country.* This dated back to 1898 when the USA had helped rescue Cuba from Spanish control. Although the island remained an independent republic, American troops were needed from time to time to maintain stability, and American financial aid and investment kept the Cuban economy ticking over. In fact there was some truth in the claim that *the USA controlled the Cuban economy*: American companies held controlling interests in all Cuban industries (sugar, tobacco, textiles, iron, nickel, copper, manganese, paper and rum), owned half the land, about three-fifths of the railways, all electricity production and the entire telephone system. The USA was the main market for Cuba's exports, of which sugar was by far the most important. All this explains why the American ambassador in Havana (the Cuban capital) was usually referred to as the second most important man in Cuba. The American connection need not have been resented so much if it had resulted in an efficiently run country, but this was not so.

2   Though Cuba was prosperous compared with other Latin American countries, *she was too dependent on the export of sugar, and the wealth of the country was concentrated in the hands of a few.* Unemployment was a serious problem; it varied from about 8 per cent of the labour force during the five months of the sugar harvest to over 30 per cent during the rest of the year. Yet there was no unemployment benefit, and the trade unions, dominated by workers who had all-the-year-round jobs in sugar mills, did nothing to help. The poverty of the unemployed was in stark contrast to the wealth in Havana and in the hands of corrupt government officials; consequently *social tensions were high.*

3   *No effective political system had been developed.* In 1952, Fulgencio Batista, who had been a leading politician since 1933, seized power in a military coup and began to rule as a dictator. He introduced no reforms, and according to historian Hugh Thomas, 'spent a lot of time dealing with his private affairs and his foreign fortunes, leaving himself too little time for affairs of state'. As well as being corrupt, his regime was also brutal.

4   Since *there was no prospect of a peaceful social revolution*, the feeling grew that violent revolution was necessary. The leading exponent of this view was Fidel Castro, a young lawyer from a middle-class background, who specialized in defending the poor. Before he came to power, Castro was more of a liberal nationalist than a communist: he wanted to rid Cuba of Batista and corruption, and to introduce limited land reforms so that all peasants would receive some land. After an unsuccessful attempt to overthrow Batista in 1953, which earned him two years in jail, Castro began a campaign of guerrilla warfare and sabotage in the cities. The rebels soon controlled the mountainous areas of the east and north and won popular support there by carrying through Castro's land reform policy.

5   *Batista's reaction played into Castro's hands.* He took savage reprisals against the guerrillas, torturing and murdering suspects. Even many of the middle classes began to support Castro as the most likely way of getting rid of a brutal dictator. Morale in Batista's poorly paid army began to crumble in the summer of 1958, after an unsuccessful attempt to destroy Castro's forces. The USA began to feel

embarrassment at Batista's behaviour and cut off arms supplies; this was a serious blow to the dictator's prestige. In September a small rebel force under Che Guevara, an Argentinian supporter of Castro, gained control of the main road across the island and prepared to move on Santa Clara. On 1 January 1959 Batista fled from Cuba, and a liberal government was set up with Castro at its head.

(b) How were Cuba's foreign relations affected?

Cuban relations with the USA did not deteriorate immediately; Castro was thought to be, at worst, a social democrat, and so most Americans were prepared to give him a chance. Before long, however, he outraged the USA by *nationalizing American-owned estates and factories*. President Eisenhower threatened to stop importing Cuban sugar, forcing Castro to sign a trade agreement with Russia. In July 1960 when the Americans carried out their threat, the USSR promised to buy Cuba's sugar, and Castro confiscated all remaining American property. As Cuba's relations with the USA worsened, those with the USSR improved: in January 1961 the USA broke off diplomatic relations with Cuba, but the Russians were already supplying economic aid. For what happened next – the Bay of Pigs invasion and the missiles crisis – see Section 7.4(b). After the missiles crisis, relations between the USA and Cuba remained cool. The attitude of other Latin American states, most of which had right-wing governments, was one of extreme suspicion; in 1962 they expelled Cuba from the Organization of American States (OAS), which only made her more dependent on the USSR.

(c) Castro and his problems

Cuba was heavily dependent on the USA – and later the USSR – buying most of her sugar exports; the economy relied far too much on the sugar industry and was at the mercy of fluctuations in world sugar prices. The whole government and administration were riddled with corruption, and in addition there was serious unemployment and poverty. The new government launched itself into tackling the problems with enthusiasm and dedication. Historian David Harkness writes that, during his first ten years, Castro took this poor and backward country by the scruff of the neck and shook it into new and radically different patterns of life. Agricultural land was taken over by the government and collective farms were introduced; factories and businesses were nationalized; attempts were made to modernize sugar production and increase output, and to introduce new industries and reduce Cuba's dependence on sugar. Social reform included attempts to improve education, housing, health, medical facilities and communications. There was equality for black people and more rights for women. There were touring cinemas, theatres, concerts and art exhibitions. Castro himself seemed to have boundless energy; he was constantly travelling around the island, making speeches and urging people to greater efforts.

By the end of the 1970s the government could claim considerable success, especially in the area of social reform. All children were now receiving some education (instead of fewer than half before 1959); sanitation, hygiene and health care were much improved, unemployment and corruption were reduced, and there was a greater sense of equality and stability than ever before. The government seemed to be popular with the vast majority of people. These successes were achieved against a background of continual harassment and attempts at destabilization by the USA. These included a trade embargo, bomb attacks on Cuban factories, oil refineries and sugar refineries. Under President Nixon (1969–74) the campaign intensified to such an extent that it amounted to US government-sponsored state terrorism. During the 1990s the economic embargo on Cuba became more stringent than ever. It was condemned by the European Union, but the Clinton administration rejected this 'interference'.

Undeterred by all this, Castro and his supporters, especially Che Guevara, did their best to spread their revolution, first into Che's native Argentina. In early 1964 this attempt was crushed by the Argentinian army. The Cubans turned their attention to Africa, helping rebels to seize power in Algeria and then becoming unsuccessfully involved in the civil war in the former Belgian Congo. In 1966 Che Guevara tried to organize a revolution in Bolivia but his expedition ended in disaster when he was captured and executed in October 1967. Turning their attention back to Africa, the Cubans backed the Marxist MPLA in Angola (1975) (see Section 25.6) and the Marxist leader Mengistu in Ethiopia (1977) (see Section 25.9). Castro was now seen as a hero by most Third World countries, though his popularity slumped when he declared his support for the Soviet invasion of Afghanistan in 1979.

The US destabilization policy and the economic embargo meant that some of Castro's economic policies had little success: the attempt to diversify industrial and agricultural output was disappointing, and so the island's economy still depended unhealthily on the quality of the sugar harvest, the world price of sugar and the willingness of the USSR and her satellites to buy up Cuba's exports. In 1980 the sugar crop was reduced by a fungus infection, while the tobacco crop was seriously affected by another fungus. This plunged the island into an economic crisis, unemployment rose again and thousands of people began to emigrate to the USA. Food rationing was introduced and the whole economy was being heavily subsidized by the USSR. By 1991 when the USSR split up and ceased to be communist, Cuba had lost its most powerful supporter.

However, the Castro regime continued to survive. During the closing years of the twentieth century the economy was boosted by a growth in tourism. Castro continued to enjoy good relations with Venezuela: in October 2000 the Venezuelan government agreed to provide Cuba with oil at favourable prices. Nevertheless, most Latin American states still viewed her as an outcast; Cuba was the only country in the Americas not invited to the third Summit of the Americas, held in Quebec in 2001. A new economic crisis developed in 2002, caused partly by drought and the consequent poor sugar harvest in 2001, and partly because the terrorist attacks of September 2001 in the USA adversely affected tourism. In February 2008 ill health forced Castro (aged 80) to hand over the presidency to his younger brother Raúl (aged 78). Since then there have been some modest improvements. In March 2008 the use of mobile phones was legalized – a measure designed to appeal to the young. Peasants are now allowed to cultivate unused land on collective farms and there have been improvements in the pricing of agricultural products that led to farmers bringing more food to market. Unfortunately hurricanes in the autumn of 2008 caused extensive damage and held up progress.

8.3   THE WARS IN VIETNAM, 1946–54 AND 1961–75

Indo-China, which consisted of three areas, Vietnam, Laos and Cambodia, was part of the French empire in south-east Asia, and was the scene of almost non-stop conflict from the end of the Second World War. In the first phase of the conflict the peoples of these areas fought for and won their independence from the French. The second phase (1961–75) began with civil war in South Vietnam; the USA intervened to prevent the further spread of communism, but eventually had to admit failure.

(a)   1946–54

From 1946 until 1954 the Vietnamese were fighting for independence from France. Indo-China was occupied by the Japanese during the war. Resistance to both Japanese and

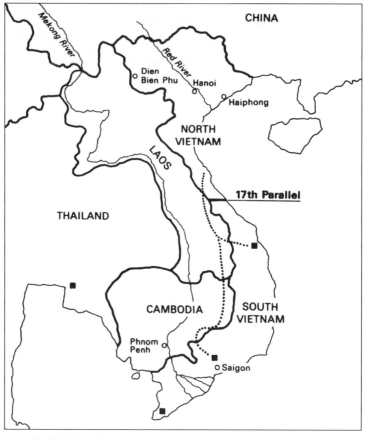

······ Ho Chi Minh Trail
■ American bases

Map 8.2   **The wars in Vietnam**

French was organized by *the League for Vietnamese Independence (Vietminh)*, led by the communist Ho Chi Minh, who had spent many years in Russia learning how to organize revolutions. The Vietminh, though led by communists, was an alliance of all shades of political opinion that wanted an end to foreign control. At the end of the war in 1945, Ho Chi Minh declared the whole of Vietnam independent. When it became clear that the French had no intention of allowing full independence, hostilities broke out, beginning an eight-year struggle which ended with the French defeat at Dien Bien Phu (May 1954). The Vietminh were successful partly because they were masters of guerrilla tactics and had massive support from the Vietnamese people, and because the French, still suffering from the after-effects of the world war, failed to send enough troops. The decisive factor was probably that from 1950 the new Chinese communist government of Mao Zedong supplied the rebels with arms and equipment. The USA also became involved: seeing the struggle as part of the Cold War and the fight against communism, the Americans supplied the French with military and economic aid; but it was not enough. However, the Americans were determined to take France's place in order to prevent the spread of communism throughout south-east Asia.

By the Geneva Agreement (1954), Laos and Cambodia were to be independent;
Vietnam was temporarily divided into two states at the 17th parallel (see Map 8.2). Ho Chi
Minh's government was recognized in North Vietnam. South Vietnam was to have a separate government for the time being, but elections were to be held in July 1956 for the
whole country, which would then become united. Ho Chi Minh was disappointed at the
partition, but was confident that the communists would win the national elections. As it
turned out, *the elections were never held*, and a repeat performance of the Korean situation seemed likely. A civil war gradually developed in South Vietnam which eventually
involved the North and the USA.

(b) What caused the civil war in South Vietnam and why did the USA become involved?

1 The South Vietnamese government under *President Ngo Dinh Diem* (chosen by a
   national referendum in 1955) refused to make preparations for the elections for the
   whole of Vietnam. The USA, which was backing his regime, did not press him for
   fear of a communist victory if the elections went ahead. US President Eisenhower
   (1953–61) was just as worried as Truman had been about the spread of communism.
   He seemed to become obsessed with *the 'domino theory'* – if there is a line of domi-
   noes standing on end close to each other and one is pushed over, it will knock over
   the next one in the line, and so on. Eisenhower thought this could be applied to
   countries: if one country in a region 'fell' to communism, it would quickly 'knock
   over' all its neighbours. However, the US attitude was a violation of the Geneva
   Agreement.
2 Although Ngo began energetically, his government soon lost popularity: he came
   from a wealthy Roman Catholic family, whereas three-quarters of the population
   were Buddhist peasants who thought themselves discriminated against. They
   demanded land reform of the type carried out in China and North Vietnam. Here
   land had been taken away from wealthy landowners and redistributed among the
   poorer people; but this did not happen in South Vietnam. Ngo also gained a reputation, perhaps not wholly deserved, for corruption, and he was unpopular with
   nationalists, who thought he was too much under American influence.
3 In 1960 various opposition groups, which included many former communist
   members of the Vietminh, formed *the National Liberation Front (NLF)*. They
   demanded a democratic national coalition government which would introduce
   reforms and negotiate peacefully for a united Vietnam. A guerrilla campaign began,
   attacking government officials and buildings; Buddhist monks had their own
   special brand of protest – committing suicide in public by setting fire to themselves.
   Ngo's credibility declined further when he dismissed all criticism – however
   reasonable – and all opposition as communist inspired. In fact the communists were
   only one section of the NLF. Ngo also introduced harsh security measures. He was
   overthrown and murdered in an army coup in November 1963, after which the
   country was ruled by a succession of generals, of whom President Nguyen Van
   Thieu lasted the longest (1967–75). The removal of Ngo left the basic situation
   unchanged and the guerrilla war continued.
4 When it became clear that Ngo could not cope with the situation, the USA decided
   to increase their military presence in South Vietnam. Under Eisenhower they had
   been supporting the regime since 1954, with economic aid and military advisers,
   and they accepted Ngo's claim that communists were behind all the trouble. Having
   failed to defeat communism in North Korea and Cuba, they felt a strong stand must
   be made. Both Kennedy and his successor Lyndon Johnson were prepared to go

Illustration 8.1   **A Vietcong suspect is executed in Saigon by Police Chief Nguyen Ngoc Loan, 1968**

further than just economic aid and advisers. In public the Americans said their intervention was to protect the independence of the Vietnamese people, but the real reason was to keep the country securely in the non-communist bloc.

5   The Americans were strengthened in their resolve by the knowledge that *the Vietcong* (as the guerrillas were now known) (see Illus. 8.1) were receiving supplies, equipment and troops from North Vietnam. Ho Chi Minh believed that such aid was justified: it was the USA and the South who were refusing to be bound by the Geneva agreements; given South Vietnam's refusal to agree to national elections, only force could unite the two halves of the country.

6   The Americans' involvement in Vietnam was different from their role in Korea where they fought as part of a UN coalition. In the intervening period, many new members, mostly former colonies of European powers, had joined the UN. These new states were critical of what they considered to be unjustified US interference in what should have been an independent country. They could not be relied on to support US action via the UN, and therefore the US had to act on its own, without UN participation.

(c)   The phases of the war

These correspond to successive American presidencies, each of which saw the introduction of new policies.

1   *John F. Kennedy (1961–3)* tried to keep American involvement down to an anti-guerrilla campaign. He sent about 16 000 'advisers' plus helicopters and other

equipment and introduced *the 'safe village' policy*, in which local peasants were moved en masse into fortified villages, leaving the Vietcong isolated outside. This was a failure because most of the Vietcong were peasants, who simply continued to operate inside the villages.

2   *Lyndon Johnson (1963–9)* was faced with a situation, according to reports from American advisers in 1964, where the Vietcong and the NLF controlled about 40 per cent of South Vietnamese villages and the peasant population seemed to support them. He assumed that the Vietcong were controlled by Ho Chi Minh and he decided to bomb North Vietnam (1965) in the hope that Ho would call off the campaign. Many historians have blamed Johnson for committing the USA so deeply in Vietnam, calling it 'Johnson's War'. Recent assessments have taken a more sympathetic view of Johnson's predicament. According to Kevin Ruane, 'far from being the hawk of legend, historians now tend to see Johnson as a man wracked with uncertainty about which direction to take on Vietnam'. He was afraid that American intervention on a large scale would bring China into the war. His real interest was his campaign for social reform – his 'great society' programme (see Section 23.1(d)). However, he inherited the situation from decisions taken by the two previous presidents – he was the unfortunate one who felt he had no alternative but to honour their commitments.

Over the next seven years *a greater tonnage of bombs was dropped on North Vietnamese cities than fell on Germany during the Second World War*. In addition, over half a million American troops arrived in the South. In spite of these massive efforts, the Vietcong still managed to unleash an offensive in February 1968 which captured something like 80 per cent of all towns and villages. Although much ground was lost later, this offensive convinced many Americans of the hopelessness of the struggle. Great pressure was put on the government by public opinion in the USA to withdraw from Vietnam. Some of his military experts told Johnson that the USA could not win the war at any reasonable cost. On 31 March 1968 Johnson therefore announced that he would suspend the bombing of North Vietnam, freeze troop levels and seek a negotiated peace. In May, peace talks opened in Paris – but no quick compromise could be reached, and the talks went on for another five years.

3   *Richard Nixon (1969–74)* realized that a new approach was needed, since public opinion would hardly allow him to send any more American troops. Early in 1969 there were half a million Americans, 50 000 South Koreans and 750 000 South Vietnamese against 450 000 Vietcong plus perhaps 70 000 North Vietnamese. *Nixon's new idea was known as 'Vietnamization'*: the Americans would rearm and train the South Vietnamese army to look after the defence of South Vietnam; this would allow a gradual withdrawal of American troops (in fact about half had been sent home by mid-1971). On the other hand, Nixon began the heavy bombing of North Vietnam again, and also began to bomb *the Ho Chi Minh Trail* through Laos and Cambodia, along which supplies and troops came from North Vietnam.

It was all to no avail: at the end of 1972 the Vietcong controlled the entire western half of the country. By now Nixon was under pressure both at home and from world opinion to withdraw. Several factors caused a revulsion of feeling against the war:

- the terrible bombing of North Vietnam, Laos and Cambodia;
- the use of chemicals to destroy jungle foliage and of inflammable napalm jelly, which burned people alive; the after-effects of the chemicals caused many babies to be born deformed and handicapped;
- the deaths of thousands of innocent civilians. The most notorious incident took place in March 1968, when American soldiers rounded up the inhabitants of

the hamlet of My Lai, including old people carrying young children; they were all shot, and buried in mass graves; between 450 and 500 people were killed.

Nixon eventually acknowledged that there was no monolithic communist plan to dominate the world. In fact relations between China and the USSR were extremely strained and there were numerous border clashes between the two in Mongolia. Nixon seized his chance to improve relations with China: trade and travel restrictions were removed, and so were the US navy patrols in the Taiwan Straits. On the Chinese side, some of Mao's generals had told him that it was time to unfreeze relations with the USA. In February 1972, Nixon paid a successful visit to Beijing.

Eventually *a ceasefire was arranged for January 1973*. It was agreed that all American troops would be withdrawn from Vietnam, and both North and South would respect the frontier along the 17th parallel. However, the Vietcong continued their campaign and without the Americans, President Thieu's government in Saigon soon collapsed as his badly led armies crumbled. In April 1975 Saigon was occupied by the North Vietnamese and Vietcong. *Vietnam was at last united and free from foreign intervention – under a communist government*. In the same year communist governments were also established in Laos and Cambodia. *The American policy of preventing the spread of communism in south-east Asia had ended in complete failure*.

(d) Why did the USA fail?

1 The main reason was that the Vietcong and the NLF had widespread support among ordinary people, who had genuine grievances against an inefficient government which failed to introduce necessary reforms. When the NLF was formed in 1960 the communists were only one of several opposition groups; by ignoring the rightness of the NLF case and choosing to prop up such an obviously deficient regime in their obsession with the fight against communism, the Americans actually encouraged the spread of communism in the South.

2 The Vietcong, like the Vietminh before them, were experts at guerrilla warfare and were fighting on familiar territory. The Americans found them much more difficult to deal with than the conventional armies they faced in Korea. With no distinguishing uniform, guerrillas could easily merge into the local peasant population. It proved impossible to stop supplies and reinforcements moving down the Ho Chi Minh Trail.

3 The Vietcong received important help from North Vietnam in the way of troops, and from China and Russia, who supplied arms. After 1970 the Russian contribution was vitally important and included rifles, machine-guns, long-range artillery, anti-aircraft missiles and tanks.

4 The North Vietnamese were dedicated to eventual victory and the unification of their country. They showed amazing resilience: in spite of appalling casualties and damage during the American bombings, they responded by evacuating city populations and rebuilding factories outside the cities.

(e) The effects of the war were wide-reaching

Vietnam was united but the cost was appalling. Between one and two million Vietnamese civilians had lost their lives and around 18 million were left homeless. The North Vietnamese army probably lost as many as 900 000 men, while the South lost 185 000.

About 48 000 American servicemen lost their lives, with a further 300 000 wounded. Around a third of the South was severely damaged by explosives and defoliants. The problems of reconstruction were enormous, and the new government's policies had unpleasant aspects such as concentration camps for opponents and no freedom of speech.

As well as being a blow to American prestige, this failure had a profound effect on American society; involvement in the war was seen in many circles as a terrible mistake, and this, together with the Watergate scandal, which forced Nixon to resign (see Section 23.4), shook confidence in a political system that could allow such things to happen. War veterans, instead of being treated as heroes, often found themselves shunned. Future American governments would have to think very carefully before committing the country so deeply in any similar situation. The war was a victory for the communist world, though both the Russians and Chinese reacted with restraint and did not boast about it to any great extent. This perhaps indicated that they wished to relax international tensions, though they now had another powerful force on their side in the Vietnamese army.

8.4 CHILE UNDER SALVADOR ALLENDE, 1970–3

In September 1970 Salvador Allende, a Marxist doctor of medicine from a middle-class background, won the presidential election as leader of a left-wing coalition of communists, socialists, radicals and social democrats; it called itself Unidad Popular (UP). It was a narrow victory, with Allende winning 36 per cent of the votes against the 35 per cent of his nearest rival. But it was enough to make him president, the world's first Marxist leader to be voted into power through a democratic election. Although it lasted only three years, Allende's government is worth looking at in some detail because it is still the only one of its kind and it shows the sort of problems likely to be faced by a Marxist government trying to function within a democratic system.

(a) How did Allende come to be elected?

Chile, unlike most other South American states, had a tradition of democracy. There were three main parties or groups of parties:

- the Unidad Popular, on the left;
- the Christian Democrats (also left-inclined);
- the National Party (a liberal/conservative coalition).

The army played little part in politics, and the democratic constitution (similar to that of the USA, except that the president could not stand for re-election immediately) was usually respected. The election of 1964 was won by Eduardo Frei, leader of the Christian Democrats, who believed in social reform. Frei began vigorously: inflation was brought down from 38 per cent to 25 per cent, the rich were made to pay their taxes instead of evading them, 360 000 new houses were built, the number of schools was more than doubled, and some limited land reform was introduced: over 1200 private holdings which were being run inefficiently were confiscated and given out to landless peasants. He also took over about half the holdings in the American-owned copper mines, with suitable compensation. The American government admired his reforms and poured in lavish economic aid.

By 1967, however, the tide was beginning to turn against Frei: the left thought his land reforms too cautious and wanted full nationalization of the copper industry (Chile's most important export), whereas the right thought he had already gone too far. In 1969 there was a serious drought in which a third of the harvest was lost; large quantities of food had to be imported, causing inflation to soar again. There were strikes of copper miners demanding higher wages and several miners were killed by government troops. Allende made skilful use of this ammunition during the 1970 election campaign, pointing out that Frei's achievements fell far short of his promises. Allende's coalition had a much better campaign organization than the other parties and could get thousands of supporters out on the streets. Allende himself inspired confidence: elegant and cultured, he appeared the very opposite of the violent revolutionary. Appearances were not deceptive: he believed that communism could succeed without a violent revolution. In the 1970 election 36 per cent of the voters were in favour of trying his policies.

(b) Allende's problems and policies

The problems facing the new government were enormous: inflation was running at over 30 per cent, unemployment at 20 per cent, industry was stagnating and 90 per cent of the population lived in such poverty that half the children under 15 suffered from malnutrition. Allende believed in a redistribution of income, which would enable the poor to buy more and thereby stimulate the economy. All-round wage increases of about 40 per cent were introduced and firms were not allowed to increase prices. The remainder of the copper industry, textiles and banks were nationalized, and Frei's land redistribution speeded up. The army was awarded an even bigger pay rise than anybody else to make sure of keeping its support. In foreign affairs, Allende restored diplomatic relations with Castro's Cuba, China and East Germany.

Whether Allende's policies would have succeeded in the long run is open to argument. Certainly he retained his popularity sufficiently for the UP to win 49 per cent of the votes in the 1972 local elections and to slightly increase their seats in the 1973 elections for Congress. However, the Allende experiment came to an abrupt and violent end in September 1973.

(c) Why was he overthrown?

Criticism of the government gradually built up as Allende's policies began to cause problems.

- *Land redistribution caused a fall in agricultural production*, mainly because farmers whose land was due to be taken stopped sowing and often slaughtered their cattle (like the Russian *kulaks* during collectivization – see Section 17.2(c)). This caused food shortages and further inflation.
- Private investors were frightened off and *the government became short of funds to carry out social reforms* (housing, education and social services) as rapidly as it would have liked.
- *Copper nationalization was disappointing*: there were long strikes for higher wages, production went down and the world price of copper fell suddenly by about 30 per cent, causing a further decrease in government revenue.
- Some communists who wanted a more drastic Castro-style approach to Chile's problems grew impatient with Allende's caution. They refused to make allowances for the fact that he did not have a stable majority in parliament; they formed the Movement of the Revolutionary Left (MIR), which embarrassed the non-violent UP by seizing farms and evicting the owners.
- The USA disapproved strongly of Allende's policies and did everything in their power to undermine Chile's economy. Other South American governments were nervous in case the Chileans tried to export their 'revolution'.

Looming above everything else was the question of *what would happen in September 1976 when the next presidential election was due.* Under the constitution, Allende would not be able to stand, but no Marxist regime had ever let itself be voted out of power. The opposition feared, perhaps with justification, that Allende was planning to change the constitution. As things stood, any president finding his legislation blocked by Congress could appeal to the nation by means of a referendum. With sufficient support Allende might be able to use the referendum device to postpone the election. It was this fear, or so they afterwards claimed, which caused the opposition groups to draw together and take action before Allende did. They organized a massive strike, and having won the support of the army, the right staged a military coup. It was organized by leading generals, who set up a military dictatorship in which *General Pinochet* came to the fore. Left-wing leaders were murdered or imprisoned and Allende himself was reported to have committed suicide. However, the cause of death has been controversial, many of his supporters claiming that he was gunned down in the presidential palace. In 2011 Chilean TV reported that a newly discovered document proved beyond doubt that he had been assassinated. The American Central Intelligence Agency (CIA), helped by the Brazilian government (a repressive military regime), played a vital role in the preparations for the coup, as part of its policy of preventing the spread of communism in Latin America. There is evidence that the CIA had been considering a coup as soon as Allende won the election in 1970. There is no doubt that the Nixon administration had done its best to destabilize the Allende government over the next three years by undermining the economy. Nixon himself was reported as saying that they must 'make the Chilean economy scream'.

The new Chilean regime soon provoked criticism from the outside world for its brutal treatment of political prisoners and its violations of human rights. However, the American government, which had reduced its economic aid while Allende was in power, stepped up its assistance again. The Pinochet regime had some economic success and by 1980 had brought the annual inflation rate down from around 1000 per cent to manageable proportions. Pinochet was in no hurry to return the country to civilian rule. He eventually allowed presidential elections in 1989, when the civilian candidate he supported was heavily defeated, winning less than 30 per cent of the votes. Pinochet permitted the winner, Christian Democrat leader Patricio Aylwin, to become president (1990), but the constitution (introduced in 1981) allowed Pinochet himself to remain Commander-in-Chief of the Armed Forces for a further eight years. During his 17 years as president, around 3000 people were killed or 'disappeared', while tens of thousands were tortured, imprisoned or driven into exile.

Pinochet duly stepped down in 1998, but his retirement did not work out as he had planned. On a visit to London later that year, he was arrested and held in Britain for 16 months after the Spanish government requested his extradition to face charges of torturing Spanish citizens in Chile. He was eventually allowed to return to Chile on medical grounds in March 2000. However, one of his most bitter opponents, Ricardo Lagos, had just been elected president (January 2000) – the first socialist president since Allende. Pinochet soon found himself facing over 250 charges of human rights abuses, but in July 2001 the Chilean Court of Appeal decided that the general, now aged 86, was too ill to stand trial. He died in 2006 at the age of 91. (For further developments in Chile see Section 26.4(e).)

8.5 MORE UNITED STATES INTERVENTIONS

Vietnam, Cuba and Chile were not the only countries in which the USA intervened during the first half of the Cold War. Working through the Central Intelligence Agency (CIA), the American State Department was active in an astonishing number of states in the cause of preserving freedom and human rights, and above all, preventing the spread of communism.

Often the regimes that were labelled as communist and targeted for removal were simply pursuing policies which went against American interests. US activities were carried out sometimes in secret, leaving the American people largely unaware of what was going on, or, as in the case of major military interventions, were presented as necessary surgical actions against the cancer of communism. Techniques included attempts to carry out assassinations, rigging of elections, organizing and financing acts of terrorism, economic destabilization and, in the last resort, full-scale military intervention.

Recently several former members of the State Department and the CIA, for example William Blum and Richard Agee, and a number of other writers, including the internationally renowned linguistics expert Noam Chomsky, have produced detailed accounts of how the leaders of the USA tried to build up their influence and power in the world by exercising control over such countries as Iran, Guatemala, Costa Rica, Indonesia, Guyana, Iraq, Cambodia, Laos, Ecuador, the Congo/Zaire, Brazil, the Dominican Republic, Ghana, Uruguay, Bolivia, East Timor, Nicaragua and many more. There is insufficient space to examine all these cases, but a few examples will illustrate how US influence reached out into most parts of the world. (For US involvement in Latin America, see Section 26.1.)

(a) South-east Asia

The area known as Indo-China consists of Vietnam, Laos and Cambodia. All three states gained their independence from France by the Geneva agreements of 1954 (see Section 8.3 for what happened in Vietnam).

In *Laos* after independence, there was conflict between the right-wing government backed by the USA, and various left-wing groups led by the Pathet Lao, a left-wing nationalist party which had fought in the struggle against the French. At first the Pathet Lao showed itself willing to take part in coalition governments in an attempt to bring about peaceful social change. The USA saw the Pathet Lao as dangerous communists: the CIA and the State Department between them arranged a series of interventions which by 1960 had removed all left-wingers from important positions. The left turned to armed force and the CIA responded by gathering an army of 30 000 anti-communists from all over Asia to crush the insurgents. Between 1965 and 1973 the US air force carried out regular bombing raids over Laos, causing enormous casualties and devastation. It was all to no avail: American intervention strengthened the resolve of the left; following the American withdrawal from Vietnam and south-east Asia, and the communist takeover in Cambodia, the Laotian right gave up the struggle and their leaders left the country. In December 1975 the Pathet Lao took control peacefully and the Lao People's Democratic Republic was proclaimed (see Section 21.4).

In *Cambodia* there was American involvement in a coup that overthrew the regime of Prince Sihanouk in 1970; the bombing campaigns which preceded the coup left the Cambodian economy in ruins. American intervention was followed by five years of civil war, which ended when Pol Pot and the Khmer Rouge took power (see Section 21.3). During the Vietnam War of 1965–73 the USA used *Thailand* as a base from which the bombing of North Vietnam took place. Eventually the American presence in Thailand was so massive that they seemed to have taken the country over. There was considerable opposition from Thais who resented the way in which their country was being used, but all criticism was treated as communist-inspired; over 40 000 American troops were active in trying to suppress opposition guerrilla fighters and in training Thai government forces. In August 1966 the *Washington Post* reported that in US government circles there was a strong feeling that 'continued dictatorship in Thailand suits the United States, since it assures the continuation of American bases in the country, and that, as a US official put it bluntly, "is our real interest in this place"'.

(b) Africa

The USA took a great interest in Africa, where the late 1950s and 1960s was the era of decolonization and the emergence of many newly independent states. At the end of the Second World War the Americans had put pressure on the European states that still owned colonies, to grant them independence as soon as possible. They claimed that in view of the growing nationalist movements in Africa and Asia, attempts to hang on to colonies would encourage the development of communism. Another reason for the US attitude was that Americans viewed the newly emerging nations as potential markets in which they could trade and establish both economic and political influence. In the Cold War atmosphere, the worst crime any new government could commit, in American eyes, was to show the slightest hint of left-wing or socialist policies and any sympathy with the USSR.

In June 1960 *the Congo* (formerly the Belgian Congo) became an independent state with Patrice Lumumba as prime minister. The country depended heavily on its exports of copper, but the copper-mining industry, situated mainly in the eastern province of Katanga, was still controlled by a Belgian company. Some leading Americans also had financial interests in the company. Lumumba talked about 'economic independence' for the Congo, which the Belgians and Americans took to mean 'nationalization'. The Belgians and the CIA encouraged Katanga to declare itself independent from the Congo so that they could keep control of the copper industry. Lumumba appealed for help first of all to the UN and then to the USSR. This was a fatal mistake: the CIA and the Belgians encouraged Lumumba's opponents, so that he was dismissed and later assassinated (January 1961); the CIA was deeply involved. After 1965 the USA supported the corrupt and brutal regime of General Mobutu, several times sending troops to suppress rebels. It seemed that no internal excess was too much, provided Mobutu acted as a friend of the USA. He remained in power until May 1997 (see Section 25.5).

Ghana became independent in 1957 under the leadership of Kwame Nkrumah. He was socialist in outlook and wanted to steer a middle way between the western powers and the communist bloc. This meant forming good relations with both sides. When he began to forge links with the USSR, China and East Germany, alarm bells rang in Washington. The CIA was active in Ghana and was in contact with a group of army officers who opposed Nkrumah's increasingly undemocratic style. In 1966, while Nkrumah was away on a visit to China, the army, backed by the CIA, launched a coup and he was forced into exile (see Section 25.2).

(c) The Middle East

The Middle East was an important area, serving as a sort of crossroads between the western nations, the communist bloc and the Third World countries of Asia and Africa. Its other importance is that it produces a large proportion of the world's oil. The USA and the states of western Europe were anxious to maintain some influence there, both to block the spread of communism and to keep some control over the region's oil supplies. The Eisenhower administration (1953–61) issued a statement which became known as the Eisenhower Doctrine, declaring that the US was prepared to use armed force to assist any Middle Eastern country against armed aggression from any country controlled by international communism. At different times since 1945 the USA has intervened in most of the Middle East states, destabilizing or overthrowing governments which it chose to define as 'communist'.

In 1950 the Shah (ruler) of *Iran* signed a defence treaty with the USA directed against the neighbouring USSR, which had been trying to set up a communist government in northern Iran. In 1953 the prime minister, Dr Mussadiq, nationalized a British-owned oil company. The USA and the British organized a coup, which removed Mussadiq and restored the Shah to full control. He remained in power for the next 25 years, fully backed and supported by Washington, until he was forced out in January 1979 (see Section 11.1(b)).

Iraq came in for constant attention from the USA. In 1958 General Abdul Kassem overthrew the Iraqi monarchy and proclaimed a republic. He was in favour of reform and modernization, and although he himself was not a communist, the new atmosphere of freedom and openness encouraged the growth of the Iraqi Communist Party. This made Washington uneasy; the State Department was further perturbed in 1960 when Kassem was involved in setting up the Organization of Petroleum Exporting Countries (OPEC), which aimed to break the control of western oil companies over the sale of Middle East oil. The CIA had been trying to destabilize the country for several years – by encouraging a Turkish invasion, financing Kurdish guerrillas who were agitating for more autonomy and attempting to assassinate Kassem. In 1963 they were successful – Kassem was overthrown and killed in a coup backed by the CIA and Britain.

From 1979 the USA financed and supplied Saddam Hussein, who became Iraqi leader in 1968, backing him against the new anti-American government in Iran. After the long and inconclusive Iran–Iraq War (1980–8; see Section 11.9), Saddam's forces invaded and conquered Kuwait (August 1990), only to be driven out again by UN forces, of which by far the largest contingent was the American one (see Section 11.10). In 2003 the Americans, with British help, finally overthrew and captured Saddam (see Section 12.4(f) for further developments).

8.6 DÉTENTE: INTERNATIONAL RELATIONS FROM THE 1970S TO THE 1990S

The word 'détente' is used to mean a permanent relaxation of tensions between East and West. The first real signs of détente could be seen in the early 1970s. With one or two blips along the way, détente eventually led on to the end of the Cold War.

(a) Reasons for détente

As the nuclear arsenals built up, both sides became increasingly fearful of a catastrophic nuclear war in which there could be no real winner. Both sides were sickened by the horrors of Vietnam. In addition, countries had their own individual motives for wanting détente.

- *The USSR was finding the expense of keeping up with the Americans crippling.* It was essential to reduce defence spending so that they could devote more resources to bringing living standards up to western levels, both in the USSR and in the satellite states, all of which were suffering economic difficulties. In 1968 Russian troops were sent to Prague to deal with disturbing developments in Czechoslovakia, when Alexander Dubček tried to introduce 'communism with a human face'. There was unrest, especially in Poland in the early 1970s, which threatened to destabilize the communist bloc. At the same time the Russians were on bad terms with China, and did not want to be left out when relations between China and the USA began to improve in 1971.
- *The Americans were beginning to realize that there must be a better way of coping with communism than the one which was having so little success in Vietnam.* Clearly there were limits to what their military power could achieve. Some Congressmen and Senators were even beginning to talk of a return to 'isolationism'.

- *The Chinese were anxious about their isolation,* nervous about American intentions in Vietnam (after what had happened in Korea) and not happy about their worsening relations with the USSR.
- *The nations of western Europe were worried because they would be in the front line if nuclear war broke out.* Willi Brandt, who became Chancellor of West Germany in 1969, worked for better relations with eastern Europe, a policy known as *Ostpolitik.*

(b) The USSR and the USA

They had already made progress with the 'hotline' telephone link and the agreement to carry out only underground nuclear tests (both in 1963). An agreement signed in 1967 banned the use of nuclear weapons in outer space. The first major breakthrough came in 1972 when the two countries signed *the Strategic Arms Limitation Treaty, known as SALT 1,* which decided how many ABMs, ICBMs and SLBMs each side could have (see Section 7.4(a) and (c)); there was no agreement about MIRVs. The agreement did not reduce the amount of armaments but *it did slow down the arms race.* Presidents Brezhnev and Nixon had three summit meetings, negotiations opened for a further treaty to be known as SALT 2 and the USA began to export wheat to Russia.

Another important step was *the Helsinki Agreement (July 1975),* in which the USA, Canada, the USSR and most European states accepted the European frontiers which had been drawn up after the Second World War (thus recognizing the division of Germany). The communist countries promised to allow their peoples 'human rights', including freedom of speech and freedom to leave the country.

However, détente did not proceed without some setbacks. This was especially true in 1979 when NATO became nervous at the deployment of 150 new Russian SS-20 missiles. NATO decided to deploy over 500 Pershing and Cruise missiles in Europe by 1983 as a deterrent to a possible Russian attack on western Europe. At the same time the US Senate decided not to accept a SALT 2 treaty which would have limited numbers of MIRVs. When the Russians invaded Afghanistan on Christmas Day 1979 and replaced the president with one more favourable to them, all the old western suspicions of Russian motives revived.

The next few years are sometimes referred to as 'the second Cold War'. *Both sides spent the first half of the 1980s building up their nuclear arsenals,* and US President Reagan (1981–9) apparently gave the go-ahead for a new weapons system, *the Strategic Defence Initiative (SDI), also known as 'Star Wars'.* This was intended to use weapons based in space to destroy ballistic missiles in flight.

Détente gathered momentum again thanks to the determination of the new Soviet leader, Mikhail Gorbachev (1985–91). In November 1985 he had a meeting with Reagan in Geneva; this went well and they issued a joint statement that 'nuclear war cannot be won and must never be fought'. The signs were that détente was back on course. Then in April 1986 there was a disastrous accident at the Chernobyl nuclear power station in the Ukraine. This caused a great wave of anti-nuclear feeling in the USSR and Gorbachev decided that measures to reduce nuclear dangers were absolutely vital. In October 1986 he invited Reagan to a summit meeting at Reykjavik and proposed a 15-year timetable for a 'step-by-step process for ridding the earth of nuclear weapons'. The Americans responded to some extent, though Reagan was not prepared to abandon his Star Wars project. At the next summit, held in Washington (December 1987), a historic breakthrough was made: *Reagan and Gorbachev formally signed the INF (Intermediate-Range Nuclear Forces) Treaty.*

- All land-based intermediate-range (300 to 3000 miles) nuclear weapons were to be scrapped over the next three years. This meant 436 American and 1575 Soviet warheads, and would include all Russian missiles in East Germany and Czechoslovakia, and all American Cruise and Pershing missiles based in western Europe.
- There were strict verification provisions so that both sides could check that the weapons were actually being destroyed.

However, all this amounted, at most, to only 4 per cent of existing stocks of nuclear weapons, and there was the stumbling block of Reagan's Star Wars, which he was still not prepared to give up, even though it was only at the planning stage. Nor did the agreement include British and French weapons. The UK prime minister Margaret Thatcher was determined that Britain should keep its own nuclear arsenal, and planned to develop Trident missiles, which were more sophisticated than Cruise missiles. Nevertheless, *this INF Treaty was an important turning point in the nuclear arms race, since it was the first time any weapons had been destroyed.*

By 1985 the USSR was seriously embarrassed by its involvement in Afghanistan. Although there were over 100 000 Soviet troops in the country, they found it impossible to subdue the ferocious Islamic guerrillas; it was a drain on their resources and a blow to their prestige. The hostility of China, the suspicion of Islamic states all over the world and repeated condemnations by the UN convinced Gorbachev it was time to pull out. It was eventually agreed that the Russians would begin withdrawing their troops from Afghanistan on 1 May 1988, provided the Americans stopped sending military aid to the Afghan resistance movement. In June 1988 Reagan went to Moscow to discuss the timetable for implementing the INF Treaty.

(c) China and the USA

China and the USA had been extremely hostile towards each other since the Korean War and seemed likely to remain so while the Americans backed Chiang Kai-shek and the Nationalists in Taiwan, and while the Chinese backed Ho Chi Minh. However, in 1971 the Chinese unexpectedly invited an American table-tennis team to visit China. Following the success of that visit, the USA responded by calling off their veto of Chinese entry into the UN. *Communist China was therefore allowed to become a member of the UN in October 1971.* President Nixon, looking for a bold initiative for which his presidency would be remembered, decided he would visit China himself. Chairman Mao agreed to receive him and the visit took place in February 1972. Though Mao was reported to have told Zhou Enlai that the USA was 'like an ape moving towards becoming a human being', the meeting led to a resumption of diplomatic relations. President Ford also paid a successful visit to Beijing (Peking) in 1975. There was still the problem of Taiwan to sour the relationship: though Chiang himself died in 1975, his supporters still occupied the island, and the communists would not be happy until it was brought under their control. Relations improved further in 1978 when Democrat President Carter decided to withdraw recognition of Nationalist China. However, this caused a row in the USA, where Carter was accused of betraying his ally.

The climax of détente between China and the USA came early in 1979 when *Carter gave formal recognition of the People's Republic of China*, and ambassadors were exchanged. Good relations were maintained during the 1980s. The Chinese were anxious that détente with the USA should continue, because of their conflict with Vietnam (Russia's ally), which had begun in 1979. In 1985 an agreement was signed on nuclear cooperation. Things suddenly took a turn for the worse in June 1989 when the Chinese government used troops to disperse a student demonstration in Tiananmen Square, Beijing (Peking). The government was afraid that the demonstration might turn into a revolution which could overthrow Chinese communism. At least a thousand students were killed and many later executed, and this brought worldwide condemnation. Tensions rose again in 1996 when the Chinese held 'naval exercises' in the straits between the Chinese mainland and Taiwan, in protest at the Taiwanese democratic elections just about to be held.

(d)   Relations between the USSR and China

Relations between the USSR and China deteriorated steadily after 1956. They had earlier signed a treaty of mutual assistance and friendship (1950), but later the Chinese did not approve of Khrushchev's policies, particularly his belief in 'peaceful coexistence', and his claim that it was possible to achieve communism by methods other than violent revolution. This went against the ideas of Lenin, leader of the 1917 Russian communist revolution, and so the Chinese accused the Russians of *'revisionism' – revising or reinterpreting the teachings of Marx and Lenin to suit their own needs*. They were angry at Khrushchev's 'soft' line towards the USA. In retaliation the Russians reduced their economic aid to China.

The ideological argument was not the only source of trouble: there was also a frontier dispute. During the nineteenth century Russia had taken over large areas of Chinese territory north of Vladivostok and in Sinkiang province, which the Chinese were now demanding back, so far without success. Now that China herself was following a 'softer' policy towards the USA, it seemed that the territorial problem was the main bone of contention. At the end of the 1970s both Russia and China were vying for American support, against each other, for the leadership of world communism. To complicate matters further, Vietnam now supported Russia. When the Chinese attacked Vietnam (February 1979), relations reached rock bottom. The Chinese attack was partly in retaliation for Vietnam's invasion of Kampuchea (formerly Cambodia) in December 1978, which overthrew the Khmer Rouge government of Pol Pot, a protégé of China, and partly because of a frontier dispute. They withdrew after three weeks, having, as Beijing put it, 'taught the Vietnamese a lesson'. *In 1984 the Chinese set out their grievances against the USSR*:

- the presence of Russian troops in Afghanistan;
- Soviet backing of the Vietnamese troops in Kampuchea;
- the Soviet troop build-up along the Chinese frontiers of Mongolia and Manchuria.

Mikhail Gorbachev was determined to begin a new era in Sino-Russian relations. Five-year agreements on trade and economic co-operation were signed (July 1985) and regular contact took place between the two governments. A formal reconciliation took place in May 1989 when Gorbachev visited Beijing. Also in 1989 Vietnam withdrew its troops from Kampuchea, and so their relations with China improved.

8.7   THE COLLAPSE OF COMMUNISM IN EASTERN EUROPE AND THE END OF THE COLD WAR: INTERNATIONAL RELATIONS TRANSFORMED

(a)   August 1988 to December 1991

Remarkable events happened in eastern Europe in the period August 1988 to December 1991. Communism was swept away by a rising tide of popular opposition and mass demonstrations, far more quickly than anybody could ever have imagined.

- The process began in Poland in August 1988 when the 'Solidarity' trade union organized huge anti-government strikes. These eventually forced the government to allow free elections, in which the communists were heavily defeated (June 1989). Revolutionary protests rapidly spread to all the other Russian satellite states.
- Hungary was the next to allow free elections, in which the communists again suffered defeat.
- In East Germany, communist leader Eric Honecker wanted to disperse the demonstrations by force, but he was overruled by his colleagues; by the end of 1989 the communist government had resigned. Soon the Berlin Wall was breached, and, most astonishing of all, *in the summer of 1990, Germany was re-united.*
- Czechoslovakia, Bulgaria and Romania had thrown out their communist governments by the end of 1989, and multi-party elections were held in Yugoslavia in 1990 and in Albania in the spring of 1991.
- By the end of December 1991, the USSR itself had split up into separate republics and Gorbachev had resigned. Communist rule in Russia was over after 74 years.

(See Sections 10.6 and 18.3 for the reasons behind the collapse of communism in eastern Europe.)

(b)   How were international relations affected?

Many people in the west thought that with the collapse of communism in eastern Europe, the world's problems would miraculously disappear. But nothing could have been further from the truth and a range of new problems surfaced.

1   *The Cold War was over*
The most immediate result was that the former USSR and its allies were no longer seen by the West as the 'enemy'. In November 1990 the countries of NATO and the Warsaw Pact signed a treaty agreeing that they were 'no longer adversaries', and that none of their weapons would ever be used except in self-defence. The Cold War was over, and Gorbachev must take much of the credit for bringing it to an end. His determination to work for disarmament broke the stalemate and impressed Reagan, who also deserves much credit for responding so positively to Gorbachev's initiatives. The end of the Cold War was an enormous step forward. However …

2   *New conflicts soon arose*
These were often caused by nationalism. During the Cold War, the USSR and the USA, as we have seen, kept tight control, by force if necessary, over areas where their vital interests might be affected. Now, a conflict which did not directly affect the interests of East or West would probably be left to find its own solution, bloody or otherwise. Nationalism, which had been suppressed by communism, soon re-emerged in some of the former states of the USSR and elsewhere. Sometimes disputes were settled peacefully, for example in Czechoslovakia, where Slovak nationalists insisted on breaking away to form a separate state of Slovakia. However, war broke out between Azerbaijan and Armenia (two former republics of the USSR) over disputed territory. There was fighting in Georgia (another former Soviet republic) where the people of the north wanted to form a separate state.

Most tragic of all was Yugoslavia, which broke up into five separate states – Serbia (with Montenegro), Bosnia–Herzegovina, Croatia, Slovenia and Macedonia. Soon a complex civil war broke out in which Serbia tried to grab as much territory as possible from Croatia. In Bosnia, Serbs, Croats and Muslims fought each other in an attempt to set up states of their own. This increasingly bitter struggle dragged on for almost four years until a ceasefire was arranged in November 1995 (see Section 10.7). So at a time when the states of western Europe were moving into closer union with the European Community (see Section 10.8), those of eastern Europe were breaking up into even smaller national units.

3   Supervision of nuclear weapons

Another fear, now that the Russians and the USA were less willing to act as 'policemen', was that *countries with what the powers considered to be unstable or irresponsible governments might use nuclear weapons* – countries like, for example, Iraq, Iran and Libya. One of the needs of the 1990s therefore, was better international supervision and control of nuclear weapons, and also of biological and chemical weapons.

4   Economic problems

All the former communist states faced another problem – how to deal with the economic collapse and intense poverty left over from the communist 'command' economies, and how to change to 'free-market' economies. They needed a carefully planned and generous programme of financial help from the West. Otherwise it would be difficult to create stability in eastern Europe. Nationalism and economic unrest could cause a right-wing backlash, especially in Russia itself, which could be just as threatening as communism was once thought to be. There was clearly cause for concern, given the large number of nuclear weapons still in existence in the region. There was the danger that Russia, desperate to raise money, might sell off some of its nuclear weapons to 'unsuitable' governments.

5   The re-unification of Germany created some problems

The Poles were very suspicious of a united and powerful Germany, fearing that it might try to take back the former German territory east of the rivers Oder and Neisse, given to Poland after the Second World War. Germany also found itself providing refuge for people fleeing from disturbances in other states of Europe; by October 1992, at least 16 000 refugees a month were entering Germany. This gave rise to violent protests from right-wing neo-Nazi groups who believed that Germany had problems enough of its own – especially the need to modernize the industry and amenities of the former East Germany – without admitting foreigners.

6   Relations between the western allies

The disappearance of communism affected relations between the western allies, the USA, western Europe and Japan. They had been held together by the need to stand firm against communism, but now differences emerged over trade and the extent to which the USA and Japan were prepared to help solve the problems of eastern Europe. For instance, during the war in Bosnia, relations between the USA and the states of western Europe became strained when the USA refused to provide troops for the UN peacekeeping forces, leaving the burden to other member states. The overriding fact now was that the USA was left as the world's only superpower; it remained to be seen how Washington would choose to play its new role on the world stage.

FURTHER READING

Blum, W., *Killing Hope: US Military and CIA Interventions Since World War II* (Zed Books, 2003).
Cawthorne, N., *Vietnam – A War Lost and Won* (Arcturus, 2003).
Foss, C., *Fidel Castro* (Sutton, 2006).
Gaddis, J. L., *The Cold War: A New History* (Allen Lane, 2006).

Hoffman, D., *The Dead Hand: Reagan, Gorbachev and the Untold Story of the Cold War Arms Race* (Icon Books, 2011).

Isaacs, J. and Downing, T., *Cold War: for Forty-Five Years the World Held its Breath* (Abacus, 2008).

Kapcia, A., *Cuba in Revolution: A History since the 1950s* (Reaktion, 2008).

Lowe, P., *The Korean War* (Macmillan, 2000).

MacMillan, M., *Seize the Hour: When Nixon met Mao* (John Murray, 2006).

Matlock, J. F., *Reagan and Gorbachev: How the Cold War Ended* (Random House, 2004).

McCauley, M., *Russia, America and the Cold War, 1949-1991* (Longman, 2nd edition, 2008).

Ruane, K., *The Vietnam Wars* (Manchester University Press, 2000).

Scott, L., *The Cuban Missile Crisis and the Threat of Nuclear War* (Continuum, 2007).

Young, J. W., *The Longman Companion to Cold War and Détente* (Longman, 1993).

QUESTIONS

1 (a) Explain why war broke out in Korea in June 1950 and why the USA became involved?

(b) What were the outcomes and the effects of the war in Korea?

2 Why was there a period of détente during the 1970s and 1980s, and in what ways did détente manifest itself?

3 Explain why the Cold War came to an end, and show how this affected international relations.

There is a document question about the USA and the war in Vietnam on the website.

The United Nations Organization

SUMMARY OF EVENTS

The United Nations Organization (UNO) officially came into existence in October 1945 after the Second World War. It was formed to replace the League of Nations, which had proved incapable of restraining aggressive dictators like Hitler and Mussolini. In setting up the UNO, the great powers tried to eliminate some of the weaknesses which had handicapped the League. The UN Charter was drawn up in San Francisco in 1945, and was based on proposals made at an earlier meeting between the USSR, the USA, China and Britain, held at Dumbarton Oaks (USA) in 1944. *The aims of the UN are*:

- to preserve peace and eliminate war;
- to remove the causes of conflict by encouraging economic, social, educational, scientific and cultural progress throughout the world, especially in under-developed countries;
- to safeguard the rights of all individual human beings, and the rights of peoples and nations.

In spite of the careful framing of the Charter, the UN was unable to solve many of the problems of international relations, particularly those caused by the Cold War. On the other hand it played an important role in a number of international crises by arranging ceasefires and negotiations, and by providing peacekeeping forces. Its successes in non-political work – care of refugees, protection of human rights, economic planning and attempts to deal with problems of world health, population and famine – have been enormous.

9.1 THE STRUCTURE OF THE UNITED NATIONS ORGANIZATION

There are now seven main organs of the UN:

- the General Assembly
- the Security Council
- the Secretariat
- the International Court of Justice
- the Trusteeship Council
- the Economic and Social Council
- the International Criminal Court (inaugurated in March 2003).

(a) The General Assembly

This is the meeting together of the representatives from all the member nations; each member can send up to five representatives, though there is only one vote per nation. It meets once a year, starting in September and remaining in session for about three months, but special sessions can be called in times of crisis by the members themselves or by the Security Council. Its function is to discuss and make decisions about international problems, to consider the UN budget and what amount each member should pay, to elect the Security Council members and to supervise the work of the many other UN bodies. *Decisions do not need a unanimous vote as they did in the League Assembly.* Sometimes a simple majority is enough, though on issues which the Assembly thinks are very important, a two-thirds majority is needed. These include decisions about admitting new members or expelling existing members, and about actions to be taken to maintain peace. All speeches and debates are translated into six official UN languages – English, French, Russian, Chinese, Spanish and Arabic.

(b) The Security Council

This sits in permanent session and its function is to deal with crises as they arise, by whatever action seems appropriate, and if necessary by calling on members to take economic or military action against an aggressor. The Council must also approve applications for UN membership, which then require a two-thirds majority in a vote of acceptance by the General Assembly. The Council began with eleven members, *five of them permanent* (*China, France, USA, USSR and Britain*), and the other six elected by the General Assembly for two-year terms. In 1965 the number of non-permanent members was increased to ten. Decisions need at least nine of the 15 members to vote in favour, but these must include all five permanent members; this means that *any one of the permanent members can veto a decision and prevent any action being taken.* In practice it has gradually been accepted that abstention by a permanent member does not count as a veto, but this has not been written into the Charter.

In order to secure some action in case of a veto by one of the permanent members, the General Assembly (at the time of the Korean War in 1950) introduced *the 'Uniting for Peace' resolution*; this stated that if the Security Council's proposals were vetoed, the Assembly could meet within 24 hours and decide what action to take, even military intervention if necessary. In cases like this, a decision by the Assembly would only need a two-thirds majority. Again this new rule was not added to the Charter, and the USSR, which used the veto more often than any other member, always maintained that a Security Council veto should take precedence over a General Assembly decision. Nevertheless, the Assembly acted in this way many times, ignoring Russian protests.

In 1950 a problem arose when the new communist People's Republic of China applied for UN membership. The USA vetoed the application, so that the Republic of China (Taiwan) retained its membership and its permanent seat on the Security Council. The USA blocked communist China's application every year for the next 20 years. In 1971, in an effort to improve relations with communist China, the USA at last refrained from vetoing the application; consequently the General Assembly voted that the People's Republic of China should take over Taiwan's membership and permanent Security Council seat.

(c) The Secretariat

This is the 'office staff' of the UN and it consists of over 50 000 employees. They look after the administrative work, preparing minutes of meetings, translations and information.

It is headed by the Secretary-General, who is appointed for a five-year term by the Assembly on the recommendation of the Security Council. In order to ensure some degree of impartiality, he is not from one of the major powers. He acts as the main spokesperson for the UN and is always at the forefront of international affairs, trying to sort out the world's problems. So far the post has been held by:

Trygve Lie of Norway (1946–52)
Dag Hammarskjöld of Sweden (1952–61)
U Thant of Burma (1961–71)
Kurt Waldheim of Austria (1971–81)
Javier Pérez de Cuellar of Peru (1981–91)
Boutros Boutros-Ghali of Egypt (1991–6)
Kofi Annan of Ghana (1996–2006)
Ban Ki-moon of South Korea (since 2006)

(d)　The International Court of Justice

The International Court of Justice at The Hague (in the Netherlands) has 15 judges, all of different nationalities, elected for nine-year terms (five retiring every third year) by the Assembly and the Security Council jointly. It adjudicates in disputes between states; a number of cases have been successfully dealt with, including a frontier dispute between Holland and Belgium and a disagreement between Britain and Norway over fishing limits. In other cases, however, it was not so successful. In 1984 for example, Nicaragua sued the USA for mining its harbours; the Court judged in favour of Nicaragua and ordered the USA to pay compensation. The USA refused to accept the verdict, and no further action was taken. Although in theory the Security Council has the power to take 'appropriate measures' to enforce the Court's decisions, it has never done so. The Court can only operate successfully when both parties to a dispute agree to accept the verdict, whichever way it should happen to go.

(e)　The Trusteeship Council

This replaced the League of Nations Mandates Commission, which had originally come into existence in 1919 to keep an eye on the territories taken away from Germany and Turkey at the end of the First World War. Some of these areas (known as *mandated territories* or *mandates*) had been handed over to the victorious powers, and their job was to govern the territories and prepare them for independence (see Sections 2.8 and 2.10). The Trusteeship Council did its job well and by 1970 most of the mandates had gained their independence (see Sections 11.1(b) and Chapter 24).

However, *Namibia remained a problem, since South Africa refused to give the area independence*. South Africa, ruled by a government representing the white minority of the population, was unwilling to give independence to a state right on its own frontier that would be ruled by a government representing its black African majority. The UN repeatedly condemned South Africa for its attitude; in 1971 the International Court of Justice ruled that South Africa's occupation of Namibia was a breach of international law and that South Africa must withdraw immediately. South Africa ignored the UN, but as the other states of Africa gradually gained independence under black governments, it became more difficult for South Africa to maintain both its position in Namibia and its own white minority rule (see Section 25.6(b–c) and 25.8(e)). At last in 1990 the pressure of black African nationalism and world opinion forced South Africa to release its grip on Namibia.

(f) The Economic and Social Council (ECOSOC)

This has 27 members, elected by the General Assembly, with one-third retiring each year. It organizes projects concerned with health, education and other social and economic matters. Its task is so enormous that *it has appointed four regional commissions (Europe, Latin America, Africa, Asia and the Far East)*, as well as commissions on population problems, drugs problems, human rights and the status of women. ECOSOC also co-ordinates the work of an astonishing array of other commissions and specialized agencies, around 30 in all. Among the best known are the International Labour Organization (ILO), the World Health Organization (WHO), the Food and Agriculture Organization (FAO), the United Nations Educational, Scientific and Cultural Organization (UNESCO), the United Nations Children's Fund (UNICEF) and the United Nations Relief and Works Agency (UNRWA). The scope of ECOSOC expanded in such a remarkable way that by 1980 more than 90 per cent of the UN's annual expenditure was devoted to ECOSOC activities (see Section 9.5).

(g) The International Criminal Court (ICC)

The idea of an International Criminal Court to try individuals accused of crimes against humanity was first discussed by a League of Nations convention in 1937, but nothing came of it. The Cold War prevented any further progress until, in 1989, it was suggested again as a possible way of dealing with drug-traffickers and terrorists. Progress towards the creation of a permanent court was again slow, and it was left to the Security Council to set up two special war crimes tribunals to try individuals accused of committing atrocities in 1994 in Rwanda and in 1995 in Bosnia. The most high-profile case was that of Slobodan Milošević, the former Yugoslav president (see Section 10.7), who was extradited from Belgrade and handed over to UN officials in the Netherlands. His trial opened in July 2001 in The Hague; he faced charges of committing crimes against humanity in Bosnia, Croatia and Kosovo. He was the first former head of state ever to be brought before an international court of justice. The trial dragged on for five for almost five years until he died of a heart attack before a verdict was reached.

Meanwhile, in July 1998 an agreement known as the Rome Statute was signed by 120 member states of the UN to create a permanent court to deal with war crimes, genocide and other crimes against humanity. The new court, consisting of 18 elected judges, was formally inaugurated in March 2003, and was based in The Hague. However, the US government did not like the idea that some of its citizens might be tried in the court – particularly Americans acting as peacekeepers who might find themselves open to 'politicized prosecutions'. Although the Clinton administration had signed the 1998 agreement, President Bush insisted that the signature should be withdrawn (May 2002). Consequently the USA did not recognize the ICC and by June 2003 had signed separate agreements with 37 states promising that no US personnel would be handed over to the ICC for trial. In some cases the USA threatened to withdraw economic or military aid if the state refused to comply with its wishes.

9.2 HOW DIFFERENT IS THE UNITED NATIONS FROM THE LEAGUE OF NATIONS?

(a) The UN has been more successful

There are some important differences which have tended to make the UN a more successful body than the League.

- The UN spends much more time and resources on economic and social matters and its scope is much wider than that of the League. All the specialized agencies, with the exception of the International Labour Organization (founded in 1919), were set up in 1945 or later.
- The UN is committed to safeguarding individual human rights, which the League did not get involved in.
- Changes in the procedures of the General Assembly and the Security Council (especially the 'Uniting for Peace' resolution), and the increased power and prestige of the Secretary-General, have enabled the UN, on occasion, to take more decisive action than the League ever achieved.
- The UN has a much wider membership and is therefore more of a genuine world organization than the League, with all the extra prestige that this entails. Both the USA and the USSR were founder-members of the UN, whereas the USA never joined the League. Between 1963 and 1968 no fewer than 43 new members joined the UN, mainly the emerging states of Africa and Asia, and by 1985 membership had reached 159; the League never had more than 50 members. Later, many of the former member states of the USSR joined, and by 1993 the total had reached 183. In 2002, East Timor, which had at last gained its independence from Indonesia with UN help, became the 191st member. Montenegro joined in 2006 and in July 2011 the newly independent Republic of South Sudan became the 193rd member.

(b) Some of the weaknesses of the League remain

Any one of the five permanent members of the Security Council can use its power of veto to prevent decisive action being taken. Like the League, the UN has no permanent army of its own and has to use forces belonging to its member states (see Section 9.6).

9.3 HOW SUCCESSFUL HAS THE UN BEEN AS A PEACEKEEPING ORGANIZATION?

Although it has had mixed success, it is probably fair to say that *the UN has been more successful than the League in its peacekeeping efforts*, especially in crises which did not directly involve the interests of the great powers, such as the civil war in the Congo (1960–4) and the dispute between the Netherlands and Indonesia over West New Guinea. On the other hand, it has often been just as ineffective as the League in situations – such as the Hungarian rising of 1956 and the 1968 Czech crisis – where the interests of one of the great powers – in this case the USSR – seemed to be threatened, and where the great power decided to ignore or defy the UN. The best way to illustrate the UN's varying degrees of success is to examine some of the major disputes in which it has been involved.

(a) West New Guinea (1946)

In 1946 the UN helped to arrange independence from Holland for the Dutch East Indies, which became Indonesia (see Map 24.3). However, no agreement was reached about the future of West New Guinea (West Irian), which was claimed by both countries. In 1961 fighting broke out; after U Thant had appealed to both sides to reopen negotiations, it was agreed (1962) that the territory should become part of Indonesia. The transfer was organized and policed by a UN force. In this case the UN played a vital role in getting negotiations off the ground, though it did not itself make the decision about West Irian's future.

(b) Palestine (1947)

The dispute between Jews and Arabs in Palestine was brought before the UN in 1947. After an investigation, the UN decided to divide Palestine, setting up the Jewish state of Israel (see Section 11.2). This was one of the UN's most controversial decisions, and it was not accepted by the majority of Arabs. The UN was unable to prevent a series of wars between Israel and various Arab states (1948–9, 1967 and 1973), though it did useful work arranging ceasefires and providing supervisory forces, while the UN Relief and Works Agency cared for the Arab refugees.

(c) The Korean War (1950–3)

This was the only occasion on which the UN was able to take decisive action in a crisis directly involving the interests of one of the superpowers. When South Korea was invaded by communist North Korea in June 1950, the Security Council immediately passed a resolution condemning North Korea, and called on member states to send help to the South. However, this was possible only because of the temporary absence of the Russian delegates, who would have vetoed the resolution if they had not been boycotting Security Council meetings (since January of that year) in protest at the failure to allow communist China to join the UN. Although the Russian delegates returned smartly, it was too late for them to prevent action going ahead. Troops of 16 countries were able to repel the invasion and preserve the frontier between the two Koreas along the 38th parallel (see Section 8.1).

Though this was claimed by the West as a great UN success, it was in fact very much an American operation – the vast majority of troops and the Commander-in-Chief, General MacArthur, were American, and the US government had already decided to intervene with force the day before the Security Council decision was taken. Only the absence of the Russians enabled the USA to turn it into a UN operation. This was a situation not likely to be repeated, since the USSR would take good care to be present at all future Council sessions.

The Korean War had important results for the future of the UN: one was the passing of *the 'Uniting for Peace' resolution*, which would permit a Security Council veto to be bypassed by a General Assembly vote. Another was the launching of *a bitter attack by the Russians on Secretary-General Trygve Lie* for what they considered to be his biased role in the crisis. His position soon became impossible and he eventually agreed to retire early, to be replaced by Dag Hammarskjöld.

(d) The Suez Crisis (1956)

This arguably showed the UN at its best. When President Nasser of Egypt suddenly nationalized the Suez Canal, many of whose shares were owned by the British and French, both these powers protested strongly and sent troops 'to protect their interests' (see Section 11.3). At the same time the Israelis invaded Egypt from the east; the real aim of all three states was to bring down President Nasser. A Security Council resolution condemning force was vetoed by Britain and France, whereupon the General Assembly, by a majority of 64 votes to 5, condemned the invasions and called for a withdrawal of troops. In view of the weight of opinion against them, the aggressors agreed to withdraw, provided the UN ensured a reasonable settlement over the canal and kept the Arabs and Israelis from slaughtering each other. A UN force of 5000, made up of troops from ten different countries, moved in, while the British, French and Israelis went home. The prestige of the UN and of Dag Hammarskjöld, who handled the operation with considerable skill, was greatly enhanced, though American and Russian pressure was also important in bringing about a ceasefire. However, the UN was not so successful in the 1967 Arab–Israeli conflict (see Section 11.4).

(e)   The Hungarian Rising (1956)

This took place at the same time as the Suez Crisis, and showed the UN at its most ineffective. When the Hungarians tried to exert their independence from Russian control, Soviet troops entered Hungary to crush the revolt. The Hungarian government appealed to the UN, but the Russians vetoed a Security Council resolution calling for a withdrawal of their forces. The General Assembly passed the same resolution and set up a committee to investigate the problem; but the Russians refused to co-operate with the committee and no progress could be made. The contrast with Suez was striking: there, Britain and France were willing to bow to international pressure; the Russians simply ignored the UN, and nothing could be done.

(f)   Civil war in the Congo (1960–4)

Here the UN mounted its most complex operation to date (see Section 25.5), except for Korea. When the Congo (known as Zaire since 1971) dissolved into chaos immediately after gaining independence, a UN force numbering over 20 000 at its largest managed to restore some sort of precarious order. A special UN Congo Fund was set up to help with the recovery and development of the ravaged country. *But the financial cost was so high that the UN was brought close to bankruptcy*, especially when the USSR, France and Belgium refused to pay their contributions towards the cost of the operations, because they disapproved of the way the UN had handled the situation. The war also cost the life of Dag Hammarskjöld, who was killed in a plane crash in the Congo.

(g)   Cyprus

Cyprus has kept the UN busy since 1964. A British colony since 1878, the island was granted independence in 1960. In 1963 civil war broke out between the Greeks, who made up about 80 per cent of the population, and the Turks. A UN peacekeeping force arrived in March 1964; an uneasy peace was restored, but it needed 3000 UN troops permanently stationed in Cyprus to prevent Greeks and Turks tearing each other apart. That was not the end of the trouble, though: in 1974 the Greek Cypriots tried to unite the island with Greece. This prompted the Turkish Cypriots, helped by invading Turkish army troops, to seize the north of the island for their own territory. They went on to expel all Greeks who were unfortunate enough to be living in that area. The UN condemned the invasion but was unable to remove the Turks. UN forces did at least achieve a ceasefire and are still policing the frontier between Greeks and Turks. However, the UN has still not been successful in finding an acceptable constitution or any other compromise. The most recent attempt – the Annan Plan of 2004 – was accepted by the Turks but rejected by the Greeks.

(h)   Kashmir

In Kashmir the UN found itself in a similar situation to the one in Cyprus. After 1947, this large province, lying between India and Pakistan (see Map 24.1) was claimed by both states. Already in 1948 the UN had negotiated a ceasefire after fighting broke out. At this point the Indians were occupying the southern part of Kashmir, the Pakistanis the northern part, and for the next 16 years the UN policed the ceasefire line between the two zones. When Pakistani troops invaded the Indian zone in 1965, a short war developed, but once again the UN successfully intervened and hostilities ceased. The original dispute still remained, however, and in 1999 there were violent clashes as Pakistanis again unsuccessfully invaded the Indian zone. There seemed little prospect of the UN or any other agency finding a permanent solution.

(i) The Czechoslovak crisis (1968)

This was almost a repeat performance of the Hungarian rising 12 years earlier. When the Czechs showed what Moscow considered to be too much independence, Russian and other Warsaw Pact troops were sent in to enforce obedience to the USSR. The Security Council tried to pass a motion condemning this action, but the Russians vetoed it, claiming that the Czech government had asked for their intervention. Although the Czechs denied this, there was nothing the UN could do in view of the USSR's refusal to co-operate.

(j) The Lebanon

While civil war was raging in the Lebanon (1975–87) matters were further complicated by a frontier dispute in the south of the country between Lebanese Christians (aided by the Israelis) and Palestinians. In March 1978 the Israelis invaded South Lebanon in order to destroy Palestinian guerrilla bases from which attacks were being made on northern Israel. In June 1978 the Israelis agreed to withdraw, provided the UN assumed responsibility for policing the frontier area. *The United Nations Interim Force in Lebanon (UNIFIL)*, consisting of about 7000 troops, was sent to South Lebanon. It supervised the Israeli withdrawal and had some success in maintaining relative peace in the area; but it was a constant struggle against frontier violations, assassinations, terrorism and the seizing of hostages (see Section 11.8(b)).

During the early 1990s a new enemy began to harass Israel from bases in South Lebanon: this was the Muslim Shi'ite group known as Hezbollah, which, according to the Israeli government, was backed by Iran and Syria. In retaliation the Israelis launched a major attack on South Lebanon (April 1996) and occupied most of the region until 1999. Once again UNIFIL helped to supervise an Israeli withdrawal and the force was increased to around 8000. In 2002, as the region seemed calmer than for many years, UNIFIL was reduced to some 3000. UNIFIL worked hard to strengthen the Lebanese army, providing training and equipment. Eventually the two forces were able to work together to maintain stability, though a permanent solution still seemed far off. In July 2006 Hezbollah ambushed an Israeli patrol; eight Israeli soldiers were killed and two taken prisoner. The Israelis responded immediately: demanding the return of the captured soldiers, they blockaded Lebanon from the sea, bombed Beirut and destroyed Hezbollah's headquarters. Hezbollah retaliated by firing rockets into Israel at a rate of over a hundred a day. It was mid-August before the UN succeeded in arranging a ceasefire. UNIFIL was increased to 12 000 and there was relative calm for the next four years. Early in 2011 violent incidents began again. The Israelis were still refusing to move out of a small area around the village of Gharjah, north of the withdrawal line agreed in 2006.

There were several exchanges of fire between the Lebanese army and the Israeli Defence Force, terrorist attacks on UNIFIL itself and the firing of rockets into Israel.

(k) The Iran–Iraq War (1980–8)

The UN was successful in bringing an end to the long-drawn-out war between Iran and Iraq. After years of attempting to mediate, the UN at last negotiated a ceasefire, though admittedly they were helped by the fact that both sides were close to exhaustion (see Section 11.9).

9.4 UN PEACEKEEPING SINCE THE END OF THE COLD WAR

The end of the Cold War unfortunately did not mean the end of potential conflict: there were a number of disputes still rolling on, which had originated many years earlier; the Middle East continued to be volatile, and there were more problems in south-east Asia and Africa. Between 1990 and 2003 the UN undertook well over 30 peacekeeping operations; at the peak of their involvement, in the mid-1990s, there were over 80 000 troops on active service, from 77 countries. A few examples illustrate the growing complexity of the problems facing the UN and the increasing obstacles making success more difficult.

(a) The 1991 Gulf War

UN action during the Gulf War of 1991 was impressive. When Saddam Hussein of Iraq sent his troops to invade and capture the tiny, but extremely rich, neighbouring state of Kuwait (August 1990), the UN Security Council warned him to withdraw or face the consequences. When he refused, a large UN force was sent to Saudi Arabia. In a short and decisive campaign, Iraqi troops were driven out, suffering heavy losses, and Kuwait was liberated (see Section 11.10). However, critics of the UN complained that Kuwait had received help only because the West needed her oil supplies; other small nations, which had no value to the West, had received no help when they were invaded by larger neighbours (for example East Timor, taken over by Indonesia in 1975).

(b) Cambodia/Kampuchea

Problems in Cambodia (Kampuchea) dragged on for nearly 20 years, but eventually the UN was able to arrange a solution. In 1975 the Khmer Rouge, a communist guerrilla force led by Pol Pot, seized power from the right-wing government of Prince Sihanouk (see Section 21.3). Over the next three years Pol Pot's brutal regime slaughtered about a third of the population, until in 1978 a Vietnamese army invaded the country. They drove out the Khmer Rouge and set up a new government. At first the UN, prompted by the USA, condemned this action, although many people thought Vietnam had done the people of Cambodia a great service by getting rid of the cruel Pol Pot regime. But it was all part of the Cold War, which meant that any action by Vietnam, an ally of the USSR, would be condemned by the USA. The end of the Cold War enabled the UN to organize and police a solution. Vietnamese forces were withdrawn (September 1989), and after a long period of negotiations and persuasion, elections were held (June 1993), won by Prince Sihanouk's party. The result was widely accepted (though not by what was left of the Khmer Rouge, which refused to take part in the elections), and the country gradually began to settle down.

(c) Mozambique

Mozambique, which gained independence from Portugal in 1975, was torn by civil war for many years (see Section 24.6(d)). By 1990 the country was in ruins and both sides were exhausted. Although a ceasefire agreement had been signed in Rome (October 1992) at a conference organized by the Roman Catholic Church and the Italian government, it was not holding. There were many violations of the ceasefire and there was no way that elections could be held in such an atmosphere. The UN now became fully involved, operating a programme of demobilizing and disarming the various armies, distributing humanitarian relief and preparing for elections, which took place successfully in October 1994. Joachim Chissano of FRELIMO was elected president and re-elected for a further term in 1999.

(d) Somalia

Somalia disintegrated into civil war in 1991 when the dictator Siad Barré was overthrown. A power struggle developed between rival supporters of Generals Aidid and Ali Mohammed; the situation was chaotic as food supplies and communications broke down and thousands of refugees were fleeing into Kenya. The Organization of African Unity (OAU) asked for UN help, and 37 000 UN troops, mainly American, arrived (December 1992) to safeguard the aid and to restore law and order by disarming the 'warlords'. However, the warlords, especially Aidid, were not prepared to be disarmed, and UN troops began to suffer casualties. The Americans withdrew their troops (March 1994), and the remaining UN troops were withdrawn in March 1995, leaving the warlords to fight it out. It was a humiliating backdown; but in fact the UN had set itself an impossible task from the beginning – to forcibly disarm two extremely powerful armies which were determined to carry on fighting each other, and to combine this with a humanitarian relief programme. At the same time the UN took no action in the civil war and genocide taking place in Rwanda in 1994 (see Section 25.7). UN military interventions had most chance of success when, as in Korea in 1950–3 and the 1991 Gulf War, UN troops actively supported one side against the other.

(e) Bosnia

A similar situation developed in Bosnia (see Section 10.7(c)). In the civil war between Bosnian Muslims and Serbs, the UN failed to send enough troops to impose law and order. This was partly because both the European Community and the USA were reluctant to get involved. There was further humiliation for the UN in July 1995 when they were unable to prevent Serb forces from capturing two towns – Srebrenica and Zepa – which the Security Council had designated as safe areas for Muslims. UN helplessness was under-lined when the Serbs went on to murder around 8000 Muslim men in Srebrenica.

(f) Iraq – the overthrow of Saddam Hussein

In March 2003 the USA and Britain launched an invasion of Iraq, on the grounds that they intended to get rid of its weapons of mass destruction and to free the Iraqi people from the brutal regime of Saddam Hussein (see Section 12.4). UN weapons inspectors had already spent months in Iraq searching for weapons of mass destruction, but had found nothing of any significance. The attack went ahead even though the UN Security Council had not given its authorization. The USA and Britain had tried to push a resolution through the

Council approving military action, but France, Russia, China and Germany wanted to allow Saddam more time to co-operate with the weapons inspectors. When it became clear that France and Russia were prepared to veto any such resolution, the USA and Britain resolved to go ahead unilaterally, without putting the resolution to a Security Council vote. They claimed that Saddam's violations of earlier UN resolutions were a justification for war.

The US and British action was a serious blow to the prestige of the UN. Secretary-General Kofi Annan, speaking at the opening of the annual session of the General Assembly in September 2003, said that their action had brought the UN to 'a fork in the road'. Until then, all states needed the authorization of the Security Council if they intended to use force beyond the normal right of self-defence, as prescribed by Article 51 of the UN Charter. However, if states continued to act unilaterally and pre-emptively against a perceived threat, that would present a fundamental challenge to the entire principles of world peace and stability on which the UN was based, and which it had been striving to achieve, however imperfectly, for the last 58 years. This, he said, could only set precedents resulting in 'a proliferation of the unilateral and lawless use of force'.

9.5 WHAT OTHER WORK IS THE UN RESPONSIBLE FOR?

Although it is the UN's role as peacekeeper and international mediator which most often gets into the headlines, the majority of its work is concerned with its less spectacular aims of safeguarding human rights and encouraging economic, social, educational and cultural progress throughout the world. There is only enough space in this book to look at a few examples.

(a) The Human Rights Commission

This works under the supervision of ECOSOC and tries to ensure that all governments treat their people in a civilized way. *A 30-point Universal Declaration of Human Rights* was adopted by the General Assembly in 1948; this means that every person, no matter what country he or she lives in, should have certain basic rights, *the most important of which are the rights to*:

- a standard of living high enough to keep him (or her) and his family in good health;
- be free from slavery, racial discrimination, arrest and imprisonment without trial, and torture;
- have a fair trial in public and to be presumed innocent until proved guilty;
- move about freely in his/her country and be able to leave the country;
- get married, have children, work, own property and vote in elections;
- have opinions and express them freely.

Later the Commission, concerned about the plight of children in many countries, produced *a Declaration of the Rights of the Child (1959). Foremost among the rights every child should be able to expect are*:

- adequate food and medical care;
- free education;
- adequate opportunity for relaxation and play (to guard against excessive child labour);
- protection from racial, religious and any other type of discrimination.

All member governments are expected to produce a report every three years on the state of human rights in their country. However, the problem for the UN is that many states do not produce the reports and they ignore the terms of the Declarations. When this happens, all the UN can do is publicize countries where the most flagrant violations of human rights take place, and hope that pressure of world opinion will influence the governments concerned. For example, the UN campaigned against *apartheid* in South Africa (see Section 25.8) and against General Pinochet's brutal treatment of political prisoners in Chile (see Section 8.4(c)). Mary Robinson (a former president of the Irish Republic), who was UN Commissioner for Human Rights from 1997 until 2002, worked hard to raise world awareness of the problems by naming and shaming guilty states. Unfortunately she made some powerful enemies by her outspoken criticism of their human rights records – among them Russia, China and the USA (all permanent members of the Security Council). Secretary-General Annan was pleased with her work and wanted her to serve another term as Commissioner. However, she was replaced by Sergio Vieira de Mello, and it was widely reported that her second term had been blocked by the USA.

(b)   The International Labour Organization (ILO)

The ILO operates from its headquarters in Geneva. *It works on the principles that*:

- every person is entitled to a job;
- there should be equal opportunities for everybody to get jobs, irrespective of race, sex or religion;
- there should be minimum standards of decent working conditions;
- workers should have the right to organize themselves into unions and other associations in order to negotiate for better conditions and pay (this is known as collective bargaining);
- there should be full social security provision for all workers (such as unemployment, health and maternity benefits).

The ILO does excellent work providing help for countries trying to improve working conditions, and it was awarded the Nobel Peace Prize in 1969. It sends experts out to demonstrate new equipment and techniques, sets up training centres in developing countries and runs the International Centre for Advanced Technology and Vocational Training in Turin (Italy), which provides vital high-level training for people from all over the Third World. Again though, the ILO, like the Human Rights Commission, is always faced with the problem of what to do when governments ignore the rules. For example, many governments, including those of communist countries, and of Latin American countries such as Chile, Argentina and Mexico, would not allow workers to organize trade unions.

(c)   The World Health Organization (WHO)

The WHO is one of the UN's most successful agencies. It aims to bring the world to a point where all its peoples are not just free of disease, but are 'at a high level of health'. One of its first jobs was to tackle a cholera epidemic in Egypt in 1947 which threatened to spread through Africa and the Middle East. Quick action by a UN team soon brought the epidemic under control and it was eliminated in a few weeks. The WHO now keeps a permanent cholera vaccine bank in case of further outbreaks, and wages a continual battle against other diseases such as malaria, tuberculosis and leprosy. The Organization provides money to train doctors, nurses and other health workers for developing countries, keeps governments informed about new drugs and provides free contraceptive pills for women in Third World countries.

One of its most striking achievements was to eliminate smallpox in the 1980s. At the same time it seemed well on the way towards eliminating malaria, but during the 1970s a new strain of malaria appeared which had developed a resistance to anti-malaria drugs. Research into new anti-malaria drugs became a WHO priority. In March 2000 it was reported that the problem of tuberculosis was growing worse – killing two million people every year.

The most serious world health problem in recent years has been the AIDS epidemic. The WHO has done excellent work collecting evidence and statistics, producing reports and putting pressure on pharmaceutical companies to reduce prices of drugs to treat the condition. In June 2001 the UN global AIDS fund was set up, which aimed to raise $10 billion a year to fight the disease (see Section 28.5 for more details about AIDS).

(d)   The Food and Agriculture Organization (FAO)

The FAO aims to raise living standards by encouraging improvements in agricultural production. It was responsible for introducing new varieties of maize and rice which have a higher yield and are less susceptible to disease. FAO experts show people in poor countries how to increase food production by the use of fertilizers, new techniques and new machinery, and cash is provided to fund new projects. Its main problem is having to deal with emergencies caused by drought, floods, civil war and other disasters, when food supplies need to be rushed into a country as quickly as possible. The Organization has done an excellent job, and there is no doubt that many more people would have died from starvation and malnutrition without its work.

(e)   The United Nations Educational, Scientific and Cultural Organization (UNESCO)

Operating from its headquarters in Paris, UNESCO does its best to encourage the spread of literacy; it also fosters international co-operation between scientists, scholars and artists in all fields, working on the theory that *the best way to avoid war is by educating people's minds in the pursuit of peace*. Much of its time and resources are spent setting up schools and teacher-training colleges in under-developed countries. Sometimes it becomes involved in one-off cultural and scientific projects. For example, it organized an International Hydrological Decade (1965–75), during which it helped to finance research into the problem of world water resources. After the 1968 floods in Florence, UNESCO played an important part in repairing and restoring damaged art treasures and historic buildings. During the 1980s UNESCO came under criticism from western powers which claimed that it was becoming too politically motivated (see Section 9.6(c)).

(f)   The United Nations Children's Emergency Fund (UNICEF)

UNICEF was founded originally in 1946 to help children left homeless by the Second World War. It dealt with this problem so efficiently that it was decided to make it a permanent agency and the word 'emergency' was dropped from its title (1953). Its new function was *to help improve the health and living standards of children all over the world, especially in poorer countries*. It works closely with the WHO, setting up health centres, training health workers and running health education and sanitation schemes. In spite of these efforts it was still a horrifying fact that in 1983, 15 million children died under the age of 5, a figure equivalent to the combined under-5 population of Britain, France, Italy, Spain and West Germany. In that year UNICEF launched its 'child health revolution' campaign, which was designed to reduce the child death rate by simple methods such as encouraging breastfeeding (which is more hygienic than bottle-feeding) and immunizing babies against common diseases such as measles, diphtheria, polio and tetanus.

(g)   The United Nations Relief and Works Agency (UNRWA)

This agency was set up in 1950 to deal with the problem of Arab refugees from Palestine who were forced to leave their homes when Palestine was divided up to form the new state of Israel (see Section 11.2). UNRWA did a remarkable job providing basic food, clothing, shelter and medical supplies. Later, as it became clear that the refugee camps were going to be permanent, it began to build schools, hospitals, houses and training centres to enable refugees to get jobs and make the camps self-supporting.

(h)   Financial and economic agencies

1   The International Monetary Fund (IMF)
The IMF is designed to foster co-operation between nations in order to encourage the growth of trade and the full development of nations' economic potential. It allows short-term loans to countries in financial difficulties, provided that their economic policies meet with the IMF's approval and that they are prepared to change policies if the IMF thinks it necessary. By the mid-1970s many Third World nations were heavily in debt (see Section 27.2), and in 1977 the IMF set up an emergency fund. However, there was a great deal of resentment among the poorer nations when the IMF Board of Governors (dominated by the rich western countries, especially the USA, which provide most of the cash) began to attach conditions to the loans. Jamaica and Tanzania, for example, were required to change their socialist policies before loans were allowed. This was seen by many as unacceptable interference in the internal affairs of member states.

2   The International Bank for Reconstruction and Development (the World Bank)
This provides loans for specific development projects, such as building dams to generate electricity, and introducing new agricultural techniques and family planning campaigns. Again though, the USA, which provides the largest share of the cash for the bank, controls its decisions. When Poland and Czechoslovakia applied for loans, they were both refused because they were communist states. Both of them resigned from the Bank and from the IMF in disgust, Poland in 1950 and Czechoslovakia in 1954.

3   The General Agreement on Tariffs and Trade (GATT)
This agreement was first signed in 1947 when member states of the UN agreed to reduce some of their tariffs (taxes on imports) in order to encourage international trade. Members continue to meet, under the supervision of ECOSOC, to try and keep tariffs as low as possible throughout the world. In January 1995 the GATT became the World Trade Organization (WTO). Its aim was to liberalize and monitor world trade and to resolve trade disputes.

4   The United Nations Conference on Trade and Development (UNCTAD)
The conference first met in 1964 and soon became a permanent body. Its role is to encourage the development of industry in the Third World and to pressurize rich countries into buying Third World products.

(i)   The Office for the Coordination of Humanitarian Affairs (OCHA)

This began life originally as the Department of Humanitarian Affairs, set up in 1991 to enable the UN to respond more effectively to natural disasters and 'complex emergencies' (the UN phrase for human disasters caused by wars and other political events). Its functions were expanded in 1998 to include the co-ordination of responses to all humanitarian disasters and projects for human development; at the same time it assumed its present title OCHA. It had a staff of some 860 members, some based in New York, some in Geneva and some working in the field.

Much valuable relief work was done in a whole series of crisis situations caused by earthquakes, hurricanes and floods; help was mainly needed in poor countries with less developed infrastructures and high population densities. UN statistics suggested that in 2003 alone, some 200 million victims of natural disasters and 45 million victims of 'complex emergencies' received aid, either supplied directly or organized by the UN. However, a recurring criticism of the UN's role was that it lacked the power and the resources to operate as effectively as it might.

The greatest challenge to OCHA came at the beginning of 2005 in what became known as the tsunami disaster. On Boxing Day 2004, two huge earthquakes occurred in the Indian Ocean, triggering off a series of massive tidal waves known as *tsunami.* No effective warning system existed, and within hours the tsunami were battering the shores of many countries around the Indian Ocean, including Indonesia, India, the Maldive Islands, Sri Lanka, Thailand, Malaysia and even Somalia on the east coast of Africa. It soon became apparent that this was a catastrophe of the highest magnitude; at least 150 000 people were killed and thousands more were missing. Worst affected were Indonesia, Sri Lanka and Thailand, where, in some coastal areas, entire towns and villages had been destroyed. A massive and complex relief operation was needed immediately, but the problems to be faced were overwhelming.

The response from around the world was heartening: ordinary people gave unstintingly to the appeals for money; foreign governments promised enormous amounts of cash; 11 states sent troops, ships and aircraft; over 400 non-government agencies and charities such as Christian Aid, the Red Cross, Red Crescent, the Salvation Army, Oxfam and Médecins sans Frontières got involved within a few days. An Oxfam spokesman said that the UN was doing as good a job as anybody could reasonably expect in the horrific circumstances, and that they were grateful for the plain-speaking leadership of Mr Jan Egeland, the UN Emergency Relief Coordinator, and of Secretary-General Kofi Annan. But there was a long-term operation ahead: after saving tens of thousands of people from death by starvation and disease, the next step was to rebuild communities and restore infrastructures.

9.6   VERDICT ON THE UNITED NATIONS ORGANIZATION

The UN has been in existence for well over half a century, but it is still nowhere near achieving its basic aims. The world is still full of economic and social problems; acts of aggression and wars continue. *The UN's failures were caused to some extent by weaknesses in its system.*

(a)   The lack of a permanent UN army

This means that it is difficult to prevail upon powerful states to accept its decisions if they choose to put self-interest first. If persuasion and the pressure of world opinion fail, the UN has to rely on member nations to provide troops to enable it to enforce decisions. For example, the USSR was able to ignore UN demands for the withdrawal of Russian troops from Hungary (1956) and Afghanistan (1980). UN involvement in Somalia (1992–5) and Bosnia (1992–5) showed the impossibility of the UN being able to stop a war when the warring parties were not ready to stop fighting. The USA and Britain were determined to attack Iraq in 2003 without UN authorization, and the UN could do nothing about it, especially now that the USA was the world's only superpower – by far the most powerful state in the world.

(b) When should the UN become involved?

There is a problem about exactly when the UN should become involved during the course of a dispute. Sometimes it hangs back too long, so that the problem becomes more difficult to solve; sometimes it hesitates so long that it scarcely becomes involved at all; this happened with the war in Vietnam (see Section 8.3) and the war in Angola (see Section 25.6). This left the UN open to accusations of indecision and lack of firmness. It caused some states to put more faith in their own regional organizations such as NATO for keeping the peace, and many agreements were worked out without involving the UN; for example, the end of the Vietnam War, the Camp David peace between Israel and Egypt in 1979 (see Section 11.6) and the settlement of the Rhodesia/Zimbabwe problem in the same year (see Section 24.4(c)).

At this time, critics were claiming that the UN was becoming irrelevant and was no more than an arena for propaganda speeches. Part of the problem was that the Security Council was hampered by the veto which its permanent members could use. Although the 'Uniting for Peace' resolution could offset this to some extent, the veto could still cause long delays before decisive action was taken. If a potential aggressor knew that his forces would be met by a UN armed force, equipped and mandated to fight, this would be a powerful disincentive; for example if a UN force had been deployed on the Kuwait side of the Iraqi–Kuwait frontier in 1990, or on the Croatian side of the Serbia–Croatia border in 1991, hostilities might well have been prevented from breaking out.

(c) The increasing membership of the UN from the 1970s

The increasing membership of the UN during the 1970s brought new problems. By 1970 members from the Third World (Africa and Asia) were in a clear majority. As these nations began to work more and more together, it meant that only they could be certain of having their resolutions passed, and it became increasingly difficult for both Western and Communist blocs to get their resolutions through the General Assembly. The western nations could no longer have things all their own way and they began to criticize the Third World bloc for being too 'political'; by this, they meant acting in a way the West disapproved of. For example, in 1974 UNESCO passed resolutions condemning 'colonialism' and 'imperialism'. In 1979 when the Western bloc introduced a General Assembly motion condemning terrorism, it was defeated by the Arab states and their supporters.

Friction reached crisis point in 1983 at the UNESCO General Congress. Many western nations, including the USA, accused UNESCO of being inefficient and wasteful and of having unacceptable political aims. What brought matters to a head was a proposal by some communist states for the internal licensing of foreign journalists. According to the USA, this would lead to a situation in which member states could exercise an effective censorship of each other's media organizations. Consequently the Americans announced that they would withdraw from UNESCO on 1 January 1985, since it had become 'hostile to the basic institutions of a free society, especially a free market and a free press'. Britain and Singapore withdrew in 1986 for similar reasons. Britain rejoined in 1997 and the USA followed in 2002.

(d)   There is a waste of effort and resources among the agencies

Some of the agencies sometimes seem to duplicate each other's work. Critics claim that the WHO and the FAO overlap too much. The FAO was criticized in 1984 for spending too much on administration and not enough on improving agricultural systems. GATT and UNCTAD even seem to be working against each other: GATT tries to eliminate tariffs and anything else that restricts trade, whereas UNCTAD tries to get preferential treatment for the products of Third World countries.

(e)   Shortage of funds

Throughout its history the UN has always been short of funds. The vast scope of its work means that it needs incredibly large sums of money to finance its operations. It is entirely dependent on contributions from member states. Each state pays a regular annual contribution based on its general wealth and ability to pay. In addition, members pay a proportion of the cost of each peacekeeping operation, and they are also expected to contribute towards the expenses of the special agencies. *Many member states refused to pay* from time to time, either because of financial difficulties of their own, or as a mark of disapproval of UN policies; 1986 was a bad year financially: no fewer than 98 of its members owed money, chief among them being the USA, which withheld more than $100 million until the UN reformed its budgeting system and curbed its extravagance. The Americans wanted the countries that gave most to have more say in how the money was spent, but most smaller members rejected this as undemocratic. As one of Sri Lanka's delegates put it: 'in our political processes at home, the wealthy do not have more votes than the poor. We should like this to be the practice in the UN as well.'

In 1987 changes were introduced giving the main financial contributors more control over spending, and the financial situation soon improved. However, expenses soared alarmingly in the early 1990s as the UN became involved in a series of new crises, in the Middle East (Gulf War), Yugoslavia and Somalia. In August 1993 the Secretary-General, Dr Boutros-Ghali, revealed that many states were well in arrears with their payments. He warned that unless there was an immediate injection of cash from the world's rich states, all the UN's peacekeeping operations would be in jeopardy. Yet the Americans and Europeans felt that they already paid too much – the USA (with about 30 per cent), the European Community (about 35 per cent) and Japan (11 per cent) paid three-quarters of the expenses, and there was a feeling that there were many other wealthy states which could afford to contribute much more than they were doing.

In spite of all these criticisms, it would be wrong to write the UN off as a failure, and there can be no doubt that the world would be a far worse place without it.

- It provides a world assembly where representatives of around 190 nations can come together and talk to each other. Even the smallest nation has a chance to make itself heard in a world forum.
- Although it has not prevented wars, it has been successful in bringing some wars to an end more quickly, and has prevented further conflict. A great deal of human suffering and bloodshed have been prevented by the actions of the UN peacekeeping forces and refugee agencies. At the present time (2012) there are around 85 000 UN peacekeepers in action across the world.

- The UN has done valuable work investigating and publicizing human rights violations under repressive regimes like the military governments of Chile and Zaire. In this way it has slowly been able to influence governments by bringing international pressure to bear on them.
- Perhaps its most important achievement has been to stimulate international co-operation on economic, social and technical matters. Millions of people, especially in poorer countries, are better off thanks to the work of the UN agencies. It continues to involve itself in current problems: UNESCO, the ILO and the WHO are running a joint project to help drug addicts and there has been a series of 15 conferences on AIDS in an attempt to co-ordinate the struggle against this terrible scourge, particularly in Africa (see Section 28.4).

9.7 WHAT ABOUT THE FUTURE OF THE UN?

Many people thought that with the end of the Cold War, most of the world's problems would disappear. In fact, this did not happen; during the 1990s there seemed to be more conflicts than ever before, and the world seemed to be less and less stable. Obviously there was still a vitally important role for the UN to play as international peacekeeper, and many people were anxious for the UN to reform and strengthen itself.

Kofi Annan, who became Secretary-General in December 1996, had gained an excellent reputation over the previous few years as head of UN peacekeeping operations. He was well aware of the organization's weaknesses and was determined to do something about them. He ordered a thorough review of all UN peace operations; the resulting report, published in 2000, recommended, among other things, that the UN should maintain permanent brigade-size forces of 5000 troops, which would be ready for immediate deployment, commanded by military professionals. The spread of terrorism, especially with the September 2001 attacks on New York, prompted Annan, now in his second term as Secretary-General, to produce his *Agenda for Further Change* (September 2002). This was a plan for reforms to strengthen the UN's role in fighting terrorism, and it included a much-needed streamlining of the cumbersome budget system. These things take time, but none of the suggested reforms is beyond the bounds of possibility.

The really serious problem, which had been brewing ever since the end of the Cold War and the emergence of the USA as sole superpower, was about the future relationship between the UN and the USA. Tensions began to mount as soon as the Bush administration took office in 2001: within its first year the new government rejected the 1972 Anti-Ballistic Missile Treaty, the 1997 Kyoto Protocol (which aimed to limit the emission of greenhouse gases) and the Rome Statute of the new UN International Criminal Court, as well as Security Council offers of a resolution authorizing a war against terrorism (this was because it prefers to conduct its own self-defence in whatever way it chooses). Tensions reached a climax in March 2003, when the US government, aided and abetted by the UK, decided to attack Iraq, *without UN authorization and against the wishes of the majority of UN members*. The USA was so disproportionately powerful that it could ignore the UN and act as it pleased unless the UN delivered the outcome it wanted.

An important American technique in its quest to control the UN was to secure the appointment of a sympathetic Secretary-General. A prime example was Kofi Annan, Secretary-General from 1996 until 2006, who whole heartedly supported the American line on every major UN involvement except one – Iraq. In a book published in November 2006 to mark the end of Annan's two terms as Secretary-General, James Traub chronicles his rise to the top. Since 1993 Annan had been in charge of all UN peacekeeping operations under Secretary-General Boutros-Ghali. However, Dr Boutros-Ghali had displeased Washington by refusing to send a UN mission into Somalia and delaying the NATO bombing of Serbia. In both cases Annan had supported the American line. In 1996 all the signs were that Boutros-Ghali would have his mandate extended for another five years. But President Clinton was determined to get rid of him; it was relentless pressure from the Clinton administration that got Kofi Annan chosen instead of Boutros-Ghali. Consequently when NATO launched its bombing attack on Yugoslavia early in 1999, instead of condemning it as a blatant violation of the UN Charter – which it most certainly was – Annan announced that it was a legitimate action.

However, the attack on Iraq in 2003 (see Section 12.4) was more difficult for Annan. When the joint US and British operation against Iraq was launched without a second Security Council Resolution authorizing the attack, Annan was eventually forced to admit that the invasion had been illegal. When he was asked in a BBC interview, 'Are you bothered that the US is becoming an unrestrainable, unilateral superpower?' he replied: 'I think in the end everybody is concluding that it is best to work together with our allies.' That innocent remark sums up the whole situation: the challenge for the UN over the coming years is to find a way to harness and make use of the power and influence of the USA instead of being impeded or stampeded by it.

FURTHER READING

Bailey, S., *The United Nations* (Macmillan, 1989).
Meisler, S., *United Nations: The First Fifty Years* (Atlantic Monthly Press, 1997).
Meisler, S., *Kofi Annan: A Man of Peace in a World of War* (Wiley, 2007).
Mingst, K. A. and Karns, M. P., *The United Nations in the Post-Cold War Era* (Westview Press, 2000).
Roberts, A. and Kingsbury, B., *United Nations, Divided World* (Oxford University Press, 1993).
Traub, J., *The Best Intentions: Kofi Annan and the UN in the Era of American World Power* (Bloomsbury, 2006).

QUESTIONS

1 'There can be little doubt that the social, economic and humanitarian work of the UN has been far more successful and valuable than its peacekeeping role.' Assess the validity of this verdict on the work of the United Nations Organization.
2 'The UN has only been successful in resolving conflict when one of the superpowers has intervened to support it.' How far would you agree with this view?
3 To what extent would it be true to say that the UN has been more successful in dealing with conflicts since 1990 than it was during the Cold War?

There is a document question about the UN and the 1956 crisis in Hungary on the website.

Chapter

10

The two Europes, East and West since 1945

SUMMARY OF EVENTS

At the end of the Second World War in 1945, Europe was in turmoil. Many areas, especially in Germany, Italy, Poland and the western parts of the USSR, had been devastated, and even the victorious powers, Britain and the USSR, were in serious financial difficulties because of the expense of the war. There was a huge job of reconstruction to be done, and many people thought that the best way to go about this was by a joint effort. Some even thought in terms of a united Europe, rather like the United States of America, in which the European states would come together under a federal system of government. However, Europe soon split into two over the American Marshall Plan to promote recovery in Europe (see Section 7.2(e)). The nations of western Europe gladly made use of American aid, but the USSR refused to allow the countries of eastern Europe to accept it, for fear that their own control over the area would be undermined. From 1947 onwards the two parts of Europe developed separately, kept apart by Joseph Stalin's 'iron curtain'.

The states of western Europe recovered surprisingly quickly from the effects of the war, thanks to a combination of American aid, an increase in the world demand for European products, rapid technological advances and careful planning by governments. Some moves took place towards unity, including the setting up of NATO and the Council of Europe (both in 1949), and the European Economic Community (EEC) in 1957. In Britain, enthusiasm for this type of unity developed more slowly than in other countries for fear that it would threaten British sovereignty. The British decided not to join the EEC when it was first set up in 1957; when they changed their minds in 1961, the French vetoed their entry, and it was 1972 before it was finally agreed that Britain could become a member.

Meanwhile the communist states of eastern Europe had to be content to be satellites of the USSR. They, too, moved towards a sort of economic and political unity with the introduction of the Molotov Plan (1947), the formation of the Council for Mutual Economic Assistance (COMECON) in 1949 and the Warsaw Pact (1955). Until his death in 1953 Stalin tried to make all these states as much like the USSR as possible, but after 1953 they began to show more independence. Yugoslavia under Tito had already developed a more decentralized system in which the communes were an important element. Poland and Romania successfully introduced variations, but the Hungarians (1956) and the Czechs (1968) went too far and found themselves invaded by Soviet troops and brought to heel. During the 1970s the states of eastern Europe enjoyed a period of comparative prosperity, but in the 1980s they felt the effects of world depression.

Dissatisfaction with the communist system began to grow; in a short period from mid-1988 until the end of 1991, communism collapsed in the USSR and in all the states of eastern Europe except Albania, where it survived until March 1992. Germany, which had been divided into two separate states, one communist and one non-communist, since soon after the war (see Section 7.2(h)), was reunified (October 1990), becoming once again the most powerful state in Europe. With the end of communism, Yugoslavia sadly disintegrated into a long civil war (1991–5).

In the west the European Community, which from 1992 was known as the European Union, continued to function successfully. Many of the former communist states began to apply to join the Union; in 2004 there were 25 members, and in 2007 the total reached 27 with the addition of Bulgaria and Romania. But the enlargement brought its own problems.

10.1 THE STATES OF WESTERN EUROPE

Shortage of space allows only a brief look at the three most influential states in mainland Europe.

(a) France

Under the Fourth Republic (1946–58) France was politically weak, and though her industry was modernized and flourishing, agriculture seemed to be stagnating. Governments were weak because the new constitution gave the president very little power. There were five major parties and this meant that governments were coalitions, which were constantly changing: in the 12 years of the Fourth Republic there were 25 different governments, which were mostly too weak to rule effectively. There were a number of disasters:

- French defeat in Indo-China (1954) (see Section 8.3(a));
- failure in Suez (1956) (see Section 11.3);
- rebellion in Algeria, which brought the government down in 1958.

General de Gaulle came out of retirement to lead the country; he introduced a new constitution giving the president more power (which became the basis of the Fifth Republic), and gave Algeria independence. With the Cold War continuing, De Gaulle successfully demonstrated that France was a strong, independent power, not a weak country in decline. He built France's own nuclear deterrent, withdrew French forces from NATO command, condemned the USA's war in Vietnam, criticized Israeli behaviour in the Middle East and vetoed Britain's entry into the Common Market. De Gaulle retired in 1969 after a wave of strikes and demonstrations protesting against, among other things, the authoritarian and undemocratic nature of the regime.

The Fifth Republic continued to provide stable government under the next two presidents, both right-wingers – Georges Pompidou (1969–74) and Valéry Giscard d'Estaing (1974–81). François Mitterand, the socialist leader, had a long period as president, from 1981 until 1995, when Jacques Chirac of the right-wing RPR (Rassemblement pour la République) was elected president for the next seven years. The dominant issues in France in the 1990s were the continuing recession and unemployment, doubts about France's role in the European Community (there was only a very small majority in September 1992 in favour of the Maastricht Treaty (see Section 10. 4(h)) and uneasiness about the reunified Germany. When Chirac's new prime minister, Alain Juppé, began cutbacks to get the French economy into shape for the introduction of the euro – the new European currency – which was due to take place in 2002, there were widespread protest demonstrations and strikes (December 1995).

It was no surprise when there was a swing towards the left in the parliamentary elections of May 1997. Chirac's conservative coalition lost its majority in parliament, and the socialist leader, Lionel Jospin, became prime minister. His policies were designed to reduce the budget deficit to no more than 3 per cent of GDP (Gross Domestic Product), as required by the European Community for entry into the new currency. They failed to arouse much enthusiasm; in the presidential elections of 2002, the general apathy of the voters allowed Jospin to be beaten into third place, leaving Chirac and the right-wing nationalist, Jean-Marie le Pen, to fight it out in the run-off. Chirac won easily, taking 80 per cent of the votes, but his second term as president (2002–7) was not a success. In a referendum held early in 2005, the electorate overwhelmingly rejected proposals for a new European Constitution, in spite of the government's wall-to-wall campaign in its favour. Later in the year there was a wave of riots in poorer areas of cities throughout the country protesting against the high level of youth unemployment. This was followed by a series of strikes and demonstrations against a new government policy designed to enable employers to take on young workers on a temporary basis instead of giving them job security. After two months of chaos, Chirac was forced to drop the plan. As the presidential election of 2007 approached, the Socialist Party was looking forward to victory.

However, unexpectedly, the Socialist candidate, Ségolène Royal, was heavily defeated by the Centre-Right candidate, Nicolas Sarkozy. Inexperienced in front-line politics, Royal fought a lacklustre campaign, while Sarkozy impressed the electorate with promises of greater security on the streets, tough policies on crime and immigration and a clean break from the Chirac era in order to reverse the increasingly obvious national decline. Unfortunately, from the autumn of 2008, the Sarkozy presidency was dominated by the aftermath of the great financial collapse in the USA, which plunged the whole EU into an ongoing economic crisis (see Section 27.7). The presidential election of 2012 was won by the socialist candidate, François Hollande.

(b) The German Federal Republic (West Germany)

Set up in 1949, the German Federal Republic enjoyed a remarkable recovery – an 'economic miracle' – under the conservative government of Chancellor Konrad Adenauer (1949–63). It was achieved partly thanks to the Marshall Plan, which brought substantial American investment into the country. This enabled the rebuilding of German industry to accelerate and provided funds for the installation of the latest up-to-date plant and equipment. The government encouraged the ploughing back of profits into industry rather than distributing them as higher dividends or higher wages (which happened in Britain). Taxation was reduced, which meant that people had more money to spend on manufactured goods; rationing and other controls were either reduced or removed altogether. Events abroad contributed to the German recovery; for example, the war in Korea (1950–1) produced a demand for exactly the type of high-quality goods that the Germans were so good at producing. Industrial recovery was so complete that by 1960 West Germany was producing 50 per cent more steel than the united Germany in 1938, and unemployment was less than a quarter of a million. The German people themselves must take much of the credit for their determination and ingenuity that enabled their country not only to recover from the catastrophe of military defeat, but also to enjoy arguably the most successful economy in Europe. All classes shared in the prosperity; pensions and children's allowances were geared to the cost of living, and 10 million new dwellings were provided.

The new constitution encouraged the trend towards a two-party system, which meant there was a better chance of strong government. The two major parties were:

- the Christian Democrats (CDU) – Adenauer's conservative party;
- the Social Democrats (SDP) – a moderate socialist party.

There was a smaller liberal party – the Free Democratic Party (FDP). In 1979 the Green Party was founded, with a programme based on ecological and environmental issues.

Adenauer's CDU successors, Ludwig Erhard (1963–6) and Kurt Georg Kiesinger (1966–9), continued the good work, though there were some setbacks and a rise in unemployment. This caused support to swing to the SDP, who stayed in power, with FDP support, for 13 years, first under Willi Brandt (1969–74) and then under Helmut Schmidt (1974–82). After the prosperous 1970s, West Germany began to suffer increasingly from the world recession. By 1982 unemployment had shot up to 2 million; when Schmidt proposed increasing spending to stimulate the economy, the more cautious FDP withdrew support and Schmidt was forced to resign (October 1982). A new right-wing coalition of the CDU and the Bavarian Christian Social Union (CSU) was formed, with FDP support, and the CDU leader, Helmut Kohl, became Chancellor. Recovery soon came – statistics for 1985 showed a healthy economic growth rate of 2.5 per cent and a big export boom. By 1988 the boom was over and unemployment rose to 2.3 million. However, Kohl managed to hold on to power, and had the distinction of becoming the first Chancellor of the reunified Germany in October 1990 (see Section 10.6(e)).

Reunification brought enormous problems for Germany – the cost of modernizing the east and bringing its economy up to western standards placed a big strain on the country. Billions of Deutschmarks were poured in and the process of privatizing state industries was begun. Kohl had promised to revive the east without raising taxes, and to make sure that 'nobody after unification will be worse off'. Neither of these pledges proved to be possible: there were tax increases and cuts in government spending. The economy stagnated, unemployment rose and the process of revival took much longer than anybody had anticipated. After 16 years the voters at last turned against Kohl; in 1998 the SDP leader Gerhard Schröder became chancellor.

The economy remained the greatest challenge facing the new chancellor. The government failed to improve the situation significantly, and Schröder was only narrowly re-elected in 2002. In the summer of 2003 unemployment reached 4.4 million – 10.6 per cent of the registered workforce. At the end of the year the budget deficit exceeded the 3 per cent ceiling for participation in the euro. France had the same problem. Both states were let off with a warning, but the situation did not bode well. Germany's finance minister admitted that the target of balancing the budget by 2006 could not be achieved without another 'economic miracle'.

In the elections of 2005 the CDU/CSU group won a very narrow victory, but lacking a majority in the Bundestag, had to form a coalition with its ally, the FDP, and the main opposition party, the SPD. Schröder stepped down and Angela Merkel, the CDU leader and a politician from the former East Germany, became the first woman Chancellor. There was an economic upswing in the period 2006–7, unemployment fell, and the resulting increase in tax revenues helped to absorb some of the budget deficit. And then came the great crash of 2008, which soon plunged Germany once again into a deep recession. In the elections of September 2009 the SPD suffered its worst ever performance and was forced to drop out of the coalition. The FDP increased its vote significantly and this enabled Merkel to continue as Chancellor. Observers attributed her popularity to her unpretentious manner, her fairness and her common-sense approach. It was obvious that she could not be held responsible for the economic crisis and she seemed to be the leader most likely to restore stability. In office she had been much more moderate than in opposition, when she had taken a tough right-wing stance, criticizing, among other things, excessive welfare dependence. In fact there seemed little to choose between her and Schröder.

(c) Italy

The new Republic of Italy began with a period of prosperity and stable government under de Gasperi (1946–53), but then many of the old problems of the pre-Mussolini era reappeared:

with at least seven major parties, ranging from communists on the left to the neo-fascists on the far right, it was impossible for one party to win a majority in parliament. The two main parties were:

- the communists (PCI);
- the Christian Democrats (DC).

The Christian Democrats were the dominant party of government, but they were constantly dependent on alliances with smaller parties of the centre and left. There was a series of weak coalition governments, which failed to solve the problems of inflation and unemployment. One of the more successful politicians was the socialist Bettino Craxi, who was prime minister from 1983 to 1987; during this time both inflation and unemployment were reduced. But as Italy moved into the 1990s the basic problems were still the same.

- There was a north–south divide: the north, with its modern, competitive industry, was relatively prosperous, while in the south, Calabria, Sicily and Sardinia were backward, with a much lower standard of living and higher unemployment.
- The Mafia was still a powerful force, now heavily involved in drug dealing, and it seemed to be getting stronger in the north. Two judges who had been trying Mafia cases were assassinated (1992), and it seemed as though crime was out of control.
- Politics seemed to be riddled with corruption, with many leading politicians under suspicion. Even highly respected leaders like Craxi were shown to have been involved in corrupt dealings (1993), while another, Giulio Andreotti, seven times prime minister, was arrested and charged with working for the Mafia (1995).
- There was a huge government debt and a weak currency. In September 1992, Italy, along with Britain, was forced to withdraw from the Exchange Rate Mechanism and devalue the lira.

Politically, the situation changed radically in the early 1990s, with the collapse of communism in eastern Europe. The PCI changed its name to the Democratic Party of the Left (PDS), while the DC broke up. Its main successor was the Popular Party (PPI). The centre-ground shrank and there was an increasing polarization between left and right. As the 1990s progressed, attention focused on several issues: the campaign for electoral reform (several attempts at which failed), concern at the escalating number of illegal immigrants (who, it was alleged, were being smuggled in by Mafia groups) and the drive to get the economy healthy enough to join the euro in 2002.

May 2001 saw a general election which brought to an end over six years of centre-left governments. Silvio Berlusconi, a media magnate reputed to be the richest man in Italy, was elected prime minister of a right-wing coalition. He promised to deliver, over the next five years, lower taxes, a million new jobs, higher pensions and better amenities. He was a colourful and controversial leader who was soon facing accusations of bribery and various other financial misdemeanours. There seemed to be some doubt as to whether he would be able to complete his term as prime minister, but these were dispelled when his government passed legislation which, in effect, granted him immunity from prosecution while he was in office. With a short interval during which the socialist Romano Prodi was prime minister (2006–8), he survived in office until November 2011. However, things started to go badly wrong soon after he returned to power in 2008. The economy was showing increasing signs of strain – there was hardly any growth at all and there was a huge national debt of €1.5 trillion. As the eurozone crisis deepened, Berlusconi lost his majority in parliament and resigned.

(a) Reasons for wanting more unity

In every country in western Europe there were people who wanted more unity. They had different ideas about exactly what sort of unity would be best: some simply wanted the nations to co-operate more closely; others (known as 'federalists') wanted to go the whole hog and have a federal system of government like the one in the USA. The reasons behind this thinking were:

- The best way for Europe to recover from the ravages of war was for all the states to work together and help each other by pooling their resources.
- The individual states were too small and their economies too weak for them to be economically and militarily viable separately in a world now dominated by the superpowers, the USA and the USSR.
- The more the countries of western Europe worked together, the less chance there would be of war breaking out between them again. It was the best way for a speedy reconciliation between France and Germany.
- Joint action would enable western Europe more effectively to resist the spread of communism from the USSR.
- The Germans were especially keen on the idea because they thought it would help them to gain acceptance as a responsible nation more quickly than after the First World War. Then, Germany had been made to wait eight years before being allowed to join the League of Nations.
- The French thought that greater unity would enable them to influence German policies and remove long-standing worries about security.

Winston Churchill was one of the strongest advocates of a united Europe. In March 1943 he spoke of the need for a Council of Europe, and in a speech in Zurich in 1946 he suggested that France and West Germany should take the lead in setting up 'a kind of United States of Europe'.

(b) First steps in co-operation

The first steps in economic, military and political co-operation were soon taken, though the federalists were bitterly disappointed that a United States of Europe had not materialized by 1950.

1 The Organization for European Economic Co-operation (OEEC)
This was set up officially in 1948, and was the first initiative towards economic unity. It began as a response to the American offer of Marshall Aid, when Ernest Bevin, the British Foreign Secretary, took the lead in organizing 16 European nations (see Section 7.2(e)) to draw up a plan for the best use of American aid. This was known as the European Recovery Programme (ERP). The committee of 16 nations became the permanent OEEC. Its first function, successfully achieved over the next four years, was to apportion American aid among its members, after which it went on, again with great success, to encourage trade among its members by reducing restrictions. It was helped by the United Nations General Agreement on Tariffs and Trade (GATT), whose function was to reduce tariffs, and by the European Payments Union (EPU): this encouraged trade by improving the system of payments between member states, so that each state could use its own

currency. The OEEC was so successful that trade between its members doubled during the first six years. When the USA and Canada joined in 1961 it became the Organization for Economic Co-operation and Development (OECD). Later, Australia and Japan joined.

2   The North Atlantic Treaty Organization (NATO)

NATO was created in 1949 (see Section 7.2(i) for a list of founder members) as a mutual defence system in case of an attack on one of the member states. In most people's minds, the USSR was the most likely source of any attack. NATO was not just a European organization – it also included the USA and Canada. The Korean War (1950–3) caused the USA to press successfully for the integration of NATO forces under a centralized command; a Supreme Headquarters Allied Powers Europe (SHAPE) was established near Paris, and an American general, Dwight D. Eisenhower, was made Supreme Commander of all NATO forces. Until the end of 1955, NATO seemed to be developing impressively: the forces available for the defence of Western Europe had been increased fourfold, and it was claimed by some that NATO had deterred the USSR from attacking West Germany. However, problems soon arose: the French were not happy about the dominant American role; in 1966 President de Gaulle withdrew France from NATO, so that French forces and French nuclear policy would not be controlled by a foreigner. Compared with the communist Warsaw Pact, NATO was weak: with 60 divisions of troops in 1980, it fell far short of its target of 96 divisions, whereas the Communist bloc could boast 102 divisions and three times as many tanks as NATO.

3   The Council of Europe

Set up in 1949, this was the first attempt at some sort of political unity. Its founder members were Britain, Belgium, the Netherlands, Luxembourg, Denmark, France, Eire, Italy, Norway and Sweden. By 1971 all the states of western Europe (except Spain and Portugal) had joined, and so had Turkey, Malta and Cyprus, making 18 members in all. Based at Strasbourg, it consisted of the foreign ministers of the member states, and an Assembly of representatives chosen by the parliaments of the states. It had no powers, however, since several states, including Britain, refused to join any organization which threatened their own sovereignty. It could debate pressing issues and make recommendations, and it achieved useful work sponsoring human rights agreements; but it was a grave disappointment to the federalists.

10.3   THE EARLY DAYS OF THE EUROPEAN COMMUNITY

Known in its early years as the European Economic Community (EEC) or the Common Market, the Community was officially set up under the terms of the Treaty of Rome (1957), signed by the six founder members – France, West Germany, Italy, the Netherlands, Belgium and Luxembourg.

(a)   Stages in the evolution of the Community

1   Benelux

In 1944 the governments of Belgium, the Netherlands and Luxembourg, meeting in exile in London because their countries were occupied by the Germans, began to plan for when the war was over. They agreed to set up the Benelux Customs Union, in which there would be no tariffs or other customs barriers, so that trade could flow freely. The driving force behind it was Paul-Henri Spaak, the Belgian socialist leader who was prime minister of Belgium from 1947 to 1949; it was put into operation in 1947.

2 The Treaty of Brussels (1948)

By this treaty, Britain and France joined the three Benelux countries in pledging 'military, economic, social and cultural collaboration'. While the military collaboration eventually resulted in NATO, the next step in economic co-operation was the ECSC.

3 The European Coal and Steel Community (ECSC)

The ECSC was set up in 1951, and was the brainchild of Robert Schuman, who was France's Foreign Minister from 1948 to 1953. Like Spaak, he was strongly in favour of international co-operation, and he hoped that involving West Germany would improve relations between France and Germany and at the same time make European industry more efficient. Six countries joined: France, West Germany, Italy, Belgium, the Netherlands and Luxembourg.

All duties and restrictions on trade in coal, iron and steel between the six were removed, and a High Authority was created to run the community and to organize a joint programme of expansion. However, the British refused to join because they believed it would mean handing over control of their industries to an outside authority. The ECSC was such an outstanding success, even without Britain (steel production rose by almost 50 per cent during the first five years), that the six decided to extend it to include production of all goods.

4 The EEC

Again it was Spaak, now foreign minister of Belgium, who was one of the main driving forces. The agreements setting up the full EEC were signed in Rome in 1957 and they came into operation on 1 January 1958. The six countries would gradually remove all customs duties and quotas so that there would be free competition and a common market. Tariffs would be kept against non-members, but even these were reduced. The treaty also mentioned improving living and working conditions, expanding industry, encouraging the development of the world's backward areas, safeguarding peace and liberty, and working for a closer union of European peoples. Clearly something much wider than just a common market was in the minds of some of the people involved; for example, Jean Monnet, a French economist who was Chairman of the ECSC High Authority, set up an action committee to work for a United States of Europe. Like the ECSC, the EEC was soon off to a flying start; within five years it was the world's biggest exporter and biggest buyer of raw materials and was second only to the USA in steel production. Once again, however, Britain had decided not to join.

(b) The machinery of the European Community

- *The European Commission* was the body which ran the day-to-day work of the Community. Based in Brussels, it was staffed by civil servants and expert economists, who took the important policy decisions. It had strong powers so that it would be able to stand up against possible criticism and opposition from the governments of the six members, though in theory its decisions had to be approved by the Council of Ministers.
- *The Council of Ministers* consisted of government representatives from each of the member states. Their job was to exchange information about their governments' economic policies and to try to co-ordinate them and keep them running on similar lines. There was a certain amount of friction between the Council and the Commission: the Commission often seemed reluctant to listen to the advice of the Council, and it kept pouring out masses of new rules and regulations.
- *The European Parliament*, which met at Strasbourg, consisted of 198 representatives chosen by the parliaments of the member states. They could discuss issues and

make recommendations, but had no control over the Commission or the Council. In 1979 a new system of choosing the representatives was introduced. Instead of being nominated by parliaments, they were to be elected directly, by the people of the Community (see Section 10.4(b)).

- *The European Court of Justice* was set up to deal with any problems that might arise out of the interpretation and operation of the Treaty of Rome. It soon became regarded as the body to which people could appeal if their government was thought to be infringing the rules of the Community.

- Also associated with the EEC was *EURATOM*, an organization in which the six nations pooled their efforts towards the development of atomic energy.

In 1967 the EEC, the ECSC and EURATOM formally merged and, dropping the word 'economic', became simply the European Community (EC).

(c) Britain holds back

It was ironic that, although Churchill had been one of the strongest supporters of the idea of a unified Europe, when he became prime minister again in 1951, he seemed to have lost any enthusiasm he might have had for Britain's membership of it. Anthony Eden's Conservative government (1955–7) decided not to sign the 1957 Treaty of Rome. There were several reasons for the British refusal to join. The main objection was that if they joined the Community they would no longer be in complete control of their economy. The European Commission in Brussels would be able to make vital decisions affecting Britain's internal economic affairs. Although the governments of the other six states were prepared to make this sacrifice in the interests of greater overall efficiency, the British government was not. There were also fears that British membership would damage their relationship with the British Commonwealth as well as their so-called 'special relationship' with the USA, which was not shared by the other states of Europe. Most British politicians were afraid that economic unity would lead to political unity, and the loss of British sovereignty.

On the other hand, Britain and some of the other European states outside the EEC were worried about being excluded from selling their goods to EEC members because of the high duties on imports from outside the Community. Consequently, in 1959 Britain took the lead in organizing a rival group, the European Free Trade Association (EFTA) (see Map 10.1). Britain, Denmark, Norway, Sweden, Switzerland, Austria and Portugal agreed gradually to abolish tariffs between themselves. Britain was prepared to join an organization like EFTA because there was no question of common economic policies and no Commission to interfere with the internal affairs of states.

(d) Britain decides to join

Within less than four years from the signing of the Treaty of Rome, the British had changed their minds and announced that they wished to join the EEC. Their reasons were the following:

- By 1961 it was obvious that the EEC was an outstanding success – without Britain. Since 1953 French production had risen by 75 per cent while German production had increased by almost 90 per cent.

- Britain's economy was much less successful – over the same period British production had risen by only about 30 per cent. The British economy seemed to be

Map 10.1 **Economic unions in Europe, 1960**

stagnating in comparison with those of the Six, and in 1960 there was a balance of payments deficit of some £270 million.

- Although EFTA had succeeded in increasing trade among its members, it was nothing like as successful as the EEC.
- The Commonwealth, in spite of its huge population, had nothing like the same purchasing power as the EEC. The British prime minister, Harold Macmillan, now thought that there need not be a clash of interest between Britain's membership of the EEC and trade with the Commonwealth. There were signs that the EEC was prepared to make special arrangements to allow Commonwealth countries and some other former European colonies to become associate members. Britain's EFTA partners might be able to join as well.
- Another argument in favour of joining was that once Britain was in, competition from other EEC members would stimulate British industry to greater effort and efficiency. Macmillan also made the point that Britain could not afford to be left out if the EEC developed into a political union.

The job of negotiating Britain's entry into the EEC was given to Edward Heath, an enthusiastic supporter of European unity. Talks opened in October 1961, and although there were some difficulties, it came as a shock when the French president, Charles de Gaulle, broke off negotiations and vetoed Britain's entry (1963).

(e) Why did the French oppose British entry into the EEC?

- De Gaulle claimed that Britain had too many economic problems and would only weaken the EEC. He also objected to any concessions being made for the Commonwealth, arguing that this would be a drain on Europe's resources. Yet the EEC had just agreed to provide aid to France's former colonies in Africa.
- The British believed that de Gaulle's real motive was his desire to continue dominating the Community. If Britain came in, she would be a serious rival.
- De Gaulle was not happy about Britain's 'American connection', believing that because of these close ties with the USA, Britain's membership would allow the USA to dominate European affairs. It would produce, he said, 'a colossal Atlantic grouping under American dependence and control'. He was annoyed that the USA had promised to supply Britain with Polaris missiles but had not made the same offer to France. He was determined to prove that France was a great power and had no need of American help. It was this friction between France and the USA that eventually led de Gaulle to withdraw France from NATO (1966).
- Finally there was the problem of French agriculture: the EEC protected its farmers with high tariffs (import duties) so that prices were much higher than in Britain. Britain's agriculture was highly efficient and subsidized to keep prices relatively low. If this continued after Britain's entry, French farmers, with their smaller and less efficient farms, would be exposed to competition from Britain and perhaps from the Commonwealth.

Meanwhile the EEC success story continued, without Britain. The Community's exports grew steadily, and the value of its exports was consistently higher than its imports. Britain, on the other hand, usually had a balance of trade deficit, and in 1964 was forced to borrow heavily from the IMF to replenish rapidly dwindling gold reserves. Once again, in 1967, de Gaulle vetoed Britain's application for membership.

(f) The Six becomes the Nine (1973)

Eventually, on 1 January 1973, Britain, along with Eire and Denmark, was able to enter the EEC and the Six became the Nine. Britain's entry was made possible because of two main factors:

- President de Gaulle had resigned in 1969 and his successor, Georges Pompidou, was more friendly towards Britain.
- Britain's Conservative prime minister, Edward Heath, negotiated with great skill and tenacity, and it was fitting that, having been a committed European for so long, he was the leader who finally took Britain into Europe.

The main developments and problems after the Six became the Nine in 1973 were the following.

(a)   The Lomé Convention (1975)

From the beginning the EC was criticized for being too inward-looking and self-centred, and for apparently showing no interest in using any of its wealth to help the world's poorer nations. This agreement, worked out in Lomé, the capital of Togo in West Africa, did something to offset criticism, though many critics argued that it was too little. It allowed goods produced in over 40 countries in Africa and the Caribbean, mostly former European colonies, to be brought into the EEC free of duties; it also promised economic aid. Other poor Third World countries were added to the list later.

(b)   Direct elections to the European parliament (1979)

Although it had been in existence for over 20 years by this time, the EC was still remote from ordinary people. One reason for introducing elections was to try to arouse more interest and bring ordinary people into closer contact with the affairs of the Community.

The first elections took place in June 1979, when 410 Euro-MPs were chosen. France, Italy, West Germany and Britain were allowed 81 each, the Netherlands 25, Belgium 24, Denmark 16, Eire 15 and Luxembourg 6. The turnout varied widely from state to state. In Britain it was disappointing – less than a third of the British electorate were interested enough to bother going along to vote. In some other countries, however, notably Italy and Belgium, the turnout was over 80 per cent. Overall, in the new European parliament, the right-wing and centre parties had a comfortable majority over the left.

Elections were to be held every five years; by the time the next elections came along in 1984, Greece had joined the Community. Like Belgium, Greece was allowed 24 seats, bringing the total to 434. Overall, in the European parliament the parties of the centre and right still kept a small majority. The turnout of voters in Britain was again disappointing at only 32 per cent, whereas in Belgium it was 92 per cent and in Italy and Luxembourg it was over 80 per cent. However, in these three countries it was more or less compulsory to vote. The highest turnout in a country where voting was voluntary was 57 per cent in West Germany.

(c)   The introduction of the Exchange Rate Mechanism (ERM) (1979)

This was introduced to link the currencies of the member states in order to limit the extent to which individual currencies (the Italian lira, the French, Luxembourg and Belgian franc and the German mark) could change in value against the currencies of other members. A state's currency could change in value depending on how well its domestic economy was performing: a strong economy usually meant a strong currency. It was hoped that linking the currencies would help to control inflation and lead eventually to a single currency for the whole of the EC. Initially Britain decided not to take the pound sterling into the ERM; she made the mistake of joining in October 1990, when the exchange rate was relatively high.

(d) Community membership grows

In 1981 Greece joined, followed by Portugal and Spain in 1986, bringing the total membership to 12 and the Community population to over 320 million. (These countries had not been allowed to join earlier because their political systems were undemocratic – see Chapter 15, Summary of events.) Their arrival caused new problems: they were among the poorer countries of Europe and their presence increased the influence within the Community of the less industrialized nations. From now on there would be increasing pressure from these countries for more action to help the less developed states and so improve the economic balance between rich and poor nations. Membership increased again in 1995 when Austria, Finland and Sweden, three relatively wealthy states, joined the Community. For further increases, see Section 10.8.

(e) Britain and the EC budget

During the early years of their membership, many British people were disappointed that Britain did not seem to be gaining any obvious benefit from the EC. The Irish Republic (Eire), which joined at the same time, immediately enjoyed a surge of prosperity as her exports, mainly agricultural produce, found ready new markets in the Community. Britain, on the other hand, seemed to be stagnating in the 1970s, and although her exports to the Community did increase, her imports from the Community increased far more. Britain was not producing enough goods for export at the right prices. Foreign competitors could produce more cheaply and therefore captured a larger share of the market. The statistics of Gross Domestic Product (GDP) for 1977 are very revealing; GDP is the cash value of a country's total output from all types of production. To find out how efficient a country is, economists divide the GDP by the population of the country, which shows how much is being produced per head of the population. Figure 10.1 shows that Britain was

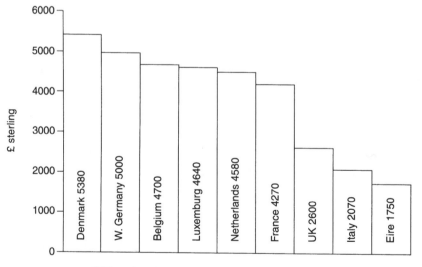

GDP per head of the population in 1977, shown in £ sterling

Figure 10.1   **Statistics of GDP per head of the population (1977)**

Source: based on J. B. Watson, *Success in Modern World History Since 1945*, John Murray (1989), p. 150.
© Margaret Watson 1989. Reproduced by permission of Hodder Education.

economically one of the least efficient nations in the EC, while Denmark and West Germany were top of the league.

A major crisis erupted in 1980 when Britain discovered that her budget contribution for that year was to be £1209 million, whereas West Germany's was £699 million and France only had to pay £13 million. Britain protested that her contribution was ridiculously high, given the general state of her economy. The difference was so great because of the way the budget contribution was worked out: this took into consideration the amount of import duties received by each government from goods coming into that country from outside the EC; a proportion of those duties received had to be handed over as part of the annual budget contribution. Unfortunately for the British, they imported far more goods from the outside world than any of the other members, and this was why her payment was so high. After some ruthless bargaining by Britain's prime minister, Margaret Thatcher, a compromise was reached: Britain's contribution was reduced to a total of £1346 million over the next three years.

(f) The 1986 changes

Encouraging developments occurred in 1986 when all 12 members, working closely together, negotiated some important changes which, it was hoped, would improve the EC. They included:

- a move to a completely free and common market (no restrictions of any kind on internal trade and movement of goods) by 1992;
- more EC control over health, safety, protection of the environment and protection for consumers;
- more encouragement for scientific research and technology;
- more help for backward regions;
- the introduction of majority voting on many issues in the Council of Ministers; this would prevent a measure from being vetoed just by one state which felt that its national interests might be threatened by that measure;
- more powers for the European parliament so that measures could be passed with less delay. This meant that the domestic parliaments of the member states were gradually losing some control over their own internal affairs.

Those people who favoured a federal United States of Europe were pleased by the last two points, but in some of the member states, especially Britain and Denmark, they stirred up the old controversy about national sovereignty. Mrs Thatcher upset some of the other European leaders when she spoke out against any movement towards a politically united Europe: 'a centralized federal government in Europe would be a nightmare; co-operation with the other European countries must not be at the expense of individuality, the national customs and traditions which made Europe great in the past'.

(g) The Common Agricultural Policy (CAP)

One of the most controversial aspects of the EC was its Common Agricultural Policy (CAP). In order to help farmers and encourage them to stay in business, so that the Community could continue to produce much of its own food, it was decided to pay them subsidies (extra cash to top up their profits). This would ensure them worthwhile profits and at the same time would keep prices at reasonable levels for the consumers. This was such a good deal for the farmers that they were encouraged to produce far more than could be sold. Yet the policy was continued, until by 1980 about three-quarters of the entire EC budget was being paid out each year in subsidies to farmers. Britain, the Netherlands and West Germany pressed for a limit to be placed on subsidies, but the French government was reluctant to agree to this because it did not want to upset French farmers, who were doing very well out of the subsidies.

In 1984, maximum production quotas were introduced for the first time, but this did not solve the problem. By 1987 the stockpiling of produce had reached ludicrous proportions. There was a vast wine 'lake' and a butter 'mountain' of one and a half million tonnes – enough to supply the entire EC for a year. There was enough milk powder to last five years, and storage fees alone were costing £1 million a day. Efforts to get rid of the surplus included selling it off cheaply to the USSR, India, Pakistan and Bangladesh, distributing butter free of charge to the poor within the Community, and using it to make animal feed. Some of the oldest butter was burnt in boilers.

All this helped to cause a massive budget crisis in 1987: the Community was £3 billion in the red and had debts of £10 billion. In a determined effort to solve the problem, the EC introduced a harsh programme of production curbs and a price freeze to put a general squeeze on Europe's farmers. This naturally caused an outcry among farmers, but by the end of 1988 it was having some success and the surpluses were shrinking steadily. Member states were now beginning to concentrate on preparing for 1992 when the intro-duction of the single European market would bring the removal of all internal trading barriers, and, some people hoped, much greater monetary integration.

(h)　Greater integration: the Maastricht Treaty (1991)

A summit meeting of all the heads of the member states was held in Maastricht (Netherlands) in December 1991, and an agreement was drawn up for 'a new stage in the process of creating an even closer union among the peoples of Europe'. Some of the points agreed were:

- more powers for the European parliament;
- greater economic and monetary union, to culminate in the adoption of a common currency (the euro) shared by all the member states, around the end of the century;
- a common foreign and security policy;
- a timetable to be drawn up of the stages by which all this would be achieved.

Britain objected very strongly to the ideas of a federal Europe and monetary union, and to a whole section of the Treaty known as *the Social Chapter*, which was a list of regulations designed to protect people at work. There were rules about:

- safe and healthy working conditions;
- equality at work between men and women;
- consulting workers and keeping them informed about what was going on;
- protection of workers made redundant.

Britain argued that these measures would increase production costs and therefore cause unemployment. The other members seemed to think that proper treatment of workers was more important. In the end, because of British objections, the Social Chapter was removed from the Treaty and it was left to individual governments to decide whether or not to carry them out. The rest of the Maastricht Treaty, without the Social Chapter, had to be ratified (approved) by the national parliaments of the 12 members, and this had been achieved by October 1993.

The French, Dutch and Belgian governments supported the Treaty strongly because they thought it was the best way to make sure that the power of the reunified Germany was contained and controlled within the Community. The ordinary people of the Community were not as enthusiastic about the Treaty as their leaders. The people of Denmark at first voted against it, and it took determined campaigning by the government before it was approved by a narrow majority in a second referendum (May 1993). The Swiss people voted not to join the Community (December 1992), and so did the Norwegians; even in the French referendum the majority in favour of Maastricht was tiny. In Britain, where the government would not allow a referendum, the Conservatives were split over Europe and the Treaty was approved only by the narrowest of majorities in parliament.

By the mid-1990s, after almost 40 years of existence, the European Community (known since 1992 as the European Union) had been a great success economically and had fostered good relations between the member states, but there were vital issues to be faced:

- How much closer could economic and political co-operation become?
- The collapse of communism in the states of eastern Europe brought with it a whole new scenario. Would these states (Map 10.2) want to join the European Union, and if so, what should be the attitude of the existing members? In April 1994, Poland and Hungary formally applied for membership.

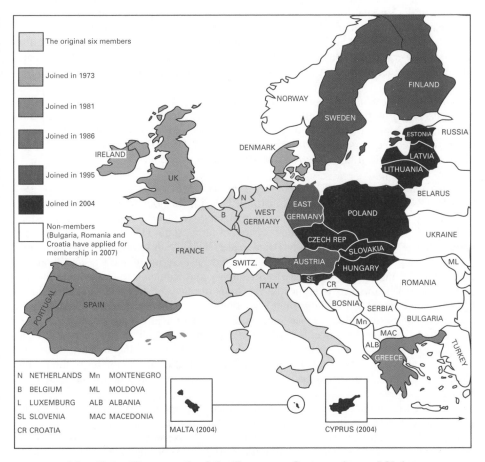

Map 10.2 **The growth of the European Community and Union**

10.5 COMMUNIST UNITY IN EASTERN EUROPE

The communist countries of eastern Europe were joined in a kind of unity under the leadership of the USSR. The main difference between the unity in eastern Europe and that in the west was that the countries of eastern Europe were forced into it by the USSR (see Section 7.2(d), (e), (g)), whereas the members of the EC joined voluntarily. By the end of 1948 there were nine states in the Communist bloc: the USSR itself, Albania, Bulgaria, Czechoslovakia, East Germany, Hungary, Poland, Romania and Yugoslavia.

(a) Organization of the Communist bloc

Stalin set about making all the states into carbon copies of the USSR, with the same political, economic and educational systems, and the same Five Year Plans. All had to carry out the bulk of their trade with Russia, and their foreign policies and armed forces were controlled from Moscow.

1   The Molotov Plan
This was the first Russian-sponsored step towards an economically united Eastern bloc. The idea of the Russian foreign minister, Molotov, it was a response to the American offer of Marshall Aid (see Section 7.2(e)). Since the Russians refused to allow any of their satellites to accept American aid, Molotov felt they had to be offered an alternative. The Plan was basically a set of trade agreements between the USSR and its satellites, negotiated during the summer of 1947; it was designed to boost the trade of eastern Europe.

2   The Communist Information Bureau (Cominform)
This was set up by the USSR at the same time as the Molotov Plan. All the communist states had to become members and its aim was political: to make sure that all the governments followed the same line as the government of the USSR in Moscow. To be communist was not enough; it had to be Russian-style communism.

3   The Council for Mutual Economic Assistance (COMECON)
COMECON was set up by the USSR in 1949. The aim was to help plan the economies of the individual states. All industry was nationalized (taken over by the state), and agriculture was collectivized (organized into a system of large, state-owned farms). Later, Nikita Khrushchev (Russian leader 1956–64) tried to use COMECON to organize the Communist bloc into a single, integrated economy; he wanted East Germany and Czechoslovakia to develop as the main industrial areas, and Hungary and Romania to concentrate on agriculture. However, this provoked hostile reactions in many of the states and Khrushchev had to change his plans to allow more variations within the economies of the different countries. The Eastern bloc enjoyed some success economically, with steadily increasing production. However, their average GDP (see Section 10.4(e) for an explanation of GDP) and general efficiency were below those of the EC. Albania had the doubtful distinction of being the most backward country in Europe. In the 1980s the economies of the Eastern bloc states experienced difficulties, with shortages, inflation and a fall in the standard of living.

Even so, the Communist bloc had a good record in social services; in some eastern European countries, health services were as good as, if not better than those in some EC countries. For example, in Britain in 1980 there was, on average, one doctor for every 618 people; in the USSR there was one doctor for every 258 people, and in Czechoslovakia the figure was 293. Only Albania, Yugoslavia and Romania had a worse ratio than Britain's.

4   The Warsaw Pact (1955)

The Warsaw Pact was signed by the USSR and all the satellite states except Yugoslavia. They promised to defend each other against any attack from outside; the armies of the member states came under overall Russian control from Moscow. Ironically, the only time Warsaw Pact troops took part in joint action was against one of their own members – Czechoslovakia – when the USSR disapproved of Czech internal policies (1968).

(b)   Tensions in the Eastern bloc

Although there were some disagreements in the EC about problems like the Common Agricultural Policy and the sovereignty of the individual states, these were not as serious as the tensions which occurred between the USSR and some of her satellite states. In the early years of the Cominform, Moscow felt it had to clamp down on any leader or movement which seemed to threaten the solidarity of the Communist bloc. Sometimes the Russians did not hesitate to use force.

1   Yugoslavia defies Moscow

Yugoslavia was the first state to stand up against Moscow. Here, the communist leader, Tito, owed much of his popularity to his successful resistance against the Nazi forces occupying Yugoslavia during the Second World War. In 1945 he was legally elected as leader of the new Yugoslav Republic and so he did not owe his position to the Russians. By 1948 he had fallen out with Stalin. He was determined to follow his own brand of communism, not Stalin's. He was against over-centralization (everything being controlled and organized from the centre by the government). He objected to Stalin's plan for the Yugoslav economy and to the constant Russian attempts to interfere in Yugoslavia's affairs. He wanted to be free to trade with the west as well as with the USSR. Stalin therefore expelled Yugoslavia from the Cominform and cut off economic aid, expecting that the country would soon be ruined economically and that Tito would be forced to resign. However, Stalin had miscalculated: Tito was much too popular to be toppled by outside pressures, and so Stalin decided it would be too risky to invade Yugoslavia. Tito was able to remain in power and *he* continued to operate communism in his own way. This included full contact and trade with the west and acceptance of aid from the International Monetary Fund (IMF).

The Yugoslavs began to reverse the process of centralization: industries were denationalized, and instead of being state-owned, they became public property, managed by workers' representatives through councils and assemblies. The same applied in agriculture: the communes were the most important unit in the state. These were groups of families, each group containing between 5000 and 100 000 people. The elected Commune Assembly organized matters to do with the economy, education, health, culture and welfare. The system was a remarkable example of ordinary people playing a part in making the decisions which closely affected their own lives, both at work and in the community. It achieved much because workers had a personal stake in the success of their firm and their commune. Many Marxists thought this was the way a genuine communist state should be run, rather than the over-centralization of the USSR.

There were some weaknesses, however. One was workers' unwillingness to sack colleagues; another was a tendency to pay themselves too much. These led to over-employment and high costs and prices. Nevertheless, with its capitalist elements (like wage differentials and a free market), this was an alternative Marxist system which many developing African states, especially Tanzania, found attractive.

Khrushchev decided that his wisest course of action was to improve relations with Tito. In 1955 he visited Belgrade, the Yugoslav capital, and apologized for Stalin's actions. The breach was fully healed the following year when Khrushchev gave his formal approval to Tito's successful brand of communism.

2 Stalin acts against other leaders

As the rift with Yugoslavia widened, Stalin arranged for the arrest of any communist leaders in the other states who attempted to follow independent policies. He was able to do this because most of these other leaders lacked Tito's popularity and owed their positions to Russian support in the first place. This did not make the way they were treated any less outrageous.

- *In Hungary*, the Foreign Minister László Rajk and Interior Minister János Kádár, both anti-Stalin communists, were arrested. Rajk was hanged, Kádár was put in jail and tortured, and about 200 000 people were expelled from the Party (1949).
- *In Bulgaria*, the prime minister, Traichko Koslov, was arrested and executed (1949).
- *In Czechoslovakia*, the Communist Party general secretary, Rudolf Slánský, and ten other cabinet ministers were executed (1952).
- *In Poland*, Communist Party leader and Vice-President Władysław Gomułka was imprisoned because he had spoken out in support of Tito.
- *In Albania*, communist premier Koçi Xoxe was removed and executed because he sympathized with Tito.

3 Khrushchev: 'different roads to socialism'

After Stalin's death in 1953 there were signs that the satellite states might be given more freedom. In 1956 Khrushchev made a remarkable speech at the Twentieth Communist Party Congress. The speech soon became famous, since Khrushchev used it to criticize many of Stalin's policies and seemed prepared to concede that there were 'different roads to socialism' (see Section 18.1(a)). He healed the rift with Yugoslavia and in April 1956 he abolished the Cominform, which had been annoying Russia's partners ever since it was set up in 1947. However, events in Poland and Hungary soon showed that there were sharp limits to Khrushchev's new toleration …

(c) Crisis in Poland

There was a general strike and a massive anti-government and anti-Soviet demonstration in Posen (Poznán) in June 1956. The banners demanded 'bread and freedom' and the workers were protesting against poor living standards, wage reductions and high taxes. Although they were dispersed by Polish troops, tension remained high throughout the summer. In October, Russian tanks surrounded Warsaw, the Polish capital, though as yet they took no action. In the end the Russians decided to compromise: Gomułka, who had earlier been imprisoned on Stalin's orders, was allowed to be reappointed as First Secretary of the Communist Party. It was accepted that Polish communism could develop in its own way provided that the Poles went along with Russia in foreign affairs. The Russians obviously felt that Gomułka could be trusted not to stray too far. Relations between the two states continued reasonably smoothly, although the Polish version of communism would definitely not have been acceptable to Stalin. For example, the collectivization of agriculture was introduced very slowly, and probably only about 10 per cent of farmland was ever collectivized. Poland also traded with countries outside the communist bloc. Gomułka remained in power until he resigned in 1970.

(d) The Hungarian Revolution (1956)

The situation in Hungary ended very differently from the one in Poland. After Stalin's death (1953), the pro-Stalin leader, Rákosi, was replaced by a more moderate communist, Imry Nagy. However, Rákosi continued to interfere and overthrew Nagy (1955). From then on resentment steadily built up against the government until it exploded in a full-scale rising (October 1956). Its causes were many:

- There was hatred of Rákosi's brutal regime, under which at least 2000 people had been executed and 200 000 others had been put in prisons and concentration camps.
- Living standards of ordinary people were getting worse while hated Communist Party leaders were living comfortable lives.
- There was intense anti-Russian feeling.
- Khrushchev's speech at the Twentieth Congress and Gomułka's return to power in Poland encouraged the Hungarians to resist their government.

Rákosi was overthrown, Nagy became prime minister, and the popular Roman Catholic Cardinal Mindszenty, who had been in prison for six years for anti-communist views, was released.

Until this point the Russians seemed prepared to compromise as they had done in Poland. But then Nagy went too far: he announced plans for a government including members of other political parties and talked of withdrawing Hungary from the Warsaw Pact. The Russians would not allow this: if Nagy had his way, Hungary might become a non-communist state and cease to be an ally of the USSR. It would encourage people in other eastern bloc states to do the same. Russian tanks moved in, surrounded Budapest, the Hungarian capital, and opened fire (3 November). The Hungarians resisted bravely and fighting lasted two weeks before the Russians brought the country under control. About 20 000 people were killed and another 20 000 imprisoned. Nagy was executed, although he had been promised a safe-conduct, and perhaps as many as 200 000 fled the country for the West. The Russians installed János Kádár as the new Hungarian leader. Although he had once been imprisoned on Stalin's orders, he was now a reliable ally of Moscow, and he stayed in power until 1988.

(e) The crisis in Czechoslovakia (1968)

After their military intervention in Hungary, the Russians did not interfere so directly anywhere until 1968, when they felt that the Czechs were straying too far from the accepted communist line. In the meantime they had allowed considerable variations within the states, and sometimes did not press unpopular plans. For example, Yugoslavia, Albania and Romania continued with their own versions of communism. In 1962, when Khrushchev suggested that each satellite state should concentrate on producing one particular product, the Hungarians, Romanians and Poles, who wanted to develop an all-round economy, protested strongly and the idea was quietly dropped. Provided no policies were introduced which threatened Communist Party domination, the Russians seemed reluctant to interfere. In the mid-1960s it was the turn of the Czechs to see how far they could go before the Russians called a halt. Their government was run by a pro-Moscow communist, Antonin Novotny, and opposition gradually escalated, for several reasons.

- The Czechs were industrially and culturally the most advanced of the Eastern bloc peoples, and they objected to the over-centralized Russian control of their economy. It seemed senseless, for example, that they should have to put up with poor quality iron ore from Siberia when they could have been using high-grade ore from Sweden.

- Between 1918 and 1938, when Czechoslovakia was an independent state, the Czechs had enjoyed great freedom, but now they resented all the restrictions on personal liberty; newspapers, books and magazines were heavily censored (that is, they could only print what the government allowed), and there was no freedom of speech; anybody who criticized the government could be arrested.
- When people tried to hold protest marches, they were dispersed by the police, whose methods were violent and brutal.

Matters came to a head in January 1968 when Novotny was forced to resign and Alexander Dubček became First Secretary of the Communist Party. He and his supporters had a completely new programme.

- The Communist Party would no longer dictate policy.
- Industry would be decentralized; this means that factories would be run by works councils instead of being controlled from the capital by party officials.
- Instead of farms being collectivized (owned and run by the state), they would become independent co-operatives.
- There should be wider powers for trade unions.
- More trade would take place with the west and there would be freedom to travel abroad; the frontier with West Germany, which had been closed since 1948, was immediately thrown open.
- There was to be freedom of speech and freedom for the press; criticism of the government was encouraged. Dubček believed that although the country would remain communist, the government should earn the right to be in power by responding to people's wishes. He called it 'socialism with a human face'.
- He was very careful to assure the Russians that Czechoslovakia would stay in the Warsaw Pact and remain a reliable ally.

During the spring and summer of 1968 this programme was carried into operation. The Russians became more and more worried by it, and in August there was a massive invasion of Czechoslovakia by Russian, Polish, Bulgarian, Hungarian and East German troops. The Czech government decided not to resist so as to avoid the sort of bloodshed which had occurred in Hungary in 1956. The Czech people tried to resist passively for a time by going on strike and holding peaceful anti-Russian demonstrations, but in the end the government was forced to abandon its new programme. The following year Dubček was replaced by Gustáv Husák, a communist leader who did as Moscow told him and so managed to stay in power until 1987.

The Russians intervened because Dubček was going to allow freedom of speech and freedom for the press, which was bound to lead to similar demands throughout the Soviet bloc. The Russians dared not risk this happening in case it led to mass protests and uprisings in the USSR itself. There was pressure for Russian action from some other communist leaders, especially those in East Germany, who were afraid that protests might spread over the frontier into Germany from Czechoslovakia. Soon afterwards, Leonid Brezhnev, the Russian leader who had ordered the invasion, announced what he called *the Brezhnev Doctrine*: this said that intervention in the internal affairs of any communist country was justified if socialism (by which he meant communism) was threatened. However, there had been some disturbing signs for the Soviet leadership: the Romanian government had been impressed by Dubček's policies and was looking forward to closer relations with Prague; consequently they refused to take part in the invasion. Yugoslavia and China also condemned the invasion.

(f) The communist bloc moves towards collapse

Although the states of eastern Europe seemed on the surface to be firmly under Russian control, resentment against Moscow's hard line simmered on, especially in Poland and Czechoslovakia.

- In Poland, Gomułka was forced to resign after a series of riots (1970), and his replacement, Gierek, also resigned (1980) following industrial unrest, food shortages and strikes in the port of Gdansk and other cities. The new government was forced to allow the formation of an independent trade union movement, known as Solidarity. The Russians moved troops up to the Polish frontier, but no invasion took place this time, perhaps because they had just sent troops into Afghanistan and were unwilling to risk another military involvement so soon.
- The Helsinki Agreements (1975) caused problems in the communist bloc. These agreements were signed at a conference in Helsinki (the capital of Finland) by every nation in Europe (except Albania and Andorra) and also by Canada, the USA and Cyprus. They promised to work for increased co-operation in economic affairs and peacekeeping, and to protect human rights. Before very long, people in the USSR and other communist states were accusing their governments of failing to allow basic human rights.
- In Czechoslovakia a human rights group calling itself Charter 77 was formed (in 1977), and during the 1980s it became more outspoken in its criticisms of the Husák government. In December 1986 a spokesman for the group said: 'while Husák lives, political stagnation will reign supreme; once he has gone, the party will explode'.
- By this time all the communist states were suffering serious economic problems, much worse than those in the EC. Although not many people in the west realized it at the time, communism and the Communist bloc were fast approaching collapse and disintegration.

10.6 WHY AND HOW DID COMMUNISM COLLAPSE IN EASTERN EUROPE?

In the short period between August 1988 and December 1991, communism in eastern Europe was swept away. Poland was the first to reject communism, closely followed by Hungary and East Germany and the rest, until by the end of 1991 even Russia had ceased to be communist, after 74 years. Why did this dramatic collapse take place?

(a) Economic failure

Communism as it existed in eastern Europe was a failure economically. It simply did not produce the standard of living which should have been possible, given the vast resources available. The economic systems were inefficient, over-centralized and subject to too many restrictions; all the states, for example, were expected to do most of their trading within the Communist bloc. By the mid-1980s there were problems everywhere. According to Misha Glenny, a BBC correspondent in eastern Europe,

> the Communist Party leaderships refused to admit that the working class lived in more squalid conditions, breathing in more damaged air and drinking more toxic water, than western working classes ... the communist record on health, education, housing, and a range of other social services has been atrocious.

Increasing contact with the west in the 1980s showed people how backward the east was in comparison with the west, and suggested that their living standards were falling even further. It showed also that it must be their own leaders and the communist system that were the cause of all their problems.

(b) Mikhail Gorbachev

Mikhail Gorbachev, who became leader of the USSR in March 1985, started the process which led to the collapse of the Soviet Empire. He recognized the failings of the system and he admitted that it was 'an absurd situation' that the USSR, the world's biggest producer of steel, fuel and energy, should be suffering shortages because of waste and inefficiency (see Section 18.3 for the situation in the USSR). He hoped to save communism by revitalizing and modernizing it. He introduced new policies of *glasnost* (openness) and *perestroika* (economic and social reform). Criticism of the system was encouraged in the drive for improvement, provided nobody criticized the Communist Party. He also helped to engineer the overthrow of the old-fashioned, hardline communist leaders in Czechoslovakia, and he was probably involved in plotting the overthrow of the East German, Romanian and Bulgarian leaders. His hope was that more progressive leaders would increase the chances of saving communism in Russia's satellite states.

Unfortunately for Gorbachev, once the process of reform began, it proved impossible to control it. The most dangerous time for any repressive regime is when it begins to try and reform itself by making concessions. These are never enough to satisfy the critics, and in Russia, criticism inevitably turned against the Communist Party itself and demanded more. Public opinion even turned against Gorbachev because many people felt he was not moving fast enough.

The same happened in the satellite states: the communist leaderships found it difficult to adapt to the new situation of having a leader in Moscow who was more progressive than they were. The critics became more daring as they realized that Gorbachev would not send Soviet troops in to fire on them. With no help to be expected from Moscow, when it came to the crisis, none of the communist governments was prepared to use sufficient force against the demonstrators (except in Romania). When they came, the rebellions were too widespread, and it would have needed a huge commitment of tanks and troops to hold down the whole of eastern Europe simultaneously. Having only just succeeded in withdrawing from Afghanistan, Gorbachev had no desire for an even greater involvement. In the end it was a triumph of 'people power': demonstrators deliberately defied the threat of violence in such huge numbers that troops would have had to shoot a large proportion of the population in the big cities to keep control.

(c) Poland leads the way

General Jaruzelski, who became leader in 1981, was prepared to take a tough line: when Solidarity (the new trade union movement) demanded a referendum to demonstrate the strength of its support, Jaruzelski declared martial law (that is, the army took over control), banned Solidarity and arrested thousands of activists. The army obeyed his orders because everybody was still afraid of Russian military intervention. By July 1983 the government was in firm control: Jaruzelski felt it safe to lift martial law and Solidarity members were gradually released. But the underlying problem was still there: all attempts to improve the economy failed. In 1988 when Jaruzelski tried to economize by cutting government subsidies, protest strikes broke out because the changes sent food prices up. This time Jaruzelski decided not to risk using force; he knew that there would be no backing from Moscow, and realized that he needed opposition support to deal with the economic crisis. Talks opened in February 1989 between the communist government, Solidarity and other opposition groups (the Roman Catholic Church had been loud in its criticisms). By April 1989, sensational changes in the constitution had been agreed:

- Solidarity was allowed to become a political party;
- there were to be two houses of parliament, a lower house and a senate;
- in the lower house, 65 per cent of the seats had to be communist;
- the senate was to be freely elected – no guaranteed communist seats;
- the two houses voting together would elect a president, who would then choose a prime minister.

In the elections of June 1989, Solidarity won 92 out of the 100 seats in the senate and 160 out of the 161 seats which they could fight in the lower house. A compromise deal was worked out when it came to forming a government: Jaruzelski was narrowly elected president, thanks to all the guaranteed communist seats in the lower house, but he chose a Solidarity supporter, Tadeusz Mazowiecki, as prime minister – the first non-communist leader in the eastern bloc (August). Mazowiecki chose a mixed government of communists and Solidarity supporters.

The new constitution proved to be only transitional. After the collapse of communism in the other east European states, further changes in Poland removed the guaranteed communist seats, and in the elections of December 1990, Lech Wałęsa, the Solidarity leader, was elected president. The peaceful revolution in Poland was complete.

(d) The peaceful revolution spreads to Hungary

Once the Poles had thrown off communism without interference from the USSR, it was only a matter of time before the rest of eastern Europe tried to follow suit. In Hungary even Kádár himself admitted in 1985 that living standards had fallen over the previous five years, and he blamed poor management, poor organization and outdated machinery and equipment in the state sector of industry. He announced new measures of decentralization – company councils and elected works managers. By 1987 there was conflict in the Communist Party between those who wanted more reform and those who wanted a return to strict central control. This reached a climax in May 1988 when, amid dramatic scenes at the party conference, Kádár and eight of his supporters were voted off the Politburo, leaving the progressives in control.

But as in the USSR, progress was not drastic enough for many people. Two large opposition parties became increasingly active. These were the liberal Alliance of Free Democrats, and the Democratic Forum, which stood for the interests of farmers and peasants. The Hungarian communist leadership, following the example of the Poles, decided to go peacefully. Free elections were held in March 1990, and in spite of a change of name to the Hungarian Socialist Party, the communists suffered a crushing defeat. The election was won by the Democratic Forum, whose leader, József Antall, became prime minister.

(e) Germany reunited

In East Germany, Erich Honecker, who had been communist leader since 1971, refused all reform and intended to stand firm, along with Czechoslovakia, Romania and the rest, to keep communism in place. However, Honecker was soon overtaken by events:

- Gorbachev, desperate to get financial help for the USSR from West Germany, paid a visit to Chancellor Kohl in Bonn, and promised to help bring an end to the divided Europe, in return for German economic aid. In effect he was secretly promising freedom for East Germany (June 1989).
- During August and September 1989, thousands of East Germans began to escape to the west via Poland, Czechoslovakia and Hungary, when Hungary opened its frontier with Austria.
- The Protestant Church in East Germany became the focus of an opposition party called New Forum, which campaigned to bring an end to the repressive and atheistic communist regime. In October 1989 there was a wave of demonstrations all over East Germany demanding freedom and an end to communism.

Honecker wanted to order the army to open fire on the demonstrators, but other leading communists were not prepared to cause widespread bloodshed. They dropped Honecker, and his successor Egon Krenz made concessions. The Berlin Wall was breached (9 November 1989) and free elections were promised.

When the great powers began to drop hints that they would not stand in the way of a reunited Germany, the West German political parties moved into the East. Chancellor Kohl staged an election tour, and the East German version of his party (CDU) won an overwhelming victory (March 1990). The East German CDU leader, Lothar de Maizière, became prime minister. He was hoping for gradual moves towards reunification, but again the pressure of 'people power' carried all before it. Nearly everybody in East Germany seemed to want immediate union.

The USSR and the USA agreed that reunification could take place; Gorbachev promised that all Russian troops would be withdrawn from East Germany by 1994. France and Britain, who were less happy about German reunification, felt bound to go along with the flow. Germany was formally reunited at midnight on 3 October 1990. In elections for the whole of Germany (December 1990) the conservative CDU/CSU alliance, together with their liberal FDP supporters, won a comfortable majority over the socialist SDP. The communists (renamed the Party of Democratic Socialism – PDS) won only 17 of the 662 seats in the Bundestag (lower house of parliament). Helmut Kohl became the first Chancellor of all Germany since the Second World War.

(f) Czechoslovakia

Czechoslovakia had one of the most successful economies of eastern Europe. She traded extensively with the west and her industry and commerce remained buoyant throughout the 1970s. But during the early 1980s the economy ran into trouble, mainly because there had been very little attempt to modernize industry. Husák, who had been in power since 1968, resigned (1987), but his successor, Miloš Jakeš, did not have a reputation as a reformer. Then things changed suddenly in a matter of days, in what became known as the Velvet Revolution. On 17 November 1989 there was a huge demonstration in Prague, at which many people were injured by police brutality. Charter 77, now led by the famous playwright Václav Havel, organized further opposition, and after Alexander Dubček had spoken at a public rally for the first time since 1968, a national strike was declared. This was enough to topple the communist regime: Jakes resigned and Havel was elected president (29 December 1989).

(g) The rest of eastern Europe

The end of communism in the remaining states of eastern Europe was less clear-cut.

1 Romania

In Romania the communist regime of Nicolae Ceauşescu (leader since 1965) was one of the most brutal and repressive anywhere in the world. His secret police, the Securitate, were responsible for many deaths. When the revolution came, it was short and bloody: it began in Timisoara, a town in western Romania, with a demonstration in support of a popular priest who was being harassed by the Securitate. This was brutally put down and many people were killed (17 December 1989). This caused outrage throughout the country, and when, four days later, Ceauşescu and his wife appeared on the balcony of Communist Party headquarters in Bucharest to address a massed rally, they were greeted with boos and shouts of 'murderers of Timisoara'. Television coverage was abruptly halted and Ceauşescu abandoned his speech. It seemed as though the entire population of Bucharest now streamed out onto the streets. At first the army fired on the crowds and many were killed and wounded. The following day the crowds came out again; but by now the army was refusing to continue the killing, and the Ceauşescu had lost control. They were arrested, tried by a military tribunal and shot (25 December 1989).

The hated Ceauşescu had gone, but many elements of communism remained in Romania. The country had never had democratic government, and opposition had been so ruthlessly crushed that there was no equivalent of the Polish Solidarity and Czech Charter 77. When a committee calling itself the National Salvation Front (NSF) was formed, it was full of former communists, though admittedly they were communists who wanted reform. Ion Iliescu, who had been a member of Ceauşescu's government until 1984, was chosen as president. He won the presidential election of May 1990, and the NSF won the elections for a new parliament. They strongly denied that the new government was really a communist one under a different name.

2 Bulgaria

In Bulgaria the communist leader Todor Zhivkov had been in power since 1954. He had stubbornly refused all reforms, even when pressurized by Gorbachev. The progressive communists decided to get rid of him. The Politburo voted to remove him (December 1989) and in June 1990 free elections were held. The communists, now calling themselves the Bulgarian Socialist Party, won a comfortable victory over the main opposition party, the Union of Democratic Forces, probably because their propaganda machine told people that the introduction of capitalism would bring economic disaster.

3 Albania

Albania had been communist since 1945 when the communist resistance movement seized power and set up a republic; so, as with Yugoslavia, the Russians were not responsible for the introduction of communism. Since 1946 until his death in 1985 the leader had been Enver Hoxha, who was a great admirer of Stalin and copied his system faithfully. Under its new leader, Ramiz Alia, Albania was still the poorest and most backward country in Europe. During the winter of 1991 many young Albanians tried to escape from their poverty by crossing the Adriatic Sea to Italy, but most of them were sent back. By this time student demonstrations were breaking out, and statues of Hoxha and Lenin were overturned. Eventually the communist leadership bowed to the inevitable and allowed free elections. In 1992 the first non-communist president, Sali Berisha, was elected.

4 Yugoslavia

The most tragic events took place in Yugoslavia, where the end of communism led to civil war and the break-up of the country (see Section 10.7).

(h) Eastern Europe after communism

The states of eastern Europe faced broadly similar problems: how to change from a planned or 'command' economy to a free economy where 'market forces' ruled. Heavy industry, which in theory should have been privatized, was mostly old-fashioned and uncompetitive; it had now lost its guaranteed markets within the communist bloc, and so nobody wanted to buy shares in it. Although shops were better stocked than before, prices of consumer goods soared and very few people could afford to buy them. The standard of living was even lower than under the final years of communism, and very little help was forthcoming from the west. Many people had expected a miraculous improvement, and, not making allowances for the seriousness of the problems, they soon grew disillusioned with their new governments.

- The East Germans were the most fortunate, having the wealth of the former West Germany to help them. But there were tensions even here: many West Germans resented the vast amounts of 'their' money being poured into the East, and they had to pay higher taxes and suffer higher interest rates. The easterners resented the large numbers of westerners who now moved in and took the best jobs.
- In Poland the first four years of non-communist rule were hard for ordinary people as the government pushed ahead with its reorganization of the economy. By 1994 there were clear signs of recovery, but many people were bitterly disappointed with their new democratic government. In the presidential election of December 1995, Lech Wałęsa was defeated by a former Communist Party member, Aleksander Kwaśniewski.
- In Czechoslovakia there were problems of a different kind: Slovakia, the eastern half of the country, demanded independence, and for a time civil war seemed a strong possibility. Fortunately a peaceful settlement was worked out and the country split into two – the Czech Republic and Slovakia (1992).
- Predictably, the slowest economic progress was made in Romania, Bulgaria and Albania, where the first half of the 1990s was beset by falling output and inflation.

(For later developments in eastern Europe see Section 10.8.)

10.7 CIVIL WAR IN YUGOSLAVIA

Yugoslavia was formed after the First World War, and consisted of the pre-First World War state of Serbia, plus territory gained by Serbia from Turkey in 1913 (containing many Muslims), and territory taken from the defeated Habsburg Empire. It included people of many different nationalities, and the state was organized on federal lines. It consisted of six republics – Serbia, Croatia, Montenegro, Slovenia, Bosnia-Herzegovina and Macedonia. There were also two provinces – Vojvodina and Kosovo – which were associated with Serbia. Under communism and the leadership of Tito, the nationalist feelings of the different peoples were kept strictly under control, and people were encouraged to think of themselves primarily as Yugoslavs rather than as Serbs or Croats. The different nationalities lived peacefully together, and had apparently succeeded in putting behind them memories of the atrocities committed during the Second World War. One such atrocity was when Croat and Muslim supporters of the fascist regime set up by the Italians to rule Croatia and Bosnia during the war were responsible for the murder of some 700 000 Serbs.

However, there was still a Croat nationalist movement, and some Croat nationalist leaders, such as Franjo Tudjman, were given spells in jail. Tito (who died in 1980) had left careful plans for the country to be ruled by a collective presidency after his death. This would consist of one representative from each of the six republics and one from each of the two provinces; a different president of this council would be elected each year.

(a) Things begin to go wrong

Although the collective leadership seemed to work well at first, in the mid-1980s things began to go wrong.

- The economy was in trouble, with inflation running at 90 per cent in 1986 and unemployment standing at over a million – 13 per cent of the working population. There were differences between areas: for example, Slovenia was reasonably prosperous while parts of Serbia were poverty-stricken.
- Slobodan Milošević, who became president of Serbia in 1988, bears much of the responsibility for the tragedy that followed. He deliberately stirred up Serbian nationalist feelings to increase his own popularity, using the situation in Kosovo. He claimed that the Serbian minority in Kosovo were being terrorized by the Albanian majority, though there was no definite evidence of this. The Serbian government's hardline treatment of the Albanians led to protest demonstrations and the first outbreaks of violence. Milošević remained in power after the first free elections in Serbia in 1990, having successfully convinced the voters that he was now a nationalist and not a communist. He wanted to preserve the united federal state of Yugoslavia, but intended that Serbia should be the dominant republic.
- By the end of 1990 free elections had also been held in the other republics, and new non-communist governments had taken over. They resented Serbia's attitude, none more so than Franjo Tudjman, former communist and now leader of the right-wing Croatian Democratic Union and president of Croatia. He did all he could to stir up Croatian nationalism and wanted an independent state of Croatia.
- Slovenia also wanted to become independent, and so the future looked bleak for the united Yugoslavia. Only Milošević opposed the break-up of the state, but he wanted it kept on Serbian terms and refused to make any concessions to the other nationalities. He refused to accept a Croat as president of Yugoslavia (1991) and used Yugoslav federal cash to help the Serb economy.
- The situation was complicated because each republic had ethnic minorities: there were about 600 000 Serbs living in Croatia – about 15 per cent of the population – and about 1.3 million Serbs in Bosnia-Herzegovina – roughly a third of the population. Tudjman would give no guarantees to the Serbs of Croatia, and this gave Serbia the excuse to announce that she would defend all Serbs forced to live under Croatian rule. War was not inevitable: with statesmanlike leaders prepared to make sensible concessions, peaceful solutions could have been found. But clearly, if Yugoslavia broke up, with men like Milošević and Tudjman in power, there was little chance of a peaceful future.

(b) The move to war: the Serb–Croat War

Crisis-point was reached in June 1991 when Slovenia and Croatia declared themselves independent, against the wishes of Serbia. Fighting seemed likely between troops of the Yugoslav federal army (mainly Serbian) stationed in those countries, and the new Croatian and Slovenian militia armies, which had just been formed. Civil war was avoided in Slovenia mainly because there were very few Serbs living there. The EC was able to act as mediator, and secured the withdrawal of Yugoslav troops from Slovenia.

However, it was a different story in Croatia, with its large Serbian minority. Serbian troops invaded the eastern area of Croatia (eastern Slavonia) where many Serbs lived, and other towns and cities, including Dubrovnik on the Dalmatian coast, were shelled. By the end of August 1991 they had captured about one-third of the country. Only then, having captured all the territory he wanted, did Milošević agree to a ceasefire. A UN force of 13 000 troops – UNPROFOR – was sent to police the ceasefire (February 1992). By this time the international community had recognized the independence of Slovenia, Croatia and Bosnia-Herzegovina.

(c) The war in Bosnia-Herzegovina

Just as hostilities between Croatia and Serbia were dying down, an even more bloody struggle was about to break out in Bosnia, which contained a mixed population – 44 per cent Muslim, 33 per cent Serb and 17 per cent Croat. Bosnia declared itself independent under the presidency of the Muslim Alija Izetbegović (March 1992). The EC recognized its independence, making the same mistake as it had done with Croatia – it failed to make sure that the new government guaranteed fair treatment for its minorities. The Bosnian Serbs rejected the new constitution and objected to a Muslim president. Fighting soon broke out between Bosnian Serbs, who received help and encouragement from Serbia, and Bosnian Muslims. The Serbs hoped that a large strip of land in the east of Bosnia, which bordered onto Serbia, could break away from the Muslim-dominated Bosnia and become part of Serbia. At the same time Croatia attacked and occupied areas in the north of Bosnia where most of the Bosnian Croats lived.

Atrocities were committed by all sides, but it seemed that the Bosnian Serbs were the most guilty. They carried out 'ethnic cleansing', which meant driving out the Muslim civilian population from Serb-majority areas, putting them into camps, and in some cases murdering all the men. Such barbarism had not been seen in Europe since the Nazi treatment of the Jews during the Second World War. Sarajevo, the capital of Bosnia, was besieged and shelled by the Serbs, and throughout the country there was chaos: two million refugees had been driven out of their homes by 'ethnic cleansing' and not enough food and medical supplies were available.

The UN force, UNPROFOR, did its best to distribute aid, but its job was very difficult because it had no supporting artillery or aircraft. Later the UN tried to protect the Muslims by declaring Srebrenica, Zepa and Gorazde, three mainly Muslim towns in the Serb-majority region, as 'safe areas'; but not enough troops were provided to defend them if the Serbs decided to attack. The EC was reluctant to send any troops and the Americans felt that Europe should be able to sort out its own problems. However, they did all agree to put economic sanctions on Serbia to force Milošević to stop helping the Bosnian Serbs. The war dragged on into 1995; there were endless talks, threats of NATO action and attempts to get a ceasefire, but no progress could be made.

During 1995 crucial changes took place which enabled a peace agreement to be signed in November. Serb behaviour eventually proved too much for the international community:

- Serb forces again bombarded Sarajevo, killing a number of people, after they had promised to withdraw their heavy weapons (May).
- Serbs seized UN peacekeepers as hostages to deter NATO air strikes.
- Serbs attacked and captured Srebrenica and Zepa, two of the UN 'safe areas', and at Srebrenica they committed perhaps the ultimate act of barbarism, killing about 8000 Muslims in a terrible final burst of 'ethnic cleansing' (July).

After this, things moved more quickly:

1   The Croats and Muslims (who had signed a ceasefire in 1994) agreed to fight together against the Serbs. The areas of western Slavonia (May) and the Krajina (August) were recaptured from the Serbs.

2   At a conference in London attended by the Americans, it was agreed to use NATO air strikes and to deploy a 'rapid reaction force' against the Bosnian Serbs if they continued their aggression.

3   The Bosnian Serbs ignored this and continued to shell Sarajevo; 27 people were killed by a single mortar shell on 28 August. This was followed by a massive NATO bombing of Bosnian Serb positions, which continued until they agreed to move their weapons away from Sarajevo. More UN troops were sent, though in fact the UN position was weakened because NATO was now running the operation. By this time the Bosnian Serb leaders, Radovan Karadžić and General Mladić, had been indicted by the European Court for war crimes.

4   President Milošević of Serbia had now had enough of the war and wanted to get the economic sanctions on his country lifted. With the Bosnian Serb leaders discredited in international eyes as war criminals, he was able to represent the Serbs at the conference table.

5   With the Americans now taking the lead, a ceasefire was arranged, and Presidents Clinton and Yeltsin agreed to co-operate on peace arrangements. A peace conference met in the USA at Dayton (Ohio) in November and a treaty was formally signed in Paris (December 1995):

- Bosnia was to remain one state with a single elected parliament and president, and a unified Sarajevo as its capital.
- The state would consist of two sections: the Bosnian Muslim/Croat federation and the Bosnian Serb republic.
- Gorazde, the surviving 'safe area', was to remain in Muslim hands, linked to Sarajevo by a corridor through Serb territory.
- All indicted war criminals were banned from public life.
- All Bosnian refugees, over two million of them, had the right to return, and there was to be freedom of movement throughout the new state.
- 60 000 NATO troops were to police the settlement.
- It was understood that the UN would lift the economic sanctions on Serbia.

There was general relief at the peace, though there were no real winners, and the settlement was full of problems. Only time would tell whether it was possible to maintain the new state (Map 10.3) or whether the Bosnian Serb republic would eventually try to break away and join Serbia.

(d)   Conflict in Kosovo

There was still the problem of Kosovo, where the Albanian majority bitterly resented Milošević's hardline policies and the loss of much of their local provincial autonomy. Non-violent protests began as early as 1989, led by Ibrahim Rugova. The sensational events in Bosnia diverted attention away from the Kosovo situation, which was largely ignored during the peace negotiations in the USA in 1995. Since peaceful protest made no impression on Milošević, more radical Albanian elements came to the forefront with the formation of the Kosovo Liberation Army (KLA). By 1998 the situation had reached the proportions of civil war, as the Serb government security forces tried to suppress the KLA. In the spring of 1999 Serb forces unleashed a full-scale offensive, committing atrocities against the Albanians. These were widely reported abroad and the world's attention at last focused on Kosovo.

Map 10.3   **The Bosnian Peace Settlement**

When peace negotiations broke down, the international community decided that something must be done to protect the Albanians of Kosovo. NATO forces carried out controversial bombing attacks against Serbia, hoping to force Milošević to give way. However, this only made him more determined: he ordered a campaign of ethnic cleansing which drove hundreds of thousands of ethnic Albanians out of Kosovo and into the neighbouring states of Albania, Macedonia and Montenegro. NATO air strikes continued, and by June 1999, with his country's economy in ruins, Milošević accepted a peace agreement worked out by Russia and Finland. He was forced to withdraw all Serb troops from Kosovo; many of the Serb civilian population, afraid of Albanian reprisals, went with them. Most of the Albanian refugees were then able to return to Kosovo. A UN and NATO force of over 40 000 arrived to keep the peace, while UNMIK (UN Mission to Kosovo) was to supervise the administration of the country until its own government was capable of taking over.

At the end of 2003 there were still 20 000 peacekeeping troops there, and the Kosovars were becoming impatient, complaining of poverty, unemployment, and corruption among the members of UNMIK.

(e)   The downfall of Milošević

By 1998, Milošević had served two terms as president of Serbia, and the constitution prevented him from standing for a third term. However, he managed to hold on to power by getting the Yugoslav federal parliament to appoint him president of Yugoslavia in 1997 (though Yugoslavia by then consisted only of Serbia and Montenegro). In May 1999 he was indicted by the International Criminal Tribunal for Former Yugoslavia (at the Hague in the Netherlands), on the grounds that as president of Yugoslavia, he was responsible for crimes against international law committed by federal Yugoslav troops in Kosovo.

Public opinion gradually turned against Milošević during 2000, because of economic difficulties, food and fuel shortages and inflation. The presidential election of September 2000 was won by his chief opponent, Vlojislav Koštunica, but a constitutional court declared the result null and void. Massive anti-Milošević demonstrations took place in the capital, Belgrade. When crowds stormed the federal parliament and took control of the TV stations, Milošević conceded defeat and Kostunica became president. In 2001, Milošević was arrested and handed over to the International Tribunal in The Hague to face the war crimes charges. His trial opened in July 2001 and he chose to conduct his own defence. No verdict had been reached when he died in March 2006.

However, the new government was soon struggling to cope with Milošević's legacy: an empty treasury, an economy ruined by years of international sanctions, rampant inflation and a fuel crisis. The standard of living fell dramatically for most people. The parties which had united to defeat Milošević soon fell out. In the elections at the end of 2003 the extreme nationalist Serbian Radicals emerged as the largest single party, well ahead of Koštunica's party, which came second. The leader of the Radicals, Vojislav Šešelj, who was said to be an admirer of Hitler, was in jail in The Hague awaiting trial on war crimes charges. The election result was a great disappointment to the USA and the EU, which were both hoping that extreme Serb nationalism had been eradicated. In July 2008 Radovan Karadžić, the former Bosnian Serb leader, was arrested after 13 years in hiding and sent to The Hague to be tried for war crimes.

10.8 EUROPE SINCE MAASTRICHT

With the continued success of the European Union, more states applied to join. In January 1995, Sweden, Finland and Austria became members, bringing the total membership to 15. Only Norway, Iceland and Switzerland of the main western European states remained outside. Important changes were introduced by *the Treaty of Amsterdam*, signed in 1997. This further developed and clarified some of the points of the 1991 Maastricht agreement: the Union undertook to promote full employment, better living and working conditions, and more generous social policies. The Council of Ministers was given the power to penalize member states which violated human rights; and the European parliament was given more powers. The changes came into effect on 1 May 1999.

(a) Enlargement and reform

As Europe moved into the new millennium, the future looked exciting. The new European currency – the euro – was introduced in 12 of the member states on 1 January 2002. And there was the prospect of a gradual enlargement of the Union. Cyprus, Malta and Turkey had made applications for membership, and so had Poland and Hungary, all of whom hoped to join in 2004. Other countries in eastern Europe were keen to join – including the Czech Republic, Slovakia, Estonia, Latvia, Lithuania, Croatia, Slovenia, Bulgaria and Romania. There seemed every chance that sooner or later the Union would double in size. This prospect raised a number of issues and concerns.

- It was suggested that most of the former communist states of eastern Europe were so economically backward that they would be unable to join on equal terms with the advanced members such as Germany and France.
- There were fears that the Union would become too large: this would slow down decision-making and make it impossible to get consensus on any major policy.
- The federalists, who wanted closer political integration, believed that this would become almost impossible in a Union of some 25 to 30 states, unless a two-speed

Europe emerged. States in favour of integration could move rapidly towards a federal system similar to the one in the USA, while the rest could move more slowly, or not at all, as the case might be.

- There was a feeling that the Union's institutions needed reforming to make them more open, more democratic and more efficient – in order to speed up policy-making. The Union's prestige and authority took a severe blow in March 1999 when a report revealed widespread corruption and fraud in high places; the entire Commission of 20 members was forced to resign.

(b)   The Treaty of Nice

It was to address the need for reform, in preparation for enlargement, that the *Treaty of Nice* was agreed in December 2000 and formally signed in February 2001; it was scheduled to come into operation on 1 January 2005.

- New voting rules were to be introduced in the Council of Ministers for the approval of policies. Many areas of policy had required a unanimous vote, which meant that one country could effectively veto a proposal. Now most policy areas were transferred to a system known as 'qualified majority voting' (QMV); this required that a new policy needed to be approved by members representing at least 62 per cent of the EU population, and the support of either a majority of members or a majority of votes cast. However, taxation and social security still required unanimous approval. The membership of the Council was to be increased: the 'big four' (Germany, UK, France and Italy) were each to have 29 members instead of 10, while the smaller states had their membership increased by roughly similar proportions – Ireland, Finland and Denmark, 7 members instead of 4; and Luxembourg, 4 members instead of 2. When Poland joined in 2004, it would have 27 members, the same number as Spain.
- The composition of the European parliament was to be changed to reflect more closely the size of each member's population. This involved all except Germany and Luxembourg having fewer MEPs than previously – Germany, by far the largest member with a population of 82 million, was to keep its 99 seats, Luxembourg, the smallest with 400 000, was to keep its 6 seats. The UK (59.2 million), France (59 million) and Italy (57.6 million) were each to have 72 seats instead of 87; Spain (39.4 million) was to have 50 seats instead of 64, and so on, down to Ireland (3.7 million), which would have 12 seats instead of 15. On the same basis, provisional figures were set for the likely new members: for example Poland, with a population similar in size to that of Spain, would also have 50 seats, and Lithuania (like Ireland with 3.7 million) would have 12 seats.
- The five largest states, Germany, UK, France, Italy and Spain, were to have only one European commissioner each instead of two. Each member state would have one commissioner, up to a maximum of 27, and the president of the Commission was to have more independence from national governments.
- 'Enhanced co-operation' was to be allowed. This meant that any group of eight or more member states which wanted to move to greater integration in particular areas would be able to do so.
- A German–Italian proposal was accepted that a conference should be held to clarify and formalize the constitution of the EU, by 2004.
- A plan for a European Union Rapid Reaction Force (RRF) of 60 000 troops was approved, to provide military back-up in case of emergency, though it was stressed that NATO would still be the basis of Europe's defence system. This did not please

the French president, Jacques Chirac, who wanted the RRF to be independent of NATO. Nor did it please the USA, which was afraid that the EU defence initiative would eventually exclude the USA. In October 2003, as discussions were taking place in Brussels on how best to proceed with EU defence plans, the US government complained that it was being kept in the dark about Europe's intentions, claiming that the EU plans 'represented one of the greatest dangers to the transatlantic relationship'. It seemed that although the Americans wanted Europe to take on more of the world's defence and anti-terrorist burden, it intended this to be done under US direction, working through NATO, not independently.

Before the Treaty of Nice could be put into operation in January 2005, it had to be approved by all 15 member states. It was therefore a serious blow when, in June 2001, Ireland voted in a referendum to reject it. Ireland had been one of the most co-operative and pro-European members of the Union; but the Irish resented the fact that the changes would increase the power of the larger states, especially Germany, and reduce the influence of the smaller states. Nor were they happy at the prospect of Irish participation in peacekeeping forces. There was still time for the Irish to change their minds, but the situation would need careful handling if voters were to be persuaded to back the agreement. When the European Commission president, Romano Prodi of Italy, announced that enlargement of the Union could go ahead in spite of the Irish vote, the Irish government was outraged. His statement prompted accusations from across the Union that its leaders were out of touch with ordinary citizens.

(c) Problems and tensions

Instead of a smooth transition to an enlarged and united Europe in May 2004, the period after the signing of the Treaty of Nice turned out to be full of problems and tensions. Some had been foreseen, but most of them were quite unexpected.

- Predictably, the divisions widened between those who wanted a much closer political union – a sort of United States of Europe – and those who wanted a looser association in which power remained in the hands of the member states. Chancellor Gerhard Schröder of Germany wanted a strong European government with more power given to the European Commission and the Council of Ministers, and a European Union constitution embodying his vision of a federal system. He was supported by Belgium, Finland and Luxembourg. On the other hand, Britain felt that political integration had gone far enough, and did not want the governments of the individual states to lose any more of their powers. The way forward was through closer co-operation between the national governments, not through handing control over to a federal government in Brussels or Strasbourg.
- The terrorist attacks of 11 September 2001 in the USA threw the EU into confusion. The EU leaders were quick to declare solidarity with the USA and to promise all possible co-operation in the war against terrorism. However, foreign and defence issues were areas where the EU was not well equipped to take rapid collective action. It was left to the leaders of individual states – Schröder, Chirac and UK prime minister Blair – to take initiatives and promise military help against terrorism. This in itself was resented by the smaller member states, which felt they were being by-passed and ignored.
- The attack on Iraq by the USA and the UK in March 2003 (see Section 12.4) caused new tensions. Germany and France were strongly opposed to any military action not authorized by the UN; they believed that it was possible to disarm Iraq by peaceful

means, and that war would cause the deaths of thousands of innocent civilians, destroy the stability of the whole region and hamper the global struggle against terrorism. On the other hand, Spain, Italy, Portugal and Denmark, together with the prospective new members – Poland, Hungary and the Czech Republic – were in favour of Britain's joint action with the USA. American Defence Secretary Donald Rumsfeld dismissed the German and French opposition, claiming that they represented 'old Europe'. An emergency European Council meeting was held in Brussels in February, but it failed to resolve the basic differences: the UK, Italy and Spain wanted immediate military action while France and Germany pressed for more diplomacy and more weapons inspectors. This failure to agree on a unified response to the Iraq situation did not bode well for the prospects of formulating a common foreign and defence policy, as required by the new EU constitution due to be debated in December 2003.

- A rift of a different sort opened up over budgetary matters. In the autumn of 2003 it was revealed that both France and Germany had breached the EU rule, laid down at Maastricht, that budget deficits must not exceed 3 per cent of GDP. However, no action was taken: the EU finance ministers decided that both states could have an extra year to comply. In the case of France, it was the third consecutive year that the 3 per cent ceiling had been breached. This bending of the rules in favour of the two largest member states infuriated the smaller members. Spain, Austria, Finland and the Netherlands opposed the decision to let them off. It raised a number of questions: what would happen if smaller countries broke the rules – would they be let off too? If so, wouldn't that make a mockery of the whole budgetary system? Was the 3 per cent limit realistic anyway in a time of economic stagnation?

- The most serious blow – in December 2003 – came when a summit meeting in Brussels collapsed without reaching agreement on the new EU constitution, which was designed to streamline and simplify the way the Union worked. Disagreement over the issue of voting powers was the main stumbling block.

Failure to agree on the new constitution was not a total disaster; the enlargement of the EU was still able to go ahead as planned on 1 May 2004; the ten new members were the Czech Republic, Cyprus, Estonia, Hungary, Latvia, Lithuania, Malta, Poland, Slovakia and Slovenia. But it was clear that the future of the Union was going to be fraught with problems. With some 25 or more members to deal with, the main issue was how to balance the interests of the smaller and larger states. Happily, most of the problems seemed to have been overcome when, in June 2004, a Constitutional Treaty was drawn up, to be presented to member states for ratification. The new constitution was something of a triumph: it brought together the confusing hotchpotch of previous treaties, and made for much smoother decision-making. It appeared to allow the national parliaments rather more powers than previously – for example, there was a procedure for members to leave the Union if they chose to; and states kept their veto on taxation, foreign policy and defence. The areas over which the EU had overriding control were competition policy, customs, trade policy and protection of marine life. The dispute over the voting system was also resolved: for a measure to pass, it must be supported by at least 15 countries representing 65 per cent of the EU's total population of 455 million; at least four countries with 35 per cent of the population would be required to block a measure. This was a safeguard to prevent the biggest countries from riding roughshod over the interests of the smaller ones. Spain, which had protested strongly that the previous proposals disadvantaged the smaller members, was happy with the compromise. The next problem was to get the new constitution ratified by all the members, and this would involve at least six national referendums. Unfortunately in 2005 it was rejected by Dutch and French voters, and it was decided that there should be a 'period of reflection'.

Eventually a new agreement was drawn up, preserving many of the reforms of the previous constitution but amending the ones that had raised objections. Signed by all 27 member states at Lisbon in December 2007, the stated aim of the treaty was 'to complete the process started by the Treaty of Amsterdam [1997] and by the Treaty of Nice [2001] with a view to enhancing the efficiency and democratic legitimacy of the Union and to improving the coherence of its actions'.

10.9 THE EUROPEAN UNION IN CRISIS

In a referendum held in June 2008 well over half the Irish voters rejected the Lisbon Treaty. The Germans and French, who were mainly responsible for the form of the treaty, were furious. The Germans threatened Ireland with expulsion from the EU, and President Sarkozy announced that the Irish must hold a second referendum. Before this took place, the economic situation in Europe had changed dramatically: in September 2008 in the USA there occurred the worst financial collapse since the Wall Street Crash of 1929 (see Section 27.7–8). The effects soon spread to Europe; by the end of 2008 the demand for European exports had contracted alarmingly, and one by one the member states of the EU plunged into recession. Worst affected were Spain and Ireland, the two countries which had enjoyed the highest growth rates in the EU since the introduction of the euro in 2002. As Perry Anderson explains:

> The crisis struck hardest of all in Ireland, where output contracted by 8.5 per cent between the first quarters of 2008 and 2009, and the fiscal deficit soared to over 15 per cent of GDP. Though a probable death warrant for the regime in place at the next polls, in the short run the debacle of the Celtic Tiger was a diplomatic godsend to it. Amid popular panic the government could now count on frightening voters into accepting Lisbon, however irrelevant it might be to the fate of the Irish economy.

In October 2009 Irish voters obligingly approved the Lisbon Treaty, which came into effect on 1 December 2009.

(For further developments in the eurozone financial crisis, see Section 27.7.).

(a) The future of the European Union

All these problems should not be allowed to lead to the conclusion that the EU is a failure. Whatever happens in the future, nothing can take away the fact that since 1945, the countries of western Europe have been at peace with each other. It seems unlikely that they will ever go to war with each other again, if not absolutely certain. Given Europe's war-torn past, this is a considerable achievement, which must be attributed in large measure to the European movement.

However, the Union's development is not complete: over the next half-century Europe could become a united federal state, or, more likely, it could remain a much looser organization politically, albeit with its own reformed and streamlined constitution. Many people hope that the EU will become strong and influential enough to provide a counterbalance to the USA, which in 2004 seemed in a position to dominate the world and convert it into a series of carbon copies of itself. Already the EU had demonstrated its potential. With the 2004 enlargement, the EU economy could rival that of the USA both in size and cohesion. The EU was providing well over half the world's development aid – far more than the USA – and the gap between EU and US contributions was growing all the time. Even some American observers acknowledged the EU's potential; Jeremy Rifkin wrote:

'Europe has become the new "city upon a hill". … We Americans used to say that the American Dream is worth dying for. The new European Dream is worth living for.'

The EU has shown that it is prepared to stand up to the USA. In March 2002 plans were announced to launch a European Galileo space-satellite system to enable civilian ships and aircraft to navigate and find their positions more accurately. The USA already had a similar system (GPS), but it was mainly used for military purposes. The US government protested strongly against the EU proposal on the grounds that the European system might interfere with US signals. The French president, Chirac, warned that if the USA was allowed to dominate space, 'it would inevitably lead to our countries becoming first scientific and technological vassals, then industrial and economic vassals of the US'. The EU stood its ground and the plan went ahead. According to Will Hutton, 'the US wanted a complete monopoly of such satellite ground positioning systems. … the EU's decision is an important declaration of common interest and an assertion of technological superiority alike: Galileo is a better system than GPS.'

Clearly the enlarged EU has vast potential, though it will need to deal with some serious weaknesses. The Common Agricultural Policy continues to encourage high production levels at the expense of quality, and causes a great deal of damage to the economies of the developing world; this needs attention, as does the whole system of food standards regulation. The confusing set of institutions needs to be simplified and their functions formalized in a new constitution. And perhaps most important – EU politicians must try to keep in touch with the wishes and feelings of the general public. They need to take more trouble to explain what they are doing, so that they can regain the respect and trust of Europe's ordinary citizens. In a move which boded well for the future, the European parliament voted by a large majority in favour of José Manuel Barroso, the former prime minister of Portugal, as the next president of the European Commission. The new president had pledged himself to reform the EU, to bring it closer to its largely apathetic citizens, to make it fully competitive and to give it a new social vision. His five-year term of office began in November 2004 and in September 2009 he was granted a second five-year term.

However, by that time the EU was facing two further problems: immigration and the deepening economic crisis. Increasing immigration into the EU, about half of which consisted of Muslims, led to racial and religious tensions; some observers were writing about the 'battle at the borders' to control and reduce the number of immigrants. By 2009 there were estimated to be between 15 and 18 million Muslim migrants in the richer western states of the EU. This might seem a small number out of a total population of perhaps 370 million, but what many people found worrying was that the birth rate among the native populations was declining, while that of the Muslims was increasing, especially in the big cities. In Brussels over half the children born every year were from Muslim immigrants. In Amsterdam there were more practising Muslims than either Protestants or Catholics. According to Perry Anderson, in 2009 the overall inflow of migrants into Europe was some 1.7 million a year.

Poverty and unemployment in these communities is nearly always above the national average and discrimination pervasive. In a number of countries – France, Denmark, the Netherlands and Italy have been the most prominent to date – political parties have arisen whose appeal has been based on xenophobic opposition to it. The new diversity has not fostered harmony. It has stoked conflict.

Given the wave of terrorism perpetrated by Muslim extremists during the first decade of the twenty-first century (see Section 12.2–3), it was hardly surprising that some observers talked about the impending war between Islam and the West. The problems of immigration and unemployment were linked: the optimistic view was that if and when the economy of Europe recovered and there was full employment, tensions would fade and Muslims and Christians would be able to live together in harmony – multiculturalism could triumph after all!

However, in 2009, this seemed a forlorn hope – the crisis deepened and some economists were predicting that the euro was beyond salvation; some even thought the EU itself might disintegrate. In February 2012 Angela Merkel, the German Chancellor, said that Europe was facing its gravest test for decades, and she predicted that 2012 would be worse than 2011. All governments were trying to cut costs by introducing unpopular austerity measures. Greece had 'manipulated' its borrowing figures to make them look less than they actually were, in order to be allowed to join the euro (2001). The consequence was that Greek debts were enormous, and for much of 2011 and 2012 the government seemed to be on the verge of defaulting. This could have disastrous effects on banks and on the economies of other countries that had traded with Greece. Hungary's currency, the forint, was in free fall, while Italy, Ireland, Spain and Portugal had huge debts and could only borrow more at high rates of interest. And everywhere unemployment was rising, averaging over 10 per cent throughout the EU.

FURTHER READING

Anderson, P., *The New Old World* (Verso, 2011 edition).

Ash, T. G., *In Europe's Name: Germany and the Divided Continent* (Jonathan Cape, 1993).

Brown, A., *The Rise and Fall of Communism* (Bodley Head, 2009).

Hix, S., *The Political System of the European Union* (Palgrave Macmillan, 2nd edition, 2005).

Hutton, W., *The World We're In* (Little, Brown, 2003).

Judah, T., *Kosovo: War and Peace* (Yale University Press, 2002).

Judt, T., *Postwar: A History of Europe Since 1945* (Vintage, 2010).

Laqueur, W., *The Last Days of Europe* (Thomas Dunne, 2007).

Mahoney, D. J., *De Gaulle: Statesmanship, Grandeur and Modern Democracy* (Greenwood, 1996).

Milward, A. S., *The European Rescue of the Nation-State* (Routledge, 2nd edition, 2000).

Naimark, N. M. and Case, H. (eds), *Yugoslavia and Its Historians: Understanding Balkan Wars of the 1990s* (Stanford University Press, 2002).

Pittaway, M., *Eastern Europe: States and Societies (1945–2000)* (Hodder/Edward Arnold, 2002).

Rifkin, J., *The European Dream* (Polity Press, 2004).

Service, R., *Comrades: Communism, A World History* (Palgrave Macmillan, 2007).

Shawcross, W., *Dubček and Czechoslovakia, 1968–1990* (Hogarth, 1990).

Wheaton, B. and Kavan, Z., *The Velvet Revolution: Czechoslovakia, 1988–91* (Westview Press, 1992).

Young, J. W., *Cold War Europe, 1945–1989: A Political History* (Longman, 1991).

QUESTIONS

1 Assess the evidence for and against the view that the European Economic Community became stronger after its enlargement in 1973.

2 Why and in what ways did the states of western Europe see closer relations with each other after the Second World War?

3   In what ways and for what reasons did Britain's attitude to Europe change during the period 1945 to 1991?

4   Assess the reasons why two German states emerged between 1945 and 1949.

5   How similar were the causes and consequences of the Hungarian uprising of 1956 and the Prague Spring of 1968?

◥   There is a document question about the collapse of communism in East Germany on the website.

11 Conflict in the Middle East

SUMMARY OF EVENTS

The area known as the Middle East has been one of the world's most troubled regions, especially since 1945. Wars and civil wars have raged almost non-stop, and there has hardly been a time when the whole region was at peace. The Middle East consists of Egypt, the Sudan, Jordan, Syria, Lebanon, Iraq, Saudi Arabia, Kuwait, Iran, Turkey, the Yemen republics, the United Arab Emirates and Oman (see Map 11.1). Most of these states, except Turkey and Iran, are peopled by Arabs; Iran, though not an Arab state, contains many Arabs living in the area around the northern end of the Persian Gulf. The Middle East also contains the small Jewish state of Israel, which was set up by the United Nations in 1948 in Palestine.

The creation of Israel in Palestine, an area belonging to the Palestinian Arabs, outraged Arab opinion throughout the world (other Arab states outside the Middle East are Morocco, Algeria, Tunisia and Libya). The Arabs especially blamed Britain, who, they felt, had been more sympathetic to the Jews than to the Arabs; most of all they blamed the USA, which had supported the idea of a Jewish state very strongly. The Arab states refused to recognize Israel as a legal state and they vowed to destroy it. Although there were four short wars between Israel and the various Arab states (1948–9, 1956, 1967 and 1973), Arab attacks failed, and Israel survived. However, the conflict between Israel and the Palestinians dragged on; even at the end of the first decade of the twenty-first century, no permanent peace agreement had been reached.

The Arab desire to destroy Israel tended for much of the time to overshadow all other concerns. However, two other themes ran through Middle East affairs which became mixed up with the anti-Israel struggle:

- the desire of some Arabs to achieve political and economic unity among the Arab states;
- the desire of many Arabs to put an end to foreign intervention in their countries.

The Middle East attracted a lot of attention from both western and communist powers, because of its strategic position and rich oil resources. In addition, there were a number of conflicts involving individual Arab states:

- There was civil war in the Lebanon which lasted for close on 15 years from 1975.
- There was a war between Iran and Iraq lasting from 1980 until 1988.
- In the First Gulf War (1990–1) Iraqi troops invaded Kuwait and were driven out again by an international coalition led by the USA.

Interpretations of the Middle East situation vary depending on whose viewpoint one looks at. For example, many British politicians and journalists regarded Colonel Nasser

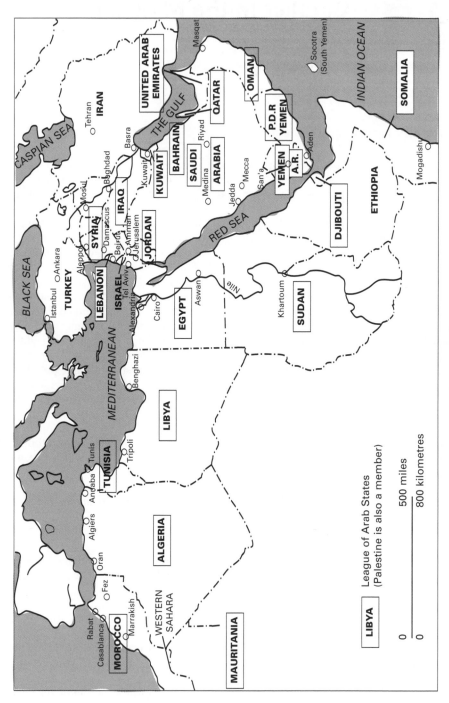

Map 11.1 The Middle East and North Africa

LIBYA League of Arab States
(Palestine is also a member)

0   500 miles
0   800 kilometres

(Egyptian leader 1954–70) as some kind of dangerous fanatic who was almost as bad as Hitler. On the other hand, most Arabs thought he was a hero, the symbol of the Arab people's move towards unity and freedom.

11.1 ARAB UNITY AND INTERFERENCE FROM THE OUTSIDE WORLD

(a) Arabs have several things in common

They all speak the Arabic language, they are nearly all Muslims (followers of the religion known as Islam), except for about half the population of Lebanon, who are Christian; and most of them wanted to see the destruction of Israel so that the Palestinian Arabs could have back the land which they feel is rightfully theirs. Many Arabs wanted to see the unity carried much further into some sort of political and economic union, like the European Community. As early as 1931 an Islamic conference in Jerusalem put out this announcement: 'The Arab lands are a complete and indivisible whole ... all efforts are to be directed towards their complete independence, in their entirety and unified.'

Several attempts were made to increase unity among the Arab states.

- *The Arab League, founded in 1945*, included Egypt, Syria, Jordan, Iraq, Lebanon, Saudi Arabia and Yemen; membership later expanded to include 20 states in 1980. However, it achieved very little politically and was constantly hampered by internal squabbles.
- In the mid-1950s Arab unity (sometimes known as pan-Arabism, 'pan' meaning 'all') received a boost with *the energetic leadership of Colonel Gamal Abdel Nasser of Egypt*, who gained enormous prestige in the Arab world after the 1956 Suez Crisis (see Section 11.3). In 1958 Syria joined Egypt to form *the United Arab Republic*, with Nasser as president. However, this only lasted until 1961 when Syria withdrew because of resentment at Nasser's attempts to dominate the union.
- After Nasser's death in 1970, his successor, President Sadat, organized a loose union between Egypt, Libya and Syria, known as *the Federation of Arab Republics*; but it never amounted to much.

In spite of their similarities, there were too many points on which the Arab states disagreed for unity ever to be really close. For example:

- Jordan and Saudi Arabia were ruled (and still are) by fairly conservative royal families who were often criticized for being too pro-British by the governments of Egypt and Syria, which were pro-Arab nationalist as well as socialist.
- The other Arab states fell out with Egypt in 1979 because Egypt signed a separate peace treaty with Israel (see Section 11.6). This caused Egypt to be expelled from the Arab League.

(b) Interference in the Middle East by other countries

- British and French involvement in the Middle East stretched back many years. Britain ruled Egypt from 1882 (when British troops invaded it) until 1922, when the country was given semi-independence under its own king. However, British troops still remained in Egypt and the Egyptians had to continue doing what Britain wanted. By the Versailles settlement at the end of the First World War, Britain and France were given large areas of the Middle East taken from the defeated Turks, to

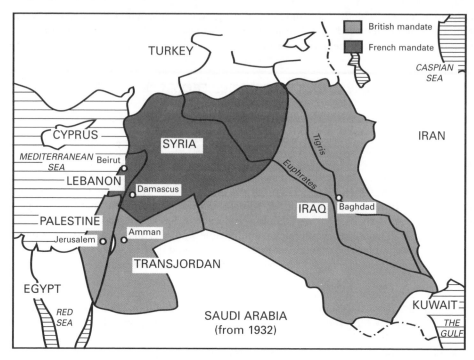

Map 11.2 **Areas given to Britain and France as mandates at the end of the First World War**

look after as mandates. Map 11.2 shows which areas were involved. Although Britain gave independence to Iraq (1932) and to Jordan (1946), both remained pro-British. France gave independence to Syria and Lebanon (1945) but hoped to maintain some influence in the Middle East.

- The Middle East held a very important strategic position in the world – it acted as a sort of crossroads between the western nations, the communist bloc and the Third World countries of Africa and Asia.
- At one time the Middle East produced over a third of the world's oil supplies, the main producers being Iran, Iraq, Saudi Arabia and Kuwait. In the days before North Sea oil was available, and before the advent of nuclear power, the European nations were heavily dependent on oil supplies from the Middle East and wanted to make sure that the oil-producing states had friendly governments which would sell them oil cheaply.
- The lack of unity among the Arab states encouraged other countries to intervene in the Middle East.

Most of the Arab states had nationalist governments which bitterly resented western influence. *One by one, governments that were thought to be too pro-West were swept away and replaced by regimes which wanted to be non-aligned*; this meant being free to act independently of both East (Communist bloc) and West.

1 Egypt
At the end of the Second World War, British troops stayed on in the canal zone (the area around the Suez Canal). This was to enable Britain to control the canal, in which over half

the shares were owned by the British and French. In 1952 a group of Egyptian army officers, tired of waiting for the British to leave, overthrew Farouk, the King of Egypt (who was thought not to be firm enough with the British), and seized power themselves. *By 1954 Colonel Nasser had become president* and his policy of standing up to Britain soon led to the Suez War of 1956 (see Section 11.3 for full details). This brought complete humiliation for Britain and was the end of British influence in Egypt.

2 Jordan

King Abdullah had been given his throne by the British in 1946. He was assassinated in 1951 by nationalists who felt that he was too much under Britain's thumb. His successor, King Hussein, had to tread very carefully to survive. He ended the treaty which allowed British troops to use bases in Jordan (1957), and all British troops were withdrawn.

3 Iraq

King Faisal of Iraq and his prime minister, Nuri-es-Said, were pro-British; in 1955 they signed an agreement with Turkey (*the Baghdad Pact*) to set up a joint defence and economic policy. Pakistan, Iran and Britain also joined, Britain promising to help Iraq if she was attacked. The British humiliation in the 1956 Suez War encouraged the anti-British movement in Iraq to act: Faisal and Nuri-es-Said were murdered and Iraq became a republic (1958). The new government was sympathetic towards Egypt and it withdrew Iraq from the Baghdad Pact. This marked the end of Britain's attempt to play a major role in Arab affairs.

4 Iran

Important changes were taking place in Iran, the only Middle East state which had a frontier with the USSR. In 1945 the Russians tried to set up a communist government in northern Iran, the part that bordered on the USSR and which had a large and active communist party. The western-educated Shah (ruler) of Iran, Reza Pahlevi, resisted the Russians and signed a defence treaty with the USA (1950); they provided him with economic and military aid, including tanks and jet fighters. The Americans saw the situation as part of the Cold War – Iran was yet another front where they thought it vital to prevent a communist advance. However, there was a strong nationalist movement in Iran which resented all foreign influence. Feelings soon began to turn against the USA and against Britain too. This was because Britain held a majority of the shares in *the Anglo-Iranian Oil Company* and its refinery at Abadan. It was widely felt that the British were taking too much of the profits, and in 1951 the Premier of Iran, Dr Mussadiq, nationalized the company (took it under the control of the Iranian government). However, most of the world, encouraged by Britain, boycotted Iran's oil exports and Mussadiq was forced to resign. In 1954 a compromise was reached in which British Petroleum was allowed 40 per cent of the shares. Iran now took 50 per cent of the profits, which the Shah was able to use for a cautious modernization and land reform programme.

This was not enough for the left and for the devout Muslims. They resented the Shah's close ties with the USA, which they considered to be an immoral influence on their country. They also suspected that a large slice of the country's wealth was finding its way into his private fortune. In January 1979 he was forced to leave the country, and *an Islamic republic was set up* under a religious leader, the Ayatollah (a sort of High Priest) Khomeini. Like Nasser, he wanted his country to be non-aligned.

(a) Why did the creation of the state of Israel lead to war?

1   The origin of the problem went back almost 2000 years to the year AD 71, *when most of the Jews were driven out of Palestine, which was then their homeland, by the Romans*. In fact, small communities of Jews stayed behind in Palestine, and over the following 1700 years there was a gradual trickle of Jews returning from exile. Until the end of the nineteenth century, however, there were never enough Jews to make the Arabs, who now looked on Palestine as their homeland, feel threatened.

2   In 1897 some Jews living in Europe founded *the World Zionist Organization* at Basle in Switzerland. Zionists were people who believed that Jews ought to be able to go back to Palestine and have what they called 'a national homeland'; in other words, a Jewish state. Jews had recently suffered persecution in Russia, France and Germany, and a Jewish state would provide a safe refuge for Jews from all over the world. The problem was that *Palestine was inhabited by Arabs* who were understandably alarmed at the prospect of losing their land to the Jews.

3   Britain became involved in 1917, when the foreign minister, Arthur Balfour, announced that *Britain supported the idea of a Jewish national home in Palestine*. After 1919, when Palestine became a British mandate, large numbers of Jews began to arrive in Palestine, and the Arabs protested bitterly to the British that they wanted an independent Palestine for the Arabs, and an end to the immigration of Jews.

    The British government stated (1922) that there was no intention of the Jews occupying the whole of Palestine and that there would be no interference with the rights of the Palestinian Arabs. Balfour himself said in his declaration: 'nothing shall be done which may prejudice the civil and religious rights of the existing non-Jewish communities in Palestine'. The British hoped to persuade Jews and Arabs to live together peacefully in the same state; they failed to understand the deep religious gulf between the two; and they failed to keep Balfour's promise.

4   Nazi persecution of Jews in Germany after 1933 caused a flood of refugees, and by 1940 about half the population of Palestine was Jewish. From 1936 onwards there were violent protests by Arabs and an uprising, which the British suppressed with some brutality, killing over 3000 Arabs. *In 1937 the British Peel Commission proposed dividing Palestine into two separate states*, one Arab and one Jewish, but the Arabs rejected the idea. The British tried again in 1939, offering an independent Arab state within ten years, and Jewish immigration limited to 10 000 a year; this time the Jews rejected the proposal.

5   *The Second World War made the situation much worse*: there were hundreds of thousands of Jewish refugees from Hitler's Europe desperately looking for somewhere to go. In 1945 the USA pressed Britain to allow 100 000 Jews into Palestine; this demand was echoed by David Ben Gurion, one of the Jewish leaders, but the British, not wanting to offend the Arabs, refused.

6   The Jews, after all that their race had suffered at the hands of the Nazis, were determined to fight for their 'national home'. They began a terrorist campaign against both Arabs and British; one of the most spectacular incidents was the blowing up of the King David Hotel in Jerusalem, which the British were using as their headquarters; 91 people were killed and many more injured. The British responded by arresting Jewish leaders and by turning back ships such as the *Exodus*, crammed with Jews intending to enter Palestine.

7   *The British, weakened by the strain of the Second World War, felt unable to cope*. Ernest Bevin, the Labour foreign secretary, asked the United Nations to deal with

the problem, and in *November 1947, the UN voted to divide Palestine*, setting aside roughly half of it to form an independent Jewish state. Early in 1948 the British decided to come out altogether and let the UN carry out its own plan. Although fighting was already going on between Jews and Arabs (who bitterly resented the loss of half of Palestine), the British withdrew all their troops. In May 1948 Ben Gurion declared the independence of the new state of Israel. It was immediately attacked by Egypt, Syria, Jordan, Iraq and Lebanon.

(b)   Who was to blame for the tragedy?

- *Most of the rest of the world seemed to blame Britain for the chaos in Palestine.* Many British newspapers which supported the Conservative Party also criticized Bevin and Britain's Labour government for its handling of the situation. It was said that British troops should have stayed on to ensure that the partition of Palestine was carried out smoothly. The Arabs accused the British of being pro-Jewish, for letting far too many Jews into Palestine in the first place, and for causing them to lose half their homeland. The Jews accused the British of being pro-Arab, for trying to limit Jewish immigration.
- *Bevin blamed the USA for the chaos*, and there is some evidence to support his case. It was US President Truman who pressured Britain to allow 100 000 extra Jews to go to Palestine in April 1946. Although this was bound to upset the Arabs even more, Truman refused to provide any American troops to help keep order in Palestine, and refused to allow any more Jews to enter the USA. It was Truman who rejected *the British Morrison Plan (July 1946)*, which would have set up separate Arab and Jewish provinces under British supervision. It was the Americans who pushed the plan for partition through the UN, even though all the Arab nations voted against it; this was bound to cause more violence in Palestine.
- *Some historians have defended the British*, pointing out that they were trying to be fair to both sides, and that in the end, it was impossible to persuade both Arabs and Jews to accept a peaceful solution. The British withdrawal was understandable: it would force the Americans and the UN to take more responsibility for the situation they had helped create. It would save the British, who since 1945 had spent over £100 million trying to keep the peace, further expense which they could ill afford.

(c)   The war and its outcome

Most people expected the Arabs to win easily, but against seemingly overwhelming odds, *the Israelis defeated them and even captured more of Palestine than the UN partition had given them*. They ended up with about three-quarters of Palestine plus the Egyptian port of Eilat on the Red Sea. The Israelis won because they fought desperately, and many of their troops had gained military experience fighting in the British army during the Second World War (some 30 000 Jewish men volunteered to fight for the British). The Arab states were divided among themselves and poorly equipped. The Palestinians themselves were demoralized, and their military organization had been destroyed by the British during the uprisings of 1936–9.

The most tragic outcome of the war was that the Palestinian Arabs became the innocent victims: they had suddenly lost three-quarters of their homeland, and the majority were now without a state of their own. Some were in the new Jewish state of Israel; others found themselves living in the area – known as the West Bank – occupied by Jordan. After some Jews had slaughtered the entire population of an Arab village in Israel, nearly a million

Arabs fled into Egypt, Lebanon, Jordan and Syria, where they had to live in miserable refugee camps. The city of Jerusalem was divided between Israel and Jordan. The USA, Britain and France guaranteed Israel's frontiers, but the Arab states did not regard the ceasefire as permanent. They would not recognize the legality of Israel, and they regarded this war as only the first round in the struggle to destroy Israel and liberate Palestine.

11.3 THE SUEZ WAR OF 1956

(a) Who was to blame for the war?

It is possible to blame different countries depending on one's point of view.

- The Arabs blamed the Israelis, who actually began hostilities by invading Egypt.
- The communist bloc and many Arab states blamed Britain and France, accusing them of imperialist tactics (trying to keep control in the Middle East against the wishes of the Arab nations) by attacking Egypt. They accused the Americans of encouraging Britain to attack.
- The British, French and Israelis blamed Colonel Nasser of Egypt for being anti-Western. However, even the Americans thought that Britain and France had over-reacted by using force, and most British historians agree.

1 *Colonel Nasser, the new ruler of Egypt*, was aggressively in favour of Arab unity and independence, including the liberation of Palestine from the Jews; almost everything he did irritated the British, Americans or French:

- He organized guerrilla fighters known as *fedayeen* ('self-sacrificers') to carry out sabotage and murder inside Israel, and Egyptian ships blockaded the Gulf of Aqaba leading to the port of Eilat, which the Israelis had taken from Egypt in 1949.
- In 1936 Britain had signed an agreement with Egypt which allowed the British to keep troops at Suez. This treaty was due to expire in 1956, and Britain wanted it renewed. Nasser refused and insisted that all British troops should withdraw immediately the treaty ended. He sent help to the Algerian Arabs in their struggle against France (see Section 24.5(c)), prodded the other Arab states into opposing the British-sponsored Baghdad Pact, and forced King Hussein of Jordan to dismiss his British army chief of staff.
- He signed an arms deal with Czechoslovakia (September 1955) for Russian fighters, bombers and tanks, and Russian military experts went to train the Egyptian army.

2 *The Americans were outraged at this*, since it meant that the West no longer controlled arms supplies to Egypt. Egypt now became part of the Cold War: any country which was not part of the Western alliance and which bought arms from Eastern Europe was, in American eyes, just as bad as a communist country. It was seen as a sinister plot by the Russians to 'move into' the Middle East. The Americans therefore cancelled a promised grant of $46 million towards the building of a dam at Aswan (July 1956); their intention was to force Nasser to abandon his new links with the communists.

3 *Crisis point was reached when Nasser immediately retaliated by nationalizing the Suez Canal*, intending to use the income from it to finance the dam. Shareholders in the canal, the majority of whom were British and French, were promised compensation.

4   *Anthony Eden, the British Conservative prime minister, took the lead at this point.* He believed that Nasser was on the way to forming a united Arabia under Egyptian control and communist influence, which could cut off Europe's oil supplies at will. He viewed Nasser as another Hitler or Mussolini, and according to historian Hugh Thomas, 'saw Egypt through a forest of Flanders poppies and gleaming jackboots'. He was not alone in this: Churchill remarked: 'We can't have this malicious swine sitting across our communications', and the new Labour leader, Hugh Gaitskell, agreed that Nasser must not be appeased in the way that Hitler and Mussolini had been appeased in the 1930s. Everybody in Britain ignored the fact that Nasser had offered compensation to the shareholders and had promised that the ships of all nations (except Israel) would be able to use the canal.

5   Secret talks took place between the British, French and Israelis and a plan was hatched: Israel would invade Egypt across the Sinai peninsula, whereupon British and French troops would occupy the canal zone on the pretext that they were protecting it from damage in the fighting. Anglo-French control of the canal would be restored, and the defeat, it was hoped, would topple Nasser from power.

Recent research has shown that the war could easily have been avoided and that Eden was more in favour of getting rid of Nasser by peaceful means. In fact there was a secret Anglo-American plan (*Omega*) to overthrow Nasser using political and economic pressures. In mid-October 1956, Eden was still willing to continue talks with Egypt. He had called off the military operation and there seemed a good chance of compromise being reached over control of the Suez Canal. However, Eden was under pressure from several directions to use force. MI6 (the British Intelligence Service) and some members of the British government, including Harold Macmillan (chancellor of the exchequer), urged military action. Macmillan assured Eden that the USA would not oppose a British use of force. In the end, it was probably pressure from the French government which caused Eden to opt for a joint military operation with France and Israel.

(b)   Events in the war

The war began with the planned Israeli invasion of Egypt (29 October). This was a brilliant success, and within a week the Israelis had captured the entire Sinai peninsula. Meanwhile the British and French bombed Egyptian airfields and landed troops at Port Said at the northern end of the canal. *The attacks caused an outcry from the rest of the world*, and the Americans, who were afraid of upsetting all the Arabs and forcing them into closer ties with the USSR, refused to support Britain, although they had earlier hinted that support would be forthcoming. At the United Nations, Americans and Russians for once agreed: they demanded an immediate ceasefire, and prepared to send a UN force. With the pressure of world opinion against them, *Britain, France and Israel agreed to withdraw*, while UN troops moved in to police the frontier between Egypt and Israel.

(c)   The outcome of the war

It was a complete humiliation for Britain and France, who achieved none of their aims, and *it was a triumph for President Nasser.*

- The war failed to overthrow Nasser, and his prestige as the leader of Arab nationalism against interfering Europeans was greatly increased; for the ordinary Arab people, he was a hero.

- The Egyptians blocked the canal, the Arabs reduced oil supplies to western Europe, where petrol rationing was introduced for a time, and Russian aid replaced that from the USA.
- The British action soon lost them an ally in Iraq, where premier Nuri-es-Said came under increasing attack from other Arabs for his pro-British attitude; he was murdered in 1958.
- Britain was now weak and unable to follow a foreign policy independently of the USA.
- The Algerians were encouraged in their struggle for independence from France which they achieved in 1962.

The war was not without success for Israel: although she had been compelled to hand back all territory captured from Egypt, she had inflicted heavy losses on the Egyptians in men and equipment, which would take years to make good. For the time being the *fedayeen* raids ceased and Israel had a breathing space in which to consolidate. Following Britain's humiliation, the Israelis now looked towards the USA as their chief supporter.

11.4 THE SIX-DAY WAR OF 1967

The Arab states had not signed a peace treaty at the end of the 1948–9 war and were still refusing to give Israel official recognition. In 1967 they joined together again in a determined attempt to destroy Israel. The lead was taken by Iraq, Syria and Egypt.

(a) The build-up to war

1 *In Iraq*, a new government came to power in 1963 which was influenced by the ideas of *the Ba'ath Party* in neighbouring Syria. Supporters of the Ba'ath (meaning 'resurrection') believed in Arab independence and unity and were left-wing in outlook, wanting social reform and better treatment for ordinary people. They were prepared to co-operate with Egypt, and in June 1967 their president, Aref, announced: 'Our goal is clear – to wipe Israel off the map.'

2 *In Syria*, political upheavals brought the Ba'ath Party to power in 1966. It supported *El Fatah, the Palestinian Liberation Movement*, a more effective guerrilla force than the *fedayeen*. Founded in 1957, Fatah eventually became the core section of the Palestine Liberation Organization (PLO), with Yasser Arafat as one of its leaders. The Syrians also began to bombard Jewish settlements from the Golan Heights, which overlooked the frontier.

3 *In Egypt*, Colonel Nasser was immensely popular because of his leadership of the Arab world and his attempts to improve conditions in Egypt with his socialist policies. These included limiting the size of farms to 100 acres and redistributing surplus land to peasants. Attempts were made to industrialize the country, and over a thousand new factories were built, almost all under government control. *The Aswan Dam project* was vitally important, providing electricity, and water for irrigating an extra million acres of land. After early delays at the time of the Suez War in 1956, work on the dam eventually got under way and the project was completed in 1971. With all going well at home and the prospect of effective help from Iraq and Syria, Nasser decided that the time was ripe for another attack on Israel. He began to move troops up to the frontier in Sinai and closed the Gulf of Aqaba.

4 *The Russians encouraged Egypt and Syria* and kept up a flow of anti-Israeli propaganda (because Israel was being supported by the USA). Their aim was to increase

their influence in the Middle East at the expense of the Americans and Israelis. They hinted that they would send help if war came.

5   *Syria, Jordan and Lebanon* also massed troops along their frontiers with Israel, while contingents from Iraq, Saudi Arabia and Algeria joined them. Israel's situation seemed hopeless.

6   *The Israelis decided that the best policy was to attack first rather than wait to be defeated.* They launched a series of devastating air strikes, which destroyed most of the Egyptian air force on the ground (5 June). Israeli troops moved with remarkable speed, capturing the Gaza Strip and the whole of Sinai from Egypt, the rest of Jerusalem and the West Bank from Jordan, and the Golan Heights from Syria. The Arabs had no choice but to accept a UN ceasefire order (10 June), and it was all over in less than a week. *Reasons for the spectacular Israeli success were*: the slow and ponderous Arab troop build-up which gave the Israelis plenty of warning, Israeli superiority in the air, and inadequate Arab preparations and communications.

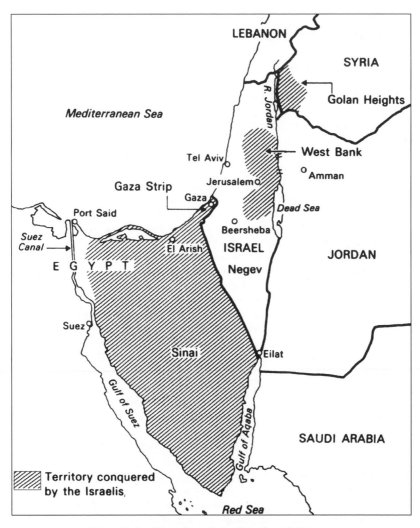

Map 11.3   **The situation after the 1967 war**

(b) Results of the war

1 *For the Israelis it was a spectacular success*: this time they had ignored a UN order to return the captured territory; this acted as a series of buffer zones between Israel and the Arab states (see Map 11.3), and meant that it would be much easier to defend Israel. However, it did bring a new problem – how to deal with about a million extra Arabs who now found themselves under Israeli rule. Many of these were living in the refugee camps set up in 1948 on the West Bank and in the Gaza Strip.

2 *It was a humiliation for the Arab states*, and especially for Nasser, who now realized that the Arabs needed outside help if they were ever to free Palestine. The Russians had been a disappointment to Nasser and had sent no help. To try and improve their relations with Egypt and Syria, the Russians began to supply them with modern weapons. Sooner or later the Arabs would try again to destroy Israel and liberate Palestine. The next attempt came in 1973 with the Yom Kippur War.

11.5 THE YOM KIPPUR WAR OF 1973

(a) Events leading up to the war

Several things combined to cause the renewed conflict.

1 *Pressure was brought to bear on the Arab states by the Palestine Liberation Organization (PLO)* under its leader Yasser Arafat, for some further action. When very little happened, a more extreme group within the PLO, called the Popular Front for the Liberation of Palestine (PFLP), embarked on a series of terrorist attacks to draw world attention to the grave injustice being done to the Arabs of Palestine. They hijacked airliners and flew three of them to Amman, the capital of Jordan, where they were blown up (1970). This was embarrassing for King Hussein of Jordan, who now favoured a negotiated peace, and in September 1970 he expelled all PLO members based in Jordan. However, terrorist attacks continued, reaching a horrifying climax when some members of the Israeli team were murdered at the 1972 Munich Olympics.

2 *Anwar Sadat, the president of Egypt since Nasser's death in 1970, was becoming increasingly convinced of the need for a negotiated peace settlement with Israel.* He was worried that PLO terrorism would turn world opinion against the Palestinian cause. He was prepared to work either with the USA or with the USSR, but he hoped to win American support for the Arabs, so that the Americans would persuade the Israelis to agree to a peace settlement. However, the Americans refused to get involved.

3 *Sadat, together with Syria, decided to attack Israel again, hoping that this would force the Americans to act as mediators.* The Egyptians were feeling more confident because they now had modern Russian weapons and their army had been trained by Russian experts.

(b) The war began on 6 October 1973

Egyptian and Syrian forces attacked early on the feast of Yom Kippur, a Jewish religious festival, hoping to catch the Israelis off guard. After some early Arab successes, the Israelis, using mainly American weapons, were able to turn the tables. They succeeded in hanging on to all the territory they had captured in 1967 and even crossed the Suez Canal into Egypt. In one sense Sadat's plan had been successful – both the USA and the USSR decided it was time to intervene to try to bring about a peace settlement. Acting with UN co-operation, they organized a ceasefire, which both sides accepted.

(c)   The outcome of the war

The end of the war brought a glimmer of hope for some sort of permanent peace. Egyptian and Israeli leaders came together (though not in the same room) in Geneva. The Israelis agreed to move their troops back from the Suez Canal (which had been closed since the 1967 war), which enabled the Egyptians to clear and open the canal in 1975 (but not to Israeli ships).

An important development during the war was that the Arab oil-producing states tried to bring pressure to bear on the USA and on western European states which were friendly to Israel, by reducing oil supplies. This caused serious oil shortages, especially in Europe. At the same time producers, well aware that oil supplies were not unlimited, looked on their action as a way of preserving resources. With this in mind, *the Organization of Petroleum Exporting Countries (OPEC)* began to raise oil prices substantially. This contributed to inflation and caused an energy crisis in the world's industrial nations.

11.6   CAMP DAVID AND THE EGYPTIAN–ISRAELI PEACE, 1978–9

(a)   Why did the two sides begin to talk to each other?

1   President Sadat had become convinced that *Israel could not be destroyed by force*, and that it was foolish to keep on wasting Egypt's resources in fruitless wars; but it took great courage to be the first Arab leader to meet the Israelis face to face. Even to talk with Israeli leaders meant conceding that Egypt recognized the lawful existence of the state of Israel. He knew that the PLO and the more aggressive Arab states, Iraq and Syria, would bitterly resent any approach. In spite of the dangers, Sadat offered to go to Israel and talk to the Knesset (Israeli parliament).
2   *The Israelis were suffering economic problems*, partly because of their enormous defence expenditure, and partly because of a world recession. The USA was pressing them to settle their differences with at least some of the Arabs. They accepted Sadat's offer; he visited Israel in November 1977, and Menachem Begin, the Israeli prime minister, visited Egypt the following month.
3   *President Carter of the USA played a vital role* in setting up formal negotiations between the two sides, which began in September 1978 at Camp David (near Washington).

(b)   The peace treaty and its aftermath

With Carter acting as intermediary, the talks led to a peace treaty being signed in Washington in March 1979. *The main points agreed were*:

•   The state of war that had existed between Egypt and Israel since 1948 was now ended;

- Israel promised to withdraw its troops from Sinai;
- Egypt promised not to attack Israel again and guaranteed to supply her with oil from the recently opened wells in southern Sinai;
- Israeli ships could use the Suez Canal.

The treaty was condemned by the PLO and most other Arab states (except Sudan and Morocco) and there was clearly a long way to go before similar treaties could be signed by Israel with Syria and Jordan. World opinion began to move against Israel and to accept that the PLO had a good case; but when the USA tried to bring the PLO and Israel together in an international conference, the Israelis would not co-operate. In November 1980 Begin announced that *Israel would never return the Golan Heights to Syria*, not even in exchange for a peace treaty; and *they would never allow the West Bank to become part of an independent Palestinian state*; that would be a mortal threat to Israel's existence. At the same time, resentment mounted among West Bank Arabs at the Israeli policy of establishing Jewish settlements on land owned by Arabs. Many observers feared fresh violence unless Begin's government adopted a more moderate approach.

The peace also seemed threatened for a time when *President Sadat was assassinated* by some extremist Muslim soldiers while he was watching a military parade (October 1981). They believed that he had betrayed the Arab and Muslim cause by doing a deal with the Israelis. However, Sadat's successor, Hosni Mubarak, bravely announced that he would continue the Camp David agreement.

For most of the 1980s the Arab–Israeli feud was overshadowed by the Iran–Iraq War (see Section 11.9), which occupied much of the Arab world's attention. But beginning in December 1987 there were massive demonstrations by Palestinians living in the refugee camps of the Gaza Strip and the West Bank (see Map 11.3). The *intifada* ('shaking off'), as it was known, was a long campaign of civil disobedience involving strikes, non-payment of taxes, and an attempt to boycott Israeli products. They were protesting against repressive Israeli policies and the brutal behaviour of Israeli troops in the camps and in the occupied territories. An Israeli clampdown failed to quell the *intifada*, which continued for over three years. The Israelis' tough methods earned them UN and worldwide condemnation.

11.7   PEACE BETWEEN ISRAEL AND THE PLO

The election of a less aggressive government (Labour) in Israel in June 1992 raised hopes for better relations with the Palestinians. Prime Minister Yitzak Rabin and Foreign Minister Shimon Peres both believed in negotiation, and were prepared to make concessions in order to achieve a lasting peace. Yasser Arafat, the PLO leader, responded and talks opened. But there was so much mutual suspicion and distrust after all the years of hostility that progress was difficult. However, both sides persevered and by early 1996, remarkable changes had taken place.

(a)   The peace accord of September 1993

This, the first major breakthrough, took place at a conference in Oslo, and became known as *the Oslo Accords. It was agreed that*:

- Israel formally recognized the PLO;
- the PLO recognized Israel's right to exist and promised to give up terrorism;

- the Palestinians were to be given limited self-rule in Jericho (on the West Bank) and in part of the Gaza Strip, areas occupied by Israel since the 1967 war. Israeli troops would be withdrawn from these areas.

Extremist groups on both sides opposed the agreement. The Popular Front for the Liberation of Palestine still wanted a completely independent Palestinian state. Israeli settlers on the West Bank were against all concessions to the PLO. However, the moderate leaders on both sides showed great courage and determination, especially Yossi Beilin, the Israeli deputy foreign minister, and Mahmoud Abbas (also known as Abu Mazen), one

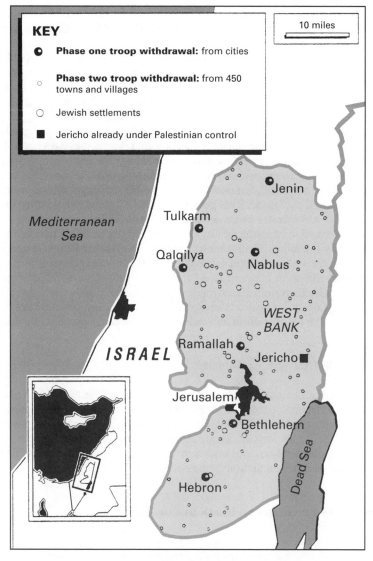

Map 11.4 **The Israeli–Palestinian Agreement, 1995**

Source: *The Guardian*, 25 September 1995

of Arafat's advisers. Two years later they took an even more momentous step forward, building on the Oslo Accords.

(b)   Self-rule for the Palestinians (September–October 1995)

- Israel agreed to withdraw its troops from most of the West Bank (except Hebron), in stages over several years, handing over both civil and security powers to the PLO. This would end Israeli control of the areas they had held since 1967 (see Map 11.4). The areas would then remain demilitarized.
- The areas would be ruled by a parliament or Palestinian Council of 88 members, to be elected early in 1996 by all West Bankers and Arab residents of Jerusalem aged over 18. East Jerusalem was to be the capital.
- All Palestinian prisoners held by Israel (about 6000) would be released, in three phases.

Most of the world's leaders welcomed this brave attempt to bring peace to the troubled region. But once again extremists on both sides claimed that their leaders were guilty of 'shameful surrender'. Tragically, Prime Minister Yitzhak Rabin was assassinated by an Israeli fanatic shortly after addressing a peace rally (4 November 1995). Peres became prime minister; the murder caused a revulsion of feeling against the extremists and the agreement was gradually put into operation. In January 1996, King Hussein of Jordan paid an official public visit to Israel for the first time, 1200 Palestinian prisoners were released and talks opened between Israel and Syria. The promised elections were held; although the extremists urged people to boycott them, there was an encouragingly large turnout of over 80 per cent. As expected, Yasser Arafat became the new Palestinian president and his supporters were in a large majority in the newly elected parliament. This government was expected to hold office until 1999, when, it was hoped, a permanent peace agreement would have been reached.

However, the situation changed rapidly during the spring of 1996: four suicide bombings, carried out by the militant Palestinian group Hamas (Islamic Resistance Movement), claimed 63 lives; the militant Shiite Islamic group Hezbollah (Party of God), based in Lebanon, shelled villages in northern Israel from southern Lebanon. All this enabled the hardline Likud leader Binyamin Netanyahu, who denounced Labour policy as 'too soft' towards the Palestinians, to win a narrow victory in the election of May 1996. This dismayed much of the outside world and threw the whole peace process into doubt.

11.8   CONFLICT IN THE LEBANON

Originally part of the Ottoman (Turkish) Empire, Lebanon (see Map 11.5) was made a French mandate at the end of the First World War and became fully independent in 1945. It soon became a prosperous state, making money from banking and from serving as an important outlet for the exports of Syria, Jordan and Iraq. However, in 1975 civil war broke out, and although all-out war ended in 1976, chaos and disorder continued right through the 1980s as different factions struggled to gain influence.

(a)   What caused civil war to break out in 1975?

1   Religious differences
The potential for trouble was there from the beginning, since the country was *a bewildering mixture of different religious groups*, some Muslim, some Christian, which had developed independently, separated from each other by mountain ranges.

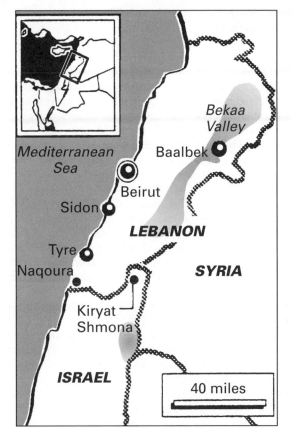

Map 11.5 **The Lebanon**

Source: *The Guardian*, May 1996

There were four main Christian groups:

- Maronites (the wealthiest and most conservative);
- Greek Orthodox;
- Roman Catholics;
- Armenians.

There were three Muslim groups:

- Shia – the largest group, mainly poor working class;
- Sunni – a smaller group, but wealthier and with more political influence than the Shia;
- Druze – a small group living in the centre of the country, mainly peasants.

There was a long history of hatred between Maronites and Druze, but this seemed to be kept in check by the carefully framed constitution, which tried to give fair representation to all groups. The president was always a Maronite, the prime minister a Sunni, the speaker (chairman of parliament) a Shia, and the army chief of staff a Druze. Of the 43 seats in parliament, the Maronites were allowed 13, Sunni 9, Shia 8, Greek Orthodox 5, Druze 3, Roman Catholics 3 and Armenians 2.

2   The presence of Palestinian refugees from Israel

This complicated the situation even more. By 1975 there were at least half a million of them living in squalid camps away from the main centres of population. The Palestinians were not popular in Lebanon because they were continually involved in frontier incidents with Israel, provoking the Israelis to hit back at the Palestinians in southern Lebanon. In particular the Palestinians, being left-wing and Muslim, alarmed conservative and Christian Maronites, who looked on the Palestinians as a dangerous destabilizing influence. By 1975 the PLO had its headquarters in Lebanon, and this meant that Syria, the chief supporter of the PLO, was constantly interfering in Lebanon's affairs.

3   A dispute between Muslims and Christians over fishing rights (1975)

The delicate balance between Muslims and Christians was upset in 1975 by a dispute over fishing rights. It began as an apparently minor incident, but it escalated when some Palestinians sided with the Muslims, and a group of right-wing Christians, known as the *Phalange*, began to attack Palestinians. Soon a full-scale civil war developed: the Maronites saw it as a chance to expel the Palestinians who had formed an alliance with the Druze (long-term enemies of the Maronites).

It is probably impossible to discover with complete certainty which side was responsible for the escalation of the war. Both sides claimed that the original fishing dispute could have been settled easily, and each blamed the other for escalating the violence. Either way, the PLO were certainly involved: the Phalangists claimed that PLO guerrillas had fired on a church where some party leaders were attending mass; the PLO claimed that the Phalangists started it by attacking a bus carrying Palestinians.

For a time it looked as though the Druze would win, but this alarmed the Israelis, who threatened to invade Lebanon. The Syrians did not want this to happen, and so in 1976 President Assad of Syria sent troops into the Lebanon to keep the PLO under some sort of control. Order was restored and it was a setback for the Druze and the PLO. It was the Syrians who now controlled Lebanon; Yasser Arafat, the PLO leader, had to agree to withdraw his troops from the area around Beirut (the capital of Lebanon).

(b)   Chaos continues

It was over ten years before something approaching peace was restored in Lebanon, as *different conflicts raged in different places.*

1   *In the south, bordering on Israel, fighting soon broke out between Palestinians and Christians.* The Israelis seized this opportunity to send troops in to help the Christians. A small semi-independent Christian state of Free Lebanon was declared under Major Haddad. The Israelis supported this because it acted as a buffer zone to protect them from further Palestinian attacks. The Palestinians and Muslims counter-attacked, and although by 1982 there were 7000 UNIFIL (United Nations Interim Force in the Lebanon) troops in the area, it was a constant struggle to keep the peace.

2   *In 1980 there was a short struggle between supporters of the two main Maronite groups* (the Gemayel and Chamoun families), which was won by the Gemayels.

3   *In 1982, in reprisal for a Palestinian attack on Israel, Israeli troops invaded Lebanon and penetrated as far as Beirut,* while Israeli planes bombed the Palestinian refugee camps of Sabra and Shatila. For a time the Gemayels, supported

by the Israelis, were in control of Beirut. During this period the Palestinians were expelled from Beirut, and from then on the PLO was divided. The hardliners went to Iraq and the rest dispersed into different Arab countries, where they were, on the whole, not welcome. The Israelis withdrew and a multinational force (made up of troops from the USA, France, Italy and Britain) took their place to maintain the peace. However, a spate of attacks and suicide bombings forced them to withdraw.

4   In 1984 an alliance of Shia militia (known as Amal) and Druze militia, backed by Syria, drove President Gemayel out of Beirut. Then the Shia and Druze themselves came to blows in a struggle for control of West Beirut. Yasser Arafat used the general confusion to rearm his Palestinians in the refugee camps.

At the end of 1986 the situation was extremely complex:

- Shiite Amal militia, backed by Syria, alarmed at the renewed strength of the PLO, which seemed likely to set up a state within a state, were besieging the refugee camps, hoping to starve them into surrender.
- At the same time an alliance of Druze, Sunni and communists was trying to drive Amal out of West Beirut. Another more extreme Shia group, known as Hezbollah (Party of God), which was backed by Iran, was also involved in the struggle.
- Early in 1987 fierce fighting again erupted between Shia and Druze militia for control of West Beirut. Several European and American hostages were seized, including Terry Waite, the Archbishop of Canterbury's special envoy, who had gone to West Beirut to try to negotiate the release of some earlier hostages.
- With the country apparently in a state of total disintegration, President Assad of Syria, responding to a request from the Lebanese government, again sent his troops and tanks into West Beirut (February 1987). Within a week, calm had been restored.

(c)   Peace at last

Although assassinations of leading figures continued, the situation gradually stabilized. *In September 1990 important changes were introduced in the country's constitution, giving the Muslims fairer representation.* The membership of the National Assembly was increased to 108, equally divided between Christians and Muslims. The government, with Syrian help, gradually restored its authority over more and more of the country and managed to get most of the militia armies disbanded. The government also succeeded in getting all the Western hostages released, the last of them in June 1992. All this was very much because of the Syrian presence; in May 1991 the two states signed a treaty of 'brotherhood and co-ordination'. However, this was strongly criticized by the Israelis, who claimed that the treaty marked the 'virtual annexation of Lebanon by Syria'. Israeli troops remained in southern Lebanon to safeguard their northern frontier.

(d)   The July War of 2006

The Israelis eventually removed their troops from southern Lebanon, but not until 2000. However, they still occupied an area known as the Sheba'a farms, which, so they claimed, was part of Syria, and therefore there was no need for Israeli troops to move out. Hezbollah insisted that the Sheba'a farms belonged to Lebanon, and therefore Israel must withdraw. Many observers suspected that both Hezbollah and Syria, which supported Hezbollah, were using the situation as a pretext to justify continued hostility to Israel. They wanted to show support for the Palestinians, who were now involved in the second *intifada*. The dispute simmered on until in July 2006 Hezbollah decided to test Israel's reactions and at the same time help Hamas, which was being attacked by Israel: they ambushed an Israeli patrol. In total, eight Israeli soldiers were killed and two were taken prisoner. Hezbollah believed that Israel would be too busy with Hamas to retaliate. They were sadly mistaken. In fact Israel had been looking for an excuse to destroy Hezbollah, and the USA was urging them to take action, as part of the general 'war on terror'.

The very day after the attack on the patrol, the Israeli response began. The Lebanese coast was blockaded, and air strikes put Beirut airport out of action and destroyed Hezbollah's headquarters. After a few days, Israeli ground troops invaded. It soon became clear that Israel intended to destroy Hezbollah's fighting ability by bombing its arsenal of rockets, killing its leaders, cutting it off from its supply lines and from its supporters. This did not prevent Hezbollah from retaliating by firing rockets into Israel at an average of over a hundred a day for the 34 days that the war lasted. But Israeli bombing did enormous damage to civilians and their property in southern Lebanon, and if anything, increased support for Hezbollah. In August 2006 the UN succeeded in arranging a ceasefire, but not before over a thousand Lebanese civilians and some 200 Hezbollah fighters had been killed and around a million civilians made homeless. On the Israeli side 118 soldiers and around 40 civilians were killed. Hezbollah claimed victory, but privately they admitted that it was a hollow victory and that had they known what Israel's response would be, it would never have kidnapped the soldiers. For Israel it left a rare taste of defeat; the ground invasion was poorly organized and ineffective, and it somewhat dented Israel's reputation for invincibility. David Hirst, in his book about Lebanon, concludes that what was meant to be a demonstration of strength by Israel turned out to be an almost comic illustration of ineffectuality. It seemed that Israel had learned nothing from the 1982 Lebanon War.

11.9 THE IRAN–IRAQ WAR, 1980–8

The Middle East and the Arab world were thrown into fresh confusion in September 1980 when Iraqi troops invaded Iran.

(a) Iraq's motives

President Saddam Hussein of Iraq had several motives for launching the attack.

- *He was afraid of militant Islam spreading across the border into Iraq from Iran.* Iran had become an Islamic republic in 1979 under the leadership of the Ayatollah Khomeini and his fundamentalist Shiite Muslim supporters. They believed that the country should be run according to the Islamic religion, with a strict moral code enforced by severe punishments. According to Khomeini, 'in Islam the legislative power to establish laws belongs to God Almighty'. The population of Iraq was mainly Sunni Muslim, but there was a large Shia minority. Saddam, whose government was non-religious, was afraid that the Shias might rise up against him, and he had some of their leaders executed early in 1980. The Iranians retaliated by launching raids across the frontier.
- *The Iraqis claimed that the Iranian border province of Khuzestan should rightfully belong to them.* This was an area peopled largely by Arabs, and Saddam hoped that they would rally to support Iraq (most Iranians were Persians, not Arabs).
- *There was a long-standing dispute over the Shatt-el-Arab waterway.* This was an important outlet for the oil exports of both countries, and it formed part of the

frontier between the two states. The Shatt-el-Arab had once been completely under Iraqi control, but five years earlier the Iranian government had forced Iraq to share control of it with Iran.

- *Saddam thought that the Iranian forces would be weak and demoralized so soon after the fundamentalist takeover*, so he expected a quick victory. It soon became clear that he had miscalculated badly.

(b)   The war drags on

The Iranians quickly organized themselves to deal with the invasion, which began with the Iraqi seizure of the disputed waterway. The Iranians replied with mass infantry attacks against heavily fortified Iraqi positions. On paper Iraq seemed much the stronger, being well supplied with Soviet tanks, helicopter gunships and missiles, and some British and American weapons as well. However, the Iranian revolutionary guards, inspired by their religion, and ready to become martyrs, fought with fanatical determination; eventually they too began to get modern equipment (anti-aircraft and anti-tank missiles) from China and North Korea (and secretly from the USA). As the war dragged on, Iraq concentrated on strangling Iranian oil exports, which paid for their arms supplies; Iran meanwhile captured Iraqi territory, and early in 1987 their troops were only ten miles from Basra, Iraq's second most important city, which had to be evacuated. By this time the territorial dispute had become lost in the deeper racial and religious conflict: Khomeini had sworn never to stop fighting until his Shia Muslim fundamentalists had destroyed the 'godless' Saddam regime.

The war had important international repercussions.

- *The stability of the entire Arab world was threatened.* The more conservative states – Saudi Arabia, Jordan and Kuwait – gave cautious support to Iraq; but Syria, Libya, Algeria, South Yemen and the PLO were critical of Iraq for starting the war at a time when, they believed, all Arab states should have been concentrating on the destruction of Israel. The Saudis and the other Gulf states, suspicious of Khomeini's fundamentalist brand of Islam, wanted to see Iran's ability to dominate the Persian Gulf controlled. As early as November 1980 an Arab summit conference in Amman (Jordan), to draw up new plans for dealing with Israel, failed to get off the ground because the anti-Iraq states, led by Syria, refused to attend.
- *The attacks on Iran's oil exports threatened the energy supplies of the West*, and at various times brought American, Russian, British and French warships into the region, raising the international temperature. In 1987 the situation took a more dangerous turn as oil tankers, whatever their nationality, were threatened by mines; which side was responsible for laying them was open to debate.
- *The success of Iran's Shia fundamentalist troops, especially the threat to Basra, alarmed the non-religious Arab governments*, and many Arabs were afraid of what might happen if Iraq was defeated. Even President Assad of Syria, at first a strong supporter of Iran, was worried in case Iraq split up and became another Lebanon; this could well destabilize Syria itself. An Islamic conference held in Kuwait (January 1987) was attended by representatives of 44 nations; but Iran's leaders refused to attend, and no agreement could be reached on how to bring the war to an end.
- The war entered a new and even more terrible phase towards the end of 1987 when both sides began to bombard each other's capital cities, Tehran (Iran) and Baghdad (Iraq), causing thousands of deaths.

(c)   The end of the war, 1988

Although neither side had achieved its aims, the cost of the war, both economically and in human lives, was telling heavily. Both sides began to look for a way to end the fighting, though for a time they continued to pour out propaganda; Saddam talked about 'total victory' and the Iranians demanded 'total surrender'. The UN became involved, did some straight talking to both sides, and succeeded in arranging a ceasefire (August 1988). This was monitored by UN troops, and against all expectations, the truce lasted. Peace negotiations opened in October 1988 and terms were finally agreed in 1990.

11.10   THE GULF WAR, 1990–1

Even before he had accepted the peace terms at the end of the Iran–Iraq War, Saddam Hussein began his next act of aggression. His forces invaded and quickly occupied the small neighbouring state of Kuwait (August 1990).

(a)   Saddam Hussein's motives

- His real motive was probably to get his hands on the wealth of Kuwait, since he was seriously short of cash after the long war with Iran. Kuwait, though small, had valuable oil wells, which he would now be able to control.
- He claimed that Kuwait was historically part of Iraq, though in fact Kuwait had existed as a separate territory – a British protectorate – since 1899, whereas Iraq had not been created until after the First World War.
- He did not expect any action from the outside world now that his troops were firmly entrenched in Kuwait, and he had the strongest army in the region. He thought Europe and the USA were reasonably amenable to him since they had supplied him with arms during his war with Iran. After all, the USA had been supporting him all the way through his war against the Iranian regime that had overthrown the Shah, an American ally. The Americans valued him as a stabilizing influence within the region and in Iraq itself – they had taken no action when Saddam had suppressed the Shias, nor when he brutally crushed the Kurds (who were demanding an independent state) in the north of Iraq, in 1988.

(b)   The world unites against Saddam Hussein

Once again, as in the case of Iran, Saddam had miscalculated. President Bush of the USA took the lead in pressing for action to remove the Iraqis from Kuwait. The UN placed trade sanctions on Iraq, cutting off her oil exports, her main source of income. Saddam was ordered to remove his troops by 15 January 1991, after which the UN would use 'all necessary means' to clear them out. Saddam hoped that this was all bluff and talked of 'the mother of all wars' if they tried to throw him out. But Bush and Margaret Thatcher had decided that Saddam's power must be curbed; he controlled too much of the oil that the industrial west needed. Fortunately for Britain and the USA, Saudi Arabia, Syria and Egypt were also nervous about what Saddam might do next, so they supported the UN action.

In spite of frantic diplomatic efforts, *Saddam Hussein felt that he could not lose face by withdrawing from Kuwait*, though he knew that an international force of over 600 000 had been assembled in Saudi Arabia. More than thirty nations contributed with troops, armaments or cash; for example the USA, Britain, France, Italy, Egypt, Syria and Saudi Arabia provided troops; Germany and Japan donated cash. When the 15 January deadline passed, *Operation Desert Storm* was launched against the Iraqis.

The campaign, in two parts, was quickly successful. First came a series of bombing attacks on Baghdad (the Iraqi capital), whose unfortunate citizens again suffered heavy casualties, and on military targets such as roads and bridges. The second phase, the attack on the Iraqi army itself, began on 24 February. *Within four days the Iraqis had been driven out of Kuwait and routed.* Kuwait was liberated and Saddam Hussein accepted defeat. However, although Iraq lost many troops (some estimates put Iraqi dead at 90 000 compared with less than 400 for the allies), Saddam was allowed to withdraw with much of his army intact. The retreating Iraqis were at the mercy of the allies, but Bush called a ceasefire, afraid that if the slaughter continued, the allies would lose the support of the other Arab nations.

(c) The aftermath of the war – Saddam Hussein survives

The war had unfortunate consequences for many of the Iraqi people. It was widely expected outside Iraq that after this humiliating defeat, Saddam Hussein would soon be overthrown. There were uprisings of Kurds in the north and Shia Muslims in the south, and it seemed as though Iraq was breaking up. However, the allies had left Saddam enough troops, tanks and aircraft to deal with the situation, and both rebellions were ruthlessly crushed. At first nobody intervened: Russia, Syria and Turkey had Kurdish minorities of their own and did not want the rebellion spreading over from Iraq. Similarly a Shiite victory in southern Iraq would probably increase the power of Iran in that region, and the USA did not want that. But eventually world opinion became so outraged at Saddam's continued ruthless bombings of his people that the USA and Britain, with UN backing, declared the areas 'no-fly zones', and used their air power to keep Saddam's aircraft out. And so Saddam Hussein remained in power.

The war and its aftermath were very revealing about the motives of the West and the great powers. Their primary concern was not with international justice and moral questions of right and wrong, but with their own self-interest. They only took action against Saddam in the first place because they felt he was threatening their oil supplies. Often in the past when other small nations had been invaded, no international action had been taken. For example, when East Timor was occupied by neighbouring Indonesia in 1975, the rest of the world ignored it, because their interests were not threatened. After the Gulf War, Saddam, who on any assessment must rank as one of the most brutal dictators of the century, was allowed to remain in power because the West thought that his survival was the best way of keeping Iraq united and the region stable.

11.11 ISRAELIS AND PALESTINIANS FIGHT AGAIN

(a) The failure of the Oslo Accords

Binyamin Netanyahu, Israeli prime minister from May 1996 until May 1999, never accepted the agreements reached in Oslo. He spent much of his time in office trying to backtrack from the commitments made by the previous Israeli government and allowed the building of large Jewish settlements on the outskirts of Jerusalem, which would cut off Arab villages on the eastern side of Jerusalem from the rest of the West Bank. This only caused more violent protests from the Palestinians; Yasser Arafat released some Hamas activists from jail and suspended security co-operation with Israel. US president Clinton tried to keep the peace process on course by calling both sides together at Camp David in October 1998, but little progress was made. Netanyahu, facing recession and rising unemployment, called an election in May 1999. In the contest for prime minister, the candidate of the Labour Party (now calling itself 'One Israel') was Ehud Barak, a retired general. He campaigned on promises of economic growth and a renewed drive for peace, and he won a decisive victory.

Barak's victory raised great hopes: he wanted a comprehensive peace settlement which included Syria (which had not signed a peace treaty with Israel after the 1973 war) as well as the Palestinians, and he tried hard to achieve one. Sadly his efforts failed.

- Although the Syrians agreed to talk, negotiations finally broke down in March 2000 when they insisted that there should be a return to the pre-Six-Day-War frontiers before any further talks could take place. Barak could not agree to this without alienating a majority of Israelis.
- In spite of this, in May 2000 Barak went ahead with his election promise to withdraw Israeli troops from southern Lebanon, where they had remained policing a security zone since 1985.
- Barak offered to share Jerusalem with the Palestinians, but Arafat refused to compromise and continued to demand full Palestinian sovereignty in East Jerusalem.

By the summer of 2000, Barak's government was falling apart, many of his supporters feeling that he was making too many concessions to the Arabs and getting nothing in return. An American-sponsored summit meeting at Camp David in July failed.

Clinton made one last effort to bring peace before his term as president ended. (The new president, George W. Bush, was due to take office on 20 January 2001.) At a meeting in the White House (in December 2000) he announced his new plan to representatives of both sides. It moved some way towards accommodating Palestinian demands: it required the Israelis to withdraw completely from Gaza and from about 95 per cent of the West Bank, and there was to be an independent Palestinian state. With regard to Jerusalem, 'the general principle is that Arab areas are Palestinian and Jewish ones are Israeli'. At a conference held at Taba in Egypt to discuss the plan (January 2001), agreement seemed tantalizingly close; only the question of Jerusalem remained as a major obstacle, but neither side would compromise over this critical issue. The Oslo peace process had well and truly foundered.

(b)   The problem of Jerusalem

The Oslo Accords had by-passed several vital questions, such as the status of Jerusalem, the right of return of the 1948 refugees, and the future of the Jewish settlements in the areas occupied by Israel since 1967. The intention was that these thorny problems would be negotiated towards the end of a five-year transition period, but the first time they were discussed in detail was at Clinton's Camp David summit in July 2000.

The original UN intention when Israel was created was that Jerusalem should be under international control. However, the fighting of 1948–9 ended with Jordan ruling East Jerusalem and Israel occupying West Jerusalem. This position remained until the 1967 Six-Day War, when Israel captured East Jerusalem, along with the entire West Bank, from Jordan; it is still occupied by the Israelis today. *The problem is that Jerusalem has great symbolic and emotional significance for both sides.* For the Jews, Jerusalem was their ancient capital city, and they believe that Temple Mount was the site of their Temple in biblical times. For the Muslims, Jerusalem, known as Al-Haram al-Sharif, is the site from which the Prophet Muhammad ascended into heaven.

The Israelis were determined to hold on to Jerusalem; they took over Arab land and built new Jewish settlements, in violation of international law. International opinion and the UN repeatedly condemned these Israeli activities. However, in 1980 the Knesset (the Israeli parliament) passed the Jerusalem Law which stated that 'Jerusalem, complete and unified, is the capital of Israel.' This provoked a storm of criticism from moderate Israelis who thought it was unnecessary, from world opinion, and from the UN Security Council which passed a resolution reprimanding Israel. Even the USA, which almost always supported Israel, abstained on this vote. This is why the 1995 agreements, which for the first time recognized the possibility of Jerusalem being divided, were such a major breakthrough. It also explains why the Palestinians were so bitterly disappointed when Netanyahu dropped the idea, following the assassination of Yitzak Rabin (see Section 11.7(b)). When Clinton's Camp David summit failed in July 2000, another outbreak of violence was inevitable.

(c) Sharon and the intifada

On 28 September 2000, Ariel Sharon, the leader of the opposition Likud party, surrounded by a large contingent of security men, paid a highly publicized visit to Temple Mount in Jerusalem. He claimed that he was going to deliver 'a message of peace'. But to most of the rest of the world it seemed that this was a gesture to emphasize Israeli sovereignty over the whole of Jerusalem, and even a deliberate attempt to provoke violence, which would end the peace process. If this was indeed his motive, he was all too successful. His visit sparked off riots which spread from Temple Mount across the entire West Bank and Gaza, and among Arabs in Israel. It soon turned into *a full-scale uprising, which became known as the al-Aqsa (Jerusalem) intifada ('shaking-off')*. After the failure of Clinton's final attempts to bring peace, in January 2001, Sharon was elected prime minister, defeating Barak, who was seen as being too fond of offering concessions to Yasser Arafat (February 2001).

Sharon immediately announced that there would be no further negotiations while violence continued. His aim was to control the intifada by a combination of tough military action and international pressure. The Israelis started to build a protective wall around the West Bank; they claimed it was purely defensive, but unfortunately for the Palestinians, a number of their villages were trapped on the Israeli side of the barrier, which also included Jewish settlements built on Arab land. The more drastic the military action taken by Israel, the less international support it got. *For the next three years the tragic cycle of suicide bombings, massive Israeli retaliations, and short ceasefires interspersed with fruitless international efforts at mediation, continued unabated.* For example:

- A Hamas suicide bomber killed five Israelis in Netanya, a popular seaside resort. The Israelis responded with 16 air strikes, killing 16 Palestinians on the West Bank (May 2001).
- In August 2001 Israelis assassinated Abu Ali Mustafa, deputy leader of the Popular Front for the Liberation of Palestine (PFLP), in Ramallah, the seat of the Palestinian Authority.
- Following the 11 September terrorist attacks on the USA, President Bush took steps to prevent the Palestine issue becoming mixed up in his 'war on terrorism'. He announced new plans for peace, including an independent Palestinian state with East Jerusalem as its capital.
- The PFLP assassinated the Israeli tourism minister, a hardline anti-Palestinian and friend of Sharon (October 2001).
- Hamas suicide bombers killed 25 Israelis in Haifa and Jerusalem; ten others were killed when a bomb exploded in a bus. Israel responded by occupying Ramallah, and surrounding Arafat's headquarters. Arafat condemned terrorism and called for

an immediate ceasefire; Hamas called a halt to the suicide bombings (December 2001). The ceasefire lasted just over four weeks.

- During the early months of 2002, fighting became more vicious. After Palestinian gunmen had killed six Israeli soldiers near Ramallah, the Israelis occupied two large Palestinian refugee camps at Nablus and Jenin. The Palestinians carried out more attacks, and the Israelis sent 150 tanks and 20 000 troops into the West Bank and the Gaza Strip and attacked Arafat's compound in Ramallah once again. It seemed that Sharon was doing everything he possibly could to injure Arafat, short of actually having him directly assassinated. There was heavy fighting in the Jenin refugee camp, and the Palestinians claimed that Israeli forces had carried out a massacre. The UN sent a team to investigate these claims, but the Israelis refused to let them in (February–April 2002). In March the UN for the first time endorsed the idea of an independent Palestinian state; UN secretary-general Annan accused Israel of the 'illegal occupation' of Palestinian land.

- Nevertheless the UN team collected sufficient information to publish a report on conditions in the West Bank and Gaza (referred to as 'the Occupied Territories'), in September 2002. It charged Israel with causing a humanitarian catastrophe among the Palestinians: the economy had been destroyed, unemployment stood at 65 per cent, half the population was living on less than $2 a day, schools and houses had been bulldozed and demolished, people deported and curfews imposed; ambulances were being prevented from passing roadblocks.

- The USA and Israel saw Yasser Arafat as the main obstacle to progress, since he would make no significant concessions and was either unwilling or unable to bring a lasting halt to Palestinian attacks. Having failed to kill him in the attacks on his compound, the Israeli leadership tried to sideline him by refusing to meet him and demanding the appointment of another leader to represent the Palestinians in negotiations. Consequently, in March 2003, Mahmoud Abbas was appointed to the newly created post of prime minister, although Arafat remained president, and continued to be the real power in the Palestinian Authority.

(d) The 'road map' for peace?

This new peace plan was drawn up originally in December 2002 by representatives of the European Union, Russia, the UN and the USA. Formal discussion had been delayed by the Israeli general election of January 2003 (won by Sharon), by the war in Iraq, and by US and Israeli insistence that they would only deal with Abbas rather than Arafat. At last, on 30 April 2003 it was formally presented, separately, to Abbas and Sharon. *The 'road map' aimed to achieve a final settlement of the entire Palestinian–Israeli conflict by the end of 2005. Its basic points were*:

- the creation of an independent, democratic and viable Palestinian state existing side by side in peace and security with Israel and its other neighbours;
- there should be 'an unconditional cessation of violence' by both sides, a freeze on new Israeli settlements, the dismantling of all the 'illegal' ones built since Sharon came to power in March 2001 and a new Palestinian constitution and elections – all to be achieved by the end of May 2003;
- after the Palestinian elections, there would be an international conference to draw up the provisional frontiers of the new state – by the end of 2003;
- over the next two years – up to the end of 2005 – Israel and Palestine would negotiate final details such as the remaining settlements, refugees, the status of Jerusalem, and the frontiers.

The 'road map' was accepted in principle by both the Palestinians and the Israelis, although Sharon had a number of reservations; for example, he would not recognize the right of Palestinian refugees to return to their former homes in Israel. The Israeli cabinet voted narrowly in favour of the plan, the first time that they had countenanced the idea of a Palestinian state which would include some of the territory they had occupied since the Six-Day War in 1967. Referring to the West Bank and the Gaza Strip, Sharon made a historic statement: 'To keep 3.5 million people under occupation is bad for us and for them. I have come to the conclusion that we have to reach a peace agreement.'

(e) What brought about the Israeli change of attitude?

Sharon's change of heart did not come totally out the blue: already in November 2002 he had persuaded his Likud party to accept that an eventual Palestinian state was now inevitable and that 'painful concessions' would have to be made once violence ended. Fighting on this platform, Likud won the general election of January 2003, and Sharon remained prime minister. A combination of reasons caused him to relinquish his hardline vision of a Greater Israel stretching from the Mediterranean to the River Jordan, and including the whole of Jerusalem.

- After almost three years of violence, even Sharon began to realize that his policy was not working. The ferocity and determination of the Palestinian resistance astonished and dismayed most Israelis. Although international opinion condemned Palestinian suicide bombings, the disproportionate Israeli responses were even more unpopular; it was the Palestinian underdogs who won the sympathy of the rest of the world, except the USA, which almost invariably supported and financed Israel.
- Moderate Israeli opinion had turned against the hardline approach and many Israelis were horrified at events such as the 'massacre' in the Jenin refugee camp. Yitzhak Laor, an Israeli writer and poet, wrote: 'There's no doubt that Israel's "assassination policy" – its killing of senior politicians – has poured petrol on the fire. ... The bulldozer, once the symbol of the building of a new country, has become a monster, following the tanks, so that everybody can watch as another family's home, another future disappears. ... Enslaving a nation, bringing it to its feet, simply doesn't work.' One estimate suggested that 56 per cent of Israelis supported the 'road map'.
- Even President Bush eventually began to lose patience with Sharon. The USA denounced the attacks on Arafat's headquarters and told Sharon to withdraw his troops from the West Bank, pointing out that his attacks on the Palestinians were threatening to destroy the American-led coalition against the Taliban regime in Afghanistan and Osama bin Laden. Bush was afraid that unless he did something to curb Sharon, the Arab states – Egypt, Jordan and Saudi Arabia – might withdraw from the coalition. Bush also threatened to reduce US aid to Israel. Sharon's first reaction was anger and defiance, but in the end he had to listen – a gradual withdrawal of troops from the West Bank got under way.
- Population trends have been suggested as another possible influence on Sharon. At the beginning of 2004 the population of Israel and Palestine was around 10 million – 5.4 million Jews and 4.6 million Arabs. At current rates of population growth, the number of Palestinian Arabs would overtake the number of Jews in the next six to ten years; within 20 years, this trend would threaten the very existence of the Jewish state. This is because, if it is a genuinely democratic state, which the Israelis claim to want, the Palestinians must have equal voting rights, and would therefore be in a majority. The best solution for both sides would be peace, and the creation of two separate states, as soon as possible.

(f)   Difficult times ahead

Although both sides had accepted the 'road map' in principle, there were still grave doubts about exactly where it was leading. By the spring of 2004 no progress had been made to implement any of the points, and the plan was well behind schedule. In spite of all efforts, it had proved impossible to achieve a lasting ceasefire; violence continued and Mahmoud Abbas resigned in exasperation, blaming the Israelis for acting 'provocatively' every time the Palestinian militant groups – Hamas, Islamic Jihad and Fatah – began a ceasefire. He was also involved in a power struggle with Arafat, who would not give him full powers to negotiate in his own way. He was replaced by Ahmed Qurie, who had been involved in the Oslo discussions in 1993.

In October 2003 some Israeli critics of Sharon, including Yossi Beilin (who had also been involved in the Oslo Peace Accords), held talks with some Palestinian leaders and together they produced *a rival, unofficial peace plan.* This was launched with great publicity at a ceremony in Geneva in December, and was welcomed as a sign of hope. The Israelis made some concessions: Jerusalem would be divided and incorporated in the Palestinian state, Israel would give up sovereignty over Temple Mount, and would abandon about 75 per cent of the Jewish settlements in the West Bank; these would be incorporated in the new Palestinian state. However, in return the Palestinians were required to give up the right of return for refugees and to accept financial compensation. For the vast majority of the Palestinians, this issue was at the heart of the conflict, and they could never willingly submit to such an agreement. For the Israelis, the abandonment of so many settlements was equally anathema. The stalemate continued during 2004.

(g)   Why did the peace process stall in this way?

Basically the reason was that although the 'road map' and the so-called Geneva Accords represented some concessions by the Israelis, they did not go nearly far enough. Several vital points were omitted which the Palestinians had a right to expect would be included.

- There was no real acknowledgement that the Israeli presence in Gaza and the West Bank was an illegal occupation and had been since 1967. Israel ignored a UN order to evacuate all territory captured during the Six-Day War (including the Golan Heights, taken from Syria).
- Frontiers were referred to as 'provisional'. Palestinians suspected that Sharon's idea was to have a weak Palestinian state made up of a number of enclaves separated from each other by Israeli territory, and therefore easily dominated by the Israelis.
- There was the thorny problem of Israeli settlements. The 'road map' mentioned the dismantling of 'illegal' settlements built since March 2001, which numbered about 60. This implied that all the earlier settlements – almost 200 of them, housing over 450 000 people, half of them in or near East Jerusalem, the rest in the West Bank and Gaza – were legal. But these were also arguably illegal, having been built on occupied territory. There was no mention in the 'road map' of these being dismantled.
- There was no reference to the massive security wall, 347 km long, being built by the Israelis in the West Bank, stretching from north to south, and looping round to include some of the larger Israeli settlements. The wall cut through Palestinian lands and olive groves, in some places cutting the Palestinians off from the farms which provided their livelihood. It was estimated that when the wall was finished, 300 000 Palestinians would be trapped in their townships, unable to get to their land.

- Above all there was the question of the refugees and their dream of returning to their pre-1948 homelands, a desire formulated in a number of UN resolutions. On the Israeli side, they believed that if the Palestinian dream became reality, that would destroy their own particular dream – the Jewish state.

In January 2004, Sharon announced that if no progress was made towards a negotiated peace, Israel would go ahead and impose its own solution. They would withdraw from some settlements and relocate the Jewish communities. Frontiers would be redefined to create a separate state of Palestine, but it would be smaller than that envisaged in the 'road map'. The situation was thrown into chaos once again in March 2004 when the Israelis assassinated Sheikh Ahmed Yassin, the founder and leader of Hamas.

Later that month Sharon announced his new unilateral solution: the Israelis would dismantle their settlements in the Gaza Strip, but keep control of all but a token four of the settlements on the West Bank. Although this was a fundamental shift away from the 'road map' by the Israelis, it received unqualified support from President Bush, who said that it was unrealistic to expect a full Israeli withdrawal from land occupied during the 1967 war, and equally unrealistic for Palestinian refugees to expect to return 'home'. Predictably this caused complete outrage across the Arab world; tensions were further inflamed in April 2004 when the Israelis assassinated Dr al-Rantissi, Sheikh Yassin's successor, and warned that Yasser Arafat could be the next target. This provoked a violent response from Palestinian militants; the Israelis retaliated by launching an attack on the Rafah refugee camp in Gaza, killing some 40 people, including children.

Yasser Arafat appeared to be extending an olive branch when he told an Israeli newspaper that he recognized Israel's right to remain a Jewish state and was prepared to accept the return of only a fraction of the Palestinian refugees. This offer was unpopular with Palestinian militants, and there was no positive response from the Israelis.

Meanwhile the International Court of Justice at The Hague had been considering the legality of the West Bank security wall; the Palestinians were delighted when the court ruled (July 2004) that the barrier was illegal, and that the Israelis should demolish it and compensate the victims. However, Prime Minister Sharon rejected the court's decision, saying that Israel had a sacred right to fight terrorists in whatever ways were necessary. The Israelis showed further defiance with an announcement that they planned to build a new settlement near Jerusalem, which would surround Palestinian East Jerusalem and make it impossible for East Jerusalem to become the capital of a Palestinian state. This violated Israel's agreement in the 'road map' not to build any more settlements; the announcement provoked condemnation from the rest of the world, except the USA, which gave tacit approval.

The situation changed with the death of Yasser Arafat in December 2004. The Palestinian prime minister, Mahmoud Abbas (also known as Abu Mazen), who was the leader of Fatah, won a decisive victory in the election for a new president, taking about 70 per cent of the votes (January 2005). He was a moderate who had constantly opposed violence; consequently President Bush of the USA, who had refused to deal with Arafat, signalled his willingness to meet the new president, and urged both the Palestinians and Israel to reduce tension and move towards peace. Later in 2005 the Israelis obligingly withdrew their troops from Gaza, along with thousands of Jews who had settled in the territory. However, Israel still controlled the Gaza Strip's land borders as well as its territorial waters and its airspace, so that it was effectively isolated, except for its short frontier with Egypt.

By the end of 2005 Abbas was seen as weak and ineffective by all sides – Palestinians, Israelis and Americans. *In January 2006 Hamas won a majority in the Palestinian elections for the legislature, with 74 seats to 58 for the opposition* (mainly supporters of the more moderate Fatah). The Israelis announced that no further peace talks could take place while 'terrorists' were in power. In July 2006 the Israelis unsuccessfully tried to destroy Hezbollah, which had just ambushed an Israeli patrol on their frontier with southern Lebanon (see Section 11.8 (d)). Meanwhile, the more moderate Palestinian party, Fatah, refused to accept the January election result and violence broke out; by the spring of 2007 something approaching a Palestinian civil war between Fatah and Hamas supporters seemed to be under way. There is evidence that the USA was financing Fatah and Abbas, who was still president, in the hope of destroying Hamas. Another complicating factor was that Egypt distrusted Hamas, which was an offshoot of the Muslim Brothers, Egypt's largest opposition group to President Mubarak. By the end of 2007 Palestine was split in two: the West Bank ruled by Fatah, and the Gaza Strip ruled by Hamas. The two areas were separated by Israeli territory and communication between the two was often difficult (see Map 11.3). However, in November 2007, in an attempt to get the peace process moving again, Abbas met Israeli prime minister Ehud Olmert in Annapolis (USA). Bur Hamas was not invited to take part in the talks, and so, not surprisingly, no progress was made.

Israel refused to negotiate with Hamas, and did all they could to destabilize the Hamas regime in Gaza, although they had been democratically elected. The blockade of Gaza, which had been intensified since Hamas took over, aimed to prevent the entry of goods of all types, including food, and to cut fuel supplies. Early in 2008 a group of aid agencies reported that the population of the strip were having to survive on less than a quarter of the volume of supplies they had been importing at the end of 2005. A six-month truce was agreed beginning in June 2008 – Hamas promised to stop firing rockets into Israel, while Israel undertook to ease its stranglehold on Gaza. However, by the end of 2008 the situation in Gaza had not improved; there was very little evidence of a relaxation in the blockade; in fact conditions were said to be worse than at any time since the Israeli occupation began in 1967. Fuel shortages and lack of spare parts were having a disastrous effect on treatment of sewage, water supply and medical facilities; in short, Gaza was in the grip of a humanitarian crisis. Even a retired general of the Israeli Defence Force (Gaza Division), Shmuel Zakai, was critical of his own government. He claimed that they had made a central error by failing to take advantage of the truce to improve the economic conditions of the Palestinians. 'You cannot just land blows,' he said, 'leave the Palestinians in Gaza in the economic distress they're in, and expect that Hamas will sit around and do nothing.' The Israelis also violated the truce in November 2008 when troops entered Gaza and killed six members of Hamas. In response Hamas launched Qassam rockets and Grad missiles into Israel.

According to Henry Siegman, formerly a director of the American Jewish Congress, at this point Hamas 'offered to extend the truce, but only on condition that Israel ended its blockade. Israel refused. It could have met its obligations to protect its citizens by agreeing to ease the blockade, but it didn't even try.' In fact, the opposite happened: the Israelis began a propaganda campaign against Hamas 'terrorism', and closed Gaza to journalists. *On 27 December 2008 they launched a major air attack on Gaza targeting weapons depots; a week later ground troops invaded the territory.* After 22 days the Israelis called a ceasefire. But damage from the aerial bombardment was indiscriminate and disastrous: 15 out of 27 hospitals were put out of action or destroyed, together with schools, police stations, mosques, factories and Hamas government buildings. About 10 000 small family farms were destroyed, which badly disrupted food supplies over the next few months. Out of 110 primary healthcare facilities, 43 were badly damaged. Altogether over 1000 Palestinians were killed and about 5000 injured; 50 000 were left homeless, half a million had no running water and a million were left without electricity. Much of the Gaza Strip was left in ruins. On the other side, 13 Israelis were killed. Amnesty International later confirmed that the Israelis had used white phosphorous shells made in the USA. These cause fires that are extremely difficult to extinguish: when the UN compound in Gaza City was hit, the fires destroyed hundreds of tons of emergency food and medicines which were about to be distributed to hospitals and medical centres.

Following the ceasefire, the blockade of Gaza continued, although the Israelis did allow in some humanitarian medical aid. However, the Red Cross reported that the blockade was still damaging the economy and that there was a shortage of basic medical supplies. Israel justified the attacks and the continued blockade on the need to protect their people from rockets. But Henry Siegman claims that this is a lie: 'it cannot be said that Israel launched its assaults to protect its citizens from rockets. It did so to protect its right to continue the strangulation of Gaza's population. Everyone seems to have forgotten that Hamas declared an end to suicide bombings and rocket fire when it decided to join the Palestinian political process, and largely stuck to it for more than a year.'

The Israelis blithely ignored the mounting international criticism flooding in from most parts of the world (except from the USA), calling on them to ease or lift the blockade. In July 2010 British prime minister David Cameron warned: 'humanitarian goods and people must flow in both directions. Gaza cannot and must not be allowed to remain a prison camp'; to which the Israeli embassy in London retorted: 'the people of Gaza are the prisoners of the terrorist organisation Hamas. The situation in Gaza is the direct result of Hamas rules and priorities.' Eventually it was Egypt which relented and partially opened its frontier with Gaza, but only for people, not supplies. In February 2011 the UN reported that Israel had co-operated to some extent between January 2009 and June 2010 by allowing fuel and cooking gas into Gaza, but added that this had not resulted in any significant improvement in people's livelihoods.

Then in May 2011 there was a dramatic change in the situation: following months of protest demonstrations and increasing violence, President Hosni Mubarak of Egypt resigned (see Section 12.7(c)). Not long before this, US president Obama had described him as 'a stalwart ally, in many respects, to the United States … a force for stability and good' in the Middle East. Yet many people had viewed Mubarak as one of the most brutal dictators in the region. One of his main opponents was the Muslim Brotherhood, who had close associations with Hamas. Egypt immediately opened its border with Gaza completely. There was great rejoicing as the people of Gaza began to look forward to better times ahead. But this was somewhat premature: in November 2012 Israel launched a series of air attacks on Gaza, claiming that their action was in retaliation for hundreds of rockets recently fired from Gaza into Israel. Lasting for eight days, the Israeli attacks killed over 160 Palestinians, including many children, and destroyed several military sites in Gaza. Five Israelis were killed. Egypt's president, Mohamed Morsi, helped to broker a ceasefire. Both sides claimed victory, but there was still no commitment by Israel to end their blockade of Gaza. Until that point was reached, it seemed likely that Hamas would continue its rocket campaign.

FURTHER READING

Aburish, S. K., *Arafat: From Defender to Dictator* (Bloomsbury, 1999).

Aburish, S. K., *Nasser: The Last Arab* (Duckworth, 2005 edition).

Chomsky, N. and Pappe, I., *Gaza in Crisis: Reflections on Israel's War against the Palestinians* (Penguin, 2011).

Cohn-Sherbok, D. and El-Alami, D. S., *The Palestinian–Israeli Conflict: A Beginner's Guide* (One World, 3rd edition, 2008).

Dawisha, A., *Arab Nationalism in the 20th Century: From Triumph to Despair* (Princeton University Press, new edition, 2005).

Hirst, D., *Beware of Small States: Lebanon, Battleground of the Middle East* (Faber, 2010).

Kyle, K., *Suez: Britain's End of Empire in the Middle East* (Tauris, Reprint edition, 2011).

Milton-Edwards, B. & Farrell, S., *Hamas: The Islamic Resistance Movement* (Polity, 2010).

Osman, T., *Egypt on the Brink: from Nasser to Mubarak* (Yale University Press, revised edition, 2011).

Roy, S., *Hamas and Civil Society in Gaza* (Princeton University Press, 2011).

Schlaim, A., *Israel and Palestine: Reappraisals, Revisions, Refutations* (Verso, 2010).

Siegman, H., 'Israel's Lies' in *London Review of Books* (29 January 2009.),

Tripp, C., *A History of Iraq* (Cambridge University Press, 3rd edition, 2007).

QUESTIONS

1   Why and with what results did the Arabs and Israelis fight the wars of 1967 and 1973?
2   'Terrorism and violence rather than peaceful diplomacy.' How far would you agree with this view of the activities of the PLO in the Middle East in the period 1973 to 1995?
3   How successful was President Nasser as leader of Egypt?
4   'The USA and the USSR intervened in the Middle East in the period 1956 to 1979 purely to preserve political and economic stability in the region.' How valid do you think this view is?
5   Assess the reasons why the Six-Day War of 1967 was followed by the Yom Kippur War only three years later.
6   To what extent have the violent actions of some Palestinians been the main obstacle to the establishment of a Palestinian state?

There is a document question about the USA and the 1990–1 Gulf War on the website.

Chapter 12

The new world order and the war against global terrorism

SUMMARY OF EVENTS

When communism collapsed in eastern Europe and the USSR broke up in 1991, the Cold War came to an end. *The USA was left as the world's only superpower.* Following its victory over communism, the USA was full of confidence and pride in the superiority of its way of life and its institutions. Optimists thought that the world could now look forward to a period of peace and harmony, during which the USA, which saw itself as the land of freedom and benevolence, would lead the rest of the world forward, wherever necessary, into democracy and prosperity. In addition, wherever necessary, the USA would act as the world's policeman, keeping 'rogue states' under control and making them toe the line. Francis Fukuyama, professor of political economy at Johns Hopkins University, even argued that the world had reached 'the end of history', in the sense that History, seen as the development of human societies through various forms of government, had reached its climax in modern liberal democracy and market-oriented capitalism.

However, the new world order turned out to be quite different. Much of the rest of the world did not wish to be led anywhere by the USA, and disagreed with the USA's world-view. Since it was so powerful both militarily and economically, it was difficult for small countries to challenge the USA in conventional ways. To the extremists, it seemed that terrorism was the only way to strike at the USA and its allies.

Terrorism was nothing new – anarchists were responsible for many assassinations around the turn of the nineteenth and twentieth centuries; during the late nineteenth and the twentieth centuries there had been many terrorist organizations, but these were mostly localized, carrying out their campaigns in their own areas. There were, for example, ETA, which wanted a Basque state completely independent of Spain; and the IRA, which wanted Northern Ireland united with the Irish Republic.

It was in the 1970s that terrorists began to act outside their own territories. For example, in 1972 Arab terrorists killed 11 Israeli athletes at the Munich Olympics; and there was a series of bomb explosions on aircraft. In the 1980s it became clear that the USA was the chief target:

- there was an attack on the American embassy in Beirut (Lebanon) in 1983;
- an American airliner flying from Frankfurt to New York crashed onto the Scottish town of Lockerbie after a bomb had exploded on board (1988);
- a bomb exploded in the World Trade Center in New York in February 1993;
- US embassies in Kenya and Tanzania were attacked in 1998;
- there was an attack on the American battleship *Cole* in port at Aden in the Yemen (2000).

The culmination of this campaign was the terrible events of 11 September 2001 when the World Trade Center in New York was completely destroyed (see Illus. 12.1). The blame for

Illustration 12.1 **New York, 11 September 2001: a fiery blast rocks the south tower of the World Trade Center as the hijacked United Airlines flight 175 from Boston crashes into the building**

this attack was placed on al-Qaeda (meaning 'the Base'), an Arab organization led by *Osama bin Laden*, which was campaigning against Western or anti-Islamic interests. US president George W. Bush immediately announced 'a declaration of war on terrorism'. His aims were to overthrow the Taliban (students) regime in Afghanistan, which was thought to be aiding and abetting al-Qaeda, to capture Osama bin Laden and to destroy al-Qaeda. Bush also threatened to attack and overthrow any regime that encouraged or harboured terrorists. First on the list was to be Saddam Hussein of Iraq, and action was also threatened against Iran and North Korea – three states which, according to Bush, formed an 'axis of evil'.

The Taliban regime in Afghanistan was quickly overthrown (October 2001) and a national government led by Hamid Kharzai was put in place, supported by NATO troops. The USA, with British help, then moved on to deal with Iraq, where *Saddam Hussein was also overthrown (April–May 2003)* and later captured. Although these regimes were removed relatively easily, it proved much more difficult to replace them with viable, stable administrations which could bring peace and prosperity to their troubled countries. In Afghanistan the Taliban soon regrouped and in 2003 they began a new insurgency. NATO troops and the native Afghan army struggled to control the insurgency, but the violence continued and in 2012 Afghanistan was still in a state of civil war. And so the 'war on terror' continued.

At the same time there was increasing tension between the Islamic republic of Iran and the West. Since 1979 when the American-backed regime of the Shah Reza Pahlevi was overthrown in the Islamic revolution, Iran had been viewed with suspicion, partly because they were pursuing a nuclear programme. Although the Iranians insisted that their nuclear power was intended only for peaceful purposes – mainly to produce electricity - the West was convinced that they were planning to manufacture nuclear weapons. By early 2012 there was talk of American and Israeli pre-emptive strikes to destroy Iran's nuclear plants.

Meanwhile sensational events were taking place in other part of the Middle East and across North Africa. Beginning in Tunisia in December 2010, a series of anti-government protests and demonstrations quickly spread through the entire region. In little over a year the governments of Tunisia, Egypt, Libya and Yemen were overthrown and several other countries were forced to introduce important reforms and improvements, in a movement that became known as the 'Arab Spring'.

12.1 THE NEW WORLD ORDER

Soon after the US 'victory' in the Cold War, various American spokesmen announced that the USA was looking forward to a new era of peace and international co-operation. They implied that the USA, the world's only superpower – all-powerful and unchallengeable – was now committed to good works; support for international justice, liberty and human rights; the eradication of poverty; and the spread of education, health and democracy throughout the world. Understandably, Americans were full of pride in their country's achievements; in 1997 David Rothkopf, a minister in the Clinton administration, wrote: 'The Americans should not deny the fact that of all the nations in the history of the world, theirs is the most just, the most tolerant and the best model for the future.'

And yet, instead of being universally loved and admired, the USA, or rather US governments, ended up being hated so violently in certain quarters that people were driven to commit the most terrible acts of terrorism in protest against the USA and its system. How did this happen? *How did the post-Cold War era, which seemed so full of hope, turn out to be so full of hatred and horror?* In simple terms, there were millions of people in many countries of the world who did not share the advantages of the prosperous American lifestyle; nor did they see much evidence that the USA was genuinely trying to do anything to narrow the gap between the poor and the wealthy, or to fight for justice and human rights.

Many American writers were aware of the dangers of this situation. Nicholas Guyatt, in his book *Another American Century*, published in 2000, pointed out that

many people around the world are frustrated by the complacency and impenetrability of the US, and by the fact that the apparent absence of political solutions to this (such as a genuinely multilateral and independent United Nations) is likely to drive many towards radical and extreme measures ... [there are] large and dangerous pockets of resentment towards the US around the world, grounded not in fundamentalism or insanity but in a real perception of the imbalance of power, and a real frustration at the impotence of political means of change.

'As long as the US remains insulated from the effects of its actions', he concluded, 'it will have little sense of the true desperation they produce in others.'

What were these actions of the USA that caused such desperation in others? Clearly there was a complex combination of actions and policies which led to such extreme reactions.

- *US foreign policy continued along the same interventionist course as during the Cold War.* For example, in December 1989 at least 2000 civilians were killed when US forces invaded and bombed Panama. This was an operation designed to arrest Manuel Noriega, the Panamanian military leader who was the power behind the presidents of Panama during the 1980s. He had worked for the CIA and had been backed by the US government until 1987, when he was accused of drug trafficking and money laundering. The heavy-handed US operation resulted in his capture and removal to the USA to stand trial. The Organization of American States proposed a resolution 'to deeply regret the military intervention in Panama'. The resolution was approved by a vote of 20 to1, the one being the USA.
- During the 1990s the Americans helped to suppress left-wing movements in Mexico, Colombia, Ecuador and Peru. In 1999 they took part in the controversial bombing of Serbia. Twice – in 1989 and 2001 – American agents intervened in the Nicaraguan elections, the first time to defeat the left-wing government, the second time to prevent the left returning to power. This sort of policy was bound to cause resentment, especially now that it could not be justified as part of the campaign against the advance of global communism. In the words of William Blum (in *Rogue State*): 'The enemy was, and remains, any government or movement, or even individual, that stands in the way of the expansion of the American Empire.'
- At other times *the USA failed to intervene in situations where international opinion hoped for a decisive US role*. In Rwanda in 1994 the USA was reluctant to play a full part, since no direct US interests were involved and intervention on a sufficiently large scale would have been expensive. Because of the delays, some half a million people were massacred. As Nicholas Guyatt puts it: 'Reluctant to give up its central role in world affairs but unwilling to commit troops and money for UN operations, the USA atrophied the cause of peacekeeping just as the situation in Rwanda required a flexible and dynamic response.' The other main example of US failure was the Arab–Israeli conflict: although the USA became involved in trying to bring peace, they were clearly on the side of Israel. George W. Bush refused to deal with Yasser Arafat, regarding him as nothing but a terrorist. This US failure to bring about a just settlement of the conflict is probably the main reason for the bitter Arab and Muslim hostility.
- *The USA often failed to support the United Nations.* In 1984 for example, President Ronald Reagan talked about the importance of international law and order: 'without law', he said, 'there can only be chaos and disorder'. However, the previous day he had rejected the verdict of the International Court of Justice which condemned the USA for its unlawful use of force by its mining of harbours in Nicaragua. Later the court ordered the USA to pay compensation to Nicaragua, but the government refused and increased its financial support to the mercenaries who were trying to destabilize the democratically elected Nicaraguan government. The UN was unable to enforce its decision.
- The USA had a long history of vetoing Security Council resolutions and opposing General Assembly resolutions. A few examples demonstrate the US attitude. In

1985 the USA was the only country to vote against a resolution proposing new policies for improving the safeguarding of human rights (voting was 130 for, 1 against). Similarly in 1987, the USA was the only member to vote against a resolution aimed at strengthening communication services in the Third World (voting was 140 for, 1 against). In 1996, at a World Food Summit organized by the UN, the USA refused to endorse a general view that it was everyone's right 'to have access to safe and nutritious food'. As Noam Chomsky succinctly puts it (in *Hegemony or Survival*): 'When the UN fails to serve as an instrument of American unilateralism on issues of elite concern, it is dismissed.' The USA even voted against UN proposals on the control of terrorism, presumably because it wanted to fight terrorism in its own way. All this – before 11 September – could only result in a weakening of the UN and of international law. In the words of Michael Byers, 'international law as applied by the US increasingly bears little relationship to international law as understood anywhere else ... It is possible that ... the US is in fact attempting to create new, exceptional rules for itself alone.'

- *President George W. Bush was less than enthusiastic about some of the agreements entered into by previous administrations.* During his first year in office – and before 11 September – he rejected the 1972 Anti-Ballistic Missile Treaty, withdrew from the 1997 Kyoto Protocols on climate change, halted the new diplomatic contacts with North Korea and refused to co-operate in discussions about the control of chemical weapons.

- *The US economy was so powerful that decisions taken in Washington and New York had worldwide repercussions.* With the increasing globalization of the world's economy, American companies had interests all over the world. The Americans kept firm control over the World Bank and the International Monetary Fund, so that states applying for loans had to make sure that their internal policies were acceptable to the USA. In 1995 the new president of the World Bank, James Wolfensohn, announced that he wanted the Bank to do more to promote debt relief, good government, education and health in the Third World. But Washington opposed this, arguing for strict austerity. In fact, according to Will Hutton, 'the international financial system has been shaped to extend US financial and political power, not to promote the world public good'. By the end of 2002 it was clear that the USA was pursuing what some observers described as 'an imperial grand strategy' leading to a new world order in which it 'runs the show'.

12.2 THE RISE OF GLOBAL TERRORISM

(a) How do we define 'terrorism'?

Ken Booth and Tim Dunne, in their recent book *Worlds in Collision*, offer this definition:

> Terrorism is a method of political action that uses violence (or deliberately produces fear) against civilians and against civilian infrastructure in order to influence behaviour, to inflict punishment or to exact revenge. For the perpetrators, the point is to make the target group afraid of today, afraid of tomorrow and afraid of each other. Terrorism is an act, not an ideology. Its instruments are assassination, mass murder, hijacking, bombing, kidnapping and intimidation. Such acts can be committed by states as well as private groups.

There are problems with any definition of terrorism. For example, are people engaged in a legitimate struggle for independence, like the Mau Mau in Kenya (see Section 24.4(b)) and the African National Congress in South Africa (see Section 25.8), terrorists or revolutionaries and freedom fighters? In the 1960s Nelson Mandela was regarded as a terrorist by the white governments of South Africa and kept in jail for 27 years; now he is respected and revered by both blacks and whites all over the world. What about Yasser Arafat, the Palestinian leader? President Bush refused to meet him because, according to the Americans, he was nothing but a terrorist. Yet when the Israeli government carried out similar attacks to those perpetrated by the Palestinians, this was classified not as terrorism, but as legitimate actions of a government against terrorism. Clearly it depends which side you are on, and which side wins in the end.

(b) Terrorist groups

Some of the best-known terrorist organizations were based in the Middle East:

The *Abu Nidal Organization (ANO)* was one of the earliest groups to make itself felt. Formed in 1974, it was an offshoot of Yasser Arafat's Palestinian Liberation Organization (PLO), which was thought not to be sufficiently aggressive. The ANO was committed to a completely independent Palestinian state; it had bases in Lebanon and Palestine (in some of the refugee camps) and it drew support from Syria, Sudan, and at first from Libya. It was responsible for operations in about 20 different countries, including attacks on airports in Rome and Vienna (1985), and a number of aircraft hijackings. Since the early 1990s the ANO has been less active.

Hezbollah (Party of God), also known as *Islamic Jihad (Holy War)*, was formed in Lebanon in 1982 after the Israeli invasion (see Section 11.8(b)). Mainly Shia Muslims, they claimed to be inspired by the Ayatollah Khomeini, the ruler of Iran. They aimed to follow his example by setting up an Islamic state in Lebanon; they also wanted to expel the Israelis from all the occupied territories in Palestine. Hezbollah was thought to be responsible for several attacks on the US embassy in Beirut during the 1980s, and for seizing a number of Western hostages in 1987, including Terry Waite, a special peace envoy sent by the Archbishop of Canterbury. In the 1990s they began to extend their sphere of operations, attacking targets in Argentina – the Israeli embassy (1992) and later an Israeli cultural centre (1994).

Hamas (Islamic Resistance Movement) was formed in 1987 with the aim of setting up an independent Islamic state of Palestine. It tried to combine armed resistance to Israel with political activity, by running candidates for some of the Palestinian Authority elections. Hamas has massive support in the West Bank and the Gaza Strip; in the last few years it has specialized in suicide bomb attacks against Israeli targets.

Al-Qaeda (the Base) was the most famous terrorist group during the early years of the twenty-first century. Consisting mainly of Sunni Muslims, it was formed towards the end of the 1980s as part of the struggle to expel the Soviet forces which had invaded Afghanistan in 1979 (see Section 8.6(b)). Since this could be portrayed as part of the Cold War, al-Qaeda was actually financed and trained by the USA, among other Western countries. After the Russian withdrawal from Afghanistan was completed (February 1989), al-Qaeda extended its horizons. It began a general campaign in support of the establishment of Islamic governments. The special target was the non-religious conservative regime in Saudi Arabia, Osama bin Laden's homeland, which was supported by the USA and garrisoned by American troops. Al-Qaeda's aim was to force the Americans to withdraw their troops so that an Islamic regime would be able to come to power. A secondary aim was to bring an end to US support for Israel. The organization is thought to have around 5000 members, with cells in many countries.

Perhaps the best-known terrorist group outside the Middle East has been *the Tamil Tigers* in Sri Lanka. They were Hindus living in the north and east of Sri Lanka, whereas the majority of the island's population were Buddhist. The Tigers campaigned since the early 1980s for an independent homeland, using suicide bombings, assassinations of leading politicians, and attacks on public buildings and Buddhist shrines. By the 1990s they had over 10 000 troops and the struggle had reached civil-war proportions. Their most notorious action was the assassination of the Indian prime minister, Rajiv Ghandi, in India in 1991. A truce was arranged in 2001, and although it was broken several times, by 2003 there were encouraging signs that a peaceful settlement could be found.

Probably the most successful terrorist group was *the African National Congress (ANC)* in South Africa. Originally formed in 1912, it only adopted violent methods in the early 1960s when *apartheid* became more brutal. After a long campaign, the white supremacist government eventually succumbed to pressure from world opinion as well as from the ANC. Nelson Mandela was released (1990), and multiracial elections were held (1994). Mandela, the former 'terrorist', became the first black president of South Africa. There have been scores of other organizations, for example *the Tupamaru Revolutionary Movement* in Peru, which aims to rid the country of US influence; *the Islamic Group* in Algeria, which aims to set up an Islamic state in place of the existing non-religious government; and *the National Liberation Army* in Bolivia, which aims to rid the country of US influence.

(c) Terrorism becomes global and anti-American

It was in the early 1970s that terrorist groups began to operate outside their own countries. In 1972 there was the murder of 11 Israeli athletes at the Munich Olympics, carried out by a pro-Palestinian group calling itself Black September. Gradually it became clear that the main target of the outrages was the USA and its interests. After the downfall of the US-backed Shah of Iran early in 1979, there was a great wave of anti-American feeling in the region. In November 1979 a large army of several thousand Iranian students attacked the American embassy in the capital, Tehran, and seized 52 Americans, who were held hostage for almost 15 months. The demands of the country's new ruler, the Ayatollah Khomeini, included handing over the ex-Shah so that he could face trial in Iran, and an acknowledgement by the USA of its guilt for all its interference in Iran prior to 1979. Only when the USA agreed to release $8 million of frozen Iranian assets were the hostages allowed to return home. This incident was seen as a national humiliation by the Americans and showed the rest of the world that there were limits to the power of the USA. But at least the hostages were not harmed; after that, the anti-American acts became more violent.

- In 1983 the Middle East became the focus of attention as resentment grew at the extent of American interests and interventions in the region. Especially unpopular was US support of Israel, which had invaded the Lebanon in 1982. In April 1983 a truck carrying a huge bomb was driven into the US embassy in Beirut, the Lebanese capital. The building collapsed, killing 63 people. In October 1983 a similar attack was carried out on the headquarters of the US marines in Beirut, killing 242 people. The same day another suicide lorry was driven into a French military base in Beirut; this time 58 French soldiers were killed. In December, action switched to Kuwait City, where a lorry packed with explosives was driven into the US embassy, killing four people. All four attacks were organized by Islamic Jihad, probably backed by Syria and Iran.
- Shortly before Christmas 1988 an American airliner carrying 259 people en route for New York blew up and crashed onto the Scottish town of Lockerbie, killing all those on board and 11 people on the ground. No organization claimed responsibility but

suspicion fell on Iran and Syria. Later it shifted to Libya; eventually the Libyan government handed over two men suspected of planting the bomb. In January 2000 both were tried in a Scottish court sitting in special session in Holland; one was found guilty of killing the 270 victims and sentenced to life imprisonment, the other man was acquitted. However, many people believe that the conviction was dubious – the evidence was extremely thin – and that Syria and Iran were the real culprits.

- In February 1993 a bomb exploded in the basement of the World Trade Center in New York, killing six people and injuring several hundred.

- American interests in Africa were the next target: on the same day – 7 August 1998 – bomb attacks were launched against the US embassies in Nairobi (Kenya) and Dar-es-Salaam (Tanzania). In total, 252 people were killed and several thousand injured; but the vast majority of the victims were Kenyans, and only 12 of those killed were Americans. The Americans were convinced that al-Qaeda was responsible for the attacks, especially when the Islamic Army Organization, which was thought to be closely connected to Osama bin Laden, issued a statement claiming that the bombings were in revenge for injustices which the USA had committed against Muslim states; the statement also threatened that this was just a beginning – there would be even more attacks and the USA would meet a 'black fate'.

- President Bill Clinton ordered immediate retaliation – the Americans fired cruise missiles at complexes in Afghanistan and Sudan, which were said to be producing chemical weapons. However, this tactic seemed to backfire. One of the sites bombed turned out to be an ordinary pharmaceutical factory, and there was a violent anti-American reaction throughout the Middle East.

- October 2000 brought a new sort of terrorist action – the attack on the American destroyer *Cole*, which was refuelling in the port of Aden (in Yemen) on its way to the Persian Gulf. Two men rammed a small boat packed with explosives into the side of the ship, apparently hoping to sink it. They failed, but the explosion did blow a large hole in the *Cole*'s side, killing 17 sailors and injuring many more. The damage was easily repaired, but once again it was a humiliation that the world's supposedly most powerful nation had been unable to defend its property adequately in hostile regions. The message from the Islamic states was clear: 'We do not want you here.' Would the USA take heed and change its policies?

(c) Has the USA been guilty of terrorism?

If we accept that a definition of 'terrorism' should include acts committed by states as well as by individuals and groups, then we have to ask the question: which states have been guilty of terrorism, in the sense that their governments have been responsible for some or even all the terrorist activities mentioned – assassinations, mass murders, hijackings, bombings, kidnappings and intimidation? The list of candidates is a long one; the most obvious must be Nazi Germany, the USSR under Stalin, Communist China, the South African *apartheid* regime, Chile during the Pinochet regime, Cambodia under Pol Pot and Milošević's Serbia. But what about the shocking claim that the USA has also been guilty of terrorism? The accusation has been made not just by Arabs and Latin American left-wingers, but by respected Western commentators and by Americans themselves. It is linked to the question of why there have been so many terrorist acts directed against the USA.

Twenty years ago very few people in the West would have thought of asking such a question. But since the end of the Cold War, and especially since the 11 September attacks, there has been a radical reappraisal by a number of writers of the US role in international affairs since the end of the Second World War. Their motive in most cases is a genuine desire to find explanations as to why US government policies have aroused so much hostility. According to William Blum in his book *Rogue State*:

> From 1945 until the end of the century, the United States attempted to overthrow more than 40 foreign governments, and to crush more than 30 populist–nationalist movements struggling against intolerable regimes. In the process, the US caused the end of life for several million people, and condemned many millions more to a life of agony and despair.

Sections 8.4–5 gave examples of such US actions in South America, South-East Asia, Africa and the Middle East; the first section of this chapter showed that US foreign policy continued on essentially the same lines after 1990.

Noam Chomsky (a professor at the Massachusetts Institute of Technology) pointed out (in his book *Rogue States*) that often 'terrorist' acts against the USA were committed in retaliation for US actions. For example, it seems highly likely that the destruction of the American airliner over Lockerbie in 1988 was a retaliation for the shooting down of an Iranian airliner by the Americans, with the loss of 290 lives, a few months earlier. Similar American acts which precipitated retaliation were the bombings of Libya in 1986 and the shooting down of two Libyan aircraft in 1989; in these instances, however, the Americans could claim that their actions were in retaliation for earlier Libyan outrages. One of the most horrific acts of terrorism was a car bomb placed outside a mosque in Beirut in March 1985. It was timed to explode as worshippers left after Friday prayers: 80 innocent people were killed, including many women and children, and over 200 were seriously injured. The target was a suspected Arab terrorist, but he was unhurt. It is now known that the attack was organized by the CIA with help from British intelligence. Sadly, these were the sorts of action which were likely to turn ordinary Muslims into 'fanatical' terrorists. In 1996, Amnesty International reported:

> Throughout the world, on any given day, a man, woman or child is likely to be displaced, tortured, killed or 'disappeared', at the hands of governments or armed political groups. More often than not, the United States shares the blame.

Lloyd Pettiford and David Harding (in *Terrorism: The New World War*) conclude that American foreign policies must take much of the blame for the increase in terrorism, since 'the US seems totally determined to ensure that the whole world is opened up to its unrestricted access and that any alternative form of society be regarded as strictly against the rules'. Noam Chomsky claims (in *Who are the Global Terrorists?*) that Washington created

> an international terror network of unprecedented scale and employed it worldwide with lethal and long-lasting effects. In Central America, terror guided and supported by the US reached its most extreme levels. ... It is hardly surprising that Washington's call for support in its war of revenge for September 11 had little resonance in Latin America.

12.3   11 SEPTEMBER 2001 AND THE 'WAR ON TERROR'

(a)   The 11 September attacks

Early in the morning of 11 September 2001, four airliners on internal flights in the USA were hijacked. The first one was deliberately crashed into the 110-storey North Tower of the World Trade Center in New York. A quarter of an hour later the second plane crashed into the South Tower; about an hour after the impact the entire South Tower collapsed into a vast heap of rubble, severely damaging surrounding buildings; after another 25 minutes the North Tower also disintegrated. In the meantime a third plane was flown into the Pentagon, the building near Washington that housed the US Department of Defense, and the fourth plane missed its intended target and crashed in a rural area of Pennsylvania, not far from Pittsburgh. It was the most stunning atrocity ever experienced on US soil: it cost the lives of around 2800 people in the World Trade Center, well over a hundred in the Pentagon building, and some 200 who were passengers on the aircraft, including the hijackers. Television cameras filmed the second plane flying into the South Tower and the collapse of the towers, and these images, shown over and over again, only added to the horror and disbelief around the world at what was happening. Nor was it only Americans who were killed: it emerged that citizens of over forty foreign countries were among the victims, either in the buildings or as passengers on the aircraft.

Although no organization claimed responsibility for the attacks, the US government assumed that Osama bin Laden and al-Qaeda were guilty. Certainly it must have been carried out by educated professionals with considerable financial backing, like the members of al-Qaeda, who were known to number perhaps 5000 highly-trained activists. Recovering quickly from the initial shock, President Bush announced that the USA would hunt down and punish not only the perpetrators of what he called 'these acts of war', but also those who supported and harboured them. The outrages were condemned by most of the world's governments, although there were reports of Palestinians and other Muslim groups celebrating at the humiliation of the USA. President Saddam Hussein of Iraq was reported as saying that the USA was 'reaping the thorns of its foreign policy'.

(b)   Bush and the 'war against terrorism'

The American government immediately tried to build on the worldwide sympathy in order to create a coalition to fight terrorism. NATO condemned the outrages and stated that an attack on one member state would be treated as an attack on all 19 members; each country would be required to assist, if necessary. Within a short time a coalition of states was put together to enable the terrorists' assets to be frozen and to collect wide-ranging intelligence; some of the countries promised to help with military action against the terrorists and against the Taliban government of Afghanistan, which was accused of sheltering al-Qaeda and Osama bin Laden. Some of Bush's statements during this period were disturbing to other governments. For example, he stated that countries were 'either with us or against us' – implying that the right to remain neutral did not exist. He also spoke of 'an axis of evil' in the world, which would have to be dealt with; the 'evil' states were Iraq, Iran and North Korea. This opened up the possibility of a long series of military operations, with the USA playing the part of 'world policeman' or 'playground bully', depending on which side you were on.

This caused some alarm, and not only in the three states named. Chancellor Gerhard Schröder of Germany stated that although Germany was prepared to 'make appropriate military facilities' available to the USA and its allies, he did not consider that there was a state of war with any particular country; and he added that 'we are not in a war with the Islamic world either'. This cautious response was because of doubts about whether a direct attack on Afghanistan was justified in international law. As Michael Byers (an expert in international law at Duke University, North Carolina) explains:

> in order to maintain the coalition against terrorism, the US military response had to be necessary and proportionate. This meant that the strikes had to be carefully targeted against those believed to be responsible for the atrocities in New York and Washington.

But if the US singled out Osama bin Laden and al-Qaeda as its targets, it would have run up against the widely held view that terrorist attacks, in and of themselves, did not justify military responses against sovereign states.

It was for this reason that the USA widened its claim of self-defence to include the Taliban government of Afghanistan, which was accused of supporting the terrorist acts. Accordingly, the UN Security Council passed two resolutions which did not authorize military action under the UN Charter, but allowed it *as the right of self-defence in customary international law*. The USA then issued an ultimatum to the Taliban demanding that they hand over bin Laden and some of his colleagues directly to the US authorities. When this was rejected by the Taliban, the scene was set for the use of force, though Mullah Zaeef, one of the Taliban leaders, issued a press release strongly condemning the attacks and calling for those responsible to be brought to justice. No doubt he knew what to expect when he added: 'We want America to be patient and careful in their actions.'

(c) Background to the attack on Afghanistan

The history of the previous 30 years in Afghanistan had been extremely violent and confused. In 1978 a left-wing government seized power and began a modernization programme. However, in a country where Islamic authority was strong, changes such as equal status for men and women and the secularization of society were seen as an affront to Islam. Opposition was fierce, and civil war soon broke out. In 1979 Soviet troops entered the country to support the government; they were afraid that if the regime was overthrown by a fundamentalist Muslim revolution, like the one in Iran in January 1979, this would stir up the millions of Muslims who were Soviet citizens and destabilize those republics with substantial Muslim populations.

The USSR expected a short campaign, but the US government treated it as part of the Cold War and sent extensive aid to the Muslim opposition in Afghanistan. There were several rival Muslim groups, but they all worked together – known collectively as the *Mujahideen* – to drive out the Russians. By 1986 the Mujahideen (meaning 'those who wage *jihad*') were receiving large amounts of weaponry via Pakistan from the USA and China, the most important of which were ground-to-air missiles, which had a devastating effect on the Afghan and Soviet air forces. One of the organizations fighting with the Mujahideen was al-Qaeda, led by Osama bin Laden, who, ironically, received training, weapons and cash from the USA.

Eventually Mikhail Gorbachev, the Soviet leader, realized that he was in a similar situation to the one in which the Americans had found themselves in Vietnam. He had to acknowledge that the war in Afghanistan could not be won, and by February 1989 all Soviet troops had been withdrawn. Left to fend for itself, the socialist government of Afghanistan survived until 1992 when it was finally overthrown. The Mujahideen formed a coalition government, but the country soon fell into total chaos as the rival factions fought for power. During the later 1990s the faction known as 'the Taliban' (meaning 'students') gradually took control of the country, driving out rival groups area by area. The Taliban were a conservative Muslim faction made up of Pashtuns, the ethnic group in the south-east of the country, especially in the province of Kandahar. By the end of 2000 they controlled most of the country except the north-west, where they were opposed by the rival ethnic groups – Uzbeks, Tajiks and Hazara – known as the 'Northern Alliance'.

The Taliban regime aroused international disapproval because of its extreme policies.

- Women were almost totally excluded from public life, and were prevented from continuing as teachers and doctors and in other professions.

- Harsh criminal punishments were introduced. For example, women were often publicly beaten for showing their ankles. Mass executions took place in public in the Ghazi football stadium.
- Its cultural policies seemed unreasonable: for example, music was banned. There was worldwide dismay when the regime ordered the destruction of two huge statues of Buddha carved into rocks and dating from the fourth and fifth centuries AD. Cultural experts regarded them as unique treasures, but the Taliban blew them up, claiming that they were offensive to Islam.
- The government allowed the country to be used as a refuge and training ground for Islamic militants, including Osama bin Laden.
- Because of a combination of the ravages of years of civil war and three consecutive years of drought, the economy was in ruins. There were severe food shortages as refugees, who could no longer sustain themselves on the land, flocked into the cities. Yet when the UN tried to distribute food supplies in Kabul, the capital, the government closed their offices down. They objected to foreign influence and to the fact that Afghan women were helping with the relief work.

Very few states recognized the Taliban regime, and its unpopularity provided a boost to the American plan to use force against it. On the other hand the Taliban succeeded in eliminating much of the corruption endemic in Afghan ruling circles, and they restored security on the roads. Writing in 2010, a British journalist, James Fergusson, who spent 14 years in Afghanistan, argued that

the Taliban were never as uniformly wicked as they were routinely made out to be – and nor are they now. ... The Taliban made some terrible mistakes, and I do not condone them. But I am also certain that we need a better understanding of how and why they made these mistakes before we condemn them.

(d) The Taliban overthrown

A joint US and UK operation against Afghanistan was launched on 7 October 2001. Taliban military targets and al-Qaeda camps were attacked with cruise missiles fired from ships. Later, American long-range bombers carried out raids on the centre of Kabul. Meanwhile troops of the Northern Alliance began an offensive against Taliban positions in the north-west. On 14 October the Taliban offered to hand bin Laden over to an intermediary state, though not directly to the USA. In return they demanded that the USA should stop the bombing. However, President Bush rejected this offer and refused to negotiate. At first the Taliban forces put up strong resistance, and at the end of the month they still controlled most of the country. During November, under pressure from the continued US air attacks and the Northern Alliance forces, the Taliban began to lose their grip. On 12 November they abandoned Kabul and were soon driven from their main power base – the province of Kandahar. Many fled into the mountains or over the border into Pakistan. The USA continued to bomb the mountain region, hoping to flush out bin Laden and his al-Qaeda fighters, but without success.

The USA and its allies had achieved one of their aims: the unpopular Taliban regime had gone; but bin Laden remained elusive and was still a free man in 2004. On 27 November 2001 a peace conference met in Bonn (Germany), under the auspices of the United Nations, to decide on a new government for Afghanistan. It was not easy to bring peace to this troubled country. Early in 2004 the central government of President Hamid Karzai in Kabul was struggling to impose its authority over troublesome warlords in the north. He was supported by US troops who were still pursuing the 'war on terror', and by

NATO troops, who were trying to keep the peace and help rebuild the country. But it was an uphill task; the most ominous development was that the Taliban had regrouped in the south and over the border in Pakistan, financed partly by rising heroin production. UN officials were worried that Afghanistan might once again turn into a 'rogue state' in the hands of drug cartels. As the violence continued, even the aid agencies came under attack. In the summer of 2004 the Médecins sans Frontières organization, which had been active in Afghanistan for a quarter of a century, decided to pull out; this was a serious blow for ordinary Afghans.

Nevertheless, the promised elections, held in November 2004, were able to go ahead largely peacefully, in spite of threats of violence from the Taliban. President Karzai was elected for a 5-year term; he won 55.4 per cent of the votes, which was not as much as he had hoped, but enough for him to claim that he now had legitimacy and a mandate from the people (for what happened next, see Section 12.5).

(e) Is the 'war on terror' a struggle between Islam and the West?

From the beginning of his campaign, Osama bin Laden claimed that it was part of a world-wide contest between the West and Islam. As early as 1996 he had issued a *fatwa* (a religious command) to all Muslims that they were to kill US military personnel in Somalia and Saudi Arabia. In 1998 he extended the *fatwa*: 'To kill Americans and their allies, civilian and military, is an individual duty for every Muslim who can do it in any country in which it is possible to do it.' When the attack on Afghanistan began, he tried to present it, not as a war against terrorism, but as a war against Afghanistan and against Islam in general. He urged Muslims living in countries whose governments had offered to help the USA to rise up against their leaders. He talked about revenge for the 80 years of humiliation which Muslims had suffered at the hands of the colonial powers: 'what America is tasting now is only a copy of what we have tasted'. Bin Laden's deputy, Ayman al-Zawahiri, said that 11 September had divided the world into two sides: 'the side of the believers and the side of infidels. Every Muslim has to rush to make his religion victorious.'

(f) What was bin Laden hoping to achieve from his campaign?

- He had special interests in Saudi Arabia, the country where he was brought up and educated. After his exploits fighting the Soviet forces in Afghanistan, he returned to Saudi Arabia, but soon clashed with the government, a conservative monarchy which, he felt, was too subservient to the USA. He believed that as a Muslim country, Saudi Arabia should not have allowed the deployment of US and other Western troops on its territory during the Gulf War of 1991, because this was a violation of the Holy Land of Islam (Mecca and Medina, the two most holy cities in Islam, are both situated in Saudi Arabia). The government took away his Saudi citizenship and he was forced to flee to the Sudan, which had a fundamentalist Muslim regime. Bin Laden therefore hoped to get rid of the American military bases, which were still in Saudi Arabia at the beginning of 2001. Secondly, he wanted to achieve the overthrow of the Saudi government and its replacement by an Islamic regime.
- By this time the Saudi regime was beginning to feel concerned as its popularity dwindled. Many of the younger generation were suffering unemployment and sympathized with bin Laden's anti-Americanism; this prompted the government to try to reduce its co-operation with the USA. Although it condemned the 11 September attacks, it was reluctant to allow US military aircraft to use its bases, and it took no active part in the campaign against Afghanistan. This annoyed the USA,

which proceeded to remove almost all its troops from Saudi Arabia and set up a new headquarters in Qatar. Bin Laden's first aim had been achieved, and the second looked distinctly possible as unrest increased and al-Qaeda groups operating in Saudi Arabia became stronger. There were an increasing number of attacks on compounds housing foreign personnel. Without American troops to prop them up, the Saudi regime seemed likely to face a difficult time.

- He hoped to force a settlement in the Israeli–Palestinian conflict: he supported the creation of a Palestinian state, and, ideally, wanted the destruction of the state of Israel. This had not been achieved by 2011, when bin Laden was killed by American agents while living in hiding in Pakistan. A settlement of any kind seemed remote, unless the USA were to decide to use its political and financial influence over Israel.

- He hoped to provoke a worldwide confrontation between the Islamic world and the West, so that ultimately all foreign troops and influence in the Muslim and Arab world would be eliminated. Some observers believe this was the reason he planned the 11 September attacks on the USA: he calculated that the Americans would respond with disproportionate violence, which would unite the Muslim world against them. Once Western influence and exploitation had been eliminated, the Muslim states could concentrate on improving conditions and alleviating poverty in their own way, and they would be able to introduce Sharia law – the ancient law of Islam – which, they claimed, had been supplanted by foreign influence.

(For a further discussion of the 'clash of civilizations' between the West and the Islamic world see Section 28.4.)

12.4 THE DOWNFALL OF SADDAM HUSSEIN

(a) Background to the attack on Iraq

After his defeat in the first Gulf War (1990–1), Saddam Hussein was allowed to remain in power (see Section 11.10(c)). He defeated uprisings of Kurds in the north and Shia Muslims in the south, where he was especially brutal in his treatment of the rebels. When refugees fled into the marshes, Saddam had the marshland drained, and many thousands of Shia were killed. He had already used chemical weapons in his war against Iran and against the Kurds, and was known to have a biological weapons programme. By 1995 Iraq had a well-advanced nuclear weapons programme. Although they were reluctant to remove Saddam Hussein because of the chaos that might follow, the USA and the UK tried to restrain him by continuing the trade embargo placed on Iraq by the UN soon after Iraqi forces invaded Kuwait. In 2000 these sanctions had been in place for ten years, but they seemed to have had little effect on Saddam; it was the ordinary people of Iraq who suffered because of shortages of food and medical supplies. In September 1998 the director of the UN relief programme in Iraq, Denis Halliday, resigned, saying that he could no longer carry out such an 'immoral and illegal' policy. In 1999, UNICEF reported that since 1990 over half a million children had died from malnutrition and lack of medicines as a direct result of sanctions.

However, sanctions did ensure that Saddam allowed inspections of his nuclear sites by members of the International Atomic Energy Agency (IAEA), authorized by a UN Security Council resolution. It was discovered that the Iraqis had all the components necessary to manufacture nuclear warheads, and that construction was actually under way. In 1998 the IAEA team destroyed all Saddam's nuclear sites and took away the equipment. At this point, however, there was no talk of removing Saddam from power, since he was keeping the Kurds and Shias under control, and thereby preventing the destabilization of the region.

(b) The USA and UK prepare to attack

The warning signals came with President Bush's State of the Union address in January 2002 when he referred to the world's rogue states, which were a threat because of their 'weapons of mass destruction' (WMD). He described them as an 'axis of evil'; the states named were Iraq, Iran and North Korea. It soon became clear that the USA, encouraged by its relatively easy victory in Afghanistan, was about to turn its attentions to Iraq. The US media began to try to convince the rest of the world that Saddam Hussein presented a serious threat and that the only remedy was a 'regime change'. *The justifications put forward by the Americans for an attack on Iraq were the following*:

- Saddam had chemical, biological and nuclear weapons, and was working on a programme to produce ballistic missiles which could fly more than 1200 km (thus breaking the 150 km limit); these were the missiles necessary for the delivery of weapons of mass destruction.
- The entire world situation had changed since 11 September (9/11); the war against terrorism required that states which supported and encouraged terrorist organizations should be restrained.
- Iraq was harbouring terrorist groups, including members of al-Qaeda, which had a training camp specializing in chemicals and explosives. Iraqi intelligence services were co-operating with the al-Qaeda network, and together they presented a formidable threat to the USA and its allies.
- The longer action was delayed, the greater the danger would become. Khidir Hamza, an Iraqi exile who had worked on his country's nuclear programme, told the USA in August 2002 that Saddam would have useable nuclear weapons by 2005. Some supporters of war compared the situation with the 1930s, when the appeasers failed to stand up to Hitler and allowed him to become too powerful.

(c) Opposition to the war

Although UK prime minister Tony Blair pledged support for a US attack on Iraq, there was much less enthusiasm in the rest of the world than there had been for the campaign against the Taliban in Afghanistan. There were massive anti-war demonstrations in the UK, Australia and many other countries, and even in the USA itself. *Opponents of the war made the following points.*

- Given that all his nuclear facilities had been destroyed in 1998 and that even more stringent trade sanctions had been imposed, it was highly unlikely that Saddam had been able to rebuild his facilities for producing WMD. Scott Ritter, the chief UN weapons inspector in Iraq, stated (in September 2002) that 'Since 1998 Iraq has been fundamentally disarmed. 90–95 per cent of Iraq's weapons of mass destruction have been verifiably eliminated. This includes all of the factories used to produce chemical, biological and nuclear weapons, and long-range ballistic missiles; the associated equipment of these factories; and the vast majority of products coming out of these factories.' Clearly Iraq was much less of a threat in 2002 than it had been in 1991. There was a feeling that the dangers had been exaggerated by exiled Iraqi opponents of Saddam, who were doing their utmost to pressure the USA into removing him.

- Even if Saddam had all these WMD, it was most unlikely that he would dare to use them against the USA and its allies. Such an attack by Saddam would certainly have ensured his rapid overthrow. Nor had Saddam invaded another state, as he had in 1990, therefore that justification could not be used for an attack on Iraq.
- There was insufficient evidence that Iraq was harbouring al-Qaeda terrorists. US military intervention would make the situation worse by fostering even more violent anti-Western feeling. Congressional reports published in 2004 concluded that critics of the war had been right: Saddam had no stocks of weapons of mass destruction and there were no links between Saddam, al-Qaeda and 9/11.
- War should be the last resort; more time should be given for the UN inspectors to complete their search for WMD. Any military action should be sanctioned by the UN.
- It was suggested that the real motives of the USA were nothing to do with the war against terrorism. It was simply a case of the world's only superpower blatantly extending its control more widely – 'maintaining global US pre-eminence'. A group of leading Republicans (the party of President Bush) had already in 1998 produced a document urging President Clinton to pursue a foreign policy that would shape the new century in a way 'favourable to American principles and interests'. They suggested 'the removal of Saddam Hussein's regime from power'. If Clinton failed to act, 'the safety of American troops in the region, of our friends and allies like Israel, and the moderate Arab states, and a significant proportion of the world's supply of oil will all be put at hazard. ... American policy cannot continue to be crippled by a misguided insistence on unanimity in the UN security council.' Having recently removed most of their forces from Saudi Arabia, the Americans would find Iraq the perfect substitute, enabling the USA to continue exercising control over the region's oil supplies.

(d)   The United Nations and the war

In view of the doubts being expressed, and under pressure from Tony Blair, President Bush decided to give the UN a chance to see what it could achieve. In November 2002 the UN Security Council approved a resolution (1441) calling on Saddam Hussein to disarm or 'face serious consequences'. The text was a compromise between the USA and the UK on one side, and France and Russia (who opposed a war) on the other. The resolution did not give the USA full authority to attack Iraq, but it clearly sent a strong message to Saddam as to what he might expect if he failed to comply. The Security Council would assess any failure by Iraq to comply with the new more stringent inspection demands. Iraq accepted the resolution and Hans Blix and his team of 17 weapons inspectors arrived back in the country after an absence of four years.

Bush and Blair were impatient at the delay, and in January 2003 Blair began to push for a second Security Council resolution which would authorize an attack on Iraq. Bush stated that although he would be happy with a second resolution, he did not consider it necessary; he argued that Resolution 1441 already gave the USA authority to attack Saddam. The USA, UK and Spain pressed for another resolution, while France, Russia and China were adamant that the weapons inspectors should be given more time before military action was taken. By the end of February 2003, Blix was reporting that the Iraqis were co-operating and had agreed to destroy some missiles which had been discovered. The USA, UK and Spain dismissed this information as a 'delaying tactic' by Saddam, although, in fact, early in March, Iraq began destroying missiles; this was described by Blix as 'a substantial measure of disarmament'. President Georges Chirac of France now made it clear that he would veto any Security Council resolution authorizing war against Iraq (10 March).

However, the Americans dismissed the objections of France and Germany contemptuously as 'old Europe' – out of touch with current trends. The USA, UK and Spain were determined to go ahead: they issued a joint ultimatum to Saddam giving him 48 hours to leave Iraq. When this was ignored, US and UK forces began air attacks and an invasion of southern Iraq from Kuwait (20 March). The USA claimed that 30 countries had agreed to join their coalition, though in the event, only the UK and Australia made any military contribution. As the invasion began, American historian Arthur Schlesinger wrote in the *Los Angeles Times*:

> The president has adopted a policy of 'anticipatory self-defence' that is alarmingly similar to the policy that Japan employed at Pearl Harbor, on a date which, as an earlier American president said it would, lives in infamy. Franklin D. Roosevelt was right, but today it is we Americans who live in infamy. ... The global wave of sympathy that engulfed the United States after 9-11 has given way to a global wave of hatred of American arrogance and militarism ... even in friendly countries, the public regards Bush as a greater threat to peace than Saddam Hussein.

(e) Saddam Hussein overthrown

Initially the invading forces made slower progress than had been expected, since some units of Iraqi troops put up strong resistance. US forces were hampered by the fact that Turkey had refused to allow US units to take up positions on its territory. This meant that it was impossible for the USA to mount a significant advance on Baghdad from the north. Forces advancing from the south were hampered by heavy desert sandstorms. By the end of March the expected swift victory had not yet been achieved; it was announced that the number of US troops would be doubled to 200 000 by the end of April. Meanwhile the assault on Baghdad by heavy bombers and cruise missiles continued. It emerged later that during the first four weeks of the attack, as many as 15 000 Iraqis were killed, of whom about 5000 were civilians.

International reaction to the invasion was mainly unfavourable. There were protest demonstrations throughout the Arab world, where the US action was seen simply as a blatant empire-building enterprise. An Iranian spokesman said it would lead to 'the total destruction of security and peace', while Saudi Arabia called for military occupation of Iraq to be avoided. Condemnation also came from Indonesia (which had the largest Muslim population in the world), Malaysia, France, Germany and Russia. However, a few countries expressed support, including the Philippines, Spain, Portugal and the Netherlands; so did some of the former communist states of eastern Europe, notably Poland. This surprised many people, but the reason for it was simple: the USA had enormous prestige in their eyes because of the vital role it had played in the defeat of communism.

In early April the sheer weight and strength of the invaders began to tell. Iraqi units began to desert and resistance collapsed. US troops captured Baghdad, while the British took Basra, the main city in the south. On 9 April it was announced that Saddam's 24-year dictatorship was over, and the world was treated to television pictures of an American tank toppling a statue of Saddam in Baghdad, cheered on by a jubilant crowd (see Illus. 12.2). Saddam himself disappeared for the time being, but was captured in December 2003. On 1 May, President Bush declared that the war was over.

(f) The aftermath

The events of the year following the overthrow of Saddam were not what President Bush had been hoping for. *No weapons of mass destruction were found.* Worse than that, in

Illustration 12.2 **The sculpted head of Saddam Hussein sits in the middle of the road in Baghdad, Iraq, 10 April 2003**

January 2004 Paul O'Neill, a former US Treasury secretary who was sacked at the end of 2002 because he disagreed with the rest of the cabinet over Iraq, made some sensational revelations. He claimed that Bush had been determined to oust Saddam as far back as January 2001 when he took office, and that 11 September provided a convenient justification. Talk of the threat of weapons of mass destruction was merely a cover, since the cabinet knew perfectly well that Saddam had no such weapons of any significance. Thus the main justification for the war given by Bush and Blair seemed to have been invalidated.

As the US and UK occupation of Iraq went on, *the Iraqis, most of whom had at first been grateful for the removal of Saddam, became impatient.* There seemed little evidence of attempts at 'nation-building' by the Americans, whose methods of keeping order were often insensitive. Nor did they seem to have any clear plan for the future of Iraq.

Inevitably, anti-American feeling grew and by June 2003 armed resistance was well under way. At first attacks were carried out just by Saddam loyalists, but they were soon joined by other groups: nationalists who wanted their country to be free and independent, and Sunni Muslims who wanted some kind of Islamic state.

In the Arab world outside Iraq *there was a wave of anti-Americanism*. Militants flocked into the country to support their fellow Muslims against the USA, which they viewed as the great enemy of Islam. The violence escalated as suicide bombers, using the tactics of Hamas and Hezbollah, targeted UN headquarters, police stations, the Baghdad Hotel, Iraqis who co-operated with the Americans, and American military personnel; by the end of 2003, 300 American soldiers had been killed – since President Bush declared the war to be over. So although al-Qaeda fighters were probably not active in Iraq before the invasion, they certainly were in its aftermath. The Americans hoped that the capture of Saddam would bring about a reduction of violence, but it seemed to make little difference.

What did the resistance movement want? A spokesman for one of the nationalist groups said: 'We do not want to see our country occupied by forces clearly pursuing their own interests, rather than being poised to return Iraq to the Iraqis.' One of the things that infuriated Iraqis was the way in which American companies were being awarded contracts for reconstruction work in Iraq, to the exclusion of all other contractors.

It seemed as though the whole focus of international attention was directed towards Iraq. What happened there would have repercussions throughout the Middle East and the whole sphere of international relations. The dangers were enormous:

- In a country where there were so many different religious, ethnic and political groups, what hope was there that a strong government with a working majority would emerge from elections? If the country were to descend into civil war, like the Lebanon during the years 1975–87, what action would the Americans take?
- The al-Qaeda organization had been strengthened by the increase in anti-American and anti-Western feeling. There were also a number of new networks of Islamic militants, with bases in Europe as well as the Middle East. In 2004, London was named as an important centre for recruiting, fundraising and the manufacture of false documents. Islamic militant cells were reported in Poland, Bulgaria, Romania and the Czech Republic. Terrorist attacks continued: even before the Iraq War, a bomb exploded on the resort island of Bali (part of Indonesia) killing almost 200 people, many of them Australian holidaymakers (October 2002). Indonesia was again the target in August 2003 when a bomb blast outside a US-owned hotel in Jakarta (the capital) killed ten Muslims, but only one European.
- The next target was Turkey, where Istanbul suffered four suicide-bomb attacks in five days. Two went off outside Jewish synagogues, one near the London-based HSBC bank, while the fourth badly damaged the British consulate, killing the UK consul-general. The attacks on UK targets were timed to coincide with a visit to London by President Bush. Altogether in the four attacks, for which al-Qaeda was blamed, around 60 people were killed, most of them local Turkish Muslims.
- In March 2004, some 200 people were killed in Madrid in multiple bomb attacks on four morning rush-hour trains. At first it was thought by the Spanish government to be the work of ETA – the Basque separatist movement; but it later became clear that the terrorists responsible were a Moroccan group allied to al-Qaeda; they had presumably acted in retaliation for the fact that Spain had supported the USA and UK in their attack on Iraq. The attacks had unexpected political results: in the Spanish general election held three days later, the government of José María Aznar, which had supported the war and had sent troops to Iraq, was defeated by the socialists, who had opposed the war. Only four weeks later, the new prime minister, José Luis Zapatero, withdrew all Spanish troops from Iraq.

- It was London's turn in July 2005, when four Muslim suicide bombers killed 52 people and injured almost 800 more on three Underground trains and a bus.
- While the Palestinian–Israeli dispute remained unsolved and American troops were in Iraq, there seemed little chance of an end to the 'war against terrorism'. Some observers suggested, as a first step, the withdrawal of American and British personnel from Iraq and their replacement by an interim UN administration backed by UN troops – from any country except the USA and the UK! In this way, the move towards democracy could be planned carefully, a constitution could be drawn up and elections conducted under UN auspices.

In 2004 most of the seasoned observers of the Middle East were saying the same thing: the USA, the world's most powerful state, must listen to what moderate Iraqis were saying if it wanted to avoid complete chaos in Iraq and the Middle East, and the prospect of another Vietnam. The situation continued to deteriorate; in April the Americans were faced with a full-scale Shia uprising led by the radical cleric Muqtada al-Sadr, who wanted Iraq to become a Shia Islamic state. The Americans suffered further embarrassment and worldwide condemnation when stories emerged of Iraqi prisoners being tortured, abused and humiliated by American soldiers. Many Iraqis were transferred to the US detention centre at Guantánamo Bay in Cuba, and there were regular newspaper reports of torture, unfair trials and suicides. In 2003, 117 prisoners were transferred to Guantánamo, joining over 600 detainees from several countries already there. Although President Barack Obama talked of closing the centre, it was still functioning at the beginning of 2012, when there were 171 inmates from 20 countries. It had taken over six years of detentions at Guantánamo before the US Supreme Court ruled (June 2008) that detainees had the right to challenge the legitimacy of their detention in the US federal court. Since then 38 men have been released after the court declared their detention illegal.

One of President Bush's main concerns was that he was due to face re-election in November 2004. It was important for him to bring the American involvement in Iraq to an end before then, if possible. It was decided to transfer authority to the Iraqis at the end of June 2004. The handover of power to an Iraqi interim government went ahead as planned, and some attempt was made to include representatives of all the different Iraqi groups. For example, the prime minister, Ayad Allawi, was a secular Shiite and leader of the Iraqi National Accord party; the president, Ajil al-Yawer, was a Sunni; there were two vice-presidents, one a Kurd, the other a leader of the Shiite Islamist Da'wa party. The UN Security Council unanimously approved a timetable for Iraq to move towards genuine democracy. Direct democratic elections to a Transitional National Assembly were to be held no later than the end of January 2005. The Assembly would draw up a permanent constitution, under the terms of which a new democratic government was to be elected by the end of 2005. This went ahead as planned, and in the elections of December 2005, almost 77 per cent of eligible Iraqis actually voted.

The Shiite Islamic Iraqi Alliance emerged as the largest group, while the Kurdistan Alliance came second; altogether 12 different groups were represented, but ominously, most Sunni Muslims boycotted the elections. This meant that the Shia majority, who had been oppressed under Saddam, were now in a strong position, although they would need to form alliances with some of the smaller parties, since many important decisions required a two-thirds majority in parliament.

Unfortunately violence continued as Sunni militants, who included many Saddam supporters, fought Shias, and insurgents attacked American and British forces which were still there, ostensibly to support the Iraqi army. It was now clear that the Americans had made a bad mistake when, almost as soon as the occupation began, they had disbanded the Iraqi army. This meant that there were large numbers of men with military training with nothing to do except join in the insurgency against the foreigners. The situation also attracted al-Qaeda supporters from outside Iraq, who were experts at terrorist acts and were quick to seize the opportunity to strike at the detested Americans. In 2007 President Bush sent more troops to Iraq, bringing the total American force to 150 000. For a time it seemed as though this 'surge', as it was called, was managing to reduce the violence; consequently in June 2009 American troops were formally withdrawn from the streets of Baghdad. Predictably, violence soon increased again, with bombings, shootings and kidnappings everyday occurrences. Before long, however, Iraqi security forces, trained by the Americans, seemed to be getting the upper hand, and by the end of 2009 the government reported that civilian deaths were at the lowest level since the invasion in 2003. In December 2011 the war was formally declared to be over, and American troops withdrew into Kuwait, fulfilling the commitment that President Obama had given at the beginning of his presidency.

Sadly, however, within a few weeks, the bright new democratic state that was meant to take over from the Saddam dictatorship was in grave difficulties. Various sectarian conflicts which had lain dormant for many years had now erupted again, and warlords and militias seemed to be out of control. In January 2012 the prime minister, Nouri al-Maliki, a Shia, accused the vice-president, Tariq al-Hashemi, a Sunni, of organizing terrorist attacks. A warrant was issued for his arrest, forcing him to flee into the Kurdish area in northern Iraq. This was seen by the Sunnis as the beginning of Maliki's campaign to eliminate non-Shia rivals one by one, in order to strengthen the Shia grip on power. The Sunnis responded with a wave of attacks: in January alone 170 people were killed in car and suicide bombings. The dead were mainly Shia Muslims, some of them pilgrims travelling to visit holy sites. Although the level of violence was not as serious as in the dark days of 2006, Iraq was still facing a crisis. There seemed to be three possible ways forward:

- Partition the country into three separate states – for the Shia, the Sunnis and the Kurds. This would delight the Kurds, who have large oil reserves in their territory; but it would mean the end of the state of Iraq.
- Introduce a federal system in which the regions have more control over their internal affairs and Baghdad's power is much less. The two Sunni areas of Anbar and Diyyala are strongly in favour of this solution.
- Continue with the present system and try to make it work more efficiently. Malaki favours this alternative because that would preserve Shia control, always providing that the other groups can be forced or persuaded to co-operate.

There were economic problems, too. In August 2009 the *New York Times* reported that Iraq's rich agricultural system had been completely devastated during the American and British occupation. During the 1980s Iraq was self-sufficient in producing wheat, rice, fruit, vegetables, sheep and poultry. They exported textiles and leather goods, including shoes. 'Slowly, Iraq's economy has become based almost entirely on imports and a single commodity, oil.' In 2010 oil exports made up around 95 per cent of Iraq's revenue; this left the country vulnerable and dependent on highly volatile markets.

12.5 THE CONTINUING WAR IN AFGHANISTAN

President Karzai was elected in 2004 for a five-year term, and his task was a difficult one. His new slogan was 'national participation'. He aimed to build a government of moderates, and he immediately launched a campaign to sideline the warlords, to clean up the drug trafficking, and to persuade farmers to switch to other crops instead of growing opium poppies. But as the Taliban insurgency gathered pace, so did the return to opium as the main cash crop. By 2007 about half the country's gross domestic product came from illegal drugs. The attempts by NATO forces to control the crop only led to further violence. By this time it was clear to many observers that it was highly unlikely that the Taliban could be defeated militarily; Karzai himself admitted that he had tried without success to open negotiations with the Taliban. His first message to newly elected US President Obama was a heartfelt plea to stop the bombing of civilians. This was soon after coalition troops had bombed a wedding party in Kandahar, allegedly killing 40 people. There was no reply from the White House. Some NATO members were beginning to think about reducing their troop numbers in the coalition force.

Presidential elections were due in 2009 and were held amid a major security operation mounted by the International Security Assistance Force (ISAF), established by the UN Security Council. There was a low turnout at only about 30 per cent; in some areas in the south the turnout was almost non-existent. In one district in Helmand province, four British soldiers were killed for the sake of just 150 votes. Karzai won a narrow victory over his main rival, Abdullah Abdullah, but the whole process was marred by massive fraud on all sides, most of all on behalf of Karzai, much to NATO's embarrassment. Meanwhile Taliban military successes continued and in many areas they set up shadow administrations with their own law courts. Karzai again called for peace talks with Taliban leaders, but this scandalized other opposition leaders who believed that the Taliban would insist on scrapping the democratic constitution. As violence continued, US president Obama announced the deployment of another 30 000 troops in Afghanistan in 2010, to stay for two years.

In May 2011 Osama bin Laden was killed by a US special operations unit. He had been living in hiding for some years with his family and al-Qaeda members in a large purpose-built compound in Pakistan. The American unit travelled by helicopters from Afghanistan, shot bin Laden and several others, and then flew out again, taking bin Laden's body with them. The assassination brought mixed reactions: there were celebrations across the USA, though a poll taken shortly afterwards showed that 60 per cent of those polled were afraid that it would increase the danger of terrorist attacks in America. A leader of the Muslim Brotherhood in Egypt said that the death of bin Laden completed the NATO mission in Afghanistan, and therefore all foreign troops should be withdrawn. One of the Hamas leaders in Gaza condemned the killing, describing bin Laden as 'an Arab holy warrior'. The government of Pakistan was criticized in the West because it had given shelter and protection to bin Laden (which it denied), and by Arabs for allowing the Americans into the country to carry out the killing.

The USA and NATO paid no heed to the Egyptian advice about withdrawing from Afghanistan. The war continued and by the end of 2011 the Taliban had acquired the support of another insurgent group, the Haqqani Network. This was based in the Waziristan area of Pakistan and operated across the frontier into Afghanistan. In response the Americans were training and arming local tribal militias in the hope that they would police their own communities. However, local people and the Taliban were soon complaining that these militias were out of control and were operating above the law. This did not bode well for the coalition forces, since it was to get rid of out-of-control militias that the Taliban came into being in 1994. Outright military victory over the insurgents seemed less and less likely. Even with the extra NATO troops in action there were still not enough of them to establish real security. A NATO summit meeting was held in Lisbon in November 2011 at which secret plans were drawn up for troop withdrawals. David Cameron publicly promised that all 10 000 UK troops would be withdrawn by 2015. By this time Washington had signalled its support for President Karzai's attempts to begin talks with the Taliban, though President Obama himself was not keen on starting direct talks. His problem was that, thanks to all the earlier misinformation and propaganda by US politicians and the media, most Americans made no distinction between the Taliban and al-Qaeda and therefore regarded both of them as nothing but terrorists; with an election due in November 2012 he needed to be careful not to be seen to be appeasing terrorists. James Fergusson sums the situation up very well, though not everybody will agree with his conclusion:

> At least the possibility of talks is firmly on the table now – and neither side can afford to ignore indefinitely the wishes of the war-weary Afghan people, who have suffered more than any other group in this conflict. At least 11,400 civilians have been killed since 2001, and the casualty rate is still accelerating. No wonder 83 per cent of Afghans are now in favour of talks. Who would not choose compromise and the chance of peace over continued war, poverty and corruption? The alternative is to persevere with a war that looks increasingly unwinnable. If ordinary Afghans are ready to give the Taliban the benefit of the doubt, is it not time that the West did too?

12.6 THE PROBLEM OF IRAN

(a) The Islamic Republic

After the revolution of 1979 and the overthrow of the Shah, the charismatic Ayatollah Khomeini became leader. As a Shia Muslim cleric, he was soon able to transform the revolution, which had started as a protest movement against the Shah, into an Islamic revolution, culminating in an Islamic republic. But first there were sensational events. There was widespread fear in Iran that the Americans would try to restore the Shah to the throne, as they had done once before in 1953. In November 1979 a party of radical Khomeini supporters attacked the American embassy in Tehran and took 66 Americans hostage. Most of them were not released until early in 1981, after long negotiations and a failed rescue attempt in which eight Americans were killed and six helicopters lost. The two main characteristics of Islamic government, at least in Khomeini's view, were the primacy of divine law over all citizens, and the principle of democracy. However, in practice this meant that Khomeini acted as an autocratic ruler and became the symbol of opposition to the less desirable aspects of Western civilization and culture. Unfortunately most of Khomeini's time in power was dominated by the war with Iraq (see Section 11.9), which lasted from 1980 until 1989. At the end of it Iran was in a sorry state: the economy was in ruins, vital revenue from oil sales had been lost, much of industry had been put out of action and inflation was running at over 30 per cent. Khomeini died in 1989, before the attack on Iraq and the downfall of Saddam Hussein in 1991.

The new president, Ali Akbar Rafsanjani, was able to take some advantage from this war. It meant that Iraq was removed from the political equation of the region for the time being, and it enabled Iran to rebuild and recover from the destruction of the earlier war. He won in the 1992 elections and shared power with the religious leader, Ayatollah Ali Khamenei. The economy gradually recovered, there were great improvements in public services, education and literacy and the government did its best to encourage birth control. But on the negative side, women were discriminated against regularly, wages were low and poverty widespread. In foreign affairs Iran was extremely hostile towards the USA and supported Hezbollah. In retaliation President Clinton condemned the Iranians on the grounds that they were organizing terrorism and harbouring terrorists. Meanwhile the Iranians were busy rearming and were considering developing nuclear weapons. It was felt that this was justified by the fact that so far Israel was the only state in the Middle East to possess nuclear armaments, so Iran needed them to act as a deterrent.

The 1997 presidential election was won by Muhammad Khatami, a more moderate leader than Rafsanjani; Khatami was in favour of liberalization and reform. He brought a more relaxed approach to both domestic and foreign policy. His government was more tolerant towards ordinary people: he believed in freedom of expression and punishments were less severe. He was soon popular with the unemployed and with the younger generation, many of whom were tired of the strict religious regime of the Ayatollahs. Abroad he improved relations with the European Union and with the Arab states. He even adopted a gentler attitude towards the USA. However, he was hampered by the intolerant religious right and also by the slump in the world price of oil, which made up around 90 per cent of revenue from Iran's exports. Khatami was re-elected in 2001 but had to face increasing opposition from the conservative clergy in parliament who did their best to undermine his efforts at reform. Liberal newspapers were banned and in the end Khatami was able to achieve very little. His support dwindled and in July 2003 there were anti-government demonstrations in Tehran. Lack of progress resulted in a steady growth of political apathy among the younger generation.

The presidential election of 2005 was won by Mahmoud Ahmadinejad, who had previously been Mayor of Tehran. He had caused controversy by reversing many of the reforms introduced by earlier mayors. According to Hooman Majd, an Iranian writer now resident in the USA, Ahmadinejad was a president in the 'common man' style. He represented the superstitions and prejudices of the ordinary Iranian – fiercely nationalist and conservative, but somewhat anti-clerical. 'At times,' Majd writes, 'he has seemed to be almost taunting the mullahs and ayatollahs.' However, he did kiss the Ayatollah Khamenei's hand during his authorization ceremony, to show that he acknowledged his superior status. Ahmadinejad soon set about reversing the few reforms that Khatami had managed to achieve. His foreign policy was uncompromising: Iran resumed its nuclear programme (see the next section), which he defended at the UN General Assembly soon after his election. Yet his domestic policies were not as successful as many had hoped. For example, his 2005 promise to put Iran's oil wealth 'on the people's dinner table or picnic rug' had not been kept by the time the next election arrived in 2009. The best that had been achieved in that direction was the distribution to the poor of surplus potatoes from government stocks. This provoked only ridicule: during the 2009 election campaign, opposition supporters carried banners which read: 'Death to Potatoes'.

President Mahmoud Ahmadinejad won the election of June 2009, taking 63 per cent of votes cast. The result was immediately challenged; millions of people simply did not believe it, and the regime was accused of fraud. Anti-government demonstrations began soon after the result was announced and within a few days, millions of people were on the streets, many of them dressed in green. The opposition became known as the Green Movement. Khamenei applauded the election result and warned that serious repercussions would follow if the streets were not cleared. When this was ignored, troops fired on the crowds and attacked a section of Tehran University where some of the Green leaders were based. Over a hundred young people were killed in one day. At least one highly respected jurist, Hossein Ali Montazeri, declared that the election was null and void and that Ahmadinejad had no authority. Demonstrations continued into 2010, but the regime did not panic. The Greens were eventually outnumbered, outmanoeuvred and overwhelmed. Gradually attention focused on external events, including the threat of Israeli expansion and American protests at Iran's nuclear programme. For a time this rallied support behind the regime, but in February 2011 thousands of Green supporters defied a government ban and staged a massive demonstration in support of the 'Arab Spring' uprisings in Tunisia and Egypt. The fact that both these regimes were ousted later in the year did nothing to calm the Islamic republic.

In the spring of 2012 the situation was confused. People were tired of all the restrictions on civil liberty, for which they blamed the government. There were also economic problems caused by US and EU sanctions imposed in protest against Iran's nuclear programme. Most Iranians blamed the USA for this; American talk of attacks on their nuclear installations stimulated the Iranians' feelings of patriotism. Russia and China both supported Iran;

President Vladimir Putin of Russia claimed that the West's real motive was to overthrow the Islamic republic. One of the US aims was to spread democracy around the world; yet Iran already had a more or less functioning democracy and a democratically elected government, flawed though the 2009 election might well have been.

(b) Iran and its nuclear programme

Iran already had nuclear technology before the 1979 revolution. An atomic research centre was set up in 1967 under the auspices of Tehran University. The Shah himself was keen for Iran to have nuclear power, and in 1974 the Atomic Energy Organization of Iran (AEOI) was founded. The Shah insisted that the nuclear programme was for entirely peaceful purposes, and Iran signed the Non-Proliferation Treaties (NPT) which said that countries which already had nuclear weapons (the USA, the USSR, China, France and Britain) could keep them, but no other country could join. In return they would supply peaceful economic technology and would themselves move towards disarmament. The government of the new Islamic republic stopped the nuclear programme on the grounds that it was far too expensive and required foreign expertise to operate. Ayatollah Khomeini wanted Iran to be able to 'go it alone'. Before long, however, there were serious power shortages and the government was forced to announce a U-turn. But the situation had changed: following the kidnappings at the American embassy in Tehran in November 1979, the USA imposed economic and military sanctions on Iraq and put pressure on the International Atomic Energy Association (IAEA) not to get involved with Iran. In 1988 Ali Akbar Rafsanjani, who at that point was chairman of the Iranian parliament, appealed to Iranian scientists working abroad to come home – it was their patriotic duty to work on the nuclear programme. The government continued to insist publicly that it had no plans to acquire nuclear weapons.

Nevertheless, as David Patrikarakos points out (in *Nuclear Iran: The Birth of an Atomic State*):

> Iran certainly had reason to want a bomb. It was extremely unpopular with one of the world's two superpowers and fighting a war with Iraq. The international community's silence about Iraq's invasion and its subsequent use of chemical weapons, as well as the tacit US and near universal Arab support of Iraq during the war, all seemed to confirm that Iran could trust no one. It is likely that Iran launched a covert weapons programme about this time.

He goes on to explain that during the 1990s the nuclear programme began to concentrate on uranium enrichment and plutonium production, both classic ways of making a bomb. The government also resolved that by 2005, at least 20 per cent of Iran's energy should come from nuclear power. In 1990 Iran signed nuclear co-operation agreements with Russia and China. By 2000 the AEOI was secretly well under way with its uranium-enriching programme at the nuclear plant at Arak.

However, not all Iranians were happy at the direction their nuclear programme was taking. In August 2002 an opposition group made public details of the Arak plant and of another nuclear site at Natanz. There was immediate consternation in the West, which was now convinced that Iran was on the verge of producing a nuclear weapon. Britain, France and Germany, encouraged by the USA, demanded that Iran should give up uranium enrichment, which was the quickest way of making a nuclear bomb. The request was rejected and since 2005 Iran has refused to negotiate about it. *President Ahmadinejad mounted a strong defence of Iran's policy at the UN General Assembly in 2005. He denounced what he called the West's 'nuclear apartheid';* throughout his two terms as president (2005–13) he seemed to delight in irritating the Americans by making the enrichment programme into an icon of patriotism.

In fact, although support for the nuclear programme was more or less universal in Iran, there were disagreements over whether it should concentrate on producing bombs or whether the priority should be the production of electricity. During the 2009 election campaign there was criticism of Ahmadinejad's deliberately confrontational style which, it was felt, only further antagonized the West. Although he won the election, possibly fraudulently, many observers felt that he had become isolated and diminished. According to the IAEA, at the end of 2011 Iran had enough uranium at the Natanz site to make four nuclear bombs, but it admitted that there was no definite proof that they had actually produced a bomb. The Iranians insisted that the enriched uranium was intended for medical isotopes. By February 2012 the IAEA's tone had changed. An inspection in January had shown that the Iranians had experimented on making warhead designs and they had also significantly stepped up the production of enriched uranium. They had not co-operated fully with the investigation and had refused to allow inspectors to visit certain sites. Even so, *there was still no incontrovertible evidence of weapons production,* and some experts believed that working on its own, Iran would be unable to make a bomb before 2015 at the earliest.

Tensions mounted as threats and counter-threats flew around. The USA was said to have drawn up plans to attack Iran's nuclear sites. Iran announced that oil exports would be cut off to any country that backed the USA. This caused panic in Europe and sent petrol prices soaring. Israel threatened to make a pre-emptive strike against Iran, and Iran responded by promising to attack any country that allowed bombers of whatever nationality to use their bases for attacks on Iran.

12.7 THE ARAB SPRING

The series of anti-government protests and demonstrations known as the Arab Spring began in **Tunisia** on 18 December 2010; in less than a month, president Zine El Abidine Ben Ali had fled to Saudi Arabia after 23 years in power (14 January 2011). Encouraged by the rapid success of the revolution in Tunisia, a wave of unrest and violence swept across North Africa and the Middle East in countries where the lack of democracy had enabled leaders to stay in power for many years. In **Egypt** president Hosni Mubarak resigned (14 February 2011) after 30 years in control. In **Algeria** the government survived after agreeing to allow more civil liberties and to end the state of emergency which had been in operation for 19 years (April 2011). King Abdullah II of **Jordan** responded to protests by sacking two consecutive prime ministers and promising reforms, though there was still dissatisfaction with the slow progress of change. President Omar Al-Bashir of **the Sudan** was forced to announce that he would not stand for re-election when his term ran out in 2015. In **Yemen** President Ali Abdullah Saleh hung on through almost a year of demonstrations and shootings, and an assassination attempt that left him seriously injured. Finally he was forced to stand down, though not before close on 2000 people had been killed. The agreement allowed him and his family safe passage into Saudi Arabia (November 2011). Even the apparently completely stable, ultra-conservative **Saudi Arabia** saw a few gentle protests which prompted the elderly King Abdullah to promise reforms. In **Bahrain,** a small island off the coast of Saudi Arabia, beginning in March 2011, there was a series of violent pro-democracy protests by the majority Shia who felt discriminated against by the ruling Sunni al-Khalifa dynasty. Reconciliation talks began in July and King Hamad promised reforms. But actual progress was slow, and civil war was still raging in January 2013.

Eventually the revolutionary protests spread to two of the largest states in the region – Libya and Syria. In **Libya** Colonel Muammar Gaddafi had been in power for 42 years and had expressed support for both Ben Ali and Hosni Mubarak before they were forced out. Time was running out for Gaddafi too: in October 2011 he was captured and killed in cold blood by revolutionaries, but it had taken a full-scale civil war in which around 30 000 people lost their lives. **Syria** had been ruled by the Baathist regime since 1963 and the state of emergency imposed at that time was still in place. Serious uprisings began in March 2011 when some children were arrested and allegedly tortured for writing anti-government slogans on walls in the southern city of Daraa. Protests rapidly spread to the capital, Damascus, and to other cities, including Homs. President Bashar al-Assad showed very little willingness to make concessions – security forces responded harshly and army tanks stormed several cities. By the end of 2011 the most determined opposition was concentrated in Homs, the third largest city in Syria with a population of about a million. Here the district of Baba Amr was occupied and controlled by revolutionaries. But in February 2012 Assad ordered a deadly all-out attack on Baba Amr, arousing condemnation and calls for him to step down from the West and from the UN. These were ignored, and in early March the revolutionaries were driven out of Homs. The situation is still ongoing.

(a) What caused the Arab Spring?

There were a whole host of causes and motives behind the protests. The lack of genuine democracy in most countries, except Iran and Turkey, meant that dictators and absolute monarchs had been able to stay in power for long periods, like Colonel Gaddafi, who had ruled Libya for 40 years. Inevitably there was corruption at the top levels, concentration of wealth in the hands of the ruling classes, and human rights violations. In the last couple of decades there had been some progress in most of these countries. Living standards had risen, education had become more widespread and the younger generation was computer-literate. This only added to the problem: these educated young people resented the lack of opportunities and jobs, the immense gap between the wealthy elite and the rest of the population, and the corruption, and now they had the skills, using social networking internet sites, to organise strikes and demonstrations more effectively. High food prices in 2010 caused great hardship among the already poverty-stricken unemployed workers. It was no coincidence that a number of the leaders under attack, including President Hosni Mubarak of Egypt, Colonel Muammar Gaddafi of Libya and President al-Assad of Syria, were pro-western dictators supported by the USA. Events in Tunisia leading to the rapid overthrow of President Zine el Abidine Ben Ali in January 2011 sparked off similar protests and uprisings that made up the Arab Spring. A closer look at four of these will show examples of the different forms and outcomes that occurred across the region.

(b) Tunisia

In December 2010 a young college graduate, Mohammed Bouazizi, who had been unable to find a job, was trying to sell fruit and vegetables at a roadside stand in the town of Sidi Bouzid. But he had no permit because they were expensive, and the police confiscated his goods. Driven to desperation, on 17 December he doused himself with petrol and set himself alight on the street. Although he was alive when passers-by managed to extinguish the flames, he was badly burned and died a month later. There were immediate protest demonstrations which quickly spread to other towns. In the capital, Tunis, demonstrators attacked police cars and set government buildings on fire. Their grievances were the high unemployment rate which stood at 30 per cent for those between 15 and 29, rising prices, general lack of freedom of expression and the obvious wealth and extravagant lifestyle of the president and his family. Tensions were increased when Wikileaks released a secret cable sent from the US embassy in Tunis to Washington. This talked of corruption at the highest levels and claimed that the Ben Ali family ran the country like a kind of Mafia.

President Ben Ali appeared on television vowing to punish all rioters, though he did promise that more jobs would be created. He also complained that riots would damage the tourist industry, one of Tunisia's main sources of income. Tunisia had no oil revenue, which meant that the government could not afford to buy off the protesters by raising wages, paying unemployment benefit and building new homes, as King Abdullah of Saudi Arabia did. Consequently demonstrations and riots continued and at least 200 people were killed by police and security forces. With no prospect of an end to the violence, Ben Ali decided it was time to leave: on 14 January 2011, after 23 years in power, he fled the country and took refuge in Saudi Arabia.

A caretaker government was hurriedly put together, consisting mainly of members of Ben Ali's party (the Constitutional Democratic Rally – RCD) plus five members of opposition groups, with Mohammed Ghannouchi as prime minister. With the government still dominated by the 'old gang', very little progress could be made, and protests continued. The five new members soon resigned in exasperation, and on 27 January Ghannouchi reshuffled his government. All the RCD members were dropped, except Ghannouchi himself, who remained prime minister. The party was eventually dissolved and its assets were seized. But by this time the momentum was so strong that none of these moves satisfied the protesters. At the end of February Ghannouchi at last acknowledged defeat and resigned. A former opposition leader, Beji Caid el Sebsi, became prime minister; one of his first actions was to release all political prisoners, and almost immediately the situation became calmer.

In October 2011 people were allowed to vote for representatives to a constituent assembly which would draw up a new constitution. Ennahda, a moderate Islamist party, emerged as the largest single grouping. They formed a coalition with two smaller secular parties, Ettakatol and the Congress for the Republic Party. In December the new interim government elected Moncef Marzouki as president for one year. He was a secularist and a highly respected figure mainly because of his fearless opposition to Ben Ali. In 1994 he had been imprisoned for having tried to run against Ben Ali in the presidential election. After his release he was forced to go into exile in France. As president he would share power with Prime Minister Hamali Jebali of Ennahda. Many secularists were unhappy about this, complaining that the Islamists would undermine Tunisia's liberal values. However, Ennahda denied any such intention and insisted that they would rule in the same way as the successful moderate Islamic government in Turkey. In January 2012, as Tunisia celebrated the first anniversary of Ben Ali's overthrow, there were still serious problems facing the new government. The main one was high unemployment – the national average was just under 20 per cent, but in some inland areas as high as 50 per cent.

(c) Egypt

There were many similarities between the Egyptian and Tunisian uprisings. Hosni Mubarak had been president in Egypt even longer than Ben Ali in Tunisia. Mubarak had come to power in 1981 after the assassination of the Egyptian President Anwar Sadat. Although he had been re-elected numerous times, only the 2005 election had been contested. In the parliamentary elections of November 2010 the moderate Islamic group, the Muslim Brotherhood, lost almost all its seats. They claimed that the election had been rigged, and it left Mubarak's party in almost total control. The next presidential election was due in September 2011 and it seemed clear that Mubarak would win. On 17 January 2011 a man set fire to himself outside parliament in Cairo, emulating the example of Mohammed Bouazizi in Tunisia, who was now seen as a martyr. Six more self-immolations soon followed and Mohamed El Baradei, an opposition leader and former UN nuclear weapons inspection chief, warned that this could unleash a 'Tunisia-style explosion'. Activists began to organize a national 'day of anger' to protest about unemployment, poor living standards, the tough methods of the security forces and the lack of genuine democracy.

On 25 January 2011 the protest was launched: in Tahrir Square in Cairo, and in other cities there were the largest demonstrations seen for a generation, and their demand was simple – 'Mubarak resign'. In response Mubarak ordered a crackdown. Security forces attacked the protesters, using tear gas and beatings, and hundreds were arrested. After four days of violence Mubarak appeared on television and announced that he had sacked his government, that he was committed to democracy, but that he would continue as president. This did nothing to satisfy the protesters, and on 30 January, as the crowds gathered in Tahrir Square to defy a night-time curfew, El Baradei called on the president to step down immediately. El Baradei was now in a strong position; he had gained the support of the Muslim Brotherhood and other opposition groups and he called on the army to negotiate about a regime change, raising the possibility of the army playing a role in government.

By this time the USA and the EU were seriously concerned about the situation. President Mubarak was seen as an invaluable ally in the Middle East. So long as he remained in power, he would keep out the Islamists. 'What we don't want', said Hilary Clinton, the American secretary of state, 'are radical ideologies to take control of a very large and important country in the Middle East.' Yet they had to admit that the Egyptian people had genuine grievances. Both Americans and Europeans agreed that Egypt needed political reform and an orderly transition to democratic government. There seems no doubt that this decision was communicated to Mubarak himself and the first step in the transition must be the resignation of the president himself, though not necessarily immediately. Consequently on 1 February 2011, the 82-year-old Mubarak announced that he would stand down – but not yet! He would stay until the end of his term in September, so that he could oversee the transition himself. Even that was too long for the protesters, who were still camped in their thousands in Tahrir Square and made no effort to disperse. The following day thousands of Mubarak supporters invaded the square, attacking the activists with clubs, knives, bats, spears and whips, some of them riding camels and horses. Casualties were high, but the attackers failed to dislodge the protesters, who seemed to grow in number. Since the protests had begun in January about 800 people had lost their lives. This time the regime tried to bribe the revolutionaries by announcing wage and pensions increases of 15 per cent. For the first time in 30 years a vice-president, Omar Suleiman, was appointed. On 10 February Mubarak announced that he had handed over all presidential powers to the vice-president. Again it was all to no avail; as one spokesman said: 'Our main object is for Mubarak to step down. We don't accept any other concessions.' With his main supporter, the USA, becoming more and more restive at the apparent stalemate, Mubarak finally bowed to the inevitable: Suleiman announced that Mubarak had resigned and had handed power over the armed forces of Egypt (11 February 2011). A *Guardian* newspaper report described the scene as the news was broadcast: 'A few moments later a deafening roar swept central Cairo. Protesters fell to their knees and prayed, wept and chanted. Hundreds of thousands of people packed into Tahrir Square, the centre of the demonstrations, waving flags, holding up hastily written signs declaring victory, and embracing soldiers.'

The military immediately dissolved parliament and suspended the constitution, and on 4 March appointed a civilian, Essam Sharaf, as prime minister. But there was a long way to go before complete calm could be restored and a democratic and stable system introduced. The new government began well: Mubarak's National Democratic party was dissolved and its assets taken over by the state. The hated state security agency, which was responsible for most of the human rights violations, was abolished and the 30-year state of emergency was lifted. A trouble-free referendum was held in which 77 per cent of voters supported changes to the constitution which would enable genuinely democratic elections to be held for parliament and the presidency within the next six months. But it gradually became clear that the generals had decided to keep permanent control. When further demonstrations were held protesting about the slow progress of reforms, the army clamped down again, arresting thousands and injuring several hundred people in Tahrir Square (29 June). Mubarak's emergency laws were reintroduced, causing yet more protests. The announcement that elections would be held on 28 November did nothing to soothe the opposition. They were convinced that any elections would be fixed to enable remnants of the old regime to stay in power.

In October 2011 there was an ominous new development. Between 10 and 15 per cent of Egypt's 82 million population are Coptic Christians. In the past they had often been attacked by Muslim fundamentalists, although Mubarak had been sympathetic towards them. During the anti-Mubarak demonstrations, Muslims and Christians had worked together and protected each other. Now there began a series of anti-Christian riots and attacks on churches in Cairo and Alexandria. It was reported that in some places soldiers had stood by and watched, or had even encouraged the attackers. Christians held a protest march in Cairo and were attacked by security forces; 24 Christians were killed and at least 500 injured. The Muslim Brotherhood, a moderate Islamist party, condemned the attacks on churches and criticized the military government for the lack of progress towards democracy. Consequently, the promised elections went ahead peacefully on 28 November, and as expected, the Muslim Brotherhood Freedom and Justice party won more seats than any other party in parliament. Together with the other smaller Islamist groups they formed a clear majority over the more liberal political groups that had emerged during the uprisings. The main function of this parliament, which was due to meet in March 2012, was to draw up a new constitution. However, the Supreme Council of the Armed Forces (SCAF) announced that they, and not the MPs, would have the final say over the new constitution. This naturally brought them into confrontation with the Muslim Brotherhood, and violent clashes followed in Tahrir Square. But the army had its way: under the new arrangements the president was to have much less power. In the presidential election of June 2012, the Muslim Brotherhood candidate, Mohammed Morsi, won a narrow victory. It was not long before he took steps to bring the army under control: in August 2012 he dismissed two of the most powerful military men, making it clear that he intended to ensure that Egypt moved towards an effective democracy.

(d) Libya

Leading a small group of junior officers, Colonel Muammar Gaddafi seized power in Libya in 1969 in a bloodless coup. They took their opportunity when King Idris of Libya, who was regarded as being too pro-West, was away in Turkey for medical treatment. The Libyan Arab Republic was proclaimed and Gaddafi remained at the head of the government until his overthrow in 2011. Libya was fortunate to have large oil reserves, and Gaddafi, who described himself as a socialist, began to spend much of the oil revenues on policies to modernize and develop the country. By 1990 the Libyans could claim that their country was the most advanced in Africa. Everything was centrally planned: there were job-creation schemes, welfare programmes providing free education and healthcare; there were more hospitals and more doctors. There were vast housing projects – in some areas the populations of entire villages living in mud-hut-style shanty towns were moved into new modern homes complete with electricity, running water and even satellite television. Women were given equal rights with men, the literacy rate rose from something like 12 per cent to nearer 90 per cent and the child mortality rate fell to only 15 per thousand live births, whereas the average for Africa was about 125 per thousand. Libya had the highest overall living standards in Africa, and it was achieved without any foreign loans.

In spite of all this success Gaddafi still had his critics. He was much less popular in the east of the country, which lagged behind the rest in social and economic progress. There were poverty-stricken areas without fresh water and efficient sewage systems. Gaddafi was accused of spending too much of Libya's income on his own family and his close circle of supporters, all of whom had conspicuously lavish lifestyles. He also faced hostility from abroad: during the 1970s it emerged that Gaddafi had stocks of chemical weapons, including nerve gas. He was known to be trying to buy weapons of mass destruction from China and later from Pakistan, though without success. The USA and the West were suspicious of his intentions, especially as he was known to be financing militant anti-Western Islamist and Communist organizations and made no secret of the fact that he was supplying the IRA with bombs. In 1984 the UK broke off diplomatic relations with Libya after a protest demonstration by anti-Gaddafi Libyans outside the Libyan embassy in London ended in violence. Shots were fired from inside the embassy, killing a British policewoman. Libya was now viewed as a pariah state by the USA and the West, and many countries imposed economic sanctions. More bomb outrages followed, including an attack on a nightclub in Berlin. Gaddafi denied any involvement in this incident, but US president Ronald Reagan used it as the pretext for bombing Tripoli, the Libyan capital, and Benghazi in the east, killing around a hundred civilians. A series of tit-for-tat incidents continued, culminating in the destruction of the American airliner over Lockerbie, Scotland in December 1988 (see Section 12.2(c)).

The collapse of the USSR and the fall of communism in eastern Europe changed the international situation. Gaddafi had usually been able to count on the support of the USSR in his anti-Western stance. Now he decided that it would be wise to try to improve relations with the West. He agreed to hand over two men alleged to have planted the bomb on the American airliner, and in 1999 they went on trial. He also promised to pay $2.7 billion as compensation to the victims' families, and this had mostly been paid by 2003. The UN responded by lifting the trade and financial sanctions on Libya. Then in December 2003 Libya promised to renounce weapons of mass destruction and Gaddafi invited the International Atomic Energy Authority (IAEA) to inspect and dismantle their nuclear installations. It was no coincidence that this offer came after Saddam Hussein of Iraq had been overthrown by the Americans and British. US president George W. Bush claimed that it was a direct consequence of the war in Iraq, and it seems likely that Gaddafi was afraid that, given half a chance, they would overthrow him too. In 2004 the IAEA inspectors were shown Libya's stockpiles of chemical weapons, including mustard gas, and allowed to visit nuclear installations. Relations between Libya and the West gradually improved: Gaddafi had successful meetings with several European leaders, and was even hugged by Tony Blair! In July 2009 he attended the G8 Summit in Italy where he met US president Barack Obama. Western countries had their own motives for working with Libya – mainly that they wanted Libyan oil and opportunities of lucrative investment in Libya.

It was ironic that at a time when Gaddafi was co-operating with the USA in the war on terror, and was beginning to be regarded as an ally, his popularity among Libyans was on the wane. During the 1990s he had faced increasing opposition from Islamist extremists known as the Libyan Islamic Fighting Group, which tried to assassinate him in 1996. Gaddafi then began passing anti-terrorist information to the American CIA and the British Secret Service. After some German anti-terrorist agents working in Libya were killed by al-Qaeda members, Gaddafi ordered the arrest of Osama bin Laden. During the presidency of George W. Bush (2001–9) the relationship became closer – the CIA began sending suspected terrorists to Libya, where they would be tortured to make them confess. This was known as the 'extraordinary rendition' programme; some of those 'rendered' were Libyan opponents of Gaddafi and some of them were members of extremist Islamist groups. But all was not well with the Libyan economy – falling gas prices led to rising unemployment, and around Benghazi in eastern Libya there was resentment that the people were still not sharing in the general prosperity; nor were they likely to, in the present economic crisis.

It was in February 2011 that anti-government protesters in Benghazi, encouraged by the news from Tunisia and Egypt, decided to launch their campaign. Benghazi, in the neglected east of the country, is Libya's second largest city. Unemployment was disproportionately high, especially among men aged 18 to 34. The protesters, who were mostly unarmed, demanded jobs, opportunities and political freedoms and the demonstrations were peaceful. However, after four days Gaddafi decided that brute force was the way to deal with the problem. Troops fired on the unarmed crowds, killing at least 230 people. Saif al-Islam, one of Gaddafi's sons, appeared on television and blamed the violence on extremist Islamists. He warned that there would be a civil war if order was not restored. In fact, there was very little evidence of Islamist involvement. Appeasement of the protesters might have been a more successful option. Gaddafi's brutal assault only made the crowds more angry and more determined to continue. Nor was it just the masses who were horrified at the violence: Libya's representative to the Arab League and the ambassador to China both resigned; the latter called on the army to intervene on the side of the protesters and urged all the diplomatic staff to resign. Leaders of the uprising in the east announced that they would halt all oil exports within 24 hours unless the authorities stopped their violent suppression, a move that would be disastrous for the economy. By the end of February 2011 much of eastern Libya was under rebel control and an interim government, the Transitional National Council, had been set up in Benghazi. The USA, Britain and France called for Gaddafi to step down, claiming that he had 'lost the legitimacy to lead'.

Gaddafi had no intention of standing down. By mid-March his forces had counterattacked and were on the outskirts of Benghazi. Civilian deaths numbered many thousands and Gaddafi warned that no mercy would be shown to any civilians in Benghazi who resisted. The UN Security Council voted in favour of taking all necessary action, including air strikes against Gaddafi forces in order to protect civilians. There was no mention of sending in ground troops, or of forcing Gaddafi from power. A coalition of the USA, European states and the Arab League was formed, and eventually NATO took overall control of the operation. NATO airstrikes targeted Gaddafi's troops surrounding Benghazi and forced them to withdraw, leaving their bombed tanks behind. The rebels then went on the offensive, advancing westwards towards Tripoli, only to be met by another Gaddafi counter-attack which recaptured most of the territory. Early in April the rebels received a boost when Moussa Koussa, for over 30 years one of Gaddafi's closest aides, defected to Britain. Stalemate was reached when the rebels managed to hold on to Ajdabiya. Meanwhile another combat zone had developed in the west where Gaddafi forces were besieging the port of Misrata, the third largest city in Libya. On 30 April Gaddafi offered a ceasefire and called for talks with NATO, but the rebels rejected the offer; they could not believe that the offer was genuine.

The civil war dragged on through the summer of 2011. NATO air strikes continued to keep up the pressure on the Gaddafi regime. Several countries, including the UK, officially recognized the National Transitional Council (NTC) as the legitimate government of Libya, claiming that it 'had proved its democratic credentials'. At times, however, there were ominous developments that did not bode well for the future, if and when Gaddafi departed. There were divisions among the different militias fighting for the rebel cause: on 30 July the most senior rebel commander, General Abdel Fatah Younis, was was shot dead by members of a militia linked to Islamists. In Britain there was criticism of the government's recognition of the NTC. There were fears that the NTC was full of potential for disunity and that 'the Libyan conflict would end with a government we don't like'.

Throughout August rebel forces attacked Tripoli and at the end of the month they forced their way in and captured Gaddafi's walled citadel and fortified compound. There had been fierce fighting as hundreds of Gaddafi loyalist snipers continued to resist. Gaddafi and many of his officials had withdrawn to his birthplace, the coastal town of Sirte. He refused to surrender and his diehard supporters put up a brave fight. The inevitable end came on 20 October when NTC troops finally gained control of Sirte. Gaddafi himself was captured and killed. His 42-year rule was over.

The removal of Gaddafi remains a controversial affair. In the USA, Britain and much of western Europe, it was welcomed as a triumph for NATO and the UN, and a significant milestone in their campaign to spread democracy around the world. For the liberal democrat revolutionaries of Libya it meant the overthrow of an autocratic tyrant. Gaddafi was said by Western leaders to have forfeited his right to rule because of the brutal way he had suppressed peaceful demonstrations and slaughtered his own people. After 42 years of Gaddafi's rule the people of Libya were not much further forward in political terms than they had been in 1969 when he seized power. Most Libyans now saw NATO as their saviour, and were looking forward to a democratic future.

However, some countries, including China, Russia, Brazil, India, Germany and Turkey, as well as many Western observers, held a rather different view. They believed that NATO should not have intervened and that the civil war should have been allowed to take its course. It was argued that Gaddafi still had a considerable measure of support, as witnessed by the huge demonstration of Gaddafi loyalists in Tripoli on 1 July and the fierce resistance that his forces put up. After all, he had given the Libyan people arguably the highest overall standard of living in Africa, with an annual per capita income of $12 000. There is evidence that reports of brutal behaviour by Gaddafi forces, including the bombing of peaceful demonstrators in Tripoli, were greatly exaggerated and may well have been rebel propaganda. It is now widely accepted that the Libyan government was not responsible for Lockerbie and the Berlin nightclub bombings; the reason why they agreed to pay compensation was not an admission of guilt, it was the Libyan government's attempt to 'buy peace'. Yet because of NATO's intervention, the combined uprising, civil war and then NATO bombing to 'protect civilians' killed around 30 000 people, left tens of thousands seriously wounded and caused massive damage to Libya's infrastructure.

According to some observers, contrary to what western political leaders claimed, there was a viable alternative that was never seriously attempted – a negotiated peace. Hugh Roberts (who was director of the International Crisis Group's North Africa Project from 2002 until 2007, and again during the Libyan civil war in 2011) explains how, on 10 March 2011, the International Crisis Group (ICG) put forward a plan for a settlement. This involved setting up a contact group made up of representatives from Libya's neighbouring states, who would help to arrange a ceasefire, and then bring the two sides together for negotiations leading to a peaceful settlement. An international peacekeeping force would be deployed once the ceasefire had been agreed. This was before the UN voted to approve military intervention; but only a few days later, before there was time to act on the ICG plan, the Security Council voted to take 'all necessary measures' to protect civilians. In the words of Hugh Roberts:

> By inserting 'all necessary measures' into the resolution, London, Paris and Washington licensed themselves, with NATO as their proxy, to do whatever they wanted whenever they wanted in the full knowledge that they would never be held to account, since as permanent veto-holding members of the Security Council, they are above all laws.

However, the resolution did also demand a ceasefire and an end to all attacks on civilians, as a prelude to negotiations. Gaddafi, whose forces at that point were on the outskirts of

Benghazi, immediately announced a ceasefire and proposed a dialogue. As Hugh Roberts put it: 'what the Security Council demanded and suggested, he provided in a matter of hours'. The offer was immediately rejected by one of the senior rebel commanders, Khalifa Haftar, on the grounds that Gaddafi could not be trusted, and the Western powers simply accepted this. A week later Turkey announced that it had held talks with both sides and offered to help negotiate a ceasefire. Gaddafi once again agreed, but the NTC rejected the offer and demanded the resignation of Gaddafi before they would agree to a ceasefire. Gaddafi offered to call a ceasefire three more times – in April, May and June – and each time the offer was rejected. No pressure was brought on the NTC, no doubt because the mission of the Western powers was regime change.

Even before Gaddafi was so unceremoniously killed, there were disturbing signs for the West that genuine democracy might not be the outcome of the civil war after all. When Gaddafi claimed that al-Qaeda was involved in the uprising, he was probably exaggerating. But in fact the revolution did stir up and mobilize the Islamists. For example, when the NTC chairman, Mustafa Abdul Jalil, made his first trip from Benghazi to Tripoli, he announced that all legislation of the future NTC government would be based on the Islamic Sharia law. The newly appointed military commander of Tripoli was none other than Abdul Hakim Belhadj, a former leader of the Libyan Islamic Fighting Group. This extremist group had waged a terrorist campaign against Gaddafi and the Libyan state throughout the 1990s and had provided hundreds of recruits for al-Qaeda. The worry for genuine Libyan democrats and for the West, once the war was over, was that the various factions and militias that had combined to overthrow the Gaddafi regime now battled among themselves for control. By December 2011 the Libyan national army, commanded by Gaddafi's former generals, was finding it very difficult to disarm the militias, each of which controlled its own area. The militias were intensely suspicious of the intentions of the NTC, which was dominated by people from the east of the country. The NTC was acting secretively: although a cabinet had been appointed, nobody knew who its members were and its meetings were held in secret. When it was announced that the oil and economic ministries were being moved from Tripoli to Benghazi, there were anti-NTC protests across the country. In the background there was the possibility of an Islamist resurgence, with the Libyan Islamic Fighting Group setting up a Taliban-style government. There was a long way to go before the Libyan people would be able to enjoy real democracy. However, during the first half of 2012 the situation became calmer, and the first elections for over 40 years were able to take place in July 2012. These passed off reasonably peacefully, except in the east where supporters of a federal state were demanding more seats in the national congress. Against expectations, the moderate National Forces Alliance won a comfortable victory, and its leader, Mahmoud Jibril, who had acted as interim prime minister for a time, became president. This was in marked contrast to what had happened in Tunisia and Egypt, where Islamists gained control. Mahmoud Jibril said he wanted to work with all parties in a grand coalition and rejected claims from some clerics that his party was too secular for the Islamists to work with. The next step was to prepare for parliamentary elections in 2013, and in the meantime the Jibril government concentrated on gaining control of the various militias still operating outside the law.

The difficulties involved in this task were clearly illustrated on 11 September 2012, the anniversary of the al-Qaeda attacks on the USA. A gang attacked the American consulate in Benghazi with guns and grenades, killing four Americans, including Chris Stevens, the American ambassador, who happened to be on a visit from Tripoli. It was believed that the attack was triggered by the showing on YouTube of the trailer for an American film called *The Innocence of Muslims*, which was extremely insulting to the prophet Muhammad. There were anti-American protests about the film in Egypt, Algeria, Tunisia, Gaza, Lebanon, Afghanistan, Iran and in most other Muslim states. It was thought that the

Benghazi attack was carried out by an extremist Islamic militia called Ansar al-Sharia ('supporters of Sharia law') (see Section 28.4(c)) for further details). The killings overshadowed an important political event that took place the following day: the Libyan parliament elected a new president, Mustafa Abu-Shakour of the National Front Party. He narrowly defeated Mahmoud Jibril, the US-backed candidate, who had been expected to win.

(e) Saudi Arabia

In Saudi Arabia, a kingdom dominated by Sunni Muslims and run under strict fundamentalist laws, the situation was rather different. There were mild protests, mainly in the east of the country where a majority of the population are Shia. On the whole the 86-year-old King Abdullah was popular, although his rule was autocratic in the extreme, and unemployment was high, especially among young men. He was quick to respond, promising a multi-billion-pound programme of reforms. A total of 60 000 new jobs were created in the security forces, a clever move which helped to reduce unemployment as well as making the regime safer. The monthly minimum wage was raised to £500 and there was to be unemployment benefit of £160 a month. Half a million apartments were to be built for people on low incomes and more money was to be given to hospitals. All this was possible because, thanks to the oil revenue, the Saudi royal family were extremely wealthy.

There was another festering grievance in Saudi Arabia – women were denied civic freedoms, were not allowed to vote or play any public role, could not leave the house unless accompanied by a male member of the family, and were not allowed to drive. In September 2011 the king announced that women would be able to vote and stand as candidates in municipal elections from 2015. They would also be able to serve as members of the Shura council, a body that supervised legislation. This was apparently warmly received, but there was disappointment that women still could not drive; Saudi Arabia was the only country in the world where women were banned from driving. A campaign was launched in which dozens of women deliberately broke the rule. One woman was arrested and sentenced to ten lashes, but King Abdullah overruled the sentence.

Things were thrown into confusion in October 2011 when Crown Prince Sultan, King Abdullah's younger half-brother and heir to the throne, died, leaving Prince Nayef as the likely successor to King Abdullah. He was in charge of the security forces, an ultra-conservative and the man responsible for sending Saudi troops into neighbouring Bahrain the previous March to help crush the pro-reform demonstrations. King Abdullah himself was in poor health and there were serious doubts about what would happen to his reforms if and when Prince Nayef took over.

And so in 2012 'the new world order' was still far from settled. The 'Arab Spring' states were in a transitional phase and it was by no means clear where they would end up. It remained to be seen whether or not the 'war of civilizations' would materialize fully, or whether militant Islamic fundamentalism, as some predicted, would be eclipsed as moderate Muslims grew tired of its strict rules and restraints and its treatment of women. Taliban aggression in Afghanistan, where NATO troops were being killed every day, and al-Qaeda's activities in Pakistan continued to present a formidable challenge to the West. Many observers were moving towards the conclusion that dialogue between the two sides must come eventually (see Section 28.4(c) for further comment on the world situation in 2012).

FURTHER READING

Blum, W., *Killing Hope: US Military and CIA Interventions since World War II* (Zed Books, 2003).

Blum, W., *Rogue State: A Guide to the World's only Superpower* (Zed Books, new edition, 2006).

Booth, K. and Dunne, T. (eds) *Worlds in Collision: Terror and the Future of Global Order* (Palgrave Macmillan, 2002).

Bradley, J. R., *After the Arab Spring: How Islamists Hijacked the Middle East Revolts* (Palgrave Macmillan, 2012).

Chomsky, N., *Rogue States* (Penguin, 2000).

Chomsky, N., *Hegemony or Survival: America's Quest for Global Dominance* (Holt, 2004).

Chomsky, N., *Hopes and Prospects* (Penguin, 2011).

Cruz, R. D. and Tarzi, A. (eds) *The Taliban and the Crisis of Afghanistan* (Harvard University Press, 2009).

Dabashi, H., *The Arab Spring: The End of Postcolonialism* (Zed Books, 2012).

Fergusson, J., *Taliban* (Corgi, 2011).

Guyatt, N., *Another American Century?: The United States and the World Since 9/11* (Zed Books, 2004).

Hashemi, N. and Postel, D. (eds) *The People Reloaded: The Green Movement and the Struggle for Iran's Future* (Melville House, 2011).

Hutton, W., *The World We're In* (Abacus, 2003).

Kagan, R., *The World America Made* (Knopf, 2012).

Majd, H., *The Ayatollahs' Democracy: An Iranian Challenge* (Allen Lane, 2011).

Patrikarakos, D., 'Doing it by ourselves: Iran's nuclear programme', *London Review of Books* (1 December 2011).

Patrikarakos, D., *Nuclear Iran: The Birth of an Atomic State* (I. B. Tauris, 2012).

Pettiford, L. and Harding, D., *Terrorism: The New World War* (Capella, 2003).

Roberts, H., 'Who said Gaddafi had to go?', *London Review of Books* (17 November 2011).

Stewart, R., 'Why are we in Afghanistan?', *London Review of Books* (9 July 2009).

Tariq Ali, *Bush in Babylon: the Recolonisation of Iraq* (Verso, 2004).

QUESTIONS

1 Examine the evidence for and against the view that in the early twenty-first century, the world was witnessing a 'civilization struggle' between Islam and the West.

2 Explain why the ending of the Cold War was not followed by a period of world peace and stability.

3 Explain why Afghanistan has played such an important role in international relations since 1979.

◥ There is a document question about the USA and the New World Order on the website.

Part

II

The Rise of Fascism and Governments of the Right

Italy, 1918–45: the first appearance of fascism

SUMMARY OF EVENTS

The unification of Italy was only completed in 1870, and the new state suffered from economic and political weaknesses. The First World War was a great strain on her economy, and there was bitter disappointment at her treatment by the Versailles settlement. Between 1919 and 1922 there were five different governments, all of which were incapable of taking the decisive action that the situation demanded. In 1919, *Benito Mussolini founded the Italian fascist party*, which won 35 seats in the 1921 elections. At the same time there seemed to be a real danger of a left-wing revolution; in an atmosphere of strikes and riots, the fascists staged a 'march on Rome', which culminated in King Victor Emmanuel inviting Mussolini to form a government (October 1922); he remained in power until July 1943.

Gradually Mussolini took on the powers of a dictator and attempted to control the entire way of life of the Italian people. At first it seemed as though his authoritarian regime might bring lasting benefits to Italy, and he won popularity with his successful foreign policy (see Section 5.2). Later he made the fatal mistake of entering the Second World War on the side of Germany (June 1940), even though he knew Italy could not afford involvement in another war. After the Italians suffered defeats by the British, who captured Italy's African possessions and occupied Sicily, they turned against Mussolini. He was deposed and arrested (July 1943), but was rescued by the Germans (September) and set up as a puppet ruler in northern Italy, backed by German troops. In April 1945, as British and American troops advanced northwards through Italy towards Milan, Mussolini tried to escape to Switzerland but was captured and shot dead by his Italian enemies (known as 'partisans'). His body was taken to Milan and strung up by the feet in a public square – an ignominious end for the man who had ruled Italy for 20 years.

13.1 WHY WAS MUSSOLINI ABLE TO COME TO POWER?

(a) Disillusionment and frustration

In the summer of 1919 there was a general atmosphere of disillusionment and frustration in Italy, caused by a combination of factors:

1 Disappointment at Italy's gains from the Versailles settlement
When Italy entered the war the Allies had promised her Trentino, the south Tyrol, Istria, Trieste, part of Dalmatia, Adalia, some Aegean islands and a protectorate over Albania. Although she was given the first four areas, the rest were awarded to other states, mainly Yugoslavia; Albania was to be independent. The Italians felt cheated in view of their valiant efforts during the war and the loss of close on 700 000 men. Particularly irritating

was their failure to get Fiume (given to Yugoslavia), though in fact this was not one of the areas which had been promised to them. Gabriele d'Annunzio, a famous romantic poet, marched with a few hundred supporters and occupied Fiume before the Yugoslavs had time to take it. Some army units deserted and supported d'Annunzio, providing him with arms and ammunition, and he began to have hopes of overthrowing the government. However, in June 1920, after d'Annunzio had held out in Fiume for 15 months, the new prime minister, Giovanni Giolitti, decided that the government's authority must be restored. He ordered the army to remove d'Annunzio from Fiume – a risky move, since he was viewed as a national hero. The army obeyed orders and d'Annunzio surrendered without a fight, but it left the government highly unpopular.

2   The economic effects of the war

The effects of the war on the economy and the standard of living were disastrous. The government had borrowed heavily, especially from the USA, and these debts now had to be repaid. As the lira declined in value (from 5 to the dollar in 1914 to 28 to the dollar in 1921) the cost of living increased accordingly by at least five times. There was massive unemployment as heavy industry cut back its wartime production levels, and 2.5 million ex-servicemen had difficulty finding jobs.

3   Growing contempt for the parliamentary system

Votes for all men and proportional representation were introduced for the 1919 elections. Although this gave a fairer representation than under the previous system, it meant that there was a large number of parties in parliament. After the election of May 1921, for example, there were at least nine parties represented, including liberals, nationalists, socialists, communists, the Catholic popular party and fascists. This made it difficult for any one party to gain an overall majority, and coalition governments were inevitable. No consistent policy was possible as five different cabinets with shaky majorities came and went. There was growing impatience with a system that seemed designed to prevent decisive government.

(b)   There was a wave of strikes in 1919 and 1920

The industrialization of Italy in the years after unification led to the development of a strong socialist party and trade unions. Their way of protesting at the mess the country was in was to organize a wave of strikes in 1919 and 1920. These were accompanied by rioting, looting of shops and occupation of factories by workers. In Turin, factory councils reminiscent of the Russian soviets (see Section 16.2(c) point 2) were appearing. In the south, socialist leagues of farmworkers seized land from wealthy landowners and set up co-operatives. The government's prestige sank even lower because of its failure to protect property; many property-owners were convinced that a left-wing revolution was at hand, especially when the Italian Communist Party was formed in January 1921. But in fact the chances of revolution were receding by then: the strikes and factory occupations were fizzling out, because although workers tried to maintain production, claiming control of the factories, it proved impossible (suppliers refused them raw materials and they needed engineers and managers). In fact the formation of the Communist Party made a revolution less likely because it split the forces of the left; nevertheless the fear of a revolution remained strong.

(c)   Mussolini attracted widespread support

Mussolini and the fascist party were attractive to many sections of society because as he himself said, he aimed to rescue Italy from feeble government and give the country a

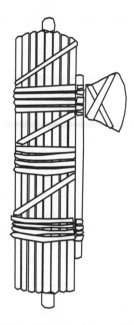

Figure 13.1   **The fascist symbol**

political system that would provide stable and strong government. Mussolini (born 1883), the son of a blacksmith in the Romagna, had a varied early career, working for a time as a stonemason's mate and then as a primary-school teacher. Politically he began as a social-ist and made a name for himself as a journalist, becoming editor of the socialist newspa-per *Avanti*. He fell out with the socialists because they were against Italian intervention in the war, and started his own paper, *Il Popolo d'Italia*. In 1919 he founded the fascist party with a socialist and republican programme, and he showed sympathy with the factory occupations of 1919–20. The local party branches were known as *fasci di combattimento* (fighting groups) – the word *fasces* meant the bundle of rods with protruding axe which used to symbolize the authority and power of the ancient Roman consuls (see Fig. 13.1). At this stage the fascists were anti-monarchy, anti-Church and anti-big business.

The new party won no seats in the 1919 elections; this, plus the failure of the factory occupations, caused Mussolini to change course. He came out as the defender of private enterprise and property, thus attracting much needed financial support from wealthy busi-ness interests. Beginning in late 1920, black-shirted squads of fascists regularly attacked and burned down local socialist headquarters and newspaper offices and beat up socialist councillors. By the end of 1921, even though his political programme was vague in the extreme, he had gained the support of property-owners in general, because they saw him as a guarantee of law and order and as a protector of their property (especially after the formation of the Communist Party in January 1921). Having won over big business, Mussolini began to make conciliatory speeches about the Roman Catholic Church; Pope Pius XI swung the Church into line behind Mussolini, seeing him as a good anti-commu-nist weapon. When Mussolini announced that he had dropped the republican part of his programme (September 1922), even the king began to look more favourably on the fascists. In the space of three years Mussolini had swung from the extreme left to the extreme right. Some of the working class supported the fascists, though probably a major-ity, especially among industrial workers, supported parties of the left.

(d) Lack of effective opposition

The anti-fascist groups failed to co-operate with each other and made no determined efforts to keep the fascists out. The communists refused to co-operate with the socialists, and Giovanni Giolitti (prime minister from June 1920 to July 1921) held the elections of May 1921 in the hope that the fascists, still unrepresented in parliament, would win some seats and then support his government. He was willing to overlook their violence, feeling that they would become more responsible once they were in parliament. However, they won only 35 seats whereas the socialists took 123. Clearly there should have been no question of a fascist takeover, though the number of fascist squads throughout the country was increasing rapidly. The socialists must take much of the blame for refusing to work with the government to curb fascist violence; a coalition of Giolitti's nationalist bloc and the socialists could have made a reasonably stable government, thus excluding the fascists. But the socialists would not co-operate, and this caused Giolitti to resign in exasperation and despair. The socialists tried to use the situation to their own advantage by calling a general strike in the summer of 1922.

(e) The attempted general strike, summer 1922

This played into the hands of the fascists, who were able to use it to their advantage: they announced that if the government failed to quell the strike, they would crush it themselves. When the strike failed through lack of support, Mussolini was able to pose as *the saviour of the nation from communism*, and by October 1922 the fascists felt confident enough to stage their 'march on Rome'. As about 50 000 blackshirts converged on the capital, while others occupied important towns in the north, the prime minister, Luigi Facta, was prepared to resist. But King Victor Emmanuel III refused to declare a state of emergency and instead, invited Mussolini, who had remained nervously in Milan, to come to Rome and form a new government, which he obligingly did, arriving by train. Afterwards the fascists fostered the myth that they had seized power in a heroic struggle, but it had been achieved legally by the mere threat of force, while the army and the police stood aside.

The role of the king was important: he made the crucial decision not to use the army to stop the blackshirts, though many historians believe that the regular army would have had little difficulty in dispersing the disorderly and poorly armed squads, many of which arrived by train. The march was an enormous bluff which came off. The reasons why the king decided against armed resistance remain something of a mystery, since he was apparently reluctant to discuss them. Suggestions include:

- lack of confidence in Facta;
- doubts about whether the army, with its fascist sympathies, could be relied on to obey orders;
- fears of a long civil war if the army failed to crush the fascists quickly.

There is no doubt that the king had a certain amount of sympathy with the fascist aim of providing strong government, and he was also afraid that some of the generals might force him to abdicate in favour of his cousin, the duke of Aosta, who openly supported the fascists. Whatever the king's motives, the outcome was clear: Mussolini became the first ever fascist premier in history.

It is important to try to define what the term 'fascist' stood for, because it was later applied to other regimes and rulers, such as Hitler, Franco (Spain), Salazar (Portugal) and Perón (Argentina), which were sometimes quite different from the Italian version of fascism. Nowadays there is a tendency among the left to label as 'fascist' anybody who holds right-wing views. The fact that fascism never produced a great theoretical writer who could explain its philosophies clearly in the way that Marx did for communism makes it difficult to pin down exactly what was involved. Mussolini's constantly changing aims before 1923 suggest that his main concern was simply to acquire power; after that he seems to have improvised his ideas as he went along. It eventually emerged that the type of fascism that Mussolini had in mind included certain basic features:

- *A stable and authoritarian government.* The Italian fascist movement was a reaction to the crisis situation outlined above that made stable democratic government impossible, just at the time when strong and decisive leadership was needed. An authoritarian government would arouse and mobilize the great mass of ordinary people, and would control as many aspects of people's lives as possible, with strong discipline. One aspect of this was *the 'corporate state'*. This was a way of promoting efficiency by setting up a separate organization of workers and employers for each branch of the economy. Each 'corporation' had a government official attached to it. In practice it was a good way of controlling the workforce.
- *Extreme nationalism.* An emphasis on the rebirth of the nation after a period of decline; building up the greatness and prestige of the state, with the implication that one's own nation is superior to all others.
- *A one-party state was essential.* There was no place for democratic debate, because that made decisive government impossible and held up progress. Only fascism could provide the necessary dynamic action to guarantee Italy a great future. It also involved the cult of the great charismatic leader who would guide and inspire the nation to great things. Mussolini did not see himself as a prime minister or president – instead he took the title *il Duce* ('the leader'), in the same way that Hitler called himself *Führer*. Fascism was especially hostile to communism, which explains much of its popularity with big business and the wealthy.
- *Economic self-sufficiency (autarky).* This was vitally important in developing the greatness of the state; the government must therefore direct the economic life of the nation (though not in the Marxist sense of the state owning factories and land.
- *Great use was made of all the latest modern forms of propaganda* – uniforms, marches, songs and displays, all to demonstrate that fascists were a completely new and dynamic alternative to the boring, old-fashioned traditional parties, and to mobilize mass support behind the heroic leader.
- *Military strength and violence* were an integral part of the fascist way of life. In domestic affairs they were prepared to use extreme violence against opponents. Mussolini himself also gave the impression that they would pursue an aggressive foreign policy; he once remarked: 'Peace is absurd: fascism does not believe in it.' Hence the Italian fascists fostered the myth that they had seized power by force, when in fact Mussolini had been invited to form a government by the king.

13.3   MUSSOLINI TRIES TO INTRODUCE THE FASCIST STATE

There was no sudden change in the system of government and state institutions; at first Mussolini was merely the prime minister of a coalition cabinet in which only four out of twelve ministers were fascists, and he had to move cautiously. However, the king had given him special powers to last until the end of 1923, to deal with the crisis. His black-shirt private army was legalized, becoming the National State Voluntary Militia (MVSN). The Accerbo Law (November 1923) changed the rules of general elections. From now on the party which got most votes in a general election would automatically be given two-thirds of the seats in parliament. As a result of the next election (April 1924) the fascists and their supporters came out with 404 seats while the opposition parties could manage only 107. The right-wing success can be explained partly by the general desire for a strong government which would put the country back on its feet again, after the weak minority governments of the preceding years. But there is no doubt that there was a good deal of violence and fraud during the election which prevented many people from voting freely.

Beginning in the summer of 1924, using a mixture of violence and intimidation, and helped by divisions among his opponents, Mussolini gradually developed Italian govern-ment and society along fascist lines. At the same time he consolidated his own hold over the country, which was largely complete, at least politically, by 1930. However, he still seems to have had no 'revolutionary' ideas about how to change Italy for the better; in fact it is difficult to avoid the conclusion that his main interest was simply to increase his own personal power by whatever methods were appropriate at the time.

(a) Only the fascist party was allowed

Persistent opponents of the regime were either exiled or murdered, the most notorious case being the murder of Giacomo Matteotti, the socialist leader in the Italian parliament, who was stabbed to death. Soon after the 1924 election Matteotti made a speech in parliament complaining about the fraud and violence, and demanding that the election be declared invalid. Mussolini was furious, and there can be little doubt that he was responsible for having Matteotti killed. Later, another opposition leader, the liberal-conservative Giovanni Amendola, was beaten to death by fascist thugs. The fascists' popularity levels slumped dramatically in the aftermath of these outrages; the party seemed likely to split, as many moderates felt that their tactics had gone too far. Even Mussolini thought his regime was likely to be overthrown. However, nobody seemed to have the nerve to take the lead and try to unite the opposition against the fascists. Mussolini survived, partly because he was still seen as a guarantee against a communist and socialist takeover. After 1926, when Mussolini felt more secure, violence was much reduced and the Italian system was never as brutal as the Nazi regime in Germany.

Further changes in the constitution meant that:

- the prime minister (Mussolini) was responsible only to the king, not to parliament (1925);
- the prime minister could rule by decree, which meant that new laws did not need to be discussed by parliament (1926);
- the electorate was reduced from about 10 million to 3 million (the wealthiest).

Although parliament still met, all important decisions were taken by the Fascist Grand Council, which always did as Mussolini told it. In effect Mussolini, who now adopted the title *il Duce*, was a dictator.

(b) Changes in local government

Elected town councils and mayors were abolished and towns were run by officials appointed from Rome. In practice the local fascist party bosses (known as *ras*) often had as much power as the government officials.

(c) Education supervised

Education in schools and universities was closely supervised. Teachers had to wear uniforms and take an oath of loyalty to the regime; new textbooks were written to glorify the fascist system. Children were encouraged to criticize any teachers who lacked enthusiasm for the party. Children and young people were encouraged to join government youth organizations such as the *Gioventu Italiana del Littorio (GIL)*; this had branches for both boys and girls aged 6 to 21 and organized sports and military parades. Then there was a special organization for young boys aged 6 to 8 known as 'Sons of the Wolf' which also tried to indoctrinate them with the brilliance of the *Duce* and the glories of war. From 1937 membership of one of these organizations was compulsory. The other main message emphasized was total obedience to authority; this was deemed necessary because everything was seen in terms of struggle – 'Believe, Obey, Fight!'

(d) Employment policies

The 'Corporate State' was one of the key elements of the Fascist system. The government claimed that it was designed to promote co-operation between employers and workers and to end class warfare. Fascist-controlled unions had the sole right to negotiate for the workers, and both unions and employers' associations were organized into corporations, and were expected to work together to settle disputes over pay and working conditions. Strikes and lockouts were not allowed. By 1934 there were 22 corporations each dealing with a separate industry; each one included a government official among its members, and there was a minister of corporations in charge of the whole system. Mussolini himself acted as the first minister of corporations from 1926 until 1929. In this way Mussolini hoped to control workers and direct production and the economy. To compensate for their loss of freedom, workers were assured of such benefits as free Sundays, annual holidays with pay, social security, sports and theatre facilities and cheap tours and holidays.

(e) An understanding was reached with the pope

The Papacy had been hostile to the Italian government since 1870 when all the territory belonging to the Papacy (Papal States) had been incorporated in the new kingdom of Italy. Though he had been sympathetic towards Mussolini in 1922, Pope Pius XI disapproved of the increasing totalitarianism of fascist government (the fascist youth organizations, for example, clashed with the Catholic scouts). Mussolini, who was probably an atheist himself, was nevertheless well aware of the power of the Roman Catholic Church, and he put himself out to win over Pius, who, as the Duce well knew, was obsessed with the fear of communism. The result was *the Lateran Treaty of 1929*, by which Italy recognized the Vatican City as a sovereign state, paid the pope a large sum of money as compensation for all his losses, accepted the Catholic faith as the official state religion, made religious instruction compulsory in all schools and left the Church free to continue its spiritual mission without interference from the government. In return the Papacy recognized the kingdom of Italy, and promised not to interfere in politics. *Some historians see the ending of the long breach between Church and State as Mussolini's most lasting and worthwhile achievement.*

(f)   Propaganda and censorship

Great importance was attached to propaganda in the attempt to brainwash the Italian people into accepting fascist values and culture. The government tried, with some success, to keep a close control over the press, radio, theatre and the cinema. Strict press censorship was enforced: anti-fascist newspapers and magazines were banned or their editors were replaced by fascist supporters. A Ministry of Popular Culture was set up in 1937 to mastermind the campaign to spread the fascist message, suggesting perhaps that for the last 15 years the campaign had been less successful than had been hoped. The main points for emphasis were the cult of Mussolini, the hero and the man of action, always in uniform; and the celebration of military greatness. People were bombarded with slogans such as 'Mussolini is always right.' The military glories of ancient Rome were constantly extolled, with the implication that fascism would bring more military glory.

(g)   Racial policy

For much of his time in power Mussolini showed little interest in any so-called problems to do with race. He had certainly not shown any signs of anti-Jewishness. At one time he had even encouraged Zionism because he thought it might be useful for embarrassing the British. Many leading members of the fascist party were Jews, and he had several times insisted that there was no such thing as a Jewish problem in Italy. He was very critical of the Nazis' anti-Semitism. On the other hand he had also claimed that certain races were superior to others. He suggested that the Italians belonged to an Aryan race that was superior to such nationalities as Spaniards and Greeks, as well as to the Africans in the Italian territories of Abyssinia and Libya. He seemed to be more worried about what he called the 'Levantines', by which he meant the slaves brought in during the time of the Roman Empire. He was afraid that as their descendants intermarried with the pure Aryans over many generations, a wrong impression of the Italian national character would be given to the rest of the world. As late as September 1937 he said that the Jews in Italy were no problem; after all, there were at most only about 70 000 of them. In the summer of 1939, however, Mussolini announced the introduction of anti-Jewish laws on the same lines as the Nazi laws. In view of his earlier pronouncements most people were shocked by this sudden change. The reasons for the change were simple. Following the hostile reception from France and Britain of the Italian invasion of Abyssinia in 1935 and their imposition of economic sanctions on Italy, Mussolini found himself being pushed towards an alliance with Hitler. In 1936 he reached an understanding with Hitler, known as the Rome–Berlin Axis, and in 1937 he joined the Anti-Comintern Pact with Germany and Japan (see Section 5.2(b)), which was directed against Communism. After a four-day visit to Germany in 1937 Mussolini realized the political expediency of aligning Italy with Germany as closely as possible. As he moved towards the full alliance with Germany – the Pact of Steel – signed in May 1939, Mussolini moved quickly to emulate Hitler, in what was simply a cynical, tactical move. There was another motive for the policy change, or so Mussolini claimed: the possession of territory in Africa (Abyssinia and Libya) meant that it was important for Italians to emphasize their domination over Africans and Arabs, and make sure that they showed the respect due to people of a superior race. In July 1938 the Charter of Race was published which claimed that Arabs, Africans *and Jews* were all inferior races. He began by urging people not to employ Jews and to sack those already in jobs. Then the press were told to report that Jews had managed to get themselves into important and influential positions and must be ousted before they sent Italy into decline. This policy was not popular with the general public, but when the pope protested strongly, the press was ordered to print articles justifying the persecution of Jews and to ignore the pope. As the Second World War got under way Mussolini appointed Giovanni Prezioso, a well-known journalist and virulent anti-Semite, to supervise the racial policy. They agreed that all Jews must be expelled from Europe. Although they knew that the Nazis were systematically murdering Jews, including women and children, they still ordered thousands of Italian Jews to be deported to Germany. Again this policy was extremely unpopular and some officials either sabotaged orders or simply refused to carry them out.

How totalitarian was Mussolini's system?

It seems clear that in spite of his efforts *Mussolini did not succeed in creating a completely totalitarian system* in the Fascist sense of there being 'no individuals or groups not controlled by the state'; nor was it as all-pervasive as the Nazi state in Germany. He never completely eliminated the influence of the king or the pope. In spite of the cult of Mussolini as il Duce, the king remained head of state, and was able to dismiss Mussolini in 1943. The Roman Catholic Church remained an extremely powerful institution and it provided the Italian people with an alternative focus of loyalty; there was no way that Mussolini could sideline it, and there were several clashes between the two even after the signing of the Lateran Treaty. The pope became highly critical of Mussolini when he began to persecute Jews in the later 1930s. The historian and philosopher Benedetto Croce and other university professors were constant critics of fascism and yet they survived, apparently because Mussolini was afraid of hostile foreign reaction if he had them arrested. They would certainly not have been tolerated in Nazi Germany. A more accurate description of Mussolini's system would be authoritarian rather than totalitarian. Even fascist sympathizers admitted that the corporative system was not a success either in controlling production or in eliminating class warfare. According to historian Elizabeth Wiskemann, 'on the whole the big industrialists only made gestures of submission and in fact bought their freedom from the fascist state by generous subscriptions to Fascist party funds'. Most of the important decisions on the economy were taken by the government in consultation with business leaders, and the workers themselves had very little say. It was the workers who had to make all the concessions – agree not to strike and give up their own trade unions – while the big employers enjoyed considerable freedom of action. In fact the corporate state was little more than a propaganda exercise and a way of controlling the workers. As far as the mass of the population was concerned, it seems that they were prepared to tolerate fascism while it appeared to bring benefits, but soon grew tired of it when its inadequacies were revealed by its failures during the Second World War.

13.4 WHAT BENEFITS DID FASCISM BRING FOR THE ITALIAN PEOPLE?

What really mattered to ordinary people was whether the regime's policies were effective or not. Did Mussolini rescue Italy from weak government as he had promised, or was he, as some of his critics alleged at the time, just a windbag whose government was as corrupt and inefficient as previous ones?

(a) A promising beginning

Much of fascist policy was concerned with the economy, though Mussolini knew very little about economics. The big drive was for self-sufficiency (*autarky*), which was thought to be essential for a 'warrior-nation'. A great nation must not be dependent on any other nations for vital commodities like raw materials and food supplies. He liked to see things in terms of struggle – hence the various 'Battles', for the lira, for wheat and for births. The early years seemed to be successful, or so the government propaganda told people.

1   *Industry was encouraged* with government subsidies where necessary, so that iron and steel production doubled by 1930 and artificial silk production increased tenfold. By 1937, production of hydro-electric power had doubled.

2   *The 'Battle for the Lira'.* Mussolini believed that Italy must have a strong currency if it wanted to be a strong state. He revalued the lira at 90 to the pound sterling instead of 150 (1926). This had mixed results: it helped some industries, notably steel and chemicals, by making imported raw materials cheaper. But unfortunately it made Italian exports more expensive on the world market and led to reduced orders, especially in the cotton industry. Many factories were on a three-day week and workers suffered wage reductions of between 10 and 20 per cent – *before* the world economic crisis that started in 1929.

3   *The 'Battle for Wheat'* encouraged farmers to concentrate on wheat production and raised tariffs (import duties) on imported wheat as part of the drive for self-sufficiency. Again this had mixed results: by 1935, wheat imports had been cut by 75 per cent, and Italy was close to achieving self-sufficiency in wheat production. This policy was popular with the wealthy cereal-growing farmers of the north; but time showed that there were some unexpected side effects (see below).

4   *The 'Battle for Births'*, launched in 1927, was a campaign to increase the birth rate. Mussolini believed that a population of 40 million was too small for a country aiming to be a great power; they simply wouldn't have enough soldiers! The target was to double the birth rate and raise the population to 60 million by 1950; this was to be achieved by taxing unmarried men heavily, giving tax relief and promotion at work for men with large families and paying generous family allowances. There were severe penalties for abortions. He specified 12 children as the ideal number for a family. This was one of Mussolini's complete failures. Apparently young married couples did not find this package attractive enough, and the birth rate actually fell.

5   *A programme of land reclamation was launched* in 1928, involving draining marshes, irrigation, and planting forests in mountainous areas, again as part of the drive to improve and increase agricultural yield. The great showpiece were the reclaimed Pontine Marshes near Rome.

6   *An impressive public works programme* was designed, among other things to reduce unemployment. It included the building of motorways, bridges, blocks of flats, railway stations, sports stadiums, schools and new towns on reclaimed land; a start was made on electrifying main railway lines, and the great fascist boast was that Mussolini had made the trains run on time. Even sportsmen did well under fascism – the Italian soccer team won the World Cup twice – in 1934 and 1938!

7   *The 'after-work'* (Dopolavoro) *organization* provided the Italian people with things to do in their leisure time. There were cheap holidays, tours and cruises, and *Dopolavoro* controlled theatres, dramatic societies, libraries, orchestras, brass bands and sporting organizations. Mobile cinemas were provided which were useful for putting out propaganda. Very poor families could get welfare support from *Dopolavoro*. All this was partly to appease the workers for the loss of their trade unions and the right to strike, and it was genuinely popular. However, most

historians seem to agree that, as a propaganda exercise, it failed to arouse genuine enthusiasm for the fascist system.

8   To promote the image of Italy as a great power, Mussolini pursued a virile foreign policy (see Section 5.2), although in the later 1920s and early 1930s he was much more cautious.

However, the promise of the early years of Mussolini's rule was in many ways never fulfilled.

(b)   Unsolved problems

Even before Italy became involved in the Second World War, it was clear that fascism had not solved many of her problems.

1   *Little had been done to remedy Italy's basic shortage of raw materials* – coal and oil – and much more effort could have been made to develop hydro-electric power. In spite of the modest increase in iron and steel production, Italy could not even match a small state like Belgium (see Table 13.1). By 1940 it was clear that Italy had failed to become self-sufficient in coal, oil and steel, which was essential if Mussolini was serious about waging war. This failure meant that Italy became increasingly dependent economically on Nazi Germany.

2   *Although the 'Battle of Wheat' was a victory, it was achieved only at the expense of dairy and arable farming*, whose output fell; the climate in the south is suited much better to grazing and orchards than to growing wheat, and these would have been much more lucrative for the farmers. As a result, agriculture remained inefficient and farm labourers the poorest class in the country. Their wages fell by between 20 and 40 per cent during the 1930s. Italy still had what is known as a 'dualist economy' – the north was industrial and comparatively prosperous, while the south was largely agricultural, backward and poverty-stricken. In 1940 the wealthiest one per cent of the population still owned 40 per cent of all the land. The attempt at self-sufficiency had been a dismal failure. More than that, it had caused an unpopular shortage of consumer goods and had greatly increased Italy's national debt.

3   *The Great Depression, which began in 1929 with the Wall Street Crash in the USA (see Section 22.6), made matters worse.* Exports fell further and unemployment rose to 1.1 million, yet the Duce refused to devalue the lira until 1936. Instead, wages and salaries were cut, and although the cost of living was falling because of the Depression, wages fell more than prices, so that workers suffered a fall of over 10

Table 13.1   **Italian iron and steel output (in million tons)**

	Iron			Steel		
	1918	1930	1940	1918	1930	1940
Italy	0.3	0.5	1.0	0.3	0.5	1.0
Belgium	–	3.4	1.8	–	3.4	1.9
Germany	11.9	9.7	13.9	15.0	11.5	19.0
USA	39.7	32.3	43.0	45.2	41.4	60.8

per cent in real wages. Particularly frustrating for industrial workers was that they had no way of protesting, since strikes were illegal and the unions weak. The economy was also hampered by the sanctions placed on Italy by the League of Nations after the invasion of Ethiopia in 1935. Some banks were in difficulties because struggling manufactures were unable to repay their loans.

4 *Another failing of the government was in social services*, where there was nothing approaching a 'welfare state'. There was no official government health insurance until 1943, and only an inadequate unemployment insurance scheme, which was not improved even during the Depression.

5 *The regime was inefficient and corrupt*, so that many of its policies were not carried out. For example, in spite of all the publicity about the land reclamation, only about one-tenth of the programme had been carried out by 1939 and work was at a standstill even before the war began. Immense sums of money disappeared into the pockets of corrupt officials. Part of the problem was that Mussolini tried increasingly to do everything himself; he refused to delegate because he wanted total control. But it was impossible for one man to do so much, and it placed an intolerable burden on him. According to his biographer Dennis Mack Smith, 'by trying to control everything, he ended by controlling very little … although he gave out a constant stream of orders, he had no way of checking that they were carried out. As officials knew this, they often only pretended to obey, and took no action at all.'

13.5 OPPOSITION AND DOWNFALL

The conclusion has to be that after the first flush of enthusiasm for Mussolini and his new system, the average Italian can have felt little lasting benefit from the regime, and disenchantment had probably set in long before the Second World War started. And yet there was not a great deal of overt opposition to him. This was partly because it was difficult to conduct an organized opposition in parliament, and there were heavy punishments for opponents and critics; fear of the political police tended to drive serious opposition underground, though they were much less repressive and brutal than Hitler's Gestapo. Also the Italians had a tradition of accepting whatever happened politically with a minimum of fuss and lots of resignation. In spite of all the problems, Mussolini could usually rely on the support of the traditional elites – the king and aristocracy, and wealthy landlords and industrialists, because he was their best insurance against the communists. The government continued to control the media, which kept on telling people that Mussolini was a hero.

(a) Why was Mussolini eventually overthrown?

- *Entry into the Second World War on Germany's side was a disastrous mistake.* The majority of Italians were against it; they already disapproved when Mussolini began to sack Jews from important jobs (1938), and they felt that Italy was becoming a German satellite. The Italian takeover of Abyssinia (Ethiopia) was popular with the public, though they had made heavy weather of that (see Section 5.2(b)). But the Second World War was a different matter altogether. Mussolini had failed to modernize the economy sufficiently to support a prolonged war; in fact, Italy was incapable of waging a major war; the army was equipped with obsolete rifles and artillery; there were only a thousand planes and no heavy tanks. The declaration of war on the USA (December 1941) horrified many of Mussolini's right-wing supporters (such as industrialists and bankers), who resented the closer economic controls which wartime brought. As for the general public, Mussolini had failed to convert them to his aims of European war and conquest. All the propaganda about reviving the glories of ancient Rome had failed to arouse any fighting spirit or military enthusiasm.

- *The general public suffered hardships.* Taxes were increased to pay for the war, there was food rationing, massive inflation and a 30 per cent fall in real wages. After November 1942 there were British bombing raids on major cities. By March 1943, unrest showed itself in strikes in Milan and Turin, the first since 1922.
- After a few early successes, *the Italians suffered a string of defeats* culminating in the surrender of all Italian troops in North Africa (May 1943) (see Section 6.4, 5 and 6).
- *Mussolini seemed to have lost his touch.* He was suffering from a stomach ulcer and nervous strain. All he could think of was to sack some of the ministers who had criticized him. Breaking point came with the Allied capture of Sicily (July 1943). Many of the fascist leaders themselves realized the lunacy of trying to continue the war, but Mussolini refused to make peace because that would have meant deserting Hitler. The Fascist Grand Council turned against Mussolini, and the king dismissed him. Nobody lifted a finger to save him, and fascism disappeared.

(b)   Verdict on Italian fascism

This is still a very controversial topic in Italy, where memories of personal experiences are strong. Broadly speaking *there are two interpretations of the fascist era.*

1   It was a temporary aberration (a departure from normal development) in Italian history, the work solely of Mussolini; historian A. Cassels calls it 'a gigantic confidence trick perpetrated on the Italian nation by Benito Mussolini – an artificial creation of Mussolini'.
2   Fascism grew naturally from Italian history; the environment and the circumstances shaped the rise and success of fascism, not the reverse.

Most historians now accept the second theory, that the roots of fascism lay in traditional Italian society and that the movement grew to fruition in the circumstances after the First World War. The Italian historian Renzo de Felice argued that fascism was primarily a movement of 'an emerging middle class', which was keen to challenge the traditional, liberal, ruling class for power. He claimed that the movement achieved a great deal – especially the modernizing of Italy's economy, which was very backward in 1918. On the other hand, British historian Martin Blinkhorn does not accept this claim about the economy and argues that de Felice has not paid enough attention to 'the negative and brutal side of Fascism'.

The most recent revisionist trend among Italian historians is to portray Mussolini once more as an inspirational leader who could do nothing wrong until he made the fatal mistake of entering the Second World War. There is a tendency to gloss over all the outrages of Italian fascism, with an element of nostalgia. A new biography by British writer Nicholas Farrell, published in 2003, takes the same line, arguing that Mussolini deserves to be remembered as a great man. He claims that not only did Mussolini save Italy from anarchy and communist subversion, but his domestic policies brought great benefits to the Italian people and improved their living standards. Other genuine successes were the ending of the historic quarrel between the Roman Catholic Church and the state and the popular *Dopolavoro,* which continued after the war under another name. Farrell also suggests that if Britain and France had handled Mussolini with more care in the years

1935 to 1940, he might well have been persuaded to join the allied side during the Second World War. After all, in 1934 when Hitler made his first attempt to take over Austria, Mussolini was the only European leader to stand up to Hitler. There is no knowing how much bloodshed might have been avoided if this had happened. Farrell even suggests that if Anthony Eden, the British foreign secretary, had not shown such anti-Italian prejudice, the Second World War might have been avoided.

This interpretation provoked mixed reviews. Some welcomed it as a long overdue revision of the dictator's career, though the majority were critical, finding Farrell's arguments unconvincing. Most were more likely to go along with the verdict of the great Italian historian Benedetto Croce, who dismissed fascism as 'a short-term moral infection'.

FURTHER READING

Blinkhorn, M., *Mussolini and Fascist Italy* (Routledge, 3rd edition, 2006).
Bosworth, R. J. B., *Mussolini* (Bloomsbury, 2011).
De Felice, R., *Interpretations of Fascism* (Harvard University Press, 1977).
Farrell, N., *Mussolini: A New Life* (Phoenix, 2005).
Mack Smith, D., *Mussolini* (Phoenix, 2002).

QUESTIONS

1 'It was the fear of communism that was mainly responsible for Mussolini coming to power in Italy in 1922, and for staying there so long.' Explain whether you agree or disagree with this view.

2 In what ways and with what success did Mussolini try to introduce a totalitarian form of government in Italy?

3 How successful were Mussolini's domestic policies up to 1940?

4 Explain why Mussolini launched the 'Battle for Wheat' in 1925.

5 Explain why you agree or disagree with the view that between 1925 and 1939 Mussolini's economic policies were very successful.

6 How important was the appeal of fascist ideology to so many Italians in explaining why Mussolini was made prime minister in October 1922?

7 Explain why racism became a more important part of Italian fascism in the 1930s.

8 How successful was Mussolini's regime in crushing cultural diversity in Italy in the years 1923 to 1940?

9 Explain why Mussolini launched the 'Battle for Births' in 1927.

10 'Fascist social policies gained widespread support for Mussolini in the 1920s and 1930s'. Explain why you agree or disagree with this view.

There is a document question about the differing interpretations of fascism on the website.

14 Germany, 1918–45: the Weimar Republic and Hitler

SUMMARY OF EVENTS

As Germany moved towards defeat in 1918, public opinion turned against the government, and in October, the Kaiser, in a desperate bid to hang on to power, appointed Prince Max of Baden as Chancellor. He was known to be in favour of a more democratic form of government in which parliament had more power. But it was too late: in November revolution broke out, the Kaiser escaped to Holland and abdicated, and Prince Max resigned. Friedrich Ebert, leader of the left-wing Social Democrat Party (SPD), became head of the government. In January 1919 a general election was held, the first completely democratic one ever to take place in Germany. The Social Democrats emerged as the largest single party and Ebert became the first president of the republic. They had some Marxist ideas but believed that the way to achieve socialism was through parliamentary democracy.

The new government was by no means popular with all Germans: even before the elections the communists had attempted to seize power in *the Spartacist Rising (January 1919)*. In 1920, right-wing enemies of the republic occupied Berlin (the Kapp *Putsch*). The government managed to survive these threats and several later ones, including *Hitler's Munich Beer-Hall Putsch (1923)*.

By the end of 1919 a new constitution had been agreed by the National Assembly (parliament), which was meeting in Weimar because Berlin was still torn by political unrest. This Weimar constitution (sometimes called the most perfect democratic constitution of modern times, at least on paper) gave its name to *the Weimar Republic*, and lasted until 1933, when it was destroyed by Hitler. It passed through three phases:

1 *1919 to the end of 1923* A period of instability and crisis during which the republic was struggling to survive.
2 *From the end of 1923 to the end of 1929* A period of stability in which Gustav Stresemann was the leading politician. Thanks to *the Dawes Plan of 1924*, by which the USA provided huge loans, Germany seemed to be recovering from her defeat and was enjoying an industrial boom.
3 *October 1929 to January 1933* Instability again; the world economic crisis, beginning with the Wall Street Crash in October 1929, soon had disastrous effects on Germany, producing six and a half million unemployed. The government was unable to cope with the situation and by the end of 1932 the Weimar Republic seemed on the verge of collapse.

Meanwhile Adolf Hitler and his National Socialist German Workers' Party (Nazis – NSDAP) had been carrying out a great propaganda campaign blaming the government for all the ills of Germany, and setting out Nazi solutions to the problems. In January 1933, President Hindenburg appointed Hitler as Chancellor, and soon afterwards Hitler saw to it that democracy ceased to exist; the Weimar Republic was at an end, and from then until

April 1945, Hitler was the dictator of Germany. Only defeat in the Second World War and the death of Hitler (30 April 1945) freed the German people from the Nazi tyranny.

14.1 WHY DID THE WEIMAR REPUBLIC FAIL?

(a) It began with serious disadvantages

1 *It had accepted the humiliating and unpopular Versailles Treaty* (see Section 2.8), with its arms limitations, reparations and war-guilt clause, and was therefore always associated with defeat and dishonour. German nationalists could never forgive it for that.

2 *There was a traditional lack of respect for democratic government* and a great admiration for the army and the 'officer class' as the rightful leaders of Germany. In 1919 the view was widespread that the army had not been defeated: it had been betrayed – 'stabbed in the back' – by the democrats, who had needlessly agreed to the Versailles Treaty. What most Germans did not realize was that it was General Ludendorff who had asked for an armistice while the Kaiser was still in power (see Section 2.6(b)). However, the 'stab in the back' legend was eagerly fostered by all enemies of the republic.

3 *The parliamentary system introduced in the new Weimar constitution had weaknesses*, the most serious of which was that it was based on a system of proportional representation, so that all political groups would be fairly represented. Unfortunately there were so many different groups that no party could ever win an overall majority. For example, in 1928 the *Reichstag* (lower house of parliament) contained at least eight groups, of which the largest were the Social Democrats with 153 seats, the German National Party (DNVP) with 73, and the Catholic Centre Party (Zentrum) with 62. The German Communist Party (KPD) had 54 seats, while the German People's party (DVP – Stresemann's liberal party) had 45. The smallest groups were the Bavarian People's Party with 16, and the National Socialists, who only had 12 seats. A succession of coalition governments was inevitable, with the Social Democrats having to rely on co-operation from left-wing liberals and the Catholic Centre. No party was able to carry out its programme.

4 *The political parties had very little experience of how to operate a democratic parliamentary system*, because before 1919 the Reichstag had not controlled policy; the Chancellor had the final authority and was the one who really ruled the country. Under the Weimar constitution it was the other way round – the Chancellor was responsible to the Reichstag, which had the final say. However, the Reichstag usually failed to give a clear lead because the parties had not learned the art of compromise. The communists and nationalists did not believe in democracy anyway, and refused to support the Social Democrats. The communist refusal to work with the SPD meant that no strong government of the left was possible. Disagreements became so bitter that some of the parties organized their own private armies, for self-defence to begin with, but this increased the threat of civil war. The combination of these weaknesses led to more outbreaks of violence and attempts to overthrow the republic.

(b) Outbreaks of violence

1 The Spartacist Rising
In January 1919 the communists tried to seize power in what became known as *the Spartacist Rising* (Spartacus was a Roman who led a revolt of slaves in 71 BC). Inspired

by the recent success of the Russian Revolution, and led by Karl Liebknecht and Rosa Luxemburg, they occupied almost every major city in Germany. In Berlin, President Ebert found himself besieged in the Chancellery. The government managed to defeat the communists only because it accepted the help of the *Freikorps* These were independent volunteer regiments raised by anti-communist ex-army officers. It was a sign of the government's weakness that it had to depend on private forces, which it did not itself control. The two communist leaders did not receive a fair trial – they were simply clubbed to death by *Freikorps* members.

2   The Kapp Putsch (March 1920)

This was an attempt by right-wing groups to seize power. It was sparked off when the government tried to disband the *Freikorps* private armies. They refused to disband and declared Dr Wolfgang Kapp as Chancellor. Berlin was occupied by a *Freikorps* regiment and the cabinet fled to Dresden. The German army (*Reichswehr*) took no action against the *Putsch* (coup, or rising) because the generals were in sympathy with the political right. In the end the workers of Berlin came to the aid of the Social Democrat government by calling a general strike, which paralysed the capital. Kapp resigned and the government regained control. However, it was so weak that nobody was punished except Kapp, who was imprisoned, and it took two months to get the *Freikorps* disbanded. Even then the ex-members remained hostile to the republic and many later joined Hitler's private armies.

3   A series of political assassinations took place

These were mainly carried out by ex-*Freikorps* members. Victims included Walter Rathenau (the Jewish Foreign Minister) and Gustav Erzberger (leader of the armistice delegation). When the government sought strong measures against such acts of terrorism, there was great opposition from the right-wing parties, who sympathized with the criminals. Whereas the communist leaders had been brutally murdered, the courts let right-wing offenders off lightly and the government was unable to intervene. In fact, throughout Germany, the legal and teaching professions, the civil service and the *Reichswehr* tended to be anti-Weimar, which was a crippling handicap for the republic.

4   Hitler's Beer-Hall Putsch

Another threat to the government occurred in November 1923 in Bavaria, at a time when there was much public annoyance at the French occupation of the Ruhr (see Section 4.2(c)) and the disastrous fall in the value of the mark (see below). Hitler, helped by General Ludendorff, aimed to take control of the Bavarian state government in Munich, and then lead a national revolution to overthrow the government in Berlin. However, the police easily broke up Hitler's march, and the 'Beer-Hall *Putsch*' (so-called because the march set out from the Munich beer hall in which Hitler had announced his 'national revolution' the previous evening) soon fizzled out. Hitler was sentenced to five years' imprisonment but served only nine months (because the Bavarian authorities had some sympathy with his aims).

5   Private armies expand

The violence died down during the years 1924 to 1929 as the republic became more stable, but when unemployment grew in the early 1930s, *the private armies expanded* and regular street fights occurred, usually between Nazis and communists. All parties had their meetings broken up by rival armies and the police seemed powerless to prevent it happening.

All this showed that the government was incapable of keeping law and order, and respect for it dwindled. An increasing number of people began to favour a return to strong, authoritarian government, which would maintain strict public order.

(c) Economic problems

Probably the crucial cause of the failure of the republic was the economic problems which plagued it constantly and which it proved incapable of solving permanently.

1 *In 1919 Germany was close to bankruptcy* because of the enormous expense of the war, which had lasted much longer than most people expected.
2 *Attempts to pay reparations instalments made matters worse.* In August 1921, after paying the £50 million due, Germany requested permission to suspend payments until her economy recovered. France refused, and in 1922 the Germans claimed they were unable to make the full annual payment.
3 *In January 1923 French troops occupied the Ruhr* (an important German industrial area) in an attempt to seize goods from factories and mines. The German government ordered the workers to follow a policy of passive resistance, and German industry in the Ruhr was paralysed. The French had failed in their aim, but the effect on the German economy was catastrophic – galloping inflation and the collapse of the mark. The rate of exchange at the end of the war was 20 marks to the dollar, but even before the Ruhr occupation, reparations difficulties had caused the mark to fall in value. Table 14.1 shows the disastrous decline in the mark.

By November 1923 the value of the mark was falling so rapidly that a worker paid in mark notes had to spend them immediately: if he waited until the following day, his notes would be worthless (see Illus. 14.1). It was only when the new Chancellor, Gustav Stresemann, introduced a new currency known as the *Rentenmark*, in 1924, that the financial situation finally stabilized.

This financial disaster had profound effects on German society: the working classes were badly hit – wages failed to keep pace with inflation and trade union funds were wiped out. Worst affected were the middle classes and small capitalists, who lost their savings; many began to look towards the Nazis for improvement. On the other hand, landowners and industrialists came out of the crisis well, because they still owned their material wealth – rich farming land, mines and factories. This strengthened the control of big business over the German economy. Some historians have even suggested that the inflation was deliberately engineered by wealthy industrialists with this aim in mind. The accusation is impossible to prove one way or the other, though the currency and the economy did recover remarkably quickly.

The economic situation improved dramatically in the years after 1924, largely thanks to *the Dawes Plan* of that year (so called after the American General Dawes, who chaired the conference), which provided an immediate loan from the USA equivalent to £40

Table 14.1 **The collapse of the German mark, 1918–23**

	Date	*Marks required in exchange for £1*
November	1918	20
February	1922	1 000
June	1922	1 500
December	1922	50 000
February	1923	100 000
November	1923	21 000 000 000

Illustration 14.1 **Hyperinflation in Germany: boys making kites out of worthless banknotes in the early 1920s**

million, relaxed the fixed reparations payments and in effect allowed the Germans to pay what they could afford. French troops withdrew from the Ruhr. The currency was stabilized, there was a boom in such industries as iron, steel, coal, chemicals and electricals, and wealthy landowners and industrialists were happy to tolerate the republic, since they were doing well out of it. Germany was even able to pay her reparations instalments under the Dawes Plan. During these relatively prosperous years, *Gustav Stresemann was the dominant political figure.* Although he was Chancellor only from August until November 1923, he remained as foreign minister until his death in October 1929, thus providing vital continuity and a steadying hand.

The work of the Dawes Plan was carried a stage further by *the Young Plan, drawn up in October 1929* by the Allied Reparations Commission, under the leadership of an American financier, Owen Young. This reduced the reparations total from £6600 million to £2000 million, to be paid in annual instalments over 59 years. There were other successes for the republic in foreign affairs, thanks to the work of Stresemann (see Section 4.1), and it seemed stable and well established. But behind this success there remained some fatal weaknesses which were soon to bring disaster.

4   The prosperity was much more dependent on the American loans than most people realized. If the USA were to find itself in financial difficulties so that it was forced to stop the loans, or worse still, demand that they be paid back quickly, the German economy would be shaken again. Unfortunately this is exactly what happened in 1929.

5   Following the Wall Street Crash (October 1929), a world economic crisis developed (see Section 22.6). The USA stopped any further loans and began to call in many of the short-term loans already made to Germany. This caused a crisis of confidence in the currency and led to a run on the banks, many of which had to close. The industrial boom had led to worldwide over-production, and German exports, along with those of other countries, were severely reduced. Factories had to close, and by the middle of 1931 unemployment was approaching 4 million. Sadly for Germany, Stresemann, the politician best equipped to deal with the crisis, died of a heart attack in October 1929 at the early age of 51.

6   The government of Chancellor Brüning (Catholic Centre Party) reduced social services, unemployment benefit and the salaries and pensions of government officials, and stopped reparations payments. High tariffs were introduced to keep out foreign foodstuffs and thus help German farmers, while the government bought shares in factories hit by the slump. However, these measures did not produce quick results, though they did help after a time; unemployment continued to rise and by the spring of 1932 it stood at over 6 million. The government came under criticism from almost all groups in society, especially industrialists and the working class, who demanded more decisive action. The loss of much working-class support because of increasing unemployment and the reduction in unemployment benefit was a serious blow to the republic. By the end of 1932 the Weimar Republic had thus been brought to the verge of collapse. Even so, it might still have survived if there had been no other alternative.

(d)   The alternative – Hitler and the Nazis

Hitler and the Nazi Party offered what seemed to be an attractive alternative just when the republic was at its most ineffective. The fortunes of the Nazi Party were linked closely to the economic situation: the more unstable the economy, the more seats the Nazis won in the *Reichstag*, as Table 14.2 shows. In the election of July 1932, with unemployment standing at over 6 million, the Nazis became the largest single party, winning 230 seats out of 608.

There is no doubt that the rise of Hitler and the Nazis, fostered by the economic crisis, was one of the most important causes of the downfall of the republic.

Table 14.2   **Nazi electoral success and the state of the economy, 1924–32**

Date		Seats	State of economy
March	1924	32	Still unstable after 1923 inflation
December	1924	14	Recovering after Dawes Plan
	1928	12	Prosperity and stability
	1930	107	Unemployment mounting – Nazis second largest party
July	1932	230	Massive unemployment – Nazis largest single party
November	1932	196	First signs of economic recovery

(e) What made the Nazis so popular?

1   *They offered national unity, prosperity and full employment* by ridding Germany of what they claimed were the real causes of the troubles – Marxists, the 'November criminals' (the people who had agreed to the armistice in November 1918 and later the Versailles Treaty), Jesuits, Freemasons and Jews. Increasingly the Nazis sought to lay the blame for Germany's defeat in the First World War and all her subsequent problems on the Jews. Great play was made in Nazi propaganda with the 'stab in the back' myth – the idea that the German armies could have fought on but were betrayed by the traitors who had surrendered unnecessarily.

2   *They promised to overthrow the Versailles settlement*, which was so unpopular with most Germans, and to build Germany into a great power again. This would include bringing all Germans (in Austria, Czechoslovakia and Poland) into the *Reich*.

3   *The Nazi private army, the SA* (Sturmabteilung – *Storm Troopers), was attractive* to young people out of work; it gave them a small wage and a uniform.

4   Wealthy landowners and industrialists encouraged the Nazis because *they feared a communist revolution* and they approved of the Nazi policy of hostility to communists. There is some controversy among historians about how far this support went. Some German Marxist historians claim that from the early 1920s the Nazis were financed by industrialists as an anti-communist force, that Hitler was, in effect, 'a tool of the capitalists'. But historian Joachim Fest believes that the amounts of money involved have been greatly exaggerated, and that though some industrialists were secretly in favour of Hitler becoming Chancellor, it was only *after* he came to power that funds began to flow into the party coffers from big business.

5   *Hitler himself had extraordinary political abilities.* He possessed tremendous energy and willpower and a remarkable gift for public speaking, which enabled him to put forward his ideas with great emotional force. He used the latest modern communication techniques – mass rallies, parades, radio and film; he travelled all over Germany by air. Many Germans began to look towards him as some sort of Messiah (saviour) figure. A full version of his views and aims was set out in his book *Mein Kampf (My Struggle)*, which he wrote in prison after the Beer-Hall Putsch.

6   *The striking contrast between the governments of the Weimar Republic and the Nazi Party impressed people.* The former were respectable, dull and unable to maintain law and order; the latter promised strong, decisive government and the restoration of national pride – an irresistible combination.

7   *Without the economic crisis, however, it is doubtful whether Hitler would have had much chance of attaining power.* It was the widespread unemployment and social misery, together with the fear of communism and socialism, that gained the Nazis mass support, not only among the working class (recent research suggests that between 1928 and 1932 the Nazis attracted over 2 million voters away from the socialist SPD), but also among the lower middle classes – office-workers, shop-keepers, civil servants, teachers and small-scale farmers.

In July 1932, then, the Nazis were the largest single party, but Hitler failed to become Chancellor, partly because the Nazis still lacked an overall majority (they had 230 seats out of 608 in the Reichstag), and because he was not yet quite 'respectable' – the conservative President Hindenburg viewed him as an upstart and refused to have him as Chancellor. Given these circumstances, *was it inevitable that Hitler would come to power?* This is still a matter for disagreement among historians. Some feel that by the autumn of 1932 nothing could have saved the Weimar Republic, and that consequently nothing could have kept Hitler out. Others believe that the first signs of economic improvement could be seen, and that it should have been possible to block Hitler's progress. In fact Brüning's policies seem to have started to pay off, though he himself had been replaced as Chancellor by Franz von Papen (Conservative/Nationalist) in May 1932. This theory seems to be supported by the election results of November 1932, when the Nazis lost 34 seats and about 2 million votes, which was a serious setback for them. It seemed that perhaps the republic was weathering the storm and the Nazi challenge would fade out. However, at this point a further influence came into play, which killed off the republic by letting Hitler into power legally.

(f)   Hitler becomes Chancellor (January 1933)

In the end it was political intrigue that brought Hitler to power. A small clique of right-wing politicians with support from the *Reichswehr* decided to bring Hitler into a coalition government with the Nationalists. The main conspirators were Franz von Papen and General Kurt von Schleicher. Their reasons for this momentous decision were:

- They were afraid of the Nazis attempting to seize power by a *Putsch*.
- They believed they could control Hitler better *inside* the government than if he remained outside it, and that a taste of power would make the Nazis modify their extremism.
- The Nationalists had only 37 seats in the *Reichstag* following the elections of July 1932. An alliance with the Nazis, who had 230 seats, would go a long way towards giving them a majority. The Nationalists did not believe in genuine democracy: they hoped that, with Nazi co-operation, they would be able to restore the monarchy and return to the system that had existed under Bismarck (Chancellor 1870–90), in which the Reichstag had much less power. Though this would destroy the Weimar Republic, these right-wing politicians were prepared to go ahead because it would give them a better chance of controlling the communists, who had just had their best result so far in the July election, winning 89 seats.

There was some complicated manoeuvring involving Papen, Schleicher and a group of wealthy businessmen; President Hindenburg was persuaded to dismiss Brüning and appoint Papen as Chancellor. They hoped to bring Hitler in as Vice-Chancellor, but he would settle for nothing less than being Chancellor himself. In January 1933 therefore, they persuaded Hindenburg to invite Hitler to become Chancellor with Papen as Vice-Chancellor, even though the Nazis had by then lost ground in the elections of November 1932. Papen still believed Hitler could be controlled, and remarked to a friend: 'In two months we'll have pushed Hitler into a corner so hard that he'll be squeaking.'

Hitler was able to come to power legally therefore, because all the other parties, including the *Reichswehr*, were so preoccupied with the threat from the communists that they did not sufficiently recognize the danger from the Nazis, and so failed to unite in opposition to them. It ought to have been possible to keep the Nazis out – they were losing ground and had nowhere near an overall majority. But instead of uniting with the other parties to exclude them, the Nationalists made the fatal mistake of *inviting* Hitler into power.

Could the Weimar Republic have survived?
Although there were signs of economic improvement by the end of 1932, it was perhaps inevitable, at that point, that the Weimar Republic would collapse, since the powerful conservative groups and the army were prepared to abandon it, and replace it with a conservative, nationalist and anti-democratic state similar to the one that had existed before 1914. In fact it is possible to argue that the Weimar Republic had already ceased to

exist in May 1932 when Hindenburg appointed Papen as Chancellor with responsibility to him, not to the *Reichstag*.

Was it inevitable that Hitler and the Nazis would come to power?
The majority view is that this need not have happened; Papen, Schleicher, Hindenburg and the others must take the blame for being prepared to invite him into power, and then failing to control him. According to Ian Kershaw, Hitler's most recent biographer:

> There was no inevitability about Hitler's accession to power ... a Hitler Chancellorship might have been avoided. With the corner turning of the economic Depression, and with the Nazi movement facing potential break-up if power were not soon attained, the future – even under an authoritarian government – would have been very different. ... In fact, political miscalculation by those with regular access to the corridors of power rather than any action on the part of the Nazi leader played a larger role in placing him in the Chancellor's seat. ... The anxiety to destroy democracy rather than the keenness to bring the Nazis to power was what triggered the complex development that led to Hitler's Chancellorship.

However, there were some people in Germany, even on the right, who had misgivings about Hitler's appointment. Kershaw tells us that General Ludendorff, who had supported Hitler at the time of the 1923 Munich *Putsch*, now wrote to Hindenburg: 'You have delivered up our holy German Fatherland to one of the greatest demagogues of all time. I solemnly prophesy that this accursed man will cast our Reich into the abyss and bring our nation to inconceivable misery. Future generations will damn you in your grave for what you have done.'

14.2   WHAT DID NATIONAL SOCIALISM STAND FOR?

What it did *not* mean was nationalization and the redistribution of wealth. The word 'socialism' was included only to attract the support of the German workers, though it has to be admitted that Hitler did promise a better deal for workers. In fact it bore many similarities to Mussolini's fascism (see Section 13.2). *The movement's general principles were:*

1   It was more than just one political party among many. *It was a way of life dedicated to the rebirth of the nation.* All classes in society must be united into a 'national community' (*Volksgemeinschaft*) to make Germany a great nation again and restore national pride. Since the Nazis had the only correct way to achieve this, it followed that all other parties, especially communists, must be eliminated.
2   Great emphasis was laid *on the ruthlessly efficient organization of all aspects of the lives of the masses* under the central government, in order to achieve greatness, with violence and terror if necessary. The state was supreme; the interests of the individual always came second to the interests of the state, that is, *a totalitarian state* in which propaganda had a vital role to play.
3   Since it was likely that greatness could only be achieved by war, *the entire state must be organized on a military footing.*
4   *The race theory was vitally important* – mankind could be divided into two groups, Aryans and non-Aryans. The Aryans were the Germans, ideally tall, blond, blue-eyed and handsome; they were the master race, destined to rule the world. All the rest, such as Slavs, coloured peoples and particularly Jews, were inferior. They were to be excluded from the 'national community', along with other groups who

were considered unfit to belong, including gypsies and homosexuals. The Slavs were destined to become the slave race of the Germans.

All the various facets and details of the Nazi system sprang from these four basic concepts. There has been great debate among historians about whether National Socialism was *a natural development of German history, or whether it was a one-off, a distortion of normal development.* Many British and American historians argued that it was a natural extension of earlier Prussian militarism and German traditions. Historian Shelley Baranowski goes along with this interpretation (in *Nazi Empire*, 2010). She points out that before the First World War Germany's African colonies, including Tanganyika, Namibia, Cameroon and Togo, were difficult to control, and that Prussian military doctrine held that the complete destruction of all enemy forces must be the prime objective of any war. In the case of rebellious colonies, this became mixed in with racist elements, producing a genocidal mentality. In Tanganyika, following unrest and uprisings, almost half a million Africans were killed, some by deliberate starvation. An uprising in Namibia was dealt with in the same way. Similar trends were apparent during the First World War, after the defeat of the Russians. In March 1918 Germany gained control of former Russian territories containing a large proportion of Russia's coal, iron-ore and oil resources. In the few months before Germany's own surrender, German troops suppressed all nationalist movements in these territories with great brutality, treating the Slav inhabitants as second-class citizens. Baranowski suggests that Nazi brutality in eastern Europe doing the Second World War was a revival and continuation of the Germans' pre-First-World-War attitudes, as was the creation of the concentration camps in 1933 for opponents of the Nazis. However, she does stop short of arguing that the Germans in general had developed a genocidal mentality that led directly to the Holocaust. As she puts it: 'The deliberate scouring of a whole continent, and potentially the entire surface of the globe for Jews to be carried off to assembly-line extermination in gas chambers or killing pits had no precedent.'

Marxist historians believed that National Socialism and fascism in general were the final stage and culmination of western capitalism, which was bound to collapse because of its fatal flaws. British historian R. Butler, writing in 1942, believed that 'National Socialism is the inevitable reappearance of Prussian militarism and terror, as seen during the 18th century.' Sir Lewis Namier, a Polish Jew who settled in Britain and became an eminent historian, was understandably bitter:

> Attempts to absolve the German people of responsibility are unconvincing. And as for Hitler and his Third Reich, these arose from the people, indeed from the lower depths of the people. … Friends of the Germans must ask themselves why individual Germans become useful, decent citizens, but in groups, both at home and abroad, are apt to develop tendencies that make them a menace to their fellow-men? (*Avenues of History*)

On the other hand, German historians like Gerhard Ritter and K. D. Bracher stressed the personal contribution of Hitler, arguing that Hitler was striving to break away from the past and introduce something completely new. National Socialism was therefore a grotesque departure from the normal and logical historical development. This is probably the majority view and it is one that found favour in Germany, since it meant that the German people, contrary to what Namier claimed, *can* be absolved from most of the blame.

Ian Kershaw recognizes that there are elements of both interpretations in Hitler's career. He points out that

> the mentalities which conditioned the behaviour both of the elites and the masses, and which made Hitler's rise possible, were products of strands of German political culture

that were plainly recognizable in the twenty years or so before the First World War. ...
Most of the elements of political culture that fed into Nazism were peculiarly German.

However, Kershaw is also clear that Hitler was not the logical, inevitable product of long-term trends in German culture and beliefs. Nor was he a mere accident in German history: 'without the unique conditions in which he came to prominence, Hitler would have been nothing. ... He exploited the conditions brilliantly.'

14.3 HITLER CONSOLIDATES HIS POWER

Hitler was an Austrian, the son of a customs official in Braunau-am-Inn on the German border. He had hoped to become an artist but failed to gain admittance to the Vienna Academy of Fine Arts, and afterwards spent six down-and-out years living in Vienna dosshouses and developing his hatred of Jews. In Munich, Hitler had joined Anton Drexler's tiny German Workers' Party (1919), which he soon took over and transformed into the National Socialist German Workers' Party (NSDAP). Now, in January 1933, he was Chancellor of a coalition government of National Socialists and nationalists, but he was not yet satisfied with the amount of power he possessed: Nazis held only three out of eleven cabinet posts. He therefore insisted on a general election in the hope of winning an overall majority for the Nazis.

(a) The election of 5 March 1933

The election campaign was an extremely violent one. Since they were now in government, the Nazis were able to use all the apparatus of state, including the press and radio, to try and whip up a majority. They had a great advantage in that Hermann Goering, one of the leading Nazis, had been appointed minister of the interior for Prussia, the largest and most important German state. This meant that he controlled the police. He replaced senior police officers with reliable Nazis, and 50 000 auxiliary policemen were called up, most of them from the SA and the SS (*Schutzstaffeln* – Hitler's second private army, formed originally to be his personal bodyguard). They had orders to avoid hostility towards the SA and SS but to show no mercy to communists and other 'enemies of the state'. They were given permission to use firearms if necessary. Meetings of Nazis and nationalists were allowed to go ahead without interference, but communist and socialist political meetings were wrecked and speakers were beaten up, while police looked the other way. The nationalists went along with all this because they were determined to use the Nazis to destroy communism once and for all.

(b) The Reichstag fire

The climax of the election campaign came on the night of 27 February when the Reichstag was badly damaged by a fire, apparently started by a young Dutch anarchist called Marinus van der Lubbe, who was arrested, tried and executed for his pains. It has been suggested that the SA knew about van der Lubbe's plans, but allowed him to go ahead and even started fires of their own elsewhere in the building with the intention of blaming it on the communists. There is no conclusive evidence of this, but what is certain is that the fire played right into Hitler's hands: *he was able to use the fire to stir up fear of communism and as a pretext for the banning of the party*. Some four thousand communists were arrested and imprisoned. However, in spite of all their efforts, the Nazis still failed to win an overall majority in the 5 March election. With almost 90 per cent of the electorate voting, the Nazis won 288 out of the 647 seats, 36 short of the magic figure – 324 – needed for an overall majority. The nationalists again won 52 seats. Hitler was still dependent on the support of Papen and Hugenberg (leader of the nationalists). This turned out to be the Nazis' best performance in a 'free' election, and they never won an overall majority. It is worth remembering that even at the height of their electoral triumph the Nazis were supported by only 44 per cent of the voting electorate.

14.4   HOW WAS HITLER ABLE TO STAY IN POWER?

(a)   The Enabling Law, 23 March 1933

Hitler was not satisfied with the election result. He was determined that he must be depen-dent on nobody except his Nazi party. While President Hindenburg was still in shock after the Reichstag fire, Hitler apparently persuaded him that emergency legislation was vital to prevent a communist uprising. Known as the Enabling Law, this legislation was forced through the Reichstag on 23 March 1933, and it was this that provided the legal basis of Hitler's power. It stated that the government could introduce laws without the approval of the Reichstag for the next four years, could ignore the constitution and could sign agree-ments with foreign countries. All laws would be drafted by the Chancellor and come into operation the day they were published. This meant that Hitler was to be the complete dicta-tor for the next four years, but since his will was now law, he would be able to extend the four-year period indefinitely. He no longer needed the support of Papen and Hugenberg; the Weimar constitution had been abandoned. Such a major constitutional change needed approval by a two-thirds majority, yet the Nazis hadn't even a simple majority.

How did the Nazis get the Enabling Bill through the Reichstag?
The method was typical of the Nazis. Since the election, the whole country had experi-enced a wave of unprecedented Nazi violence directed at political opponents and at Jews. Jewish synagogues were attacked and trashed by Hitler's brownshirts (SA), and there were countless beatings and murders. Hundreds more were arrested and sent to newly set-up concentration camps (see Illus. 14.2). On 23 March, the day of the Enabling Law vote, The Kroll Opera House (where the Reichstag had been meeting since the fire) was surrounded by Hitler's private armies. MPs had to push their way through solid ranks of SS troops to get into the building. The 81 communist MPs had either been arrested or were in hiding. Some of the socialists were simply not allowed to pass. Inside the building, rows of brown-shirted SA troops lined the walls, and the SS could be heard chanting outside: 'We want the Bill, or fire and murder.' It took courage to vote against the Enabling Bill in such surroundings. When the Catholic Centre Party decided to vote in favour of the Bill, the result was a foregone conclusion. Only the Social Democrats spoke against it, and it passed by 441 votes to 94 (all Social Democrats). The Nazi aim of killing off parliamen-tary democracy had been achieved, and by means that could in no way be called 'legal'. The Papen/Schleicher/Hindenburg plan to control Hitler had failed completely, and Ludendorff's prophecy was beginning to become reality.

(b)   *Gleichschaltung*

Having effectively muzzled the *Reichstag,* Hitler immediately set about sidelining the Chancellery and the ministries. This was achieved by a policy known as *Gleichschaltung* (forcible co-ordination), which turned Germany into a totalitarian or fascist state. The

Illustration 14.2 **Jewish people being taken to a concentration camp**

government tried to control as many aspects of life as possible, using a huge police force and the notorious State Secret Police, the *Gestapo (Geheime Staatspolizei)*. It became dangerous to oppose or criticize the government in any way. *The main features of the Nazi totalitarian state were*:

1 All political parties except the National Socialists were banned, so that Germany became *a one-party state* like Italy and the USSR. The Catholic Centre Party actually dissolved itself a week before the official ban was introduced!

2 The separate state parliaments (*Länder*) still existed but lost all power. Most of their functions were taken over by *a Nazi Special Commissioner*, appointed in each state by the Berlin government, who had complete power over all officials and affairs within his state. There were no more state, provincial or municipal elections.

3 *The civil service was purged*: all Jews and other suspected 'enemies of the state' were removed, so that it became fully reliable.

4 *Trade unions, a likely source of resistance, were abolished*, their funds confiscated and their leaders arrested. They were replaced by *the German Labour Front*, to which all workers had to belong. The government dealt with all grievances, and strikes were not allowed.

5 *The education system was closely controlled* so that children could be indoctrinated with Nazi opinions. School textbooks were often rewritten to fit in with Nazi theory, the most obvious examples being in history and biology. History was distorted to fit in with Hitler's view that great things could only be achieved by force. Human biology was dominated by the Nazi race theory. Teachers, lecturers and professors were closely watched to make sure they did not express opinions

which strayed from the party line, and many lived in fear in case they were reported to the Gestapo by children of convinced Nazis.

6   The system was supplemented by *the Hitler Youth*, which all boys had to join at 14; girls joined *the League of German Maidens*. The regime was deliberately trying to destroy traditional bonds such as loyalty to the family: children were taught that their first duty was to obey Hitler, who took on the title *Führer* (leader, or guide). The favourite slogan was 'the Führer is always right'. Children were even encouraged to betray their parents to the *Gestapo*, and many did so. These youth organizations worked on the assumption that the Nazi regime would remain in power for many generations; there was much talk of 'the thousand-year Reich'. This is why the present generation of young people had to be thoroughly indoctrinated to provide a firm foundation for the regime. The vital element was: they must become steeped in militaristic values. In a speech in Nuremberg in September 1935, Hitler told the crowd: 'What we look for from our German youth is different from what people wanted in the past. In our eyes, the German youth of the future must be slim and slender, swift as the greyhound, tough as leather, and hard as Krupp steel. We must educate a new type of man so that our people are not ruined by the symptoms of degeneracy of our day.'

7   *There was a special policy concerned with the family.* The Nazis were worried that the birth rate was declining, and therefore 'racially pure' and healthy families were encouraged to have more children. Family planning centres were closed down and contraceptives banned. Mothers who responded well were awarded medals – the Cross of Honour of the German Mother; a mother of eight children gained a gold medal, six children a silver medal, and four children a bronze medal. On the other hand, people who were considered 'undesirable' were discouraged from having children. These included Jews, gypsies, and people deemed to be physically or mentally unfit. In 1935, marriages between Aryans and Jews were forbidden; over 300 000 people who were designated as 'unfit' were forcibly sterilized to prevent them having children.

8   *All communications and the media were controlled by the minister of propaganda, Dr Joseph Goebbels.* Leni Riefenstahl, a brilliant young film director, was invited personally by Hitler to work for the Nazis; she made an impressive film of the 1934 Nuremberg party rally. Using 30 cameras and a crew of 120, she produced a documentary the like of which had never been seen before. When it was released in March 1935 under the title *Triumph of the Will*, it was widely acclaimed; it even won a gold medal at the Venice Film Festival in 1935. But it was more than an ordinary documentary. In the words of Richard J. Evans, the 'will' in question was 'not only that of the German people, but also and above all, the will of Hitler, whom her cameras almost invariably portrayed standing alone. ... In the final stages of the film the screen was filled with columns of marching stormtroopers, and black-shirted, steel-helmeted SS men, leaving audiences no room for doubt. It was a propaganda film designed to convince Germany and the world of the power, strength and determination of the German people under Hitler's leadership.' No further films were made about Hitler himself – *Triumph of the Will* had said it all. However, the state gradually increased its control over the cinema so that only feature films approved by the regime could be shown.

    Radio, newspapers, magazines, books, theatre, music and art were all supervised. The government made cheap radios available so that by 1939 over 70 per cent of German households owned a 'wireless' set. But as John Traynor puts it: 'While people may have appreciated the material benefit this represented, we cannot know for certain what they came to think of the relentless message that poured constantly from their radio set.' A national book-burning day was held on

10 May 1933 when thousands of books by Jewish, socialist and other 'suspect' writers were publicly burned on huge bonfires in Germany's university cities. By the end of 1934 about 4000 books were on the forbidden list because they were 'un-German'. It was impossible to perform the plays of Bertolt Brecht (a communist) or the music of Felix Mendelssohn and Gustav Mahler (they were Jewish). American jazz was popular with young people, but Hitler hated it and tried to exclude it from Germany. But it was so widespread in nightclubs and dance halls that it proved impossible to eliminate it completely.

Hitler had a special interest in art, having once tried to make a career as an artist. He was soon announcing that it was time for a new type of art – German art. The idea that art was international must be rejected out of hand because it was decadent and Jewish. A wide variety of artists was condemned and their works removed from galleries. They included Jewish, abstract, left-wing, modernist and all foreign artists, whatever their style. Hitler even condemned the French impressionists simply because they were not German. On 20 March 1939 about 5000 condemned paintings and drawings were burnt on a massive bonfire outside the central fire station in Berlin. Artists, writers and scholars were continually harassed until it became pointless to produce any artwork that did not win the approval of the regime, and it was impossible to express any opinion which did not fit in with the Nazi system. By these methods public opinion could be moulded and mass support assured, or so the Nazis hoped.

9 *The economic life of the country was closely organized.* Although the Nazis (unlike the communists) had no special ideas about the economy, they did have some basic aims: *to eliminate unemployment and to make Germany self-sufficient by boosting exports and reducing imports, a policy known as 'autarky'.* The idea was to put the economy onto a war footing, so that all the materials necessary for waging war could be produced, as far as possible, in Germany itself. This would ensure that Germany would never again be hamstrung by a trade blockade like the one imposed by the Allies during the First World War. The centrepiece of the policy was the Four-Year Plan introduced in 1936 under the direction of Hermann Goering, the head of the *Luftwaffe* (the German air force). Policies included:

- telling industrialists what to produce, depending on what the country needed at that moment; and closing factories down if their products were not required;
- moving workers around the country to places where jobs existed and labour was needed;
- encouraging farmers to increase agricultural yields;
- controlling food prices and rents;
- manipulating foreign exchange rates to avoid inflation;
- introducing vast schemes of public works – slum clearance, land drainage and *autobahn* (motorway) building;
- forcing foreign countries to buy German goods, either by refusing to pay cash for goods bought from those countries, so that they had to accept German goods instead (often armaments), or by refusing permission to foreigners with bank accounts in Germany to withdraw their cash, so that they had to spend it in Germany on German goods;
- manufacturing synthetic rubber and wool and experimenting to produce petrol from coal in order to reduce dependence on foreign countries;
- increasing expenditure on armaments; in 1938–9 the military budget accounted for 52 per cent of government spending. This was an incredible amount for 'peacetime'. As Richard Overy puts it: 'this stemmed from

Hitler's desire to turn Germany into an economic and military superpower before the rest of the world caught up'.

10   *Religion was brought under state control*, since the churches were a possible source of opposition. At first Hitler moved cautiously with both Roman Catholics and Protestants.

- **The Roman Catholic Church**
  In 1933 Hitler signed an agreement (known as the *Concordat*) with the pope, in which he promised not to interfere with German Catholics in any way; in return they agreed to dissolve the Catholic Centre Party and take no further part in politics. But relations soon became strained when the government broke the Concordat by dissolving the Catholic Youth League because it rivalled the Hitler Youth. When the Catholics protested, their schools were closed down. By 1937 Catholics were completely disillusioned with the Nazis, and Pope Pius XI issued an Encyclical (a letter to be read out in all Roman Catholic churches in Germany) in which he condemned the Nazi movement for being 'hostile to Christ and his Church'. Hitler was unimpressed, however, and thousands of priests and nuns were arrested and sent to concentration camps.

- **The Protestant Churches**
  Since a majority of Germans belonged to one or other of the various Protestant groups, Hitler tried to organize them into a '*Reich* Church' with a Nazi as the first *Reich* bishop. But many pastors (priests) objected and a group of them, led by Martin Niemoller, protested to Hitler about government interference and about his treatment of the Jews. Once again the Nazis were completely ruthless – Niemoller and over 800 other pastors were sent to concentration camps (Niemoller himself managed to survive for eight years until he was liberated in 1945). Hundreds more were arrested later and the rest were forced to swear an oath of obedience to the Führer.
  Eventually the persecutions appeared to bring the churches under control, but resistance continued, and the churches were the only organizations to keep up a quiet protest campaign against the Nazi system. For example, in 1941 some Catholic bishops protested against the Nazi policy of killing mentally handicapped and mentally ill people in German asylums. Over 70 000 people were murdered in this 'euthanasia' campaign. Hitler publicly ordered the mass killings to be stopped, but evidence suggests that they still continued.

11   *Above all, Germany was a police state*. The police, helped by the SS and the Gestapo, tried to prevent all open opposition to the regime. The law courts were not impartial: 'enemies of the state' rarely received a fair trial, and *the concentration camps* introduced by Hitler in 1933 were full. The main ones before 1939 were Dachau near Munich, Buchenwald near Weimar and Sachsenhausen near Berlin. They contained 'political' prisoners – communists, Social Democrats, Catholic priests, Protestant pastors. Other persecuted groups were homosexuals and above all, Jews; perhaps as many as 15 000 homosexual men were sent to the camps, where they were made to wear pink triangle badges.
    However, recent research in Germany has shown that the police state was not as efficient as used to be thought. The Gestapo was understaffed; for example, there were only 43 officials to police Essen, a city with a population of 650 000. They had to rely heavily on ordinary people coming forward with information to

denounce others. After 1943, as people became more disillusioned with the war, they were less willing to help the authorities, and the Gestapo's job became more difficult.

12 *The worst aspect of the Nazi system was Hitler's anti-Semitic (anti-Jewish) policy.* There were only just over half a million Jews in Germany, less than one per cent of the total population, but Hitler decided to use them as scapegoats for everything – the humiliation at Versailles, the depression, unemployment and communism. He began by talking in terms of racial purity – the Aryan race, especially the Germans, must be kept free from contamination by the non-Aryan Jews. This is why they must be cleared out of Germany. In 1925 he wrote in his book *Mein Kampf* (My Struggle) about the time in Vienna when he was converted to anti-Semitism. He saw:

> a phenomenon in a black caftan and wearing black sidelocks. ... The longer I gazed at this strange countenance, the more the question shaped itself in my brain: is this a German? ... As soon as I began to investigate the matter, Vienna appeared to me in a new light: was there any shady undertaking, any form of foulness, especially in cultural life, in which at least one Jew did not participate? In putting the probing knife to that kind of abscess one immediately discovered, like a maggot in a putrescent body, a little Jew who was often blinded by the sudden light.

Ian Kershaw suggests that this was probably a dramatization, since he was known to have been reading anti-Semitic newspapers before he went to live in Vienna. In fact the Jewish community played an important role in the cultural, scientific and business life of Germany, but Hitler would allow them no credit for that. In many speeches before he became Chancellor he spoke about them in the most extreme language. As soon as he became Chancellor, his supporters took it as a licence to begin persecuting the Jews. However, when the government declared a boycott of Jewish shops for 1 April 1933, the expected mass support was not forthcoming. The general public seemed apathetic, and some people even showed sympathy for the Jewish shops. Hitler decided that restraint was called for; clearly people's main concerns were elsewhere. Consequently further boycotts were cancelled and the focus moved to attempts to strengthen the economy.

By 1935 Hitler's attitude had hardened again and he claimed that there was a world Jewish/communist plot to take control. He seemed to assume that communism was a Jewish movement, probably because many of the leading Russian Bolsheviks were Jewish. This, Hitler believed, would plunge the world into a new Dark Age, unless the Germans were able to thwart the plot. Lots of Germans were in such a desperate situation that they were prepared to accept the propaganda about the Jews and were not sorry to see thousands of them removed from their jobs as lawyers, doctors, teachers and journalists. Robert Gellately (in *Backing Hitler,* 2001) shows that many ordinary Germans actively participated in the atrocities against the Jews, helped themselves to stolen Jewish property and happily took jobs vacated by Jews. Gotz Aly also asked the question: 'What drove ordinary Germans to tolerate and commit historically unprecedented crimes against humanity?' His answer is that ordinary Germans co-operated in genocide because they benefited from it in material terms. The anti-Jewish campaign inside Germany was given legal status by *the Nuremberg Laws* (1935), which deprived Jews of their German citizenship, forbade them to marry non-Jews (to preserve the purity of the Aryan race), and ruled that even a person with only one Jewish grandparent must be classed as a Jew.

Until 1938 Hitler still proceeded relatively cautiously with the anti-Jewish policy, probably because he was concerned about unfavourable foreign reaction. Later the campaign became more extreme. In November 1938, he authorized what became known as

Kristallnacht (the 'Night of Broken Glass'), a vicious attack on Jewish synagogues and other property throughout the whole country. When the Second World War began, the plight of the Jews deteriorated rapidly. They were harassed in every possible way; their property was attacked and burnt, shops looted, synagogues destroyed, and Jews themselves herded into concentration camps. Eventually the terrible nature of what Hitler called his 'Final Solution' of the Jewish problem became clear: *he intended to exterminate the entire Jewish race.* During the war, as the Germans occupied such countries as Czechoslovakia, Poland and western Russia, he was able to lay his hands on non-German Jews as well. It is believed that by 1945, out of a total of 9 million Jews living in Europe at the outbreak of the Second World War, about 5.7 million had been murdered, most of them in the gas chambers of the Nazi extermination camps. The *Holocaust*, as it became known, was the worst and most shocking of the many crimes against humanity committed by the Nazi regime (see Section 6.8 for full details).

(c) Hitler's policies were popular with many sections of the German people

It would be wrong to give the impression that Hitler hung on to power simply by terrorizing the entire nation. True, if you were a Jew, a communist or a socialist, or if you persisted in protesting and criticizing the Nazis, you would run into trouble; but many people who had no great interest in politics could usually live quite happily under the Nazis. This was because Hitler took care to please many important groups in society. Even as late as 1943, when the fortunes of war had turned against Germany, Hitler somehow retained his popularity with ordinary people. Gotz Aly (in *Hitler's Beneficiaries,* 2007) argues that the Nazis were as much socialist as they were nationalist, and that they genuinely tried to make life better for ordinary Germans. Hitler told a reporter that his ambition was to raise the general standard of living and make the German people rich.

1   His arrival in power in January 1933 caused a great wave of enthusiasm and anticipation after the weak and indecisive governments of the Weimar Republic. *Hitler seemed to be offering action and a great new Germany.* He was careful to foster this enthusiasm by military parades, torchlight processions and firework displays, the most famous of which were the huge rallies held every year in Nuremberg, which seemed to appeal to the masses.

2   *Hitler was successful in eliminating unemployment.* This was probably the most important reason for his popularity with ordinary people. When he came to power the unemployment figure still stood at over 6 million, but by the end of 1935 it had dropped to just over two million, and by 1939 it was negligible. *How was this achieved?* The public works schemes provided thousands of extra jobs. A large party bureaucracy was set up now that the party was expanding so rapidly, and this provided thousands of extra office and administrative posts. There were purges of Jews and anti-Nazis from the civil service and from many other jobs connected with law, education, journalism, broadcasting, the theatre and music, leaving large numbers of vacancies. Conscription was reintroduced in 1935. Rearmament was started in 1934 and gradually speeded up. Thus Hitler had provided what the unemployed had been demanding in their marches in 1932: work and bread (*Arbeit und Brot*).

3   *Care was taken to keep the support of the workers* once it had been gained by the provision of jobs. This was important because the abolition of trade unions still rankled with many of them. The Strength through Joy Organization (*Kraft durch Freude*) provided benefits such as subsidized holidays in Germany and abroad, cruises, skiing holidays, cheap theatre and concert tickets and convalescent homes.

Gotz Aly looked at documents from the former East German archives which show in detail that the Nazis passed scores of laws extending and increasing social security provision, doubling workers' holiday entitlement, with pay, and making it more difficult for landlords to increase rents and evict tenants. According to Aly, the Nazi dictatorship was built not on terror but on a mutual calculation of interest between leaders and people.

4 *Wealthy industrialists and businessmen were delighted with the Nazis* in spite of the government's interference with their industries. This was partly because they now felt safe from a communist revolution, and because they were glad to be rid of trade unions, which had constantly pestered them with demands for shorter working hours and increased wages. In addition they were able to buy back at low prices the shares they had sold to the state during the crisis of 1929–32, and there was promise of great profits from the public works schemes, rearmament and other orders which the government placed with them.

5 *Farmers, though doubtful about Hitler at first, gradually warmed towards the Nazis* as soon as it became clear that farmers were in a specially favoured position in the state because of the declared Nazi aim of self-sufficiency in food production. Prices of agricultural produce were fixed so that they were assured of a reasonable profit. Farms were declared to be hereditary estates, and on the death of the owner, had to be passed on to his next of kin. This meant that a farmer could not be forced to sell or mortgage his farm to pay off his debts, and was welcomed by many farmers who were heavily in debt as a result of the financial crisis.

6 *Hitler gained the support of the Reichswehr (army)*, which was crucial if he was to feel secure in power. The *Reichswehr* was the one organization which could have removed him by force. Yet by the summer of 1934, Hitler had won it over:

- Although some of the generals thought that Hitler was a contemptible upstart, on the whole the officer class was well-disposed towards him because of his much publicized aim of setting aside the restrictions of the Versailles Treaty by rearmament and expansion of the army to its full strength.
- There had been a steady infiltration of National Socialists into the lower ranks, and this was beginning to work through to the lower officer classes.
- the army leaders were much impressed by Hitler's handling of the troublesome SA in the notorious *Rohm Purge* (also known as 'the Night of the Long Knives') of 30 June 1934.

The background to this was that the SA, under their leader Ernst Röhm, a personal friend of Hitler from the early days of the movement, was becoming an embarrassment to the new Chancellor. Röhm wanted his brownshirts to be merged with the *Reichswehr* and himself made a general. Hitler knew that the aristocratic *Reichswehr* generals would not hear of either; they considered the SA to be little more than a bunch of gangsters, while Röhm himself was known to be a homosexual (which was frowned on in army circles as well as officially among the Nazis) and had criticized the generals in public for their stiff-necked conservatism. There were also divisions within Nazi ranks: some leading Nazis, including Gregor Strasser and Röhm himself, repeatedly urged Hitler to be more radical and socialist in his policies. Again, this was something that would not be to the taste of the Nationalists and the army. Röhm had enemies in the party; Hermann Goering and Heinrich Himmler, who were both busy building up their own power bases, also felt that Röhm was getting too powerful. Himmler told Hitler that Röhm was planning to use his SA to seize power from Hitler (see Illus. 14.3). Apparently this caused Hitler to make up his mind – for all these reasons Röhm must be removed.

Illustration 14.3 **Hitler and the *Sturmabteilung* (SA) at a Nuremberg Rally**

Hitler's solution to the problem was typical of Nazi methods – ruthless but efficient; he used one of his private armies to deal with the other. Rohm and most of the SA leaders were murdered by SS troops, and Hitler seized the opportunity to have a number of other enemies and critics murdered who had nothing to do with the SA. For example, two of Papen's advisers were shot dead by the SS because ten days earlier Papen had made a speech at Marburg criticizing Hitler. Papen himself was probably saved only by the fact that he was a close friend of President Hindenburg. It is thought that at least 400 people were murdered during that one night or soon afterwards. Hitler justified his actions by claiming that they were all plotting against the state.

The German historian Lothar Machtan, in his book *The Hidden Hitler* (2000), suggested that Hitler was a homosexual who had a series of relationships with young men during his early days in Vienna and Munich, which Röhm and his friends knew all about. If Machtan is right, then another explanation for the purge was the need for Hitler to safeguard his reputation, as the rift between himself and Röhm widened. 'Hitler's principal motive for taking action against Röhm and associates was fear of exposure and blackmail. ... The elimination of witnesses and evidence – *that* was the real purpose of this act of terrorism.'

Whatever Hitler's true motives, *the purge had important results*: the *Reichswehr* were relieved to be rid of the troublesome SA leaders and impressed by Hitler's decisive handling of the problem. When President Hindenburg died only a month later, the *Reichswehr* agreed that Hitler should become president as well as Chancellor (though he preferred to be known as the *Führer*). The *Reichswehr* took an oath of allegiance to the *Führer*.

7 *Finally, Hitler's foreign policy was a brilliant success.* With each successive triumph, more and more Germans began to think of him as infallible (see Section 5.3).

14.5 NAZISM AND FASCISM

There is sometimes confusion about the meaning of the terms 'Nazism' and 'fascism'. Mussolini started the first fascist party, in Italy; later the term was used, not entirely accurately, to describe other right-wing movements and governments. In fact, each brand of so-called 'fascism' had its own special features; in the case of the German Nazis, there were many similarities with Mussolini's fascist system, but also some important differences.

(a) Similarities

- Both were intensely anti-communist and, because of this, drew a solid basis of support from all classes.
- They were anti-democratic and attempted to organize a totalitarian state, controlling industry, agriculture and the way of life of the people, so that personal freedom was limited.
- They attempted to make the country self-sufficient.
- They emphasized the close unity of all classes working together to achieve these ends.
- Both emphasized the supremacy of the state, were intensely nationalistic, glorifying war, and the cult of the hero/leader who would guide the rebirth of the nation from its troubles.

(b) Differences

- Fascism never seemed to take root in Italy as deeply as the Nazi system did in Germany.
- The Italian system was not as efficient as that in Germany. The Italians never came anywhere near achieving self-sufficiency and never eliminated unemployment; in fact unemployment rose. The Nazis succeeded in eliminating unemployment, though they never achieved complete autarky.
- The Italian system was not as ruthless or as brutal as that in Germany and there were no mass atrocities, though there were unpleasant incidents like the murders of Matteotti and Amendola.
- Italian fascism was not particularly anti-Jewish or racist until 1938, when Mussolini adopted the policy to emulate Hitler.
- Mussolini was more successful than Hitler with his religious policy after his agreement with the pope in 1929.
- Finally, their constitutional positions were different: the monarchy still remained in Italy, and though Mussolini normally ignored Victor Emmanuel, the king played a vital role in 1943 when Mussolini's critics turned to him as head of state. He was able to announce Mussolini's dismissal and order his arrest. Unfortunately there was nobody in Germany who could dismiss Hitler.

There are conflicting views about this. Some argue that Hitler's regime brought many benefits to the majority of the German people. Others believe that his whole career was a complete disaster and that his so-called successes were a myth created by Joseph Goebbels, the Nazi minister of propaganda. Taking the argument a step further, some German historians claim that Hitler was a weak ruler who never actually initiated any policy of his own.

(a) Successful?

One school of thought claims that the Nazis were successful up to 1939 because they provided many benefits of the sort mentioned above in Section 14.4(c), and developed a flourishing economy. Hence Hitler's great popularity with the masses, which endured well on into the 1940s, in spite of the hardships of the war. If only Hitler had succeeded in keeping Germany out of war, so the theory goes, all would have been well, and his Third Reich might have lasted a thousand years (as he boasted it would).

(b) Only superficially successful?

The opposing view is that Hitler's supposed successes were superficial and could not stand the test of time. The so-called 'economic miracle' was an illusion; there was a huge budget deficit and the country was, technically, bankrupt. Even the superficial success was achieved by methods unacceptable in a modern civilized society:

- Full employment was achieved only at the cost of a brutal anti-Jewish campaign and a massive rearmament programme.
- Self-sufficiency was not possible unless Germany was able to take over and exploit large areas of eastern Europe belonging to Poland, Czechoslovakia and Russia.
- Permanent success therefore depended on success in war; thus there was no possibility of Hitler keeping out of war (see also Section 5.3(a)).
- Nor was there much evidence of any improvement in the standard of living of ordinary people, which Hitler claimed was one of his main aims. As Richard J. Evans points out: 'Most statistical investigations are agreed that the economic situation of the majority of middle-class wage-earners did not markedly improve between 1933 and 1939.' As concentration on rearmament increased, there were shortages of food and other important goods; in fact the per capita consumption of many basic food-stuffs declined in the mid-1930s. Any wage increases came about only through working longer hours.

The conclusion must therefore be, as Alan Bullock wrote in his biography of Hitler, that

> Recognition of the benefits which Hitler's rule brought to Germany needs to be tempered by the realization that for the Fuhrer – and for a considerable section of the German people – these were by-products of his true purpose, the creation of an instrument of power with which to realize a policy of expansion that in the end was to admit no limits.

Even the policy of preparedness for war failed; Hitler's plans were designed to be completed during the early 1940s, probably around 1942. In 1939 Germany's economy was not ready for a major war, although it was strong enough to defeat Poland and France. However, as Richard Overy points out, 'the large programmes of war production were not yet complete, some barely started. ... The German economy was caught in 1939 midway through the transformation anticipated ... as Hitler ruefully reflected some years later, militarization had been "mismanaged".' Adam Tooze argues that Hitler resisted pressure from his advisers to prepare for a long war because he believed that Germany had no chance of winning a long war. In fact, in the first year of the war most of the increased military expenditure went on the production of aircraft, artillery and ammunition for the war in the West, which was expected to be fairly short. Only then would preparations be made for the attack on Russia.

(c)   The Hitler myth

Given that all Hitler's work ended in disastrous failure, this raises a number of questions: for example, why was he so popular for so long? Was he genuinely popular, or did people merely put up with Hitler and the Nazis through fear of what would happen to them if they complained too loudly? Was his popular image just a myth created by Goebbels's propaganda machine?

There can be no doubt that Hitler's achievements in foreign affairs were extremely popular; with each new success – announcement of rearmament, remilitarization of the Rhineland, the *Anschluss* with Austria and the incorporation of Czechoslovakia into the Reich, it seemed that Germany was reasserting its rightful position as a great power. This was where Goebbels's propaganda probably had its greatest impact on public opinion, building up Hitler's image as the charismatic and infallible Messiah who was destined to restore the greatness of the Fatherland. Even though there was little enthusiasm for war, Hitler's popularity reached new heights in the summer of 1940 with the rapid defeat of France.

There is evidence too that Hitler himself was genuinely popular, although some sections of the Nazi party were not. Gotz Aly argued that ordinary Germans genuinely believed Hitler's promise that he would raise their living standards and many of them had personal experience of improvement. Ian Kershaw, in his earlier work, *The Hitler Myth*, showed that Hitler was seen as being somehow above the unpleasantness of day-to-day politics, and people did not associate him with the excesses of the more extreme party members. The middle and propertied classes were grateful that Hitler had restored law and order; they even approved of the concentration camps, believing that communists and other 'anti-social troublemakers' deserved to be sent there. The propaganda machine helped, by portraying the camps as centres of re-education where undesirables were turned into useful citizens.

However, Richard J. Evans (in *The Third Reich in Power,* 2006) does not go along with the view that Hitler enjoyed widespread support after his first few years in power. He believes that the endless propaganda – in the newspapers, over the radio, in the cinema and in the theatre – together with the experiments in education, the limits on what types of culture were allowed and the constant military parades and Nazi celebrations simply led to boredom and escapism after the initial novelty wore off. Evans argues that the relative lack of opposition can be at least partly explained by the fact that people developed survival strategies, keeping clear of politics and immersing themselves in private, family and church life. Fear of arrest and violence were still the main reason why the vast majority of people merely tolerated the Nazis There can be no doubt that it was difficult and risky to criticize the regime; the government controlled all the media, so that the normal channels of criticism that exist in a modern democratic society were not available to ordinary Germans. Anyone who tried even to initiate discussion about Nazi policies risked the threats of informers, the Gestapo and the concentration camps.

It was during 1941 that Hitler's image became seriously tarnished. As the war dragged on, and Hitler declared war on the USA, doubts about his infallibility began to creep in. The realization gradually dawned that the war could not be won. In February 1943, as news of the German surrender at Stalingrad spread, a group of students at Munich university courageously issued a manifesto: 'The nation is deeply shaken by the destruction of the men of Stalingrad ... the World War 1 corporal has senselessly and irresponsibly driven three hundred and thirty thousand German men to death and ruin. Führer, we thank you!' Six of the leaders were arrested by the Gestapo and executed, and several others were given lengthy jail sentences. After that the majority of people remained loyal to Hitler, and there was no popular uprising against him. The only significant attempt to overthrow him was made by a group of army leaders in July 1944; after the failure of that plot to blow Hitler up, the general public remained loyal to the bitter end, partly through fear of the consequences if they were seen to have turned against the Nazis, and partly through fatalism and resignation.

(d) A weak dictator?

It was the German historian Hans Mommsen, writing in 1966, who first suggested that Hitler was a 'weak dictator'. He meant, apparently, that in spite of all the propaganda about the charismatic leader and the man of destiny, Hitler had no special programme or plan, and simply exploited circumstances as they occurred. Martin Broszat, in his 1969 book *The Hitler State*, developed this theme further, arguing that many of the policies attributed to Hitler were in fact instigated or pressed on him by others and then taken up by Hitler.

The opposite view, that Hitler was an all-powerful dictator, also has its strong proponents. Norman Rich, in *Hitler's War Aims* (vol. 1, 1973), believed that Hitler was 'master in the Third Reich'. Eberhard Jäckel has consistently held to the same interpretation ever since his first book about Hitler appeared in 1984 (*Hitler in History*): he used the term 'monocracy' to describe Hitler's 'sole rule'.

In his recent massive, two-volume biography of Hitler, Ian Kershaw suggests a 'half-and-half' interpretation. He emphasizes the theory of 'working towards the Führer' – a phrase used in a speech in 1934 by a Nazi official who was explaining how government policy took shape:

> It is the duty of every single person, to attempt in the spirit of the Führer to work towards him. Anyone making mistakes will notice it soon enough. But the one who works correctly towards the Führer along his lines and towards his aim, will in future have the finest reward of suddenly one day attaining the legal confirmation of his work.

Kershaw explains how this worked: 'initiatives were taken, pressures created, legislation instigated – all in ways which fell into line with what were taken to be Hitler's aims, and without the dictator necessarily having to dictate. ... In this way, policy became increasingly radicalized.' The classic example of this way of working was the gradual introduction of the Nazi campaign against the Jews (see Section 6.8). It was a method of working which had the advantage that if any policy went wrong, Hitler could dissociate himself from it and blame somebody else.

In practice, therefore, this was hardly the method of a 'weak dictator'. Nor did he always wait for people to 'work towards him'. When occasion demanded it, he was the one who took the initiative and got what he wanted; for example, all his early foreign policy successes, the suppression of the SA in 1934, and the decisions that he took in 1939–40 during the early part of the war, when he reached the peak of his popularity – there was nothing weak about any of this. People who knew him well recognized how he became more 'masterful' as his confidence grew. Otto Dietrich, Hitler's Press Chief, described in his memoirs how Hitler changed: he 'began to hate objections to his views and doubts on their infallibility. ... He wanted to speak, but not to listen. He wanted to be the hammer, not the anvil.'

Clearly Hitler could not have carried out Nazi policies without the support of many influential groups in society – the army, big business, heavy industry, the law courts and the civil service. But equally, without Hitler at the head, much of what happened during those terrible 12 years of the Third Reich would have been unthinkable. Ian Kershaw provides this chilling verdict on Hitler and his regime:

> Never in history has such ruination – physical and moral – been associated with the name of one man. ... Hitler's name justifiably stands for all time as that of the chief instigator of the most profound collapse of civilization in modern times. ... Hitler was the main instigator of a war leaving over 50 million dead and millions more grieving their lost ones and trying to put their shattered lives together again. Hitler was the chief inspiration of a genocide the like of which the world had never known. ... The Reich whose glory he had sought lay at the end wrecked. ... The arch-enemy, Bolshevism, stood in the Reich capital itself and presided over half of Europe.

FURTHER READING

Aly, G., *Hitler's Beneficiaries: How the Nazis Bought the German People* (Verso, 2007).

Baranowski, S., *Nazi Empire: German Colonialism and Imperialism from Bismarck to Hitler* (Cambridge University Press, 2010).

Broszat, M., *The Hitler State* (Longman, 1983).

Bullock, A., *Hitler: A Study in Tyranny* (Penguin, 1990 edition).

Burleigh, M., *The Third Reich: A New History* (Macmillan, 2001).

Evans, R. J., *The Coming of the Third Reich* (Penguin Allen Lane, 2003).

Evans, R. J., *The Third Reich in Power* (Penguin Allen Lane, 2006).

Fest, J., *Hitler* (Penguin, new edition, 1982).

Fest, J., *The Face of the Third Reich: Portraits of the Nazi Leadership* (Tauris Parke, 2011).

Friedlander, S., *The Years of Extermination: Nazi Germany and the Jews 1939–1945* (Weidenfeld & Nicolson, 2007).

Gellately, R., *Backing Hitler: Consent and Coercion in Nazi Germany* (Oxford University Press, 2001).

Henig, R., *The Weimar Republic* (Routledge, 1998).

Housden, M., *Hitler: Study of a Revolutionary* (Routledge, 2000).

Kershaw, I., *Hitler, 1889–1936: Hubris* (Penguin/Allen Lane, 1998).

Kershaw, I., *Hitler, 1936–1945: Nemesis* (Penguin/Allen Lane, 2000).

Machtan, L., *The Hidden Hitler* (Perseus Press, 2000).

Mommsen, H. (ed.) *The Third Reich between Vision and Reality* (Oxford University Press, 2001).

Namier, L., *Avenues of History* (Hamish Hamilton, 1952).

Overy, R. J., *The Dictators* (Allen Lane, 2004).

Tooze, A., *The Wages of Destruction: The Making and Breaking of the Nazi Economy* (Penguin, 2007).

Traynor, J., *Mastering Modern German History* (Palgrave Macmillan, 2008).

Wright, J., *Gustav Stresemann: Weimar's Greatest Statesman* (Oxford University Press, 2002).

1 Describe how the Weimar government and constitution came into existence after the end of the First World War, and explain why the Republic was so unstable in the years 1919 to 1923.

2 'The political instability of the Weimar Republic in the years 1919 to 1923 was largely the result of flaws in the constitution.' Explain why you agree or disagree with this interpretation of events.

3 How far would you agree that it was political intrigue rather than the economic situation that enabled Hitler to come to power in Germany in January 1933?

4 How far was the popularity of Nazi ideology responsible for the success of the Nazi Party in the elections of 1930 to 1932?

   (a) Explain why Hitler introduced the Enabling Law in March 1933.

   (b) 'Hitler's dictatorship was complete by August 1934 and it was achieved entirely by legal means.' Explain why you agree or disagree with this view.

5 To what extent did Hitler bring about a political, economic and social revolution in Nazi Germany in the years 1933 to 1939?

6 (a) Explain why the Nazis encouraged membership of the Hitler Youth and the League of German Maidens.

   (b) 'In the years 1933 to 1939 there was support for the Nazis from all sections of German society.' Explain why you agree or disagree with this view.

7 (a) Explain why the Nazis wanted control over the media.

   (b) How far would you agree or disagree with the view that the various forms of Nazi propaganda had very little impact on the German people by 1939?

8 How far would you agree that the main reason for Hitler's persecution of the Jews was that he was committed to racial purity?

▶ There is a document question about how the Nazi state was run on the website.

Chapter

15 Japan and Spain

SUMMARY OF EVENTS

During the 20 years after Mussolini's March on Rome (1922), many other countries, faced with severe economic problems, followed the examples of Italy and Germany and turned to fascism or right-wing nationalism.

In **Japan** the democratically elected government, increasingly embarrassed by economic, financial and political problems, fell under the influence of the army in the early 1930s. The military soon involved Japan in war with China, and later took the country into the Second World War with its attack on Pearl Harbor (1941). After a brilliant start, the Japanese eventually suffered defeat and devastation when the two atomic bombs were dropped, the first on Hiroshima and the second on Nagasaki. After the war Japan returned to democracy and made a remarkable recovery, soon becoming one of the world's most powerful states economically. During the 1990s the economy began to stagnate; it seemed as though the time had come for some new economic policies.

In **Spain** an incompetent parliamentary government was replaced by General Primo de Rivera, who ruled from 1923 until 1930 as a sort of benevolent dictator. The world economic crisis brought him down, and in an atmosphere of growing republicanism, King Alfonso XIII abdicated, hoping to avoid bloodshed (1931). Various republican governments failed to solve the many problems facing them, and the situation deteriorated into civil war (1936–9) with the forces of the right fighting the left-wing republic. The war was won by the right-wing Nationalists, whose leader, General Franco, became head of the government. He kept Spain neutral during the Second World War, and stayed in power until his death in 1975, after which the monarchy was restored and the country gradually returned to democracy. In 1986 Spain became a member of the European Union.

Portugal also had a right-wing dictatorship – Antonio Salazar ruled from 1932 until he had a stroke in 1968. His *Estado Novo* (New State) was sustained by the army and the secret police. In 1974 his successor was overthrown and democracy returned to Portugal. Although all three regimes – in Japan, Spain and Portugal – had many features similar to the regimes of Mussolini and Hitler, such as a one-party totalitarian state, death or imprisonment of opponents, secret police and brutal repression, they were not, strictly speaking, fascist states: they lacked the vital element of mass mobilization in pursuit of the rebirth of the nation, which was such a striking feature in Italy and Germany.

Many South American politicians were influenced by fascism. Juan Perón, leader of **Argentina** from 1943 until 1955 and again in 1973–4, and Getulio Vargas, who led *Estado Novo* (New State) in **Brazil** from 1939 until 1945, were two of those who were impressed by the apparent success of Fascist Italy and Nazi Germany. They adopted some of the European fascist ideas, especially the mobilization of mass support. They won huge support from the poor working classes in the mass union movement. But they weren't really like Mussolini and Hitler either. Their governments can best be summed up as a combination of nationalism and social reform. As historian Eric Hobsbawm puts it (in his

The Age of Extremes): 'European fascist movements destroyed labour movements, the Latin American leaders they inspired, created them.'

15.1 JAPAN BEFORE THE SECOND WORLD WAR

(a)   In 1918 Japan was in a strong position in the Far East

Japan's close contact with the West dated back to 1853, when the American Commodore Matthew Perry sailed into Yokohama harbour with four battleships and demanded that Japan should open up trade with the USA. Over the next five years Japan had little choice but to sign trade treaties with several Western countries. It was clear that the Western powers had imperialist designs on Japan, and the signing of these treaties was regarded by the Japanese as a great national humiliation. Gradually a determination to modernize and strengthen the country developed. Beginning in 1868 with the restoration of the Meiji emperor, the Japanese embarked on a policy of building railways, improving the road system, starting modern industries, like cotton and silk manufacture, and introducing a more democratic parliamentary system, modelled on Germany's constitution. For the first time in over two and a half centuries Japan became a unified and centralized empire. The government decided that the best way to prevent the western powers from treating Japan in the same way as China was to occupy neighbouring territories; first Korea and then Manchuria were 'colonized', but this caused two wars, first with China (1894–95) and then with Russia (1904–5). Japan was victorious in both wars; in the case of Russia, this was the first time that an Asian country had defeated one of the European great powers. It meant that Japan was now the dominant power in the Far East. A military alliance had already been signed with Britain in 1902, and when the First World War broke out in 1914, Japan entered the war on the side of Britain. Their main contribution was to seize German colonies and bases in China. Japan was represented at the Versailles peace conference in 1919, became a member of the League of Nations and was officially recognized as one of the 'Big Five' world powers. Japan now had a powerful navy, a well-trained and well-equipped army and a great deal of influence in China.

Japan had also benefited economically from the First World War, while the states of Europe were busy fighting each other. Japan took advantage of the situation both by providing the Allies with shipping and other goods, and by stepping in to supply orders, especially in Asia, which the Europeans could not fulfil. During the war years, the exports of Japanese cotton cloth almost trebled, while their merchant fleet doubled in tonnage. Politically the course seemed set fair for democracy when in 1925 all adult males were given the vote. Hopes were soon dashed: at the beginning of the 1930s the army assumed control of the government.

(b)   Why did Japan become a military dictatorship?

During the 1920s problems developed, as they did in Italy and Germany, which democratically elected governments seemed incapable of solving.

1   Influential elite groups began to oppose democracy
Democracy was still relatively new in Japan; it was during the 1880s that the emperor gave way to the growing demands for a national assembly, in the belief that it was constitutions and representative government which had made the USA and the countries of western Europe so successful. Gradually a more representative system was introduced consisting of a house of appointed peers, a cabinet of ministers appointed by the emperor, and a Privy

Council whose function was to interpret and safeguard the new constitution, which was formally accepted in 1889. It provided for an elected lower house of parliament (the Diet); the first elections were held and the Diet met in 1890. However, the system was far from democratic and the emperor retained enormous power: he could dissolve the Diet whenever he felt like it, he took decisions about war and peace, he was commander-in-chief of the armed forces, and he was regarded as 'sacred and inviolable'. But the Diet had one great advantage: it could initiate new laws, and consequently the cabinet found that it was not as susceptible to their will as they had expected.

At first the elite groups in society were content to give the government free rein, but after the First World War they began to be more critical. Especially troublesome were the army and the conservatives, who were strongly entrenched in the house of Peers and in the Privy Council. They seized every opportunity to discredit the government. For example, they criticized Baron Shidehara Kijuro (foreign minister 1924–7) for his conciliatory approach to China, which he thought was the best way to strengthen Japan's economic hold over that country. The army was itching to interfere in China, which was torn by civil war, and considered Shidehara's policy to be 'soft'. They were strong enough to bring the government down in 1927 and reverse his policy.

2 Corrupt politicians

Many politicians were corrupt and regularly accepted bribes from big business; sometimes fighting broke out in the lower house (the Diet) as charges and counter-charges of corruption were flung about. The system no longer inspired respect, and the prestige of parliament suffered.

3 The trade boom ended

When economic problems were added to the political ones, the situation became serious. The great trading boom of the war years lasted only until the middle of 1921, when Europe began to revive and recover lost markets. In Japan, unemployment and industrial unrest developed, and at the same time farmers were hit by the rapidly falling price of rice caused by a series of bumper harvests. When farmers and industrial workers tried to organize themselves into a political party, they were ruthlessly suppressed by the police. Thus the workers, as well as the army and the right, gradually became hostile to a parliament which posed as democratic, but allowed the left to be suppressed, and accepted bribes from big business.

4 The world economic crisis

The world economic crisis beginning in 1929 (see Section 22.6) affected Japan severely. Exports shrank disastrously and other countries introduced or raised tariffs against Japanese goods to safeguard their own industries. One of the worst affected trades was the export of raw silk, which went mostly to the USA. The period after the Wall Street Crash was no time for luxuries, and the Americans drastically reduced their imports of raw silk, so that by 1932 the price had fallen to less than one-fifth of the 1923 figure. This was a further blow for Japanese farmers, since about half of them relied for their livelihood on the production of raw silk as well as rice. There was desperate poverty, especially in the north, for which factory workers and peasants blamed the government and big business. Most of the army recruits were peasants; consequently the rank-and-file as well as the officer class were disgusted with what they took to be weak parliamentary government. As early as 1927, many officers, attracted by fascism, were planning to seize power and introduce a strong nationalist government.

5 The situation in Manchuria

Matters were brought to a head in 1931 by the situation in Manchuria, a large province of China, with a population of 30 million, in which Japan had valuable investments and trade.

The Chinese were trying to squeeze out Japanese trade and business, which would have been a severe blow to a Japanese economy already hard hit by the depression. To preserve their economic advantages, Japanese army units invaded and occupied Manchuria (September 1931) without permission from the government. When Prime Minister Inukai criticized extremism, he was assassinated by a group of army officers (May 1932); not surprisingly, his successor felt he had to support the army's actions.

For the next 13 years the army more or less ran the country, introducing similar methods to those adopted in Italy and Germany: ruthless suppression of communists, assassination of opponents, tight control of education, a build-up of armaments and an aggressive foreign policy which aimed to capture territory in Asia to serve as markets for Japanese exports. This led to an attack on China (1937) and participation in the Second World War in the Pacific (see Section 6.2(c), Maps 6.4 and 5.1 for Japanese conquests). Some historians blame Emperor Hirohito who, though he deplored the attack on Manchuria, refused to become involved in political controversy, afraid to risk his orders for a withdrawal being ignored. Historian Richard Storry claims that 'it would have been better for Japan and for the world if the risk had been taken'. He believes that Hirohito's prestige was so great that the majority of officers would have obeyed him if he had tried to restrain the attacks on Manchuria and China. When the Second World War began, it seems that the emperor genuinely wanted to stay out of it, and hesitated over whether or not to sign an alliance with Nazi Germany. However, after the early successes of the German *Blitzkrieg* he agreed to the alliance, and eventually, to the attack on Pearl Harbor (see Section 6.2(c)), thereby giving the military the chance to achieve their ambition – to continue with the conquest of China and south-east Asia.

The war began successfully for the Japanese: by May 1942 they had captured Hong Kong, Malaya, Singapore and Burma (all belonging to Britain), the Dutch East Indies, the Philippines and two American possessions – Guam and Wake Island. There seemed no way of stopping them. However, it became clear that the attack on Pearl Harbor was not quite the success it had seemed at first. It did not destroy the American aircraft carriers which were out at sea, and it was the aircraft carriers that were to prove the vital element in Japan's defeat. In June the Americans, using planes from three aircraft carriers, inflicted a severe defeat on the Japanese at Midway Island (see Section 6.3(a)). This proved to be a crucial turning point in the war, with Japan suffering a series of reverses over the next over the next three years. It was a long and bitter struggle which ended in August 1945 with the Japanese surrender after the Americans had dropped two atomic bombs, one on Hiroshima and the second on Nagasaki. Japan's ambitions of a great empire were dashed and the country and its economy were largely in ruins.

15.2 JAPAN RECOVERS

At the end of the Second World War the Japanese were defeated; their economy was in ruins with a large proportion of their factories and a quarter of their housing destroyed by bombing (see Sections 6.5(f) and 6.6(d)). Until 1952 the country was occupied by Allied troops, mostly American, under the command of General MacArthur. For the first three years the Americans aimed to make sure the Japanese could never again start a war – they were forbidden to have armed forces and were given a democratic constitution under which ministers had to be members of the Diet (parliament). The Emperor Hirohito was allowed to remain on the throne, but in a purely symbolic role. Nationalist organizations were disbanded and the armaments industry was dismantled. People who had played leading roles during the war were removed, and an international tribunal was set up to deal with those accused of war crimes. The wartime prime minister, Tojo, and six others were executed, and 16 men were given life sentences.

The Americans did not at this stage seem concerned to restore the Japanese economy. During 1948 the American attitude gradually changed: as the Cold War developed in Europe and the Kuomintang crumbled in China, they felt the need for a strong ally in south-east Asia and began to encourage Japanese economic recovery. From 1950 industry recovered rapidly and by 1953 production had reached the 1937 levels. American occupying forces were withdrawn in April 1952 (as had been agreed by the *Treaty of San Francisco* the previous September) though some American troops remained for defence purposes.

(a) How was Japan's rapid recovery possible?

1 *American help was vital in the early years of Japanese recovery.* The USA decided that an economically healthy Japan would be a strong bulwark against the spread of communism in south-east Asia. The Americans believed that it was important to move Japan away from the semi-feudal and hierarchical system, which was restrictive of progress. For example, half the agricultural land was owned by wealthy landlords who lived in the cities and rented small plots out to tenants, most of whom were little more than subsistence farmers. *A land-reform plan was introduced* which took much of the land away from the landlords and sold it to the tenants at reasonable rates, creating a new class of owner–farmers. This was a great success: the farmers, helped by government subsidies and regulations which kept agricultural prices high, became a prosperous and influential group. The Americans helped in other ways too: Japanese goods were allowed into American markets on favourable terms and the USA supplied aid and new equipment.

2 *The Korean War (1950–3) gave an important boost to Japan's recovery.* Japan was ideally placed to act as a base for the United Nations forces involved in Korea; Japanese manufacturers were used to provide a wide range of materials and supplies. The close relationship with the USA meant that Japan's security was well taken care of; this meant that Japan was able to invest in industry all the cash that would otherwise have been spent on armaments.

3 Much of Japan's industry had been destroyed during the war; this enabled *the new factories and plants to start afresh with all the latest technology*. In 1959 the government decided to concentrate on high-technology goods both for the home market and for export. The domestic consumer market was helped by another government initiative started in 1960, which aimed to double incomes over the next decade. The demands of the export market led to the construction of larger and faster transport ships. Japanese products gained a reputation for high quality and reliability and were highly competitive in foreign markets. Throughout the 1960s, Japanese exports expanded at an annual rate of over 15 per cent. By 1972 Japan had overtaken West Germany to become the world's third largest economy, specializing in shipbuilding, radio, television and hi-fi equipment, cameras, steel, motorcycles, motor cars and textiles.

4 *Recovery was helped by a series of stable governments.* The dominant party was the Liberal-Democratic Party (LDP); it was conservative and pro-business in character, and it had the solid support of the farmers who had benefited from the land reform carried through by the Americans. They were afraid that their land would be nationalized if the socialists came to power; so the LDP was consistently in government from 1952 until 1993. The main opposition was provided by the Japan Socialist Party, which changed its name to the Social Democratic Party of Japan in 1991; it drew most of its support from workers, trade unions and a large slice of the city population. There were two smaller socialist parties and the Japan Communist

Party. This fragmentation of the left was one of the reasons for the LDP's continued success.

(b)   Japanese recovery was not without its problems

1   *There was a good deal of anti-American feeling in some quarters.*

- Many Japanese felt inhibited by their close ties with the USA.
- They felt that the Americans exaggerated the threat from communist China; they wanted good relations with China and the USSR but this was difficult with Japan so firmly in the American camp.
- The renewal of the defence treaty with the USA in 1960 caused strikes and demonstrations.
- There was resentment among the older generation at the way in which Japanese youth culture was taking on all things American, which were seen as a sign of 'moral decay'.

2   *Another problem was working-class unrest at long working hours and overcrowded living conditions.* As industry expanded, workers flocked into the industrial areas from the countryside; the rural population fell from about 50 per cent of the total in 1945, to only 20 per cent in 1970. This caused severe overcrowding in most towns and cities, where flats were tiny compared with those in the West. As property prices rose, the chances of ordinary workers being able to buy their own homes virtually disappeared. As cities grew larger, there were serious problems of congestion and pollution. Commuting times became longer; male workers were expected to dedicate themselves to the 'firm' or the 'office culture', and leisure time dwindled.

3   *During the early 1970s the high economic growth rate came to an end.* A variety of factors contributed to this. Japanese competitiveness in world markets declined in certain industries – particularly shipbuilding and steel. Concerns about the growing problems of urban life led to some questioning of the assumption that continuing growth was essential for national success. The economy was disrupted by fluctuating oil prices; in 1973–4 the Organization of Petroleum Exporting Countries (OPEC) raised their oil prices, partly in order to conserve supplies. The same happened in 1979–81, and on both occasions Japan suffered recessions. One Japanese response to this was to increase investment in the generation of nuclear power.

4   *Japan's prosperity aroused some hostility abroad.* There were constant protests from the USA, Canada and western Europe that the Japanese were flooding foreign markets with their exports while refusing to buy a comparable amount of imports from their customers. In response Japan abolished or reduced import duties on almost 200 commodities (1982–3) and agreed to limit car exports to the USA (November 1983); the French themselves restricted imports of cars, televisions and radios from Japan. To compensate for these setbacks the Japanese managed to achieve a 20 per cent increase in exports to the European Community between January and May 1986.

In spite of these problems, there is no doubt that in the mid-1980s the Japanese economy was still a staggering success; the total Gross National Product (GNP) amounted to about one-tenth of world output. With its huge export trade and relatively modest domestic consumption, Japan enjoyed an enormous trade surplus, was the world's leading net creditor nation and gave away more in development aid than any other country. Inflation was well under control at below 3 per cent and unemployment was relatively low at less than 3 per cent of the working population (1.6 million in 1984). The Japanese success story was symbolized by a remarkable engineering feat – a tunnel 54 kilometres long linking Honshu (the largest island) with Hokkaido to the north. Completed in 1985, it had taken 21 years to build and was the world's longest tunnel. Another new development which continued into the 1990s was that Japanese manufacturers were beginning to set up car, electronics and textile factories in the USA, Britain and western Europe; Japanese economic success and power seemed without limit.

(c) Economic and political change: 1990–2004

During the early 1990s the strange paradox of the Japanese economy became more obvious: domestic consumption began to stagnate; statistics showed that the Japanese were now consuming less than the Americans, British and Germans, because of higher Japanese prices, wage increases which lagged behind inflation, and the exorbitant cost of property in Japan. It was the export trade which continued to earn the Japanese their massive surpluses. The 1980s had been a time of feverish speculation and government overspending in order, it was claimed, to improve the country's infrastructure. However, this led to a severe recession in 1992–3 and left the public finances in an unhealthy state.

As economic growth slowed down and then stagnated, worker productivity declined and industry became less competitive. Although unemployment was low by Western standards, layoffs became more common and the traditional Japanese policies of jobs for life and company paternalism began to be abandoned. Industrialists began to produce more goods in other countries outside Japan in order to remain competitive. By the end of the century there were worrying signs: Japan had moved into a recession and there seemed little prospect of an end to it. The statistics were discouraging; the trade surplus was shrinking rapidly and exports were falling – the first six months of 2001 showed the largest export fall on record. By the end of the year industrial production had fallen to a 13-year low. Worse still, unemployment had risen to 5.4 per cent, an unheard of level since the 1930s.

As American historian and Japanese expert R. T. Murphy put it (in 2002):

The Japanese government has been presiding for a decade now over a stagnant economy, a ruined financial system and a demoralized citizenry. ... Japan finds itself unable to rethink the economic policies pursued since the immediate postwar years. Those policies – export like mad and hoard foreign exchange earnings – were so obvious they required no political discussion. But now that the policies must be reordered [given that there is reduced demand for Japanese exports] Japan is waking up to the melancholy reality that it is unable to change course.

He lays the blame for this on the bureaucracy and the debt-laden banking community, which, he says, are insulated from any kind of government interference and control, and have been guilty of 'disastrous irresponsibility'.

There were important changes on the political scene. In the early 1990s, the LDP, which had held power since 1952, suffered a series of unpleasant shocks when some of its members were involved in corruption scandals. There were many resignations and in the election of July 1993, the LDP lost its majority to a coalition of opposition parties. There was a period of political instability, with no fewer than four different prime ministers in the year following the election. One of them was a socialist, the first left-wing prime minister since 1948. However, the LDP kept a foothold in government by forming a surprise coalition with the Social Democratic Party of Japan (formerly the Japan Socialist

Party). At the end of 1994 the other opposition parties also formed a coalition, calling themselves the New Frontier Party. The LDP remained in government through to the elections of 2001, in which it scored yet another victory, this time in coalition with the New Conservative Party and a Buddhist party.

15.3 SPAIN

(a) Spain in the 1920s and 1930s

The constitutional monarchy under Alfonso XIII (king since 1885) was never very efficient and reached rock bottom in 1921 when a Spanish army, sent to put down a revolt led by Abd-el-Krim in Spanish Morocco, was massacred by the Moors. In 1923 General Primo de Rivera seized power in a bloodless coup, with Alfonso's approval, and ruled for the next seven years. The king called him 'my Mussolini', but though Primo was a military dictator, he was not a fascist. He was responsible for a number of public works – railways, roads and irrigation schemes; industrial production developed at three times the rate before 1923; most impressive of all, he succeeded in ending the war in Morocco (1925).

When the world economic crisis reached Spain in 1930, unemployment rose, and Primo and his advisers bungled the finances, causing depreciation of the currency. The army withdrew its support, whereupon Primo resigned. In April 1931 municipal elections were held in which the Republicans won control of all the large cities. As huge crowds gathered on the streets of Madrid, Alfonso decided to abdicate to avoid bloodshed, and a republic was proclaimed. The monarchy had been overthrown without bloodshed, but unfortunately the slaughter had merely been postponed until 1936.

(b) Why did civil war break out in Spain in 1936?

1 The new republic faced some serious problems

- Catalonia and the Basque provinces (see Map 15.1) wanted independence.
- The Roman Catholic Church was bitterly hostile to the republic, which in return disliked the Church and was determined to reduce its power.
- It was felt that the army had too much influence in politics and might attempt another coup.
- There were additional problems caused by the depression: agricultural prices were falling, wine and olive exports declined, land went out of cultivation and peasant unemployment rose. In industry, iron production fell by a third and steel production by almost half. It was a time of falling wages, unemployment and declining standards of living. Unless it could make some headway with this final problem, the republic was likely to lose the support of the workers.

2 Right-wing opposition

The left's solutions to these problems were not acceptable to the right, which became increasingly alarmed at the prospect of social revolution. The dominant grouping in the *Cortes* (parliament), the socialists and middle-class radicals, began energetically:

- Catalonia was allowed some self-government.
- An attack was made on the Church – Church and State were separated, priests would no longer be paid by the government, Jesuits were expelled, other orders could be dissolved and religious education in schools ceased.

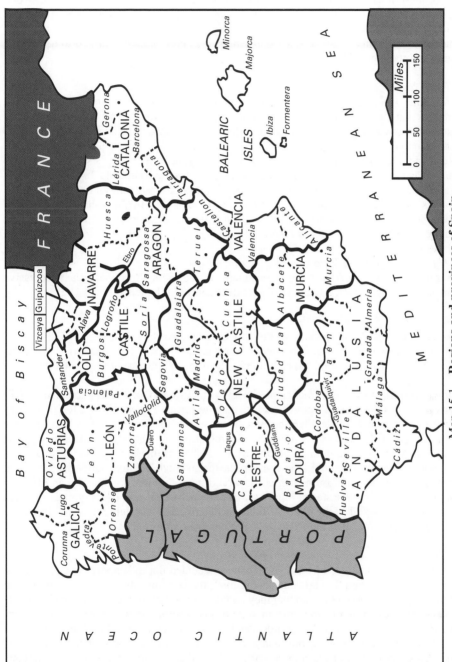

Map 15.1 **Regions and provinces of Spain**

- A large number of army officers were compulsorily retired.
- A start was made on the nationalization of large estates.
- Attempts were made to raise the wages of industrial workers.

Each of these measures infuriated one or other of the right-wing groups – Church, army, landowners and industrialists. In 1932 some army officers tried to overthrow the prime minister, Manuel Azaña, but the rising was easily suppressed, as the majority of the army remained loyal at this stage. A new right-wing party, the *Ceda*, was formed to defend the Church and the landlords.

3   Left-wing opposition
The republic was further weakened by opposition from two powerful left-wing groups, the anarchists and the syndicalists (a group of powerful trade unions), who favoured a general strike and the overthrow of the capitalist system. They despised the socialists for co-operating with the middle-class groups. They organized strikes, riots and assassinations. Matters came to a head in January 1933 when some government guards set fire to houses in the village of Casas Viejas near Cadiz, to smoke out some anarchists. In total 25 people were killed, which lost the government much working-class support, and caused even the socialists to withdraw support from Azaña, who resigned. In the following elections (November 1933) the right-wing parties won a majority, the largest group being the new Catholic *Ceda* under its leader Gil Robles.

4   The actions of the new right-wing government
The actions of the new right-wing government were designed to reverse the progressive elements of Azaña's policies, and understandably aroused the left to fury. They

- cancelled most of Azaña's reforms;
- interfered with the working of the new Catalan government; and
- refused to allow the Basques self-government. This was a serious error, since the Basques had supported the right in the elections, but now switched to the left.

As the government moved further right, the left-wing groups (socialists, anarchists, syndicalists and now communists) drew closer together to form a *Popular Front*. Revolutionary violence grew: anarchists derailed the Barcelona–Seville express, killing 19 people; there was a general strike in 1934 and there were rebellions in Catalonia and Asturias. The miners of Asturias fought bravely but were crushed ruthlessly by troops under the command of General Franco. In the words of historian Hugh Thomas, 'after the manner in which the revolution had been quelled, it would have required a superhuman effort to avoid the culminating disaster of civil war. But no such effort was forthcoming.' Instead, as the financial, as well as the political situation deteriorated, the right fell apart, and in the elections of February 1936 the *Popular Front* emerged victorious.

5   The new government turned out to be ineffective
The left-wing socialists, led by Largo Caballero, decided not to support the government, since it was largely middle-class and 'bourgeois'; the communists supported him, hoping that the government would fail so that they could seize power. In fact, Caballero had made no plans for a revolution of this sort, in spite of his revolutionary language. The government seemed incapable of keeping order, and crisis point came in July 1936 when Calvo Sotelo, the leading right-wing politician, was murdered by members of the Republican guard. This terrified the right and convinced them that revolution was imminent. They decided that *the only way to restore order was by a military dictatorship*. A group of army leaders, chiefly Generals Mola and Sanjurjos, conspiring with the right, especially with the

new fascist *Falange* party of José Antonio de Rivera (Primo's son), had already planned a military takeover. Using Calvo Sotelo's murder as a pretext, they began a revolt in Morocco, where General Franco soon assumed the leadership. They claimed to be fighting to restore law and order and to defend the Church against the godless communists. The civil war had begun.

(c) The civil war, 1936–9

By the end of July 1936, the right, calling themselves *Nationalists*, controlled much of the north, where they set up their capital at Burgos, and the area around Cadiz and Seville in the south. However, the risings in Madrid and Barcelona, the two most important cities, had been suppressed. This meant that the plan to take over the whole country in one fell swoop had failed, leaving the *Republicans* in control of the centre and north-east, including Madrid and Barcelona. The military strengths of the two sides seemed to be fairly evenly balanced with about half the army, air force and navy remaining on the side of the Republic.

The struggle was a bitter one in which both sides committed terrible atrocities. The Church suffered horrifying losses at the hands of the Republicans, with over 6000 priests and nuns murdered. When the Nationalists captured Republican areas, they killed thousands of Republican leaders and supporters. According to Hugh Thomas, the Nationalists murdered 75 000 people, the Republicans 55 000. Together with those killed in battle, the total deaths in the war reached around half a million. The Nationalists were helped by Italy and Germany, who sent arms and men, together with food supplies and raw materials. Mussolini provided 70 000 troops and Hitler sent tanks and allowed his air force to practice bombing undefended civilian targets. The most notorious of these attacks took place in April 1937 when around a hundred bombers of the German Condor Legion destroyed the defenceless Basque market town of Guernica, killing 1600 people.

The Republicans received some help from Russia in the form of troops, tanks and planes, but France and Britain refused to intervene. In fact all the powers – Germany, Italy, Britain, France and the USSR – had given an undertaking to remain neutral, but only Britain and France kept the agreement. The Republicans were also helped by some 40 000 foreign volunteers from over fifty nations. These International Brigades were organized and deployed by the Russians, working from a base in Paris. The Nationalists slowly but surely wore down the Republicans, capturing Barcelona and the whole of Catalonia in January 1939. Only Madrid remained in Republican hands and the war ended in March 1939 when Madrid surrendered to Franco's forces (Map 15.2).

Reasons for the Nationalist victory

- Franco was extremely skilful in holding together the various right-wing groups (army, Church, monarchists and Falangists) so that they worked as a single military and political unit, with one central aim – to crush the godless republicans.
- The Republicans were much less united, and anarchists and communists actually fought each other for a time in Barcelona. At first things seemed to go well. Largo Caballero was the head of the Popular Front government and the communists announced that they were postponing the revolution in order to work with socialists and republicans to defeat the hated fascists (they labelled all the Nationalist groups as fascists). Even the anarchists joined the government. But gradually the unity began to fall apart. The communists themselves were divided: some were Stalinists and some were Trotskyites (known by their initials as POUM). Disagreements developed in Barcelona, and the Stalinists came to blows with the other two groups. Caballero was replaced by the socialist Juan Negrín.

HELPING NATIONALISTS
15,000 German troops plus the Condor Legion
20,000 Portuguese troops
50,000 Italian troops

AREAS CAPTURED BY THE NATIONALISTS
By end of 1937
By end of 1938
By Spring 1939

FRANCE

Guernica

Barcelona

PORTUGAL

Madrid

Valencia

This area held out until the war ended, March 1939

HELPING REPUBLICANS
500 Russian troops
40,000 International Brigade troops (foreign volunteers)

Seville

Granada

Cadiz

Almeria

SPANISH MOROCCO

0   200 km

Original Nationalist attack

Map 15.2   **The Spanish Civil War, 1936–9**

- The extent of foreign help for the Nationalists was probably decisive, especially in the early part of the war. For example, Mussolini provided the transport aircraft to bring Franco's army across to Spain from Morocco, after Franco had decided it was too risky to bring them by sea.

(d) Franco in power

In the immediate aftermath of the war, thousands of republicans fled the country, many of them crossing the frontier into France. But thousands more were captured by Nationalist forces and imprisoned. It is estimated that between 1939 and 1943 about 150 000 of them were executed. Meanwhile General Franco, taking the title *Caudillo* (leader), set up a government which was similar in many ways to those of Mussolini and Hitler. It was marked by repression, military courts and mass executions. But in other ways it was not fascist: for example, the regime supported the Church, which was given back its control over education and other areas. That would never have happened in a true fascist state. Franco amalgamated all the right-wing parties under the Falange label, and all other parties and trade unions were banned. Franco himself ruled as a dictator. There was a strict censorship of all media and anyone who criticized the regime was likely to be arrested and sent to a concentration camp. Persistent critics faced the death penalty.

Franco was also shrewd enough to keep Spain out of the Second World War, though Hitler expected Spanish help and tried to persuade Franco to get involved. When Hitler and Mussolini were defeated, Franco survived and ruled Spain until his death in 1975. As Spain moved into the 1950s the regime became less violent, but it continued to be repressive. Franco tried to enforce a rigid nationalism based on traditional Spanish culture. For example, bullfighting and flamenco were encouraged, but the Sardana, the national dance of Catalonia, was banned because it was 'not Spanish'. The use of the Galician, Catalan and Basque languages in official documents was forbidden. The Roman Catholic Church became the established state Church once again and regained many of the privileges that it had lost under the Republic. For example, all civil servants had to be Catholic, and non-church weddings, divorce, contraceptives and abortion were forbidden. Homosexuality and prostitution were criminal offences. All the Republic's legislation designed to improve the position of women in society was cancelled. Now women could not become judges or university professors and could not testify in trials. The civil war had left the economy in ruins and Franco did not help matters by insisting on isolating Spain economically, as far as possible, from the rest of the world. However, the USA and the IMF persuaded him to change to a more free-market economy. In the mid-1950s the economy slowly began to revive.

During the 1960s Franco gradually relaxed the repressiveness of his regime: military courts were abolished, workers were allowed a limited right to strike and elections were introduced for some members of parliament (though political parties were still banned). Much was done to modernize Spanish agriculture and industry and the economy was helped by Spain's growing tourist industry. By the time Franco died at the age of 82 in 1975, most people had begun to enjoy a higher standard of living than ever before. Eventually Franco came to be regarded as standing above politics. He was preparing Alfonso XIII's grandson, Juan Carlos, to succeed him, believing that a conservative monarchy was the best way of keeping Spain stable. When Franco died, Juan Carlos became king, and soon showed that he was in favour of a return to all-party democracy. The first free elections were held in 1977. Later, under the leadership of socialist Prime Minister Felipe González, Spain joined the European Community (January 1986). The economy seemed to be flourishing at first; tourism was a huge revenue earner, and during the early years of the twenty-first century there was a massive boom in house and property building. But following the great financial meltdown of 2008 (see Section 27.7) the euro-zone found itself in serious crisis; Spain's housing and property market collapsed, and Spain, along with Portugal, the Irish Republic and worst of all Greece, was left heavily in debt and needing help from the European Central Bank.

FURTHER READING

Beasley, W. E., *Japanese Imperialism, 1894–1945* (Oxford University Press, 1987).

Beasley, W. E., *The Rise of Modern Japan since 1850* (Phoenix, new edition, 2001).

Beevor, A., *The Battle for Spain: The Spanish Civil War, 1936–1939* (Phoenix, 2007 edition).

Bolloten, B., *The Spanish Civil War: Revolution and Counter-Revolution* (North Carolina University Press, 1991).

Gordon, A., *A Modern History of Japan from Tokugawa Times to the Present* (Oxford University Press, 2008 edition).

Jansen, M. B., *The Making of Modern Japan* (Harvard University Press, 2002 edition).

Murphy, R. T., 'Looking to Game Boy', *London Review of Books* (3 January 2002).

Payne, S. G., *The Franco Regime, 1936–1975* (Wisconsin University Press, new edition, 2011).

Preston, P., *The Spanish Civil War: Reaction, Revolution and Revenge* (Harper, 2006).
Preston, P., *Franco: A Biography* (Fontana, 2011 edition).
Quiroga, A., *Making Spaniards: Primo de Rivera and the Nationalization of the Masses, 1923–1930* (Palgrave Macmillan, 2007).
Storry, R., *A History of Modern Japan* (Penguin, 1990 edition).
Thomas, H., *The Spanish Civil War* (Penguin, fourth edition, 2003).
Williams, B., *Modern Japan* (Longman, 1987).

QUESTIONS

1　How far would you agree that it was the world economic crisis which caused Japan to fall under military rule in the early 1930s?
2　'Japan's recovery after the Second World War was not without its associated problems.' How far do you agree with this view?
3　Explain what changes and problems were experienced by Japan in the years after 1990.
4　Assess the reasons for the outbreak of civil war in Spain in 1936.
5　How far would you agree that it was mainly help from outside that made the Nationalist victory in the Spanish Civil War possible?

◤ There is a document question about the Spanish Civil War on the website.

Part

III

Communism – Rise and Decline

Russia and the revolutions, 1900–24

SUMMARY OF EVENTS

In the early years of the twentieth century, Russia was in a troubled state. Nicholas II, who was Tsar (emperor) from 1894 until 1917, insisted on ruling as an autocrat (someone who rules a country as he sees fit, without being responsible to a parliament), but had failed to deal adequately with the country's many problems. Unrest and criticism of the government reached a climax in 1905 with the Russian defeats in the war against Japan (1904–5); there was a general strike and an attempted revolution, which forced Nicholas to make concessions (the October Manifesto). These included the granting of *an elected parliament* (the *Duma*). When it became clear that the *Duma* was ineffective, unrest increased and culminated, after disastrous Russian defeats in the First World War, in two revolutions, both in 1917.

- The first revolution (February/March) overthrew the Tsar and set up a moderate *provisional government*. When this coped no better than the Tsar, it was itself overthrown by a second uprising:
- *the Bolshevik revolution* (October/November).

The new Bolshevik government was shaky at first, and its opponents (known as the Whites) tried to destroy it, causing a bitter civil war (1918–20). Thanks to the leadership of Lenin and Trotsky, the Bolsheviks (Reds) won the civil war, and, now calling themselves communists, were able to consolidate their power. Lenin began the task of leading Russia to recovery, but he died prematurely in January 1924.

16.1   AFTER 1905: WERE THE REVOLUTIONS OF 1917 INEVITABLE?

(a)   Nicholas II tries to stabilize his regime

Nicholas survived the 1905 revolution because:

- his opponents were not united;
- there was no central leadership (the whole thing having flared up spontaneously);
- most of the army remained loyal;
- he had been willing to compromise at the critical moment by issuing the October Manifesto, promising concessions. These included allowing an elected parliament (Duma); granting basic civil liberties to the population – freedom of conscience, of speech, of assembly and of association; universal suffrage in elections for the Duma; no law could begin to operate without the approval of the Duma.

The Manifesto appeared to grant many of the demands of the moderate liberal reformers, so that tsarism now had a breathing space in which Nicholas had an excellent opportunity to make a constitutional monarchy work, and to throw himself on the side of the moderate reformers. However, there were other demands not addressed in the Manifesto, for example:

- improvements in industrial working conditions and pay;
- cancellation of redemption payments – these were annual payments to the government by peasants in return for their freedom and some land, following the abolition of serfdom in 1861: although peasants had received their legal freedom, these compulsory payments had reduced over half the rural population to dire poverty;
- an amnesty for political prisoners.

Unfortunately Nicholas seems to have had very little intention of keeping to the spirit of the October Manifesto, having agreed to it only because he had no choice.

1 *The First Duma (1906)* was not democratically elected, for although all classes were allowed to vote, the system was rigged so that landowners and the middle classes would be in the majority. Even so, it put forward far-reaching demands such as confiscation of large estates; a genuinely democratic electoral system, and the right of the *Duma* to approve the Tsar's ministers; the right to strike and the abolition of the death penalty. This was far too drastic for Nicholas, who had the *Duma* dispersed by troops after only ten weeks. He was apparently heard to remark that if things continued to go on like this, 'we should find ourselves close to being a democratic republic. That would be senseless and criminal.'
2 *The Second Duma (1907)* suffered the same fate, after which Nicholas changed the voting system, depriving peasants and urban workers of the vote.
3 *The Third Duma (1907–12) and the Fourth Duma (1912–17)* were much more conservative and therefore lasted longer. Though on occasion they criticized the government, they had no power, because the Tsar controlled the ministers and the secret police.

Some foreign observers were surprised at the ease with which Nicholas ignored his promises and was able to dismiss the first two *Dumas* without provoking another general strike. The fact was that the revolutionary impetus had subsided for the time being, and many leaders were either in prison or in exile.

This, together with the improvement in the economy beginning after 1906, has given rise to some controversy about whether or not the 1917 revolutions were inevitable. The traditional liberal view was that although the regime had obvious weaknesses, there were signs that shortly before the First World War broke out, living standards were improving, and that given time, the chances of revolution would have diminished. The strengths were beginning to outweigh the weaknesses, and so the monarchy would probably have survived if Russia had kept out of the war. The Soviet view was that, given the Tsar's deliberate flouting of his 1905 promises, there was bound to be a revolution sooner or later. The situation was deteriorating again *before* Russia's involvement in the First World War; therefore the inevitable completion of the 'unfinished' revolution of 1905–6 could not be long delayed.

(b) Strengths of the regime

1 The government seemed to recover remarkably quickly, with most of its powers intact. Peter Stolypin, prime minister from 1906 to 1911, introduced strict repressive

measures, with some 4000 people being executed over the next three years. But he also brought in some reforms *and made determined efforts to win over the peasants*, believing that, given 20 years of peace, there would be no question of revolution. Redemption payments were abolished and peasants were encouraged to buy their own land; about 2 million had done so by 1916 and another 3.5 million had emigrated to Siberia where they had their own farms. As a result, there emerged a class of comfortably-off peasants (*kulaks*) on whom the government could rely for support against revolution, or so Stolypin hoped.

2   As more factories came under the control of inspectors, there were *signs of improving working conditions*; as industrial profits increased, the first signs of a more prosperous workforce could be detected. In 1912 a workers' sickness and accident insurance scheme was introduced.

3   In 1908 a programme was announced to bring about *universal education within ten years*; by 1914 an extra 50 000 primary schools had been opened.

4   At the same time *the revolutionary parties seemed to have lost heart*; they were short of money, torn by disagreements, and their leaders were still in exile.

(c) Weaknesses of the regime

1   Failure of the land reforms
By 1911 it was becoming clear that Stolypin's land reforms would not have the desired effect, partly because the peasant population was growing too rapidly (at the rate of 1.5 million a year) for his schemes to cope with, and because farming methods were too inefficient to support the growing population adequately. The assassination of Stolypin in 1911 removed one of the few really able tsarist ministers and perhaps the only man who could have saved the monarchy.

2   Industrial unrest
There was a wave of industrial strikes set off by the shooting of 270 striking gold miners in the Lena goldfields in Siberia (April 1912). In all there were over 2000 separate strikes in that year, 2400 in 1913, and over 4000 in the first seven months of 1914, *before* war broke out. Whatever improvements had taken place, they were obviously not enough to remove all the pre-1905 grievances.

3   Government repression
There was little relaxation of the government's repressive policy, as the secret police rooted out revolutionaries among university students and lecturers and deported masses of Jews, thereby ensuring that both groups were firmly anti-tsarist. The situation was particularly dangerous because the government had made the mistake of alienating three of the most important sections in society – peasants, industrial workers and the intelligentsia (educated classes).

4   Revival of the revolutionary parties
As 1912 progressed, the fortunes of the various revolutionary parties, especially *the Bolsheviks and Mensheviks*, revived. Both groups had developed from an earlier movement, the Social Democrat Labour Party, which was Marxist in outlook. Karl Marx (1818–83) was a German Jew whose political ideas were set out in the *Communist Manifesto* (1848) and *Das Kapital* (*Capital*) (1867). He believed that economic factors were the real cause of historical change, and that workers (proletariat) were everywhere exploited by capitalists (middle-class bourgeoisie); this means that when a society became fully industrialized, the workers would inevitably rise up against their exploiters and take

control themselves, running the country in their own interests. Marx called this 'the dictatorship of the proletariat'. When this point was reached there would be no further need for the 'state', which would consequently 'wither away'.

One of the Social Democrat leaders was *Vladimir Lenin*, who helped to edit the revolutionary newspaper *Iskra* (The Spark). It was over an election to the editorial board of *Iskra* in 1903 that the party had split into Lenin's supporters, *the Bolsheviks* (the Russian word for 'majority'), and the rest, *the Mensheviks* (minority).

- *Lenin and the Bolsheviks* wanted a small, disciplined party of professional revolutionaries who would work full-time to bring about revolution; because the industrial workers were in a minority, Lenin believed they must work with the peasants as well, and get them involved in revolutionary activity.
- *The Mensheviks*, on the other hand, were happy to have party membership open to anybody who cared to join; they believed that a revolution could not take place in Russia until the country was fully industrialized and industrial workers were in a big majority over peasants; they had very little faith in co-operation from peasants, who were actually one of the most conservative groups in society. The Mensheviks were the strict Marxists, believing in a proletarian revolution, whereas Lenin was the one moving away from Marxism. In 1912 appeared the new Bolshevik newspaper *Pravda* (Truth), which was extremely important for publicizing Bolshevik ideas and giving political direction to the already developing strike wave.
- *The Social Revolutionaries* were another revolutionary party; they were not Marxists – they did not approve of increasing industrialization and did not think in terms of a proletarian revolution. After the overthrow of the tsarist regime, they wanted a mainly agrarian society based on peasant communities operating collectively.

5 The royal family discredited

The royal family was discredited by a number of scandals. It was widely suspected that Nicholas himself was a party to the murder of Stolypin, who was shot by a member of the secret police in the Tsar's presence during a gala performance at the Kiev opera. Nothing was ever proved, but Nicholas and his right-wing supporters were probably not sorry to see the back of Stolypin, who was becoming too liberal for their comfort.

More serious was the royal family's association with Rasputin, a self-professed 'holy man', who made himself indispensable to the Empress Alexandra by his ability to help the ailing heir to the throne, Alexei. This unfortunate child had inherited haemophilia from his mother's family, and Rasputin was able, on occasion, apparently through hypnosis and prayer, to stop the bleeding when Alexei suffered a haemorrhage. Eventually Rasputin became a real power behind the throne, but attracted public criticism by his drunkenness and his numerous affairs with court ladies. Alexandra preferred to ignore the scandals and the *Duma*'s request that Rasputin be sent away from the court (1912).

(d) The verdict?

The weight of evidence seems to suggest therefore that events were moving towards some sort of upheaval before the First World War broke out. There was a general strike organized by the Bolsheviks in St Petersburg (the capital) in July 1914 with street demonstrations, shootings and barricades. The strike ended on 15 July, a few days before the war began; the government still controlled the army and the police at this point and might well have been able to hold on to power, but writers such as George Kennan and Leopold

Haimson believed that the tsarist regime would have collapsed sooner or later even without the First World War to finish it off. More recently, Sheila Fitzpatrick takes a similar view: 'The regime was so vulnerable to any kind of jolt or setback that it is hard to imagine that it could have survived long, even without the war.'

On the other hand, some recent historians are more cautious. Christopher Read thinks the overthrow of the monarchy was by no means inevitable, and that the situation in the years immediately before 1914 could have continued indefinitely, provided there was no war. Robert Service agrees: he argues that although Russia was in a condition of 'general brittleness', although it was a 'vulnerable plant, it was not doomed to suffer the root-and-branch revolution of 1917. What made that kind of revolution possible was the protracted, exhausting conflict of the First World War.' Soviet historians of course continued to argue to the end that revolution was historically inevitable: in their view, the 'revolutionary upsurge' was reaching a climax in 1914, and the outbreak of war actually delayed the revolution.

(e)   War failures made revolution certain

Historians agree that Russian failures in the war made revolution certain, causing troops and police to mutiny, so that there was nobody left to defend the autocracy. The war revealed the incompetent and corrupt organization and the shortage of equipment. Poor transport organization and distribution meant that arms and ammunition were slow to reach the front; although there was plenty of food in the country, it did not get to the big cities in sufficient quantities, because most of the trains were being monopolized by the military. Bread was scarce and very expensive.

Norman Stone has shown that the Russian army acquitted itself reasonably well, and Brusilov's 1916 offensive was an impressive success (see Section 2.3(c)). However, Nicholas made the fatal mistake of appointing himself supreme commander (August 1915); his tactical blunders threw away all the advantages won by Brusilov's offensive, and drew on himself the blame for later defeats, and for the high death rate.

By January 1917, most groups in society were disillusioned with the incompetent way the Tsar was running the war. The aristocracy, the *Duma*, many industrialists and the army were beginning to turn against Nicholas, feeling that it would be better to sacrifice him to avoid a much worse revolution that might sweep away the whole social structure. General Krimov told a secret meeting of *Duma* members at the end of 1916: 'We would welcome the news of a *coup d'état*. A revolution is imminent and we at the front feel it to be so. If you decide on such an extreme step, we will support you. Clearly there is no other way.'

16.2   THE TWO REVOLUTIONS: FEBRUARY/MARCH AND OCTOBER/ NOVEMBER 1917

The revolutions are still known in Russia as the February and October Revolutions. This is because the Russians were still using the old Julian calendar, which was 13 days behind the Gregorian calendar used by the rest of Europe. Russia adopted the Gregorian calendar in 1918. The events which the Russians know as the February Revolution began on 23 February 1917 (Julian), which was 8 March outside Russia. When the Bolsheviks took power on 25 October (Julian), it was 7 November elsewhere. In this section, the Julian calendar is used for internal events in Russia, and the Gregorian calendar for international events such as the First World War, until 1 February 1918.

(a) The February Revolution

The first revolution began on 23 February when bread riots broke out in Petrograd (St Petersburg). The rioters were quickly joined by thousands of strikers from a nearby armaments factory. The Tsar sent orders for the troops to use force to end the demonstrations, and 40 people were killed. Soon, however, some of the troops began to refuse to fire at the unarmed crowds and the whole Petrograd garrison mutinied. Mobs seized public buildings, released prisoners from jails and took over police stations and arsenals. The *Duma* advised Nicholas to set up a constitutional monarchy, but he refused and sent more troops to Petrograd to try to restore order. This convinced the *Duma* and the generals that Nicholas, who was on his way back to Petrograd, would have to go. Some of his senior generals told Nicholas that the only way to save the monarchy was for him to renounce the throne. On 2 March, in the imperial train standing in a siding near Pskov, the Tsar abdicated in favour of his brother, the Grand Duke Michael. Unfortunately nobody had made sure that Michael would accept the throne, so when he refused, the Russian monarchy came to an end.

Was it a revolution from above or below, organized or spontaneous? This has been the subject of some controversy among historians. George Katkov thought that the conspiracy among the elite was the decisive factor – nobles, *Duma* members and generals forced Nicholas to abdicate in order to prevent a real mass revolution developing. W. H. Chamberlin, writing in 1935, came to the opposite conclusion: 'it was one of the most leaderless, spontaneous, anonymous revolutions of all time'. The revolution from below by the masses was decisive, because it threw the elite into a panic; without the crowds on the streets, there would have been no need for the elite to act. None of the traditional liberal historians thought the revolutionary parties had played a significant role in organizing the events.

Soviet historians agreed with Chamberlin that it was a revolution from below, but they did not accept that it was spontaneous. On the contrary, they made out a strong case that the Bolsheviks had played a vital role in organizing strikes and demonstrations. Many recent Western historians have supported the theory of a mass uprising organized from below, but not necessarily one organized by the Bolsheviks. There were many activists among the workers who were not affiliated to any political group. Historians such as Christopher Read, Diane Koenker and Steve Smith have all shown that workers were motivated by economic considerations rather than politics. They wanted better conditions, higher wages and control over their own lives; in the words of Steve Smith, 'it was an outburst of desperation to secure the basic material needs and a decent standard of living'.

(b) The provisional government

Most people expected the autocracy of the tsarist system to be replaced by a democratic republic with an elected parliament. The *Duma*, struggling to take control, set up a mainly liberal *provisional government* with Prince George Lvov as prime minister. In July he was replaced by Alexander Kerensky, a moderate socialist. But the new government was just as perplexed by the enormous problems facing it as the Tsar had been. On the night of 25 October a second revolution took place, which overthrew the provisional government and brought the Bolsheviks to power.

(c) Why did the provisional government fall from power so soon?

1   It took the unpopular decision to continue the war, but *the June offensive, Kerensky's idea, was another disastrous failure*. It caused the collapse of army morale and discipline, and sent hundreds of thousands of deserting troops streaming home.

2   *The government had to share power with the Petrograd soviet,* an elected committee of soldiers' and workers' representatives, which tried to govern the city. It had been elected at the end of February, before the Tsar's abdication. Other soviets appeared in Moscow and all the provincial cities. When the Petrograd soviet ordered all soldiers to obey only the soviet, it meant that in the last resort, the provisional government could not rely on the support of the army.

3   *The government lost support because it delayed elections,* which it had promised, for a Constituent Assembly (parliament), arguing that these were not possible in the middle of a war when several million troops were away fighting. *Another promise not kept was for land reform* – the redistribution of land from large estates among peasants. Tired of waiting, some peasants started to seize land from landlords. The Bolsheviks were able to use peasant discontent to win support.

4   Meanwhile, thanks to a new political amnesty, *Lenin was able to return from exile in Switzerland* (April). The Germans allowed him to travel through to Petrograd in a special 'sealed' train, in the hope that he would cause further chaos in Russia. After a rapturous welcome, he urged (in his *April Theses*) that the Bolsheviks should cease to support the provisional government, that all power should be taken by the soviets, and that Russia should withdraw from the war.

5   *There was increasing economic chaos,* with inflation, rising bread prices, lagging wages and shortages of raw materials and fuel. Industry was severely handicapped by a shortage of investment. In the midst of all this, Lenin and the Bolsheviks put forward what seemed to be a realistic and attractive policy: a separate peace with Germany to get Russia out of the war, all land to be given to the peasants, workers' control in the factories and more food at cheaper prices.

6   *The government lost popularity because of the 'July Days'.* On 3 July there was a huge demonstration of workers, soldiers and sailors, who marched on the Tauride Palace where both the provisional government and the Petrograd soviet were meeting. They demanded that the soviet should take power, but the members refused to take the responsibility. The government brought loyal troops from the front to restore order and accused the Bolsheviks of trying to launch an uprising; it was reported, falsely, that Lenin was a German spy. At this, the popularity of the Bolsheviks declined rapidly; Lenin fled to Finland and other leaders were arrested. But about 400 people had been killed during the violence, and Prince Lvov, who was deeply shocked by the July Days, resigned. He was replaced by Alexander Kerensky. It is still not absolutely clear who was responsible for the events of the July Days. American historian Richard Pipes is convinced that Lenin planned the whole affair from the beginning; Robert Service, on the other hand, argues that Lenin was improvising, 'testing the waters' to discover how determined the provisional government was. The demonstration was probably spontaneous in origin, and Lenin soon decided that it was too early to launch a full-scale uprising.

7   *The Kornilov affair embarrassed the government* and increased the popularity of the Bolsheviks. General Kornilov, the army commander-in-chief, viewed the Bolsheviks as traitors; he decided it was time to move against the soviet, and he brought troops towards Petrograd (August). However, many of his soldiers mutinied and Kerensky ordered Kornilov's arrest. Army discipline seemed on the verge of collapse; public opinion swung against the war and in favour of the Bolsheviks, who were still the only party to talk openly about making a separate peace. By October they had won a majority over the Mensheviks and Social Revolutionaries (SRs) in both the Petrograd and Moscow soviets, though they were in a minority in the country as a whole. Leon Trotsky (who had just become a Bolshevik in July) was elected Chairman of the Petrograd soviet.

8   In mid-October, *urged on by Lenin, the Petrograd soviet took the crucial decision to attempt to seize power.* He was strongly supported by Joseph Stalin and Yakov Sverdlov, who had assumed the leadership while Lenin was absent in Finland. But it was Leon Trotsky who made most of the plans, which went off without a hitch. During the night of 25–26 October, Bolshevik Red Guards and troops loyal to the Petrograd Soviet took over important buildings, including telegraph offices and the railway station, and surrounded the Winter Palace. Later the provisional government ministers were arrested, except Kerensky, who managed to escape. It was almost a bloodless coup, enabling Lenin to announce that the provisional government had been overthrown.

The Bolsheviks knew exactly what they were aiming for, and were well disciplined and organized, whereas the other revolutionary groups were in disarray. The Mensheviks, for example, thought that the next revolution should not take place until the industrial workers were in a majority in the country. Lenin and Trotsky believed that both revolutions could be combined into one, and so, after years of disagreement, they were able to work well together. However, the Mensheviks and the Social Revolutionaries still believed that this revolution should have been delayed until the industrial workers were more numerous. They walked out of the Second Congress of Soviets, leaving Lenin and the Bolsheviks to set up a new Soviet government with himself in charge. It was to be called the Council of People's Commissars, or Sovnarkom for short.

(d) Coup or mass insurrection?

The official Soviet interpretation of these events was that the Bolshevik takeover was the result of a mass movement: workers, peasants and most of the soldiers and sailors were attracted by the revolutionary politics of the Bolsheviks, which included peace, land for the peasants, worker control, government by the soviets and self-determination for the different nationalities in the Russian Empire. Lenin was a charismatic leader who inspired his party and the people. Soviet historians have pointed out that in only 16 out of 97 major centres did the Bolsheviks have to use force in order to assert their authority. It was important for the Bolsheviks, or Communists, as they became known later, to emphasize the popular nature of the revolution because that gave the regime its legitimacy.

The traditional liberal interpretation put forward by Western historians rejected the Soviet view. They refused to accept that there was any significant popular support for the Bolsheviks, who were simply a minority group of professional revolutionaries who used the chaos in Russia to take power for themselves. They were successful because they were well organized and ruthless. According to Adam Ulam, 'the Bolsheviks did not seize power in this year of revolutions. They picked it up. ... Any group of determined men could have done what the Bolsheviks did in Petrograd in October 1917: seize the few key points of the city and proclaim themselves the government.' Richard Pipes is the most recent historian to re-state the traditional interpretation. In his view, the October revolution was due almost entirely to Lenin's overwhelming desire for power.

The libertarian interpretation takes a completely different line. Libertarians believe that the October revolution was the result of a popular uprising, which had very little to do with the Bolsheviks. The masses were not responding to Bolshevik pressure, but to their own aspirations and desires; they had no need of the Bolsheviks to tell them what they wanted. Alexander Berkman claimed that 'the shop and factory committees were the pioneers in labour control of industry, with the prospect of themselves, in the near future, managing the industries'. For the libertarians the tragedy was that the Bolsheviks hijacked the popular revolution: they pretended that their aims were the same as those of the masses, but in reality they had no intention of allowing factory committees any power, and they did not believe in genuine democracy and freedom. Just as the masses were about to take power for themselves, it was wrenched from their hands by the Bolsheviks.

Revisionist interpretations have concentrated on what was happening among ordinary people; their conclusions were wide-ranging. However, they all agree that there was great political awareness among ordinary people, many of whom were involved in trade unions and the soviets. In some places they seem to have been influenced by the Bolsheviks; in Kronstadt, the island naval base off Petrograd, the Bolsheviks were the largest group in the local soviet. In June 1917 it was their influence which caused the Kronstadt soviet to pass a resolution condemning 'this pernicious war' and the Kerensky offensive.

The revisionist interpretations are the ones most widely accepted nowadays, although Richard Pipes continues to cling to the traditional views. More evidence has become available since the end of communist rule in the USSR, when millions of files were thrown open in the previously closed archives. There seems no doubt that by October 1917 the masses were broadly in favour of a government by the soviets, of which there were some 900 by that time, throughout Russia. Christopher Read believes that 'the revolution was constantly driven forward by the often spontaneous impulse given to it from the grass roots'. Robert Service (in *Lenin: A Biography*) stresses the role of Lenin; he thinks there can be no doubt that Lenin wanted power and used the potentially revolutionary situation brilliantly. 'His every pronouncement was directed towards encouraging the "masses" to exercise initiative. His wish was for the Bolsheviks to appear as a party that would facilitate the making of Revolution by and for the people.' So in fact the Bolsheviks did have popular backing, even though it was fairly passive, for their October *coup*, because the popular movement thought it was going to get government by the soviets.

Although the circumstances were right and there was hardly any resistance to the Bolsheviks, it still needed that small group of people with the nerve and the resolve to use the situation. This was the contribution that Lenin and Trotsky made – they judged to perfection the point of maximum unpopularity of the provisional government, and then they actually 'made' the revolution happen. It would not have been possible without the masses – it was the popular movement which determined that there would be so little resistance, but equally, it would not have been possible without Lenin and Trotsky.

(e) Lenin and the Bolsheviks consolidate their control

The Bolsheviks were in control in Petrograd as a result of their coup, but in some places the takeover was not so smooth. Fighting lasted a week in Moscow before the soviet won control, and it was the end of November before other cities were brought to heel. Country areas were more difficult to deal with, and at first the peasants were only lukewarm towards the new government. They preferred the Social Revolutionaries, who also promised them land and who saw the peasants as the backbone of the nation, whereas the Bolsheviks seemed to favour industrial workers. Very few people expected the Bolshevik government to last long because of the complexity of the problems facing it. As soon as the other political groups recovered from the shock of the Bolshevik coup, there was bound to be some determined opposition. At the same time they had somehow to extricate Russia from the war and then set about repairing the shattered economy, while at the same time keeping their promises about land and food for the peasants and workers.

16.3 HOW SUCCESSFULLY DID LENIN AND THE BOLSHEVIKS DEAL WITH THEIR PROBLEMS (1917–24)?

(a) Lack of majority support

The Bolsheviks had nothing like majority support in the country as a whole. One problem therefore was how to keep themselves in power and yet allow free elections. One of Lenin's first decrees nationalized all land, including former crown estates and land belonging to the church, without compensation, so that it could be redistributed among the peasants and, so he hoped, win their support. The decree on workers' control gave industrial workers authority over their managers and was intended to reduce unrest and strikes in factories. Another decree limited the working day in factories to eight hours. Other decrees included granting self-determination to every national group, nationalizing banks, large factories and mines, and cancelling all debts incurred by the tsarist government and the Provisional government. One major concession that Lenin and Trotsky were prepared to make was to allow some Left Social Revolutionaries to act as junior partners in the government, because they had far more support than the Bolsheviks in rural areas. At the same time they took steps to deal with any opposition. The government claimed the right to close down hostile newspapers and journals, and set up a new security police force. This had the mind-blowing name – the Extraordinary Commission for Combating Sabotage and Counter-Revolution, usually known as the Cheka. Its leader was Felix Dzierzynski.

Lenin knew that he would have to allow elections, since he had criticized Kerensky so bitterly for postponing them; but he sensed that a Bolshevik majority in the Constituent Assembly was highly unlikely. Kerensky had arranged elections for mid-November, and they went ahead as planned. Lenin's worst fears were realized: the Bolsheviks won 175 seats out of about 700, but the Social Revolutionaries (SRs) won 370; the Mensheviks won only 15, Left Social Revolutionaries 40, various nationality groups 80 and Kadets (Constitutional Democrats who wanted genuine democracy) 17.

Under a genuine democratic system, the SRs, who had an overall majority, would have formed a government under their leader, Viktor Chernov. However, Lenin was determined that the Bolsheviks were going to stay in power; there was no way in which he was going to hand it over to the SRs, or even share it, after the Bolsheviks had done all the hard work of getting rid of the Provisional Government. After some anti-Bolshevik speeches at the first meeting of the Constituent Assembly (January 1918), it was dispersed by Bolshevik Red Guards and not allowed to meet again. Lenin's justification for this undemocratic action was that it was really the highest form of democracy: since the Bolsheviks knew what the workers wanted, they had no need of an elected parliament to tell them. The Assembly must take second place to the Congress of Soviets and Sovnarkom (the Council of People's Commissars); this was a sort of cabinet which had Lenin as its chairman. Armed force had triumphed for the time being, but opposition was to lead to civil war later in the year.

(b) The war with Germany

The next pressing problem was how to withdraw from the war. An armistice between Russia and the Central Powers had been agreed in December 1917, but long negotiations followed during which Trotsky tried, without success, to persuade the Germans to moderate their demands. *The Treaty of Brest–Litovsk (March 1918)* was cruel: Russia lost Poland, Estonia, Latvia and Lithuania, the Ukraine, Georgia and Finland; this included a third of Russia's farming land, a third of her population, two-thirds of her coalmines and

Map 16.1   **Russian losses by the Treaty of Brest–Litovsk**

half her heavy industry (Map 16.1). This was a high price to pay, and all the other parties condemned it; the Left Socialist Revolutionaries walked out of Sovnarkom. However, Lenin insisted that it was worth it, pointing out that Russia needed to sacrifice space in order to gain time to recover. He probably expected Russia to get the land back anyway when, as he hoped, the revolution spread to Germany and other countries.

(c)   The drift towards violence

Almost immediately after the October revolution, the Bolsheviks began to resort to coercion in order to get things done and to stay in power. This raises the question, much debated by historians, of *whether Lenin had violent intentions from the beginning, or whether he was pushed into these policies against his will by the difficult circumstances.*

Soviet and Marxist historians played down the violence and claimed that the Bolsheviks had no choice, given the uncompromising attitude of their enemies. After the signing of the Treaty of Brest–Litovsk, the SRs left Petrograd and moved eastwards to Samara on the

Volga. They set up an alternative government which launched a campaign of assassination and terror, before the civil war started. According to Christopher Hill,

> there was no wholesale suppression of the opposition press during the six months immediately after the Bolshevik revolution, and no violence against political opponents, because there was no need for it. The death sentence was even abolished at the end of October, though Lenin thought this very unrealistic.

The members of the provisional government who had been arrested were almost all released after promising 'not to take up arms against the people any more'. Lenin himself remarked in November 1917: 'We do not use the sort of terror as was used by the French revolutionaries who guillotined unarmed people, and I hope we shall not have to use it.' However, *circumstances became increasingly difficult.*

- *By January 1918 there were severe food shortages in Petrograd and Moscow* and some other cities. Lenin was convinced that the better-off peasants (*kulaks*) were hoarding huge quantities of grain in protest against the low payments that they were receiving. They hoped to force the government to increase their payments. There is plenty of evidence that this was indeed the case. Lenin's new secret police, the Cheka, were given the job of dealing with grain hoarders and speculators. 'There will be no famine in Russia', Lenin said in April 1918, 'if stocks are controlled and any breach of the rules is followed by the harshest punishment – the arrest and shooting of takers of bribes and swindlers.'
- After the signing of the humiliating Treaty of Brest–Litovsk (March 1918), *the loss of Ukraine, a vitally important source of wheat, made the food situation worse.*
- *The left-wing Social Revolutionaries did their best to wreck the treaty, and began a campaign of terror.* They assassinated the German ambassador and a leading Bolshevik member of the Petrograd soviet, and there was some evidence that they were attempting either to seize power for themselves or to spark off a popular uprising to force the Bolsheviks to change their policies.
- On 30 August 1918, the head of the Petrograd Cheka was assassinated, and later the same day a woman shot Lenin twice with a revolver at point-blank range. He was wounded in the neck and one of his lungs, but seemed to make a quick recovery.

All these events can be taken as evidence that it was the desperate situation, rather than any inherent ideological motive, which drove Lenin and the Bolsheviks into retaliating with violence.

The problem was that however well-intentioned the Bolsheviks were, *Lenin's reasoning was fatally flawed in two vital respects.*

1 Karl Marx had predicted that the collapse of capitalism would take place in two stages: first, the middle-class bourgeois capitalists would overthrow the autocratic monarchy and set up systems of parliamentary democracy. Secondly, when industrialization was complete, the industrial workers (proletariat), who were now in a majority, would overthrow the bourgeois capitalists and set up a classless society – the 'dictatorship of the proletariat'. The first stage had taken place with the February revolution. The Mensheviks believed that the second stage could not occur until Russia was fully industrialized and the proletariat was in a majority. However, Lenin insisted that in Russia's case, the two revolutions – bourgeois and proletarian – could be successfully telescoped together; this was why he had launched the October coup – the opportunity was too good to be missed! This had given rise to the situation in which the Bolsheviks were in power before their most reliable supporters – the

industrial workers – had become a large enough class to sustain them. This left the Bolsheviks as a minority government, uncomfortably dependent on the largest, but most self-interested class in Russian society – the peasants.

2 Lenin expected that a successful revolution in Russia would occur as part of a European or even a worldwide socialist revolution. He was convinced that revolutions would quickly follow in central and western Europe, so that the new Soviet government would be supported by sympathetic neighbouring governments. None of this had happened, so Russia was left isolated, facing a capitalist Europe which was deeply suspicious of the new regime.

Both internally and externally, therefore, the regime was under pressure from the forces of counter-revolution. Law and order seemed to be breaking down and local soviets simply ignored the government's decrees. If the Bolsheviks intended to stay in power and rebuild the country, regrettably they would more than likely have to resort to violence to achieve anything significant.

Traditional liberal historians reject this interpretation; they believe that Lenin and Trotsky, though perhaps not all the Bolshevik leaders, were committed to the use of violence and terror from the beginning. Richard Pipes claims that Lenin regarded terror as an absolutely vital element of revolutionary government and was prepared to use it as a preventive measure, even when no active opposition to his rule existed. Why else did he set up the *Cheka* early in December 1917, at a time when there was no threat of opposition and no foreign intervention? He points out that in a 1908 essay on the failure of the French revolutionaries, Lenin had written that the main weakness of the proletariat was 'excessive generosity – it should have exterminated its enemies instead of trying to exert moral influence over them'. When the death penalty was abolished, Lenin was highly indignant, retorting: 'This is nonsense, how can you make a revolution without executions?'

(d) The 'Red Terror'

Whatever the intentions of the Bolsheviks, there is no doubt that violence and terror became widespread. The Red Army was used to enforce the procurement of grain from peasants who were thought to have surpluses. During 1918 the *Cheka* suppressed 245 peasant uprisings and 99 in the first seven months of 1919. Official *Cheka* figures show that during the course of these operations over 3000 peasants were killed and 6300 executed; in 1919 there were over 3000 more executions, but the actual death toll was probably much higher. Social Revolutionaries and other political opponents were rounded up and shot. One of the most disturbing features of this 'Red Terror' was that many of those arrested and executed were not guilty of any particular offence, but were accused of being 'bourgeois'; this was a term of abuse, applied to landowners, priests, businessmen, employers, army officers and professional people. They were all labelled 'enemies of the people' as part of the government's campaign of class war.

One of the worst incidents of the terror was the murder of the ex-Tsar Nicholas and his family. In the summer of 1918 they were being kept under guard in a house in Ekaterinburg in the Ural Mountains. By that time the civil war was in full swing; the Bolsheviks were afraid that White forces, which were advancing towards Ekaterinburg, might rescue the royal family, who would then become a focus for all the anti-Bolshevik forces. Lenin himself gave the order for them to be killed, and in July 1918 the entire family, together with members of their household, were shot by members of the local *Cheka*. Their graves were only discovered after the collapse of the Soviet Empire. In 1992 some of the bones were subjected to DNA analysis, which proved that they were indeed the remains of the Romanovs.

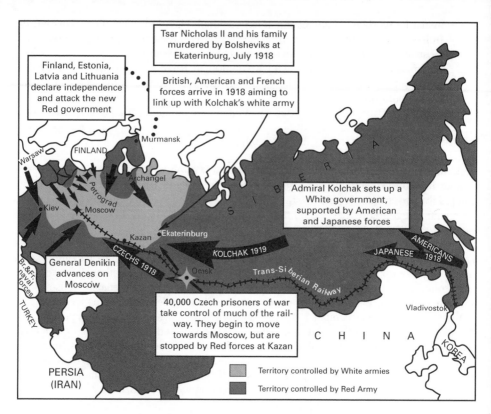

Map 16.2   **Civil war and interventions in Russia, 1918–22**

(e)   Civil war

By April 1918, armed opposition to the Bolsheviks was breaking out in many areas (see Map 16.2), leading to civil war. The opposition (known as the Whites) was a mixed bag, consisting of Social Revolutionaries, Mensheviks, ex-tsarist officers and any other groups which did not like what they had seen of the Bolsheviks. There was great discontent in the countryside, where peasants hated the food-procurement policies of the government; even the soldiers and workers, who had supported the Bolsheviks in 1917, resented the high-handed way in which the Bolsheviks treated the soviets (elected councils) all over Russia. One of the Bolshevik slogans had been 'ALL POWER TO THE SOVIETS'. Naturally, people had expected that every town would have its own soviet, which would run the town's affairs and local industry. Instead, officials (known as commissars) appointed by the government arrived, supported by Red Guards; they threw Social Revolutionary and Menshevik members out of the soviets, leaving Bolshevik members in control. It soon turned into dictatorship from the centre instead of local control. The slogan of the government's opponents became 'LONG LIVE THE SOVIETS AND DOWN WITH THE COMMISSARS'. Their general aim was not to restore the Tsar, but simply to set up a democratic government on Western lines.

In Siberia, Admiral Kolchak, former Black Sea Fleet commander, set up a White government; General Denikin was in the Caucasus with a large White army. Most bizarre of all, the Czechoslovak Legion of about 40 000 men had seized long stretches of the Trans-Siberian Railway in the region of Omsk. These troops were originally prisoners taken by the Russians from the Austro-Hungarian army, who had then changed sides after the March revolution and fought for the Kerensky government against the Germans. After Brest-Litovsk the Bolsheviks gave them permission to leave Russia via the Trans-Siberian Railway to Vladivostok, but then decided to disarm them in case they co-operated with the Allies, who were already showing interest in the destruction of the new Bolshevik government. The Czechs resisted with great spirit and their control of the railway was a serious embarrassment to the government.

The situation was complicated by the fact that Russia's allies in the First World War intervened to help the Whites. They claimed that they wanted a government which would continue the war against Germany. When their intervention continued even after the defeat of Germany, it became clear that their aim was to destroy the Bolshevik government, which was now advocating world revolution. The USA, Japan, France and Britain sent troops, who landed at Murmansk, Archangel and Vladivostok. The situation seemed grim for the Bolsheviks when, early in 1919, Kolchak (whom the Allies intended to place at the head of the next government) advanced towards Moscow, the new capital. However, Trotsky, now Commissar for War, had done a magnificent job creating the well-disciplined Red Army, based on conscription and including thousands of experienced officers from the old tsarist armies. Kolchak was forced back and later captured and executed by the Reds. The Czech Legion was defeated, and Denikin, advancing from the south to within 250 miles of Moscow, was forced to retreat; he later escaped with British help.

By the end of 1919 it was clear that the Bolsheviks (now calling themselves communists) would survive. As the White armies began to suffer defeats, the interventionist states lost interest and withdrew their troops. In 1920 there was an invasion of Ukraine by Polish and French troops, which forced the Russians to hand over part of Ukraine and White Russia (the Treaty of Riga, 1921). From the communist point of view, however, the important thing was that they had won the civil war. Lenin was able to present it as a great victory, and it did much to restore the government's prestige after the humiliation of Brest–Litovsk. *There were a number of reasons for the communist victory.*

1   *The Whites were not centrally organized.* Kolchak and Denikin failed to link up, and the nearer they drew to Moscow, the more they strained their lines of communication. They lost the support of many peasants both by their brutal behaviour, and because peasants feared that a White victory would mean the loss of their newly acquired land.

2   *The Red Armies had more troops.* After the introduction of conscription, they had almost 3 million men in arms, outnumbering the Whites by about ten to one. They controlled most of the modern industry and so were better supplied with armaments, and had the inspired leadership of Trotsky.

3   Lenin took decisive measures, known as *war communism*, to control the economic resources of the state. All factories of any size were nationalized, all private trade banned, and food and grain were seized from peasants to feed town workers and troops. This was successful at first since it enabled the government to survive the civil war, but it had disastrous results later.

4   Lenin was able to present the Bolsheviks *as a nationalist government fighting against foreigners*; and even though war communism was unpopular with the peasants, the Whites became even more unpopular because of their foreign connections.

(f)   Effects of the civil war

The war was a terrible tragedy for the Russian people – *there was an enormous cost in human lives and suffering.* Taking into account those killed in the Red Terror, in the military action, and in the White anti-Jewish pogroms; those who died from starvation and those who perished from dysentery and in the typhus and typhoid epidemics, the total number of deaths was at least 8 million – more than four times the number of Russian deaths in the First World War (1.7 million). The economy was in ruins and the rouble was worth only one per cent of its value in October 1917.

At the end of the war *important changes had taken place in the communist regime.* Economically it became more centralized, as state control was extended over all areas of the economy. Politically, the regime became militarized and even brutalized. *The question that has occupied historians is whether it was the crisis of the civil war which forced these changes on the government, or whether they would have taken place anyway because of the nature of communism.* Was this the inevitable drive towards socialism?

Robert C. Tucker argues that the civil war *was* responsible for the political developments. He believes that it brutalized the Party and gave its members a siege mentality which they found it difficult to break away from. It made centralization, strict discipline and mobilization of the population in order to achieve the regime's targets an integral part of the system. Tucker also points out that already, at the height of the civil war, there were signs of Lenin's more 'liberal' thinking, which he was able to put into practice during the period of the New Economic Policy (NEP). For example, in May 1919 Lenin wrote a pamphlet in which he explained that the main obstacle to the achievement of socialism in Russia was the culture of backwardness left over from centuries of tsarist rule. According to Lenin, the best way to change this was not by forcible means, but by education, which unfortunately would take a long time.

Other historians argue that the civil war was one of the influences which brutalized the communist regime, but that it was not the only one. Christopher Read makes the point that the Bolsheviks were products of the tsarist environment, which had itself been extremely authoritarian; tsarist governments had never hesitated to use extreme methods against their enemies. It was only a few years since Stolypin had executed around 4000 opponents. 'In the prevailing circumstances', argues Read, 'it is hard to see why opposition should be tolerated when the Russian tradition was to eradicate it as heresy.' Among the older generation of liberal historians, Adam Ulam argued that violence and terror were an integral part of communism, and claimed that Lenin actually welcomed the civil war because it gave him an excuse to use more violence.

There is the same debate about the economic features of war communism: were nationalization and state control of the economy central to communist aims and ideals, or were they forced on the government by the need to harness the economy to the war effort? Even Soviet historians differ in their interpretations of this. Some believe that the Party had a basic plan for nationalizing the major industries as soon as possible: hence the nationalization of banks, railways, shipping and hundreds of large factories by June 1918. Others believe that what Lenin really hoped for was a mixed economy in which some capitalist activity would be allowed. Alec Nove came to the very sensible conclusion that 'Lenin and his colleagues were playing it by ear. ... We must allow for the interaction of Bolshevik ideas with the desperate situation in which they found themselves.'

(g) Lenin and the economic problems

From early 1921 Lenin faced the formidable task of rebuilding an economy shattered by the First World War and then by civil war. War communism had been unpopular with the peasants, who, seeing no point in working hard to produce food which was taken away from them without compensation, simply produced enough for their own needs. This caused severe food shortages aggravated by droughts in 1920–1. In addition, industry was almost at a standstill. In March 1921 a serious naval mutiny occurred at Kronstadt, the island naval base just off St Petersburg. This was suppressed only through prompt action by Trotsky, who sent troops across the ice on the frozen sea.

The mutiny seems to have convinced Lenin that a new approach was needed, to win back the faltering support of the peasants; this was vitally important since peasants formed a large majority of the population. He put into operation what became known as *the New Economic Policy (NEP)*. Peasants were now allowed to keep surplus produce after payment of a tax representing a certain proportion of the surplus. This, plus the reintroduction of private trade, revived incentive, and food production increased. Small industries and trade in their products were also restored to private ownership, though heavy industry such as coal, iron and steel, together with power, transport and banking, remained under state control. Lenin also found that often the old managers had to be brought back, as well as such capitalist incentives as bonuses and piece-rates. Foreign investment was encouraged, to help develop and modernize Russian industry.

There is the usual debate among historians about Lenin's motives and intentions. Some Bolsheviks claimed that the Kronstadt mutiny and peasant unrest had no bearing on the decision to change to NEP; that in fact they had been on the point of introducing an earlier version of NEP when the outbreak of the civil war prevented them. To confuse matters further, some of the other communist leaders, especially Kamenev and Zinoviev, disapproved of NEP because they thought it encouraged the development of *kulaks* (wealthy peasants), who would turn out to be the enemies of communism. They saw it as a retreat from true socialism.

Did Lenin intend NEP as a temporary compromise – a return to a certain amount of private enterprise until recovery was assured; or did he see it as a return to something like the correct road to socialism, from which they had been diverted by the civil war? It is difficult to be certain one way or the other. What is clear is that Lenin defended NEP vigorously: he said they needed the experience of the capitalists to get the economy blooming again. In May 1921 he told the Party that NEP must be pursued 'seriously and for a long time – not less than a decade and probably more'. They had to take into account the fact that instead of introducing socialism in a country dominated by industrial workers – the true allies of the Bolsheviks – they were working in a backward, peasant-dominated society. Therefore NEP was not a retreat – it was an attempt to find an alternative road to socialism in less than ideal circumstances. It would require a long campaign of educating the peasants in the benefits of agrarian co-operatives so that force would not be necessary; this would lead to the triumph of socialism. Roy Medvedev, a dissident Soviet historian, was convinced that these were Lenin's genuine intentions, and that if he had lived another 20 years (to the same age as Stalin), the future of the USSR would have been very different.

NEP was moderately successful: the economy began to recover and production levels were improving; in most commodities they were not far off the 1913 levels. Given the territorial losses at the end of the First World War and the war with Poland, this was a considerable achievement. Great progress was made with the electrification of industry, one of Lenin's pet schemes. Towards the end of 1927, when NEP began to be abandoned, the ordinary Russian was probably better off than at any time since 1914. Industrial workers who had a job were being paid real wages and they had the benefits of NEP's new social legislation: an eight-hour working day, two weeks' holiday with pay, sick and unemployment pay and healthcare. The peasants were enjoying a higher standard of living than in 1913. The downside of NEP was that unemployment was higher than before, and there were still frequent food shortages.

(h) Political problems were solved decisively

Russia was now the world's first communist state, the Union of Soviet Socialist Republics (USSR); power was held by the Communist Party, and no other parties were allowed. *The main political problem now for Lenin was disagreement and criticism within the Communist Party.* In March 1921 Lenin banned 'factionalism' within the Party. This meant that discussion would be allowed, but once a decision had been taken, all sections of the Party had to stick to it. Anybody who persisted in holding a view different from the official party line would be expelled from the Party. During the rest of 1921 about one-third of the Party's members were 'purged' (expelled) with the help of the ruthless Cheka; many more resigned, mainly because they were against NEP. Lenin also rejected the claim of the trade unions that they should run industry. Trade unions had to do as the government told them, and their main function was to increase production.

The governing body in the Party was known as the 'Politburo'. During the civil war, when quick decisions were required, the Politburo got into the habit of acting as the government, and they continued to do so when the war was over. Control by Lenin and the Communist Party was now complete (for his successes in foreign affairs see Section 4.3(a) and (b)). However, the 'dictatorship of the proletariat' was nowhere in evidence; nor there any prospect of the state 'withering away'. Lenin defended this situation on the grounds that the working class were exhausted and weak; this meant that the most advanced workers and their leaders – the Communist Party – must rule the country for them.

In May 1922 Lenin suffered a stroke; after this he gradually grew weaker, and was forced to take less part in the work of government. He later suffered two more strokes, and died in January 1924 at the early age of 53. His work of completing the revolution by introducing a fully communist state was not finished, and the successful communist revolutions which Lenin had predicted in other countries had not taken place. This left the USSR isolated and facing an uncertain future. Although his health had been failing for some time, Lenin had made no clear plans about how the government was to be organized after his death, and this meant that a power struggle was inevitable.

16.4   LENIN – EVIL GENIUS?

(a)   Lenin remains a controversial figure

After his death the Politburo decided that Lenin's body should be embalmed and put on display in a glass case in a special mausoleum, to be built in Red Square in Moscow. The Politburo members, especially Joseph Stalin, encouraged the Lenin cult for all they were worth, hoping to share in his popularity by presenting themselves as Lenin's heirs, who would continue his policies. No criticism of Lenin was allowed, and Petrograd was renamed Leningrad. He became revered almost as a saint, and people flocked to Red Square to view his remains as though they were religious relics.

Some historians admire him: A. J. P. Taylor claimed that 'Lenin did more than any other political figure to change the face of the twentieth-century world. The creation of Soviet Russia and its survival were due to him. He was a very great man and even, despite his faults, a very good man.' Some revisionist historians also took a sympathetic view. Moshe Lewin, writing in 1968, portrayed Lenin as having been forced unwillingly into policies of violence and terror, and in his last years, in the face of ill health and the evil ambitions of Stalin, struggling unsuccessfully to steer communism into a more peaceful and civilized phase.

These interpretations are at opposite poles from what some of his contemporaries thought, and also from the traditional liberal view which sees Lenin as a ruthless dictator who paved the way for the even more ruthless and brutal dictatorship of Stalin. Alexander

Potresov, a Menshevik who knew Lenin well, described him as an 'evil genius' who had a hypnotic effect on people that enabled him to dominate them. Richard Pipes can find scarcely a single good word to say about Lenin. He emphasizes Lenin's cruelty and his apparent lack of remorse at the great loss of life which he had caused. The success of the Bolshevik seizure of power in October 1917 was nothing to do with social forces – it was simply because Lenin lusted after power.

Robert Service probably presents the most balanced view of Lenin. He concludes that Lenin was certainly ruthless, intolerant and repressive, and even seemed to enjoy unleashing terror. But although he sought power, and believed that dictatorship was desirable, power was not an end in itself. In spite of all his faults, he was a visionary: 'Lenin truly thought that a better world should and would be built, a world without repression and exploitation, a world without even a state. ... It was his judgement, woeful as it was, that the Dictatorship of the Proletariat would act as midwife to the birth of such a world.' He points out that with the introduction of NEP, the situation began to settle down. 'The Cheka's resources were limited and its repressive functions somewhat moderated. Religion was openly practised. Age-old peasant customs were left undisturbed. Whole sections of economic activity were released from state ownership.' Perhaps it was one of the great tragedies of the twentieth century that Lenin died prematurely before his vision could be realized. Nevertheless his achievements make him one of the great political figures of the last century. In the words of Robert Service: 'He led the October revolution, founded the USSR and laid down the rudiments of Marxist–Leninism. He helped to turn a world upside down.'

(b) Leninism and Stalinism

One of the most serious charges laid against Lenin by his critics is that he bears the responsibility for the even greater excesses and atrocities of the Stalin era. Was Stalinism merely a continuation of Leninism, or did Stalin betray Lenin's vision of a society free from injustice and exploitation? During the early years of the Cold War, Western historians held the 'straight line' theory – that Stalin simply continued Lenin's work. It was Lenin who destroyed the multi-party system when he suppressed the Constituent Assembly. He created the highly authoritarian structures of the Bolshevik Party, which became the structures of government, and which Stalin was able to make full use of in his collectivization policies and his purges (see Sections 17.2–3). It was Lenin who founded the *Cheka*, which became the dreaded KGB under Stalin, and it was Lenin who destroyed most of the powers of the trade unions.

Revisionist historians take a very different view. Moshe Lewin, Robert C. Tucker and Stephen F. Cohen argue that there was a fundamental discontinuity between Lenin and Stalin – things changed radically under Stalin. Stephen Cohen points out that Stalin's treatment of the peasants was quite different from Lenin's merely coercive policies: Stalin waged a virtual civil war against the peasantry, 'a holocaust by terror that victimized tens of millions of people for 25 years'. Lenin was against the cult of the individual leader, whereas Stalin began his own personality cult. Lenin wanted to keep the Party bureaucracy as small and manageable as possible, but Stalin enlarged it. Lenin encouraged discussion and got his way by persuading the Politburo; Stalin allowed no discussion or criticism and got his way by having opponents murdered. In fact, during the 'Great Terror' of 1935–9, Stalin actually destroyed Lenin's Communist Party. According to Robert Conquest, 'it was in cold blood, quite deliberately and unprovokedly, that Stalin started a new cycle of suffering'.

Robert Suny provides this clear summing up of Leninism and its relationship to Stalinism:

Devoted to Karl Marx's vision of socialism, in which the working class would control the machines, factories and other sorts of wealth production, the communists led by Lenin believed that the future social order would be based on the abolition of unearned social privilege, the end of racism and colonial oppression, the secularization of society, and the empowerment of working people. Yet within a generation Stalin and his closest comrades had created one of the most vicious and oppressive states in modern history.

FURTHER READING

Acton, E., *Rethinking the Russian Revolution* (Edward Arnold, 1990).
Berkman, A., *The Russian Tragedy* (Consortium Books, 1989 edition).
Brown, A., *The Rise and Fall of Communism* (Vintage, 2010).
D'Encausse, H. C., *Lenin* (Holmes & Meier, 2001).
Ferro, M., *Nicholas II: The Last of the Tsars* (Viking, 1991).
Figes, O., *A People's Tragedy: The Russian Revolution, 1891–1924* (Penguin edition, 1998).
Fitzpatrick, S., *The Russian Revolution* (Oxford University Press, 3rd edition, 2008).
Hill, C., *Lenin and the Russian Revolution* (Penguin, 1971 edition).
Lewin, M., *The Making of the Soviet System* (New Press, 1994).
Lewin, M., *Lenin's Last Struggle* (Michigan University Press, 2005).
Lieven, D. C. B., *Nicholas II: Emperor of All the Russias* (John Murray, 1996).
Lincoln, W. B., *Red Victory: A History of the Russian Civil War, 1918–21* (Da Capo, 1999).
Lowe, N., *Mastering Twentieth Century Russian History* (Palgrave Macmillan, 2002).
Massie, R. K., *The Romanovs: The Final Chapter* (Random House, 1995).
McCauley, M., *The Rise and Fall of the Soviet Union* (Longman, 2nd edition, 2007).
Nove, A., *An Economic History of the USSR* (Penguin, 3rd edition, 1992).
Pipes, R., *The Russian Revolution, 1899–1919* (Harvill, 1993).
Pipes, R., *Russia under the Bolshevik Regime, 1919–1924* (Harvill, 1997 edition).
Radzinsky, E., *Rasputin* (Weidenfeld & Nicolson, 2000).
Read, C., *From Tsar to Soviets: The Russian People and their Revolution,1917–21* (Oxford University Press, 1996).
Read, C., *Lenin: A Revolutionary Life* (Routledge, 2005).
Service, R., *The Russian Revolution 1900–1927* (Macmillan, 3rd edition, 1999).
Service, R. *Lenin: A Biography* (Macmillan, 2000).
Service, R., *Stalin: A Biography* (Macmillan, 2004).
Service, R., *Comrades: A World History of Communism* (Macmillan, 2007).
Service, R., *Trotsky: A Biography* (Macmillan, 2010).
Smith, S. A., *Red Petrograd: Revolution in the Factories, 1917–1918* (Cambridge University Press, 1983).
Suny, R. G., *The Soviet Experiment* (Oxford University Press, 2nd edition, 2010).
Ulam, A. B., *Lenin and the Bolsheviks* (Fontana/Collins, 1965).
Volkogonov, D., *Lenin: Life and Legend* (Free Press, 1994).
Wood, A., *The Origins of the Russian Revolution, 1861–1917* (Routledge, 3rd edition, 2003).
Yakovlev, A., *A Century of Violence in Soviet Russia* (Yale University Press, 2002).

QUESTIONS

1 Explain why the tsarist regime was able to survive the 1905 revolution but was overthrown in February/March 1917.

2   How far would you agree that the February/March revolution which overthrew the Russian monarchy was a 'spontaneous uprising'?

3   'The Bolsheviks did not seize power, they picked it up; any group of determined men could have done what the Bolsheviks did in Petrograd in October 1917' (Adam Ulam). Explain to what extent you agree or disagree with this view.

4   How far was popular dissatisfaction with the Provisional Government responsible for its overthrow in October/November 1917?

5   How far did the Tsar Nicholas II fulfil the promises made in the 1905 October Manifesto by the outbreak of war in 1914)

6   How far was Russia a modernized industrial state by 1914?

7   How far would you agree that the impact of the First World War on Russia was the main reason for the downfall of Nicholas II in 1917?

8   How far would you agree that Lenin's leadership was the main reason for the success of the Bolshevik Revolution in 1917?

9   In what ways, and with what success, did Lenin's policies attempt to solve the problems facing Russia at the beginning of 1918?

10 Assess the reasons why the Bolsheviks were victorious in the civil war by 1921.

There is a document question about differing views of Lenin on the website.

Chapter 17

The USSR and Stalin, 1924–53

SUMMARY OF EVENTS

When Lenin died in January 1924, it was widely expected that Trotsky would take over as leader, but a complex power struggle developed from which Stalin emerged triumphant by the end of 1929. He remained the dominant figure in the USSR, in effect a dictator, right through the Second World War and until his death in 1953 at the age of 73. Immense problems faced communist Russia, which was still only a few years old when Lenin died in January 1924. Industry and agriculture were underdeveloped and inefficient, there were constant food shortages, pressing social and political problems and – many Russians thought – the danger of another attempt by foreign capitalist powers to destroy the new communist state. Stalin made determined efforts to overcome all these problems: he was responsible for the following:

- Five Year Plans to revolutionize industry, carried out between 1928 and 1941;
- collectivization of agriculture, which was completed by 1936;
- introduction of *a totalitarian regime* which, if anything, was even more ruthless than Hitler's system in Germany.

All his policies aroused criticism among some of the 'Old Bolsheviks', especially the speed of industrialization and the harsh treatment of peasants and industrial workers. However, Stalin was determined to eliminate all opposition; in 1934 he began what became known as 'the Purges', in which, over the next three years, some two million people were arrested and sentenced to execution or imprisonment in a labour camp for 'plotting against the Soviet state'. There was a vast network of these camps, known as the 'Gulag'. It is estimated that perhaps as many as ten million people 'disappeared' during the 1930s, as all criticism, opposition and possible alternative leaders were eliminated and the ordinary population were terrorized into obedience.

Yet brutal though Stalin's methods were, they seem to have been successful, at least to the extent that when the dreaded attack from the West eventually came, in the form of a massive German invasion in June 1941, the Russians were able to hold out, and eventually end up on the winning side, though at a terrible cost (see Sections 6.2, 6.3 and 6.9). The western part of the country, which had been occupied by the Germans, was in ruins, and many people would have been happy to see the end of Stalin. But he was determined that his dictatorship and the one-party state should continue. There was a return to the harsh policies, which had been relaxed to some extent during the war.

17.1 HOW DID STALIN GET TO SUPREME POWER?

Joseph Djugashvili (he took the name 'Stalin' – man of steel – soon after joining the Bolsheviks in 1904) was born in 1879 in the small town of Gori in the province of

Illustration 17.1   **Joseph Stalin**

Georgia. His parents were poor peasants; his father, a shoemaker, had been born a serf. Joseph's mother wanted him to become a priest and he was educated for four years at Tiflis Theological Seminary, but he hated its repressive atmosphere and was expelled in 1899 for spreading socialist ideas. After 1917, thanks to his outstanding ability as an administrator, he was quietly able to build up his own position under Lenin. When Lenin died in 1924, Stalin was Secretary-General of the Communist Party and a member of the seven-man Politburo, the committee which decided government policy (see Illus. 17.1).

At first it seemed unlikely that Stalin would become the dominant figure; Trotsky called him 'the party's most eminent mediocrity ... a man destined to play second or third fiddle'. The Menshevik Nikolai Sukhanov described him as 'nothing more than a vague, grey blur'. Lenin thought him stubborn and rude, and suggested in his will that Stalin should be removed from his post. 'Comrade Stalin has concentrated enormous power in his hands,' he wrote, 'and I am not sure he always knows how to use that power with sufficient caution. ... He is too crude, and this defect becomes unacceptable in the position of General-Secretary. I therefore propose to comrades that they should devise a means of removing him from this job.'

The most obvious successor to Lenin was Leon Trotsky, an inspired orator, an intellectual and a man of action – the organizer of the Red Armies. The other candidates were the 'old' Bolsheviks who had been in the Party since the early days: Lev Kamenev (head of the Moscow party organization), Grigori Zinoviev (head of the Leningrad party organization and the Comintern) and Nikolai Bukharin, the rising intellectual star of the Party. However, circumstances arose which Stalin was able to use to eliminate his rivals.

(a) Trotsky's brilliance worked against him

It aroused envy and resentment among the other Politburo members. He was arrogant and condescending, and many resented the fact that he had only joined the Bolsheviks shortly before the November revolution. During Lenin's illness, he was bitterly critical of Kamenev, Zinoviev and Bukharin, who were acting as a triumvirate, accusing them of having no plan for the future and no vision. The others therefore decided to run the country jointly: collective action was better than a one-man show. They worked together, doing all they could to prevent Trotsky from becoming leader. By the end of 1924 almost all his support had disappeared; he was even forced to resign as Commissar for Military and Naval Affairs, though he remained a member of the Politburo.

(b) The other Politburo members underestimated Stalin

They saw him as nothing more than a competent administrator; they ignored Lenin's advice about removing him. They were so busy attacking Trotsky that they failed to recognize the very real danger from Stalin and they missed several chances to get rid of him. In fact Stalin had great political skill and intuition; he had the ability to cut through the complexities of a problem and focus on the essentials; and he was an excellent judge of character, sensing people's weaknesses and exploiting them. He knew that both Kamenev and Zinoviev were good team members but lacked leadership qualities and sound political judgement. He simply had to wait for disagreements to arise among his colleagues in the Politburo; then he would side with one faction against another, eliminating his rivals one by one until he was left supreme.

(c) Stalin used his position cleverly

As Secretary-General of the Party, a position he had held since April 1922, Stalin had full powers of appointment and promotion to important jobs such as secretaries of local Communist Party organizations. He quietly filled these positions with his own supporters, while at the same time removing the supporters of others to distant parts of the country. The local organizations chose the delegates to national Party Conferences, and so the Party Conferences gradually filled with Stalin's supporters. The Party Congresses elected the Communist Party Central Committee and the Politburo; thus by 1928 all the top bodies and congresses were packed with Stalinites, and he was unassailable.

(d) Stalin used the disagreements to his own advantage

Disagreement over policy arose in the Politburo partly because Marx had never described in detail exactly how the new communist society should be organized. Even Lenin was vague about it, except that 'the dictatorship of the proletariat' would be established – that is, workers would run the state and the economy in their own interests. When all opposition had been crushed, the ultimate goal of a classless society would be achieved, in which, according to Marx, the ruling principle would be: 'from each according to his ability, to each according to his needs'. With the New Economic Policy (NEP; see Section 16.3(g)) Lenin had departed from socialist principles, though whether he intended this as a temporary measure until the crisis passed is still open to debate. Now the right wing of the Party, led by Bukharin, and the left, whose views were most strongly put by Trotsky, Kamenev and Zinoviev, fell out about what to do next:

1   Bukharin thought it important to consolidate Soviet power in Russia, based on a prosperous peasantry and with a very gradual industrialization; this policy became known as *'socialism in one country'*. Trotsky believed that they must work for revolution outside Russia – *permanent revolution*. When this was achieved, the industrialized states of western Europe would help Russia with her industrialization. Kamenev and Zinoviev supported Bukharin in this, because it was a good pretext for attacking Trotsky.

2   *Bukharin wanted to continue NEP*, even though it was causing an increase in the numbers of wealthy peasants, *kulaks* (fists), so called because they were said to hold the ordinary peasants tightly in their grasp. Some even employed poor peasants as labourers, and were therefore regarded as budding capitalists and enemies of communism. Bukharin's opponents, who now included Kamenev and Zinoviev, wanted to abandon NEP and concentrate on rapid industrialization at the expense of the peasants.

Stalin, quietly ambitious, seemed to have no strong views either way at first, but on the question of 'socialism in one country' he came out in support of Bukharin, so that Trotsky was completely isolated. Later, when the split occurred between Bukharin on the one hand, and Kamenev and Zinoviev, who were feeling unhappy about NEP, on the other, Stalin supported Bukharin. One by one, Trotsky, Kamenev and Zinoviev were voted off the Politburo, replaced by Stalin's yes-men, and expelled from the Party (1927); eventually Trotsky was exiled from the USSR and went to live in Istanbul in Turkey.

Stalin and Bukharin were now the joint leaders, but Bukharin did not survive for long. The following year Stalin, who had supported NEP and its great advocate, Bukharin, ever since it was introduced, now decided that NEP must go – he claimed that the *kulaks* were holding up agricultural progress. When Bukharin protested, he too was voted off the Politburo (1929), leaving Stalin supreme. Stalin's critics claimed that this was a cynical change of policy on his part, designed simply to eliminate Bukharin. To be fair to Stalin, it does seem to have been a genuine policy decision; NEP had begun to falter and was not producing the necessary amounts of food. Robert Service makes the point that Stalin's policies were actually popular with the vast majority of party members, who genuinely believed that the *kulaks* were blocking progress to socialism and getting rich while the industrial workers went short of food.

17.2   HOW SUCCESSFUL WAS STALIN IN SOLVING RUSSIA'S ECONOMIC PROBLEMS?

(a)   What were Russia's economic problems?

1   Although Russian industry was recovering from the effects of the First World War, *production from heavy industry was still surprisingly low*. In 1929 for example, France, which did not rank as a leading industrial power, produced more coal and steel than Russia, while Germany, Britain and especially the USA were streets ahead. Stalin believed that a rapid expansion of heavy industry was essential to enable Russia to deal with the attack which he was convinced would come sooner or later from the western capitalist powers, who hated communism. Industrialization would have the added advantage of increasing support for the government, because *it was the industrial workers who were the communists' greatest allies*: the more industrial workers there were in relation to peasants (whom Stalin saw as the enemies of socialism), the more secure the communist state would

be. One serious obstacle to overcome, however, was lack of capital to finance expansion, since foreigners were unwilling to invest in a communist state.

2 *More food would have to be produced*, both to feed the growing industrial population and to provide a surplus for export (the only way that the USSR could earn foreign capital and profits for investment in industry). Yet the primitive agricultural system, which was allowed to continue under NEP, was incapable of providing such resources. By the beginning of 1928 there were food shortages in the cities and there seemed to be a real danger of famine by the end of the winter unless something drastic was done.

(b) The Five Year Plans for industry

Although he had no economic experience whatsoever, Stalin seems to have had no hesitation in plunging the country into a series of dramatic changes designed to overcome the problems in the shortest possible time. In a speech in February 1931 he explained why: 'We are 50 or 100 years behind the advanced countries. We must make good this distance in 10 years. Either we do it or we shall be crushed.' NEP had been permissible as a temporary measure, but must now be abandoned: both industry and agriculture must be taken firmly under government control.

Industrial expansion was tackled by a series of *Five Year Plans*, the first two of which (1928–32 and 1933–7) were said to have been completed a year ahead of schedule, although in fact neither of them reached the full target. The third Plan (1938–42) was cut short by the USSR's involvement in the Second World War. The first Plan concentrated on heavy industries – coal, iron, steel, oil and machinery (including tractors), which were scheduled to triple output. The two later Plans provided for some increases in consumer goods as well as in heavy industry. It has to be said that in spite of all kinds of mistakes and some exaggeration of the official Soviet figures, the Plans were a remarkable success: by 1940 the USSR had overtaken Britain in iron and steel production, though not yet in coal, and was within reach of Germany (see Tables 17.1 and 17.2).

Hundreds of factories were built, many of them in new towns east of the Ural Mountains where they would be safer from invasion. Well-known examples are the iron and steel works at Magnitogorsk, tractor works at Kharkov and Gorki, a hydro-electric dam at Dnepropetrovsk and the oil refineries in the Caucasus. This proved to be an inspired decision: on 22 June 1941 the Germans invaded Russia and soon overran the western parts of the USSR. Without the new industry, the war would have been quickly lost (see Sections 6.2(b), 6.3(c) and 6.7).

How was all this achieved?

The cash was provided almost entirely by the Russians themselves, with no foreign investment. Some came from grain exports, some from charging peasants heavily for the use of

Table 17.1 **Industrial expansion in the USSR: production in millions of tons**

	1900	*1913*	*1929*	*1938*	*1940*
Coal	16.0	36.0	40.1	132.9	164.9
Pig-iron	2.7	4.8	8.0	26.3	14.9
Steel	2.5	5.2	4.9	18.0	18.4

Table 17.2 **Industrial production in the USSR compared with other great powers, 1940**

	Pig-iron	Steel	Coal	Electricity (in billion kilowatts)
USSR	14.9	18.4	164.6	39.6
USA	31.9	47.2	395.0	115.9
Britain	6.7	10.3	227.0	30.7
Germany	18.3	22.7	186.0	55.2
France	6.0	16.1	45.5	19.3

government equipment, and the ruthless ploughing-back of all profits and surpluses. Hundreds of foreign technicians were brought in and great emphasis was placed on expanding education in colleges and universities, and even in factory schools, to provide a whole new generation of skilled workers. In the factories, the old capitalist methods of piecework and pay differentials between skilled and unskilled workers were used to encourage production. Medals were given to workers who achieved record output; these were known as *Stakhanovites*, after Alexei Stakhanov, a champion miner who, in August 1935, supported by a well-organized team, managed to cut 102 tons of coal in a single shift (by ordinary methods even the highly efficient miners of the Ruhr in Germany were cutting only 10 tons per shift).

Unfortunately the Plans had their drawbacks. Ordinary workers were ruthlessly disciplined: there were severe punishments for bad workmanship, people were accused of being 'saboteurs' or 'wreckers' when targets were not met, and given spells in forced labour camps. Primitive housing conditions and a severe shortage of consumer goods (because of the concentration on heavy industry), on top of all the regimentation, must have made life grim for most workers. As historian Richard Freeborn pointed out (in *A Short History of Modern Russia*): 'It is probably no exaggeration to claim that the First Five Year Plan represented a declaration of war by the state machine against the workers and peasants of the USSR who were subjected to a greater exploitation than any they had known under capitalism.' However, by the mid-1930s things were improving as benefits such as medical care, education and holidays with pay became available. Another major drawback with the Plans was that many of the products were of poor quality. The high targets forced workers to speed up and this caused shoddy workmanship and damage to machinery.

In spite of the weaknesses of the Plans, Martin McCauley (in *Stalin and Stalinism*) believes that 'the First Five-Year Plan was a period of genuine enthusiasm, and prodigious achievements were recorded in production. The impossible targets galvanized people into action, and more was achieved than would have been the case had orthodox advice been followed.' Alec Nove leaned towards a similar view; he argued that, given the industrial backwardness inherited from the tsarist period, something drastic was needed. 'Under Stalin's leadership an assault was launched ... which succeeded in part but failed in some sectors. ... A great industry was built ... and where would the Russian army have been in 1942 without a Urals–Siberian metallurgical base?' Nove acknowledged, however, that Stalin made vast errors – he tried to go too far much too fast, used unnecessarily brutal methods and treated all criticism, even when it was justified, as evidence of subversion and treason.

(c) The collectivization of agriculture

The problems of agriculture were dealt with by the process known as 'collectivization'. The idea was that small farms and holdings belonging to the peasants should be merged to form large collective farms (*kolkhoz*) jointly owned by the peasants. There were two main reasons for Stalin's decision to collectivize.

- The existing system of small farms was inefficient, and seemed unable to satisfy the increasing demand for food, especially in the growing industrial cities. However, large farms, under state direction, and using tractors and combine harvesters, would vastly increase grain production, or so the theory went.
- He wanted to eliminate the class of prosperous peasants (*kulaks*), which NEP had encouraged, because, he claimed, they were standing in the way of progress. The real reason was probably political: Stalin saw the *kulaks* as the enemy of communism. 'We must smash the *kulaks* so hard that they will never rise to their feet again.'

The policy was launched in earnest in 1929, and had to be carried through by sheer brute force, so determined was the resistance in the countryside. It proved to be a disaster, and it took Russia at least half a century to recover. There was no problem in collectivizing landless labourers, but all peasants who owned any property at all, whether they were *kulaks* or not, were hostile to the plan, and had to be forced to join by armies of party members, who urged poorer peasants to seize cattle and machinery from the *kulaks* to be handed over to the collectives. *Kulaks* often reacted by slaughtering cattle and burning crops rather than allow the state to take them. Peasants who refused to join collective farms were arrested and taken to labour camps, or shot. When newly collectivized peasants tried to sabotage the system by producing only enough for their own needs, local officials insisted on seizing the required quotas. In this way, well over 90 per cent of all farmland had been collectivized by 1937.

In one sense Stalin could claim that collectivization was a success: it allowed greater mechanization, which did achieve a substantial increase in production in 1937. The amount of grain taken by the state increased impressively and so did grain exports: 1930 and 1931 were excellent years for exports, and although the amounts fell sharply after that, they were still far higher than before collectivization. On the other hand, so many animals had been slaughtered that it was 1953 before livestock production recovered to the 1928 figure, and the cost in human life and suffering was enormous.

The truth was that total grain production did not increase at all (except for 1930) – in fact it was less in 1934 than it had been in 1928. *The reasons for this failure were*:

- The best producers – the *kulaks* – were excluded from the collective farms. Most of the party activists who came from the cities to organize collectivization did not know much about agriculture.
- Many peasants were demoralized after the seizure of their land and property; some of them left the *kolkhoz* to look for jobs in the cities. With all the arrests and deportations, this meant that there were far fewer peasants to work the land.
- The government did not at first provide sufficient tractors; since many peasants had slaughtered their horses rather than hand them over to the *kolkhoz*, there were serious problems in trying to get the ploughing done in time.
- Peasants were still allowed to keep a small private plot of their own; they tended to work harder on their own plots and do the minimum they could get away with on the *kolkhoz*.

Table 17.3 **Grain and livestock statistics in the USSR**

Actual grain harvest (in million tons)									
1913	*1928*	*1929*	*1930*	*1931*	*1932*	*1933*	*1934*	*1936*	*1937*
80.1	73.3	71.7	83.5	69.5	69.6	68.4	67.6	56.1	97.4

Grain taken by the state (in million tons)					
1928	*1929*	*1930*	*1931*	*1932*	*1933*
10.8	16.1	22.1	22.8	18.5	22.6

Grain exported (in million tons)					
1927–8	*1929*	*1930*	*1931*	*1932*	*1933*
0.029	0.18	4.76	5.06	1.73	1.69

Livestock in the the USSR (in millions)								
	1928	*1929*	*1930*	*1931*	*1932*	*1933*	*1934*	*1935*
Cattle	70.5	67.1	52.5	47.9	40.7	38.4	42.2	49.3
Pigs	26.0	20.4	13.6	14.4	11.6	12.1	17.4	22.6
Sheep & goats	146.7	147.0	108.8	77.7	52.1	50.2	51.9	61.1

A combination of all these factors led to famine, mainly in the countryside, during 1932–3, especially in Ukraine. Yet 1.75 million tons of grain were exported during that same period while over 5 million peasants died of starvation. Some historians have even claimed that Stalin welcomed the famine, since, along with the 10 million *kulaks* who were removed or executed, it helped to break peasant resistance. Certainly it meant that for the first time the state had taken important steps towards controlling the countryside. The government could get its hands on the grain without having to be constantly haggling with the peasants. No longer would the *kulaks* hold the socialist state to ransom by causing food shortages in the cities; it was the countryside which would suffer now if there was a bad harvest. The statistics in Table 17.3 give some idea of the scale of the problems created.

17.3 POLITICS AND THE PURGES

(a) Political problems

During the 1930s Stalin and his closest allies gradually tightened their grip on the Party, the government and the local party organizations, until by 1938 all criticism and disagreement had been driven underground. Although his personal dictatorship was complete, Stalin did not feel secure; he became increasingly suspicious, trusted nobody and seemed to see plots everywhere. The main political issues during these years were:

1 By the summer of 1930, the government's popularity with the general public had fallen sharply because of collectivization and the hardships of the First Five Year Plan. There was growing opposition to Stalin in the Party; a document known as the 'Ryutin Platform' (after one of the Moscow party leaders) was circulated, advocating

a slowdown in industrialization, more gentle treatment of the peasants and the removal of Stalin (described as 'the evil genius of the Revolution') from the leadership, by force if necessary. However, Stalin was equally determined that political opponents and critics must be eliminated once and for all.

2 A new constitution was needed to consolidate the hold of Stalin and the Communist Party over the whole country.

3 Some of the non-Russian parts of the country wanted to become independent, but Stalin, although he was non-Russian himself (he was born in Georgia), had no sympathy with nationalist ambitions and was determined to hold the union together.

(b) The Purges and the Great Terror, 1934–8

The first priority for Stalin was to deal with the opposition. During the early part of 1933 more party members began to call for the break-up of collective farms, the return of powers to the trade unions and the removal of Stalin. But Stalin and his allies in the Politburo would have none of it and they voted for a purge of dissident party members. By the end of 1933, over 800 000 had been expelled, and a further 340 000 were expelled in 1934. There were over 2 million people in prisons and forced labour camps. As yet, however, nobody was executed for opposing Stalin; Sergei Kirov (the Leningrad party boss and ally of Stalin) and Sergo Ordzhonikidze (Stalin's fellow-Georgian and staunch ally) both voted against the death penalty. However, Ordzhonikidze later committed suicide when he became aware of the full horror of what was happening.

In December 1934 Kirov was shot dead by Leonid Nikolaev, a young Communist Party member. Stalin announced that a wide-ranging plot had been uncovered to assassinate himself and Molotov (the prime minister) as well. The murder was used as the pretext for launching further purges against anybody that Stalin distrusted. It seems likely that Stalin himself organized Kirov's murder, perhaps because he suspected him of plotting to take over the leadership himself. Historian Robert Conquest (in *The Great Terror: A Reassessment*) calls the murder 'the crime of the century, the keystone of the entire edifice of terror and suffering by which Stalin secured his grip on the soviet peoples'. From 1936 until 1938 this campaign intensified to such an extent that it became known as 'the Great Terror'. The number of victims is still in dispute, but even the more modest estimates put the total executed and sent to labour camps at well over three million in the years 1937–8 alone.

Hundreds of important officials were arrested, tortured, made to confess to all sorts of crimes, of which they were largely innocent (such as plotting with the exiled Trotsky or with capitalist governments to overthrow the Soviet state), and forced to appear in a series of 'show trials' at which they were invariably found guilty and sentenced to death or labour camp. Those executed included M. N. Ryutin (author of the Ryutin Platform), all the 'Old Bolsheviks' – Zinoviev, Kamenev and Bukharin – who had helped to make the 1917 revolution; the commander-in-chief of the Red Army, Tukhachevsky, 13 other generals and about two-thirds of the army's top officers. Millions of innocent people ended up in labour camps (estimates range from 5 million to around 8 million). Even Trotsky was sought out and murdered in exile in Mexico City (1940).

What were Stalin's motives for such an extraordinary policy? The traditional view is that Stalin was driven by his immense lust for power; once he had achieved supreme power he would stop at nothing to hold on to it. Robert Conquest suggested that Stalin's Terror has to be looked at as a mass phenomenon rather than in terms of individuals; even Stalin could hardly have had personal grudges against several million people; nor could they all have been plotting against him. Stalin's motive was to frighten the great mass of the population into uncomplaining obedience by deliberately arresting and shooting a given proportion of that society, whether they were guilty of any crime or not.

Revisionist historians have tried to shift the blame to some extent away from Stalin. J. Arch Getty argues that the Purges were a form of political infighting at the top. He plays down the role of Stalin and claims that it was the obsessive fears of all the leaders which generated the Terror. Sheila Fitzpatrick suggests that the Purges must be seen in the context of continuing revolution; the circumstances were abnormal – all revolutions are faced by constant conspiracies designed to destroy them, so abnormal responses can be expected.

Some of the most recent evidence to emerge from the Soviet archives seems to bear out the traditional view. Dmitri Volkogonov came to the conclusion that Stalin simply had an evil mind and lacked any moral sense. It was Stalin who gave the orders to Nikolai Yezhov, head of the NKVD (as the secret police were now called), about the scale of the repressions, and it was Stalin who personally approved long lists of people to be executed. After he had announced the end of the Terror, Stalin made Yezhov the scapegoat, accusing him and his subordinates of going too far. Yezhov was a 'scoundrel' who was guilty of great excesses, and he and most of his staff were arrested and shot. In this way Stalin diverted responsibility for the Terror away from himself, and so managed to keep some of his popularity.

The Purges were successful in eliminating possible alternative leaders and in terrorizing the masses into obedience. The central and local government, government in the republics, the army and navy and the economic structures of the country had all been violently subdued. Stalin ruled unchallenged with the help of his supporting clique – Molotov, Kaganovich, Mikoyan, Zhdanov, Voroshilov, Bulganin, Beria, Malenkov and Khrushchev – until his death in 1953.

But the consequences of the Purges and the Terror were serious.

- Historians are still arguing about how many people fell victim to the Purges. But whichever statistics you accept, the cost in human lives and suffering is almost beyond belief. Robert Conquest gave relatively high figures: just for the years 1937–8 he estimated about 7 million arrests, about a million executions and about 2 million deaths in the labour camps. He also estimated that of those in the camps, no more than 10 per cent survived. Official KGB figures released in the early 1990s show that in the same period there were 700 000 executions, and that at the end of the 1930s there were 3.6 million people in labour camps and prisons. Ronald Suny points out that if you add the 4 million to 5 million people who perished in the famine of 1932–3 to the total figures of those executed or exiled during the 1930s, 'the total number of lives destroyed runs from ten to eleven million'.
- Lenin's old Bolshevik Party was the main victim; the power of the Bolshevik elite had been broken and eliminated.
- Many of the best brains in the government and in industry had disappeared. In a country where numbers of highly educated people were still relatively small, this was bound to hinder progress.
- The purge of the army disrupted the USSR's defence policies at a time of great international tension, and contributed to the disasters of 1941–2 during the Second World War.

(c)   The new constitution of 1936

In 1936, after much discussion, a new and apparently more democratic constitution was introduced. It described the USSR as 'a socialist state of workers and peasants' resulting from 'the overthrow of the landlords and capitalists'. It stated that everyone, including 'former people' (ex-nobles, *kulaks*, priests and White Army officers), was allowed to vote by secret ballot to choose members of a national assembly known as *the Supreme Soviet*. However, this met for only about two weeks in the year, when it elected a smaller body, *the Praesidium*, to act on its behalf. The Supreme Soviet also chose *the Council of People's Commissars*, a small group of ministers of which Stalin was the secretary. *In fact the democracy was an illusion*: the elections, to be held every four years, were not competitive – there was only one candidate to vote for in each constituency, and that was the Communist Party candidate. It was claimed that the Communist Party represented everybody's interests. The aim of the candidates was to get as near as possible to 100 per cent of the votes, thereby showing that the government's policies were popular.

The constitution merely underlined the fact that Stalin and the Party ran things. Although it was not specifically stated in the constitution, the real power remained with the Politburo, the leading body of the Communist Party, and with its general secretary, Joseph Stalin, who acted as a dictator. There was mention of 'universal human rights', including freedom of speech, thought, the press and religion; the right to employment and to public assembly and street demonstrations. But in reality, anybody who ventured to criticize Stalin was quickly 'purged'. Not surprisingly, very few people in the USSR took the 1936 constitution seriously.

(d) Holding the union together

In 1914, before the First World War, the tsarist empire included many non-Russian areas – Poland, Finland, the Ukraine, Belorussia (White Russia), Georgia, Armenia, Azerbaijan, Kazakhstan, Kirghizia, Uzbekistan, Turkmenistan, Tajikistan and the three Baltic states of Estonia, Latvia and Lithuania. Poland and the three Baltic republics were given independence by the Treaty of Brest–Litovsk (March 1918). Many of the others wanted independence too, and at first the new Bolshevik government was sympathetic to these different nationalities. Lenin gave Finland independence in November 1917.

However, some of the others were not prepared to wait: by March 1918, Ukraine, Georgia, Armenia and Azerbaijan had declared themselves independent and soon showed themselves to be anti-Bolshevik. Stalin, who was appointed commissar (minister) for nationalities by Lenin, decided that these hostile states surrounding Russia were too much of a threat; during the civil war they were all forced to become part of Russia again. By 1925 there were six Soviet republics – Russia itself, Transcaucasia (consisting of Georgia, Armenia and Azerbaijan), Ukraine, Belorussia, Uzbekistan and Turkmenistan.

The problem for the communist government was that 47 per cent of the population of the USSR were non-Russian, and it would be difficult to hold them all together if they were bitterly resentful of rule from Moscow. Stalin adopted a two-handed approach, which worked successfully until Gorbachev came to power in 1985:

- on the one hand, national cultures and languages were encouraged and the republics had a certain amount of independence; this was much more liberal than under the tsarist regime, which had tried to 'Russianize' the empire;
- on the other hand, it had to be clearly understood that Moscow had the final say in all important decisions. If necessary, force would be used to preserve control by Moscow.

When the Ukrainian Communist Party stepped out of line in 1932 by admitting that collectivization had been a failure, Moscow carried out a ruthless purge of what Stalin called 'bourgeois nationalist deviationists'. Similar campaigns followed in Belorussia, Transcaucasia and Central Asia. Later, in 1951, when the Georgian communist leaders tried to take Georgia out of the USSR, Stalin had them removed and shot.

(e)   Was Stalin's regime totalitarian?

The traditional western democratic view held by historians such as Adam Ulam and Robert Conquest was that Stalin's regime was totalitarian, in many ways like Hitler's Nazi regime in Germany. A 'perfect' totalitarian regime is one in which there is dictatorial rule in a one-party state which totally controls all activities – economic, political, social, intellectual and cultural – and directs them towards achieving the state's goals. The state attempts to indoctrinate everybody with the party ideology and to mobilize society in its support; both mental and physical terror, and violence are used to crush opposition and keep the regime in power. As we have seen, there was ample evidence of all these characteristics at work in Stalin's system.

However, during the 1970s, 'revisionist' Western historians, among whom Sheila Fitzpatrick was one of the leaders, began to look at the Stalin period from a social viewpoint. They criticized the 'totalitarian' historians on the grounds that they ignored social history and presented society as the passive victim of government policies, whereas, in fact, there was a great deal of solid support for the system from the many people who benefited from it. These included all the officials in the party state bureaucracy and trade unions, the new managerial classes and key industrial workers – the new elite. The social historians suggested that to some extent these people were able to show 'initiatives from below', and even negotiate and bargain with the regime, so that they were able to influence policy. A further twist occurred during the 1980s when a group of historians, notably J. Arch Getty, claimed that the 'totalitarian' historians had exaggerated Stalin's personal role; they suggested that his system was inefficient and chaotic.

The 'totalitarian' writers criticized Arch Getty and his colleagues on the grounds that they were trying to whitewash Stalin and to gloss over the criminal aspects of his policies. The latter in turn accused the totalitarianists of Cold War prejudice – refusing to recognize that anything good could come out of a communist system.

From the new evidence emerging from the archives, it is now possible to arrive at a more balanced conclusion – there are elements of truth in both interpretations. It is impossible to ignore the central role of Stalin himself; all the evidence suggests that after 1928 it was Stalin's policy preferences which were carried out. On the other hand, the regime did not completely ignore public opinion – even Stalin wanted to be popular and to feel that he had the support of the new elite groups. There is ample evidence too that although the regime had totalitarian aims, in practice it was far from successful. Streams of orders came from the top which would have been obeyed without question in a genuine totalitarian state; yet in the USSR, peasants and workers found plenty of ways of ignoring or evading unpopular government orders. The more the government tried to tighten controls, the more counter-productive its efforts often became, and the greater the tensions between central and regional leaderships.

Clearly the Stalinist system was over-centralized, disorganized, inefficient, corrupt, sluggish and unresponsive. But at the same time, it was extremely efficient at operating terror and purges – nobody was safe. Whatever else it was, everyday life under Stalin was never 'normal'. According to Robert Service (in *Comrades,* 2007), 'the USSR was a listening state with an insatiable curiosity, in which maids, porters and drivers were routinely employed to file reports'. It seems clear that many people, perhaps even a majority of the population, lived a kind of double existence. At work and in public they were careful to mouth all the correct opinions and on no account to make the slightest criticism of the regime. Only at home with the family or among the most trustworthy friends would anybody be foolish enough to express their private thoughts and say what they really thought of Comrade Stalin.

However much they might try, ordinary people in the USSR could not avoid contact with the state – being educated, finding a job, getting promotion, marrying and bringing up children, finding somewhere to live, shopping, travelling, sport, reading literature, going to the theatre and concerts, enjoying the visual arts, practising their religion, reading the news, listening to the radio – in all these activities people came up against the state. This was because the communists had a mission: to eradicate 'backwardness'. The Soviet state must become modernized and socialist, and the new Soviet citizen must be educated and 'cultured'. It was the duty of artists, musicians and writers to play their part in this transformation: they were to attack 'bourgeois' values by producing works of 'socialist realism' which glorified the Soviet system. In the words of Stalin, they were to be 'engineers of the human soul', helping to indoctrinate the population with socialist values. Even the Moscow Dinamo football team was run by the NKVD.

(a)   A hard life

Although the ideals were impressive, all the evidence suggests that the most striking point about everyday life in the early 1930s was that everything, including food, seemed to be in short supply. This was partly because of the concentration on heavy industry at the expense of consumer goods, and partly because of famine and bad harvests. In 1933 the average married worker in Moscow consumed less than half the amount of bread and flour consumed by his counterpart around 1900. In 1937, average real wages were only about three-fifths of what they had been in 1928.

The rapid growth of the urban population – which increased by 31 million between 1926 and 1939 – caused serious housing shortages. Local soviets controlled all the housing in a town; they had the power to evict residents and move new residents into already occupied houses. It was common for middle-class families living in large houses to be told that they were taking up too much space and to find their home transformed into a 'communal apartment' as perhaps two or three other families were moved in. Kitchens, bathrooms and toilets were shared between families, and most large houses had people living in corridors and under staircases. Even less fortunate were the workers who lived in barracks. In the new industrial city of Magnitogorsk in 1938, half the housing consisted of barracks, which was the usual accommodation for unmarried workers and students. City conditions generally were poor; most of them lacked efficient sewage systems, running water, electric light and street lights. Moscow was the exception – here the government made a real effort to make the capital something to be proud of.

One of the most annoying aspects of life for ordinary people was the existence of special elite groups such as party members, government officials in the bureaucracy (these were known as *nomenklatura*), successful members of the intelligentsia, engineers, experts and Stakhanovites. They escaped the worst of the hardships and enjoyed many privileges – they had bread delivered to their homes instead of having to queue for hours to buy a loaf, and they were allowed lower prices, better living accommodation and the use of *dachas* (country houses). This resulted in a 'them and us' attitude, and ordinary people felt aggrieved that they were still the underdogs.

(b)   Signs of improvement

In a speech in November 1935 Stalin told his audience of Stakhanovites: 'life has become better, life has become more joyous'. This was not entirely wishful thinking: food supplies improved and all rationing was abolished in 1936. The provision of cheap meals in factory canteens and free work clothes was a great help. Education and healthcare were free, and the number of schools and medical centres was increasing. The government worked hard at the concept of state paternalism – the idea that the population were like children, who must be looked after, protected and guided by the state, which acted as a sort of guardian. The state provided more facilities for leisure: by the end of the 1930s there were close on 30 000 cinemas, there were sports facilities for players and spectators, and there were public gardens and culture parks. The largest and most famous was Gorky Park in Moscow, named after Maxim Gorky, one of Stalin's favourite writers. Most towns of any size had a theatre and a library.

Another important aspect of the state's role was to encourage what the Russians called *kul'turnost'* – 'culturedness'. This involved taking care over one's appearance and personal hygiene. Some industrial enterprises ordered that all engineers and managers should be clean-shaven and have their hair neatly cut. Conditions in barracks were improved by the use of partitions, so that each person had his own space. Other signs of culture were sleeping on sheets, eating with a knife and fork, avoiding drunkenness and bad language and not beating your wife and children. According to Stephen Kotkin, the cultured person was one who had learned to 'speak Bolshevik': he knew how to conduct himself in the workplace, stopped spitting on the floor, could make a speech and propose a motion; and he could understand the basic ideas of Marxism.

'Culturedness' was extended to shopping: at the end of 1934 over 13 000 new bread shops opened across the country; the assistants wore white smocks and caps and had lessons in how to be polite to customers. Strict new sanitary regulations were brought in and loaves had to be wrapped. This campaign for 'cultured trade' spread to every shop in the country, from the largest Moscow department store to the smallest bread shop.

(c) The state, women and the family

The 1930s were a difficult time for many families because of the 'disappearance' of so many men during collectivization, the famine and the Purges. There was a high desertion and divorce rate, and millions of women were left as the sole breadwinner in the family. During the rapid industrialization of the 1930s more than 10 million women became wage earners for the first time; the percentage of women at work rose from 24 per cent to 39 per cent of the total paid workforce. By 1940 about two-thirds of the workforce in light industry were women and many were even engaged in heavier jobs such as construction, lumbering and machine-building, which were traditionally thought of as men's work.

The government faced the dilemma that it needed women to provide much of the workforce for the industrialization drive, while at the same time it wanted to encourage and strengthen the family unit. One way of coping was to build more day-care centres and nurseries for children – the number of places doubled in the two years 1929–30. In the mid-1930s new laws were passed encouraging women to have as many children as possible; abortion was made illegal except in cases where the mother's life was in danger; maternity leave of up to 16 weeks was allowed and there were to be various subsidies and other benefits for pregnant women. Even so, this placed a heavy burden on working-class and peasant women, who were expected to produce children, take jobs, increase output and look after the household and family.

Things were different for wives of the elite, and for educated women, either married or single, who had professional jobs. They were seen by the state as part of its campaign to 'civilize' the masses. The Wives' Movement, as it became known, began in 1936; its aim was to raise the culturedness of the people the wives came into contact with, particularly those in their husbands' workplaces. Their main duty was to make a comfortable home life for their husbands and families. Towards the end of the 1930s, as war began to seem more likely, the Wives' Movement encouraged women to learn to drive lorries, shoot, and even to fly planes, so that they would be ready to take men's places if they had to go to war.

(d) Education

One of the greatest achievements of the Stalinist regime was the expansion of free, mass education. In 1917 under half the population could be described as literate. In January 1930 the government announced that by the end of the summer, all children aged 8 to 11 must be enrolled in schools. Between 1929 and 1931 the number of pupils increased from 14 million to around 20 million; it was in rural areas, where education had been patchy, that most of the increase took place. By 1940 there were 199 000 schools, and even the most remote areas of the USSR were well provided. Many new training colleges were set up to train the new generation of teachers and lecturers. According to the census of 1939, of people aged between 9 and 49, 94 per cent in the towns and 86 per cent in rural areas were literate. By 1959 these percentages had increased to 99 and 98, respectively.

Of course the regime had an ulterior motive – education was the way by which it could turn the younger generation into good, orthodox Soviet citizens. Religion and other 'bourgeois' practices were presented as superstitious and backward. Ironically, the education experts decided that a return to traditional teaching methods would be better than the experimental, more relaxed techniques tried in the 1920s. These had included the abolition of examinations and punishments, and an emphasis on project work. This was now reversed: teachers were given more authority and were to impose strict discipline, examinations were brought back and more teaching time was to be spent on mathematics and science.

(e) Religion

Lenin, Stalin and the other Bolshevik leaders were atheists who accepted Marx's claim that religion was merely an invention of the ruling classes to keep the people docile and under control – the 'opium of the masses'. Lenin had launched a savage attack on the Orthodox Church, seizing all its lands, schools and church buildings, and having hundreds of priests arrested. After Lenin's death the regime became more tolerant towards religious groups. Many priests were sympathetic towards communist ideals, which, after all, do have some similarities to Christian teachings about the poor and oppressed. There seemed a good chance of complete reconciliation between Church and State; with careful handling the Church could have been useful in helping to control the peasants. However, many militant young communists continued to believe that religion was a 'harmful superstition'. A 'League of Militant Godless' was formed, their aim being to persecute the clergy and eliminate religion, as far as possible.

Relations deteriorated disastrously during Stalin's regime. Many priests courageously opposed collectivization, so Stalin secretly instructed local party organizations to attack churches and priests. Hundreds of churches and cemeteries were vandalized and literally thousands of priests were killed. The number of working priests fell from about 60 000 in 1925 to under 6000 by 1941. The slaughter was not confined to Christians: hundreds of Muslim and Jewish leaders also fell victim. The campaign was relentless: by 1941 only one in 40 church buildings was still functioning as a place of worship. For the Bolsheviks, communism was the only religion, and they were determined that people should worship the communist state instead of God.

The anti-religious campaign caused outrage, especially in rural areas where priests, mullahs, shamans and rabbis were popular and respected members of the local communities. During the Second World War, State and Church were to some extent reconciled. In 1942, with the war going badly for the Russians, and both Leningrad and Moscow under attack from the Germans, Stalin decided that religion had a role to play after all, as a force for patriotism. An understanding was reached with Christians, Jews and Muslims that past differences would be forgotten in their joint struggle against the invader. Churches, mosques and synagogues were allowed to reopen, and by most accounts, the religious groups played a vital role in maintaining morale among the general public.

(f) Literature and the theatre

The years 1928 to 1931 became known as 'the Cultural Revolution', when the regime began to mobilize writers, artists and musicians to wage a cultural war against 'bourgeois intellectuals'. At first there were two rival groups of writers; the dedicated communists were members of the All-Russian Association of Proletarian Writers (RAPP) and were committed to 'socialist realism'. The other group were the non-communists, who wanted to keep politics out of literature; they were labelled dismissively by the communists as 'fellow-travellers'. They were members of the All-Russian Union of Writers (AUW), and they included most of the leading writers who had made their names before the revolution. RAPP did not approve of the AUW's attitude and accused some of its members of publishing anti-Soviet works abroad. They were found guilty and the government dissolved the AUW, replacing it with a new organization – the All-Russian Union of Soviet Writers (AUSW). About half the former members of the AUW were refused admission to the new union, which was a serious blow for them, since only union members were allowed to publish.

This left RAPP as the dominant literary organization, but it soon fell foul of Stalin. Its members believed in portraying society as it really was, with all its faults, whereas Stalin wanted it portrayed as he would like it to be. In 1930 Stalin announced that nothing could be published which went against the party line or showed the Party in a poor light. When some RAPP members failed to respond to this clear warning, Stalin disbanded both RAPP and the new AUSW, replacing them with one organization – the Union of Soviet Writers, chaired by Maxim Gorky, whose works Stalin admired. Andrei Zhdanov emerged as the politician most involved in the arts; opening the first Congress of Soviet Writers in 1934, he announced that their guiding principle must be 'the ideological remoulding and re-education of the toiling people in the spirit of socialism'.

Among the most popular new works were Nikolai Ostrovsky's novel *How the Steel was Tempered* (1934) and Mikhail Sholokov's *Virgin Soil Upturned*, which dealt with collectivization. There were other works of lesser quality, sometimes known as 'five-year plan' novels, in which the heroes were ordinary people who bravely achieved their targets in spite of all kinds of obstacles, like the train driver who overcame all the efforts of wreckers and saboteurs and repeatedly brought his train in on time. They were not great literature, but arguably they served a purpose – they were easily understood, they raised morale and they inspired people to greater efforts.

Writers who did not succeed in producing the right kind of socialist realism ran the risk of arrest. Stalin himself sometimes read novels in typescript and would add comments and suggest changes which the authors were expected to take note of. In the later 1930s many writers were arrested and kept in labour camps for long periods or even executed. Among the best-known victims were the poet Osip Mandelstam, who had written a poem criticizing Stalin; he was sent to a labour camp, where he died. Evgenia Ginsburg spent 18 years in prison and labour camps after being accused of organizing a writers' terrorist group. Some of the best writers, like the poet Anna Akhmatova and the novelist Boris Pasternak, either stopped work altogether or kept their new work locked away. Pasternak's great novel *Dr Zhivago* was published abroad only after Stalin's death. Mikhail Bulgakov's wonderful novel *The Master and Margarita* lay unpublished for years until after Stalin's death. Soon after Khrushchev came to power in 1956 the authorities announced that at least 600 writers had perished in prisons or labour camps during Stalin's rule.

Theatre people also came under attack: a number of actors, actresses and ballet dancers were sent to labour camps. The most famous victim was the great experimental director Vsevolod Meyerhold. In 1938 his theatre in Moscow was closed down on the grounds that it was 'alien to Soviet art'; Meyerhold himself was arrested, tortured and later shot, and his wife, a well-known actress, was found stabbed to death in their flat.

Ironically, after all the obsession with 'socialist realism', after the first flush of the Cultural Revolution in the early 1930s, the regime decided to reinstate nineteenth-century classical Russian literature. Pushkin, Tolstoy, Gogol, Turgenev and Chekhov were back in fashion. The government had decided that after all, these were 'revolutionary democrats'.

(g) Art, architecture and music

Artists, sculptors and musicians were all expected to play their part in 'socialist realism'. Abstract art was rejected and paintings were expected to portray workers straining every muscle to fulfil their targets, scenes from the revolution or the civil war, or Revolutionary leaders. They were to be photographic in style and finely detailed. There was a steady flow of paintings of Lenin and Stalin, and worker scenes with titles like *The Steelworker* and *The Milkmaids*. Sculptors were limited to producing busts of Lenin and Stalin, and architecture deteriorated into the uninspiring and dull, with grandiose neoclassical façades and featureless tower blocks.

Music followed a similar pattern to literature. The committed communist members of the Russian Association of Proletarian Musicians (RAPM) condemned what they described as the 'modernism' of western music. This included not only the atonal 12-note music of the Austrians Schoenberg, Webern and Berg, but also jazz, music hall-style 'light' music, and even the foxtrot. However, in the mid-1930s the regime relaxed its attitude towards non-classical music, and jazz, dance and 'light' music were permitted.

The USSR had two outstanding classical composers who had achieved international reputations by the 1930s – Sergei Prokofiev and Dmitri Shostakovich. Prokofiev had left Russia soon after the Revolution but decided to return in 1933. He was especially successful at producing music of high quality which could be readily appreciated by ordinary people – his ballet *Romeo and Juliet* and his musical story for children, *Peter and the Wolf*, were highly popular with audiences and the authorities. Shostakovich was not so successful: his first opera, *The Nose*, based on a short story by Gogol, was condemned and banned by RAPM (1930). His second opera, *Lady Macbeth of Mtsensk*, was well received by audiences and critics in 1934 and ran for over 80 performances in Leningrad and over 90 in Moscow. Unfortunately, in January 1936 Stalin himself went to a performance in Moscow and walked out before the end. Two days later a devastating article, thought to have been written by Stalin himself, appeared in *Pravda*; the opera was dismissed as 'a cacophony, crude and vulgar' and Shostakovich's work was banned. Basically, Stalin thought it had no good tunes that you could hum on the way home. Badly shaken, Shostakovich expected to be arrested; for some reason he was spared, though he remained in official disgrace for some time. He was saved from a spell in the Gulag probably because Maxim Gorky, one of Stalin's favourites, defended him, pointing out that some of his music was much more tuneful than the opera.

After the *Lady Macbeth* incident, the American ambassador in Moscow noted that 'half the artists and musicians in Moscow are having nervous prostration, and the others are trying to imagine how to write and compose in a manner to please Stalin'. Apparently Stalin, who was a great lover of ballet, liked music which was approachable, tuneful and inspiring, like that of the great nineteenth-century Russian composers Tchaikovsky and Rimsky-Korsakov. Shostakovich redeemed himself with his *Fifth Symphony* (1937), a fine piece of music which also fulfilled the requirements of the regime.

(h) The cinema

Stalin, like Lenin, considered that film was probably the most important form of communication; he loved films and had a private cinema in the Kremlin and one in his *dacha*. He demanded that Soviet films should be 'intelligible to the millions', telling a simple but powerful story. In 1930 Boris Shumyatsky was given the job of modernizing the film industry; he aimed to make films which were genuinely entertaining as well as being full of 'socialist realism'. Unfortunately, he was hampered by the arrival of sound films – these were more expensive to make, and there was a language problem in a country where so many different languages were spoken. Another difficulty was the almost impossible demands of the regime, which wanted film-makers to incorporate so many different and sometimes contradictory themes into their work – proletarian values, classless Soviet nationalism, the problems of ordinary people, the heroic exploits of the revolutionaries and the glorious communist future.

In 1935 Shumyatsky went to Hollywood to look for new ideas; he decided that the USSR needed a Soviet equivalent of Hollywood and chose the Crimea as the best site. But the government refused to provide the necessary finance and the project never got off the ground. Stalin was not satisfied with Shumyatsky's progress, and in 1938 he was arrested and shot. In spite of all these problems, over 300 Soviet films were made between 1933 and 1940, some of which were of high quality. There was a huge increase in the number of cinemas during the same period – from about 7000 to around 30 000.

Not all of these films found favour with Stalin, who became so obsessed that he vetted many scripts himself. He had to be satisfied that they successfully put over the message that life in the USSR was better and happier in every way than anywhere else in the world. Sergei Eisenstein failed to repeat his great masterpieces of the 1920s – *Strike*, *Battleship Potemkin* and *October* – until in 1938 he salvaged his reputation with his great patriotic film *Alexander Nevsky*. This told the story of the invasion of Russia by Teutonic knights in medieval times and their defeat. Given the international situation at the time, this hit exactly the right note with the censors; it gave a clear warning as to what the Germans could expect if they invaded Russia again.

17.5   STALIN'S FINAL YEARS, 1945–53

(a)   The aftermath of the war

The Soviet victory in the Second World War was only achieved by enormous sacrifices of human life, far in excess of the losses of all the other participants put together. There were 6.2 million military personnel dead, 15 million wounded, and 4.4 million captured or missing. On top of that there were about 17 million civilian deaths, giving a total Soviet war dead not far short of 25 million. The areas occupied by the Germans were left in ruins; 25 million people were homeless. In effect, the entire modernization programme of the Five Year Plans had to be started all over again in the western parts of the country. Stalin saw the victory as the ultimate vindication of his entire system of government; it had passed the sternest test imaginable – total war. As far as he was concerned, the Russian people now faced another challenge – the battle to rebuild the Soviet Union.

(b) Stalin's last battles

Any Soviet citizens who were expecting more freedom and a more relaxed way of life as a reward for their superhuman efforts during the war were quickly disillusioned. *Stalin was well aware of the growing unrest and the desire for radical change.* Peasants were disgusted with the tiny wages paid on the collectives and were beginning to take land back and farm it for themselves. Industrial workers were protesting about low wages and rising food prices. People in the newly acquired areas – the Baltic states and western Ukraine (see Map 17.1) – bitterly resented Soviet rule and resorted to armed resistance. Stalin was utterly ruthless: nationalist risings were crushed and about 300 000 people deported from western Ukraine. The population of the labour camps more than doubled to about 2.5 million. Peasants and industrial workers once again came under military-style discipline.

Stalin saw enemies everywhere. Soviet soldiers who had been captured by the Germans were seen as tainted, potential traitors. It seems beyond belief that 2.8 million Red Army soldiers, who had survived appalling treatment in Hitler's prison camps, returned to their homeland only to be arrested by the NKVD. Some were shot, some were sent to the Gulag and only about a third were allowed home. One of Stalin's motives for sending so many people to labour camps was to ensure a constant supply of cheap labour for coalmines and other projects. Another category of 'tainted' people were those who had come into Allied hands during the final months of the war. They were now suspect because they had seen that life in the west was materially better than in the USSR. About 3 million of them were sent to labour camps.

The task of rebuilding the country was tackled by the Fourth Five Year Plan (1946–50), which, if the official statistics are to be believed, succeeded in restoring industrial production to its 1940 levels. The outstanding achievement was considered to be the explosion in Kazakhstan, in August 1949, of the first Soviet atomic bomb. However, the great failure of the Plan was in agriculture: the 1946 harvest was less than that of 1945, resulting in famine, starvation and reports of cannibalism. Peasants were leaving the collectives in droves to try to find jobs in industry. Production of all agricultural commodities was down. Even in 1952 the grain harvest reached only three-quarters of the 1940 harvest. As Alec Nove commented: 'How could it be tolerated that a country capable of making an atomic bomb could not supply its citizens with eggs?'

Stalin also launched *the battle to re-establish control over the intelligentsia*, who, Stalin felt, had become too independent during the war years. Beginning in August 1946, Zhdanov, the Leningrad party boss, led the attack. Hundreds of writers were expelled from the union; all the leading composers were in disgrace and their music banned. The campaign continued into the early 1950s, though Zhdanov himself died of a heart attack in August 1948. After Zhdanov's death, Stalin carried out a purge of the Leningrad party organization, who were all arrested, found guilty of plotting to seize power, and executed.

The final act in the drama was the so-called Doctors' Plot. In November 1952 13 Moscow doctors, who had treated Stalin and other leaders at different times, were arrested and accused of conspiring to kill their eminent patients. Six of the doctors were Jewish and this was the signal for an outburst of anti-Semitism. By this time nobody felt safe. There is evidence that Stalin was working up to another major purge of leading figures in the party, with Molotov, Mikoyan and Beria on the list. Fortunately for them, Stalin died of a brain haemorrhage on 5 March 1953.

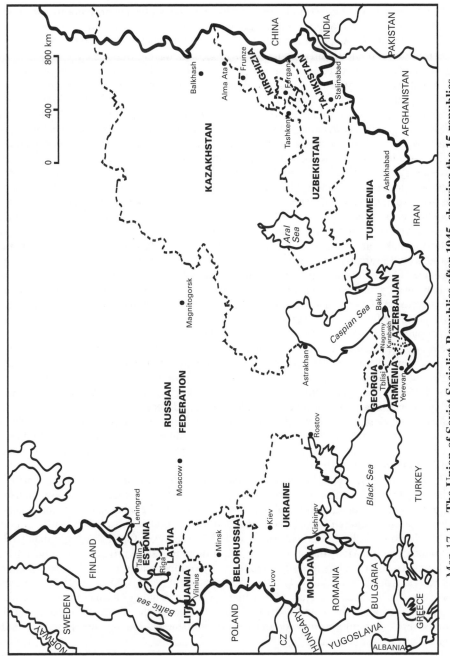

Map 17.1 **The Union of Soviet Socialist Republics after 1945, showing the 15 republics**

(c) Assessments of Stalin

When Stalin's death was announced there was widespread and apparently genuine grief; as he lay in state, thousands of people flocked to see his body, which was later embalmed and placed in a glass case next to Lenin. For 25 years the public had been brainwashed into regarding him as a kind of god, whose opinion on every subject was correct. However, *his reputation in the USSR soon went into decline* when Khrushchev delivered his sensational speech at the Twentieth Party Congress in 1956, denouncing Stalin's excesses. In 1961 Stalin's body was removed from the mausoleum and buried beneath the Kremlin wall.

How does one begin to assess a phenomenon like Stalin, who was responsible for so many dramatic changes but whose methods were so unorthodox and brutal? *Some historians have found positive things to say.* Sheila Fitzpatrick points out that under Stalin the USSR 'was at its most dynamic, engaging in social and economic experiments that some hailed as the future becoming manifest and others saw as a threat to civilization'. Collectivization, the rapid industrialization, the new constitution, the rise of the new bureaucracy, the spread of mass education and social services – all these can be traced directly or indirectly to Stalin. Martin McCauley and Alec Nove believe that the situation was so desperate when he came to power that only extraordinary methods could have brought success. The supreme justification of Stalin and his methods is that he made the USSR powerful enough to defeat the Germans. Geoffrey Roberts argues that in spite of all Stalin's mistakes and his brutality that caused the deaths of millions of people, without him Russia would probably have lost the war with Nazi Germany – his leadership was irreplaceable. The regime was certainly extremely popular with the top and middle ranks of the bureaucracy, in the various ministries, in the army and navy, and in the security forces. These were people who had risen from the working classes; they owed their privileged positions to Stalin, and they would do their utmost to defend the Soviet state. Stalin was also popular with the majority of ordinary people.

How did such a brutal leader come to enjoy such popularity? The answer is that he was adept at manipulating public opinion; he rarely admitted to making a mistake and always shifted the blame on to somebody else. He succeeded in giving the impression that injustices would be put right if only he knew about them. Even some of his critics admit that during the war he did much to keep morale high, and deserves some credit for the Soviet victory. After their victory over the Germans, millions of Russians genuinely saw Stalin as a heroic leader who had saved his country. The public believed what it was told, was taken in by the 'cult of personality' and was deeply shocked by Khrushchev's 'de-Stalinization' speech in 1956.

There is no disguising the fact that the policies at best had only mixed success. Collectivization was a disaster; industrial modernization was a success in heavy industry and armaments and enabled the USSR to win the war. On the other hand, Soviet industry failed to produce enough household goods, and much of what was produced was of poor quality. Living standards and real wages in 1953 were lower for most people than when Stalin took control. Many historians believe that more industrial progress could have been made with conventional methods, perhaps even by simply continuing NEP. Even the claim that Russia won the war thanks to Stalin is disputed. In fact his mistakes almost lost the war in the early stages. He ignored warnings of the impending German invasion, which resulted in the loss of the western part of Russia; he ignored the advice of his commanders with the result that millions of soldiers were taken prisoner. Arguably therefore, the USSR won the war *in spite of* Stalin.

The worst aspect of Stalinism was that it was responsible for about 20 million deaths, over and above the victims of the war. This happened during collectivization, the famine of 1932–3, the Purges and the Great Terror. During the war he uprooted and deported millions of Volga Germans, Crimean Tartars, Chechens and other nationalities in case they tried to co-operate with the invading Germans. Thousands died on the way, and thousands more perished when they were abandoned at their destinations without any accommodation. Stalin always made sure that other members of the Politburo signed death warrants as well as himself. There were huge numbers of people, from those at the top right down to interrogators, torturers, guards and executioners, who were willing to carry out the orders. Local party bosses – little Stalins – often initiated their own terrors from below. Alexander Yakovlev, the former Soviet ambassador to Canada and later a close colleague of Gorbachev and a Politburo member, recently published an account of the terror and violence which took place during the communist regime. He was once a committed Marxist, but the more he learned about the past, and the longer he experienced life at the top, the more disgusted he became at the corruption, lies and deceit at the heart of the system. Convinced that communism was not reformable, he played an important role, along with Gorbachev, in destroying the system from the inside. He estimates the number of victims of communism after 1917 at between 60 million and 70 million.

Some historians argue that Stalin was paranoid; psychologically unbalanced. Khruschchev seemed to think so; he claimed that Stalin was a 'very distrustful man, sickly suspicious'. On the other hand Roy Medvedev believes that Stalin was perfectly sane, but coolly ruthless, one of the greatest criminals in human history, whose main motives were inordinate vanity and lust for power. Fifty years after his death, more information is available from recently opened Soviet archives, though it is clear that many vital records have been destroyed, probably deliberately. Revisionist historians like Arch Getty still maintain that Stalin had no overall plan for terror. Getty believes that the Terror developed out of the anxieties of the entire ruling elite: 'Their fears of losing control, even of losing power, led them into a series of steps to protect their position: building a unifying cult around Stalin.' So for Getty, Stalin was not the master criminal, he was just one among the rest of the elite taking the necessary measures to stay in power.

(d) Was Stalinism a continuation of Leninism?

The current trend among Russian historians is to demonize both Stalin and Lenin. Alexander Yakovlev condemns both of them and produces ample evidence of their crimes: Stalin simply carried on from Lenin. However, it is important to compare their policies in more detail. Leninism was a complex mixture of a basic ideology, a particular style of leadership and government and a programme of policies:

- Lenin's ideology and political style were based on the Marxist concept of 'the dictatorship of the proletariat'. However, Lenin also believed that a tightly disciplined party was needed to guide the proletariat after the successful revolution. Under the supervision of the Party, the people would run their own affairs working through the soviets. This was seen as the highest form of democracy: since the Party and the soviets were mainly made up of members of the proletariat, they would know what was best for the people. Lenin also believed that this could only survive and work in Russia if it was accompanied by revolutions in some of the more advanced countries, such as Germany. Towards the end of his life, however, Lenin suggested that NEP would improve people's lives so much that 'permanent revolution' would not be necessary. This brought him closer to Stalin's theory of 'socialism in one country'. Dmitri Volkogonov stresses that both Lenin and Stalin were violent and brutal in their methods, Lenin during the Civil War and Stalin's treatment of the kulaks and the 'Great Terror' of the 1930s.
- Nevertheless, there were clear differences between the two: Irina Pavlova maintains that it was only under Stalin that the party apparatus, the bureaucracy,

became all-powerful and synonymous with the state. Stalinism could in no way be described as democratic; the new constitution of 1936, with it elections for the Supreme Soviet and its lists of human rights, did nothing to change the fact that Stalin was much more of a dictator then Lenin ever was. While it is true that Lenin used violence, Christopher Read argues that the counter-revolutionary forces were so powerful that the Bolsheviks had no choice if they were to survive. They simply continued to use the same methods that the Tsars had used for centuries. On the other hand, Stalin was under no such threat, and could have used alternative methods of dealing with the opposition, instead of killing hundreds of thousands of innocent people. Moreover, even at the height of the Civil War, as Robert Tucker points out, Lenin was already thinking about how to deal with Russia's culture of backwardness, and deciding that the best method was by education, not violence. Trotsky claimed that Stalinism grew out of this backward political culture, not from Lenin's party, which was essentially democratic.

- As for actual policies, Stalin claimed that collectivization and the Five Year Plans for industry were a natural development from Lenin's NEP, since Lenin himself had said that although NEP would last a long time, it would not continue forever. Stalinists argue that the First Five Year Plan was similar to Lenin's War Communism. But in fact there was nothing inevitable about Stalinism: a different leader, Bukharin for example, could have caused the system left by Lenin to have evolved in a completely different way. Bukharin envisaged that private farming should be replaced by farming co-operatives, but that it should be done slowly and certainly not in the violent way that collectivization brought. It was important to win over the peasants so that future peace would be based on an alliance between peasants and industrial workers (hence the hammer and sickle on the Russian flag). In any case, rule by one man was anti-Leninist – it went directly against the idea of rule by the Party on behalf of the working class. In fact there was a clear break between Lenin and Stalin. Many western historians believe that Stalin hijacked the Revolution and betrayed the idealism of Marx and Lenin. Instead of a new, classless society in which everybody was free and equal, ordinary workers and peasants were just as exploited as they had been under the Tsars. The Party had taken the place of the capitalists, and enjoyed all the privileges – the best houses, country retreats and cars. Instead of Marxism, socialism and the 'dictatorship of the proletariat', there was merely Stalinism and the dictatorship of Stalin. Perhaps the fairest conclusion on Stalin and Stalinism is the one by Martin McCauley: 'Whether one approves or disapproves of it, it was a truly remarkable phenomenon, one that profoundly marked the twentieth century. One can only approve of it if one suspends moral judgement' (see also Section 16.4(b)).

FURTHER READING

Applebaum, A., *A History of the Soviet Camps* (Penguin/Allen Lane, 2003).
Brown, A., *The Rise and Fall of Communism* (Vintage, 2010).
Conquest, R., *The Great Terror: A Reassessment* (Pimlico, 2008).
Figes, O., *The Whisperers: Private Life in Stalin's Russia* (Penguin/Allen Lane, 2007).
Fitzpatrick, S., *Everyday Stalinism: Ordinary Life in Extraordinary Times. Soviet Russia in the 1930s* (Oxford University Press, 2001).
Freeborn, R., *A Short History of Modern Russia* (Hodder & Stoughton, 1966).
Getty, J.A., *The Road to Terror: Stalin and the Self-Destruction of the Bolsheviks* (Yale University Press, 2010).

Ilic, M. (ed.) *Stalin's Terror Revisited* (Palgrave Macmillan, 2006).

Lovell, S., *The Shadow of War: Russia and the USSR, 1941 to the Present* (Wiley-Blackwell, 2011).

Lowe, N., *Mastering Twentieth Century Russian History* (Macmillan, 2002).

McCauley, M., *The Rise and Fall of the Soviet Union, 1917–1991* (Longman, 3rd edition, 2007).

McCauley, M., *Stalin and Stalinism* (Longman, 3rd edition, 2008).

Medvedev, R. A., *Let History Judge: The Origins and Consequences of Stalinism* (Oxford University Press, 1989).

Medvedev, Z. A. and R. A., *The Unknown Stalin* (I. B. Tauris, 2005).

Merridale, C., *Moscow Politics and the Rise of Stalin* (Macmillan, 1990).

Montefiori, S. S., *Stalin: The Court of the Red Tsar* (Phoenix, 2007).

Roberts, G., *Stalin's Wars: From World War to Cold War (1939–1953)* (Yale University Press, 2006).

Sakwa, R., *The Rise and Fall of the Soviet Union, 1917–1991* (Routledge, 1999).

Service, R., *Stalin: A Biography* (Macmillan, 2004).

Service, R., *Comrades: A World History of Communism* (Macmillan, 2007).

Service, R., *Trotsky: A Biography* (Macmillan, 2010).

Suny, R G., *The Soviet Experiment* (Oxford University Press, 1998).

Suny, R. G., *The Cambridge History of Russia, vol. 3: The Twentieth Century* (Cambridge University Press, 2006).

Tucker, R.C., *Stalin in Power: The Revolution from Above* (Norton, 1992).

Volkogonov, D., *Stalin: Triumph and Tragedy* (Phoenix, 2000).

Yakovlev, A., *A Century of Russian Violence in Soviet Russia* (Yale University Press, 2002).

QUESTIONS

1 How important were the divisions among his opponents in explaining Stalin's rise to supreme power during the 1920s?

2 How accurate is it to talk about the 'Stalin Revolution' in economic and political affairs in the USSR during the period 1928 to 1941?

3 To what extent did the lives of ordinary people in the USSR improve or worsen as a result of Stalin's policies during the period 1928 to 1941?

4 'Agriculture was always the basic weakness of the Soviet economy.' Assess the validity to this view of the Soviet economy during the Stalin years.

5 'Stalin's power during the 1930s was based almost entirely on terror.' How far would you agree with this view?

6 How effective were the Five Year Plans in creating a successful economy in the USSR up to 1941?

7 How far would you agree that Stalinism was just a continuation of Leninism?

There is a document question about Stalin, the *kulaks* and collectivization on the website.

Chapter 18

Continuing communism, collapse and aftermath, 1953 to the present

SUMMARY OF EVENTS

This long period falls into four phases:

1953–64
After Stalin's death, *Nikita Khrushchev* gradually emerged as the dominant leader. He began a de-Stalinization policy and introduced new measures to strengthen the Soviet economy and reform the bureaucracy. In 1962 the USSR came to the brink of war with the USA over the Cuban missiles crisis. Khrushchev's colleagues turned against him and he was forced to retire into private life in October 1964.

1964–85
This was a period of stagnation and decline, during which *Leonid Brezhnev* was the leading figure.

1985–91
Mikhail Gorbachev tried to reform and modernize Russian communism and to encourage similar progress in the satellite states of eastern Europe. However, he proved unable to control the rising tide of criticism directed at communism, and in 1989–90, non-communist governments were established in most of the states of eastern Europe (see Section 8.7). When Gorbachev failed to keep his promises of economic reform and higher living standards, the people of the USSR turned against communism and he lost power to *Boris Yeltsin*. The Communist Party was declared illegal, the USSR broke up into 15 separate states and Gorbachev resigned as president of the USSR (December 1991).

1991–2012
Boris Yeltsin was president of Russia, which was now a separate state, from 1991 until his resignation at the end of December 1999. After the collapse of communism, Russia was plunged into chaos as successive governments tried desperately to introduce new economic and political systems. The problems were vast: inflation, unemployment, poverty, trouble in Chechnya and clashes between Yeltsin and parliament. In 2000, *Vladimir Putin* became president and was re-elected for a second term in March 2004. The constitution did not allow a president two terms, so in 2008 Putin's close supporter, Medvedev, was elected president with Putin as prime minister. In the 2012 elections, in spite of declining popularity and allegations of electoral fraud, Putin was elected president for a third term.

(a) The rise of Khrushchev, 1953–7

With the departure of Stalin, the situation was similar to that after Lenin's death in 1924: there was no obvious candidate to take charge. Stalin had allowed no one to show any initiative in case he developed into a dangerous rival. The leading members of the Politburo, or Praesidium, as it was now called, decided to share power and rule as a group. Malenkov became chairman of the Council of Ministers, Khrushchev party secretary, and Voroshilov chairman of the Praesidium. Also involved were Beria, the chief of the secret police, Bulganin and Molotov. Gradually Nikita Khrushchev began to emerge as the dominant personality. The son of a peasant farmer, he had worked as a farm labourer and then as a mechanic in a coalmine before going to technical college and joining the Communist Party. Beria, who had an atrocious record of cruelty as chief of police, was executed, probably because the others were nervous in case he turned against them. Malenkov resigned in 1955 after disagreeing with Khrushchev about industrial policies, but it was significant that in the new relaxed atmosphere, he was not executed or imprisoned.

Khrushchev's position was further strengthened by *an amazing speech which he delivered at the Twentieth Communist Party Congress (February 1956) strongly criticizing various aspects of Stalin's policies*. He:

- condemned Stalin for encouraging the cult of his own personality instead of allowing the Party to rule;
- revealed details about Stalin's purges and the wrongful executions of the 1930s, and criticized his conduct of the war;
- claimed that socialism could be achieved in ways other than those insisted on by Stalin;
- suggested that peaceful coexistence with the west was not only possible but essential if nuclear war was to be avoided.

Why did Khrushchev make this attack on Stalin? It was a risky step to take, bearing in mind that he and most of his colleagues owed their positions to Stalin and had gone along with his worst excesses without protest. Khrushchev genuinely believed that the truth about Stalin's crimes would have to come out sooner or later, and that it would be better if the Party took the initiative itself and confronted the issue before it was forced into it by public pressure. This argument enabled him to secure the approval of his colleagues for him to deliver the speech, and then he used the opportunity cleverly for his own political ends. He emphasized that he had only joined the Politburo in 1939, giving the clear impression that his seniors – Malenkov, Molotov, Kaganovitch and Voroshilov – were all infinitely more responsible for the bloodletting than he was. His publicly condemning Stalin's behaviour in this way made it more difficult for any future leader to attempt to imitate him. Khrushchev genuinely felt, too, that Stalin's system had held up progress and stifled initiative; he wanted to get things back on the track that Lenin would have followed, and rule as an enlightened dictator.

Khrushchev was not quite supreme yet; Molotov and Malenkov believed his speech was too drastic and would encourage unrest (they blamed him for the Hungarian revolution of October 1956), and they tried to force him out of office. However, as party secretary, Khrushchev, like Stalin before him, had been quietly filling key positions with his own supporters, and since he could rely on the army, it was Molotov and Malenkov who found themselves compulsorily retired (June 1957). After that, Khrushchev was fully responsible for all Russian policy until 1964. But he never wielded as much power as

Stalin; the Central Committee of the Party was ultimately in charge, and it was the Party which voted him out in 1964.

(b) Khrushchev's problems and policies

In spite of Russia's recovery during Stalin's last years, there were a number of serious problems: the low standard of living among industrial and agricultural workers, and the inefficiency of agriculture, which was still a long way from providing all Russia's needs. Khrushchev was fully aware of the problems both at home and abroad and was keen to introduce important changes as part of *a general de-Stalinization policy.*

1 Industrial policy
Industry continued to be organized under the Five Year Plans, with Number Six starting in 1955; for the first time the concentration was more on light industries producing consumer goods (radios, TV sets, washing machines and sewing machines) in an attempt to raise living standards. To reduce over-centralization and encourage efficiency, over a hundred Regional Economic Councils were set up to make decisions about and organize their local industries. Managers were encouraged to make profits instead of just meeting quotas, and wages depended on output.

All this certainly led to an improvement in living standards: a vast housing programme was started in 1958; there were wage increases, a minimum wage, tax cuts on low incomes, a shorter working week, increases in pensions and disability allowances, and the abolition of all tuition fees in secondary and higher education. Between 1955 and 1966 the number of radios per thousand of the population increased from 66 to 171, TV sets from 4 to 82, refrigerators from 4 to 40 and washing machines from 1 to 77. However, this was a long way behind the USA, which in 1966 could boast no fewer than 1300 radios, 376 TV sets, 293 refrigerators, and 259 washing machines per thousand. Of course, much depends on how one measures progress, but it was Khrushchev himself who rashly boasted that the gap between Russia and America would be closed within a few years.

After the initial improvement, economic growth began to slow down, partly because the Regional Councils were inefficient, and partly because insufficient investment took place. This was because of the enormous cost of the armaments programme and the advanced technological and space programmes. The achievement which gained most publicity both at home and abroad was the first manned orbit of the earth by Uri Gagarin (1961).

2 Agricultural policy
One of the most serious problems left behind by Stalin was the inefficient state of agriculture. Collectivization had not achieved the ambitious targets set for it by Stalin; the main priority therefore was somehow to increase food production. Because of his peasant background, Khrushchev considered himself an expert on farming matters. He toured the countryside meeting peasants and talking about their problems, which no previous Russian ruler had ever taken the trouble to do. His special brainchild was *the Virgin Lands Scheme* (started 1954), which involved cultivating for the first time huge areas of land in Siberia and Kazakhstan. The scheme was implemented by tens of thousands of young volunteers, with the government providing over 100 000 new tractors. Khrushchev also aimed to increase yields from the collective farms: peasants were allowed to keep or sell crops grown on their private plots, their taxes were lowered and the government increased its payments for crops from the collectives, thus providing incentives to produce more.

By 1958 there was a dramatic increase in total farm output, which rose by 56 per cent; between 1953 and 1962 grain production rose from 82 million tons to 147 million, and all this helped to improve the standard of living. But then things began to go wrong; the 1963 grain output was down to 110 million tons, mainly because of the failure of the virgin lands scheme. Critics in the Party complained that too much was being spent on agriculture to the detriment of industry; Khrushchev had to give way, and the supply of agricultural equipment dwindled. But the main problem was that much of the land was of poor quality, not enough fertilizers were used, because they were expensive, and the exhausted soil began to blow away in dust storms. In general there was still too much interference in agriculture from local party officials, and it remained the least efficient sector of the economy. The Russians had to rely on grain imports, often from the USA and Australia; this humiliation contributed to Khrushchev's downfall in October 1964.

3 Political, social and cultural changes

There were important changes in all these areas. Khrushchev favoured a more relaxed approach in general and the period became known as the 'thaw'. In politics this included a return to party control instead of Stalin's personality cult. Khrushchev was careful not to act too much like a dictator for fear of laying himself open to similar charges. There was a reduction in secret police activities; after the execution of the sinister Beria, sacked politicians and officials were allowed to retire into obscurity instead of being tortured and shot. The labour camps began to empty and many people were rehabilitated. Unfortunately this was too late for some people: Nadezhda Mandelstam received a letter addressed to her husband Osip, informing him that he had been rehabilitated; sadly, he had died in a labour camp in 1938.

There was more freedom for ordinary people, and a higher standard of living. It was estimated that in 1958 at least 100 million people were living below the poverty line, but in 1967 this had fallen to about 30 million; the improvement was due mainly to the introduction of a minimum wage.

There was more freedom for writers, for whom Khrushchev had great respect. Ilya Ehrenburg caused a stir with the publication of *The Thaw*, a novel full of criticisms of the Stalin era (1954). Anna Akhmatova, Bulgakov and Meyerhold were rehabilitated. Alexander Solzhenitsyn's novel *One Day in the Life of Ivan Denisovich*, about an innocent man sentenced to hard labour, drew on his own experiences of eight years in a camp. The simple test of Khrushchev's reaction to a new work was: if it attacked Stalin and his system, it would be approved; if it attacked the Party or present aspects of Soviet life, it would be denounced and banned. Some writers overstepped the mark and found themselves disgraced and expelled from the writers' union. But at least they did not end up in labour camps.

The 'thaw' also had its limits in other areas; for example, Khrushchev decided that the Orthodox Church was gaining too much influence in Soviet life. Thousands of churches were closed down and it was illegal to hold gatherings in private houses without permission; since this was never granted for religious meetings, it became extremely difficult for Christians to worship. In 1962 when some factory workers at Novocherkassk went on strike and organized a demonstration in protest against increases in meat and dairy prices, tanks and troops were called in. Troops fired into the crowd, killing 23 people and injuring dozens more; 49 people were arrested and five of the ringleaders were executed.

4 Foreign affairs

Following his Twentieth Party Congress speech, Khrushchev aimed for *peaceful coexistence and a thaw in the Cold War* (see Section 7.3), and seemed prepared to allow different 'roads to socialism' among the satellite states of eastern Europe. However, these departures from strict Marxist–Leninist ideas (including his encouragement of profit and wage incentives) laid him open to Chinese accusations of *revisionism* (see Section 8.6(d)). In addition, encouraged by his speech, Poland and Hungary tried to break free from Moscow's grip. Khrushchev's reaction to the developments in Hungary, where the 'rising' was brutally crushed, showed how limited his toleration was (see Sections 9.3(e) and 10.5(d)). The greatest crisis of all came in 1962 when the USSR clashed with the USA over the question of the Russian missiles in Cuba (see Section 7.4).

(c) Khrushchev's fall

In October 1964 the Central Committee of the Party voted Khrushchev into retirement on the grounds of ill health; in fact, although he was 70, his health was perfectly good. The real reasons were probably the failure of his agricultural policy (though he had been no less successful than previous governments in this), his loss of prestige over the Cuban missiles crisis (see Section 7.4(b)), and the widening breach with China, which he made no attempt to heal. He had offended many important groups in society: his attempts to make the Party and the government more efficient and decentralized brought him into conflict with the bureaucracy, whose privileged positions were being threatened. The military disapproved of his cuts in defence spending and his attempts to limit nuclear weapons. Perhaps his colleagues were tired of his extrovert personality (once, in a heated moment at the United Nations, he took off his shoe and hammered the table with it) and felt he was taking too much on himself. Without consulting them he had just tried to win the friendship of President Nasser of Egypt by awarding him the Order of Lenin at a time when he was busy arresting Egyptian communists. Khrushchev had become increasingly aggressive and arrogant, and at times seemed to have developed the 'cult of personality' almost as much as Stalin.

In spite of his failures, many historians believe that Khrushchev deserves considerable credit; his period in power has been described as 'the Khrushchev revolution'. He was a man of outstanding personality: a tough politician and yet at the same time impulsive and full of warmth and humour. After Stalin's grim remoteness, his more approachable and human style was more than welcome; he deserves to be remembered for the return to comparatively civilized politics (at least inside Russia). Alec Nove believed that the improvement in living standards and his social policies were perhaps his greatest achievements. Others see his 'peaceful coexistence' policy and his willingness to reduce nuclear weapons as a remarkable change in attitude.

Martin McCauley sees Khrushchev as a kind of heroic failure, a man with a noble vision, whose success was only modest because he was let down by the greed and concern for their own positions of those in authority. Powerful vested interests in the Party and the state administration did everything they could to delay his attempts to decentralize and 'return power to the people'. Dmitri Volkogonov, who was not a great admirer of any of the Soviet leaders, wrote that Khrushchev had achieved the virtually impossible: as a product of the Stalinist system, 'he had undergone a visible change in himself and in a fundamental way also changed society. However much his successor, Brezhnev, may have sympathized with Stalinism, he could not bring himself to restore it; the obstacles placed in his way by Khrushchev proved insurmountable.'

18.2 THE USSR STAGNATES, 1964–85

(a) The Brezhnev era

After Khrushchev's departure, three men, Kosygin, Brezhnev and Podgorny, seemed to be sharing power. At first Kosygin was the leading figure and the chief spokesman on foreign affairs, while Brezhnev and Podgorny looked after home affairs. In the early 1970s Kosygin was eclipsed by Brezhnev after a disagreement over economic policies. Kosygin pressed for more economic decentralization, but this was unpopular with the other leaders, who claimed that it encouraged too much independence of thought in the satellite states, especially Czechoslovakia. Brezhnev established firm personal control by 1977, and he remained leader until his death in November 1982. Reform disappeared from the agenda; most of Khrushchev's policies were abandoned and serious economic problems were ignored. Brezhnev and his colleagues were less tolerant of criticism than Khrushchev; anything that threatened the stability of the system or encouraged independent thinking was stifled, and this applied to the states of eastern Europe as well. Brezhnev's main concern seems to have been to keep the *nomemklatura* (the ruling elite and the bureaucracy) happy.

1   Economic policies

Economic policies maintained wage differentials and profit incentives, and some growth took place, but the rate was slow. The system remained strongly centralized, and Brezhnev was reluctant to take any major initiatives. By 1982 therefore, much of Russian industry was old-fashioned and in need of new production and processing technology. There was concern about the failure of the coal and oil industries to increase output, and the building industry was notorious for slowness and poor quality. Low agricultural yield was still a major problem – not once in the period 1980–4 did grain production come anywhere near the targets set. The 1981 harvest was disastrous and 1982 was only slightly better, throwing Russia into an uncomfortable dependence on American wheat. It was calculated that in the USA in 1980 one agricultural worker produced enough to feed 75 people, while his counterpart in Russia could manage only enough to feed 10.

The one section of the economy which was successful was the production of military hardware. By the early 1970s the USSR had caught up with the USA in numbers of intercontinental missiles, and had developed a new weapon, the anti-ballistic missile (ABM). Unfortunately, the arms race did not stop there – the Americans continued to produce even more deadly missiles, and at each step, the USSR strained to draw level again. *This was the basic problem of the Soviet economy – defence spending was so vast that the civilian areas of the economy were deprived of the necessary investment to keep them up to date.*

2   The Eastern bloc

The Eastern bloc states were expected to obey Moscow's wishes and to maintain their existing structure. When liberal trends developed in Czechoslovakia (especially the abolition of press censorship), a massive invasion took place by Russian and other Warsaw Pact troops. The reforming government of Dubček was replaced by a strongly centralized, pro-Moscow regime (1968) (see Section 10.5(e)). Soon afterwards Brezhnev declared the so-called *Brezhnev Doctrine*: according to this, intervention in the internal affairs of any communist country was justified *if socialism in that country was considered to be threatened.* This caused some friction with Romania, which had always tried to maintain some independence, refusing to send troops into Czechoslovakia and keeping on good terms with China. The Russian invasion of Afghanistan (1979) was the most blatant application of the doctrine, while more subtle pressures were brought to bear on Poland (1981) to control the independent trade union movement, Solidarity (see Section 10.5(f)).

3   Social policy and human rights

Brezhnev genuinely wanted the workers to be better-off and more comfortable, and there is no doubt that life improved for most people during these years. Unemployment was almost eliminated and there was a full programme of social security. The increasing amount of accommodation enabled millions of people to move from communal apartments to single-family flats.

However, personal freedom became more limited. For instance, by 1970 it was impossible to get any writings published which were critical of Stalin. Historians such as Roy

Medvedev and Viktor Danilov had their latest books banned, and Alexander Solzhenitsyn, after the success of *One Day in the Life of Ivan Denisovich*, found that his next two novels, *The First Circle* and *Cancer Ward*, were rejected. He was expelled from the writers' union, which meant that it was impossible for him to publish in the USSR.

The KGB (secret police) were now using a new technique to deal with 'troublemakers' – they were confined in psychiatric hospitals or mental asylums, where some were kept for many years. In May 1970 the biologist and writer Zhores Medvedev, Roy's twin brother, was locked up in a mental hospital and diagnosed as suffering from 'creeping schizophrenia'; the real reason was that his writings were considered to be anti-Soviet. This sort of treatment made reform-minded intellectuals more determined to persevere. A Human Rights Committee was formed by the physicists Andrei Sakharov and Valeri Chalidze, to protest about conditions in labour camps and prisons, and to demand free speech and all the other rights promised in the constitution. Writers began to circulate works in typescript around their little groups, a practice known as *samizdat* – self-publishing.

The Human Rights Committee gained a new weapon in 1975 when the USSR, along with the USA and other nations, signed the Helsinki Final Treaty. Among other things, this provided for economic and scientific cooperation between East and West, as well as full human rights. Brezhnev claimed to be in favour of the treaty, and appeared to make important concessions about human rights in the USSR, but in fact little progress was made. Groups were set up to check whether the terms of the agreement were being kept, but the authorities put them under intense pressure. Their members were arrested, imprisoned, exiled or deported, and finally the groups were dissolved altogether. Only Sakharov was spared, because he was so internationally renowned that there would have been a worldwide outcry had he been arrested. He was sent into internal exile in Gorky and later in Siberia.

4   Foreign policy

'Peaceful coexistence' was the only Khrushchev initiative which was continued during the Brezhnev period. The Russians were anxious for détente, especially as relations with China deteriorated almost to the point of open warfare in 1969. But after 1979 relations with the West deteriorated sharply as a result of the Russian invasion of Afghanistan. Brezhnev continued to advocate disarmament but presided over a rapid increase in Soviet armed forces, particularly the navy and the new SS-20 missiles (see Section 7.4(c)). He stepped up Soviet aid to Cuba and offered aid to Angola, Mozambique and Ethiopia.

(b)   Androppov and Chernenko

After Brezhnev's death in 1982, Russia was ruled for a short period by two elderly and ailing politicians – Yuri Andropov (November 1982–February 1984) and then Konstantin Chernenko (February 1984–March 1985). Head of the KGB until May 1982, Andropov immediately launched a vigorous campaign to modernize and streamline the Soviet system. He began an anti-corruption drive and introduced a programme of economic reform, hoping to increase production by encouraging decentralization. Some of the older party officials were replaced with younger, more go-ahead men. Unfortunately Andropov was dogged by ill health and died after little more than a year in office.

The 72-year-old Chernenko was a more conventional type of Soviet politician; he owed his rise to the fact that for many years he had been Brezhnev's personal assistant, and he was already terminally ill when he was chosen as next leader by the Politburo. Clearly the majority wanted somebody who would abandon the anti-corruption campaign and leave them in peace. There was no relaxation in the treatment of human rights activists. Sakharov was still kept in exile in Siberia (where he had been since 1980), in spite of appeals by western leaders for his release. Members of an unofficial trade union, support-ers of a group 'for the establishment of trust between the USSR and the USA' and members of unofficial religious groups were all arrested. This was how Dmitri Volkogonov (in *The Rise and Fall of the Soviet Empire*) summed up Chernenko's 13 months in power: 'Chernenko was not capable of leading the country or the party into the future. His rise to power symbolized the deepening of the crisis in society, the total lack of positive ideas in the party, and the inevitability of the convulsions to come.'

18.3 GORBACHEV AND THE END OF COMMUNIST RULE

Mikhail Gorbachev, who came to power in March 1985, was, at 54, the most gifted and dynamic leader Russia had seen for many years. He was determined to transform and revi-talize the country after the sterile years following Khrushchev's fall. He intended to achieve this by *modernizing and streamlining the Communist Party* with new policies of *glasnost* (openness) and *perestroika* (restructuring – of the Party, the economy and the government). The new thinking soon made an impact on foreign affairs, with initiatives on détente, relations with China, a withdrawal from Afghanistan and ultimately the ending of the Cold War in late 1990 (see Section 8.6).

Gorbachev outlined what was wrong at home in a speech to the Party Conference in 1988: the system was too centralized, leaving no room for local individual initiative. It was a 'command' economy, based almost completely on state ownership and control, and weighted strongly towards defence and heavy industry, leaving consumer goods for ordi-nary people in short supply. *Gorbachev did **not** want to end communism; he wanted to replace the existing system, which was still basically Stalinist, with a socialist system which was humane and democratic.* He sincerely believed that this could be achieved within the framework of the Marxist–Leninist one-party state. He did not have the same success at home as abroad. His policies failed to provide results quickly enough, and led to the collapse of communism, the break-up of the USSR, and the end of his own political career.

(a) Gorbachev's new policies

1 Glasnost

Glasnost was soon seen in areas such as *human rights and cultural affairs*. Several well-known dissidents were released, and the Sakharovs were allowed to return to Moscow from internal exile in Gorky (December 1986). Leaders like Bukharin, who had been disgraced and executed during Stalin's purges of the 1930s, were declared innocent of all crimes. *Pravda* was allowed to print an article criticizing Brezhnev for overreacting against dissidents, and a new law was introduced to prevent dissidents from being sent to mental institutions (January 1988). Important political events like the Nineteenth Party Conference in 1988 and the first session of the new Congress of People's Deputies (May 1989) were televised.

In cultural matters and the media generally, there were some startling developments. In May 1986 both the Union of Soviet Film-makers and the Union of Writers were allowed to sack their reactionary heads and elect more independent-minded leaders. Long-banned anti-Stalin films and novels were shown and published, and preparations were made to publish works by the great poet Osip Mandelstam, who died in a labour camp in 1938.

There was a new freedom in news reporting: in April 1986, for example, when a nuclear reactor at Chernobyl in the Ukraine exploded, killing hundreds of people and releasing a massive radioactive cloud which drifted across most of Europe, the disaster was discussed with unprecedented frankness. The aims of this new approach were to use the media to publicize the inefficiency and corruption which the government was so anxious to stamp out, to educate public opinion and to mobilize support for the new policies. *Glasnost* was encouraged provided nobody criticized the Party itself.

2 Economic affairs

Important changes were soon afoot. In November 1986 Gorbachev announced that 1987 was to be 'the year for broad applications of the new methods of economic management'. Small-scale private enterprise such as family restaurants, family businesses making clothes or handicrafts or providing services such as car and television repairs, painting and decorating and private tuition, was to be allowed, and so were workers' co-operatives up to a maximum of 50 workers. One motive behind this reform was the desire to provide competition for the slow and inefficient services provided by the state, in the hope of stimulating a rapid improvement. Another was the need to provide alternative jobs as patterns of employment changed over the following decade: it was clear that as more automation and computerization were introduced into factories and offices, the need for manual and clerical workers would decline.

Another important change was that responsibility for quality control throughout industry as a whole was to be taken over by independent state bodies rather than factory management. The most important part of the reforms was *the Law on State Enterprises (June 1987)*; this removed the central planners' total control over raw materials, production quotas and trade, and made factories work to orders from customers.

3 Political changes

These began in January 1987 when Gorbachev announced moves towards democracy within the Party. Instead of members of local soviets being *appointed* by the local Communist Party, they were to be *elected by the people*, and there was to be a choice of candidates (though not of parties). There were to be secret elections for top party positions, and elections in factories to choose managers.

During 1988 dramatic changes in central government were achieved. The old parliament (Supreme Soviet) of around 1450 deputies only met for about two weeks each year. Its function was to elect two smaller bodies – the Praesidium (33 members) and the Council of Ministers (71 members). It was these two committees which took all important decisions and saw that policies were carried out. Now the Supreme Soviet was to be replaced by a Congress of People's Deputies (2250 members), whose main function was to elect a new and much smaller Supreme Soviet (450 representatives), which would be a proper working parliament, sitting for about eight months a year. The chairman of the Supreme Soviet would be head of state.

Elections went ahead, and the first Congress of People's Deputies met in May 1989. Well-known figures elected included Roy Medvedev, Andrei Sakharov and Boris Yeltsin. This was a dramatic comeback for Yeltsin, who had been sacked as Moscow first secretary and forced to resign from the Politburo by the conservatives (traditionalists) in the Party in November 1987. During the second session (December 1989) it was decided that reserved seats for the Communist Party should be abolished. Gorbachev was elected president of the Soviet Union (March 1990), with two councils to advise and help him: one contained his own personal advisers, the other contained representatives from the 15 republics. These new bodies completely sidelined the old system, and it meant that the Communist Party was on the verge of losing its privileged position. At the next election, due in 1994, even Gorbachev would have to stand and put himself to the test of a popular vote.

(b) What went wrong with Gorbachev's policies?

1 Opposition from radicals and conservatives
As the reforms got under way, Gorbachev ran into problems. Some party members, such as Boris Yeltsin, were more radical than Gorbachev, and felt that the reforms were not drastic enough. They wanted a change to a western-style market economy as quickly as possible, though they knew this would cause great short-term hardship for the Russian people. On the other hand, the conservatives, like Yegor Ligachev, felt that the changes were too drastic and that the Party was in danger of losing control. This caused a danger-ous split in the Party and made it difficult for Gorbachev to satisfy either group. Although he had some sympathy with Yeltsin's views, he could not afford to side with Yeltsin against Ligachev, because Ligachev controlled the party apparatus.

The conservatives were in a large majority, and when the Congress of People's Deputies elected the new Supreme Soviet (May 1989), it was packed with conservatives; Yeltsin and many other radicals were not elected. This led to massive protest demonstra-tions in Moscow, where Yeltsin was a popular figure, since he had cleaned up the corrupt Moscow Communist Party organization. Demonstrations would not have been allowed before Gorbachev's time, but *glasnost* – encouraging people to voice their criticisms – was now in full flow, and was beginning to turn against the Communist Party.

2 The economic reforms did not produce results quickly enough
The rate of economic growth in 1988 and 1989 stayed exactly the same as it had been in previous years. In 1990 national income actually fell, and continued to fall – by about 15 per cent – in 1991. Some economists think that the USSR was going through an economic crisis as serious as the one in the USA in the early 1930s.

A major cause of the crisis was the disastrous results of the Law on State Enterprises. The problem was that wages were now dependent on output, but since output was measured by its value in roubles, factories were tempted not to increase overall output, but to concentrate on more expensive goods and reduce output of cheaper goods. This led to higher wages, forcing the government to print more money to pay them with. Inflation soared, and so did the government's budget deficit. Basic goods such as soap, washing-powder, razor-blades, cups and saucers, TV sets and food were in very short supply, and the queues in the towns got longer.

Disillusion with Gorbachev and his reforms rapidly set in, and, having had their expec-tations raised by his promises, people became outraged at the shortages. In July 1989 some coal miners in Siberia found there was no soap to wash themselves with at the end of their shift. 'What kind of a regime is it', they asked, 'if we can't even get washed?' After stag-ing a sit-in, they decided to go on strike; they were quickly joined by other miners in Siberia, in Kazakhstan and in the Donbass (Ukraine), the biggest coalmining area in the USSR, until half a million miners were on strike. It was the first major strike since 1917. The miners were well disciplined and organized, holding mass meetings outside party headquarters in the main towns. They put forward detailed demands, 42 in all. These included better living and working conditions, better supplies of food, a share in the prof-its and more local control over the mines. Later, influenced by what was happening in Poland (where a non-communist president had just been elected – see Section 10.6(c)), they called for independent trade unions like Poland's Solidarity, and in some areas they demanded an end to the privileged position of the Communist Party. The government soon gave way and granted many of the demands, promising a complete reorganization of the industry and full local control.

By the end of July the strike was over, but the general economic situation did not improve. Early in 1990 it was calculated that about a quarter of the population was living below the poverty line; worst affected were those with large families, the unemployed and pensioners. *Gorbachev was fast losing control of the reform movement which he had started*, and the success of the miners was bound to encourage the radicals to press for even more far-reaching changes.

3 Nationalist pressures

These also contributed towards Gorbachev's failure and led to the break-up of the USSR. The Soviet Union was a federal state consisting of 15 separate republics, each with its own parliament. The Russian republic was just one of the 15, with its parliament in Moscow (Moscow was also the meeting place for the *federal* Supreme Soviet and Congress of People's Deputies). The republics had been kept under tight control since Stalin's time, but *glasnost* and *perestroika* encouraged them to hope for more powers for their parliaments and more independence from Moscow. Gorbachev himself seemed sympathetic, provided that the Communist Party of the Soviet Union (CPSU) remained in overall control. However, once started, demands got out of hand.

- *Trouble began in Nagorno-Karabakh*, a small Christian autonomous republic within the Soviet republic of Azerbaijan, which was Muslim. The parliament of Nagorno-Karabakh asked to become part of neighbouring Christian Armenia (February 1988), but Gorbachev refused. He was afraid that if he agreed, this would upset the conservatives (who opposed internal frontier changes) and turn them against his entire reform programme. Fighting broke out between Azerbaijan and Armenia, and Moscow had clearly lost control.
- *Worse was to follow in the three Baltic soviet republics of Lithuania, Latvia and Estonia*, which had been taken over against their will by the Russians in 1940. Independence movements, denounced by Gorbachev as 'national excesses', had been growing in strength. In March 1990, encouraged by what was happening in the satellite states of eastern Europe, Lithuania took the lead by declaring itself independent. The other two soon followed, though they voted to proceed more gradually. Moscow refused to recognize their independence.
- Boris Yeltsin, who had been excluded from the new Supreme Soviet by the conservatives, made a dramatic comeback when he was elected president of the parliament of the Russian republic (Russian Federation) in May 1990.

4 Rivalry between Gorbachev and Yeltsin

Gorbachev and Yeltsin were now bitter rivals, disagreeing on many fundamental issues.

- *Yeltsin believed that the union should be voluntary*: each republic should be independent but also have joint responsibilities to the Soviet Union as well. If any republic wanted to opt out, as Lithuania did, it should be allowed to do so. However, Gorbachev thought that a purely voluntary union would lead to disintegration.
- Yeltsin was now completely disillusioned with the Communist Party and the way the traditionalists had treated him. He thought the Party no longer deserved its privileged position in the state. Gorbachev was still hoping against hope that the Party could be transformed into a humane and democratic organization.
- On the economy, Yeltsin thought the answer was a rapid changeover to a market economy, though he knew that this would be painful for the Russian people. Gorbachev was much more cautious, realizing that Yeltsin's plans would cause massive unemployment and even higher prices. He was fully aware of how unpopular he was already; if things got even worse, he might well be overthrown.

(c) The coup of August 1991

As the crisis deepened, Gorbachev and Yeltsin tried to work together, and Gorbachev found himself being pushed towards free, multi-party elections. This brought bitter attacks from Ligachev and the conservatives, who were already outraged at the way Gorbachev had 'lost' eastern Europe without putting up a fight, and worst of all, had allowed Germany to be reunited. In July 1990, Yeltsin resigned from the Communist Party. Gorbachev was now losing control: many of the republics were demanding independence, and when Soviet troops were used against nationalists in Lithuania and Latvia, the people organized massive demonstrations. In April 1991, Georgia declared independence: it seemed that the USSR was falling apart. However, the following month Gorbachev held a conference with the leaders of the 15 republics and persuaded them to form a new voluntary union in which they would be largely independent of Moscow. The agreement was to be formally signed on 20 August 1991.

At this point a group of hardline communists, including Gorbachev's vice-president, Gennady Yanayev, decided they had had enough, and launched a coup to remove Gorbachev and reverse his reforms. On 18 August, Gorbachev, who was on holiday in the Crimea, was arrested and told to hand over power to Yanayev. When he refused, he was kept under house arrest while the coup went ahead in Moscow. The public was told that Gorbachev was ill and that an eight-member committee was now in charge. They declared a state of emergency, banned demonstrations and brought in tanks and troops to surround public buildings in Moscow, including the White House (the parliament of the Russian Federation), which they intended to seize. Gorbachev's new union treaty, which was due to be signed the following day, was cancelled.

However, the coup was poorly organized and the leaders failed to have Yeltsin arrested. He rushed to the White House, and, standing on a tank outside, condemned the coup and called on the people of Moscow to rally round in support. The troops were confused, not knowing which side to support, but none of them would make a move against the popular Yeltsin. It soon became clear that some sections of the army were sympathetic to the reformers. By the evening of 20 August, thousands of people were on the streets, barricades were built against the tanks and the army hesitated to cause heavy casualties by attacking the White House. On 21 August the coup leaders admitted defeat, and they were eventually arrested. Yeltsin had triumphed and Gorbachev was able to return to Moscow. But things could never be the same again, and the failed coup had important consequences.

- The Communist Party was disgraced and discredited by the actions of the hardliners. Even Gorbachev was now convinced that the Party was beyond reform and he soon resigned as party general secretary; the Party was banned in the Russian Federation.
- Yeltsin was seen as the hero and Gorbachev was increasingly sidelined. Yeltsin ruled the Russian Federation as a separate republic, introducing a drastic programme to move to a free-market economy. When Ukraine, the second largest Soviet republic, voted to become independent (1 December 1991), it was clear that the old USSR was finished.
- Yeltsin was already negotiating for a new union of the republics. This was joined first by the Russian Federation, Ukraine and Belorussia (8 December 1991), and eight other republics joined later. The new union was known as the Commonwealth of Independent States (CIS). Although the member states were fully independent, they agreed to work together on economic matters and defence.
- These developments meant that Gorbachev's role as president of the USSR had ceased to exist, and he resigned on Christmas Day 1991.

(d)   Assessment of Gorbachev

At the time of his downfall, and for some years afterwards, a majority of people in Russia dismissed him as a failure, though for different reasons. The conservatives, who thought the USSR and the Party still had a lot to offer, saw him as a traitor. Radical reformers thought he had stayed with communism too long, trying to reform the unreformable. Ordinary people thought he was incompetent and weak, and had allowed their standard of living to decline.

However, there can be no question that Gorbachev was one of the outstanding leaders of the twentieth century, although his career was a mixture of brilliant successes and disappointing failures. Some historians see him as the real successor of Lenin, and believe that he was trying to get communism back on the track intended for it by Lenin before it was hijacked by Stalin, who twisted and perverted it. The two main disappointments were his failure to streamline the economy, and his complete misunderstanding of the nationalities problem, which led to the break-up of the USSR.

On the other hand, his achievements were enormous. Archie Brown sums them up:

> He played the decisive part in allowing the countries of Eastern Europe to become free and independent. He did more than anyone else to end the Cold War between East and West. He initiated fundamental rethinking about the political and economic systems he inherited and about better alternatives. He presided over the introduction of freedom of speech, freedom of the press, freedom of association, religious freedom and freedom of movement, and left Russia a *freer country* than it had been in its long history.

He began by believing that the Communist Party could be reformed and modernized, and that once this was achieved, there could be no better system. But he discovered that the majority of the Party – the elite and the bureaucracy – were resisting change for their own selfish reasons; the whole system was riddled with racketeers, black-market operators and all kinds of corruption. This discovery led Gorbachev to change his aims: if the Party refused to reform itself, then the Party would have to lose its dominant role. He achieved that goal peacefully, without bloodshed, which was remarkable in the circumstances. His achievement, especially in foreign affairs, was enormous. His policies of *glasnost* and *perestroika* restored freedom to the people of the USSR. His policies of reducing military expenditure, détente and withdrawal from Afghanistan and eastern Europe made a vital contribution to the ending of the Cold War.

(e)   Was the communist system reformable?

Could Russian communism have survived if Gorbachev had followed different policies? Many Russians are convinced that it could, and that if the USSR had followed the same path as China, it would still be communist today. The argument is that both Russia and China needed reform in two areas – the Communist Party and government, and the economy. Gorbachev believed these could only be achieved one at a time, and chose to introduce the political reforms first, without any really fundamental economic innovations. The Chinese did it the other way round, introducing economic reform first (see Section 20.3) and leaving the power of the Communist Party unchanged. This meant that although the people suffered economic hardship, the government retained tight control over them, and in the last resort was prepared to use force against them, unlike Gorbachev.

Vladimir Bukovsky, a reformer and social democrat, explained where Gorbachev went wrong: 'His only instrument of power was the Communist Party, but his reforms weakened precisely that instrument. He was like the proverbial man sawing off the branch on which he was sitting. There could be no other outcome except what happened.' If Gorbachev had put into operation a carefully worked-out programme of economic reform designed to last ten years, arguably the situation could have been saved.

Other observers argue that the Communist Party was beyond reform. They point out that any political system or party which enjoys a long, uninterrupted period in power becomes arrogant, complacent and corrupt. Both Khrushchev and Gorbachev tried to reform the *nomenklatura*, and both failed, because the elite, the bureaucracy in the government and the economic system, were solely concerned to further their own careers and refused to respond to the changing circumstances. In theory, reform should have been possible, but it might have been necessary to use force, as the Chinese government did in Tiananmen Square. Given Gorbachev's extreme reluctance to resort to force, the prospects for success would not seem promising.

(f) The legacy of communism

Any regime in power for over 70 years is bound to leave its marks, both good and bad, on the country. Most historians seem to feel that the achievements of communism are outweighed by its ill effects. And yet no system could have survived for so long by force alone. One important achievement was that the system brought benefits in the form of promotion, and reasonably well-paid jobs with privileges, to large numbers of people from 'lower-class' backgrounds who had been excluded from such things under the tsarist regime. Education and literacy became more widespread; Soviet 'culture' was encouraged and so was sport; the performing arts, especially music, were subsidized by the state, and science was given special prominence and funding. Perhaps the greatest achievement of communism was that it played a vital role in defeating the evil regime of Hitler and the Nazis. After Stalin's death, although in one sense the country stagnated, the system brought a certain stability and an improved standard of living for the majority of its people.

On the other hand, the Soviet system left behind a whole range of problems which would be extremely difficult for the succeeding regime to cope with. The whole system was rigid and over-centralized, initiative had been stifled for generations and the bureaucrats opposed any radical changes. The country was overburdened with its vast military expenditure. Boris Yeltsin had played an important part in destroying the Soviet system. Would he be able to do any better?

18.4 THE AFTERMATH OF COMMUNISM, YELTSIN, PUTIN AND MEDVEDEV

Yeltsin's eight years as president of Russia were packed with incident as he and his successive prime ministers tried to transform the country into a political democracy with a market economy, in the shortest time possible.

(a) Yeltsin, Gaidar and 'shock therapy'

Boris Yeltsin's problem was daunting: how best *to dismantle the command economy and transform Russia into a market economy* by privatizing the inefficient, subsidized state industries and agriculture. Yeltsin was hugely popular, but this would only last if he could improve the people's living standards. He chose as his vice-president Yegor Gaidar, a young economist who was influenced by the theories of the Western monetarists (see Section 23.5(b)). He convinced Yeltsin that the necessary changes could be achieved in one year, beginning with 'price liberalization' and going on to privatize almost the entire economy. It would be difficult for about six months, but he assured Yeltsin that things would then stabilize and people's lives would gradually improve.

This 'shock therapy', as it was called, began in January 1992 with the removal of price controls from about 90 per cent of goods, and the ending of government subsidies to industry. Prices rose steeply and kept on rising after the first six months. By the end of the year prices were, on average, 30 times higher than at the beginning; there were plenty of goods in the shops but most people could not afford to buy them. The situation was disastrous, since wages did not keep pace with prices; as sales fell, factory workers were laid off, and over a million people lost their jobs. Thousands were homeless and were forced to live in tents outside the towns. Many people had to rely on food parcels sent from abroad.

When the privatization programme began, it seemed as though the intention was for all big state industries and collective farms to be transferred to the joint ownership of all the people. Every citizen was given vouchers to the value of 10 000 roubles as their share, and there were plans for workers to be able to buy shares in their enterprise. However, none of this happened; 10 000 roubles was the equivalent of about £35 – a minute amount at a time of rapid inflation; nor could most workers afford to buy shares. What happened was that managers were able to buy up and accumulate enough vouchers to take over the ownership of their plant. This continued until by the end of 1995 most of the former state industry had fallen into the hands of a relatively small group of financiers, who became known as the 'oligarchs'. They made enormous profits, but from government subsidies, which were reintroduced, rather than from the market. Instead of reinvesting their profits in industry, as the government intended, they transferred them into Swiss bank accounts and foreign investments. Total investment in Russia fell by two-thirds.

Long before this stage was reached, Yeltsin's popularity had dwindled. Two of his former supporters, Alexander Rutskoi and Ruslan Khasbulatov, led the opposition in the Supreme Soviet and forced Yeltsin to dismiss Gaidar, replacing him with Viktor Chernomyrdin. In January 1993 he reintroduced some controls on prices and profits, but at the end of 1993, after two years of 'shock therapy', according to one report: 'Our country has been thrown back two centuries to the "savage era" of capitalism.' As a first experience of any kind of 'democracy', it was a grave disappointment for the vast majority of people. In the words of Daniel Beer, 'the Yeltsin government presided over an economic collapse so vast and devastating that for most Russians the term became synonymous with chaos and the plunder of state property (that is, society's) by a small clique of robber barons. ... By 1993 Russians were bitterly referring to *dermocracy* – *dermo* being the Russian for "shit".' Sadly, corruption, fraud, bribery and criminal activity became part of everyday life in Russia. Another report, prepared for Yeltsin early in 1994, estimated that *criminal mafias had gained control of between 70 and 80 per cent of all business and banking*. One Russian writer, Alexander Chubarov, recently described the government's policies as 'deformed capitalism'. It was an attempt to create in six months the sort of market capitalism which had taken generations to evolve in the West.

(b) Opposition and the 'civil war' in Moscow

The leading politicians lacked experience of democracy as well as of how to organize a market economy. At first there were no properly organized political parties on the western model, and the constitution, a leftover from the Soviet era, was unclear about the division of powers between president and parliament. However, in November 1992 the Communist Party was legalized again, and other groups began to form, although Yeltsin himself did not have a supporting party. *A majority in parliament strongly opposed Yeltsin's policies and tried to get rid of him*, but in a referendum in April 1993, 53 per cent of voters expressed approval of his social and economic policies. Yeltsin's success surprised many, and suggested that although he was unpopular, people had even less confidence in the alternatives.

Yeltsin now tried to neutralize parliament by producing a new constitution, making parliament subordinate to the president. Khasbulatov and Rutskoi were determined not to succumb. They rushed to the White House, where the Supreme Soviet met, and barricaded themselves in, together with hundreds of deputies, journalists and supporters. After a few days the building was surrounded by troops loyal to Yeltsin; some supporters of parliament attacked the mayor of Moscow's headquarters and a television station, whereupon Yeltsin ordered the troops to storm the White House (3 October 1993). Eventually the deputies surrendered, though not before around 200 had been killed, some 800 wounded and the White House badly damaged. Yeltsin's new constitution was narrowly approved in a referendum (December 1993). In elections for the new lower house of parliament (the *Duma*), Yeltsin's supporters won only 70 seats out of 450 whereas the Communist bloc won 103. This was a clear rebuff for Yeltsin, *but his power was not affected since the new constitution allowed him to dismiss parliament and rule by decree if he chose to.*

Although he had great power, Yeltsin knew that he could not afford to ignore public opinion completely, especially since presidential elections were due in 1996. He tried to avoid confrontation with the *Duma* and relations improved. Meanwhile the move towards privatization continued and the creation of a new, wealthy property-owning class was completed. Yet the state treasury seemed to benefit very little from these sales; what had happened was that, in effect, the state enterprises had been sold off to former managers, entrepreneurs, bankers and politicians at knock-down prices. Strangely, Yeltsin, who had once been the scourge of corrupt officials in Moscow, did very little to restrain his underlings. *For most people there were no obvious signs of improvement*: prices continued to rise during 1995; the number of people living in poverty, unemployment and the death rate increased; and the birth rate declined. The situation had not been helped by the outbreak of war with the Chechen republic in December 1994.

(c) Conflict in Chechnya, 1994–6

The Chechens are an Islamic people numbering about one million, who live in the area north of Georgia, inside the borders of the Russian republic. They were never happy under Russian control; they resisted communist rule during its early years and the civil war, and they resisted collectivization. During the Second World War Stalin accused them of collaborating with the Germans; the entire nation was brutally deported to Central Asia, and thousands died on the way. In 1956 Khrushchev allowed the Chechens to return to their homeland, and their autonomous republic was restored.

When the USSR broke up, Chechnya declared itself an independent republic under the leadership of Jokhar Dudaev. After attempts to persuade them to rejoin the Russian Federation failed, Yeltsin decided to use force against them. Reasons given were that their declaration of independence was illegal and that Chechnya was being used as a base from which criminal gangs were operating throughout Russia. In December 1994, 40 000 Russian troops invaded Chechnya. To their surprise there was fierce resistance before the Chechen capital, Grozny, was captured in February 1995. All round the world, television viewers saw shocking images of Russian tanks rolling through the ruined city. But the Chechens would not surrender and continued to harass the Russians with guerrilla attacks. In the summer of 1996, by the time the Chechens had succeeded in recapturing Grozny, the Russians had lost 20 000 men. The *Duma* had voted overwhelmingly against military action and the general public did not support the war. As the elections drew nearer, Yeltsin decided to compromise and a ceasefire was signed (May 1996). The Russians agreed to withdraw their troops, the Chechens promised to set up a government acceptable to Moscow and there was to be a cooling-off period of five years. However, the Chechens did not drop their demands for independence, and fighting started again long before five years had elapsed.

(d) Elections: December 1995 and June/July 1996

Under the terms of the new constitution, elections for the *Duma* were to be held in December 1995 and the presidential election in June 1996. The results of the *Duma* elections were disappointing for the government, which was still unpopular. Yeltsin and his supporters won only 65 seats out of the 450, whereas the Communist Party, led by Gennady Zyuganov, took 157 seats; together with their allies, they could muster 186 seats, by far the largest grouping. There was obviously much residual support and nostalgia for the old days of the USSR and strong government. In a genuinely democratic system the communists would have taken a leading role in the next government; but this did not happen: Yeltsin remained president for the time being at least. The big question was: would the communist candidate win the presidential election the following June?

Almost immediately, the politicians began to prepare for the June election. Yeltsin's popularity rating was so low that some of his advisers wanted him to cancel the election and resort to force if necessary. However, to his credit he allowed it to go ahead, and over 20 candidates registered for the first round, including the communist leader Zyuganov and Mikhail Gorbachev. Early opinion polls put Zyuganov as the likely winner, causing consternation in the West at the prospect of a return to communism. However, Yeltsin and his supporters rallied well; he had suffered a heart attack in the summer of 1995 but now he seemed to find new energy, and toured the country promising everything to everybody. His greatest boost came when the ceasefire was signed in Chechnya shortly before the election.

Zyuganov also presented an attractive programme, but he lacked Yeltsin's personal charisma and failed to distance himself sufficiently from Stalin. In the first round Yeltsin won a narrow victory with 35 per cent of the votes to Zyuganov's 32 per cent; Gorbachev received barely 1 per cent of the votes. In spite of his ill health, Yeltsin's team continued to campaign vigorously; in the second round he won a decisive victory over Zyuganov, taking 54 per cent of the votes. It was a remarkable victory, considering his low popularity at the beginning of the campaign and the fact that the economic situation was only just beginning to improve. The reason for Yeltsin's victory was not so much that people liked him, but that they liked the alternative even less. If the communists had put forward genuine social democrat policies, Zyuganov might well have won. But Zyuganov was not a social democrat; he made no secret of his admiration for Stalin, and this was a fatal mistake. When it came to the push, the majority of Russians could not bring themselves to vote a Stalinist-type communist back into power. They gritted their teeth and voted for the lesser of two evils.

(e) Yeltsin's second term, 1996–9

As Yeltsin began his second term as president, it seemed that at last things had reached a turning point: inflation had fallen to only 1 per cent a month, and for the first time since 1990, production ceased to fall. *But the promise was not fulfilled.* The great weakness of the economy was lack of investment, without which no significant expansion could take place. In the autumn of 1997, external events had an adverse effect on Russia. There was a series of financial crises and disaster in the Asian 'tiger' economies – Thailand, Singapore and South Korea – which affected stock markets all over the world. There was a fall in the world price of oil because of overproduction, which was a disaster for the Russians, since oil was their greatest export earner. The projected profits for 1998 were wiped out, foreign investors withdrew their funds and the Central Bank was forced to devalue the rouble (August 1998). It was another financial catastrophe in which millions of people had their savings and capital rendered worthless.

With the government floundering, the *Duma* suggested a new prime minister, Evgeny Primakov, a distinguished economic scientist and veteran communist who believed that the state should continue to play an important role in organizing the economy. To the surprise of most people, Yeltsin agreed to appoint Primakov, who planned to reduce imports, prevent capital from leaving the country, attract foreign investment and root out corruption. Almost before his policies had begun, the economic situation quickly improved. The world oil price recovered, devaluation made foreign imports too expensive, and this provided a boost for Russian industry. The government could afford to pay the arrears of wages and pensions, and the crisis passed. Opinion polls showed that 70 per cent of the voters approved of Primakov's policies. After only eight months, however, Yeltsin sacked him (May 1999), claiming that a younger and more energetic man was needed (Primakov was almost 70). It was rumoured that the real reason was Primakov's determination to eradicate corruption; many influential people who had gained their wealth and power by corrupt means put pressure on Yeltsin to dismiss Primakov. However, his dismissal caused consternation among ordinary Russians and Yeltsin's popularity rating fell to only 2 per cent. Yet Yeltsin's regime was certainly not a complete failure. By his programme of privatizations and allowing what passed for competitive elections, he had laid the foundations of a new Russian-style capitalism for the twenty-first century. Certainly in the eyes of the US Clinton administration, he had done as well as could be expected in such a rapid transition from communism to capitalism.

(f) Enter Putin

In preparation for the *Duma* election set for December 1999 and the next presidential election (June 2000), Yeltsin appointed as prime minister Vladimir Putin, the director of the security police, and a former KGB leader. The constitution prevented Yeltsin from standing for a third term, so he wanted to make sure that the candidate of his choice became next president. If a president were to retire before the end of his term, the constitution stipulated that the prime minister would automatically become president for three months, during which time presidential elections must be held. Opinion polls suggested that Primakov might well be elected next president, but events in September 1999 changed the situation dramatically. There was a series of bomb explosions in Moscow; two large apartment blocks were blown up and over 200 people killed. Putin claimed that the Chechen rebels were responsible and he ordered an all-out attack on the Chechen separatists. This time public opinion, outraged by the bomb attacks, was in favour of the war. Putin impressed people by his decisive handling of the situation and his determination to wipe out the warlords.

The renewed war in Chechnya worked in favour of Putin and his party – the Unity bloc. In the *Duma* elections Primakov's supporters won only 12 per cent of the seats, Putin's Unity bloc 24 per cent and the communists 25 per cent. On 31 December 1999 Yeltsin resigned as president, confident that his candidate, Putin, would be next president. As acting president Putin immediately pulled off a master stroke: his Unity bloc formed an alliance in the *Duma* with the communists and a few other smaller groups, giving the pro-Putin bloc a majority, something which Yeltsin had never achieved. In the presidential election held in March 2000, Putin won outright on the first ballot, taking 53 per cent of the votes; once again Zyuganov came second.

(g) Putin's first term, 2000–4

Putin had a reputation for political acumen and the ability to get things done. He was determined to stamp out corruption – to destroy the oligarchs as a class, as he put it – to develop a strictly controlled market economy, to restore law and order and to bring an end to the war in Chechnya. He was able to get his new measures approved by the *Duma* thanks to the continuing alliances formed after the December 1999 elections, and he achieved considerable success.

- Two of the most influential 'oligarchs', Vladimir Gusinsky and Boris Berezovsky, who between them controlled most of Russia's television companies and had been critical of Putin, were both removed from their positions and threatened with arrest on corruption charges. Both men decided to leave the country, and state control over the television network was re-established. In 2003 a third business tycoon, Mikhail Khodorkovsky, once said to be the wealthiest man in Russia, was arrested and jailed.
- New regulations for political parties meant that no party with fewer than 10 000 members would be allowed to take part in national elections. This reduced the number of parties from 180 to about 100, and the great advantage for the government was that it would prevent wealthy oligarchs from financing their own groups of supporters. In October 2001, Putin scored another success when his Unity party merged with one of its largest rivals, the Fatherland movement; together they were set to become the majority group in the *Duma*.
- The economy continued to recover, production increased and Russia continued to benefit from the high world price of oil, though this began to fall at the end of 2001. The federal budget moved into surplus and the government was able to service its debts without any more borrowing. Putin felt that the recovery was still precarious and he continued with more economic liberalization policies.
- In contrast to the Yeltsin presidency, Putin cultivated a 'strong-man' image. He was firm and authoritative, and he could be ruthless if the situation required it. As a precaution, the budget of the secret police (the FSB – successor to the KGB) was trebled, and an increasing number of important positions in the government administration apparatus were filled by people with a background in the security services.

Putin also had less successful experiences. When the nuclear submarine *Kursk* sank mysteriously in the Barentz Sea with the loss of all 118 crew members (August 2000), the government came under criticism for its unimpressive handling of the tragedy. Putin failed to bring a decisive end to the conflict in Chechnya, and terrorist bomb outrages continued. In October 2002 a group of between 40 and 50 armed and masked Chechens occupied the Dubrovka Theatre in Moscow, and took some 850 members of the audience hostage. They demanded the withdrawal of all Russian troops from Chechnya and an end to the Second Chechen War. After two and a half days, neither side would make any concessions, so government troops pumped noxious gas into the theatre through the ventilation system and then launched an attack. They killed 39 of the rebels, but unfortunately 129 hostages were also killed, most of them by the toxic gas. Again the government came under criticism for its handling of the crisis, especially from doctors. They claimed that they would have been able to save more of the hostages if the government had not refused to disclose the name of the gas used. To make matters worse, estimates published in the summer of 2003 suggested that one-third of the population were still living below the poverty line.

However, Putin's personal popularity remained high among the general public, enabling him to face the elections of 2003–4 with confidence. He had achieved a great deal for the Russian people, especially through his tax and pensions reforms. Most people were delighted with his attacks on the 'oligarchs', the economy was flourishing and foreign investors were showing interest in Russia again.

It was no surprise when in the *Duma* elections of December 2003, Putin's United Russia party won a massive 222 seats out of the 450. The real surprise was the poor showing of Zyuganov's Communist Party, which lost almost half its MPs and was left with only 53 seats. Some observers believed that this marked the end of the road for the communists, who had provided the only real political opposition to the government. One reason for the communists' poor showing was the creation of a new party – *Rodina* (Motherland) – only four months before the elections. This was a nationalist party pledged to raise company taxation and return to ordinary people the fortunes made by the oligarchs in their shady privatization deals. *Rodina* took most of its votes from the communists and ended up with 37 MPs, who would vote for Putin.

Analysts pointed out that Putin was developing distinct authoritarian tendencies: *Rodina* had been deliberately founded by the Kremlin in the hope of taking support away from the communists, as part of Putin's strategy for 'controlled democracy'. In other words, he was trying to create a parliament 'in his own image'. If he could secure a two-thirds majority in the *Duma*, he would be able to change the constitution to allow himself a third term as president. Clearly democracy in Russia was in the balance.

In the presidential election of March 2004, President Putin won a sweeping victory, taking 71 per cent of the votes cast. His nearest rival was the Communist candidate, Nikolai Kharitonov, but he gained only 13.7 per cent. Observers from the Council of Europe reported that the election had failed to meet healthy democratic standards. In particular, it was alleged that rival candidates had not been allowed fair access to the state-controlled media, and that there had been no genuine pre-election political debate. However, President Putin dismissed these criticisms; he promised to press ahead with economic reform and to safeguard democracy.

(h) Putin's second term, 2004–8

There was a tragic early reminder of the Chechen situation when, on 1 September 2004, the traditional start of the Russian school year, a group of heavily-armed Chechen guerrillas occupied a school in the town of Beslan, in North Ossetia, and took around 1100 children and adults hostage. They demanded an end to the Second Chechen War and the complete withdrawal of all Russian troops from Chechnya. After three days Russian security forces stormed the building, using tanks and rockets. This soon ended the crisis, but not before over 300 people had been killed, including 186 children. The government was criticized for its handling of the situation on the grounds that excessive force was used. Alexander Litvinenko, a former member of the KGB, claimed that it was an 'inside job', that the security services had organized the hostage-taking to keep public opinion anti-Chechen and to justify stricter security measures. Soon afterwards Putin introduced tougher anti-terrorist laws and increased the powers of the security forces. In June 2006 the Duma passed a new law which gave the FSB (successor to the KGB) authority to send commandos abroad to assassinate 'terrorist groups'; this power was to be used only at the discretion of the president.

Litvinenko had a history of criticizing the government and the security services: in 1998 he accused FSB bosses of ordering the murder of the oligarch Boris Berezovsky. This led to Litvinenko's arrest on charges of 'exceeding his authority'. The charges were dropped, but in 2000 he took refuge in the UK where he worked as a journalist and acted as a 'consultant' for the British intelligence services. In 2002 he published a book in which he accused the FSB of organizing the series of terrorist attacks that were blamed on the Chechens, in order to justify the Second Chechen War and bring Putin to power. This was dangerous stuff, and his comments on the Beslan crisis proved to be the final straw. In November 2006 Litvinenko was killed in London by a rare radioactive poison, Polonium 210. Investigations suggested that the poison had been administered by Andrey Lugovoy, a Russian security agent, who was charged with the murder. The UK authorities requested his extradition from Russia, but this was refused. Although the UK government did not directly blame the Russian government, there was a clear inference that the murder was indeed sponsored by the Russian state. In 2007 another Russian exile, Alex Goldfarb, with the collaboration of Litvinenko's widow, Marina, published a book containing compelling evidence that Putin himself must have ordered the murder. Nor was this the first time a critic of the Putin regime had been murdered. A few weeks earlier, in October 2006, Anna Politskovskaya, a journalist and writer, was shot dead in the lift of her apartment block. She had been a long-time critic of the Chechen War, and in 2004 had published a book, *Putin's Russia,* in which she claimed that Russia still had elements of the police state, or mafia state. On the more positive side, as Putin began his second term as president, *the economic situation was looking bright.* Oil prices were rising: around £28 a barrel in 2000, they now stood at £40 a barrel, and by the end of 2006 they had reached over £60. By this time Russia was the largest producer of gas in the world, and the second largest exporter of oil after Saudi Arabia. As Europe becomes more dependent on fuel supplies from Russia, this could well strengthen Moscow's influence and leverage. *The economy had grown steadily by over 6 per cent a year since Putin became president in 2000.* Another contributor to the success story was the software-manufacturing industry: in 2006 exports of software were worth $1.5 billion as opposed to only £128 million in 2001. This success was encouraging more foreign investment. There were plans to use some of the increased revenue to improve living standards. In 2005 the National Priority Projects were announced, designed to improve the health system, education, housing and agriculture, including wage increases for health workers and teachers.

However, Putin decided to use much of the cash to build up a large reserve fund to protect against a fall in oil prices. This meant less government investment and stagnation in the economic reform programme. To make matters worse, Russia was hard-hit by the 2008–9 world financial crisis, which cut off the flow of cheap credit and investment from the West. Fortunately Putin's $90-billion reserve fund helped Russia to cope, and by the end of 2009 the economy was growing again. On the downside, the National Priority Projects suffered. Under the Soviet system, universities and academies were well financed, as were the arts – orchestras, theatres, film studios and publishers. Admittedly, there was a price to pay in the form of strict censorship, but following the 1998 economic crisis, this funding had been drastically reduced – for example, the budget for higher education had been slashed to only 12 per cent of the 1989 level. By 2008, in spite of its promises, the government had largely failed to reverse these cuts. Average wages of lecturers and teachers were only two-thirds of the national rate. Even the Ministry of Education reported that only 20 per cent of institutions of higher education had retained the high standards that were the norm under the Soviet system. The state now provides less than a third of their funding. The same is true of the health service: although this is still free, the care is far inferior to that provided under the communists. To get the best and quickest treatment, patients must pay. Probably worst affected are the elderly; although prices have rocketed, pensions have not increased. In most Russian towns and cities, old people can be seen on street corners trying to sell bits of produce, fruit and vegetables, as they struggle to make ends meet. Understandably, many ordinary Russians look back on post-Stalinist Soviet times with nostalgia, in spite of its drawbacks.

During 2007 there were a number of protest demonstrations, known as Dissenters' Marches, in Moscow, St Petersburg, Nizhny Novgorod and Samara, but later demonstrations were met by police, and overt public support soon dwindled. Although by the end of 2008 there was much hostility to the Putin regime, most of it was in private, and there was very little public criticism. This was partly because the government kept tight control of the media, and journalists and writers were afraid of meeting the same fate as Anna Politskovskaya and Alexander Litvinenko. There was another reason too: according to Perry Anderson:

> it is the knowledge, which can only be half-repressed, that the liberal intelligentsia is compromised by its own part in bringing to being what it now so dislikes. By clinging to Yeltsin long after the illegality and corruption of his rule were plain, in the name of defence against a toothless Communism, it destroyed its credibility in the eyes of the population, only to find that Yeltsin had landed it with Putin.

The constitution did not allow Putin to stand for a third consecutive term, so he chose his close friend and ally, Dmitri Medvedev, as the United Russia presidential candidate. Before the election, Medvedev announced that if he won, he would choose Putin as his prime minister. Their election slogan was 'Together We Win'. In March 2008 Medvedev won a sweeping victory, taking around 70 per cent of the popular vote. His nearest rival, the Communist leader, Gennady Zyuganov, received just under 18 per cent. In spite of the dissatisfaction with falling living standards, it seemed that Putin's personal popularity was still sufficient to win elections. Whatever his faults, he and his United Russia party were still more attractive than any of the alternatives.

(i)   Putin and Medvedev, 2008–12

The day after he became president in May 2008, Medvedev duly appointed Putin as prime minister. The State Duma approved the appointment by 392 votes to 56; only the communists voted against. Clearly Putin would continue to be extremely influential, and journalists soon labelled the new government the 'tandemocracy'. They were soon faced with a crisis – *The South Ossetia War*. When the USSR broke up, Georgia became independent. But South Ossetia and Abkhazia soon declared themselves independent of Georgia, and were supported by Russia. Georgia refused to accept this, and the conflict dragged on. In August 2008 Georgian troops suddenly invaded South Ossetia. Medvedev reacted swiftly – Russian forces counter-attacked and after five days of heavy fighting, the Georgians were driven out. Russia officially recognized South Ossetia and Abkhazia as independent states. Medvedev's decisive handling of the crisis was popular with most Russians, though the Western media, especially in the USA, sided with Georgia. Towards the end of 2008 Russia began to feel the effects of the world financial crisis (see Section 27.7). Fortunately the government was able to use the large surplus accumulated earlier to bail out any banks that were in difficulties, and to help struggling companies with generous loans. Even so GDP fell by around 10 per cent in 2009, and the economy only began to move forward again in 2010. The reserve fund had been emptied and this delayed various reform and modernization programmes. Medvedev's main aim was to reduce Russia's dependence on income from oil and gas exports by diversifying into nuclear technology and pharmaceuticals, and by further developing information technology and software production. In January 2011 Medvedev admitted that one of his other key policies – to eliminate corruption – had so far been a failure. As the time approached for the next Duma and presidential elections, there was great speculation as to whether Medvedev would stand for re-election or step down in favour of Putin. There had been rumours of a breach between the two. However, in September 2011, Medvedev announced that he would not stand again and he officially proposed Vladimir Putin as the United Russia party candidate. In the Duma elections held on 4 December 2011, United Russia suffered something of a setback. Their share of the vote was below 50 per cent for the first time; it actually fell from 64 per cent in 2007 to 49 per cent, and the party lost 77 seats, down from 315 to 238, out of a total of 450. The Communists took 37 of these seats, going up from 57 to 92. Of the two smaller parties, Just Russia won 64 seats and the Liberal Democrats 56. Putin and Medvedev's party had lost their two-thirds majority, although they still had a small overall majority. The election was followed by protest demonstrations in Moscow and St Petersburg claiming widespread electoral fraud and demanding annulment of the results. These were followed by even larger demonstrations in support of the government. In March 2012 the presidential election brought a decisive victory for Putin, who took 63 per cent of the votes, against 17 per cent for Gennady Zyuganov, the Communist leader, who came second of the five candidates. On 7 May 2012, Vladimir Putin was inaugurated as president for the third time. Although there were more protests about irregularities at polling stations, there could be no doubt that Putin was still remarkably popular. He defended what he called his 'managed democracy' on the grounds that this was the most suitable type of democracy for Russia, because the country had no history of Western-style democracy. And a majority of people evidently agreed. Putin was set to continue in power, either as president or as prime minister, for the foreseeable future. No matter what the state of the nation, and in spite of numerous protest demonstrations, he seemed to be unassailable.

FURTHER READING

Anderson, P., 'Russia's Managed Democracy', *London Review of Books* (25 January 2007).

Aron, L., *Boris Yeltsin: A Revolutionary Life* (HarperCollins, 2001 edition).

Brown, A., *The Gorbachev Factor* (Oxford University Press, 1996).

Brown, A., *Seven Years That Changed the World: Perestroika in Perspective* (Oxford University Press, 2008).

Brown, A., *The Rise and Fall of Communism* (Vintage, 2010).

Goldfarb, A. and Litvinenko, M., *Death of a Dissident: The Poisoning of Alexander Litvinenko* (Simon & Schuster, 2007).

Kozlov, V., *Sedition: Everyday Resistance in the Soviet Union under Khrushchev and Brezhnev* (Yale University Press, 2011).

Lowe, N., *Mastering Twentieth Century Russian History* (Palgrave Macmillan, 2002).

McCauley, M., *The Rise and Fall of the Soviet Union, 1917–1991* (Longman, 3rd edition, 2007).

Medvedev, R., *Post-Soviet Russia: A Journey Through the Yeltsin Era* (Columbia University Press, 2000).

Politkovskaya, A., *Putin's Russia* (Harvill, 2004).

Sakwa, R., *The Rise and Fall of the Soviet Union, 1917–1991* (Routledge, 1999).

Sakwa, R., *The Quality of Freedom: Khodorkovsky, Putin and the Yukos Affair* (Oxford University Press, 2009).

Sakwa, R., *The Crisis of Russian Democracy: The Dual State, Factionalism and the Medvedev Succession* (Cambridge University Press, 2010).

Service, R., *Comrades: A World History of Communism* (Macmillan, 2007).

Taubman, W., *Khrushchev: The Man and his Era* (Free Press, new edition, 2005).

Tompson, W. J., *Khrushchev: A Political Life* (Macmillan, 1995).

Tompson, W. J., *The Soviet Union Under Brezhnev, 1964–1982* (Longman, 2003)

Triesman, D. S., *The Return: Russia's Journey from Gorbachev to Medvedev* (Simon Spotlight, 2010).

1 Khrushchev believed that communism in the USSR could be reformed and modernized and made more efficient. How far had this been achieved by 1970?

2 'The USSR remained politically and socially stable in the years 1964 to 1982 despite the policies of the Brezhnev era.' How far would you agree with this view?

3 Consider the view that if Gorbachev had followed different policies, the USSR could have survived, in the same way that communism survived in China.

4 'It was Gorbachev's reluctance to commit himself to sufficiently radical changes that led to the break-up of the Soviet Union.' Assess the validity of this view.

5 Explain why the collapse of the USSR was followed by serious economic and political problems.

6 'Putin's Russia may well have been a police state, but at least he rescued the country from the chaos of the Yeltsin years.' How far do you think this is a fair comment on both presidents?

There is a document question about Khrushchev's promises for the future on the website.

Chapter 19

China, 1900–49

SUMMARY OF EVENTS

China had a long history of national unity and since the mid-seventeenth century had been ruled by the Manchu or Ch'ing dynasty. However, during the 1840s, the country moved into a troubled period of foreign interference, civil war and disintegration, which lasted until the communist victory in 1949.

The last emperor was overthrown in 1911 and a republic was proclaimed. The period 1916 to 1928, known as *the Warlord Era*, was one of great chaos, as a number of generals seized control of different provinces. A party known as the *Kuomintang (KMT)*, or Nationalists, was trying to govern China and control the generals, who were busy fighting each other. The KMT leaders were Dr Sun Yat-sen, and after his death in 1925, General Chiang Kai-shek. The Chinese Communist Party (CCP) was founded in 1921, and at first it co-operated with the KMT in its struggle against the warlords. As the KMT gradually established control over more and more of China, it felt strong enough to do without the help of the communists, and it tried to destroy them. The communists, under their leader Mao Zedong (Mao Tse-tung), reacted vigorously, and after escaping from surrounding KMT forces, they embarked on the 6000-mile Long March (1934–5) to form a new power base in northern China.

Civil war dragged on, complicated by Japanese interference, which culminated in a full-scale invasion in 1937. When the Second World War ended in defeat for the Japanese and their withdrawal from China, the KMT and the CCP continued to fight each other for control of China. Chiang Kai-shek received help from the USA, but in 1949 it was Mao and the communists who finally triumphed. Chiang and his supporters fled to the island of Taiwan (Formosa). Mao Zedong quickly established control over the whole of China, and he remained leader until his death in 1976.

19.1 REVOLUTION AND THE WARLORD ERA

(a) Background to the revolution of 1911

In the early part of the nineteenth century China kept itself very much separate from the rest of the world; life went on quietly and peacefully with no great changes, as it had done since the Manchus took over in the 1640s. However, in the mid-nineteenth century China found itself faced by a number of crises. The prolonged period of relative peace had led to a rapid increase in the population – between 1741 and 1841 the population rose from 140 million to 410 million. This made it difficult to produce enough food for subsistence, forcing many peasants to turn to robbery and banditry as a means of survival. The ensuing chaos encouraged foreigners, especially Europeans, *to force their way into China* to take advantage of trading possibilities. The British were first on the scene, fighting and defeating the Chinese in the Opium Wars (1839–42). They forced China to hand over Hong Kong and to allow them to trade at certain ports. Other western nations followed, and eventually these 'barbarians', as the Chinese regarded them, had rights and concessions in about 80 ports and other towns.

Next came *the Taiping Rebellion (1850–64)*, which spread all over southern China. It was partly a Christian religious movement and partly a political reform movement, which aimed to set up a 'Heavenly Kingdom of Great Peace' (*Taiping tianguo*). The movement was eventually defeated, not by the Manchu government troops, which proved to be ineffective, but by newly-formed regional armies. The failure of the government forces was a serious blow to the authority of the Ch'ing dynasty. It left them dependent on regional armies that they did not control. This began the process in which provinces began to assert their independence from the central government in Beijing (Peking), culminating in the Warlord Era (1916–28).

China was defeated in a war with Japan (1894–5) and forced to hand over territory, including the large island of Formosa. By the end of 1898 Britain, Germany, France and Russia had leased large areas of land from the Chinese government which they proceeded to treat as if they were no longer Chinese territory. There was a story in circulation that outside a British-run park in Shanghai, there was a sign reading NO DOGS OR CHINESE. The sign never actually existed, but the story showed the outrage felt by ordinary Chinese people at the intrusive foreign presence in their country. A Chinese uprising – *the Boxer Rising* – against foreign influence took place in 1898–1900, but it was defeated by an international army, and the Empress Tz'u-hsi was forced to pay massive compensation for damage done to foreign property in China. More territory was lost to Japan as a result of the Japanese victory in the Russo-Japanese War (1904–5), and China was clearly in a sorry state.

In the early years of the twentieth century thousands of young Chinese travelled abroad and were educated there. They returned with radical, revolutionary ideas of overthrowing the Manchu dynasty and westernizing China. Some revolutionaries, like Dr Sun Yat-sen, wanted a democratic state modelled on the USA.

(b) The 1911 revolution and the Twenty-One Demands (1915)

The government tried to respond to the new radical ideas by introducing reforms, promising democracy and setting up elected provincial assemblies. However, this only encouraged the provinces to distance themselves still further from the central government, which was now extremely unpopular. *The revolution began among soldiers in Wuchang in October 1911, and most provinces quickly declared themselves independent of Beijing.*

The government, ruling on behalf of the child emperor Puyi (who was only 5 years old), in desperation sought help from a retired general, Yuan Shikai, who had been commander of the Chinese Northern Army, and still had a lot of influence with the generals. However, the plan backfired: Yuan, who was still only in his early fifties, turned out to have ambitions of his own. He did a deal with the revolutionaries – they agreed to his becoming the first president of the Chinese republic in return for the abdication of Puyi and the end of the Manchu dynasty. With the support of the army, Yuan ruled as a military dictator from 1912 until 1915.

Meanwhile the Japanese sought to take advantage of the upheaval in China and the outbreak of the First World War. A few days after the war began they demanded that Germany should hand over all their rights in the Chinese Shantung peninsula to Japan. This was followed up in January 1915 by *Japan's Twenty-One Demands to China*. These were divided into five groups. First they wanted Chinese approval of Japan's concessions in Shantung (seized from the Germans), including the right to build railways and to begin new mines; similar rights in south Manchuria; in Hanyehping, the right to continue developing the coal mines at Wuhan; similar rights in Fukien province; and finally the demand that China should accept Japanese 'advisers' in political, economic and military matters, and must allow the police forces in some large cities to be jointly organized by Japanese and Chinese. As soon as the demands became public there was a wave of anti-Japanese feeling and a boycott of Japanese goods. Yuan delayed accepting the demands until the Japanese eventually agreed to drop the final group. An agreement accepting the rest was signed on 25 May 1915. In fact the agreement made very little difference to the situation: it simply restated the concessions that Japan already had. It was group five of the demands that revealed Japan's motives. Acceptance of those would have reduced China almost to a colony or a protectorate of Japan. However, Japan had another strategy in mind: they knew that Yuan had developed a desire to become emperor, and in return for his acceptance of the demands, they secretly promised that they would support him in his ambitions. A new emperor who owed his position to Japanese support would be an excellent alternative method of controlling China. In December 1915 it was announced that there was to be a return to the monarchy in the person of Yuan himself, who would become emperor on 1 January 1916. This turned out to be a fatal mistake: most people saw the ending of the new republic as a backward step, and his support dwindled rapidly. The army turned against him and forced him to abdicate. He died in October 1916.

(c) The Warlord Era (1916–28)

The abdication and death of Yuan Shikai removed the last person who seemed capable of maintaining some sort of unity in China. The country now disintegrated into literally hundreds of states of varying sizes, each controlled by a warlord and his private army. As they fought each other, it was the ordinary Chinese peasants who suffered untold hardships (see Illus. 19.1). However, *two important positive developments took place during this period.*

- The May the Fourth Movement began on that date in 1919 with a huge student demonstration in Beijing, protesting against the warlords and against traditional Chinese culture. The movement was also anti-Japanese, especially when the 1919 Versailles settlement officially recognized Japan's right to take over Germany's concessions in Shantung province. It was this humiliation at the hands of Japan that seemed to stir up the whole country to support the movement. Thousands of university students went on strike at the failure of the government to protest strongly enough at Versailles. Once again there was a boycott of Japanese goods. This was popular with Chinese industrialists, who benefited from the boycott; they supported the students, many of whom had been jailed, while factory workers and railway workers went on strike in sympathy. It was a remarkable show of mass patriotism. The government finally had no choice but to give way: the students were released; the ministers who had signed the Twenty-One Demands agreement in 1915 were sacked, and the Chinese delegation at Versailles refused to sign the peace treaty.
- The other problems addressed by May the Fourth Movement – the need to tame the warlords, and the desire to modernize Chinese culture – took longer to achieve. However, as the Kuomintang or Nationalist Party gradually grew stronger, they succeeded in bringing the warlords under control by 1928. Chinese culture was partly based on the teachings of the Chinese philosopher, Confucius, who died in 478 BC. He had developed his philosophy during a period of anarchy in China and it was designed to solve the problems of how best to organize society so that all could live together in peace. He stressed the necessity for loyalty in all relationships

Illustration 19.1 **A street execution in China in 1927, towards the end of the Warlord Era**

and for the strict upbringing of children. 'Let the ruler be a ruler, the subject a subject, the father a father, and a son a son.' If people acted properly according to their place in society, then the moral integrity and social harmony of the nation would be restored. For centuries Chinese emperors and rulers had embraced Confucianism because it justified their autocratic and conservative rule. After the 1911 revolution and May the Fourth 1919, some writers began to produce questioning and challenging works calling for modernization in politics, science and individual rights in place of traditional Confucianism. But the practical effect of these writings was limited; the warlords were totally unmoved by this new thinking, and Chiang's Nationalists suppressed intellectual and political freedom after they had set up their government in Nanjing in the late 1920s. They even promoted Confucianism because of its conservatism and because it was a good means of distinguishing themselves from Mao and the communists. It was not until the student protests of 1989 that the May the Fourth ideas surfaced again (see Section 20.3).

19.2 THE KUOMINTANG, DR SUN YAT-SEN AND CHIANG KAI-SHEK

(a) The Kuomintang

The main hope for the survival of a united China lay with the Kuomintang, or National People's Party, formed in 1912 by Dr Sun Yat-sen. He had trained as a doctor in Hawaii and Hong Kong and lived abroad until the 1911 revolution. He was dismayed by the disintegration of China and wanted to create a modern, united, democratic state. Returning to China after the revolution, he succeeded in setting up a government at Canton in southern China (1917). His ideas were influential but he had very little power outside the Canton area. The KMT was not a communist party, though it was prepared to co-operate with the communists, and developed its own party organization along communist lines, as well as building up its own army. Sun himself summarized his aims as *the Three Principles*:

nationalism – to rid China of foreign influence and build the country into a strong and united power, respected abroad.

democracy – China should not be ruled by warlords, but by the people themselves, after they had been educated to equip them for democratic self-government.

land reform – sometimes known as 'the people's livelihood'; this was vague – although Sun announced a long-term policy of economic development and redistribution of land to the peasants and was in favour of rent restraint, he was opposed to the confiscation of landlords' property.

Sun gained enormous respect as an intellectual statesman and revolutionary leader, but when he died in 1925 little progress had been made towards achieving the three principles, mainly because he was not himself a general. Until the KMT armies were built up, he had to rely on alliances with sympathetic warlords, and he had difficulty exercising any authority outside the south.

(b) Chiang Kai-shek

General Chiang Kai-shek became leader of the KMT after Sun's death. He had received his military training in Japan before the First World War, and being a strong nationalist, joined the KMT. At this stage the new Russian Soviet government was providing help and guidance for the KMT in the hope that Nationalist China would be friendly towards Russia. In 1923 Chiang spent some time in Moscow studying the organization of the Communist Party and the Red Army. The following year he became head of the Whampoa Military Academy (near Canton), which was set up with the help of Russian cash, arms and advisers to train officers for the KMT army. However, in spite of his Russian contacts, Chiang was not a communist. In fact he was more right-wing than Sun Yat-sen and became increasingly anti-communist, his sympathies lying with businessmen and landowners. Soon after becoming party leader, he removed all left-wingers from leading positions in the Party, though for the time being he continued the KMT alliance with the communists.

In 1926 he set out on *the Northern March* to destroy the warlords of central and northern China. Starting from Canton, the KMT and the communists had captured Hankow, Shanghai and Nanking by 1927. The capital, Beijing, was taken in 1928. Much of Chiang's success sprang from massive local support among the peasants, who were attracted by communist promises of land. The capture of Shanghai was helped by a rising of industrial workers organized by *Zhou En-lai*, a member of the KMT and also a communist.

During 1927 Chiang decided that the communists were becoming too powerful. In areas where communists were strong, landlords were being attacked and land seized; it was time to destroy an embarrassing ally. All communists were expelled from the KMT and a terrible 'purification movement' was launched in which thousands of communists, trade union and peasant leaders were massacred; some estimates put the total murdered as high as 250 000. The communists had been checked, the warlords were under control and Chiang was the military and political leader of China.

The Kuomintang government proved to be a great disappointment for the majority of the Chinese people. Chiang could claim to have achieved Sun's first principle, nationalism, but relying as he did on the support of wealthy landowners, no moves were made towards democracy or land reform, though there was some limited progress with the building of more schools and roads.

19.3 MAO ZEDONG AND THE CHINESE COMMUNIST PARTY

(a) The early years

The party had been officially founded in 1921; at first it consisted mostly of intellectuals and had very little military strength, which explains why it was willing to work with the KMT. Mao Zedong, who was present at the founding meeting, was born in Hunan province (1893) in south-east China, the son of a prosperous peasant farmer. After spending some time working on the land, Mao trained as a teacher, and then moved northwards to Beijing where he worked as a library assistant at the university, a centre of Marxist studies. Later he moved back to Hunan and built up a reputation as a skilful trade union and peasant association organizer. After the communist breach with the KMT, Mao was responsible for changing the Party's strategy: they would concentrate on winning mass support among the peasants rather than trying to capture industrial towns, where several communist insurrections had already failed because of the strength of the KMT. In 1931 Mao was elected chairman of the Central Executive Committee of the Party, and from then on, he gradually consolidated his position as the real leader of Chinese communism. The Chinese Soviet Republic was proclaimed at Juichin in 1931, and on 7 November 1931 the first All-China Congress of Soviets was held there. It was attended by delegates from 15 soviet areas.

Mao and his supporters spent most of their energies on survival as Chiang carried out five 'extermination campaigns' against them between 1930 and 1934. They took to the mountains between Hunan and Kiangsi provinces and concentrated on building up the Red Army. However, early in 1934 Mao's base area was surrounded by KMT armies poised for the final destruction of Chinese communism. Mao decided that the only chance of survival was to break through Chiang's lines and set up another power base somewhere else. In October 1934 the breakthrough was achieved and almost 100 000 communists set out on the remarkable *Long March*, which was to become part of Chinese legend. They covered about 6000 miles in 368 days (see Map 19.1) and, in the words of American journalist Edgar Snow:

> crossed 18 mountain ranges, 5 of which were snow-capped, and 24 rivers. They passed through 12 different provinces, occupied 62 cities, and broke through enveloping armies of 10 different provincial warlords, besides defeating, eluding, or out-manoeuvring the various forces of government troops sent against them.

Eventually the 20 000 survivors found refuge at Yenan in Shensi province: this was the last surviving communist base in China and was controlled by the guerrilla leader Kao Kang. The Shensi communists, not entirely willingly, accepted Mao as leader, and a new base and a soviet were organized. Mao was able to control the provinces of Shensi and Kansu. However, according to writers Jung Chang and Jon Halliday in their book *Mao: The Unknown Story,* published in 2005, the march was vastly exaggerated and was in fact nothing like as heroic as legend claimed. They even suggested that Mao's 'breakout' in October 1934 was actually permitted by Chiang Kai-shek because he preferred the communists to be in the north where he could box them in while he extended the KMT control over the south-west. This interpretation was welcomed by Mao's critics, but historians generally gave a more balanced judgement: while agreeing that there had been some exaggeration in accounts of the march in order to show Mao and the communists in the best possible light, they rejected the Jung Chang/Halliday interpretation as 'more fantasy than fact'. *During the ten years following the Long March the communists continued to gain support, while Chiang and the KMT steadily lost popularity.*

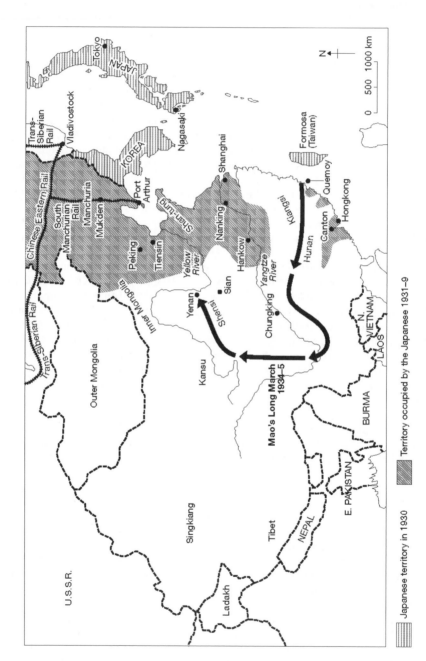

Map 19.1 **China after the First World War**

Japanese territory in 1930

Territory occupied by the Japanese 1931–9

(b)   Why did Mao and the communists gain support?

1   The inefficiency and corruption of the KMT in government
The KMT had little to offer in the way of reform, spent too much time looking after the interests of industrialists, bankers and landowners, and made no effective attempts to organize mass support. This provided the main opportunity for Mao and the communists to win support.

2   There was little improvement in factory conditions
Poor industrial working conditions continued, in spite of laws designed to remove the worst abuses, such as child labour in textile mills. Often these laws were not applied: there was widespread bribery of inspectors and Chiang himself was not prepared to offend his industrial supporters.

3   There was no improvement in peasant poverty
In the early 1930s there was a series of droughts and bad harvests which caused widespread famine in rural areas. At the same time there was usually plenty of rice and wheat being hoarded in the cities by profiteering merchants. In addition there were high taxes and forced labour. In contrast, the land policy followed in areas controlled by the communists was much more attractive: at first in the south, they seized the estates of rich landlords and redistributed them among the peasants. After the temporary truce with the KMT during the war with Japan, the communists compromised, and confined themselves to a policy of restricting rents and making sure that even the poorest labourers got a small piece of land. This less drastic policy had the advantage of winning the support of the smaller landowners, as well as the peasants.

4   Chiang's 'New Life Movement' was controversial
In the early 1930s Chiang began to advocate a return to the traditional values of Confucianism, the traditional Chinese religion. In 1934 he introduced the New Life Movement which, he claimed, was a unique secular, rational and modern Chinese version of Confucianism. It was meant to mobilize the population and to revive the country's 'innate morality', thereby helping to create a healthy society and a strong and united country. However, in the words of historian Rana Mitter: 'The movement was not ultimately successful, as its formal prescriptions, including not spitting in the street, and queuing up in an orderly fashion, came over as trivial in comparison with the much larger issues of national coherence which dogged twentieth-century China.' Unfortunately many May the Fourth supporters and other modern progressive thinkers protested that this was another backward step designed to return China to its oppressive imperial past.

5   The KMT put up no effective resistance to the Japanese
This was the crucial factor in the communist success. The Japanese occupied Manchuria in 1931 and were obviously preparing to bring the neighbouring provinces of northern China under their control. Chiang seemed to think it was more important to destroy the communists than to resist the Japanese, and moved into south Shensi to attack Mao (1936). Here a remarkable incident took place: Chiang was taken prisoner by some of his own troops, mostly Manchurians, who were incensed at the Japanese invasion. They demanded that Chiang should turn against the Japanese, but at first he was unwilling. Only after the prominent communist Zhou En-lai came to see him at Sian did he agree to a fresh alliance with the CCP and a national front against the Japanese.

The new alliance brought great advantages for the communists: the KMT extermination campaigns ceased for the time being and consequently the CCP was secure in its Shensi base. When full-scale war broke out with Japan in 1937, the KMT forces were quickly defeated and most of eastern China was occupied by the Japanese as Chiang retreated westwards. This enabled the communists, undefeated in Shensi, to present themselves as patriotic nationalists, leading an effective guerrilla campaign against the Japanese in the north. This won them massive support among the peasants and middle classes, who were appalled at Japanese arrogance and brutality. Whereas in 1937 the CCP had 5 base areas controlling 12 million people, by 1945 this had grown to 19 base areas controlling 100 million people.

However, a recent biographer of Chiang Kai-shek, Jay Taylor, has suggested that he deserves more credit than the Americans and British have given him. For example, the American General Stilwell used to refer to him as 'Peanut', while the British Field-Marshal Lord Alanbrooke described him as 'a cross between a pine-marten and a ferret'. Without trying to ignore Chiang's brutality and his mistakes, Taylor argues that, given the enormity of the problems facing him, he governed the country with reasonable skill and certainly understood the challenges facing him far better than his American advisers did.

19.4 THE COMMUNIST VICTORY, 1949

(a) China and the Second World War

When the war began, Chiang Kai-shek was in a dilemma: China had already been in a state of undeclared war with Japan since 1937, yet he had great admiration for Japan's ally Germany, and for the German military tradition. It was only after the German defeat at Stalingrad in 1942–3 that he decided to commit China to the Allied side. However, relations between China and the USSR were strained because of Chiang's campaigns against the communists, so that Stalin refused to take part in any meeting at which Chiang was present. As an encouragement, in January 1943 the USA, Britain and several other states renounced their territorial rights and concessions in China (though Britain insisted on keeping Hong Kong), and promised that Manchuria and Formosa would be returned to China after the war. The irony was that most of these territories were occupied by the Japanese at the time – unless Japan could be defeated, none of it would happen. Nevertheless the agreements were important because they showed that at last China was being treated as an equal among the great powers, and was promised a permanent seat on the Security Council of the United Nations.

The Japanese reaction to these developments was to launch an offensive by troops moved from Manchuria. Striking southwards from the Yangtse Valley, they eventually reached the frontier with Indochina, cutting off the south-east coast from the interior. The Nationalist forces were disorganized and ineffective, and their sporadic attempts to repel the Japanese advance were swept aside. Fortunately for the Chinese, time was running out for the Japanese in other areas (see Section 6.6(e)). In August 1945 the atomic bombs were dropped on Hiroshima and Nagasaki, and within a few days Japan surrendered. The Chinese contribution to the defeat of Japan had been to keep hundreds of thousands of Japanese troops bogged down in what was, for them, only a sideshow.

(b) Victory for the communists was still not inevitable

When the Japanese were defeated in 1945, the KMT and the CCP became locked in the final struggle for power. Many observers, especially in the USA, hoped and expected that Chiang would be victorious. The Americans helped the KMT to take over all areas previously occupied by the Japanese, except Manchuria, which had been captured by the Russians a few days before the war ended. Here the Russians obstructed the KMT and allowed CCP guerrillas to move in. In fact the apparent strength of the KMT was deceptive: in 1948 the ever-growing communist armies were large enough to abandon their guerrilla campaign and challenge Chiang's armies directly. As soon as they came under direct pressure, the KMT armies began to disintegrate. In January 1949 the communists took Beijing, and later in the year, Chiang and what remained of his forces fled to the island of Taiwan, leaving Mao Zedong in command of mainland China. In October 1949, standing at Tiananmen (the Gate of Heavenly Peace) in Beijing, Mao proclaimed the new People's Republic of China with himself as both Chairman of the CCP and president of the republic.

(c) Reasons for the CCP triumph

The communists continued to win popular support by their restrained land policy, which varied according to the needs of particular areas: some or all of a landlord's estate might be confiscated and redistributed among the peasants, or there might simply be rent restriction; communist armies were well disciplined and communist administration was honest and fair.

On the other hand the KMT administration was inefficient and corrupt, much of its American aid finding its way into the pockets of officials. Its policy of paying for the wars by printing extra money resulted in galloping inflation, which caused hardship for the masses and ruined many of the middle class. Its armies were poorly paid and were allowed to loot the countryside; subjected to communist propaganda, the troops gradually became disillusioned with Chiang and began to desert to the communists. The KMT tried to terrorize the local populations into submission, but this only alienated more areas. Chiang also made some tactical blunders: like Hitler, he could not bear to order retreats and consequently his scattered armies were surrounded, and often, as happened at Beijing and Shanghai, surrendered without resistance, totally disillusioned.

Finally the CCP leaders, Mao Zedong and Zhou En-lai, were shrewd enough to take advantage of KMT weaknesses and were completely dedicated. The communist generals, Lin Biao, Chu Teh and Ch-en Yi, had prepared their armies carefully and were more competent tactically than their KMT counterparts.

FURTHER READING

Bergère, M-C., *Sun Yat-sen* (Stanford University Press, 2000).

Felber, R. (ed.), *The Chinese Revolution in the 1920s: Triumph and Disaster* (Routledge, 2002).

Fenby, J., *Generalissimo: Chiang Kai-shek and the China he Lost* (Free Press, 2005 edition).

Fenby, J., *The Penguin History of Modern China, 1850–2009* (Penguin/Allen Lane, 2009).

Fenby, J., *Tiger Head, Snake Tails: China Today, How it Got There and Where it is Heading* (Simon & Schuster, 2012).

Jung Chang and J. Halliday, *Mao: The Unknown Story* (Cape, 2005).

Lynch, M., *China: From Empire to People's Republic* (Hodder & Stoughton, 1995).

Martin, M., *Strange Vigour: a Biography of Sun Yat-Sen* (Read Books, 2006).

Mitter, R., *A Bitter Revolution: China's Struggle with the Modern World* (Oxford University Press, 2004).

Snow, E., *Red Star Over China : The Rise of the Red Army* (Read Books, 2006 edition).

Taylor, J., *The Generalissimo: Chiang Kai-shek and the Struggle for Modern China* (Harvard University Press, 2011).

Wilbur, C. M., *The Nationalist Revolution in China, 1923–1928* (Cambridge University Press,1984).

1   Explain why there was a revolution in China in 1911 and assess the consequences of that revolution.
2   Explain why it took the Nationalists (Kuomintang) so long to establish their authority over China after the revolution of 1911.
3   'Chiang Kai-shek was popular during the second half of the 1920s, but after he came to power, his Kuomintang government proved to be a disappointment to the majority of Chinese people.' How far would you agree that this is a fair assessment of the career of Chiang Kai-shek?
4   'The communist victory in 1949 was due as much to the shortcomings of the Kuomintang as it was to the leadership of Mao Zedong.' How far would you agree with this assessment?
5   Assess the view that popular support was the main reason why the communists were able to achieve power in China in 1949.

There is a document question about the communist victory in China on the website.

China since 1949: the communists in control

SUMMARY OF EVENTS

After the communist victory over the Kuomintang in 1949, Mao Zedong set about rebuilding a shattered China. At first he received Russian advice and aid, but in the late 1950s relations cooled and Russian economic aid was reduced. In 1958 Mao introduced *the 'Great Leap Forward'*, in which communism was adapted – not altogether successfully – to meet the Chinese situation, with the emphasis on decentralization, agriculture, communes and contact with the masses. Mao became highly critical of the Russians, who, in his view, were straying from strict Marxist–Leninist principles and following the 'capitalist road' in both foreign and domestic affairs. During the 1960s these disagreements caused a serious rift in world communism, which was only healed after Mikhail Gorbachev became Russian leader in 1985. With *the Cultural Revolution (1966–9)*, Mao tried successfully to crush opposition within the Party and to keep China developing along Marxist–Leninist lines.

After Mao's death in 1976, there was a power struggle from which Deng Xiaoping emerged as undisputed leader (1981). Much less conservative than Mao, Deng was responsible for some important policy changes, moderating Mao's hardline communism and looking towards Japan and the capitalist West for ideas and help. This aroused resentment among the Maoist supporters, who accused Deng of straying along the 'capitalist road'; in 1987 they forced him to slow down the pace of his reforms.

Encouraged by Gorbachev's *glasnost* policy in the USSR, student protests began in Tiananmen Square in Beijing in April 1989, continuing through into June. They demanded democracy and an end to corruption in the Communist Party. On 3–4 June the army moved in, attacked the students, killing hundreds, and restored order. The communists had regained control. The economic reforms continued with some success, but there was no political reform. Deng Xiaoping continued as supreme leader until his death (at the age of 92) in 1997. The first few years of the new century saw more economic changes, including the opening up of the party to capitalists. By 2012, with the Communist Party still supreme, it seemed that China might soon supplant the USA as the world's most powerful nation.

20.1 HOW SUCCESSFUL WAS MAO IN DEALING WITH CHINA'S PROBLEMS?

(a) Problems facing Mao

The problems facing the People's Republic in 1949 were complex, to say the least. The country was devastated after the long civil war and the war with Japan: railways, roads, canals and dykes had been destroyed and there were chronic food shortages. Industry was backward, agriculture was inefficient and incapable of feeding the poverty-stricken masses and inflation seemed out of control. Mao had the support of the peasants and many of the middle class, who were disgusted by the miserable performance of the Kuomintang, but it was essential for him to improve conditions if he were to hold on to their support. To control and organize such a vast country with a population of at least 600 million must have been a superhuman task. Yet Mao succeeded, and China today, whatever its faults, is still very much his creation. He began by looking closely at Stalin's methods and experimented, by a process of trial and error, to find which would work in China and where a special Chinese approach was necessary.

(b) The constitution of 1950 (officially adopted 1954)

This included the National People's Congress (the final authority for legislation), whose members were elected for four years by people over 18. There was also a State Council and the Chairman of the Republic (both elected by the Congress), whose function was to make sure that laws were carried out and that the administration of the country went ahead. The State Council chose the Political Bureau (Politburo), which took all the main decisions. The whole system was, of course, dominated by the Communist Party, and only party members could stand for election. The constitution was important because it provided China with a strong central government for the first time for many years, and it has remained largely unchanged (see Fig. 20.1).

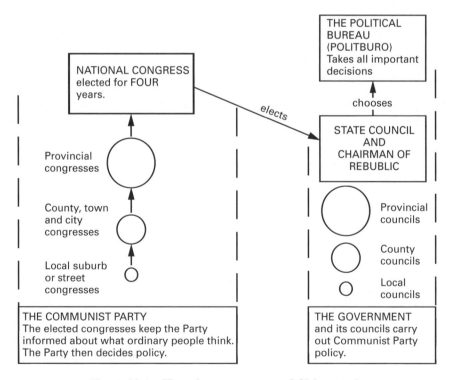

Figure 20.1 **How the government of China works**

(c) Agricultural changes

These transformed China from a country of small, inefficient private farms into one of large co-operative farms like those in Russia (1950–6). In the first stage, land was taken from large landowners and redistributed among the peasants, no doubt with violence in places. Some sources mention as many as two million people killed, though historian Jack Gray, writing in 1970, when Mao was still alive, claimed that 'the redistribution of China's land was carried out with a remarkable degree of attention to legality and the minimum of physical violence against landlords'. Recently, however, during the atmosphere of good-will and openness surrounding the 2008 Beijing Olympics, the Chinese authorities decided to declassify some secret archives and make them available for historians. These show that the official accounts of a number of events and policies do not tell the whole truth; achievements were exaggerated and unpleasant events were either toned down or not reported at all. Professor Frank Dikotter of the University of Hong Kong has shown that in some areas there were very few wealthy landowners, since the land was already fairly equally divided between the peasants. What actually happened was that their land was taken away from them and redistributed to communist party activists, with considerable violence, torturing and execution. One document from the Hebei archives reported that:

> When it comes to the ways in which people are killed, some are buried alive, some are executed, some are cut to pieces, and among those who are strangled or mangled to death, some of the bodies are hung from trees or doors.

By 1956, whatever the methods used, about 95 per cent of all surviving peasants were in collective farms with joint ownership of the farm and its equipment.

(d) Industrial changes

These began with the government nationalizing most businesses. In 1953 it embarked on a Five Year Plan concentrating on the development of heavy industry (iron, steel, chemicals and coal). The Russians helped with cash, equipment and advisers, and the plan had some success. Before it was complete, however, Mao began to have grave doubts as to whether China was suited to this sort of heavy industrialization. On the other hand he could claim that under his leadership the country had recovered from the ravages of the wars: full communications had been restored, inflation was under control and the economy was looking much healthier.

(e) The Hundred Flowers campaign (1957)

This seems to some extent to have developed out of industrialization, which produced a vast new class of technicians and engineers. The party *cadres* (groups who organized the masses politically and economically – the collectivization of the farms, for example, was carried out by the cadres) believed that this new class of experts would threaten their authority. The government, feeling pleased with its progress so far, decided that open discussion of the problems might improve relations between cadres and experts or intellectuals. 'Let a hundred flowers bloom and a hundred schools of thought contend', said Mao, calling for constructive criticism. Unfortunately he got more than he had anticipated as critics attacked:

- the cadres for incompetence and over-enthusiasm;
- the government for over-centralization;

- the Communist Party for being undemocratic; some suggested that opposition parties should be allowed.

Mao hurriedly called off the campaign and clamped down on his critics, insisting that his policies were right. The campaign showed how much opposition there still was to communism and to the uneducated cadres, and it convinced Mao that a drive was needed to consolidate the advance of socialism; so in 1958 he called for the 'Great Leap Forward'.

(f) The Great Leap Forward

Mao felt that something new and different was needed to meet China's special problems – something not based on Russian experience. The Great Leap Forward involved further important developments in both industry and agriculture, in order to increase output (agriculture in particular was not providing the required food) and to adapt industry to Chinese conditions. Its most important features were:

1 The introduction of communes. These were units larger than collective farms, containing up to 75 000 people, divided into brigades and work teams with an elected council. They ran their own collective farms and factories, carried out most of the functions of local government within the commune and undertook special local projects. One typical commune in 1965, for example, contained 30 000 people, of which a third were children at school or in crèches, a third were housewives or elderly, and the rest were the workforce. This included a science team of 32 graduates and 43 technicians. Each family received a share of the profits and also had a small private plot of land.
2 A complete change of emphasis in industry. Instead of aiming for large-scale works of the type seen in the USSR and the West, much smaller factories were set up in the countryside to provide machinery for agriculture. Mao talked of 600 000 'backyard steel furnaces' springing up, organized and managed by the communes, which also undertook to build roads, canals, dams, reservoirs and irrigation channels.

At first it looked as though the Great Leap might be a failure: there was some opposition to the communes, a series of bad harvests (1959–61) and the withdrawal of all Russian aid following the breach between Russia and China. All this, coupled with the lack of experience among the cadres, caused hardship in the years 1959–63; statistics which emerged later suggested that some 20 million people may have died prematurely as a result of hardships, especially the disastrous famine of 1959–60, caused by the Great Leap. Even Mao's prestige suffered and he was forced to resign as Chairman of the People's Congress (to be succeeded by Liu Shaoqi), though he remained Chairman of the Communist Party. Professor Dikotter's researches in the newly opened archives reveal that the situation was much worse than the official account shows. Towards the end of the Great Leap Forward, special teams were sent out to discover the extent of the disaster around the country. Their findings included reports on peasant resistance during the collectivization campaign, reports about mass murders, confessions of leaders responsible for millions of deaths and reports about working conditions. In the words of Professor Dikotter:

What comes out of this massive and detailed dossier is a tale of horror in which Chairman Mao emerges as one of the greatest mass murderers in human history, responsible for the premature deaths of at least 45 million people between 1958 and 1962. It is not merely the extent of the catastrophe that dwarfs earlier estimates, but also the manner in which many people died: between two and three million victims were tortured to death or summarily killed, often for the slightest infraction. When a boy stole a handful of grain in a Hunan village, local boss Xiong Dechang, forced his father to bury him alive. The father died of grief a few days later. … The killing of slackers, weaklings, those too ill to work, or otherwise unproductive elements, increased the overall food supply for those who contributed to the regime through their labour. At one meeting Mao announced: 'It is better to let half the people die so that the other half can eat their fill'.

However, in the long term the importance of the Great Leap became clear. According to the official account, by the early 1970s both agricultural and industrial production had increased substantially, and China was at least managing to feed its massive population without any further famine (which had rarely happened under the KMT). The communes proved to be a successful innovation. They were much more than merely collective farms – they were an efficient unit of local government and they enabled the central government in Beijing to keep in touch with local opinion. They seemed to be the ideal solution to the problem of running a vast country while at the same time avoiding the over-centralization that stifles initiative. The crucial decision had been taken that China would remain predominantly an agricultural country with small-scale industry scattered around the countryside. The economy would be labour-intensive (relying on massive numbers of workers instead of using labour-saving machines). Given the country's enormous population, this was arguably the best way of making sure that everybody had a job, and it enabled China to avoid the growing unemployment problems of the highly industrialized western nations. Other genuine benefits were the spread of education and welfare services and a reduction in infant mortality, which fell from 203 per thousand births in 1949 to 84 by the end of the 1960s. There was also a definite improvement in the position of women in society. Again, however, the true picture may well not be quite so rosy as it appears. In 2012 Jonathan Fenby, an expert in Chinese affairs, making use of the latest research, claimed that Mao 'had brought the country to its knees' and that China was virtually bankrupt in 1976 when Mao died.

(g) The Cultural Revolution (1966–9)

This was Mao's attempt to keep the revolution and the Great Leap on a pure Marxist–Leninist course, and to hit back at what he considered to be an over-bureaucratic party leadership under his deputy, Liu Shauqi. In the early 1960s, when the success of the Great Leap was by no means certain, opposition to Mao grew. Right-wing members of the Party believed that incentives (piecework, greater wage differentials and larger private plots, which had been creeping in in some areas) were necessary if the communes were to function efficiently. They also felt that there should be an expert managerial class to push forward with industrialization on the Russian model, instead of relying on the cadres. Even Deng Xiaoping, one of Mao's most loyal supporters, had grave doubts about the wisdom of the Great Leap. But to the Maoists, these ideas were totally unacceptable; it was exactly what Mao was condemning among the Russians, whom he dismissed as 'revisionists' taking the 'capitalist road'. The Party must avoid the emergence of a privileged class who would exploit the workers; it was vital to keep in touch with the masses.

Between 1963 and 1966 there was a great public debate between the rightists (including Liu Shaoqi and Deng Xiaoping) and the Maoists about which course to follow. Mao, using his position as Chairman of the Party to rouse the young people, launched a desperate campaign to 'save' the revolution. In this Great Proletarian Cultural Revolution, as he called it, Mao appealed to the masses. His supporters, the Red Guards (mostly students), toured the country arguing Mao's case, and carrying their Little Red Books containing the thoughts of Chairman Mao. In some areas schools, and later factories, were closed down, as young people were urged to move into the countryside and work on farms. If questioned, they were required to say that they would like to spend their whole lives on the farm, whether it was true or not. It was an incredible propaganda exercise in which Mao was trying to renew revolutionary fervour.

Unfortunately it brought chaos and something close to civil war. Once the student masses had been roused, they denounced and physically attacked anybody in authority, not just critics of Mao. Teachers, professionals, local party officials, all were targets; millions of people were disgraced and ruined. By 1967 the extremists among the Red Guards were almost out of control, and Mao had to call in the army, commanded by Lin Biao, to restore order. Mao, privately admitting that he had made mistakes, in public blamed his advisers and the Red Guard leaders. Many were arrested and executed for 'committing excesses'. At the party conference in April 1969 the Cultural Revolution was formally ended, and Mao was declared free of all blame for what had happened. Later, Mao blamed Defence Minister Lin Biao (his chosen successor), who had always been one of his most reliable supporters, for the over-enthusiasm of the Red Guards. Some sources claim that Mao decided to make Lin Biao the scapegoat because he was trying to manoeuvre Mao into retiring. He was accused of plotting to assassinate Mao (which was highly unlikely), and was killed in an air crash in 1971 while trying to escape to the USSR, or so the official reports claimed.

The Cultural Revolution caused great disruption, ruined millions of lives and probably held up China's economic development by ten years. And yet in spite of that, there was probably some economic recovery in the last few years before Mao's death. Certainly China had made great strides since 1949. Nevertheless, Jonathan Fenby's recent verdict on Mao was damning:

> In general, China had been laid low by his experiments. Poverty was institutionalized. Much of the country was still in a pre-industrial stage. Productivity had slumped. Urban wages were half what they had been under the Nationalist Republic. It took six months' pay to buy a sewing machine. In Guangdong 90 per cent of would-be army recruits were rejected on grounds of size or health. … Productive people were demoralized. Trade was tiny. If there was equality in the People's Republic, it was the equality of poverty.

The most surprising development in Mao's policies during his last years was in foreign affairs when Mao and Zhou En-lai decided it was time to improve relations with the USA (see Section 8.6 (a) and (c)).

20.2 LIFE AFTER MAO

(a) A power struggle followed the death of Mao in 1976

There were three main contestants to succeed Mao: Hua Guofeng, named by Mao himself as his successor; Deng Xiaoping, who had been sacked from his position as general secretary of the Party during the Cultural Revolution for allegedly being too liberal; and a group known as the Gang of Four, led by Jiang Qing, Mao's widow, who were extremely militant Mao supporters, more Maoist than Mao himself. Jiang Qing did her best to muscle in and sideline Hua. But she was extremely unpopular with most sections of Chinese society, and it was said that she suffered from an 'empress syndrome'. When the Gang attempted to stage a coup, this gave Hua an excuse to have them arrested. Meanwhile Deng Xiaoping kept very much in the background, and Hua seemed set to become Supreme Leader.

Hua was keen to press ahead with industrialization and he introduced an ambitious ten-year plan which included an increase in oil production. But things soon went wrong: a large oil rig collapsed with the loss of scores of lives; expensive imported technology and insufficient exports resulted in the biggest trade gap since the mid-1950s; and inflation cancelled out wage increases. Hua Guofeng was blamed for the failures and Deng seized the chance to get rid of him. In 1980 the Politburo decided that Hua 'lacks the political and organizational ability to be the Chairman of the Party'. Hua was forced to resign, leaving the 73-year-old Deng as undisputed leader (June 1981).

In the words of Robert Service: 'Deng was as hard as teak. He endured as many demotions as promotions at Mao's hand since the 1950s. His son was crippled from the waist down after leaping from a window to escape physical maltreatment in the Cultural Revolution. Deng was forthright about the need for change … and he knew he had no time to waste if he wanted to make the changes he wanted.' As a gesture of open criticism of Mao and his policies, the Gang of Four were put on trial for 'evil, monstrous and unpardonable crimes' committed during the Cultural Revolution. They were all found guilty and sentenced to life imprisonment. The Central Committee of the Party (CCP) issued a 'Resolution' condemning the Cultural Revolution as a grave 'Left' error for which Mao himself was chiefly responsible. However, Mao was praised for his successful efforts to 'smash the counter-revolutionary Lin Biao clique'. As historian Steve Smith explained: 'By pinning the blame on one man in this fashion, the Resolution sought to exculpate the "overwhelming majority" of CCP leaders who were said to have been on the right side in the struggle. The Resolution thus underwrote a shift of authority within the CCP from a single leader to a collective leadership.'

(b) There was a period of dramatic policy changes

This new phase began in June 1978 as Deng Xiaoping gained the ascendancy. Deng somehow succeeded in persuading the Politburo that changes were vital, after all the upheavals and crises caused by the Great Leap Forward and then the Cultural Revolution.

1   Many changes introduced during the Cultural Revolution were reversed: the revolutionary committees set up to run local government were abolished and replaced by more democratically elected groups. Property confiscated from former capitalists was returned to survivors, and there was more religious freedom and greater freedom for intellectuals to express themselves in literature and the arts.

2   In economic matters Deng and his protégé Hu Yaobang wanted technical and financial help from the West in order to modernize industry, agriculture, science and technology. Loans were accepted from foreign governments and banks, and contracts signed with foreign companies for the supply of modern equipment. In 1980 China joined the International Monetary Fund (IMF) and the World Bank. On the home front, permission was given for the setting up of private industrial companies. State farms were given more control over planning, financing and profits; bonuses, piece-rates and profit-sharing schemes were encouraged; the state paid higher prices to the communes for their produce and reduced taxes in order to stimulate efficiency and output. These measures had some success – grain output reached a record level in 1979, and many peasants became prosperous.

As so often happens, this reform programme led to demands for more radical reform.

(c) Demands for more radical reform: the Democracy Wall

In November 1978 there was a poster campaign in Beijing and other cities, often in support of Deng Xiaoping. Soon there were massive demonstrations demanding more drastic changes, and early in 1978 the government felt obliged to ban marches and poster campaigns. However, there still remained what was called the 'Democracy Wall' in Beijing, where the public could express itself with huge wall posters (*Dazibao*); During 1979 the posters displayed there became progressively more daring, attacking Chairman Mao and demanding a wide range of human rights:

- the right to criticize the government openly;
- representation for non-communist parties in the National People's Congress;
- freedom to change jobs and to travel abroad;
- abolition of the communes.

This infuriated Deng, who had approved the Democracy Wall in the first place only because most of the posters were criticizing the Gang of Four. Now he launched a fierce attack on the leading dissidents, accusing them of trying to destroy the socialist system. Several were arrested and given prison sentences of up to 15 years. In November 1979 the Democracy Wall was abolished altogether. Law and order and party discipline were restored. 'Without the party', Deng remarked, 'China will retrogress into divisions and confusions.'

(d) Modernization and its problems

Following the first flush of reforming zeal and the embarrassment of the Democracy Wall, the pace slowed considerably. But Deng, together with his two protégés, Hu Yaobang (party general secretary) and Zhao Ziyang (prime minister), was determined to press ahead with modernization as soon as possible.

Zhao Ziyang had won a reputation as a brilliant administrator in Sichuan province where he was responsible for an 80 per cent increase in industrial production in 1979. He also began experiments, later extended to the whole country, to break up the communes so as to give peasants control of individual plots. The land, although still officially owned by the state, was divided up and allocated to individual peasant households, which would be allowed to keep most of the profits. This was successful in raising agricultural production, and the standard of living for many people improved. In December 1984 Zhao announced that compulsory state purchase of crops was to be abandoned; the state would continue to buy staple products, but in much smaller quantities than before. Prices of surplus grain, pork, cotton and vegetables would be allowed to fluctuate on the open market.

By this time, however, modernization, and what Deng called the move to 'market socialism', were having some unfortunate side effects. Although exports increased by 10 per cent during 1984, imports increased by 38 per cent, leaving a record trade deficit of $1100 million, and causing a sharp fall in China's foreign exchange reserves. The government tried with some success to control imports by placing heavy duties on all imported goods except vital raw materials and microchip equipment (80 per cent on cars and 70 per cent on colour televisions and video players). Another unwelcome development was that the annual rate of inflation began to rise, reaching 22 per cent in 1986.

(e) The thoughts of Deng Xiaoping

Apparently not unduly worried by these trends, the 82-year-old Deng explained his ideas for the future in a magazine article of November 1986. His main aim was to enable his people to get richer. By the year 2000, if all went well, the average annual income per head should have risen from the equivalent of £280 to somewhere near £700, and China's production should have doubled. 'To get rich is not a crime', he added. He was happy with the way agricultural reform was going, but emphasized that in industry, sweeping decentralization was still needed. The Party must withdraw from administrative tasks, issue fewer instructions and allow more initiative at the lower levels. Only capitalist investment could create the conditions in which China could become a prosperous, modernized state. His other main theme was China's international role: to lead a peace alliance of the rest of the world against the dangerous ambitions of the USA and the USSR. Nothing, he said, could possibly alter the course he had set for his country.

20.3 TIANANMEN SQUARE, 1989 AND THE CRISIS OF COMMUNISM

(a) The crisis of 1987

In spite of his radical words, Deng always had to keep an eye on the traditional, conservative or Maoist members of the Politburo, who were still powerful and might be able to get rid of him if his economic reforms failed or if party control seemed to be slipping. Deng was doing a clever balancing act between the reformers like Zhao Ziyang and Hu Yaobang on the one hand, and the hardliners like Li Peng on the other. Deng's tactics were to encourage criticism from students and intellectuals, but only up to a point: enough to enable him to drop some of the oldest and most inefficient party bureaucrats. If the criticism looked like getting out of hand, it had to be stopped (as had happened in 1979) for fear of antagonizing the hardliners.

In December 1986 there was a series of student demonstrations supporting Deng Xiaoping and the 'Four Modernizations' (agriculture, industry, science and defence), but urging a much quicker pace and, ominously, more democracy. After the students ignored a new ban on wall posters and a new rule requiring five days' notice for demonstrations, Deng decided that this challenge to party control and discipline had gone far enough, and the demonstrators were dispersed. However, it had been enough to alarm the hardliners, who forced the resignation of the reformer Hu Yaobang as party general secretary. He was accused of being too liberal in his political outlook, encouraging intellectuals to demand greater democracy and even some sort of opposition party. Although this was a serious blow to Deng, it was not a complete disaster since his place was taken by Zhao Ziyang, another economic reformer, but one who had so far kept clear of controversial political ideas; however, Li Peng, a hardline supporter of order and authority, took Zhao's place as prime minister, and he demanded a clampdown on all further protests.

Zhao soon announced that the government had no intention of abandoning its economic reform programme, and promised new measures to speed up financial reform, and at the same time, a clampdown on 'bourgeois intellectuals' who threatened party control. This highlighted the dilemma facing Deng and Zhao: was it possible to offer people a choice in buying and selling and yet deny them any choice in other areas such as policies and political parties? Many western observers thought it was impossible to have one without the other (and so did Gorbachev in the USSR), and by the end of January 1987 there were signs that they could be right. On the other hand, if the economic reforms proved successful, Deng and Zhao could turn out to be right.

(b) Tiananmen Square, 1989

Unfortunately for Deng and Zhao, the economic reforms ran into problems during 1988 and 1989. Inflation went up to 30 per cent, and wages, especially of state employees (such as civil servants, party officials, police and soldiers), lagged well behind prices. Probably encouraged by Gorbachev's political reforms, and the knowledge that he was to pay a visit to Beijing in mid-May 1989, student demonstrations began again in Tiananmen Square on 17 April; they were demanding political reform, democracy and an end to Communist Party corruption. On 4 May, Zhao Ziyang said that the students' 'just demands would be met', and allowed the press to report the demands; but this outraged Deng. The demonstrations continued throughout Gorbachev's visit (15–18 May, to mark the formal reconciliation between China and the USSR) and into June, with sometimes as many as 250 000 people occupying the square and surrounding streets. The scene was vividly described by John Simpson (in *Despatches from the Barricades*, Hutchinson, 1990), the Foreign Affairs editor of the BBC, who was there for much of the time:

> There was a new spirit of courage and daring. ... There was a sense of liberation, that just to be in the Square was a statement in itself. People smiled and shook my hand ... everyone, it seemed, listened to the BBC's Chinese language service. The gentleness, the smiles and the headbands were irresistibly reminiscent of the big rock concerts and the anti-Vietnam demonstrations in the 1960s. There was the same certainty that because the protesters were young and peaceful the government must capitulate. ... Food was delivered on a regular basis. Ordinary people responded with generosity to requests for bottled water. ... Hundreds of thousands of people had decided to join in on the side which seemed certain to win. The major avenues of Peking were blocked with bicycles, cars, lorries, buses and flatbed trucks all heading for the Square, filled with people cheering, singing, playing musical instruments, waving flags, enjoying themselves. The racket of it all could be heard streets away. ... Victory seemed a foregone conclusion; how could any government resist a popular uprising of this magnitude?

It certainly began to look very much as though the government had lost control and might soon give way to the demands. Behind the scenes, however, a power struggle was going on in the Politburo between Zhao Ziyang and the hardline Li Peng, the prime minister. Li Peng, with the support of Deng Xiaoping, eventually won. On 20 May Deng declared martial law, and sent Li Peng to negotiate with the protesters. When negotiations failed, thousands of troops were brought in, and on 3–4 June the army, using paratroopers, tanks and infantry, attacked the students, killing between 1500 and 3000 of them (see Illus. 20.1). Tiananmen Square was under government control again, and demonstrations in other large cities were also dispersed, though with less bloodshed. The protest leaders were sentenced to long terms in labour camps. Zhao Ziyang was removed from his position as party chief and replaced by Jiang Zemin, a more 'middle of the road' politician. The hardliners were triumphant and Prime Minister Li Peng became the leading figure, when the 85-year-old Deng stepped down as premier in November 1989.

There was worldwide condemnation of the massacres, but Deng and the hardliners were convinced that they had taken the right decision. They felt that to have given way to the students' demands for democracy would have caused too much disruption and confusion; one-party control was needed to supervise the transition to a 'socialist market economy'. Later, events in the USSR seemed to prove them right: when Mikhail Gorbachev tried to introduce economic and political reforms both at the same time, he failed; the Communist Party lost control, the economic reforms were a disaster, and the USSR broke up into 15 separate states (see Section 18.3). Whatever the rest of the world thought about the Tiananmen Square massacres, the Chinese leadership could congratulate itself on avoiding Gorbachev's mistakes and preserving communism in China at a time when it was being swept away in eastern Europe.

Illustration 20.1 **Tanks advance in Tiananmen Square, Beijing, June 1989; the man was pulled away by bystanders**

20.4 THE CHANGING FACE OF COMMUNISM IN CHINA

China's leaders were deeply disturbed by the collapse of communism in eastern Europe. Although they had clamped down on any political changes, Deng Xiaoping, Li Peng and Jiang Zemin were still committed to progressive 'open door' economic policies. Deng often warned that disaster awaited countries where reform proceeded too slowly. He hoped that a successful economy which enabled more and more people to become prosperous would make people forget their desire for 'democracy'. During the 1990s the economy was booming; from 1991 to 1996 China led the world, with average GDP increases of 11.4 per cent, and living standards were rising fast. Eastern and southern China were especially prosperous: cities were growing rapidly, there was significant foreign investment and there were plenty of consumer goods for sale. On the other hand, some of the remote western provinces were not sharing in the prosperity.

A new Five Year Plan, unveiled in March 1996, aimed to keep the economic boom on course by increasing grain production, keeping average GDP growth at 8 per cent, and spreading wealth more evenly among the regions. Although Deng Xiaoping died in 1997, Jiang Zemin, who became the next president, could be relied on to continue his policies in spite of criticism from the party hardliners. Public unrest had all but disappeared, partly because of China's economic success, and partly because of the government's ruthless treatment of dissidents. Jiang was determined to launch an assault on corruption within the Party; this was mainly to please the hardliners, who blamed the widespread corruption on Deng's capitalist reforms; it would also help to silence the dissidents who had made corruption one of their favourite targets. In 2000 there was a series of trials of high-ranking officials, several of whom were found guilty of fraud and accepting bribes; some were executed and others received long prison sentences. The government even organized an exhibition in Beijing to show how well it was dealing with corruption.

Jiang's next step (May 2000) was to announce what he called *the Three Represents*, an attempt to define what the CCP stood for, and also to emphasize that no matter how much the economic system might change, there would be no dramatic political changes, and certainly no moves towards democracy, so long as he was in control. He pointed out that the CCP represented three main concerns – to look after:

- China's development and modernization;
- China's culture and heritage;
- the interests of the vast majority of the Chinese people.

To help make good the claim that the Party genuinely represented all the people, Jiang announced (July 2001) that it was now open to capitalists. The hardliners, who still clung to the idea that communist parties were there for the good of the working class, criticized this move. However, Jiang thought it was reasonable since the capitalists had been responsible for most of China's recent economic success, and he pressed ahead regardless. Many of the capitalists were delighted to join, since party membership gave them access to political influence. Restrictions were relaxed on trade unions: workers were now allowed to protest to employers about problems of safety, poor working conditions and long working hours. More good news came with the announcement that Beijing was to host the 2008 Summer Olympics.

(a) Leadership changes

Jiang Zemin, general secretary of the Party and president of China, together with several others among the older leaders, were due to step down from their posts at the Sixteenth Congress of the CCP, to be held in November 2002, the first to take place since 1997. In his final speech as general secretary, the 76-year-old Jiang voiced his determination that the CCP must remain in absolute power, and that this would involve broadening the power base of the Party so that all classes would be represented. 'Leadership by the Party', he said, 'is the fundamental guarantee that the people are the masters of the country and that the country is ruled by law.' With that, Jiang retired as general secretary, though he was to remain president until the National People's Congress met in March 2003. Hu Jintao was elected CCP general secretary in place of Jiang.

The National People's Congress saw the completion of the sweeping leadership changes. Hu Jintao was chosen as the new president and he appointed Wen Jiabao as prime minister or premier. Wen had a reputation as a progressive, and was considered lucky to have survived the purges after the Tiananmen Square massacres in 1989. It was not long before the new leadership announced some important changes, both economic and political.

- Parts of some of China's largest state-owned enterprises were to be sold off to foreign or private companies; some smaller companies were allowed to become private. However, the government emphasized that it was committed to retaining control of many large industries (November 2003).
- In December 2003, six independent candidates were allowed to stand in local elections in Beijing for the district legislature. They were standing against over 4000 official CCP candidates, so that even if all six were elected, their impact would be minimal. However, it was an interesting departure from the usual practice.

Meanwhile China's economic success continued, despite an outbreak of the deadly SARS (severe acute respiratory syndrome) virus during the early summer of 2003, which infected over 5000 people and killed around 350. Statistics showed that during 2003 the economy had expanded by over 8 per cent, its fastest rate for six years; this was thought to be largely the result of a shift towards consumer spending. The government claimed that it had created over 6 million jobs during the year. Many of the new factories were foreign-owned – multinational firms could hardly wait to set up business in China in order to exploit the cheap labour. By 2010 China had become the world's largest manufacturer and exporter. It was the largest maker of steel and the biggest user of energy. In the words of Jonathan Fenby:

> The last major state on earth to be ruled by a Communist party plays a pivotal role in the global supply chain, assembling goods for foreign firms at prices they could not achieve at home. It has the largest monetary reserves of any country, topping $2.3 trillion. Its cheap labour, cheap capital, productivity and sheer competitiveness have exported price deflation to the rest of the globe, while its voracious appetite for raw materials laps up oil from Africa, the Middle East and Latin America, iron ore from Brazil, coal and more ore from Australia, timber from Russia, and key metals from wherever they are mined. … Growth and modernization have transformed society and demographics. Average annual per capita income has soared from 528 yuan in the early 1980s to 18,100 in urban areas and 5900 in the countryside. (The 2010 exchange rates were £1 = 10 yuan, $1 = 6.4 yuan, 1 euro = 8.7 yuan.)

Nevertheless, there were many areas of concern.

- Prosperity was not evenly spread: incomes and living standards were improving steadily for the two-fifths of the total population of 1.3 billion who lived in towns and cities; but millions of rural Chinese, especially in the west of China, were still struggling on or below the poverty line. According to UN statistics, more than 200 million Chinese were still living in 'relative poverty', while over 20 million were living in 'absolute poverty'. It was estimated that around 300 million people had no access to clean drinking water. At the other end of the scale, almost one million people were reported to be millionaires (in terms of dollars or sterling).
- The economy was expanding so fast that it was in danger of moving into over-production, which could lead to a reduction in sales and a slump. For example, in 2009 excess capacity stood at 28 per cent in steel production and at 33 per cent in aluminium. It seems likely that within a few years car companies will have 20 per cent too much plant.
- China's success caused strained relations with the USA, where manufacturers were feeling the competition from cheaper Chinese goods. Washington blamed the Chinese for the loss of millions of US jobs, complaining, with some justification, that the yuan was being deliberately undervalued in order to give Chinese exports an unfair advantage.
- Chinese banks were suffering from problems of overlending and bad debts. They had been guilty of overspending on a huge range of building projects in the main cities, new roads and railways, and what was deemed to be the world's largest engineering project – the Three Gorges Dam. Many of the state-run companies which received the loans have failed to repay. In 2004 the Chinese government was forced to bail out two of the largest state-owned banks – the Bank of China and China Construction Bank – to the tune of £24.6 billion.
- In spite of all the economic progress, the government continued to oppose any demands for political change. Anybody who complained publicly or staged a

protest demonstration would be ruthlessly suppressed. In fact China had signed an agreement accepting UN advice on how to improve its justice and police systems, and promising to improve its human rights record (November 2000). However, in February 2001, Amnesty International complained that China was actually increasing its use of torture in the questioning of political dissidents, Tibetan nationalists and members of Falun Gong (a semi-religious organization which practised meditation, and which had been banned in 1999 on the grounds that it was a threat to public order). Dissidents were making more use of the internet, setting up websites and communicating with each other by email; the government therefore began a determined clampdown on 'internet subversion', persuading Google and others not to include politically sensitive material in their coverage of China.

- As the decade progressed, discontent grew, especially among peasants in the countryside. They had done well from the break-up of the communes and had made good profits from selling much of their harvests. But now they were being taxed heavily and were also being exploited by local governments which illegally seized their land and sold it to offset their debts. In 2004 there were no fewer than 74 000 'mass incidents' or public protests against a wide variety of malpractice – lack of democracy, high taxes, high prices, corruption in high places and safety scandals. The government stepped up its repressive policies and by 2012 it was estimated that between 5 and 6 million dissidents were being held in labour camps. Many of them had been tortured.

Wen Jiabao was the only leading politician to show any sympathy with these dissenters. He publicly called for political and legal reform, and the need to respect people's rights – including the ownership rights of farmers. But Hu Jintao had developed a consensus style of government in which, although different power groups exist, they restrain each other, so that only mutually beneficial policies are followed, and no real reforming progress can be made. Some commentators even think that Wen's performance, as Jonathan Fenby puts it, 'is all part of an orchestrated campaign to dangle the possibility of reform that will never be delivered'. Meanwhile the economy continued to perform well. In 2008–9, when the rest of the world was suffering from the global financial crisis (see Section 27.7), China seemed to emerge relatively unscathed. As the global economy continued in crisis, it was reported in 2011 that President Sarkozy of France, emerging from a summit meeting discussing how to save the eurozone, immediately telephoned Beijing to ask for help. The cry went up around Europe and the Americas: 'Will China save the world?'

(b)   What of the future?

Hu Jintao and Wen Jiabao were due to reach the end of their term in office in 2012. Determined to go out on a high, in 2011 they introduced another Five Year Plan, to be completed in 2015. This aimed to increase spending on research and development (R&D) so that China could move away from low-cost manufacturing and into more advanced industrial production. For example, work was in progress to produce a 220-seat airliner, to be flying by 2016, and a preliminary agreement had been signed with Ryanair, the low-cost airline. In 2012 China had 13 nuclear power stations, and was planning to have at least 120 by 2020. A Chinese astronaut had already walked in space, and there were plans to land a man on the moon by 2020.

All this raises many questions. Will China overtake the USA as the world's greatest power? If the Chinese 'economic miracle' continues, will this plunge Europe and the USA into mass unemployment and ruin? And does it also mean that the Chinese political system is more efficient than western-style democracy? There has been no shortage of people willing to answer that question. The American political scientist Francis Fukuyama argues that China's one-party system enables decisive action to be taken, avoiding 'the delays of a messy democratic process'. The financier George Soros believes that China has 'not only a more vigorous economy, but actually a better-functioning government than the United States'.

On the other hand, some western and Chinese observers take the opposite view. Critics argue that with the falling birth rate, demand will inevitably decline, leaving China with a large over-capacity problem; money has been wasted on vast infrastructure projects that will never bring any return, and there is an enormous problem of non-performing loans. Perhaps the most serious weakness is the steadily increasing social tensions. Ai Weiwei, the well-known Chinese artist, compared the country to 'a runner sprinting very fast – but he has a heart condition'. But when he voiced his concerns publicly, he was arrested for 'economic crimes' in 2011. Others critics point to the increasing disparity between rich and poor, and between countryside and city, the poor quality and the rising expense of health care, and the vast amount of corruption. In 2011 there were a staggering 180 000 'collective protest incidents'. Roderick MacFarquhar, writing in 2011, argued that it was as though China were sitting on some massive geological fault which must one day split wide open, plunging the whole country into ruin. By the autumn of 2012 there were ominous signs as exports began to fall and large stockpiles of coal, steel and cars were reported, and many firms producing cheap clothing for export collapsed. One sales manager lamented: 'I feel like a blossoming summer has turned into a dull winter. In 2008 we didn't feel the crisis at all. This year we do feel that the crisis has really struck.'

As China moved towards October 2012, preparations were under way for the handover of power after Hu and Wen stand down. The likely candidates seemed to be Xi Jinping, the party secretary in Shanghai, and Li Keqiang, a close associate of Hu. But behind the scenes there were competing factions, each with ambitions. For example, Bo Xilai of Chongqing seemed to have leadership ambitions. He became party secretary in Chongqing in 2007 and was responsible for what became known as the Chongqing experiment. According to Professor Wang Hui of Tsinghua University in Beijing:

> The Chongqing model operated within China's existing political institutions and development structures which emphasise attracting business and investment, but involved quite distinctive social reforms. Large-scale industrial and infrastructural development went hand in hand with an ideology of greater equality – officials were instructed to 'eat the same, live the same, work the same' as the people – and an aggressive campaign against organized crime. Open debate and political participation were encouraged, and policies adjusted accordingly. No other large-scale political and economic programme has been carried out so openly since the reform era began in 1978 soon after Mao's death.

During 2011 the movement spread to Beijing, and it seemed that Bo and his policies had won the support of Xi Jinping. Unfortunately for Bo, this all coincided with decisions by Hu and Wen to put political reform on hold and to tighten up bureaucracy and control from the centre. The idea of different local models ran counter to this trend. Bo had also made the mistake of suggesting that the Chongqing model compared in importance with Mao's Cultural Revolution. This gave Wen the chance to announce that the Chongqing reforms would lead to a repeat of the chaos caused by the Cultural Revolution. Therefore it must be condemned and placed on the list of subjects not available for public discussion. In March 2012 Bo was sacked as Chongqing party secretary on the grounds of corruption. In reality the government's aim was to clamp down on political freedom so that it would be easier to continue pressing ahead with their unpopular neo-liberal policies. At the same time it got rid of a dangerous leadership rival. In fact Jonathan Fenby, in his reply to Professor Wang Hui (in the *London Review of Books*, 24 May 2012), is convinced that this was the real reason why Bo was removed. 'He had simply become too big for his boots ahead of the selection of a new Politburo Standing Committee at the Communist Party Congress later this year. When word spread that he sought the internal security portfolio on the Standing Committee, his downfall was guaranteed.' His ruin seemed complete when, in September 2012, he was expelled from the Communist Party.

In November 2012, at the party congress in the Great Hall of the People in Beijing, Hu Jintao formally handed power over to the next leader, Xi Jinping. China had certainly changed in the ten years since Hu came to power. In 2002 it was the world's sixth largest economy, now it is the second. For the first time it has become an urban nation, with just over half of its 1.4 billion people living in cities. However, Premier Xi Jinping and his prime minister, Li Keqiang, face serious problems. The economy is unhealthy, and many experts are advising that China's state-owned enterprises should be privatized. But there is little sign of any such radical changes on the agenda. There is considerable social unrest, caused by the widening gap between rich and poor, the widespread corruption within the communist party, and the revelations that many of the party leaders and their families have amassed huge personal fortunes. According to Bo Zhiyue, a research fellow at the National University of Singapore, 'corruption within the Chinese Communist Party is so rampant ... if they don't do anything about this they will lose credibility very quickly. ... Eventually the credibility deficit will become so huge that it could mean the collapse of the CCP as the ruling party' (*Guardian*, 9 November 2012).

FURTHER READING

Chang-tai Hung, *Mao's New World* (Cornell University Press, 2010).

Dikotter, F., *Mao's Great Famine: The History of China's Most Devastating Catastrophe* (Bloomsbury, 2010).

Fenby, J., *The Penguin History of Modern China* (Penguin, 2009).

Fenby, J., *Tiger Head, Snake Tails: China Today, How it Got There and Where it is Heading* (Simon & Schuster, 2012).

Fewsmith, J., *China after Tiananmen* (Cambridge University Press, 2008).

Friedberg, A., *A Contest for Supremacy: China, America and the Struggle for Mastery in Asia* (Norton, 2011).

Garnaut, J., *The Rise and Fall of the House of Bo* (Penguin, 2012).

Gittings, J., *The Changing Face of China* (Oxford University Press, 2005).

Karl, R. E., *Mao Zedong and China in the Twentieth Century* (Duke University Press, 2010).

MacFarquhar, R., *The Politics of China* (Cambridge University Press, 2011).

Mitter, R., *A Bitter Revolution: China's Struggle with the Modern World* (Oxford University Press, 2004).

Service, R. *Comrades – A World History of Communism* (Macmillan, 2007).

Smith, S. A., 'China: Coming to Terms with the Past', *History Today* (December 2003).

Vogel, E. F., *Deng Xiaoping and the Transformation of China* (Harvard University Press, 2011).

Wang Hui, 'The Rumour Machine: On the dismissal of Bo Xilai', *London Review of Books* (10 May 2012).

QUESTIONS

1   'A total and unmitigated disaster.' How far would you agree with this comment on the policies of Mao Zedong and the Chinese Communist Party during the period 1949–60?
2   'The Cultural Revolution of 1966–9 was an attempt by Mao Zedong to protect his own power and position rather than a genuine battle of ideas.' To what extent do you think this is a fair verdict on Mao's Cultural Revolution?
3   'Neither in his economic nor in his political outlook could Deng Xiaoping be considered to be a liberal.' How far would you agree with this view?
4   Assess the reasons why the policies of Deng Xiaoping led to a period of crisis in 1987–9. How successfully did Deng deal with the crisis?

There is a document question about Mao Zedong's Cultural Revolution on the website.

Chapter 21

Communism in Korea and south-east Asia

SUMMARY OF EVENTS

In Korea and some of the countries of south-east Asia, foreign occupation, among other factors, had led to the development of communist parties, which were usually in the forefront of resistance and which played a vital role in the campaign for independence.

- **Korea** was under Japanese rule for most of the first half of the twentieth century and regained its independence when Japan was defeated at the end of the Second World War. However, it was divided into two separate states – the North was communist, the South non-communist. After the war of 1950–3, the two states remained strictly separate; North Korea, one of the most secretive and little-known states in the world, has remained communist until the present day.
- The area known as **Indo-China** was under French control, and consisted of three countries: **Vietnam**, **Cambodia** and **Laos**. At the end of the Second World War, instead of gaining their independence, as they had expected in view of France's defeat, they found that the French intended to behave as though nothing had happened and to reimpose their colonial rule. Vietnam and Laos, unlike Cambodia, were not content to sit back and wait for the French to withdraw. They fought a long campaign, in which the communist parties of both countries played a prominent part. In 1954 the French admitted defeat, and all three states became completely independent.

Tragically, this did not bring a more peaceful era.

- **Communist North Vietnam** became involved in a long conflict with **South Vietnam** (1961–75), which became part of the Cold War. There was massive American involvement in support of South Vietnam. Thanks to Chinese help, North Vietnam was victorious, but both states were devastated by the war. In 1975 the two Vietnams were united under communist rule, a situation which has lasted until the present day.
- **Cambodia** succeeded in remaining relatively peaceful until 1970, under the semi-autocratic rule of Prince Sihanouk. Eventually the country found itself dragged into the Vietnam War. It suffered five years of catastrophic heavy bombing by the USA, followed by four years of rule by the bloodthirsty communist Pol Pot and his Khmer Rouge regime. By the time he was overthrown in 1979, thanks to the intervention of Vietnamese communist forces, Cambodia had probably suffered as much devastation as Vietnam. For the next ten years a more moderate communist government with Vietnamese backing ran Cambodia, after which the country returned to something like democratic rule, with Prince Sihanouk again playing a leading role.

- **Laos** also had a turbulent history. Soon after independence, civil war broke out between right and left, until it too suffered the same fate as Cambodia – it was drawn into the Vietnam War in spite of its desire to remain neutral, and had to endure indiscriminate US bombing. At the end of 1975 the communist Pathet Lao organization took power, and is still in control of the country today.

21.1 NORTH KOREA

(a) The communist regime established

Korea had been under Japanese occupation and rule since 1905, following the Japanese victory in the Russo-Japanese War of 1904–5. There was a strong Korean nationalist movement, and at a conference held in Cairo in 1943, the USA, the UK and China promised that when the war was over, a united, independent Korea would be created. As defeat loomed for Japan early in 1945, it seemed that at last a free Korea was a distinct possibility.

Unfortunately for the Koreans, things did not work out as they had hoped: three weeks before the Japanese surrendered, the USSR declared war on Japan (8 August 1945). This brought a new element into the equation; the Russians had for many years wanted to gain influence in Korea, and their entry into the war meant that they too would have a say in Korea's future. Russian troops in Manchuria were closest to Korea, and were able to move into the north of the country even before the Japanese officially surrendered on 2 September. Soviet forces worked closely with Korean communists and nationalists, and the Japanese occupying armies were quickly disarmed. The Korean People's Republic was proclaimed, and *the communist leader, Kim Il-sung, soon emerged as the dominant political figure.* Supported by Soviet troops, Kim, who had been trained in the USSR, began to introduce his own version of Marxism–Leninism into the new state.

Meanwhile, the Americans, who were worried that the entire Korean peninsula was about to be taken over by the Russians, hastily sent troops to occupy the south. It was the Americans who proposed that the division between north and south should be along the 38th parallel. *In the south, Dr Syngman Rhee emerged as the leading politician.* He was strongly nationalist and anti-communist, and was determined to bring about a united Korea free of communism. In response, Stalin poured massive Russian aid into the north, transforming it into a powerful military state well able to defend itself against any attack from the south. In 1948 Stalin withdrew Soviet troops, and the Democratic People's Republic of Korea was proclaimed, with Kim Il-sung as premier. North Korea therefore had an independent communist government before the communist victory in China. The following year, after Mao Zedong became Chinese leader, the independent North Korea was given official diplomatic recognition by China, the USSR and the communist states of eastern Europe.

(b) One state or two?

The dominating question in the immediate post-war period was: *what had become of the Allied promise of a united Korea?* Ideally, the Americans wanted a united, anti-communist and pro-Western Korea, while the Russians, and after 1949 the Chinese, wanted a unified Korea which was communist. However, neither the USA nor the USSR wanted to become closely involved; given the entrenched positions of both Kim and Rhee, the dilemma seemed insoluble. It was therefore agreed that the problem be handed over to the United Nations, which undertook to organize elections for the whole country as a first step towards unifying the peninsula.

Kim refused to hold elections in North Korea, because the population of the north was much smaller than that of the south, so that the communists would be in a minority in the country as a whole. However, elections were held in the south; the new National Assembly chose Rhee as first president of the Republic of Korea. North Korea responded by holding its own elections, which resulted in Kim's victory. Both leaders claimed to speak for the whole country. In June 1949 the Americans thankfully withdrew their troops from South Korea, where Rhee was becoming an embarrassment because of his corrupt and authoritarian rule, which was almost as extreme as Kim's in the north. But *the withdrawal of all foreign troops left a potentially unstable and dangerous situation.*

Only a year later, on 25 June 1950, after a number of border clashes, North Korean forces invaded South Korea. Rhee's armies quickly began to fall apart, and the communists seemed poised to unite the country under their government in Pyongyang. The immediate reasons why Kim launched the attack are still a matter for debate among historians (see Section 8.1). What is certain is that by the time a peace agreement was signed in 1953, at least 4 million Koreans had lost their lives, and the peninsula was destined to remain divided for the foreseeable future into two heavily armed and mutually suspicious states.

(c) North Korea after the war

Thanks to Chinese help, Kim and his regime had survived. Once the war was over he concentrated on eliminating all remaining domestic opposition – first the non-communist groups, and then all rivals for the leadership within the Korean Communist Party. Having made himself into an absolute ruler, he remained in power, apparently unassailable, for the next 40 years, until his death in 1994. Although he was a communist, he had his own ideas about exactly what that meant, and he did not merely imitate the USSR and China.

- He began a programme of industrialization, and the collectivization of agriculture, aiming for self-sufficiency in all areas of the economy, so that North Korea would not be dependent on help from either of its great communist allies. Ironically, however, he accepted considerable aid from both of them, which enabled the economy to expand rapidly during the first ten years after the war. Living standards improved and the future under Kim's regime looked promising.
- Great emphasis was placed on building up the country's military strength after the disappointing performance in the second half of the war. The army and air force were increased in size and new military airfields were built. Kim never abandoned the dream of bringing the south under his control.
- The whole of society was strictly regimented in pursuit of self-sufficiency; the state controlled everything – the economic plans, the labour force, the resources, the military and the media. Kim's propaganda system was geared towards building up his personality cult as the great infallible leader of his people. The government's total control of the media and communications with the outside world meant that North Korea was probably the most isolated, secretive and closed state in the world.
- In the mid-1960s the principle of self-sufficiency was officially defined as consisting of four themes: 'autonomy in ideology, independence in politics, self-sufficiency in economy, and self-reliance in defence'.
- Kim continued his anti-south campaign, attempting to destabilize the government of the south in a variety of ways, the most outrageous of which was an attempt, which failed, by North Korean commandos to murder the South Korean president (1968). With the development of détente in the early 1970s, and the improving relations between East and West, the North called off its campaign and began talks with the south. In July 1972 it was announced that both sides had agreed to work peacefully

for unification. However, the North's policy was erratic: sometimes Kim suspended all discussions; in 1980 he proposed a federal state in which both North and South would have equal representation; in 1983 several leading South Koreans were killed in a bomb explosion; in 1987 a South Korean airliner was destroyed by a time bomb. Then in 1991, high-level talks were held which led to the announcement of a joint renunciation of violence and nuclear weapons. However, it seemed as though no genuine progress could be made while Kim was still in charge.

- During the second half of the 1960s North Korea's economy ran into difficulties for a number of reasons. The rift between the USSR and China, which gradually widened from 1956 onwards, placed Kim in a difficult position. Which side should he support? At first he stayed pro-Soviet, then he switched his allegiance to China, and finally tried to be independent of both. When he moved away from Moscow at the end of the 1950s the USSR sharply reduced its aid; in 1966 at the beginning of Mao's Cultural Revolution, the Chinese cut off their aid. After that, none of Kim's development plans reached their targets. Another serious weakness was the excessive expenditure on heavy industry and armaments. Consumer goods and luxuries were considered to be of secondary importance. There was a rapid population increase, which put a strain on agriculture and the food industries generally. Living standards fell; life for most people was hard and conditions basic. During the 1980s the economy recovered but in the early 1990s, as aid from Russia disappeared, there were more difficulties.

(d)   Life under Kim Jong-il

In 1980 Kim Il-sung ('Great Leader') made it clear that he intended his son Kim Jong-il (soon to be known as 'Dear Leader'), who had been acting as Party Secretary, to be his successor. The younger Kim gradually took over more of the day-to-day work of government, until his father died of a heart attack in 1994 at the age of 82. By this time North Korea was facing crisis. The economy had deteriorated further during the previous ten years, the population had increased threefold since 1954 and the country was on the verge of famine. Yet enormous amounts of cash had been spent developing nuclear weapons and long-range missiles. With the collapse of the USSR, North Korea had lost one of the few states which might be expected to show some sympathy with its plight.

Kim Jong-il, who was more open-minded and progressive than his father, was forced into drastic action. *He accepted that North Korea needed to move away from its isolationism* and aimed to improve relations with the south and with the USA. In 1994 he agreed to shut down North Korea's plutonium-producing nuclear-reactor plants in return for the provision of alternative sources of energy – two light-water nuclear reactors for the generation of electricity – by an international consortium known as KEDO (Korean Peninsula Energy Development Organization), involving the USA, South Korea and Japan. The Clinton administration was sympathetic, agreeing to ease US economic sanctions against North Korea; in return, Kim suspended his long-range missile tests (1999). In June 2000 President Kim Dae-jung of South Korea visited Pyongyang and soon afterwards a number of North Korean political prisoners who had been held in the south for many years were released. Even more startling, in October, American secretary of state Madeleine Albright paid a visit to Pyongyang and had positive talks with Kim. North Korea reopened diplomatic relations with Italy and Australia. In 2001 Kim, who had gained a reputation as something of a recluse, paid state visits to China and Russia, where he met President Putin, and promised that his missile testing would remain in suspension at least until 2003.

Meanwhile the situation inside North Korea continued to deteriorate. In April 2001 it was reported that following the severe winter, there were serious food shortages, with most people surviving on 200 grams of rice a day. In response, Germany immediately promised to send 30 000 tonnes of beef. In May the deputy foreign minister presented a horrifying report to a UNICEF conference about conditions in his country. Between 1993 and 2000, mortality rates for children under 5 had risen from 27 to 48 per thousand; per capita Gross National Product had fallen from $991 per year to $457; the percentage of children being vaccinated against diseases such as polio and measles fell from 90 to 50 per cent; and the percentage of the population with access to safe water fell from 86 to 53. In 2001 North Korea received almost $300 million-worth of food aid from the European Union, the USA, Japan and even from South Korea.

In July 2002 a programme of limited economic reform was introduced: the currency was devalued and food prices were allowed to rise in the hope that this would encourage an increase in agricultural production. Food rationing was to be phased out and a family-unit farming system was introduced for the first time since collectivization. At the end of 2003 reports indicated that living conditions inside North Korea were showing signs of improvement. However, by the summer of 2005 there were soldiers in the paddy fields to make sure that every grain of rice was handed over to the state procurement agency. There was even a ban on private selling of produce from kitchen gardens. At the same time there was disturbing information about the existence of large numbers of labour camps in the north of the country containing thousands of political prisoners, and where torture and execution were common – a situation reminiscent of Stalin's gulag system in the USSR.

(e) North Korea, USA and the nuclear confrontation

On top of all the economic problems, *relations with the USA took a sudden turn for the worse when George W. Bush came to power there in January 2001*. The new president seemed reluctant to continue the sympathetic approach begun by the Clinton regime. After the 11 September atrocities he issued threats against what he called 'the axis of evil', by which he meant Iraq, Iran and North Korea. *The confrontation with the USA developed over the question of whether or not North Korea possessed nuclear weapons.* The Americans suspected that they did, but the North Koreans claimed that their nuclear-reactor plants were to provide electricity. The behaviour of both sides, especially North Korea, was inconsistent, and the dispute was still ongoing in 2012. The problem arose from the lack of progress with the KEDO project agreed in 1994. Work was not even started on the promised light-water reactors; the Americans accused Kim of not completing the promised shutdown of his existing nuclear plants, while the North Koreans protested that work on the new light-water reactors must start before they shut down their own reactors. In August 2002 work actually began on the first of the light-water reactors. The Americans then demanded that Korea allow inspectors from the International Atomic Energy Agency (IAEA) to inspect its existing nuclear facilities, but the Koreans refused and blamed the USA for the delay in building the reactors. The Americans imposed technology sanctions on the North Koreans and accused them of supplying ballistic missile parts to Yemen.

After a meeting with the Japanese prime minister, Yurichiro Koizimi, Kim conceded that he would allow the inspectors in. However, when this failed to produce a positive response from the USA, it was announced that North Korea would restart its nuclear power plant at Yongbyon, which had been closed since 1994. The USA then declared the KEDO project to be null and void, although Japan and South Korea were prepared to go ahead with it. The Americans, who were also threatening war against Iraq, continued their hardline stance, claiming that the USA was capable of winning two large-scale wars in different areas at the same time (December 2002). The North Koreans responded by announcing their withdrawal from the Nuclear Non-Proliferation Treaty (NPT) signed in 1970, though they insisted that they had no plans to make nuclear weapons. What they really wanted, their ambassador told the UN, was a non-aggression pact with the USA. This the Americans refused, claiming that the Koreans already had at least two nuclear bombs. At about the same time the UN World Food Programme reported that there were serious shortages of basic foods and medicines in North Korea, and appealed for contributions of grain.

January 2003 brought a sudden change in US policy: President Bush, probably under pressure from Japan and South Korea, who were anxious to see the crisis resolved, offered to resume food and fuel aid to North Korea if it dismantled its nuclear weapons programme. The Koreans insisted that they had no nuclear weapons and had no intention of making any, and said they were ready to allow the USA to send its own inspectors to verify the claims. However, in April 2003 a spokesman for the North Korean foreign ministry claimed that they already had nuclear weapons and would shortly have enough plutonium for eight more nuclear warheads. This gave rise to widespread international speculation and discussion over whether or not the North Koreans really did have nuclear weapons; the majority view seemed to be that they did not, and that their tactics were designed to force the USA to make concessions, such as economic aid and a non-aggression agreement. Another theory was that, given the recent American and British attack on Iraq, Kim wanted to make Bush think twice before he took on North Korea as well.

Although some members of Bush's administration made hostile remarks about Kim Jong-il, the president himself was anxious to calm things, especially as American forces were becoming embroiled in an increasingly difficult situation in Iraq. In August 2003 the Americans softened their approach in talks with the North Koreans: instead of demanding that the nuclear programme be scrapped completely before US aid would be resumed, they now signified that a step-by-step approach to dismantling nuclear facilities would be acceptable and would be matched by 'corresponding steps' from the American side. Later Bush announced that the USA would continue to finance the KEDO project and was prepared to offer North Korea assurances of security in exchange for a verifiable scrapping of its nuclear weapons programme. North Korea replied that it was ready to consider Bush's proposals (October 2003). Then in February 2005 the government announced that it now had nuclear weapons, and in October 2006 it claimed to have successfully exploded a nuclear device underground, without any radiation leak.

In 2009 relations between North and South Korea became strained after the north carried out more nuclear tests, and even more so in 2010 when it was revealed that North Korea had opened a new uranium enriching plant. There were several clashes between the two naval forces, and then in March 2010 a South Korean corvette, the *Cheonan,* was sunk by a torpedo fired from a North Korean submarine, with the loss of 46 lives. In November 2010 the South Korean island of Yeonpyeong was bombarded by North Korean shells and rockets. There was considerable damage to both military and civilian property, and four people were killed. The North Koreans claimed that the south had fired first, and in fact the incident took place during the annual joint South Korean–US military and naval exercise in and around the Yellow Sea, off the west coast of South Korea. The North Korean government regards this as part of the preparations for an eventual invasion of their territory, and every year tensions rose in case the exercise turned out to be the real thing.

In December 2011 Kim Jong-il, the Dear Leader, died of a heart attack and his third son, Kim Jong-un, was named as the next Supreme Leader. It seemed likely that he would continue with broadly the same policies as his father. His administration got off to a disappointing start when, in April 2012, a rocket that was meant to send an observational satellite into orbit broke up and crashed into the Yellow Sea shortly after lift-off.

21.2 VIETNAM

(a) The struggle for independence

Vietnam, together with Laos and Cambodia, was part of the French Empire in south-east Asia, known as the Indochinese Union, which was established in 1887. In many ways the French were good colonial administrators; they built roads and railways, schools and hospitals, and even a university in Hanoi, in the north of Vietnam. But there was very little industrialization; most of the people were poor peasants for whom life was a struggle. During the 1930s, protest movements began to emerge, but these were unceremoniously suppressed by the French authorities. The French attitude encouraged nationalist and revolutionary feelings and brought *a rush of support for the new Vietnamese Communist Party, formed by Ho Chi Minh in 1929.* Ho Chi Minh had spent time in France, China and the USSR; he had always been a committed nationalist, but after his travels abroad, he became a committed communist as well. *His dream was a united Vietnam under communist rule.* During the 1930s, however, there seemed little hope of breaking free from French control.

The French defeat in Europe in June 1940 raised hopes of Vietnamese independence, but these were soon dashed when Japanese forces moved into Indochina. When the nationalists and communists launched a full-scale uprising in the south of Vietnam, the French (now under orders from the Vichy government and therefore technically on the same side as Germany and Japan) and Japanese worked together and the rising was brutally crushed. With the communist movement almost wiped out in the South, Ho Chi Minh moved to the north and organized the communist and nationalist resistance movement, the League for the Independence of Vietnam, known as 'Vietminh'.

The Vietminh were forced to bide their time until the tide turned against the Japanese. In the summer of 1945, with the Japanese defeat imminent (they surrendered on 14 August), Ho Chi Minh prepared to seize the initiative before the French returned. Vietminh forces and supporters took over Hanoi, Saigon and most of the large towns, and in September 1945 the Democratic Republic of Vietnam was proclaimed with Ho Chi Minh as president. Unfortunately the declaration proved to be premature. It had been agreed among the Allies that when the war ended, the southern half of Vietnam should come under British and French administration. When British forces moved in, it was decided that French control should be restored as soon as possible.

Unbelievably, the British used Japanese troops who were still in Vietnam after their government had surrendered, and who had still not been disarmed, to suppress the Vietminh in the south. The British were anxious not to deprive their ally of its colonies, since this might encourage a general trend towards decolonization, in which Britain might also lose its empire. By the end of the year, order had been restored and some 50 000 French troops had arrived to take control. At this time, before the Cold War developed, the Americans were appalled at what had happened, since they had promised to liberate the people of Indo-China. As J. A. S. Grenville points out (in *The Collins History of the World in the Twentieth Century*), this was

> one of the most extraordinary episodes of the post-war period. If the south had been permitted to follow the north and the independence of the whole of Indo-China had been accepted by the British, the trauma of the longest war in Asia, which led to at least 2.5 million deaths and untold misery, might have been avoided.

At first the French seemed prepared to compromise. They controlled the south but recognized the independence of the Vietnamese Republic in the north, provided it remained within the French Union. However, during the summer of 1946 it became increasingly clear that the French had no intention of allowing the north genuine independence. Ho Chi Minh therefore demanded complete independence for the whole of Vietnam. The French rejected this, and hostilities began when they shelled the northern port of Haiphong, killing thousands of Vietnamese civilians. After eight years of bitter struggle, the French were finally defeated at Dien Bien Phu (1954); the Geneva Agreements recognized the independence of Ho Chi Minh's North Vietnam, but for the time being the area south of the 17th parallel of latitude was to be controlled by an international commission of Canadians, Poles and Indians. The commission was to organize elections for the whole country in July 1956, after which Vietnam would be united.

(b)   The two Vietnams

All the indications were that the Vietminh would win the national elections, but once again their hopes were dashed. The elections never took place: *with the Cold War in full swing, the Americans were determined to prevent Vietnam becoming united under a government with strong communist connections.* They backed Ngo Dinh Diem, a nationalist and anti-communist, for the leadership of the south. In 1955 he proclaimed the Vietnam Republic, with himself as president of a strongly anti-communist regime; elections had disappeared from the agenda.

By this time, both Vietnams were in a sorry state, devastated by almost a decade of fighting. Ho Chi Minh's government in Hanoi received aid from the USSR and China and began to introduce socialist policies of industrialization and the collectivization of agriculture. President Ngo Dinh Diem's government in Saigon became increasingly unpopular, causing more people to join the communists or Vietcong, who were enthusiastically backed by the North. (For subsequent developments and the Vietnam War of 1961–75 see Section 8.3.)

(c)   The Socialist Republic of Vietnam isolated

The government of the new Socialist Republic of Vietnam, officially proclaimed in July 1976, with its capital at Hanoi, faced daunting problems. The country had hardly known peace for over 30 years. Large parts of the north had been devastated by American bombings, and throughout the country millions of people were homeless. Their inspirational leader, Ho Chi Minh, had died in 1969. Clearly, recovery would be a struggle.

- The government began to extend its centralized command-economy policies to the south, abolishing capitalism and collectivizing farm land. But this aroused serious opposition, especially in the great business and commercial centre of Saigon (which was renamed Ho Chi Minh City). Many people refused to co-operate and did their utmost to sabotage the new socialist measures. The cadres, whose job was to go out into the countryside to organize collectivization, were often unwilling and incompetent. This, together with the corruption which was rife among party officials, turned the whole process into a disaster.
- There were serious divisions among the top party leaders over how long pure Marxist–Leninist policies should be continued. Some wanted to follow China's example and experiment with elements of capitalism; but the hardliners condemned these ideas as sacrilegious.
- In the late 1970s the country suffered from major floods and drought, which, together with collectivization problems and the rapid increase in population, caused

serious food shortages. Hundreds of thousands of people fled the country, some on foot to Thailand and Malaya, and others by sea (the 'boat people').

- Vietnamese foreign policy was expensive and brought the county into conflict with its neighbours. The regime aimed to form alliances with the new left-wing governments in Laos and Cambodia (Kampuchea). When Pol Pot's Khmer Rouge government in Cambodia refused the offer of a close relationship and persisted with provocative border raids, Vietnam invaded and occupied most of the country (December 1978). The Khmer Rouge were driven out and replaced by a pro-Vietnamese government. However, the Khmer Rouge were not finished: they began a guerrilla war against the new regime, and the Vietnamese were forced to send some 200 000 troops to maintain their ally in power. To make matters worse, Pol Pot was a protégé of the Chinese, who were furious at Vietnam's intervention. In February 1979 they launched an invasion of northern Vietnam; they inflicted considerable damage in the frontier area, although they did not escape unscathed as the Vietnamese mounted a spirited defence. The Chinese withdrew after three weeks, claiming to have taught the Vietnamese a sharp lesson. After that, the Chinese supported the Khmer Rouge guerrillas, and the USA, Japan and most of the states of Western Europe imposed a trade embargo on Vietnam. It was a bizarre situation in which the USA and its allies continued to support Pol Pot, one of the most grotesque and brutal dictators the world had ever seen.

By the mid-1980s Vietnam was almost completely isolated; its neighbours in the Association of South-East Asian Nations (ASEAN) were all hostile and supported the resistance movement in Cambodia, and even the USSR, which had consistently backed Vietnam against China, was drastically reducing its aid.

(d)   Vietnam changes course

In 1986 Vietnam was in serious crisis. Internationally isolated, the regime had a vast permanent army of around one million, which was cripplingly expensive to maintain; it had still not succeeded in introducing a viable socialist economy in the south. With the deaths of the older party leaders, younger members were able to convince the party of the need for drastic policy changes, and in particular the need to extricate themselves from Cambodia. At the Third National Congress of the Communist Party (December 1986), a leading economic reformer, Nguyen Van Linh, was appointed as general secretary. He introduced a new doctrine known as *Doi Moi*, which meant *renewing the economy, as the Chinese had already begun to do, by moving towards the free market*, in an attempt to raise living standards to the level enjoyed by Vietnam's neighbours.

Agreement was at last reached over Cambodia: Vietnamese troops were withdrawn in September 1989 and the task of finding a permanent settlement was handed over to the UN (see next section). This was a great relief for the regime, since it freed vast sums of revenue which could now be invested in the economy. Even so, economic progress was slow, and it was several years before the population felt much benefit. One of the problems was the rapidly growing population, which reached almost 80 million at the end of the century (in 1950 it had been around 17 million).

Signs of progress were more obvious during the early years of the new century. In July 2000 the country's first stock exchange was opened in Ho Chi Minh City, and important steps were taken towards reconciliation with the USA. A trade agreement was signed allowing American goods to be imported into Vietnam in exchange for lower duties on Vietnamese goods entering the USA; in November, President Clinton paid a visit to Vietnam as part of a publicity drive to encourage closer business and cultural ties.

In 2001 the Communist Party appointed a new general secretary, Nong Duc Manh. This was the country's most powerful leadership post. Nong had a reputation as a reformer and modernizer; one of his first announcements was that he was aiming for Vietnam to become an industrialized power by 2020. A new target of a 7.5 per cent annual growth rate was announced for the next five years. Equality was to be given to the private sector of the economy; according to a government directive, 'all economic sectors are important components of the socialist-oriented market economy'. In an attempt to reduce corruption, all party and government officials were required to declare publicly their assets and interests. Work began on a new hydro-electric scheme in the north, which would both provide power and help to control flooding. Another encouraging development was the expansion of tourism – it was revealed that over two million people had visited the country in 2000. In December 2002 it was announced that the economy had almost reached its target, growing by 7 per cent during the year. Industrial production had risen by 14 per cent, which was mainly due to a sharp increase in the manufacture of motor-cycles and cars. In October 2003, the UN World Food Programme welcomed Vietnam's first ever contribution – a consignment of rice for Iraq. *Vietnam was now an international donor of aid instead of having to be a recipient.*

At the same time, Vietnam was becoming less isolated. In 2001, as well as closer relations with the USA, links were formed with Russia, China and the ASEAN countries. President Putin of Russia paid a visit and agreement was reached about economic co-operation and sales of Russian arms. There were visits from the Chinese leaders Hu Jintao and Li Peng, and Vietnam hosted several meetings of the Association of South-East Asian Nations.

Although Vietnam seemed to have successfully reformed its command economy, following the Chinese model, very little change took place in the political system. Vietnam remained a one-party state, with the Communist Party dominating and controlling everything. For example, in the elections held in May 2002, 498 MPs were elected from 759 candidates; 51 of those elected were not members of the Communist Party and two were described as 'independents'. However, all the candidates had to be vetted and approved by the Party; no other political parties were allowed, and although the newly elected National Assembly might be more critical of ministers than previously, there was no possibility of the communists being defeated.

In 2002 and 2003 there were disturbing reports of human rights abuses, especially persecution of religious groups, including Buddhists and Christians. A Protestant evangelical Christian group known as the Montagnards were the main target. Their members complained of beatings, torture and detention on charges of 'reactionary behaviour'. Churches were burnt down and at least one Christian was beaten to death. Several hundred fled into Cambodia, where they lived in refugee camps. The Vietnamese government demanded that they should be sent back to Vietnam. By the end of 2003, Vietnam's foreign relations were beginning to suffer: the USA and the European Union made official protests about the persecution and the USA offered asylum to the Montagnards. However, the Vietnamese government rejected the protests and claimed that the reports were 'totally false and slanderous'. Nong was chosen for a second five-year term in 2006.

21.3 CAMBODIA/KAMPUCHEA

(a) Prince Sihanouk

Before the Second World War, Cambodia was a French protectorate with its own king, Monivong (reigned 1927–41), although the French allowed him very little power. Monivong was succeeded by his 18-year-old grandson Norodom Sihanouk, but from 1941 until 1945 Cambodia was under Japanese occupation. In March 1945, as the Japanese defeat became inevitable, *Sihanouk proclaimed Cambodia an independent state*; however, French troops soon returned, and he had to accept a reversion to the position that had existed before the war. Sihanouk was a shrewd politician; he believed that French rule would not survive long and was prepared to bide his time rather than use force. While the struggle for independence raged in neighbouring Vietnam, *Cambodia was relatively peaceful*. He placed himself at the head of the nationalist movement, avoided involvement in any political party, and soon won respect and popularity with a wide cross-section of Cambodian society.

In 1954, after the French defeat in Vietnam, the Geneva Conference recognized the independence of Cambodia, and Sihanouk's government as the rightful authority. Although he was immensely popular with ordinary people as the architect of peace and independence, many of the intelligentsia resented his growing authoritarianism. *The opposition included pro-democracy groups and the Communist Party, formed in 1951, which eventually became known as the Communist Party of Kampuchea.* Sihanouk founded his own political party, 'the People's Socialist Community', and in March 1955 he took the remarkable step of abdicating in favour of his father, Norodom Suramarit, so that he himself could play a full part in politics, as plain Mr Sihanouk (though he continued to be popularly known as Prince Sihanouk).

His new party won a total landslide victory in the subsequent elections, taking every seat in the National Assembly. Prince Sihanouk took the title of prime minister, and when his father died in 1960, he became head of state, but did not take the title of king. Given his continuing popularity, the opposition parties, especially the communists (now calling themselves *the Khmer Rouge*), made very little headway, and Sihanouk remained in power for the next 15 years. His rule succeeded in being authoritarian and benign at the same time, and *the country enjoyed a period of peace and reasonable prosperity* while, for much of this time, Vietnam was torn by civil war.

Unfortunately, Sihanouk's foreign policy antagonized the USA. He distrusted US motives and suspected that Thailand and South Vietnam – both American allies – had designs on Cambodia. He tried to remain neutral in international affairs; he avoided accepting American aid and was encouraged in this attitude by President de Gaulle of France, whom he admired. As the war in Vietnam escalated, Sihanouk realized that the Vietnamese communists were likely to win in the end; he agreed to allow the Vietnamese communists to use bases in Cambodia, as well as the Ho Chi Minh trail through Cambodian territory, which the Vietminh used for moving troops and supplies from the communist north to the south. Since he was powerless to prevent this anyway, it seemed the most sensible policy. However, the Americans started to bomb Cambodian villages near the border with Vietnam, and consequently in May 1965 Sihanouk broke off relations with the USA. At the same time he began to move towards a closer relationship with China.

(b) Prince Sihanouk overthrown: Cambodia at war (1970–5)

In the late 1960s Sihanouk's popularity waned. Right-wingers resented his anti-American stance and his collaboration with the Vietnamese communists, while the left and the communists opposed his authoritarian methods. The communists, under the leadership of *Saloth Sar (who later called himself Pol Pot)*, a teacher in Phnom Penh, the capital, before he left to organize the Party, were becoming stronger. In 1967 they provoked an uprising among peasants in the north of the country, which frightened Sihanouk into thinking that a communist revolution was imminent. He overreacted, using troops to quell the uprising; villages were burned, and suspected troublemakers were murdered or imprisoned without trial. He further discredited himself with the left by reopening diplomatic relations with the USA. Clashes between Cambodian communist guerrillas (the Khmer Rouge) and Sihanouk's army increased, becoming almost daily events.

Worse still, the new American president, Richard Nixon, and his security adviser Henry Kissinger began large-scale bombings of Vietnamese bases in Cambodia. As the communists moved deeper inside the country, the bombers followed and Cambodian civilian casualties mounted. By 1970 the leading anti-communists decided that drastic action was needed. In March 1970, while Sihanouk was visiting Moscow, General Lon Nol and his supporters, backed by the Americans, staged a coup. Sihanouk was overthrown; he took refuge in Beijing, and Lon Nol became head of the government.

Lon Nol's period in power (1970–5) was a disaster for Cambodia. He had rashly promised to drive Vietcong forces out of the country, but this drew Cambodia into the thick of the Vietnam War. Almost immediately American and South Vietnamese troops invaded eastern Cambodia, while over the next three years, heavy US bombing pounded the countryside, destroying hundreds of villages. However, the Americans failed to destroy either the Vietcong or Pol Pot's Khmer Rouge, both of which continued to harass American forces. Even Sihanouk's supporters joined the struggle against the invaders.

In January 1973, peace came to Vietnam, but the Americans continued a massive aerial bombardment of Cambodia, in a final attempt to prevent the Khmer Rouge from coming to power. During March, April and May 1973, the tonnage of bombs dropped on Cambodia was more than double that of the whole of the previous year. Yet the USA and Cambodia were not at war, and no American troops were being threatened by Cambodians. Cambodia's infrastructure, such as it was, and its traditional economy, were all but destroyed. After the Americans called off the bombings, the civil war continued for a further two years, as the Khmer Rouge gradually closed in on Lon Nol's government in Phnom Penh. In April 1975, Lon Nol's regime collapsed, the Khmer Rouge entered the capital, and *Pol Pot became the ruler of Cambodia.*

(c) Cambodia under the Khmer Rouge

The new government called the country 'Democratic Kampuchea', a completely inappropriate term, in view of what happened over the next four years. Prince Sihanouk, who had worked with the Khmer Rouge during the previous five years, returned home from Beijing, expecting to be well received by Pol Pot. Instead he was placed under house arrest and forced to watch helplessly as Pol Pot exercised total power. The Khmer Rouge caused even more misery for the unfortunate people of Cambodia by trying to introduce doctrinaire Marxist/Leninist principles almost overnight without adequate preparation. In the words of Michael Leifer:

> Under the leadership of the fearsome Pol Pot, a gruesome social experiment was inaugurated. Cambodia was transformed into a primitive agricultural work camp combining the worst excesses of Stalin and Mao in which around a million people died from execution, starvation and disease.

The communists ordered the population of Phnom Penh and other cities to move out, live in the countryside and wear peasant working clothes. Within a short time, the urban centres were virtually empty, and thousands of people were dying in what amounted to forced marches. The aim was to collectivize the entire country immediately, in order to double the rice harvest. Even Mao had taken years to get to this stage in China. But the party cadres whose job it was to organize the transformation were inexperienced and incompetent and most city dwellers were helpless in rural settings. The whole operation was a disaster and conditions became unbearable. At the same time, money, private property, shops and markets were abolished, and schools, hospitals and monasteries closed. Pol Pot's next move was to launch a campaign of genocide against all educated Cambodians and against anybody he thought might be capable of leading opposition. The result – an entire generation of educated people was either killed or driven into exile. In his controversial 2005 biography of Pol Pot, Philip Short argues that these atrocities were not the product of either a sociopathic dictator or his Marxist ideology, but of Cambodian popular culture which had a long history of violent extremism. During Pol's own schooldays in the 1950s, naughty children were severely beaten and their wounds exposed to red ants. Previous royalist and republican governments had regularly tortured, raped and murdered on a huge scale. In the words of Tim Stanley in his review of the biography:

> Short is correct that there is something so uniquely insane about the Khmer genocide that national character is the only way of understanding its eccentric development. Neighbouring Vietnam and Laos experienced war and terror at the same time but never attempted such a radical social solution.

As his paranoia increased, hundreds of Pol Pot's more moderate supporters began to turn against him. Many were executed and many more fled to Thailand and Vietnam. These included *Hun Sen*, a former Khmer Rouge military commander, who organized an anti-Pol Pot army of Cambodian exiles in Vietnam. Some estimates put the total of those who died in the notorious 'killing fields' as high as 2 million; just over a third of the total population of 7.5 million disappeared. The tragedy was, as J. A. S. Grenville puts it, that 'if the Americans had not turned against Sihanouk, one of the cleverest and wiliest of south-east Asian leaders, Cambodia might have been spared the almost unbelievable horrors that followed'.

Eventually Pol Pot contributed to his own downfall: he tried to cover up the failings of his economic policies by adopting a brash nationalistic foreign policy. This caused unnecessary tensions with Vietnam, whose government was anxious for a close relationship with its communist neighbour. After a number of border incidents and provocations by the Khmer Rouge, the Vietnamese army invaded Cambodia and drove out the Pol Pot regime (January 1979). They installed a puppet government in Phnom Penh, in which *Hun Sen was a leading figure*. Most of the country was occupied by Vietnamese troops until 1989. Meanwhile, Pol Pot and a large army of Khmer Rouge guerrillas retreated into the mountains of the south-west and continued to cause trouble. *The new regime was a great improvement on Pol Pot's murderous government, but it was not recognized by the USA and most other countries*. According to Anthony Parsons (see Further Reading for Chapter 9), the UK permanent representative at the UN,

> instead of receiving a public vote of thanks from the UN for ridding Cambodia of a latter-day combination of Hitler and Stalin, and saving the lives of countless Cambodians, the Vietnamese found themselves on the receiving end of draft resolutions in January and March 1979 calling for a cease-fire and the withdrawal of 'foreign forces'.

However, the USSR supported Vietnam and vetoed the resolutions, so no further action was taken. The reason for the UN's anti-Vietnam stance was that the USA and the non-communist states of south-east Asia were more afraid of a powerful Vietnam than they were of the Khmer Rouge. For the sake of their own interests they would have preferred to see Pol Pot's regime continue in power.

(d)   After Pol Pot: the return of Prince Sihanouk

The new government in Phnom Penh consisted mainly of moderate communists who had deserted Pol Pot. Uncertainty about what might happen under the new regime caused perhaps half a million Cambodians, including former communists and members of the intelligentsia, to leave the country and take refuge in Thailand. As it turned out, although it was kept in power by Vietnamese troops, *the government could claim considerable success over the next ten years.* The extreme Khmer Rouge policies were abandoned, people were allowed to return to the towns and cities, schools and hospitals reopened, and Buddhists were allowed to practise their religion. Later, money and private property were restored, the economy settled down and trade started up again.

The government's main problem was opposition from resistance groups operating from over the border in Thailand. There were three main groups: the Khmer Rouge, who were still a formidable force of some 35 000; Prince Sihanouk and his armed supporters, numbering about 18 000; and the non-communist National Liberation Front led by Son Sann, who could muster around 8000 troops. In 1982 the three groups formed a joint government-in-exile with Sihanouk as president and Son Sann as prime minister. The UN officially recognized them as the rightful government, but they received very little support from ordinary Cambodians, who seemed happy with the existing regime in Phnom Penh. Hun Sen became prime minister in 1985, and the opposition made no headway.

The situation changed towards the end of the 1980s as it became clear that Vietnam could no longer afford to keep a large military force in Cambodia. For a time there was the frightful possibility that the Khmer Rouge might seize power again when the Vietnamese withdrew. But the other two opposition groups, as well as Hun Sen, were determined not to let this happen. They all agreed to take part in talks organized by the UN. The ending of the Cold War made it easier to reach a settlement, and *agreement was reached in October 1991.*

- There was to be a transitional government known as the Supreme National Council, consisting of representatives of all four factions, including the Khmer Rouge.
- UN troops and administrators were to help prepare the country for democratic elections in 1993.

The Supreme National Council elected Prince Sihanouk as president, and a large UN team of 16 000 troops and 6000 civilians arrived to demobilize the rival armies and make arrangements for the elections. Progress was far from easy, mainly because the Khmer Rouge, which saw its chances of regaining power slipping away, refused to co-operate or take part in the elections.

Nevertheless the elections went ahead in June 1993; the royalist party led by Prince Ranariddh, Sihanouk's son, emerged as the largest group, with Hun Sen's Cambodian People's Party (CCP) second. Hun Sen, who had difficulty forgetting his undemocratic past, refused to give up power. The UN found a clever solution by setting up a coalition government with Ranariddh as first prime minister and Hun Sen as second prime minister. *One of the first acts of the new National Assembly was to vote to restore the monarchy, and Prince Sihanouk became king and head of state once again.*

From this point onwards the political history of Cambodia consisted largely of a bizarre feud between the royalists and the supporters of Hun Sen. In July 1997, Hun Sen, with the elections of July 1998 in mind, removed Ranariddh in a violent coup; the prince was tried and found guilty, in absentia, of attempting to overthrow the government. He had apparently been trying to enlist help from what was left of the Khmer Rouge. However, he was pardoned by his father, the king, and was able to take part in the 1998 elections. This time,

Hun Sen's CPP emerged as the largest single party, but lacking an overall majority, they once again joined together in an uneasy coalition with the royalists.

As for the Khmer Rouge, their support gradually dwindled; in 1995 many of them had accepted the government's offer of an amnesty. *In 1997 Pol Pot was arrested by other Khmer Rouge leaders and sentenced to life imprisonment*. He died the following year. The question of how to deal with the surviving members of the Pol Pot regime caused controversy. There was a general feeling that they should be prosecuted for crimes against humanity, but there was no consensus about how this should be done. The UN, supported by King Sihanouk, wanted them tried by an international tribunal; Hun Sen wanted them dealt with by the Cambodian legal system, but the UN felt that this lacked the expertise to carry out effective prosecutions. No progress was made.

Meanwhile the country remained calm; in 2000 the economy seemed well balanced, inflation was under control and tourism was becoming increasingly important, with almost half a million foreign visitors during the year. In 2001 the World Bank provided financial aid for the government but, significantly, urged Hun Sen to make more determined efforts to eliminate corruption. In the autumn and winter of 2002–3 there were serious food shortages after extremes of drought and flooding caused the rice crop to fail.

At the same time the leading politicians were preparing for the elections due in July 2003. They were to be contested by three main parties: Hun Sen's Cambodian People's Party, Ranariddh's royalist party, and a liberal opposition group led by Sam Rangsi. The months before the election were marked by a spate of assassinations of leading members of all three parties; 31 people died, and tensions continued between Prime Minister Hun Sen and the royal family. *The result of the July election led to a constitutional crisis*: the CPP won 73 of the 123 seats in the National Assembly, the lower house of the Cambodian parliament; the royalists 26 and the Sam Rangsi party 24. This left the CPP nine seats short of the two-thirds majority needed to form a government. Foreign observers reported that the CPP had been guilty of violent intimidation and had also used 'a more subtle strategy of coercion and intimidation'. The two smaller parties refused to join a coalition with the CPP unless Hun Sen resigned, but he consistently refused.

In the months following the election, the violence and assassinations continued; the victims were either members or well-known supporters of the opposition parties. Hun Sen simply continued to run the country and was still in power in 2012. The country was in a far from healthy state. Although there had been some economic growth since 2006, Cambodia still relied on foreign aid for about half the government's budget. According to a report by the International Food Policy Research Institute, *in 2009 the country ranked alongside the poorest nations in Africa for deficiencies in nutrition.* One of the problems was that, whereas Vietnam and Thailand attract multi-million-dollar foreign investment, very few Western investors would even consider Cambodia, because of the violence and the high crime rate. Vast sums of money are still needed for healthcare, basic education and infrastructure.

21.4 LAOS

(a) Independence and civil war

Laos, the third country in former French Indo-China, was organized as a French protectorate with its capital at Vientiane. After the Japanese occupation during the Second World War, the French gave Laos a measure of self-government under King Sisavang Vong, but all important decisions were still taken in Paris. Many of the Lao leaders were satisfied with limited independence, but in 1950 the convinced nationalists formed a new movement known as the *Pathet Lao* (Land of the Lao People), to fight for full independence.

The Pathet Lao worked closely with the Vietminh in Vietnam, who were also fighting the French, and they were strong in the north of the country in the provinces adjoining North Vietnam.

The 1954 Geneva Accords, which ended French rule in Indo-China, decided that *Laos should continue to be ruled by the royal government*. However, it also allowed what it called regroupment zones in northern Laos, where the Pathet Lao forces could assemble. Presumably the intention was that they would negotiate with the royal government about their future. But the outcome was inevitable: the Pathet Lao, with its strong left-wing connections and its continuing links with communist North Vietnam, was unlikely to remain at peace for long with a right-wing royalist government. In fact a fragile peace did survive until 1959, but then fighting broke out between left and right, and continued off and on until it became part of the much larger conflict in Vietnam. *During these years Laos was divided into three groups*:

- the Pathet Lao – mainly communist, backed by North Vietnam and China;
- the right-wing anti-communists and royalists, backed by Thailand and the USA;
- a neutralist group led by *Prince Souvanna Phouma*, which tried to bring peace by creating a coalition of all three factions, each of which would be left in control of the areas that they held.

In July 1962 a fragile coalition government of all three groups was formed, and for a time it seemed that Laos might be able to remain neutral in the developing conflict in Vietnam. The USA was unhappy with this situation because it meant that the communist Pathet Lao controlled key areas of Laos which bordered on Vietnam (and through which the Ho Chi Minh trail would later pass). The Americans poured in vast amounts of financial aid for the Laotian Royal Army and *in April 1964 the neutralist coalition government was overthrown by the right, with CIA backing*. A new government of mainly right-wingers and a few neutralists was formed; the Pathet Lao were excluded, although they were still strong in their areas. Since they were well organized and well equipped, they soon began to extend their control further.

As the war in Vietnam escalated, Laos began to suffer the same fate as Cambodia. Between 1965 and 1973 more than two million tons of US bombs were dropped on Laos, more than were dropped on Germany and Japan during the Second World War. At first the attacks were mainly on provinces controlled by the Pathet Lao; as support for the Pathet Lao increased and their control extended further, so the American bombings spread over more of the country. An American community worker in Laos later reported that 'village after village was levelled; countless people were buried alive by high explosives, or burnt alive by napalm and white phosphorous, or riddled by anti-personnel bomb pellets'.

Peace returned to Laos only in 1973 with the withdrawal of the Americans from Vietnam. The three factions signed an agreement in Vientiane setting up another coalition, with Souvanna Phouma as the leader. However, the Pathet Lao gradually extended their control over more of the country. In 1975, when the North Vietnamese took over South Vietnam, and the Khmer Rouge gained control in Cambodia, the right-wing forces in Laos decided to throw in the towel and their leaders left the country. The Pathet Lao were able to take power, and in December 1975 they *declared the end of the monarchy and the beginning of the Lao People's Democratic Republic*.

(b)   The Lao People's Democratic Republic

The communist Lao People's Revolutionary Party (LPRP), which took control in 1975, stayed in power for the rest of the century and still seemed secure in 2004. For 20 years before they came to power, their leaders had worked in close co-operation with their allies in Vietnam, and it was only to be expected that the two governments would follow similar paths. In Laos the communists introduced farming collectives and brought trade, and what little industry there was, under government control. They also imprisoned several thousand political opponents in what were called re-education camps. The country and the economy were slow to recover from the ravages of the previous 15 years, and thousands of people – some estimates put the total at around 10 per cent of the population – left the country to live in Thailand.

Fortunately, the government was prepared to compromise its strict Marxist principles; in the mid-1980s, following the example of China and Vietnam, the collectivization programme was abandoned and replaced by groups of family-run farms. State control over business and industry was relaxed, market incentives were introduced and private investment was invited and encouraged. UN statistics suggested that by 1989 the economy of Laos was performing better than those of Vietnam and Cambodia in terms of Gross National Product per head. The Party still kept full political control, but after the introduction of a new constitution in 1991, people were allowed more freedom of movement. The fact that the government, like those of China and Vietnam, had abandoned its communist or socialist economic policies raised the interesting question of whether or not it still *was* a communist regime. The leaders still seemed to think of themselves and describe themselves as having communist political systems, and yet their economic restructuring had left them with very few specifically socialist attributes. They could just as well be called simply 'one-party states'.

At the end of the century Laos was still a one-party state, with a mixed economy which was performing disappointingly. In March 2001, President Khamtai Siphandon admitted that the government had so far failed to bring about the hoped-for increase in prosperity. He outlined an impressive 20-year programme of economic growth and improved education, health and living standards. Impartial analysts pointed out that the economy was precarious, foreign aid to Laos had doubled over the previous 15 years, and the International Monetary Fund had just approved a loan of $40 million to help balance the budget for the year.

None of this made any difference to the National Assembly elections held in February 2002. There were 166 candidates for the 109 seats, but all except one were members of the LPRP. The state-run media reported that there had been a 100 per cent turnout and the Party continued blithely in power. Nevertheless, *dissatisfaction with the lack of progress was beginning to cause some unrest.* In July 2003 an organization called the Lao Citizens' Movement for Democracy held demonstrations and mini-uprisings in ten provinces. In October another group, calling itself the Free Democratic People's Government of Laos (FDPGL), exploded a bomb in Vientiane and claimed responsibility for 14 other explosions since 2000. They announced that their aim was to overthrow 'the cruel and barbarian LPRP'. The pressure was on for the Party to deliver reform and prosperity without too much delay. In 2006 a new leader came to power: Choummaly Sayasone was chosen as Communist Party general secretary and president of Laos.

FURTHER READING

Buzo, A., *The Guerilla Dynasty: Politics and Leadership in North Korea* (I. B. Tauris, 1999).
Chandler, D. P., *A History of Cambodia* (Westview, 4th edition, 2007).
Dae-sook Suh, *Kim Il Sung: The North Korean Leader* (Columbia University Press, 1995).
Hayton, B., *Vietnam: Rising Dragon* (Yale University Press, 2011).

Kiernan, B., *The Pol Pot Regime: Race, Power and Genocide in Cambodia* (Yale University Press, 3rd edition, 2008).
Liefer, M., *Dictionary of the Modern Politics of South-East Asia* (Routledge, 1996).
Service, R., *Comrades: A World History of Communism* (Macmillan, 2007).
Short, P., *Pol Pot: Anatomy of a Nightmare* (John Murray, 2005).
Stanley, T., 'A Question of Identity', *History Today* (July 2011).
Stuart-Fox, M., *A History of Laos* (Cambridge University Press, 1997).

QUESTIONS

1 Explain how Korea came to be divided into two separate states during the period 1945–53.
2 'Half a century of disaster for the people of North Korea.' How far would you agree with this verdict on Kim Il-sung's period of rule in North Korea?
3 What problems faced the government of Vietnam in the years following its unification in 1976? How and with what success did the government's policies change after 1986?
4 Assess the contribution of Prince Sihanouk to the development of Cambodia in the years 1954 to 1970. Explain why he was overthrown in March 1970.
5 Trace the steps by which Cambodia/Kampuchea became a victim of the Cold War in the period 1967 to 1991.
6 Explain why and how Laos came under communist rule in the period 1954 to 1975. How successful had the government been in rebuilding Laos by the end of the twentieth century?

◤ There is a document question about Cambodia and Prince Sihanouk and their relations with the USA on the website.

Part IV

The United States of America

The USA before the Second World War

SUMMARY OF EVENTS

During the second half of the nineteenth century, the USA experienced remarkable social and economic changes.

- The Civil War (1861–5) between North and South brought the *end of slavery in the USA and freedom for the former slaves*. However, many whites, especially in the South, were reluctant to recognize black people (African Americans) as equals and did their best to deprive them of their new rights. This led to *the beginning of the Civil Rights movement*, although it had very little success until the second half of the twentieth century.
- *Large numbers of immigrants began to arrive from Europe*, and this continued into the twentieth century. Between 1860 and 1930 over 30 million people arrived in the USA from abroad.
- *There was a vast and successful industrial revolution*, mainly in the last quarter of the nineteenth century. The USA entered the twentieth century on a wave of business prosperity. By 1914 she had easily surpassed Britain and Germany, the leading industrial nations of Europe, in output of coal, iron and steel, and was clearly a rival economic force to be reckoned with.
- Although industrialists and financiers did well and made their fortunes, *prosperity was not shared equally among the American people*. Immigrants, blacks and women often had to put up with low wages and poor living and working conditions. This led to *the formation of labour unions and the Socialist Party, which tried to improve the situation for the workers*. However, big business was unsympathetic, and these organizations had very little success before the First World War (1914–18).

Although the Americans came late into the First World War (April 1917), *they played an important part in the defeat of Germany and her allies*; Democrat President *Woodrow Wilson* (1913–21) was a leading figure at the Versailles Conference, and the USA was now one of the world's great powers. However, after the war the Americans decided not to play an active role in world affairs, a policy known as *isolationism*. It was a bitter disappointment for Wilson when the Senate rejected both the Versailles settlement and the League of Nations (1920).

After Wilson came three Republican presidents: Warren Harding (1921–3), who died in office; Calvin Coolidge (1923–9) and Herbert C. Hoover (1929–33). Until 1929 the country enjoyed a period of great prosperity, though not everybody shared in it. The boom ended suddenly with *the Wall Street Crash* (October 1929), which led to the Great Depression, or world economic crisis, only six months after the unfortunate Hoover's inauguration. The effects on the USA were catastrophic: by 1933 almost 14 million people were out of work and Hoover's efforts failed to make any impression on the crisis. Nobody was surprised when the Republicans lost the presidential election of November 1932.

The new Democrat president, *Franklin D. Roosevelt*, introduced policies known as *the New Deal* to try and put the country on the road to recovery. Though it was not entirely successful, the New Deal achieved enough, together with the circumstances of the Second World War, to keep Roosevelt in the White House (the official residence of the president in Washington) until his death in April 1945. He was the only president to be elected for a fourth term.

22.1 THE AMERICAN SYSTEM OF GOVERNMENT

The American Constitution (the set of rules by which the country is governed) was first drawn up in 1787. Since then, 26 extra points (Amendments) have been added; the last one, which lowered the voting age to 18, was added in 1971.

The USA has a federal system of government

This is a system in which a country is divided up into a number of states. There were originally 13 states in the USA; by 1900 the number had grown to 45 as the frontier was extended westwards. Later, five more states were formed and added to the union (see Map 22.1); these were Oklahoma (1907), Arizona and New Mexico (1912), and Alaska and Hawaii (1959). Each of these states has its own state capital and government and they share power with the federal (central or national) government in the federal capital, Washington. Figure 22.1 shows how the power is shared out.

The federal government consists of three main parts:

Congress: known as the legislative part, which makes the laws;
President: known as the executive part; he carries out the laws;
Judiciary: the legal system, of which the most important part is *the Supreme Court*.

(a) Congress

1 *The federal parliament, known as Congress, meets in Washington and consists of two houses*:

- the House of Representatives
- the Senate

Members of both houses are elected by universal suffrage. The House of Representatives (usually referred to simply as 'the House') contains 435 members, elected for two years, who represent districts of roughly equal population. Senators are elected for six years, one third retiring every two years; there are two from each state, irrespective of the population of the state, making a total of 100.

2 *The main job of Congress is to legislate (make the laws)*. All new laws have to be passed by a simple majority in both houses; treaties with foreign countries need a two-thirds vote in the Senate. If there is a disagreement between the two houses, a joint conference is held, which usually succeeds in producing a compromise proposal, which is then voted on by both houses. Congress can make laws about taxation, currency, postage, foreign trade and the army and navy. It also has the

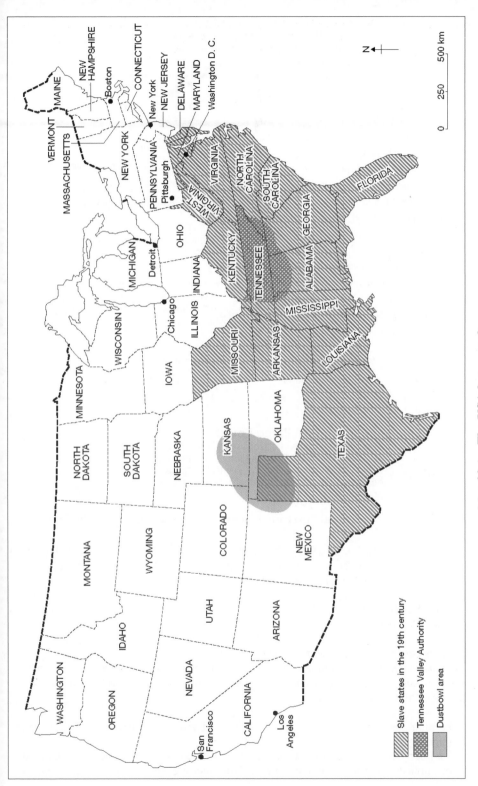

Map 22.1 **The USA between the wars**

Source: D. Heater, *Our World This Century* (Oxford, 1992), p. 97

Slave states in the 19th century

Tennessee Valley Authority

Dustbowl area

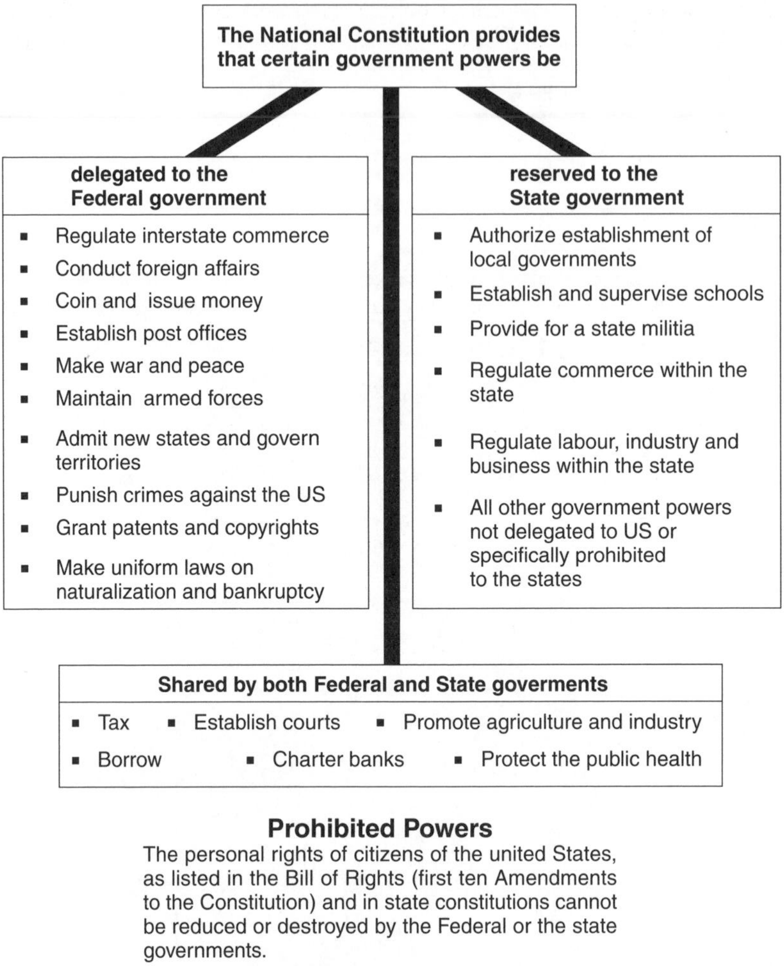

```
                  ┌──────────────────────────────┐
                  │  The National Constitution    │
                  │  provides that certain        │
                  │  government powers be         │
                  └──────────────────────────────┘
```

delegated to the Federal government	reserved to the State government
■ Regulate interstate commerce	■ Authorize establishment of local governments
■ Conduct foreign affairs	■ Establish and supervise schools
■ Coin and issue money	■ Provide for a state militia
■ Establish post offices	■ Regulate commerce within the state
■ Make war and peace	
■ Maintain armed forces	■ Regulate labour, industry and business within the state
■ Admit new states and govern territories	■ All other government powers not delegated to US or specifically prohibited to the states
■ Punish crimes against the US	
■ Grant patents and copyrights	
■ Make uniform laws on naturalization and bankruptcy	

Shared by both Federal and State goverments

■ Tax	■ Establish courts	■ Promote agriculture and industry
■ Borrow	■ Charter banks	■ Protect the public health

Prohibited Powers

The personal rights of citizens of the united States, as listed in the Bill of Rights (first ten Amendments to the Constitution) and in state constitutions cannot be reduced or destroyed by the Federal or the state governments.

Figure 22.1   **How the federal government and the states divide powers in the USA**

power to declare war. In 1917, for example, when Woodrow Wilson decided it was time for the USA to go to war with Germany, he had to ask Congress to declare war.

3   *There are two main parties represented in Congress*:

- Republicans
- Democrats

Both parties contain people of widely differing views.

The Republicans have traditionally been a party which has a lot of support in the North, particularly among businessmen and industrialists. The more conservative of the two parties, its members believed in:

- keeping high tariffs (import duties) to protect American industry from foreign imports;
- a *laissez-faire* approach to government: they wanted to leave businessmen alone to run industry and the economy with as little interference from the government as

possible. Republican Presidents Coolidge (1923–9) and Hoover (1929–33), for example, both favoured non-intervention and felt that it was not the government's job to sort out economic and social problems.

The Democrats have drawn much of their support from the South, and from immigrants in the large cities of the North. They have been the more progressive of the two parties: Democrat presidents such as Franklin D. Roosevelt (1933–45), Harry S. Truman (1945–53) and John F. Kennedy (1961–3) wanted the government to take a more active role in dealing with social and economic problems.

However, the parties are not as united or as tightly organized as political parties in Britain, where all the MPs belonging to the government party are expected to support the government all the time. In the USA, party discipline is much weaker, and votes in Congress often cut across party lines. There are left- and right-wingers in both parties. Some right-wing Democrats voted against Roosevelt's New Deal even though he was a Democrat, while some left-wing Republicans voted for it. But they did not change parties, and their party did not throw them out.

(b)   The President

The President is elected for a four-year term. Each party chooses its candidate for the presidency and the election always takes place in November. The successful candidate (referred to as the 'President elect') is sworn in as President the following January. The powers of the President appear to be very wide: he (or she) is Commander-in-Chief of the armed forces, controls the civil service, runs foreign affairs, makes treaties with foreign states, and appoints judges, ambassadors and the members of the cabinet. With the help of supporters among the Congressmen, the President can introduce laws into Congress and can veto laws passed by Congress if he or she does not approve of them.

(c)   The Supreme Court

This consists of nine judges appointed by the President, with the approval of the Senate. Once a Supreme Court judge is appointed, he or she can remain in office for life, unless forced to resign through ill health or scandal. The court acts as adjudicator in disputes between President and Congress, between the federal and state governments, between states, and in any problems which arise from the constitution.

(d)   The separation of powers

When the Founding Fathers of the USA (among whom were George Washington, Benjamin Franklin, Alexander Hamilton and James Madison) met in Philadelphia in 1787 to draw up the new Constitution, one of their main concerns was to make sure that none of the three parts of government – Congress, President and Supreme Court – became too powerful. *They deliberately devised a system of 'checks and balances' in which the three branches of government work separately from each other* (see Figure 22.2). The President and his cabinet, for example, are not members of Congress, unlike the British prime minister and cabinet, who are all members of parliament. Each branch acts as a check on the power of the others. This means that the President is not as powerful as he might appear: since elections for the House are held every two years and a third of the Senate is elected every two years, a President's party can lose its majority in one or both houses after he or she has been in office only two years.

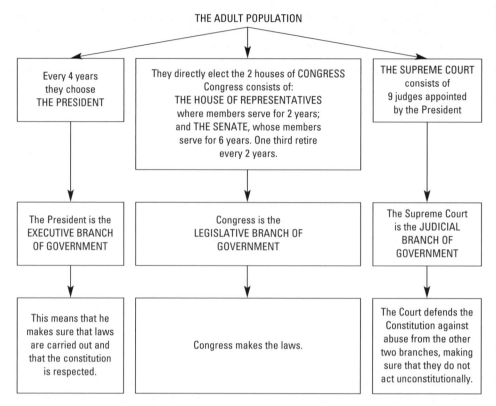

THE ADULT POPULATION

| Every 4 years they choose THE PRESIDENT | They directly elect the 2 houses of CONGRESS Congress consists of: THE HOUSE OF REPRESENTATIVES where members serve for 2 years; and THE SENATE, whose members serve for 6 years. One third retire every 2 years. | THE SUPREME COURT consists of 9 judges appointed by the President |

| The President is the EXECUTIVE BRANCH OF GOVERNMENT | Congress is the LEGISLATIVE BRANCH OF GOVERNMENT | The Supreme Court is the JUDICIAL BRANCH OF GOVERNMENT |

| This means that he makes sure that laws are carried out and that the constitution is respected. | Congress makes the laws. | The Court defends the Constitution against abuse from the other two branches, making sure that they do not act unconstitutionally. |

Figure 22.2   **The three separate branches of the US federal government**

Although the President can veto laws, Congress can over-rule this veto if it can raise a two-thirds majority in both houses. Nor can the President dissolve Congress; it is just a question of hoping that things will change for the better at the next set of elections. On the other hand, Congress cannot get rid of the President unless it can be shown that he or she has committed treason or some other serious crime. In that case the President can be threatened with *impeachment* (a formal accusation of crimes before the Senate, which would then carry out a trial). It was to avoid impeachment that Richard Nixon resigned in disgrace (August 1974) because of his involvement in the Watergate Scandal (see Section 23.4). A President's success has usually depended on how skilful he is at persuading Congress to approve his legislative programme. The Supreme Court keeps a watchful eye on both President and Congress, and can make life difficult for both of them by declaring a law 'unconstitutional', which means that it is illegal and has to be changed.

22.2   INTO THE MELTING POT: THE ERA OF IMMIGRATION

(a)   A huge wave of immigration

During the second half of the nineteenth century there was a huge wave of immigration into the USA. People had been crossing the Atlantic to settle in America since the seventeenth century, but in relatively small numbers. During the entire eighteenth century the total immigration into North America was probably no more than half a million; *between 1860 and 1930 the total was over 30 million.* Between 1840 and 1870 the Irish were the predominant immigrant group. After 1850 Germans and Swedes arrived in vast numbers, and by 1910 there were at least 8 million Germans in the USA. Between 1890 and 1920 it was the turn of Russians, Poles and Italians to come flooding in. Table 22.1 shows in detail the numbers of immigrants arriving in the USA and where they came from.

Peoples' motives for leaving their home countries were mixed. Some were attracted by the prospect of jobs and a better life. They hoped that if they could come through the 'Golden Door' into the USA, they would escape from poverty. This was the case with the Irish, Swedes, Norwegians and Italians. Persecution drove many people to emigrate; this was especially true of the Jews, who left Russia and other eastern European states in their millions after 1880 to escape pogroms (organized massacres). Immigration was much reduced after 1924 when the US government introduced annual quotas. Exceptions were still made, however, and during the 30 years following the end of the Second World War, a further 7 million people arrived.

Having arrived in the USA, many immigrants soon took part in a second migration, moving from their ports of arrival on the east coast into the Midwest. Germans, Norwegians and Swedes tended to move westwards, settling in such states as Nebraska, Wisconsin, Missouri, Minnesota, Iowa and Illinois. This was all part of a general American move westwards: the US population west of the Mississippi grew from only about 5 million in 1860 to around 30 million in 1910.

(b)   What were the consequences of immigration?

- The most obvious consequence was the increase in population. It has been calculated that if there had been no mass movement of people to the USA between 1880 and the 1920s, the population would have been 12 per cent lower than it actually was in 1930.
- Immigrants helped to speed up economic development. Economic historian William Ashworth calculated that without immigration, the labour force of the USA would have been 14 per cent lower than it actually was in 1920, and 'with fewer people, much of the natural wealth of the country would have waited longer for effective use'.
- The movement of people from countryside to town resulted in the growth of huge urban areas, known as 'conurbations'. In 1880 only New York had over a million inhabitants; by 1910, Philadelphia and Chicago had passed that figure too.
- The movement to take jobs in industry, mining, engineering and building meant that the proportion of the population working in agriculture declined steadily. In 1870, about 58 per cent of all Americans worked in agriculture; by 1914 this had fallen to 14 per cent, and to only 6 per cent in 1965.
- The USA acquired the most remarkable mixture of nationalities, cultures and religions in the world. Immigrants tended to concentrate in the cities, though many Germans, Swedes and Norwegians moved westwards in order to farm. In 1914 immigrants made up over half the population of every large American city, and there were some 30 different nationalities. This led idealistic Americans to claim with pride that the USA was a 'melting pot' into which all nationalities were thrown and melted down, to emerge as a single, unified American nation. In fact this seems to have been something of a myth, certainly until well after the First World War. Immigrants would congregate in national groups living in city ghettos. Each new wave of immigrants was treated with contempt and hostility by earlier immigrants, who feared for their jobs. The Irish, for example, would often refuse to work with Poles and Italians. Later the Poles and Italians were equally hostile to Mexicans. Some writers have said that the USA was not really a 'melting pot' at all; as historian Roger Thompson puts it,

Table 22.1 US population and immigration, 1851–1950

	1851–60	1861–70	1871–80	1881–90	1891–1900	1901–10	1911–20	1921–30	1931–40	1941–50	Quota per annum (1951)
Total population (census year 1860, 1870, etc.)	31 443	39 818	50 156	62 948	75 995	91 972	105 711	122 775	131 669	150 697	154
Total immigration	2 598	2 315	2 812	5 247	3 688	8 795	5 736	2 478	528	1 035	
Selected countries of origin:											
Ireland (N & S)	914	436	437	655	388	339	146	221	13	28[b]	18[b]
Germany	952	787	718	1 453	505	341	144	412	118[c]	227	26
Austria		8	73	354	593	2145	454	33	8	25	1
Hungary							443	31		3	
England	247	222	438	645	217	388	250	157	22	112	66(UK)
Italy	9	12	56	307	652	2046	1 110	455	68	58	6
Sweden	21[a]	38	116	392	226	250	95	97	4	11	3
Poland	1	2	13	52	97		5	228	17	8	7
Russia		3	39	213	505	1 597	921	62	1	1	3
China	41	64	123	62	15	21	21	30	5	17	0

a Includes Norway for this decade
b Eire only
c Includes Austria
Source: Roger Thompson, *The Golden Door* (Allman & Son, 1969), p. 309

the country was 'more like a salad bowl, where, although a dressing is poured over the ingredients, they nonetheless remain separate'.

- There was growing agitation against allowing too many foreigners into the USA, and there were demands for the 'Golden Door' to be firmly closed. The movement was racial in character, claiming that America's continuing greatness depended on preserving the purity of its Anglo-Saxon stock, known as White Anglo-Saxon Protestants (WASPS). This, it was felt, would be weakened by allowing the entry of unlimited numbers of Jews and southern and eastern Europeans. From 1921 the US government gradually restricted entry, until it was fixed at 150 000 a year in 1924. This was applied strictly during the depression years of the 1930s when unemployment was high. After the Second World War, restrictions were gradually relaxed; the USA took in some 700 000 refugees escaping from Castro's Cuba between 1959 and 1975 and over 100 000 refugees from Vietnam after the communists took over South Vietnam in 1975.

22.3 THE USA BECOMES ECONOMIC LEADER OF THE WORLD

(a) Economic expansion and the rise of big business

In the half-century before the First World War, a vast industrial expansion took the USA to the top of the league table of world industrial producers. The statistics in Table 22.2 show that already in 1900 they had overtaken most of their nearest rivals.

This expansion was made possible by the rich supplies of raw materials – coal, iron ore and oil – and by the spread of railways. The rapidly increasing population, much of it from immigration, provided the workforce and the markets. Import duties (tariffs) protected American industry from foreign competition, and it was a time of opportunity and enterprise. As American historian John A. Garraty puts it: 'the dominant spirit of the time encouraged businessmen to maximum effort by emphasising progress, glorifying material wealth and justifying aggressiveness'. The most successful businessmen, like Andrew Carnegie (steel), John D. Rockefeller (oil), Cornelius Vanderbilt (shipping and railways), J. Pierpoint Morgan (banking) and P. D. Armour (meat), made vast fortunes and built up huge industrial empires which gave them power over both politicians and ordinary people.

Table 22.2 **The USA and its chief rivals, 1900**

	USA	nearest rival
Coal production (tons)	262 million	219 million (Britain)
Exports (£)	311 million	390 million (Britain)
Pig-iron (tons)	16 million	8 million (Britain)
Steel (tons)	13 million	6 million (Germany)
Railways (miles)	183 000	28 000 (Germany)
Silver (fine oz)	55 million	57 million (Mexico)
Gold (fine oz)	3.8 million	3.3 million (Australia)
Cotton production (bales)	10.6 million	3 million (India)
Petroleum (metric tons)	9.5 million	11.5 million (Russia)
Wheat (bushels)	638 million	552 million (Russia)

Source: J. Nichol and S. Lang, *Work Out Modern World History* (Macmillan, 1990).

(b)   The great boom of the 1920s

After a slow start, as the country returned to normal after the First World War, the economy began to expand again: industrial production reached levels which had hardly been thought possible, doubling between 1921 and 1929 without any great increase in the numbers of workers. Sales, profits and wages also reached new heights, and *the 'Roaring Twenties'*, as they became known, gave rise to the popular image of the USA as the world's most glamorous modern society. There was a great variety of new things to be bought – radio sets, refrigerators, washing machines, vacuum cleaners, smart new clothes, motorcycles, and above all, motor cars. At the end of the war there were already 7 million cars in the USA, but by 1929 there were close on 24 million; Henry Ford led the field with his Model T. Perhaps the most famous of all the new commodities on offer was the Hollywood film industry, which made huge profits and exported its products all over the world. By 1930 almost every town had a cinema. And there were even new forms of music and dance; the 1920s are also sometimes known as *the Jazz Age* as well as the age of the daring new dances – the Charleston and the Turkey Trot.

What caused the boom?

1   *It was the climax of the great industrial expansion of the late nineteenth century*, when the USA had overtaken her two greatest rivals, Britain and Germany. The war gave American industry an enormous boost: countries whose industries and imports from Europe had been disrupted bought American goods, and continued to do so when the war was over. The USA was therefore the real economic victor of the war.

2   *The Republican governments' economic policies contributed to the prosperity in the short term.* Their approach was one of *laissez-faire*, but they did take two significant actions:

- the Fordney–McCumber tariff (1922) raised import duties on goods coming into America to the highest level ever, thus protecting American industry and encouraging Americans to buy home-produced goods;
- a general lowering of income tax in 1926 and 1928 left people with more cash to spend on American goods.

3   *American industry was becoming increasingly efficient*, as more mechanization was introduced. More and more factories were adopting the moving production-line methods first used by Henry Ford in 1915, which speeded up production and reduced costs. Management also began to apply F. W. Taylor's 'time and motion' studies, which saved more time and increased productivity.

4   *As profits increased, so did wages* (though not as much as profits). Between 1923 and 1929 the average wage for industrial workers rose by 8 per cent. Though this was not spectacular, it was enough to enable some workers to buy the new consumer luxuries, often on credit.

5   *Advertising helped the boom and itself became big business during the 1920s.* Newspapers and magazines carried more advertising than ever before, radio commercials became commonplace and cinemas showed filmed advertisements.

6   *The motor-car industry stimulated expansion* in a number of allied industries – tyres, batteries, petroleum for petrol, garages and tourism.

7   *Many new roads were built* and mileage almost doubled between 1919 and 1929. It was now more feasible to transport goods by road, and the numbers of trucks registered increased fourfold during the same period. Prices were competitive and this meant that railways and canals had lost their monopoly.

8   *Giant corporations* with their methods of mass production played an important part in the boom by keeping costs down. Another technique, encouraged by the government, was the trade association. This helped to standardize methods, tools and prices in smaller firms making the same product. In this way the American economy became dominated by giant corporations and trade associations, using mass-production methods for the mass consumer.

(c)   Free and equal?

Although many people were doing well during the 'Roaring Twenties', the wealth was not shared out equally; there were some unfortunate groups of people who must have felt that their freedom and their liberty did not extend very far. In fact, in many ways it was an age of intolerance.

1   Farmers were not sharing in the general prosperity
They had done well during the war, but during the 1920s prices of farm produce gradually fell. Farmers' profits dwindled and farm labourers' wages in the Midwest and the agricultural South were often less than half those of industrial workers in the north-east. The cause of the trouble was simple – farmers, with their new combine harvesters and chemical fertilizers, were producing too much food for the home market to absorb. This was at a time when European agriculture was recovering from the war and when there was strong competition from Canada, Russia and Argentina on the world market. It meant that not enough of the surplus food could be exported. The government, with its *laissez-faire* attitude, did hardly anything to help. Even when Congress passed the McNary–Haugen Bill, designed to allow the government to buy up farmers' surplus crops, President Coolidge twice vetoed it (1927 and 1928) on the grounds that it would make the problem worse by encouraging farmers to produce even more.

2   Not all industries were prosperous
Coal mining, for example, was suffering competition from oil, and many workers were laid off.

3   The black population was left out of the prosperity
In the South, where the majority of black people lived, white farmers always laid off black labourers first. About three-quarters of a million moved north during the 1920s looking for jobs in industry, but they almost always had to make do with the lowest-paid jobs, the worst conditions at work and the worst slum housing. Black people also had to suffer the persecutions of the *Ku Klux Klan*, the notorious white-hooded anti-black organization, which had about 5 million members in 1924. Assaults, whippings and lynchings were common, and although the Klan gradually declined after 1925, prejudice and discrimination against black people and against other coloured and minority groups continued (see Section 22.5).

4   Hostility to immigrants
Immigrants, especially those from eastern Europe, were treated with hostility by descendants of the original white settlers who came from Britain and the Netherlands. These WASPS – White Anglo-Saxon Protestants – felt under threat from the enormous numbers of immigrants. These included Catholic Irish and Italians and Orthodox and Jewish Russians, together with Poles and Hungarians. It was thought that, not being Anglo-Saxon, these people were threatening the American way of life and the greatness of the American nation. In 1924 the Johnson–Reed Act set an annual quota of 150 000 immigrants.

5 Super-corporations

Industry became increasingly monopolized by large trusts or super-corporations. By 1929 the wealthiest 5 per cent of corporations took over 84 per cent of the total income of all corporations. Although trusts increased efficiency, there is no doubt that they kept prices higher, and wages lower than was necessary. They were able to keep trade unions weak by forbidding workers to join. The Republicans, who were pro-business, did nothing to limit the growth of the super-corporations because the system seemed to be working well.

6 Widespread poverty in industrial areas and cities

Between 1922 and 1929, real wages of industrial workers increased by only 1.4 per cent a year; 6 million families (42 per cent of the total) had an income of less than $1000 a year. Working conditions were still appalling – about 25 000 workers were killed at work every year and 100 000 were disabled. After touring working-class areas of New York in 1928, Congressman La Guardia remarked: 'I confess I was not prepared for what I actually saw. It seemed almost unbelievable that such conditions of poverty could really exist.' In New York City alone there were 2 million families, many of them immigrants, living in slum tenements that had been condemned as firetraps.

7 The freedom of workers to protest was extremely limited

Strikes were crushed by force, militant trade unions had been destroyed and the more moderate unions were weak. Although there was a Socialist Party, there was no hope of it ever forming a government. After a bomb exploded in Washington in 1919, the authorities whipped up a 'Red Scare'; they arrested and deported over 4000 citizens of foreign origin, many of them Russians, who were suspected of being communists or anarchists. Most of them, in fact, were completely innocent.

8 Prohibition was introduced in 1919

This 'noble experiment', as it was known, was the banning of the manufacture, import and sale of all alcoholic liquor. It was the result of the efforts of a well-meaning pressure group before and during the First World War, which believed that a 'dry' America would mean a more efficient and moral America. But it proved impossible to eliminate 'speakeasies' (illegal bars) and 'bootleggers' (manufacturers of illegal liquor), who protected their premises from rivals with hired gangs, who shot each other up in gunfights. Organized crime was rife and gang violence became part of the American scene, especially in Chicago. It was there that Al Capone made himself a fortune, much of it from speakeasies and protection rackets. It was there too that the notorious St Valentine's Day Massacre took place in 1929, when hitmen hired by Capone arrived in a stolen police car and gunned down seven members of a rival gang who had been lined up against a wall.

The row over Prohibition was one aspect of *a traditional American conflict between the countryside and the city*. Many country people believed that city life was sinful and unhealthy, while life in the country was pure, noble and moral. President Roosevelt's administration ended Prohibition in 1933, since it was obviously a failure and the government was losing large amounts of revenue that it would have collected from taxes on liquor.

9 Women not treated equally

Many women felt that they were still treated as second-class citizens. Some progress had been made towards equal rights for women: they had been given the vote in 1920, the birth control movement was spreading and more women were able to take jobs. On the other hand, these were usually jobs men did not want; women were paid lower wages than men for the same job, and education for women was still heavily slanted towards preparing them to be wives and mothers rather than professional career women.

22.4 SOCIALISTS, TRADE UNIONS AND THE IMPACT OF WAR AND THE RUSSIAN REVOLUTIONS

(a) Labour unions during the nineteenth century

During the great industrial expansion of the half-century after the Civil War, *the new class of industrial workers began to organize labour unions to protect their interests.* Often the lead was taken by immigrant workers who had come from Europe with experience of socialist ideas and trade unions. It was a time of trauma for many workers in the new industries. On the one hand there were the traditional American ideals of equality, the dignity of the worker and respect for those who worked hard and achieved wealth – 'rugged individualism'. On the other hand there was a growing feeling, especially during the depression of the mid-1870s, that workers had lost their status and their dignity. Hugh Brogan neatly sums up the reasons for their disillusionment:

> Diseases (smallpox, diphtheria, typhoid) repeatedly swept the slums and factory districts; the appalling neglect of safety precautions in all the major industries; the total absence of any state-assisted schemes against injury, old age or premature death; the determination of employers to get their labour as cheap as possible, which meant, in practice, the common use of under-paid women and under-age children; and general indifference to the problems of unemployment, for it was still the universal belief that in America there was always work, and the chance of bettering himself, for any willing man.

As early as 1872 *the National Labor Union* (the first national federation of unions) led a successful strike of 100 000 workers in New York, demanding an eight-hour working day. In 1877 *the Socialist Labor Party* was formed, its main activity being to organize unions among immigrant workers. In the early 1880s an organization called *the Knights of Labor* became prominent. It prided itself on being non-violent, non-socialist and against strikes, and by 1886 it could boast more than 700 000 members. Soon after that, however, it went into a steep decline. A more militant, though still moderate, organization was *the American Federation of Labor (AFL)*, with Samuel Gompers as its president. Gompers was not a socialist and did not believe in class warfare; he was in favour of working with employers to get concessions, but equally he would support strikes to win a fair deal and improve the workers' standard of living.

When it was discovered that on the whole, employers were not prepared to make concessions, *Eugene Debs* founded a more militant association – *the American Railway Union* (ARU) – in 1893, but that too soon ran into difficulties and ceased to be important. Most radical of all were *the Industrial Workers of the World (known as the Wobblies)*, a socialist organization. Started in 1905, they led a series of actions against a variety of unpopular employers, but were usually defeated (see Section (c)). None of these organizations achieved very much that was tangible, either before or after the First World War, though arguably they did draw the public's attention to some of the appalling conditions in the world of industrial employment. *There were several reasons for their failure.*

- *The employers and the authorities were completely ruthless in suppressing strikes*, blaming immigrants for what they called 'un-American activities' and labelling them as socialists. Respectable opinion regarded unionism as something unconstitutional which ran counter to the cult of individual liberty. The general middle-class public and the press were almost always on the side of the employers, and the authorities had no hesitation in calling in state or federal troops to 'restore order' (see the next section).

- *The American workforce itself was divided*, the skilled workers against the unskilled, which meant that there was no concept of worker solidarity; the unskilled worker simply wanted to become a member of the skilled elite.
- *There was a division between white and black workers*; most unions refused to allow blacks to join, and told them to form their own unions. For example, blacks were not allowed to become members of the new ARU in 1894, although Debs wanted to bring everybody in. In retaliation the black unions often refused to co-operate with the whites, and allowed themselves to be used as strike-breakers.
- *Each new wave of immigrants weakened the union movement*; they were willing to accept lower wages than established workers and so could be used as strike-breakers.
- *In the early years of the twentieth century, some union leaders, especially those of the AFL, were discredited*: they were becoming wealthy, paying themselves large salaries, and seemed to be on suspiciously close terms with employers, while ordinary union members gained very little benefit and working conditions hardly improved. The union lost support because it concentrated on looking after skilled workers; it did very little for unskilled, black and women workers, who began to look elsewhere for protection.
- Until after the First World War it was the American farmers, not the industrial workers, who made up a majority of the population. Later it was the middle class, white-collar workers, who narrowly became the largest group in American society.

(b)   The unions under attack

The employers, fully backed by the authorities, soon began to react vigorously against strikes, and the penalties for strike leaders were severe. In 1876 a miners' strike in Pennsylvania was crushed and ten of the leaders (members of a mainly Irish secret society known as the Molly Maguires) were hanged for allegedly committing acts of violence, including murder. The following year there was a series of railway strikes in Pennsylvania; striking workers clashed with police, and the National Guard was brought in. The fighting was vicious: two companies of US infantry had to be called in before the workers were finally defeated. Altogether that year, about 100 000 railway workers had gone on strike, over a hundred were killed, and around a thousand sent to jail. The employers made a few minor concessions, but the message was clear: *strikes would not be tolerated*.

Ten years later nothing had changed. In 1886, organized labour throughout the USA campaigned for an eight-hour working day. There were many strikes and a few employers granted a nine-hour day to dissuade their workers from striking. However, on 3 May, police killed four workers in Chicago. The following day, at a large protest meeting in Haymarket Square, a bomb exploded in the middle of a contingent of police, killing seven of them. Who was responsible for the bomb was never discovered, but the police arrested eight socialist leaders in Chicago. Seven of them were not even at the meeting; but they were found guilty and four were hanged. The campaign failed.

Another strike, which became legendary, took place in 1892 at the Carnegie steelworks in Homestead, near Pittsburgh. When the workforce refused to accept wage reductions, the management laid them all off and tried to bring in strike-breakers, protected by hired detectives. Almost the entire town supported the workers; fighting broke out as crowds attacked the detectives, and several people were killed. Eventually troops were brought in and both the strike and the union were broken. The strike leaders were arrested and charged with murder and treason against the state, but the difference this time was that sympathetic juries acquitted them all.

In 1894 it was the turn of Eugene Debs and his American Railway Union. Outraged by the treatment of the Homestead workers, he organized a strike of workers at the Pullman

Palace Car Company's Chicago plant, who had just had their wages reduced by 30 per cent. ARU members were ordered not to handle Pullman cars, which meant in effect that all passenger trains in the Chicago area were brought to a standstill. Strikers also blocked tracks and derailed wagons. Once again, federal troops were brought in, and 34 people were killed; the strike was crushed and nothing much more was heard from the ARU. In a way Debs was fortunate: he was only given six months in prison, and during that time, he later claimed, he was converted to socialism.

(c) Socialism and the Industrial Workers of the World (IWW)

A new and more militant phase of labour unionism began in the early years of the twentieth century, with the formation of the IWW in Chicago in 1905. Eugene Debs, who was by this time the leader of the Socialist Party, was at the inaugural meeting, and so was 'Big Bill' Haywood, a miners' leader, who became the main driving force behind the IWW. It included socialists, anarchists and radical trade unionists; their aim was to form 'One Big Union' to include all workers across the country, irrespective of race, sex or level of employment. Although they were not in favour of starting violence, they were quite prepared to resist if they were attacked. They believed in strikes as an important weapon in the class war; but strikes were not the main activity: 'they are tests of strength in the course of which the workers train themselves for concerted action, to prepare for the final "catastrophe" – the general strike which will complete the expropriation of the employers'.

This was fighting talk, and although the IWW never had more than 10 000 members at any one time, *employers and property owners saw them as a threat to be taken seriously*. They enlisted the help of all possible groups to destroy the IWW. Local authorities were persuaded to pass laws banning meetings and speaking in public; gangs of vigilantes were hired to attack IWW members; leaders were arrested. In Spokane, Washington, in 1909, 600 people were arrested and jailed for attempting to make public speeches in the street; eventually, when all the jails were full, the authorities relented and granted the right to speak.

Undeterred, the IWW continued to campaign, and over the next few years members travelled around the country to organize strikes wherever they were needed – in California, Washington State, Massachusetts, Louisiana and Colorado, among other places. One of their few outright successes came with a strike of woollen weavers in Lawrence, Massachusetts, in 1912. The workers, mainly immigrants, walked out of the factories after learning that their wages were to be reduced. The IWW moved in and organized pickets, parades and mass meetings. Members of the Socialist Party also became involved, helping to raise funds and make sure the children were fed. The situation became violent when police attacked a parade; eventually state militia and even federal cavalry were called in, and several strikers were killed. But they held out for over two months until the mill owners gave way and made acceptable concessions.

However, successes like this were limited, *and working conditions generally did not improve*. In 1911 a fire in a New York shirtwaist factory killed 146 workers, because employers had ignored the fire regulations. At the end of 1914 it was reported that 35 000 workers had been killed that year in industrial accidents. Many of those sympathetic to the plight of the workers began to look towards the Socialist Party and political solutions. A number of writers helped to increase public awareness of the problems. For example, Upton Sinclair's novel *The Jungle* (1906) dealt with the disgusting conditions in the meat-packing plants of Chicago, and at the same time succeeded in putting across the basic ideals of socialism.

By 1910 the party had some 100 000 members and Debs ran for president in 1908, though he polled only just over 400 000 votes. *The importance of the socialist movement was that it publicized the need for reform and influenced both major parties*, which acknowledged, however reluctantly, that some changes were needed, if only to steal the socialists' thunder and beat off their challenge. Debs ran for president again in 1912, but by that time the political scene had changed dramatically. The ruling Republican Party had split: its more reform-minded members set up *the Progressive Republican League* (1910) with a programme that included the eight-hour day, prohibition of child labour, votes for women and a national system of social insurance. It even expressed support for labour unions, provided they were moderate in their behaviour. The Progressives decided to run former president *Theodore Roosevelt* against the official Republican candidate William Howard Taft. The Democrat Party also had its progressive wing, and their candidate for president was *Woodrow Wilson*, a well-known reformer who called his programme the 'New Freedom'.

Faced with these choices, the American Federation of Labor stayed with the Democrats as the most likely party to actually carry out its promises, while the IWW supported Debs. With the Republican vote divided between Roosevelt (4.1 million) and Taft (3.5 million), Wilson was easily elected president (6.3 million votes). Debs (900 672) more than doubled his previous vote, indicating that support for socialism was still increasing despite the efforts of the progressives in both major parties. During Wilson's presidency (1913–21) a number of important reforms were introduced, including a law forbidding child labour in factories and sweatshops. More often than not, however, it was the state governments which led the way; for example, by 1914, nine states had introduced votes for women; it was only in 1920 that women's suffrage became part of the federal constitution. Hugh Brogan sums up Wilson's reforming achievement succinctly: 'By comparison with the past, his achievements were impressive; measured against what needed to be done, they were almost trivial.'

(d)   The First World War and the Russian revolutions

When the First World War began in August 1914, Wilson pledged, to the relief of the vast majority of the American people, that the USA would remain neutral. Having won the 1916 election largely on the strength of the slogan 'He Kept Us Out of the War', Wilson soon found that Germany's campaign of 'unrestricted' submarine warfare gave him no alternative but to declare war (see Section 2.5(c)). The Russian revolution of February/March 1917 (see Section 16.2), which overthrew Tsar Nicholas II, came at exactly the right time for the president – he talked of 'the wonderful and heartening things that have been happening in the last few weeks in Russia'. The point was that many Americans had been unwilling for their country to enter the war because it meant being allied to the most undemocratic state in Europe. Now that tsarism was finished, an alliance with the apparently democratic Provisional Government was much more acceptable. Not that the American people were enthusiastic about the war; according to Howard Zinn:

> There is no persuasive evidence that the public wanted war. The government had to work hard to create its consensus. That there was no spontaneous urge to fight is suggested by the strong measures taken: a draft of young men, an elaborate propaganda campaign throughout the country, and harsh punishment for those who refused to get in line.

Wilson called for an army of a million men, but in the first six weeks, a mere 73 000 volunteered; Congress voted overwhelmingly for compulsory military service.

The war gave the Socialist Party a new lease of life – for a short time. It organized anti-war meetings throughout the Midwest and condemned American participation as 'a crime against the people of the United States'. Later in the year, ten socialists were elected to the New York State legislature; in Chicago the socialist vote in the municipal elections rose from 3.6 per cent in 1915 to 34.7 per cent in 1917. Congress decided to take no chances – in June 1917 it passed the Espionage Act, which made it an offence to attempt to cause people to refuse to serve in the armed forces; the socialists came under renewed attack: anyone who spoke out against conscription was likely to be arrested and accused of being pro-German. About 900 people were sent to jail under the Espionage Act, including members of the IWW, which also opposed the war.

Events in Russia influenced the fortunes of the socialists. When Lenin and the Bolsheviks seized power in October/November 1917, they soon ordered all Russian troops to cease fire, and began peace talks with the Germans. This caused consternation among Russia's allies, and the Americans condemned the Bolsheviks as 'agents of Prussian imperialism'. There was plenty of public support when the authorities launched a campaign against the Socialist Party and the IWW, who were both labelled as pro-German Bolsheviks. In April 1918, 101 'Wobblies', including their leader, 'Big Bill' Haywood, were put on trial together. They were all found guilty of conspiring to obstruct recruitment and encourage desertion. Haywood and 14 others were sentenced to 20 years in jail; 33 others were given ten years and the rest received shorter sentences. The IWW was destroyed. In June 1918, Eugene Debs was arrested and accused of trying to obstruct recruitment and of being pro-German; he was sentenced to ten years in prison, though he was released after serving less than three years. The war ended in November 1918, but in that short period of US involvement, since April 1917, some 50 000 American soldiers had died.

(e) The Red Scare: the Sacco and Vanzetti case

Although the war was over, the political and social troubles were not. In the words of Howard Zinn, 'with all the wartime jailings, the intimidation, the drive for national unity, the Establishment still feared socialism. There seemed to be again the need for the twin tactics of control in the face of revolutionary challenge: reform and repression.' The 'revolutionary challenge' took the form of a number of bomb outrages during the summer of 1919. An explosion badly damaged the house of the attorney-general, *A. Mitchell Palmer*, in Washington, and another bomb went off at the great House of Morgan banking establishment on Wall Street, in New York, killing 39 people and injuring hundreds. Exactly who was responsible has never been discovered, but the explosions were blamed on anarchists, Bolsheviks and immigrants. 'This movement,' one of Wilson's advisers told him, 'if it is not checked, is bound to express itself in an attack on everything we hold dear.'

Repression soon followed. *Palmer himself whipped up the 'Red Scare'* – the fear of Bolshevism – according to some sources, in order to gain popularity by handling the situation decisively. He was ambitious, and fancied himself as a presidential candidate in the 1920 elections. In lurid language, he described the 'Red Threat', which, he said, was 'licking the altars of our churches, crawling into the sacred corners of American homes, seeking to replace the marriage vows … it is an organization of thousands of aliens and moral perverts'. Although he was a Quaker, Palmer was extremely aggressive; he leapt into the attack during the autumn of 1919, ordering raids on publishers' offices, union and socialist headquarters, public halls, private houses, and meetings of anyone who was thought to be guilty of Bolshevik activities. Over a thousand anarchists and socialists were arrested, and some 250 aliens of Russian origin were rounded up and deported to Russia. In January 1920 a further 4000 mostly harmless and innocent people were arrested, including 600 in Boston, and most of them were deported after long periods in jail.

One case above all caught the public's imagination, not only in America but worldwide: *the Sacco and Vanzetti affair*. Arrested in Boston in 1919, Nicola Sacco and Bartolomeo Vanzetti were charged with robbing and murdering a postmaster. They were found guilty, though the evidence was far from convincing, and sentenced to death. However, the trial was something of a farce; the judge, who was supposed to be neutral, showed extreme prejudice against them on the grounds that they were anarchists and Italian immigrants who had somehow avoided military service. After the trial he boasted of what he had done to 'those anarchist bastards … sons of bitches and Dagoes'.

Sacco and Vanzetti appealed against their sentences and spent the next seven years in jail while the case dragged on. Their friends and sympathizers succeeded in arousing worldwide support, especially in Europe. Famous supporters included Stalin, Henry Ford, Mussolini, Fritz Kreisler (the world-famous violinist), Thomas Mann, Anatole France and H. G. Wells. There were massive demonstrations outside the US embassy in Rome and bombs exploded in Lisbon and Paris. In the USA itself, the campaign for their release gathered momentum; a support fund was opened for their families and demonstrations were organized outside the jail where they were being held. It was all to no avail: in April 1927 the Governor of Massachusetts decreed that the guilty verdicts should stand. In August Sacco and Vanzetti were executed in the electric chair, protesting their innocence to the end.

The whole affair provided great adverse publicity for the USA; it seemed clear that Sacco and Vanzetti had been made scapegoats because they were anarchists and immigrants. There was outrage in Europe and further protest demonstrations were held after their execution. Nor were anarchists and immigrants the only classes of people who felt persecuted; black people too continued to have a hard time in the so-called classless society of the USA.

22.5 RACIAL DISCRIMINATION AND THE CIVIL RIGHTS MOVEMENT

(a) Background to the civil rights problem

During the second half of the seventeenth century the colonists in Virginia began to import slaves from Africa in large numbers to work on the tobacco plantations. Slavery survived through the eighteenth century and was still firmly in place when the American colonies won their independence and the USA was born in 1776. In the North, slavery had mostly disappeared by 1800, when one in five of the total US population was African American. In the South it lingered on because the whole plantation economy – tobacco, sugar and cotton – was based on slave labour, and Southern whites could not imagine how they could survive without it. This was in spite of the fact that one of the founding principles of the USA was the idea of freedom and equality for everybody. This was clearly stated in the 1776 Declaration of Independence:

> We hold these truths to be self-evident, that all men are created equal, and that they are endowed by their Creator with inalienable rights, that among these are Life, Liberty and the Pursuit of Happiness.

Yet when the Constitution was drawn up in 1787 it somehow succeeded in ignoring the issue of slavery. When Abraham Lincoln, who was opposed to slavery, was elected president in 1860, the eleven Southern states began to secede (withdraw) from the Union, so that they could continue slavery and maintain control over their own internal affairs. Thus the abolition of slavery and the question of states' rights were the basic causes of the Civil War.

(b) 'Black Reconstruction' after the Civil War

The Civil War between North and South (1861–5) was the most terrible conflict in American history, leaving some 620 000 men dead. As well as widespread damage, especially in the South, it also left behind deep political and social divisions. The victory of the North had two clear results: *the Union had been preserved, and slavery had been brought to an end.* The Thirteenth, Fourteenth and Fifteenth Amendments to the Constitution outlawed slavery, laid down the principle of racial equality and gave all US citizens equal protection of the law. Any state which deprived any male citizens over 21 of the right to vote would be penalized. *For a short time, black people in the South were able to vote*; many African Americans were elected to state legislatures; in South Carolina they even won a small majority; 20 became members of Congress and two were elected to the Senate. Another great step forward was the introduction of free and racially mixed schools.

The formerly dominant Southern whites found all this difficult to accept. They accused the black politicians of being incompetent, corrupt and lazy, though on the whole they were probably no more so than their white counterparts. Southern state legislatures soon began to pass what were known as the 'Black Codes'; these were laws introducing all kinds of restrictions on the freedom of the former slaves, which as near as possible restored the old slavery laws. When black people protested there were brutal reprisals; clashes occurred, and there were race riots in Memphis, Tennessee, in which 46 blacks were killed (1866). In New Orleans later the same year, the police killed around 40 people and wounded 160, mostly blacks. Violence intensified in the late 1860s and early 1870s, much of it organized by the *Ku Klux Klan.* Union troops stayed on in the South at the end of the Civil War and were able to maintain some semblance of order. But gradually the federal government in Washington, anxious to avoid another war at all costs, began to turn a blind eye to what was happening.

The real turning point came with the presidential election of November 1876. At the end of the year, with only three states in the South – Florida, South Carolina and Louisiana – still to count their votes, the Democrats looked like winning. However, if the Republican candidate, Rutherford B. Hayes, won all three, he would become president. After long and secret discussions, a shady deal was worked out: Hayes made concessions to the white South, promising extensive federal cash investment for railways, and the withdrawal of Union troops. In effect it meant abandoning the former slaves and handing back political control of the South to the whites in return for the presidency. Hayes became president in March 1877, and the period known as Black Reconstruction was over.

(c) The Ku Klux Klan and the Jim Crow laws

In their campaign to prevent blacks from gaining equal civil rights, Southern whites used violence as well as legal methods. The violence was supplied by the Ku Klux Klan ('Ku Klux' from the Greek *kuklos* – a drinking bowl), which began as a secret society on Christmas Eve 1865, in Tennessee. They claimed that they were protecting whites who were being terrorized by former slaves, and they warned that they would take revenge. They carried out a campaign of threats and terror against blacks and against whites who were sympathetic to the black cause. Lynchings, beatings, whippings and tarring and feathering became commonplace. Their aims soon became more specific; they wanted to:

- terrorize blacks to such an extent that they would be afraid to exercise their votes;
- drive them from any land which they had been able to obtain;
- intimidate and demoralize them so that they would give up all attempts to win equality.

Ordinary law-abiding white citizens who might disapprove of the Klan's activities were afraid to speak out or give evidence against its members. And so the Klan rampaged around the South in their night raids, dressed in white hoods and masks, and holding pseudo-religious ceremonies involving burning crosses. By the end of the 1870s, with its main aims apparently achieved, Klan activity decreased somewhat until the early 1920s. Even so, between 1885 and the US entry into the First World War in 1917, over 2700 African Americans were lynched in the South.

Legal weapons used by Southern whites to maintain their supremacy included the so-called *Jim Crow laws* passed by state legislatures soon after Hayes became president in 1877. These severely restricted black people's rights: various devices were used to deprive them of their vote; they were only allowed to take the worst and lowest-paid jobs; they were forbidden to live in the best areas of towns. There was worse to come: blacks were excluded from schools and universities attended by whites, and from hotels and restaurants. Even trains and buses were to have separate sections for blacks and whites. Meanwhile in the North, black people were somewhat better off in the sense that they could at least vote, though they still had to put up with discrimination in housing, jobs and education. In the South, however, at the end of the century, white supremacy seemed unassailable.

Not surprisingly, many black leaders seemed to have given up hope. One of the best known figures, *Booker T. Washington*, who had been born a slave in Virginia, believed that the best way for blacks to cope was to accept the situation passively and work hard to achieve economic success. His ideas were set out in his *'Atlanta Compromise' speech* in 1895: only when African Americans demonstrated their economic abilities and became disciplined could they hope to win concessions from the ruling whites and make political progress. He stressed the importance of education and vocational training, and in 1881 became principal of the new Tuskegee Institute in Alabama, which he developed into a major centre of black education.

(d) Civil rights in the early twentieth century

Early in the new century black people began to organize themselves. There were something like 10 million African Americans in the USA and 9 million of them lived in the South, where they were downtrodden and discouraged. However, several outstanding new leaders emerged who were prepared to risk speaking out. *W. E. B. Du Bois* was educated in the North, was the first black man to take a Ph.D. degree at Harvard, and worked as a teacher in Atlanta. He was determined to fight for full civil and political rights. He opposed the tactics of Booker T. Washington, which he thought were too cautious and moderate; he dismissed the vocational education provided at Tuskegee, claiming that it was designed to keep young black people in the old rural South, instead of providing them with the training and skills necessary for success in the new urban centres of the North. Du Bois, together with *William Monroe Trotter*, who edited a newspaper called the *Guardian* in Boston, organized a conference over the border in Canada, near Niagara Falls. This led to the formation of *the Niagara group* (1905); its founding statement set the tone for its campaign:

> We refuse to allow the impressions to remain that the Negro-American assents to inferiority, is submissive under oppression and apologetic before insults. The voice of protest of ten million Americans must never cease to assail the ears of their fellows so long as America is unjust.

In 1910 *the National Association for the Advancement of Colored People (NAACP)* was founded, with Du Bois as one of its leaders and editor of its magazine, *The Crisis*. They aimed to fight segregation through legal actions and better education – by demonstrating their abilities and skills, black people would earn respect from the whites, and gradually, it was hoped, full civil rights would follow.

A rather different approach was tried by another black leader, *Marcus Garvey*. Born in Jamaica, Garvey only moved to the USA in 1916, arriving in New York at the time of the great influx of black people who were hoping to escape from poverty in the South. He soon came to the conclusion that there was little chance of black people being treated as equals and enjoying full civil rights in the near future. So he advocated black nationalism, black pride and racial separation. Living and working in the black areas of Harlem, Garvey edited his own weekly newspaper, *Negro World*, and introduced his *Universal Negro Improvement Association*, which he had started in Jamaica in 1914. *He was a forerunner of the black nationalism* of Malcolm X and the Black Panthers, even suggesting that a return to Africa might be the best future for the black people of white-supremacist America. This idea failed to catch on, and he turned his attention to business ventures. He founded a Black Factories Corporation and the Black Star Line, a steamship company owned and operated by blacks. This collapsed in 1921 and Garvey got into financial difficulties. He was convicted of fraud and then deported, and his black nationalist movement declined. He spent the last years of his life in London.

At the time of the Red Scare just after the First World War, *the Ku Klux Klan revived*. Again it claimed self-defence as its main motive – the defence of the 'Nordic Americans of the old stock … the embattled American farmer and artisans' whose way of life was being threatened by hordes of fast-breeding immigrants. What worried them in the early 1920s was that the children of the immigrants who had entered the country between 1900 and 1914 were now coming up to voting age. The Klan rejected the 'melting pot' theory; they campaigned once more against black people, who had been moving in their thousands to live in the North, even though most of them were not exactly doing well during the 'Roaring Twenties'. They also campaigned against Italians and Roman Catholics, and against Jews. The Klan spread to the North and by 1924 could boast not far short of 5 million members. There were more harassments, beatings and lynchings; black and white mobs fought each other and racial hatred seemed as deep-seated as ever. When the federal government limited immigration to 150 000 a year in 1924, the Klan claimed the credit. The organization declined in importance after 1925, following a series of financial and sexual scandals; by 1929 membership had fallen to around one million. However, this did not mean an improvement in the lives of black people, particularly as the country was soon plunged into the Great Depression.

22.6 THE GREAT DEPRESSION ARRIVES, OCTOBER 1929

(a) The Wall Street Crash, October 1929

As 1929 opened, most Americans seemed blissfully unaware that anything serious was wrong with the economy. In 1928 President Coolidge told Congress: 'The country can regard the present with satisfaction, and anticipate the future with optimism.' Prosperity seemed permanent. The Republican Herbert C. Hoover won an overwhelming victory in the 1928 presidential election. Sadly the prosperity was built on suspect foundations and it could not last. 'America the Golden' was about to suffer a profound shock. In September 1929 the buying of shares on the New York stock exchange in Wall Street began to slow down. Rumours spread that the boom might be over, and so people rushed to sell their shares before prices fell too far. By 24 October the rush had turned into a panic and share prices fell dramatically. By 29 October – 'Black Tuesday' – thousands of people who had bought their shares when prices were high were ruined; the value of listed stocks fell catastrophically by around $30 billion.

This disaster is always remembered as the Wall Street Crash. Its effects spread rapidly: so many people in financial difficulties rushed to the banks to draw out their savings that thousands of banks had to close. As the demand for goods fell, factories closed down and unemployment rose alarmingly. The great boom had suddenly turned into the Great Depression. It rapidly affected not only the USA, but other countries as well, and so it became known as *the world economic crisis.* The Wall Street Crash did not cause the depression; it was just a symptom of a problem whose real causes lay much deeper.

(b)   What caused the Great Depression?

1   Domestic overproduction
American industrialists, encouraged by high profits and helped by increased mechanization, were *producing too many goods for the home market to absorb* (in the same way as the farmers). This was not apparent in the early 1920s, but as the 1930s approached, unsold stocks of goods began to build up, and manufacturers produced less. Since fewer workers were required, men were laid off; and as there was no unemployment benefit, these men and their families bought less. And so the vicious circle continued.

2   Unequal distribution of income
The enormous profits being made by industrialists were not being distributed equally among the workers. The average wage for industrial workers rose by about 8 per cent between 1923 and 1929, but during the same period, industrial profits increased by 72 per cent. An 8 per cent increase in wages (only 1.4 per cent in real terms) meant that there was not enough buying power in the hands of the general public to sustain the boom; they could manage to absorb goods produced for a limited time, with the help of credit, but by 1929 they were fast approaching the limit. Unfortunately manufacturers, usually super-corporations, were not prepared to reduce prices or to increase wages substantially, and so a glut of consumer goods built up.

This refusal by the manufacturers to make some compromise was short-sighted to say the least; at the beginning of 1929 there were still millions of Americans who had no radio, no electric washing machine and no car because they could not afford them. If employers had allowed larger wage increases and been content with less profit, there is no reason why the boom could not have continued for several more years while its benefits were more widely shared. Even so, a slump was still not inevitable, provided the Americans could export their surplus products.

3   Falling demand for exports
However, exports began to fall away, partly because foreign countries were reluctant to buy American goods when the Americans themselves put up tariff barriers to protect their industries from foreign imports. Although the Fordney–McCumber tariff (1922) helped to keep foreign goods out, at the same time it prevented foreign states, especially those in Europe, from making much-needed profits from trade with the USA. Without those profits, the nations of Europe would be unable to afford American goods, and they would be struggling to pay their war debts to the USA. To make matters worse, many states retaliated by introducing tariffs against American goods. A slump of some sort was clearly on the way.

4   Speculation
The situation was worsened by a great rush of *speculation* on the New York stock market, which began to gather momentum about 1926. Speculation is the buying of shares in companies; people with cash to spare chose to do this for two possible motives:

- to get the dividend – the annual sharing-out of a company's profits among its shareholders;
- to make a quick profit by selling the shares for more than they originally paid for them.

In the mid-1920s it was the second motive which most attracted investors: as company profits increased, more people wanted to buy shares; this forced share prices up and there were plenty of chances of quick profits from buying and selling shares. The average value of a share rose from $9 in 1924 to $26 in 1929. Share prices of some companies rose spectacularly: the stock of the Radio Corporation of America, for example, stood at $85 a share early in 1928 and had risen to $505 in September 1929, and this was a company which did not pay dividends.

Promise of quick profits encouraged all sorts of rash moves: ordinary people spent their savings or borrowed money to buy a few shares. Stockbrokers sold shares on credit; banks speculated in shares using the cash deposited with them. It was all something of a gamble; but there was enormous confidence that prosperity would continue indefinitely.

This confidence lasted well on into 1929, but when the first signs appeared that sales of goods were beginning to slow down, some better-informed investors decided to sell their shares while prices were still high. This caused suspicion to spread – more people than usual were trying to sell shares – something must be wrong! Confidence in the future began to waver for the first time, and more people decided to sell their shares while the going was good. And so a process of what economists call *self-fulfilling expectation* developed. This means that by their own actions, investors actually caused the dramatic collapse of share prices which they were afraid of.

By October 1929 there was a flood of people rushing to sell shares, but because confidence had been shaken, there were far fewer people wanting to buy. Share prices tumbled and unfortunate investors had to accept whatever they could get. One especially bad day was 24 October – 'Black Thursday' – when nearly 13 million shares were 'dumped' on the stock market at very low prices. By mid-1930 share prices were, on average, about 25 per cent of their peak level the previous year, but they were still falling. Rock bottom was reached in 1932, and by then the whole of the USA was in the grip of depression.

(c) How did the depression affect people?

1. To begin with, *the stock market crash ruined millions of investors* who had paid high prices for their shares. If investors had bought shares on credit or with borrowed money, their creditors lost heavily too, since they had no hope of receiving payment.

2. *Banks were in a shaky position*, having themselves speculated unsuccessfully. When, added to this, millions of people rushed to withdraw their savings in the belief that their cash would be safer at home, many banks were overwhelmed, did not have enough cash to pay everybody, and closed down for good. There were over 25 000 banks in the country in 1929, but by 1933 there were fewer than 15 000. This meant that millions of ordinary people who had had nothing to do with the speculation were ruined as their life savings disappeared.

3. As the demand for all types of goods fell, *workers were laid off and factories closed*. Industrial production in 1933 was only half the 1929 total, while unemployment stood at around 14 million. About a quarter of the total labour force was without jobs, and one in eight farmers lost all their property. There was a drop in living standards, with people queuing for bread, charity soup kitchens, evictions of

tenants who could not afford the rent, and near-starvation for many people. The 'great American dream' of prosperity for everybody had turned into a nightmare. In the words of historian Donald McCoy: 'the American people were affected as though a war had been fought from coast to coast'. There were no unemployment or sickness benefits to help out. Outside large cities, homeless people lived in camps nicknamed 'Hoovervilles' after the president who was blamed for the depression.

4 *Many other countries, especially Germany, were affected* because their prosperity depended to a large extent on loans from the USA. As soon as the crash came, the loans stopped, and the Americans called in the short-term loans they had already made. By 1931 most of Europe was in a similar plight. The depression had political results too; in many states – Germany, Austria, Japan and Britain – right-wing governments came to power when the existing regimes failed to cope with the situation.

(d) Who was to blame for the disaster?

At the time it was fashionable to blame the unfortunate President Hoover, but this is unfair. The origins of the trouble go much further back, and the Republican Party as a whole must share the blame. There were several measures the government could have taken to control the situation: they could have encouraged overseas countries to buy more American goods by lowering American tariffs instead of raising them. Decisive action could have been taken in 1928 and 1929 to limit the amount of credit which the stock market was allowing speculators. But their *laissez-faire* attitude would not allow such interference in private affairs.

(e) What did Hoover's government do to ease the depression?

Hoover tried to solve the problem by encouraging employers not to reduce wages and not to lay workers off. The government lent money to banks, industrialists and farmers to save them from bankruptcy, and urged state governors to create jobs by investing in public works schemes. After a promising beginning the policy began to falter: as the depression got worse, businesses started to break the agreement and lay men off. As for the states, they lacked sufficient funds to create any effective public works.

Hoover's attempts to help farmers were even less effective. The government began to buy up surplus grain, but this only encouraged them to produce even more, so that the government could not afford to continue the policy; the result – there was even more surplus grain, causing the price to fall further. In 1931 Hoover declared a one-year moratorium on war debts. This meant that foreign governments could miss one instalment of their debts to the USA in the hope that they would use the money saved to buy more American goods. However, this was a failure partly because at the same time the new Smoot–Hawley Tariff put import duties on agricultural produce, making them more expensive than home-grown goods, and so protect farmers from foreign competition. But this backfired: European countries retaliated by introducing their own tariffs, which prevented American farmers from exporting to Europe. Hoover's efforts made little difference – American exports in 1932 were less than a third of the 1929 total.

Hoover tried to address the problem of the mass closure of banks by setting up the National Credit Corporation. This was designed to persuade large banks to lend money to smaller banks that were in difficulties. But large banks were reluctant to lend money

Illustration 22.1 **The winner and the loser: Roosevelt waves to the cheering crowds, while defeated President Hoover looks downcast during their ride through Washington, March 1933**

for fear that the smaller banks might collapse, and be unable to pay back the loan. More effective was another new organization – the Reconstruction Finance Corporation (RFC), which was given the power to lend money to banks and provide cash for job-creation programmes. This was beginning to show results towards the end of 1932, but it was too late; the election was due in November 1932. A measure which would have been more helpful was the government making relief payments to individual families. Even in a crisis as serious as this, he was against relief payments to individuals because he believed in self-reliance and hard work, in other words, 'rugged individualism'. The idea that it was the government's job to provide for the suffering poor was complete anathema to him, because it would create what he called 'a dependency culture'. It was no surprise when the Democrat candidate, Franklin D. Roosevelt ('FDR'), easily beat Hoover in the presidential election of November 1932 (see Illus. 22.1).

22.7 ROOSEVELT AND THE NEW DEAL

The 51-year-old Roosevelt came from a wealthy New York family; educated at Harvard, he entered politics in 1910 and was Assistant Secretary to the Navy during the First World War. It seemed as though his career might be over when, at the age of 40, he was stricken with polio (1921), which left his legs completely paralysed. With tremendous determination he overcame his disability, though he was never able to walk unaided. He now brought the same determination to bear in his attempts to drag America out of the depression. He was dynamic, full of vitality and brimming with new ideas. He was a brilliant communicator – his radio talks (which he called his fireside chats) inspired confidence and won him great popularity. During the election campaign he had said: 'I pledge you, I pledge myself, to a new deal for the American people.' The phrase stuck, and his policies have always been remembered as 'the New Deal'. Right from the beginning he brought new hope when he said in his inauguration speech: 'Let me assert my firm belief that the only thing we have to fear is fear itself. This nation asks for action, and action now. ... I shall ask Congress for the power to wage war against the emergency.'

(a) What were the aims of the New Deal?

Basically Roosevelt had three aims:

- **relief**: to give direct help to the poverty-stricken millions who were without food and homes;
- **recovery**: to reduce unemployment, stimulate the demand for goods and get the economy moving again;
- **reform**: to take whatever measures were necessary to prevent a repeat of the economic disaster.

It was obvious that drastic measures were needed, and Roosevelt's methods were a complete change from those of the *laissez-faire* Republicans. He gathered advice from a small group of economists and university academics whom he called his Brain Trust. He was prepared to intervene in economic and social affairs as much as possible and to spend government cash to pull the country out of depression. The Republicans were always reluctant to take steps of this sort.

(b) What did the New Deal involve?

The measures which go to make up the New Deal were introduced over the years 1933 to 1940. Some historians have talked about a 'First' and a 'Second' New Deal starting in 1935, and even a 'Third', each with different characteristics. However, Michael Heale believes that this oversimplifies the subject. 'The Roosevelt administration', he writes, 'was never governed by a single political ideology, and its components were always pulling in different directions. Broadly, however, it is fair to say that from 1935 the New Deal moved closer to the political left in that it stumbled into an uneasy alliance with organised labour and showed a greater interest in social reform.' For the 'first hundred days' he concentrated on emergency legislation to deal with the ongoing crisis:

1 Banking and financial systems
It was important to get the banking and financial systems working properly again. This was achieved by the government taking over the banks temporarily and guaranteeing that depositors would not lose their cash if there was another financial crisis. This restored confidence, and money began to flow into the banks again. *The Securities Exchange Commission (1934)* reformed the stock exchange; among other things, it insisted that people buying shares on credit must make a down payment of at least 50 per cent instead of only 10 per cent.

2 The Farmers' Relief Act (1933) and the Agricultural Adjustment Administration (AAA)
It was important to help farmers, whose main problem was that they were still producing too much, which kept prices and profits low. Under the Act, the government paid compensation to farmers who reduced output, thereby raising prices. The AAA, under the control

of the dynamic Henry Wallace, Roosevelt's secretary of agriculture, was responsible for carrying out the policy. It had some success – by 1937 the average income of farmers had almost doubled. But its weakness was that it did nothing to help the poorer farmers, the tenant-farmers and the farm labourers, many of whom were forced to leave the land to seek a better life in the cities.

3 The Civilian Conservation Corps (CCC)
Introduced in 1933, this was a popular Roosevelt idea to provide jobs for young men in conservation projects in the countryside. By 1940 about 2.5 million had 'enjoyed' a six-month spell in the CCC, which gave them a small wage ($30 a month, of which $25 had to be sent home to the family), as well as food, clothing and shelter.

4 The National Industrial Recovery Act (1933)
The most important part of the emergency programme, the National Industrial Recovery Act, was designed to get people back to work permanently, so that they would be able to buy more. This would stimulate industry and help the economy to function normally. The Act introduced *the Public Works Administration (PWA)*, which organized and provided cash for the building of useful works – dams, bridges, roads, hospitals, schools, airports and government buildings – creating several million extra jobs. Another section of the Act set up *the National Recovery Administration (NRA)*, which abolished child labour, introduced a maximum eight-hour working day and a minimum wage, and thus helped to create more employment. Although these rules were not compulsory, employers were pressured to accept them; those who did were privileged to use an official sticker on their goods showing a blue eagle and the letters 'NRS'. The public was encouraged to boycott firms that refused to co-operate. The response was tremendous, with well over two million employers accepting the new standards.

5 The Federal Emergency Relief Administration (1933)
Further relief and recovery were provided by the Federal Emergency Relief Administration, which provided $500 million of federal cash to enable the state governments to provide relief and soup kitchens.

6 The Works Progress Administration (WPA)
Founded in 1935, this funded a variety of projects such as roads, schools and hospitals (similar to the PWA but smaller-scale projects), and the Federal Theatre Project created jobs for playwrights, artists, actors, musicians and circus performers, as well as increasing public appreciation of the arts.

7 The Social Security Act (1935)
This introduced old-age pensions and unemployment insurance schemes, to be jointly financed by federal and state governments, employers and workers. However, this was not a great success at the time, because payments were usually not very generous; nor was there any provision made for sickness insurance. The USA was lagging well behind countries such as Germany and Britain in social welfare.

8 Working conditions
Two acts encouraged trade unions and helped improve working conditions.

- *The Wagner Act (1935)*, the work of Senator Robert F. Wagner of New York, gave unions a proper legal foundation and the right to bargain for their members in any dispute with management. It also set up the National Labour Relations Board, to which workers could appeal against unfair practices by management.

- *The Fair Labour Standards Act (1938)* introduced a maximum 45-hour working week as well as a minimum wage in certain low-paid trades, and made most child labour illegal.

9   Other measures

Also included in the New Deal were such measures as *the Tennessee Valley Authority (TVA)*, which revitalized a huge area of rural America which had been ruined by soil erosion and careless farming (see Map 22.2). The new authority built dams to provide cheap electricity, and organized conservation, irrigation and afforestation to prevent soil erosion. Other initiatives included loans for householders in danger of losing their homes because they could not afford mortgage repayments; slum clearance and building of new houses and flats; increased taxes on the incomes of the wealthy; and trade agreements which at last reduced American tariffs in return for tariff reductions by the other party to the treaty (in the hope of increasing American exports). One of the very first New Deal measures in 1933 was the end of Prohibition; as 'FDR' himself remarked, 'I think this would be a good time for beer.'

(c)   Opposition to the New Deal

It was inevitable that such a far-reaching programme would arouse criticism and opposition from both right and left. Critics on the left thought that the New Deal didn't go far enough, while those on the right were horrified at the lengths to which it went.

- *Businessmen* objected strongly to the growth of trade unions, the regulation of hours and wages, and increased taxation. These would encourage socialists and communists and might even lead to revolution. In their view, governments should not interfere so massively in economic affairs, because that would only stifle private enterprise with all the new rules and taxes.
- Some of *the state governments* resented the extent to which the federal government was interfering in what they considered to be internal state affairs.
- *The Supreme Court* claimed that the president was taking on too much power; it ruled that several measures (including NRA) were unconstitutional, and this held up their operation. The nine members were all elderly and were not Roosevelt appointees. However, the Supreme Court became more amenable during Roosevelt's second term after he had appointed five more co-operative judges to replace those who had died or resigned.
- There was also opposition from *socialists*, who felt that the New Deal was not drastic enough and still left too much power in the hands of big business. One of the most vociferous critics was Huey Long, governor of Louisiana and a member of the US senate. He believed that governments should spend heavily wherever it was necessary to help the poor. In 1934 he set up a scheme in Louisiana called Share Our Wealth which planned to make sure that every family had at least $5000, a house and a car, and old-age pensions. This was to be financed by taxing the rich, and he urged Roosevelt to do something similar throughout the nation. Long was considering running for president in the 1936, but he was assassinated in September 1935.
- From about the end of 1936 there was opposition from right-wing members of his own Democratic Party. What upset them was that the New Deal led some of the new trade unions to strike. Both General Motors and US Steel were forced to give way by sit-down strikes, and this encouraged the formation of numerous new unions. Dissident Democrats joined the Republicans in Congress and blocked further important legislation.

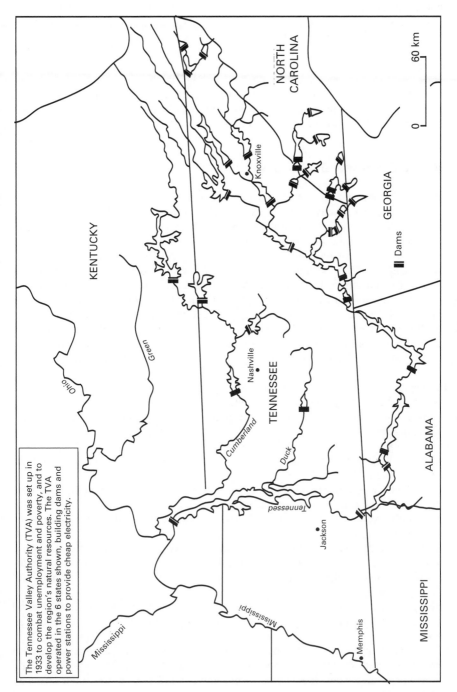

The Tennessee Valley Authority (TVA) was set up in 1933 to combat unemployment and poverty, and to develop the region's natural resources. The TVA operated in the 6 states shown, building dams and power stations to provide cheap electricity.

Map 22.2   **The Tennessee Valley Authority, 1933**

- Some people poured scorn on the wide variety of new organizations, known by their initials. Ex-president Hoover remarked: 'There are only four letters of the alphabet not now in use by the administration. When we establish the Quick Loan Corporation for Xylophones, Yachts and Zithers, the alphabet of our fathers will be exhausted.' From then on the term 'Alphabet Agencies' stuck.

Nevertheless, *Roosevelt was tremendously popular with the millions of ordinary Americans*, the 'forgotten men', as he called them, who had benefited from his policies. He had won the support of trade unions and of many farmers and black people. Although the forces of the right did their best to remove him in 1936 and 1940, Roosevelt won a crushing victory in 1936 and another comfortable one in 1940.

(d)   What did the New Deal achieve?

It has to be said that *it did not achieve all that 'FDR' had hoped*. Some of the measures failed completely or were only partially successful. The Farmers' Relief Act, for example, certainly helped farmers, but it threw many farm labourers out of work. Nor did it do much to help farmers living in parts of Kansas, Oklahoma and Texas; in the mid-1930s these areas were badly hit by drought and soil erosion, which turned them into a huge 'dustbowl' (see Map 22.1). Although unemployment was reduced to less than 8 million by 1937, it was still a serious problem. Part of the failure was due to the Supreme Court's opposition. Another reason was that although he was bold in many ways, Roosevelt was too cautious in the amounts of money he was prepared to spend to stimulate industry. In 1938 he reduced government spending, causing another recession, which sent unemployment up to 10.5 million. *The New Deal therefore did not rescue the USA from the depression; it was only the war effort which brought unemployment below the million mark in 1943.*

Still, in spite of this, Roosevelt's first eight years in office were a remarkable period. Never before had an American government intervened so directly in the lives of ordinary people; never before had so much attention been focused on an American president. *And much was achieved.*

- In the early days the chief success of the New Deal was in providing relief for the destitute and jobless, and in the creation of millions of extra jobs.
- Confidence was restored in the financial system and the government, and some historians think it may even have prevented a violent revolution.
- The public works schemes and the Tennessee Valley Authority provided services of lasting value.
- Welfare benefits such as the 1935 Social Security Act were an important step towards a welfare state. Although 'rugged individualism' was still a vital ingredient in American society, the American government had accepted that it had a duty to help those in need.
- Many of the other innovations were continued – national direction of resources and collective bargaining between workers and management became accepted as normal.
- Some historians believe that Roosevelt's greatest achievement was to preserve what might be called 'the American middle way' – democracy and free enterprise – at a time when other states, like Germany and Italy, had responded to similar crises by turning to fascism. Federal government authority over the state governments had increased and Roosevelt had put in place the structures to enable Washington to manage the economy and social policy.

(e)   The Second World War and the American economy

It was the war that finally put an end to the depression. The USA entered the war in December 1941 after the Japanese had bombed the American naval base at Pearl Harbor in the Hawaiian Islands. However, the Americans had begun to supply Britain and France with aircraft, tanks and other armaments as soon as war broke out in Europe in September 1939. 'We have the men, the skills, and above all the will', said Roosevelt. 'We must be the arsenal of democracy.' Between June 1940 and December 1941, the USA provided 23 000 aircraft.

After Pearl Harbor, production of armaments soared: in 1943, 86 000 aircraft were built, while in 1944 the figure was over 96 000. It was the same with ships: in 1939 American shipyards turned out 237 000 tons of shipping; in 1943 this had risen to nearly 10 million tons. In fact the Gross National Product (GNP) of the USA almost doubled between 1939 and 1945. In June 1940 there were still 8 million people out of work, but by the end of 1942 there was almost full employment. It was calculated that by 1945 the war effort had created 7 million extra jobs in the USA. In addition, about 15 million Americans served in the armed forces. Economically therefore, the USA did well out of the Second World War – there were plenty of jobs, wages rose steadily, and there was no decline in the standard of living as there was in Europe.

FURTHER READING

Behr, E., *Prohibition: The 13 Years that Changed America* (BBC Books, 1997).

Black, C., *Franklin Delano Roosevelt: Champion of Freedom* (Public Affairs, 2005).

Brogan, H., *The Penguin History of the United States of America* (Penguin, 2001 edition).

Cooper, W. M., *Woodrow Wilson: A Biography* (Vintage, 2011).

Heale, M. J., *Franklin D. Roosevelt: The New Deal and War* (Lancaster Pamphlets, Routledge, 1997).

Luhrssen, D. and Jeansonne, G., *A Time of Paradox: America Since 1890* (Rowman & Littlefield, 2006).

Roberts, A., *A History of the English Speaking Peoples Since 1900* (Weidenfeld & Nicolson, 2006).

Smith, J. E., *FDR* (Random House, 2008 edition).

Temkin, M., *The Sacco – Vanzetti Affair: American Trial* (Yale University Press, 2009).

White, R. D., *Kingfish: The Reign of Huey P. Long* (Random House, 2007).

Zinn, H., *A People's History of the United States* (Harper Perennial, 2010 edition).

QUESTIONS

1   Explain what impact the First World War and the Bolshevik revolution in Russia had on politics and society in the USA in the years 1914 to 1929.

2   In what ways did African Americans campaign for civil rights in the years before the Great Depression? How did they respond to the activities of the Ku Klux Klan?

3   Explain why the Palmer Raids took place in 1920. How did attitudes in the USA towards immigrants change during the years 1920 to 1929?

4   How successful were Republican policies in helping the US economy in the years 1920 to 1932?

5   Explain why unemployment was a major problem in the USA during the 1930s, and why the problem was reduced in the years 1939–43.

6   Explain why there was opposition to President Roosevelt's New Deal. How success-
    ful do you think these critics were in the period 1933 to 1941?
7   Explain why Franklin D. Roosevelt won the presidential election of 1932. How
    successful were the New Deal policies in relieving the depression in rural areas during
    the years 1933 to 1941?
8   How accurate do you think it is to talk about the 'First' and 'Second' New Deals? How
    successful had Roosevelt's policies been in solving the economic problems of the USA
    by 1941?

■ There is a document question about Roosevelt and the New Deal on the website.

23

The USA since 1945

SUMMARY OF EVENTS

When the Second World War ended in 1945, the economic boom continued as factories switched from producing armaments to producing consumer goods. Lots of new goods had appeared by this time – TV sets, dishwashers, modern record players and tape recorders – and many ordinary working people could afford to buy these luxury goods for the first time. This was the big difference between the 1950s and the 1920s, when too many people had been too poor to keep the boom going. The 1950s was the time of the *affluent society*, and in the 20 years following the end of the war, GNP increased by almost eight times. *The USA continued to be the world's largest industrial power and the world's richest nation.*

In spite of the general affluence, there were still serious problems in American society. There was a great deal of poverty and constant unemployment; black people, on the whole, were still not getting their fair share of the prosperity, did not have equal rights with whites and were treated as second-class citizens. The Cold War caused some problems for Americans at home and led to another outbreak of anti-communist feeling, like the one after the First World War. There were unhappy experiences such as the assassinations of President Kennedy in Dallas, Texas, allegedly by Lee Harvey Oswald (1963), and of Dr Martin Luther King (1968). There was the failure of American policy in Vietnam, and the forced resignation of President Nixon (1974) as a result of the Watergate scandal, which shook confidence in American society and values, and in the American system. One reaction to this state of affairs was a wave of religious revivalism that led to calls for a return to a more strict moral code. The Christian 'New Right' became influential in politics, supporting Ronald Reagan and later George W. Bush.

After 1974 both political parties took turns in power, and confidence was gradually restored. Americans could claim that with the collapse of communism in Europe and the ending of the Cold War, their country had reached the peak of its achievement; it was now the world's only remaining superpower. Many Americans believed that, wherever it was necessary, the USA, the land of liberty and democracy, would lead the rest of the world forward into an era of peace and prosperity. However, as we saw in Chapter 12, the American attitude was resented so much that many people were driven towards extreme measures – terrorism, culminating in the terrible events of 11 September 2001, when the World Trade Center in New York was destroyed. President George W. Bush issued a declaration of war on terrorism and the USA became embroiled in a long military campaign in Iraq and Afghanistan. This was still continuing in 2013, an involvement that had important effects on domestic affairs in the USA. By the end of Bush's second term in 2008, the US economy was in a state of crisis, and the Republicans were defeated in the presidential election of November 2008. The Democrat, Barack Obama, became the USA's first African American president.

The presidents of the post-war period were:

1945–53	Harry S. Truman	Democrat
1953–61	Dwight D. Eisenhower	Republican
1961–3	John F. Kennedy	Democrat
1963–9	Lyndon B. Johnson	Democrat
1969–74	Richard M. Nixon	Republican
1974–7	Gerald R. Ford	Republican
1977–81	Jimmy Carter	Democrat
1981–9	Ronald Reagan	Republican
1989–93	George Bush	Republican
1993–2001	Bill Clinton	Democrat
2001–2009	George W. Bush	Republican
2009–	Barack Obama	Democrat

23.1 POVERTY AND SOCIAL POLICIES

Ironically in the world's richest country, poverty remained a problem. Although the economy was on the whole a spectacular success story, with industry flourishing and exports booming, there was constant unemployment, which crept steadily up to 5.5 million (about 7 per cent of the labour force) in 1960. In spite of all the New Deal improvements, social welfare and pensions were still limited, and there was no national health system. It was calculated that in 1966 some 30 million Americans were living below the poverty line, and many of them were aged over 65.

(a)   Truman (1945–53)

Harry S. Truman, a man of great courage and common sense, once compared by a reporter to a bantam-weight prize fighter, had to face the special problem of returning the country to normal after the war. This was achieved, though not without difficulties: removal of wartime price controls caused inflation and strikes, and the Republicans won control of Congress in 1946. In the fight against poverty he had put forward a programme known as *the Fair Deal*, which he hoped would continue Roosevelt's New Deal. It included *a national health scheme, a higher minimum wage, slum clearance and full employment.*

However, the Republican majority in Congress threw out his proposals, and even passed, despite his veto, the Taft–Hartley Act (1947), which reduced trade-union powers. The attitude of Congress gained Truman working-class support and enabled him to win the 1948 presidential election, together with a Democrat majority in Congress. Some of the Fair Deal then became law (extension of social security benefits and an increase in the minimum wage), but Congress still refused to pass his national health and old-age pension schemes, which was a bitter disappointment for him. Many Southern Democrats voted against Truman because they disapproved of his support for black civil rights.

(b)   Eisenhower (1953–61)

Dwight D. Eisenhower had no programme for dealing with poverty, though he did not try to reverse the New Deal and the Fair Deal. Some improvements were made:

- insurance for the long-term disabled;
- financial help towards medical bills for people over 65;
- federal cash for housing;
- an extensive road-building programme, beginning in 1956, which over the next 14 years gave the USA a national network of first-class roads; this was to have important effects on people's everyday lives: cars, buses and trucks became the dominant form of transport, the motor industry received a massive boost, and this contributed towards the prosperity of the 1960s;
- more spending on education to encourage study in science and mathematics (it was feared that the Americans were falling behind the Russians, who in 1957 launched the first space satellite – Sputnik).

Farmers faced problems in the 1950s because increased production kept prices and incomes low. The government spent massive sums paying farmers to take land out of cultivation, but this was not a success: farm incomes did not rise rapidly and poorer farmers hardly benefited at all. Many of them sold up and moved into the cities.

Much remained to be done, but the Republicans were totally against national schemes such as Truman's health service, because they thought they were too much like socialism. However, some progress was made towards fairer treatment of the black population (see the next section).

(c) Kennedy (1961–3)

By the time John F. Kennedy became president in 1961, the problems were more serious, with over 4.5 million unemployed. He won the election partly because the Republicans were blamed for inflation and unemployment, and because he ran a brilliant campaign, accusing them of neglecting education and social services. He came over as elegant, articulate, witty and dynamic, and his election seemed to many people to be the beginning of a new era. He had a detailed programme which included medical payments for the poor and aged, more federal aid for education and housing, and increased unemployment and social security benefits. 'We stand today on the edge of a New Frontier', he said, and implied that only when these reforms were introduced would the frontier be crossed and poverty eliminated.

Unfortunately for Kennedy, he had to face strong opposition from Congress, where many right-wing Democrats as well as Republicans viewed his proposals as 'creeping socialism'. Hardly a single one was passed without some watering down, and many were rejected completely. Congress would allow no extra federal cash for education and rejected his scheme to pay hospital bills for elderly people. His successes were:

- an extension of social security benefits to each child whose father was unemployed;
- raising of the minimum wage from $1 to $1.25 an hour;
- federal loans to enable people to buy houses;
- federal grants to the states enabling them to extend the period covered by unemployment benefit.

Kennedy's overall achievement was limited: unemployment benefit was only enough for subsistence, and even that was only for a limited period. Unemployment still stood at 4.5 million in 1962, and soup kitchens had to be set up to feed poor families.

Illustration 23.1   **The assassination of Kennedy, 1963. Here the president slumps forward, seconds after having been shot**

(d)   Johnson (1963–9)

Kennedy's vice-president, Lyndon B. Johnson, became president when Kennedy was assassinated in Dallas, Texas, in 1963 (see Illus. 23.1). Coming from a humble background in Texas, he was just as committed as Kennedy to social reform, and achieved enough in his first year to enable him to win a landslide victory in the 1964 election. In 1964 Johnson's economic advisers fixed an annual income of $3000 for a family of two or more as the poverty line, and they estimated that over 9 million families (30 million people, nearly 20 per cent of the population) were on or below the line. Many of them were African Americans, Puerto Ricans, Native Americans (American Indians) and Mexicans. Johnson announced that he wanted to move America towards *the Great Society*, where there would be an end to poverty and racial injustice and 'abundance and liberty for all'.

Many of his measures became law, partly because after the 1964 elections the Democrats had a huge majority in Congress, and partly because Johnson was more skilful and persuasive in handling Congress than Kennedy had been.

- The *Economic Opportunity Act (1964)* provided a number of schemes under which young people from poor homes could receive job training and higher education.
- Other measures were the provision of federal money for special education schemes in slum areas, including help in paying for books and transport; financial aid for clearing slums and rebuilding city areas; and *the Appalachian Regional Development Act (1965)*, which created new jobs in one of the poorest regions.
- Full voting and civil rights were extended to all Americans, regardless of their colour (see the next section).
- Perhaps his most important innovation was *the Social Security Amendment Act (1965)*, also known as *Medicare*: this was a partial national health scheme, though it applied only to people over 65.

This is an impressive list, and yet the overall results were not as successful as Johnson would have hoped, for a number of reasons. His major problem from early 1965 was that *he was faced by the escalating war in Vietnam* (see Section 8.3). Johnson's great dilemma was how to fund both the war in Vietnam and the war on poverty. It has been suggested that the entire Great Society programme was under-financed because of the enormous expenditure on the war in Vietnam. The Republicans criticized Johnson for wanting to spend money on the poor instead of concentrating on Vietnam; they were supporters of *the strong American tradition of self-help*: it was up to the poor to help themselves and wrong to use taxpayers' money on schemes which, it was thought, would only make the poor more lazy. Thus many state governments failed to take advantage of federal offers of help. And the unfortunate president, trying to fight both wars at the same time, ended up losing in Vietnam, winning only a limited victory in the war against poverty, and damaging the US economy as well.

In the mid-1960s violence increased and seemed to be getting out of hand: there were riots in black ghettos, where the sense of injustice was strongest; there were student riots in the universities in protest against the Vietnam War. There were a number of political assassinations – President Kennedy in 1963, Martin Luther King and Senator Robert Kennedy in 1968. Between 1960 and 1967 the number of violent crimes rose by 90 per cent. Johnson could only hope that his 'war on poverty' would gradually remove the causes of discontent; beyond that he had no answer to the problem. The general discontent and especially the student protests about Vietnam ('LBJ, LBJ, how many kids have you burnt today?') caused Johnson not to stand for re-election in November 1968, and it helps to explain why the Republicans won, on a platform of restoring law and order.

(e) Nixon (1969–74)

Unemployment was soon rising again, with over 4 million out of work in 1971; their plight was worsened by rapidly rising prices. The Republicans were anxious to cut public expenditure; Nixon reduced spending on Johnson's poverty programme, and introduced a wages and prices freeze. However, social security benefits were increased, Medicare was extended to disabled people under 65, and a Council for Urban Affairs was set up to try to deal with the problems of slums and ghettos. Violence was less of a problem under Nixon, partly because protesters could now see the approaching end of America's controversial involvement in Vietnam, and because students were allowed some say in running their colleges and universities.

During the last quarter of the twentieth century, in spite of some economic success under Reagan, the underlying problem of poverty and deprivation was still there. In the world's richest country there was a permanent underclass of unemployed, poor and deprived people, the inner cities needed revitalizing, and yet federal spending on welfare, although it increased after 1981, remained well below the level of government welfare funding in western European states like Germany, France and Britain (see Section 23.5(c) for later developments).

23.2 RACIAL PROBLEMS AND THE CIVIL RIGHTS MOVEMENT

(a) The government's attitude changes

As we saw earlier (Section 22.5), African Americans were still being treated as second-class citizens right up to the Second World War. Even when American troops were travelling aboard the *Queen Mary* to fight in Europe, blacks and whites were segregated – blacks had to travel in the depths of the ship near the engine room, well away from the fresh air. However, the attitude of the nation's leaders was changing. In 1946 President Truman appointed a committee to investigate civil rights. It recommended that Congress should pass laws to stop racial discrimination in jobs and to allow blacks to vote. *What caused this change of heart?* The committee itself gave several reasons:

1   Some politicians were worried by their consciences; they felt that it was not morally right to treat fellow human beings in such an unfair way.
2   Excluding black people from top jobs was a waste of talent and expertise.
3   It was important to do something to calm the black population, who were becoming more outspoken in their demands for civil rights.
4   The USA could hardly claim to be a genuinely democratic country and leader of the 'free world' when 10 per cent of its population were denied voting and other rights. This gave the USSR a chance to condemn the USA as 'a consistent oppressor of underprivileged peoples'. The American government wanted that excuse removed.
5   Nationalism was growing rapidly in Asia and Africa. Non-whites in India and Indonesia were on the point of gaining independence. These new states might turn against the USA and towards communism if American whites continued their unfair treatment of blacks.

Over the next few years, during the Eisenhower presidency, the government and the Supreme Court introduced *new laws to bring about racial equality.*

- Separate schools for blacks and whites were illegal and unconstitutional; some black people had to be included on all juries (1954).
- Schools must be desegregated 'with all deliberate speed'; this meant that black children had to attend white schools, and vice versa.
- The 1957 Civil Rights Act set up a commission to investigate the denial of voting rights to black people.
- The 1960 Civil Rights Act provided help for blacks to register as voters; but this was not very effective, since many were afraid to register for fear of being harassed by whites.

Unfortunately laws and regulations were not always carried out. For example, whites in some Southern states refused to carry out the school desegregation order. In September 1957, when Governor Faubus of Arkansas defied a Supreme Court order by refusing to desegregate schools, President Eisenhower sent federal troops to escort nine black children into the High School at Little Rock. They were greeted outside the school by a mob of protesters who at first refused to move. The troops had to disperse them at bayonet point; the nine students entered the school escorted by 22 armed guards, who took them home again after school. The escort continued for several months afterwards. This was a symbolic victory, but Southern whites continued to defy the law, and by 1961 only 25 per cent of schools and colleges in the South were desegregated. In 1961 the Governor of Mississippi refused the application of a black student, James Meredith, to the all-white state university; he was eventually accepted the following year.

(b)   Dr Martin Luther King and the non-violent campaign for equal rights

In the mid-1950s a mass Civil Rights movement developed. *This happened for a number of reasons*:

- By 1955 a larger proportion of black people lived in the North than was the case earlier. In 1900 almost 90 per cent of all blacks lived in the Southern states, working on the plantations. By 1955 almost 50 per cent lived in Northern industrial cities, where they became more aware of political issues. A prosperous black middle class developed which produced talented leaders.
- As Asian and African states such as India and Ghana gained their independence, African Americans resented their own unfair treatment more than ever.
- Black people, whose hopes had been raised by Truman's committee, grew increasingly impatient at the slow pace and the small amount of change. Even the small advances they made aroused intense hostility among many Southern whites; the Ku Klux Klan revived and some Southern state governments banned the National Association for the Advancement of Colored People (NAACP). It was obvious that only a nationwide mass movement would have any effect.

The campaign took off in 1955 when *Dr Martin Luther King* (see Illus. 23.2), a Baptist minister, emerged as the outstanding leader of the non-violent Civil Rights movement. After a black woman, Rosa Parks, had been arrested for sitting in a seat reserved for whites on a bus in Montgomery, Alabama, a boycott of all Montgomery buses was organized. King soon found himself the chief spokesman for the boycott; as a committed Christian, he insisted that the campaign must be peaceful:

Love must be our regulating ideal. If you will protest courageously, and yet with dignity and Christian love, when the history books are written in future generations, historians

Illustration 23.2   **Dr Martin Luther King**

will have to say 'there lived a great people – a black people – who injected new dignity into the veins of civilization'.

White segregationalists responded with violence: bombs exploded in four black churches and Martin Luther King's house. The black people of Montgomery refused to be intimidated. The campaign continued and in November 1956 its goal was achieved: segregated seating was stopped on Montgomery buses. Soon afterwards the Supreme Court ruled that any segregation on public buses was unconstitutional. This was just a beginning: in 1957 the Southern Christian Leadership Conference (SCLC) was founded and King was elected as its president. Its aim was to achieve full black equality by non-violent methods. In the summer of 1957 King launched a moral reform campaign, emphasizing that if black people wished to have complete equality with whites, they must 'seek to gain the respect of others by improving on [their] shortcomings'. In a series of sermons all over the South, he criticized what some whites called 'bad niggers', meaning those who were lazy, promiscuous, slovenly, drunken, ignorant and downright criminal. Only when such people had undergone 'a process of self-purification' to produce 'a calm and loving dignity befitting good citizens', could all black people become fully equal.

The campaign of sit-ins and peaceful disobedience reached a climax in 1963 when King organized successful demonstrations against segregation in Birmingham, Alabama. The police used tear gas, clubs, dogs and water-hoses against the demonstrators, and King was arrested and briefly imprisoned. Although the campaign had attracted world attention and sympathy, and some progress had been made, there was still a long way to go before black people could enjoy equal rights with whites. The Kennedy government was sympathetic to black aspirations but was desperately trying to keep the campaign peaceful, which was becoming more difficult. As Howard Zinn points out, how could you expect blacks to remain peaceful

> when bombs kept exploding in churches, when new 'civil rights' laws did not change the root condition of black people. In the spring of 1963, the rate of unemployment for whites was 4.8 percent. For nonwhites it was 12.1 percent. According to government estimates, one-fifth of the white population was below the poverty line, and one-half of the black population was below that line. The civil rights bills emphasized voting, but voting was not a fundamental solution to racism or poverty. In Harlem, blacks who had voted for years, still lived in rat-infested slums.

A huge march on Washington was organized for August 1963, to protest at the failure to solve the problem. About a quarter of a million people, both black and white, gathered to listen to the speakers, and it was here that Martin Luther King made one of his most moving speeches. He talked about his dream of a future America in which everybody would be equal:

> I have a dream that my four little children will one day live in a nation where they will not be judged by the colour of their skin, but by the content of their character.

In 1964 King was awarded the Nobel Peace Prize. But not everything he attempted was successful. In 1966 when he led a campaign against segregated housing in Chicago, he came up against bitter white opposition and could make no progress.

King admitted that the achievements of the Civil Rights movement had not been as dramatic as he had hoped. Together with the SCLC he began the Poor People's Campaign in 1967, which aimed to alleviate poverty among black people and other disadvantaged groups such as American Indians, Puerto Ricans, Mexicans and even poor whites. They aimed to present a bill of economic rights to Congress. King also launched himself into criticism of the Vietnam War, and this upset President Johnson, who had been sympathetic to the civil rights campaign, as well as losing him some of his support among the whites. The FBI began to harass him, but he was undeterred. Still insisting on non-violence, he decided that the way forward was to have huge demonstrations lasting over a period, and was planning what he called a Poor People's Encampment to be set up in Washington to act as a permanent reminder to the government. However, tragically, in April 1968, King was assassinated by a white man, James Earl Ray, in Memphis, Tennessee, where he had gone to support a strike of refuse workers.

Dr Martin Luther King is remembered as probably the most famous of the black civil rights leaders. He was a brilliant speaker and the fact that he emphasized non-violent protest gained him much support and respect even among whites. He played a major part in the achievement of civil and political equality for black people, although, of course, others also made valuable contributions. He was not much involved, for example, in the campaign to desegregate education. He was fortunate that the presidents he had to deal with – *Kennedy (1961–3) and Johnson (1963–9) – were both sympathetic to the Civil Rights movement.* Kennedy admitted in 1963 that an African American had

> half as much chance of completing high school as a white, one-third as much chance of completing college, twice as much chance of becoming unemployed, one-seventh as much chance of earning $10,000 dollars a year, and a life expectancy which is seven years less.

Kennedy showed his good intentions by appointing the USA's first black ambassador and by presenting a Civil Rights Bill to Congress. This was delayed at first by the conservative Congress but passed in 1964 after a debate lasting 736 hours. It was a far-reaching measure: it guaranteed the vote for blacks and made racial discrimination in public facilities (such as hotels, restaurants and shops) and in jobs illegal. Again the Act was not always carried out, especially in the South, where black people were still afraid to vote.

Johnson introduced *the Voting Rights Act (1965)* to try to make sure that black people exercised their right to vote. He followed it up with another *Civil Rights Act (1968)*, which made it illegal to discriminate in selling property or letting accommodation. Again there was bitter white hostility to these reforms, and the problem was to make sure that the Acts were carried out.

(c)   The Black Muslims

Although progress was being made, many African Americans were impatient with the slow pace and began to look for different approaches to the problem. *Some black people converted to the Black Muslim faith* – a sect known as *Nation of Islam*, arguing that Christianity was the religion of the racist whites. They believed that black people were the superior race, and that whites were evil. One of the movement's best known leaders was *Malcolm X* (formerly Malcolm Little), whose father had been murdered by the Ku Klux Klan. He was a charismatic speaker and a good organizer; he dismissed the idea of racial integration and equality and claimed that the only way forward was black pride, black self-dependence and complete separation from the whites. He became extremely popular, especially among young people, and the movement grew. Its most famous convert was the world heavyweight boxing champion Cassius Clay, who changed his name to Muhammad Ali.

Malcolm X came into conflict with other Black Muslim leaders, who began to look on him as a fanatic because of his willingness to use violence. In 1964 he left the Nation of Islam and started his own organization. However, later that year his views began to change: after a pilgrimage to Mecca, he became more moderate, acknowledging that not all whites were evil. In October 1964 he converted to orthodox Islam and began to preach about the possibility of peaceful black/white integration. Tragically, the hostility between Malcolm X's movement and Nation of Islam exploded into violence, and in February 1965 he was shot dead by a group of Black Muslims in Harlem.

(d) Violent protest

More militant organizations included the Black Power movement and the Black Panther Party. *The Black Power movement* emerged in 1966 under the leadership of *Stokeley Carmichael*. He was a West Indian who had moved to the USA in 1952 and became a strong supporter of Martin Luther King. However, he was outraged by the brutal treatment suffered by civil rights campaigners at the hands of the Ku Klux Klan and other whites. The Black Power movement encouraged robust self-defence and self-determination, and 1967 saw probably the worst urban riots in American history. A total of 83 people were shot dead and hundreds were injured, the vast majority of whom were black civilians. In 1968 Carmichael began to speak out against American involvement in the Vietnam War; when he returned to the USA after a trip abroad, his passport was confiscated. He decided he could no longer live under such a repressive system; in 1969 he left the country and went to Guinea, in West Africa, where he lived until his death in 1998.

The Black Panther Party for Self-defence was founded in 1966 in Oakland, California, by *Huey Newton, Leroy Eldridge Cleaver and Bobby Searle*. Its original aim, as its name implies, was to protect people in the black ghettos from police brutality. Eventually the party became more militant and developed into a Marxist revolutionary group; *their programme included*:

- the arming of all black people;
- the exemption of blacks from military service;
- the release of all blacks from jail;
- payment of compensation to blacks for all the years of ill-treatment and exploitation by white Americans;
- practical on-the-spot help with social services for black people living below the poverty line.

They used the same methods against white people as the Ku Klux Klan had used for years against black people – arson, beatings and murders. In 1964 there were race riots in Harlem (New York) and in 1965 the most severe race riots in American history took place in the Watts district of Los Angeles; 35 people were killed and over a thousand injured. The police harassed the Panthers unmercifully, so much so that Congress ordered an investigation into their conduct. By the mid-1970s the Panthers had lost many of their leading activists, who had either been killed or were in prison. This, plus the fact that most non-violent black leaders felt that the Panthers were bringing the whole Civil Rights movement into disrepute, caused them to change tactics and concentrate on the social service aspects of their activities. By 1985 the Panthers had ceased to exist as an organized party.

(e) Mixed fortunes

By that time great progress had been made, especially in the area of voting; by 1975 there were 18 black members of Congress, 278 black members of state governments, and 120 black mayors had been elected. However, there could never be full equality until black poverty and discrimination in jobs and housing were removed. Unemployment was always higher among black people; in the big Northern cities they were still living in overcrowded slum areas known as *ghettos*, from which the whites had moved out; and a large proportion of the jail population was black. *In the early 1990s, most black Americans were worse off economically than they had been 20 years earlier.* The underlying tensions broke out in the spring of 1992 in Los Angeles: after four white policemen were acquitted of beating up a black motorist (in spite of the incident having been caught on video), crowds of black people rioted. Many were killed, thousands were injured, and millions of dollars worth of damage was done to property.

Yet at the same time, a prosperous African American middle class had emerged, and talented individuals were able to make it to the top. The best example was Colin Powell, whose parents had moved to New York from Jamaica. He had a successful career in the army and in 1989 was appointed chairman of the Joint Chiefs of Staff, the first African American to reach the highest position in the US military. In the Gulf War of 1990–1 he commanded the UN forces with distinction. After his retirement in 1993 he became involved in politics; both parties hoped he would join them, but he eventually declared himself a Republican. There was talk that he might run for president in the elections of 2000, but he chose not to. In January 2001, George W. Bush appointed him secretary of state, the US head of foreign affairs. Again he was the first African American to occupy such a vitally important post.

In 2003 it was reported that, because of higher birth rates and immigration, Hispanics or Latinos had become the largest minority group in the USA, making up 13 per cent of the total population; with a total of 37 million they had overtaken African Americans, who totalled 36.2 million (12.7 per cent). At the same time, the birth rate among the white population was falling. Demographers pointed out that if these trends continued, the political parties would be forced to take more account of the wishes and needs of both Latinos and black Americans. In the presidential election of 2000, more than 80 per cent of African American voters backed the Democrats, while in the 2002 mid-term elections, about 70 per cent of Latinos voted Democrat. In 2009 the Democrat candidate, Barack Obama, became the first African American president of the USA.

23.3 ANTI-COMMUNISM AND SENATOR MCCARTHY

(a) Anti-communist feeling

After the Second World War the USA took upon itself the world role of preventing the spread of communism; this caused the country to become deeply involved in Europe, Korea, Vietnam, Latin America and Cuba (see Chapters 7, 8, 21 and 26). There had been a strong anti-communist movement in the USA ever since the communists had come to power in Russia in 1917. In a way this is surprising, because the American Communist Party (formed in 1919) attracted little support. Even during the depression of the 1930s, when a mass swing to the left might have been expected, party membership was never more than 100 000, and there was never a real communist threat.

Some US historians argue that Senator Joseph McCarthy and other right-wingers who whipped up anti-communist feelings were trying to protect what they saw as the traditional American way of life, with its emphasis on 'self-help' and 'rugged individualism'. They thought that this was being threatened by the rapid changes in society, and by developments like the New Deal and the Fair Deal, which they disliked because they were financed by higher taxation. Many were deeply religious people, some of them fundamentalists, who wanted to get back to what they called 'true Christianity'. It was difficult for them to pinpoint exactly who was responsible for this American 'decline', and so they focused on communism as the source of all evil. The spread of communism in eastern Europe, the beginning of the Cold War, the communist victory in China (1949) and the attack on South Korea by communist North Korea (June 1950) threw the 'radical right' into a panic.

1 Troop demobilization

The rapid demobilization of American troops at the end of the war worried some people. The general wish was to 'bring the boys home' as soon as possible, and the army planned to have 5.5 million soldiers back home by July 1946. However, Congress insisted that it should be done much more quickly, and that the army should be dramatically reduced in size. By 1950 it was down to only 600 000 men, none of them fully prepared for service. This thoroughly alarmed the people, who thought that the USA should be ready to take deterrent action against communist expansion.

2 Fear of espionage

Reports of espionage (spying) prompted Truman to set up a *Loyalty Review Board* to investigate people working in the government, the civil service, atomic research and armaments (1947). During the next five years, over 6 million people were investigated; no cases of espionage were discovered, though about 500 people were sacked because it was decided that their loyalty to the USA was 'questionable'.

3 Alger Hiss and the Rosenbergs

Much more sensational were the cases of Alger Hiss and Julius and Ethel Rosenberg. Hiss, a former top official in the State Department (the equivalent of the British Foreign Office), was accused of being a communist and of passing secret documents to Moscow. He was eventually found guilty of perjury and given a five-year jail sentence (1950). The Rosenbergs were convicted of passing secret information about the atomic bomb to the Russians, though much of the evidence was doubtful. They were sentenced to death in the electric chair. They were eventually executed in 1953, in spite of worldwide appeals for mercy.

These cases helped to intensify the anti-communist feeling sweeping America, and led Congress to pass *the McCarran Act*, which required organizations suspected of being communist to supply lists of members. Many of these people were later sacked from their jobs, although they had committed no offence. Truman, who felt that things were going too far, vetoed this Act, but Congress passed it, over his veto.

4 McCarthyism

Senator Joseph McCarthy was a right-wing Republican who hit the headlines in 1950 when he claimed (in a speech at Wheeling, West Virginia, on 9 February) that the State Department was 'infested' with communists. He claimed to have a list of 205 people who were members of the Party and who were 'still working and shaping policy'. Although he could produce no evidence to support his claims, many people believed him, and he launched a campaign to root out the communists. All sorts of people were accused of being communists: socialists, liberals, intellectuals, artists, pacifists and anyone whose views did not appear orthodox were attacked and hounded out of their jobs for 'un-American activities'.

McCarthy became the most feared man in the country, and was supported by many national newspapers. McCarthyism reached its climax soon after Eisenhower's election. McCarthy won many votes for the Republicans among those who took his accusations seriously, but he went too far when he began to accuse leading generals of having communist sympathies. Some of the hearings were televised and many people were shocked at the brutal way in which he banged the table with rage and abused and bullied witnesses. Even

Republican senators felt he was going too far, and the Senate condemned him by 67 votes to 22 (December 1954). McCarthy foolishly attacked the president for supporting the Senate, but this finally ruined his reputation and McCarthyism was finished. But it had been an unpleasant experience for many Americans: at least 9 million people had been 'investigated', thousands of innocent people had lost their jobs, and an atmosphere of suspicion and insecurity had been created.

5 After McCarthy

Right-wing extremism continued even after the disgrace of McCarthy. Public opinion had turned against him not because he was attacking communists, but because of his brutal methods and because he had overstepped the mark by criticizing generals. Anti-communist feeling was still strong and Congress passed an Act making the Communist Party illegal (1954). There were also worries in case communism gained a foothold in the countries of Latin America, especially after Fidel Castro came to power in Cuba in 1959, and began nationalizing American-owned estates and factories. In response, Kennedy launched *the Alliance for Progress (1961)*, which aimed to pump billions of dollars of aid into Latin America to enable economic and social reform to be carried out. Kennedy did genuinely want to help the poor nations of Latin America, and American aid was put to good use. But other motives were important too.

- By helping to solve economic problems, the USA hoped to reduce unrest, making it less likely that communist governments would come to power in these states.
- US industry would benefit, because it was understood that much of the cash would be spent buying American goods (see Chapter 26 for full details).

(b) The military–industrial complex

Another by-product of the Cold War was what President Eisenhower called the 'military–industrial complex'. This was the situation in which the American military leaders and armaments manufacturers worked together in a partnership. The army chiefs decided what was needed, and as the arms race developed, more and more orders were placed – atomic bombs, then hydrogen bombs, and later many different types of missile (see Section 7.4). Armaments manufacturers made huge profits, though nobody was quite sure just how much, because all the dealings were secret. *It was in their interests to keep the Cold War going* – the more it intensified, the greater their profits. When the Russians launched the first space satellite (Sputnik) in 1957, Eisenhower set up *the National Aeronautics and Space Administration (NASA)*, and even more expensive orders were placed.

At any sign of a possible improvement in East–West relations, for example when Khrushchev talked about 'peaceful coexistence', the armaments manufacturers were far from happy. Some historians have suggested that the American U-2 spy plane that was shot down over Russia in 1960 was sent deliberately in order to ruin the summit conference, which was about to begin in Paris (see Section 7.3(c)). If true, this would mean that the military–industrial partnership was even more powerful than the super-corporations – so powerful that it was able to influence American foreign policy. The amounts of cash involved were staggering: in 1950 the total budget was around $40 billion, of which $12 billion was military spending. By 1960 the military budget was almost $46 billion, and that was half the country's total budget. By 1970, military spending had reached $80 billion. A Senate report found that over 2000 former top officers were employed by defence contractors, who were all making fortunes.

23.4 NIXON AND WATERGATE

Richard M. Nixon (1969–74) was Eisenhower's vice-president from 1956, and had narrowly lost to Kennedy in the 1960 election. On his election in 1969 he faced an unenviable task – what to do about Vietnam, poverty, unemployment, violence and the general crisis of confidence that was afflicting America (see Section 23.1(e) for his social policies).

(a) Foreign policy

Overseas problems, especially Vietnam, dominated his presidency (at least until 1973 when Watergate took over). After the Democrat majority in Congress refused to vote any further cash for the war, Nixon extricated the USA from Vietnam with a negotiated peace signed in 1973 (see Section 8.3(c)), to the vast relief of most of the American people, who celebrated 'peace with honour'. Yet in April 1975, South Vietnam fell to the communists; the American struggle to prevent the spread of communism in south-east Asia had ended in failure, and her world reputation was somewhat tattered.

However, *Nixon was responsible for a radical and constructive change in foreign policy* when he sought, with some success, to improve the USA's relations with the USSR and China (see Section 8.6(a–c)). His visit to meet Chairman Mao in Beijing in February 1972 was a brilliant success; in May 1972 he was in Moscow for the signing of an arms limitation treaty.

By the end of his first term in office, Nixon's achievements seemed full of promise: he had brought the American people within sight of peace, he was following sensible policies of détente with the communist world, and law and order had returned. The Americans had enjoyed a moment of glory by putting the first men on the moon (Neil Armstrong and Ed 'Buzz' Aldrin, 20 July 1969). Nixon won the election of November 1972 overwhelmingly, and in January 1973 was inaugurated for a second term. However, his second term was ruined by a new crisis.

(b) The Watergate scandal

The scandal broke in January 1973 when a number of men were charged with having broken into the Democratic Party offices in the Watergate Building, Washington, in June 1972 during the presidential election campaign. They had planted listening devices and photocopied important documents. It turned out that the burglary had been organized by leading members of Nixon's staff, who were sent to jail. Nixon insisted that he knew nothing about the affair, but suspicions mounted when he consistently refused to hand over tapes of discussions in the White House which, it was thought, would settle matters one way or the other. The president was widely accused of having deliberately 'covered up' for the culprits. He received a further blow when his vice-president, Spiro Agnew, was forced to resign (December 1973) after facing charges of bribery and corruption. He was replaced by Gerald Ford, a little-known politician, but one with an unblemished record.

Nixon was called on to resign, but refused even when it was discovered that he had been guilty of tax evasion. He was threatened with *impeachment* (a formal accusation of his crimes before the Senate, which would then try him for the offences). To avoid this, Nixon resigned (August 1974) and Ford became president. It was a tragic end to a presidency which had shown positive achievements, especially in foreign affairs, but the scandal shook people's faith in politicians and in a system which could allow such things to happen. Ford won admiration for the way in which he restored dignity to American politics, but given the recession, unemployment and inflation, it was no surprise when he lost the 1976 election to the Democrat James Earl Carter.

23.5 THE CARTER–REAGAN–BUSH ERA, 1977–93

(a) Jimmy Carter (1977–81)

Carter's presidency was something of a disappointment. He was elected as an outsider – ex-naval officer, peanut farmer, ex-Governor of Georgia, and a man of deep religious convictions; he was the newcomer to Washington who would restore the public's faith in politicians. *He managed some significant achievements. He*

- stopped giving American aid to authoritarian right-wing governments merely to keep communism out;
- co-operated with Britain to bring about black majority rule in Zimbabwe (see Section 24.4(c));
- signed a second Strategic Arms Limitation Treaty (SALT II) with the USSR in 1979;
- played a vital role in the Camp David talks, bringing peace between Egypt and Israel (see Section 11.6).

Unfortunately Carter's lack of experience of handling Congress meant that he had the same difficulties as Kennedy, and he failed to pilot the majority of his reforming programme into law. By 1980 the world recession was biting deeply, bringing factory closures, unemployment and oil shortages. He was a great disappointment to the Christian conservatives, many of whom had voted for him. They expected him to support their call for the banning of abortion and for making prayers a compulsory part of education in state schools, neither of which materialized. Apart from Camp David, Democratic foreign policy seemed unimpressive; even an achievement like SALT II was unpopular with the military leaders and the arms manufacturers, since it threatened to reduce their profits. The Christian Right saw it as a capitulation to ungodly communism. The Americans were unable to take effective action against the Russian occupation of Afghanistan (1979). Just as frustrating was their failure to free a number of American hostages seized in Tehran by Iranian students (November 1979) and held for over a year. The Iranians were trying to force the American government to return the exiled Shah and his fortune, but stalemate persisted even after the Shah's death. A combination of these problems and frustrations resulted in a decisive Republican victory in the election of November 1980. Ironically the hostages were set free minutes after the inauguration of Carter's successor (January 1981).

(b) Ronald Reagan (1981–9)

Reagan, a former film star, quickly became the most popular president since the Second World War. He was a reassuring, kindly father-figure who won a reputation as 'The Great Communicator' because of his straightforward and simple way of addressing the American public. *Americans particularly admired his determination to stand no nonsense from the Soviets* (as he called the USSR); he wanted to work for peaceful relations with them, but from a position of strength. He persuaded Congress to vote extra cash to build MX intercontinental ballistic missiles (May 1983) and deployed Cruise and Pershing missiles in Europe (December 1983). He intervened in Central America, sending financial and military aid to rebel groups in El Salvador and Nicaragua (see Section 26.3(c)), whose governments he believed to be communist-backed. He continued friendly relations with China, visiting Beijing in April 1984, but he did not meet any top Russian politicians until shortly before the presidential election of November 1984.

On the home front, Reagan brought with him some new ideas about how to run the economy. He believed that the way to restore US greatness and prosperity was by applying what was known as 'supply-side economics'. This was the theory that by lowering taxes, the government would actually draw in more revenue. Lower taxes would mean that both firms and individual consumers were left with more cash to spend on investment and on buying goods. This would encourage people to work harder, creating greater demand for goods and therefore more jobs, and this in turn would save expenditure on unemployment and welfare benefits. All this extra economic activity would produce more tax revenue for the government. Reagan was greatly impressed by the theories of American economist Milton Friedman and Friedrich Hayek, an Austrian who had set out his New Right economic ideas in his book *The Road to Serfdom*, first published in 1944. Their 'monetarist' theories opposed socialism and the welfare state on the grounds that they involved too much government interference and regulation. They argued that people should be free to run their own lives and businesses with a minimum of government regulation. Reagan's policies – 'Reaganomics', as they became known – were based on these theories. 'Government is not the solution to our problems,' he told the nation; 'government *is* the problem.' Consequently he aimed to remove restrictions on business, to reduce government spending on welfare (though not on defence), to balance the federal budget, to introduce a free-market economy, and to control the money supply in order to keep inflation low.

Unfortunately the 'Reagan revolution' got off to a bad start. For the first three years the government failed to balance the budget, partly because of a significant increase in defence spending. The 'supply-side' stimulus failed to work, the economy went into recession and unemployment rose to 10 per cent – some eleven million people were out of work. Government expenditure on welfare was inadequate at the time of greatest need, there was an adverse trade balance and the budget deficit, though not exactly out of control, was certainly enormous.

The economy began to recover in 1983 and continued to grow for the next six years. The recovery started in time for the presidential election of November 1984. Reagan could claim that his policies were working, though his critics pointed out that government spending had actually increased in all major areas including welfare and social security. The national debt had increased massively, while investment had declined. In fact the recovery had taken place *in spite of* 'Reaganomics'. Another criticism levelled at the government was that its policies had benefited the rich but increased the tax burden on the poor. According to Congressional investigations, taxes took only 4 per cent of the income of the poorest families in 1978, but over 10 per cent in 1984. In April 1984 it was calculated that, thanks to successive Reagan budgets since 1981, the poorest families had gained an average of $20 a year from tax cuts, but had lost $410 a year in benefits. On the other hand, households with the highest incomes (over $80 000 a year) had gained an average of $8400 from tax cuts and lost $130 in benefits. One of the 'supply-side' economists' most attractive predictions – that the new wealth would 'trickle down' to the poor – had not been fulfilled.

Reagan nevertheless retained his popularity with the vast majority of Americans and *won a sweeping victory in the presidential election of November 1984* over his Democratic rival, Walter Mondale, who was portrayed by the media, probably unfairly, as an unexciting and old-fashioned politician with nothing new to offer. Reagan took 59 per cent of the popular vote; at 73, he was the oldest person ever to be president.

During his second term in office, everything seemed to go wrong for him. He was dogged by economic problems, disasters, scandals and controversies.

1   Economic problems

- *Congress became increasingly worried by the rapidly growing federal budget deficit.* The Senate rejected Reagan's 1987 budget for increased defence spending at a time when they felt it was vital to reduce the deficit. Senators also complained that the cash allowed for Medicare would be 5 per cent short of the amount needed to cover rising medical costs. In the end, Reagan was forced to accept a cut in defence spending of around 8 per cent, and to spend more than he wanted on social services (February 1986).
- *There was a serious depression in the agricultural Midwest*, which brought falling prices, falling government subsidies and rising unemployment.

2   Disasters in the space programme

1986 was a disastrous year for America's space programme. The space shuttle *Challenger* exploded only seconds after lift-off, killing all seven crew members (January). A Titan rocket carrying secret military equipment exploded immediately after lift-off (April), and in May a Delta rocket failed, the third successive failure of a major space launch. This seemed likely to delay for many years Reagan's plans to develop a permanent orbital space station.

3   Foreign policy problems

- *The bombing of Libya (April 1986) provoked a mixed reaction.* Reagan was convinced that Libyan-backed terrorists were responsible for numerous outrages, including bomb attacks at Rome and Vienna airports in December 1985. After Libyan missile attacks on US aircraft, American F-111 bombers attacked the Libyan cities of Tripoli and Benghazi, killing 100 civilians. While the attack was widely applauded in most circles in the USA, world opinion on the whole condemned it as an overreaction.
- *American policy towards South Africa caused a row between president and Congress.* Reagan wanted only limited sanctions but Congress was in favour of a much stronger package to try to bring an end to apartheid, and they succeeded in overturning the president's veto (September 1986).
- The Reykjavik meeting with President Gorbachev of the USSR (October 1986) left the feeling that Reagan had been outmanoeuvred by the Soviet leader. However, failure turned to success in October 1987 with the signing of the INF (intermediate nuclear forces) Treaty (see Section 8.6(b)).

Growing dissatisfaction with the government was reflected in the mid-term Congressional elections (November 1986), when the Republicans lost many seats, leaving the Democrats with an even larger majority in the House of Representatives (260–175), and more important, now in control of the Senate (54–45). With two years of his second term still to go, Reagan was a 'lame-duck' president – a Republican faced with a Democrat Congress. He would have the utmost difficulty persuading Congress to vote him cash for policies such as Star Wars (which most Democrats thought impossible) and aid for the Contra rebels in Nicaragua; and under the Constitution, a two-thirds majority in both houses could overrule the president's veto.

4   The Irangate scandal

This was the most damaging blow to the president. Towards the end of 1986, it emerged that *the Americans had been supplying arms secretly to Iran in return for the release of*

hostages. However, Reagan had always insisted publicly that the USA would never negotiate with governments which condoned terrorism and the taking of hostages. Worse still,
it emerged that profits from the Iranian arms sales were being used to supply military aid
to the Contra rebels in Nicaragua; this was illegal, since Congress had banned all military
aid to the Contras from October 1984.

A Congressional investigation found that a group of Reagan's advisers, including his
national security chief Donald Regan, Lieutenant-Colonel Oliver North and Rear-Admiral
John Poindexter had been responsible and had all broken the law. Reagan accepted responsibility for the arms sales to Iran but not for sending funds to the Contras. It seems that he
was only dimly aware of what was going on, and was probably no longer in touch with
affairs. 'Irangate', as it was dubbed, did not destroy Reagan, as Watergate did Nixon, but
it certainly tarnished the administration's record in its last two years.

5   A severe stock market crash (October 1987)

This was brought on by the fact that the American economy was in serious trouble. There
was a huge budget deficit, mainly because Reagan had more than doubled defence spending since 1981, while at the same time cutting taxes. During the period 1981–7, the national
debt had more than doubled – to $2400 billion, and borrowing had to be stepped up simply
to pay off the massive annual interest of $192 billion. At the same time the USA had the
largest trading deficit of any leading industrialized country, and the economy was beginning to slow down as industry moved into recession. Some sources claimed that spending
cuts had left economic infrastructures and inner cities in a state of decay; apparently in some
of the worst areas, housing and infant mortality were on the same level as some Third
World black spots. On the other hand statistics from the Federal Reserve Bank told a more
positive story. During the eight years that Reagan was in office, inflation dropped from 12
percent to 4.5 percent, unemployment fell from 7.5 percent to 5.7 percent, the top rate of
personal tax fell from 70 percent to 33 percent, and 18 million new jobs were created.
Certainly Reagan somehow managed to retain his personal popularity. During 1988 the
economy and the balance of payments improved and unemployment fell. This enabled the
Republican George Bush to win a comfortable victory in the election of November 1988.

(c)   George Bush (1989–93)

George Bush, who had been Reagan's vice-president, scored *a big foreign policy success
with his decisive leadership against Saddam Hussein* after the Iraqi invasion of Kuwait
(August 1990). When the Gulf War ended in the defeat of Saddam, Bush's reputation
stood high (see Section 11.10). However, as time passed, he was increasingly criticized for
not having pressed home the advantage and for allowing the brutal Saddam to remain in
power.

Meanwhile all was not well at home: the legacy of Reaganomics was not easy to throw
off. A recession began in 1990, the budget deficit was still growing, and unemployment
increased again. During the election campaign Bush had promised, in a famous reply to
the Democrat candidate Michael Dukakis, not to raise taxes: 'Read my lips; no new taxes.'
But now he found himself forced to raise indirect taxes and reduce the number of wealthy
people exempt from tax. Although people with jobs were comfortably off materially, the
middle classes felt insecure in the face of the general trend towards fewer jobs. Among the
working classes there was a permanent 'underclass' of unemployed people, both black and
white, living in decaying inner-city ghettos with a high potential for crime, drugs and
violence. Many of these people were completely alienated from politics and politicians,
seeing little chance of help from either party. It was in this atmosphere that the election of
November 1992 brought a narrow victory for the Democrat Bill Clinton.

(a) Bill Clinton (1993–2001)

William J. Clinton, like John F. Kennedy 30 years earlier and Franklin D. Roosevelt 60 years earlier, came into the White House like a breath of fresh air. He had been a Rhodes Scholar at Oxford, and the youngest ever Governor of Arkansas, elected in 1978 at the age of 32. As president he immediately caused a stir by appointing more women to top posts in his administration than had ever been seen before. Madeleine Albright became the first woman secretary of state; a woman judge was appointed to the Supreme Court, and three other important positions were given to women.

In the presidential election, Clinton had campaigned on a programme of welfare reform and a system of universal health insurance, together with a change in direction – away from 'Reaganomics'. Unfortunately he experienced the same problems as Kennedy – how to persuade or manoeuvre the Republicans in Congress into approving his reforms. When his Health Security Bill was published, it was attacked by the insurance industry and the American Medical Association, and Congress refused to pass it. His task became even more difficult after big Republican gains in the Congressional elections of 1994. However, the uncompromising behaviour of some of the Republicans in Congress did not go down well with ordinary Americans, and Clinton's popularity increased. He did have some successes:

- Plans were introduced to reduce the huge budget deficit left over from the Reagan era.
- A complete reorganization and streamlining of the welfare system was begun.
- A minimum wage of $4.75 an hour was introduced (May 1996), and this was to increase to $5.15 in May 1997.
- The North American Free Trade Agreement was signed with Canada and Mexico, setting up a free trade area between the three states.

Clinton could also point to some solid achievements in foreign affairs. He made a positive contribution to peace in the Middle East when he brought Israeli and Palestinian leaders together in Washington in 1993; the eventual result was an agreement granting the Palestinians limited self-government in the Gaza Strip and Jericho (see Section 11.7). In 1995 he worked with President Yeltsin of Russia to try to bring an end to the war in Bosnia, the outcome being the Dayton Accords (see Section 10.7(c)).

At the same time his presidency was dogged by rumours of shady business deals which he and his wife Hillary were said to have been involved in while he was Governor of Arkansas – the so-called 'Whitewater scandal'. When two of his former business associates and the current Governor of Arkansas were convicted of multiple fraud (May 1996), the Republicans hoped that Whitewater would do to Clinton what Watergate did to Nixon – drive him from office, or at least help to bring about his defeat in the election of November 1996. However, what seemed to matter to a majority of the American people was the state of the economy; and here too Clinton was successful – *the economy began to recover and the budget deficit was reduced to more manageable proportions.* The confrontational tactics of some of the Republicans, particularly Newt Gingrich, who constantly held up Clinton's measures in Congress, probably won him sympathy, so that he was comfortably re-elected.

The great success story of Clinton's second term was the sustained economic growth, which by 1999 had set a new record for the longest period of continuous economic expansion in peacetime. Already in 1998 the budget had been balanced and there was a surplus for the first time since 1969. Other signs of the healthy economy were that the value of the stock market tripled, there was the lowest unemployment rate for almost 30 years, and the highest level of home ownership in the nation's history.

(b)   Scandal and impeachment

Rumours of financial and sexual improprieties constantly circulated during Clinton's first term as president. The attorney-general could not avoid giving the go-ahead for an investigation into the Clintons' business affairs in Arkansas. The enquiry became known as 'Whitewater', after the housing development company at the centre of the controversy; although it dragged on for several years, no conclusive evidence was found of any illegal dealings. Determined to discredit the president somehow or other, Kenneth Starr, the man conducting the enquiry, extended his investigations and eventually discovered proof that Clinton had been having an affair with Monica Lewinsky, a young intern on the White House staff. Having repeatedly denied any such involvement, the president was forced to make a public apology to the American people. The House of Representatives voted to impeach Clinton on charges of perjury and obstruction of justice, but in 1999 the Senate found him not guilty. It was a sordid business which to some extent damaged Clinton's reputation. On the other hand, his personal popularity remained high; he had achieved a great deal during his presidency, and there was a feeling that he had been the victim of unreasonable harassment at the hands of some Republicans.

(c)   The election of November 2000

The presidential election brought surprises, in more ways than one. The Democrat candidate, Al Gore (Clinton's vice-president), started out the favourite in the contest against George W. Bush (Governor of Texas and son of the former president). Yet in spite of the healthy economic situation, the voting was very close. In total votes cast over the nation as a whole, Gore beat Bush by over 500 000. But the final result depended on which candidate won Florida, the last state to declare. Florida had 25 electoral votes, and this meant that whoever won in Florida would become president. After a recount, it looked as though Bush had won, though with a majority of less than 1000. The Democrats challenged the result and demanded a manual recount on the grounds that the machine counts were not reliable. The Florida Supreme Court ordered a manual recount, and after hand-counted ballots in two counties had been included in the result, Bush's lead was reduced to under 200. At this point, the Bush camp appealed to the US Supreme Court, which had a majority of Republican judges; the court reversed the Florida Supreme Court's decision and cancelled the manual count, on the grounds that it would take too long – five weeks had passed and the presidency had still not been decided. The Supreme Court decision meant that Bush had won Florida, and with it, the presidency. He was the first president since 1888 to win the election and yet lose the nationwide popular vote. The court's action was controversial in the extreme; many people were convinced that if the manual recount had been allowed, Gore would have won.

(d)   George W. Bush's first term (2001–5)

During his first year in office, the nature of President Bush's administration quickly became clear – he was on the far right, or neo-conservative, wing of the Republican party; one analyst later described him as 'the most hard-right president since Herbert Hoover'.

Although he had campaigned as a 'compassionate conservative', he began by introducing massive tax cuts amounting to $1.35 trillion for the wealthiest citizens. He also signalled his intention to spend less on social services. He drew criticism from the European Union and other countries when he announced that the USA was withdrawing from the 1997 Kyoto Protocol, which aimed to reduce the emission of greenhouse gases (see Section 27.5(b)), and from the 1972 Anti-Ballistic Missile Treaty.

The president soon faced a testing crisis with the 11 September terrorist attacks on New York and Washington (see Section 12.3). He responded decisively, declaring war on terrorism and building up an international coalition to carry out the campaign. During the next 18 months the Taliban regime was removed from Afghanistan and Saddam Hussein was driven from power in Iraq. However, it proved more difficult to bring peace to these countries; two years after the overthrow of Saddam in April 2003, American soldiers in Iraq were still being killed by terrorists. There were reports that even in Afghanistan the Taliban were creeping back and gaining a hold in certain areas.

Meanwhile, at home the economy began to run into problems. The annual budget published in February 2004 showed that there was a deficit of well over 4 per cent of GDP (the EU ceiling was 3 per cent). Reasons for this were:

- increasing expenditure on anti-terrorist security measures and the continuing cost of the operations in Iraq;
- a fall in government revenue because of the huge tax cuts for the wealthy;
- extra credits given to farmers.

The government's policies were having mixed effects, the most striking one of which was the ever-widening gap between rich and poor. Statistics published at the end of 2003 showed that the richest one per cent of Americans owned well over 40 per cent of their nation's wealth. (For comparison, in the UK the richest 1 per cent owned 18 per cent of the total wealth.) This was not due solely to Bush's policies – it had been developing over the previous 20 years; but the trend accelerated after 2001, partly because of the tax cuts. The Centre for Public Integrity reported that every member of the Bush cabinet was a millionaire, and that its total net worth was more than ten times that of the Clinton cabinet.

At the other extreme there was increasing poverty, caused partly by rising unemployment and partly by low wages. Three million people had lost their jobs since Bush took office, and over 34 million, one in eight of the population, were living below the poverty line. Unemployment benefit was only paid for six months, and in some states – Ohio was an outstanding example – thousands of people were surviving with the help of charity food kitchens run by churches. At the end of Bush's first four years in office, the number of Americans living below the poverty line had increased by 4.3 million since he became president in January 2001.

Why was this happening in the world's richest country? The government blamed the closure of so many factories on foreign imports, and singled out China as the main culprit. The poor received only the minimum of help from the government because, basically, the Bush administration held fast to the traditional conservative American principles of *laissez-faire*: government should be kept to a minimum and should not have a direct role in alleviating poverty. Social welfare was thought to weaken self-reliance, whereas people should be encouraged to help themselves. Taxation was considered to be an unwarranted interference with individual property, and the wealthy should not feel obliged to help the poor, unless they chose to do so. The main obligation of business was to maximize profits for the benefit of shareholders; to that end, all government interference and regulation should be kept to a minimum.

Unfortunately this approach led to an 'anything goes' atmosphere, and some disturbing developments took place. In the absence of proper regulation, it was tempting for companies to 'manipulate' their accounts to show ever-increasing profits, and thereby keep their share prices rising. But this practice could not continue indefinitely; in November 2001 the energy trading company Enron went bankrupt after a series of secret deals – unknown both to the authorities and to investors – which turned out to be disastrously loss-making. Enron's chief executive and his board members had to face Congressional investigations for fraud. Several other major companies followed; tens of thousands of people lost their investments, while employees of the companies lost their retirement pensions when the pension funds disappeared.

As the election of November 2004 approached, many analysts believed that these mounting problems would bring about a Republican defeat. However, President Bush won a decisive, though still fairly close victory over his Democrat challenger, Senator John Kerry. Some 58.9 million Americans voted for Bush compared with 55.4 million for Kerry. The Republicans also increased their majority in the House of Representatives and the Senate. The growing poverty and unemployment in some states had apparently not been widespread enough to win the day for Kerry. *Other reasons suggested for the Republican victory include*:

- The Democrats failed to produce a clear campaign message setting out what the party stood for. Consequently, many voters decided it was wiser to stick with the tried and tested Bush rather than switch to Kerry, who was perceived as an unknown quantity.
- The Democrats failed to convince enough voters that they could be trusted to keep the country safe and secure.
- The Republicans were seen by the Christian right as the party that stood for moral and family values, whereas the Democrats were thought to be too sympathetic towards abortion and gay marriages.
- The Republicans were more successful than they had been in the 2000 election at galvanizing their supporters into going along to vote.

(e)   George W. Bush's second term (2005–8)

Disaster struck in the first year of President Bush's second term, just as it had in the first. This time it was Hurricane Katrina which battered the southern coast on 29 August. New Orleans was right at the centre and suffered extensive damage and flooding. Louisiana, Mississippi and Alabama were badly affected and Bush declared a state of emergency in all three states. He toured the area, ordered federal cash to be used in the recovery and rebuilding process and sent the National Guard in to help the locals. The recovery was extremely slow and Bush was criticized for the government response and the apparent incompetence of those appointed to organize the recovery programme. Some observers believe that this flawed response to Hurricane Katrina was one of the reasons for the Republican defeats in the mid-term Congressional elections of 2006, which left Bush as a 'lame-duck' president – a president faced with a hostile Congress. In the area of health and social security, Bush's record was mixed. Increased funding introduced in 2003 for the National Institute of Health (NIF) was withdrawn because of rising inflation – the first time it had been reduced for 36 years. He approved an addition to the Medicare health-insurance scheme to provide assistance towards paying for prescription medicines. However, in 2007 he vetoed the State Children's Health Insurance Programme (SCHIP), which would have extended the amount of free healthcare for the children of poor families. It was to be funded by an increase in the tax on cigarettes, and had been approved by the House of Representatives and the Senate, both of which had a Democrat majority following the 2006 Congressional elections. Bush opposed the programme because he believed it was too close to socialism.

In the early part of Bush's second term the economic situation seemed to be improving. Unemployment fell but the underlying problem was still the huge budget deficit. At a time of reduced taxation, defence and military spending were increasing, thanks to the continued campaigns in Iraq and Afghanistan, where the Taliban insurgency was assuming crisis proportions (see Section 12.5). In December 2007 the country had slipped into a recession. Unemployment rose rapidly and in just one month – February 2008 – 63 000 jobs were lost. The president tried to help by launching an aid programme in which thousands of people received a large tax rebate and some struggling businesses were given tax breaks. This was not enough to turn the tide, and all parts of the economy were affected. House sales and prices fell dramatically, and there was a sub-prime mortgage crisis when people were unable to keep up repayments. This threw mortgage lenders into difficulties and *by September 2008 the US was on the brink of the worst financial crisis since the Great Depression of the 1930s.* On 15 September 2008 Lehman Brothers, the fourth largest investment bank in the USA, filed for bankruptcy (for full details of the world financial crisis see Section 27.7). In November 2008 over half a million jobs were lost. The National Bureau of Labor reported that by the time Bush left office no fewer than 2.9 million jobs had been lost since he came to power in January 2001.

As the November 2008 presidential election drew near, the Republicans could hardly have faced a more inauspicious situation. When Bush took office in 2001 the USA had a huge budget surplus of $2 trillion. That was not counting the national debt, which stood at $5.7 trillion. However, many economists predicted that if the government – of whichever party – continued on the same path followed by Bill Clinton, the national debt should be paid off in about ten years. Bush decidedly did not continue on the Clinton road. First of all he cut taxes – a very popular move; unfortunately that meant a reduction in government revenue of $1.8 trillion. Next he declared the 'war on terror', leading to the invasion of Iraq and the operations in Afghanistan. These were extremely expensive and were financed by borrowing to the tune of $1.5 trillion. The financial crisis and the recession reduced government income still further, so that by November 2008, according to political commentator Corey Robin, 'Bush had squandered the surplus and nearly doubled the size of the debt, adding more to it than any other president in US history.'

In the election on 4 November 2008 the Democrat presidential and vice-presidential candidates, Barack Obama and Joe Biden, won a comfortable victory over Republicans John McCain and Sarah Palin. The decisive factors were the unpopularity of the Iraq war, which McCain supported and Obama opposed, and the continuing economic crisis, which was blamed on Bush. Obama campaigned on a slogan of 'Washington must change', promising universal healthcare, full employment, green policies and a USA respected instead of feared by its enemies. He also labelled McCain's programme damagingly as 'more of the same', referring to his close association with the unpopular Bush over the previous eight years. This election made history: until 2008 both president and vice-president had always been WASPS; *now the president was an African American and the vice-president was a Roman Catholic.*

(f) Barack Obama (2009–13)

The most pressing problem facing the new president was the sorry state of the economy. Wasting no time, in February 2009 he signed into law the American Recovery and Reinvestment Act. This was a plan setting aside $787 billion to rescue the economy by creating new jobs. In June 2009 General Motors filed for bankruptcy, the largest manufacturing collapse in US history. Fortunately the government was able to step in and take over 60 per cent of the business. Then in July 2010 came the Financial Reform Act, designed to reduce the power of the large banks and provide more protection for customers and investors. This was a step in the right direction, but critics argued that it did not go far enough to be certain of preventing another financial crash like that of 2008. Obama was determined to deal with the other source of discontent – the war in Iraq. His first act as president was to ask his military leaders to prepare a plan for what he called a 'responsible' withdrawal of troops from Iraq, to be completed by the end of 2011. This was achieved: the war was formally declared to be over, although it was not the end of violence, since Sunnis and Shias continued to fight each other (see Section 12.4(f)).

Unfortunately the war in Afghanistan was decidedly not over; by the middle of 2009 the Taliban had been so successful that they controlled many areas and had set up shadow governments and law courts there. Many observers were convinced that it was impossible to defeat the Taliban militarily, and that talks would have to begin. Even President Karzai of Afghanistan thought this was the only way forward. However, Obama decided to have another 'surge', and in December 2009 he ordered an extra 30 000 troops into Afghanistan with orders to 'seize' the initiative'.

Another Obama initiative concerned the Arab–Israeli problem. In a speech in Cairo in June 2009 he had promised to form a new relationship of trust and co-operation between Islam and the USA, putting behind them years of suspicion and discord, and calming the dispute with Iran over nuclear weapons. The Iranian government made no response, but most other countries welcomed the announcement. He even apologized to Muslims for American military strength, the war in Iraq, Guantánamo and colonialism. It was probably because of this initiative that President Obama was awarded the Nobel Peace Prize in October 2009. It was a great honour for him, but it drew mixed reactions – critics said it was too early for such an award, as he had not actually achieved anything yet. Then in a speech at the UN General Assembly (23 September 2010), he proposed that a separate Palestinian state should be set up within a year and requested President Netanyahu of Israel to stop allowing new Israeli settlements to be built on land destined to be part of Palestine. Predictably, the Israelis were furious: they protested strongly and sought support from the Israeli lobby in the USA. Massive pressure was put on Obama by the conservatives until he felt obliged to change his position. The next demand for statehood by the Palestinians in September 2011 was vetoed at the United Nations – by the USA! Understandably they felt betrayed, and the new 'rapprochement' between the USA and Islam was looking distinctly shaky. Nor did it help that the Guantánamo Bay prison, which in January 2009 Obama had promised would be closed within the year, was still fully operational. . In domestic affairs Obama also ran into problems: there were great objections to his healthcare reforms designed to bring some 30 million more Americans within the protection of health insurance. Eventually he was able to sign the changes into law (March 2010), but the Republicans were so determined to strike down 'Obamacare' that 26 of the states challenged the legality of parts of the legislation via the Supreme Court. This took over two years to reach a decision – in June 2012 the Court ruled that the whole of the legislation was legal. It was due to be introduced piece by piece until it became fully operational in 2018, taking the USA closer than ever before to guaranteed coverage for everybody. In the mid-term elections of November 2010 the Democrats lost 63 seats and control of the House of Representatives, probably because the economy was showing very little sign of improvement and unemployment remained static. Leading the opposition to Obama was the Tea Party movement, a conservative group which advocated reduced taxes, lower government spending and paying off some of the national debt; in other words, a return to general austerity. They took their name from the Boston Tea Party of 1773, when colonists had protested against the British tax on tea by dumping tea taken from British ships into the harbour. After months of argument, in August 2011 Obama gave way and signed an austerity bill that, among other things, reduced the pay of federal workers, cut defence spending and endorsed a more aggressive austerity programme.

It was claimed that this had saved the USA from what would have been a disastrous debt default, though others argue that Obama would never have allowed the US to default; there was money in reserve to pay its debts, and there were alternative savings that he could have made, rather than default. Whatever the truth, the euphoria was only short-lived: only four days later the ratings agency, Standard and Poor's, cut the US triple-A rating for the first time, reducing it to AA+ status. The reason –the USA had failed to tackle its massive budget deficit and its equally massive debts. There were two bright spots among the gloom, though even they were controversial. In December 2010 President Obama signed an historic law repealing the ban on gays serving openly in the military – a largely popular move, but one which appalled the religious right. In May 2011 it was announced that Osama bin Laden, the al-Qaeda leader, had been killed by American troops in Pakistan (see Section 12.5). This caused widespread celebrations in the USA but brought relations with Pakistan to an all-time low. As the USA moved towards the next presidential election in November 2012, unemployment was still high and economic recovery very slow. Most commentators predicted a close election, but in the event, Obama won a comfortable victory over his Republican challenger, Mitt Romney. One important reason for this was the changing racial makeup of the USA – African Americans and Hispanics make up a steadily increasing proportion of the population, and overwhelmingly, they support the Democrats. The Republicans' anti-gay and anti-abortion policies lost them votes, and so too did the perception that Romney, a multi-millionaire, cared more for the interests of wealthy plutocrats than for the needs of ordinary people. Controversially, many Christian-right voters turned against Romney on the grounds that, since he was a Mormon, he could not be a true Christian. In the end Obama won much support for his demand that the wealthy (those earning more than $250 000 a year) should pay more in taxes.

FURTHER READING

Ali, Tariq, *The Obama Syndrome: Surrender at Home, War Abroad* (Verso, 2011).

Black, C., *Nixon: The Invincible Quest* (Quercus, 2008).

Brogan, H., *The Penguin History of the United States of America* (Penguin, 2001 edition).

Dallek, R., *John F. Kennedy: An Unfinished Life* (Penguin, 2004).

Dallek, R., *Lyndon P. Johnson: Portrait of a President* (Penguin, 2005).

Dallek, R., *Nixon and Kissinger: Partners in Power* (Allen Lane, 2007).

Foner, N., *From Ellis Island to JFK: New York's Two Great Waves of Immigration* (Yale University Press, 2001).

Graubard, S., *The Presidents: The Transformation of the American Presidency from Theodore Roosevelt to George W. Bush* (Penguin, 2009).

Hedges, C., *American Fascists: the Christian Right and the War on America* (Cape, 2007).

Herman, A., *Joseph McCarthy* (Free Press, 2000).

Johnson, P., *A History of the American People* (Harper, 2000).

Lipset, M. and Marks, G., *It Didn't Happen Here: Why Socialism Failed in the USA* (Norton, 2001).

Maranto, R., Lansford, T. and Johnson, J. (eds) *Judging Bush* (Stanford University Press, 2009).

McCullough, D., *Truman* (Simon & Schuster, 1993).

Newton, J., *Eisenhower: The White House Years* (Doubleday, 2011).

Reeves, R., *President Nixon: Alone in the White House* (Simon & Schuster, 2002).

Roberts, A., *A History of the English Speaking Peoples Since 1900* (Weidenfeld & Nicolson, 2006).

Robin, C., 'The War on Tax', *London Review of Books* (25 August 2011).

Suri, J., *Henry Kissinger and the American Century* (Harvard University Press, 2007).

Unger, C., *The Fall of the House of Bush* (Simon & Schuster, 2007).

Woods, R. B., *Quest for Identity: America since 1945* (Cambridge University Press, 2005).

Zinn, H., *A People's History of the United States* (Harper Perennial, 2010 edition)

QUESTIONS

1 How far would you agree with the view that Johnson's administration was largely a failure because of US involvement in the Vietnam War?

2 Explain why there was such a powerful anti-communist movement in the USA in the years following the Second World War. How important was Senator Joseph McCarthy's role in the movement?

3 (a) Explain why Malcolm X left the Nation of Islam.
　(b) 'The growth of radicalism among African Americans was important in helping them to gain their civil rights during the 1960s.' Explain whether you agree or disagree with this view.

4 Explain why the March on Washington took place in 1963.

5 'The use of non-violence was the most important reason for African Americans gaining improved civil rights in the years 1960–8.' How far would you agree with this statement?

6 Critics have sometimes described the presidencies of Jimmy Carter (1977–81) and George Bush (1989–93) as completely ineffective. Explain whether you think this is a fair criticism.

7 In what ways can the Clinton administration (1993–2001) be judged a success? Explain why, in spite of his successes, Clinton was impeached towards the end of his presidency.

8 Explain what was meant by 'Reaganomics', the term used to describe President Reagan's economic policies. How successful were these policies?

9 The presidency of George W. Bush has been described as 'one long disaster'. How far do you think this verdict is justified?

There is a document question about the struggle for civil rights on the website.

Part

V

Decolonization and After

Chapter
24

The end of the European empires

SUMMARY OF EVENTS

At the end of the Second World War in 1945, the nations of Europe still claimed ownership of vast areas of the rest of the world, particularly in Asia and Africa.

- *Britain's Empire was the largest in area*, consisting of India, Burma, Ceylon, Malaya, enormous tracts of Africa and many assorted islands and other territories, such as Cyprus, Hong Kong, the West Indies, the Falkland Islands and Gibraltar.
- *France had the second largest empire*, with territories in Africa, Indo-China and the West Indies. In addition, Britain and France still held land in the Middle East, taken from Turkey at the end of the First World War. Britain held Transjordan and Palestine and France held Syria. They were known as *'mandated' territories*, which meant that Britain and France were intended to 'look after' them and prepare them for independence.
- *Other important empires* were those of the Netherlands (Dutch East Indies), Belgium (Congo and Ruanda Urundi), Portugal (Angola, Mozambique and Guinea), Spain (Spanish Sahara, Ifni, Spanish Morocco and Spanish Guinea) and Italy (Libya, Somalia and Eritrea).

Over the next 30 years, remarkable changes took place. By 1975 most of these colonial territories had gained their independence. Sometimes, as in the Dutch and French colonies, they had to fight for it against determined European resistance. The problems involved were often complex; in India there were bitter religious differences to resolve. In some areas – Algeria, Kenya, Tanganyika, Uganda and Rhodesia – large numbers of whites had settled, and they were relentlessly hostile to independence, which would place them under black rule. Britain was prepared to grant independence when it was felt that individual territories were ready for it, and most of the new states retained a link with Britain by remaining in the British Commonwealth (a group of former British-controlled nations which agreed to continue associating together, mainly because there were certain advantages to be gained from doing so).

The main British territories which gained independence, sometimes changing their names (new names in brackets), were:

India; Pakistan – 1947
Burma; Ceylon (Sri Lanka) – 1948
Transjordan (Jordan) – 1946; Palestine – 1948 (see Sections 11.1–2)
Sudan – 1956
Malaysia; Gold Coast (Ghana) – 1957

Nigeria; Somaliland (became part of Somalia); Cyprus – 1960
Tanganyika and Zanzibar (together forming Tanzania) – 1961
Jamaica; Trinidad and Tobago; Uganda – 1962
Kenya – 1963
Nyasaland (Malawi); Northern Rhodesia (Zambia); Malta – 1964
British Guiana (Guyana); Barbados; Bechuanaland (Botswana) – 1966
Aden (South Yemen) – 1967
Southern Rhodesia (Zimbabwe) – 1980

The other colonial powers were at first determined to hold on to their empires by military force. But they all gave way in the end.

The main territories gaining independence were:

French
Syria – 1946
Indo-China – 1954
Morocco; Tunisia – 1956
Guinea – 1958
Senegal; Ivory Coast; Mauretania; Niger; Upper Volta (later Burkina-Faso); Chad; Madagascar (Malagasey); Gabon; French Sudan (Mali); Cameroun (Cameroon); Congo; Oubangui-Shari (Central Africa); Togo; Dahomey (Benin from 1975) – 1960

Dutch
East Indies (Indonesia) – 1949
Surinam – 1975

Belgian
Congo (Zaire 1971–97) – 1960
Ruanda-Urundi (became two separate states: Ruanda and Burundi) – 1962

Spanish
Spanish Morocco – 1956
Guinea (Equatorial Guinea) – 1968
Ifni (became part of Morocco) – 1969
Spanish Sahara (divided between Morocco and Mauretania) – 1975

Portuguese
Guinea (Guinea-Bissau) – 1974
Angola; Mozambique – 1975
East Timor (seized by Indonesia later in 1975) – 1975

Italian
Ethiopia – 1947
Libya – 1951
Eritrea (became part of Ethiopia) – 1952
Italian Somaliland (became part of Somalia) – 1960

During the 1990s more documents dealing with decolonization became available, enabling historians to investigate more deeply the motives of the European powers in giving up their colonies and the different ways in which they carried out their withdrawals. The main debate that has developed is about the extent to which decolonization was caused by local nationalist movements, and how far it was brought about by outside political and economic considerations. Robert Holland, a leading exponent of what has become known as the '*metropolitan thesis*', believes that outside forces – metropolitan forces – were more important. He writes:

> The great colonial powers divested themselves of their subordinate possessions, not because internal pressures within their colonies left them with no other choice, but in the wake of a revisionist process whereby imperial roles came to be seen as incongruent with more 'modern' goals in the fields of foreign and economic policy.

Other historians feel that more credit must be given to the strength of local nationalist movements, and they acknowledge that in some cases the imperial power was quite simply expelled by sheer force. For example, would the British have left East and Central Africa for purely 'metropolitan' reasons if there had been no nationalist movements in these areas? Of course there is no simple answer. What can be said with certainty is that all these factors were present in varying degrees in all colonial territories.

(a) Nationalist movements

These had been in existence in many of Europe's overseas colonies, especially those in Asia, for many years before the Second World War. *Nationalists* were people who had a natural desire to get rid of their foreign rulers so that they could have a government run by people of their own nationality. Although the European powers claimed to have brought the benefits of western civilization to their colonies, there was a general feeling among colonial peoples that they were being exploited by the Europeans, who took most of the profits from their partnership. They claimed that the development and prosperity of the colonies were being held back in the interests of Europe, and that most of the colonial peoples continued to live in poverty. In India, *the Indian National Congress Party* had been agitating against British rule since 1885, while in south-east Asia, Vietnamese nationalists began to campaign against French rule during the 1920s. However, nationalism was not so strong in other areas, and progress towards independence would have been much slower without the boost provided by the Second World War. There is no doubt, however, that after the war the strength of nationalist feeling in many cases forced the colonial power to grant independence long before they had intended to do so. This often had disastrous results because the new states had not been properly prepared for independence. This was true of the British in Nigeria, the Belgians in the Congo and Rwanda-Urundi, the Spanish in Spanish Sahara and the Portuguese in Mozambique and Angola.

(b) Effects of the Second World War

The Second World War gave a great stimulus to nationalist movements in a number of ways:

- *Before the war, colonial peoples believed it would be impossible to defeat the militarily superior Europeans by force of arms.* Japanese successes in the early part of the war showed that it was possible for non-Europeans to defeat European armies. Japanese forces captured the British territories of Malaya, Singapore, Hong Kong and Burma, the Dutch East Indies and French Indo-China. Although the Japanese were eventually defeated, the nationalists, many of whom had fought against the Japanese, had no intention of tamely accepting European rule again. After all, Britain, France and Holland had failed miserably to protect their subjects, thus destroying any claim to legitimacy they might have had. If necessary, nationalists would continue to fight against the Europeans, using the guerrilla tactics they had learned fighting the Japanese. This is exactly what happened in Indo-China (see Chapter 21), the Dutch East Indies, Malaya and Burma.
- *Asians and Africans became more aware of social and political matters as a result of their involvement in the war.* Some 374 000 Africans were recruited into the British armed forces. The vast majority of them had never left their homeland before, and they were appalled at the contrast between the primitive living conditions in Africa and the relatively comfortable conditions they experienced even as members of the armed forces. Some Asian nationalist leaders worked with the Japanese, thinking that after the war there would be more chance of independence being granted by the Japanese than by the Europeans. Many of them, like Dr Sukarno in the Dutch East Indies, gained experience helping to govern the occupied areas. Sukarno later became the first president of Indonesia (1949).
- Some European policies during the war encouraged colonial peoples to expect independence as soon as the war was over. The Dutch government, shocked that people were so ready to co-operate with the Japanese in the East Indies, offered them some degree of independence as soon as the Japanese were defeated. *The 1941 Atlantic Charter* set out joint Anglo-American thinking about how the world should be organized after the war. *Two of the points mentioned were:*

  - Nations should not expand by taking territory from other nations.
  - All peoples should have the right to choose their own form of government.

  Though Churchill later said that this only applied to victims of Hitler's aggression, the hopes of Asian and African peoples had been raised.
- *The war weakened the European states*, so that in the end, they were not militarily or economically strong enough to hold on to their far-flung empires in the face of really determined campaigns for independence. The British were the first to recognize this because, as Bernard Porter pointed out:

  The British Empire had always been a cheapskate affair. Governments had never wanted to spend money on it or commit more than the minimum of personnel to it, or trouble the British people with it too much. The best way to manage things was to devolve the ruling of colonial possessions (and the expense) to settlers, or local traditional rulers (chiefs). This had its advantages but it also diluted Britain's power.

  Consequently the British responded by giving independence to India (1947). After that, British policy was to delay independence as long as possible, but to give way when the pressure became irresistible. At the same time the British concentrated on making their withdrawals 'look good'. It was important to give the impression that they were in control of the process, that it was something that they had intended all along, and that they were not 'scuttling away'. It was a further ten years before the Gold Coast became the first British territory in Africa to win independence; this became a great source of inspiration for other African colonies. As Iain Macleod (British Colonial Secretary) later put it: 'we could not possibly have held by force our territories in Africa; the march of men towards freedom cannot be halted; it can only be guided'. The French, Dutch, Spanish and Portuguese reacted differently and seemed determined to preserve their empires. But this involved them in costly military campaigns, and eventually they all had to admit defeat.

(c) Pan-Africanism

Early in the twentieth century there was an important development in African thinking which emphasized that all people of African descent, wherever they lived, were united by the same cultural and spiritual heritage. Pan-Africanism, as it became known, was first publicized by people of African origin living outside Africa. At the forefront were Marcus Garvey, a self-educated Jamaican who had founded the Universal Negro Improvement Association, and W. E. B. Du Bois, the first African American to earn a doctorate from Harvard. Gradually these ideas spread and by the end of the Second World War some African students, mainly from British colonies, had taken up pan-Africanism. Not only was it an encouragement to their ambitions of independence, it also inspired them to think beyond that. If all Africans shared the same social and cultural ties, it meant that the ultimate goal after independence must be to abandon the artificial frontiers set up by the Europeans and have a sort of federal United States of Africa along the same lines as the United States of America.

Kwame Nkrumah, who was to become the first prime minister of a semi-independent Gold Coast and then the first president of Ghana, was a strong believer in pan-Africanism. He wasted no time before organizing meetings and conferences of African leaders in which he pressed the advantages of African unification. Some states supported the idea, including Guinea, Mali and Morocco, but a majority were not impressed – having just won their independence, they saw little point in surrendering a large proportion of it by entering a huge political federation. Some of the other leaders suspected that Nkrumah was developing delusions of grandeur, seeing himself as the president of a federal Africa. Strongest in their opposition were Ethiopia and Liberia, which had been independent for generations, together with Nigeria, Sierra Leone and almost all the former French colonies. By 1963 the prospect of a United States of Africa had disappeared when a conference of African countries at Addis Ababa (Ethiopia) decided that the best way forward would be for them all to join an Organization of African Unity (OAU), a much less binding arrangement, while still displaying a sort of unity. But pan-Africanism had not been totally irrelevant – it had been an important influence on the rise of nationalist movements in many of the former colonies.

(d) Outside pressures

There were several outside pressures on the colonial powers to give up their empires. The USA, no doubt remembering that they had been the earliest part of the British Empire to declare independence (1776), was hostile to imperialism (building up empires and owning colonies). During the war, President Roosevelt made it clear that he took the Atlantic Charter to apply to all peoples, not just those taken over by the Germans. He and his successor, Truman, pressurized the British government to speed up independence for India. Peter Clarke points out that Churchill's imperialism irritated the Americans to such an extent that they were determined not to do anything that would help Britain to keep its empire. One reason given by the Americans for wanting to see the end of the European empires was that delays in granting independence to European colonies in Asia and Africa would encourage the development of communism in those areas. While there was clearly some truth in this argument in the case of Asia, Bernard Porter was convinced that in the case of Africa, there was still comparatively little communist influence. More important was the fact that the Americans looked on the newly-independent nations as potential markets into which they could force their way and establish both economic and political influence. In the eyes of the USA, imperially protected markets gave the British and other Europeans an unfair advantage.

The United Nations Organization, under American influence, came out firmly against imperialism and demanded a step-by-step programme for decolonization. The USSR also added its voice to the chorus and constantly denounced imperialism. As well as putting the European states under pressure, this encouraged nationalists all over the world to intensify their campaigns.

Almost every case was different; the following sections will look at some of the different ways in which colonies and territories gained their independence.

24.2   INDIAN INDEPENDENCE AND PARTITION

(a)   Background to independence

The British had made some concessions to the Indian nationalists even before the Second World War. The Morley–Minto reforms (1909), the Montague–Chelmsford reforms (1919) and the Government of India Act (1935) all gave the Indians more say in the government of their country. The Indians were also promised 'dominion status' as soon as the war was over. This meant becoming more or less completely independent, though still acknowledging the British monarch as head of state, like Australia. The Labour government, newly elected in 1945, wanted to show that it disapproved of exploiting the Indians and was anxious to press ahead with independence, on both moral and economic grounds. Ernest Bevin, the foreign secretary, had earlier toyed with the idea of delaying independence for a few years to enable Britain to finance a development programme for India. This idea was dropped because the Indians would be suspicious of any delay, and because Britain could not afford the expense, given its own economic difficulties. Bevin and Clement Attlee, the prime minister, therefore decided to give India full independence, allowing the Indians to work out the details for themselves.

The reasons why the British decided to grant Indian independence have been the subject of lively debate. Official sources presented it as the culmination of a process going back to the Government of India Act of 1919 – a process by which the British carefully prepared India for independence. Some Indian historians, including Sumit Sarkar and Anita Inder Singh, have challenged this view, arguing that Indian independence was never a long-term goal of the British and that the Government of India Acts of 1919 and 1935 were designed not to prepare the way for independence but to postpone it. Independence was not a gift from the British, it was 'the hard-won fruit of struggle and sacrifice'. Other historians have suggested that India was no longer of any value to Britain: instead of being a source of profit, it was now a drain on British resources. The aim of the government was therefore to get out of India in a way that did not look too much like a humiliation, and that kept India within the British financial network and Commonwealth.

Some writers have taken a middle view. Howard Brasted defended the Labour government against accusations that it made its policy up as it went along, and ended up running away from the problem. He showed that the Labour Party had drawn up a clear policy of withdrawal from India *before* the Second World War, and this was discussed by the party leader, Clement Attlee, and Jawaharlal Nehru, the Indian Congress leader, in 1938. Nehru and Gandhi knew that when Labour won the election of July 1945, Indian independence could not be far away. Sadly the progress towards independence turned out to be far more difficult than had been expected: the problems were so complex that the country ended up having to be divided into two states – India and Pakistan.

(b)   Why was the partition of India necessary?

1   Religious hostility between Hindus and Muslims
This was the main problem. Hindus made up about two-thirds of the 400 million population, and the rest were mostly Muslims. After their victories in the 1937 elections when they won eight out of the eleven states, *the Hindu National Congress Party* unwisely called on *the Muslim League* to merge with Congress. This alarmed the Muslim League, who were afraid that an independent India would be dominated by Hindus. The Muslim leader, *M. A. Jinnah*, demanded *a separate Muslim state of Pakistan*, and adopted as his slogan 'Pakistan or Perish'.

2   Compromise attempts failed
Attempts to draw up a compromise solution acceptable to both Hindus and Muslims failed. The British proposed a federal scheme in which the central government would have only limited powers, while those of the provincial governments would be much greater. This would enable provinces with a Muslim majority to control their own affairs and there would be no need for a separate state. Both sides accepted the idea in principle but failed to agree on the details.

3   Violence broke out in August 1946
This began when the viceroy (the king's representative in India), Lord Wavell, invited the Congress leader, *Jawaharlal Nehru*, to form an interim government, still hoping that details could be worked out later. Nehru formed a cabinet which included two Muslims, but Jinnah was convinced that the Hindus could not be trusted to treat the Muslims fairly. He called for a day of 'direct action' in support of a separate Pakistan. Fierce rioting followed in Calcutta, where 5000 people were killed, and it soon spread to Bengal, where Muslims set about slaughtering Hindus. As Hindus retaliated, *the country seemed on the verge of civil war.*

4   Mountbatten decides on partition
The British government, realizing that they lacked the military strength to control the situation, announced early in 1947 *that they would leave India no later than June 1948*. The idea was to try to shock the Indians into adopting a more responsible attitude. *Lord Louis Mountbatten* was sent as the new viceroy, and he soon decided that partition was the only way to avoid civil war. He realized that there would probably be bloodshed whatever solution was tried, but felt that partition would produce less violence than if Britain tried to insist on the Muslims remaining part of India. Within six weeks Mountbatten had worked out a plan for dividing the country up and for the British withdrawal. This was accepted by Nehru and Jinnah, although *M. K. Gandhi*, known as the Mahatma (Great Soul), the other highly respected Congress leader, who believed in non-violence, was still hoping for a united India. Afraid that delay would cause more violence, Mountbatten brought the date for British withdrawal forward to August 1947.

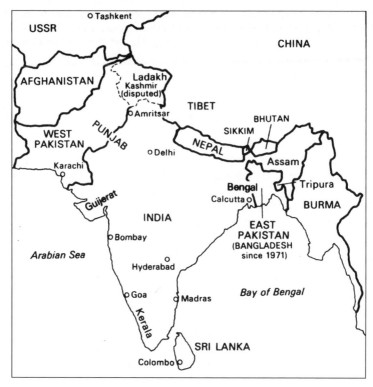

Map 24.1 **India and Pakistan**

(c) How was partition carried out?

The Indian Independence Act was rushed through the British parliament (August 1947), separating the Muslim majority areas in the north-west and north-east from the rest of India to become the independent state of Pakistan. The new Pakistan unfortunately consisted of two separate areas over a thousand miles apart (see Map 24.1). Independence day for both India and Pakistan was 15 August 1947. Problems followed immediately:

1 *It had been necessary to split the provinces of the Punjab and Bengal, which had mixed Hindu/Muslim populations.* This meant that millions of people found themselves on the wrong side of the new frontiers – Muslims in India and Hindus in Pakistan.

2 *Afraid of being attacked, millions of people headed for the frontiers*, Muslims trying to get into Pakistan and Hindus into India. Clashes occurred which developed into near-hysterical mob violence, especially in the Punjab, where about 250 000 people were murdered. Violence was not quite so widespread in Bengal, where Gandhi, still preaching non-violence and toleration, managed to calm the situation.

3 *Violence began to die down before the end of 1947, but in January 1948 Gandhi was shot dead by a Hindu fanatic* who detested his tolerance towards Muslims. It was a tragic end to a disastrous set of circumstances, but the shock somehow seemed to bring people to their senses, so that the new governments of India and Pakistan could begin to think about their other problems. From the British point of view, the government could claim that although so many deaths were regrettable,

the granting of independence to India and Pakistan was an act of far-sighted states-manship. Attlee argued, with some justification, that Britain could not be blamed for the violence; this was due, he said, 'to the failure of the Indians to agree among themselves'. V. P. Menon, a distinguished Indian political observer, believed that Britain's decision to leave India 'not only touched the hearts and stirred the emotions of India … it earned for Britain universal respect and goodwill'. Howard Brasted agreed, pointing out that a less sensitive handling of the situation by the British government could have produced an even more catastrophic bloodbath. On the other hand, A. N. Wilson believes that there could have been less violence if Mountbatten had acted differently. He should have provided peacekeeping forces to protect the migrant populations, and he should have taken more care in deciding the frontiers. Wilson writes, perhaps a trifle unfairly: 'By his superficial haste, his sheer arrogance and his inattention to vital detail … Mountbatten was responsible for as many deaths as some of those who were hanged after the Nuremberg trials.'

4 *In the longer term, Pakistan did not work well as a divided state*, and in 1971 East Pakistan broke away and became the independent state of Bangladesh.

24.3 THE WEST INDIES, MALAYA AND CYPRUS

As these three territories moved towards independence, interesting experiments in setting up federations of states were tried, with varying degrees of success. A federation is where a number of states join together under a central or federal government which has overall authority; each of the states has its own separate parliament, which deals with internal affairs. This is the type of system which works well in the USA, Canada and Australia, and many people thought it would be suitable for the British West Indies and for Malaya and neighbouring British territories.

- *The West Indies Federation was the first one to be tried*, but it proved to be a failure: set up in 1958, it only survived until 1962.
- *The Federation of Malaysia*, set up in 1963, was much more successful.
- *The British handling of independence for Cyprus unfortunately was not a success* and the island had a troubled history after the Second World War.

(a) The West Indies

Britain's West Indian possessions consisted of a large assortment of islands in the Caribbean Sea (see Map 24.2); the largest were Jamaica and Trinidad, and others included Grenada, St Vincent, Barbados, St Lucia, Antigua, the Seychelles and the Bahamas. There were also British Honduras on the mainland of Central America and British Guiana on the north-east coast of South America. Together these territories had a population of around six million. Britain was prepared in principle to give them all independence, but there were problems.

- *Some of the islands were very small, and there were doubts about whether they were viable as independent states.* Grenada, St Vincent and Antigua, for example, had populations of only about 100 000 each, while some were even smaller: the twin islands of St Kitts and Nevis had only about 60 000 between them.
- *The British Labour government felt that a federation could be the ideal way of uniting such small and widely scattered territories, but many of the territories themselves objected.* Some, like Honduras and Guiana, wanted nothing to do with a

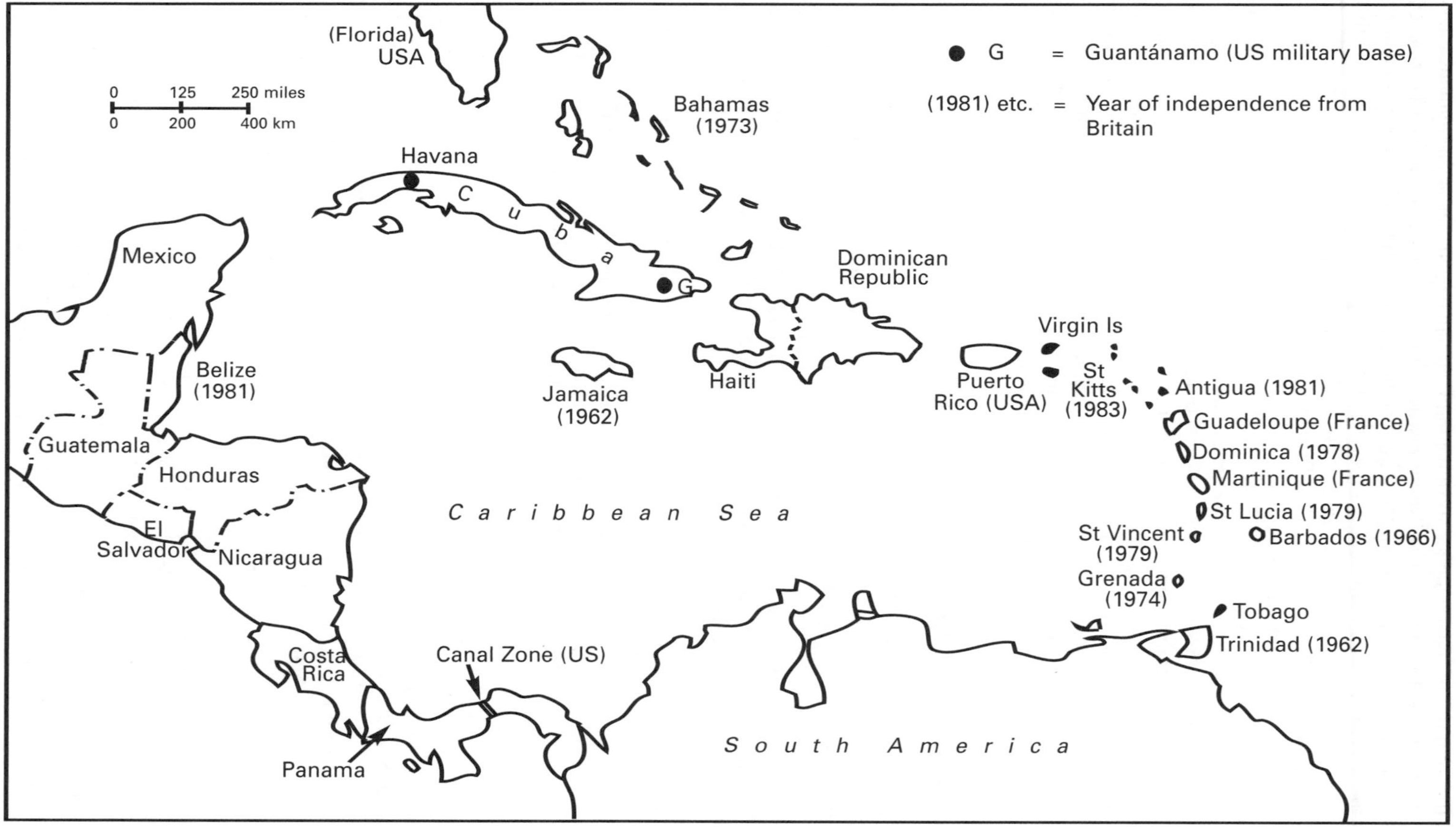
● G = Guantánamo (US military base)
(1981) etc. = Year of independence from Britain
0 125 250 miles
0 200 400 km
(Florida) USA
Bahamas (1973)
Havana
C u b a
G
Mexico
Belize (1981)
Guatemala
Honduras
El Salvador
Nicaragua
Costa Rica
Panama
Canal Zone (US)
Jamaica (1962)
Haiti
Dominican Republic
Puerto Rico (USA)
Virgin Is
St Kitts (1983)
Antigua (1981)
Guadeloupe (France)
Dominica (1978)
Martinique (France)
St Lucia (1979)
St Vincent (1979)
Barbados (1966)
Grenada (1974)
Tobago
Trinidad (1962)
C a r i b b e a n S e a
S o u t h A m e r i c a

Map 24.2 **Central America and the West Indies**

federation, preferring completely separate independence. This left Jamaica and Trinidad worried about whether they would be able to cope with the problems of the smaller islands. Some islands did not like the prospect of being dominated by Jamaica and Trinidad, and some of the smallest were not even sure they wanted independence at all, preferring to remain under British guidance and protection.

Britain went ahead in spite of the difficulties and established the West Indies Federation in 1958 (excluding British Honduras and British Guiana). But it never really functioned successfully. The one thing they all had in common – a passionate commitment to cricket – was not enough to hold them together, and there were constant squabbles about how much each island should pay into the federal budget and how many representatives they should each have in the federal parliament. When Jamaica and Trinidad withdrew in 1961, the federation no longer seemed viable. In 1962 Britain decided to abandon it and grant independence separately to all those that wanted it. By 1983 all parts of the British West Indies, except a few tiny islands, had become independent. Jamaica and Trinidad and Tobago were first, in 1962, and the islands of St Kitts and Nevis were last, in 1983. British Guiana became known as Guyana (1966) and British Honduras took the name Belize (1981). All of them became members of the British Commonwealth.

Ironically, having rejected the idea of a fully-fledged federation, they soon found that there were economic benefits to be had from co-operation. The Caribbean Free Trade Association was set up in 1968, and this soon developed into *the Caribbean Community and Common Market (CARICOM) in 1973*, which all the former British West Indies territories (including Guyana and Belize) joined.

(b) Malaya

Malaya was liberated from Japanese occupation in 1945, but there were two difficult problems to be faced before the British were prepared to withdraw.

1 *It was a complex area which would be difficult to organize.* It consisted of nine states each ruled by a sultan, two British settlements, Malacca and Penang, and Singapore, a small island less than a mile from the mainland. The population was multiracial: mostly Malays and Chinese, but with some Indians and Europeans as well. In preparation for independence it was decided to group the states and the settlements *into the Federation of Malaya (1948)*, while Singapore remained a separate colony. Each state had its own legislature for local affairs; the sultans retained some power, but the central government had firm overall control. All adults had the vote and this meant that the Malays, the largest group, usually dominated affairs.

2 *Chinese communist guerrillas led by Chin Peng, who had played a leading role in the resistance to the Japanese, now began to stir up strikes and violence against the British*, in support of an independent communist state. The British decided to declare a state of emergency in 1948, and in the end they dealt with the communists successfully, though it took time, and the state of emergency remained in force until 1960. Their tactics were to resettle into specially guarded villages all Chinese suspected of helping the guerrillas. It was made clear that independence would follow as soon as the country was ready for it; this ensured that the Malays remained firmly pro-British and gave very little help to the communists, who were Chinese.

The move towards independence was accelerated when the Malay Party, under their able leader *Tunku Abdul Rahman*, joined forces with the main Chinese and Indian groups to

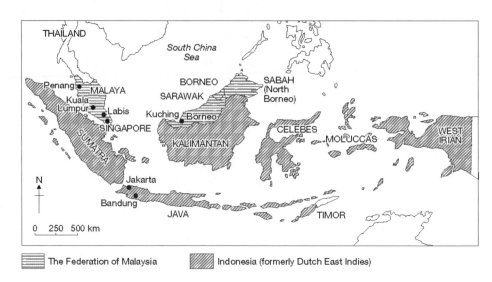

The Federation of Malaysia	Indonesia (formerly Dutch East Indies)

Map 24.3 **Malaysia and Indonesia**

form *the Alliance Party*, which won 51 out of the 52 seats in the 1955 elections. This seemed to suggest stability and the British were persuaded to grant full independence in 1957, when Malaya was admitted to the Commonwealth.

The Federation of Malaysia was set up in 1963. Malaya was running well under Tunku's leadership, and its economy, based on exports of rubber and tin, was the most prosperous in south-east Asia. In 1961, when the Tunku proposed that Singapore and three other British colonies, North Borneo (Sabah), Brunei and Sarawak, should join Malaya to form the Federation of Malaysia, Britain agreed (see Map 24.3). After a United Nations investigation team reported that a large majority of the populations concerned was in favour of the union, the Federation of Malaysia was officially proclaimed (September 1963). Brunei decided not to join, and eventually became an independent state within the Commonwealth (1984). Although Singapore decided to leave the Federation to become an independent republic in 1965, the rest of the Federation continued successfully.

(c) Cyprus

The British Labour government (1945–51) considered giving Cyprus independence, but progress was delayed by complications, the most serious of which was the mixed population – about 80 per cent were Greek-speaking Christians of the Orthodox Church, while the rest were Muslims of Turkish origin. The Greek Cypriots wanted the island to unite with Greece (*enosis*), but the Turks were strongly opposed to this. Churchill's government (1951–5) inflamed the situation in 1954 when their plans for self-government allowed the Cypriots far less power than Labour had had in mind. There were hostile demonstrations, which were dispersed by British troops.

Sir Anthony Eden, Churchill's successor, decided to drop the idea of independence for Cyprus, believing that Britain needed the island as a military base to protect her interests in the Middle East. He announced that Cyprus must remain permanently British, though the Greek government promised that Britain could retain her military bases even if *enosis* took place.

The Greek Cypriots, led by *Archbishop Makarios*, pressed their demands, while a

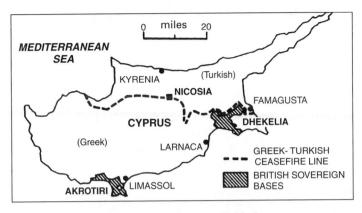

Map 24.4   **Cyprus divided**

guerrilla organization called *Eoka*, led by General Grivas, waged a terrorist campaign against the British, who declared a state of emergency (1955) and deployed about 35 000 troops to try to keep order. British policy also involved deporting Makarios and executing terrorists. The situation became even more difficult in 1958 when the Turks set up a rival organization in support of dividing the island.

Eventually, to avoid possible civil war between the two groups, Harold Macmillan, Eden's successor, decided to compromise. He appointed the sympathetic and tactful Hugh Foot as governor and he negotiated a deal with Makarios:

- The Archbishop dropped *enosis* and in return Cyprus was granted full independence.
- Turkish interests were safeguarded, Britain retained two military bases and, along with Greece and Turkey, guaranteed the independence of Cyprus.
- Makarios became the first president with a Turkish Cypriot, Fazil Kutchuk, as vice-president (1960). It seemed the perfect solution.

Unfortunately it only lasted until 1963 when civil war broke out between Greeks and Turks. In 1974 Turkey sent troops to help establish a separate Turkish state in the north, and the island has remained divided since then (Map 24.4). Turks occupy the north (roughly one-third of the island's area) and Greeks the south, with UN troops keeping the peace between the two. Many attempts were made to find agreement, but all failed. In the mid-1980s the UN began to press the idea of a federation as the most likely way of reconciling the two states, but this solution was rejected by the Greeks (1987). In April 2003 the checkpoints along the frontier between the two states were opened so that both Greek and Turkish Cypriots could cross the partition line for the first time since 1974. The island was still divided in May 2004 when the Republic of Cyprus (Greek) joined the European Union. The Turkish Republic of Northern Cyprus also voted to join, but since it was only recognized as an independent state by Turkey, it was not part of the accession agreement.

24.4   THE BRITISH LEAVE AFRICA

African nationalism spread rapidly after 1945; this was because more and more Africans were being educated in Britain and the USA, where they were made aware of racial discrimination. Colonialism was seen as the humiliation and exploitation of blacks by whites, and working-class Africans in the new towns were particularly receptive to nationalist ideas. The British, especially the Labour governments of 1945–51, were quite willing to allow independence, and were confident that they would still be able to exercise influence through trade links, which they hoped to preserve by including the new states as members of the Commonwealth. This practice of exercising influence over former colonies after independence by economic means became known as *neo-colonialism*; it became widespread in most of the new states of the Third World. Even so, the British intended to move the colonies towards independence very gradually, and the African nationalists had to campaign vigorously and often violently to make them act more quickly.

The British colonies in Africa fell into three distinct groups, which had important differences in character that were to affect progress towards independence.

WEST AFRICA: Gold Coast, Nigeria, Sierra Leone and the Gambia

Here there were relatively few Europeans, and they tended to be administrators rather than permanent settlers with profitable estates to defend. This made the move to independence comparatively straightforward.

EAST AFRICA: Kenya, Uganda and Tanganyika

Here, especially in Kenya, things were complicated by the 'settler factor' – the presence of European and Asian settlers, who feared for their future under black governments.

CENTRAL AFRICA: Nyasaland, Northern and Southern Rhodesia

Here, especially in Southern Rhodesia, the 'settler factor' was at its most serious. This was where European settlers were most firmly entrenched, owning huge and profitable estates, and confrontation between white settlers and African nationalists was most bitter.

(a) West Africa

1 The Gold Coast

The Gold Coast was the first black African state south of the Sahara to win independence after the Second World War, taking the name *Ghana (1957)*. It was achieved fairly smoothly, though not without some incident. The nationalist leader, Kwame Nkrumah, educated in London and the USA and since 1949 leader of *the Convention People's Party (CPP)*, organized the campaign for independence. There were boycotts of European goods, violent demonstrations and a general strike (1950), and Nkrumah and other leaders were imprisoned for a time. But the British, realizing that he had mass support, soon released him and agreed to allow a new constitution which included the vote for all adults; an elected Assembly; and an eleven-man Executive Council, of which eight were chosen by the Assembly.

In the 1951 elections, the first under the new constitution, the CPP won 34 seats out of 38. Nkrumah was released from prison, invited to form a government and became prime minister in 1952. This was self-government but not yet full independence. The Gold Coast had a small but well-educated group of politicians and other professionals, who, for the next five years, gained experience of government under British supervision. This experience was unique to Ghana; had it been repeated in other newly independent states, it might possibly have helped to avoid chaos and mismanagement. In 1957 Ghana, as it became known, received full independence.

2 Nigeria

Nigeria was easily the largest of Britain's African colonies, with a population of over 60 million. It was a more difficult proposition than Ghana because of its great size, and because of its regional differences between the vast Muslim north, dominated by the Hausa and Fulani tribes, the western region (Yorubas) and the eastern region (Ibos). The leading nationalist was *Nnamdi Azikiwe*, popularly known to his supporters as 'Zik'. He was educated in the USA and for a time worked as a newspaper editor in the Gold Coast. After his return to Nigeria in 1937 he founded a series of newspapers and became involved in the nationalist movement, soon gaining enormous prestige. In 1945 he showed he meant business by organizing an impressive general strike, which was enough to prompt the British to begin preparing Nigeria for independence. It was decided that a federal system would be most suitable; in 1954 a new constitution introduced local assemblies for the three regions, with a central (federal) government in Lagos, the capital. The regions assumed self-government first and the country as a whole became independent in 1960. Sadly, in spite of the careful preparations for independence, tribal differences caused civil war to break out in 1967 when the Ibos declared the eastern region independent with the name *Biafra* (see Section 25.3).

The other two British colonies in West Africa achieved independence without serious incident – Sierra Leone in 1961 and the Gambia in 1965 (see Map 24.5).

(b) East Africa

The British thought that independence for the colonies of East Africa was not so necessary as for West Africa, and that when independence did come, it would be in the form of multiracial governments, in which the European and Asian settlers would play a significant part. But during Harold Macmillan's government (1957–63) *an important change took place in British policy towards both East and Central Africa*. Macmillan had come to realize the strength of black African nationalist feeling; in a famous speech in Cape Town in 1960, he said: 'the wind of change is blowing through the continent. Whether we like it or not, this growth of national consciousness is a political fact, and our national policies must take account of it.'

1 Tanganyika

In Tanganyika the nationalist campaign was conducted by *the Tanganyika African National Union (TANU)* led by *Dr Julius Nyerere*, who had been educated at the University of Edinburgh. He insisted that the government must be African, but he also made it clear that whites had nothing to fear from black rule. Macmillan's government, impressed by Nyerere's ability and sincerity, conceded independence with black majority rule (1961). The island of Zanzibar was later united with Tanganyika, and the country took the name Tanzania (1964). Nyerere was president until his retirement in 1985.

2 Uganda

In Uganda independence was delayed for a time by tribal squabbles; the ruler (known as the kabaka) of the Buganda area objected to the introduction of democracy. Eventually a solution was found in a federal constitution which allowed the kabaka to retain some powers in Buganda. Uganda itself became independent in 1962 with *Dr Milton Obote* as prime minister.

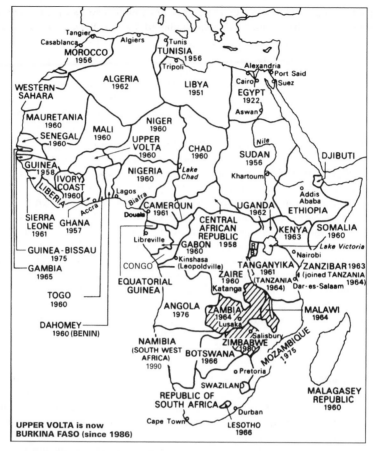

The Central African Federation 1953-63
Northern Rhodesia (Zambia), Southern Rhodesia (Zimbabwe),
Nyasland (Malawi)

R Rwanda 1962
B Burundi 1962

Map 24.5   **Africa becomes independent**

3   Kenya

Kenya was the most difficult area of East Africa to deal with because of the presence of a significant non-African population. As well as the 10 million Africans, there were some 66 000 white settlers who were violently opposed to black majority rule. There were also around 200 000 Indians and 35 000 Muslim Arabs. But it was the white settlers who had the political influence over the British government. They pointed out that they had worked hard and devoted their lives to making their farms successful, and that they now saw themselves as white Africans, and that Kenya was their homeland.

The main Kenyan African leader was *Jomo Kenyatta*; born in 1894, he was a member of the Kikuyu tribe and a veteran among African nationalists. He spent some time in Britain during the 1930s and returned to Kenya in 1947, becoming leader of the *Kenya African Unity Party (KAU)*, which consisted mostly of members of the dominant Kikuyu tribe. He hoped to win African majority rule gradually, first of all gaining more African seats on the Legislative Council. However, the more radical wing of his party – calling themselves the Forty Group – wanted to drive the British out by force, if necessary. The main African grievance was the land situation: the most fertile farming land was on the highland plateau, but only white settlers were allowed to farm there. Africans also resented the discrimination and the colour bar between blacks and whites, under which they were treated as inferior, second-class citizens. This was especially unacceptable, since many Africans had served in the army during the Second World War and had received equal treatment and respect from whites. Moreover it was clear that the whites expected to keep all their privileges even if they had to agree to independence.

The white settlers refused to negotiate with Kenyatta, and were determined to prolong their rule. They provoked a confrontation, hoping that violence would destroy the African Party. The British government was under pressure from both sides, and the white settlers were supported by certain big-business interests in Britain; even so, it did not handle the situation with much imagination. The KAU was able to make little progress, the only British concession being to allow six Africans to join the Legislative Council of 54 members.

In 1952, African impatience burst out in an uprising against the British, with attacks on European-owned farms and on black workers. It was organized by the *Mau Mau* secret society, whose members were mainly from the Kikuyu tribe. A state of emergency was declared (1952); Kenyatta and other nationalist leaders were arrested and found guilty of terrorism. Kenyatta was kept in jail for six years although he had publicly condemned violence and insisted that the KAU had not been involved in organizing the rebellion. In 1954 the British launched Operation Anvil in which 100 000 troops were deployed to flush out the terrorists (the Africans regarded themselves as freedom fighters, not terrorists).

There was a scandal in 1959 with revelations of brutal treatment of prisoners at the Hola detention camp, where savage beatings left 11 dead. However, the British government managed to hide from people at home the scale of what was going on in Kenya. It was only in 2005 that the full horrifying details were revealed in two separate books by historians David Anderson and Caroline Elkins. During the period of the emergency the British hanged more than a thousand Kikuyu, and killed some 20 000 in combat. In addition up to 100 000 died in detention camps, where there was a culture of brutality, routine beatings, killings and torture of the most grotesque kinds. One police chief later admitted that conditions in the camps were far worse than he had suffered as a prisoner of war in Japan. By contrast, less than a hundred whites were killed.

The uprising had been defeated by 1960, but by then, ironically, the British, encouraged by the 'wind of change' and by the expense of the anti-terrorist campaign, had changed their attitude. Harold Macmillan, who became prime minister in January 1957, faced up to the fact that it was impossible and indefensible to continue trying to prolong the privileged position of a group which made up no more than 5 per cent of the population. He decided to move Kenya towards independence. Africans were allowed to settle in the fertile highland plateau; restrictions were lifted on what the Kikuyus could grow, and as a result, coffee became one of the main crops. Attempts were made to increase the political role of the Africans; in 1957 elections were held for eight African seats in the Legislative Council, and the following year plans were announced to increase African membership of the council. In 1960 Africans became the majority group on the council and were given four out of ten seats in the Council of Ministers. In 1961 Kenyatta was at last released.

Progress towards independence was held up by rivalry and disagreement between the different tribal groups. While Kenyatta had been in prison, new leaders had emerged. *Tom Mboya* and *Oginga Odinga*, both members of the second largest ethnic group, the Luo, formed *the Kenya African National Union (KANU)*, which largely succeeded in uniting the Kikuyus and Luos. When Kenyatta was freed, so great was his prestige that he was immediately recognized as leader of KANU; both Kikuyus and Luos co-operated well together, and they wanted a strong, centralized government which would be dominated by their tribes. However, there were a number of smaller tribes who did not relish the idea of being controlled by Kikuyus and Luos. Led by Ronald Ngala, they formed a rival party – *the Kenya African Democratic Union (KADU)* – and they wanted a federal form of government which would enable them to have more control over their own affairs.

Both parties worked together to form a coalition government (1962), in preparation for elections to be held in May 1963. KANU won a clear majority in the elections and Kenyatta became prime minister of a self-governing Kenya. It was decided to abandon the idea of a federal system of government; Kenya became fully independent in December 1963. A year later it became a republic with Kenyatta as its first president and Odinga as vice-president. To his great credit, in spite of his harsh treatment by the British, Kenyatta favoured reconciliation; whites who decided to stay on after independence were fairly treated provided they took Kenyan citizenship, and Kenya became one of the most pro-British of the former colonies. Sadly, the tribal differences continued to cause problems after independence; the Luos believed that Kikuyus were receiving special treatment from the government and Kenyatta and Odinga fell out. Mboya was assassinated in 1969 and Odinga was sacked and spent two years in prison.

(c) Central Africa

This was the most troublesome area for Britain to deal with because this was where the settlers were most numerous and most deeply entrenched, particularly in Southern Rhodesia. Another problem was that numbers of well-educated Africans were much smaller than in West Africa because the settlers had ensured that very little money was spent on further and higher education for black Africans. Missionaries did their best to provide some education, but their efforts were often frustrated by the white governments. Alarmed at the spread of nationalism, the whites decided that their best policy was to combine resources. They persuaded Churchill's government (1953) to allow them to set up a union of the three colonies – Nyasaland and Northern and Southern Rhodesia, to be known as *the Central African Federation*. Their aim was to preserve the supremacy of the white minority (about 300 000 Europeans out of a total population of about 8.5 million). The federal parliament in Salisbury (the capital of Southern Rhodesia) was heavily weighted to favour the whites, who hoped that the federation would soon gain full independence from Britain, with dominion status.

The Africans watched with growing distrust, and their leaders, Dr Hastings Banda (Nyasaland), Kenneth Kaunda (Northern Rhodesia) and Joshua Nkomo (Southern Rhodesia) began to campaign for black majority rule. As violence developed, a state of emergency was declared in Nyasaland and Southern Rhodesia, with mass arrests of Africans (1959). However, there was much support for the Africans in Britain, especially in the Labour Party, and the Conservative colonial secretary, Iain Macleod, was sympathetic. *The Monckton Commission (1960) recommended* votes for Africans, an end to racial discrimination and the right of territories to leave the Federation.

1   Nyasaland and Northern Rhodesia
The British introduced new constitutions in Nyasaland and Northern Rhodesia which, in effect, allowed the Africans their own parliaments (1961–2). Both wanted to leave the Federation, which was therefore terminated in December 1963, signalling defeat for the settlers. *The following year Nyasaland and Northern Rhodesia became fully independent, taking the names Malawi and Zambia.*

2   Southern Rhodesia

Southern Rhodesia took much longer to deal with, and it was 1980 before the colony achieved independence with black majority rule. It was in Rhodesia, as it was now known, that the white settlers fought most fiercely to preserve their privileged position. There were fewer than 200 000 whites, about 20 000 Asians and 4 million black Africans, but *the Rhodesia Front*, a right-wing white racist party, was determined never to surrender control of the country to black African rule. The black African parties were banned.

When Zambia and Malawi were given independence, the whites assumed that Southern Rhodesia would get the same treatment, and put in a formal request for independence. The British Conservative government refused and made it clear that independence would be granted *only if the constitution was changed to allow black Africans at least a third of the seats in parliament.* Ian Smith (who became prime minister of Southern Rhodesia in April 1964) rejected this idea and refused to make any concessions. He argued that continued white rule was essential in view of the problems being faced by the new black governments in other African states, and because the Zimbabwe nationalists seemed bitterly divided. Harold Wilson, the new British Labour prime minister (1964–70), continued to refuse independence unless the constitution was changed to prepare for black majority rule. Since no compromise seemed possible, Smith declared Southern Rhodesia independent, against the wishes of Britain (a unilateral declaration of independence, or UDI), in November 1965.

There were mixed reactions to UDI:

- *At first there seemed very little Britain could do about it*, once the government had decided not to use force against the illegal Smith regime. It was hoped to bring the country to its knees by economic sanctions, and Britain stopped buying sugar and tobacco from Rhodesia.
- *The UN condemned UDI* and called on all member states to place a complete trade embargo on Rhodesia.
- *South Africa, also ruled by a white minority government, and Portugal, which still controlled neighbouring Mozambique, were sympathetic to the Smith regime* and refused to obey the Security Council resolution. This meant that Rhodesia was able to continue trading through these countries. Many other countries, while publicly condemning UDI, privately evaded the embargo; the USA, for example, bought Rhodesian chrome because it was the cheapest available. Companies and businessmen in many countries, including British oil companies, continued to break sanctions, and although the Rhodesian economy suffered to some extent, it was not serious enough to topple the Smith regime.
- *The Commonwealth was seriously shaken.* Ghana and Nigeria wanted Britain to use force, and offered to supply troops. Zambia and Tanzania hoped that economic sanctions would suffice; relations with the British became extremely cool when it seemed that they were deliberately soft-pedalling sanctions, especially as Zambia was suffering more from them than Rhodesia. When Wilson twice met Smith (aboard HMS *Tiger* in 1966 and HMS *Fearless* in 1968) to put new proposals, there was a howl of protest in case he betrayed the black Rhodesians. Perhaps fortunately for the future of the Commonwealth, Smith rejected both sets of proposals.
- *The World Council of Churches* set up a programme to combat racism (1969), and this gave encouragement and support to the nationalists both morally and financially.

In 1970 Rhodesia declared itself a republic, and the rights of black citizens were gradually whittled away until they were suffering similar treatment to that experienced by blacks in South Africa (see Section 25.8). In 1976 the first signs began to appear that the whites would have to compromise. *Why did the whites give way?*

1   *Mozambique's independence from Portugal (June 1975)* was a serious blow to Rhodesia. The new president of Mozambique, Samora Machel, applied economic sanctions and allowed Zimbabwean guerrillas to operate from Mozambique.

2   *The 'front-line states'* – which included Zambia, Botswana and Tanzania, as well as Mozambique – *supported the armed struggle* and provided training camps for the resistance movement. Thousands of black guerrillas were soon active in Rhodesia, straining the white security forces to their limits and forcing Smith to hire foreign mercenaries.

3   *The South Africans became less inclined to support Rhodesia* after their invasion of Angola (October 1975) had been called off on American orders. The Americans and South Africans were helping the rebel FNLA (National Front for the Liberation of Angola), which was trying to overthrow the ruling MPLA Party (People's Movement for Angolan Liberation), which had Russian and Cuban backing. The Americans were afraid that the USSR and Cuba might become involved in Rhodesia unless some compromise could be found; together with South Africa, they urged Smith to make concessions to the blacks before it was too late.

4   *By 1978 nationalist guerrillas controlled large areas of the Rhodesian countryside.* Farming was adversely affected as white farmers were attacked; schools in rural areas were closed and sometimes burnt down. It became clear that the defeat of the whites was only a matter of time.

Smith still tried everything he knew to delay black majority rule as long as possible. He was able to present the divisions between the nationalist leaders as his excuse for the lack of progress, and this was a genuine problem:

- **ZAPU** (the Zimbabwe African People's Union) was the party of the veteran nationalist Joshua Nkomo.
- **ZANU** (the Zimbabwe African National Union) was the party of the Reverend Ndabaningi Sithole.

These two, representing different tribes, seemed to be bitter enemies.

- **UANC** (the United African National Council) was the party of Bishop Abel Muzorewa.
- **Robert Mugabe**, leader of the guerrilla wing of ZANU, was another powerful figure, who eventually emerged as ZANU's unchallenged leader.

The divisions were reduced to some extent as a result of the 1976 Geneva Conference, when ZAPU and ZANU came together loosely in the Patriotic Front (PF). After this, the parties were referred to as **ZANU-PF** and **PF-ZAPU**.

Smith now tried to compromise by introducing his own scheme, a joint government of whites and UANC, the most moderate of the nationalist parties, with Bishop Muzorewa as prime minister. The country was to be called Zimbabwe/Rhodesia (April 1979). However, it was ZANU-PF and PF-ZAPU which had mass support and they continued the guerrilla war. Smith soon had to admit defeat and the British called *the Lancaster House Conference* in London (September–December 1979), which agreed the following points.

- There should be a new constitution which would allow the black majority to rule.
- In the new Republic of Zimbabwe, there would be a 100-seat parliament with 20 seats reserved for whites (uncontested). The remaining 80 MPs were to be elected, and it was expected that they would be black, since the vast majority of the population was black.
- Muzorewa would step down as prime minister and the guerrilla war would end.

In the elections which followed, Mugabe's ZANU won a sweeping victory, taking 57 out of the 80 black African seats. This gave him a comfortable overall majority, enabling him to become prime minister when Zimbabwe officially became independent in April 1980. The transference to black majority rule was welcomed by all African and Commonwealth leaders as a triumph of common sense and moderation. ZAPU and ZANU merged in 1987, when Mugabe became the country's first executive president. He was re-elected for a further term in March 1996, not without controversy, and was still clinging on to power in 2012, at the age of 87 (see Section 25.12).

24.5 THE END OF THE FRENCH EMPIRE

The main French possessions at the end of the Second World War were:

- Syria in the Middle East, from which they withdrew in 1946;
- Guadeloupe and Martinique (islands in the West Indies);
- French Guiana (on the mainland of South America);
- Indo-China in south-east Asia;

together with huge areas of North and West Africa:

- Tunisia, Morocco and Algeria (together known as the Maghreb);
- French West Africa;
- French Equatorial Africa;
- the large island of Madagascar off the south-east coast of Africa.

The French began by trying to suppress all nationalist agitation, regarding it as high treason.

As the 1944 Brazzaville Declaration put it:

> The colonising work of France makes it impossible to accept any idea of autonomy for the colonies or any possibility of development outside the French Empire. Even at a distant date, there will be no self-government in the colonies.

But gradually the French were influenced by Britain's moves towards decolonization, and after their defeat in Indo-China in 1954, they too were forced to bow to the 'wind of change'.

(a) Indo-China

Before the war, the French had exercised direct rule over the area around Saigon and had protectorates over Annam, Tonkin, Cambodia and Laos. A protectorate was a country which was officially independent with its own ruler, but which was under the 'protection' or guardianship of the mother country. It usually meant, in practice, that the mother country, in this case France, controlled affairs in the protectorate just as it did in a colony.

During the war, the whole area was occupied by the Japanese, and resistance was organized by the communist *Ho Chi Minh and the League for Vietnamese Independence (Vietminh)*. When the Japanese withdrew in 1945, Ho Chi Minh declared

Vietnam independent. This was unacceptable to the French, and an eight-year armed struggle began which culminated in the French defeat at Dien Bien Phu in May 1954 (see Sections 8.3(a) and 21.2–3). The defeat was a humiliating blow for the French and it caused a political crisis. The government resigned and the new and more liberal premier Pierre Mendès-France, realizing that public opinion was turning against the war, decided to withdraw.

At the Geneva Conference (July 1954) it was agreed that Vietnam, Laos and Cambodia should become independent. Unfortunately this was not the end of the troubles. Although the French had withdrawn, the Americans were unwilling to allow the whole of Vietnam to come under the rule of the communist Ho Chi Minh, and an even more bloody struggle developed (see Section 8.3(b–e)); there were also problems in Cambodia (see Section 9.4(b)).

(b) Tunisia and Morocco

Both these areas were protectorates – Tunisia had a ruler known as the bey, and Morocco had a Muslim king, Mohammed V. But nationalists resented French control and had been campaigning for real independence since before the Second World War. The situation was complicated by the presence of large numbers of European settlers. Tunisia had about 250 000 and Morocco about 300 000 of these in 1945, and they were committed to maintaining the connection with France, which guaranteed their privileged position.

1 Tunisia
In Tunisia the main nationalist group was *the New Destour* led by Habib Bourghiba. They had widespread support among both rural dwellers and townspeople who believed independence would improve their living standards. A guerrilla campaign was launched against the French, who responded by banning New Destour and imprisoning Bourghiba (1952); 70 000 French troops were deployed against the guerrillas, but failed to crush them. The French became aware of a disturbing trend: with Bourghiba and other moderate leaders in jail, the guerrilla movement was becoming more left-wing and less willing to negotiate. Under pressure at the same time in Indo-China and Morocco, the French realized that they would have to give way. With a moderate like Bourghiba at the head of the country, there would be more chance of maintaining French influence after independence. He was released from jail and Mendès-France allowed him to form a government. In March 1956 Tunisia became fully independent under Bourghiba's leadership.

2 Morocco
In Morocco the pattern of events was remarkably similar. There was a nationalist party calling itself *Istiqlal (Independence)*, and King Mohammed himself seemed to be in the forefront of opposition to the French. The new trade unions also played an important role. The French deposed the king (1953), provoking violent demonstrations and a guerrilla campaign. Faced with the prospect of yet another long and expensive anti-guerrilla war, the French decided to bow to the inevitable. The king was allowed to return and Morocco became independent in 1956.

(c) Algeria

It was here that the 'settler' factor had the most serious consequences. There were over a million French settlers (known as *pieds noirs*, 'black feet'), who controlled something like a third of all the most fertile land in Algeria, taken from the original Algerian owners during the century before 1940. The whites exported most of the crops they produced and also used some of the land to grow vines for winemaking; this meant there was less food available for the growing African population, whose standard of living was clearly falling. There was an active, though peaceful, nationalist movement led by Messali Hadj, but after almost ten years of campaigning following the end of the Second World War, they had achieved absolutely nothing.

- The French settlers would make no concessions whatsoever, continuing to dominate the economy with their large farms and treating the Algerians as second-class citizens. They firmly believed that fear of the full might of the French army would be enough to dissuade the nationalists from becoming violent.
- Algeria continued to be treated not as a colony or a protectorate, but as an extension or province of metropolitan France itself; but that did not mean that the 9 million Muslim Arab Algerians were treated as equals with ordinary French people. They were allowed no say in the government of their country. Responding to pressure, the French government allowed what appeared to be power-sharing. An Algerian assembly of 120 members was set up, though its powers were limited. But the voting was heavily weighted in favour of the Europeans: the million whites were allowed to vote for 60 members, while the other 60 were chosen by the 9 million Muslim population. Corruption on the part of the Europeans usually meant that they had a majority in the assembly.
- In spite of what had happened in Indo-China, Tunisia and Morocco, no French government dared consider independence for Algeria, since this would incur the wrath of the settlers and their supporters in France. Even Mendès-France declared: 'France without Algeria would be no France.'

Tragically, the stubbornness of the settlers and their refusal even to talk meant that the struggle would be decided by the extremists. Encouraged by the French defeat in Indo-China, a more militant nationalist group was formed – *the National Liberation Front (FLN), led by Ben Bella*, which launched a guerrilla war towards the end of 1954. At the same time, however, they promised that when they came to power, the *pieds noirs* would be treated fairly. On the other hand, the settlers were still confident that with the support of the French army they could overcome the guerrillas. The war gradually escalated as the French sent more forces. By 1960 they had 700 000 troops engaged in a massive anti-terrorist operation. *The war was having profound effects in France itself:*

- Many French politicians realized that even if the army won the military struggle, the FLN still had the support of most of the Algerian people, and while this lasted, *French control of Algeria could never be secure.*
- *The war split public opinion in France* between those who wanted to continue supporting the white settlers and those who thought the struggle was hopeless. At times feelings ran so high that France itself seemed on the verge of civil war.
- The French army, after its defeats in the Second World War and Indo-China, saw the Algerian war as a chance to restore its reputation and refused to contemplate surrender. Some generals were prepared to stage a military coup against any government that decided to give Algeria independence.
- In May 1958, suspecting that the government was about to give way, as it had in Tunisia and Morocco, Generals Massu and Salan organized demonstrations in Algiers and demanded that General de Gaulle should be called in to head a new government. They were convinced that the general, a great patriot, would never agree to Algerian independence. They began to put their plan – codenamed *Resurrection* – into operation, airlifting troops from Algiers into Paris, where it was

intended that they should occupy government buildings. Civil war seemed imminent; the government could see no way out of the deadlock and consequently resigned. De Gaulle cleverly used the media to reinforce his case; he condemned the weakness of the Fourth Republic and its 'regime of the parties', which he claimed was incapable of dealing with the problem. Then, looking back to 1940, he said: 'Not so long ago, the country, in its hour of peril, trusted me to lead it to salvation. Today, with the trials that face it once again, it should know that I am ready to assume the powers of the Republic.'

President Coty called upon de Gaulle, who agreed to become prime minister on condition that he could draw up a new constitution. This turned out to be *the end of the Fourth Republic*. Historians have had a great debate about the role of de Gaulle in all this. How much had he known about Resurrection? Had he or his supporters actually planned it themselves so that he could return to power? Was he simply using the situation in Algeria as a way of destroying the Fourth Republic, which he thought was weak? What does seem clear is that he knew about the plan and had dropped hints to Massu and Salan that if President Coty refused to allow him to take power, he would be happy for Resurrection to go ahead so that he could take power in that way.

- De Gaulle soon produced his new constitution, giving the president much more power, and he was elected president of the Fifth Republic (December 1958), a position he held until his resignation in April 1969. His enormous prestige was demonstrated when a referendum was held on the new constitution – in France itself, over 80 per cent voted in favour, while in Algeria, where Muslim Algerians were allowed to vote on equal terms with whites for the first time, over 76 per cent were in favour.

Having gained power, de Gaulle was now expected to deliver a solution. But how could he possibly achieve this when any attempt at compromise would be seen as total betrayal by the very people who had helped him to power? But de Gaulle was the great pragmatist. As the vicious fighting continued, with both sides committing atrocities, he must have realized that outright military victory was out of the question. He no doubt hoped that his popularity would enable him to force a settlement. When he showed a willingness to negotiate with the FLN, the army and the settlers were incensed; this was not what they had expected from him. Led by General Salan, they set up *l'Organisation de l'Armée Secrète (OAS) in (1961)*, which began a terrorist campaign, blowing up buildings and murdering critics both in Algeria and in France. Several times they attempted to assassinate de Gaulle; in August 1962, after independence had been granted, he and his wife narrowly escaped death when their car was riddled with bullets. When it was announced that peace talks would begin at Evian, the OAS seized power in Algeria. This was going too far for most French people and for many of the army too. When de Gaulle appeared on television dressed in his full general's uniform and denounced the OAS, the army split, and the rebellion collapsed.

The French public was sick of the war and there was widespread approval when Ben Bella, who had been in prison since 1956, was released to attend peace talks at Evian. *It was agreed that Algeria should become independent in July 1962*, and Ben Bella was elected as its first president the following year. About 800 000 settlers left the country and the new government took over most of their land and businesses. The aftermath of the struggle was savage. Algerian Muslims who had remained loyal to France, including some 200 000 who had served in the French army, were now denounced by the FLN as traitors. Nobody knows how many were executed or murdered, but some estimates put the total as high as 150 000. Some historians have criticized de Gaulle for his handling of the Algerian situation and for the enormous bloodshed that was caused. Of all the wars of independence waged against a colonial power, this was one of the most bloody. Yet, given the intransigence of the white settlers and the rebel elements of the army, and eventually that of the FLN, it is difficult to imagine any other politician who could have handled it any better. It may have been a flawed process, but arguably it was one that saved France from civil war.

(d) The rest of the French Empire

The French possessions in Africa south of the Sahara were:

- **French West Africa**, consisting of eight colonies: Dahomey, Guinea, Ivory Coast, Mauretania, Niger, Senegal, Sudan and Upper Volta;
- **French Equatorial Africa**, consisting of four colonies: Chad, Gabon, Middle Congo and Oubangui-Shari;
- a third group consisting of **Cameroun** and **Togo** (former German colonies given to France to be looked after as mandates in 1919), and the island of **Madagascar**.

French policy after 1945 was to treat these territories as if they were part of France. Yet this was a sham, since the Africans were not treated on equal terms with Europeans, and any moves towards more privileges for the Africans were opposed by the French settlers. In 1949 the French government decided to clamp down on all nationalist movements, and many nationalist leaders and trade unionists were arrested. Often they were denounced as communist agitators, though without much evidence to support the accusations.

Gradually the French were forced by events in Indo-China and the Maghreb, together with the fact that Britain was preparing the Gold Coast and Nigeria for independence, to change their policy. *In 1956 the 12 colonies of West and Equatorial Africa were each given self-government for internal affairs, but they continued to press for full independence.*

When de Gaulle came to power in 1958 he proposed a new plan, hoping to keep as much control over the colonies as possible:

- the 12 colonies would continue to have self-government, each with its own parliament for local affairs;
- they would all be members of a new union, *the French Community*, and France would take all important decisions about taxation and foreign affairs;
- all members of the community would receive economic aid from France;
- there would be a referendum in each colony to decide whether the plan should be accepted or not;
- colonies opting for full independence could have it, but would receive no French aid.

De Gaulle was confident that none of them would dare face the future without French help. He was almost right: 11 colonies voted in favour of his plan, but one, *Guinea, under the leadership of Sékou Touré, returned a 95 per cent vote against the plan*. Guinea was given independence immediately (1958), but all French aid was stopped. However, Guinea's brave stand encouraged the other 11, as well as Togo, Cameroun and Madagascar: they all demanded full independence and de Gaulle agreed. They all became independent republics during 1960. However, this new independence was not quite so complete as the new states had hoped: *de Gaulle was intent on neo-colonialism* – all the states except Guinea found that France still influenced their economic and foreign policies, and any independent action was almost out of the question.

Three French possessions outside Africa – Martinique, Guadeloupe and French Guiana – were not given independence. They continued to be treated as extensions of the mother country and their official status was 'overseas départements' (a sort of county or province). Their peoples voted in French elections and their representatives sat in the French National Assembly in Paris.

24.6 THE NETHERLANDS, BELGIUM, SPAIN, PORTUGAL AND ITALY

All these colonial powers, with the exception of Italy, were, if anything, even more determined than France to hold on to their overseas possessions. This was probably because, being less wealthy than Britain and France, they lacked the resources to sustain neo-colonialism. There was no way that they would be able to maintain the equivalent of the British Commonwealth or the French influence over their former colonies, against competition from foreign capital.

(a) The Netherlands

Before the Second World War, the Netherlands had a huge empire in the East Indies including the large islands of Sumatra, Java and Celebes, West Irian (part of the island of New Guinea) and about two-thirds of the island of Borneo (see Map 24.3). They also owned some islands in the West Indies, and Surinam on the mainland of South America, between British and French Guiana.

It was in the valuable East Indies that the first challenge came to Dutch control, even before the war. The Dutch operated in a way similar to the French in Algeria – they grew crops for export and did very little to improve the living standards of the East Indians. Nationalist groups campaigned throughout the 1930s, and many leaders, including Ahmed Sukarno, were arrested. When the Japanese invaded in 1942, they released Sukarno and others and allowed them to play a part in the administration of the country, promising independence when the war was over. With the Japanese defeat in 1945, *Sukarno declared an independent Republic of Indonesia*, not expecting any resistance from the Dutch, who had been defeated and their country occupied by the Germans. However, Dutch troops soon arrived and made determined efforts to regain control. Although the Dutch had some success, the war dragged on, and they were still a long way from complete victory in 1949, when they at last decided to negotiate. *Reasons for their decision were the following.*

- The expense of the campaign was crippling for a small country like the Netherlands.
- Outright victory still seemed a long way off.
- They were under strong pressure from the UN to reach agreement.
- Other countries, including the USA and Australia, were pressing the Dutch to grant independence so that they could exert their influence in the area, once exclusive Dutch control ended.
- The Dutch hoped that by making concessions, they would be able to preserve the link between Holland and Indonesia and maintain some influence.

The Netherlands agreed to recognize the independence of the United States of Indonesia (1949) with Sukarno as president, but not including West Irian. Sukarno agreed to a Netherlands–Indonesia Union under the Dutch crown, and Dutch troops were withdrawn. However, the following year Sukarno broke away from the Union and began to pressurize the Dutch to hand over West Irian, seizing Dutch-owned property and expelling Europeans. Eventually in 1963, the Dutch gave way and allowed West Irian to become part of Indonesia.

Important developments took place in 1965 when Sukarno was overthrown in a right-wing military coup, apparently because he was thought to be too much under the influence of communist China and the Indonesian Communist Party – the largest communist party outside the USSR and China. The USA, operating via the CIA, was involved in the coup, because they did not like Sukarno's toleration of the Communist Party, or the way in which he was acting as leader of the non-aligned and anti-imperialist movements of the Third World. The Americans welcomed Sukarno's successor, General Suharto, who obligingly introduced what he called his 'New Order'. This involved a purge of communists, during which at least half a million people were murdered, and the Communist Party was broken. The regime had all the hallmarks of a brutal military dictatorship, but there were few protests from the West because, in the Cold War atmosphere, Suharto's anti-communist campaign was perfectly acceptable. Of the other Dutch possessions, Surinam was allowed to become an independent republic in 1975; the West Indian islands were treated as part of the Netherlands, though allowed some control over their internal affairs.

(b) Belgium

Belgian control of their African possessions, the Belgian Congo and Ruanda-Urundi, ended in chaos, violence and civil war. *The Belgians thought that the best ways to preserve their control were as follows.*

- Denying the Africans any advanced education. This would prevent them from coming into contact with nationalist ideas and deprive them of an educated professional class who could lead them to independence.
- Using tribal rivalries to their advantage by playing off different tribes against each other. This worked well in the huge Congo, which contained about 150 tribes; men from one tribe would be used to keep order in another tribal area. In Ruanda-Urundi the Belgians used the Tutsi tribe to help them control the other main tribal group, the Hutu.

In spite of all these efforts, nationalist ideas still began to filter in from neighbouring French and British colonies.

1   The Belgian Congo
The Belgians seemed taken by surprise when widespread rioting broke out (January 1959) in the capital of the Congo, Leopoldville. The crowds were protesting against unemployment and declining living standards, and disorder soon spread throughout the country.

The Belgians suddenly changed their policy and announced that the Congo could become independent in six months. This was inviting disaster: the Belgians' own policies meant that there was no experienced group of Africans to which power could be handed over; the Congolese had not been educated for professional jobs – there were only 17 graduates in the entire country, and there were no African doctors, lawyers, engineers or officers in the army. *The Congolese National Movement (MNC),* led by *Patrice Lumumba*, had been in existence less than a year. The huge size of the country and the large number of tribes would make it difficult to govern. Six months was far too short a time to prepare for independence.

Why did the Belgians take this extraordinary decision?

- They were afraid of further bloodshed if they hesitated; there were over 100 000 Belgians in the country, who could be at risk.
- They did not want to face the expense of a long anti-guerrilla campaign like the one dragging on in Algeria.

- They hoped that granting independence immediately while the Congo was weak and divided would leave the new state completely helpless; it would be dependent on Belgium for support and advice, and so Belgian influence could be preserved.

The Congo became independent on 30 June 1960 with Lumumba as prime minister and Joseph Kasavubu, the leader of a rival nationalist group, as president. Unfortunately everything went wrong shortly after independence and the country was plunged into a disastrous civil war (see Section 25.5). Order was not restored until 1964.

2 Ruanda-Urundi

The other Belgian territory, *Ruanda-Urundi*, was given independence in 1962 and divided into two states – Rwanda and Burundi, both governed by members of the Tutsi tribe, as they had been throughout the colonial period. Neither of the states had been properly prepared, and after independence, both had a very unsettled history of bitter rivalry and violence between the Tutsis and the Hutus (see Section 25.7).

(c) Spain

Spain owned some areas in Africa: the largest was Spanish Sahara, and there were also the small colonies of Spanish Morocco, Ifni and Spanish Guinea. General Franco, the right-wing dictator who ruled Spain from 1939 until 1975, showed little interest in the colonies.

- When nationalist movements developed, he did not resist long in the case of *Spanish Morocco*: when the French gave independence to French Morocco (1956), Franco followed suit and Spanish Morocco became part of Morocco. The other two small colonies had to wait much longer;
- *Ifni* was allowed to join Morocco, but not until 1969;
- *Guinea* became independent as Equatorial Guinea in 1968.

Spanish Sahara

Here Franco resisted even longer, because the country was a valuable source of phosphates. Only after Franco's death in 1975 did the new Spanish government agree to release Sahara. Unfortunately the process was badly bungled: instead of making it into an independent state ruled by its nationalist party, *the Polisario Front*, it was decided to divide it between its two neighbouring states, Morocco and Mauretania. The Polisario Front, under its leader, Mohamed Abdelazia, declared the Democratic Arab Republic of Sahara (1976), which was recognized by Algeria, Libya, the communist states and India. Algeria and Libya sent help and in 1979 Mauretania decided to withdraw, making it easier for Sahara to struggle on against Morocco. However, the fact that Sahara had been officially recognized by the USSR was enough to arouse American suspicions. Just when it seemed that the Moroccans too were prepared to negotiate peace, the new American president, Ronald Reagan, encouraged them to continue the fight, stepping up aid to Morocco.

The war dragged on through the 1980s; yet another new Third World country had become a victim of superpower self-interest. In 1990 the UN proposed that a referendum should be held so that the people of Sahara could choose whether to be independent or become part of Morocco. Both sides signed a ceasefire, but the referendum was never held; during the 1990s the Polisario forces grew weaker as support was withdrawn by Algeria and Libya, mainly because they were preoccupied with their own problems. Sahara remained under Moroccan control and large numbers of Moroccan settlers began to move in. At the same time many Saharans, including Polisario fighters, moved out of the country and were forced to live in refugee camps in Algeria.

(d) Portugal

The main Portuguese possessions were in Africa: the two large areas of *Angola* and *Mozambique*, and the small West African colony of *Portuguese Guinea*. They also still owned the eastern half of the island of Timor in the East Indies. The right-wing Portuguese government of Dr Salazar blithely ignored nationalist developments in the rest of Africa, and for many years after 1945 the Portuguese colonies seemed quiet and resigned to their position. They were mainly agricultural; there were few industrial workers and the black populations were almost entirely illiterate. In 1956 there were only 50 Africans in the whole of Mozambique who had received any secondary education. Though nationalist groups were formed in all three colonies in 1956, they remained insignificant. *Several factors changed the situation.*

- By 1960 the nationalists were greatly encouraged by the large number of other African states winning independence.
- The Salazar regime, having learned nothing from the experiences of the other colonial powers, stepped up its repressive policies, but this only made the nationalists more resolute.
- Fighting broke out first in Angola (1961), where Agostinho Neto's *MPLA (People's Movement for Angolan Liberation)* was the main nationalist movement. Violence soon spread to Guinea, where Amilcar Cabral led the resistance, and to Mozambique, where the FRELIMO guerrillas were organized by Eduardo Mondlane.
- The nationalists, who all had strong Marxist connections, received economic and military aid from the Communist bloc.
- The Portuguese army found it impossible to suppress the nationalist guerrillas; the troops became demoralized and the cost escalated until by 1973 the government was spending 40 per cent of its budget fighting three colonial wars at once.
- Still the Portuguese government refused to abandon its policy; but public opinion and many army officers were sick of the wars, and in 1974 the Salazar dictatorship was overthrown by a military coup.

Soon all three colonies were granted independence: Guinea took the name Guinea-Bissau (September 1974) and Mozambique and Angola became independent the following year. This caused a serious crisis for Rhodesia and South Africa; they were now the only states left in Africa ruled by white minorities, and their governments felt increasingly threatened.

Now it was the turn of Angola to become a victim of outside interference and the Cold War. South African troops immediately invaded the country in support of UNITA (National Union for the Total Independence of Angola), while General Mobutu of Zaire, with American backing, launched another invasion in support of the FNLA (National Front for the Liberation of Angola). The Americans thought that a joint Angolan government of these two groups would be more amenable and open to western influence than the Marxist MPLA. The MPLA received aid in the form of Russian weapons and a Cuban army; this enabled them to defeat both invasion forces by March 1976, and Neto was accepted as president of the new state. This proved to be only a temporary respite – further invasions followed and Angola was torn by civil war right through into the 1990s (see Section 25.6). The South Africans also interfered in Mozambique, sending raiding parties over the border and doing their best to destabilize the FRELIMO government. Again the country was torn by civil war for many years (see Section 9.4(c)).

One other Portuguese territory deserves mention: East Timor was half of a small island in the East Indies (see Map 24.6); the western half belonged to the Netherlands and became part of Indonesia in 1949. East Timor's nationalist movement (FRETILIN) won a short civil war against the ruling group, which wanted to stay with Portugal (September 1975). The USA denounced the new government as Marxist, which was not entirely accurate; after only a few weeks, Indonesian troops invaded, overthrew the government and incorporated East Timor into Indonesia, a sequence of events vividly described in Timothy Mo's novel *The Redundancy of Courage*. The USA continued to supply military goods to the Indonesians, who were guilty of appalling atrocities both during and after the war. It is estimated that about 100 000 people were killed (one-sixth of the population) while another 300 000 were put into detention camps.

FRETILIN continued to campaign for independence, but although the UN and the EU condemned Indonesia's action, East Timor was apparently too small and too unimportant, and the nationalists too left-wing to warrant any sanctions being applied against Indonesia by the West. The USA consistently defended Indonesia's claim to East Timor and played down the violence. In November 1991, for example, 271 people were killed in Dili, the capital, when Indonesian troops attacked a pro-independence demonstration. However, this incident helped to focus international attention on the campaign against Indonesian abuses of human rights and against US and UK arms sales to Indonesia. In 1996, the Roman Catholic Bishop of Dili, Carlos Belo, and exiled FRETILIN spokesman José Ramos-Horta, were jointly awarded the Nobel Peace Prize, in recognition of their long, non-violent campaign for independence.

By 1999, with international support for East Timor mounting, and the Cold War long since over, Indonesia at last began to give way and offered to allow a referendum on 'special autonomy' for East Timor. This was organized by the UN and took place in August 1999, resulting in an almost 80 per cent vote for complete independence from Indonesia. However, the pro-Indonesian minority did their best to sabotage the elections; as voting took place, their militia, backed by Indonesian troops, did everything they could to intimidate voters and throw the whole country into chaos. After the result was announced, they ran wild in a furious outburst of revenge and destruction, killing 2000 and leaving 250 000 homeless. Violence was only ended by the arrival of a large Australian peacekeeping force.

Two years later, in August 2001, when elections were held for the Constituent Assembly, the situation was much calmer. FRETILIN won by a large majority and their

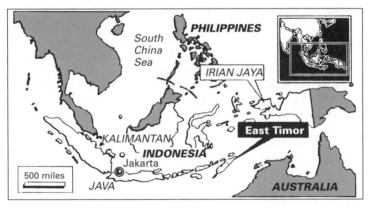

Map 24.6   **Indonesia and East Timor**

Source: *The Guardian*, 20 April 1996.

25

Problems in Africa

After achieving independence, the new African nations faced similar problems. It is not possible in the limited space available to look at events in every state in Africa. The following sections examine the problems common to all the states, and show what happened in some of the countries which experienced one or more of these problems. For example:

- *Ghana* suffered economic problems, the failure of democracy and several coups.
- *Nigeria* experienced civil war, a succession of military coups and brutal military dictatorship.
- *Tanzania* – extreme poverty.
- *The Congo* – civil war and military dictatorship.
- *Angola* – civil war prolonged by outside interference.
- *Burundi and Rwanda* – civil war and horrifying tribal slaughter.
- *South Africa* was a special case: after 1980, when Rhodesia (Zimbabwe) gained its independence, South Africa was the last bastion of white rule on the continent of Africa, and the white minority was determined to hold out to the bitter end against black nationalism. Gradually the pressures became too much for the white minority, and in May 1994 Nelson Mandela became the first black president of South Africa.
- *Liberia, Ethiopia, Sierra Leone and Zimbabwe* also had their own special problems.
- In the mid-1980s most of the countries of Africa began to experience HIV/AIDS, which by 2004 had reached pandemic proportions, especially in sub-Saharan Africa. Some 28 million people – about 8 per cent of the population – were HIV positive.

25.1 PROBLEMS COMMON TO THE AFRICAN STATES

(a) Tribal differences

They each contained a number of different tribes which had only been held together by the foreign colonial rulers and which had united in the nationalist struggle for freedom from the foreigners. As soon as the Europeans withdrew, there was little incentive to stay together, and they tended to regard loyalty to the tribe as more important than loyalty to their new nation. In Nigeria, the Congo (Zaire), Burundi and Rwanda, tribal differences became so intense that they led to civil war.

(b) They were economically under-developed

In this, they were like many other Third World states. Most African states had very little industry; this had been a deliberate policy by the colonial powers, so that Africans would have to buy manufactured goods from Europe or the USA; the role of the colonies had been to provide food and raw materials. After independence they often relied on only one or two commodities for export, so that a fall in the world price of their products was a major disaster. Nigeria, for example, relied heavily on its oil exports, which produced about 80 per cent of its annual income. There was a shortage of capital and skills of all kinds, and the population was growing at a rate of over 2 per cent a year. Loans from abroad left them heavily in debt, and as they concentrated on increasing exports to pay for the loans, food for home consumption became scarcer. All this left the African nations heavily dependent on western European countries and the USA for both markets and investment and enabled those countries to exert some control over African governments (neo-colonialism). In the atmosphere of the Cold War, some states suffered direct military intervention from countries which did not like their government, usually because they were thought to be too left-wing and under Soviet influence. This happened to Angola, which found itself invaded by troops from South Africa and Zaire because those countries disapproved of Angola's Marxist-style government.

(c) Political problems

African politicians lacked experience of how to work the systems of parliamentary democracy left behind by the Europeans. Faced with difficult problems, they often failed to cope, and governments became corrupt. Most African leaders who had taken part in guerrilla campaigns before independence had been influenced by Marxist ideas, which often led them to set up one-party states as the only way to achieve progress. In many states, such as Kenya and Tanzania, this worked well, providing stable and effective government. On the other hand, since it was impossible to oppose such governments by legal means, violence was the only answer. Military coups to remove unpopular rulers became common. President Nkrumah of Ghana, for example, was removed by the army in 1966 after two assassination attempts had failed. Where the army was unable or unwilling to stage a coup, such as in Malawi, the one-party system flourished at the expense of freedom and genuine democracy.

(d) Economic and natural disasters

In the 1980s the whole of Africa was beset by economic and natural disasters. The world recession reduced demand for African exports such as oil, copper and cobalt, and there was a severe drought (1982–5) which caused crop failures, deaths of livestock, famine and starvation. The drought ended in 1986 and much of the continent had record harvests that year. However, by this time, Africa, like the rest of the world, was suffering from a severe debt crisis, and at the same time had been forced by the International Monetary Fund (IMF) to economize drastically in return for further loans. In a number of cases the IMF prescribed the ESAP (Economic Structural Adjustment Programme) which the country had to follow. Often this forced them to devalue their currency, and reduce food price subsidies, which led to increased food prices at a time when unemployment was rising and wages were falling. Governments were also forced to cut their spending on education, health and social services as part of the austerity programme. Table 26.2 in the next chapter shows how poor most of the African states were in comparison with the rest of the world.

25.2 DEMOCRACY, DICTATORSHIP AND MILITARY GOVERNMENT IN GHANA

Kwame Nkrumah ruled Ghana from the time the country gained independence in 1957 until his removal by the army in 1966.

(a) His initial achievements were impressive

He was a socialist in outlook and wanted his people to enjoy a higher standard of living, which would come from efficient organization and industrialization. Production of cocoa (Ghana's main export) doubled, forestry, fishing and cattle-breeding expanded, and the country's modest deposits of gold and bauxite were more effectively exploited. The building of a dam on the River Volta (begun 1961) provided water for irrigation and hydro-electric power, producing enough electricity for the towns as well as for a new plant for smelting Ghana's large deposits of bauxite. Government money was provided for village projects in which local people built roads and schools.

Nkrumah also gained prestige internationally: he strongly supported *the pan-African movement*, believing that only through a federation of the whole continent could African power make itself felt. As a start, an economic union was formed with Guinea and Mali, though nothing much came of it, while his dream of an African federal state quickly faded (see Section 24.1(c)). He supported *the Organization of African Unity* (set up in 1963), and usually played a responsible role in world affairs, keeping Ghana in the Commonwealth; in 1961 Queen Elizabeth II made a state visit to Ghana. At the same time Nkrumah forged links with the USSR, East Germany and China.

(b) Why was Nkrumah overthrown?

He tried to introduce industrialization too quickly and borrowed vast amounts of capital from abroad, hoping to balance the budget from increased exports. Unfortunately Ghana was still uncomfortably dependent on cocoa exports, and a steep fall in the world price of cocoa left her with a huge balance-of-payments deficit. The smelting plant was a disappointment because the American corporation that built and owned it insisted on buying bauxite from abroad instead of using Ghanaian bauxite. There was criticism that too much money was being wasted on unnecessary projects, like the ten-mile stretch of motorway from Accra (the capital) to Tema, and some grandiose building projects.

Probably the most important reason for his downfall was that he gradually began to abandon parliamentary government in favour of a one-party state and personal dictatorship. He justified this on the grounds that the opposition parties, which were based on tribal differences, were not constructive and merely wanted more power in their own areas. They had no experience of working a parliamentary system, and as Nkrumah himself wrote: 'Even a system based on a democratic constitution may need backing up in the period following independence by emergency measures of a totalitarian kind.'

From 1959 onwards, opponents could be deported or imprisoned for up to five years without trial. Even the respected opposition leader, J. B. Danqua, was arrested in 1961 and died in prison. In 1964 all parties except Nkrumah's were banned, and even within his own party no criticism was allowed. He began to build up the image of himself as the 'father of the nation'. Slogans such as 'Nkrumah is our Messiah, Nkrumah never dies' were circulated, and numerous statues of the 'saviour' were erected. This struck many people as absurd, but Nkrumah justified it on the grounds that the population could identify itself better with a single personality as leader than with vague notions of the state. All this, plus the fact that he was believed to have amassed a personal fortune through corruption, was too much for the army, which seized control when Nkrumah was on a visit to China (1966). The American CIA gave the coup its full backing, because the USA disapproved of Nkrumah's links with communist states.

The military government promised a return to democracy as soon as a new constitution could be drawn up, complete with safeguards against a return to dictatorship. The constitution was ready in 1969 and the elections returned Dr Kofi Busia, leader of the Progressive Party, as the new prime Minister (October 1969).

(c)   Kofi Busia

Dr Busia survived only until January 1972 when he too was overthrown by the army. An academic who had studied economics at Oxford, Busia illustrates perfectly the difficulties of democratically elected politicians trying to maintain political stability in the African situation. In power in the first place only by permission of the army, he had to produce quick results. Yet the problems were enormous – rising unemployment, rising prices, the low price of cocoa on the world market, and massive debts to be repaid. Canada and the USA were prepared to wait for repayment, but other countries, including Britain, were not so sympathetic. Busia, who had a reputation for honesty, genuinely tried to keep up payments, but these were using up about 40 per cent of Ghana's export profits. In 1971 imports were limited and the currency was devalued by nearly 50 per cent. Busia was hampered by the tribal squabbles which re-emerged under conditions of democracy, and the economic situation deteriorated so rapidly that in January 1972, while he was away on a visit to London, the army announced that he had been replaced by a National Redemption Council under the leadership of Colonel Ignatius Acheampong. They too struggled with all the same problems, exacerbated by sharp rises in the price of oil and other imports.

(d)   J. J. Rawlings

As Ghana continued to flounder amid her economic problems, Acheampong was himself removed from power by General Fred Akuffo, for alleged corruption. In June 1979, a group of junior officers led by 32-year-old Jerry J. Rawlings, a charismatic air-force officer of mixed Ghanaian and Scottish parentage, seized power on the grounds that corrupt soldiers and politicians needed to be weeded out before a return to democracy. They launched what was described as a 'house-cleaning' exercise in which Acheampong and Akuffo were executed after secret trials. In July, elections were held as a result of which Rawlings returned Ghana to civilian rule with Dr Hilla Limann as president (September 1979).

Limann was no more successful than previous leaders in halting Ghana's economic decline. Corruption was still rife at all levels, and smuggling and hoarding of basic goods were commonplace. During 1981, inflation was running at 125 per cent, and there was widespread labour unrest as wages remained low. Rawlings came to the conclusion that he and some of his associates could do better. Limann was removed in a military coup (December 1981), and Flight-Lieutenant Rawlings became chairman of a Provisional National Defence Council (PNDC). He was rare among military leaders: the army did not want power, he said, but simply to be 'part of the decision-making process' which would change Ghana's whole economic and social system. Though Rawlings remained leader, the PNDC appointed a civilian government of well-known figures from political and academic circles. Ghana suffered badly from the drought in 1983, but there was ample rainfall in 1984, bringing a good maize harvest.

Reluctantly Rawlings turned to the IMF for help, and though he had to agree to their conditions (austerity measures had to be introduced), the new recovery programme soon seemed to be working. Production rose by 7 per cent, and early in 1985 inflation was down to 40 per cent. As Ghana celebrated 30 years of independence (March 1987), she was still on course for recovery, and Rawlings and his party, the National Democratic Congress (NDC), evoking memories of Nkrumah, were running an apparently successful campaign to unite the 12 million Ghanaians solidly behind them. In the early 1990s Ghana was enjoying one of the highest economic growth rates in Africa. Yet for many people there remained one big criticism: there was no progress towards representative democracy. Rawlings responded in 1991 by calling an assembly to draw up a new constitution, and promised democratic elections in 1992. These duly went ahead (November) and Rawlings himself was elected president for a four-year term, with over 58 per cent of the votes. He was both Head of State and Commander-in-Chief of the Armed Forces. He was re-elected in 1996, but the constitution did not allow him to stand again in 2000. His career had been a remarkable one; seizing power in 1981 at the age of only 36, he remained leader for some 20 years, and gave Ghana a long period of political stability and modest prosperity.

The NDC chose Vice-President J. E. A. Mills as its presidential candidate. His main opponent was John Kufuor, leader of the New Patriotic Party. Mills was expected to win, but Kufuor scored a surprise victory and took over as president in January 2001. The NDC defeat was probably caused by economic problems – there had been a fall in the world prices of cocoa and gold, which were Ghana's two main exports – and by the fact that the popular J. J. Rawlings was no longer the candidate. Kufuor continued the stability and prosperity, and in 2002 he set up a National Reconciliation Commission. He was re-elected in 2004 and remained president until the next election, in December 2008. He concentrated on diversifying Ghana's economy, modernizing agriculture and infrastructure, and encouraging private involvement. Social conditions were improved and the National Health System was reformed. In 2005 the Ghana School Feeding Programme was started – this provided a free hot meal a day for schoolchildren in the poorest areas.

Ghana continued to be regarded as one of the most stable, prosperous and generally successful democracies in the whole of Africa. Kufuor's policies won the approval of the western countries and the US Millennium Challenge Account awarded Ghana a record $500 million grant for economic development. However, Kufuor was not without his critics among whom J. J. Rawlings was prominent. The complaints were that some projects had not been carried through fully and some had been underfunded or not funded at all. In the 2008 elections the NDC candidate, J. E. A. Mills, won the narrowest of victories.

25.3 CIVIL WARS AND CORRUPTION IN NIGERIA

Superficially, Nigeria, which gained independence in 1960, seemed to have advantages over Ghana; it was potentially a wealthy state, extensive oil resources having been discovered in the eastern coastal area. The prime minister was the capable and moderate Sir Abubakar Tafawa Balewa, assisted by the veteran nationalist leader Nnamdi Azikiwe, who was made president when Nigeria became a republic in 1963. However, in 1966 the government was overthrown by a military coup, and the following year civil war broke out and lasted until 1970.

(a) What caused the civil war?

A combination of the problems mentioned in Section 25.1 led to the outbreak.

- Nigeria's tribal differences were more serious than Ghana's, and although the constitution was a federal one, in which each of the three regions (north, east and west) had its own local government, the regions felt that the central government in Lagos did not safeguard their interests sufficiently. Balewa came from the Muslim north where the Hausa and Fulani tribes were powerful; the Yorubas of the west and the Ibos of the south and east were constantly complaining about northern domination, even though Azikiwe was an Ibo.
- To make matters worse there was an economic recession. By 1964 prices had risen by 15 per cent, unemployment was rising and wages were, on average, well below what had been calculated as the minimum living wage. Criticism of the government mounted and Balewa replied by arresting Chief Awolowo, prime minister of the western region, which for a time seemed likely to break away from the federation. The central government was also accused of corruption after blatantly trying to 'fix' the results of the 1964 elections.
- In January 1966 there was a military coup carried out by mainly Ibo officers, in which Balewa and some other leading politicians were killed. After this the situation deteriorated steadily: in the north there were savage massacres of Ibos, who had moved into the region for better jobs. The new leader, General Ironsi, himself an Ibo, was murdered by northern soldiers. When a northerner, Colonel Yakubu Gowon, emerged supreme, almost all the Ibos fled from other parts of Nigeria back to the east, whose leader, Colonel Ojukwu, announced that the eastern region had seceded (withdrawn) from Nigeria to become the independent state of Biafra (May 1967). Gowon launched what he described as a 'short surgical police action' to bring the east back into Nigeria.

(b) The civil war

It took more than a short police action, as the Biafrans fought back vigorously. Britain and the USSR supplied Gowon with arms, and France supplied Biafra. It was a bitter and terrible war, in which Biafra lost more civilians from disease and starvation than troops killed in the fighting. Neither the UN, the Commonwealth, nor the Organization of African Unity was able to mediate, and the Biafrans hung on to the bitter end as Nigerian troops closed in on all sides. The final surrender came in January 1970. Nigerian unity had been preserved.

(c) Recovery after the war was remarkably swift

There were pressing problems: famine in Biafra, inter-tribal bitterness, unemployment, and economic resources strained by the war. Gowon showed considerable statesmanship in this difficult situation. There was no revenge-taking, as the Ibos had feared, and Gowon made every effort to reconcile them, persuading them to return to their jobs in other parts of the country. He introduced a new federal system of 12 states, later increased to 19, to give more recognition of local tribal differences; this was a pragmatic move in a country with so much ethnic diversity. The Nigerians were able to take advantage of rising oil prices in the mid-1970s, which gave them a healthy balance of payments position. In 1975 Gowon was removed by another army group, which probably thought he intended to return the country to civilian rule too early. Nigeria continued to prosper and the army kept its promise of a return to democratic government in 1979. Elections were held, resulting in President Shagari becoming head of a civilian government. With Nigeria's oil much in demand abroad, prosperity seemed assured and prospects for a stable government bright.

(d) Unfulfilled promise

Unfortunately disappointment was soon to follow: during 1981 the economy got into difficulties. The Nigerians had relied too heavily on oil exports; there was a fall in world oil prices, and the healthy trade balance of 1980 became a deficit in 1983. Although Shagari was elected for another four-year term (August 1983), he was removed by a military coup the following December. According to the new leader, Major-General Bukhari, the civilian government was guilty of mismanagement of the economy, financial corruption and rigging of the election. In August 1985, Bukhari became the victim of yet another coup carried out by a rival group of army officers who complained that he had not done enough to reverse the fall in living standards, rising prices, chronic shortages and unemployment. Simmering in the background was religious unrest between the largely Muslim north and the mainly Christian south.

The new president, Major-General Babangida, began energetically, introducing what he called a 'belt-tightening' campaign, and announcing plans to develop the non-oil side of the economy. He aimed to expand production of rice, maize, fish, vegetable oil and animal products, and to give special priority to steel manufacture and the assembly of motor vehicles. Following the example of Jerry Rawlings in Ghana, he declared that his military government would not remain in power 'a day longer than was absolutely necessary'. A committee of academics was set to work to produce a new constitution which could 'guarantee an acceptable and painless succession mechanism'; October 1990 was fixed as the date for a return to civilian rule. Another blow came in 1986 with a further dramatic fall in oil prices, which in June reached a record low of only $10 a barrel. This was a disaster for the government, which had based its 1986 budget calculations on a price of $23.50 a barrel. It was forced to accept a loan from the World Bank to enable the recovery programme to go ahead.

In spite of the economic problems, local and state elections were held as promised in 1990 and 1991 and there seemed a good chance of a return to democratic civilian rule; in June 1993 Chief Abiola won the presidential election. However, Babangida announced that the election had been annulled because of malpractices, although most foreign observers reported that it had been conducted fairly and peacefully. Babangida's deputy, General Sani Abacha, seized power in a bloodless coup, and Chief Abiola was later arrested.

Abacha's rule soon developed into a repressive military dictatorship with the imprisonment and execution of opposition leaders, which brought worldwide condemnation (November 1995). Nigeria was suspended from the Commonwealth and the UN applied economic sanctions; most countries stopped buying Nigerian oil and aid was suspended, which were further blows to the economy. Abacha meanwhile continued apparently unmoved, maintaining that he would hand power to a democratically elected president in 1998, or when he felt ready. Some opposition groups called for the country to be divided up into separate states; others demanded a looser federal system which would enable them to escape from the appalling Abacha regime. Corruption continued to flourish; it was reported that during Babangida's period of power, over $12 billion in oil revenues had gone missing, and this trend was maintained under Abacha. Nor were such practices confined to the political elite: there was evidence that at every level of activity, bribery was usually necessary to keep the system operating.

It seemed as though military rule might continue indefinitely; then in June 1998 Abacha died unexpectedly. He was replaced by General Abubakar, a northern Muslim, who promised a return to civilian rule as soon as was practical. Political prisoners were released, and political parties allowed to form, in preparation for elections to be held in 1999. Three main parties emerged: the People's Democratic Party (PDP), the All People's Party (a more conservative party based in the north) and the Alliance for Democracy (a mainly Yoruba party based in the south-east). The presidential election held in February 1999 was declared by a team of international observers to be fair and free; Olusegun Obasanjo of the PDP was declared the winner and he took over as president in May.

(e) Civilian rule again

President Obasanjo tried hard to make civilian rule a success; he began by retiring many of the military who had held official posts in the administration, and introduced new restrictions designed to eliminate corruption. Nigeria's international image improved and US president Clinton paid a visit in 2000, promising aid to restore the country's infrastructure, which had been allowed to fall into disrepair. However, things did not run smoothly: there was religious and ethnic violence, and the economy did not fulfil its potential.

- There was sporadic violence between different tribal groups. For example, in Nassarawa state, around 50 000 people were forced to flee from their homes after two months of fighting between the dominant Hausa tribe and the Tiv minority.
- The most serious problem was the continuous violence between Muslims and Christians. There had always been hostility between the two, but this was now further complicated by the issue of *Sharia law*. This is a system of Islamic law which imposes severe punishments, including amputation of limbs and death by stoning; for example: for theft – amputation of the right hand for a first offence, left foot for a second offence, left hand for a third, and so on. A man in the state of Zamfara lost his right hand for stealing the equivalent of £25. Punishments are especially severe on women: committing adultery and becoming pregnant outside marriage can bring a sentence of death by stoning. By the end of 2002, 12 of the 19 states – those in the north, which are mainly Muslim – had adopted Sharia law into their legal systems. Sharia was only applied to Muslims, but it was opposed by many Christians, who thought it was barbaric and medieval.

  In the other states, which have Christian majorities, there were violent clashes between Muslims and Christians. The president and the attorney-general, both Christians and southerners, were against the introduction of Sharia law, but were in a difficult situation. With the presidential election due in April 2003, they could not afford to antagonize the northern states. However, the attorney-general did go so far as to declare Sharia law illegal on the grounds that it infringed the rights of Muslims by subjecting them 'to a punishment more severe than would be imposed on other Nigerians for the same offence'. In March 2002 an appeal court overturned the death sentence imposed on a woman in Sokoto state for adultery; but in the same month, a woman in Katsina state was sentenced to death by stoning for having a child out of wedlock. Later in the year a young couple were sentenced to death for having sex outside marriage. These sentences aroused strong international protests; both the European Union and the USA expressed their concern, and the federal government of Nigeria said that it was totally opposed to such sentences.
- There was serious violence in the northern city of Kaduna following the unwise decision to stage the Miss World contest in Nigeria in December 2002. Many Muslims strongly disapproved, but in November an article appeared in the national newspaper, *This Day*, which suggested that the Prophet Mohammed himself would not have objected to the Miss World contest, and would probably have chosen a wife from among the contestants. This outraged Muslim opinion; the offices of *This Day* in Kaduna were destroyed by Muslims, and some churches were burned. Christians retaliated and over 200 people died in the rioting that followed. The Miss World contest was relocated to the UK, and the deputy governor of the northern

state of Zamfara issued a *fatwa* (formal decision) urging Muslims to kill Isioma Daniel, the writer of the article.

- Early in 2003 there were outbreaks of ethnic violence in the southern Niger delta region. This was serious because it was an important oil-producing centre; three foreign oil companies were forced to suspend operations, and Nigeria's total output of oil fell by 40 per cent.

In spite of all the problems, president Obasanjo won a convincing victory in the elections of April 2003, taking over 60 per cent of the votes; his People's Democratic Party won majorities in both houses of parliament. But things did not become any easier for him: in July the country was crippled by a general strike in protest against large increases in the price of petrol. Violence between Christians and Muslims now seemed a permanent feature of life in Nigeria; in February 2004 at least 150 people were killed in Plateau state in central Nigeria, after Muslims attacked a church and Christians took revenge. Statistics published by the UN showed that between 66 and 70 per cent of the population were living in poverty, compared with 48.5 per cent as recently as 1998. The same basic problem continues – the misuse of Nigeria's oil wealth. By 2004 the country had been exporting oil for more than 30 years, earning over $250 billion in revenue. However, ordinary people had seen very little benefit, while the ruling elites had amassed huge fortunes. In 2005 the president seemed to be making determined efforts to root out corruption. Several government ministers were sacked and even the vice-president, Atiku Abubakar, was accused of accepting bribes. During 2006 Nigerians were treated to the spectacle of their president and vice-president accusing each other of corruption and demanding the other's resignation. The constitution did not allow a president to run for more than two terms; however, the 2007 presidential election was won by Obasanjo's choice for the PDP party, the highly respected Umaru Yar'Adua.

Sadly, Yar'Adua was dogged by ill health and in November 2009 was flown to Saudi Arabia for medical treatment. Vice-President Goodluck Jonathan, a Christian, took over as acting president. Yar'Adua's death was announced in May 2010. Goodluck Jonathan was elected president in April 2011. His popularity soon plummeted when he announced the removal of a fuel subsidy, one of the few benefits that ordinary Nigerians enjoyed from their country's oil. The removal more than doubled the price of petrol from 45 cents a litre to 94 cents a litre, causing nationwide and violent protests culminating in a week-long strike. Eventually Jonathan bowed to pressure and announced that the price would be 60 cents a litre (January 2012). The unions called off the strikes but many people still believed that the price was too high. Meanwhile there was violence in the north where a radical Islamist group, Boko Haram, which wanted a separate Islamic state in the north, was blamed for a series of shootings and bombings killing around 500 people in the first of half of 2012. President Jonathan and his PDP supporters announced that they were determined to preserve the unity of Nigeria and to restore peace and security; but towards the end of the year there were reports that the government was on the verge of losing control of the north.

25.4 POVERTY IN TANZANIA

Tanganyika became independent in 1961 and was joined in 1964 by the island of Zanzibar to form Tanzania. It was ruled by Dr Julius Nyerere, leader of the Tanzanian African Nationalist Union (TANU), who had to deal with formidable problems:

- Tanzania was one of the poorest states in the whole of Africa.
- There was very little industry, few mineral resources and a heavy dependence on coffee production.

- Later, Tanzania became involved in expensive military operations to overthrow President Idi Amin of Uganda, and provided help and training for nationalist guerrillas from countries like Zimbabwe.
- On the other hand, tribal problems were not as serious as elsewhere, and the Swahili language provided a common bond.

Nyerere retired as president in 1985 (aged 63), though he remained chairman of the party until 1990. He was succeeded as president by Ali Hassan Mwinyi, who had been vice-president, and who ruled for the next ten years.

(a) Nyerere's approach and achievements

His approach was different from that of any other African ruler. He began conventionally enough by expanding the economy: during the first ten years of independence, production of coffee and cotton doubled and sugar production trebled, while health services and education expanded. But Nyerere was not happy that Tanzania seemed to be developing along the same lines as Kenya, with an ever-widening gulf between the wealthy elite and the resentful masses. His proposed solution to the problem was set out in a remarkable document known as *the Arusha Declaration*, published in 1967. The country was to be run on socialist lines.

- All human beings should be treated as equal.
- The state must have effective control over the means of production and must intervene in economic life to make sure that people were not exploited, and that poverty and disease were eliminated.
- There must be no great accumulations of wealth, or society would no longer be classless.
- Bribery and corruption must be eliminated.
- According to Nyerere, Tanzania was at war, and the enemy was poverty and oppression. The way to victory was not through money and foreign aid, but through hard work and self-reliance. The first priority was to improve agriculture so that the country could be self-sufficient in food production.

Nyerere strove hard to put these aims into practice: all important enterprises, including those owned by foreigners, were nationalized; five-year development plans were introduced. Village projects were encouraged and given aid by the government; these involved *ujamaa* ('familyhood', or self-help): families in each village pooled resources and farmed in co-operatives; these were small but viable units which operated collectively and could use more modern techniques. Foreign loans and investments as well as imports were reduced to a minimum to avoid running into debt. Politically, Nyerere's brand of socialism meant a one-party state run by TANU, but elections were still held. It seemed that some elements of genuine democracy existed, since voters in each constituency had a choice of two TANU candidates and every election resulted in a large proportion of MPs losing their seats. Nyerere himself provided dignified leadership, and with his simple lifestyle and complete indifference to wealth, he set the perfect example for the party and the country to follow. It was a fascinating experiment which tried to combine socialist direction from the centre with the African traditions of local decision-making. It tried to provide an alternative to western capitalist society with its pursuit of profit, which most other African states seemed to be copying.

(b)   Success or failure?

Despite Nyerere's achievements, it was clear when he retired in 1985 that his experiment had been, at best, only a limited success. At an international conference on the Arusha Declaration (held December 1986), President Mwinyi gave some impressive social statistics which few other African countries could match: 3.7 million children in primary school; two universities with, in total, over 4500 students; a literacy rate of 85 per cent; 150 hospitals and 2600 dispensaries; infant mortality down to 137 per thousand; life expectancy up to 52.

However, other parts of the Arusha Declaration were not achieved. Corruption crept in because many officials were not as high-minded as Nyerere himself. There was insufficient investment in agriculture so that production was far below what was expected. The nationalization of the sisal estates carried out in the 1960s was a failure – Nyerere himself admitted that production had declined from 220 000 tonnes in 1970 to only 47 000 tonnes in 1984, and in May 1985 he reversed the nationalization. From the end of 1978, Tanzania was in difficulties because of the fall in world prices of coffee and tea (her main exports), rising oil prices (which used up almost half her earnings from exports) and the expense of the war against Amin in Uganda (at least £1000 million). Although oil prices began to fall during 1981, there was soon the problem of the near-collapse of her other exports (cattle, cement and agricultural produce), which left her without foreign exchange. Loans from the IMF only brought her the added problem of how to meet the interest repayments. Tanzania was nowhere near being a socialist state, nor was it self-sufficient – two major aims of the Declaration. Nyerere's socialist experiment might have worked well in a closed economy, but unfortunately Tanzania was becoming part of the 'global village', exposed to the vagaries of the world economy.

Nevertheless Nyerere was deservedly highly respected both as an African and as a world statesman, as an enemy of apartheid in South Africa, and as an outspoken critic of the world economy and the way it exploited poor countries. He played a vital role in the overthrow of Idi Amin, the brutal dictator who ruled Uganda from 1971 until 1979. Nyerere's prestige was at its height when he was chosen as chairman of the Organization of African Unity (OAU) for 1984–5.

(c)   Tanzania after Nyerere

Nyerere's successor, President Mwinyi, while at first keeping to the one-party system, began to move away from strict government control, allowing more private enterprise and a mixed economy; he also accepted financial help from the IMF, which Nyerere had always avoided. Mwinyi was re-elected for a further five-year term in 1990; in 1992 a new constitution was introduced, allowing a multi-party system. The first major democratic elections were held in October 1995. Mwinyi was obliged to stand down after two terms as president. The ruling party, which now called itself Chama Cha Mapinduzi (CCM – the Party of the Revolution), put forward Benjamin Mkapa as its presidential candidate. He won a clear victory, with 60 per cent of the votes, and the CCM won 214 out of the 269 seats in parliament.

Tanzania's economy continued to be fragile and dependent on foreign aid. But foreign aid often came with unpleasant strings attached. In April 2000, for example, the IMF announced a debt-relief package for Tanzania, but one of the conditions was that parents had to contribute part of the fees for their children's education. This was totally unrealistic for a poor country like Tanzania and consequently the numbers of children in primary schools fell sharply. Nor was the situation helped by the spread of the HIV/AIDS virus, which infected over a million people. Care and prevention became major public health problems. At the same time, there were some promising developments. In 1999 Tanzania's first commercial gold mine went into production, and in 2000 preparations began for the mining of tanzanite, a precious stone even rarer than diamonds. As the elections of October 2000 approached, the government was troubled by a series of corruption scandals involving some of its wealthiest members, and also by nationalist sentiment in Zanzibar, which wanted more freedom from the mainland. However, the opposition parties were disorganized and seemed to have nothing better to offer; the president and his CCM won a sweeping victory – Mkapa took over 70 per cent of the votes and CCM won about 90 per cent of the seats in parliament. Foreign observers declared the elections to be free and fair, except in Zanzibar, where there were always complaints of rigging.

As Tanzania moved further into the twenty-first century, the economy began to fulfil some of its promise. President Mkapa privatized a number of state-owned corporations and introduced free-market policies, hoping that this would attract foreign investment and help towards economic expansion. The IMF and World Bank were so impressed by this that they obligingly agreed to cancel some of Tanzania's foreign debts. By the time Mkapa stepped down at the end of his second term in 2005, Tanzania was well on the way to becoming the world's third largest gold producer, and both foreign investment and tourism were increasing. However, although he had promised to put an end to corruption, he himself was accused of having, during the privatizations, illegally appropriated to himself, a coal mine. He was also criticized for spending £15 million on a private presidential jet. In the 2005 election the CCM candidate, Jakaya Kikwete, a protégé of Julius Nyerere, was elected president. He vowed to eliminate corruption and invested in the building of around 1500 new schools around the country and a new university at Dodoma, the capital. The USA gave a grant of some $700 million to help Tanzania's general development, and the UK promised £500 million towards education.

25.5 THE CONGO/ZAIRE

(a) Why and how did civil war develop?

Section 24.6(b) explained how the Belgians suddenly allowed the Congo to become independent in June 1960, with completely inadequate preparations. There was no experienced group of Africans to which power could be handed over. The Congolese had not been educated for professional jobs, very few had received any higher education and no political parties had been allowed. This did not mean that civil war was inevitable, but there were added complications.

1   There were about 150 different tribes (or ethnic groups, as they now tend to be called), which would have made the Congo difficult to hold together even with experienced administrators. Violent and chaotic elections were held in which the Congolese National Movement (MNC), led by a former post-office clerk, Patrice Lumumba, emerged as the dominant party; but there were over 50 different groups. Agreement of any sort was going to be difficult; nevertheless the Belgians handed power over to a coalition government with Lumumba as prime minister, and Joseph Kasavubu, the leader of another group, as president.

2   A mutiny broke out in the Congolese army (July 1960) only a few days after independence. This was in protest against the fact that all officers were Belgians, whereas the Africans expected instant promotion. Lumumba was deprived of the means of keeping law and order, and tribal violence began to spread.

3   The south-eastern province of Katanga, which had rich copper deposits, was encouraged by the Belgian company (Union Minière) which still controlled the

copper-mining industry, to declare itself independent under Moïse Tshombe. This was the wealthiest part of the Congo, which the new state could not afford to lose. Lumumba, unable to rely on his mutinous army, appealed to the UN to help him preserve Congolese unity, and a 3000-strong peacekeeping force soon arrived.

(b) The civil war and the role of the UN

Lumumba wanted to use UN troops to force Katanga back into the Congo, but the situation was complex. The president had already made himself unpopular with the Americans and British because of his outspoken socialism; the Americans in particular regarded him as a dangerous communist who would align the Congo on the side of the USSR in the Cold War. Many Belgians preferred an independent Katanga, which would be easier for them to influence, and they wanted to continue their control of the copper mining. Faced with all these pressures, the UN secretary-general, Dag Hammarskjöld, refused to allow a UN attack on Katanga, though at the same time he refused to recognize Katangese independence. In disgust Lumumba appealed for help to the Russians, but this horrified Kasavubu, who, supported by General Joseph Mobutu and encouraged by the Americans and Belgians, had Lumumba arrested; he and two former ministers in his government were later badly beaten and then murdered by Belgian troops. As the chaos continued, Hammarskjöld realized that more decisive UN action was needed, and although he was killed in an air crash while flying to Katanga to see Tshombe, his successor, U Thant, followed the same line. By mid-1961 there were 20 000 UN troops in the Congo; in September they invaded Katanga and in December 1962 the province admitted failure and ended its secession; Tshombe went into exile.

Though successful, UN operations had been expensive, and within a few months all their troops were withdrawn. Tribal rivalries aggravated by unemployment caused disorders to break out again almost immediately, and calm was not restored until 1965 when General Mobutu of the Congolese army, using white mercenaries and backed by the USA and Belgium, crushed all resistance and took over the government himself.

(c) General Mobutu in power

It was probably inevitable that if the Congo, with its many problems (an under-developed economy, tribal divisions and a shortage of educated people), was to stay united, a strong authoritarian government was required. Mobutu provided exactly that! There was a gradual improvement in conditions as the Congolese gained experience of administration, and the economy began to look healthier after most of the European-owned mines were nationalized.

However, in the late 1970s there were more troubles. In 1977 Katanga (now known as Shaba) was invaded by troops from Angola, apparently encouraged by the Angolan government, which resented Mobutu's earlier intervention in its affairs (see Section 24.6(d)), and by the USSR, which resented American support for Mobutu. This was a way for the USSR to make a gesture against the Americans, and yet another extension of the Cold War.

Having survived that problem, Zaire (as the country had been called since 1971) found itself in economic difficulties, mainly because of declining world copper prices, and drought which made expensive food imports necessary. Mobutu came under increasing criticism outside Zaire for his authoritarian style of government and his huge personal fortune. In May 1980 Amnesty International claimed that at least a thousand political prisoners were being held without trial and that several hundred had died from torture or starvation during

1978–9. An important new measure, the Nationality Law, was introduced in 1981. This restricted citizenship in Zaire to people who could demonstrate a family connection with the Congo at the time of the Berlin Conference of 1885. It aimed to deal with the problem dating back to the colonial era, when tens of thousands of migrant workers had moved into the Congo from neighbouring territories. The problem was exacerbated later by an influx of refugees from Uganda, Rwanda and Burundi. There was tension between the indigenous population and the immigrants, and the Nationality Law was passed in response to pressure from the indigenous Congolese. However, it was difficult to implement, and conflict between the two continued. In 1990 Mobutu allowed a multi-party system, but with himself above politics as head of state. He remained in power, but in 1995, after 30 years of his rule, he was becoming more and more unpopular with his people.

(d) The Kabilas, and civil war again

In the mid-1990s opposition to Mobutu increased. In the east of Zaire, Laurent Kabila, who had been a supporter of Patrice Lumumba, organized forces and began to move towards Kinshasa, the capital. In May 1997 Mobutu left the country and died later in the year in exile in Morocco. Laurent Kabila became president and changed the country's name from Zaire to the Democratic Republic of the Congo (DRC). If the Congolese people had expected dramatic changes in the system of government, they were soon disappointed. Kabila continued many of Mobutu's techniques – opposition politicians and journalists were arrested, political parties were banned, and elections cancelled. Some of his own supporters began to turn against him; the Banyamulenge, a people of Tutsi origin, many of whom had fought in Kabila's army, resented what they saw as his favouritism towards members of his own Luba tribe. They began a rebellion in the east (August 1998) and received support from the governments of neighbouring Uganda and Rwanda. The governments of Zimbabwe, Angola and Namibia pledged support for Kabila. With forces from six countries involved, the conflict soon developed a wider significance than just a civil war. In spite of attempts at negotiation, hostilities dragged on into the next century. Then in January 2001 Kabila was assassinated by a member of his bodyguard, who was immediately himself shot dead. His motive was unclear, though the murder was blamed on the rebels.

The ruling group quickly declared Kabila's son Joseph, the head of the Congolese military, as the next president. Joseph Kabila seemed more conciliatory than his father, promising free and fair elections and announcing that he was willing to make peace with the rebels. It was reported that since the civil war began, almost 3 million people had lost their lives, most of them from starvation and disease in the rebel area in the east. Encouraging signs soon developed:

- Restrictions on political parties were lifted (May 2001).
- The UN agreed that its peace mission should stay on in the DRC; it also welcomed the withdrawal of Namibian troops and called for other states with forces still in the DRC to withdraw them.
- Peace agreements were signed between the DRC, Rwanda and Uganda (2002), with South Africa and the UN acting as guarantors. Both sides were to withdraw troops from the eastern area of the country; a system of power-sharing was to be introduced in which Kabila remained president, with four vice-presidents chosen from the various rebel groups. The transitional power-sharing government would work towards elections in 2005.

The new transitional government was formed in July 2003; the future looked more promising than for many years, though sporadic ethnic violence continued. Especially troubled was the north-eastern province of Ituri, where there were clashes between the Hema and Lendu tribes. A major step forward was achieved in 2005 when citizenship was awarded to everybody descended from ethnic groups present in the country at the time of independence in 1960. In July 2006 elections were held for president and for the national and provincial assemblies. Joseph Kabila took 44 per cent of the vote and did particularly well in the eastern Congo. His party won 111 out of 500 seats in the national assembly. Kabila's nearest rival, Jean-Pierre Bemba Gombo, a former rebel leader, won 20 per cent of the vote and did well in western Congo. Kabila had failed to win a large enough majority and a second round of voting was held in October. In the meantime violence broke out between armies of rival supporters, but the election itself went off reasonably peacefully and was declared to have been fairly conducted. This time Kabila won decisively, taking 58 per cent of the votes and was able to form a coalition government. However, Bemba refused to accept the result, and in March 2007 he tried to seize power in Kinshasa. After fierce fighting Bemba's forces were defeated and he took refuge in the South African embassy. He was allowed to fly to Portugal but was later arrested and taken to the Netherlands where, in July 2008 an International Criminal Court charged him with war crimes.

Joseph Kabila was elected for a second term as president in December 2011, but the election was widely condemned and described as 'lacking credibility'. It was reported that the votes from almost 2000 polling stations in areas where support for the opposition candidate, Etienne Tshisekede, was strong, had been 'lost'. The election was also condemned by the 35 Roman Catholic bishops in the DRC as being full of 'treachery, lies and terror'. They called for the electoral commission to put right 'serious errors'. The Archbishop of Kinshasa even called for a campaign of civil disobedience until the election result was annulled (January 2012). Nevertheless, Kabila stayed in power and the violence continued through 2012 as various rebel groups, with help from Rwanda, tried to overthrow him. In September 2012 President Kagame of Rwanda insisted that Rwanda's intervention was to protect Rwanda business interests in the DRC and to preserve Rwanda's security.

25.6 ANGOLA: A COLD WAR TRAGEDY

(a) Civil war escalates

Section 24.6(d) described how Angola was engulfed by civil war immediately after gaining independence from Portugal in 1975. Part of the problem was that there were three different liberation movements, which started to fight each other almost as soon as independence was declared.

- The **MPLA** (People's Movement for the Liberation of Angola) was a Marxist-style party which tried to appeal across tribal divisions to all Angolans. It was the MPLA which claimed to be the new government, with its leader, Agostinho Neto, as president.
- **UNITA** (National Union for the Total Independence of Angola), with its leader Jonas Savimbi, drew much of its support from the Ovimbundu tribe in the south of the country.
- **FNLA** (National Front for the Liberation of Angola); much weaker than the other two, it drew much of its support from the Bakongo tribe in the north-west.

Alarm bells immediately rang in the USA, which did not like the look of the Marxist MPLA. The Americans therefore decided to back the FNLA (which was also supported by President Mobutu of Zaire), providing advisers, cash and armaments, and encouraged it to attack the MPLA. UNITA also launched an offensive against the MPLA. Cuba sent troops to help the MPLA, while South African troops, supporting the other two groups, invaded Angola via neighbouring Namibia in the south. General Mobutu also sent troops in from Zaire to the north-east of Angola. No doubt there would have been fighting and bloodshed anyway, but outside interference and the extension of the Cold War to Angola certainly made the conflict much worse.

(b) Angola and Namibia

The problem of Namibia also complicated the situation. Lying between Angola and South Africa, Namibia (formerly German South West Africa) had been handed to South Africa in 1919 at the end of the First World War, to be prepared for independence. The white South African government had ignored UN orders and delayed handing Namibia over to black majority rule as long as possible. The Namibian liberation movement, SWAPO (South West Africa People's Organization), and its leader, Sam Nujoma, began a guerrilla campaign against South Africa. After 1975 the MPLA allowed SWAPO to have bases in southern Angola, so it was not surprising that the South African government was so hostile to the MPLA.

(c) The Lisbon Peace Accords (May 1991)

The civil war dragged on right through the 1980s until changing international circumstances brought the possibility of peace. In December 1988 the UN managed to arrange a peace settlement, in which South Africa agreed to withdraw from Namibia provided that the 50 000 Cuban troops left Angola. This agreement went ahead: Namibia became independent under the leadership of Sam Nujoma (1990). The end of the Cold War and of communist rule in eastern Europe meant that all communist support for the MPLA ceased, all Cuban troops had gone home by June 1991, and South Africa was ready to end her involvement. The UN, the Organization of African Unity (OAU), the USA and Russia all played a part in setting up peace talks between the MPLA government of Angola and UNITA in Lisbon (the capital of Portugal). It was agreed that there should be a ceasefire followed by elections, to be monitored by the UN.

(d) The failure of the peace

At first all seemed to go well: the ceasefire held and elections took place in September 1992. The MPLA won 58 per cent (129) of the seats in parliament, UNITA only 31 per cent (70 seats). Although the presidential election result was much closer – MPLA president Jose Eduardo Dos Santos won 49.57 per cent of the votes, with Jonas Savimbi (UNITA) taking 40.07 per cent – it was still a clear and decisive victory for the MPLA.

However, Savimbi and UNITA refused to accept the result, claiming that there had been fraud, even though the elections had been monitored by 400 UN observers; the leader of the UN team reported that the election had been 'generally free and fair'. Tragically UNITA, instead of accepting defeat gracefully, renewed the civil war, which was fought with increasing bitterness. By the end of January 1994 the UN reported that there were 3.3 million refugees and that an average of a thousand people a day, mainly civilians, were dying. The UN had too few personnel in Angola to bring the fighting to an end. This time the outside world could not be blamed for the civil war: this was clearly the fault of UNITA. However, many observers blamed the USA for encouraging UNITA:

shortly before the Lisbon agreement, President Reagan had officially met Savimbi in the USA, which made him seem like an equal with the MPLA government instead of a rebel leader. At the same time the USA had not officially recognized the MPLA as the legal government of Angola, even after the elections; it was not until May 1993, six months after UNITA had resumed the war, that the USA finally gave recognition to the MPLA government.

A ceasefire was eventually negotiated in October 1994 and a peace agreement was reached in November. UNITA, which was losing the war by that time, accepted the 1992 election result, and in return was to be allowed to play a part in what would be, in effect, a coalition government. Early in 1995, 7000 UN troops arrived to help enforce the agreement and supervise the transition to peace. But incredibly, Savimbi soon began to break the terms of the agreement; financing his forces with the proceeds from illicit sales of diamonds, he continued the struggle against the government until February 2002, when he was killed in an ambush by government troops. His death changed the situation dramatically Almost immediately the new leaders of UNITA showed a willingness to negotiate. In April 2002 a ceasefire was signed, and the two sides promised to keep the terms of the 1994 agreement. The Angolan National Assembly voted in favour of extending an amnesty to all UNITA members, including fighters and civilians. The whole agreement was to be monitored by the UN. At last, with Savimbi no longer on the scene, there seemed to be a genuine chance for peace and reconstruction in Angola.

During the 27 years of its existence, Angola had not known real peace, and its development had been severely hampered. It was a potentially prosperous country, rich in oil, diamonds and minerals; the central highlands were fertile – ideal for rearing cattle and raising crops; coffee was a major product. But at the end of the twentieth century the economy was in a mess: inflation was running at 240 per cent, the war was ruinously expensive, and the vast majority of the population was living in poverty, and thousands were on the verge of starvation. Leading politicians faced accusations of corruption on a grand scale. According to the IMF over $4 billion of oil receipts had disappeared from the treasury since 1996. Human Rights Watch reported that UNITA had employed 86 000 child soldiers, and even the government forces had used 3000. The two armies between them had laid some 15 million landmines and many of these still had to be destroyed. It was calculated that about 4 million people (a third of the population) had been forced to leave their homes and were left homeless in 2002, while 1.5 million had been killed.

Angola's natural resources enabled the country to recover reasonably quickly economically. An encouraging sign was the signing of a peace deal with the separatist rebels of the Cabinda region. It was a relatively small area with a population of little more than 100 000, but it was important because about 65 per cent of Angola's oil comes from there. In September 2008 the first national elections for 16 years took place. The ruling MPLA won just over 80 per cent of the votes, while the main opposition party (UNITA) could muster only 10 per cent, giving the MPLA and president José Eduardo dos Santos a two-thirds majority in parliament. By 2010 the president's popularity was beginning to wane. One of the main criticisms was that he and his family had amassed huge personal fortunes while the country's recovery and wealth had not percolated down to ordinary people. He survived an assassination attempt in October 2010, and there was an increasing number of massive anti-government demonstrations. By September 2011 the police were using violent methods to disperse demonstrators. However, President dos Santos, now aged 70, appeared to be the comfortable winner in the election of August 2012, and thanks to a change in the constitution, he seemed set to stay in power until 2022.

The Belgians left these two small states, like the Congo, completely unprepared for independence. In both states there was an explosive mixture of two tribes – the Tutsi and the Hutu. They spoke the same language and looked very much alike, and although the Hutu were in a majority, the Tutsi were the elite ruling group, and they followed different occupations: the Tutsi raised cattle (the word 'Tutsi' actually means 'rich in cattle'), whereas the Hutu were mainly farmers growing bananas and other crops (the word 'Hutu' means 'servant)'. There was continuous tension and skirmishing between the two tribes right from independence day in 1962.

(a) Burundi

There was a mass rising of Hutus against the ruling Tutsi in 1972; this was savagely put down, and over 100 000 Hutu were killed, along with many Tutsi. Some 200 000 Tutsi fled into Tanzania. In 1988 Hutu soldiers in the Burundi army massacred thousands of Tutsi. In 1993 the country held its first democratic elections and for the first time a Hutu president was chosen. Tutsi soldiers soon murdered the new president, in October 1993, but other members of the Hutu government were able to escape. As Hutu carried out reprisal killings against Tutsi, massacre followed massacre; around 50 000 Tutsi were killed and the country disintegrated into chaos. Eventually the army imposed a power-sharing agreement: the prime minister was to be a Tutsi, the president a Hutu, but most of the power was concentrated in the hands of the Tutsi prime minister.

Fighting continued into 1996, and the Organization of African Unity, which sent a peacekeeping force (the first time it had ever taken such action), was unable to prevent the continuing massacres and ethnic cleansing. The economy was in ruins, agricultural production was seriously reduced because much of the rural population had fled, and the government seemed to have no ideas about how to end the war. The outside world and the great powers showed little concern – their interests were not involved or threatened – and the conflict in Burundi was not given much coverage in the world's media. In July 1996, the army overthrew the divided government, and Major Pierre Buyoya (a Tutsi moderate) declared himself president. He claimed that this was not a normal coup – the army had seized power in order to save lives. He had the utmost difficulty in pacifying the country; several former African presidents, including Julius Nyerere of Tanzania and Nelson Mandela of South Africa, attempted to mediate. The problem was that there were about 20 different warring groups, and it was difficult to get representatives of them all together at the same time. In October 2001 an agreement was reached at Arusha (Tanzania), with the help of Mandela. There was to be a three-year transitional period; during the first half of this, Buyoya would continue as president with a Hutu vice-president; after this, a Hutu would become president with a Tutsi vice-president. There was to be an international peacekeeping force and restrictions were to be lifted on political activity. However, not all the rebel groups had signed the Arusha agreement, and fighting continued, in spite of the arrival of South African peacekeepers.

Prospects for peace brightened in December 2002 when the main Hutu rebel party at last signed a ceasefire with the government. President Buyoya kept his side of the Arusha agreement, handing over the presidency to Domitien Ndayizeye, a Hutu (April 2003). The new president was soon able to reach a power-sharing agreement with the remaining Hutu rebel group, but the peace remained fragile. Elections for parliament in 2005 resulted in a series of victories for the ruling party, and its leader, Pierre Nkurunziza, was chosen as the next president. One of the younger generation of Hutu leaders, he described himself as a born-again Christian and was committed to restoring peace and harmony among all Burundians. He also aimed to revive the economy and develop social policy. His first achievement was to reach a ceasefire with the last of the rebel militias (2006). New policies were introduced to safeguard the rights of women and children and to provide free education for primary-school children. He was also keen to keep in touch with ordinary people, and spent a lot of time in the countryside, meeting and talking with villagers. He received several international honours including a UN peace award, and in August 2009 he was presented with the 'Model Leader for a New Africa Award' by the African Forum on Religion and Government, the first African president to be so honoured. In August 2010 President Nkurunziza was elected for a second five-year term.

(b) Rwanda

Tribal warfare began in 1959 before independence, and reached its first big climax in 1963, when the Hutu, fearing a Tutsi invasion from Burundi, massacred thousands of Rwandan Tutsi and overthrew the Tutsi government. In 1990 fighting broke out between the rebel Tutsi-dominated Rwandese Patriotic Front (Front Patriotique Rwandais – FPR), which was based over the border in Uganda, and the official Rwandan army (Hutu-dominated). This lasted off and on until 1993 when the UN helped to negotiate a peace settlement at Arusha in Tanzania, between the Rwandan government (Hutu) and the FPR (Tutsi): there was to be a more broadly-based government, which would include the FPR; 2500 UN troops were sent to monitor the transition to peace (October 1993).

For a few months all seemed to be going well, and then disaster struck. The more extreme Hutu were bitterly opposed to the Arusha peace plan, and shocked by the murder of the Hutu president of Burundi. Extremist Hutu, who had formed their own militia (the Interahamwe), decided to act. The aircraft bringing the moderate Hutu President Habyarimana of Rwanda and the Burundian president back from talks in Tanzania was brought down by a missile, apparently fired by extremist Hutu as it approached Kigali (the capital of Rwanda), killing both presidents (April 1994). With the president dead, nobody was sure who was giving the orders, and this gave the Interahamwe the cover they needed to launch a campaign of genocide. The most horrifying tribal slaughter followed; Hutu murdered all Tutsi they could lay hands on, including women and children. A favourite technique was to persuade Tutsi to take sanctuary in churches and then destroy the church buildings and the sheltering Tutsi. Even nuns and clergy were caught up in the massacre. Altogether about 800 000 Tutsi and moderate Hutu who tried to help their neighbours were brutally murdered in what was clearly a deliberate and carefully planned attempt to wipe out the entire Tutsi population of Rwanda, and it was backed by the Hutu government of Rwanda.

The Tutsi FPR responded by taking up the fight again and marching on the capital; UN observers reported that the streets of Kigali were literally running with blood and the corpses were piled high. The small UN force was not equipped to deal with violence on this scale, and it soon withdrew. The civil war and the genocide continued through into June; in addition to those killed, about a million Tutsi refugees had fled into neighbouring Tanzania and Zaire.

Meanwhile the rest of the world, though outraged and horrified by the scale of the genocide, did nothing to stop it. Historian Linda Melvern has shown how the warning signs of what was to come were ignored by all those who might have prevented the genocide. She claims that Belgium and France both knew what was being planned; as early as the spring of 1992, the Belgian ambassador told his government that extremist Hutus were 'planning the extermination of the Tutsi of Rwanda once and for all, and to crush the internal Hutu opposition'. The French continued to supply the Hutu with arms throughout the genocide;

US president Clinton knew precisely what was happening, but after the humiliation of the US intervention in Somalia in 1992, he was determined not to get involved. Linda Melvern is highly critical of the UN; she points out that UN secretary-general Boutros-Ghali knew Rwanda well and was aware of the situation, but being pro-Hutu, refused to allow arms inspections and avoided sending sufficient UN forces to deal with the problem. On the other hand, it was not just the West and the UN that turned a blind eye to the tragedy in Rwanda; the Organization of African Unity did not even condemn the genocide, let alone try to prevent it; nor did any other African states take any action or issue public condemnation. Arguably African attention was focused on the new democracy in South Africa rather than on halting the genocide in Rwanda.

By September the FPR were beginning to get the upper hand: the Hutu government was driven out and a Tutsi FPR government was set up in Kigali. But progress to peace was slow; by the end of 1996 this new government was still beginning to make its authority felt over the whole country, and refugees started to return. Eventually a power-sharing arrangement was reached, and a moderate Hutu, Pasteur Bizimungu, became president with Paul Kagame, a Tutsi, as his vice-president. This was an important concession by the Tutsi as they tried to deflect accusations of a resurgent Tutsi elitism, though in fact Kagame was the real policy decider. However, in 2000 when Bizimungu began to criticize parts of Kagame's programme, he was removed from the presidency and Kagame took over. Bizimunbu immediately founded an opposition party but the Kagame government banned it.

One of the problems facing the government was that jails were overflowing with well over 100 000 prisoners awaiting trial for involvement in the 1994 genocide. There were simply too many for the courts to deal with. In January 2003, Kagame ordered the release of around 40 000 prisoners, though it was made clear that they would face trial eventually. This caused consternation among many survivors of the massacres, who were horrified at the prospect of coming face to face with the people who had murdered their relatives.

A new constitution was introduced in 2003 providing for a president and a two-chamber parliament and established a balance of political power between Hutu and Tutsi – no party can hold more than half the seats in parliament. It also outlawed the incitement of ethnic hatred in the hope of avoiding a repeat of the genocide. In the first national elections since 1994, President Kagame won an overwhelming victory, taking 95 per cent of the votes (August 2003). However, observers reported that there were 'malpractices' in some areas, and two of the main opposition parties were banned. But at least Rwanda seemed to be enjoying a period of relative calm. In February 2004, the government introduced a new reconciliation policy: people who admitted their guilt and asked for forgiveness before 15 March 2004 would be released (except those accused of organizing the genocide). It was hoped that this, like the South African Truth and Reconciliation Commission, would help Rwandans to come to terms with the traumas of the past and move forward into a period of peace and harmony.

Certainly economic and social conditions improved during Kagame's presidency. He succeeded in reducing the amount of corruption and crime; between 2000 and 2008 per capita income doubled; almost half the country's children were receiving a full primary education, compared with 20 per cent before Kagame came to power; and there was a marked increase in life expectancy. Rwandans infected with AIDS could now receive antiretroviral drugs in health centres across the country. Exports of tea and coffee began to increase, and tourism became an important source of revenue, especially the safari parks. In 2009 Rwanda was accepted as a member of the British Commonwealth of Nations; this was an attempt to distance the country from its Belgian past. President Kagame was decisively re-elected for a further term in August 2010, although doubts were expressed by observers about how free the elections really were. During the election campaign, several opposition supporters and journalists were killed and press freedom was limited. The UN, the European Union and the USA all expressed concerns about these developments.

25.8 APARTHEID AND BLACK MAJORITY RULE IN SOUTH AFRICA

(a) The formation of the Union of South Africa

South Africa has had a complicated history. The first Europeans to settle there permanently were members of the Dutch East India Company who founded a colony at the Cape of Good Hope in 1652. It remained a Dutch colony until 1795, and during that time, the Dutch, who were known as Afrikaners or Boers (a word meaning 'farmers'), took land away from the native Africans and forced them to work as labourers, treating them as little better than slaves. They also brought more labourers in from Asia, Mozambique and Madagascar.

In 1795 the Cape was captured by the British during the French Revolutionary Wars, and the 1814 peace settlement decided that it should remain British. Many British settlers went out to Cape Colony. The Dutch settlers became restless under British rule, especially when the British government made all slaves free throughout the British Empire (1838). The Boer farmers felt that this threatened their livelihood, and many of them decided to leave Cape Colony. They moved northwards (in what became known as 'the Great Trek') and set up their own independent republics of the Transvaal and Orange Free State (1835–40). Some also moved into the area east of Cape Colony known as Natal. In the Boer War (1899–1902) the British defeated the Transvaal and the Orange Free State, and in 1910 they joined up with Cape Colony and Natal to form the Union of South Africa.

The population of the new state was mixed:

Approximately

> 70 per cent were black Africans, known as Bantus;
> 18 per cent were whites of European origin; of these about 60 per cent were Dutch, the rest British;
> 9 per cent were of mixed race, known as 'coloureds';
> 3 per cent were Asians.

Although they made up the vast majority of the population, black Africans suffered even worse discrimination than black people in the USA.

- The whites dominated politics and the economic life of the new state, and, with only a few exceptions, blacks were not allowed to vote.
- Black people had to do most of the manual work in factories, in the gold mines and on farms; the men mostly lived in barracks accommodation away from their wives and children. Black people generally were expected to live in areas reserved for them away from white residential areas. These reserved areas made up only about 7 per cent of the total area of South Africa and were not large enough to enable the Africans to produce sufficient food for themselves and to pay all their taxes. Black Africans were forbidden to buy land outside the reserves.
- The government controlled the movement of blacks by a system of pass laws. For example, a black person could not live in a town unless he had a pass showing that he was working in a white-owned business. An African could not leave the farm

where he worked without a pass from his employer; nor could he get a new job unless his previous employer signed him out officially; many workers were forced to stay in difficult working conditions, even under abusive employers.

- Living and working conditions for blacks were primitive; for example, in the gold-mining industry, Africans had to live in single-sex compounds with sometimes as many as 90 men sharing a dormitory.
- By a law of 1911, black workers were forbidden to strike and were barred from holding skilled jobs.

(b) Dr Malan introduces apartheid

After the Second World War there were important changes in the way black Africans were treated. Under Prime Minister Malan (1948–54), a new policy called *apartheid (separateness)* was introduced. This tightened up control over blacks still further. Why was apartheid introduced?

- When India and Pakistan were given independence in 1947, white South Africans became alarmed at the growing racial equality within the Commonwealth, and they were determined to preserve their supremacy.
- Most of the whites, especially those of Dutch origin, were against racial equality, but the most extreme were the Afrikaner Nationalist Party led by Dr Malan. They claimed that whites were a master race, and that non-whites were inferior beings. The Dutch Reformed Church (the official state church of South Africa) supported this view and quoted passages from the Bible which, they claimed, proved their theory. This was very much out of line with the rest of the Christian churches, which believe in racial equality. The Broederbond was a secret Afrikaner organization which worked to protect and preserve Afrikaner power.
- The Nationalists won the 1948 elections with promises to rescue the whites from the 'black menace' and to preserve the racial purity of the whites. This would help to ensure continued white supremacy.

(c) Apartheid developed further

Apartheid was continued and developed further by the prime ministers who followed Malan: Strijdom (1954–8), Verwoerd (1958–66) and Vorster (1966–78).

The main features of apartheid

1   There was complete separation of blacks and whites as far as possible at all levels. In country areas blacks had to live in special reserves; in urban areas they had separate townships built at suitable distances from the white residential areas. If an existing black township was thought to be too close to a 'white' area, the whole community was uprooted and 're-grouped' somewhere else to make separation as complete as possible. There were separate buses, coaches, trains, cafés, toilets, park benches, hospitals, beaches, picnic areas, sports and even churches. Black children went to separate schools and were given a much inferior education. But there was a flaw in the system: complete separation was impossible because over half the non-white population worked in white-owned mines, factories and other businesses. The economy would have collapsed if all non-whites had been moved to reserves. In addition, virtually every white household had at least two African servants.

2   Every person was given a racial classification and an identity card. There were strict pass laws which meant that black Africans had to stay in their reserves or in their townships unless they were travelling to a white area to work, in which case they would be issued with passes. Otherwise all travelling was forbidden without police permission.

3   Marriage and sexual relations between whites and non-whites were forbidden; this was to preserve the purity of the white race. Police spied shamelessly on anybody suspected of breaking the rules.

4   The Bantu Self-Government Act (1959) set up seven regions called Bantustans, based on the original African reserves. It was claimed that they would eventually move towards self-government. In 1969 it was announced that the first Bantustan, the Transkei, had become 'independent'. However, the outside world dismissed this with contempt since the South African government continued to control the Transkei's economy and foreign affairs. The whole policy was criticized because the Bantustan areas covered only about 13 per cent of the country's total area; over 8 million black people were crammed into these relatively small areas, which were vastly overcrowded and unable to support the black populations adequately. They became very little better than rural slums, but the government ignored the protests and continued its policy; by 1980 two more African 'homelands', Bophuthatswana and Venda, had received 'independence'.

5   Africans lost all political rights, and their representation in parliament, which had been by white MPs, was abolished.

(d)   Opposition to apartheid

1   *Inside South Africa*

Inside South Africa, opposition to the system was difficult. Anyone who objected – including whites – or broke the apartheid laws, was accused of being a communist and was severely punished under the Suppression of Communism Act. Africans were forbidden to strike, and their political party, the African National Congress (ANC), was helpless. In spite of this, protests did take place.

- Chief Albert Luthuli, the ANC leader, organized a protest campaign in which black Africans stopped work on certain days. In 1952 Africans attempted a systematic breach of the laws by entering shops and other places reserved for whites. Over 8000 blacks were arrested and many were flogged. Luthuli was deprived of his chieftaincy and put in jail for a time, and the campaign was called off.

- In 1955 the ANC formed a coalition with Asian and coloured groups, and at a massive open-air meeting at Kliptown (near Johannesburg), they just had time to announce a freedom charter before police broke up the crowd. The charter soon became the main ANC programme. It began by declaring: 'South Africa belongs to all who live in it, black and white, and no government can claim authority unless it is based on the will of the people.' It went on to demand:

  - equality before the law;
  - freedom of assembly, movement, speech, religion and the press;
  - the right to vote;
  - the right to work, with equal pay for equal work;
  - a 40-hour working week, a minimum wage and unemployment benefits;
  - free medical care;
  - free, compulsory and equal education.

Illustration 25.1 **Bodies litter the ground after the Sharpeville massacre, South Africa, 1960**

- Church leaders and missionaries, both black and white, spoke out against apartheid. They included people like Trevor Huddleston, a British missionary who had been working in South Africa since 1943.
- Later the ANC organized other protests, including the 1957 bus boycott: instead of paying a fare increase on the bus route from their township to Johannesburg ten miles away, thousands of Africans walked to work and back for three months until fares were reduced.
- Protests reached a climax in 1960 when a huge demonstration took place against the pass laws at Sharpeville, an African township near Johannesburg. Police fired on the crowd, killing 67 Africans and wounding many more (see Illus. 25.1). After this, 15 000 Africans were arrested and hundreds of people were beaten by police. This was an important turning point in the campaign: until then most of the protests had been non-violent; but this brutal treatment by the authorities convinced many black leaders that violence could only be met with violence.
- A small action group of the ANC, known as *Umkhonto we Sizwe* (Spear of the Nation), or MK, was launched; Nelson Mandela was a prominent member. They organized a campaign of sabotaging strategic targets: in 1961 there was a spate of bomb attacks in Johannesburg, Port Elizabeth and Durban. But the police soon clamped down, arresting most of the black leaders, including Mandela, who was sentenced to life imprisonment on Robben Island. Chief Luthuli still persevered with non-violent protests, and after publishing his moving autobiography *Let My People Go*, he was awarded the Nobel Peace Prize. He was killed in 1967, the authorities claiming that he had deliberately stepped in front of a train.
- Discontent and protest increased again in the 1970s because the wages of Africans failed to keep pace with inflation. In 1976, when the Transvaal authorities announced that Afrikaans (the language spoken by whites of Dutch descent) was to be used in black African schools, massive demonstrations took place at Soweto, a black township near Johannesburg. Although there were many children and young people in the crowd, police opened fire, killing at least 200 black Africans. This

time the protests did not die down; they spread over the whole country. Again the government responded with brutality: over the next six months a further 500 Africans were killed; among the victims was Steve Biko, a young African leader who had been urging people to be proud of their blackness. He was beaten to death by police (1976).

2   Outside South Africa

Outside South Africa there was opposition to apartheid from the rest of the Commonwealth. Early in 1960 the British Conservative prime minister, Harold Macmillan, had the courage to speak out against it in Cape Town; he spoke about the growing strength of African nationalism: 'the wind of change is blowing through the continent ... our national policies must take account of it'. His warnings were ignored, and shortly afterwards, the world was horrified by the Sharpeville massacre. At the 1961 Commonwealth Conference, criticism of South Africa was intense, and many thought the country would be expelled. In the end Verwoerd withdrew South Africa's application for continued membership (in 1960 it had become a republic instead of a dominion, thereby severing the connection with the British crown; because of this the government had had to apply for readmission to the Commonwealth), and it ceased to be a member of the Commonwealth.

3   The UN and OAU

The United Nations and the Organization of African Unity condemned apartheid and were particularly critical of the continued South African occupation of South West Africa (see above, Section 25.6(b)). The UN voted to place an economic boycott on South Africa (1962), but this proved useless because not all member states supported it. Britain, the USA, France, West Germany and Italy condemned apartheid in public, but continued to trade with South Africa. Among other things, they sold South Africa massive arms supplies, apparently hoping that it would prove to be a bastion against the spread of communism in Africa. Consequently Verwoerd (until his assassination in 1966) and his successor Vorster (1966–78) were able to ignore the protests from the outside world until well into the 1970s.

(e)   The end of apartheid

The system of apartheid continued without any concessions being made to black people, until 1980.

1   P. W. Botha

The new prime minister, P. W. Botha (elected 1979), realized that all was not well with the system. He decided that he must reform apartheid, dropping some of the most unpopular aspects in an attempt to preserve white control. What caused this change?

- Criticism from abroad (from the Commonwealth, the United Nations and the Organization of African Unity) gradually gathered momentum. External pressures became much greater in 1975 when the white-ruled Portuguese colonies of Angola and Mozambique achieved independence after a long struggle (see Section 24.6(d)). The African takeover of Zimbabwe (1980) removed the last of the white-ruled states which had been sympathetic to the South African government and apartheid. Now South Africa was surrounded by hostile black states, and many Africans in these new states had sworn never to rest until their fellow-Africans in South Africa had been liberated.

- There were economic problems – South Africa was hit by recession in the late 1970s, and many white people were worse off. Whites began to emigrate in large numbers, but the black population was increasing. In 1980 whites made up only 16 per cent of the population, whereas between the two world wars they had formed 21 per cent.
- The African homelands were a failure: they were poverty-stricken, their rulers were corrupt and no foreign government recognized them as genuinely independent states.
- The USA, which was treating its own black people better during the 1970s, began to criticize the South African government's racist policy.

In a speech in September 1979 which astonished many of his Nationalist supporters, the newly elected Prime Minister Botha said:

A revolution in South Africa is no longer just a remote possibility. Either we adapt or we perish. White domination and legally enforced apartheid are a recipe for permanent conflict.

He went on to suggest that the black homelands must be made viable and that unnecessary discrimination must be abolished. Gradually he introduced some important changes which he hoped would be enough to silence the critics both inside and outside South Africa.

- Blacks were allowed to join trade unions and to go on strike (1979).
- Blacks were allowed to elect their own local township councils (but not to vote in national elections) (1981).
- A new constitution was introduced, setting up two new houses of parliament, one for coloureds and one for Asians (but not for Africans). The new system was weighted so that the whites kept overall control. It came into force in 1984.
- Sexual relations and marriage were allowed between people of different races (1985).
- The hated pass laws for non-whites were abolished (1986).

This was as far as Botha was prepared to go. He would not even consider the ANC's main demands (the right to vote and to play a full part in ruling the country). Far from being won over by these concessions, black Africans were incensed that the new constitution made no provision for them, and were determined to settle for nothing less than full political rights.

Violence escalated, with both sides guilty of excesses. The ANC used the 'necklace', a tyre placed round the victim's neck and set on fire, to murder black councillors and black police, who were regarded as collaborators with apartheid. On the 25th anniversary of Sharpeville, police opened fire on a procession of black mourners going to a funeral near Uitenhage (Port Elizabeth), killing over forty people (March 1985). In July a state of emergency was declared in the worst affected areas, and it was extended to the whole country in June 1986. This gave the police the power to arrest people without warrants, and freedom from all criminal proceedings; thousands of people were arrested, and newspapers, radio and TV were banned from reporting demonstrations and strikes.

However, as so often happens when an authoritarian regime tries to reform itself, it proved impossible to stop the process of change (the same happened in the USSR when Gorbachev tried to reform communism). By the late 1980s international pressure on South Africa was having more effect, and internal attitudes had changed.

- In August 1986 the Commonwealth (except Britain) agreed on a strong package of sanctions (no further loans, no sales of oil, computer equipment or nuclear goods to

South Africa, and no cultural and scientific contacts). British prime minister Margaret Thatcher would commit Britain only to a voluntary ban on investment in South Africa. Her argument was that severe economic sanctions would worsen the plight of black Africans, who would be thrown out of their jobs. This caused the rest of the Commonwealth to feel bitter against Britain; Rajiv Gandhi, the Indian prime minister, accused Mrs Thatcher of 'compromising on basic principles and values for economic ends'.

- In September 1986 the USA joined the fray when Congress voted (over President Reagan's veto) to stop American loans to South Africa, to cut air links and to ban imports of iron, steel, coal, textiles and uranium from South Africa.
- The black population was no longer just a mass of uneducated and unskilled labourers; there was a steadily growing number of well-educated, professional, middle-class black people, some of them holding important positions, like Desmond Tutu, who was awarded the Nobel Peace Prize in 1984 and became Anglican archbishop of Cape Town in 1986.
- The Dutch Reformed Church, which had once supported apartheid, now condemned it as incompatible with Christianity. A majority of white South Africans now recognized that it was difficult to defend the total exclusion of blacks from the country's political life. So although they were nervous about what might happen, they became resigned to the idea of black majority rule at some time in the future. White moderates were therefore prepared to make the best of the situation and get the best deal possible.

2 F. W. de Klerk

The new president, F. W. de Klerk (elected 1989), had a reputation for caution, but privately he had decided that apartheid would have to go completely, and he accepted that black majority rule must come eventually. The problem was how to achieve it without further violence and possible civil war. With great courage and determination, and in the face of bitter opposition from right-wing Afrikaner groups, de Klerk gradually moved the country towards black majority rule.

- Nelson Mandela was released after 27 years in jail (1990) and became leader of the ANC, which was made legal.
- Most of the remaining apartheid laws were dropped.
- Namibia, the neighbouring territory ruled by South Africa since 1919, was given independence under a black government (1990).
- Talks began in 1991 between the government and the ANC to work out a new constitution which would allow blacks full political rights.

Meanwhile the ANC was doing its best to present itself as a moderate party which had no plans for wholesale nationalization, and to reassure whites that they would be safe and happy under black rule. Nelson Mandela condemned violence and called for reconciliation between blacks and whites. The negotiations were long and difficult; de Klerk had to face right-wing opposition from his own National Party and from various extreme, white racialist groups who claimed that he had betrayed them. The ANC was involved in a power struggle with another black party, the Natal-based Zulu Inkatha Freedom Party led by Chief Buthelezi.

3 Transition to black majority rule

In the spring of 1993 the talks were successful and a power-sharing scheme was worked out to carry through the transition to black majority rule. A general election was held and the ANC won almost two-thirds of the votes. As had been agreed, a coalition government of the ANC, National Party and Inkatha took office, with Nelson Mandela as the first black president of South Africa, two vice-presidents, one black and one white (Thabo Mbeki and F. W. de Klerk), and Chief Buthelezi as Home Affairs Minister (May 1994). A right-wing Afrikaner group, led by Eugene Terreblanche, continued to oppose the new democracy, vowing to provoke civil war, but in the end it came to nothing. Although there had been violence and bloodshed, it was a remarkable achievement, for which both de Klerk and Mandela deserve the credit, that South Africa was able to move from apartheid to black majority rule without civil war.

(f) Mandela and Mbeki

The government faced daunting problems and was expected to deliver on the promises in the ANC programme, especially to improve conditions for the black population. Plans were put into operation to raise their general standard of living – in education, housing, health care, water and power supplies and sanitation. But the scale of the problem was so vast that it would be many years before standards would show improvement for everybody. In May 1996 a new constitution was agreed, to come into operation after the elections of 1999, which would not allow minority parties to take part in the government. When this was revealed (May 1996), the Nationalists immediately announced that they would withdraw from the government to a 'dynamic but responsible opposition'. As the country moved towards the millennium, the main problems facing the president were how to maintain sound financial and economic policies, and how to attract foreign aid and investment; potential investors were hesitant, awaiting future developments.

One of Mandela's most successful initiatives was the Truth and Reconciliation Commission, which looked into human rights abuses during the apartheid regime. Assisted by Archbishop Desmond Tutu, the commission's approach was not one of taking revenge, but of granting amnesties; people were encouraged to talk frankly, and to acknowledge their crimes and ask for forgiveness. This was one of the most admirable things about Mandela, that although he had been kept in prison under the apartheid regime for 27 years, he still believed in forgiveness and reconciliation. The president decided not to stand for re-election in 1999 – he was almost 81 years old; he retired with his reputation high, almost universally admired for his statesmanship and restraint.

Thabo Mbeki, who became ANC leader and president on Mandela's retirement, had a difficult job to follow such a charismatic leader. After winning the 1999 elections, Mbeki and the ANC had to deal with mounting problems: the crime rate soared, trade unions called strikes in protest against job losses, poor working conditions and the increasing rate of privatization. The economic growth rate was slowing down: in 2001 it was only 1.5 per cent compared with 3.1 in 2000. The government came under special criticism for its handling of the AIDS epidemic. Mbeki was slow to recognize that there really was a crisis and claimed that AIDS was not necessarily linked to HIV; he refused to declare a state of emergency, as opposition parties and trade unions demanded. This would have enabled South Africa to obtain cheaper medicines, but the government seemed unwilling to spend large amounts of cash on the necessary drugs. There was uproar in October 2001 when a report claimed that AIDS was now the main cause of death in South Africa, and that if the trend continued, at least 5 million people would have died from it by 2010.

As the 2004 elections approached, there were many positive signs in the new South Africa. Government policies were beginning to show results: 70 per cent of black households had electricity, the number of people with access to pure water had increased by 9 million since 1994, and about 2000 new houses for poor people had been built. Education was free and compulsory and many black people said that they felt they now had dignity, instead of being treated like animals, as they had been under apartheid. The economic situation appeared brighter: South Africa was diversifying its exports instead of relying on gold and there was a growing tourist industry; the budget deficit had fallen sharply and inflation was down to 4 per cent. The main problems were still AIDS – it was reported that in 2005 South Africa was the country with the most HIV positive people in the world, 6.5 million; high unemployment levels and the high crime rate. However, in the election of April 2004, Mbeki was re-elected for a second and final five-year term as president and his ANC won a landslide victory, taking around two-thirds of the votes cast.

During Mbeki's second term it was the problems rather than the progress that gained most of the publicity. There was an influx of migrants and refugees, mainly from Zimbabwe, but also from Rwanda, the Congo, Somalia and Ethiopia. With unemployment already high and housing in short supply, this has caused competition for jobs and living accommodation, especially in the shanty towns that surround most large cities. In May 2008 there were serious protest riots directed against immigrants, and at least 80 people were killed. The more left-wing ANC supporters felt that there had been too little progress in the redistribution of wealth. In May 2009 South Africa's unemployment rate had reached 25 per cent and those out of work were forced to live on less than US$1.25 a day. Mbeki's second term was also marred by a feud with his vice-president Jacob Zuma. In 2005 Mbeke sacked him after Zuma was accused of corruption, including fraud and money-laundering. In December 2007 Zuma, still a very popular figure, defeated Mbeke in the election for president of the ANC. When Zuma was acquitted on the corruption charges, the ANC National Executive Committee voted that Mbeke was no longer fit to lead the country, the implication being that the charges against Zuma had been trumped up in order to get him removed. Mbeke immediately resigned and in May 2009 Zuma was elected president. He was firmly on the left-wing of the ANC and had once been a member of the South African Communist Party. Now he could rely on solid support from the trade unions and the communists. His programme included a pledge to fight poverty and narrow the poverty gap, given that South Africa was tenth in the world list of countries with the widest gap between rich and poor.

The president suffered a setback in August 2012 when police shot and killed 34 striking platinum miners at the Marikana mine, near Johannesburg. Poorly paid and working in difficult conditions, the miners were demanding wage increases from the mine-owners, a British company called Lonmin. To make matters worse, 270 miners were arrested and charged with the murder of their colleagues, on the grounds that their behaviour had caused the police action. A wave of outrage followed and President Zuma came under severe criticism for his handling of the crisis. Although the charges were later dropped, critics claimed that he was an ineffective leader, more interested in protecting the industry rather than helping the poverty-stricken miners and working to narrow the poverty gap. In December 2012 he was re-elected leader of the ANC for another five years. However, many observers see his continuing presence as the party's Achilles heel. According to the *Guardian* (18 December 2012), Zuma is 'a man steeped in corruption and personal scandal'.

25.9 SOCIALISM AND CIVIL WAR IN ETHIOPIA

(a) Haile Selassie

Ethiopia (Abyssinia) was an independent state, ruled since 1930 by the Emperor Haile Selassie. In 1935 Mussolini's forces attacked and occupied the country, forcing the Emperor into exile. The Italians joined Ethiopia to their neighbouring colonies of Eritrea and Somaliland, calling them Italian East Africa. In 1941, with British help, Haile Selassie was able to defeat the weak Italian forces and return to his capital, Addis Ababa. The wily emperor scored a great success in 1952 when he persuaded the UN and the USA to allow him to take over Eritrea, giving his landlocked country access to the sea. However, this was to be a source of conflict for many years, since Eritrean nationalists bitterly resented the loss of their country's independence.

By 1960 many people were growing impatient with Haile Selassie's rule, believing that more could have been done politically, socially and economically to modernize the country. Rebellions broke out in Eritrea and in the Ogaden region of Ethiopia, where many of the population were Somali nationalists who were keen for their territories to join Somalia (which had become independent in 1960). Haile Selassie hung on to power, without introducing any radical changes, into the 1970s. Fuelled by poverty, drought and famine, unrest finally came to a head in 1974, when some sections of the army mutinied. The leaders formed themselves into the Co-ordinating Committee of the Armed Forces and Police (known as the Derg for short), whose chairman was Major Mengistu. In September 1974, the Derg deposed the 83-year-old emperor, who was later murdered, and set itself up as the new government. Mengistu gained complete control and remained head of state until 1991.

(b) Major Mengistu and the Derg

Mengistu and the Derg gave Ethiopia 16 years of government based on Marxist principles. Most of the land, industry, trade, banking and finance were taken over by the state. Opponents were usually executed. The USSR saw the arrival of Mengistu as an excellent chance to gain influence in that part of Africa, and they provided armaments and training for Mengistu's army. Unfortunately the regime's agricultural policy ran into the same problems as Stalin's collectivization in the USSR; in 1984 and 1985 there were terrible famines, and it was only prompt action by other states, rushing in emergency food supplies, which averted disaster. Mengistu's main problem was the civil war, which dragged on throughout his period in power and swallowed up his scarce resources. In spite of the help from the USSR, he was fighting a losing battle against the Eritrean People's Liberation Front, the Tigray People's Liberation Front and the Ethiopian People's Revolutionary Democratic Front (EPRDF). By 1989 the government had lost control of Eritrea and Tigray, and Mengistu admitted that his socialist policies had failed; Marxism–Leninism was to be abandoned. The USSR deserted him; in May 1991, with rebel forces closing in on Addis Ababa, Mengistu fled to Zimbabwe and the EPRDF took power.

(c) The Ethiopian People's Revolutionary Democratic Front (EPRDF)

The new government, while maintaining some elements of socialism (especially state control of important resources), promised democracy and less centralization. The leader, Meles Zenawi, who was a Tigrayan, announced the introduction of a voluntary federation for the various nationalities; this meant that ethnic groups could leave Ethiopia if they chose, and it prepared the way for Eritrea to declare its independence in May 1993. This was one less problem for the regime to deal with, but there were many others. Most serious was the state of the economy, and yet another dreadful famine in 1994. In 1998 war broke out between Ethiopia and Eritrea over frontier disputes. Even the weather was uncooperative: in the spring of 2000 the rains failed for the third year in succession, and another famine threatened. Although a peace settlement with Eritrea was signed in December 2000, tensions remained high.

Events in 2001 suggested that Ethiopia might have turned the corner, at least economically. Prime Minister Zenawi and his EPRDF, who had easily won the national elections in May 2000, went on to register another landslide victory in the local elections in 2001. The economy grew by 6.5 per cent, the rains arrived on time and there was a good harvest. The World Bank helped by cancelling almost 70 per cent of Ethiopia's debt. Zenawi won the 2005 elections, though there were allegations of fraud followed by riots and protest demonstrations in which at least 200 people were killed. The opposition accused the police of massacring protesters, while the government blamed one of the main opposition parties, the Coalition for Unity and Democracy (CUD), for organizing the protests. In fact the majority of foreign observers declared that the elections were basically free and fair. With Zenawi in charge for the next five years, economic growth continued, but at the end of 2006 Ethiopia became involved in war with neighbouring Somalia. In the south of Somalia, bordering on Ethiopia, Islamist groups were fighting against the National Transitional Federal Government of Somalia, which was supported by the USA (see Section 25.13(b)). It was suspected that these Islamist groups had links with al-Qaeda, and Ethiopia had already allowed the USA to station military advisers at Camp Hurso, where they had spent a year training the Ethiopian army. In December 2006 the Ethiopians took the offensive, forced the Islamists to retreat and occupied the areas formerly under Islamist control. They pulled out in January 2009, leaving behind a small African Union force and a small detachment of the Somali army. But they were not strong enough to keep the Islamists at bay, and they soon began to take back control of southern Somalia. Re-elected in 2010 for a further five-year term, Zenawi died in August 2012 aged only 57. His deputy, Hailemariam Desalegn, took over, and was expected to remain prime minister until the next elections, due in 2015. However, there were fears that, since the new prime minister lacked the experience, the prestige and the charisma of Mr Zenawi, the country was in for a difficult few years.

25.10   LIBERIA – A UNIQUE EXPERIMENT

(a)   Early history

Liberia has a unique history among African states. It was founded in 1822 by an organization called the American Colonization Society, whose members thought it would be a good idea to settle freed slaves in Africa where, by rights, they ought to have been living in the first place. They persuaded several local chieftains to allow them to start a settlement in West Africa. The initial training of the freed slaves to prepare them for running their own country was carried out by white Americans, led by Jehudi Ashmun. Liberia was given a constitution based on that of the USA, and the capital was named Monrovia after James Monroe, US president from 1817 until 1825. Although the system appeared to be democratic, in practice only the descendants of American freed slaves were allowed to vote. The native Africans in the area were treated as second-class citizens, just as they were in the areas colonized by Europeans. In the late 1920s there was a scandal when the US State Department accused the Liberian government of selling large numbers of these citizens into slavery. The League of Nations carried out an investigation and in 1930 published a report showing that this was indeed the case. There were probably mixed motives: to make money for the poverty-stricken government and to get rid of trouble-makers from native tribes in the interior. The president, Charles King, was forced to resign, but a further investigation in 1935, this time by the Anti-Slavery Society, showed that the practice was still going on. One of the investigators was the British novelist, Graham Greene.

Liberia gained new importance during the Second World War because of its rubber plantations, which were a vital source of natural latex rubber for the Allies. The Americans poured cash into the country and built roads, harbours and an international airport at

Monrovia. In 1943, William Tubman of the True Whig Party – the only major political party – was elected president; he was continually re-elected and remained president until his death in 1971, shortly after his election for a seventh term. He presided over a largely peaceful country, which became a member of the UN and a founder member of the Organization of African Unity (1963). But the economy was always precarious; there was little industry and Liberia depended heavily on her exports of rubber and iron ore. Another source of income came from allowing foreign merchant ships to register under the Liberian flag. Shipowners were keen to do this because Liberia's rules and safety regulations were the most lax in the world and the registration fees among the lowest.

(b) Military dictatorship and civil war

President Tubman was succeeded by his vice-president, William Tolbert, but during his presidency things began to go badly wrong. There was a fall in the world prices of rubber and iron ore and the ruling elite came under increasing criticism for its corruption. Opposition groups developed and in 1980 the army staged a coup, led by Master Sergeant Samuel Doe. Tolbert was overthrown and executed in public along with his ministers, and Doe became head of state. He promised a new constitution and a return to civilian rule, but was in no hurry to relinquish power. Although elections were held in 1985, Doe made sure that he and his supporters won. His ruthless regime aroused determined opposition and a number of rebel groups emerged; by 1989 Liberia was engaged in a bloody civil war. The rebel armies were poorly disciplined and guilty of indiscriminate shooting and looting. In spite of efforts by neighbouring West African states which intervened in an attempt to bring peace, Doe was captured and killed (1990); but this did not end the war: two of the rebel groups, led by Charles Taylor and Prince Johnson (the man responsible for Doe's murder), fought each other for control of the country. Altogether this devastating conflict raged on for seven years; new rival factions appeared; at one point Taylor's forces invaded Sierra Leone which he accused of backing Prince Johnson who controlled the capital, Monrovia. The Organization of African Unity tried to broker talks under the chairmanship of former Zimbabwean president Canaan Banana; but it was not until 1996 that a cease-fire was agreed. Taylor succeeded in winning the support of Nigeria and announced that he wanted to be a conciliator.

Elections held in 1997 resulted in a decisive victory for Charles Taylor and the National Patriotic Front of Liberia Party. He faced an unenviable task: the country was literally in ruins, its economy was totally disrupted and its peoples were divided. Nor did the situation improve. Taylor soon found himself at odds with much of the outside world: the USA criticized his human rights record and the European Union claimed that he was helping the rebels in Sierra Leone. After the terrorist attacks of 11 September 2001, the USA accused him of harbouring members of al-Qaeda. Taylor denied all these charges and accused the USA of trying to undermine his government. The UN voted to impose a worldwide ban on the trade in Liberian diamonds.

By the spring of 2002 the country was once again in the grip of civil war as rebel forces in the north launched a campaign to overthrow Taylor. Again the ordinary people suffered appallingly: by the end of the year, 40 000 had fled the country and a further 300 000 were only kept alive by food aid from the UN. In August 2003 the UN Security Council decided to send security forces into Liberia and about a thousand Nigerian troops were airlifted into Monrovia to prevent rebel forces taking it. Taylor resigned and took refuge in Nigeria. All the various factions met and signed a peace agreement. There was to be a two-year transitional period, during which a UN force of 3500 troops from several West African countries would keep the peace. Democratic elections were held in October and November 2005 in which the final run-off was won by Ellen Johnson-Shirleaf, who became Africa's first female head of state. She had been educated at Harvard, and had worked as an economist for the World Bank.

In 2006 ex-president Charles Taylor was handed over to an international court at the Hague and charged with crimes against humanity alleged to have been committed in the 1990s when he intervened to support the rebels in the civil war in Sierra Leone. In April 2012 he was found guilty of being responsible for murder, rape, sexual slavery and conscription of child soldiers. He was sentenced to 50 years in prison. Meanwhile in 2011 president Johnson-Shirleaf was a joint winner, along with two other African female politicians from Liberia and Yemen, of the Nobel Peace Prize for their work for the safety of women and for women's rights. Later in the year she was re-elected president for a second term.

25.11 STABILITY AND CHAOS IN SIERRA LEONE

(a) Early prosperity and stability

Sierra Leone became independent in 1961 with Sir Milton Margai as leader and with a democratic constitution based on the British model. It was potentially one of the richest states in Africa, with valuable iron-ore deposits and diamonds; later gold was discovered. Sadly, the enlightened and gifted Margai, widely seen as the founding father of Sierra Leone, died in 1964. His brother, Sir Albert Margai, took over as leader, but in the election of 1967, his party (the Sierra Leone People's Party – SLPP) was defeated by the All-People's Congress (APC) and its leader Siaka Stevens. In a foretaste of the future, the army removed the new prime minister and installed a military government. This had only been in place for a year when some sections of the army mutinied, imprisoned their officers and restored Stevens and the APC to power. Stevens remained president until his retirement in 1985.

Sierra Leone under Siaka Stevens enjoyed peace and stability, but gradually the situation deteriorated in a number of ways.

- Corruption and mismanagement crept in and the ruling elite lined their own pockets at public expense.
- The deposits of iron ore ran out, and the diamond trade, which should have filled the state treasury, fell into the hands of smugglers, who siphoned off most of the profits.
- As criticism of the government increased, Stevens resorted to dictatorial methods. Many political opponents were executed, and in 1978 all political parties except the APC were banned.

(b) Chaos and catastrophe

When Stevens retired in 1985 he took care to appoint as his successor another strong man, the Commander-in-Chief of the army, Joseph Momoh. His regime was so blatantly corrupt and his economic policies so disastrous that in 1992 he was overthrown, and replaced by a group calling itself the National Provisional Ruling Council (NPRC). The new head of state, Captain Valentine Strasser, accused Momoh of bringing the country 'permanent poverty and a deplorable life', and promised to restore genuine democracy as soon as possible.

Unfortunately the country was already moving towards the tragic civil war, which was to last into the next century. A rebel force calling itself the Revolutionary United Front

(RUF) was organizing in the south, under the leadership of Foday Sankoh. He had been an army corporal who, according to Peter Penfold (a former British High Commissioner in Sierra Leone), 'brainwashed his young followers on a diet of coercion, drugs, and unrealistic promises of gold'. His forces had been causing trouble since 1991, but the violence intensified; Sankoh rejected all calls to negotiate, and by the end of 1994 the Strasser government was in difficulties. Early in 1995 there were reports of fierce fighting all over the country, although Freetown (the capital) was still calm. An estimated 900 000 people had been driven from their homes and at least 30 000 had taken refuge in neighbouring Guinea.

In desperation Strasser offered to hold democratic elections and to sign a truce with the RUF. This produced a lull in the fighting and preparations went ahead for elections to be held in February 1996. However, some sections of the army were unwilling to give up power to a civilian government, and a few days before the election they overthrew Strasser. Nevertheless, voting went ahead, though there was serious violence, especially in Freetown, where 27 people were killed. There were reports of mutinous soldiers firing at civilians as they queued up to vote, and chopping off the hands of some people who had voted. In spite of intimidation, 60 per cent of the electorate voted. The Sierra Leone People's Party (SLPP) emerged as the largest party and its leader, Ahmad Tejan Kabbah, was elected president. Enormous crowds celebrated in Freetown when the army formally handed over authority to the new president, after 19 years of one-party and military rule. President Kabbah pledged to end violence and corruption and offered to meet RUF leaders. In November 1996 he and Sankoh signed a peace agreement.

Just as it seemed that peace was about to return, the country was plunged into further chaos when a group of army officers seized power (May 1997), forcing Kabbah to take refuge in Guinea. The new president, Major Johnny Paul Koroma, abolished the constitution and banned political parties. Sierra Leone was suspended from the Commonwealth and the UN imposed economic sanctions until the country returned to democracy. Nigerian forces fighting on behalf of the Economic Community of West African States (ECOWAS) drove Koroma's military regime out and restored Kabbah (March 1998).

But this was not the end of Sierra Leone's misery. The RUF resurrected itself and was joined by troops loyal to Koroma. They advanced on Freetown, which they reached in January 1999. Then followed the most appalling events of the entire civil war: in a ten-day period about 7000 people were murdered, thousands more were raped or had their arms and legs hacked off, about a third of the capital was destroyed and tens of thousands were left homeless. Eventually Kabbah and Sankoh signed a peace agreement in Lomé, the capital of Togo (July 1999), providing for a power-sharing system and granting an amnesty for the rebels. This provoked strong criticism from human rights groups in view of the terrible atrocities committed by some of the rebels. The UN Security Council voted to send 6000 troops to Sierra Leone to supervise the implementation of peace. Unbelievably, in May 2000 Sankoh, who had become a member of Kabbah's cabinet, ordered his rebel troops to march on Freetown and overthrow the Kabbah government. This was prevented by the timely arrival of British troops sent by UK prime minister Tony Blair. In October 2000 this number had to be increased to 20 000, since many of the RUF fighters refused to accept the terms of the settlement and continued to cause havoc. British troops joined the UN forces and played an important part in the final defeat of the rebels. Sankoh was captured and died in prison in 2003. The job of disarmament was slow and difficult, but violence gradually subsided and something approaching calm was restored. In January 2002 the war was officially declared to be over; it was estimated that 50 000 people had been killed during ten years of conflict.

However, peace was fragile, and the UN kept 17 000 troops in the country, and some of the British contingent stayed in case of renewed violence. In May 2002 President Kabbah was re-elected, winning 70 per cent of the votes. In 2004 it was announced that all rebel troops had been disarmed and the UN opened a war crimes tribunal. But the country's economy was in ruins, the infrastructure needed rebuilding, and in 2003 the UN rated it as one of the five poorest countries in the world.

The constitution did not allow President Kabbah to run for a third consecutive term, and his party, the Sierra Leonean People's Party (SLPP), chose the vice-president, Solomon Berewa, as their candidate in the elections of September 2007. He was unexpectedly defeated by the All People's Party (APC) candidate, Ernest Bai Koroma. He promised that corruption would not be tolerated and that the country's resources would be used in the best interests of all citizens. Further work was done to restore the country's infrastructure and more resources were put into the healthcare system. In April 2010 a new free healthcare system was introduced for pregnant women, mothers and babies, and children under 5. In 2008, after an aircraft carrying around 700 kg of cocaine was stopped at Freetown airport, President Koroma took action against the increasing number of drug cartels, many of them from Colombia, which had started to use Sierra Leone as a base from which to ship drugs to Europe. The minister for transport was suspended and stricter punishments and longer gaol sentences were introduced for offenders. As the 2012 elections approached, there was still a long way to go before Sierra Leone came anywhere near fulfilling its potential.

25.12 ZIMBABWE UNDER ROBERT MUGABE

(a) An impressive beginning, 1980–90

Robert Mugabe, prime minister of the newly independent Zimbabwe, had been an uncompromising guerrilla leader with Marxist opinions. He soon showed that he was capable of moderation, and pledged himself to work for reconciliation and unity. This calmed the fears of the white farmers and businessmen who had remained in Zimbabwe and who were necessary for the economy to flourish. He formed a coalition government between his party, the Zimbabwe African National Union (ZANU), whose main support came from the Shona people, and Joshua Nkomo's Zimbabwe African People's Union (ZAPU), supported by the Ndebele people in Matabeleland. He kept his promise made at the Lancaster House Conference (see Section 24.4(c)) that the whites should have 20 guaranteed seats in the 100-seat parliament. Measures were introduced to alleviate the poverty of the black population – wage increases, food subsidies and better social services, health care and education. Many commentators felt that in his first few years in power, Mugabe showed great statesmanship and deserved credit for keeping his country relatively peaceful.

Nevertheless there were problems to be dealt with. The most serious in the early years was the long-standing hostility between ZANU and ZAPU. The Shona people of ZANU felt that ZAPU could have done more to help during the struggle for black majority rule. The coalition between Mugabe and Nkomo was uneasy, and in 1982 Nkomo was accused of planning a coup. Mugabe forced him to resign and had many leading members of ZAPU arrested. Nkomo's supporters in Matabeleland retaliated with violence, but were brutally suppressed. However, resistance continued until 1987 when at last the two leaders reached agreement – the so-called Unity Accord:

- ZANU and ZAPU united and became known as the Zimbabwe African National Union-Patriotic Front (ZANU-PF);
- Mugabe became executive president and Nkomo became a vice-president in a power-sharing scheme;
- reserved seats for whites in parliament were abolished.

The other worrying problem was the state of the economy. Although in years of good harvests Zimbabwe was regarded as 'the breadbasket of southern Africa', success depended heavily on the weather. During the 1980s there were more than the usual periods of drought, and the country also suffered from the high world price of oil. It was becoming clear that although Mugabe was a clever politician, his economic skills were not so impressive. Since the 1987 Unity Accord, he had been pushing to turn Zimbabwe into a one-party state. However, this was thwarted when Edgar Tekere formed his Zimbabwe Unity Movement (ZUM) in 1989. Nevertheless, in 1990 Mugabe was still immensely popular and regarded as a hero by much of the population because of his vital role in the struggle for freedom. In 1990 he was re-elected president in a landslide victory over ZUM.

(b)   The hero's image begins to tarnish

During the 1990s Zimbabwe's economic problems worsened. After the collapse of the USSR, Mugabe abandoned most of his Marxist policies and attempted to follow western free-market methods. He accepted a loan from the IMF and, very much against public opinion, agreed to abide by the Economic Structural Adjustment Programme it imposed. This involved unpopular cuts in public spending on social services and jobs. Difficulties were compounded in 1992 by a severe drought, bringing a poor harvest and food shortages. More problems were caused when squatters occupied hundreds of white-owned farms. About 4000 white farmers had stayed on in Zimbabwe after independence, and between them they owned about half the country's arable land. The government encouraged the squatters and the police gave the farmers no protection; consequently the areas occupied by squatters were not cultivated, and this added to the food supply problem. Unemployment and inflation rose and the spread of AIDS began to cause concern.

By the late 1990s unrest was growing. Mugabe's intervention to help President Laurent Kabila in the civil war in the Democratic Republic of the Congo was unpopular, since it was widely rumoured that his motive was to protect his own personal investments in that country. In November 1998 there were protest demonstrations when it was announced that Mugabe had awarded himself and his cabinet large pay increases.

(c)   Opposition increases

Around the turn of the century, opposition to the regime increased as Mugabe's rule became more repressive and dictatorial.

- In February 2000, men claiming to be veterans of the war for independence began the systematic and violent occupation of white-owned farms. This continued throughout the next four years, and was clearly a deliberate policy organized by the government. When the UK government protested, Mugabe claimed that it was the fault of the British: they had broken their promise (made during the 1979 Lancaster House Conference) to provide adequate compensation to white farmers. Britain declared itself willing to pay extra compensation provided that the confiscated land was given to ordinary peasant farmers rather than to members of Mugabe's ruling elite.
- Another proviso was that the elections due in June 2000 were free and fair. In February 2000, the people had rejected a new pro-Mugabe draft constitution, a clear indication that his popularity had dwindled. This probably led him to take whatever measures were necessary to win the June elections. Although he had agreed that they should be free and fair, he apparently did little to make sure that this happened.

There was widespread violence and intimidation of the opposition before and during the election, and international observers were severely restricted. Even so, the result was close: Mugabe's ZANU-PF won 62 seats in the 150-seat parliament, while the opposition Movement for Democratic Change (MDC) won 57. The MDC had support from trade unions and by the prominent, but mainly white Commercial Farmers' Union (CFU). However, the president had the right to nominate 30 of the 150 members, and so Mugabe maintained a comfortable majority.

- The forcible occupation of white-owned farms continued during 2001, bringing more protests from the UK and the USA. Mugabe accused the British government of running a neo-colonial and racist campaign, supporting whites against blacks. The dispute brought mixed reactions from the rest of the world. The majority of black African states expressed sympathy and support for Mugabe. President Mbeki of South Africa, on the other hand, claimed that the land seizures were a violation of the rule of law, and ought to stop; but he urged a conciliatory approach and refused to apply economic sanctions against Zimbabwe, since these would only ruin the already ailing economy. However, the EU condemned Mugabe's policy and imposed sanctions (February 2002), the Commonwealth expelled Zimbabwe for one year, and the World Bank cut off its funding because of Zimbabwe's huge debt arrears, which had risen to over $380 million.

- Meanwhile, Mugabe took steps to muzzle the mounting criticism of his policies within Zimbabwe. There was now only one independent daily newspaper, the *Daily News*, and its journalists were increasingly harassed and intimidated, as were members of the MDC. Morgan Tsvangirai, the MDC leader, was charged with plotting to overthrow the president, and the government tightened its control over TV and radio. When the Supreme Court ventured to criticize Mugabe's land policy, he sacked three of the judges and replaced them with his own nominees. As the presidential election of March 2002 approached, restrictions were tightened further. Public meetings were banned, except those of Mugabe's supporters, and it became an offence 'to undermine the authority of the president by making statements or publishing statements that provoke hostility'. No foreign observers were to be allowed into the country to monitor the elections.

During the election campaign ZANU-PF took the line that the MDC was a puppet political party being used by the West to destabilize the nationalist and fundamentally Marxist attempt to redistribute wealth in Zimbabwe. Jonathan Moyo, the Minister of Information and Publicity, accused the MDC of being unpatriotic because they supported the CFU in their attempts to derail Mugabe's land-redistribution exercise. It was no surprise when Mugabe won the election and was sworn in for a further six-year term, although he was 78 years old. He took 56 per cent of the vote while Morgan Tsvangirai could muster only 42 per cent. Tsvangirai immediately challenged the result, claiming that 'it was the biggest electoral fraud I've seen in my life'. He complained of terrorism, intimidation and harassment; tensions ran high as he demanded that the High Court overturn the result.

(d) Zimbabwe in crisis

Rejecting the opposition's accusations, President Mugabe declared a 'state of disaster' (April 2002) because of the food situation. The whole of Central Africa was suffering the effects of a prolonged drought, and the harvest was expected to be only half its usual size. Yet Mugabe continued with his controversial land-seizure policy, although agricultural experts pointed out that this would threaten the vital crop of winter wheat.

Protests against the government continued in various forms, and so did the suppression of criticism. Mugabe used almost every means possible to stay in power: war veterans, youth militias and members of the security forces were used to intimidate the opposition. In February 2003 the Cricket World Cup competition was held in Zimbabwe; in Zimbabwe's opening match, two of their players – one black and one white – wore black armbands in order, they said, to 'mourn the death of democracy in our beloved Zimbabwe. We cannot in all conscience take the field and ignore the fact that millions of our compatriots are starving, unemployed and oppressed.' They did not play for Zimbabwe again. Later in the month, 21 Christian church leaders were arrested when they tried to present a petition asking the police to behave with less violence and more regard for human rights.

But the opposition refused to be silenced; in March the MDC organized a mass protest across the whole country, demanding that Mugabe should either reform his regime or leave office. Many factories, banks and shops closed, but the government dismissed it as 'an act of terrorism'. It was reported that over 500 opposition members, including Gibson Sibanda, vice-president of the MDC, had been arrested. Supported by a number of Western countries, the MDC called for foreign intervention and appealed for the UN to get involved in future elections. They also called on neighbouring states, asking them to take a more active role in Zimbabwe's affairs. Through the regional Southern African Development Community (SADC) there were a number of attempts at mediation. Presidents Mbeki of South Africa and Obasanjo of Nigeria several times tried to persuade Mugabe to form a coalition government with the MDC, but although representatives of Mugabe and Tsvangirai held talks, no solution to the deadlock could be found. Mugabe insisted that Zimbabwe was a sovereign country which could run its own affairs without interference from other states; issues pertaining to Zimbabwe could only be solved by Zimbabweans themselves. He also argued that Western talk of human rights abuses in Zimbabwe was simply political rhetoric and part of a neo-colonial strategy to continue influencing what went on in Zimbabwe. Jonathan Moyo has linked the recent farm seizures to the 1970s war of liberation from British colonial rule. He described the farm takeovers as the third 'Chimurenga', a Shona word for the war of liberation, the first and second Chimurenga being the wars started by black natives against white settlers during the 1890s and 1970s.

When the Commonwealth summit met in Abuja (Nigeria) in December 2003, the issue which dominated the conference was whether or not Zimbabwe's suspension should be lifted. Mugabe was hoping to split the Commonwealth along black–white lines, but after intense discussion, the majority of members, including many African countries, voted to continue the suspension. Bitterly disappointed, Mugabe withdrew Zimbabwe from the Commonwealth.

The tragedy was that by the summer of 2004, as well as the dire human rights situation, Zimbabwe's economy was in a state of collapse. It was reported that since the land reform programme began, agricultural production had fallen catastrophically: in 2003 the tobacco crop fell to less than a third of the 2000 crop; worst of all, the wheat crop was less than a quarter of the total in 2000, and the numbers of cattle on commercial farms fell from 1.2 million to a mere 150 000. Although the government claimed that 50 000 black families had been settled on commercial farms, the real figure was less than 5000. Many of the best farms had been given to the president's supporters; vast amounts of fertile land were lying uncultivated because of shortages of seeds, fertilizers and agricultural machinery. In May 2004, the unemployment rate stood at over 70 per cent and the inflation rate was over 600 per cent, one of the highest in the world. The EU decision to continue sanctions for a further year did nothing to help. As usual, the main victims were Zimbabwe's poverty-stricken, oppressed and neglected people.

In spite of all this, Mugabe's ZANU-PF party won a decisive victory in the parliamentary elections of April 2005, taking 78 seats out of the 120 contested. The opposition MDC could muster only 41 seats. With the 30 seats that the president could fill with his own appointments, he would have more than the two-thirds majority needed to change the constitution. A smiling Mugabe said that he would retire when he was 'a century old'. There was less violence than during the two previous elections, and South African observers reported that the proceedings had been free and fair. However, the MDC and many European observers claimed that there had been widespread abuses, fraud and intimidation of voters; they accused the South African government of turning a blind eye to the fraud in order to discourage the MDC from resorting to violence, which would destabilize South Africa's frontier with Zimbabwe. In fact, the MDC leader, Morgan Tsvangirai, a former trade union leader, decided not to launch a legal challenge to the results and rejected calls for armed resistance. As the UK *Times* put it: 'It would be a brave group indeed which would openly confront the thugs of ZANU-PF.' In March 2007 when the MDC did criticize Mugabe and staged a protest march, Tsvangirai and several other protesters were arrested and beaten up and one of them was killed.

In 2008 both parliamentary and presidential elections were held. With the economy in dire straits, Mugabe's ZANU-PF suffered a narrow defeat by the MDC, and Mugabe himself came second to Morgan Tsvangirai in the first round of the election for president. However, Tsvangirai had narrowly failed to win the requisite 50 per cent to secure victory in the first round. A run-off took place almost two months after these results were announced. During that time ZANU-PF launched a campaign of violence against the MDC and its supporters in which 86 people were reported killed, hundreds injured and hundreds more driven from their homes. Five days before the run-off Tsvangirai announced that he had withdrawn from the contest; there was no point in running, he said, when the election would not be free and fair, and when the outcome would be decided by Mugabe himself. He claimed that his supporters risked being killed if they turned up to vote for him. Mugabe retorted that he had only withdrawn because he knew he would be humiliated in the vote. The run-off went ahead and predictably, since Tsvangirai was no longer a candidate, Mugabe took around 90 per cent of the votes. In June 2008 he was sworn in for a further term as president. There was widespread international condemnation of the result, and the African Union insisted that the only fair outcome would be the formation of a government of national unity. Talks were held between ZANU-PF and the MDC under the auspices of the Southern African Development Community (SADC), and mediated by South African president Mbeki. In September 2008 a power-sharing agreement was signed: Mugabe was to remain as president, Tsvangirai was to become prime minister, both would share control of the police and Mugabe's ZANU-PF would be in control of the army.

Over the next four years the economy at last began to make some progress, although in June 2012 an MDC report stated that 'the transport system remains in a complete shambles'; all major roads were in need of upgrading and the secondary roads were full of potholes. At the same time the UN Human Rights Commissioner reported that in spite of the unity government, polarization was still very pronounced; she expressed grave concerns that the next elections, due in 2013, could turn into a repeat of the 2008 elections. Only a week after the Commissioner's visit an MDC official was murdered by ZANU-PF supporters and several others were severely beaten. Clearly Mugabe's conception of sovereignty has more to do with the perpetuation of his own rule than the protection and well-being of his people. In the words of one of the disaffected Anglican priests, in 2012:

Zimbabweans continue to suffer under Mugabe's rule. There is general suffering across Zimbabwe, and unemployment is a serious problem in every part of the country. Moreover the involvement of the military in the politics of the country means that the idea of free and fair elections continues to be a fantasy in the minds of many Zimbabweans.

25.13 CONFUSION AND CIVIL WAR IN SOMALIA

(a) Somalia united

The territories occupied by the Somali people had been colonized in the nineteenth century by the French, British and Italians. By 1960 both Britain and Italy recognized the independence of their areas which were united to form the Republic of Somalia. There was a long history of frontier disputes between the Somalis in the south-west of the country neighbouring Kenya, and between the Somalis in the north-west of Somalia, bordering on the Ethiopian province of Ogaden, and the Ethiopian government. In 1963 a boundary commission recommended that the Somali-populated area bordering on Kenya should be included in the new Republic of Kenya. When the British government agreed to this there were protest riots across Somalia and the Somali government broke off diplomatic relations with Britain. This alarmed Ethiopia where border skirmishes had already occurred in Ogaden in 1962. The president of Sudan and the King of Morocco offered to mediate, and following talks in Khartoum, hostilities between Somalia and Ethiopia were suspended temporarily. However, sporadic border clashes continued until 1967 when President Kaunda of Zambia mediated more successfully. Meanwhile the small French colony of Djibouti, situated between Somalia and Eritrea, voted to remain separate as a member of the French Union. The French finally withdrew in 1975 and Djibouti became an independent republic in 1977. Though small, the new republic included the port of Djibouti, which was vital for the trade of the landlocked state of Ethiopia and extremely desirable for Somalia. The republic's population was mixed, consisting both of Ethiopians (Afars) and Somalis (Issas).

In October 1969 the Somali president Abdi Rashid Ali Shermarke was assassinated and the army took over, with Major-General Mohamed Siad Barre as president. The country's name was changed to the Somali Democratic Republic, but this did not solve one of its basic problems – it was divided into a large number of tribes or clans, and sub-tribes. Before independence these had only been held together by the colonial power, and after 1960 some tribes began to act more independently. The new president Siad Barre, a member of the Marehan tribe, aimed to reassert central control from the capital, Mogadishu, with himself as the uniting force. He gained the support of several other clans and introduced a programme of socialist reforms.

(b) War and civil war

In 1977, expecting help from the USA, President Siad Barre launched an ill-advised invasion of Ethiopia. When American help failed to materialize, his forces were easily driven back by the Ethiopians, who received support from the USSR and Cuba. After the Ethiopians had invaded Somalia in 1982, the country gradually deteriorated into a terrible civil war lasting well into the next century. The former British area in the north declared itself independent under President Muhammad Egal, though only Djibouti gave it official recognition. A number of tribes united and in 1991 forced Barre to leave the country. However, they immediately fell out again and continued to fight each other. The leading figures were now Muhammad Farah Aided, who was supported by Islamist groups, and Ali Mahdi Muhammad, whose forces controlled Mogadishu and who declared himself president.

Meanwhile the unfortunate population suffered famine, epidemics and drought; millions were forced to flee from their homes. At one point there were over 20 different aid agencies at work in the country. Sadly they were often terrorized and robbed by local militias, and at the end of 1992 a UN mission (known as UNOSOM) was sent to try to make sure that the aid reached the right people. This group was eventually enlarged to 28 000 (of which 8000 were from the USA) and given authority to disarm the warring factions. When this proved beyond them, the Americans decided it would be easier to back Ali Mahdi and eliminate Aided, rather than trying to bring the two together in peace talks. They were in for a great disappointment: an American force sent to arrest Aided failed to capture him and lost two helicopters and the lives of 18 teenage American soldiers. This was too much for President Clinton, who decided to pull all American troops out of Somalia. UNOSOM forces soon followed (1994). They had totally failed to disarm the militias and certainly to reunite the country. Aided was killed in 1996 but it seemed to make little difference. In reality, Somalia had no government, just a collection of warlords each ruling his own patch.

In 2000 it seemed that some progress was being made: a group of warlords met in Djibouti and set up a government, though at first it controlled only about 10 per cent of the country. In August 2004 a National Transitional Federal Parliament of 275 members was inaugurated for a five-year term and Abdullahi Yusuf Ahmed was elected president. The new government was forced to spend the first year based in Kenya, because Somalia itself was too violent, but eventually it was able to move to the town of Baidoa. More violence followed in 2006, this time caused by a group of Islamists calling themselves the Somali Islamic Courts Council (SICC). They seized Mogadishu and took control of most of the south. President Yusuf tried to reach a peace agreement with them, but no progress could be made. At this point the Ethiopian government intervened. They considered the Islamists to be a dangerous threat to their territory and to the region in general, and carried out a series of air strikes against them. Ethiopian troops joined the Somali government's struggling forces and together they regained control of Mogadishu. By the end of 2006 most of the Islamists had been forced out of Somalia. The Americans joined in, launching air strikes against the retreating Islamists whom they suspected of having links with al-Qaeda. These were widely condemned in a number of Muslim countries which claimed that the Americans had killed more ordinary Somalis than Islamist rebels.

The Islamists soon regrouped and the militant wing of the SICC, known as Al-Shabab, grew much stronger in 2007. Supported by many local warlords, they recaptured much of the south. One encouraging sign for the beleaguered government was that many moderate Muslims supported it, and when President Yusuf resigned at the end of 2008, parliament elected Sheikh Sharif Ahmed, a moderate Muslim cleric, as the next president. In 2010 Al-Shabab announced that it acknowledged allegiance to al-Qaeda and in July it claimed responsibility for a bomb blast in a restaurant at Kampala, the capital of Uganda, which killed 75 people. Ugandan forces had been helping the Somali government, and the explosion was clearly meant as a warning to any other countries that might be considering similar assistance. Even the weather was cruel to the Somalis – in the summer of 2011 there was a prolonged drought. This caused a famine in most of the south where thousands were reported to have died from malnutrition and thousands more had migrated into neighbouring Kenya and Ethiopia looking for food. The government had proved incapable of controlling the Somali pirates who had been terrorizing the seas off the coast of East Africa for many years. Since 2000 hundreds of vessels have been attacked, though only a small proportion of these resulted in successful hijackings. Many countries have joined an international task force to eliminate piracy. This had some success and the number of attacks was reduced, though in February 2012 pirates were still holding ten ships and 159 hostages. In September 2012 Sheikh Sharif Ahmed was unexpectedly defeated when MPs voted for Hassan Sheikh Mohamud as the next president. He was described as being 'a more moderate Muslim' than his predecessor. He was an academic who had once worked for UNICEF.

At the end of the twentieth century no fewer than 17 African countries were experiencing crises of various kinds, and the UN rated Sudan as probably the worst. Since 1956, southern Sudan had been ravaged by civil war between the Arab-dominated government and the African tribes, many of whom were Christians. The Africans felt they were not receiving a fair deal; they had been refused the right to secede and had not even been allowed a certain amount of independence as part of a federal state. In 1983 the government in Khartoum introduced fundamentalist Islamic law, which only exacerbated the rift between Arabs in the north and the black African tribes in the south. Government forces were strongly influenced by the National Islamic Front (NIF) while the rebels' main supporters were the Sudan People's Liberation Army (SPLA). In 1989 a group of army officers led by Omar al-Bashir overthrew the Sudanese government and took over the presidency. He was still president in 2012 though he has promised to stand down in 2015. The fighting ended in 2002, but peace was fragile, and in February 2003 rebel groups from African tribes in the Darfur region again took up arms against the government in the struggle for more land and resources. In retaliation the government used various Arab militias including the Janjaweed to disguise the fact that they were really waging an ethnic cleansing campaign against people of African origin. The government itself did nothing to stop the violence. By the summer of 2004, the situation in the Darfur region was chaotic: some estimates put the number of deaths as high as 300 000, between 3 million and 4 million people were homeless, and over 2 million were in urgent need of food and medical attention. To make matters worse, consecutive years of drought and floods had ruined tens of thousands of livelihoods, and living conditions were said to be appalling. The infrastructure was in ruins, with scores of schools and hospitals destroyed, there was no electricity, disease was rife and trade depended on barter. UN and other aid agencies were desperately trying to provide for basic survival needs; food was dropped in from planes because there were no good roads. The whole of the south was desperately backward and under-developed. Yet the country had plenty of valuable assets which were not being fully exploited: the soil was fertile and watered by the Nile – properly cultivated, it could easily provide sufficient food for the population; and there were rich oil resources.

Hopes for an improvement rose in August 2004 when the African Union began a peace-keeping mission. In January 2005 representatives of the Sudan People's Liberation Movement and the Khartoum government signed a peace deal in Nairobi, the capital of Kenya. It was agreed that Southern Sudan would be autonomous for six years, and that there would then be a referendum to decide whether it was to remain part of the Sudan. However, the new deal seemed to have little immediate effect in Darfur, where fighting continued, in spite of all international efforts to bring peace. In March 2009 the International Criminal Court issued a warrant for the arrest of President Bashir on charges of war crimes and crimes against humanity in Darfur. He continued blithely in office and in April 2010 he won the first multi-party elections to be held in Sudan since 1986. This was no surprise since most of the opposition parties boycotted the elections. The leader of the SPLM, Salva Kiir, was re-elected for another term as president of the semi-independent Darfur.

In January 2011 the referendum over the future of Darfur provided for in the 2005 peace agreement took place; 98 per cent voted in favour of independence. President Bashir accepted the result and said he would not stand for re-election at the end of his term in 2015. In July 2011 South Sudan officially became independent as Africa's 54th state. Even then tensions between the two continued, mainly over possession of oil fields and disputed frontiers. In April 2012 the South took over some disputed oil fields but withdrew after the

Sudan launched air attacks. The African Union gave the two sides three months to resolve all their issues, but the future did not look promising.

25.15 AFRICA AND ITS PROBLEMS IN THE TWENTY-FIRST CENTURY

In November 2003 the UN secretary-general Kofi Annan complained that since the terrorist attacks of 11 September 2001 on the USA, the world's attention had focused on the war against terrorism, and that Africa and its problems had been, if not exactly forgotten, then certainly neglected. Resources that might have gone to help Africa had been diverted to Afghanistan and later to Iraq, which turned out to be a much more difficult problem than the USA had expected. He appealed for $3 billion (about £1.8 billion) to help provide basic services such as food, water, medical supplies and shelter. It was pointed out in comparison that the US Congress had voted to spend $87 billion on rebuilding Iraq.

After gaining independence from Ethiopia in 1993, **Eritrea** had a difficult time. There was continuing tension with Ethiopia over the exact position of their frontiers. Border clashes broke out in 1998. Both governments seemed to be obsessed with building up large armaments in case of a full-scale border war, and spent millions of dollars which they could ill afford on warplanes and weapons. Unfortunately, as well as using up vital resources, this also took men away from the farms where they were needed for ploughing and bringing water. Fortunately a peace agreement was signed at the end of 2000. Eritrea also suffered four consecutive years of drought; the once fertile plains were barren and the wind was blowing away the topsoil. The harvest was only 10 per cent of normal, and it was estimated that 1.7 million people were unable to feed themselves. Border tensions continued and clashes between frontier forces at some stage every year, the most serious recent skirmish being in January 2010 when Eritrean forces killed 10 Ethiopians.

Tanzania had the problem of how to deal with hundreds of thousands of refugees who had fled from the civil wars in Burundi and the Democratic Republic of the Congo. Similarly in West Africa, **Guinea's** frontier areas were crammed with refugees from neighbouring Sierra Leone and Liberia. Southern Africa was feeling the effects of drought. **Malawi** was badly affected: in January 2003 the government declared a national emergency after a drought and the failure of the maize crop. Then storms and heavy rains washed away bridges and flooded riverside fields; by April the World Food Programme claimed it was feeding around 3.5 million Malawians – a third of the population. Things did not improve in 2005 when more than 4 million people had insufficient food.

Lesotho, Mozambique and Swaziland were suffering from similar problems. The outlook for the future was not encouraging: experts were predicting that unless global warming could be controlled, droughts would become progressively worse and some parts of Africa might become uninhabitable (see Section 27.5). On top of this, all the countries of Africa were suffering in different degrees from the HIV/AIDS pandemic (see Section 28.4). In fact, although the West was understandably obsessed with the threat of terrorism, Africans were most concerned about AIDS, since, by and large, it was affecting the most active generations – the 20 to 50 age group.

On the other hand, there were encouraging developments on the political and economic front. At a summit conference of the Southern African Development Community (SADC) held in Mauritius in August 2004, a new charter of regulations for the conduct of democratic elections was drawn up. This included, among other things, allowing a free press, no vote-rigging, and no violence or intimidation. There was also to be a commitment by presidents to submit themselves for re-election when their term of office ended, and not to use armed force to keep themselves in power. As a demonstration of good faith, the presidents of Tanzania, Mozambique and Namibia indicated that they would be stepping down soon. In October 2008 the African Free Trade Zone was set up with 26 members. Experts believed that this would encourage African internal trade and boost economic development, as well strengthening the bloc's bargaining power when negotiating international trade agreements.

FURTHER READING

Adejumobi, S. A., *The History of Ethiopia* (Greenwood, 2006).

Barclay, S., *Zimbabwe: Years of Hope and Despair* (Bloomsbury, 2011).

Cornelissen, S., Cheru, F. and Shaw, T. M. (eds), *Africa and International Relations in the 21st Century* (Palgrave Macmillan, 2011).

Dallaire, R., *Shake Hands With the Devil: The Failure of Humanity in Rwanda* (Random House, 2004).

Daly, M. W., *Darfur's Sorrow: The Forgotten History of a Humanitarian Disaster* (Cambridge University Press, 2010).

Davidson, B., *Black Star: A View of the Life and Times of Kwame Nkrumah* (James Currey, 2007).

Ellis, S., *The Mask of Anarchy: The Destruction of Liberia* (Hurst, 1999).

Gevisser, M., *Thabo Mbeki: The Dream Deferred* (Jonathan Ball, 2007).

Godwin, P., *The Fear: The Last Days of Robert Mugabe* (Picador, 2011).

Gumede, W. M., *Thabo Mbeki and the Battle for the Soul of the ANC* (Zed Books, second edition, 2007).

Hall, A. J., *Earth into Property: Colonization, Decolonization and Capital* (McGill University Press, 2010).

Harris, D., *Civil War and Democracy in West Africa: Sierra Leone and Liberia* (I. B. Tauris, 2011).

Harvey, R., *The Fall of Apartheid: The Inside Story from Smuts to Mbeki* (Palgrave Macmillan, 2003).

Kisangani, E. F., *Civil Wars in the Democratic Republic 1960–2010* (Lynne Rienner, 2012).

Maier, K., *This House Has Fallen: Nigeria in Crisis* (Penguin, 2002).

Mamdani, M., *Saviours and Survivors: Darfur, Politics and the War on Terror* (Pantheon, 2009).

Mamdani, M., 'The Invention of the Indigene', *London Review of Books* (20 January 2011).

Marcus, M. G., *A History of Ethiopia* (University of California Press, 2002).

Melvern, L., *A People Betrayed: The Role of the West in Rwanda's Genocide* (Zed Books, 2000).

Meredith, M., *Mugabe: Power, Plunder and the Struggle for Zimbabwe's Future* (Public Affairs, 2007).

Osagae, E. E., *Crippled Giant: Nigeria since Independence* (Indiana University Press, 1998).

Prunier, G., *Africa's World War: Congo, the Rwandan Genocide and the Making of a Continental Catastrophe* (Oxford University Press, 2009).

Sampson, A., *Nelson Mandela: The Authorised Biography* (HarperCollins, 2000).

Turner, T., *The Congo Wars: Conflict, Myth, Reality* (Zed Books, 2007).

Weigert, S. L., *Angola: A Modern Military History, 1961–2002* (Palgrave Macmillan, 2011).

1 Explain why the newly independent states in Africa suffered so many problems and assess to what extent the problems were of their own making.
2 How accurate do you think it is to describe Angola as 'a victim of the Cold War' during the years 1975 to 2002?
3 Explain why Robert Mugabe was regarded as a hero in Zimbabwe in the years 1980 to 1990, but had to face increasing opposition after 1990.
4 Assess the reasons why J. J. Rawlings was more successful as president of Ghana than Kwame Nkrumah.
5 How far would you agree that the Belgians should bear most of the responsibility for the outbreak of civil war in the Congo in 1960 and its continuation until 1965?
6 Why was apartheid in South Africa brought to an end, and how successfully did the ANC govern the country up until 2009?

◥ There is a document question about Nelson Mandela and the anti-apartheid campaign in South Africa on the website.

Chapter
26 Latin America

The area known as Latin America consists of the countries of South America, Central America including Mexico, and islands in the Caribbean Sea such as Cuba, Jamaica and Hispaniola (see Map 26.1). The latter is divided into two states – Haiti and the Dominican Republic. These states gained their independence from Spain – in the case of Brazil, from Portugal – in the early nineteenth century, and they had much in common. Spanish is spoken in most of these countries, though in Brazil Portuguese is the main language. They all shared similar difficulties: they were underdeveloped both industrially and agriculturally, and they had massive problems of poverty and illiteracy and unstable political systems. Revolutions, coups and assassinations were commonplace, and progress occurred only very slowly and unevenly. The USA provided economic aid for some of the states of Latin America, but its motives were not entirely selfless. In return the Americans expected to be able to exert political influence in order to prevent socialist or communist governments from gaining power. They had no hesitation in intervening in any Latin American country whose government was deemed unacceptable to them.

Consequently, following the end of the Second World War the USA was able to exercise a huge amount of economic, political and military influence, and Latin America found itself dragged into the Cold War. Republican presidents in particular were constantly suspicious that the USSR was trying to forge a Soviet–Latin American Axis, which would give the communists a clear advantage and pose a threat right on the USA's doorstep. US interventions to remove 'suspect' governments took place in Guatemala (1954), Cuba (1962), Brazil (1964), the Dominican Republic (1965), Chile (1970–3), Nicaragua (from 1979 onwards), Panama (1989) and Haiti (1994). However, the attempt to remove Fidel Castro from Cuba in 1962 failed miserably, and in 2012 his brother Raul was still in power (see Sections 7.4(b) and 8.2).

The international situation changed towards the end of the twentieth century with the ending of the Cold War. The demise of the communist 'enemy' – the Soviet Empire – removed the Americans' justification for their constant interventions. After half a century of US domination, Latin American states had more freedom to take control of their own affairs; no longer could the USA accuse them of aiming to become part of a communist power bloc. Venezuela was the first country to throw off US influence when, in 1998, Hugo Chávez was elected president on a programme of greater spending on social services to help alleviate poverty, and of making trading agreements with Cuba – absolute anathema to the USA! In 2002 right-wing forces backed by US finance tried to overthrow Chávez, but he survived. By this time he had become an inspiration to other Latin American voters: Brazil (2002), Argentina (2003), Chile (2005), Bolivia (2005) and Ecuador (2006) all elected presidents who, if not exactly left-wing, were determined to introduce changes that would give them greater freedom from control by Washington.

Map 26.1 **Latin America**

Chávez was re-elected in 2000 and 2006 and again in 2012. These developments had seri-ous consequences for the USA which, for one thing, was losing its economic, diplomatic and military advantages in South America. Some Latin American states began to look towards China as an important trading partner. This seemed bound to affect the US econ-omy adversely. Conversely, some of the Latin American states began to enjoy greater prosperity. By 2011, for example, Brazil was viewed, along with India, as one of the world's great emerging economies, destined soon to rival the USA and China.

(a) Problems facing the countries of Latin America

1 They were economically underdeveloped both industrially and agriculturally. Factory industries did exist (the Second World War had acted as a stimulus because manufactured goods from Europe and the USA were impossible to come by), but for all sorts of reasons, Latin American industry was still well below the level of industry in the developed countries of Europe, the USA and Japan. There was a shortage of capital, equipment and technical knowledge. Home markets were unpredictable because the vast majority of people were too poverty-stricken to provide enough purchasing power, and it was difficult to export because of competition from the advanced industrial nations. Many countries found themselves heavily dependent for exports on a limited range of products, sometimes even a single commodity. A fall in the world price of that commodity would be a major disaster. Chile relied on copper, Cuba on sugar and tobacco, and Bolivia on tin; during the 1950s, in fact, 80 per cent of all Bolivia's revenue came from tin exports. Agriculture remained backward because peasant labour was so plentiful and cheap that wealthy estate owners had no need to go to the trouble of modernizing. Peru, for example, was dominated by huge estates whose owners were all-powerful, and who ruled their peasants like feudal monarchs.

2 There was a massive rise in population mainly because of advances in medicine and hygiene and the refusal of the Roman Catholic Church to promote birth control. Peasants found their holdings were too small to support large families, but when they moved to the cities they found that jobs were scarce. Almost all the major cities were surrounded by improvised shanty towns (known as *favelas* in Brazil) that were without water, sewage disposal or electricity. The gap between rich and poor grew wider and little progress was made in eliminating poverty and illiteracy.

3 Latin American political systems were, for the most part, inadequate for dealing with such enormous problems. There was no tradition of democracy, except in Chile, and states were dominated by groups of wealthy landowners and run by military dictators (caudillos). After the Second World War democratic systems were introduced in some of the states. But when the newly elected governments tried to introduce reforms, they faced strong opposition from the landowners who were determined to protect their privileged positions. They were able to use the army either to block the reforms or to overthrow the reforming government. This happened in Guatemala (1950), Bolivia (1964), Brazil (1964), Argentina (1966) and Chile (1973).

4 Heavy investment by foreigners in industry and agriculture caused problems because much of the profit was taken out of the countries. Most of the oil in Bolivia and Venezuela, both potentially rich countries, was extracted by American-owned companies. The US Fruit Company was the biggest landowner in Guatemala, while Chilean copper mines and Cuban sugar plantations were also under US control.

(b) Solutions to the problems?

1 Several international organizations were set up to help: the Organization of American States (OAS), founded in 1948, included most of the Latin American countries and the USA. It aimed to foster inter-American co-operation and to settle disputes. The Central American Common Market (1960) had some success in reducing tariffs.

2   The United Nations helped by providing technical experts and holding conferences to discuss how underdeveloped nations might go about increasing exports.

3   The USA provided massive economic aid. President Kennedy started the 'Alliance for Progress' which aimed to pump billions of dollars into Latin America to enable economic and social reform to be carried out. However, this kind of aid did not always work out for the best, and sometimes it created extra problems. American motives were mixed: they hoped, by solving basic economic and social problems, to encourage the election of moderate reforming governments which would be popular enough to prevent communists from coming to power. Sometimes the aid was in the form of loans made on condition that a large proportion of the loan should be spent on buying US products. This did nothing to help the development of local industry and involved governments in large interest payments. Often, as with Castro's Cuba and Allende's Chile, aid would be cut short if a government unacceptable to the USA came to power. Only if the government changed would the aid be resumed. In this way the USA was able to exert political influence via economic control; on occasion, they supplied rebels with weapons to overthrow a reforming government (Guatemala, 1954), and even used 20,000 American troops to crush an attempted comeback by a reforming president (the Dominican Republic, 1965).

(c)   The crisis of the 1980s

By the early 1980s it was clear that the problems of Latin America had not been solved. Two problems in particular – those of debt and finance – had reached crisis proportions. The trouble was that, under US domination, the countries of Latin America had been obliged to follow economic policies known as 'neo-liberalism'. This involved privatization, deregulation of finance, cuts in social spending and other austerity measures. Basically this was designed to make use of a country's resources in order to benefit a wealthy elite at home, foreign investors, big business and bankers, particularly those in the USA. This had forced Latin American governments to borrow massively from foreign banks, in order to develop their amenities and industries. Many of these banks were in the USA, and the borrowing was at its height from 1973 until 1982. In 1982 the seven largest US banks made 60 per cent of their profits from the interest on loans to Third World countries, as against only 2 per cent in 1970. With the doubling of American interest rates in the period 1979–81, many of the debtor nations could not even pay the interest, let alone repay the debts, and the amount of interest they failed to pay each year was added on to the existing debt. They were forced to borrow from new sources merely to keep up the interest payments on the original loans. If a country stepped out of line, the USA did not hesitate to intervene; for example in 1991 the democratically elected president of Haiti, Jean-Bertrand Aristide, was removed in a military coup backed by the CIA after only eight months in office. Aristide was a committed Roman Catholic, a former priest, who was strongly influenced by the ideals of the Church's liberation theology. This was a style of theology which accepted many of Marx's theories (though not his atheism!). It stressed the church's mission to the poor and oppressed, based on the fact that Jesus was considered as a sympathizer with, and a liberator of the poor and downtrodden. In 2004 Aristide was removed for the second time in a similar coup. Throughout Latin America there were large numbers of priests with left-wing views and some were even supporters of revolution. Inevitably this brought them into conflict with the authorities; many were arrested and some were killed. In 1980 Bishop Oscar Romera of El Salvador was murdered by US-backed paramilitaries.

By 1985 Latin America owed some $368 billion, and there was a constant drain of capital to the USA, leaving Latin America increasingly impoverished. By 1987, as export earnings steadily declined, the situation was approaching catastrophe. *Brazil,* one of the most prosperous states with its huge natural resources, had debts of over $100 million, and in February the government announced that it was suspending interest payments. *Mexico,* which owed almost as much, was considering the possibility of repudiating its debts. Fortunately it didn't quite come to that: the IMF and the World Bank, desperate to avoid an economic catastrophe, arranged credits amounting to several billion dollars for Brazil. The Mexican government secured an annual loan for the next 30 years from the IMF and was able to reschedule its debts. Similar arrangements helped other debtor countries to survive.

There is insufficient space to consider all the countries of Latin America, but a closer look at five of them – Brazil, Venezuela, Mexico, Guatemala and Nicaragua – will demonstrate the varied Latin American experience during this period of US domination.

26.2 SOUTH AMERICA: BRAZIL AND VENEZUELA

(a) Brazil

Brazil had gained its independence from Portugal in 1825. It was a monarchy until 1889, when it became a republic. Until 1930 the country was ruled mainly by military dictatorships, but none of them succeeded in establishing a stable system. There were economic, social and political problems which caused several revolutions and attempted coups. The country began to make genuine economic progress after 1930 when the army replaced the ultra-conservative government of wealthy landowners with the more progressive and liberal President Getulio Vargas. For the first time the government took over economic planning, and Vargas was especially keen to encourage industry. Thousands of extra jobs were created, especially in electrical and steel manufacture. He soon became popular and was able to stay in power right through the Second World War. However, by this time the army was turning against him. They were worried by his popularity with the working classes and felt that he had become too powerful. In fact, he had been acting as a dictator since 1937, and no elections had taken place. The army wanted a president whom they could control, and so in 1945 Vargas was forced to step down. The army faced a dilemma when he was re-elected in 1950 for a five-year term: should they prevent him from taking office or not? Fortunately the younger army officers favoured Vargas and in the end, he was allowed to return. He stayed in power until 1954. He tried to continue acting as a dictator and once again the army grew tired of him. They accused him of corruption and incompetence and asked him to resign. Instead, he committed suicide, claiming that his death was 'a sacrifice on behalf of the Brazilian workers'.

The election of 1955 was won by Juscelino Kubitschek, whose first major action was to increase the army's pay, thereby, he hoped, guaranteeing their support. He completed his term in office in 1961, but his presidency was a disappointment. His only memorable achievement was the building of a new capital, Brasilia, and that was arguably an extravagance the country could ill afford. The winner in the 1961 presidential election was Janio Quadros, but he resigned after only seven months and the vice-president, Julio Goulart, took over. He wanted to move Brazil gradually towards democracy and proposed to give more people the right to vote. He also planned to limit the amount of profit that large multinational companies could take out of the country; the government could then use the extra revenue to help improve social conditions for the masses. Worse still – as far as the USA was concerned – he opened diplomatic relations with the USSR, promised to nationalize Brazil's oil refineries, and opposed economic sanctions against Cuba.

All this was much too radical for the army and for the right, and tension between them and Goulart's supporters looked like developing into civil war. US president Lyndon Johnson told the American ambassador in Brazil that the USA must do everything possible to help overthrow 'this left-wing government'. Goulart was accused of being a communist, though by no stretch of the imagination could this be taken seriously; in fact he was a millionaire landowner and a devout Roman Catholic. However, in April 1964 he was removed in a military coup. Fortunately there was no civil war, but it emerged later that President Johnson had ordered US naval vessels, including an aircraft carrier and two destroyers, together with ammunition and fuel, to be made ready in case the Brazilian military needed assistance. Although well-intentioned, Goulart's policies left the country in economic difficulties. He had failed to attract sufficient foreign investment which had been discouraged by the USA; inflation increased rapidly, and economic growth was minimal.

For the next 20 years Brazil was ruled by the military. For the first few years their policy was one of harsh repression: the old political parties were banned, there was a strict press censorship, opponents were arrested and the jails soon filled with political prisoners; trade unionists and left-wing students were a favourite target and there were reports of widespread torture and violent treatment of prisoners. After 1974, when General Ernesto Geisel became president, repression was gradually relaxed and it was announced that the army would return the country to full democracy, albeit slowly. During the years of military dictatorship the government had great success with its economic policies, achieving what many described as an 'economic miracle'. Faced with massive inflation and a stagnating economy, they tackled the problems by borrowing extensively from abroad. Countries that had been unwilling to lend to the Goulart government were quite happy to do business with a strong right-wing regime which had eliminated communist influence. This stimulated economic growth so that the years 1968–74 were a boom period; the annual growth rate was 10 per cent and exports quadrupled. After 1974 the growth rate fell to around 5 per cent, mainly because Brazil was having to import more of its oil supplies, much of it from Iraq. By 1980 it seemed that the good times were over: Brazil had incurred huge foreign debts, there was a slump in export markets, there was a yawning gap between rich and poor and there was widespread unrest among the rural poor in the north east of the country. In an attempt to find substitute fuels, the government, which had its own supplies of uranium, turned to nuclear power and bought reactors from West Germany. But there was no immediate improvement and in provincial elections in 1982, the government suffered significant defeats.

Faced with escalating economic and social problems, the military decided this was an appropriate time to hand power over to civilians. In 1985 the presidential electoral college chose the 75-year-old Tancredo Neves as the first civilian president for over 20 years. Sadly, he was taken ill almost immediately and died before he could be sworn in. His deputy, Jose Sarney, took over and for the next four years struggled to stabilize the economy. In February 1987 the government announced that it was suspending interest payments, but the IMF came to the rescue with credits amounting to $41 million. Brazil was able to pay the interest on time, but Sarney's emergency policies caused hyper-inflation, and in the 1989 election he was defeated by Ferdinando Collor. In an attempt to stem the rocketing inflation he introduced even more stringent policies: the currency was devalued, government expenditure was reduced, bank accounts of over 50 000 cruzeiros (about £1300 US at that time) were frozen for 18 months. This was a disastrous move since it meant that the economy was deprived of some $80 billion at a time when it was most needed. The result was a wave of business failures and massive unemployment. In the midst of the chaos Collor was accused of corruption, impeached by the Senate and forced to resign at the end of 1992.

The 1994 election was won by a coalition of right-wing groups with Francesco Cardoso as president. He had produced a *Plano Real* designed to bring inflation under control. This involved large tax increases, wage reductions for public-service workers, and the privatization of many government enterprises. This had great success in lowering inflation from a thousand per cent when the plan was first put into action, to single figures by 1997. Overseas markets began to revive and there were marked increases in exports of agricultural produce and manufactured goods. Cardoso was re-elected president in 1998. Just as it seemed that Brazil had at last achieved some sort of stability, there was another crisis. Some of its foreign customers, including Russia and south-east Asia, reduced their imports from Brazil, government spending and borrowing were still much too high, and inflation began to rise again. Once more the IMF stepped in to help stabilize the currency with massive credits of $41 billion. There was considerable unrest among the working classes, many of whom were poverty-stricken, and there was an increase in crime and violence.

The year 2002 was when things began to change, with the election of the left-wing Luis Ignacio da Silva (popularly known as 'Lula') as president. He was re-elected in 2006 and remained in power until the end of 2010. It was during this period that Brazil at last began to fulfil its promise, so that by 2011 it was viewed as potentially one of the world's leading economies (see below).

(b) Venezuela

Venezuela is one of the wealthiest states of Latin America because of its oil resources. Until 1945, however, profits went to foreign oil companies (mainly American and British) or to the small group of wealthy people who ran the country via a military dictatorship. The great mass of the population received no benefit from this wealth and remained poor and illiterate. In 1945 Romulo Betancourt, the leader of a progressive left-wing party called *Acción Democrática,* was placed in power by a group of young army officers after fierce fighting in Caracas, the capital, had led to the overthrow of the military government. Betancourt introduced a new constitution which allowed full civil rights to all citizens. A programme of land reform was introduced, heavy taxes were placed on the foreign oil companies, and plans were prepared to exclude the army from politics. These reforms were bitterly opposed by foreign companies and by rich landowners, and in 1948 Betancourt was driven out of office by an army coup.

For the next ten years the country was under ruthless military dictatorship. Political parties and trade unions were banned, and a strict press censorship was imposed. On the other hand, with the removal of Betancourt the USA was once again prepared to invest in Venezuela. American dollars flowed in and some progress was made with the building of steel plants to exploit local iron-ore deposits. Iron and steel soon became Venezuela's most valuable export, but still very little of the country's wealth filtered down to the ordinary people. In 1957 Archbishop Blanco of Caracas publicly condemned the great wealth and corruption that was rife among the country's leaders, while the majority of Venezuelans lived in poverty and often subhuman conditions. In 1958 a general strike broke out and a section of the army removed the dictator Marcos Pérez Jiménez (1952–8). Democracy was restored and Betancourt was voted back into power.

Betancourt immediately raised Venezuela's share of oil revenues to 60 per cent, but this disappointed the growing communist party which had expected him to nationalize all foreign companies. However, he proceeded cautiously, not wanting to alienate the USA in case aid was stopped. Although measures were introduced to improve education and health, his popularity gradually waned, though he was able to complete his presidency, stepping down in 1964. Democracy survived, with the presidency alternating between *Acción Democrática* and the other main group, the Christian Social Party. Venezuela was now the main supplier of oil for the Central American states and to a lesser extent for the USA, and was doing well out of the great oil boom of the early 1970s. In 1976 President

Carlos Andrés Pérez nationalized part of the oil industry and created a new state oil company known as PdVSA.

The country remained politically stable right through until the early 1980s; the government legalized the Communist Party and opened diplomatic relations with the USSR. But then there was a fall in world oil prices that adversely affected Venezuela's revenue. At the same time there were difficulties in maintaining the levels of its other main exports – iron and steel. In March 1985, President Lusinchi (*Acción Democrática),* who had been elected in 1983, complained about the 'obstinately protective policies' of industrialized nations, which 'obstruct our trade possibilities'. He was especially critical of the USA which had just announced that it would reduce imports of Venezuelan steel from 550 000 tonnes a year (about 85 per cent of its total steel exports) to 110 000 tonnes for the next five years – a disastrous blow for Venezuelan industry. By the early 1990s the country was falling into arrears with debt repayments, and the government was trying to cope by following IMF requirements: this involved reducing imports and government spending. At the same time unemployment was rising and inflation was running at not far short of 40 per cent. Throughout the period there had been very little improvement in social conditions; the early advances in education and health care had not been maintained and dire poverty was rife. There was growing discontent and riots and in 1992 Colonel Hugo Chávez, a young military officer, was so disgusted when the government sent troops into poor neighbourhoods to put down the protests that he organized a coup to overthrow the dictatorship. Although the coup failed, it brought Chávez to the public's attention and demonstrated the split in the ranks of the military.

Meanwhile the economic situation worsened and in 1994 half the country's banking system collapsed. In 1997 the government announced an expansion of gold and diamond mining in an attempt to reduce its reliance on oil. After another failed coup in 1994, Chávez decided to run for president in the 1998 election. Campaigning on a programme of increased social spending and trading agreements with Cuba, he won a convincing victory, as voters turned away from the two main parties.

26.3 MEXICO, GUATEMALA AND NICARAGUA

(a) Mexico

The Mexicans won their independence from Spain in 1821 and until 1877 they were ruled by an assortment of two emperors, several dictators and some presidents. Important events included the loss of Texas after a short war of independence in 1836. Large numbers of Americans had settled in the thinly populated northern area of Mexico, known as *Tejas.* Calling themselves Texans, they declared themselves an independent republic and defeated a Mexican army sent to suppress them. Texas became a state of the USA in 1845. Mexico was defeated again in a war with the USA (1846–8), which resulted in the loss of about one-third of Mexican territory, including the areas now known as California, New Mexico, Nevada, Utah and Arizona, together with parts of Wyoming and Colorado. However, the USA did pay Mexico $18 million and waived its debts.

From 1876 until 1910 the country was ruled, except for one short interlude, by a dictator, Porfirio Díaz. This was a period of relative stability: oil production, mining and manufacturing industries were developed, largely thanks to foreign investment, while education, health care and the country's infrastructure were improved. The problem was that most of the industry was owned by foreigners, and little of the wealth generated percolated down to the masses. When workers formed trade unions in an attempt to improve their conditions, they were quickly suppressed. Also Mexico had become uncomfortably dependent on the USA. In 1910 Díaz decided to stand for re-election, although he was 80 years old by that time. He was declared the winner by a huge majority, but the election was so blatantly fraudulent that a revolution broke out, forcing him to resign.

The following decade was extremely confused and the revolution became a civil war as revolutionaries and counter-revolutionaries fought to gain control. In 1916–17 the USA sent troops into northern Mexico against the revolutionaries, and a war between Mexico and the USA was only narrowly averted. After 1920 the party eventually known as the Institutional Revolutionary Party (PRI) gradually gained control. It was dominated by revolutionary and reformist politicians and its programme was based on economic reform designed to narrow the gap between rich and poor. The PRI remained in power until 2000. In 1938 President Lázaro Cárdenas (1934–40) nationalized the oil industry, much to the delight of the general public. However, this was not welcomed by the USA or the UK, both of which started a boycott of Mexican goods. This forced Mexico to sell oil to Nazi Germany and Fascist Italy, but after a compensation agreement was reached in November 1941, the USA was prepared to buy Mexican oil again. In fact after the USA entered the Second World War in December 1941, Mexican oil became vital. Following the sinking of some of their oil tankers by German submarines, the Mexicans joined the Allied side in 1942. An air-force squadron known as 'the Aztec Eagles' worked alongside the American Fifth Air Force in the liberation of the Philippines in 1945.

For 25 years following the end of the war, Mexico enjoyed a period of economic progress. The government invested in agriculture, fuel production, the railway system and primary education. A modest, but consistent annual growth rate averaging 3–4 per cent was achieved; Mexico became a major producer of petroleum – the sixth largest in the world; and exports of cotton, coffee and sugar were also important sources of revenue. By 1960 the number of workers employed in manufacturing industries had overtaken those working in agriculture. However, in the late 1960s the economy began to show signs of strain, partly because the government had accumulated massive external debts thanks to its extravagant borrowing. Confident that oil revenues would always be sufficient to cover interest payments, successive governments seemed to have abandoned restraint.

There was wide protest, and on 2 October 1968 troops fired on a demonstration by an estimated 10 000 students in Mexico City demanding a revolution and a return to democracy. Estimates of the numbers killed vary between 30 and 300. The government claimed that snipers among the demonstrators had fired at the army first. It later emerged that the snipers were actually members of the presidential guard who had been ordered to fire on the army in order to provoke them to attack the students. Coming as it did ten days before the Olympic Games were about to open in Mexico City, this caused grave concern about security; in response the USA sent riot control experts, weapons and ammunition to Mexico in case of further violence.

As the 1970s progressed Mexico's exports were badly hit by the world recession, leading to a shortage of capital for investment, to inflation and to difficulties in meeting interest repayments. Unemployment was rising and the gap between rich and poor continued to widen, until by 1980 it was estimated that about nine-tenths of Mexico's total wealth was owned by fewer than half a million people out of a total population of 85 million. In 1982 the government introduced desperate measures: the banks were nationalized, the currency was devalued by 70 per cent and there were drastic reductions in spending on public services. The new president, Miguel de la Madrid, elected in 1982, negotiated a deal with the IMF for a loan and a rescheduling of half the country's overseas debts of $96 billion. However, Mexico failed to fulfil the conditions attached, and in 1895 the IMF was preparing to cancel the agreement when Mexico City suffered a severe earthquake (measuring 8.1 on the Richter scale) which caused widespread damage and killed at least 7000 people. Clearly this was not the time to cause Mexico any further misery, and so the agreement went ahead. Meanwhile the PRI government was fast losing popularity and it came under further criticism for what was seen as its incompetent handling of the earthquake relief efforts. For the first time since the 1930s the party began to face challengers at elections.

Worse was to follow: in 1986 there was a sudden collapse in world oil prices and a consequent reduction in Mexico's oil revenues. There seemed a real possibility that Mexico would have to repudiate its debts. As President de la Madrid put it: 'We have reached the limit of being able to sustain this net transfer of resources to the rest of the world, which violates economic logic and is tremendously inequitable.' The more pessimistic economists were predicting the collapse of world-trading financial systems if Third World countries were to begin a mass repudiation of debts. In 1990 Mexico again had to appeal to the IMF, which saved the situation by promising relief of $3.6 billion dollars for the next 30 years, while the World Bank rescheduled its debts. The next president, Carlos Salinas (1988–94) reduced domestic spending and embarked on a policy of privatization; although this did nothing to solve the unemployment problem, it did help to bring inflation down to single figures and eliminated the budget deficit. Mexico joined the North American Free Trade Association (NAFTA), along with the USA and Canada, which came into force in January 1994. This removed tariffs on more than half of Mexico's exports to the USA and on about one-third of US exports to Mexico. All tariffs between the two countries were to be removed after 15 years. Opinions differ on whether or not this has been beneficial for Mexico. Certainly Mexican exports to the USA increased, and the country was opened up to US and Canadian investment. On the other hand, Mexican farmers suffered because imports of US agricultural produce, especially meat, increased substantially.

The year 1994 saw two shocking events which did nothing to enhance the reputation of the PRI government. First, on 1 January, there was an armed uprising in the southern province of Chiapas by the Zapatista Army of National Liberation (ZANL). Chiapas was one of the most deprived parts of Mexico; the majority of the population were poverty-stricken Mayan Indians who had no land of their own and were angered by the blatant corruption and incompetence of the ruling elite. Demanding land reform, full civil rights and genuine democracy, the Zapatistas (as they called themselves, after Emiliano Zapata, one of the leaders of the 1910 revolution) occupied several towns, setting fire to police stations and army barracks. Within a few days they were crushed by the Mexican army, suffering heavy casualties. Having decided to abandon violence, they concentrated on an internet campaign that brought them widespread publicity and growing support. Then in March 1994 the PRI candidate in the coming presidential election, Luis Donaldo Colosio, was shot dead at a political rally in Tijuana. Mario Aburto, a factory worker, was jailed for the murder, but many still believe that he was a scapegoat, and that the murder was arranged by the PRI itself. It was alleged that with his promise of drastic reforms of the corrupt political system, Colosio was breaking party ranks and therefore had to be eliminated.

Both these events frightened off investors at a time when outgoing President Salinas had just indulged in a year of high spending resulting in a huge budget deficit and inflation. This was made worse when members of his family helped themselves to enormous illicit payoffs. With falling oil prices compounding the problem, Mexico was heading for an economic crisis. The new president, Ernesto Zedillo (1994–2000), decided to devalue the peso. Within the space of one week in December 1994 the peso fell from 4 to the dollar to 7.2. With many private banks apparently on the verge of collapse, and some US banks involved in Mexico also threatened, Zedillo appealed to the IMF and the USA. US president Clinton, working with the IMF, arranged loans of around $50 billion. Economic collapse was averted and over the next six years there was a modest recovery. But the crisis had important results. In the words of Peter Calvocoressi:

The Mexican crisis called into question the ability of international finance to meet such a crisis and therewith the willingness of financiers worldwide to support Latin American governments pursuing economic policies dependent on foreign loans and investment. The collapse of the Mexican peso dismayed all Latin American countries, where economic growth was desperately needed for its own economic ends and as a prerequisite for political stability. In Mexico the gap between rich and poor widened, and insurrection became more widespread and better armed.

In fact by 2000, underneath the outward appearance of prosperity, about one-third of Mexico's population still lived below the poverty line. The PRI seemed to be in a state of stagnation and blocked all moves designed to lessen the gap between rich and poor. In the Congressional elections of 1997 the party lost control of Congress, gaining only 38 per cent of the vote. In the presidential election of 2000 the PRI candidate, Francisco Labastida, was opposed by Vicente Fox, representing the centre-right National Action Party (PAN). Fox won a comfortable victory with 43 per cent of the vote against Labastida's 36 per cent; single-party rule by the PRI had been brought to an end after 71 years.

(b) Guatemala

Situated on Mexico's southern border, Guatemala is one of the poorest states of Latin America. Its history during the twentieth century is an excellent illustration of US involvement. A Spanish colony since the mid-sixteenth century, Guatemala gained independence from Spain in 1821, andfor a short time it was part of a Mexican empire and then part of a new federal state known as the United Provinces of Central America. This broke up in 1840 when Guatemala became fully independent. Largely an agricultural state, its economy depended on exports of bananas and coffee. The population, of which about 40 per cent were Mayan Indians who did not speak Spanish, consisted mainly of landless peasants, and the country was dominated by a few wealthy landowners and the army. In the early twentieth century the USA became heavily involved in Guatemala in the form of the powerful United Fruit Company (UFC). Beginning in 1901 the UFC gradually increased its activities and investments in Guatemala until by the Second World War it controlled almost half the country's best agricultural land and was the majority share-owner in the railways and the electricity system, among other things. This meant that although this foreign involvement brought many positive developments, in the last resort the interests of the UFC came first. The classic example of this was that the UFC was reluctant to finance the building of new roads because this would reduce its profits from the railways.

In October 1944 dissatisfaction with this state of affairs reached a climax: during a general strike the long-serving military dictator, Jorge Ubico (1931–44), was forced to step down by a mixed uprising of anti-government army officers, students and liberal intellectuals. In 1945 democratic elections were held and the Christian Socialist, Juan José Arévalo, was elected president for five years. Much-needed reforms were introduced:

- Many foreign-owned estates were confiscated and the land redistributed to peasants.
- A minimum wage was introduced.
- Extensive building programmes were started, including new houses, hospitals and schools.
- Landowners were required to provide adequate housing for their farm labourers.
- The formation of political parties was allowed, and so was the formation of trade unions, although their powers were restricted.

The next president, Jacobo Arbenz, was elected in a landslide victory in 1951. He continued Arévalo's reforms, going much further. There were new social welfare programmes and wage increases for workers. Uncultivated land was taken from large estates, including those of the UFC, to be redistributed among peasants; although compensation was offered, the UFC claimed that it was not enough. Then Arbenz took one step too far: he legalized the Communist Party. This was too much for the USA: all aid to Guatemala was immediately stopped, Arbenz was accused of being a communist, and his opponents were supplied with arms and trained in neighbouring Honduras and Nicaragua by American CIA agents. Early in 1954 the USA introduced a resolution in the Organization of American States (OAS) declaring that communist domination of any state in the Western hemisphere posed a threat to the security of all member states. This was passed by 17 votes to one (Guatemala).

In June 1954 American-backed forces led by Colonel Castillo Armas invaded Guatemala from Honduras and Nicaragua, while American planes bombed Guatemala City. Although the official Guatemalan army took no part in the coup, neither did they attempt to defend Arbenz, who was forced to resign. Armas took over and became a military dictator; parliament was disbanded and leading communists were arrested. Armas was assassinated in 1957 and was replaced by another military dictator, Miguel Ydigoras. US aid was resumed and an uprising against Ydigoras was put down in 1960 with American help.

The Americans insisted on calling the overthrow of President Arbenz an 'anti-communist coup'. But there seems little doubt that the Eisenhower government overestimated the threat from communism in Guatemala. It was prepared to sacrifice the Arbenz reforming government even though it meant violating the principle of non-intervention and souring relations with the rest of Latin America. Anti-American feeling spread, and 'Yankee go home' became a common slogan throughout Latin America.

Years of military dictatorship followed the overthrow of President Arbenz, during which the opposition constantly demanded social and economic reform. For over 30 years the country was in a state of virtual civil war: left-wing groups resorted to guerrilla attacks and kidnappings and were opposed by right-wing vigilante groups; the government used death squads against people deemed to be communists. It was calculated that in four months (October 1979–January 1980) during the presidency of General Romero García, 3252 political murders had taken place. After the next election, said to have been won by a García nominee, General Guevara, a group of army officers declared that the result had been fixed, and in March 1982 they put General Ríos Montt in power. After little more than a year, in August 1983, another coup replaced Ríos Montt with yet another General, Óscar Mejía. Montt complained that the USA had put pressure on him to take action against Nicaragua, and that when he refused, they had engineered his removal in favour of somebody who would. Soon afterwards Mejía did indeed announce that he saw the Sandinista government of Nicaragua as a threat to the whole of Central America (see below). He promised a return to civilian democracy and in 1985 elections were held for a legislative assembly. The Christian Democrats emerged as clear winners with 51 out of the 100 seats, and in December their leader, Cerezo Arévalo, was elected president for five years.

Arévalo managed to tread a narrow tightrope, trying to reconcile the guerrillas and vigilantes, while the army was a baleful background presence. To complicate matters further, the economy was in crisis, the treasury was empty, and his fear was that if his reforming policies went too far, he would be removed by US intervention. Arévalo completed his full term and was replaced in 1991 by Jorge Serrano. He had some success in reversing the economic downturn and decreasing inflation, but then in May 1993 he made the mistake of suspending the constitution and dissolving Congress and the Supreme Court. He claimed that this was part of a clampdown to reduce the amount of corruption in public life; he also tried to remove civil liberties and muzzle the press. This caused an outcry from most sections of society, and the army forced him to resign. Congress reconvened and in June 1993 chose Ramiro de León, a popular civil rights leader, to complete the presidential term.

De León was keen to bring formal ending to the civil-war situation that had now dragged on for well over thirty years. The Roman Catholic Church helped the government and Congress to agree on a programme of constitutional reform which came into operation in August 1994. De León worked hard to bring about reconciliation and the United Nations became involved in the search for peace. But it was not until 1996 that the civil war was officially ended. President Álvaro Arzú of the National Advancement Party (PAN), who was elected in January 1996, had the distinction of signing a peace agreement with the main guerrilla group, Guatemalan National Revolutionary Unity (URNG). In February he had personal meetings in Mexico with the rebel leaders and a ceasefire from 20 March was agreed. In December 1996 a formal peace agreement was signed; this legalized the URNG and granted a partial amnesty to the various participants in the violence. The war was over at last, but not before some 200 000 people had been killed during those 36 years, well over half of whom were Mayan Indians, who were especially targeted because of their militancy. Although the fighting was officially over, there was inevitably a legacy of bitterness and mistrust. The congressional and presidential elections of November and December 1999 were won by the Guatemalan Republican Front (FRG), and the new president, Alfonso Portillo, faced daunting problems including a high crime rate, continued violence and corruption, and economic challenges.

(c) Nicaragua

Like Guatemala, Nicaragua was a Spanish colony from the mid-sixteenth century until it became independent in 1821; then it was part of the Mexican empire for a short time and after that it became a member of the United Provinces of Central America until 1840, when it achieved full independence. The country had a disturbed history: politically unstable, punctuated by periods of ruthless military dictatorship and plagued by foreign intervention, especially from the USA. For the remainder of the nineteenth century internal politics were dominated by the power struggle between liberals, whose main power base was in León, and the conservatives, based in Granada. The two parties alternated in power – liberals for a short period in the 1850s, conservatives from 1860 until 1993, and liberals from 1993 until 1909.

The president during this last period was José Santos Zelaya, who was responsible for some important changes. There were great improvements in education, transport (new railways were built) and communications; coffee production expanded and exports increased, and the country enjoyed a modest prosperity. He also began the building of a new and neutral capital city – Managua. This helped to reduce the long rivalry and feuding between León and Granada and between liberals and conservatives. Unfortunately Zelaya had several faults: he was violent and corrupt, and developed delusions of further grandeur. He had many of his conservative opponents arrested, tortured and executed, and he and his associates helped themselves shamelessly to the state's assets – selling privileges and concessions to foreign interests and increasing taxes, but keeping the extra revenue for themselves. And finally he had visions of a united states of Central America, with himself as president! To further this ambition he stirred up unrest in other states. In 1906 for example, his troops invaded Guatemala in an attempt to overthrow the government. When this failed he turned to Honduras and supported a rebellion there; when that failed, his troops invaded Honduras, and with help from the army of El Salvador, defeated the Hondurans and occupied the capital, Tegucigalpa. By 1909 most Nicaraguans had had enough of

Zelaya; the conservatives had hated him for years, and even his own liberal supporters had turned against him, disgusted at the corruption and the meddling in the internal affairs of other states. The USA saw him as a destabilizing influence in the region and felt that their own interests were threatened.

It was a liberal, General Juan Estrada, who decided the time had come to remove Zelaya. He organized an uprising and was supported by the USA which sent warships and marines in case the coup failed. Zelaya decided to beat a hasty retreat to Mexico, having thoughtfully emptied the treasury before leaving. However, the power struggle between liberals and conservatives broke out again, and in 1912 US marines were sent in to prop up the conservative government and restore order. They stayed until 1925, but as soon as they left violence broke out again and after only a few months US forces returned. In 1927 the Somoza family came to power with the approval of the USA and the situation gradually stabilized, partly because American troops stayed until 1933.

After that the Somoza family ruled Nicaragua with an iron fist until 1979, supported by the USA. Political opponents were exiled and each of the Somozas amassed a large fortune. On three occasions the USA was able to use Nicaraguan territory and troops for attacks on other Latin American governments that it didn't approve of – Guatemala (1954), Cuba (1961) and the Dominican Republic (1965). The last of the Somazas, Anastasio, was so blatantly corrupt that he even became an embarrassment to the USA. President Carter urged him to reform and pay more attention to human rights. This had little effect and in 1979 he was driven out by the Sandinista National Liberation Front, named after Augusto Sandinista, who had led an unsuccessful revolution in 1933 and was later murdered on the orders of Somoza. The Sandinistas had widespread support among ordinary people and from a section of the Roman Catholic Church which was highly critical of the excesses of capitalism.

The new Sandinista government immediately introduced a programme of long overdue reform: a redistribution of 5 million acres of land, including some confiscated Somoza property, to about 100,000 families, a literacy drive and health improvements which eliminated polio and reduced other diseases. There were other social and economic reforms, and in 1985 Oxfam reported that the efforts of the government and their commitment to improving the conditions of their people were exceptional. Although the Sandinistas allowed a mixed economy of state and privately owned business, the US Reagan administration which took office in 1981 saw them as dangerous communists, especially when they formed close links with Cuba. The USA did everything it could to undermine them and bring them down. All aid was stopped; the US began, and encouraged other states to join, a trade blockade and a credit squeeze against Nicaragua; and they financed the Nicaraguan Democratic Force (FDN), known as the Contras. The Contras waged a damaging guerrilla campaign, blowing up bridges, schools and health clinics and burning crops. After they had mined three harbours, the International Court of Justice condemned the American CIA's backing of the Contras and ordered them to pay compensation for damages caused; the USA rejected the ruling and refused to pay compensation.

US policy was not popular with most of Nicaragua's neighbours. A meeting of the Latin American parliament (which had been founded in 1968) was held in Guatemala City in April 1986, when 16 out of 18 members voted in favour of a motion condemning the US attitude (Honduras and El Salvador were the exceptions). The policy was controversial in the USA itself, and in March 1987, following the Irangate Scandal (see Section 23.5(b)), Congress voted that aid to the Contras should be stopped.

This provided a ray of hope for embattled Nicaragua and her president, Daniel Ortega, who had been elected in 1984 for six years. In 1987 President Óscar Arias of Costa Rica persuaded all the Central American presidents to support his peace plan for the region, an achievement that won him the Nobel Peace Prize. However, the plan proved difficult to carry out, mainly because the Reagan administration was still doing its utmost to destabilize Nicaragua. Under US pressure, both Honduras and El Salvador declined to co-operate with the peace plan. Ortega's co-operation with Castro's Cuba outraged the Americans, and during the 1990 election campaign, the Bush administration threatened that violence would continue if the Sandinistas won the election. Even so, it was a surprise when the National Opposition Union candidate, Violeta Barrios de Chamorro, became the first female president to be elected in Latin America. Ortega and the Sandinistas accepted the result and she was able to serve her six-year term. Her main achievement was to disarm some of the guerrilla groups that had been terrorising the country for years, and most of the fighting ceased. Things became more stable and some of the Sandinista social reforms were allowed to stay. But the economy was in total ruins and government debts were astronomical. Nevertheless, Ortega was again defeated in the 1996 election, this time by Arnoldo Alemán, and in the 2001 election by the National Liberal Party candidate (PLC), Enrique Bolanos.

At the turn of the century the country was still in dire straits. In 1998 there was a devastating hurricane which killed 9000 people, left around 2 million homeless and caused damage amounting to $10 billion. In 2002 former president Alemán was charged with corruption and embezzlement and later sentenced to 20 years' imprisonment. The situation was so bad that in 2004 the World Bank and the IMFI waived $4.5 billion of Nicaragua's debts. In the elections of November 2006 Daniel Ortega made a comeback: he won the presidency with 62 per cent of the vote, and the Sandinistas had a comfortable majority in parliament. But as they took office in January 2007, they faced a challenging prospect – Nicaragua had the distinction of being the poorest country in the Western hemisphere. When he stood for election for a third term in November 2011, Ortega won a landslide victory.

26.4 THE CHALLENGE TO US DOMINATION

Towards the end of the twentieth century, some Latin American states began to resist US control. As genuine democracy spread, leftish political groups organized campaigns in favour of social and economic reform. People were prepared to vote for them because their programmes were attractive: the neo-liberal-style policies favoured by the USA should be abandoned; foreign companies should be required to hand over more of their profits to the state to help tackle the poverty and inequality which were still rife throughout Latin America. Since the Cold War was over and the USSR had ceased to exist, the USA could no longer get rid of left-leaning governments on the grounds that they were aiming to form alliances with the communist bloc. The first major challenge to US influence came in 1998 when Hugo Chávez won the **Venezuelan** presidential election with 56 per cent of the vote on a programme of increased social spending and an attack on poverty.

Similar trends followed in some other important states: in 2002 the left-wing Luiz Inácio da Silva (popularly known as 'Lula') won the **Brazilian** presidential election with a programme similar to that of Hugo Chávez. The following year **Argentina** followed suit with the election of Nestor Kirschner, and in **Chile** in January 2005 the centre-left Michele Bachelet was elected – Chile's first woman president. Like-minded presidents were elected in **Bolivia** and **Ecuador** in 2006, and in the same year Daniel Ortega staged a comeback when he became president of **Nicaragua** for the second time after a gap of 16 years. Meanwhile in **Mexico** the trend seemed to be in the opposite direction: after 71 years of rule by nominally left-wing governments, voters turned to a moderately conservative party for their next president – Vicente Fox. A brief look at each of these countries should reveal how much, or how little progress has been made towards modernization.

(a) Venezuela

Although Venezuela was rich in oil, when Hugo Chávez became president in 1998 the country was facing economic problems, mainly because of a fall in world oil prices. His general aim was to free Venezuela from US influence and create a network of countries sympathetic to his project. He didn't try to abandon capitalism, but simply moved away from the type of neo-liberal capitalism favoured by the USA and other leaders, such as Margaret Thatcher in the UK. From the beginning he spoke out publicly against the USA, ending Venezuela's long-standing military ties with the USA, and giving economic support to Cuba. This provided a lifeline for the beleaguered Cuba, which had lost its main supporter when the USSR collapsed.

One of Chávez's earliest moves was to tighten control over the PdVSA, the state oil company set up in the 1970s. In recent years the company had been contributing less and less to the state treasury, while managers paid themselves vastly inflated salaries. This was immediately put right, and a Hydrocarbons Law introduced, making it illegal for any private company to own more than 50 per cent of the shares in joint oil ventures with the state. All of this upset many traditional interests – sections of the army, oil executives and right-wingers in general. An alliance of these groups, partly financed by the USA, staged street demonstrations demanding the resignation of Chávez. A group of hostile officers kidnapped him, but he was rescued by officers loyal to him, and amid massive pro- Chávez street demonstrations, he was enabled to stay in power. This proved to be the first serious blow against US influence in South America and the beginning of a new era. Large parts of the economy were taken into state control: the oil industry was fully nationalized in 2007, followed by the electricity supply and telecommunications. In 2011 the gold industry followed.

By this time Chávez had started moving much of Venezuela's gold reserves out of Western banks and into countries he counts as allies – Russia, China and Brazil. As the debt crisis in Europe worsened, more reserves were transferred to China, a move welcomed by Beijing, which had invested heavily in Venezuela. The main economic weakness was that Venezuela, the world's fifth largest oil exporter, was still overdependent on oil production, with around 90 per cent of revenue from all exports coming from oil. It meant that whenever world oil prices fell, the economy suffered. In 2009 for example, the economy shrank by around 3 per cent because of the world recession.

Another aim of the Chávez government was to help the poverty-stricken masses by spreading some of the country's wealth more widely. According to UN statistics, in 1998 when Chávez came to power, 54 per cent of the population were living below the poverty line. He introduced a social welfare programme known as the Bolivar Plan 2000 (called after the nineteenth-century revolutionary leader and founding father of Venezuela). There were plans to improve the public health-care system, housing projects, and loans to enable people to start up small businesses. Thousands of co-operatives owned by the workers were set up with government help. Extra cash was made available to tackle the AIDS epidemic. Great progress was made in securing equal rights for women, including a new rule for political parties: at least 50 per cent of election candidates had to be female. In 2008 the government announced a $111 million plan to upgrade dozens of hospitals.

There is no doubt that Chávez and his Bolivarian socialism have brought important changes to Venezuela. He has switched the country from being almost a colony of the USA, asserting its independence, and has focused on trade and co-operation agreements with other states in the region, in order to promote his vision of Latin American integration. His attempts to reduce poverty have had some success: UN statistics show that 54 per cent of the population lived in poverty in 1998 compared to 28 per cent in 2008. Clearly there is still some way to go, but these statistics suggest that if similar policies were to be continued for another ten years (until 2018), serious poverty might well have been all but eliminated. However, by 2012 the signs were not auspicious. By this time Chávez had alienated most of the business class, the Roman Catholic Church, and left-wingers who felt that he had become too authoritarian. In 2009 the Church and Human Rights Watch accused him of 'creating a climate of fear'. Chávez was due to stand for re-election in October 2012, but local elections in 2010 and 2011 showed a fall in his socialist party vote. He also had health problems, having been recently diagnosed with cancer. However, he was still seen as a hero by the majority of the working class; in spite of all these problems, plus the efforts of the USA to discredit him, he won the 2012 election comfortably.

(b) Brazil

In 2002 the voters of Brazil, sick of corrupt party politics and neo-liberal economic policies, elected as president 'Lula' da Silva of the Workers' Party. He had promised to narrow the enormous gap between rich and poor by expanding education and redistributing land, and to introduce social welfare programmes. In office he turned out to be much more moderate than he had sounded during the election campaign. Though a socialist, he felt that the economic crisis was serious enough to require non-socialist solutions. He went along with the IMF conditions, reducing public spending in return for the $41 billion credit needed to stabilize the currency. On the other hand he did introduce widespread anti-poverty programmes, and increased the minimum wage by 25 per cent. His *Bolsa Familia* programme paid modest monthly grants to poor families provided they sent their children to school and had their health checked regularly. It was estimated that by 2008 *Bolsa Familia* had helped some 7.5 million families.

Lula was not afraid to stand up to the USA if he felt strongly enough. He opposed George Bush's Free Trade Area of the Americas (FTAA) and got away with it, probably because the USA was preoccupied with the Iraq War. Instead, a trade agreement with China did much to steady the economy, and reforms were made to pensions and taxation systems, as well as a drive for administrative efficiency. New policies were devised to encourage industry, trade and exports and foreign investors were encouraged. Inflation and government debt were brought under control. This was a considerable achievement and Lula was re-elected in 2006. Brazil received an enormous boost in 2007 when the Tupi undersea oilfield was discovered, taking it into the top league of oil producers and removing the need to import oil. The surge in exports, the fall in unemployment and the general economic expansion, together with the welfare programmes, have helped to lift millions of people out of poverty, so that for the first time probably a majority of the population of over 190 million can be deemed middle-class.

The constitution did not allow Lula da Silva to stand for a third term in office, but the Workers' Party continued in power with the election of Dilma Rousseff who, in January 2011, became the first woman president of Brazil. A strong advocate of human rights, social inclusion and equal treatment for women, she had served as a minister in the da Silva cabinet. She continued Lula's policies; at the end of 2011 Brazil's economy was ranked sixth largest in the world, and experts predicted that by the end of 2012 it would probably have risen to fifth place. Since the economic crisis at the end of the twentieth century the country had made remarkable progress. It now had arguably the most advanced industrial sector in the whole of Latin America, responsible for about one-third of total GDP. Brazil is a major supplier of minerals such as iron ore, tin, manganese, uranium, copper, zinc and gold. Manufactures include motor vehicles and spare parts, aeroplanes, textiles, steel, various types of machinery, computers and petrochemicals. Agriculture is important – Brazil is the world's largest producer of sugarcane, coffee, tropical fruits and concentrated orange juice. Although agricultural produce makes up only about 7 per cent of GDP, it amounts to over 30 per cent of exports. Brazil is also active in the realms of science and technology, including agricultural research and deep-sea oil production.

Although relations with the USA are generally good, there has been a change in the nature of their relationship. Brazil was once treated very much as a subordinate; now they deal with each other almost as equals. As the Brazilian economy climbs higher in the international league table, they could easily become serious rivals in the future.

(c) Mexico

The new National Action Party (PAN) president Vicente Fox had been elected on a programme of ending government corruption and improving the economy. As a centre-right politician he was happy to have a close relationship with the USA and worked hard to improve and expand Mexico's trading partnership with the USA, and they co-operated in a campaign against drug trafficking. However, when Fox called for the frontier between Mexico and the USA to be opened so that Mexican migrant workers could move freely into the USA, the Americans rejected the idea and accused Fox of encouraging illegal immigration. On the other hand, Fox's left-wing opponents criticized him for aligning Mexico too closely with the USA. In 2002 when he proposed to visit Washington, the Mexican senate blocked the plan. Unfortunately for Fox, PAN did not have a majority in the legislature, which rejected many of his reform proposals. Farmers staged widespread protests because the government did nothing to solve agricultural problems caused by Mexico's membership of the North American Free Trade Association (NAFTA), particularly the huge increase in imports of American produce, especially meat. Fox's presidency was something of a disappointment, although he was personally popular.

The constitution did not permit a second term; the presidential election of 2006 was won by the PAN candidate, Felipe Calderón, by the narrowest of margins. His election promises included campaigns against corruption, poverty and tax evasion; and infrastructure improvements – new roads, railways, airports, dams and bridges, all of which would help to solve the unemployment problem. But again there were economic problems: the economy was heavily dependent on the cash that millions of migrant workers sent home from the USA. In 2008 the world credit crisis (see Section 27.7) caused a downturn in the US economy and in global demand generally, and this had repercussions on Mexico, which was also hard hit, suffering arguably the worst slump since the 1930s. However, a recovery was soon under way. Foreign investment began to flood in once more, so that during the first half of 2010 there was a 30 per cent increase from a year earlier. In 2012 Mexico had the second largest economy in Latin America, with about a third of its revenue coming from oil, much of which is sold to the USA. Other exports include machinery and transport equipment, various foodstuffs and live animals.

One of the great issues in Mexico and in much of Latin America is the drug-trafficking problem. Powerful cartels control the trafficking of drugs out of Latin America into the USA, a business which generates around a staggering £9 million. One of President Calderón's first actions was to declare war on drugs and deploy the army against the drug gangs. Since December 2006 an estimated 35 000 people have been killed in Mexico in drug-related violence and the country has one of the highest rates of kidnapping in the world. The president claims that his fight against the cartels is working, but still the struggle goes on. In April 2012 a summit meeting of Latin American leaders was held in Cartagena, Colombia, at which Guatemalan president Carlos Molina said that the system of merely making drugs illegal had failed, and he called for an alternative system. The summit was divided between those who advocated complete legalization of drugs and those who thought that this would be irresponsible. In Mexico critics of the president claimed that his policy of using the army against the cartels had failed and had been so expensive that more important projects, such as improving the nation's infrastructure, had been neglected. Although Mexico had the second largest economy in Latin America, there was still a long way to go before it could claim to be a genuinely 'modern' state. According to a BBC report in January 2012:

> Mexico is a nation where affluence, poverty, natural splendour and urban blight rub shoulders ... . But prosperity remains a dream for many Mexicans and the socio-economic gap remains wide. Rural areas are often neglected and huge shanty-towns ring the cities.

(d) Argentina

Argentina was ruled by a military junta from 1976 until 1983, when the country returned to democracy. The junta was responsible for thousands of deaths in what became known as the 'the dirty war' to restore order and eliminate opponents. A human rights commission charged the junta with 2300 political murders, over 10 000 political arrests and the disappearance of up to 30 000 people. In an attempt to win some popularity the junta made the mistake of invading the Malvinas Islands, held by the UK as the Falkland Islands (April 1982). Britain won an unexpected victory, recapturing the islands, and leaving Argentina with an unprecedentedly high foreign debt and inflation of around 900 per cent. There was a return to democracy for the presidential election of 1983, but the economy continued in crisis. By 1991 there were riots in protest at high food prices and unemployment. President Carlos Menem, who took office in 1991, resorted to classic neo-liberal policies: protectionist trade and business regulations were removed, strict austerity measures were introduced and there was a wave of privatizations of state-owned industries. It was all to no avail – in September 1998 Argentina moved into the worst recession for years. Ferdinando de la Rúa was elected president in 1999 and introduced more austerity measures. But the recession continued and the IMF came to the rescue twice in 2001. In November of that year the economy seemed on the verge of total collapse and there was a financial panic; in December there was serious rioting in the capital, Buenos Aires, forcing the president to resign.

After a chaotic interval, Nestor Kirchner was elected president and came to power in 2003. An admirer of Hugo Chávez and his policies in Venezuela, Kirchner was determined to make a break with the past and reject neo-liberal economics. In his public pronouncements he savagely criticized the IMF and foreign investors. He abandoned what he called 'automatic alignment' with the USA in favour of closer ties with other Latin American countries, especially Venezuela, and with Mercosur, a sort of common market and customs union set up in 1991 to encourage free trade and political co-operation. Its original members were Argentina, Brazil, Uruguay and Paraguay; Venezuela joined in 2006. Kirchner raised wages and pensions for those most in need, set up a new state-run oil company and signed energy agreements and various other trade agreements with Venezuela. He encouraged greater government involvement in the energy sector, though he stopped short of renationalizing the country's main oil company, YPF, which had been sold off to a Spanish company, Repsol, during Carlos Menem's presidency. The economy soon showed signs of recovery: Venezuela began to import cattle and agricultural machinery from Argentina, and by 2008 Argentina's exports to Venezuela had quadrupled since Kirchner came to power. The economy showed an impressive annual growth rate of about 8 per cent and in January 2006 it was announced that Argentina had paid off all remaining debts to the IMF. Kirchner also won popularity when the laws granting pardon to those accused of atrocities during the 'dirty war' were cancelled, so that in 2006 many military and police personnel who thought they were safe were arrested and put on trial. Kirchner decided not to stand for re-election in 2007, and his wife Cristina Fernández de Kirchner was elected instead. She broadly continued her husband's policies, and against the predictions of many neo-liberal economists, Argentina's boom continued. The economy maintained its 8 per cent annual growth rate, and by the time of the next election in October 2011, the poverty rate had been halved, employment had risen to a record high, and a lucrative export market had been developed in China. It was no surprise when President Fernández was easily re-elected for a second term, winning by the largest margin since democracy had been restored in 1983. Relations with the UK were threatened by the re-emergence of the Falklands question when it was announced in September 2011 that a British company would begin drilling to exploit the Falkland's offshore oil reserves in 2016.

(e) Chile

Chile had the first democratically chosen Marxist/socialist government ever, when Salvador Allende was elected president in 1970. However, he was soon overthrown and killed in a military coup backed by the CIA. General Augusto Pinochet ruled Chile for the next 17 years, and though he did much to improve Chile's economy, it was a period of brutal repression (for full details see Section 8.4). Following the return to democracy in 1990, Chile was ruled by presidents from the centre-left Coalition of Parties for Democracy (CPD). There were two Christian Democrats: Ricardo Aylwin (1990–4) and Eduardo Frei (1994–2000), son of the earlier President Eduardo Frei. Next came two socialists: Ricardo Lagos (2000–6) and then Michelle Bachelet (2006–10), Chile's first woman president. She was a former paediatrician and her father had been a victim of the Pinochet regime. Faced almost immediately with a strike by thousands of students demanding educational reforms, she calmed the situation and promised to put things right.

At first she continued her predecessor's economic policies and increased social spending. It was during her presidency that Chile began to move out of the period of transition from military dictatorship to genuine democracy. Clearly the classic neo-liberal economic policies were not sufficient to bring full recovery, and so the government broke the neo-conservative rules with a dose of state intervention: for example, the world's largest copper producer, Codelco, was taken into state hands and government control of capital was introduced, allowing the president to finance new social policies. As the next election (December 2009) approached, Bachelet's popularity level, which had dropped to around 40 per cent during the world debt crisis in 2008, had risen to 84 per cent. Unfortunately for Bachelet and the CPD, the constitution does not allow presidents to serve for two consecutive terms, and consequently a former president, Eduardo Frei, was endorsed as the CPD candidate. The main right-wing opponent was Sebastián Piñera, whom Bachelet had defeated in 2006. It was Piñera who won the presidency in the second round of voting in January 2010. His victory surprised many observers, bearing in mind the popularity of President Bachelet. However, the explanation for the CPD defeat was probably that Eduardo Frei failed to generate any enthusiasm and was seen as representing old-style politics. Piñera, on the other hand, concentrated his campaign on the need for greater government efficiency. Shortly after the January run-off, Chile was hit by a devastating earthquake that killed 500 people, left around a million homeless and caused damage estimated at between $15 and 30 billion. Unfortunately the new president was faced with the problem of dealing with the aftermath of the catastrophe.

(f) Bolivia

One of the poorest states in Latin America, after gaining independence from Spain in 1825, Bolivia had a long history of instability and military dictatorships. Since the Second

World War the Bolivian economy was controlled by the USA, which, among other things, processed all Bolivia's tin exports. In the 1950s, when the country was trying to become more self-sufficient in spite of its limited available capital, the USA insisted that this capital should be used to pay the country's foreign debts rather than to finance its own developments designed to increase revenue. In 1964 the military seized power and in 1967 the army, with the help of US advisers, easily defeated a guerrilla campaign led by Ernesto 'Che' Guevara, who was captured and murdered on CIA orders. The army stayed in control until 1982 when Bolivia returned to democracy, with a string of presidents who took care not to antagonize the USA. In 1997 Hugo Banzer, a former general and dictator-turned democrat, was elected president. He made important progress in eliminating coca production and drug trafficking, much to the delight of the USA.

The near-eradication of coca farming by 2001 was an extremely controversial issue that was to have profound effects on Bolivia's future. Coca had been an important crop in Bolivia for around 4000 years and as Nikolas Kozloff explains, it has several legal uses:

> In Bolivia and the Andes coca leaf is legally used as an infusion to make tea. The leaf is usually chewed with a bitter wood-ash paste to bring out the stimulant properties similar to caffeine or nicotine. In the Andes, visitors are commonly offered coca tea to combat altitude sickness, which can cause headache or vertigo. Coca is also used for cosmetic products and toothpaste. Outside the region, however, coca is classified as a prohibited drug. In order to convert coca leaf into cocaine, it must be combined with other ingredients and subjected to a complex chemical process.

Thousands of coca farmers became unemployed and were plunged into poverty; the coca growers' union joined with other trade unions and social interest groups to form an organization called MAS (Movement Towards Socialism), which campaigned on a platform of decriminalizing coca and nationalizing the country's natural resources. The call for nationalization of resources was a response to the unpopular privatization of water resources by foreign companies, which led to a doubling of water prices.

In December 2005 the MAS candidate, Juan Evo Morales, was elected president. An Aymara Indian, he was the first Bolivian president to come from the country's ethnic majority. He had been a leader of the coca growers' federation and was determined to do his utmost to get coca decriminalized. In September 2006 he told the UN General Assembly in New York that coca had therapeutic uses and should not be criminalized. While agreeing that it was necessary to fight drug smuggling, he insisted that prohibition of pure coca leaf was 'an historic injustice ... coca does not harm human health'. He added that criminalizing coca was simply a strategy by the USA and Europe to recolonize the Andes region. Clearly Hugo Chávez had found a courageous ally in his anti-US stand. Morales soon signed trade agreements with Venezuela and refused to have anything to do with the US-sponsored American Free Trade Area, which he described as 'an agreement to legalize the colonization of the Americas'. He added that Bolivia, Venezuela and Cuba might form 'an axis of good' in contrast to the 'axis of evil' that included the USA and its allies. Further anti-neo-liberal moves included signing new contracts with the private gas companies designed to bring in more revenue for the government; and a partial nationalization of the hydrocarbons industry. According to Noam Chomsky:

> Since the election of Morales in 2005, Bolivia's economic performance has been quite impressive. A Center for Economic and Policy Research (CEPR) study found that in the four years since Morales took office, 'economic growth has been higher than at any time during the last 30 years, averaging 4.9 percent annually. Projected GDP growth for 2009 is the highest in the hemisphere and follows its peak growth rate in 2008, along with "several programs targeted at the poorest Bolivians".

Morales was re-elected for a second term in 2009 with an increased majority, and MAS won a two-thirds majority in both houses of Congress.

(g) Ecuador

Ecuador is another of the poorest states in Latin America. It became fully independent in 1830 and was ruled by centre-right presidents until 1895, when a revolution led to half a century of more liberal governments. The army seized power in 1972, but giving way to popular demand, they returned the country to democracy in 1979. However, progress towards modernization was disappointing; successive governments failed to deliver on their promises of land reform, an end to unemployment and the provision of social services. In 1998 a fall in the world price of oil, Ecuador's main export, caused an economic crisis; inflation rose to over 40 per cent, and the poverty rate rocketed to around 70 per cent. Although the economy recovered quickly, the government became increasingly unpopular, because of its strict austerity measures together with blatant corruption among leading politicians. In 2006 there were huge protest demonstrations against a proposed free-trade agreement with the USA which was widely seen as a ploy to tighten US control over Ecuador's economy. The presidential election of November 2006 was won by the left-wing economist, Rafael Correa.

It soon became clear that the new president intended to follow the example of Chávez and Morales. He announced that 'the long neo-liberal night' had come to an end and promised an economic revolution to renegotiate the foreign debt and channel as much money as possible into health and education. Correa's first term was due to end in January 2011, but a new constitution was proposed which would weaken Congress, strengthen the powers of the president and allow him to stand for two further terms. His critics accused him of trying to make himself into a dictator, but in a referendum held in September 2008, the new constitution was approved by 64 per cent of voters. This now required a general election in April 2009. Correa was easily re-elected for a second term to last until August 2013, which could be extended to 2017 if he were to be elected again. In 2010 legislation was passed requiring foreign oil companies to renegotiate their contracts so that more of the profits went to the government, to be used in the campaign against poverty and its causes. Companies were warned that if they refused, they would be nationalized and forced out of the country.

These policies alienated various right-wing groups and in September 2010, after President Correa took the dangerous step of ending bonuses and other benefits for the police force, protest demonstrations broke out in which the police were heavily involved. Road blocks were set up and protesters invaded the National Assembly and the state-run TV station. When Correa tried to talk with police representatives, he was kidnapped and held hostage. It looked as though a coup was being attempted, and the president declared a state of emergency and called on the army to intervene. During the night an army unit rescued him from a hospital where he was being held; after fighting between the army and the police, order was restored and Correa continued in office.

By 2012 there were signs that Correa's social policies were working: both unemployment and poverty levels had fallen, and there had been vastly increased expenditure on roads, hospitals and schools. In 2011 Ecuador's economy grew by 7.8 per cent, helped by higher oil prices. Not surprisingly the president's popularity with the poor increased considerably, but the middle classes complained about rising prices and rising taxation, while human-rights groups accused him of making himself too powerful. Although the opposition was divided and relatively small in number, Correa had to contend with a largely hostile media. However, it was widely expected that he would be re-elected, if he decided to stand again in August 2013. Ecuador gained worldwide attention in the summer of 2012 when President Correa granted political asylum to Julian Assange, the founder of WikiLeaks, which publishes classified information, including US military and diplomatic documents. He was wanted for questioning in Sweden in relation to a rape investigation, and there was a strong possibility that he could be prosecuted in the USA over the WikiLeaks publication of confidential documents. The British government wanted to hand him over to Sweden, but from June 2012, with the situation locked in stalemate, Assange was living under diplomatic protection in the Ecuadorian embassy in London.

(h) Nicaragua

Taking office in January 2007, President Ortega had become less 'revolutionary' and toned down his anti-capitalist stand during his years in opposition since 1990. He claimed that he was now motivated by Christian principles rather than by Marxism. There were allegations of fraud during the election, and both the USA and the EU suspended their aid programmes to Nicaragua. Nevertheless, Ortega introduced new schemes to improve healthcare, social services, education (including a system of scholarships for poor students) and housing. Progress was slow – in 2011, towards the end of his term in office, the country was still the poorest in Latin America, with 46 per cent of the population living below the poverty line. On the other hand, private businesses had been allowed to continue without state interference, and the government could claim with some justification that the mixed economy had produced a period of sustained economic growth. According to Robin Yapp, writing in the *Telegraph* (7 October 2011), Nicaragua was 'helped by cheap oil from Hugo Chávez's Venezuela, which has helped to prop up social schemes like subsidized housing. Ortega has also been able to attract foreign investors who see Nicaragua as a safe haven compared to neighbouring Honduras or El Salvador which have the world's highest murder rates.'

Ortega has attracted considerable criticism from many sections of society. Some of his former left-wing supporters have left the party, accusing him of kowtowing to the neo-liberals simply in order to stay in power. Democrats claim that he is well on the way towards becoming a dictator like the Somozas. He certainly got the Supreme Court to cancel the ban on presidents standing for consecutive terms, enabling him to stand again in November 2011. Yet his popularity with the masses remains such that he won a comfortable victory, taking 62 per cent of the votes.

This chapter has shown how, during the early years of the twenty-first century, Latin America became one of the most fascinating regions of the world. Starting in Venezuela with the election of Hugo Chávez in 1998, a new trend began to spread across the region. This was the change from neo-liberalism to policies which allowed a country's resources to be shared more equally among the great mass of the population, and which enabled modernization to take place. Of course there were different degrees of change: the USA did its best to divide Mexico, Chile and Guatemala from the rest by making separate trade agreements with them, so that relations between the four states are reasonably cordial. Venezuela, Bolivia, Cuba, Ecuador and Argentina were the most decisive in their rejection of neo-liberalism, while Brazil, Nicaragua and Uruguay were middle of the road, with a mixture of policies.

There was another strand in this move towards modernization – the growth of regional co-operation between states. A number of institutions and organizations were set up; named after Simon Bolívar, the famous nineteenth-century revolutionary leader, the Bolivarian Alternative for the Americas (ALBA) was the creation of Chávez in 2004. In the words of Nikolas Kozloff, it was 'an initiative designed to encourage greater trade, solidarity and exchange between nations standing outside the usual market-based strictures' (i.e. outside the US orbit). Its activities went far beyond simple free-trade agreements, to include mutual economic and social assistance. For example Venezuela supplies Cuba with oil from its state-owned refineries at very reasonable prices and in return Cuba has sent thousands of doctors and teachers to work in Venezuela. Cuban doctors have also worked in Bolivia and provided medical supplies. In 2012 the membership of ALBA included Venezuela, Cuba, Bolivia, Ecuador, Nicaragua, Haiti and various small islands in the Caribbean. Discussions were well under way into the adoption of a common currency, the sucre, although there were problems with the small Caribbean islands which were already members of the Eastern Caribbean monetary union.

Another regional organization is the Union of South American Nations (UNASUR), which was set up at a meeting in the Brazilian capital in 2008. It brought together two existing customs unions – Mercosul and the Andean Community of Nations. In 2011 there were 12 member states – Argentina, Brazil, Bolivia, Chile, Colombia, Ecuador, Guyana, Paraguay, Peru, Suriname, Venezuela and Uruguay. The plan was eventually to set up a South American parliament to be situated in Cochabamba, the third largest city in Bolivia.

The Bank of the South was launched in 2009 with initial capital of $20 million, the bulk of which was supplied by Argentina, Brazil and Venezuela, with smaller contributions from Bolivia, Ecuador, Paraguay and Uruguay. The bank provides loans for approved social and infrastructure improvements to any Latin American country as an alternative to the IMF. However, some governments prefer to use smaller regional funds that are on offer, such as the Andean Development Corporation and the state-run Venezuelan Development Bank, known as BANDES. This has branches in Ecuador, Bolivia and Uruguay, and it has been especially helpful to Bolivia in financing educational programmes. Whichever of these alternatives the countries of Latin America decided to choose as a source of funding, the outcome would have been similar: the IMF was on the verge of being eclipsed as a force within the region. In a no-nonsense assessment of the situation, Jason Tockman, an expert on ALBA and Bolivia, declared that 'US influence through international financial institutions like the IMF has collapsed'.

And finally, some of the Latin American countries began a diversification of markets and investment, with China as an increasingly important partner. Venezuela, the leading oil exporter in the hemisphere, delivered quite a blow to Washington's energy policies. Having built up probably the closest relations with China of any Latin American country, Venezuela plans to export increasing amounts of oil to China as part of its effort to reduce its dependence on the openly hostile US government. In fact Latin America as a whole is increasing trade and other relations with China, in particular raw materials exporters such as Brazil, Peru and Chile. For Brazil, now often called 'the farmer of the world', China is now its largest trading partner. These increases are just part of the move toward a more diverse world that is causing considerable agitation among American planners and businessmen, who had assumed for a long time that their global domination would continue indefinitely. As Noam Chomsky explains:

The former colonies in Latin America have a better chance now than ever before to overcome centuries of subjugation, violence, repression and foreign intervention. ... These are exciting prospects for Latin America, and if the hopes can be realized, even partially, the results cannot fail to have a large-scale global impact as well.

FURTHER READING

Ali, T., *Pirates of the Caribbean: Axis of Hope* (Verso, 2006).
Castaneda, J. and Morales, M. (eds) *Tales of the Latin American Left* (Routledge, 2008).
Chomsky, N., *Hopes and Prospects* (Penguin, 2010).

Gott, R., *Hugo Chávez and the Bolivarian Revolution* (Verso, revised edition, 2011).

Grandin, G., *The Last Colonial Massacre: Latin America in the Cold War* (Chicago University Press, 2004).

Grandin, G., *Empire's Workshop: Latin America, the United States and the Rise of the New Imperialism* (Owl Books, 2006).

Harten, S., *The Rise of Evo Morales and the MAS* (Zed Books, 2011).

Jones, B., *Hugo: The Hugo Chávez Story from Mud Hut to Perpetual Revolution* (Vintage, 2009).

Kozloff, N., *Hugo Chávez: Oil, Politics and the Challenge to the US* (Palgrave Macmillan, 2006).

Kozloff, N., *Revolution! South America and the Rise of the New Left* (Palgrave Macmillan, 2008).

Raby, D. L., *Democracy and Revolution: Latin America and Socialism Today* (Pluto, 2006).

Sivak, M., *Evo Morales: The Extraordinary Rise of the First Indigenous President of Bolivia* (Palgrave Macmillan, 2010).

QUESTIONS

1   What were the problems facing the countries of Latin America at the end of the Second World War? Explain why progress in solving these problems was so slow.

2   In what ways and with what motives was the USA involved in the affairs of Latin America during the second half of the twentieth century?

3   'The Cold War was to have profound effects on the economic and political systems of Latin America.' How far do you agree?

4   'The election of Hugo Chávez as president of Venezuela in 1998 was the beginning of a left-wing revolution that was to transform Latin America over the next decade.' Explain what happened in this transformation. Do you think this statement is an accurate assessment of recent events in Latin America, or is it an exaggeration?

There is a document question about US–Latin American relations on the website.

Part

VI

Global Problems

The changing world economy since 1900

SUMMARY OF EVENTS

For much of the nineteenth century Britain led the rest of the world in industrial production and trade. In the last quarter of the century, Germany and the USA began to catch up, and by 1914 the USA was the world's leading industrial nation. The First and Second World Wars caused important changes in the world economy. The USA gained most, economically, from both wars, and it was the USA which became economically dominant as the world's richest nation. Meanwhile, Britain's economy slowly declined, and it was not improved by the fact that Britain stayed outside the European Community until 1973.

In spite of slumps and depressions, the general trend was for the relatively wealthy industrialized countries to get wealthier, while the poorer nations of Africa and Asia (known as the Third World), most of which were once colonies of the European states, became even poorer. However, some Third World countries began to industrialize and become richer, and this caused a split in the Third World bloc. During the last quarter of the twentieth century, new developments came to the forefront. Industrial production and some service industries began to move from the western nations into countries such as China and India, where labour was much cheaper. Western economic systems showed signs of faltering, and there was controversy about which was the most successful type of economy – the US model or the European model. Global warming, caused by the emission of gases such as carbon dioxide, produced problematic climate changes which threatened to do most harm to the poorer countries, which were least able to cope. During the first decade of the twenty-first century, beginning in the USA in 2008, the world suffered an unprecedented financial crisis in which, for a time, the entire capitalist system teetered on the edge of collapse. The US and various European governments saved the banking system with massive bailouts, but could not prevent the world from plunging into recession.

27.1 CHANGES IN THE WORLD ECONOMY SINCE 1900

In one sense, in 1900 there was already a single world economy. A few highly industrialized countries, mainly the USA, Britain and Germany, provided the world's manufactured goods, while the rest of the world provided raw materials and food (known as 'primary products'). The USA treated Latin America (especially Mexico) as an area of 'influence', in the same way that the European states treated their colonies in Africa and elsewhere. European nations usually decided what should be produced in their colonies: the British made sure that Uganda and the Sudan grew cotton for their textile industry; the Portuguese did the same in Mozambique. They fixed the prices at which colonial products were sold as low as possible, and also fixed the prices of manufactured goods exported to the colonies as high as possible. In other words, as historian Basil Davidson (see Further

Reading for Chapters 24 and 25) puts it: 'the Africans had to sell cheap and buy dear'. The twentieth century brought some important changes:

(a) The USA became the dominant industrial power and the rest of the world became more dependent on the USA

In 1880 Britain produced roughly twice as much coal and pig iron as the USA, but by 1900 the roles had been reversed: the USA produced more coal than Britain and about twice as much pig iron and steel. This growing domination continued right through the century: in 1945, for example, incomes in the USA were twice as high as in Britain and seven times higher than in the USSR; during the next 30 years, American production almost doubled again. What were the causes of the American success?

1 The First World War and after
The First World War and its aftermath gave a big boost to the American economy (see Section 22.3). Many countries which had bought goods from Europe during the war (such as China and the states of Latin America) were unable to get hold of supplies because the war had disrupted trade. This forced them to buy goods from the USA (and also Japan) instead, and after the war they continued to do so. The USA was the economic winner of the First World War and became even richer thanks to the interest on the war loans it had made to Britain and her allies (see Section 4.5). Only the USA was rich enough to provide loans to encourage German recovery during the 1920s, but this had the unfortunate effect of linking Europe too closely with the USA financially and economically. When the USA suffered its great slump (1929–35) (see Section 22.6), Europe and the rest of the world were also thrown into depression. In 1933, in the depth of the depression, about 25 million people were out of work in the USA and as many as 50 million in the world as a whole.

2 The Second World War
The Second World War left the USA the world's greatest industrial (and military) power. The Americans entered the war relatively late and their industry did well out of supplying war materials for Britain and her allies. At the end of the war, with Europe almost at a standstill economically, the USA was producing 43 per cent of the world's iron ore, 45 per cent of its crude steel, 60 per cent of its railway locomotives and 74 per cent of its motor vehicles (see also Section 22.7(e)). When the war was over, the industrial boom continued as industry switched to producing consumer goods, which had been in short supply during the war. Once again, only the USA was rich enough to help western Europe, which it did with Marshall Aid (see Section 7.2(e)). It was not simply that the Americans wanted to be kind to Europe: they had at least two other ulterior motives:

- a prosperous western Europe would be able to buy American goods and thus keep the great American wartime boom going;
- a prosperous western Europe would be less likely to go communist.

(b) After 1945 the world split into capitalist and communist blocs

- *The capitalist bloc* consisted of the highly developed industrial nations – the USA, Canada, western Europe, Japan, Australia and New Zealand. They believed in private enterprise and private ownership of wealth, with profit as the great motivating influence, and ideally, a minimum of state interference.

- *The communist bloc* consisted of the USSR, its satellite states in eastern Europe, and later, China, North Korea, Cuba and North Vietnam. They believed in state-controlled, centrally planned economies, which, they argued, would eliminate the worst aspects of capitalism – slumps, unemployment and the unequal distribution of wealth.

The next forty or so years seemed like a contest to find out which economic system was best. The collapse of communism in eastern Europe at the end of the 1980s (see Sections 10.6 and 18.3) enabled the supporters of capitalism to claim the final victory; however, communism still continued in China, North Korea, Vietnam and Cuba. This big contest between the two rival economic and political systems was known as *the Cold War*; it had important economic consequences. It meant that both blocs spent enormous amounts of cash on building nuclear weapons and other armaments (see Section 7.4), and on even more expensive space programmes. Many people argued that much of this money could have been better spent helping to solve the problems of the world's poorer nations.

(c)   The 1970s and 1980s: serious economic problems in the USA

After many years of continual economic success, the US began to experience problems.

- Defence costs and the war in Vietnam (1961–75) (see Section 8.3) were a constant drain on the economy and the treasury.
- There was a budget deficit every year in the late 1960s. This means that the government was spending more money than it was collecting in taxes, and the difference had to be covered by selling gold reserves. By 1971 the dollar, which was once considered to be as good as gold, was weakening in value.
- President Nixon was forced to devalue the dollar by about 12 per cent and to put a 10 per cent duty on most imports (1971).
- Rising oil prices worsened America's balance-of-payments deficit, and led to the development of more nuclear power.
- President Reagan (1981–9) refused to cut defence spending and tried new economic policies recommended by the American economist Milton Friedman. He argued that governments should abandon all attempts to plan their economies and concentrate on monetarism: this meant exercising a tight control on the money supply by keeping interest rates high. His theory was that this would force businesses to be more efficient. These were policies which Margaret Thatcher was already trying in Britain. At first the new ideas seemed to be working – in the mid-1980s unemployment fell and America was prosperous again. But the basic problem of the US economy – the huge budget deficit – refused to go away, mainly because of high defence spending. The Americans were even reduced to borrowing from Japan, whose economy was extremely successful at that time. The drain on American gold reserves weakened the dollar, and also weakened confidence in the economy. There was a sudden and dramatic fall in share prices (1987), which was followed by similar falls all over the world. In the late 1980s much of the world was suffering from a trade recession.

(d)   Japan's success

Japan became economically one of the world's most successful states. At the end of the Second World War Japan was defeated and her economy was in ruins. She soon began to

Table 27.1 **Gross National Product per head of the population in 1992**

Year	GNP
1955	200
1978	7 300
1987	15 800
1990	27 000

recover, and during the 1970s and 1980s, Japanese economic expansion was dramatic, as Table 27.1 shows. (For full details see Section 15.2.)

27.2 THE THIRD WORLD AND THE NORTH–SOUTH DIVIDE

During the 1950s the term *Third World* began to be used to describe countries which were not part of the First World (the industrialized capitalist nations) or the Second World (the industrialized communist states). The Third World states grew rapidly in number during the 1950s and 1960s as the European empires broke up and newly independent countries emerged. By 1970 the Third World consisted of Africa, Asia (except the USSR and China), India, Pakistan, Bangladesh, Latin America and the Middle East. They were almost all once colonies or mandates of European powers, and were left in an undeveloped or under-developed state when they achieved independence.

(a) The Third World and non-alignment

The Third World states were in favour of non-alignment, which means that they did not want to be too closely associated with either the capitalist or the communist bloc, and they were very suspicious of the motives of both. Prime Minister Nehru of India (1947–64) saw himself as a sort of unofficial leader of the Third World, which he thought could be a powerful force for world peace. Third World countries deeply resented the fact that both blocs continued to interfere in their internal affairs (neo-colonialism). The USA, for example, interfered unashamedly in the affairs of Central and South America, helping to overthrow governments which they did not approve of; this happened in Guatemala (1954), the Dominican Republic (1965) and Chile (1973). Britain, France and the USSR interfered in the Middle East. Frequent meetings of Third World leaders were held, and in 1979, 92 nations were represented at a 'non-aligned' conference in Havana (Cuba). By this time the Third World contained roughly 70 per cent of the world's population.

(b) Third World poverty and the Brandt Report (1980)

Economically the Third World was extremely poor. For example, although they contained 70 per cent of the world's population, Third World countries only consumed 30 per cent of the world's food, while the USA, with perhaps 8 per cent of the world's population, ate 40 per cent of the world's food. Third World people were often short of proteins and vitamins, and this caused poor health and a high death-rate. In 1980 an international group of

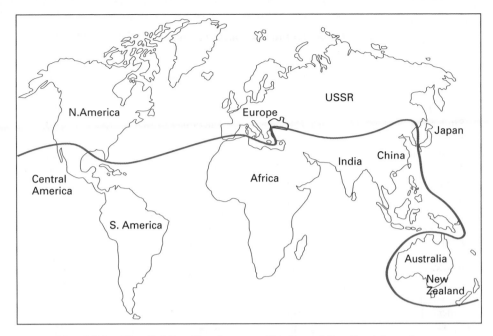

Map 27.1 **The dividing line between North and South, rich and poor**

politicians under the chairmanship of Willi Brandt (who had been chancellor of West Germany from 1967 until 1974), and including Edward Heath (prime minister of Britain 1970–4), produced a report (*the Brandt Report*) on the problems of the Third World. It said that the world could be roughly divided into two parts (see Map 27.1).

The North – the developed industrial nations of North America, Europe, the USSR and Japan, plus Australia and New Zealand.
The South – most of the Third World countries.

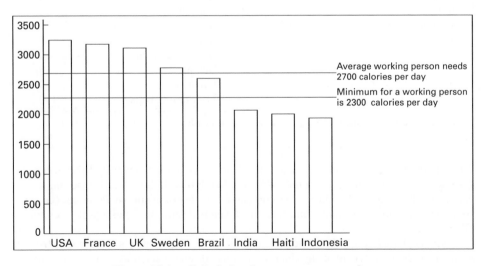

Figure 27.1 **Calorie intake per person per day**

Table 27.2   **Gross National Product per head of the population in 1992 (in US dollars)**

Japan	28 220	Libya	5 310
Taiwan	10 202	Uganda	170
Hong Kong	15 380	Rwanda	250
Singapore	15 750	Tanzania	110
South Korea	6 790	Kenya	330
North Korea	943	Zaire	220
Thailand	1 840	Ethiopia	110
Vietnam	109	Sudan	400
China	380	Somalia	150
		Zimbabwe	570
		Zambia	290
Peru	950	Nigeria	320
Bolivia	680	Mozambique	60
Paraguay	1 340	South Africa	2 670
Brazil	2 770	Algeria	2 020
Argentina	2 780		
Colombia	1 290		
Chile	2 730	India	310
Venezuela	2 900	Pakistan	410
Uruguay	3 340	Bangladesh	220
		Sri Lanka	540
Germany	21 000	Russian Fed.	2 680
France	22 300	Poland	1 960
Britain	17 760	Romania	1 090
Italy	20 510	Czechoslovakia	2 440
Switzerland	36 230		
Greece	7 180		
Spain	14 020		
Portugal	7 450	USA	23 120
Norway	25 800	Canada	20 320
Sweden	26 780	Australia	17 070
Belgium	20 880	Haiti	380
		Dominican Rep.	1 040
		Guyana	330
		Jamaica	1 340
		Trinidad & Tobago	3 940

Source: World Bank statistics, in *Europa World Year Book 1995*.

The report came to the conclusion that the North was getting richer and the South was getting poorer. This gap between the North and South is well illustrated by the statistics of calorie intake (Fig. 27.1) and by the comparison of Gross National Products (GNP) of some typical North and South countries, or 'developed' and 'low and middle' economies (Table 27.2).

GNP is calculated by taking the total money value of a country's total output from all units of production, wherever production is situated; and it includes interest, profits and dividends received from abroad. This total value is divided by the population figure, and this gives the amount of wealth produced per head of the population. In 1989–90 the GNP of the North averaged over 24 times that of the South. In 1992 a highly developed and efficient country like Japan could boast a GNP of over $28 000 per head of the population, and Norway $25 800. On the other hand, among poor African countries, Ethiopia could manage only $110 per head, the second lowest GNP in the world.

(c) Why is the South so poor?

- The South was and still is economically dependent on the North because of neo-colonialism (see Sections 24.4 and 24.7). The North expected the South to continue providing food and raw materials for them, and expected them to buy manufactured goods from the North. They did not encourage the South to develop their own industries.
- Many states found it difficult to break away from the one-product economies left behind from colonial days, because governments lacked the cash needed to diversify. Ghana (cocoa) and Zambia (copper) found themselves facing this problem. In states like Ghana, which depended for its income on exporting crops, it meant that too little food would be left for the population. Governments then had to spend their scarce money on importing expensive food. A fall in the world price of their main product would be a major disaster. In the 1970s there was a dramatic fall in the world price of such products as cocoa, copper, coffee and cotton. Table 27.3 shows the disastrous effects on the incomes, and therefore the buying power of countries such as Ghana and Cameroon (cocoa), Zambia, Chile and Peru (copper), Mozambique, Egypt and the Sudan (cotton), and Ivory Coast, Zaire and Ethiopia (coffee).
- At the same time, prices of manufactured goods continued to rise. The South had to import from the North. In spite of the efforts of the United Nations Conference on Trade and Development (UNCTAD), which tried to negotiate fairer prices for the Third World, no real improvement was achieved.
- Although a great deal of financial aid was given by the North to the South, much of it was on a business basis – the countries of the South had to pay interest.

Table 27.3 **What commodities could buy in 1975 and 1980**

	Barrels of oil	Capital ($US)
Copper (1 tonne could buy)		
1975	115	17 800
1980	58	9 500
Cocoa (1 tonne would buy)		
1975	148	23 400
1980	63	10 200
Coffee (1 tonne would buy)		
1975	148	22 800
1980	82	13 000
Cotton (1 tonne would buy)		
1975	119	18 400
1980	60	9 600

Sometimes a condition of the deal was that countries of the South had to spend aid on goods from the country which was making the loan. Some countries borrowed directly from banks in the USA and western Europe, so that by 1980 Third World countries owed the equivalent of $500 billion; even the annual interest payable was about $50 billion. Some states were forced to borrow more cash just to pay the interest on the original loan.

- Another problem for Third World countries was that their populations were increasing much faster than those in the North. In 1975 the total world population stood at about 4000 million, and it was expected to reach 6000 million by 1997. Since the population of the South was growing so much faster, a larger proportion of the world's population than ever before would be poor (see Chapter 28).
- Many Third World countries had suffered long and crippling wars and civil wars, which ravaged crops and ruined economies. Some of the worst wars were in Ethiopia, Nicaragua, Guatemala, Lebanon, the Congo/Zaire, Sudan, Somalia, Liberia, Sierra Leone, Mozambique and Angola.
- Drought was sometimes a serious problem in Africa. Niger in West Africa was badly affected: in 1974 it produced only half the food crops grown in 1970 (mainly millet and sorghum), and about 40 per cent of the cattle died. As global warming gathered pace towards the end of the century, droughts became more frequent and many countries were dependent on overseas aid to feed their people.

(d) The Brandt Report (1980) was full of good ideas

For example, it pointed out that it was in the North's interests to help the South to become more prosperous, because that would enable the South to buy more goods from the North. This would help to avoid unemployment and recession in the North. If just a fraction of the North's spending on armaments was switched to helping the South, vast improvements could be made. For example, for the price of one jet fighter (about $20 million), 40 000 village pharmacies could be set up. The Report went on to make some important recommendations which, if carried out, would at least eliminate hunger from the world:

- the rich nations of the North should aim to be giving 0.7 per cent of their national income to poorer countries by 1985 and 1.0 per cent by the year 2000;
- a new World Development Fund should be set up in which decision-making would be more evenly shared between lenders and borrowers (not like the International Monetary Fund and the World Bank, which were dominated by the USA);
- an international energy plan should be drawn up;
- there should be a campaign to improve agricultural techniques in the South, and an international food programme should be drawn up.

Did the Brandt Report change anything? Sadly, there was no immediate improvement in the general economic situation of the South. By 1985 very few countries had reached the suggested 0.7 per cent giving target. Those that did were Norway, Sweden, Denmark, the Netherlands and France; however, the USA gave only 0.24 per cent and Britain 0.11 per cent. There was a terrible famine in Africa, especially in Ethiopia and the Sudan in the mid-1980s, and the crisis in the poorer parts of the Third World seemed to be worsening. Throughout the 1990s the US economy boomed under the Clinton administration, whereas the plight of the Third World became even more serious. At the end of 2003 the UN reported that 21 Third World states, 17 of them in Africa, were in crisis because of a combination of natural disasters, AIDS, global warming and civil wars (see Section 25.15). Yet the richest 1 per cent of the world's population (around 60 million) received as much income as the poorest 57 per cent. Norway was top of the UN's league table for human development: Norwegians had a life expectancy of 78.7 years, there was a literacy rate of virtually 100 per cent, and annual income was just under $30 000. In Sierra Leone life expectancy was about 35, the literacy rate was 35 per cent and annual income averaged $470. The USA seemed to attract the most hostility and resentment on account of this imbalance of wealth; it was widely believed that the growth of terrorism – especially the 11 September attacks on the USA – was a desperate response to the failure of peaceful attempts to bring about a fairer world economic system (see Sections 12.1 and 12.2).

UN economic advisers were clear about what needed to be done. It was up to the West to remove trade barriers, dismantle its over-generous system of subsidies, provide greater debt relief, and double the amount of aid from $50 billion to $100 billion a year. This would enable poor countries to invest in clean water systems, rural roads, education and proper healthcare.

27.3 THE SPLIT IN THE THIRD WORLD ECONOMY

During the 1970s some Third World states began to become more prosperous, sometimes thanks to the exploitation of natural resources such as oil, and also because of industrialization.

(a) Oil

Some Third World states were lucky enough to have oil resources. In 1973 the members of the Organization of Petroleum Exporting Countries (OPEC), partly in an attempt to conserve oil supplies, began to charge more for their oil. The Middle East oil-producing states made huge profits, as did Nigeria and Libya. This did not necessarily mean that their governments spent the money wisely or for the benefit of their populations. One African success story, however, was provided by Libya, the richest country in Africa thanks to its oil resources and the shrewd policies of its leader, Colonel Gaddafi (who took power in 1969). He used much of the profits from oil on agricultural and industrial development, and to set up a welfare state. This was one country where ordinary people benefited from oil profits; with a GNP of £5460 in 1989, Libya could claim to be almost as economically successful as Greece and Portugal, the poorest members of the European Community.

(b) Industrialization

Some Third World states industrialized rapidly and with great success. These included Singapore, Taiwan, South Korea and Hong Kong (known as the four 'Pacific tiger' economies), and among others, Thailand, Malaysia, Brazil and Mexico.

The GNPs of the four 'tiger' economies compared favourably with those of many European Community countries. The success of the newly industrialized countries in world export markets was made possible partly because they were able to attract firms from the North who were keen to take advantage of the much cheaper labour available in the Third World. Some firms even shifted all their production to newly industrialized countries, where low production costs enabled them to sell their goods at lower prices than goods produced in the North. This posed serious problems for the industrialized nations of the North, which were all suffering high unemployment during the 1990s. It seemed that the golden days of western prosperity might have gone, at least for the foreseeable future, unless their workers were prepared to accept lower wages, or unless companies were prepared to make do with lower profits.

In the mid-1990s the world economy was moving into the next stage, in which the Asian 'tigers' found themselves losing jobs to workers in countries such as Malaysia and the Philippines. Other Third World states in the process of industrializing were Indonesia and China, where wages were even lower and hours of work longer. Jacques Chirac, the French president, expressed the fears and concerns of many when he pointed out (April 1996) that developing countries should not compete with Europe by allowing miserable wages and working conditions; he called for a recognition that there are certain basic human rights which need to be encouraged and enforced:

- freedom to join trade unions and the freedom for these unions to bargain collectively, for the protection of workers against exploitation;
- abolition of forced labour and child labour.

In fact most developing countries accepted this when they joined the International Labour Organization (ILO) (see Section 9.5(b)), but accepting conditions and keeping to them were two different things.

27.4   THE WORLD ECONOMY AND ITS EFFECTS ON THE ENVIRONMENT

As the twentieth century wore on, and the North became more and more obsessed with industrialization, new methods and techniques were invented to help increase production and efficiency. The main motive was the creation of wealth and profit, and very little attention was paid to the side effects all this was having. During the 1970s people became increasingly aware that all was not well with their environment, and that industrialization was causing several major problems:

- Exhaustion of the world's resources of raw materials and fuel (oil, coal and gas).
- Massive pollution of the environment. Scientists realized that if this continued, it was likely to severely damage the ecosystem. This is the system by which living creatures, trees and plants function within the environment and in which they are all interconnected. 'Ecology' is the study of the ecosystem.
- Global warming – the uncontrollable warming of the Earth's atmosphere caused by the large quantities of gases emitted from industry.

(a)   Exhaustion of the world's resources

- Fossil fuels – coal, oil and natural gas – are the remains of plants and living creatures which died hundreds of millions of years ago. They cannot be replaced, and are rapidly being used up. There is probably plenty of coal left, but nobody is quite sure just how much remains of the natural gas and oil. Oil production increased enormously during the twentieth century, as Figure 27.2 shows. Some experts believe that all the oil reserves will be used up early in the twenty-first century. This was one of the reasons why OPEC tried to conserve oil during the 1970s. The British responded by successfully drilling for oil in the North Sea, which made them less dependent on oil imports. Another response was to develop alternative sources of power, especially nuclear power.

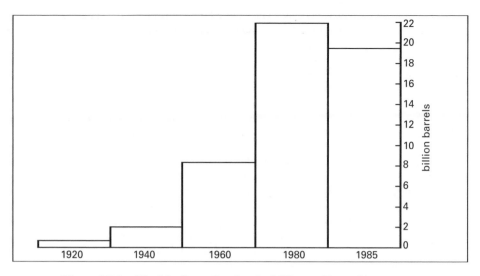

Figure 27.2 **World oil production in billions of barrels per year**

- Tin, lead, copper, zinc and mercury were other raw materials being seriously depleted. Experts suggested that these might all be used up early in the twenty-first century, and again it was the Third World which was being stripped of the resources it needed to help it escape from poverty.
- Too much timber was being used. About half of the world's tropical rainforests had been lost by 1987, and it was calculated that about 80 000 square kilometres, an area roughly the size of Austria, was being lost every year. A side effect of this was the loss of many animal and insect species which had lived in the forests.
- Too many fish were being caught and too many whales killed.
- The supply of phosphates (used for fertilizers) was being rapidly used up. The more fertilizers farmers used to increase agricultural yields in an attempt to keep pace with the rising population, the more phosphate rock was quarried (an increase of 4 per cent a year since 1950). Supplies were expected to be exhausted by the middle of the twenty-first century.
- There was a danger that supplies of fresh water might soon run out. Most of the fresh water on the planet is tied up in the polar ice caps and glaciers, or deep in the ground. All living organisms – humans, animals, trees and plants – rely on rain to survive. With the world's population growing by 90 million a year, scientists at Stanford University (California) found that in 1995, humans and their farm animals, crops and forestry plantations were already using up a quarter of all the water taken up by plants. This leaves less moisture to evaporate and therefore a likelihood of less rainfall.
- The amount of land available for agriculture was dwindling. This was partly because of spreading industrialization and the growth of cities, but also because of wasteful use of farmland. Badly designed irrigation schemes increased salt levels in the soil. Sometimes irrigation took too much water from lakes and rivers, and whole areas were turned into deserts. Soil erosion was another problem: scientists calculated that every year about 75 billion tons of soil were washed away by rain and floods or blown away by winds. Soil loss depended on how good farming practices were: in western Europe and the USA (where methods were good), farmers lost on average 17 tons of topsoil every year from each hectare. In Africa, Asia and South

America, the loss was 40 tons a year. On steep slopes in countries like Nigeria, 220 tons a year were being lost, while in some parts of Jamaica the figure reached 400 tons a year.

An encouraging sign was the setting-up of *the World Conservation Strategy* (1980), which aimed to alert the world to all these problems.

(b) Pollution of the environment – an ecological disaster?

- Discharges from heavy industry polluted the atmosphere, rivers, lakes and the sea. In 1975 all five Great Lakes of North America were described as 'dead', meaning that they were so heavily polluted that no fish could live in them. About 10 per cent of the lakes in Sweden were in the same condition. Acid rain (rain polluted with sulphuric acid) caused extensive damage to trees in central Europe, especially in Germany and Czechoslovakia. The USSR and the communist states of eastern Europe were guilty of carrying out the dirtiest industrialization: the whole region was badly polluted by years of poisonous emissions.
- Getting rid of sewage from the world's great cities was a problem. Some countries simply dumped sewage untreated or only partially treated straight into the sea. The sea around New York was badly polluted, and the Mediterranean was heavily polluted, mainly by human sewage.
- Farmers in the richer countries contributed to the pollution by using artificial fertilizers and pesticides, which drained off the land into streams and rivers.
- Chemicals known as chlorofluorocarbons (CFCs), used in aerosol sprays, refrigerators and fire extinguishers, were found to be harmful to the ozone layer which protects the Earth from the sun's harmful ultraviolet radiation. In 1979, scientists discovered that there was a large hole in the ozone layer over the Antarctic; by 1989 the hole was much larger and another hole had been discovered over the Arctic. This meant that people were more likely to develop skin cancers because of the unfiltered radiation from the sun. Some progress was made towards dealing with this problem, and many countries banned the use of CFCs. In 2001 the World Meteorological Organization reported that the ozone layer seemed to be mending.
- Nuclear power causes pollution when radioactivity leaks into the environment. It is now known that this can cause cancer, particularly leukaemia. It was shown that of all the people who worked at the Sellafield nuclear plant in Cumbria (UK) between 1947 and 1975, a quarter of those who have since died, died of cancer. There was a constant risk of major accidents like the explosion at Three Mile Island in the USA in 1979, which contaminated a vast area around the power station. When leaks and accidents occurred, the authorities always assured the public that nobody had suffered harmful effects; however, nobody really knew how many people would die later from cancer caused by radiation.

  The worst ever nuclear accident happened in 1986 at Chernobyl in Ukraine (then part of the USSR). A nuclear reactor exploded, killing 35 people and releasing a huge radioactive cloud which drifted across most of Europe. Ten years later it was reported that hundreds of cases of thyroid cancer were appearing in areas near Chernobyl. Even in Britain, a thousand miles away, hundreds of square miles of sheep pasture in Wales, Cumbria and Scotland were still contaminated and subject to restrictions. This also affected 300 000 sheep, which had to be checked for excessive radioactivity before they could be eaten. Concern about the safety of nuclear power led many countries to look towards alternative sources of power which were safer, particularly solar, wind and tide power.

One of the main difficulties to be faced is that it would cost vast sums of money to put all these problems right. Industrialists argue that to 'clean up' their factories and eliminate pollution would make their products more expensive. Governments and local authorities would have to spend extra cash to build better sewage works and to clean up rivers and beaches. In 1996 there were still 27 power-station reactors in operation in eastern Europe of similar elderly design to the one which exploded at Chernobyl. These were all threatening further nuclear disasters, but governments claimed they could afford neither safety improvements nor closure. The following description of Chernobyl from the *Guardian* (13 April 1996) gives some idea of the seriousness of the problems involved:

> At Chernobyl, the scene of the April 1986 explosion, just a few miles north of the Ukrainian capital Kiev, the prospect is bleak. Two of the station's remaining reactors are still in operation, surrounded by miles of heavily contaminated countryside. Radioactive elements slowly leach into the ground water – and hence into Kiev's drinking supply – from more than 800 pits where the most dangerous debris was buried ten years ago.

Nuclear reactors were also at risk from natural disasters. In May 2011 a huge tsunami hit the north-east coast of Japan. As well as killing thousands of people, it flooded a nuclear power station in Fukushima. First the six nuclear reactors were battered by high waves, and then the basement, where the emergency generators were situated, was submerged, disabling the entire plant. Again the ongoing problem was how best to deal with the widespread radioactive contamination. There was a great outburst of anti-government feeling when it later emerged that the authorities had ignored and then lied about reports of design weaknesses in the reactors.

(c)   Genetically modified (GM) crops

One of the economic issues that came to the forefront during the 1990s, and which developed into a political confrontation between the USA and the EU, was the growing of genetically modified crops. These are plants injected with genes from other plants which give the crops extra characteristics. For example, some crops can be made to tolerate herbicides that kill all other plants; this means that the farmer can spray the crop with a 'broad-spectrum' herbicide that will destroy every other plant in the field except his crop. Since weeds use up precious water and soil nutrients, GM crops should produce higher yields and require less herbicide than conventional crops. Some GM crops have been modified to produce a poison which kills pests that feed on them, others have been modified so that they will grow in salty soil. The main GM crops grown are wheat, barley, maize, oilseed rape, soya beans and cotton. Advocates of GM crops claim that they represent one of the greatest advances ever achieved in farming; they provide healthier food, produced in a more efficient and environmentally friendly way. Given the problem of the growing world population and the difficulties of feeding everybody, supporters see GM crops as perhaps a vital breakthrough in solving the world food problem. By 2004 they were being grown by at least 6 million farmers in 16 countries, including the USA, Canada, India, Argentina, Mexico, China, Colombia and South Africa. The main supporters of GM crops were the Americans, who were also the world's largest exporter.

However, not everybody was happy about this situation. Many people object to GM technology on the grounds that it can be used to create unnatural organisms – plants can be modified with genes from another plant or even from an animal. There are fears that genes might escape into wild plants and create 'superweeds' that cannot be killed; GM crops might be harmful to other species and also in the long term to the humans who eat them. Genes escaping from GM crops might be able to pollinate organically growing crops, which would ruin the organic farmers involved. These unfortunate farmers might find themselves being sued for having GM genes in their crops, even though they had not knowingly planted such seeds. The main objections came from Europe; although some European countries – Germany and Spain for example – grew GM crops, the amounts were small. Scientists on the whole tended to reserve judgement, claiming that there should be long field trials to show whether or not GM crops were harmful, both for the environment and for public health. Opinion polls showed that around 80 per cent of the European public had grave doubts about their safety; several countries, including Austria, France, Germany, Italy and Greece, banned imports of individual GMs either for growing or for use as food. Americans, on the other hand, insisted that the crops had been thoroughly tested and approved by the government, and that people had been eating GM foods for several years without any apparent ill effects.

Another European objection was that the GM industry was controlled by a few giant agriculture businesses, most of them American. In fact, by 2004 the American company Monsanto was producing more than 90 per cent of GM crops worldwide. The feeling was that such companies had too much control over world food production, which would enable them to exert pressure on countries to buy their products and force more traditional farmers out of the market. The controversy came to a head in April 2004 when the USA called on the World Trade Organization (WTO) to take action. The USA accused the EU of breaking WTO free-trade rules by banning GM imports without any scientific evidence to support their case.

However, by no means does everybody in the USA support GM farming. An organization called the Centre for Food Safety (CFS) has launched several cases in the Supreme Court, most notably in 2006 when a group of organic alfalfa farmers sued Monsanto for growing GM alfalfa, without first carrying out safety checks. They were afraid that their organic alfalfa would be cross-pollinated by GM alfalfa, which would make their organic alfalfa unsaleable in countries where GM crops were banned. The judgement was that the planting of GM alfalfa should stop until a full-scale investigation into possible ill effects had been carried out. A spokesman for Monsanto stated that they were confident that tests would be completed in time for the autumn planting in 2010. Encouraged by this result, the CFS organized another lawsuit against Monsanto in 2009, this time against the growing of GM sugar beet. In August 2010 a similar judgement halted the planting of GM sugar beet until the necessary tests had been completed.

At the same time not everybody in Europe was against GM farming. In Britain, for example, at the Rothamsted Agricultural Research Centre at Harpenden, experiments were being carried out with GM wheat which is resistant to several kinds of insects and should therefore need fewer pesticides. In June 2012 a group of protesters calling themselves 'Take the Flour Back' threatened to destroy the crop. Several hundred protesters, including some from France, attempted to invade the research centre, but were prevented by a large police presence. Fortunately they were persuaded to call off their plan and meet the research team for discussions. At the end of June 2012 it was revealed that recent tests in China on GM cotton crops showed that some insects were developing increased resistance to these crops, and that an increasing number of other pests were developing in and around the cotton crop, and these were affecting surrounding crops too. In other words, the early benefits were now being replaced by unexpected problems. And so the basic problem still remains: how is agriculture going to produce enough to feed the steadily growing world population, given that the amount of land suitable for agricultural production makes up only about 11 per cent of the earth's surface, and that a lot of this land is being contaminated by salt (salination), and therefore unsuitable for agriculture? Continuing global warming and rising sea levels are not likely to improve the situation (see the next section). At least there was one piece of good news in 2012 – in March it was announced that

Australian scientists had tested a new strain of wheat that could increase yields by 25 per cent in saline soils. Perhaps in the end, if the world is to survive, we shall have no choice but to accept GM produce. On the other hand it could be that scientists will succeed in producing new non-GM strains of all foodstuffs, like the Australian wheat, which will give higher yields from the same size of land area.

27.5 GLOBAL WARMING

(a) Early concerns

In the early 1970s scientists became concerned about what they called the 'greenhouse effect' – the apparently uncontrollable warming of the earth's atmosphere, or 'global warming', as it became known. It was caused by large amounts of carbon dioxide, methane and nitrous oxide, three gases produced during various industrial processes and by the burning of fossil fuels, being released into the atmosphere. These gases acted like the glass roof of a greenhouse, trapping and magnifying the sun's heat. Opinions differed about exactly what its effects would be; one alarming theory was that the ice caps, glaciers and snow in the polar regions would melt, causing the level of the sea to rise, and flooding large areas of land. It was also feared that Africa and large parts of Asia could become too hot for people to live in, and there could be violent storms and prolonged drought.

Some scientists dismissed these theories, arguing that if indeed the world was becoming warmer, it was a natural climatic change, not a man-made one. They played down the threats of flooding and drought, and accused those who suggested them of being anti-West and anti-industrialization. Industrialists themselves naturally welcomed these sympathizers, and as the debate between the two camps developed, nothing was done to reduce or control emissions of greenhouse gases.

Gradually the scientific evidence became more convincing: the Earth's average temperature was definitely increasing significantly, and the fossil-burning habits of humans were responsible for the changes. The evidence was enough to convince US vice-president Al Gore, who in 1992 wrote a pamphlet advocating international action to combat the greenhouse effect. President Clinton later proclaimed: 'We must stand together against the threat of global warming. A greenhouse may be a good place to raise plants; it is no place to nurture our children.' In June 1992 the UN organized the Earth Summit conference in Rio de Janeiro (Brazil) to discuss the situation. Representatives of 178 nations attended, including 117 heads of state; it was probably the largest gathering of world leaders in history. Most of them signed a range of treaties undertaking to protect the environment and reduce emissions of greenhouse gases.

However, signing treaties was one thing, enforcing them was quite another. For example, in 1993 when President Clinton introduced a bill to tax energy, the Republican majority in the Senate, many of whose supporters were industrialists and businessmen, threw it out. By this time many other countries were showing concern at the worsening situation. In 1995 an Intergovernmental Panel on Climatic Change produced a report outlining the probable effects of global warming and concluding that there could be little doubt that human actions were to blame.

(b) The Kyoto Convention (1997) and after

In 1997 another large international conference was held, this time in Kyoto (Japan), to work out a plan for reducing harmful emissions. It was appropriate that the conference was held in Kyoto, since, of all the industrialized countries, the Japanese had achieved most success in limiting their carbon emissions; and they had achieved it by heavy taxation on power and petrol. Statistics were worked out to show how much carbon each country was producing. The USA was by far the biggest culprit, emitting an average of 19 tons of carbon per head a year; Australia was not far behind with 16.6 tons per head. Japan emitted 9 tons per head a year, while the countries of the EU averaged 8.5 tons. On the other hand, the countries of the Third World emitted very modest amounts per head – South America 2.2 tons and Africa less than one ton.

The target set was to return global emissions to their 1990 levels by 2012. This meant that countries would have to reduce their emissions by different amounts to comply with the regulations; for example, the USA was required to reduce by 7 per cent, whereas France needed no reduction, since by 1997 the French were producing 60 per cent of their energy from nuclear power. In the end, 86 nations signed the agreement, which became known as the Kyoto Protocol. However, over the next few years this seemed to have little effect; in 2001 the Intergovernmental Panel on Climatic Change reported that climatic conditions were getting steadily worse. The 1990s was the hottest decade of the millennium and 1998 was the hottest year. In March 2001 the Kyoto Protocol was dealt a fatal blow when newly elected US President Bush announced that he would not ratify it. 'I will not accept a plan that will harm our economy and hurt American workers', he said. 'First things first are the people who live in America. That's my priority.'

Thus, early in the twenty-first century the world found itself in a situation where the USA, with no more than 6 per cent of the planet's population, was emitting a quarter of all the greenhouse gases, and would continue to do so, whatever the consequences for the rest of the world. In 2003 the effects of global warming were increasingly worrying. The UN calculated that at least 150 000 people had died during the year as a direct result of climate change – prolonged drought and violent storms. During that summer, 25 000 people died in Europe because of the unusually high temperatures. The increased warmth and the storms provided ideal breeding conditions for mosquitoes, which were spreading into mountainous areas where it had been too cold for them. Consequently the death rate from malaria increased sharply, especially in Africa. Droughts caused famine and malnutrition, so that people were more prone to catch life-threatening diseases.

(c)   What happens next?

It was clear to climatologists that drastic measures were needed if dire consequences were to be avoided. Sir John Houghton, the former head of the British Meteorological Office, compared climate change to a weapon of mass destruction: 'like terrorism, this weapon knows no boundaries. It can strike anywhere, in any form – a heatwave in one place, a drought or a flood or a storm surge in another.' It was also being suggested that the Kyoto agreement, designed when climate change was thought to be less destructive, would be insufficient to make much difference to the problem, even if it were fully implemented. The tragedy is that the world's poorest countries, which have contributed hardly anything to the build-up of greenhouse gases, are likely to be the ones most seriously affected. Recently published statistics suggested that in 2004 some 420 million people were living in countries which no longer had enough crop land to grow their own food; half a billion people lived in areas prone to chronic drought. The threats are exacerbated by the pressure of the growing world population (see Sections 28.1–3). A number of measures have been suggested:

- Professor John Schnellnhuber, director of the UK-based Tyndall Centre, which researches climate change, believes that an adaptation fund should be set up under the auspices of the UN and financed by wealthy polluters through levies based on the amount of emissions they make. The fund would be used to help poorer countries to improve their infrastructures, water industries and food production, and to cope with changes such as higher temperatures, rising river and sea levels, and tidal surges.

- A World Environment Court should be set up to enforce global agreements like the Kyoto Protocol. States must face fines large enough to deter them from breaking the rules.
- At national level, companies should be fined heavily for polluting rivers and dumping hazardous waste.
- An all-out effort should be made to develop new technologies so that 'green' power – solar, wind, tide and wave – will replace fossil fuels. Some people have suggested expanding nuclear power, an option which the French have chosen to take.

The main objections to all these alternatives are that they require fundamental changes in the way people live, and organize their countries' economies, and they will cost a lot of money to secure returns that will only become apparent in the future. A few scientists have suggested that the best thing is to do nothing at all at present, and hope that future scientists will find new and cheap methods of reducing greenhouse gases. However, in the words of Murray Sayle, 'long before that happy day, Miss Liberty may well be up to her bodice in New York harbour'. There were further worrying developments: in 2007 and 2008 a series of Gallup polls were held in 127 countries. These showed that over a third of the world's population were unaware of global warming. A survey in the USA in October 2009 showed that only 35 per cent of Republicans thought there was any reliable evidence that global warming was actually taking place. More Gallup polls in 111 countries in 2010 showed a disturbing fall in the USA and Europe in the percentage of people who thought that global warming was a serious threat. However, in Latin America the opposite was happening: an increasing number of people were worried about the effect that global warming was going to have on their families.

It was fitting that Latin America hosted the next two important conferences: the UN Climate Change Conference in Cancun, Mexico at the end of 2010, and the UN Conference on Sustainable Development in Rio de Janeiro, Brazil in June 2012. There was little to show from the Cancun Conference. There was simply an agreement, not a binding treaty, that member states would aim, as a matter of urgency, to reduce emissions of greenhouse gases sufficiently to limit global warming to 2° C. Delegates from 190 nations attended the 2012 Conference in Rio de Janeiro. Brazilian president Dilma Rousseff told the conference that Brazil had made significant progress in reducing emissions, and was now providing 45 per cent of its energy from renewable sources, mainly hydropower. UN secretary-general Ban Ki-moon pointed out that the world had not yet risen to the challenge of reducing greenhouse-gas emissions by concentrating on sustainable development. The outcome of the conference was disappointing: no specific reduction targets were set and a proposed fund of $30 billion to help the transition to a green economy was dropped from the final agreement. Koomi Naidoo, the international director of Greenpeace, described the conference as an epic failure. 'It has failed on equity, failed on ecology and failed on economy.' Ban Ki-moon summed up the situation well. He pointed out that 20 years ago there were 50 billion people in the world; today there are 75 billion. By 2030 we shall need 50 per cent more food and 45 per cent more energy than we need today. 'Let us not forget the scarcest resource of all – time. We are running out of time.' As if to underline his concern, it was announced in September 2012 that sea ice in the Arctic had shrunk to its smallest extent ever recorded. Scientists were predicting that within 20 years the Arctic Ocean would be completely ice-free in the summer months. John Sauven, the head of Greenpeace UK, warned that 'we are on the edge of one of the most significant moments in environmental history as sea ice heads towards a new record low. The loss of sea ice will be devastating, raising global temperatures that will impact on our ability to grow food, and causing extreme weather around the world.'

27.6 THE WORLD ECONOMY AT THE TURN OF THE MILLENNIUM

Since the USA was unquestionably the most powerful state economically during the last decade of the twentieth century, it was natural that the US economic system should come under close scrutiny. The EU, which some people saw as a rival power bloc to the USA, had a rather different view of how a market economy and society should be organized, in terms of international trade, care of the environment, aid and debt relief. According to British analyst Will Hutton, in his book *The World We're In* (2003): 'the relationship between the two power blocs is the fulcrum on which the world order turns. Managed skilfully, this could be a great force for good; managed badly, it could give rise to incalculable harm.'

(a) The American economic model

The US economic system evolved out of American traditions of freedom and the sanctity of property. The American right-wing attitude was that the law of private property and the freedom from government interference should be supreme. This was why the USA came into existence in the first place; people emigrated to the USA so that they could enjoy that freedom. It followed that the US federal government should interfere with people's lives as little as possible, its main function being to safeguard national security.

On the question of social welfare – to what extent the state should be responsible for the care of the poor and helpless – attitudes were divided. The right-wing or conservative attitude was based on 'rugged individualism' and self-help. Taxation was viewed as an invasion of private property, and government regulations were seen as restraints on freedom and prosperity. The liberal attitude was that 'rugged individualism' should be tempered by the idea of a 'social contract'. This held that the state should provide basic welfare in return for the respect and obedience of its citizens. Hence Roosevelt's New Deal and Johnson's Great Society – programmes introduced by Democrat administrations, which included large elements of social reform. For 16 out of the 24 years preceding 2005, the US had Republican governments which favoured the right-wing approach.

Both schools of thought had their supporters and champions in the USA. For example John Rawls, in his book *A Theory of Justice* (Oxford University Press, 1973), put forward a theory of 'justice as fairness'. He argued in favour of equality and claimed that it was the duty of government to provide welfare and some redistribution of wealth through taxation. In reply, Robert Nozick, in his book *Anarchy, State and Utopia* (Harvard University Press, 1974), argued that property rights should be strictly upheld, that there should be minimal government intervention, minimal taxation and minimal welfare and redistribution. Nozick's theories had a great influence on the New Right and were taken up by the neo-conservative branch of the Republican party. They were seen in action during the Reagan administration (1981–9), and even more so under George W. Bush (2001–9), when both taxes and welfare programmes were reduced. With neo-conservatism in the ascendant in the USA, it was only to be expected that, as the USA assumed the role of world leadership, the same principles would be extended to American international dealings; hence American reluctance to become involved in initiatives to help the Third World – on issues such as debt relief, international trade and global warming. There was no denying that the American economic system in its different variants had achieved remarkable success over the years. However, in the early twenty-first century the New Right approach was clearly faltering (see Section 23.6(d)); many liberal Americans were looking towards the European model as a potentially better way of providing a just economic and social order.

(b)   The European economic model

The economic and social systems of western, democratic Europe, which took shape after the Second World War, varied from country to country. But they all shared certain basic characteristics – provision of social welfare and public services, particularly education and health, and a reduction in inequality. It was expected that the state would take an active role in regulating business and society and in operating a tax system that redistributed income more fairly and provided the revenue to finance education and healthcare. There was also the assumption that big business had a part in the social contract – it had respon-sibilities to society and so must function in a socially acceptable way, looking after its employees, paying fair wages and taking care of the environment. Whereas in the USA the interests of shareholders were paramount, in most parts of Europe the perception was that the interests of the entire business must come first; dividends were kept relatively low so that high investment was not neglected. Trade unions were stronger than in the USA, but on the whole they operated responsibly. This system produced highly successful compa-nies and relatively fair and just societies.

Outstanding examples of successful European companies include the German car and truck manufacturer Volkswagen: some 20 per cent of the company's shares are owned by the state government of Lower Saxony, shareholders' voting rights are limited to 20 per cent and the company pays only 16 per cent of its profits as dividends – none of which would be allowed to happen in the USA. Michelin, the French tyre manufacturer, and the Finnish company Nokia, the world's largest manufacturer of mobile phones, are high-performance organizations run on similar lines to Volkswagen. Another European success story is the joint German, French and British Airbus, which can claim to be the world's most successful aircraft manufacturer, surpassing even the USA's Boeing company. Western European states have generous welfare systems financed by a combination of taxa-tion and social security contributions, and a high standard of public health and education. Even in Italy, Spain, Greece and Portugal, with their history of fascism and military dicta-torships, the social contract exists, and unemployment insurance is the highest in Europe.

Many American analysts were critical of the European system, since during the 1990s unemployment rose in Europe, while the USA enjoyed an economic boom. The Americans claimed that European problems were caused by high taxation, over-generous welfare systems, the activities of trade unions and too much regulation. Europeans blamed their difficulties on the need to keep inflation under control so that they would be able to join the single currency launched in 1999. Europeans were confident that once that hurdle had been surmounted, economic growth and job creation would recover. European confidence in their system received a boost during the Bush administration, when it was observed that all was not well with the US economy.

(c)   The American system in action

Even during the Clinton administration, the USA extended its economic principles into its global dealings. American interests usually came first, so much so that many people complained that globalization meant Americanization. Some examples were:

- During the 1990s the USA gained control of the International Monetary Fund (IMF), which meant that the Americans could decide which countries should receive aid, and could insist that governments adopted policies of which the USA approved. This happened to many Latin American countries as well as Korea, Indonesia and Thailand. Often the conditions imposed made recovery harder instead of easier. In 1995, when the World Bank suggested that debt relief was vital for some poor countries, it met stiff opposition from the USA, and its chief economist felt compelled to resign. Basically these developments meant that the USA could control the world's financial system.

- In 1994 the USA used the General Agreement on Tariffs and Trade (GATT) to force the EU to open all its voice communications (post, telephone and telegraphs) to international competition. In 1997 the World Trade Organization (WTO), which succeeded GATT in 1995, agreed that 70 countries should be opened up to US telecoms companies on American terms. By 2002 there were 180 commercial satellites orbiting in space, and 174 of them were American. The USA all but controlled the world's communications systems. It was to counter this that the EU insisted on launching its own Galileo space satellite system (see Section 10.8(d)).

- In March 2002 the Bush administration imposed import duties on foreign steel in order to protect the American steel industry. This brought bitter protests from the EU, since the function of the WTO was to encourage free trade. The USA resisted the pressure until December 2003; then, faced with threats of retaliatory duties on a wide range of American goods, President Bush cancelled the steel tariffs. In the same month, however, the US announced new tariffs on imports of textiles and television sets from China.

- In 2003 there was one positive step which benefited poorer countries: responding to worldwide protests from states suffering the worst ravages of HIV/AIDS, President Bush agreed that the patents controlling the necessary drugs should be overridden, allowing far cheaper versions to be produced for sale in the worst affected states. There was an ulterior motive, however: in return, the Americans were hoping to gain access to African oil and to set up military bases in strategic parts of the continent.

There was a long way to go before globalization produced a fair and just world in which wealth was more evenly distributed. Some observers believed that the way forward was in a reinvigorated and strengthened UN; others saw the newly enlarged EU as the best hope. The participation of the USA – the world's richest nation – was still thought to be vital. As Will Hutton put it: 'We badly need the better America back – the liberal, outward-looking and generous US that won World War II and constructed a liberal world order that in many respects has sustained us to this day.' South African president Thabo Mbeki summed up the world situation admirably in July 2003 when he wrote: 'The progressive politicians must demonstrate whether they have the courage to define themselves as progressive, recovering their historic character as champions of the poor, and break the icy ideological grip of right-wing politics. The African masses are watching and waiting.' Sadly, what happened next can hardly have been more disappointing for them. The participation of the USA was still very much in evidence, but not quite in the way the commentators hoped for.

27.7 CAPITALISM IN CRISIS

(a) Meltdown – the Great Crash of 2008

On 15 June 2007 Ben S. Bernanke, chairman of the American Federal Reserve Bank, made a long speech in which he extolled the virtues of the American financial system:

In the United States, a deep and liquid financial system has promoted growth by effectively allocating capital, and has increased economic resilience by increasing our ability to share and diversify risks both domestically and globally.

There was, he said, no possibility of a financial crisis in America. Yet, little over a year later the American system and the whole global economy seemed to be on the verge of total collapse. In fact some experts had been predicting collapse for some years, but had been proved wrong. However, in March 2008 the unthinkable happened – it was revealed that one of the oldest and most respected Wall Street investment banks, Bear Stearns, was in serious trouble. It had lost $1.6 billion when some affiliated hedge funds collapsed, but much worse, it had a problem with bad debts estimated at $220 billion. Reluctantly, US treasury secretary, Henry Paulson, decided that Bear Stearns could not be allowed to collapse, since that might inconvenience or even ruin many of the rich citizens who had entrusted their wealth to the bank. There was a rule that the US government should never bail out an investment bank, so it was arranged that another bank, J. P. Morgan, should be provided with Federal Reserve funds to enable it to take over Bear Stearns. This indirect Federal Reserve bailout of Bear Stearns saved the system from collapsing. Unfortunately, it also left the impression that any other bank that got itself into difficulties would always be able to rely on a government bailout. In financial circles this was described as 'moral hazard' – the idea that there are some investors who believe that they are 'too big to fail', and who therefore take reckless risks.

The fourth largest bank on Wall Street, Lehman Brothers, had been struggling for over a year with problems of bad debts and a shortage of capital. In August 2008 it too was on the verge of bankruptcy and no other bank was willing to bail it out. In September its European branch based in London was put into administration, but there was wide expectation in the USA that the government would come to the rescue with a Bear Stearns-type deal. But this time there was to be no bailout – Tim Geithner of the Federal Reserve of New York state announced that there was 'no political will' for a Federal rescue. Lehman Brothers was allowed to go bankrupt; it was the largest US company until then ever to go bust. The collapse sent shock waves around the world, and share prices plummeted. Why was Lehman Brothers allowed to collapse? Government and state financial bosses like Paulson and Geithner were determined that there should be no such thing as 'moral hazard' – state takeovers should not become a habit, because it was seen as state capitalism. In a country that almost worshipped free-market capitalism, the idea that private companies and banks should be subsidized or taken over by the government was sacrilege. One leading financier remarked: 'I just think it is disgusting; this is not American.'

Unfortunately, the crisis worsened rapidly and the government found it impossible to maintain its free-market stance. Another struggling investment bank, Merrill Lynch, was taken over by the Bank of America (BOA). Then came the biggest sensation so far: a giant insurance company, American International Group (AIG), asked the government for a loan of $40 billion to stave off bankruptcy. Like the failing investment banks, AIG had too many bad or 'toxic' debts, as they were now being called. The government was in a dilemma: AIG was so big and had done so much business with most of the major financial institutions worldwide, that if it were allowed to collapse the repercussions would be catastrophic. Consequently it was decided that AIG should be bailed out with a government loan of $85 billion, although the state took an 80 per cent stake in the company. In effect, the US government had nationalized AIG, though the word itself was never used.

The UK banking system was already in trouble before the US crisis began, mainly because the Bank of England was reluctant to pump money into the system and failed to reduce interest rates on borrowing. The UK mortgage bank, Northern Rock, which had been forced to reduce its lending because of its own dependence on short-term borrowing (see below (**b**)*3*), collapsed in September 2007. It was eventually nationalized at a cost of some £100 billion. In September 2008 Halifax Bank of Scotland (HBOS) was saved from collapse when it was taken over by Lloyds TSB for £12 billion in a deal arranged by British prime minister Gordon Brown. However, its share price fell rapidly, so that only a few weeks later its value had slumped to £4 billion. This brought Lloyds TSB to its knees as well and it too had to be rescued by the government. Royal Bank of Scotland (RBS) was partly nationalized, so that it became 83 per cent taxpayer-owned. Shares in European banks followed suit; Fortis, the huge Dutch–Belgian bank, lost almost half its value in just a few days and was taken into joint ownership by the two governments. In Germany, France, the Irish Republic and Iceland similar bailouts were taking place. And most of this happened in just a few days in September 2008. The situation was exacerbated by millions of ordinary depositors rushing to withdraw their funds from the banks. Lending between banks had more or less dried up because the inter-bank lending rates (known as LIBOR) were prohibitive.

By the time the crisis passed, the US Treasury had acquired stakes in several more major financial institutions, including Goldman Sachs, Morgan Stanley, J. P. Morgan Chase, and two mortgage underwriters, Freddie Mac and Fannie Mae. The function of these last two institutions was not to provide mortgages directly to house-buyers, but to act as an insurance by underwriting mortgages given by other banks. Much of the help was provided under the Bush administration's Troubled Asset Relief Program (TARP) and later by the Obama administration's Public–Private Investment Program. According to an official report in July 2009, TARP had saddled the taxpayers of the USA with a debt of $27.3 trillion. By that time the crisis had developed into a global recession. The whole bailout operation was extremely controversial. President Bush was accused of being un-American and of introducing socialism. To get the TARP approved by Congress it was necessary to attach several conditions: limits on executive pay, a cap on dividends and the right of the government to take stakes in the ailing banks.

(b) What were the causes of the great crash?

Paul Mason, economics editor of the BBC *Newsnight* programme, sums up the causes of the crisis neatly in his book *Meltdown* (2010):

> If you exalt the money-changers, exhort them to make more money and hail the ascendancy of speculative finance as a 'golden age', this is what you get. The responsibility for what happened must lie, as well as with any banker found to have broken the law, with regulators, politicians and the media who failed to hold them up to scrutiny.

He argues that the system known as neo-liberalism that had been in operation for the last quarter of a century was mainly responsible for the catastrophe. In the words of Sir Keith Joseph, a UK Conservative supporter of the free-market system, neo-liberalism involved 'the strict and unflinching control of money supply, substantial cuts in tax and public spending and bold incentives and encouragements to the wealth creators'.

Beginning in the last decade of the twentieth century, globalization played an important role, as national economies became interlinked as never before. In the 20 years after 1990 the world's labour force doubled and with the increase in migration, became global. China and the former Soviet bloc joined the world economy. The greater availability of labour brought a fall in real wages in the leading western economies, including the USA, Japan and Germany. Yet consumption grew, made possible by a massive increase in credit and the heyday of the credit-card era. The credit boom seemed sustainable at first but after 2000 the debts began to run out of control. At the same time capital flowed around as western financiers began to invest abroad more than ever before, and this caused a huge rise in global imbalances. For example, China's foreign currency reserves grew from $150 billion in 1999 to $2.85 trillion in 2010; but between 1989 and 2007 the US deficit increased from $99 billion to $800 billion. So long as the US housing boom continued, the situation was just about sustainable, but once house prices began to falter, chaos was unleashed as the amount of toxic debts soared. To look at the steps towards meltdown in more detail:

1   The deregulation of the US banking industry in 1999–2000
In November 1999 the US Congress passed an act designed to promote economic growth through competition and freedom. This cancelled the regulation, dating from the Depression of the 1930s, that prevented investment banks from handling the savings and deposits of the general public, and meant that they now had access to far larger funds. Banks were also allowed to act as insurance companies. A year later futures and all other derivatives were exempted from being classified as gambling and all attempts to regulate the derivatives market were declared illegal. Probably the most common type of derivatives are futures; a future is a contract in which you agree to buy something at a future date, but at a price decided on now. The hope is that in the meantime the price will go up, enabling you to sell it again at a profit. The actual contract between the two parties can itself be sold and resold several times before the agreed date. However, there is a risk involved: in the meantime the price might fall, but you still have to pay the agreed price. Another type of derivative develops when observers start betting among themselves on whether the original contract will be fulfilled. The option derivative is similar to a future except that you simply agree the option to buy, rather than actually buying the commodity itself.

The deregulation, together with the spread of the latest computer technology, was certainly a 'bold incentive and encouragement' to the bankers who now had a free hand to indulge in all these types of speculation. It enabled the derivatives market to become global, and foreign-exchange dealing increased rapidly. In the two years leading up to the crash, there was a massive rush of money into derivatives and currency trading. The statistics are staggering: in 2007 the total value of the world's stock market companies was $63 trillion; but the total value of derivative investments stood at $596 trillion – eight times the size of the real economy. It was as though there were two parallel economies – the real economy and a kind of phantom or fantasy economy which only existed on paper. Admittedly, not all the derivative dealings were speculative, but enough of them were risky to cause concern among perceptive financiers. As early as 2002 Warren Buffett, probably the world's most successful investor, warned that derivatives were a time bomb, financial weapons of mass destruction, because in the last resort, neither banks nor governments knew how to control them. Paul Mason concludes that since the end of the 1990s, 'this new global finance system has injected gross instability into the world economy'. By October 2008, even Alan Greenspan, a former chairman of the Federal Reserve, who had always claimed that banks could be trusted to regulate themselves, was forced to admit that he had been wrong. By the time the crisis peaked, some 360 banks had received capital from the US government.

2   Sub-prime mortgages and the collapse of the US housing market
The long-running housing boom in the USA reached a peak towards the end of 2005. House prices had been rising steadily and had reached levels that could not be sustained. Too many houses had been built, demand gradually fell and so did prices. The unfortunate thing was that many houses, especially during the latter stages of the boom, had been bought using sub-prime mortgages. These are mortgages lent to borrowers who have a high risk of being unable to keep up the payments, and for that reason sub-prime borrowers have to pay a higher interest rate. As house prices were rising, mortgage providers were able to repossess houses whose buyers defaulted on their mortgage payments, and make a

profit from selling them on. When house prices began to fall, many lenders foolishly continued to push sub-prime mortgages, and suffered heavy losses when the buyers defaulted. The more careful mortgage providers took out insurance to underwrite their loans, so insurance companies like AIG, Freddie Mac and Fannie Mae were faced with huge payouts. Niall Ferguson, in one of his 2012 Reith Lectures, suggested that Freddie and Fannie should take a large slice of the blame for the crisis, because they encouraged people who really couldn't afford to do so to take out mortgages.

Another of the practices that contributed to the meltdown was known as collateral debt obligation (CDOs). This was the packaging together of different debts and bonds for sale as assets; a package might include sub-prime mortgages, credit-card debts and any kind of debt, and anybody buying the package would hope to receive reasonable interest payments. In fact since the year 2000, buyers, which included investment banks, pension funds and building societies, had been receiving interest payments on average between 2 and 3 per cent higher than if the debts had not been bundled up. But then several things went wrong – houses prices fell by around 25 per cent, more people defaulted on the mortgage payments than had been expected, unemployment rose, and many people were unable to pay off their credit-card debts. One estimate put the likely losses to buyers at $3.1 trillion.

3 Leverage, short selling and short-termism
These were other tactics in which banks indulged in order to make money, and which eventually ended in disaster. Leverage is using borrowed money to increase your assets which can then be sold at a profit when the value increases. Lehman was guilty of this, having a very high leverage level of 44. This means that every $1 million owned by the bank had been stretched by borrowing so that they were able to buy assets valued at $44 million. In a time of inflation like the period 2003–6, these assets could be sold at a comfortable profit. But it was gamble, because only a small downward movement in the value of the assets would be enough to break the bank. As John Lanchester explains:

> Lehman made gigantic investments in the property market, not just in the now notorious sub-prime mortgages, but also to a huge extent in commercial property. In effect, Fuld [Richard Fuld, head of Lehman Brothers] allowed his colleagues to bet the bank on the US property market. We all know what happened next.

As US house prices collapsed and the number of mortgage defaulters soared, Lehman was left with debts of $613 billion. In the words of Warren Buffett: 'when the tide goes out it reveals those who are swimming naked'.

Short selling is a strange process in which the investor first borrows, for a fee, shares from a bank or other institution which is not planning to sell the shares itself. The investor then sells the shares in the hope that their price will fall. If and when this happens, he buys the shares back, returns them to the owner and keeps the difference. It is the company whose shares are being sold and bought that suffers, as illustrated by the plight of Morgan Stanley. As the crisis deepened investors began to move their money out. In three days 10 per cent of the cash on Morgan Stanley's books was withdrawn. The share price began to fall and this was the signal for short sellers to unload their Morgan Stanley shares, sending the share price plunging further.

Short-termism is the common banking practice of lending money for long terms and borrowing it for short terms – you issue a long-term loan and fund it by short-term borrowing yourself. When lending between banks dried up in September 2008 following the rush of depositors to withdraw cash, many banks were unable to pay out. This was because they had lent too much out on long-term loans which they could not get back immediately, and had failed to keep to the rule that they must hold a large enough 'cushion' to fall back on.

Many banks tried to get round this regulation by setting up a sort of 'shadow' banking system. Paul Mason explains how the system worked:

> The essence of the shadow banking system is that it is designed to get round the need for any capital cushion at all. Almost everybody in the shadow system was 'borrowing short' by buying a piece of paper on the vast international money market, and then 'lending long' by selling a different piece of paper into that same money market. So it was basically just traditional banking: but they were doing it with no depositors, no shareholders and no capital cushion to fall back on. They were pure intermediaries. They did it by exploiting a loophole in the regulations to create two kinds of off-balance sheet companies known as 'conduits' and 'structured investment vehicles' (SIVs). ... The conduits were set up by banks in offshore tax havens. The bank would, theoretically, be liable for any losses, but it did not have to show this on its annual accounts.

Incredible as it may seem, all this was kept secret from investors, which didn't matter when all was running smoothly. But there was one huge flaw in the system: it could only work as long as bankers continued to buy and sell everything on offer. As soon as short-term credit was no longer available, bankers could not fund their long term loans, and inevitably some pieces of paper became unsaleable.

4   Regulators and credit-rating agencies failed to do their job satisfactorily
Since 2000, thanks to the actions of both the US and UK governments, regulation of the banking system had been exercised with what can only be described as a light touch. The politicians were apparently happy to continue this non-interventionist attitude since bankers had played an important part in achieving the consumer boom and full employment. They mistakenly believed that bankers could therefore be trusted not to do anything too risky. The credit-rating agencies were the second line of defence against high risk. The three main agencies are Standard and Poor's, Moody's and Fitch. Their job is to carry out a risk-assessment process on banks, companies and assets and award grades showing investors whether or not it would be safe to do business with them. The safest gets an AAA rating, while BB or less indicates a high-risk institution or commodity. Between 2001 and 2007 the amount of money paid to the three main credit rating agencies doubled, reaching a total of $6 billion. Yet an official report published in July 2007 was highly critical of the work of the rating agencies. They were accused of being unable to show convincing evidence that their methods of assessment were reliable, especially in the case of CDOs. They were unable to cope with the vast increase in the amount of new business that they were called on to do since 2000. Many critics saw the whole system as suspect: the fact that institutions and sellers of bonds actually paid for their own ratings invited 'collusion'; if they gave the correct ratings, they risked upsetting the banking business and losing market share. As a result, no decisive action was taken until it was too late. For example, it was only a matter of hours before the British HBOS collapsed in September 2008 that Standard and Poor's downgraded it, and even then the comforting phrase, 'but the outlook is stable', was added.

(c)   The aftermath of the crash

Although the capitalist financial system had been saved from total collapse, the consequences of the crisis were clearly going to be felt for a long time. As the money supply dried up, demand for goods fell, and across the world, manufacturing industry slumped. Many of the weakest companies went to the wall and unemployment rocketed. In the USA in the first few months of 2009 it was calculated that around half a million jobs a month were being lost. The great exporting nations like China, Japan, South Korea and Germany suffered huge falls in exports. Although central bank interest rates were almost zero in the USA and Britain, nobody was investing to try to stimulate the still declining economy. Attempts to deal with this problem included:

- Fiscal stimulus provided by governments and central banks. As early as November 2009 the Chinese government had decided to supply cash worth $580 billion over the next two years to fund various environmental projects. Banks were encouraged to lend vast sums of money, guaranteed by the state, to fund other projects. Millions of new jobs were created, and within a few months China's economic growth rate had recovered and surpassed its previous high point. The main problem was the uncertainty about how risky those massive bank loans were.

  In the USA, newly elected Democrat president Barack Obama's fiscal stimulus of $787 billion went into operation in February 2009. It was a controversial move because the Republican party was totally against it; even in a crisis as serious as this, they believed that the state should not be expected to provide help. A right-wing Republican group calling themselves the Tea Party Movement launched an anti-stimulus protest campaign encouraging Republican state governors not to accept stimulus money. Although the US economy did begin to grow again towards the end of 2009 and continued slowly through 2010, there were still 15 million unemployed at the end of the year.

  In the EU the effects of the crisis varied among its 27 member states. They experienced different degrees of recession, though the average growth reduction at the end of 2009 was 4.7 per cent. The three Baltic states fared the worst, suffering full-scale slump: Estonia's GDP fell by 14 per cent, Lithuania's by 15 per cent and Latvia's by 18 per cent. France did best, losing only 3 per cent of GDP. Most states borrowed heavily in order to launch fiscal-stimulus packages. For example, in 2009 France's borrowing was equivalent to 8 per cent of GDP and Britain's was 11 per cent. These amounts were quite small compared with America's and China's, but in the case of France they were successful: as early as August 2009 the French economy was growing again. The problem was that they were all left with massive national debts. Those countries which had signed up to the Maastricht Agreement of 1991 (see Section 10.4(h)) had broken the rules that borrowing must not exceed 3 per cent of GDP and total debt must be limited to 60 per cent of GDP.

- Quantitative easing (QE). This was the practice, first thought of by John Maynard Keynes back in the 1930s, of increasing the amounts of cash in circulation by 'printing money'. In fact nowadays banks do not actually print new notes; the central banks simply invent or create more money which is added into their reserves, and then used to buy up government debts. The UK was the first to use QE in March 2009 when a modest £150 billion was 'created', and this to some extent helped to put demand back into the system. According to Paul Mason, 'Britain's "pure" QE strategy saw it inject around 12 per cent of GDP into the economy. The Bank of England estimates this should, over a period of three to four years, filter through into a 12 per cent increase in the money supply and thus in demand.' The USA adopted QE soon after Britain. However, the European Central Bank rejected QE on the grounds that it would threaten the stability of the euro. It was argued that simply making more of the existing money available to eurozone banks and buying AAA-rated bonds would be sufficient to stimulate demand. But demand was not sufficiently stimulated and consequently the value of the euro was weakened. By the end of 2009 the eurozone was in big trouble as the cost of all the fiscal stimulus and bank bailouts had to be faced. Some economists were already predicting that the zone was on the verge of break-up. In fact some economists and politicians *hoped* it would break up, so this seemed an unmissable opportunity!

(d) The eurozone in crisis

The financial crisis in Greece sparked things off. In October 2009 the newly elected social-democrat government discovered that the country's budget deficit – which stood at 6 per cent according to the previous government – was in reality 12.7 per cent. Over half its actual debt, with a little assistance from Goldman Sachs, had been moved into the shadow-banking system, 'off balance sheet'. It later emerged that there were serious flaws in the Greek system that had allowed massive tax evasion and other corrupt practices, such as pensions still being paid to families of the deceased. The immediate problem was that Greece had financed its national debt with short-term loans, a quarter of which were due for repayment in 2010. How were they going to find the necessary €50 billion? The first step was to introduce strict austerity policies – cuts in pensions, wages and social services and a campaign to eliminate tax evasion. Eventually in May 2010 the eurozone banks and the IMF agreed a loan of €110 billion to Greece, provided they fulfilled the austerity programme. This was extremely unpopular with the Greeks, and resulted in strikes and two general elections over the next two years. By the autumn of 2011 there seemed a real danger that Greece would default on its debts. Worried about the disastrous effects this might have on other members of the eurozone, leaders agreed to write off half of Greece's debts to private creditors.

Meanwhile some other eurozone countries had also got themselves too heavily in debt. In November 2011 the Republic of Ireland had to be helped with a bailout of €85 billion. Portugal, which had suffered crippling competition from Germany and China, was on the verge of bankruptcy. In July 2011 Moody's had downgraded Portugal's debt to 'junk' status, and in October it too received an IMF bailout. Portugal had the lowest GDP per capita in western Europe and in March 2012 the unemployment rate was around 15 per cent. By August 2011 Spain and Italy had drifted into the danger zone. Paul Mason explains what happened next (in *Why It's Kicking Off Everywhere: The New Global Revolutions* (2012)):

> The European Central Bank was forced to break its own rules and start buying up the debt of these two massive, unbailable economies. The dilemma throughout the euro crisis has been clear: whether to impose losses from south European bad debts onto north European taxpayers, or onto the bankers who had actually lent the money to these bankrupt countries in the first place. The outcome was always a function of the level of class struggle. By hitting the streets, Greek people were able to force Europe to impose losses on the bankers; where opposition remained within traditional boundaries – the one-day strike, the passive demo – it was the workers, youth and pensioners who took the pain. Meanwhile Europe itself was plunged into institutional crisis. Monetary union without fiscal union had failed.

27.8 THE WORLD ECONOMIES IN 2012

At the turn of the millennium 'globalization' had been the buzzword. It seemed to promise huge benefits for the world – increased connectivity between countries, faster growth, greater transfer of knowledge and wealth, and perhaps even a fairer distribution of wealth. Economists talked about the 'BRIC' countries, meaning Brazil, Russia, India and China. These were the world's fastest growing and largest emerging market economies, and between them they contained almost half the world's population. Many economists were predicting that it was only a matter of time before China became the largest economy in the world, probably some time between 2030 and 2050. Goldman Sachs believed that by 2020 all the BRIC countries would be in the world's top 10 economies, and that by 2050 they would be the top four, with China in first place. The USA was expected to have been relegated to fifth place.

There were differing views about actual details of how this scenario would play out. In 2008 the BRIC countries held a summit conference. Many analysts got the impression that they had ulterior motives of turning their growing economic strength into some kind of political power. They could carve out the future economic order between themselves. China would continue to dominate world markets in manufactured goods, India would specialize in providing services, while Russia and Brazil would be the leading suppliers of raw materials. By working together in this way the BRIC states can present an effective challenge to the entrenched interests and systems of the West. However, the fact that these four countries have very little in common could mean that any economic and political co-operation would only be temporary, or rather artificial. Once China becomes the world's largest economy, it might not need the other three. In that case it could be China and the USA that work together to lead the global economy.

It was not immediately obvious how the 2008 meltdown would affect the BRIC nations. Many economists believed it would be possible for them to 'decouple' themselves from the West and continue growing. This turned out not to be the case and many commentators began to doubt whether globalization had been a 'good thing' after all. It seemed as if it had made the world economy less stable, more volatile, and more vulnerable to the danger of a crisis in one country infecting the rest of the world. A brief survey of the world's leading states shows that, unfortunately, very few were able to avoid the contagion. As a report from Crédit Suisse said: 'We may not be at the brink of a new global recession, but we are even less likely to be at the threshold of a global boom.'

(a) China

As we saw earlier, the financial crisis of 2008 caused an immediate drop in China's exports. China launched a great spending spree in 2008 and 2009 to improve the country's infrastructure and launch a number of environmental projects. This seemed to work at first and China's growth rate soon recovered. However, this policy was continued through 2010 and 2011 when the total investment was an unprecedented 49 per cent of China's GDP. There were several problems with this state of affairs. Most observers believed that there was a limit to the number of roads, airports and high-rise flats that China could keep on building, and they feared that there had been an unsustainable building bubble that was about to burst, just as similar bubbles burst earlier in the USA, Spain and Portugal. The concentration on domestic consumption and reduced demand from overseas meant that exports, and therefore revenue from exports, were continuing to decline, and the growth rate was slowing. The Chinese themselves were extremely nervous about their own vulnerability in view of the continuing crisis in the eurozone. So much so that in June 2012, along with India, they contributed tens of billions of dollars to the IMF's emergency fund for tackling the EU's ongoing problems.

(b) Brazil

Like China, Brazil initially responded well to the 2008 economic crisis, launching a massive property-building project. This created thousands of new jobs and unemployment fell to its lowest level for many years. Domestic demand continued at a high level. The economy continued to grow, receiving a huge boost with the discovery of more oil and gas reserves off the coast. By 2012 Brazil had become the world's ninth largest oil producer, and was hoping eventually to become the fifth largest. It had overtaken Britain and was now rated to be the sixth largest economy in the world. Other good news was that poverty was decreasing – over the last few years, the incomes of the poorest 50 per cent of the population have increased by almost 70 per cent. Brazil will host the 2014 soccer World Cup and the 2016 Summer Olympics will take place in Rio de Janeiro.

However, the latest reports suggest that all is not well in Brazil. House prices in Rio have trebled since 2008, causing mortgage borrowing to rocket and raising the prospect of yet another crash if and when the housing bubble should burst. Since some of Brazil's main exports included raw materials and oil to China, the slow-down in Chinese exports of manufactured goods and the general decline in global demand did not bode well for Brazil's export trade, especially taking into account the 30 per cent fall in oil prices. Domestic demand fell as consumer confidence waned, and all the analysts were predicting a dramatic slowdown in growth.

(c)   India

India's economy had been expanding rapidly and words like 'dynamic' and 'rampaging Asian tiger' had been used to describe it. However, as the financial crisis hit the USA and Europe, demand for Indian goods plummeted and was still falling in 2012. In fact, Indian exports fell by a further 3 per cent in the year from May 2011 to May 2012. As the economy slowed down, investors began to desert India, preferring something safer, like the US dollar. This sent the value of the rupee plunging until in June 2012 it reached a record low against the dollar. In theory this should help Indian exports, which would be cheaper; but on the other hand it made India's imports more expensive, and this pushed up the cost of living, making even essentials difficult to afford. In addition India had further problems: much of its infrastructure was in a dilapidated state, and businesses complained of being hampered by corruption, bribery and unnecessary bureaucracy. The country's current account deficit stood at $49 billion in June 2011 and was estimated to be $72 billion at the end of 2012, which would be over four per cent of India's GDP. According to Morgan Stanley, a sustainable deficit ought to be no more than two per cent of GDP. Standard and Poor's and Fitch both reduced their ratings of the Indian economy to 'negative', though Moody's continued to rate it as 'stable'. Clearly India had failed to 'decouple' itself from the problems of the eurozone. Desperate for the eurozone crisis to be resolved, in June 2012 India joined China in making a substantial contribution to the IMF's emergency fund.

(d)   Russia

Up until 2008 the Russian economy enjoyed ten years of spectacular growth thanks mainly to high oil prices. GDP increased tenfold, and by 2008 revenues from oil and gas were worth around $200 billion, about one-third of total revenue. The fact that the economy was so dependent on the price of oil meant that there could be no 'decoupling' from the rest of the world's economic problems. The rapid fall in oil prices and in demand for oil had a disastrous effect on Russia: in 2008 the price per barrel plunged from $140 to $40, causing a drastic fall in revenue. The foreign credits that Russian banks and businesses had relied on quickly dried up, leaving many firms unable to pay their debts. The government was forced to help them by providing $200 billion to increase liquidity in the Russian banking sector. The Russian Central Bank also spent a third of its $600 billion international currency reserve fund to slow down the devaluation of the rouble. Fortunately, by the middle of 2009 the slump had bottomed out and the economy began to grow again. In 2011, as well as becoming the world's leading oil producer, surpassing Saudi Arabia, Russia also became the second largest producer of natural gas and the third largest exporter of steel and aluminium. The high price of oil in 2011 helped the recovery and enabled Russia to reduce the large budget deficit that had accrued during the lean period in 2008 and early 2009.

However, recognizing the danger of being too dependent on oil, the government successfully encouraged the expansion of other areas. In 2012 Russia was the world's second largest producer of armaments, including military aircraft, after the USA, and the IT industry had a year of record growth. Companies making nuclear power plants were expanding, and several plants were exported to China and India. In 2012 statistics showed that Russia was the third richest country in the world in terms of cash reserves; inflation had been reduced and unemployment had fallen. Nor was the expansion confined to Moscow and St Petersburg; other cities, including Nizhny Novgorod, Samara and Volgograd (formerly Stalingrad), were playing an important role in the diversification of industry. Of the four BRIC nations Russia was clearly the strongest economically.

(e) The USA

Unemployment, which had stood at 15 per cent at the end of 2010, continued to fall, but only slowly. Fitch ratings agency estimated that President Obama's fiscal stimulus packages boosted US GDP by 4 per cent over the following two years. However, according to a *Guardian* report (27 June 2012), 'the US economy is still limping along with very slow growth and a high rate of unemployment. Although the economy has been expanding for three years, the level of GDP is still only 1 per cent higher than it was nearly five years ago. Recent data shows falling real personal incomes, declining employment gains, and lower retail sales.' Another problem was that, although mortgage interest rates were low, house prices have continued to fall and in 2012 were 10 per cent lower in real terms than they were two years ago.

At the end of June 2012 the Organization for Economic Co-operation and Development (OECD), the Paris-based group of independent economists from 34 countries, produced its biannual report on the US economy. This confirmed that the US recovery remained fragile and pointed out that two of the main problems were record long-term unemployment and the widening gap between the poor and the wealthy. About 5.3 million Americans, 40 per cent of unemployed people, have been out of work for six months or more. Poverty in the US is worse than in Europe, and of the 34 OECD member states, only Chile, Mexico and Turkey rank higher in terms of income inequality. The report also suggested measures to remedy the situation:

- Equalize tax rates by ending tax breaks for the very wealthy – in other words, make the rich pay more. Earlier in 2012 the government proposed a measure to make sure that everyone making more than a million dollars a year pays at least 30 per cent in tax. Predictably, this was strongly opposed by the Republicans.
- Provide more investment for education and innovation, and more training programmes to get the long-term unemployed back to work.
- Increase gas prices to help reduce the use of fossil fuels.
- The government should reduce spending, but only gradually, rather than make drastic cuts; these might discourage business investment and slow growth even further.

How the situation would develop depended very much on the results of the presidential and congressional elections held in November 2012. Tax cuts for the wealthy introduced during the Bush administration were due to end on 31 December 2012. Another hangover from the Bush era was that automatic spending cuts would be applied at the end of 2012. The cuts involved, dubbed 'the fiscal cliff', would amount to $1.2 trillion.

(e) The European Union

In the summer of 2012 the future looked uncertain. In June there were tense elections in Greece when the party that was prepared to continue the austerity policy won a narrow victory over the socialist party that resented having austerity forced on the country by outsiders, and was determined to abandon the euro. And so the euro survived again. There was also resentment in some of the more economically successful north European states, especially in Germany, at having to bail out what many saw as the 'feckless, reckless and lazy' south. The most likely outcome seemed to be that the taxpayers of northern Europe would bail out the south and would, in effect, take control of overall eurozone economic policy, so that the eurozone would become much closer to being a fiscal union, and therefore, to some extent, a political union as well. Of course the governments of southern Europe resisted losing overall control of their economic policies; but without a bailout of some sort – the eurozone seemed likely to disintegrate.

On the other hand, many economists and financiers believed that the euro must be saved. In September 2012 Mario Draghi, the president of the European Central Bank (ECB), announced: 'We say that the euro is irreversible. So, unfounded fears of reversibility are just that – unfounded fears.' It was felt that the collapse of the euro would throw the entire global economy into chaos. Certainly Germany wanted the euro saved, because the cheap euro benefited German exports, whereas a strong Deutschmark would do considerable damage to their exports. Hopes for the survival of the euro revived in September 2012 when Mario Draghi unveiled a rescue plan that involved the ECB buying up the bonds of Spain and Italy, the two eurozone countries after Greece most heavily in debt. Those governments could then request a bailout from the ECB which would be granted, provided they agreed to implement strict austerity measures. The announcement of the plan received a glowing reception across most of Europe; stock markets soared on both sides of the Atlantic, and so did confidence in the euro's survival. This was sufficient to bring down borrowing costs for Spain and Italy, and their future seemed brighter. Even the Germans agreed to go along with the scheme. At first the German Bundesbank condemned the whole idea as 'tantamount to financing governments by printing banknotes'. But eventually, after pressure from Chancellor Merkel and Mario Draghi himself, followed a few days later by the approval of the German constitutional court, the Bundesbank, albeit rather grudgingly, agreed to back the plan. The European Stability Mechanism (ESM), as it was now known, was poised to go into operation with the creation of a rescue fund of €500 billion.

FURTHER READING

Archer, D. and Rahmstorf, S., *The Climate Crisis* (Cambridge University Press, 2009).
Brandt, W., *World Armament and World Hunger* (Gollancz, 1986).
The Brandt Report: North-South, A Programme for Survival (Pan, 1980).
Cohan, W., *Money and Power: How Goldman Sachs Came to Rule the World* (Allen Lane, 2011).
Giddens, A., *The Politics of Climate Change* (Polity, 2nd edition, 2011).
Harvey, D., *The Enigma of Capital and the Crises of Capitalism* (Profile, 2010).
Hulme, M., *Why We Disagree About Climate Change* (Cambridge University Press, 2009).

Hutton, W., *The World We're In* (Abacus, 2003).
Hutton, W., *The Writing on the Wall: China and the West in the 21st Century* (Abacus, 2008).
Kenwood, G., Lougheed, A. and Graff, M., *Growth of the International Economy, 1820–2012* (Routledge, 2012).
Lanchester, J., 'Cityphobia', *London Review of Books* (23 October 2008).
Lanchester, J., 'The Great British Economy Disaster', *London Review of Books* (11 March 2010).
Lanchester, J., 'On the Global Economy, *London Review of Books* (8 September 2011).
Laqueur, W., *After the Fall: The End of the European Dream and the Decline of a Continent* (Thomas Dunne, 2012).
Lloyd, J., *The Protest Ethic: How the Anti-Globalisation Movement Challenges Social Democracy* (Demos, 2001).
Mason, P., *Meltdown: The End of the Age of Greed* (Verso, 2010 edition).
Mason, P., *Why It's Kicking Off Everywhere: The New Global Revolutions* (Verso, 2012).
Mattick, P., *Business As Usual: The Economic Crisis and the Failure of Capitalism* (Reaktion Books, 2011).
McDonald, L., *A Colossal Failure of Common Sense: The Incredible Inside Story of the Collapse of Lehman Brothers* (Ebury, 2009).
Moss, N., *Managing the Planet: The Politics of the New Millennium* (Earthscan, 2009).
Peston, R., *Who Runs Britain: and Who's to Blame for the Economic Mess We're in?* (Hodder, 2008).
Posner, R. A., *A Failure of Capitalism* (Harvard University Press, 2009).
Rifkin, J., *The European Dream: How Europe's Vision of the Future is Eclipsing the American Dream* (Polity, 2004).
Tett, G., *Fool's Gold: How Unrestrained Greed Corrupted a Dream, Shattered Global Markets and Unleashed a Catastrophe* (Abacus, 2010).
Victor, D. G., *The Collapse of the Kyoto Protocol and the Struggle to Slow Global Warming* (Princeton University Press, 2004).

QUESTIONS

1 What is meant by the term 'North–South divide'? What attempts have been made since 1980 to close the gap between North and South, and how successful have they been?
2 Assess the reasons why global warming is seen as such a serious problem for the world's future. To what extent do you think it is the twenty-first century's major problem?
3 Explain why there was a 'crisis of capitalism' in the decade leading up to 2012.

There is a document question about pollution and global warming on the website.

28

The world's population

SUMMARY OF EVENTS

Before the seventeenth century the world's population increased very slowly. It has been estimated that by 1650 the population had doubled since the year AD 1, to about 500 million. Over the next 200 years the rate of increase was much faster, so that by 1850 the population had more than doubled to 1200 million (1.2 billion). After that, the population growth accelerated so rapidly that people talked about a population 'explosion'; in 1927 it reached the 2 billion mark. By the year 2000 it had passed 6 billion and at the end of 2011 it reached 7 billion. In 2003 the UN calculated that if the population continued to increase at the same rate, the global total would be somewhere between 10 billion and 14 billion by 2050, depending on how effectively family planning campaigns were carried out. It was also estimated, given the much lower birth rates in the developed world, that almost 90 per cent of the people would be living in the poorer countries. During the 1980s the spread of HIV/AIDS reached pandemic proportions; most countries in the world were affected, but again it was the poor nations of the Third World which suffered worst. This chapter examines the causes of the population 'explosion', the regional variations, the consequences of all the changes, the attempts at population control and the impact of AIDS.

28.1 THE INCREASING WORLD POPULATION SINCE 1900

(a) Statistics of population increase

It is easy to see from the steeply climbing population total in Figure 28.1 why people talk about a population 'explosion' in the twentieth century. Between 1850 and 1900 the world's population was increasing, on average, by 0.6 per cent every year. During the next 50 years the rate of increase averaged 0.9 per cent a year; it was after 1960 that the full force of the 'explosion' was felt, with the total world population increasing at the rate of 1.9 per cent a year, on average. In 1990 the population was increasing by roughly a million every week, and the total had reached 5300 million. In 1994 there was an increase of 95 million, the biggest ever increase in a single year so far. In 1995 the record was broken again, as the total population grew by 100 million to 5750 million. According to the Population Institute in Washington, 90 per cent of the growth was in poor countries 'torn by civil strife and social unrest'. During 1996 a further 90 million were added to the population, and by 2000 the global total was well past 6 billion. It topped the 7 billion mark at the end of 2011.

However, there were important regional variations within the general population increase. Broadly speaking, the industrialized nations of Europe and North America had their most rapid increase before the First World War; after that their rate of increase slowed considerably. In the less developed, or Third World nations of Africa, Asia and Latin America, the rate of population increase accelerated after the Second World War,

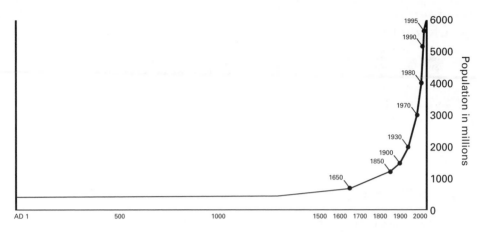

Figure 28.1   **World population increases from AD 1 to 1995**

and it was in these areas that population growth caused the most serious problems. The growth rate began to slow down in some Latin American countries after 1950, but in Asia and Africa the rate continued to increase. Figure 28.2, which is based on statistics provided by the United Nations, shows:

1   The percentage rates at which the world's population grew between 1650 and 1959.
2   The percentage rates of population increase in the different continents during the periods 1900–50 and 1950–9.

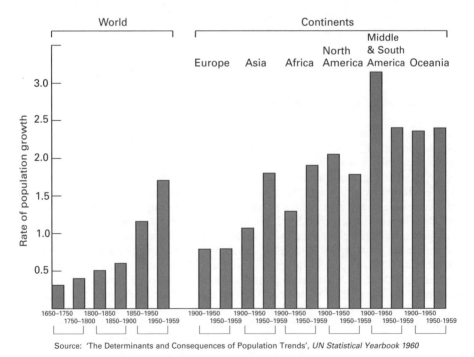

Source: 'The Determinants and Consequences of Population Trends', *UN Statistical Yearbook 1960*

Figure 28.2   **Rate of population growth by regions**

(b) Reasons for the population increase

The population increase in Europe and North America in the later part of the nineteenth and the early twentieth centuries had several causes.

- Increasing industrialization, economic growth and prosperity meant that the necessary resources were available to sustain a larger population, and the two seemed to go hand in hand.
- There was a great improvement in public health, thanks to advances in medical science and sanitation. The work of Louis Pasteur and Joseph Lister in the 1860s on germs and antiseptic techniques helped to reduce the death rate. At the same time, the big industrial cities introduced piped water supplies and drainage schemes, which all helped to reduce disease.
- There was a decline in infant mortality (the number of babies who died before the age of 1). Again this was mainly thanks to medical improvements, which helped to reduce deaths from diseases such as scarlet fever, diphtheria and whooping cough, which were so dangerous to young babies. The improvement in some countries can be seen in Table 28.1, which shows how many babies per thousand born, died within their first year.
- Immigration helped to swell the population of the USA and, to a lesser extent, some other countries on the continents of America, such as Canada, Argentina and Brazil. In the 100 years after 1820, some 35 million people entered the USA; in the last few years before 1914 they were arriving at a rate of a million a year (see Section 22.2).

After 1900 the growth rate in Europe began to slow down, mainly because more people were using modern contraceptive techniques. Later, the economic depression of the 1930s discouraged people from having as many children.

The rapid population growth after 1945 in Third World countries had three main causes:

- *Modern medical and hygiene techniques* began to make an impact for the first time; the child mortality rate fell and people lived longer, as killer diseases like smallpox, malaria and typhoid were gradually brought under control.
- *At the same time, the vast majority of the population made no attempt to limit their families by using contraceptives.* This was partly through ignorance and partly because contraceptives were too expensive for ordinary people to buy. The Roman Catholic Church said that contraception was forbidden for its members, on the grounds that it prevented the natural creation of new lives, and was therefore sinful. Since the Roman Catholic Church was strong in Central and South America, its teaching had important effects. The population growth rate for many countries in these areas was over 3 per cent per annum. The average for the whole of Latin America was 2.4 per cent in 1960, whereas the average for Europe was only 0.75 per cent. *An increase of 2 per cent per annum means that the population of that*

Table 28.1 **Deaths within one year of birth, per thousand births**

	England	Switzerland	France	Italy	Austria
1880–90	142	165	166	195	256
1931–38	52	43	65	104	80

country doubles in about 30 years. This happened in Brazil and Mexico in the 30 years up to 1960.

- Many Third World countries have a long tradition of people *having as many children as possible to combat high infant mortality*, in order to make sure their family continues. Some cultures, Muslims, for example, attach great value to having many sons. The same attitudes persisted in spite of the reduction in infant mortality.

28.2 CONSEQUENCES OF THE POPULATION EXPLOSION

(a) The industrializing nations of Europe and North America

The population growth of the nineteenth century helped to stimulate further economic development. There was a plentiful workforce and more people to buy goods, and this encouraged more investment and enterprise. Nor were there any great problems about feeding and educating these growing numbers, because prosperity meant that the necessary resources were available. Later on, there were unexpected effects on the age structure of the population in the developed nations. This was especially true in Europe where, because of the very low birth rates and longer life expectancy, a growing proportion of the population was over 65. By the 1970s, in countries such as Sweden, France and Britain, about 15 per cent of the population were over 65. In the early 1990s, with this proportion still increasing, questions were being asked about whether state welfare systems would be able to afford to pay pensions to all old people if this trend continued into the twenty-first century.

(b) The Third World

The rapid population growth caused serious problems: some countries, like India, Pakistan and Bangladesh, became overcrowded and there was insufficient land to go round. This forced people to move into towns and cities, but these were already overcrowded and there were not enough houses or jobs for all the new arrivals. Many people were forced to live on the streets; some cities, especially those in Latin America, were surrounded by shanty-towns and slums which had no proper water supply, sanitation or lighting.

(c) It became increasingly difficult to feed the population

All areas of the world succeeded in increasing their food production during the late 1960s and 1970s, thanks to what became known as the 'green revolution'. Scientists developed new strains of heavy-cropping rice and wheat on short, fast-growing stems, helped by fertilizers and irrigation schemes. For a time, food supplies seemed to be well ahead of population growth; even a densely populated country like India was able to export food, and China became self-sufficient. In the USA crop yields increased threefold between 1945 and 1995, and the Americans were able to export surplus crops to over a hundred countries. However, in the mid-1980s, with the world's population growing faster than ever, the 'green revolution' was running into problems and scientists became concerned about the future.

- A point had been reached beyond which crop yields could not be increased any further, and there was a limit to the water supply, topsoil and phosphates for fertilizers (see Section 27.4(a)).

- A survey carried out by scientists at Stanford University (California) in 1996 found that the amount of farmland available was dwindling because of industrialization, the spread of cities and soil erosion. They calculated that the number of mouths to feed in the USA would double by 2050.

There seemed no way in which food production could be doubled from less land. In 1996, on average there were 1.8 acres of cropland to each American and the US diet was made up of 31 per cent animal products. By 2050 there was likely to be only 0.6 of an acre per head. The Stanford scientists came to the conclusion that the solution was for people everywhere to eat less meat; it was suggested that by 2050 the US diet would probably be about 85 per cent vegetarian. Matters were made worse in parts of Africa (Ethiopia, Angola, Mozambique and Somalia) during the 1980s and 1990s by drought and civil wars, which played a part in causing severe food shortages and tens of thousands of deaths from starvation.

(d) Resource shortages in the Third World

Third World governments were forced to spend their valuable cash to feed, house, and educate their growing populations. But this used up resources which they would have preferred to spend on industrializing and modernizing their countries, and so their economic development was delayed. The general shortage of resources meant that the poorest countries also lacked sufficient cash to spend on healthcare. Following a meningitis epidemic in the African state of Niger, Save the Children reported (April 1996) that one-sixth of the world's population – over 800 million people – had no access to healthcare. Health systems in many poorer countries were collapsing, and the situation was becoming worse because richer countries were reducing aid. The report estimated that it cost at least $12 a person a year to provide basic healthcare; but 16 African countries (including Niger, Uganda, Zaire, Tanzania, Mozambique and Liberia) plus Bangladesh, India, Pakistan, Nepal and Vietnam were spending much less than that. In comparison, Britain was spending the equivalent of $1039 (£723). In fact Zaire was spending only 40c per head a year, while Tanzania managed 70c. This meant that simple immunization against easily preventable diseases was not being carried out in these countries. Widespread epidemics could be expected before the end of the century, and a rise in the child mortality rate. When the AIDS epidemic spread, around the turn of the century, it was clear that Africa in particular would be in dire crisis. Another disturbing fact was that almost all these states were spending vastly more per head on defence than on healthcare.

28.3 ATTEMPTS AT POPULATION CONTROL

For many years people had been giving serious thought to the question of controlling the population before the world became too overcrowded and impossible to live in. Soon after the First World War, scientists in a number of countries first began to be concerned at the population growth and felt that it was a problem that should be studied at international level. The first *World Population Congress* was held in Geneva in 1925, and the following year an *International Union for the Scientific Study of Population* was set up in Paris. As well as scientists, the organization also included statisticians and social scientists who were concerned about the probable economic and social effects if the world's population continued to grow. They did valuable work collecting statistics and encouraging governments to improve their data systems, so that accurate information about population trends could be collected.

Illustration 28.1 Posters from India and Africa encouraging people to use birth control and limit families to three children

(a) The United Nations Population Commission

When the United Nations Organization was set up in 1945, a Population Commission was included among its many agencies. When the Third World population began to 'explode' during the 1950s, it was the UN which took the lead in encouraging governments to introduce birth-control programmes. India and Pakistan set up family-planning clinics to advise people about the various methods of birth control available, and to provide them with cheap contraceptives. Huge publicity campaigns were launched with government posters recommending a maximum of three children per family (see Illus. 28.1). Many African governments recommended a maximum of three children, while the Chinese government went further and fixed the legal maximum at two children per family. But progress was very slow: ancient practices and attitudes were difficult to change, especially in countries like India and Pakistan. In the Roman Catholic countries of South America, the Church continued to forbid artificial birth control.

(b) How successful were the campaigns?

The best that can be said is that in parts of Asia the population growth rate was beginning to fall slightly during the 1980s; but in many African and Latin American countries it was still rising. Table 28.2 shows what could be achieved with the spread of birth control.

Table 28.3 shows the 1986 populations and growth rates of various regions, compared with the 1950–9 growth rates. The most rapid growth rate in 1986 was in Africa, where some countries had rates of over 3 per cent per year. The table also reveals how serious the problem of overcrowding was in some areas where there were on average over a hundred people to every square kilometre. This was not so serious in the developed nations of Europe, which had the prosperity and resources to support their populations; but in the poorer nations of Asia, it meant grinding poverty. Bangladesh was probably the world's most crowded country with an average of 700 people to every square kilometre. The population growth rates of Bangladesh and Britain provide a startling comparison: at the present growth rates, Bangladesh will double its population of 125 million in less than 30 years, but Britain's population of 58.6 million will take 385 years to double in size. The Population Institute predicted (December 1995) that, with effective birth control, the global population could stabilize by 2015 at about 8 billion. However, without effective promotion of family planning, the total could well have reached 14 billion by 2050. With the population of Europe and North America growing so slowly, it meant that an ever-increasing proportion of the world's population would be poor.

Table 28.2 **Use of contraceptives and the birth rate**

	% of married women using contraceptives, 1986	*Fall in the % birth-rate, 1978–86*
India	35	4.5 > 3.2
China	74	3.2 > 2.1
Colombia (S. America)	65	4.3 > 2.6
South Korea	70	3.5 > 1.6
Kenya	under 20	4.6 constant
Pakistan	under 20	4.6 constant

Table 28.3 **Population growth rates and density**

	1986 population (millions)	% growth rate 1950–9 (annual)	% growth rate 1980–5 (annual)	1986 population density per sq km
N. America	266	1.75	0.9	12
Europe	493	0.75	0.3	100
USSR	281	1.4	1.0	13
Oceania	25	2.4	1.5	3
Africa	572	1.9	2.9	19
Latin America	414	2.4	2.3	20
E. Asia	1264	1.5	1.2	105
S. Asia	1601	2.2	2.2	101
World total	4916	1.7	1.5	36

On the other hand, some historians feel that the fears about the population explosion have been exaggerated. Paul Johnson, for example, believes that there is no need to panic; once Asia, Latin America and Africa become more successfully industrialized, living standards will rise, and this economic betterment, along with more effective use of contraception, will slow down the birth rate. According to Johnson, the example of China is most encouraging: 'The most important news during the 1980s, perhaps, was that the population of China appeared virtually to have stabilised.'

However, the case of China raises another issue: how far should a government go in its efforts to control population? In 1978 a group of scientists calculated that unless Chinese women were limited to one child each, China would face disaster – the country's resources would simply not be sufficient to feed the population. Conversely, if the one woman one-child limit could be achieved, then the Chinese would become prosperous and assume their rightful place among the world's leading nations. In 1980 the government duly announced the one-child policy. Historian Matthew Connelly describes what happened next:

> This was the most coercive phase in the whole history of China's one-child policy. ... All women with one child were to be inserted with a stainless steel, tamper-resistant IUD [intra-uterine device], all parents with two or more children were to be sterilized, and all unauthorized pregnancies terminated. There was not even a pro forma injunction to avoid coercion. ... In 1983 more than 16 million women and more than 4 million men were sterilized in China, nearly 18 million women were inserted with IUDs, and over 14 million underwent abortions.

There was widespread criticism of this policy in China itself. The All-China Women's Federation demanded an end to 'infanticide and the abuse of women'. There was outrage among Roman Catholics and pro-life supporters around the world, especially in the USA. Eventually the Chinese government softened the policy, but claimed that it had been successful, and was therefore justified. Now that China's population has stabilized and the birth rate is even falling, this means that there are fewer people to share the available resources; therefore standards of living should rise and poverty should be reduced. However, some observers point out that although this in itself is a great achievement, it does not solve the problems facing the ecosystem. Matthew Connelly explains why, using as an example some Asian countries which adopted population control policies:

If Asians have only 2.1 children, but also air conditioning and automobiles, they will have a greater impact on the global ecosystem than a billion more subsistence farmers … [because] they tend to consume more of everything per capita, whether fuel, or water, or wide open spaces.

This was borne out in a joint report by a group of scientists from 105 institutions published shortly before the Earth Summit Conference of July 2012. This confirmed that one of the main causes of the rapid rise in consumption was 'the growing middle class in developed countries and the very lavish lifestyles of the very rich across the planet'. American biologist Paul Ehrlich put it this way: 'The current redistribution of wealth from poor to rich must be halted, and overconsumption by the rich must be controlled with programs such as those that transformed consumption patterns in the United States when it entered World War II.' Former World Bank economist Aklog Birara suggested that

the world can no longer afford to follow the same economic and social model of insatiable demand and concentration of consumption and wealth in a few hands. I cannot imagine that the rest of the world would tolerate continuation of 20 per cent of humanity consuming 80 per cent of the world's goods and services, while one-fifth of the poorest consume only 1.3 per cent. Is this not what triggered the Arab Spring and is likely to trigger Springs in the rest of the poorest and most repressed countries?

This last point was taken up by Paul Liotta and James Miskel, who highlight another worrying aspect of the still growing population; the growth of huge cities with populations of over 10 million. They calculate that by 2025 there will be at least 27 of these megacities around the globe. In Africa, Asia, the Middle East and South America these massive concentrations of people inevitably include a large proportion of poverty-stricken havenots. In the authors' words: 'Crowded masses within these unaccommodating spaces will have literally nowhere else to go; if left to their own devices by inept or uncaring governments, collective rage, despair and hunger will inevitably erupt.' They argue that megacities are attracting terrorists and various types of criminal gangs; unless governments meet this challenge by taking effective counter-measures, some of them will present a serious security threat to the rest of the world.

As the world population reached 7 billion at the end of 2011, the majority view was still that efforts to reduce population growth in areas like Africa must not be relaxed. Greater efforts should be made to provide contraceptives to everybody in the developing world who wants them; and greater use of the internet should be made to spread information about the various methods of birth control.

28.4   THE POPULATION INCREASE AND ISLAMISM

(a)   Samuel Huntington and the 'clash of civilizations'

Another aspect of population growth that many Western observers found threatening was that many of the states where the population was increasing most rapidly were Muslim. It was believed that by 2020 the total Muslim population would far outweigh the non-Muslims in the West, bearing in mind also that many Muslims actually lived in the West. It was in a 1992 lecture that the American political commentator, Samuel Huntington, first proposed the 'clash of civilizations' theory. He later elaborated the theory in his book *The Clash of Civilizations and the Remaking of World Order* (1996). He argued that with the end of the Cold War, the clash of ideologies was also over, and that in the future, the great conflicts would be between different cultures and civilizations. The USA would be 'the primary bastion, agent, champion and defender of Western civilization' against whatever challenges presented themselves. He also pointed out that the rise of the West had depended more on military force than cultural persuasion. 'The West won the world not by the superiority of its ideas or values or religion (to which few members of other civilizations were converted) but rather by its superiority in applying organized violence. Westerners often forget this fact; non-Westerners never do.'

At the time Huntington was writing, it was becoming increasingly clear that Islamism was the main challenge to Western liberal values – stable democracy, regard for human rights, and capitalist free-market economies. The Iranian revolution of 1979, which overthrew the pro-American government of the Shah Reza Pahlevi (see Section 11.1(b)) and set up an Islamic republic, was regarded by many in the West as a dangerous manifestation of the threat from Islamic fundamentalism. Even more so when Iranian students kidnapped over 50 Americans and held them hostage for 444 days, in an attempt to force the US to hand over the former Shah who was living in exile in the USA. Then in October 1981 President Sadat of Egypt was assassinated by members of a militant Islamic group, the Egyptian Islamic Jihad, because they thought he was too pro-American and he had made peace with the Israelis (see Section 11.7). Islamism came to be regarded by many in the West as synonymous with terrorism, as a whole series of attacks took place on American targets (see Section 12.2(c)): US embassies in Beirut and Kuwait (1983 – carried out by Islamic Jihad), the US embassies in Nairobi (Kenya) and Dar-es-Salaam (Tanzania – both in 1988), the destruction of the airliner over Scotland with the loss of 270 lives (1988), a bomb explosion in the World Trade Center in New York (1993), the damaging of the destroyer *Cole* in harbour in Yemen (2000) and the following year the climax of 9/11 with the destruction of the World Trade Center in New York (see Section 12.3). Many Americans condemned Islam as a whole, calling Muslims 'a colossal threat' and 'a failed faith and civilization', and claiming that Muslims everywhere 'lack the liberal gene'. As President Bush launched his 'war against terrorism' with the attack on Afghanistan, announcing that countries were 'either with us or against us', it looked as though Huntington's predictions were about to become reality.

However, Raymond Baker (see *Further Reading*) argues that such blanket condemnations of Islam ignore some of the most influential Islamic thinkers of the last half-century, who have put forward a vision of Islam that champions 'rationality, science, education, tolerance, social justice, democracy and political participation. In Turkey, for example, democracy has worked successfully and Islamists have done well in elections. Compared with other parties, "they are perceived by the population to be greatly supportive of local communities".' In Palestine, the militant Hamas Party won the election fairly in 2006; but the USA, claiming to be committed to democracy, were most reluctant to accept the voters' verdict (see Section 11.11(g)). Certainly many respected Muslim writers had already rejected the 'clash of civilizations' theory. Abdullahi Ahmed An-Na'im, a professor of law in Atlanta, USA, and formerly of the University of Khartoum (Sudan), argued that 'all the governments of predominantly Islamic countries have clearly and consistently acted in consideration of their own economic, political or security interests. What is happening everywhere is simply the politics of power, as usual, not the manifestation of a clash of civilizations.' During the 1990s the UN and NATO actually supported Muslims in Kosovo and Bosnia (see Section 10.7), as well as in Somalia and Chechnya. In the aftermath of the 9/11 attacks on the USA, some Muslim states sided with the Americans and offered their support. Pakistan provided vital help, and its president, Pervez Musharraf, condemned Pakistani extremists for bringing Islam into disrepute. Thus Pakistan received considerable financial aid from the USA in return for its co-operation, as did Kazakhstan, Tajikistan and Uzbekistan. Another Muslim, Ziauddin Sardar, wrote (*Observer,* 16 September 2001) that 'Islam cannot explain the actions of the suicide hijackers, just as Christianity cannot explain the gas chambers, or Catholicism the bombing at Omagh. They are acts beyond belief by people who long ago abandoned the path of Islam.' He insisted that terrorist actions were completely alien to the faith and reasoning of Islam; it was a war against a small group of Muslim terrorists [al-Qaeda] and the rogue states that were harbouring them.

Other writers have made the point that Islamism, like Christianity, is far from being a united entity. There are at least three major divisions of Islam and many subdivisions and groups. Paul Berman (in *Terror and Liberalism*, 2004 edition), an American political and cultural critic, argues that distinct cultural boundaries do not exist – there is no 'Islamic civilization', nor a 'Western civilization', and that the evidence for a civilization clash is therefore not convincing. Edward Said pointed out that the Islamic world numbers over a billion people, includes dozens of countries, societies, traditions, languages and, of course, an infinite number of different experiences. It is therefore simply false to treat them all as a monolithic entity called Islamists, who are inherently violent, who are anti-modern and anti-liberal, who do not believe in democracy and who want to turn the clock back to the seventh century, when Islam began. Noam Chomsky has dismissed the whole theory as being merely a new justification for the USA 'for any atrocities that they wanted to carry out'. The USA needed a new threat on which to lay the blame for their interventionist policies, now that the Soviet Union was no longer a viable threat. And indeed one example of this: the invasion of Iraq was blamed on al-Qaeda and Saddam Hussein's non-existent weapons of mass destruction, when in fact the real reason for the attack was to enable the USA to protect their oil supplies.

(b)   Islamism and its beliefs and principles

Founded by the Prophet Mohammed (570–632) in Mecca, Islam (meaning 'submission', because Muslims submit themselves to the will of God) soon spread throughout Arabia. At its furthest extent it reached across North Africa and into Southern Spain, Malaya, Indonesia, Turkey and eastern Europe, following the capture of Constantinople (Istanbul) in 1453. Mohammed claimed to have received messages from the angel Gabriel, which were written down by his followers, and formed the Muslim holy book, the Koran. This contains the Five Pillars of Islam, the five basic obligatory acts: saying the creed, daily prayers, giving alms for the poor, fasting during Ramadan and making the pilgrimage to Mecca at least once. In addition, Muslims must follow Islamic law, which deals with virtually every aspect of life and society.

As with Christianity, there are several different denominations:

- **Sunni:** these are the largest denomination, making up over 80 per cent of all Muslims. There are several divisions within the Sunnis, some moderate and peaceful, others more extreme, such as Salafi and Jihadists (who believe in a holy war).
- **Shia:** they are the second largest group, making up more than 10 per cent of the total. They share many of the core beliefs and practises of Islam with Sunnis; but the main division occurred over the question of who was the true successor to Mohammed himself. Sunnis believe that Mohammed did not appoint a successor, and that God's choice for the next leader would be shown through an election. Shias, on the other hand, believe that Mohammed appointed his son-in-law, Ali ibn Abi Talib, and that therefore he was the first Imam (leader). This means that the Caliphs elected after Mohammed's death are not regarded as legitimate leaders by Shias. Sunnis and Shias also disagree on which hadiths (reports about Mohammed's words and actions) are the most important. To complicate matters further, Shias themselves have several divisions, including Zaidis, Alawites, Twelvers and Druze.

In Iraq Shia are the majority group; after the war in 2003, the militant Sunnis launched an uprising against both the Shia and the foreign occupiers (see Section 12.4(f)).

- **Sufis:** Sufism is a branch of Islam that focuses on the more spiritual aspects of religion. It began as a reaction against the wealthy lifestyles of many leading Muslims. Sufis tried to lead simple and austere lives of service to others, aiming for spiritual perfection and a direct experience of God.

Most Islamists agree that Islam must be involved in politics. They believe that in some way governments must incorporate Muslim principles, concepts and traditions into their policies. One of their central goals is to introduce sharia (Islamic) law in countries that they control. Some believe in achieving this peacefully, but others are prepared to use violence. The West's conception of Islamism is probably skewed by the fact that the media tends to focus on violent groups such as al-Qaeda, whereas some of the most popular, dynamic and influential Islamists, such as the Muslim Brotherhood in Egypt, the Islamic Action Front in Jordan and the Justice and Benevolence movement in Morocco, get less attention. In Morocco the media has focused on an extremist Salafi group which in May 2003 carried out horrific bombings that killed 45 people. Compared with that, Justice and Benevolence is moderate and benign.

(c)   The situation in 2012

In September 2012, anti-American and anti-Western protests swept through the Muslim world following the showing on YouTube of an American film, *The Innocence of Muslims.* This was extremely insulting to the prophet Mohammed. The protests began in Libya where Islamists attacked the US consulate and killed four Americans, including the US ambassador. It emerged that the attacks had been carried out by an Islamist militia known as Ansar al-Sharia (supporters of Sharia law). As the anti-West protests, many of them violent, spread around the globe, it seemed that the world was on the brink of the long-predicted great civilizations clash.

Then events took an unexpected turn. In Libya counter-protests began to appear, demanding that the militias, which were operating outside government control, should be disbanded. The Jihadist formations Ansar al-Sharia and Abu Salem, together with several other militias, agreed to disband and hand over their weapons, claiming that they had decided their role was over. This left a number of active militias that would take time to deal with, but it was a move in the right direction. It demonstrated clearly what many writers had been arguing for the last 20 years: that the majority of Muslims are moderate and peace-loving, and those in the Third World are facing the usual problem – the struggle to feed their families. They probably have neither the time nor the inclination to take part in a struggle between rival civilizations. The terrorists represent just one strand of militant Islamic fundamentalism, which is intolerant and anti-modern. In fact, all religions have their fanatics, whose extreme beliefs often contradict the very religions they claim to embrace. Francis Fukuyama, writing in 2002, argued that the idea of the theocratic Islamic state is appealing in theory, but that the reality is less appealing:

Those who have actually had to live under such regimes, for example, in Iran or Afghanistan, have experienced stifling dictatorships whose leaders are more clueless than most on how to overcome the problems of poverty and stagnation. … Even as the September 11th events unfolded, there were continuing demonstrations in Tehran and many other Iranian cities on the part of tens of thousands of young people fed up with the Islamic regime and wanting a more liberal political order.

This does not mean, of course, that Muslims do not have genuine grievances. The root cause that lay behind much of the terrorism was Third World poverty, human rights abuses and the ever-widening gap between rich and poor. On the one hand there was the Western capitalist system, thriving on profit-led globalization (though less so after the 2008 financial crisis) and its ruthless exploitation of the rest of the world. On the other hand there was the Third World, which saw itself as marginalized and deprived, and where all manner of problems were rife – famine, drought, AIDS, crippling debts and corrupt governments which abused human rights and failed to share the wealth of their countries among ordinary citizens. Some of these governments, such as President Mubarak's regime in Egypt, were supported by the West, because they were good at suppressing potential terrorists. The problem with the so-called 'war on terrorism' was that it had concentrated on military and police action, with not much evidence of successful aid and nation-building. In Muslim and Arab eyes, the whole situation is epitomized in the Arab–Israeli conflict. On the one hand there is Israel, wealthy, heavily armed, guilty of violating UN resolutions and supported by the USA. On the other hand there are the Palestinians, marginalized, deprived of their land, poverty-stricken and without much hope of improvement. Until these problems are addressed seriously, it is unlikely that the Muslim world and the West can ever be on close terms.

27.5 THE HIV/AIDS EPIDEMIC

(a) The beginnings

In the early 1980s AIDS (Acquired Immune Deficiency Syndrome) was thought to be a disease that mainly affected homosexual men; some people called it the 'gay plague'. Another group which contracted the disease were people who used unsterilized syringes to inject themselves with drugs. At first it was in the wealthy countries of the West, particularly the USA, that most cases were reported, but after governments had launched campaigns about sexual health and the use of condoms to prevent the transmission of HIV (Human Immunodeficiency Virus), the outbreaks seemed to have been brought under control. The widespread use of anti-retroviral (ARV) drugs therapy slowed down the development of the virus and enabled people to live much longer.

It was something of a shock when, during the 1990s, the world became aware that the disease had spread to the poorest countries in the world, and that in Africa it had reached epidemic proportions. Scientists now know that it takes an average of eight to ten years for HIV infection to develop into full-blown AIDS, which was why the virus was able to spread so widely before it was recognized. The epidemic also spread to India, China and the countries of the former USSR. Tony Barnett and Alan Whiteside, in their recent book *AIDS in the 21st Century* (2002), showed how each epidemic was different: in *China* the main causes were contaminated needles and the practice of selling blood at state-run blood collection points in the early 1990s. The World Health Organization (WHO) estimated that two-thirds of injections given in China were unsafe and that much of the collected blood plasma was infected. When the symptoms of AIDS began to appear, local officials tried to suppress the news. It was only in 2003 that the government admitted publicly that over a million of its citizens were HIV-positive; the infection was increasing by 30 per cent a year and 10 million could be affected by 2010. In *Russia* and *Ukraine* the highest rates were among injecting drug-users, especially those in prison. Experts calculate that once HIV enters the general population and infects around 5 per cent of adults, a general epidemic is likely to follow, as it has in southern Africa.

(b) AIDS in southern Africa

The first cases to be reported in Africa were in a fishing village in south-west Uganda, in the mid-1980s. The HIV virus spread rapidly, transmitted mainly by unprotected hetero-sexual sex. Governments were slow to realize the significance of what was happening and aid agencies made no provision for dealing with the disease in their assistance programmes. It was in 2001 that a report by the International Crisis Group (ICG) sounded alarm bells. It said that the impact of HIV on Africa was as though it was involved in a major war. The report concentrated on Botswana, but it warned that the impact of AIDS on Africa as a whole was likely to be devastating within just a few years, if nothing was done about it. The report was not exaggerating: in 2001, 3 million people died from the disease in Africa, and 5 million became infected. By 2003 it was estimated that 29.4 million people were living with HIV or AIDS in Africa, and this was about 70 per cent of the global total. A further 3 million people died from the virus in Africa during 2003.

By that year HIV prevalence levels had risen to horrifying proportions. In Botswana and Swaziland, almost 40 per cent of adults were living with the virus or with full-blown AIDS, and the percentage was almost as high in Zimbabwe. In South Africa the prevalence level was 25 per cent. Life expectancy in southern Africa, which had reached the sixties by 1990, had fallen again to the lower forties; in Zimbabwe it was down to 33. One of the tragic side effects of the pandemic was the huge numbers of children left without parents. In Uganda there were over a million orphans; the WHO estimated that by 2010 there were likely to be 20 million AIDS orphans in Africa. There were economic effects too: a substantial proportion of the labour force was being lost, with all its skills and experience. This was being felt especially in farming and food production, while the deaths of so many young women was an irreplaceable loss to the domestic economy and to child-rearing. At the same time there was an increased demand for people to nurse the sick and care for orphaned children.

Why was the epidemic so much worse in southern Africa?

HIV was able to spread more quickly in conditions of poverty, where there was very little access to information and education about the virus and how to prevent it spreading. Widespread hunger reduced resistance to the disease and accelerated the progress from HIV to AIDS. Nor were any of the expensive anti-retroviral drugs available for Africans. The large number of civil wars in Africa produced thousands of refugees, who were often cut off from their normal healthcare services. In emergency situations like these, there was a greater danger of the HIV virus being spread through contaminated blood. Most African governments took a long time to acknowledge what was happening, partly because of the stigma attached to the disease: the belief that it was caused by homosexual sex and the general reluctance to discuss sexual habits. South Africa itself was one of the slowest to take action, mainly because President Mbeki refused to accept the link between HIV and AIDS.

(c) What is being done to combat AIDS?

The experts know what needs to be done to bring the AIDS epidemic under control: people must be persuaded to have safe sex and use condoms; and somehow governments must be able to provide cheap ARV treatment. Brazil is one country where the campaign has slowed down the spread of the disease. In Africa, governments have concentrated on the so-called 'ABC' message: 'Abstain from sex. Be faithful to one partner, and if you cannot, use a Condom.' Uganda provides the great African success story; the government admitted to the WHO in 1986 that they had some AIDS cases, and President Museveni personally took charge of the campaign, travelling round from village to village to talk about the problem and what should be done. Uganda was the first country in Africa to launch the ABC campaign and provide cheap condoms for its people. People were encouraged to come forward voluntarily for testing. The programme was financed jointly by the government, by aid agencies and by religious organizations and churches. Uganda's meagre resources were strained to the limits, but the campaign worked, even though very few people had access to ARV drugs: Uganda's HIV prevalence rate had peaked at 20 per cent in 1991, but by the end of 2003 it had fallen to about 5 per cent. The epidemic had passed its acute stage, but the problem of orphaned children was just reaching its height.

Elsewhere in Africa and China, governments were slow off the mark and the epidemic took a firmer hold, reaching crisis proportions in 2003. Some African countries were beginning to follow Uganda's example. In Malawi, President Muluzi set up an AIDS commission and appointed a special minister to deal with the problem. But huge sums of money are needed to finance the necessary three-pronged attack on HIV/AIDS across Southern Africa:

- ABC campaigns or some equivalent;
- anti-retroviral drugs – these are much cheaper now, since pharmaceutical companies gave way to political pressure and allowed drugs to be supplied more cheaply to poorer countries;
- healthcare systems and infrastructures, which in most poor states need modernizing in order to cope with the magnitude of the problem; more doctors and nurses are required.

There are several international agencies trying to deal with the disease, the most important being the UN's Global Fund to Fight AIDS, TB and Malaria; the World Health Organization (WHO); and UNAIDS. In December 2003, UN secretary-general Kofi Annan complained that he was 'angry, distressed and helpless'; 1 December was World AIDS Day, but the outlook was bleak. Reports from all over the Third World showed that the war against the disease was being lost; the virus was still spreading and 40 million people were living with HIV. The UN Fund said it would need £7 billion by 2005 and the WHO wanted £4 billion. Many wealthy countries have given generously; the USA, for example, has promised $15 billion over the next five years, but insists that the money be spent in the way it specifies. The Bush administration favoured programmes which promoted abstinence against those that advocated the use of condoms. The Roman Catholic Church also continues to oppose the use of condoms, even though scientists have shown that it is the best means of prevention available. No wonder Kofi Annan was angry; 'I am not winning the war', he said, 'because I don't think the leaders of the world are engaged enough.'

By 2012 well over 30 million people had died from AIDS since the first cases were identified in 1981. An estimated 1.8 million of them died in 2010 alone, two-thirds of them in southern Africa, where nearly 15 million children were left orphaned. In the same year around 2.7 million people became infected with HIV. According to the WHO, the attempts to control the epidemic have been intensified; from 2002–8 spending on the campaign in low- and middle-income countries increased sixfold. Since 2008 spending has not increased, but at least the level has been maintained. In May 2012 the WHO published a plan of priority action for the next two years: focusing on HIV prevention, encouraging people who might be at risk to get themselves tested regularly, providing even wider access to cheap ARV drugs and improving and modernizing healthcare systems, especially in southern Africa. There were some encouraging signs: more people than ever before were receiving ARV treatment, the annual number of AIDS deaths had declined and the global percentage of people infected with HIV seemed to have stabilized. However, the UN agencies warn that recent achievements should not lead to complacency; on no account should efforts be relaxed. In fact in eastern Europe infection rates were still rising; and in the USA in June 2012 more than one million people were living with HIV, but probably 20 per cent of them didn't know they were infected.

FURTHER READING

Baker, R., 'Degrading Democracy: American Empire, Islam and Struggles for Freedom in the Arab Islamic World', in S. Shehata, S. (ed.), *Islamic Politics in the Middle East* (Routledge, 2012).

Berman, P., *Terror and Liberalism* (Norton, 2004 edition).

Connelly, M. J., *Fatal Misconception: The Struggle to Control World Population* (Harvard University Press, 2008).

Barnett, D. and Whiteside, A., *AIDS in the 21st Century: Disease and Globalisation* (Palgrave Macmillan, 2002).

Epstein, H., *The Invisible Cure: Africa, the West, and the Fight Against AIDS* (Viking, 2007).

Fassin, D., *When Bodies Remember: Experiences and Politics of Aids in South Africa* (University of California Press, 2007).

Liotta, P. H. and Miskel, J. F., *The Real Population Bomb: Megacities, Global Securities and the Map of the Future* (Potomac Books, 2012).

QUESTIONS

1   Explain the causes and consequences of the rapid growth in the world's population during the twentieth century.
2   What methods were used to try to control population growth in the second half of the twentieth century, and why did some of them arouse criticism?
3   Why was it that in the second half of the twentieth century the rate of population growth in Europe slowed down, while in Africa and other Third World areas it accelerated?

◤   There is a document question about the HIV/AIDS epidemic on the website.

Index

Italy *cont.*
and the peace settlement   41
problems after 1918   31, 295
Mussolini comes to power in   295–8
under Mussolini   299–306
foreign policy between the wars   72–5
during Second World War   89, 94, 100,
101, 104–5
since 1945   189–90, 661
and decolonization   559
Ivory Coast   553

Jackel, Eberhard   87
Jamaica   537–9, 605
Japan   3, 4, 7
before the First World War   336
during First World War   336
between the wars   336–8
and China   69, 70–2, 118, 336–8,
421–2
and League of Nations   43, 48
invasion of Manchuria   43, 48, 69, 70,
337–8
and USA   52–3, 338–40
during Second World War   31, 89–90,
96–100, 108–10, 117–19, 338
since 1945   338–42, 650
Jaruzelski, General Woyciech   208–9,
647
Java   554
Jerusalem   248–9
Jews   172, 225–40, 247–55
under Hitler   111–17, 325–6
Jiang Quing   436
Jiang Zemin   440–2
Jim Crow Laws   487–8
Jinnah, M.A.   535
Johnson, Lyndon B.   612
social policies   504–5
and Vietnam   151, 153
Johnson, Paul   674
Johnson-Shirleaf, Ellen   594–5
Jonathan, Goodluck   571
Jordan   229
Jospin, Lionel   187–8
Jung Chang   425

Kabbah, Tejan   596
Kabila, Joseph   576–7
Kabila, Laurent   576
Kádár, János   204, 205, 209
KADU   546

Kagame, Paul   577, 582
Kamenev, Lev   367, 373–5, 380
Kampuchea   *see* Cambodia
KANU   545–6
Kapp Putsch (1920)   311
Karadžić, Radovan   217
Karzai, Hamid   259, 268–9, 277–8
Kasavubu, Joseph   574
Kashmir   173–4
Katanga (Shaba)   574–5
Kaunda, Kenneth   546, 602
Kellogg–Briand Pact (1928)   54
Kennan, George   129
Kennedy, John F.   137, 152–3, 611
assassination of   501, 504
social policies   503
Kennedy, Robert   139, 505
Kenya   264, 544–6
Kenyatta, Jomo   544–6
Kerensky, Alexander   356–8
Kershaw, Ian   82, 87, 112, 317, 318–19,
325, 332–3
Keynes, J.M.   41, 54
Khatami, Muhammad   279–80
Khmer Rouge   175, 456, 458–60, 462
Khomeini, Ayatollah   244–5, 262, 279
Khrushchev, Nikita   137–9, 203, 381,
396–400
criticism of Stalin   204, 397
Kikwete, Jakaya   574
Kim Dae Jung   451
Kim Il Sung   143–5, 449
Kim Jong Il   451–3
Kim Jong-un   455
King, Dr Martin Luther   505, 506–9
Kirchner, Cristina Fernández de   626–7
Kirchner, Nestor   622, 626
Kirov, Sergei   380
Kissinger, Henry   459
Kohl, Helmut   189
Kolchak, Admiral Alexander   364–5
kolkhozy   378
Korea
North   448–53
South   449–53, 643
war in (1950–3)   143–6, 172, 450
Kornilov, General Vladimir   357
Koroma, Ernest Bai   597
Koroma, Johnny Paul   596
Kosovo   215–16
Kosygin, Alexander   400–1
Krenz, Egon   210

Niemoller, Pastor Martin   324
Nigeria   543, 567–71
  civil war in   567–8
Nixon, Richard M.   153–5, 157, 162, 514
  social policies   505
  and Watergate   514–15
Nkomo, Joshua   546, 548, 598
Nkrumah, Kwame   542, 565–6
Normandy Landings (1944)   104
North American Free Trade Association
  (NAFTA)   617, 625
North Borneo   see Sabah
Northern Rhodesia   see also Zambia
  546
Northern Rock   655
North–South Divide   638–44
Norway   89, 90–1, 132, 192, 194, 201
Nove, Alec   400
nuclear disarmament   139–40, 161–2
nuclear power   281–2, 644, 646–7
nuclear weapons   136–40, 161, 165, 270,
  281–2, 453
Nujoma, Sam   578
Nuremberg Laws (1935)   325
Nyasaland   see also Malawi   546
Nyerere, Dr Julius   543, 571–3

OAS (Organisation de l'Armée Secrète)
  552–3
OAU (Organization of African Unity)   573,
  582, 587, 594
Obama, Barack   276–8, 523–5, 656, 660
Obasanjo, Olusegun   570–1
Obote, Dr Milton   543
October Manifesto (1905)   351–2
Oder–Neisse Line   126–7
Odinga, Oginga   545–6
oil   624, 645
  in Third World   614–17, 629, 643
OPEC (Organization of Petroleum Exporting
  Countries)   237, 643–5
Operation Overlord (1944)   104–5
Ortega, Daniel   621–2, 630
Oslo Peace Accords (1993)   238–40,
  247–8
Ostpolitik   161
Overy, Richard   381

Pact of Steel (1939)   75
Pakistan   670
  creation of   535–7

Palestine   230–2, 237–40, 247–55
  self-rule in (1995)   240
Palestine Liberation Organization (PLO)
  234–6
pan-Africanism   533
Panama   260, 608
Papen, Franz von   316–17, 328
Paris   91, 105, 106
Pass Laws   583–4, 585
Pasteur, Louis   669
Pathet Lao   462–3
Paulson, Henry   655
peaceful coexistence   133, 399, 402
Pearl Harbor   89, 96–8, 338
perestroika   208, 403
Persia   see Iran
Peking   see Beijing
Perón, Juan   335
Pétain, Marshal Henri   24, 27, 91, 93
Petrograd   see also Leningrad   356–9, 361
Piłsudski, Józef   63
Pinochet, General Augusto   157, 627
Pipes, Richard   357, 358, 359, 363
Pius XI, Pope   301–2
Poincaré, Raymond   56
Poland   62–3
  during Second World War   89, 90, 111
  end of communism in   164, 207, 208–9,
    212
  and Hitler   70, 82–3
  since 1945   204
Polisario Front   556–7
Polish Corridor   75, 77, 83
pollution   644, 646–7
Pol Pot   175, 456, 458–60, 462
Pompidou, Georges   187
Popular Front for the Liberation of Palestine
  (PFLP)   236, 239, 249
population, growth and problems   669–71
  and AIDS/HIV   679–82
  control of   671–5
  and Islamism   675–9
  statistics   667–8
Portugal   132, 143, 194, 198, 220, 335, 661
  and decolonization   557–9, 612
  and Zimbabwe   547–8
Potsdam Conference (1945)   126
Powell, Colin   511
Primakov, Evgeny   413
Princip, Gavrilo   11
Prodi, Romano 219
Prohibition (USA)   480